# Public Policy and Higher Education

## Second Edition

Edited by

Cheryl D. Lovell, Ph.D.
Toni E. Larson, Ph.D.
Diane R. Dean, Ed.D.
David L. Longanecker, Ph.D.

**Learning Solutions**

New York   Boston   San Francisco
London   Toronto   Sydney   Tokyo   Singapore   Madrid
Mexico City   Munich   Paris   Cape Town   Hong Kong   Montreal

Pearson Learning Solutions, 501 Boylston Street, Suite 900, Boston, MA 02116
A Pearson Education Company
www.pearsoned.com

Printed in the United States of America

10  9  8  7  6

2009220066

DC/LP

ISBN 10: 0-558-41406-0
ISBN 13: 978-0-558-41406-1

# Table of Contents

CHAPTER 7   TEACHER PREPARATION

# A Note to the Reader

This Second Edition of *Public Policy and Higher Education* is a new contribution to the Association for the Study of Higher Education (ASHE) Reader Series. It is intended to assist both scholars and practitioners in understanding the intricate relationship between colleges and universities and the federal and state governments that have oversight and often governance responsibilities with and over the postsecondary institutions. We also believe this volume will greatly contribute to current and future scholarship, giving faculty and graduate students an in-depth view of this important relationship. Equally important, we believe this Reader will serve as an important reference for the policymakers and staff members who navigate both the higher education terrain and the policy world to make decisions that best serve the public. As with the First Edition (1997), the selected readings come from a multidisciplinary approach including publications from the fields of higher education, political science, public administration, public policy, and policy analysis. This broader approach allows a more thorough presentation of the topics related to public policy and higher education.

Volumes are often updated with new readings and we would welcome your feedback and suggestions for future editions to this Reader. Please send your comments and suggestions to any of the four editors below regarding this ASHE Reader:

Cheryl D. Lovell, Ph.D.
Associate Dean, Morgridge College
of Education and Professor of
Higher Education
University of Denver
2450 S. Vine St.
Denver, CO 80208

Toni E. Larson, Ph.D.
Executive Director, Independent
Higher Education of Colorado
1177 Grant St., #102
Denver, CO 80203

Diane R. Dean, Ed.D.
Assistant Professor, Higher Education
Administration & Policy
Campus Box 5900
Illinois State University
Normal, Illinois 61790-5900

David L. Longanecker, Ph.D.
Executive Director, Western
Interstate Commission for Higher
 Education (WICHE)
3035 Center Green Dr, Suite 200
Boulder, CO 80301

# Introduction

## Public Policy and Higher Education

What is the relationship between the campus and the capitol and how can the two work together for the benefit of all? State and federal policymakers, staff members, faculty, and campus administrators alike ask these important questions on a daily basis. Each of the many stakeholders affected by postsecondary public policy has a unique story to tell, one that adds to the rich and complex understandings of how public policy is made.

Even the cover of this Reader is intentionally designed to reflect the connections, integration, and nexus of the two worlds of higher education and public policy. The vision of the capitol and the statehouse in the upper left and bottom right photos are clear symbols of the policy world that must connect and interact with the higher education world represented in the top right and bottom left photos. The top right and bottom left photos are especially important as they represent college students who are the center and focus of this important connection of these two worlds. Our work in the postsecondary policy arena is focused on improving systems of education through policy and through official enactments designed to allow our colleges and universities to thrive at what they do best, that of preparing generations of educated professionals who will be our leaders now and in the future. It is critical that we have strong relations from the campus level to the statehouse level and on to the federal level. This Reader will provide a solid foundation for those who are interested in these relationships and how to access them, facilitate them, and work proactively in them.

## The Organization of the Reader

This *Second Edition* of *Public Policy and Higher Education* presents readers with (1) two introductory essays on the themes and readings of this volume: "The Foundations of Public Policy and Higher Education" written by Toni Larson and Cheryl Lovell and "Current Issues in Public Policy and Higher Education" written by Diane Dean; and (2) an extended bibliography of other key readings published since the *First Edition* (1997).

This Reader continues to provide one of the few comprehensive works on public policy and higher education. Most publications cover the areas of higher education and public policy separately. Few attempt to address both as this Reader does. As we noted in the *First Edition*, this original Reader began as course packets for four courses in public policy and higher education in the Higher Education Program at the University of Denver. The *First Edition* contributed substantially to faculty and students who needed one volume for use with policy courses in higher education programs. Since that original volume, the scholarship and resulting literature base on postsecondary public policy has grown substantially. This *Second Edition* represents the benefits of the greatly expanded literature base.

Understanding public policy and higher education as two worlds that revolve together in the same demanding universe requires a comprehensive background best achieved through a team approach. We assembled a team of editors who hail from and understand each of these worlds as separate entities, and yet also see and understand the symbiotic whole they create together. Our editorial team includes two faculty who research and study these interconnected worlds of public policy and higher education, Drs. Cheryl Lovell and Diane Dean; and two practitioners of the policy world, Drs. Toni Larson and David Longanecker, who daily confront the public policy process and use it as a tool to address issues faced by the higher education community. While our faculty members teach and research, they also have extensive backgrounds in practice-based policy work with Dr. Lovell coming from the National Center for Higher Education Management Systems (NCHEMS), the State Higher Education Executive Officers (SHEEO), and the Florida Board of Regents before beginning her role as a faculty member in the Higher Education Program at the University of Denver. Dr. Dean also has experience in campus-based financial management at Teachers College, Columbia University. She has written extensively on areas of educational reform and student success, and has been an associate with the National Center for Public Policy and Higher Education. She brings a wealth of campus-based experiences in administration, policy, and research to the project. Our current policy practitioners Toni Larson and David Longanecker contribute an enormously deep background in higher education public policy. Dr. Larson, as Executive Director of Independent Higher Education of Colorado and based on her long involvement with the National Association of Independent Colleges and Universities, brings a vital understanding of policy issues as they affect the independent sector. Dr. Longanecker has had extensive state and federal policy posts, including the current Executive Director of Western Interstate Commission for Higher Education (WICHE), prior Assistant Secretary of Education for the US Department of Education, and prior Executive Director of the Colorado Commission for Higher Education. Both of our current policy practitioners have numerous publications and research projects as well. The resulting team, who both studies and works in the postsecondary public policy arena, moved this *Second Edition* forward with a comprehensive focus, an analytical view, and a good sense of practicality.

Our work was guided by our extensive scholarly and practical knowledge about public policy and higher education as well as our desire to (1) create a text that provides foundational reading important for understanding the meaning of public policy; (2) clarify how public policy research and analysis in higher education have similar roots yet are separate in purpose and interpretation; and (3) explore current contemporary public policy issues facing higher education. Each of these ideas constituted themes for the selection of readings. Due to space limitation we could not include many valuable readings. Therefore, an extensive bibliography of related readings to aid those who desire additional research is also included.

# Dedication

The Editors want to express our sincere appreciation and respect to Dr. Len Foster and to Dr. Barbara Townsend by dedicating this Reader to their memory. Both were valuable members of our ASHE community and both are deeply missed.

# Dedication

# Acknowledgments

This Reader continues to be among the few volumes that focus on the nexus between public policy and higher education. Accurately addressing this relationship necessitates the merging of several different perspectives. Therefore the editors of this book brought together diverse publications to provide a broad background on postsecondary public policy. The bulk of the work on vetting publications for inclusion in this *Second Edition* was made possible by our top notch Advisory Board. The Advisory Board evaluated many more readings than space will allow for inclusion in this Reader. We express our warm appreciation and thanks for their time and contributions.

| | |
|---|---|
| Julie Bell | National Conference of State Legislatures |
| Margarita Benitez | The Education Trust |
| Robert O. Berdahl | University of Maryland |
| Cheryl Blanco | Southern Regional Education Board |
| Marilee Bresciani | San Diego State University |
| Ellen E. Chaffee | Valley City University |
| Frances Contreras | University of Washington |
| Joni E. Finney | University of Pennsylvania |
| Barbara E. Lee | Rutgers University |
| Paul Lingenfelter | State Higher Education Executive Officers |
| Mario Martinez | University of Nevada |
| Michael McLendon | Vanderbilt University |
| Kathryn Mohrman | Arizona State University |
| Michael A. Olivas | University of Houston |
| Travis Reindle | Jobs for the Future |
| Frank Schmidtlein | University of Maryland |
| Kathleen Shaw | Pennsylvania Department of Education |
| Jane Wellman | The Delta Cost Project |
| Mimi Wolverton | University of Nevada |
| Fredericks Volkwein | Pennsylvania State University |
| Ami Zusman | University of California |

Many other colleagues graciously sent us materials and suggestions for consideration. Faculty colleagues shared relevant course syllabi and readings, and administrator colleagues made insights on the practical side of the postsecondary public policy work, and many others offered suggested readings. We appreciate their efforts to make this Reader useful for students and faculty in higher education programs as well as for administrators, state officials, and policy analysts who assist in policymaking.

This *Second Edition* would not be possible without the support, guidance, and extensive contributions of Dr. Edward Hines, Professor Emeritus, Illinois State University. While his name is not listed as an Editor for this *Second Edition*, he did play a major role in this project. We are truly grateful to him for his contributions and support.

We are also especially indebted to Brandi Van Horn, a Research Analyst with the Western Interstate Commission for Higher Education (WICHE) and a doctoral student in the Higher Education Program at the University of Denver who also contributed extensively to this book through bibliographic searches, by keeping meticulous notes from our various meetings and conversations, and for moving the project forward with gently persistent inquires to see if there was something else she could be doing on the project. Also a warm thank you to Brianna Hovendick who was a graduate student in the Library and Information Science Program at the University of Denver for her wonderful technical assistance with creating our electronic portfolio site that enabled our Advisory Board to review and rate the many manuscripts.

The editors express deep appreciation to the various publishers that have allowed their manuscripts to be included in this collection of readings on postsecondary public policy. We appreciate their efforts to allow reproduction for the benefit of the ASHE membership. Finally, the editors would like to thank Len Foster, ASHE Reader Series editor and the editorial board who selected our proposal and endorsed this project.

# Acknowledgments

Grateful acknowledgment is made to the following sources for permission to reprint material copyrighted or controlled by them:

"Between Planning and Politics: Intellect Vs. Interaction as Analysis," by Aaron Wildavsky, reprinted from *Speaking Truth to Power: The Art and Craft of Policy Analysis* (1973), Aspen Law and Business.

"Wrapping Things Up," by J. W. Kingdon, reprinted from *Agendas, Alternatives, and Public Policies*, Second Edition (1995), HarperCollins.

"The Need for Better Theories," by P. A. Sabatier, reprinted from *Theories of the Policy Process*, Second Edition (2007), by permission of Perseus Books Group.

"The Nature of the Policy Process," by Randall B. Ripley, reprinted from *Policy Analysis in Political Science* (1985), Nelson-Hall Publishers.

"The Federal Government and Higher Education," by Lawrence E. Gladieux, Arthur M. Hauptman, and Laura Greene Knapp, reprinted from *Higher Education in American Society*, edited by P. G. Altback, R. O. Berdahl, and J. P. Gumport (2005), Johns Hopkins University Press.

"Policy Environments and System Design: Understanding State Governance Structures," by Kathy Reeves Bracco et al., reprinted from *The Review of Higher Education* 23, no. 1 (1999), Johns Hopkins University Press.

"Are The States and Public Higher Education Striking a New Bargain?" by David W. Breneman, reprinted from *AGB Public Policy Paper Series* 4, no. 4 (June 2004), Association of Governing Boards of Universities and Colleges.

"Effects of Key State Policies on Private Colleges and Universities: Sustaining Private-Sector Capacity in the Face of Higher Education Access Challenge," by Fred Thompson and William Zumeta, reprinted from *Economics of Education Review* 20, no. 6 (2001), Elsevier Ltd.

"Higher Education Policies and Representation," by C. E. Cook, reprinted from *Lobbying for Higher Education: How Colleges and Universities Influence Federal Policy* (1998), by permission of Vanderbilt University Press.

"Policy Scholars Are from Venus; Policy Makers are from Mars," by Robert Birnbaum, reprinted from *The Review of Higher Education* 23, no. 2 (winter 2000), Johns Hopkins University Press.

"The Study of Public Policy," by James E. Anderson, reprinted from *Public Policy-Making* (1975), Praeger Publishers/Greenwood Publishing Group, Inc.

"The Science of Muddling Through," by Charles E. Lindblom, reprinted from *Public Administration Review* 19, no. 2 (1959), American Society for Public Administration.

"The Scientific Method, Social Science, and Policy Analysis," by Lewis G. Irwin, reprinted from *The Policy Analyst's Handbook: Rational Problem Solving in a Political Word* (2003), M. E. Sharpe, Inc., Publisher.

"Innovation & Diffusion Models in Policy Research," by Francis Stokes Berry and William D. Berry, reprinted from *Theories of the Policy Process*, Second Edition, edited by P.S. Sabatier (2007), by permission of Perseus Books Group.

"Substance Vs. Politics: Through the Dark Mirror of Governance Reform," by D. W. Leslie and R. J. Novak, reprinted from *Educational Policy* 17, no. 1 (2003), by permission of Sage Publications.

"Understanding the Relationship of Federal Policies and Community Colleges: A Proposed Analytical Policy Framework," by Cheryl D. Lovell, reprinted from *Journal of Applied Research in the Community College* 7, no. 2 (2000), New Forums Press, Inc.

"Conducting Policy Analysis in Higher Education," by Judith I. Gill and Laura Saunders, reprinted from *Developing Effective Policy Analysis in Higher Education* 14, no. 4 (1992), Jossey-Bass Publishers, Inc.

"Claiming Common Ground: State Policymaking for Improving College Readiness and Success," by Patrick M. Callan et al. (March 2006).

"Reluctant Partners, Problem Definition, and Legislative Intent: K-16 Policy for Latino College Success," by Maricela Oliva, reprinted from *Journal of Hispanic Higher Education* 3, no. 2 (2004), by permission of Sage Publications, Inc.

"A Typology of Federal and State Programs Designed to Promote College Enrollment," by Laura W. Perna et al., reprinted from *Journal of Higher Education* 79, no. 3 (2008), Journal of Higher Education.

"Effectiveness of Statewide Articulation Agreements on the Probability of Transfer: A Preliminary Policy Analysis," by Gregory M. Anderson, Jeffery C. Sun, and Mariana Alfonso, reprinted from *The Review of Higher Education* 29, no. 3 (2006), Johns Hopkins University Press.

"Access to What? Mission Differentiation and Academic Stratification in U.S. Public Higher Education," by Michael N. Bastedo and Patricia J. Gumport, reprinted from *Higher Education* 46, no. 3 (2003), Kluwer Academic Publishers.

"Minority Enrollment Demand for Higher Education at Historically Black Colleges and Universities from 1976 to 1998: An Empirical Analysis," by Macki Sissoko and Liang-Rong Shiau, reprinted from *The Journal of Higher Education* 76, no. 2 (2005), Journal of Higher Education.

"Patterns of Finance: Revolution, Evolution, or More of the Same?" by D. Bruce Johnson, reprinted from *The Review of Higher Education* 21, no. 3 (1998), Johns Hopkins University Press.

"Equity and Efficiency of Community College Appropriations: The Role of Local Financing," by Alicia C. Dowd and John L. Grant, reprinted from *The Review of Higher Education* 29, no. 2 (2005), Johns Hopkins University Press.

"Affordability: Obtaining and Making Sense of Information about How Students, Families, and States Pay for Higher Education," by Joni E. Finney and Patrick J. Kelly, reprinted from *Change* 36, no. 4 (2004), Taylor and Francis, Inc.

"The Causes and Consequences of Public College Tuition Inflation," by Michael Mumper and Melissa L. Freeman, reprinted from *Higher Education: Handbook of Theory and Research* 20, edited by J.C. Smart (2005), Springer Science and Business Media.

"Hitting Home: The Case for Making Opportunity Affordable," by Travis Reindl (2007), by permission of author.

"Federal Financial Aid: How Well Does It Work?" by Sarah E. Turner, reprinted from *Higher Education: Handbook of Theory and Research* 16 (2001), Springer Science and Business Media.

# PART I

## *FOUNDATIONS OF PUBLIC POLICY AND HIGHER EDUCATION*

# The Integration of Higher Education and Public Policy: A Complex and Often Misunderstood Nexus

## by TONI E. LARSON AND CHERYL D. LOVELL

This section of the Reader contains classic, historic contributions relating to the nature of policy, political theory, and specific readings on policy inquiry and analysis. With these readings we believe there is a foundation that will provide the reader with general and subtle understandings of the complex dynamics of higher education as it interacts with the policymaking process. This section of the Reader is divided into three major parts: (a) What is policy?, (b) the arenas of policymaking, and (c) the processes or methods of policy inquiry.

## What is Policy?

This section begins with definitions, concepts, and foundational readings that provide an overview of public policymaking. Insights into the encompassing environment of policymaking, in which our higher education institutions are only one component, will be presented as well. Generally speaking, it is helpful to understand that public policy is an interdisciplinary field of inquiry that draws upon research in the social sciences and it is most often associated with the political science discipline and the study of public administration.

A generalized definition of public policy is the collection of policies embodied in constitutions, statutes, rules, and regulations that have been enacted by various governments at some level. These are official acts the government enacts according to formal rules for adoption of policies. Another school of thought, however, would include the less formal actions and interpretations taken by government agents as well. Thus public policy is not always completely evident. It is subject to a variety of forces that act upon the official language adopted through various processes such as lawmaking and rulemaking. Public policy is complex and seldom clear cut.

Acknowledging that interpretation is an underlying element of public policy, certain common themes run through various definitions of public policy. Public policy allows authoritative actors to use their power and influence to follow a course of action with the intent of achieving a particular public purpose. It provides a framework for a collective course of action that attempts to provide a solution to a societal problem or situation. Public policies allocate resources and/or reflect values. They are adopted through a formalized process with the action being generally accepted.

From these general definitions of public policy, it is useful to turn to the readings included in this "Foundation Section" to gain a deeper understanding of the various views of policy from a historical and contemporary point of view. Wildavsky's book, *The Art and Craft of Policy Analysis* (1973), offers a good beginning for expanding one's knowledge on public policy, particularly in the chapter

"Between Planning and Politics," where he leans toward the rational approach to policy. He thinks of policy analysis as a hybrid that uses both the intellect and social interaction to guide policy. Politics is about preferences and social interaction as well as planning, which is about intellectual design. The reading discusses the rationality of politics, planning, and policy analysis. It further explains such concepts as system, efficiency, coordination, and consistency.

With Wildavsky's thinking in mind, it is useful to read Kingdon's chapter "Wrapping Things Up," found in his book, *Agendas, Alternatives, and Public Policies* (1995). Kingdon describes the two major pre-decision policy processes as "agenda setting" and "alternative specification" and the importance of key participants in both of these activities. He further elaborates on the separate streams of problems, policies, and politics and the fact that for a while these streams are separate only to be joined later at some critical juncture. "Policy entrepreneurs" are the actors willing to take certain proposals to the public arena and attempt to see them to fruition. According to Kingdon, the policy process is somewhat random but there is also a degree of pattern as "evident in three fundamental sources: Processes within each stream, processes that structure couplings, and general constraints on the system" (p. 206).

Following Kingdon is Sabatier's framework for policymaking. He believes for any one policy an extremely complex set of circumstances can be identified that brought it about. Sabatier states, in *Theories of the Policy Process* (2007), that these circumstances involve hundreds of interest groups, a significant period of time, the complexity of government itself, technical disputes, and values. He states that we have little choice but to simplify presuppositions and that there are two different strategies for doing so. One of these is done in an implicit, ad hoc fashion, the other in a scientific manner. He then presents several different frameworks based on a set of four criteria. To be considered a framework for the development of policy, each must meet the criteria of being (1) a scientific theory, (2) the subject of "recent conceptual development and/or empirical testing," (3) a theory that explains much of the policy process, and (4) a framework that addresses a broad set of factors (p. 8).

Further, Ripley emphasizes the importance of context, or the setting in which any one policy is found. Policy has a lot to do with the environment inside and outside government. Environmental elements include policies and programs already in place, statements given, and actions taken regarding those policies, program results, and relationships among key actors. Using these elements, Ripley in *Policy Analysis in Political Science* (1985), provides a model of the policy making process at the national level. The stages of policymaking identified by Ripley include agenda setting, goal formulation and legitimation, program implementation, evaluation, and decisions about the future.

## Policymaking and Arenas of Policymaking

How and why policymakers adopt new or revise old policies is an extremely complicated process, and one that is not totally understood. As a basic premise, the need for new or different policies occurs because of interlocking changes within the current environment. Situations change and policies to address the changing circumstances are needed.

Policymaking is a complex course of loosely coupled relationships and nonlinear weaving among various environmental components, actors, and processes. Idea formation or agenda setting, policymaking or alternative selection, policy implementation, and evaluation exist within an environment that is constantly changing. The actors in this complex arena include institutions, organizations, interest groups, individuals, opinion leaders, and political leaders. Ideas are transmitted through a variety of sources: media, reports, diffusion, replication, informal communication, and discourse. Ultimately stakeholders bring an issue to the official policymaking arena where a solution is selected from among various alternatives for implementation and evaluation. This policymaking process is intended to result in a decision for the public good.

There are several theories and concepts about the ways in which ideas to change or create new policies rise to the political surface for consideration and adoption; there are also various ways in which policymakers decide which policy should be selected. After some change in the environment, individuals, opinion leaders, political leaders, interest groups, coalitions, organizations, agencies, corporations, and institutions begin to generate ideas to adjust to the change. The ideas for a change in a policy area come from a variety of sources and through a variety of processes. For example, ideas come to people through experience, lesson drawing, opinion, ideology, intuition, judgment, discourse, and research and analysis.

Additionally, various theories have been developed to explain the adoption of ideas. Among the commonly known theories and concepts used to explain how policies are developed and selected are included here:

1. rational choice—relying on the outcome of "the unplanned result of everybody fighting for his or her own self interest" (Stone, 1988, p. xi);
2. bounded rationality (Simon, 1957)—acting with limited (bounded) knowledge thus satisficing rather than maximizing (Birnbaum, 1988);
3. muddling through or incrementalism (Lindblom, 1959)—choosing in a random fashion based on small goals and limited alternatives;
4. mixed scanning (Etzioni, 1967)—combining "fundamental 'rationalistic' decision making with incrementalism" (Stone, 1988, p. 306);
5. garbage can (Cohen, March, & Olsen, 1972)—using a solution that has been around for awhile, one that is waiting for a problem to appear to which it can be applied;
6. cybernetic (Morgan, 1986)—steering a course to avoid obstacles;
7. opportunism—taking advantage of a situation to promote a long sought goal;
8. diffusion—adopting policy from others; and
9. punctuated equilibrium (Baumgartner & Jones, 1991)—policy change "alternates between incremental drift and rapid, major shifts of existing arrangements" (Van Der Slik, 2001, p. 28).

These theories all help to explain a part of the policymaking process. Experience, opinion, intuition, judgment, ideology, discourse, lesson drawing, research, and influence in the forms of persuasion, bargaining, collaboration, and power need to be factored into describing what policies are discussed and selected. These concepts are, of course, much more complex than what is presented here. Even in their abbreviated form, however, their description contributes to an understanding of how policies are chosen and changed. These theories and concepts help us understand why people select the policies they do. They help us understand the complexity of policy selection. In reality it is no doubt true that none of the theories or concepts act in isolation. Like the policymaking process itself, interaction, complexity, and murkiness are the rule.

Policymakers have a variety of tools available to them to implement the policies they have adopted. Among the tools available for policymakers are those ranging from non-coercive to coercive: being supportive of the change, requesting voluntary compliance, encouraging partnerships, setting the agenda or framework, using persuasion, using general incentives, providing recognition for compliance, providing for increased funding, providing for increased subsidies, providing for performance funding, reducing the amount and complexity of regulations, reducing the bureaucracy, providing for compulsory compliance, mandating pre- and post-audits, providing for enforcement, increasing regulations, establishing penalties for noncompliance, and implementing line item budgeting. When and how these policy instruments or tools are employed depends upon a variety of factors including the reasons behind a policy shift, the amount of support that exists for the change, the speed with which the change needs to be implemented, past experience with the various policy instruments, and the desired effect.

We now turn to the specific application of policymaking at different levels of government and activities. The first reading in the section on policymaking and arenas of policymaking is from *Higher Education in American Society* (2005). The chapter of particular interest regarding higher education policymaking at the federal level is "The Federal Government and Higher Education" by Gladieux, Hauptman, and Knapp. Higher education is primarily the responsibility of state government, but the federal government plays an important role in the areas of student financial aid, student loans, and funds for research and development. Also, included in this work are discussions of nontraditional and graduate student aid, tax policies, and federal regulations, as well as access and affordability. This reading provides a good overview of the role of the federal government and its affect on higher education.

Bracco, Richardson, Callan, and Finney (1999) apply policymaking to the state arena of government in "Policy Environments and System Design: Understanding State Governance Structures," as they look "at the impact of structure, leadership, and context on system performance" (p. 24).

The first sections of the paper describe the methodology used and provide a review of the relevant literature. This is followed by a description of the framework used in the study; subsequently the framework is applied to three states, Michigan, Georgia, and Illinois. These three states are illustrative of the major different characteristics of governance systems. Michigan has a planning agency, Georgia has a consolidated governing board, and Illinois has a coordinating board. In a newly developed framework, the authors discuss the two dimensions critical to understanding a state system. They are the interaction between a policy environment and the use of market forces and "a system design which determines provider responsibilities, capacities, and linkages to each other and to elected leaders" (p. 43). Misalignment of these factors can bring about a poorly functioning system of higher education.

A further exploration at the state level of policymaking is presented by Breneman (2004) in "Are the States and Public Higher Education Striking a New Bargain." Here he asks the question "Is the relationship between states and higher education changing?" In the face of declining support from state budgets, increasingly higher tuitions, and more reliance on foundation endowments, public higher education institutions appear to be becoming more on their own. Breneman analyzes experiments leading to more independence in seven states: Colorado, Florida, Oregon, South Carolina, Texas, Virginia, and Washington. In general, these states have provided greater flexibility to higher education in one or more areas, including tuition setting, reduced regulatory burden, performance contracts, and vouchers. The various proposals are all basically reduce to "(1) considerable tuition increases, (2) greater independence for institutions from the state, and (3) state subsidies increasingly directed to students rather than to institutions" (p. 12). Breneman warns that without care these experiments could result in a more stratified system of higher education.

Next we turn to a reading that explores the effect of policy at the state level on private institutions of higher education. In their article "Effects of Key State Policies on Private Colleges and Universities," Thompson and Zumeta (2001) conclude that some public policies threaten the health of private colleges and universities. Those policies mainly are significant tuition-price differences and low levels of funding for student financial aid, particularly need-based aid. Thus, examined in this work are the variables of tuition, state-funded student aid, and public institution density, with density being "computed by dividing the number of public and private collegiate institutions in each state in each of the relevant years by the state's population" (Appendix A). Two types of analyses are used to address the issues raised in this work. A regression model is used to show the "effect of public sector tuition and state student aid on private college and university enrollment." Market segmentation models are also used. Besides addressing the private college arena, this article demonstrates how modeling can be used in policy inquiry/analysis. As the authors conclude, "it is desirable for policymakers to have access to empirical analysis that sheds light on the relationship between state policies and enrollments in private higher education."

In a further exploration of the policymaking process, it is important to note that lobbyists can play an important role as Cook discusses in "Higher Education Policies and Representation." She observes that until fairly recently advocacy on the part of higher education officials was seen as a dirty business. However, Cook makes the case that it has become extremely important for higher education officials to participate in the policymaking process, both legislatively and administratively. She puts forth the premise that in "1995–96 a paradigm shift occurred." Higher education participants became much more involved in the process. The higher education community needs to ensure that the federal government continues to be a positive force with policies supportive of higher education. Cook makes the point that even given the importance of higher education, federal policymaking has been piecemeal with the role of the national government as rather ambiguous. Over time the role of the federal government as in relationship to higher education has expanded; funding and regulation have increased.

Finally, there is much discussion about linking academic research to policymaking. Just how much should researchers be involved in policymaking and how much should they tailor their research to the needs of policymakers are questions to consider. Birnbaum puts forth what he labels four "misleading assumptions" regarding "higher education policy scholarship and policy making." These misleading assumptions are (1) it is possible for policymakers to agree on policy problems and the type of research that should be done to address the problems; (2) policy scholars are not engaged in policy related work; (3) policymakers are not influenced by policy research; and (4) more policy research would improve policymaking (p.120). In his article "Policy Scholars Are from Venus; Policy Makers Are from Mars," Birnbaum examines these assumptions. He goes on to say that policy scholars and policymakers are from two different and distinct cultures and that research may never be able to fully address the needs of policymakers. Policy research and policymaking are both independent variables; they are not reliant on one another. Birnbaum concludes "that there is little scholars can do to make higher education policy scholarship more immediately useful to policymakers" (p. 127). Since we cannot know what policy issues will be relevant in the future, it is best if policy research agendas are driven by the interest of the researchers. The accumulation of interest-driven research over time will inform policy debates.

## Policy Research and Policy Analysis

Policy research and policy analysis are two forms used to explore and examine policy issues. Policy analysis is the form most likely to be used in public policymaking. Policy analysis is important to the adoption of public policies because it provides a process to guide decision-making and implementation; it is action oriented. The aim of policy analysis is to improve and inform the solution of public problems. Policy research, on the other hand, is more explanatory and descriptive and focuses on background and historical information regarding an issue. It does not provide information necessary for the selection of the best course of action to address a public policy; however, it does give the policy researcher a good idea of the history and how we arrived at the point in the issue we are at today.

The components of policy analysis allow the policy actors to understand the issue and its background, to identify the problem to be addressed, to identify alternative solutions to the problem, to establish criteria for evaluating the identified alternatives, to evaluate the solutions, and to select the best alternative based on established criteria. Other forms of policy-related exploration would include policy evaluation, which is answering the question of what the effect of a current policy is, and exploration of the policymaking process itself. Cross-cultural and cross-institutional understanding is another form of policy exploration. Several tools are available for use by the analyst to help provide information regarding the selected alternatives. Among them are cost/benefit analysis, social cost/benefit analysis, tradeoff analysis, and systems analysis. The problem always confronted by a public policy analyst is that issues are not static. Issues exist in a dynamic and constantly changing world.

In any case policy research, analysis, and evaluation provide numerous advantages and opportunities. These forms of analyses and exploration can (1) bring to light various alternatives to a public policy issue; (2) help policy makers to ask the right questions; (3) point out the need for positive change and action; (4) provide information and advice; (5) help to make sense of things; (6) promote discourse in a democratic society; (7) bring an authoritative voice to a chaotic, political world; (8) establish credibility; (9) provide a way of talking about the topic; and (10) help to keep the debate honest. But even given all these advantages of good analyses, one dilemma faced by policy analysts is finding ways to attract the attention of policymakers. One of the most promising suggestions is for researchers and analysts to address issues of current concern to policymakers though as Birnbaum suggests, this may not be as easy as we had hoped. Policymakers often accept relevant information enthusiastically—the problem being, is the information timely? What are the needs of policymakers? What are the emerging issues that might be of interest? Of equal importance is ensuring that the information is written with the policymaker in mind.

The first reading in this subsection provides a general discussion of various facets of public policy and policymaking. Anderson was among the first authors to discuss the nature of policymaking and to provide an approach to policy research. In "The Study of Public Policy," he states that policy should be studied for scientific, professional, and political reasons. A functional definition of policy given by the author is that it is "a purposive course of action followed by an actor or set of actors in dealing with a problem or matter of concern." Anderson subscribes to the school that believes public policies are enactments (not "informal actions") of the branches of government in the form of statutes, executive orders or edicts, rules, and judicial interpretations. Definitions of policy demands, policy decisions, policy statements, policy outputs, and policy outcomes are given.

The definition section of the chapter is followed by a discussion of how enactments come about and theories of decision making. Anderson identifies the rational, incremental, and mixed-scanning theories as ways of looking at how policies come into being. He then points out that these theories should be placed in the context of the environment. He goes on to discuss various system theories as ways of approaching policy analysis and identifies the stages of policy development as problem formation, formulation, adoption, implementation, and evaluation.

Lindblom is another of the classic writers in the field of policymaking. The work included in this Reader is well known among those interested in the topic. Explored are two different concepts of policy formulation. Lindblom states that democracies change policies primarily through incremental adjustments. Change seldom happens through large steps. "The Science of 'Muddling Through'" is one of the classic works regarding policy where Lindblom compares two different approaches to policy formulation, the "branch method," and the "root method." The branch method, also referred to as the "successive limited comparison" approach, builds from current situations; the root method, also referred to as the "rational-comprehensive" approach, starts anew each time. The author contends that the branch method is more realistic, that the root approach is in reality impossible. The branch approach uses small incremental steps, building on current policies to help limit the field of possibilities, and incorporating the human factor in the process. The main thrust of the article is a critique of the rational-comprehensive (root) approach. The critique addresses evaluation and empirical analysis (values), relations between means and ends, the test of "good" policy, non-comprehensive analysis, relevance and realism, and succession of comparisons and discusses the limitations of each in the root approach.

A more practical approach to policy analysis, one that can be used by analysts when exploring a policy issue, is presented in Irwin's chapter (2003) "The Scientific Method, Social Science, and Policy Analysis." Here he explains three "sequential and nested processes" that confront the analyst. The first of these is the scientific method, the elements of which are question identification, answer theorizing, and confirmation through reasoning and observation. "The basic goal of the scientific method is *empirical analysis*" (p. 4). Irwin makes the point that applying the scientific method to the world of social science is a difficult task at best. The challenge of uncertainty is the main reason. The world of human beings and their activities is very unpredictable. After a discussion of empirical analysis (questions of "is") and normative concerns (questions of "ought") and some of the challenges faced by a policy analyst, Irwin turns to a description of a framework for a policy analysis project. Irwin's framework is a nine-step process, beginning with problem identification and ending with implementation, supervision, and assessment of results. He makes the point that no analyst can fully evaluate an issue or problem.

Another aspect of policy research and policy analysis are the theories of policy adoption and the diffusion theory. Berry and Berry (2007) acknowledge that most policymaking is incremental but that at some point in time there was a "nonincremental *innovation*," or in other words, a new program was adopted by a government. "New" is defined as any program new to the government adopting it. In this work we find a discussion of the diffusion theory, another way of looking at how issues make it to agendas and how policymaking occurs. In "Innovation and Diffusion Models in Policy Research," the authors review "the dominant theories of government innovation in the public policy literature" (p. 223). Much reliance is placed on models of both individual and organizational innovation. "There are two principal forms of explanation for the adoption of a new program by a state: internal determinants and diffusion models" (p. 224). The authors describe both and after a discussion of each, they examine the methodologies used to test them. Many of the early studies were "single-explanation," that is they looked at either internal determinants or diffusion, and have been deemed by the authors to be highly flawed. Berry and Berry developed a model that shows the effects of both factors simultaneously. They find this model to be a much more satisfactory explanation of government innovation.

A case study approach to policy analysis is found in "Substance vs. Politics: Through the Dark Mirror of Governance Reform" (2003). Leslie and Novak present a critique of current methods of inquiry suggesting that improvements are needed. Further, an issue of continuing interest and importance to higher education is explored, that of governance. The authors report on five case studies that explore changes in higher education governance structures in particular states. Leslie and Novak conclude that each case was unique but that there was "a discernable shift toward decentralization and a more reasoned balance of authority between central board control and institutional discretion" (p. 116). Politics and political leaders were important factors in the reforms. The authors suggest that using "qualitative heuristics" and applying them to multiple case studies might achieve a richer analysis of higher education policy issues. They argue that the existing methods of inquiry are insufficient to support adequate understanding.

A simpler view of understanding the impact of the policymaking process is presented in the article by Lovell (2000) "Understanding the Relationship of Federal Policies and Community Colleges: A Proposed Analytical Policy Framework," where she developed a policy framework to be used to understand the relationship to and influence of federal policies. In this analysis, the impact is to community colleges; however, the analytical framework could be used to understand the broader impact of federal policies to any sector of higher education. Very little is written about the "effect" side of the policymaking process, and we thought this brief example would keep the reader focused not only on the policymaking aspects but also on the implications side to the policy actions.

Another example that lays out a practical approach to policy analysis is by Gill and Saunders. The main thrust of the work by these two authors is to "lay out a road map for the policy analyst" and to present a way to improve policy analysis. In the chapter "Conducting Policy Analysis in Higher Education" (1992), they discuss the tools of policy analysis, how to do policy analysis, and the written report. The tools of policy analysis are the "iterative process, intuition and judgment, and the advice and opinions of others." How to do policy analysis includes diagnosing the problem (defining objectives, understanding the environment, identifying boundaries and limits, and an initial statement) and "unraveling the policy analysis knot" (four basic components which are the policy issue, environment, implementation, alternatives or recommendations). As pointed out by the authors, policy analysis is not a linear process and the analyst must be open to changing circumstances. Policy analysis is an iterative process requiring the analyst to continually reevaluate the contents of her/his work.

From the readings on the definitions of policy, the arenas of policymaking, and the research and analysis of policy we believe we have provided a foundation on which to better understand the context of the current policy issues facing higher education that are included in Section II of this Reader.

## References

Baumgartner, F. R., & Jones, B. D. (1991). Agenda dynamics and policy subsystems. *Journal of Politics, 53*(4), 1044–1074.

Cohen, M. D., March, J. G., & Olsen, J. (1972). A garbage can model of organizational choice. *Administrative Quarterly, 17*, 1–25.

Etzioni, A. (1967). Mixed scanning: A third approach to decision-making. *Public Administration Review, 27*, 385–392.

Lindblom, C. E. (1959). The science of 'muddling through.' *Public Administration Review, 19*, 79–88.

Morgan, D. R., & England, R. E. (1988). The two faces of privatization. *Public Administration Review, 48*(6), 979–987.

Simon, H. A. (1957). *Administrative behavior: A study of decision-making process in administrative organization* (2nd ed.). New York: Macmillan.

Stone, D. (1988). *Policy paradox and political reason.* Harper Collins.

Van Der Slik, J. R. (2001). *Intruding on academe: The assertion of political control in Illinois.* Carbondale and Edwardsville, IL: Southern Illinois University Press.

# CHAPTER 1:
# WHAT IS POLICY?

# Between Planning and Politics: Intellect vs. Interaction as Analysis

## Aaron Wildavsky

Professors and policy analysts share one thing at least: they prefer explanations depending on latent rather than manifest functions—theories that are not obvious because they can account for action more profound than the specific behavior to be explained. After all, if things are just as they seem on the surface, who needs theorists? These academic scribblers have differed critically, however, in their evaluation of the mysterious mechanisms that guide society.

Beginning with the two Adams—Ferguson and Smith—the "invisible hand" of self-interest was found to guide buyers and sellers to serve each other, and hence society at large, without anyone necessarily intending this serendipitous outcome. The results before us (increase in national income, bread and butter on the table, each without conscious central coordination) and the theory (each actor trying to make a better deal) are on different levels. A closer look shows that this (in)famous theory is based on the superiority of social interaction over intellectual cogitation. The interactions in economic markets, where alterations in outcomes go on all the time, lead to better results than central direction by one mind that decides everything once and for all. Observe that it is not conscious intent but actual outcomes, even (perhaps especially) when unintended, which provide the criteria of success.

Let me recapitulate: motives may be base; outcomes can be unintended; intelligence is interactive. If self-interest is the motive, where (after all, Adam Smith was a professor of moral philosophy) does virtue come in? Through exchange! Morality does not depend on what motivates individual actions but on the results of social interaction. How are collective objectives set? They aren't; collective objectives are by-products of individual interactions. No one sets out to make the nation richer or to achieve a decent distribution of income. If these come about, they are not the results of public objectives but rather the collective consequences of private acts. Individuals make decisions; their social exchanges make outcomes.[1] How is intelligence brought to bear on human activity? By many minds interacting. How is coordination of these multitudes accomplished? Pretty much as crowds are coordinated when crossing streets; by each individual adjusting to the others. Coordination does not require a coordinator; coordination takes place so long as there is mutual benefit in the individual transaction.

Just as constitutions are written to guard against previous predators, so, too, theories react to the past as well as point to the future. Adam Smith saw himself as a radical critic of the mercantilist doctrine that justified a vast variety of state interventions in economic life.[2] As the doctrines of his school became the prevailing wisdom, they were in turn challenged by succeeding generations who found Smith's ideas self-centered, reactive, and fatalistic. His "hidden hand" had four unappealing aspects: (1) its motivation—selfishness over altruism; (2) its passivity—resultants instead of decisions; (3) its irrationality—interaction rather than intellect; and (4) its unpredictability—the future had become fate.

The secret was out. That hidden hand was a mailed fist. Capitalism was a legalized form of robbery, an institutionalized exploitation. Law, government, philosophy, all were rationalizations of capitalist class interests who owned the means of production. What else could one expect of a corrupt class that made a virtue out of evil by elevating self-interest to a moral principle?

Who, then, should be the repository of communal interests? If virtue resided in everyman alone, anarchy was the result. People were good but contaminated by a selfish state. They needed liberation not only from capitalism but from all forms of state power. Where the people collectively exercised their power through the state—for it was the people as a whole who represented virtue—the regime was called democratic socialism. When the masses did not recognize their own interests—failed, on their own, as Lenin said, to develop a revolutionary consciousness but instead retained the false consciousness of bourgeois reformism inculcated by the capitalist class—virtue resided in a revolutionary fragment. This vanguard of the proletariat, able to cleanse its consciousness of illusion, became the Communist Party.

Under socialism men would control their own destiny; fatalism would be replaced by conscious collective coordination. The name for this enterprise was scientific socialism. It was socialist in that, as the fraternal community of the dispossessed, it spoke in the name of all. It was scientific in professing a historical, developmental theory of society, which explained where it had come from and predicted where it would go (or where socialists would take it). Scientific socialism fused modern consciousness and medieval community. In the name of all, a collective consciousness, acting as one mind, would make rationality serve fraternity. And, best of all, the end would be known at the beginning because of planning.

Of special importance to students of policy analysis, however, is a difference among socialist traditions. As the participants themselves were wont to say, social democrats were likely to sacrifice socialism to democracy but their communist rivals would give up democracy for socialism. Social democracy therefore legitimized social interaction as a mode of decision making in politics. Once political forces are allowed free rein, including party competition, there cannot be one correct solution apart from the consent of the political actors. Politics becomes part of planning. The parties must establish and maintain rules (or conventions) for the give-and-take, bargaining, and negotiation by which political decisions must be made. It is essential also that they accept these decisions, apart from whether they wholly approve of the outcome, because they cannot expect to prevail on every occasion. Decisions no longer can be correct but can only be acceptable in that the criteria for truth are established by agreement through social interaction.

Between capitalism and socialism, then, between choice through social interaction and intellectual cogitation, where does policy analysis come in? Policy analysis is an effort to combine elements from the two traditions—infusing social interaction with intellectual direction and vice versa. I shall approach this attempt at synthesis by trying to clarify these opposing tendencies in the form of ideal models of pure intellect (called planning), and pure interaction (called politics).

If interaction does not demand common objectives, can our actions make sense if they are not goal-directed? They can. Do objectives have any place in policy analysis? They do. Efforts to modify intellect by interaction raise doubts about whether policy can be rational. I argue that it can. But can it also be moral? Applying social interaction in analysis of policy leads one to wonder whether one must morally accept whatever comes forth from this pulling and hauling. No. Must a collective conscience, then, guide all interaction? That depends on how we interpret the conversion of individual preferences into collective choices.

Consider the implications of Jung's wise words: "If a man is capable of leading a responsible life himself, then he is also conscious of his duties to the community." The intuitive meaning is clear enough: people who meet their immediate obligations to family and friends are those also more likely to recognize their implication in wider matters to which they ought to contribute. Obligation is learned most readily at home. At the communal level, however, this argument presupposes a compatibility between the individual and the collective that is open to challenge. Suppose what is good for General Motors (or for you and me) is not necessarily good for the country, and that such a clash of interests rends the fabric of society. Do citizens, then, have any right to base actions (that is, to do analysis) on selfish motives? It is argued that selfishness can serve society; in the clash of interests, citizens must give up part of what they have to get part of what they want; this exchange moderates their demands and, willy-nilly, serves others. If their motives were altruistic, the critical response goes, the general interest would have been paramount, and vulgar trades would be less necessary. To trade in values is to lose virtue. From this viewpoint, analysis would seem to be immoral, either because good motives would make it unnecessary to trade or because better motives would forbid it. We had better discuss this further, for if individual interests and collective exchanges are ruled out, policy analysis will be prohibited.

## Exchange

Analysis is based on exchange: what individuals or groups will give up for what they can get. If we can get what we want without ceding anything, then we are either in a condition of perfect freedom—no obstacles to the realization of desires—or of absolute constraint—no movement can take place, because (all desires being absolute) nothing can be given up. Either there is no need to think because all desires are compatible, or there is no point in thinking because it can lead to no action. Neither thought leading to action, nor action influencing thought, makes sense.

The fundamental objection to exchange is that its motivation is seen as immoral. By reducing mankind to mere individual wants, citizens become sybarites: self-centered, indulgent, materialistic bundles of appetites—mouths without morals. Empathy gives way to selfishness. The citizen in a democracy, who should be an active contributor, becomes instead an apathetic ingestor driven by purely personal desires. Economic man, who recognizes no goals transcending himself, makes decisions that affect others thinking only of his own private profit. Democratic choice becomes perverted into the sum of individual choices based on materialist motivations. If exchange is dirty, policy analysis is culturally contaminated.

It is not always clear whether the objection is to exchange or to the motivation behind it. If the motivation were collective rather than individual, if its objective were moral and not material, would it then be all right to give up one thing for another? If justice for all could not be achieved, could more justice for some (as in preferential hiring of minorities) be traded off, in the vulgar jargon of the profession, for less to others? If the object of a political community were to inculcate virtue in its citizens by establishing and enforcing norms of proper conduct, could one consider that some means of obtaining virtue might be sacrificed in order to obtain others?

A nice example of this objection to exchange is the requirement that proposed federal government programs contain environmental impact statements showing absence of significantly adverse consequences before action can take place. Protecting the environment becomes a constraint around which other interests must work; that is, it becomes part of the objectives that must be satisfied in all other policies. We can describe the environment with the phrase fashionable in the sixties; it is a nonnegotiable demand. A reasonably rich society undoubtedly has room to accommodate the environmental consideration. Suppose, however, more than one objective becomes a nonnegotiable (nonexchangeable) constraint? There is now a requirement for inflationary impact statements, and few would argue that reducing inflation is unimportant. Recent proposals also call for impact statements on health, safety, education, and employment. Now the plot thickens. Where nothing is allowed to vary, everything remains constant. If all or most basic values are untouchable, change becomes impossible. The environment must remain sacrosanct, yet energy must be saved; how, then, can auto exhaust devices (which use more gas) be justified? If energy must be conserved and nuclear proliferation halted, how can one justify abandoning breeder reactors—which increase energy but also the opportunity to make nuclear explosives? Evidently, exchanges for good causes are being made. Once one escapes this *reductio ad absurdum* by saying that only comparatively few values must remain nonnegotiable, we are back again to exchange.

## Motivation

Perhaps it is not exchange itself but the bad motives that lie behind it that are found objectionable. Mandeville's dictum—private vices, public virtues—may be rejected if we hold that public virtue reduces private vices. By acting for community and common interest, it is thought, public life may be elevated.

Motives, however, are (almost) always mixed. The question of which motive should prevail, therefore, is often crucial to public policy. Suppose some doctors make excessive income from medicaid for the poor. Should programs be designed to prevent their abuses, programs that make life difficult for doctors who behave honorably? Obviously, profiteering cannot be allowed. Or can it, *if* our objective is not only to deter the few but help the many? The moral of the story may take more palatable form if we consider people who are called "welfare cheats" because they deceive the government in order to receive payments. Should governmental programs be designed to catch cheaters, if this means also (as it does) denying or delaying welfare for the honest majority who need it? Just as citizens have varying motives, governmental programs that are meant to serve them also exhibit multiple motivation.

To suggest that anyone believes justice can be achieved and virtue inculcated by fiat (down with self-interest and up with community!) would be absurd. Everyone knows that governments that choose public over private interests often achieve neither and may even end up elevating a favored few in the name of the many. Clearly there is an empirical question about which sort of motivation leads to the best ends. The reverse—how can justice and virtue be achieved if they are not explicitly recognized as the proper wellspring of human motivation?—is more nearly arguable.

This argument has two components that are of the utmost importance for analyzing policy. One is that motives must be acceptable, and the other that justice must be knowable. Another way of putting it is that results, however good, do not count if they lack justification according to motives acknowledged to be good. If it is intentions rather than consequences of our actions that matter, evaluation of public policy would be about internal states. We would ask if intentions were good rather than looking to external effects and asking if accomplishments have been realized.

Evaluation of intentions would require knowledge of how to achieve justice (or other ultimate goals) because it would then be appropriate that good motives be distinguished from bad motives just as good results are differentiated from bad results. If intent were equivalent to accomplishment, good motives always would be the harbinger of good deeds.

President Jimmy Carter's presentation of his energy program illustrates the contemporary importance of good motives and conscious intent. Conscious emphasis on good motives is evident from his reiteration of the theme that the burden of conservation and cost would be shared fairly under his programs. After the Organization of Petroleum Exporting Countries (OPEC) raised the price of oil many times over, the federal government, to prevent precipitous price increases in the United States, controlled the price of old oil at less than half its price abroad. Now one way to encourage conservation is to let the domestic price of crude oil rise to the price it would bring if sold abroad. If oil were valued within the United States at the international price, motorists, home-owners, industrialists, indeed, all consumers of oil would take steps to reduce consumption, or switch to alternatives if that made sense. But the solution has two fatal flaws. For one thing, oil companies would profit by selling their old oil at new prices, widely considered unfair; for another, unseen hands—namely, market prices—would be determining what America would do.

On the surface, President Carter's oil policy appeared anomalous: old domestic crude remained price controlled while—on top of this subsidy to bring the price down—a substantial tax on oil was recommended, a tax that would, in effect, bring the domestic price up to the international price. What's the difference between letting the market set the price and setting a similar price by taxes? Nothing and everything: nothing in that the economic consequences are equivalent; everything in that when the government sets the price it is acting with conscious intent rather than appearing to give way to impersonal forces. Instead of letting the oil companies make money and taxing it away afterward, the government gets its share first. The important thing for us to understand from this example is the two ways in which decisions are made: interaction among people or intellectual determination of what would be just and effective.

Here is the distinction we have been seeking between intellectual and interactive modes of analysis—between analysis as an intellectual construct and analysis as a product of social interaction of which thought is but a part. If analysis is a social phenomenon, based on interaction among interests, then analysis must stem from a variety of motivations, not all of which are necessarily good. Nor, without knowledge of means and ends—what is good for man and how to achieve it—would it be either desirable or possible to completely control man's motives and aspirations or make them equivalent. But contingency is a condition of life. Only if analysis were solely a product of the mind and that mind knew the difference between good and evil and could therefore integrate motives and aspirations, could policy be judged by intention rather than execution.

# Planning and Politics

Let us call analysis as an intellectual construct "pure planning" and analysis as social interaction "pure politics" or hereafter, in short, planning and politics. Here planning is defined as current action to secure future consequences; the more future consequences planners control, the better they have planned.[3] Planning, therefore, requires causal knowledge theories of society to predict the paths of the complex sequences of desired actions and power to sustain this effort. Once conflict is admitted over whose preferences are to prevail (there being ineradicable differences between the needs, wants, desires, and hence preferences of people), comprehensive national economic and social planning fails either from intellectual presumption or political persuasion. Planners do not have adequate knowledge or power. The more planning fails to secure intended results, the more it tries to become relevant by accommodating itself to social forces. Consequently, by shortening time horizons (annual plans), by reducing the need for prediction (adaptive planning), and by limiting coercion (indicative plans, which merely point the way), planning becomes indistinguishable from whatever means of decision it was meant to supplant.

## Planning

Suppose, however, to sharpen the contrast, we say planning does have perfect knowledge and power in a context without conflict and thus deserves its new nametag, "pure planning." With compatible (indeed, mutually supportive) desires and preferences, there could be right or wrong solutions to all problems. Reason would reign supreme. Decisions would be made as if a single mind were supporting a single set of preferences. Nor would there be need for error correction because, with knowledge, there would be no error. Dissent would either be unnecessary, in the absence of conflict, or uncalled for, because the Grand Planners would know what is right; acting in the common interest, their motives are above suspicion. Hence, also, there would be no need to hedge them about with restrictions on term of office or extent of authority. Centralization and comprehensiveness would be valued because they are possible and desirable. Attributes that might lead to further differentiation, such as race, religion, class, ethnicity, sex, and language, would be discouraged; after all, why worry about diverse viewpoints or alternative hypotheses when there is only one right way and that is discoverable by reason? Ends do justify means. If ends are in harmony, and means are always appropriate to them, what else would justify means if not ends? To get an answer to that question, we must leave planning and turn to politics.

## Politics

Politics is about preferences. The point about preferences is that they are not ultimately knowable, either by those who profess them or by those who propose to act for those who prefer them. Because there is no one source of ultimate wisdom, no one knows people's preferences better than they, themselves, do. And, hoping to learn, people reserve the right to change preferences frequently to suit their experience. Ends or objectives, therefore, are held to be provisional—to be modified by experience or to accommodate others.

> Political choice is never purely a matter of being for this program or against that policy. It is always partly a matter of being willing to compromise and adjust desires to various conflicting factions. Therefore, as soon as any group's wishes are revealed everyone else's wishes may, and indeed normally do, shift. . . . Priorities, that is, depend upon estimates of preference distributions. They may change whenever any particular set of preferences becomes known, and they never exist as entities separate and apart from their strategic possibility of enactment. Political options must always be understood to include some commitment to the decision-making process itself and to the value of agreement.[4]

The criterion of choice in planning is obvious—the one policy known to be right—but what is the correct criterion for politics? That there is no correct criterion. Does this mean that whatever is done is right? Hardly. It does mean that short of agreement no one is authoritatively able to say another alternative is better.

What takes the place of the correct criterion? An incorrect one? Not quite. Correction of error. All politicians and political institutions are considered, Martin Landau said, risky actors.[5] Power in American politics, for example, is limited in time and tenure, so that no one can impose a truth without opposition. Power is divided through the separation of powers, subdivided through federalism, and checks and balances are multiplied at every level. Conflict is desired (both to use the self-interest of one group or institution to counter the others and to refine preferences under pressure) and feared (because it may undermine the understanding that decisions will be considered acceptable, providing they get through corrective procedures giving everyone a chance to be heard, allowing parties to alternate in office, specifying due process, and so on).

The political equivalent of original sin is that men and the institutions they create are fallible if not fallacious and error-prone if not erroneous. They must be hedged with restraints, especially when they are sure they are right. It is hard to say whether criticism is valued more for its constructive aspects—making improvements—than for its destructive ones—exposing error. In practice, however, if there must be a choice, destructive criticism is preferable; procedures must be pursued in the realization that no one knows ultimate ends. All the more reason, then, to protect criticism politically. A decentralization of authority, the very untidiness of politics that contrasts with the neatness of planning, allows for alternatives rejected at one time and place to be available at others, should they have been passed over by mistake.

Politics does not consider preferences to be finally formed, as in planning, but to be undergoing continual reformulation. Personal preferences are not infallible, coming *ex cathedra*, as it were, from *homo politicus*, but they must be presentable, regarded as coming from a person who is entitled to them.

Political preferences are personal. They belong to a person (group or organization) until that person changes them. If the charge of "false consciousness" (propaganda, advertising, and indoctrination that make people mistake their true interests) merely meant that people did not realize they should have other preferences, it might be seen as just another effort at suasion. Surely, if we knew better, we might feel differently. But if false consciousness means that there are others with "true consciousness," who know what is better for us than we do, then we have been stripped of our political persona. Politics declines and planning takes over.


## Comparison

Both politics and planning, at least in their modern manifestations, claim as their territory the general welfare of citizens. One shows this through interaction, the other through cogitation. The choice would seem to lie in whether one expects better or worse outcomes from intellectual or from interactive modes of decision making.

Wait a minute! Haven't I turned the usual understanding upside down? Isn't it governmental planning that is commonly considered to be social, and economic markets and pluralistic politics that are said to be individualistic? Yes, of course, but no, not necessarily. An important distinction is to be made between the *locus of decision* and the *mode of calculation*. As larger proportions of the national product are redistributed through the government, or as government owns and operates more of industry, no doubt government is an increasingly important locus of decision. Because individual citizens are not directly deciding for themselves, but through government, such decisions commonly are called collective. The locus or site or arena of decision is collective. My interest, however, is policy analysis—recognition, reformulation, and resolution of problems. Looked at as modes of calculation, markets and politics are social because they are based on interaction among many minds. Planning, by contrast, is pursued as if there were but one collective mind whose intellectual operations posed and solved problems. As suggested in Table 1, politics and markets share the same analytic style: decisions are made through social mechanisms—exchange and bargaining by many minds—aimed at correcting error and securing agreement (rather than avoidance of error and a single proper choice) and administered by reacting to the other participants rather than by sending down orders and expecting obedience. As for the style of policy analysis, appearances are deceiving: politics appears to be individual but is in fact social, whereas planning seems to be social but actually is single-minded.

**Table 1. Alternative Styles of Policy Analysis**

|  | Social interaction | Intellectual cogitation |
|---|---|---|
| Institutions | Markets and politics | Planning |
| Calculations | Partial | Comprehensive |
| Calculators | Many minds interacting | Single-minded decision |
| Decision making | Exchange and bargaining | Comprehending and deciding |
| Error | Correction | Avoidance |
| Criteria | Agreement | Right |
| Administration | Reactions | Orders |

If we accept this socially interactive view of markets and politics, what is one to make of common criticism that these institutions prejudice decision making? Markets accept the prevailing distribution of income when some say public policy should be designed to make it more egalitarian. Politics, others say, leads those who have less to use government as a lever for redistributing income to themselves, in effect expropriating property that doesn't belong to them. Monopolies let manipulators of markets administer prices for their own benefit, and political parties mobilize masses to monopolize government, denying minorities the medium to express their own message. Where there is agreement that these conditions (and their subsequent consequences) break the rules for decent decision making, they are regarded as imperfections in the respective arenas and institutions. Rules for regulating interaction (such as conditions for allowing monopoly or of specifying who may vote) are subject to change, both through evaluation and intervention, so as to improve interaction. Social interaction may be preferred to intellectual cogitation as a style of analysis without the need to accept only current modes. Indeed, the stress on correcting error suggests that alteration in interaction is desirable.

Of course, I do not pretend that planning or politics exist in pure essence; they are ideal types, designed to display differences when they are pushed to extremes. What happens, however, if they are merged? If the reader will allow me my preference for two-thirds politics and one-third planning, this hybrid of social interaction and intellectual cogitation may be called policy analysis.

## Analysis

If analysis were purely intellectual, analysts would be everything, or if analysis were purely interactive, analysts would be nothing. Are we faced, then, with a choice between mind without matter or force without foresight? No. Our task is to develop a hybrid, called policy analysis, which uses intellect to help guide rather than replace social interaction. This peculiar amalgam called policy analysis may be better understood if we ask why either pure planning or pure politics alone are unsatisfactory as modes of making collective choices.

The effects of interaction may not be visible to participants. They may have to be identified mainly through intellectual constructs, for direct observation has severe limits. When many agencies are operating numerous programs in any area of policy, which they are most of the time nowadays, it may be hard to connect acts with consequences. Efforts of agencies to act and observe what happens may be unsuccessful without theories to tell them how things are connected. Agencies can hope, of course, that if other agencies are adversely affected by these consequences, they will act to correct them. This sort of defensive action, which Lindblom calls mutual partisan adjustment, is a major rationale in favor of social interaction as a mode of decision making. Unfortunate consequences for other actors need not be predicted if those who already have suffered can take effective corrective action. Instead of having to figure out what various groups want, or will accept—as if it all had to be done in and by a single mind—policy preferences are registered directly through interaction on actual programs. Aside from whether, without analysis, anyone knows what is happening and what might be done about it, turning consequences over to others raises fundamental questions about the basis for social interaction.

A political system in which all interests are fairly represented would work differently from one in which important ones are left out or occupy a weak position. The outcomes of political processes cannot be considered apart from their design, which is an intellectual construct as well as a social fact. Outcomes may be altered not only by seeking them directly but also indirectly by redesigning interaction (who participates under what rules).

Action outside the rules (monopoly, for instance) may not be socially desirable. The classical conditions of the marketplace—competition, information, internalization of costs—must be satisfied for prices to represent optimal choices. If not, governmental intervention may be justified to restore competition, to provide as public information that which is not in the interest of any firm to supply privately, and to arrange compensation when the behavior of one party imposes burdens on another that, like pollution, cannot be alleviated through the marketplace. All these market imperfections depend upon theoretical schemes for recognition and for correction.

Dependence upon social interaction is inappropriate, moreover, when the acknowledged objective is that nothing should happen. The purpose of analysis of nuclear warfare is precisely to ensure that the main hypothesis need never be tested.[6] The trouble with experience is that one needs so much of it. The attraction of analysis is that one need not live through everything.

At first glance, the purely intellectual mode seems ideally suited to policy analysis, which seeks to bring intelligence to bear on policy. But this identity is achieved at the cost of triviality. Instead of innumerable minds, each with somewhat different perspectives, there is really only one. Instead of conflict there is consensus. Instead of problem solving, in short, there is suppression of problems. Everyone either gets what he wants, or has to want what he gets. Thought is made supreme at the expense of having anything worth thinking about.

When planning is infused with politics, however, social forces guide intelligence. The danger, of course, is that interest will overwhelm intellect. By being tied to power, intellect becomes the handmaiden of power, the excuse for inexcusable behavior. Autonomy is exalted above reciprocity. The alternative, however, is worse: when intellect alone is powerful, there can be neither autonomy, because the Great Planner is always right, nor reciprocity, because the good of all has been determined by intellect, not by interaction. My conclusion is that policy analysis makes more sense as an aid to (rather than substitute for) the politics of social interaction.

The way things stand, however, the world does not appear to be suffering from a surfeit of intelligence. Usually things work the other way around: social forces use analysis to advance as well as to understand their own interests. The task of policy analysis, therefore, is the weighty and ancient one of speaking truth to power.

For policy analysis to modify pure politics (if social interaction automatically produced social welfare there would be no need for intelligence), it must expect to lose more often than it wins. And this is as it should be. Who said analysts possess wisdom? False prophets abound now as before. Who said analysts exemplify virtue? They have interests of their own, and they are also part of social life that is suspect. And who expects social forces to give way without much travail? There is a place for the voice of experience, which says "show me!" to self-deluded theorists.

Yet there is something to be said for invoking intelligence. Aside from the small victories and larger number of defeats, analysis, not in one instance but in many, not at one time but over decades, performs a critical function. Citizens must be able to decide what is in their interest, to interpret their own experience in some way they can explain to themselves. This requires thought. When that thought leads them to reinterpret their experience so as to shift their notion of what is problematic, policy analysis, accepted as a body of thought about public policy, may be more influential than is apparent from isolated acts.

Practitioners of policy analysis seek to have it neither absorbed into social interaction nor substituted for it. Analysis supplements social interaction by using the theoretical mode to formulate and test hypotheses that can help bring precision to the judgment of decision makers. Analysis uses social interaction both to understand what is happening and to suggest how it might be altered. Studies of political feasibility, for instance, may help with the allocation of analytic time: which programs are most worth pursuing because change is possible. The purpose of studying feasibility, however, is not to equate the feasible with the desirable but may also be to make the desirable do-able. Merely to say that something should be done—without saying anything about how—is an abdication of responsibility.[7] But it is one thing to notice organizational resistance to change, still another to use this understanding to help bring out necessary changes. The purpose of analysis is improvement—how to get from a worse to a better place—not to curse the fates.

If analysis is to aid judgment, it must simplify calculations. The world in the analyst's models must abstract from the overwhelming complexity of experience. Otherwise, experience itself would be a better guide. Analysis makes use of social forces to simplify calculations about preferences. The alternative would be to invent preferences and imagine interaction. To do so would be morally wrong—the people already involved are the best experts on how they feel—and intellectually obtuse—that is, to reinvent the wheel.

A difficulty with health policy—how we should seek to restrain exploding medical costs—illustrates the question of calculation because there is now no alternative to governmental regulation. One approach is to apply controls to each doctor, patient, and hospital for each service and capital cost. This form of direct regulation, covering hundreds of millions of transactions, would involve almost every person in the United States. Implementation would become intolerable. Obviously, if anyone is to understand what they are doing, the social relationships among doctors, patients and hospitals (rather than their individual transactions) have to be regulated. One alternative is to set much higher deductibles for private insurance and governmental subsidies, forcing cost consciousness on consumers. But this alternative is politically unfeasible today because most people are not willing to pay much more in direct costs for a service they believe is their due. In the long run, one might hope to persuade people to take greater responsibility for their own health. Right now, however, private solutions are not possible, nor will Americans accept a wholly governmental system by abolishing private medicine. If these interpretations are reasonable, government must move in with regulations that create incentives for the actors to consider cost as part of their everyday transactions. Hospitals might be given fixed budgets,[8] depending on the number and kinds of patients, and left to decide what mix of services should be offered. Regulating social interaction appears to be a better way of doing analysis than is minute control of mass behavior.

Here I am again appearing to accept miserable motives by founding analysis on manipulating self-interest rather than on expanding altruism. Surely, a critic would say, giving rein to brute empiricism—nudging interactions this way or that—is no substitute for a more rational and humane health policy. Have I, then, by emphasizing interaction, subordinated intellect? Is there a larger role for rationality than I have been prepared to admit? That depends on what rationality is about—intelligence, interaction, or both.

## Rationality

In the world of action we know that politics and planning—social interaction and intellectual design—coexist. Problems are discovered, solved, and reformulated both by interchange among organized actors and by their efforts to guide events along paths they anticipate in their minds. Not only our thoughts but our institutions may be conceived of as attempts to increase the probability of some desired outcomes and decrease the probability of others. Once we abandon pure planning, which occurs only in the mind, or pure politics, in which action carries its own (and only) interpretation, intention commingles with interaction. What are we to make of the rationality, of the conscious design, in policy analysis?

1. Rationality is real.
2. Rationality is relative.
3. Rationality is retrospective as well as prospective.
4. Rationality is a property of politics as well as of planning.

I shall begin by arguing that politics follow the same form as planning; any differences do not reflect commonly considered components of rational choice. The substantial difference is that the norms of planning: efficiency, comprehensiveness, and others have no content, and the norms of politics: agreement, bargaining, and so on, do. Because of their inherent ambiguity, I shall argue further, objectives absent in the present are retrospectively rationalized into the past. We then act as if we once knew what we were doing and, therefore, can be trusted to know what to do next. Nor is retrospective rationalization (we act, review the effects of what we have done, and then decide what our objectives really were) necessarily a bad thing because it enables us to (re)create a past as we make a future. If rationality can be retrospective as well as prospective, then it follows that planning and politics, as they are practiced, do not differ with respect to reason.

## Politics and Planning are Equally (Ir)Rational[9]

Once human ignorance and recalcitrance are reintroduced into planning and unlimited knowledge and power are taken away, so that planning has to cope with politics, planners must revise what they do in order to take account of events they can neither predict nor control. When planning is placed amid continual adjustment to a changing world, it becomes hard to distinguish from any other method of decision. By making planning reasonable we render it inseparable from the techniques of decision it was designed to supplant. One plans the way one governs; one does the best possible at the time hoping that future information will make for improvement as circumstances change. Some call this adaptive planning; others call it muddling through. Under the criteria of adaptation, almost any way of making decisions in a social context can be considered to be planning.[10] One cannot, for instance, discuss democracy for long without using the words goal, alternative, appraisal, objective, which are at the heart of almost any contemporary definition of planning.

May electoral democracy then be considered a mode of planning? The United States does not seek to achieve goals stated in a national plan. Yet that does not mean the country has no goals for its decision makers to aim at. There are institutions—the Federal Reserve Board, Council of Economic Advisers, Office of Management and Budget, congressional committees, among many—whose task is to find goals and policies that embody these goals. Specific pieces of legislation are dedicated to full employment, ending or mitigating the effects of pollution, building highways, expanding recreational opportunities, improving agricultural productivity, on and on. When goals conflict, new decisions must be made on how much of each to try to achieve. Moreover, these goals are related to ultimate objectives. The Preamble to the Constitution states national goals, and the body presents an institutional plan for achieving them. The government of the United States seeks to achieve domestic prosperity and to protect its interest overseas; while these broad objectives remain constant the intermediate goals change in response to forces in society.

West Churchman (in *The Systems Approach*)[11] postulates that planning has to do with multi-stage decision making and "hence it must study (1) a decision maker who (2) chooses among alternative courses of action in order to reach (3) certain first-stage goals, which lead to (4) other-stage objectives." It is easy to parallel this model for electoral democracy as the operation of (1) the electorate which (2) chooses from a group of candidates in order to reach (3) certain first-stage goals, which lead to (4) the implicit goals of the society at large. Table 2 illustrates more thoroughly the parallels between models of the planning system and the electoral system. Please notice the close correspondence not only between the broad outlines of the two systems, but also between the components that comprise the system.

Similar comparisons could be made between the system of planning and that of legislation and administration. Consider a recent description of how public policy is made: "Generically, one can identify at least six different steps in the process of making government policy—publicizing a problem, initiating a search for a solution, evaluating alternative solutions, choosing a solution or a combination of solutions, implementing the measures decided upon, and finally, evaluating the consequences of a measure."[12] At this level of description there appears to be no significant difference between the United States (and almost any other government, for that matter) and societies that engage in planning.

In reality, planning is not defended for what it accomplishes but for what it symbolizes—rationality. Planning is conceived to be the way in which intelligence is applied to social problems. The efforts of planners are presumably better than other people's because they result in policy proposals that are systematic, efficient, coordinated, and consistent. Words like these convey the superiority of planning, and the virtue of planning is that it embodies universal criteria of rational choice.

## The Imperatives

Key words appear over and over: planning is good because it is *systematic* rather than random, *efficient* rather than wasteful, *coordinated* rather than helter-skelter, *consistent* rather than contradictory, and above all, *rational* rather than unreasonable. For deeper understanding of why planning is preferred, consider these norms as instructions to decision makers, observing what they do.

**Table 2**[13]

| The planning system (PS) | The electoral democratic system |
|---|---|
| **Program 1: Legitimacy** | **Program 1: Legitimacy** |
| Relationship between the planning system (PS) and the decision makers<br>(a) Justification (why the PS should exist and its role)<br>(b) Staffing the PS and establishing responsibility and authority<br>(c) The communication subsystem<br>   (1) Persuasion (selling the PS)<br>   (2) Mutual education<br>   (3) Politics identifying and changing the power structure of the organization<br>(d) Implementation (installing the plan) | Relationship between the constitution, etc, and the electorate<br>(a) Justification (why democracy should exist and its role)<br>(b) Designing the institutions of democracy and establishing responsibility and authority<br>(c) The communication subsystem<br>   (1) Persuasion (e.g., the Federalist, etc.)<br>   (2) Public schools and media<br>   (3) Politics (constitutional amendments, judiciary)<br>(d) Implementation (setting up the institutions and operating them) |
| **Program 2: Analysis** | **Program 2: Analysis** |
| Measurement (identification, classification, prediction, etc.)<br>(a) Identifying the decision makers, and customers of the larger system<br>(b) Discovering and inventing the alternatives<br>(c) Identifying the first-stage goals<br>(d) Identifying the ultimate objectives<br>(e) Measuring the effectiveness of each alternative for each first stage goal<br>(f) Measuring the effectiveness of each first-stage goal for ultimate objectives<br>(g) Estimating the optimal alternative | Measurement (identification, classification, prediction, etc.)<br>(a) Identifying interest groups, setting the franchise, etc.<br>(b) Selecting candidates for office<br>(c) Identifying and lobbying for first-stage goals and policies<br>(d) Identifying the ultimate aims of society (e.g., Goal for Americans, Bill of Rights, etc.)<br>(e) Assessing the candidate and his policy platform<br>(f) Assessing the effectiveness of policies for ultimate objectives (e.g., the Vietnam war as protecting democracy)<br>(g) Voting for the candidates of one's choice |
| **Program 3: Testing** *(verifying the plan)* | **Program 3: Testing** *(does the democracy work?)* |
| (a) Simulation and parallel testing<br>(b) Controlling the plan once implemented | (a) Comparison with other nations, self-appraisal by the citizenry<br>(b) Checks and balances, news media, public debate, the opposition |

Table adapted from student paper by Owen McShane

## System

What does it mean to say that decisions should be made in a systematic manner? A word like "careful" will not do because planners cannot be presumed to be more careful than other people. Perhaps "orderly" is better; it implies a checklist of items to be taken into account, but anyone can make a list. "Systematic" as a designation implies further that one knows the right variables in the correct order to put into the list, and can specify their relationships. The essential meaning of systematic, therefore, is having qualities of a system—that is, a series of variables whose interactions are known and whose outputs can be predicted from knowledge of their inputs. System is another word for theory or model, a device explaining and predicting events in the real world in a way that permits manipulation.[14] To say that one is being systematic, consequently, implies that one has causal knowledge, whether one does or does not.

## Efficiency

Modern man has a deeply rooted belief that objectives should be attained at the lowest cost. Who can quarrel with that? But technical efficiency should never be considered in a vacuum. It does not tell you where to go, but only that you should arrive there (or go part of the way) with the least effort. The great questions are: efficiency for whom and for what? Some goals (destroying other nations in nuclear war, decreasing the living standards of the poverty-stricken in order to benefit the wealthy) one does not wish achieved at all, let alone efficiently. Efficiency, therefore, raises once more the prior question of objectives.

Stress on efficiency assumes agreed-upon objectives. Knowledge of the general welfare, to which the plan is supposed to contribute, turns out to be one of its major assumptions. Without this knowledge, planners would have no legitimacy to tell others what part they should play in this grand scheme.

## Coordination

Coordination is one of the golden words of our time. Offhand, I can think of no way in which the word is used that implies disapproval. Policies should be coordinated; they should not run every which way. No one wants his child described as uncoordinated. Many of the world's ills are attributed to lack of coordination in government.

But what does it mean? Policies should be mutually supportive rather than contradictory. People should not work at cross-purposes. Participants in any activity should contribute to a common purpose at the appropriate time and in the right amount to achieve coordination. A should facilitate B in order to achieve C. From this intuitive sense of coordination four important (and possibly contradictory) meanings can be derived.

If there is a common objective, then efficiency requires that it be achieved with the smallest input of resources. When these resources are supplied by a number of actors (hence the need for coordination), they must all contribute their proper share at the correct time. If their actions turn out to be efficient, it means they contributed just what they should have, no more, no less.

Coordination then equals efficiency, which is highly prized because achieving it means avoiding bad things: duplication, overlapping, and redundancy. These are bad because they result in unnecessary effort, expending resources that might be used more effectively for other purposes. But now we complicate matters by introducing another criterion that is (for good reason) much less talked about when planning is discussed. I refer to reliability, the probability that a function will be performed. Heretofore we have assumed that reliability was subsumed in the definition of efficiency. It has been discussed as if the policy in mind had to work only once. Yet we all know that major problems of designing policies can depend on the need to have them go on working at a set level of reliability. For this reason, as Martin Landau brilliantly demonstrates, redundancy is built into most human enterprises.[15] We ensure against failure by having adequate reserves and by creating several mechanisms to perform a task in the event one should fail. Telling us simply to avoid duplication, therefore, gives us no useful instruction. We need to know how much and what kind of redundancy to build into our programs. To coordinate one must be able to get others to do things they do not want to do. Participants in a common enterprise may act in a contradictory fashion because of ignorance. But when shown how they fit into the scheme of things, they can generally be expected to behave properly. If we moderate the assumption that a common purpose is involved, however, and admit the possibility (indeed the likelihood of conflict over goals, then coordination becomes another word for coercion. Because actors A and B disagree with goal C, they can be coordinated only by being told what to do, and then doing it. Coordination then becomes a form of coercion.

When bureaucrats tell one another to coordinate a policy, they mean that it should be cleared with other official participants who have some stake in the matter. This is a way of sharing the blame if things go wrong (each initial on the documents being another hostage against retribution). Because they cannot be coerced, their consent must be obtained. Bargaining has to take place to reconcile the differences; thus the policy may be modified, even at the cost of compromising its original purpose. In this sense coordination is another word for consent.

Coordination means achieving efficiency and reliability, consent and coercion. Telling other people to achieve coordination, therefore, does not tell them whether to coerce or bargain or stipulate what mixture of efficiency and reliability to attempt. An apt illustration is "consistency."

## Consistency

Do not run in all directions at once. Consistency may be conceived of as vertical (over a series of periods extending into the future) or horizontal (at a moment in time). Vertical consistency requires that the same policy be pursued for a time, horizontal consistency that it mesh with others at the same time. The former requires continuity of a powerful regime able to enforce its preferences; the latter, tremendous knowledge of how policies affect one another. These are demanding prerequisites. One requires rigidity to ensure continuity, the other, flexibility to achieve accommodation with other policies. Be firm, be pliant, are hard directions to follow simultaneously.

The divergent directions implied suggest that the virtue of consistency should not be taken for granted. It may well be desirable to pursue one task with energy and devotion but it may also prove valuable to hedge one's bets. Consistency secures a higher payoff for success but also imposes a steeper penalty for failure. If several divergent policies are being pursued in the same area they may interfere with each other but the chance may be greater that one will succeed. Like other admonitions, this one, "Be consistent" has its opposing proverb "Don't put all your eggs in one basket."

Consistency is not wholly compatible with adaptation. Although it may be desirable to pursue a steady course, it is also prudent to adapt to changing circumstances. There is the model of the unchanging objective pursued along numerous detours and tactical retreats but never abandoned and ultimately achieved. There is also the model of learning in which experience leads men to alter their objectives as well as the means of attaining them. They may come to believe the cost is too high or they may learn they prefer a different outcome. Apparent inconsistency may turn out to be a change in objectives. If both means and ends, policies and objectives, are changing simultaneously, consistency may turn out to be a will o' the wisp that eludes one's grasp.[16]

The resulting inconsistency may not matter so much, however, as long as alternative courses of action are thoroughly examined at each point of decision from this follows the usual advice to consider alternatives. Which ones? How many? Answers here depend on the inventiveness of planners, the acknowledged constraints, and the resources (in time, talent, and money) that can be spent on each. Though it used to be popular to say that all alternatives should be compared systematically, it has become evident that this method will not work. Knowledge is lacking and the cost is too high. The more diverse the society, by religion, race, class, region, the broader the span of alternatives likely to be considered and the more difficult it will be to secure agreement about their desirability. The number of alternatives considered should be infinite if the dimensions of the problem (such as time, money, skill, and size) are continuous.

Let us suppose that only a small number of alternatives will be considered. Which among the many should receive attention? Unfortunately no rules are written to tell us when to intervene in which possible decisions and how much time to devote to each.

We have gone a long way from the simple advice to consider alternatives. Now we know that this command does not tell anyone which decisions should interest him, how many alternatives he should consider, how much time and attention to devote to them, or whether he knows enough to make the whole enterprise worthwhile. To say that alternatives should be considered is to suggest that something better must exist without being able to isolate it.

## Rationality

If rationality means achieving one's goals in the optimal way, it refers here to technical efficiency, the principle of least effort. Paul Diesing argues,[17] however, that one can conceive of several levels of rationality for different aspects of society: the rationality of legal norms and of social structures; political rationality, which affects the maintenance of structures for decision; and economic rationality, devoted to increasing national wealth.

Strict economic rationality means getting the most national income out of an investment. The end is to increase real gross national product (GNP), no matter who receives it; the means is an investment expenditure, no matter who pays for it. To be economically rational is to increase growth to its maximum. What is good for the political system, however, may not be good for the economy and vice versa. The political effects of raising national income may differ according to who gets the increase or whether this increase strengthens or weakens governmental institutions. An analysis of public policy that does not consider incompatibilities among the different realms of rationality is bound to be partial and misleading.

Rationality is used also in the broader sense of reason. The rational man has goals that he tries to achieve by being systematic, efficient, consistent, and so on. Because rationality in the sense of reason has no independent meaning, it can have only such validity as imparted by the criteria that tell us what reasonable action is about. The injunction to plan (Think!) is empty. The key terms associated with it are proverbs or platitudes. Pursue goals! Consider alternatives! Obtain knowledge! Exercise power! Obtain consent! Or be flexible but do not alter your course. These imperatives have a noncontroversial ring to them, in part because they contain no operational guidance.

## "Retrospection"

By "rational," it should now be clear, we mean something like intended, designed, or purposeful. Something happens because it is supposed to. Rational behavior is action appropriately calculated to achieve a desired state of affairs. Yet we have seen that this definition is so broad it readily fits the disjunctive and disorderly world of politics. So-called norms of rationality, moreover, are devoid of content in that they do not tell anyone what to choose. No doubt the difficulty lies in confusing the wrongly reasonable—specifying alternatives, comparing them, and so on—with the really rational—securing intended results, with all that is implied of knowledge and power. Instead of analysis connecting instruments of policy to its objectives, we are offered criteria of what would constitute rationality on the supposition that actions embodying them will prove efficacious. Instead of devices for correcting errors, we get norms alleged to be errorless. In a way, this self-protective behavior is not surprising: why risk failure—which lies in comparing intentions with results—when one cannot ever fail if the success of a norm lies in its form?

Herbert Simon has made a valiant effort to save rationality.[18] By introducing "bounded rationality," Simon argues that people are intendedly rational, their behavior is goal-directed but, because their ability to calculate is limited and the world is complex, they do less well than they would like. Human rationality being bounded, people who would like to maximize end up "satisficing," that is, being satisfied with a solution sufficient to get them past the present decision. With this, I have no quarrel. Rationality is treated as a relationship between means and ends, which, because of human limitations, is necessarily circumscribed. There is, in a word, a little rationality, though not a whole lot.

## Intention and Inference

For present purposes, however, I would like to open up the question of intention: what do rational actors intend to do? Move toward their goals. But in what direction? How can we be goal-directed if we don't know what our goal is until we get there?

We are able to choose as we go along, so that we have the opportunity to choose objectives not only before we act but afterward, too. Actions are undertaken; along the way they intersect others, which together cause consequences—some of which may be attributed to what has just been done, others which belong to external causes, still others which are unexplained. This multiplicity and ambiguity may be used selectively to make the objectives we attribute to the past serve our aims for the future.

Any action can be related to a number of possible objectives. When the number of hospital beds is curtailed it may be related to reducing costs, decreasing unnecessary surgery, increasing income for doctors and hospitals, increasing control over the mix of surgical procedures, or improving the quality of care. The meaning of an act does not necessarily inhere in it like a sign naming a railway station; it must be inferred. This inference can take place only after the act—and numerous others related to it—are safely in the past. At that time there is no single self-evident "there there" for goal direction. It is possible always to invoke a number of possible goals as connected to the action. No one need be surprised, therefore, at retrospective rationalization, which is done to increase the coherence of past actions. We make sense of our past by considering future needs. The multiple potential in each act gives us opportunities, not only before we act but also after, when we know more about how to present ourselves and our objectives.

Karl Weick, whose theorizing has helped me make sense of organizational objectives, holds:

> Rationality seems better understood as a post-decision rather than a pre-decision occurrence. Rationality makes sense of what has been, not what will be. It is a process of justification in which past deeds are made to appear sensible to the actor himself and to those other persons to whom he feels accountable. It is difficult for a person to be rational if he does not know precisely what it is that he must be rational about. He can create rationality only when he has available some set of actions which can be viewed in several ways. It is possible for actors to make elaborate, detailed statements of their plans. However, the error comes if we assume that these plans then control their behavior. If we watch closely, it will become clear that the behavior is under the control of more determinants than just the vocally stated plan. And at the conclusion of actions, it will never be true that the plan as first stated will have been exactly accomplished. But something will have been accomplished, and it is this something, and the making sense of this something, that constitute rationality.[19]

All is not lost. Once we recognize that rationality has much in common with "rationalization," it may yet be saved. Rationality is like a rocker that goes both forward and back; it tries by intention and is saved by rationalization. One acts first and makes sense of it later. We rewrite history from present motives. By attributing new motivational meaning to what we have done, we try to learn what we ought to be doing. We get three strikes before we're out, the first by acting in the present, the second by interpreting the past into the present, and the third by imagining the future as if it had occurred already so that we can correct and control it before it happens. Is this, one wonders, an example of creativity or of hypocrisy?

## Retrospective Rationalization

The word "rationalize" or "rationalization" has at least two distinct meanings. One, according to Webster, is "to make conformable to principles satisfactory to reason." Here the question is whether reason resides in form or in function, in procedures or in consequences. The other meaning is deceitful: "To attribute (one's actions) to rational and creditable motives without adequate analysis of the true motives." Obviously, if I meant deceit, I should have said so. A word is needed that expresses our ability to make what we have done conform to reason as we understand it after we have acted. "Rationalization" has that meaning.

The word "rationalization" is often modified by "mere" as if it were only a poor excuse disconnected from real motivations. To rationalize, however, carries also the connotation of relating apparently disparate elements of behavior so as to make sense of them after, as well as before, we act. In this way, retrospective rationalization (hereinafter called "retrospection") is essential in policy analysis.

Retrospection is a method of incorporating the past into the present that we wish to become our future. For as the times change so also do the values we wish to turn into future objectives. Why, it is these very objectives, retrospection tells us, that we have been pursuing all along—dormant, asleep but still alive, immanent in our acts, ready for resurrection. Retrospection links what we now think we should do with what we ought to have done. Rationalization allows us to reformulate our problems without rejecting our past. If we want to act as analysts in prospect, we must also be able to make sense of our public lives in retrospect.

When social scientists speak of goal-directed behavior they mean that they try to understand and predict behavior as if it were geared to securing this or that objective. This is the origin of maximization models. Thus one speaks of maximizing sales or profits or budgets or survival or whatever. A successful prediction or explanation, however success is defined, does not mean that the true motive was discerned but only that the behavior produced in the model was similar to that observed in the world. Without a good fit between the model and observed behavior, that model must be reformulated (retrofitted, engineers say) to do better. Other objectives must now be introduced to produce a better fit. What is this but a retrospection of results?

Two stories, one far away in Nepal and the other near in the United States will show the potential of retrospection. Years ago in Nepal, I observed that bureaucrats in the field were reluctant to spend governmental funds allotted to them. Underspending authorized amounts was a major difficulty. Because studies of budgeting follow the desire of agencies to spend (often they are called spending agencies), I thought the difficulty could not lie with bad bureaucrats who, engaged in repetitive activities, must know what they are about, but with simple social scientists who assumed the wrong motivation. Investigation revealed that in the old regime of the Rana Prime Ministers, budgetary authorizations required numerous rules for proper accounting, which, if not punctiliously met, resulted in a fine of seven times the amount in question. Caution in spending was plainly advisable. Often, in the ordinary course of events, it is difficult to determine what is or is not correct accounting. Suppose a tractor was called from its home station to a farm and broke down there. Who was responsible for the repair, the station or the farm? Only if officials had connections, with the protection this implies, would they risk taking responsibility for the expenditure. Hence the tractor would remain unrepaired for months or years until higher authorities removed the risk by assigning accounting responsibility for repair.[20]

Was spending a bureaucratic objective or wasn't it? Yes, it was—but not the only one. Spending was an objective until it ran afoul of risk. It became possible to reformulate the problem from irrationality among field bureaucrats to inappropriate incentives applied by the government. It turned out further that the king and his advisors did not want to solve the problem as formulated, because their spending was tied to an even stronger objective—preventing unauthorized expenditure. How did they resolve this duality? In the usual way: they pressed alternatively on each front (one year spending and the next, accounting) without ever resolving the tension. Was their behavior rational? It depends on which motive you are willing to assign them at what time. Whenever the powers that be want to change, they will be able to choose what their objectives were as well as what they will be.

President Carter said the nation had a physical shortage of oil and that, therefore, the American people must support policies requiring sacrifice. Informed opinion was not agreed about the truth of such a shortage nor will we decide that here. Let us, instead, ask about the consequences of deciding after the fact that there had or had not been a shortage. If there was no oil shortage, there was little rationale for asking people to conserve or to pay higher taxes. If there is no shortage, why are prices so high? Either American oil companies are profiteering, which calls for attacks on them, or the foreign oil cartel, OPEC, is price gouging, which calls for an attack on it. Both approaches are unsatisfactory for a president who wishes to show that he is peaceful abroad and a protector of private enterprise at home. If, however, it could be argued that the world would run out of petroleum, the preferences of ecologists (who want less use for the environment's sake) and of business (which wants less use for cost's sake) could be reconciled under a motif of national unity. By making the one essential to the other, President Carter was trying retrospectively to rationalize the conflict between conservation and consumption. Amid massive change "Retrospection" is a bridge between experiences and future policies to maintain meaning within a recognizable universe.

## Reprise

Policy analysis, as I conceive it, is about change in patterns of social interaction. How does change happen? By joining planning to politics, social interaction gives analysis a historical outlook made up of the past pattern of agreements, including agreements to disagree until next time. From the organized actors, the constituent elements of this interaction, analysis gets its abiding interest in incentives to alter their behavior. And planning helps analysis bring intelligence to interaction, by rationalizing movement to a different pattern that may lead to improved future outcomes.

The trouble with social interaction is that you don't know how it will turn out in advance. People can't be trusted to be predictable. Lord knows what they'll do next, as the saying goes, for we surely don't. Accepting the consequences of social interaction is not only hard on the nerves but may be disquieting to a sense of justice. Who ever said that the way things turn out when we bid and bargain is how they ought to be? Not I. If the decks are stacked, the dealer always wins. Enter intellect to guide behavior and motivate morality. Intellect, however, can also be imperious; it can make things turn out right by rigging the rules. By limiting aspirations to internal consistency, intellect can always plead itself innocent of contamination with consequences. So long as reason is about right rules rather than right results, it remains internally consistent and externally vacuous. How can principles of rationality be reasonable if they are not operational?

If rationality is about results, however, how are results to be judged? By relating outcomes to objectives. Yet objectives are as much produced by social interaction as by intellectual postulation. There may be disagreements about what the original objectives were. In any event, we know objectives are likely to be multiple, conflicting, and vague. A way is needed to try out objectives posthumously, so to speak, after the act or, at least, as we go along. Rationality, therefore, is as much (or more) retrospective as it is prospective. Retrospection is a species of policy midwifery through which objectives are revamped to fit new conceptions of what is problematic and hence worthy of attempted solution. Retrospection is how we change without saying so.

Of what, then, does rationality consist? If reason is reduced to intention—the launching of glorious objectives and breath-taking procedures—then the reasonable becomes irrational, productive of cruel (and possibly unusual) consequences. Rationality is a reflexive relationship between acts and consequences, either one being used to justify the other. Sometimes we seek and subsequently achieve objectives postulated in advance; at other times we learn to change objectives as we act; occasionally we examine consequences and decide these were the results we should have wanted to achieve. Thus, if rationality can be retrospective as well as prospective, it can also be interactive as well as intellectual.

Where does one find social interaction and intellectual cogitation? Everywhere and nowhere: everywhere in that they are important components of choice in designing policies; nowhere in that they do not come labeled as such like the products of a sausage machine. With or without brand labels, they are independent of us. Because these categories do not force themselves upon us, however, we see them only where we choose. Therefore, it is important to view cogitation and interaction as general phenomena, operating at different levels, which can be made manifest when convenient. Our interest extends to the institutions through which policies are made and the doctrines (ideologies, if you prefer) on which they are based as well as the policies themselves. That is why I will illustrate here the tension between interaction and cogitation within institutions (the "Bias toward Federalism" is, in fact, a rule for resolving this tension), among doctrines (opportunity costs are calculated interactively and merit wants by cogitation), and among policies as the environmentalist drama is played out in "Ritual and Rationality, Economy and Environment."

## Notes

1.  Adam Smith, *The Wealth of Nations*, Andrew Skinner, ed. (Harmondsworth, Middlesex, Eng.: Pelican Books, 1970); Adam Ferguson, *An Essay on the History of Civil Society, 1767*, Duncan Forbes, ed. (Edinburgh: Edinburgh University Press, 1966).

2.  Aaron Wildavsky, with Frank Levy and Arnold Meltsner, *Urban Outcomes* (Berkeley and Los Angeles: University of California: Press, 1974).

3.  Aaron Wildavsky, "If Planning Is Everything, Maybe It's Nothing," *Policy Sciences*, Vol. 4, No. 2 (June 1973), pp. 127–153.

4.  Elaine Mates, "Paradox Lost—Majority Rule Regained," *Ethics*, Vol. 84, No. 1 (October 1973), p. 49

5.  Martin Landau, "Federalism, Redundancy and System Reliability," from *The Federal Polity in Publius*, Vol. 3, No. 2 (1973), pp. 173–196.

6.  Aaron Wildavsky, "Practical Consequences of the Theoretical Study of Defense Policy," *Public Administration Review*, Vol. 25, No. 1 (March 1965), pp. 90–103.

7.  Giandomenico Majone, "On the Notion of Political Feasibility," *European Journal of Political Research*, Amsterdam: Elsevier Scientific, Vol. 3 (1975); Arnold J. Meltsner, "Political Feasibility and Policy Analysis," *Public Administration Review*, Vol. 32, No. 6 (November/December 1972), pp. 859–867.

8.  Stuart H. Altman and Sanford L. Weiner, "Constraining the Medical Care System: Regulation as a Second Best Strategy," Working Paper #73 (Berkeley: Graduate School of Public Policy, University of California, 1977).

9.  Aaron Wildavsky, "If Planning Is Everything, Maybe It's Nothing," *Policy Sciences*, Vol. 4, No. 2 (June 1973), pp. 127–153.

10. Imre Lakatos, "History of Science and Its Rational Reconstructions," from *Boston Studies in the Philosophy of Science* VIII, 1970; Roger C. Buck and Robert S. Cohen, eds. (Dordrecht, Holland: D. Reidel, 1970), pp. 91–136; Paul Feyerabend, *Against Method* (Atlantic Highlands, N.J.: Humanities Press, 1975); Giandomenico Majone, "Policies as Theories," paper presented at the joint European Consortium for Political Research Workshops, Louvain, 1976.

11. C. West Churchman, *The Systems Approach* (New York: Delacorte Press, 1969), p. 150.

12. Richard Rose, "The Variability of Party Government: A Theoretical and Empirical Critique," *Political Studies*, Vol. 17, No. 4 (December 1969), p. 415.

13. Aaron Wildavsky, "If Planning Is Everything, Maybe It's Nothing," *Policy Sciences*, Vol. 4, No. 2 (June 1972), pp. 127–153.

14. See David Berlinski, "Systems Analysis," *Urban Affairs Quarterly*, Vol. 7, No. 1 (September 1970), pp. 104–126.

15. Martin Laudau, "Redundancy, Rationality and the Problem of Duplication and Overlap," *Public Administration Review*, Vol. 29, No. 4 (July/August 1969), pp. 346–358.

16. It is, by the way, often difficult to know when actions are inconsistent. Leaving aside obtaining accurate information, there are serious conceptual problems. Policies often are stated in general terms that leave ample scope for varying interpretations of their intent. Ambiguity sometimes performs a valuable political function by enabling people (who might otherwise disagree if everything was made clear) to get together. There cannot then be a firm criterion against which to judge consistency. There is also the question of conflicting perspectives among actors and observers. The observers may note an apparent commitment to a certain level and type of investment and see it vitiated by diversion of funds to wage increases. To the observer this means inconsistency. The actor, however, may feel consistent in pursuing his goal of political support. Given any two policies that lead to conflicts among two values one can always find a third value by which they are reconciled. Investment seemed to bring support when it was announced, and so, subsequently, does spending for other purposes when its turn comes. The actors' values may be rephrased as "the highest possible investment so long as it does not seriously affect immediate political support." In view of the pressures to meet the needs of different people variously situated in society, most decisions undoubtedly are made on such contingent basis. This is what it means to adapt to changing circumstance. As the goals of actors shift with time, consistency becomes a moving target, difficult to hit at best, impossible to locate at worst.

17. Paul Diesing, *Reason in Society: Five Types of Decisions and Their Social Conditions* (Urbana: University of Illinois Press, 1962).

18. Herbert Simon, "Cognitive Limits on Rationality." See also the demonstration that "satisficing" is compatible with prevailing doctrines of decision making under uncertainty in M. A. H. Dempster and Aaron Wildavsky, "Yes, Virginia, There Is No Magic Size for an Increment," in *The Political Economy of Spending: A Predictive Theory in the United States Federal Budgetary Process* (in progress).

19. Karl E. Weick, *The Social Psychology of Organizing* (Reading, Mass.: Addison-Wesley, 1969), p. 38.

20. Aaron Wildavsky, "Why Planning Fails in Nepal," *Administrative Science Quarterly*, Vol. 17, No. 4 (December 1972), pp. 508–528.

# Wrapping Things Up

## J. W. KINGDON

This book has considered why some subjects rise on governmental agendas while other subjects are neglected, and why people in and around government pay serious attention to some alternatives at the expense of others. The book is not about how presidents, members of Congress, or other authoritative figures make their final decisions. Instead, we have been occupied with understanding why participants deal with certain issues and neglect others. This chapter summarizes and ties together what we have learned.

Two major predecision processes have occupied us: agenda setting and alternative specification. A governmental agenda is a list of subjects to which officials are paying some serious attention at any given time. Thus an agenda-setting process narrows the set of subjects that could conceivably occupy their attention to the list on which they actually do focus. Obviously, there are agendas within agendas. They range from highly general agendas, such as the list of items occupying the president and his immediate inner circle, to rather specialized agendas, including the agendas of such subcommunities as biomedical research or waterway transportation. Subjects that do not appear on a general agenda may be very much alive on a specialized agenda.

The process of alternative specification narrows the large set of possible alternatives to that set from which choices actually are made. This distinction between agenda and alternatives proves to be very useful analytically, and we have returned to it repeatedly.

Why do some subjects rise on agendas while others are neglected? Why do some alternatives receive more attention than others? Some of our answers to these questions concentrate on participants: We uncover who affects agendas and alternatives, and why they do. Other answers explore the processes through which these participants affect agendas and alternatives. We have conceived of three streams of processes: problems, policies, and politics. People recognize problems, they generate proposals for public policy changes, and they engage in such political activities as election campaigns and pressure group lobbying. Each participant—president, members of Congress, civil servants, lobbyists, journalists, academics, etc.—can in principle be involved in each process (problem recognition, proposal formation, and politics). Policy is not the sole province of analysts, for instance, nor is politics the sole province of politicians. In practice, though, participants usually specialize in one or another process to a degree. Academics are more involved in policy formation than in politics, for instance, and parties are more involved in politics than in drafting detailed proposals. But conceptually, participants can be seen as different from processes.

Each of the participants and processes can act as an impetus or as a constraint. As an impetus, the participant or process boosts a subject higher on an agenda, or pushes an alternative into more active consideration. A president or congressional committee chair, for instance, decides to emphasize a subject. Or a problem is highlighted because a disaster occurs or because a well-known indicator changes. As a constraint, the participant or process dampens consideration of a subject or alternative. Vigorous pressure group opposition to an item, for instance, moves it down the list of priorities or even off the agenda. As an administration emphasizes its priorities, for another example, it limits people's ability to attend to other subjects. Concerns over budgetary costs of an item can also make its serious consideration quite unlikely.

# Agenda Setting

How are governmental agendas set? Our answer has concentrated on three explanations: problems, politics, and visible participants.

## Problems

Why do some problems come to occupy the attention of governmental officials more than other problems? The answer lies both in the means by which those officials learn about conditions and in the ways in which conditions become defined as problems. As to means, we have discussed indicators, focusing events, and feedback. Sometimes, a more or less systematic indicator simply shows that there is a condition out there. Indicators are used to assess the magnitude of the condition (e.g., the incidence of a disease or the cost of a program), and to discern changes in a condition. Both large magnitude and change catch officials' attention. Second, a focusing event—a disaster, crisis, personal experience, or powerful symbol—draws attention to some conditions more than to others. But such an event has only transient effects unless accompanied by a firmer indication of a problem, by a preexisting perception, or by a combination with other similar events. Third, officials learn about conditions through feedback about the operation of existing programs, either formal (e.g., routine monitoring of costs or program evaluation studies) or informal (e.g., streams of complaints flowing into congressional offices).

There is a difference between a condition and a problem. We put up with all kinds of conditions every day, and conditions do not rise to prominent places on policy agendas. Conditions come to be defined as problems, and have a better chance of rising on the agenda, when we come to believe that we should do something to change them. People in and around government define conditions as problems in several ways. First, conditions that violate important values are transformed into problems. Second, conditions become problems by comparison with other countries or other relevant units. Third, classifying a condition into one category rather than another may define it as one kind of problem or another. The lack of public transportation for handicapped people, for instance, can be classified as a transportation problem or as a civil rights problem, and the treatment of the subject is dramatically affected by the category.

Problems not only rise on governmental agendas, but they also fade from view. Why do they fade? First, government may address the problem, or fail to address it. In both cases, attention turns to something else, either because something has been done or because people are frustrated by failure and refuse to invest more of their time in a losing cause. Second, conditions that highlighted a problem may change—indicators drop instead of rise, or crises go away. Third, people may become accustomed to a condition or relabel a problem. Fourth, other items emerge and push the highly placed items aside. Finally, there may simply be inevitable cycles in attention; high growth rates level off, and fads come and go.

Problem recognition is critical to agenda setting. The chances of a given proposal or subject rising on an agenda are markedly enhanced if it is connected to an important problem. Some problems are seen as so pressing that they set agendas all by themselves. Once a particular problem is defined as pressing, whole classes of approaches are favored over others, and some alternatives are highlighted while others fall from view. So policy entrepreneurs invest considerable resources bringing their conception of problems to officials' attention, and trying to convince them to see problems their way. The recognition and definition of problems affect outcomes significantly.

## Politics

The second family of explanations for high or low agenda prominence is in the political stream. Independently of problem recognition or the development of policy proposals, political events flow along according to their own dynamics and their own rules. Participants perceive swings in national mood, elections bring new administrations to power and new partisan or ideological distributions to Congress, and interest groups of various descriptions press (or fail to press) their demands on government.

Developments in this political sphere are powerful agenda setters. A new administration, for instance, changes agendas all over town as it highlights its conceptions of problems and its proposals, and makes attention to subjects that are not among its high priorities much less likely. A national mood that is perceived to be profoundly conservative dampens attention to costly new initiatives, while a more tolerant national mood would allow for greater spending. The opposition of a powerful phalanx of interest groups makes it difficult—not impossible, but difficult—to contemplate some initiatives.

Consensus is built in the political stream by bargaining more than by persuasion. When participants recognize problems or settle on certain proposals in the policy stream, they do so largely by persuasion. They marshal indicators and argue that certain conditions ought to be defined as problems, or they argue that their proposals meet such logical tests as technical feasibility or value acceptability. But in the political stream, participants build consensus by bargaining—trading provisions for support, adding elected officials to coalitions by giving them concessions that they demand, or compromising from ideal positions that will gain wider acceptance.

The combination of national mood and elections is a more potent agenda setter than organized interests. Interest groups are often able to block consideration of proposals they do not prefer, or to adapt to an item already high on a governmental agenda by adding elements a bit more to their liking. They less often initiate considerations or set agendas on their own. And when organized interests come into conflict with the combination of national mood and elected politicians, the latter combination is likely to prevail, at least as far as setting an agenda is concerned.

## Visible Participants

Third, we made a distinction between visible and hidden participants. The visible cluster of actors, those who receive considerable press and public attention, include the president and his high-level appointees, prominent members of Congress, the media, and such elections-related actors as political parties and campaigners. The relatively hidden cluster includes academic specialists, career bureaucrats, and congressional staffers. We have discovered that the visible cluster affects the agenda and the hidden cluster affects the alternatives. So the chances of a subject rising on a governmental agenda are enhanced if that subject is pushed by participants in the visible cluster, and dampened if it is neglected by those participants. The administration—the president and his appointees—is a particularly powerful agenda setter, as are such prominent members of Congress as the party leaders and key committee chairs.

At least as far as agenda setting is concerned, elected officials and their appointees turn out to be more important than career civil servants or participants outside of government. To those who look for evidences of democracy at work, this is an encouraging result. These elected officials do not necessarily get their way in specifying alternatives or implementing decisions, but they do affect agendas rather substantially. To describe the roles of various participants in agenda setting, a fairly straightforward top-down model, with elected officials at the top, comes surprisingly close to the truth.

# Alternative Specification

How is the list of potential alternatives for public policy choices narrowed to the ones that actually receive serious consideration? There are two families of answers: (1) Alternatives are generated and narrowed in the policy stream; and (2) Relatively hidden participants, specialists in the particular policy area, are involved.

## Hidden Participants: Specialists

Alternatives, proposals, and solutions are generated in communities of specialists. This relatively hidden cluster of participants includes academics, researchers, consultants, career bureaucrats, congressional staffers, and analysts who work for interest groups. Their work is done, for instance, in planning and evaluation or budget shops in the bureaucracy or in the staff agencies on the Hill.

These relatively hidden participants form loosely knit communities of specialists. There is such a community for health, for instance, which includes analogous subcommunities for more specialized areas like the direct delivery of medical services and the regulation of food and drugs. Some of these communities, such as the one for transportation, are highly fragmented, while others are more tightly knit. Each community is composed of people located throughout the system and potentially of very diverse orientations and interests, but they all share one thing: their specialization and acquaintance with the issues in that particular policy area.

Ideas bubble around in these communities. People try out proposals in a variety of ways: through speeches, bill introductions, congressional hearings, leaks to the press, circulation of papers, conversations, and lunches. They float their ideas, criticize one another's work, hone and revise their ideas, and float new versions. Some of these ideas are respectable, while others are out of the question. But many, many ideas are possible and are considered in some fashion somewhere along the line.

## The Policy Stream

The generation of policy alternatives is best seen as a selection process, analogous to biological natural selection. In what we have called the policy primeval soup, many ideas float around, bumping into one another, encountering new ideas, and forming combinations and recombinations. The origins of policy may seem a bit obscure, hard to predict and hard to understand or to structure.

While the origins are somewhat haphazard, the selection is not. Through the imposition of criteria by which some ideas are selected out for survival while others are discarded, order is developed from chaos, pattern from randomness. These criteria include technical feasibility, congruence with the values of community members, and the anticipation of future constraints, including a budget constraint, public acceptability, and politicians' receptivity. Proposals that are judged infeasible—that do not square with policy community values, that would cost more than the budget will allow, that run afoul of opposition in either the mass or specialized publics, or that would not find a receptive audience among elected politicians—are less likely to survive than proposals that meet these standards. In the process of consideration in the policy community, ideas themselves are important. Pressure models do not completely describe the process. Proposals are evaluated partly in terms of their political support and opposition, to be sure, but partly against logical or analytical criteria as well.

There is a long process of softening up the system. Policy entrepreneurs do not leave consideration of their pet proposals to accident. Instead, they push for consideration in many ways and in many forums. In the process of policy development, recombination (the coupling of already-familiar elements) is more important than mutation (the appearance of wholly new forms). Thus entrepreneurs, who broker people and ideas, are more important than inventors. Because recombination is more important than invention, there may be "no new thing under the sun" at the same time that there may be dramatic change and innovation. There is change, but it involves the recombination of already-familiar elements.

The long softening-up process is critical to policy change. Opportunities for serious hearings, the policy windows we explored in Chapter 8, pass quickly and are missed if the proposals have not already gone through the long gestation process before the window opens. The work of floating and refining proposals is not wasted if it does not bear fruit in the short run. Indeed, it is critically important if the proposal is to be heard at the right time.

## Coupling and Windows

The separate streams of problems, policies, and politics each have lives of their own. Problems are recognized and defined according to processes that are different from the ways policies are developed or political events unfold. Policy proposals are developed according to their own incentives and selection criteria, whether or not they are solutions to problems or responsive to political considerations. Political events flow along on their own schedule and according to their own rules, whether or not they are related to problems or proposals.

But there come times when the three streams are joined. A pressing problem demands attention, for instance, and a policy proposal is coupled to the problem as its solution. Or an event in the political stream, such as a change of administration, calls for different directions. At that point, proposals that fit with that political event, such as initiatives that fit with a new administration's philosophy, come to the fore and are coupled with the ripe political climate. Similarly, problems that fit are highlighted, and others are neglected.

## Decision Agendas

A complete linkage combines all three streams—problems, policies, and politics—into a single package. Advocates of a new policy initiative not only take advantage of politically propitious moments but also claim that their proposal is a solution to a pressing problem. Likewise, entrepreneurs concerned about a particular problem search for solutions in the policy stream to couple to their problem, then try to take advantage of political receptivity at certain points in time to push the package of problem and solution. At points along the way, there are partial couplings: solutions to problems, but without a receptive political climate; politics to proposals, but without a sense that a compelling problem is being solved; politics and problems both calling for action, but without an available alternative to advocate. But the complete joining of all three streams dramatically enhances the odds that a subject will become firmly fixed on a decision agenda.

Governmental agendas, lists of subjects to which governmental officials are paying serious attention, can be set solely in either problems or political streams, and solely by visible actors. Officials can pay attention to an important problem, for instance, without having a solution to it. Or politics may highlight a subject, even in the absence of either problem or solution. A decision agenda, a list of subjects that is moving into position for an authoritative decision, such as legislative enactment or presidential choice, is set somewhat differently. The probability of an item rising on a decision agenda is dramatically increased if all three elements—problem, policy proposal, and political receptivity—are linked in a single package. Conversely, partial couplings are less likely to rise on decision agendas. Problems that come to decisions without solutions attached, for instance, are not as likely to move into position for an authoritative choice as if they did have solutions attached. And proposals that lack political backing are less likely to move into position for a decision than ones that do have that backing.

A return to our case studies in Chapter 1 illustrates these points. With aviation deregulation, awareness of problems, development of proposals, and swings of national mood all proceeded separately in their own streams. Increasingly through the late 1960s and early 1970s, people became convinced that the economy contained substantial inefficiencies to which the burdens of government regulation contributed. Proposals for deregulation were formed among academics and other specialists, through a softening-up process that included journal articles, testimony, conferences, and other forums. In the 1970s, politicians sensed a change in national mood toward increasing hostility to government size and intrusiveness. All three of the components, therefore, came together at about the same time. The key to movement was the coupling of the policy stream's literature on deregulation with the political incentive to rein in government growth, and those two elements with the sense that there was a real, important, and increasing problem with economic inefficiency.

The waterway user charge case illustrates a similar coupling. A proposal, some form of user charge, had been debated among transportation specialists for years. The political stream produced an administration receptive to imposing a user charge. This combination of policy and politics was coupled with a problem—the necessity, in a time of budget stringency, to repair or replace aging facilities like Lock and Dam 26. Thus did the joining of problem, policy, and politics push the waterway user charge into position on a decision agenda.

By contrast, national health insurance during the Carter years did not have all three components joined. Proponents could argue that there were real problems of medical access, though opponents countered that many of the most severe problems were being addressed through Medicare, Medicaid, and private insurance. The political stream did produce a heavily Democratic Congress and an administration that favored some sort of health insurance initiative. It seemed for a time that serious movement was under way. But the policy stream had not settled on a single, worked-up, viable alternative from among the many proposals floating around. The budget constraint, itself a severe problem, and politicians' reading of the national mood, which seemed to be against costly new initiatives, also proved to be too much to overcome. The coupling was incomplete, and the rise of national health insurance on the agenda proved fleeting. Then the election of Ronald Reagan sealed its fate, at least for the time being.

Success in one area contributes to success in adjacent areas. Once aviation deregulation passed, for instance, government turned with a vengeance to other deregulation proposals, and passed several in short order. These spillovers, as we have called them, occur because politicians sense the payoff in repeating a successful formula in a similar area, because the winning coalition can be transferred, and because advocates can argue from successful precedent. These spillovers are extremely powerful agenda setters, seemingly bowling over even formidable opposition that stands in the way.

## Policy Windows

An open policy window is an opportunity for advocates to push their pet solutions or to push attention to their special problems. Indeed, advocates in and around government keep their proposals and their problems at hand, waiting for these opportunities to occur. They have pet solutions, for instance, and wait for problems to float by to which they can attach their solutions, or for developments in the political stream that they can use to their advantage. Or they wait for similar opportunities to bring their special problems to the fore, such as the appearance of a new administration that would be concerned with these problems. That administration opens a window for them to bring greater attention to the problems about which they are concerned.

Windows are opened by events in either the problems or political streams. Thus there are problems windows and political windows. A new problem appears, for instance, creating an opportunity to attach a solution to it. Or such events in the political stream as turnover of elected officials, swings of national mood, or vigorous lobbying might create opportunities to push some problems and proposals to the fore and dampen the chances to highlight other problems and proposals.

Sometimes, windows open quite predictably. Legislation comes up for renewal on a schedule, for instance, creating opportunities to change, expand, or abolish certain programs. At other times, windows open quite unpredictably, as when an airliner crashes or a fluky election produces an unexpected turnover in key decision makers. Predictable or unpredictable, open windows are small and scarce. Opportunities come, but they also pass. Windows do not stay open long. If a chance is missed, another must be awaited.

The scarcity and the short duration of the opening of a policy window create a powerful magnet for problems and proposals. When a window opens, problems and proposals flock to it. People concerned with particular problems see the open window as their opportunity to address or even solve these problems. Advocates of particular proposals see the open window as the opportunity to enact them. As a result, the system comes to be loaded down with problems and proposals. If participants are willing to invest sufficient resources, some of the problems can be resolved and some of the proposals enacted. Other problems and proposals drift away because insufficient resources are mobilized.

Open windows present opportunities for the complete linkage of problems, proposals, and politics, and hence opportunities to move packages of the three joined elements up on decision agendas. One particularly crucial coupling is the link of a solution to something else. Advocates of pet proposals watch for developments in the political stream that they can take advantage of, or try to couple their solution to whatever problems are floating by at the moment. Once they have made the partial coupling of proposal to either problem or politics, they attempt to join all three elements, knowing that the chances for enactment are considerably enhanced if they can complete the circle. Thus they try to hook packages of problems and solutions to political forces, packages of proposals and political incentives to perceived problems, or packages of problems and politics to some proposal taken from the policy stream.

## Entrepreneurs

Policy entrepreneurs are people willing to invest their resources in return for future policies they favor. They are motivated by combinations of several things: their straightforward concern about certain problems, their pursuit of such self-serving benefits as protecting or expanding their bureaucracy's budget or claiming credit for accomplishment, their promotion of their policy values, and their simple pleasure in participating. We have encountered them at three junctures: pushing their concerns about certain problems higher on the agenda, pushing their pet proposals during a process of softening up the system, and making the couplings we just discussed. These entrepreneurs are found at many locations; they might be elected officials, career civil servants, lobbyists, academics, or journalists. No one type of participant dominates the pool of entrepreneurs.

As to problems, entrepreneurs try to highlight the indicators that so importantly dramatize their problems. They push for one kind of problem definition rather than another. Because they know that focusing events can move subjects higher on the agenda, entrepreneurs push to create such things as personal viewings of problems by policy makers and the diffusion of a symbol that captures their problem in a nutshell. They also may prompt the kinds of feedback about current governmental performance that affect agendas: letters, complaints, and visits to officials.

As to proposals, entrepreneurs are central to the softening-up process. They write papers, give testimony, hold hearings, try to get press coverage, and meet endlessly with important and not-so-important people. They float their ideas as trial balloons, get reactions, revise their proposals in the light of reactions, and float them again. They aim to soften up the mass public, specialized publics, and the policy community itself. The process takes years of effort.

As to coupling, entrepreneurs once again appear when windows open. They have their pet proposals or their concerns about problems ready, and push them at the propitious moments. In the pursuit of their own goals, they perform the function for the system of coupling solutions to problems, problems to political forces, and political forces to proposals. The joining of the separate streams described earlier depends heavily on the appearance of the right entrepreneur at the right time. In our case study of Health Maintenance Organizations in Chapter 1, Paul Ellwood appeared on the scene to link his pet proposal (HMOs) to the problem of medical care costs and to the political receptivity created by the Nixon administration casting about for health initiatives. The problems and political streams had opened a window, and Ellwood cleverly took advantage of that opportunity to push his HMO proposal, joining all three streams in the process.

The appearance of entrepreneurs when windows are open, as well as their more enduring activities of trying to push their problems and proposals into prominence, are central to our story. They bring several key resources into the fray: their claims to a hearing, their political connections and negotiating skills, and their sheer persistence. An item's chances for moving up on an agenda are enhanced considerably by the presence of a skillful entrepreneur, and dampened considerably if no entrepreneur takes on the cause, pushes it, and makes the critical couplings when policy windows open.

## Conclusion

The ideas we have explored in the pages of this book have a few important properties which it is appropriate to highlight as we draw to a close. These properties fall into two general categories: the differences between our model of these processes and other notions, and the places of randomness and pattern.

### Other Notions

The ideas developed in this book are quite unlike many other theories that could have captured our attention. For example, events do not proceed neatly in stages, steps, or phases. Instead, independent streams that flow through the system all at once, each with a life of its own and equal with one another, become coupled when a window opens. Thus participants do not first identify problems and then seek solutions for them; indeed, advocacy of solutions often precedes the highlighting of problems to which they become attached. Agendas are not first set and then alternatives generated; instead, alternatives must be advocated for a long period before a short-run opportunity presents itself on an agenda. Events do not necessarily proceed in similar order in several different case studies; instead, many things happen separately in each case, and become coupled at critical points.

Other notions have elements of truth, and do describe parts of the processes, but they are incomplete. A pressure model, for instance, does describe parts of the political stream, but ideas are as important as pressure in other parts of the processes. Agenda items do not necessarily start in a larger systemic or public arena and transfer to a formal or governmental agenda; indeed, the flow is just as often in the reverse direction. As we argued in Chapter 4, a concentration on origins does not take us very far because ideas come from many locations, nobody has a monopoly on leadership or prescience, and tracing origins involves an infinite regress. We were drawn to the importance of combinations rather than single origins, and to a climate of receptivity that allows ideas to take off. Also in Chapter 4, we portrayed comprehensive-rational and incremental models as incomplete. Participants sometimes do approach their decisions quite comprehensively and decide quite rationally, but the larger process is less tidy. Incrementalism does describe the slow process of generating alternatives, and often does describe small legislative and bureaucratic changes stretching over many years, but does not describe agenda change well. Thus, in addition to arguing for one way of looking at the policy formation world, we have argued what the world does *not* look like.

## On Randomness and Pattern

We still encounter considerable doses of messiness, accident, fortuitous coupling, and dumb luck. Subjects sometimes rise on agendas without our understanding completely why. We are sometimes surprised by the couplings that take place. The fortuitous appearance or absence of key participants affect outcomes. There remains some degree of unpredictability.

Yet it would be a grave mistake to conclude that the processes explored in this book are essentially random. Some degree of pattern is evident in three fundamental sources: processes within each stream, processes that structure couplings, and general constraints on the system.

First, processes operating within each stream limit randomness. Within the problems stream, not every problem has an equal chance of surfacing. Those conditions that are not highlighted by indicators, focusing events, or feedback are less likely to be brought to the attention of governmental officials than conditions that do have those advantages. Furthermore, not all conditions are defined as problems. Conditions that do not conflict with important values or that are placed in an inappropriate category are less likely to be translated into problems than conditions that are evaluated or categorized appropriately. In the policy stream, not every proposal surfaces. Selection criteria make patterns out of initial noise. Proposals that meet such standards as technical feasibility, value acceptability, public acquiescence, politicians' receptivity, and budgetary stringency are more likely to survive than those that fail to meet such standards. In the political stream, not every environment or event is equally likely. Some groups lack the resources that others have, some swings of national mood (e.g., to socialism) are unlikely, and some types of turnover of elected officials are more likely than others.

Second, some couplings are more likely than others. Everything cannot interact with everything else. For one thing, the timing of an item's arrival in its stream affects its ability to be joined to items in other streams. A window may open, for instance, but a solution may not be available at that time in the policy stream, so the window closes without a coupling of solution to problem or politics. Or a proposal may be ready in the policy stream, but the political conditions are not right for it to be pushed, again limiting the coupling possibilities. In addition to timing, germaneness limits the coupling possibilities. Not all solutions have an equal possibility of being discussed with all problems. Instead, participants have some sense of what would constitute an appropriate solution to a problem. There is some room for different solutions being hooked to a given problem or different problems being hooked to a given solution, but participants also set some limits on the appropriate couplings. Finally, the appearance of a skillful entrepreneur enhances the probability of a coupling. Potential couplings without entrepreneurs are less likely because they fail for lack of someone willing to invest resources in them.

Third, there are various constraints on the system, limits that provide a basic structure within which the participants play the games we have described.[1] The political stream provides many of these constraints. Participants sense some boundaries that are set on their actions by the mood of the mass public, and narrower boundaries set by the preferences of specialized publics and elected politicians. As I have argued elsewhere, governmental officials sense these limits and believe they must operate within them.[2] The budget imposes constraints as well. Costly proposals are not likely to be addressed in times of economic contraction or budget stringency, but might be more likely to receive attention in more robust times. Various rules of procedure, including the constitution, statutes, prescribed jurisdictions, precedents, customary decision-making modes, and other legal requirements, all impose structures on the participants. Finally, the scarcity of open windows constrains participants. They compete for limited space on agendas, and queue up for their turn. Even the selection criteria used by specialists in the policy stream anticipate these constraints.

These various types of pattern—dynamics internal to each stream, limits on coupling possibilities, and more general constraints—help us understand why some items never rise on policy agendas. Chapter 1 set forth several such items in health and transportation in the late 1970s. Some of them, such as long-term care and mental health, remained low, not because participants would not recognize real problems there but because they had little sense for alternatives that might be available as solutions. Some agenda items, such as buses, did not have powerful constituencies behind them in the political stream and failed to receive attention for lack of such advocates. Items such as rail nationalization failed because of powerful opposition. Others were not prominent on health and transportation agendas because systems of specialization and jurisdiction limited their movement. Items like direct delivery of medical care and food and drug regulation were indeed high on certain specialized agendas, but not on the larger health agenda. Finally, some items like environmental impact and transportation safety had been prominent earlier, but were played out by the time of these interviews, according to dynamics we explored when examining why problems fade. Thus this study helps to understand not only the appearance of some items on agendas, but also the failure of other items to appear.

Finally, it should be noted that all of our ideas are probabilistic. I have tried to adhere to such formulations as "the chances are improved or lessened" and "these events are more likely than others." In describing these processes, hard-and-fast rules and the specification of conditions that *must* be met seem less fruitful than a quotation of odds. Constraints, for instance, are not absolutes. Instead, they are conditions that make some events highly unlikely and other events more likely to occur. They do impose structure on the system, but it is structure that still allows room for some gray areas and some unpredictability. A budget constraint, for instance, is subject to some interpretation in the light of knowledge gaps and participants' values, but its operation still does make attention to some proposals at some points in time highly unlikely.

Thus we have made some progress in understanding the vague and imprecise phenomena we wanted to understand at the beginning of our journey. To the extent that our vision is still obscured, the world itself may be somewhat opaque. But further research and thinking beyond what is presented in this book may also allow us to see more clearly.

## Notes

1. For a good discussion of constraints, see Roger W. Cobb and Charles D. Elder, "Communications and Public Policy," in Dan Nimmo and Keith Sanders, eds., *Handbook of Political Communications* (Beverly Hilis: Sage, 1981), pp. 402–408.

2. John W. Kingdon, *Congressmen's Voting Decisions*, 3rd ed. (Ann Arbor: University of Michigan Press, 1989), Chapter 12.

# The Need for Better Theories

## PAUL A. SABATIER

In the process of public policymaking, problems are conceptualized and brought to government for solution; governmental institutions formulate alternatives and select policy solutions; and those solutions get implemented, evaluated, and revised.

## Simplifying a Complex World

For a variety of reasons, the policy process involves an extremely complex set of elements that interact over time:

1.  There are normally hundreds of actors from interest groups, governmental agencies, legislatures at different levels of government, researchers, journalists, and judges involved in one or more aspects of the process. Each of these actors (either individual or corporate) has potentially different values/interests, perceptions of the situation, and policy preferences.
2.  This process usually involves time spans of a decade or more, as that is the minimum duration of most policy cycles, from emergence of a problem through sufficient experience with implementation to render a reasonably fair evaluation of a program's impact (Kirst and Jung 1982; Sabatier and Jenkins-Smith 1993). A number of studies suggest that periods of twenty to forty years may be required to obtain a reasonable understanding of the impact of a variety of socioeconomic conditions and to accumulate scientific knowledge about a problem (Derthick and Quirk 1985; Baumgartner and Jones 1993; Eisner 1993).
3.  In any given policy domain, such as air pollution control or health policy, there are normally dozens of different programs involving multiple levels of government that are operating, or are being proposed for operation, in any given locale, such as the state of California or the city of Los Angeles. Since these programs deal with interrelated subjects and involve many of the same actors, many scholars would argue that the appropriate unit of analysis should be the policy subsystem or domain, rather than a specific governmental program (Hjern and Porter 1981; Ostrom 1983; Sabatier 1986; Rhodes 1988; Jordan 1990).
4.  Policy debates among actors in the course of legislative hearings, litigation, and proposed administrative regulations typically involve very technical disputes over the severity of a problem, its causes, and the probable impacts of alternative policy solutions. Understanding the policy process requires attention to the role that such debates play in the overall process.
5.  A final complicating factor in the policy process is that most disputes involve deeply held values/interests, large amounts of money, and, at some point, authoritative coercion. Given these stakes, policy disputes seldom resemble polite academic debates. Instead, most actors face enormous temptations to present evidence selectively, to misrepresent the position of their opponents, to coerce and discredit opponents, and generally to distort the situation to their advantage (Riker 1986; Moe 1990a, 1990b; Schlager 1995).

In short, understanding the policy process requires knowledge of the goals and perceptions of hundreds of actors throughout the country involving possibly very technical scientific and legal issues over periods of a decade or more while most of those actors are actively seeking to propagate their specific "spin" on events.

Given the staggering complexity of the policy process, the analyst must find some way of simplifying the situation in order to have any chance of understanding it. One simply cannot look for, and see, everything. Work in the philosophy of science and social psychology has provided persuasive evidence that perceptions are almost always mediated by a set of presuppositions. These perform two critical mediating functions. First, they tell the observer what to look for; that is, what factors are likely to be critically important versus those that can be safely ignored. Second, they define the categories in which phenomena are to be grouped (Kuhn 1970; Lakatos 1971; Brown 1977; Lord, Ross, and Lepper 1979; Hawkesworth 1992; Munro et al. 2002).

To understand the policy process, for example, most institutional rational choice approaches tell the analyst (1) to focus on the leaders of a few critical institutions with formal decisionmaking authority, (2) to assume that these actors are pursuing their material self-interest (e.g., income, power, security), and (3) to group actors into a few institutional categories, for example, legislatures, administrative agencies, and interest groups (Shepsle 1989; Scharpf 1997). In contrast, the advocacy coalition framework tells the analyst to assume (1) that belief systems are more important than institutional affiliation, (2) that actors may be pursuing a wide variety of objectives, which must be measured empirically, and (3) that one must add researchers and journalists to the set of potentially important policy actors (Sabatier and Jenkins-Smith 1993). Thus, analysts from these two different perspectives look at the same situation through quite different lenses and are likely to see quite different things, at least initially.

## Strategies for Simplification

Given that we have little choice but to look at the world through a lens consisting of a set of simplifying presuppositions, at least two quite different strategies exist for developing such a lens. On the one hand, the analyst can approach the world in an implicit, ad hoc fashion, using whatever categories and assumptions that have arisen from his or her experience. This is essentially the method of common sense. It may be reasonably accurate for situations important to the analyst's welfare in which she or he has considerable experience. In such situations, the analyst has both the incentive and the experience to eliminate clearly invalid propositions. Beyond that limited scope, the commonsense strategy is likely to be beset by internal inconsistencies, ambiguities, erroneous assumptions, and invalid propositions, precisely because the strategy does not contain any explicit methods of error correction. Since its assumptions and propositions remain implicit and largely unknown, they are unlikely to be subjected to serious scrutiny. The analyst simply assumes they are, by and large, correct—insofar as he or she is even cognizant of their content.

An alternative strategy is that of science. Its fundamental ontological assumption is that a smaller set of critical relationships underlies the bewildering complexity of phenomena. For example, a century ago Darwin provided a relatively simple explanation—summarized under the processes of natural selection—for the thousands of species he encountered on his voyages. The critical characteristics of science are that (1) its methods of data acquisition and analysis should be presented in a sufficiently public manner that they can be replicated by others; (2) its concepts and propositions should be clearly defined and logically consistent and should give rise to empirically falsifiable hypotheses; (3) those propositions should be as general as possible and should explicitly address relevant uncertainties; and (4) both the methods and concepts should be self-consciously subjected to criticism and evaluation by experts in that field (Nagel 1961; Lave and March 1975; King, Keohane, and Verba 1994). The overriding strategy can be summarized in the injunction: Be clear enough to be proven wrong. Unlike "common sense," science is designed to be self-consciously error seeking, and thus self-correcting.

A critical component of that strategy—derived from principles 2–4 above—is that scientists should develop clear and logically interrelated sets of propositions, some of them empirically falsifiable, to explain fairly general sets of phenomena. Such coherent sets of propositions have traditionally been termed theories.

Elinor Ostrom has developed some very useful distinctions among three different sets of propositions (see Chapter 2 of this volume). (1) In her view, a "conceptual framework" identifies a set of variables and the relationships among them that presumably account for a set of phenomena. The framework can provide anything from a modest set of variables to something as extensive as a paradigm. It need not identify directions among relationships, although more developed frameworks will certainly specify some hypotheses. (2) A "theory" provides a denser and more logically coherent set of relationships. It applies values to some of the variables and usually specifies how relationships may vary depending upon the values of critical variables. Numerous theories may be consistent with the same conceptual framework. (3) A "model" is a representation of a specific situation. It is usually much narrower in scope, and more precise in its assumptions, than the underlying theory. Ideally, it is mathematical. Thus, frameworks, theories, and models can be conceptualized as operating along a continuum involving increasing logical interconnectedness and specificity but decreasing scope.

One final point: Scientists should be aware of, and capable of applying, several different theoretical perspectives—not just a single one (Stinchcomb 1968; Loehle 1987). First, knowledge of several different perspectives forces the analyst to clarify differences in assumptions across frameworks, rather than implicitly assuming a given set. Second, multiple perspectives encourage the development of competing hypotheses that should ideally lead to "strong inference" (Platt 1964), or at least to the accumulation of evidence in favor of one perspective over another. Third, knowledge and application of multiple perspectives should gradually clarify the conditions under which one perspective is more useful than another. Finally, multiple perspectives encourage a comparative approach: Rather than asking if theory X produces statistically significant results, one asks whether theory X explains more than theory Y.

Consistent with this multiple-lens strategy, the original edition of this volume discussed seven conceptual frameworks. A few of them—notably, institutional rational choice—have given rise to one or more theories, and virtually all have spawned a variety of models seeking to explain specific situations.

## Theoretical Frameworks of the Policy Process

### The Stages Heuristic

Until the mid-1980s, the most influential framework for understanding the policy process—particularly among American scholars—was the "stages heuristic," or what Nakamura (1987) termed the "textbook approach." As developed by Lasswell (1956), Jones (1970), Anderson (1975), and Brewer and deLeon (1983), it divided the policy process into a series of stages—usually agenda setting, policy formulation and legitimation, implementation, and evaluation—and discussed some of the factors affecting the process within each stage. The stages heuristic served a useful purpose in the 1970s and early 1980s by dividing the very complex policy process into discrete stages and by stimulating some excellent research within specific stages—particularly agenda setting (Cobb, Ross, and Ross 1976; Kingdon 1984; Nelson 1984) and policy implementation (Pressman and Wildavsky 1973; Hjern and Hull 1982; Mazmanian and Sabatier 1983).

Beginning in the late 1980s, however, the stages heuristic was subjected to some devastating criticisms (Nakamura 1987; Sabatier 1991; Sabatier and Jenkins-Smith 1993):

1. It is not really a causal theory since it never identifies a set of causal drivers that govern the policy process within and across stages. Instead, work within each stage has tended to develop on its own, almost totally without reference to research in other stages. In addition, without causal drivers there can be no coherent set of hypotheses within and across stages.
2. The proposed sequence of stages is often descriptively inaccurate. For example, evaluations of existing programs affect agenda setting, and policy formulation/legitimation occurs as bureaucrats attempt to implement vague legislation (Nakamura 1987).
3. The stages heuristic has a very legalistic, top-down bias in which the focus is typically on the passage and implementation of a major piece of legislation. This focus neglects the interaction of the implementation and evaluation of numerous pieces of legislation—none of them preeminent—within a given policy domain (Hjern and Hull 1982; Sabatier 1986).
4. The assumption that there is a single policy cycle focused on a major piece of legislation oversimplifies the usual process of multiple, interacting cycles involving numerous policy proposals and statutes at multiple levels of government. For example, abortion activists are currently involved in litigation in the federal courts and most state courts, in new policy

proposals in Washington and most of the states, in the implementation of other proposals at the federal and state levels, and in the evaluation of all sorts of programs and proposed programs. They're also continually trying to affect the conceptualization of the problem. In such a situation—which is common—focusing on "a policy cycle" makes very little sense.

The conclusion seems inescapable: The stages heuristic has outlived its usefulness and needs to be replaced with better theoretical frameworks.

## More Promising Theoretical Frameworks

Fortunately, over the past twenty years a number of new theoretical frameworks of the policy process have been either developed or extensively modified. The 1999 edition of this book sought to present some of the more promising ones and to assess the strengths and limitations of each.[1]

Following are the criteria utilized in selecting the frameworks to be discussed. They strike me as relatively straightforward, although reasonable people may certainly disagree with my application of them:

1.  Each framework must do a reasonably good job of meeting the criteria of a scientific theory; that is, its concepts and propositions must be relatively clear and internally consistent, it must identify clear causal drivers, it must give rise to falsifiable hypotheses, and it must be fairly broad in scope (i.e., apply to most of the policy process in a variety of political systems).
2.  Each framework must be the subject of a fair amount of recent conceptual development and/or empirical testing. A number of currently active policy scholars must view it as a viable way of understanding the policy process.
3.  Each framework must be a positive theory seeking to explain much of the policy process. The theoretical framework may also contain some explicitly normative elements, but these are not required.
4.  Each framework must address the broad sets of factors that political scientists looking at different aspects of public policymaking have traditionally deemed important: conflicting values and interests, information flows, institutional arrangements, and variation in the socioeconomic environment.

By means of these criteria, seven frameworks were selected for analysis in the 1999 edition of this book. Following is a brief description and justification for each selection.

*The Stages Heuristic.* Although I have doubts that the stages heuristic meets the first and second criteria above, there is certainly room for disagreement on whether it meets the second. In particular, implementation studies appeared to undergo a revival in the late 1990s (Lester and Goggin 1998). Even were that not the case, I have spent so much time criticizing the stages heuristic that simple fairness required me to provide a forum for its defense. Peter deLeon, one of the earliest proponents of the heuristic, volunteered to be the spokesperson.

*Institutional Rational Choice.* Institutional rational choice is a family of frameworks focusing on how institutional rules alter the behavior of intendedly rational individuals motivated by material self-interest. Although much of the literature on institutional rational choice focuses on rather specific sets of institutions, such as the relationships between Congress and administrative agencies in the United States (Moe 1984; Shepsle 1989; Miller 1992), the general framework is extremely broad in scope and has been applied to important policy problems in the United States and other countries (Ostrom 1986, 1990; Ostrom, Schroeder, and Wynne 1993; Ostrom, Gardner, and Walker 1994; Scholz, Twombley, and Headrick 1991; Chubb and Moe 1990; Dowding 1995; Scharpf 1997). It is clearly the most developed of all the frameworks in this volume and is arguably the most utilized in the United States and perhaps in Germany. Elinor Ostrom agreed to write the chapter for this volume.

*Multiple-Streams.* The multiple-streams framework was developed by John Kingdon (1984) based upon the "garbage can" model of organizational behavior (Cohen, March, and Olsen 1972). It views the policy process as composed of three streams of actors and processes: a problem stream consisting of data about various problems and the proponents of various problem definitions; a policy stream involving the proponents of solutions to policy problems; and a politics stream consisting of elections and elected officials. In Kingdon's view, the streams normally operate independently of each other, except when a "window of opportunity" permits policy entrepreneurs to couple the various streams. If the entrepreneurs are successful, the result is major policy change. Although the multiple-streams framework is not always as clear and internally consistent as one might like, it appears to be applicable to a wide variety of policy arenas and was cited about eighty times annually in the Social Science Citation Index. John Kingdon is the obvious author for this chapter; however, he declined. I then selected Nikolaos Zahariadis, who had utilized the multiple-streams framework extensively in his own research (Zahariadis 1992, 1995, 2003).

*Punctuated-Equilibrium Framework.* Originally developed by Baumgartner and Jones (1993), the punctuated-equilibrium (PE) framework argues that policymaking in the United States is characterized by long periods of incremental change punctuated by brief periods of major policy change. The latter come about when opponents manage to fashion new "policy images" and exploit the multiple policy venues characteristic of the United States. Originally developed to explain changes in legislation, this framework has been expanded to include some very sophisticated analyses of long-term changes in the budgets of the federal government (Jones, Baumgartner, and True 1998). The PE framework clearly meets all four criteria, at least for systems with multiple policy venues. The chapter for this volume is coauthored by its original proponents, Frank R. Baumgartner and Bryan D. Jones, together with James L. True.

*The Advocacy Coalition Framework.* Developed by Sabatier and Jenkins-Smith (1988, 1993), the advocacy coalition framework (ACF) focuses on the interaction of advocacy coalitions—each consisting of actors from a variety of institutions who share a set of policy beliefs—within a policy subsystem. Policy change is a function of both competition within the subsystem and events outside the subsystem. The framework spends a lot of time mapping the belief systems of policy elites and analyzing the conditions under which policy-oriented learning across coalitions can occur. It has stimulated considerable interest throughout the countries of the Organization for Economic Cooperation and Development (OECD)—including some very constructive criticism (Schlager 1995). Paul Sabatier and Hank C. Jenkins-Smith are clearly qualified to assess the implications of these recent applications.

The frameworks discussed thus far have all focused on explaining policy change within a given political system or set of institutional arrangements (including efforts to change those arrangements). The next two frameworks seek to provide explanations of variation across a large number of political systems.

*Policy Diffusion Framework.* The policy diffusion framework was developed by Berry and Berry (1990, 1992) to explain variation in the adoption of specific policy innovations, such as a lottery, across a large number of states (or localities). It argues that adoption is a function of both the characteristics of the specific political systems and a variety of diffusion processes. Recently, Mintrom and Vergari (1998) integrated this framework with the literature on policy networks. The diffusion framework has thus far been utilized almost exclusively in the United States. It should, however, apply to variation among countries or regions within the European Union, the OECD, or any other set of political systems. The authors of the chapter in this volume were Frances Stokes Berry and William D. Berry, the original developers of the framework.

*The Funnel of Causality and Other Frameworks in Large-N Comparative Studies.* Finally, we turn to a variety of frameworks that were extremely important in the United States in the 1960s and 1970s in explaining variation in policy outcomes (usually budgetary expenditures) across large numbers of states and localities (Dye 1966, 1991; Sharkansky 1970; Hofferbert 1974). These began as very simple frameworks seeking to apportion the variance among background socioeconomic conditions, public opinion, and political institutions—although they became somewhat more sophisticated over time (Mazmanian and Sabatier 1981; Hofferbert and Urice 1985). Although interest in this approach has declined somewhat in the United States, it is still popular in OECD countries, particularly for explaining variation in social welfare programs (Flora 1986; Klingeman, Hofferbert, and Budge 1994; Schmidt 1996). The author for this chapter is William Blomquist. Although he has contributed to this literature (Blomquist 1991), he is not a major proponent—and thus differs from all the other chapter authors. He was selected because I expected him to be critical of the "black box" features of this framework and to seek to integrate it with other literatures, particularly institutional rational choice. Although those expectations were never communicated to him, he wound up doing a superb job of fulfilling them.

## What's New in the Second Edition?

The first (1999) edition of this book has been quite successful. It has sold about 1,000 copies per year for seven years. It has generally received favorable reviews (Dudley 2000; Parsons 2000; Radaelli 2000; Skogstad 2001; Theodoulou 2001). It has substantially accomplished what it set out to do: namely, to provide first-rate introductions to a set of the most promising theories of the policy process, together with some insightful comparisons.

Nevertheless, the first edition has been subjected to at least two major criticisms. First, it has been justly taken to task for its "overwhelming focus on the American literature" (Skogstad 2001). All of the authors were American. The only chapter that referenced a significant non-American literature was Ostom, whose IAD framework has largely been used in developing countries. Several of the chapters—particularly those covering the ACF and punctuated equilibrium—implicitly assumed that the basic features of American pluralism (multiple venues, majoritarian rule, weak political parties, politicized bureaucracies) were the norm everywhere. There was no acknowledgment of corporatist and authoritarian regimes, which are prevalent in many European and developing countries.

Second, the first edition was criticized for its narrow selection criteria, particularly for only including frameworks that followed scientific norms of clarity, hypothesis-testing, acknowledgement of uncertainty, etc. Since I am unequivocally a social scientist, this criticism fell on deaf ears (Sabatier 2000). A related criticism was that the first edition ignored social constructionist frameworks, largely on grounds that they don't follow scientific norms. But Helen Ingram and Anne Schneider convinced me that their particular constructionist framework (Schneider and Ingram 1997) met those norms and thus ought to be included in the book.

The second edition addresses these criticisms in a number of ways. In reaction to the charge of American chauvinism, the new edition:

- Adds a new chapter on network analysis written by two Europeans, Hanspeter Kriesi and Silke Adam of the University of Zurich. They were selected over possible competitors (e.g., Knoke and Laumann) because their concepts and arguments are clearer.[2]
- Adds new chapters on network analysis and social construction, both of which are very prominent topics in the European and Commonwealth literature.
- Revises several chapters—particularly those covering the ACF and PE—to no longer assume American pluralism as the norm. Most other chapters increased their coverage of the non-American literature.

As for the neglect of social construction, the new edition adds a chapter on that topic by Ingram and Schneider.

Given my doubts about the utility of the stages heuristic and the need to find space for two more promising frameworks, the chapter on the stages heuristic has been deleted from the second edition.

Finally, since one indicator of a viable research program is evidence that scholars beyond those who initiate the program expand it to other contexts, I have encouraged contributors to this volume to include in their chapter a table or appendix listing published studies employing the model/framework in different situations.' Most of the authors have chosen to do so, although the format utilized varies substantially from chapter to chapter.

## Plan of the Book

With respect to each of the eight theoretical frameworks selected for discussion, I have asked one of its principal proponents to present a brief history, to discuss its underlying principles and propositions, to analyze recent empirical evidence and revisions, to evaluate the strengths and limitations of the framework, and to suggest directions for future development.

After this introductory chapter, the next major section contains analyses of three frameworks that differ substantially concerning their assumptions of individual and collective rationality. Institutional rational choice frameworks assume that policy actors are "intendedly rational"; that is, they seek to realize a few goals efficiently but must overcome some obstacles (including imperfect information) to do so. The assumption is that policy problems and options are relatively well defined, but ascertaining the probable consequences of those alternatives is problematic. In contrast, Kingdon's multiple-streams model assumes that most policy situations are cloaked in "ambiguity," that is, lacking clear problem definitions and goals. In addition, serendipity and chance play a major role in the multiple-streams framework. In the Ingram and Schneider social construction approach, actors' perceptions of reality are strongly influenced by "social constructions" of the worthiness (virtue) and power of various target populations.

The third section presents three frameworks that seek to explain policy change over fairly long periods of time within a policy subsystem/domain: the punctuated-equilibrium framework of Jones et al., the advocacy coalition framework of Sabatier et al., and the policy network analysis of Kriesi et al. Although these three frameworks have similar dependent variables, they differ in several respects—most notably, in the relative importance of the general public versus policy elites, the model of the individual, and the importance of institutional context.

The fourth section contains two frameworks that typically seek to explain variation in policy decisions across large numbers of political systems. I had considered combining these into a single chapter but decided against it for two reasons. First, the diffusion models discussed by Berry and Berry are really a significant addition to the traditional set of state/local system variables discussed by Sharkansky/Dye/Hofferbert. Second, I very much wanted to have a critique of the "black box" character of the Sharkansky et al. models on the record, which I knew I could count on from Blomquist.

The final section contains two concluding chapters. The first is a comparison of the various theoretical frameworks, including comparisons of their dependent variables, the critical independent variables, the strengths and weaknesses of each, and some speculations about how they might be integrated and/or more clearly differentiated. The author is Edella Schlager, who has already revealed herself to be extremely talented at this sort of comparative analysis (Schlager 1995; Schlager and Blomquist 1996). In the last chapter, I suggest several strategies for advancing the state of policy theory.

The goal of this book is to advance the state of policy theory by presenting several of the more promising frameworks and by inviting the reader to compare the strengths and limitations of each. At the end of the day, the reader will hopefully have a repertoire of two or three frameworks that she or he is familiar with and adept at employing.

## Notes

1. Just to show that my tastes are not totally idiosyncratic, the list of "synthetic theories" developed by Peter John (1998) includes the advocacy coalition framework, punctuated equilibrium, and multiple streams. Earlier in the book, he includes socioeconomic approaches, institutions, rational choice, and ideas. I have grouped most of the last into a constructivist paradigm in the next section. My list also overlaps considerably those of Parsons (1996) and Muller and Surel (1998).

2. For example, in Knoke et al. (1996) "interest" is used both for "a topic of concern" and a "goal" (p. 13). In addition, the critical discussion of organization interests in specific settings (pp. 21–22) is quite confusing. In contrast, Kriesi's work (Kriesi and Jegen 2001) is very clear.

3. I wish to thank Bill Berry for clarifying this argument.

## References

Anderson, James. 1975. *Public Policy-Making*. New York: Praeger.

Baumgartner, Frank, and Bryan Jones. 1993. *Agendas and Instability in American Politics*. Chicago: University of Chicago Press.

Berry, Frances Stokes, and William Berry. 1990. "State Lottery Adoptions as Policy Innovations: An Event History Analysis." *American Political Science Review, 84*(June), 397–415.

___. 1992. "Tax Innovation in the States: Capitalizing on Political Opportunity." *American Journal of Political Science, 36*(August), 715–742.

Blomquist, William. 1991. "Exploring State Differences in Groundwater Policy Adoptions, 1980–89." *Publius, 21*, 101–115.

Brewer, Gary, and Peter deLeon. 1983. *The Foundations of Policy Analysis*. Monterey, CA: Brooks/Cole.

Brown, Harold. 1977. *Perception, Theory, and Commitment*. Chicago: University of Chicago Press.

Chubb, John, and Terry Moe. 1990. *Politics, Markets, and America's Schools*. Washington, D.C.: Brookings Institution.

Cobb, Roger, Jennie-Keith Ross, and Marc Ross. 1976. "Agenda Building as a Comparative Political Process." *American Political Science Review, 70*(March), 126–138.

Cohen, Michael, James March, and Johan Olsen. 1972. "A Garbage Can Model of Organizational Choice." *Administrative Science Quarterly, 17*(March), 1–25.

Derthick, Martha, and Paul Quirk. 1985. *The Politics of Deregulation*. Washington, D.C.: Brookings Institution.

Dowding, Keith. 1995. "Model or Metaphor? A Critical Review of the Policy Network Approach." *Political Studies, 43*(March), 136–159.

Dudley, Geoffrey. 2000. "New Theories and Policy Discontinuities." *Journal of European Public Policy, 7*, 122–126.

Dye, Thomas. 1966. *Politics, Economics, and Public Policy*. Chicago: Rand McNally.

___. 1991. *Politics in States and Communities*, 7th ed. Englewood Cliffs, NJ: Prentice-Hall.

Eisner, Marc A. 1993. *Regulatory Politics in Transition*. Baltimore, MD: Johns Hopkins University Press.

Flora, Peter, ed. 1986. *Growth to Limits: The Western European Welfare States Since World War II*. Berlin: deGruyter.

Hawkesworth, Mary. 1992. "Epistemology and Policy Analysis." In William Dunn and Rita Kelly, eds., *Advances in Policy Studies*, pp. 295–329. New Brunswick, NJ: Transaction Books.

Hjern, Benny, and Chris Hull. 1982. "Implementation Research as Empirical Constitutionalism." *European Journal of Political Research, 10*, 105–115.

Hjern, Benny, and David Porter. 1981. "Implementation Structures: A New Unit of Administrative Analysis." *Organization Studies, 2*, 211–227.

Hofferbert, Richard. 1974. *The Study of Public Policy*. Indianapolis, IN: Bobbs-Merrill.

Hofferbert, Richard, and John Urice. 1985. "Small-Scale Policy: The Federal Stimulus Versus Competing Explanations for State Funding for the Arts." *American Journal of Political Science, 29*(May), 308–329.

John, Peter. 1998. *Analyzing Public Policy*. London: Pinter.

Jones, Bryan, Frank Baumgartner, and James True. 1998. "Policy Punctuations: U.S. Budget Authority, 1947–1995." *Journal of Politics, 60*(February), 1–33.

Jones, Charles. 1970. *An Introduction to the Study of Public Policy*. Belmont, CA: Wadsworth.

Jordan, A. G. 1990. "Sub-Governments, Policy Communities, and Networks." *Journal of Theoretical Politics, 2*, 319–338.

King, Gary, Robert Keohane, and Sidney Verba. 1994. *Designing Social Inquiry*. Princeton, NJ: Princeton University Press.

Kingdon, John. 1984. *Agendas, Alternatives, and Public Policies*. Boston: Little, Brown.

Kirst, Michael, and Richard Jung 1982. "The Utility of a Longitudinal Approach in Assessing Implementation." In Walter Williams, ed., *Studying Implementation*, pp. 119–148. Chatham, NJ: Chatham House.

Klingemann, Hans-Dieter, Richard Hofferbert, and Ian Budge. 1994. *Parties, Policies, and Democracy*. Boulder, CO: Westview Press.

Knoke, David, Franz Pappi, Jeffrey Broadbent, and Yutaka Tsujinaka. 1996. *Comparing Policy Networks*. Cambridge, UK: Cambridge University Press.

Kriesi, H., and M. Jegen. 2001. "The Swiss Energy Policy Elite." *European Journal of Political Research, 39*, 251–287.

Kuhn, Thomas. 1970. *The Structure of Scientific Revolutions*, 2d ed. Chicago: University of Chicago Press.

Lakatos, Imre. 1971. "History of Science and Its Rational Reconstruction." In R. C. Buck and R. S. Cohen, eds., *Boston Studies in the Philosophy of Science*, pp. 91–122. Dordrecht, The Netherlands: D. Reidel.

Lasswell, Harold. 1956. *The Decision Process*. College Park, MD: University of Maryland Press.

Lave, Charles, and James March. 1975. *An Introduction to Models in the Social Sciences*. New York: Harper & Row.

Lester, James, and Malcolm Goggin. 1998. "Back to the Future: The Rediscovery of Implementation Studies." *Policy Currents, 8*(3), 1–10.

Loehle, Craig. 1987. "Hypothesis Testing in Ecology: Psychological Aspects and the Importance of Theory Maturation." *Quarterly Review of Biology, 62*, 397–409.

Lord, Charles, Lee Ross, and Mark Lepper. 1979. "Biased Assimilation and Attitude Polarization: The Effects of Prior Theories on Subsequently Considered Evidence." *Journal of Personality and Social Psychology, 37,* 2098–2109.

Mazmanian, Daniel, and Paul Sabatier. 1981. "A Multivariate Model of Public Policy-Making." *American Journal of Political Science, 24*(August), 439–468.

___. 1983. *Implementation and Public Policy.* Glenview, IL: Scott Foresman. (Reissued in 1989 by University Press of America.)

Miller, Gary. 1992. *Managerial Dilemmas.* Cambridge, England: Cambridge University Press.

Mintrom, Michael, and Sandra Vergari. 1998. "Policy Networks and Innovation Diffusion: The Case of State Educational Reform." *Journal of Politics, 60*(February), 120–148.

Moe, Terry. 1984. "The New Economics of Organization." *American Journal of Political Science, 28*(November), 739–777.

___. 1990a. "Political Institutions: The Neglected Side of the Story." *Journal of Law, Economics, and Organization, 6,* 215–253.

___. 1990b. "The Politics of Structural Choice." In Oliver Williamson, ed., *Organization Theory: From Chester Bernard to the Present and Beyond,* pp. 116–153. Oxford: Oxford University Press.

Muller, Pierre, and Yves Surel. 1998. *L'analyse des politiques publiques.* Paris: Montchrestien.

Munro, Geoffrey D., Peter H. Ditto, Lisa K. Lockhart, Angela Fagerlin, Mitchell Gready, and Elizabeth Peterson. 2002. "Biased Assimilation of Socio-political Arguments." *Basic and Applied Social Psychology, 24,* 15–26.

Nagel, Ernest. 1961. *The Structure of Science.* New York: Harcourt, Brace, & World.

Nakamura, Robert. 1987. "The Textbook Process and Implementation Research." *Policy Studies Review, 1,* 142–154.

Nelson, Barbara. 1984. *Making an Issue of Child Abuse.* Chicago: University of Chicago Press.

Ostrom, Elinor. 1983. "A Public Service Industry Approach to the Study of Local Government Structure and Reform." *Policy and Politics, 11,* 313–341.

___. 1986. "An Agenda for the Study of Institutions." *Public Choice, 48,* 3–25.

___. 1990. *Governing the Commons.* Cambridge, England: Cambridge University Press.

Ostrom, Elinor, Roy Gardner, and James Walker. 1994. *Rules, Games, and Common-Pool Resources.* Ann Arbor, MI: University of Michigan Press.

Ostrom, Elinor, Larry Schroeder, and Susan Wynne. 1993. *Institutional Incentives and Sustainable Development.* Boulder, CO: Westview Press.

Parsons, Wayne. 1996. *Public Policy: An Introduction to the Theory and Practice of Policy Analysis.* London: Elgar, Aldershot.

___. 2000. "When Dogs Don't Bark." *Journal of European Public Policy, 7,* 126–130.

Platt, John. 1964. "Strong Inference." *Science, 146*(October), 347–353.

Pressman, Jeffrey, and Aaron Wildavsky. 1973. *Implementation.* Berkeley, CA: University of California Press.

Raddaelli, Claudio. 2000. "Public Policy Comes of Age." *Journal of European Public Policy, 7,* 130–135.

Rhodes, R. A. W. 1988. *Beyond Westminster and Whitehall.* London: Unwin & Hyman.

Riker, William. 1986. *The Art of Political Manipulation.* New Haven, CT: Yale University Press.

Sabatier, Paul. 1986. "Top-Down and Bottom-Up Models of Policy Implementation: A Critical and Suggested Synthesis." *Journal of Public Policy, 6*(January), 21–48.

___. 1991. "Toward Better Theories of the Policy Process." *PS: Political Science and Politics, 24*(June), 147–156.

___. 2000. "Clear Enough to Be Wrong." *Journal of European Public Policy, 7,* 1335–140.

Sabatier, Paul, and Hank Jenkins-Smith, eds. 1988. "Special Issue: Policy Change and Policy-Oriented Learning: Exploring an Advocacy Coalition Framework." *Policy Sciences, 21,* 123–272.

___. 1993. *Policy Change and Learning: An Advocacy Coalition Approach.* Boulder, CO: Westview Press.

Scharpf, Fritz. 1997. *Games Policy Actors Play.* Boulder, CO: Westview Press.

Schlager, Edella. 1995. "Policy-Making and Collective Action: Defining Coalitions within the Advocacy Coalition Framework." *Policy Sciences, 28,* 243–270.

Schlager, Edella, and William Blomquist. 1996. "Emerging Political Theories of the Policy Process: Institutional Rational Choice, the Politics of Structural Choice, and Advocacy Coalitions." *Political Research Quarterly, 49*(September), 651–672.

Schmidt, Manfred. 1996. "When Parties Matter." *European Journal of Political Research, 30*(September), 155–183.

Schneider, Anne, and Helen Ingram. 1997. *Policy Design for Democracy.* Lawrence, KS: University Press of Kansas.

Schneider, Mark, Paul Teske, Michael Mintrom, and Sam Best. 1993. "Establishing the Micro Foundations for Macro-Level Theory." *American Political Science Review, 87*, 702–716.

Scholz, John, James Twombley, and Barbara Headrick. 1991. "Street Level Political Controls over Federal Bureaucrats." *American Political Science Review, 85*(September), 829–858.

Sharkansky, Ira. 1970. *Policy Analysis in Political Science*. Chicago: Markham

Shepsle, Kenneth. 1989. "Studying Institutions: Some Lessons from the Rational Choice Approach." *Journal of Theoretical Politics, 1*, 131–147.

Skogstad, Grace. 2001. Review of *Theories of the Policy Process*, by Paul A. Sabatier. *Canadian Journal of Political Science, 34*, 419–420.

Stinchcombe, Arthur. 1968. *Constructing Social Theories*. Chicago: University of Chicago Press.

Theodoulou, Stella. 2001. Review of *Theories of the Policy Process*, by Paul A. Sabatier. *American Political Science Review, 95*, 107–1008.

Zahariadis, Nikolaos, 1992. "To Sell or Not to Sell? Telecommunications Policy in Britain and France." *Journal of Public Policy, 12*, 355–376.

___. 1995. *Markets, States, and Public Policy: Privatization in Britain and France*. Ann Arbor, MI: University of Michigan Press.

___. 2003. *Ambiguity and Choice in Public Policy*. Washington, D.C.: Georgetown University Press.

# The Nature of the Policy Process

## RANDALL B. RIPLEY

The policy process is complicated, and the analyst must seek to simplify it. The generic form of simplification used by social scientists, including political scientists, is a model. These models—or simplifications of a very complicated set of processes—can take many different forms, ranging from the purely verbal to the purely mathematical. All of them, however, have the same purpose: to render what is incredibly complex and idiosyncratic in any individual case into a set of relationships that are both simpler and more recurrent. Model makers aim at both understandable patterned description and, sometimes without thinking about it, at explanation (what causes what). This chapter represents my own efforts to "model" in several ways the policy process at the national level in the United States. I will try to make a complicated set of processes understandable in terms of patterns that tend to recur, and I will offer some comments about explanation.

This chapter focuses on models that lay out various stages of policy activity. These models include stages in the policy process that include both political activities and intellectual activities that occur simultaneously (much like the discussion in chapter 1 of the six major policy-related activities and the potential roles of political scientists at each stage). These stages also deal, either implicitly or explicitly, with the policy "products" that emerge over time. And, of course, the ordering of the stages has chronological implications about what might be expected and in what order by anyone looking at the policy process.

A second kind of modeling enterprise starts with the notions that different kinds of policies, differentiated by some broad categorical scheme, are the product of different kinds of political patterns and/or that, when different things are at stake, different kinds of policies help generate different kinds of patterns of political relationships and influence.

Relationships running in both directions (that is, from patterns of interaction to types of policy and from types of policy to patterns of interaction) may be present simultaneously and may reinforce each other. This whole area of exploration will be the subject of chapter 3.

In the rest of this chapter I will look at the utility, limits, and purposes of models in general. Second, I will lay out a simple model for the understanding of policy. Third, I will consider more complicated visions of the U.S. national policy process, and finally, I will summarize in descriptive fashion the flow of policy activities and products of which students of the national policy process in the United States should be aware.

## Models: Utility, Purposes, and Limits

Models are not neutral. The choices of what factors seem important to include (and, conversely, what can be excluded) may be shaped, consciously or unconsciously, by ideology or any of a thousand other influences over the mind of the person constructing the model. In short, the general vision of political life is both empirically and theoretically derived. This vision is likely to be included in a model of the policy process.

## Utility and Purpose

The major utility of any model is that it simplifies complex reality in ways that can be readily understood. The trick is knowing what level of simplification is appropriate. If a model adheres to too many of the attributes of reality it is seeking to summarize, it becomes unwieldy and too like the original. If, on the other hand, the model becomes too simple and omits too much, it is no longer recognizable enough to be useful in understanding reality.

Modelers of anything face the same general problem. Consider those who want to model railroads. They must choose a scale that allows trains, yards, mainlines, surrounding countryside, and other attributes in and around the real thing to be portrayed sufficiently to give the sense of reality, but with obvious distortions. They must decide what is essential. That usually comes down to preferences for details on cars, especially on locomotives. What is gained in detail is lost in space and vice versa. Ultimately, the scale chosen by any individual modeler becomes a matter of aesthetic taste based, in part, on a judgment of the nature of a satisfactory model. Choices of levels of abstraction and detail in models of political and policy processes partake of the same mix of judgment and aesthetics.

## Limits

A specific limit on models of the policy process that needs to be mentioned is that any model (particularly the "flow chart" or "box and arrow" type you will find in this book) is likely to make the world of policy too ordered, too predictable, and too rational. Regardless of the form of the model used, it needs to be realized that:

- The chronology implied in any model of the policy process is only rough at best. Stages may occur "out of order," simultaneously, or in other ways that are not tidy chronologically.
- The boundaries between different stages are blurred and not readily discernible to either participants or analysts in completely clear or consistent ways.

## A Simple Model of the Policy Process

As we begin to examine some possible models of the policy process, we must be constantly aware of the purpose of such examinations. Such models are useful in either designing research or in appreciating the studies of others, because they point the reader to the appropriate clusters of variables and to the appropriate relationships between those variables. A model of general applicability and with few variable clusters inevitably points out only the most important variables and the most gross level of relationships to which the observer or researcher must be sensitive. But such a model, although not immediately useful for guiding specific and focused empirical research, is useful in a broader sense because it suggests a general overall vision of the factors that the political science policy analyst must take into account in making sense out of policy phenomena. Thus, we begin with Figure 1, which portrays the most general model of the policy process.

There are several fairly important ideas embedded in this figure. First, note that the environment and the perceptions of environment on the part of policy actors are partially independent and partially intersecting. Environmental factors can be important even if not perceived by policy actors. Likewise, perceptions—regardless of how accurate or inaccurate they may be—may have independent weight. Analysts define environmental variables in analyzing policy and in trying to figure out what causes certain kinds of policy responses. Some of those analytical constructs have considerable validity, and some of them reveal pressures and forces in society that help explain substantial portions of subsequent policy activity. This is true even if, in some cases, the policy actors themselves are not aware totally, or even aware at all, of the environmental factors that analysts find to be important.

It is also important to note that policy actors move on the basis of their own perceptions. These perceptions include some of the environmental factors that analysts determine to be important. But

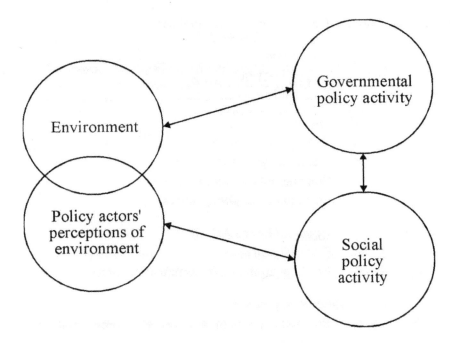

**Figure 1. General Model of the Policy Process**

the perceptions may also be of events, trends, and factors that analysts cannot find systematically important but, in the day-to-day decisions by influential actors that shape outcomes in detail, are quite important.

The analyst must pay attention, then, to environmental variables that are uncovered and structured by analytical procedures. But he or she must also pay attention to the perceptions of policy actors as distinct from the analyst's constructs. Actors' perceptions are also "independent variables" that can and usually do have considerable importance in explaining subsequent policy activity.

A second idea that has some importance is that policy activity occurs both in the government and in society. Political scientists interested in policy all too often assume that the activity of government and of governmental actors (members of Congress, presidents, bureaucrats, justices) is all that needs to be studied. To be sure, governmental policy activity is important and requires careful analysis. But equally important is the activity in society that helps shape the general nature of any policy activity. For example, a health clinic may be built by the government, but without the societal activity of individuals choosing to use the clinic nothing much happens. Society and government interact within the context of environment in determining the totality of policy activity. In subsequent discussion I will distinguish between different types of policy activity, but the general point that there are both societal and governmental dimensions to any study of policy should not be missed.

It is worth noting that the arrows, which signify influence or in a rough sense causation, run in both directions between all of the variable clusters. This suggests not just that environment and policy actors' perceptions of the environment "cause" subsequent policy activity in the government and society but that policy activity in both government and society helps shape both the environment and (especially) policy actors' perceptions of it. Likewise, the governmental and societal dimensions of policy activity affect each other.

The notion of "subsequent" policy activity is, in some ways, misleading. The use of such language suggests that there is a single linear passage of time in which some events take place before some other events and that there are variables that are causative (or independent) and other variables that are resultant (or dependent). Such relationships can be analyzed. In fact, there is no simple linear chronology because all phenomena are constantly present and constantly changing through time, and these changes can have many different chronological relationships to each other. Thus, environment at Time 1 may help "cause" governmental policy activity at Time 2, which may have

**Table 1. Major Factors for Inclusion in a General Model of the U.S. Policy Process**

I.    *Environment*
    A.    Outside government
    B.    Inside government
    C.    Specific policies and programs
    D.    Perceptions of policy actors

II.    *Governmental Policy Activity*
    A.    Policy statements
    B.    Policy actions (implementation actions)

III.    *Societal Policy Activity*
    A.    Societal implementation (usage of programs)
    B.    Policy/program results

impact on societal policy activity at Time 3, which in turn may help shape the environment at Time 4, and so on. Even this abstract example is too simple, since it implies that there are predictable cycles of what variables are to be considered independent and dependent at any given time. That may not be altogether true, although the analyst sometimes has to pretend it is true in order to impose some order on an otherwise hopelessly complicated set of relationships.

## More Complicated Models of the U.S. Policy Process

### Major Factors to Consider

Let's look again at the very simple set of relationships portrayed in Figure 1. That figure lays out three major clusters of factors (variables) that a policy analyst needs to consider. Those clusters can be elaborated a bit in order to develop a more sophisticated, specific, and practical design for conducting any individual inquiry. Table 1 presents an overview of one such elaboration. In the paragraphs that follow I will discuss the major concepts.

*Environment: That Outside Government.* The first facet of the environment of importance to the policy analyst is the general environment external to government. This signifies that all policy decisions are set in the context of general external environmental factors and that these factors are likely to influence a good deal of what else happens.

The external environment is of two broad types. First, the environment can be described as a series of patterns involving a variety of economic, social, and political factors, including patterns of beliefs and values. These patterns are the constructs of social observers and analysts. For example, unemployment is a genuine feature of the external environment that has the potential for exerting an influence over a good deal else that goes on in the policy process. But the specific form in which unemployment is described—based on a monthly rate broken into population sectors (white males, black teenagers, female heads of household, and so on)—is the construct of social scientists (in this case, economists). Many features of society are in the same mold: they are real, to be sure, but the form of their description is an invention of social scientists. Patterns of portions of the external environment might involve such factors as public opinion, party strength in society, the nature of political coalitions in society, and a great variety of economic and social conditions.

The second type of broad environment is best described as random events. These are not the external constructs of social scientists, even in descriptive form. They are simply events—both natural and those made by people—that occur and have some policy relevance. Major natural disasters (earthquakes, floods, hurricanes, and so on), for example, usually occasion some kind of policy response. Acts of terrorism, national or international, also trigger responses. The analyst needs to acknowledge that such events occur, are generally unpredictable, and have policy consequences that must be analyzed.

*Environment: That Inside Government.* A second major facet of the environment of importance to the policy analyst is the general internal environment. "Internal" refers to the inside of government in both a structural sense and a process sense. The goverptnment has a particular structure and a particular set of operative processes at any given time. These facts have general policy consequences, as do the pattern of relationships between governmental units and nongovernmental interests. Features of the general internal environment that might require systematic attention by an analyst include characteristics of agency structure in the bureaucracy or of subcommittee structure in Congress; characteristics of personnel in agencies or subcommittees; and characteristics of decision-making processes in pieces of the bureaucracy or of Congress.

*Environment: That Related to Specific Policies and Programs.* A third major facet of the environment of direct relevance to policy analysis is the specific environment in which any particular policy or program is set. While any individual policy or program is set in the general external and general internal environments described above, any individual policy or program is also set in a context of previous statements and actions. These statements and actions may be in earlier iterations of the policy or program itself, they may be in relation to related forerunner programs, or, at minimum, they describe the context in which the program was formed. No policy or program emerges without some sort of history. If it is an ongoing program or policy, the history is that of the policy or program itself. Even new policies or programs have a prehistory that helps shape the actions, results, and other phenomena at any given time. The notion of incrementalism—that policies and programs tend to change only in small units at any time—is based on the notion, in part, that the specific policy and program environment is a powerful explanatory factor. In short, what occurs in any given time period is a close variant of what existed in the previous time period.

*Environment: Perception of Environments by Policy Actors.* All aspects of the environment are subject to some sort of perception (or ignorance) on the part of policy actors. Those perceptions, in a sense, become independent of the phenomena perceived. Thus, both the phenomena and the perceptions can and often do have independent weight in a policy process. The perceptions are most important in helping determine what policy decisions get made. The phenomena—regardless of the accuracy or inaccuracy of perceptions—have the most weight in helping determine what the policies adopted can and cannot accomplish.

*Governmental Policy Activity: Policy Statements.* The first major form of governmental policy activity of concern to a policy analyst is the set of activities and processes that result in policy statements. Policy statements are declarations of intent on the part of the government (or a portion of the government) to do something. This declaration is sometimes highly visible, as in a statement by the president or in the passage by Congress of an important new statute. This declaration can also be invisible to most of the public, as in a statement by a bureau chief to an important lobbyist for the bureau's clients. Different levels and different parts of the government may make conflicting policy statements simultaneously. Even the same participant in the policy process may make conflicting statements within a relatively short period of time.

Policy statements may be either intragovernmental or societal in nature. In the former case, they represent an orientation toward the future of specific units of government within the governmental structure. In the latter case, they represent an orientation to what the unit of government will seek to do in society. The latter policy statements are of interest to policy analysts. The former are of primary interest to students of public administration in a more restricted sense.

*Governmental Policy Activity: Policy Actions.* Policy actions are what the government does as distinguished from what it says it is going to do, sometimes with many and conflicting or unclear voices. Policy actions can also be called implementation actions. Such actions are what happens, typically, after laws are passed authorizing a program, a Policy, a benefit, or some kind of tangible governmental output. The set of activities that follow policy statements constitute implementation activities. Implementation activities (to be explored in more detail in chapter 5) include the acquisition of resources needed for action, interpretation of laws (usually through writing regulations), planning for action, organizing action, and providing benefits and services.

*Societal Policy Activity: Societal Implementation.* Societal implementation refers to patterns of usage or nonusage of programs and intended benefits on the part of those eligible to partake. Or, in a coercive program, such as the draft, societal implementation would refer to such matters as registration rates and evasion rates. In a program conferring benefits—a publicly funded job training program, for example—the rate of usage of training slots for individuals and the nature of the users would both be matters of interest to the policy analyst. Who's involved? Who benefits? It needs to be recognized that not all of those who are eligible may actually show up and take part or benefit in whatever way they are supposed to benefit.

*Societal Policy Activity: Policy/Program Results.* The results of any policy or program also involve society. The central point of the governing enterprise is—or should be—to have some felicitous impact on society through a variety of policies and programs. The analyst needs to sort out what those impacts or results are and, above all, how they are to be explained. Why? is the central question in the analysis of results, just as it is in the analysis of any part of the policy process.

While the analyst needs to look for evidence of the intended results or consequences of a policy or program actually occurring, he or she also needs to look for unintended consequences. In some ways, it is useful if the consequences of nonactions or "paths not taken" can also be discerned. All of this is complicated and tricky. The whole question of how to evaluate policy and program impact will occupy us again in chapter 6.

*Relationships Between Major Factors.* As Figure 1 suggests, all major clusters of policy related variables interact with each other. When the major variable clusters are elaborated, as in the discussion accompanying Table 1, the relationships of any one cluster to all others should be investigated. The world of policy, in fact, seems to be structured that way. In a more practical vein, however, social and political research cannot pay attention to all important factors and relationships in any single study. Therefore, a subset of factors and relationships will be selected for closer analysis in any given study. A few examples of studies using subsets of the basic collection of factors and relationships will indicate the strengths and weaknesses of the particular choices that are made.

The point to be underscored through these illustrations is that any given set of choices about what to study and what not to study in considering policy and policy-relevant variables has both costs and benefits. Practicalities of time, money, and brainpower limit any study. Different choices of what to study and what to exclude are appropriate depending on what needs to be examined with the most care.

*Example A: A Perceptual-Process Model.* A model stressing the impact of the perceptions of the policy-relevant environment on the part of policy actors and characteristics of governmental processes on policy actions has been used to investigate the development of four specific federal programs in the economic and human resource development area in the mid-1960s to early 1970s period (Ripley, 1972). The general model used to structure the research is diagrammed in Figure 2. The point of this example is not to summarize the research findings but to assess the strengths and weaknesses of focusing on these particular variables in trying to explain policy actions.

The model was used, essentially, in analyzing data that can best be described as four case studies of the programs of the Economic Development Administration, of the Job Corps, for Appalachia, and for Model Cities that were systematically compared. The empirical content of the four cases was partly based on judgments—those of the author and those of people involved in decision making for the programs. This model seems best adapted to studies that might be characterized as decision-making studies. The strengths of the model (or more accurately, the strengths of relying on the factors assumed to be most important for purposes of the model) can be summarized briefly:

1.  This model allows examination, understanding, and explanation (in a loose sense) of agenda building. In the study cited, the model was applied to the four programs noted above, all of

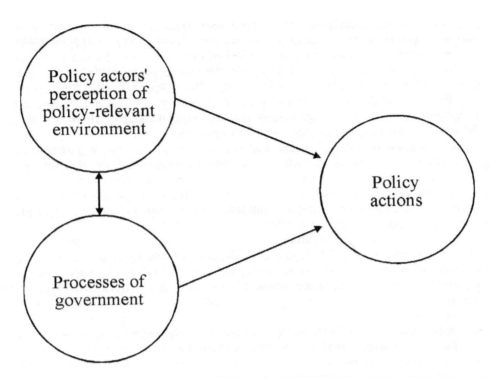

**Figure 2. A Perceptual-Process Model for Investigating Policymaking**

which were created between 1964 and 1966. Thus, the initial stage of the process—agenda building—could be examined in a comparative framework. This is useful since there is relatively little systematic study of agenda building even though it is important (see chapter 4 for more discussion of this point; see also Kingdon, 1984).

2. This model allows examination, understanding, and explanation of initial policy actions (also policy statements). The earliest stages of creating a policy and implementing it are amenable to use of these particular clusters of important factors.

3. This model accommodates detailed variations in policy actions. These variations might be washed out in a different kind of model and/or a model relying on different kinds of data. Detailed variations might seem trivial, but if policies do not differ a great deal from each other over time (which is often, although not always, the case in the United States), then relatively small variations are or can be important.

4. This model is particularly strong in assessing decision making—not just the content of decisions themselves. A number of approaches to policy studies assume that the content of decisions is all that matters. This model suggests that the manner of decision making also helps produce different kinds of policy actions.

This way of examining policy has some definite limitations:

1. It does not seem particularly suited to dealing with policy results.

2. It may be limited to comparative case studies. And, of course, case studies detailed enough to be worth analysis can be produced only in limited quantities. Therefore, the data base (or the N) is, by design and of necessity, fairly limited.

3. This model—particularly the reliance on perceptions of policy-relevant environment on the part of policy actors—has limited longitudinal utility. Typically, perceptual data have to come from interviews or a combination of interviews and documentary sources. Yet, trying to get interviewees to reconstruct their perceptions for times past is generally unrewarding. They have forgotten the past, or they look at the past through the eyes with which they see the world in the present (which produces distortions, although not necessarily deliberate), or they deliberately distort what they claim to have thought in the past for one or more of many possible reasons.

4. Data collection is costly because considerable detail has to be gathered and because interviewing in general, which is a technique required for collecting some of the appropriate data, is expensive in terms of both time and financial support.

5. As already implied in some of the points above, the scope of this kind of policy study is limited. As scope expands, detail (and in that sense, rigor) is almost surely going to have to be sacrificed.

This type of model is a good example of the mix of strengths and weaknesses that any particular choice of model is likely to impose on the study of policy. The person or persons doing the study should be aware of those strengths and weaknesses and choose the model best suited to the purpose.

*Example B: A Structural Model.* One more example will help underscore the general points made above. A submodel focusing on the impact of patterned parts of both the external and internal environment on policy actions and, at least in principle, on policy results in society has here been labeled a structural model (see Ripley and Franklin, 1975, for an example of its use, primarily in explaining dollars available to individual federal agencies that compete in a budget process over time). The general model employed for such a study is portrayed in Figure 3. Perceptions and processes are omitted. They are replaced by patterned parts of the external environment, by patterned structures inside the government, and by previous policy actions. This model, like the previous example, seeks to explain policy actions. But it goes about seeking those explanations in a very different way. Again, some fairly clear strengths and weaknesses are attached to this way of investigating policy. In some ways, they present a mirror image of the strengths and weakness outlined for the first submodel.

The strengths can be summarized in three points:

1. This model is more suitable for investigating ongoing programs than the other model, which is more suitable for investigating new programs in their early stages. The model rests on assumptions and can be made to incorporate research techniques appropriate to continuing programs, some of them with long histories. Policy actions in such programs and results stemming from them can, in principle, be investigated using this model.

2. This model can be used in connection with data collection priorities that allow both considerable rigor and a large scope (that is, many programs) simultaneously.

3. The first two points imply that this approach to the study of policy allows a long period of time to be covered. People's (policy actors') memories are not a source of data, so relevant policy data can, in principle, be reconstructed for the past from documentary sources. There

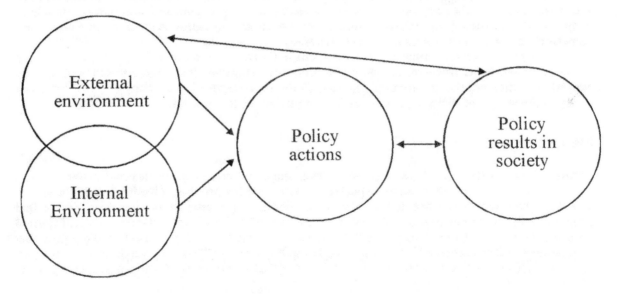

**Figure 3. A Structural Model for Investigating Policymaking**

are, of course, the usual problems in finding comparable data in documentary sources, but the problems do not lie in the decay of people's memories, the distortion of their memories, or the unavailability of the people.

This submodel also has definite limitations:

1. It is not suited to addressing agenda building. It is best at handling ongoing, established programs.
2. It does not examine fine variations in programs; rather, it looks at aggregate program data, which inevitably produces a concern for fairly gross variations.
3. It has no way of probing for, including, or accounting for the various factors (political, psychological, perceptual) that go into the making of any specific decision. It simply assumes these will somehow "wash out" when the aggregate level is investigated.

I do not offer these two examples of models to suggest that one is better than the other in every case, nor am I under any illusion that two examples exhaust the universe of possibilities. But I want to make the point as clearly as I can that analysts have to make choices about what they can study and how they will go about their work. These choices are at many levels and at many points in time. But the first critical choice is to specify a model. Any choice inevitably includes some concerns and excludes others. A choice of a model (or submodel, if you prefer) can shape the nature of the data to be collected and, ultimately, may affect the analytical techniques to be used. The choices of model, data, and analytic techniques influence each other. A good analyst will understand the intricacies and interactions of these choices. A sloppy one will make choices and thereby be forced into additional choices without necessarily knowing or understanding that fact.

## Stages of the Policy Process

Numerous treatments of the policy process lay out stages of that process, with various nominal labels attached, in order to help organize discussion and analysis. Such stage-oriented discussions do not form the direct basis for hypothesizing causal relationships, although such hypotheses may emerge. Rather, they are rough chronological and logical guides for observers who want to see important activities in some ordered pattern or sequence. Such organizational helpers are useful and, in fact, essential for anyone trying to plow through the complexities of policy making and policy analysis. At best, such maps—even with their rough spots and simplifications—lend some clarity to the observer/reader/student as he or she grapples with a complicated and sometimes murky set of interactions and processes.

I see no point to repeating a lot of different authors' versions of policy stages. There are many versions. Most of them have some similarities. Many analysts agree pretty well on the central activities requiring attention. Instead, in the final pages of this chapter, I will offer my guide to the stages of the policy process for the readers of this volume.

### Major Stages

Figure 4 lays out the basic flow of policy stages, major functional activities that occur in those stages, and the products that can be expected at each stage if a product is forthcoming. Naturally, a policy process may be aborted at any stage. Beginning a process does not guarantee that products will emerge or that a stage will be "completed" and so lead to the next stage. Figure 4 presents the general flow of stages, activities, and products that can be expected in a policy that is generated and transformed into a viable and ongoing program. "Stages" are the names attached to major clusters of activities that result in identifiable products if they reach conclusion. "Functional activities" are the major subroutines of actions and interactions engaged in by policy actors. "Products" are the output, or end result, of any general stage.

*Agenda setting.* Somehow the organs of government must decide what they will pay attention to. The stage at which this decision is made in any given policy area is here called agenda setting. Thousands of issues are constantly vying for inclusion on the governmental agenda. Only some of them make it at any given time. The form in which they come on the agenda can vary over time

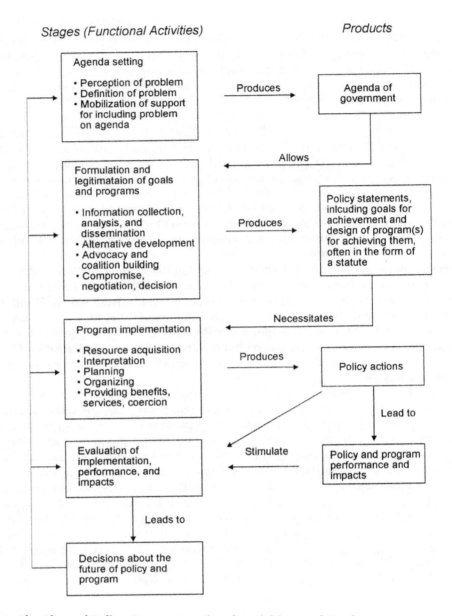

Stages (Functional Activities)                                    Products

**Figure 4. The Flow of Policy Stages, Functional Activities, and Products**

and influence subsequent concrete decisions. The functional activities in the agenda-setting stage include the necessity for some individuals and/or groups to perceive a problem to exist, to decide the government should be involved in the problem, to define the problem, and to mobilize support for including the problem on the governmental agenda.

Competition enters these activities in several ways. First, different people compete to attract the attention of governmental actors for inclusion of any specific problem on the agenda. There is not a fixed number of agenda item " 'slots" available at any one time. On the other hand, the capacity for the government to include items on its action agenda at any point in time is not unlimited. Second, even within the groups and among individuals concerned with a general issue area there will be competition over the specific definition of the problem and, subsequently, competition over which groups and views to mobilize and how to do it.

*Formulation and Legitimation of Goals and Programs.* Not all agenda items receive specific treatment in the form of decisions about policies and programs. Not all of them even get translated into a form that allows specific formulation and legitimation activities to take place. But if an item on the agenda is treated in any concrete way, the next step is for it to become the subject of formulation and legitimation.

Formulation and legitimation are complex activities that involve four major sets of functional activities, each complex in its own right. Part of formulating alternatives and then choosing one alternative for possible ratification is collecting, analyzing, and disseminating information for purposes of assessing alternatives and projecting likely outcomes and for purposes of persuasion.

Alternative development is one of the successor sub-routines to the one dealing with information. Another is advocacy, in which different persons and groups advocate different points of views and alternatives and seek to build supporting coalitions in support of their views and their preferred alternative. Finally, usually as a result of compromise and negotiation, a decision is reached. If the compromise and negotiation process breaks down, no decision is reached.

The generic products of the formulation and legitimation stage are policy statements (declarations of intent, including some form of goal statement) and the design of programs for making the intent concrete and pursuing achievement of the goals. Both the goals and the program designs may be vague and sketchy. Grandiose goal statements that lack clarity are usually the result of the compromise process. Too much specificity and clarity might prevent compromise of forces that don't really agree on fundamental concrete goals and aspirations. If the goals are raised to a more general and murky level, they can attract the support of persons and groups that might otherwise disagree.

Reasons for lack of specificity and clarity in program design are more numerous. Partly it is a matter of not proliferating details that might also proliferate disagreements, and partly it is a matter of time on the part of Congress, since program designs usually appear first in a statute. Congress must address hundreds, even thousands, of agenda items in any given two-year period. The members cannot fool with any one too long. Throughout the course of history, Congress has gotten into the habit of delegating administrative power to the president and/or to the agencies and secretaries concerned to flesh out rudimentary program designs. From the early 1930s to 1983, Congress could hedge its bets by inserting some form of legislative veto in a statute, which in effect made the president or agency check with Congress before proceeding with some specific actions. The Supreme Court ruled this invention unconstitutional in mid-1983. This ruling may force Congress to fill in a few more details some of the time, but it is doubtful if it will have more effect than that. The pressures producing extensive delegation by Congress will not change.

*Program Implementation.* The next stage (assuming that a policy has been stated and a program created) is program implementation. In order to implement a program, resources need to be acquired. The law needs to be interpreted, usually in written regulations and then in elaborations of those regulations. A variety of planning activities typically take place. Various organizing routines are part of implementation. Finally, the payoff-routines of providing benefits, services, and/or coercion (whatever the tangible manifestation of the program) are developed. All of these activities, although they sound more dull than advocacy and negotiation, are political. Conflict and disagreement can erupt. Various techniques of conflict resolution are necessarily brought into play. Policy actions are the products of the various routines and activities that comprise the program implementation stage.

*Evaluation of Implementation, Performance, and Impacts.* After policy actions lead to various kinds of results (what I call performance and impact), evaluation of both the actions (implementation) and the results (performance and impacts) takes place. The word evaluation often conjures up an image of "objective" social scientists applying rigorous analytic techniques and letting the chips fall where they may. Some of that may transpire. But, as used in this book, evaluation is a much broader concept and refers to the assessment of what has happened or, in many cases, what is thought to have happened. The "what" can refer to implementation, to short-run results (performance), or to long-run results (impacts). That assessment takes place constantly and is done by all kinds of people—officials of all descriptions, interest groups, legislators, researchers inside the government, and researchers outside the government. Some evaluation is completely based on political instincts and judgments. A good deal is based on a mix of a little information (often anecdotal) and political judgments. Some (a small portion) is based on systematic analysis of fairly extensive information (data).

Policy analysts coming from political science or any other discipline have a role to play in evaluation of implementation, performance, and impacts. But they should realize that their form of evaluation is only one form and that probably it is less politically relevant than almost any other form of evaluation that takes place. Not too much should be expected in terms of attention to or subsequent actions based on evaluation. On the other hand, evaluation should not be written off entirely. It has a place. I will return to this theme later in the book.

*Decisions about the Future of the Policy and Program.* The evaluative processes and conclusions, in all of their diversity, lead to one or more of many decisions about the future (or nonfuture) of the policy and program being evaluated. The necessity for such decisions means that the cycle can be entered again at any of its major stages. Conceivably, a problem will be taken off the agenda either because it has been "solved" or because it is viewed as no longer relevant. Or the nature of its most salient features as an agenda item may be changed. Thus, decisions about the future might reset the cycle to the agenda-setting stage.

Those decisions may lead back to policy formulation and legitimation. The necessity or legitimacy of keeping an item on the agenda may not be questioned, but legislative (statutory) revisions may be viewed as necessary or desirable, at least by some actors. Thus, the cycle is reentered somewhere in the activity cluster comprising formulation and legitimation. In some cases, decisions about the future may not require new legislation or amendments to existing legislation, but they may require some adjustments in program implementation.

## Principal Limits on and Utility of a Stage Conception of the Policy Process

Remember when looking at the policy process as a succession of stages that any such conception is artificial. It may also not be true to what happens. It has a logical appeal, and it is presented chronologically, but chronological reality as it emerges in any case may vary significantly from what the stage-based model says "should" happen in a specific order. The process can be stopped at any point, and, in most cases, the policy process is truncated at some fairly early stage. Only some fairly modest subsets of all possible policies go through the entire process. And the process can be reentered or reactivated at any point and at any time.

In short, reality is messy. Models, particularly a nice listing of stages with an implied tidy chronology, are not messy. In a collision between tidiness and untidiness the analyst must not be so struck by the values of order as to force reality into a model in which it might not fit.

These are only caveats, however. The utility of organizing data and thoughts about complicated reality in this way is great. It allows the analyst to look for patterns and, more important, to explain the causes of different patterns.

Each of the major clusters of policy products contained in Figure 4 imply the beginning questions that are likely to be central to political scientists who are functioning as policy analysts:

1. The agenda generates the questions: To what does the government pay attention? Why?
2. Policy statements generate the questions: What does the government say it will do? Why?
3. Policy actions generate the questions: What does the government do? Why? How well does it do it?
4. Policy and program performance and impact generate the questions: What differences do government actions make? Why? How well do the programs work? Why?

These are not elaborately worded questions, but they contain the essence of the policy analytic enterprise. Clear answers are hard to come by, especially when they go beyond a fairly simple descriptive level.

## Summary

1. Models in general are a useful device for portraying complex reality, including the policy process, in understandable form.
2. The simplest and most general model of the policy process introduces the interrelated concepts of environment, policy actors' perceptions of environment, governmental policy activity, and societal policy activity as the most important.

3.  A more complicated model of the policy process necessarily distinguishes between different aspects of the environment, two types of governmental policy activity (policy statements and policy actions), and two types of societal policy activity (societal implementation and policy and program results).
4.  The major policy stages are: (1) agenda setting; (2) formulation and legitimation of goals and programs; (3) program implementation; and (4) evaluation of implementation, performance, and impacts.

## References

Kingdon, John W. *Agendas, Alternatives, and Public Policies*. Boston, Mass.: Little, Brown, 1984.

Ripley, Randall B., and Grace A. Franklin, eds. *Policy-Making in the Federal Executive Branch*. New York: Free Press, 1975.

# CHAPTER 2:
## ARENAS OF POLICYMAKING

# The Federal Government and Higher Education

## Lawrence E. Gladieux, Arthur M. Hauptman, and Laura Greene Knapp

## Introduction

The framers of the U.S. Constitution lodged no specific responsibility for education with the national government, yet the federal influence on American colleges and universities has been enduring and pervasive. From sponsorship of land-grant colleges in the nineteenth century to the underwriting of student loans and university-based research and development in the twentieth century, the federal government has actively and extensively supported higher education to serve a variety of national purposes.

Today the federal government provides less than 15 percent of all college and university revenues. But in two types of spending, direct aid to students and funds for R&D, federal outlays far exceed those of the states, industry, and other donors. Higher education is also affected by federal tax policies, both in the financing of institutions and in family and student financing of the costs of attendance. Moreover, as a condition of federal spending and tax support, Congress and executive agencies of the government impose a variety of rules and mandates on postsecondary institutions and students.

The federal impact on campuses and on students is substantial, diverse, and constantly changing. It is the product of deeply rooted traditions but also short-term decisions. This chapter analyzes the federal government's relationship to higher education, beginning with the historical underpinnings and current means and dimensions of support. It then discusses issues in student aid, research support, tax policy, and regulation, and concludes with thoughts on federal policy directions for the balance of the 1990s.

## The Responsibility for Higher Education in the American System

That the states have the basic responsibility for education at all levels is an American tradition. The Tenth Amendment, reserving powers not delegated to the central government to the states, coupled with the fact that "education" is nowhere mentioned in the Constitution, pointed toward a secondary role for the federal government in this field. While some of the founding fathers urged a national system of education run by the federal government, the majority favored state, local and private control, perhaps with a national university to cap the system. All proposals to establish such a university in the capital city failed, despite the fervent support of George Washington and several of his successors in the presidency. To this day the federal government does not directly sponsor institutions of higher learning apart from the military academies and a few institutions serving special populations. Still, early federal policy was crucial in promoting higher education as an adjunct of western migration and public land development in the late eighteenth and nineteenth centuries. The Morrill Land-Grant College Act of 1862, for example, fostered the creation and development of what are now some of the nation's great public and private universities.[1]

Federal investment in university-based R&D and in student aid via the GI Bill soared following World War II. Beginning with the Soviet challenge of Sputnik, Congress created a variety of aid-to-education programs in the late 1950s and 1960s, and by the 1970s the federal government became the largest source of direct assistance to individual students for financing their college expenses. Fundamentally, however, federal expenditures have remained supplementary to state subsidies and private support of higher learning. Terry Sanford, former governor of North Carolina, U.S. Senator, and president of Duke University, once put it this way:

> The money for the extras came from the national funds. . . . This is the glamour money. . . . It is needed, it has improved the quality. . . . It is proper to remember, however, for all the advantages brought by the extras, the train was put on the track in the first place by the states, and continues to be moved by state fuel and engineers.[2]

Over the past two centuries, the states have moved with varying speed to create and expand public systems of higher education and, more recently, to assist private colleges and universities or to purchase educational services from them. Today the major public support for postsecondary institutions continues to come from the states. Figure 1, which shows the sources of funding for higher education in 1990, demonstrates the continuing hegemony of the states in this regard.

The traditional division of responsibilities between the federal and state governments was reaffirmed in the early 1970s when Congress debated and ultimately rejected proposals for general-purpose federal institutional aid. In passing the 1972 amendments to the Higher Education Act:

> Congress pulled up short of a plan that amounted to federal revenue sharing with institutions of higher education—across-the-board general operating support distributed on the basis of enrollments. It was unwilling to underwrite the entire system without reference to any national objective other than preserving and strengthening educational institutions. . . . The responsibility for general support of institutions, it was decided, should continue to rest with the states.[3]

This is not to say that the federal government has been unconcerned about the health and capacity of institutions. Certain types of institutions have received special federal attention because of their particular contributions to the national interest. Major research and graduate-oriented universities, particularly their medical schools, are one such category. They are supported by grants and contracts from multiple federal agencies. The historically black colleges are also beneficiaries of federal institution-based support, primarily through programs authorized under Title III of the Higher Education Act.

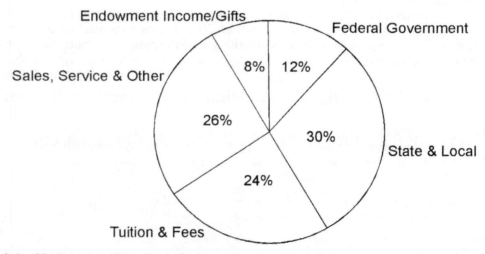

Source: Arthur M. Hauptman, *Higher Education Finance Issues in the Early 1990s* (New Brunswick, NJ.: Consortium for Policy Research in Education, Rutgers University, 1993).

**Figure 1. Sources of Revenue to Higher Education Institutions, FY 1990**

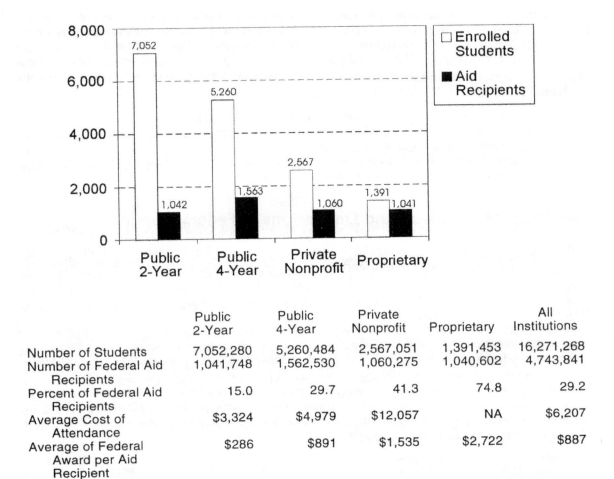

| | Public 2-Year | Public 4-Year | Private Nonprofit | Proprietary | All Institutions |
|---|---|---|---|---|---|
| Number of Students | 7,052,280 | 5,260,484 | 2,567,051 | 1,391,453 | 16,271,268 |
| Number of Federal Aid Recipients | 1,041,748 | 1,562,530 | 1,060,275 | 1,040,602 | 4,743,841 |
| Percent of Federal Aid Recipients | 15.0 | 29.7 | 41.3 | 74.8 | 29.2 |
| Average Cost of Attendance | $3,324 | $4,979 | $12,057 | NA | $6,207 |
| Average of Federal Award per Aid Recipient | $286 | $891 | $1,535 | $2,722 | $887 |

Source: 1990 National Postsecondary Student Aid Study. Cost of attendance (tuition, fees, room and board) data from: *Digest of Education Statistics: 1990* (U.S. Department of Education) and *The College Cost Book 1989–90* (The College Board, 1989).

**Figure 2. Enrolled Students and Federal Aid Recipients, 1989–90 Academic Year**

In addition, a few federal programs address institutional capacity for research. These include the National Institutes of Health's Biomedical Research Support Grants and the National Science Foundation's Institutional Development Program. Other federal funding goes to support the arts and humanities, occupational and vocational education, international exchanges and studies, the provision of military training, and other purposes. Although the amounts are relatively small they are significant for some institutions and certain parts of the education community.

Student aid also represents an indirect subsidy that affects nearly every institution in the country.[4] As shown in Figure 2, about a third of the 16 million-plus students who attend postsecondary education each year are estimated to receive some federal aid, in the form of grants, loans, or work-study. The aid programs benefit all sectors of postsecondary education, but the rate of student participation is by far the highest in proprietary schools (75 percent), followed by private non-profit colleges (41 percent), public four-year institutions (30 percent), and public two-year institutions (15 percent). The vigorous politics surrounding congressional reauthorization and revision of the student aid programs in 1980, 1986, and 1992 attests to the high stakes involved for postsecondary institutions. Representatives of the various sectors—two-year, four-year, public, private, proprietary—struggled over scores of amendments that determined who got what under Title IV of the Higher Education Act.

In sum, while federal education monies are much sought after, the historical limitations on the federal role continue to prevail in the 1990s. The states retain the fundamental responsibility for higher education, primarily through provision of operating support for public systems of colleges and universities. The federal role is to provide particular kinds of support to meet perceived national objectives, generally without distinguishing between public and nonpublic recipients. The federal government:

- purchases services and supports research capacity of universities;
- fills some gaps (e.g., in college library support, foreign language and area studies, and health professions development); and
- directs the bulk of its aid to students rather than to institutions, with the aim of removing barriers facing individuals who aspire to higher education.

## Overview: Mechanisms and Dimensions of Federal Support

In the nineteenth century, states served as intermediaries in federal patronage of higher education. Proceeds from the sale of public lands provided endowments that helped the states establish and finance the early land-grant institutions, agricultural extension programs, and other forerunners of today's comprehensive colleges and universities. The federal grants to the states were broad and carried few restrictions.

Toward the beginning of the twentieth century, however, the pattern began to change. Federal support became piecemeal and started going directly to institutions themselves, bypassing state governments. In recent decades, nearly all federal monies have been channeled to institutions (or to departments, schools, and faculty members within institutions) or to individual students.

For this reason, a federal-state "partnership" in supporting higher education is meaningful only in a general sense. In fact, there is virtually no conscious meshing of funding purposes and patterns between the two levels of government. By and large the federal activity proceeds independently. One observer has concluded:

> With a few modest exceptions, federal postsecondary spending arrangements make no attempt to stimulate state spending, to compensate for differences in state wealth or effort, or to give state governments money to allot as they see fit.[5]

Nor, it might be added, would it be easy to implement a program or funding formula that would effectively achieve any combination of such objectives.

The federal government's activities affecting higher education are so decentralized and so intermixed with other policy objectives that simply trying to enumerate the programs and tally the total investment is problematic. Creation of the U.S. Department of Education in 1979 consolidated only about a fourth of the more than 400 programs that existed then, and less than a third of total federal expenditures for higher education—not substantially more than were encompassed by the old Office of Education in the U.S. Department of Health, Education, and Welfare. The remaining programs and funds are still scattered across a number of federal agencies, from the Departments of Defense, Energy, Agriculture, Transportation, and Health and Human Services to the Veterans Administration, Environmental Protection Agency, National Aeronautics and Space Administration, and Smithsonian Institution. This diffuse pattern within the executive branch is mirrored in Congress, where committee responsibilities tend to follow agency structures. Thus the fragmentary nature of federal influence and support for higher education seems likely to persist.

Table 1 provides an overview of federal support for higher education. In fiscal year 1992, federal spending totaled $29 billion, with 43 percent of this amount going for the cost of student aid, 50 percent for university-based R&D, and the balance for assorted categorical assistance and payments to colleges and universities. The more than $12 billion spent on the student aid programs is considerably less than the amount of aid actually made available to students (see Table 2), because the federal government guarantees and subsidizes private loans and requires non-federal matching in certain other programs.

**Table 1. Estimated Federal Financial Assistance to Higher Education
by Type and Source Fiscal Year 1992 (dollars in millions)**

| Source | Amount | Percentage |
|---|---|---|
| *Student Aid* | | |
| Department of Education | $10,124 | |
| Department of Veterans Affairs | 810 | |
| ROTC scholarships and other military assistance | 537 | |
| Health professions scholarships/fellowships and training program | 839 | |
| Programs for Native Americans | 78 | |
| Other Scholarship/ Fellowship Programs | 12 | |
| Subtotal | 12,400 | 42.7% |
| *Research and Development* | 14,652 | 50.4 |
| *Other Institutional Support* | | |
| Department of Education | 687 | |
| Special Institutions | 345 | |
| Military academies | 193 | |
| National Science Foundation | 310 | |
| International Education/Cultural Exchange | 223 | |
| Other | 255 | |
| Subtotal | 2,013 | 6.9 |
| *Total Federal Aid* | $29,065 | 100.0% |

*Source:* National Center for Education Statistics, *Digest of Education Statistics: 1992*, Washington, D.C.: U.S. Department of Education, 1992, Table 347.

*Note:* Some figures differ from those in Tables 2 and 5. Student aid here includes federal program costs only for FY 1992; Table 2 gives total aid available to students for academic year 1991–92, including the volume of borrowing generated by federal loan guarantees and subsidies, as well as amounts contributed by states and institutions. Military training assistance is included here but not in Table 2. Research and development figures include federal obligations for research and development centers administered by colleges and universities, unlike comparable figures in Table 5.

# Student Aid

## Legislative History

From the land-grant college movement to the GI-Bill experience following World War II, public policy has progressively extended educational opportunity to new groups in society. In recent decades a major current in this policy stream has been federal aid to students. In 1963, the federal government invested around $200 million in student aid through the then-fledgling National Defense Student Loan program and a handful of graduate fellowships. Thirty years later, in the academic year 1992–93, the federal government generated an estimated $25 billion for students in postsecondary education, through either direct appropriations or loan guarantees and subsidies. After adjusting for inflation, that is almost a 25-fold increase. During the same period, enrollments also increased, but only about three-fold.

The growth of student assistance over the past quarter century is especially remarkable in light of the controversy surrounding the issue of federal student aid during the 1950s and 1960s. Congress had approved college benefits for military veterans under the GI-Bill but balked at general scholarships to undergraduates, whether based on financial need or on academic merit. Resistance to giving students a "free ride" doomed one such proposal after another in Congress during the Eisenhower and Kennedy years.

The breakthrough came in the mid-1960s. As part of the "Great Society" under President Johnson, the Higher Education Act of 1965 embodied, for the first time, an explicit federal commitment to equalizing college opportunities for needy students. Programs were designed to identify the college-eligible poor and to facilitate their access with grants, replacing contributions their families could not afford to make. Colleges and universities that wanted to participate in the new grant program were required to make "vigorous" efforts to identify and recruit students with "exceptional financial need."

With the 1965 legislation, a new dynamic began to shape the federal role in higher education. Earlier federal support had been prompted by specific national concerns: fostering a democratic citizenry, sponsoring research in the national interest, meeting perceived personnel shortages in the economy, compensating those who had served the country in wartime, and promoting international understanding. In the same vein, scientific and military preparedness was the spark for the National Defense Education Act of 1958. The 1960s did not change the national-interest focus of federal aid to education, but did put the spotlight on a broader moral imperative: removing inequitable barriers to individual opportunity. Also in 1965, Congress added a new benefit to the Social Security program that allowed children of deceased, disabled, or retired parents eligible for Social Security to receive benefits as dependents while they attended college.

Appropriations for student aid grew in the late 1960s, while other forms of federal support, such as construction of academic facilities, gradually faded in importance. In 1972, Congress and the Nixon administration converged with separate proposals for elaborating and greatly expanding the federal commitment to student assistance. Amendments to the Higher Education Act created Basic Educational Opportunity Grants as a floor of direct support for all needy students. Now called Pell Grants, this program in 1992–93 provided over $6 billion to more than 4 million students enrolled in postsecondary education and training.

The 1972 legislation also created the State Student Incentive Grant (SSIG) program to provide federal matching funds for need-based state scholarship programs. Twenty-eight states had already inaugurated scholarships to students, but the federal stimulus of SSIG helped prompt the rest of the states to launch need-based aid programs of their own. Likewise during the 1970s, an increasing number of states responded to federal incentives to help generate credit financing for students through federally guaranteed loans. Pell and SSIG rounded out the federal commitment to student aid, which during the 1960s had already come to include College Work-Study, Supplemental Educational Opportunity Grants (SEOG), National Defense Loans (now called Perkins Loans), and Guaranteed Student Loans (now called Stafford Loans). Assistance was generally targeted at low- and moderate-income students. But in the late 1970s pressure mounted for broadening the base of eligibility for student aid. Proposals for college tuition tax credits built a head of steam in Congress and, to ward them off, the Carter administration went along with a legislative package that resulted in the Middle Income Student Assistance Act (MISAA) of 1978. MISAA liberalized eligibility for Pell grants and opened subsidized loans to students regardless of income or need. Shortly thereafter, Congress let the special allowance to banks participating in the guaranteed-loan program float with Treasury-bill rates, assuring a favorable return for lenders in the program.

The legislative expansion continued through the Education Amendments of 1980, which further liberalized need analysis for student aid, shielded the guaranteed-loan program from cost controls, and established two additional loan programs called Parent Loans for Undergraduate Students (PLUS) and Supplemental Loans for Students (SLS). Then came the 1980 elections and a new administration determined to shrink domestic social spending. While public and congressional reaction blocked wholesale cutbacks in student aid, the growth era in student assistance was clearly over. Many provisions of the Higher Education Act as amended in 1980 were repealed or delayed, guaranteed-loan eligibility was tightened, Social Security benefits for students were phased out, appropriations levelled off, and the purchasing power of federal student aid declined.

## Recent Trends and Issues

Table 2 shows the amounts of aid available to students by source in 1992–93 compared to 1980–81. Notwithstanding the retrenchment of the early Reagan years, the federal government continues to supply the lion's share of assistance. As illustrated in Figure 3, the constant-dollar value of federal assistance gradually rebounded toward the end of the 1980s and was slightly higher in 1992–93 than in 1980–81. Several factors at work over the past decade, however, have diluted the impact of federal support in making college affordable.

- Tuition and other costs of attendance in higher education have risen faster than federal aid. At the same time, as shown in Table 3, tuition in both public and private colleges has out-paced per capita disposable personal income and median family income.
- The available aid has been spread over a larger student population, including a substantially increased number of students enrolled in short-term training offered by proprietary schools. Today students in proprietary schools account for about 20 percent of Pell Grants and Stafford Loans.[6]
- The emphasis in federal aid has shifted from grants to loans. Loans accounted for 20 percent of federal aid in 1975–76 and 64 percent in 1992–93, while grant aid has dropped from 76 percent to 33 percent over the same period. The shift in the grant-loan balance has been the result of several factors: the winding down of Vietnam-era veterans educational benefits, the phasing out of Social Security student benefits, the substantial growth of federally guaranteed student borrowing beginning in the late 1970s, and erosion of the Pell Grants' real value over time.[7]

By contrast, in the 1970s the growth in federal aid outstripped growth in tuition and growth in the eligible student population; grant aid was more common than borrowing, especially for low-income students; and family income levels generally rose faster than tuition. All these trends adversely affected college affordability in the 1980s and into the 1990s.

## The Grant-Loan Issue

The growing predominance of loan financing, a factor frequently cited in relation to the decline of minority and low-income college enrollees, has turned the federal policy commitment to equal opportunity 180 degrees from its origins. The Higher Education Act of 1965 sought to help the disadvantaged through need-based grants, while helping middle-class families through government-guaranteed but minimally subsidized private bank loans. Today, guaranteed loans are far and away the largest source of aid, even for the lowest-income students. Guaranteed loans provide almost $15 billion in aid annually—two and a half times the size of the Pell Grant program that was meant to be the system's foundation.

When Congress reauthorized the student aid programs in both 1986 and 1992, a major focus of concern was the grant-loan imbalance. Yet the policy drift toward a loan-centered financial aid system remains unchecked. A key proposal in the 1992 reauthorization was to turn the Pell Grant into an entitlement or mandated spending program with automatic increases for inflation. But the Bush administration opposed such a change, arguing there were already too many federal entitlements, one reason the federal budget had become so hard to control. Republicans in Congress backed the administration on the issue, as did Budget Committee leaders from both parties in both the House and Senate. So the Pell entitlement provision was withdrawn from the legislation before final passage.

After the Pell entitlement failed, Congress followed a path of less resistance in boosting the dollar ceilings in the existing loan programs. Since loans, unlike Pell Grants, already operate as an entitlement, all eligible students are assured access to funds up to authorized levels. The legislation does raise the authorized maximum Pell Grant, but without the entitlement provision, actual funding levels will depend on annual appropriations. And there has been a widening gap between the authorized and actual Pell maximum in recent years.

The reauthorization bill also establishes an unsubsidized loan option not restricted by need. This is intended to make loans available to those in the middle-income range who have been squeezed out of eligibility for the regular guaranteed loan. The new loans will be less of a drain on the federal budget in that the government will not pay the interest costs while the borrower is in school.

All told, the principal impact of the 1992 legislation is clear: far from correcting the grant-loan imbalance, it will expand borrowing capacity for students and parents at all income levels in the years ahead.

**Table 2. Aid Awarded to Postsecondary Students by Program,
1980–81 and 1992–93 (dollars in millions)**

| Program | Academic Year 1980–81 | 1992–93 | Percentage Change (in constant dollars) |
|---|---|---|---|
| *Federally Supported Programs* | | | |
| Generally Available Aid | | | |
| Pell Grants | 2,387 | 6,162 | 56.9 |
| SEOG | 368 | 630 | 4.0 |
| SSIG | 72 | 70 | −41.0 |
| CWS | 660 | 760 | −30.0 |
| Perkins Loans (NDSL) | 694 | 897 | −21.4 |
| ICL | 0 | 5 | N/A |
| Stafford and PLUS/SLS | 6,202 | 14,998 | 46.9 |
| Subtotal | 10,383 | 23,522 | 37.7 |
| Specially Directed Aid | | | |
| Social Security | 1,883 | 0 | −100.0 |
| Veterans | 1,714 | 971 | −65.6 |
| Military | 201 | 384 | 16.6 |
| Other Grants | 122 | 160 | −19.8 |
| Other Loans | 62 | 418 | 307.9 |
| Subtotal | 3,982 | 1,934 | −70.5 |
| *Total Federal Aid* | 14,365 | 25,456 | 7.7 |
| *Nonfederal Aid* | | | |
| State Grant Programs | 801 | 2,126 | 61.3 |
| Institutional and Other Aid | 1,625 | 6,971 | 160.8 |
| *Total Federal, State, and Institutional Aid* | 16,791 | 34,554 | 25.1 |

*Source:* Washington Office of the College Board, *Trends in Student Aid: 1983 to 1993* (Washington, D.C.: Washington Office of the College Board, 1993).

**Table 3. Tuition Fees and Income, 1980–81 to 1991–92**

| | Public Four-Year | Public Two-Year | Private Four-Year | Private Two-Year | Personal (Per Capita) | Median Family |
|---|---|---|---|---|---|---|
| 1980–81 | 804 | 391 | 3,617 | 2,413 | 8,424 | 21,023 |
| 1981–82 | 909 | 434 | 4,113 | 2,605 | 9,240 | 22,388 |
| 1982–83 | 1,031 | 473 | 4,639 | 3,008 | 9,721 | 23,433 |
| 1983–84 | 1,148 | 528 | 5,093 | 3,099 | 10,350 | 24,674 |
| 1984–85 | 1,228 | 584 | 5,556 | 3,485 | 11,257 | 26,433 |
| 1985–86 | 1,318 | 641 | 6,121 | 3,672 | 11,863 | 27,735 |
| 1986–87 | 1,414 | 660 | 6,658 | 3,684 | 12,474 | 29,458 |
| 1987–88 | 1,537 | 706 | 7,116 | 4,161 | 13,081 | 30,970 |
| 1988–89 | 1,646 | 730 | 7,722 | 4,817 | 14,109 | 32,191 |
| 1989–90 | 1,780 | 756 | 8,396 | 5,196 | 14,973 | 34,213 |
| 1990–91 | 1,888 | 824 | 9,083 | 5,570 | 15,898 | 35,353 |
| 1991–92 | 2,134 | 962 | 9,841 | 5,784 | 16,318 | 35,939 |
| Pct. Chg. from 1980–81 to 1991–92 | 165% | 146% | 172% | 140% | 94% | 71% |

*Source:* Washington Office of the College Board, *Trends in Student Aid 1983 to 1993* (Washington, D.C.: Washington Office of the College Board, 1993).

*Note:* Income data are for the calendar year in which the academic year begins.

## Providing Flexibility in Loan Repayment

While the shift to loans continues, policy makers hope to mitigate the potentially adverse effects on students' career choices and on equity of access to higher education by providing greater flexibility in repayment. The 1992 legislation offers graduated and extended repayment terms to some categories of borrowers, and the Clinton administration is committed to pursuing a policy of allowing students to repay loans as a percentage of their future income through the Internal Revenue Service. The majority of borrowers will probably continue to repay without difficulty on the standard ten-year amortized basis. But for those students who know in advance that they want to pursue relatively low-paying service occupations, as well as those who later fall on hard times, alternative repayment schemes will probably become increasingly important in the 1990s.

### Linking Student Aid and Service

The Clinton administration is also committed to expanding opportunities for students to pay for their education through performance of service to the nation or community. While falling well short of the ambitious program the President had initially proposed, legislation passed in 1993 aims to enable up to 100,000 individuals to earn postsecondary education or training benefits by serving in areas of public need for up to two years. The benefits could be used either to pay post-service educational expenses or to repay educational debts already incurred.

The Clinton service initiative has many historical antecedents, including the Civilian Conservation Corps of the 1930s, the Peace Corps, VISTA, the National Health Service Corps, and a number of loan forgiveness and deferment provisions written into student aid legislation over the past 30 years. The new program seeks to strengthen the linkage between service and college aid—and even in its modified form, would do so on a much larger scale than previously attempted. Critics charge that the program will mainly benefit middle-class students, and that appropriations for it will inevitably cut into the base of funding for Pell Grants and other need-based aid focused on the disadvantaged.

### Reforming the Student Loan Process

One way the Clinton administration intends to pay for the national service program is to capture savings from student loan reform. The Clinton plan, as modified and approved by Congress in the

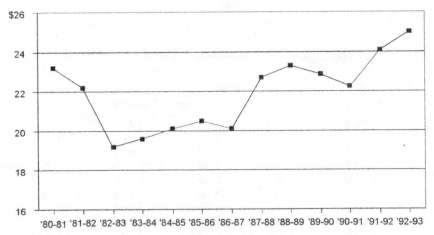

Source: Washington Office of the College Board. Trends in Student Aid: 1983 to 1993 (Washington, D.C.: Washington Office of the College Board, 1993).

Note: Base year used for constant dollar conversions is 1992.

**Figure 3. Amount of Federal Financial Aid, 1980–81 through 1992–93
(In Billions of Constant Dollars)**

deficit-reduction package of 1993, calls for creation of a system of direct federal lending through postsecondary institutions, replacing at least in part the current program which relies on private banks and other financial intermediaries for loan capital. The aim is to squeeze excess subsidies out of the existing student loan structure, ultimately reducing federal costs by at least an estimated $1 billion a year while at the same time lowering interest expense to students and parents. The Student Loan Reform Act became law as part of the Clinton deficit-reduction package of 1993. The question is whether the federal government can make a successful conversion to direct lending; an under-staffed Department of Education faces a major challenge in launching the new program, and doing so without disruption and increased complexity for students.

## Widening Eligibility for Student Aid

As in the late 1970s, Congress in the early 1990s wanted to extend federal assistance to more of the middle class. So the 1992 reauthorization law incorporates new federal standards for determining family and student ability to pay, and these standards are being used not only to award federal need-based grants and subsidized loans but a substantial portion of state and institutional aid as well. The new federal standards expand calculated need by several billion dollars. But while the new law promises much on paper, there is little prospect of a corresponding increase in available funds from the federal government, states or institutions. The likely effect will be to shift scarce dollars up the economic ladder, at the expense of disadvantaged, truly needy students and families.

## Helping Nontraditional Students

At the same time, many policymakers and analysts worry that the existing aid system, designed primarily for families whose dependent children attend college full-time, is not sensitive to the wide-ranging needs and circumstances of nontraditional students. Increasing numbers of adults beyond traditional college age are returning to higher education for a second chance, retraining, and mid-career change. They often attend less than full-time and have continuing family and work responsibilities while in school.

Whether and how to support these students will be an ongoing policy concern in the 1990s. It may be that conventional aid programs are not the best way to reach nontraditional students. Expanding eligibility of independent adult students for aid will reduce the dollars available to dependent students from low-income families. And need-based grants and loans may not fit with the needs of many nontraditional students attending on a sporadic basis. Policymakers may need to consider new mechanisms outside the traditional forms of student assistance, including incentives to employers for facilitating and supporting employee training and retraining.

## Graduate Student Assistance[8]

The bulk of federal student aid goes to undergraduates, and the policy debates in Washington focus largely on issues of educational access and choice at the undergraduate level. Yet a portion of the aid available through the loan and work-study programs goes to graduate and professional students. Federal support for graduate students also comes in the form of research assistantships, fellowships, and traineeships, and much of this support is built into the funding of R&D administered by institutions. Table 4 compares estimated amounts of financial aid for undergraduate and graduate students in 1989–90 by source—federal, state, institutional, and private.

Overall, fellowship and other grant money for graduate students has declined since the 1960s, and universities have looked to alternative sources. The federal work-study program, for example, requires only 20 percent matching and has been increasingly used to fund teaching assistants. But the most common recourse for filling the gap has been student borrowing. Federally guaranteed loans have become an integral part of financing graduate and professional education, and many privately sponsored supplemental loan programs have been created to serve students in high-cost fields such as the health professions. It is at this level that concerns about mounting student indebtedness become most acute, especially among students who have already accumulated substantial loan obligations as undergraduates.

**Table 4. Estimated Financial Assistance for Undergraduate and Graduate Students 1989–90 Academic Year (current dollars in millions)**

| | Undergraduate Amount | Students Percent | Graduate Amount | Students Percent |
|---|---|---|---|---|
| *Federal Sources* | | | | |
| Title IV Grants | $5,392 | 21.2% | $2 | 0.0% |
| College Work Study | 607 | 2.4 | 56 | 0.7 |
| Federal Loans | 7,710 | 30.4 | 3,178 | 38.1 |
| Other Federal Grants | 22 | 0.1 | 42 | 0.5 |
| Other Types of Federal Aid | 286 | 1.1 | 43 | 0.5 |
| Subtotal | 14,015 | 55.2 | 3,321 | 39.8 |
| | | | | |
| *State Sources* | | | | |
| Grants | 2153 | 8.5 | 104 | 1.2 |
| Loans | 268 | 1.1 | 15 | 0.2 |
| Work Study | 42 | 0.2 | 4 | 0.1 |
| Other | 342 | 1.3 | 32 | 0.4 |
| Subtotal | 2,805 | 11.0 | 155 | 1.9 |
| | | | | |
| *Institutional Sources* | | | | |
| Grants | 4,389 | 17.3 | 1,057 | 12.7 |
| Loans | 150 | 0.6 | 13 | 0.2 |
| Work Study | 371 | 1.5 | 20 | 0.2 |
| Assistantships | 0 | 0.0 | 1,564 | 18.7 |
| Other | 397 | 1.6 | 1,174 | 14.1 |
| Subtotal | 5,306 | 20.9 | 3,829 | 45.9 |
| | | | | |
| *Private Sources* | | | | |
| Employer Provided Aid | 535 | 2.1 | 441 | 5.3 |
| Grants/Scholarships | 1,350 | 5.3 | 182 | 2.2 |
| Loans | 428 | 1.7 | 262 | 3.1 |
| Other | 961 | 3.8 | 153 | 1.8 |
| Subtotal | 3,273 | 12.9 | 1,038 | 12.4 |
| | | | | |
| *Total Assistance* | $25,400 | 100.0% | $8,350 | 100.0% |

*Source:* Data are from the *National Postsecondary Student Aid Study* (National Center for Education Statistics, and U.S. Department of Education). Special analyses were conducted by the Washington Office of the College Board.

*Note:* Graduate research assistantships funded through federal research grants to institutions may appear under Institutional Sources rather than Federal Sources because of the way the data were collected by the National Postsecondary Student Aid Study. Thus, federal graduate assistantships are understated and institutional graduate assistantships are overstated in this table.

Traditionally, graduate institutions and departments have awarded aid primarily on the basis of academic merit. But recent financing trends have created a dual system. Research assistantships and what remains of fellowship support from federal and private sources continue to be awarded on competitive academic criteria, whereas the great proportion of subsidized work, loan, and other aid to graduate and professional students is directed to students according to their financial need.

In general, graduate students are experiencing increased difficulty financing their education when financial rewards accruing to an advanced degree, especially in traditional academic disciplines, are uncertain at best. Many observers worry about the quality and numbers of students pursuing graduate work, and about the adequacy of federal policies to meet national needs for highly trained personnel in the 1990s and beyond.

## Beyond Financial Aid

Whatever the federal policy and commitment to helping students meet postsecondary costs, policy makers increasingly recognize that student aid dollars alone are not sufficient to ensure greater access to higher education by under-represented groups. Too many variables other than finance—quality of prior schooling, family attitudes, motivation, awareness of opportunities—help to determine college participation. Earlier, larger, and sustained interventions in the education pipeline are necessary.

This need is addressed at the federal level through the so-called TRIO programs of counseling, outreach, and special support services for the disadvantaged, created as a complement to the student aid programs in the original Higher Education Act. Congressional appropriations for the TRIO program grew even during the most difficult fiscal years of the 1980s, but funding of these efforts still falls far short of the need. Also in this vein, the 1992 reauthorization of the law calls for additional initiatives inspired by Eugene Lang's "I Have a Dream" movement in cities around the country, which seeks to mentor disadvantaged junior high students, widen their horizons, and see them through to high school graduation and postsecondary opportunities.

## Access to What?

For most of the past quarter century, federal policy under Title IV of the Higher Education Act has consistently emphasized access. The ideal that was forged in the mid-1960s—equalizing postsecondary opportunities by removing financial barriers for needy individuals—remains paramount. But high default rates on guaranteed student loans and widely publicized problems of program abuse have raised nagging questions. Are dollars being directed effectively to those who really need help and have a reasonable chance of benefitting from the education and training that is being subsidized? What assurances does the federal government have regarding the quality and utility of such education and training? Is it provided at reasonable cost? Do federal aid recipients complete their programs in a reasonable period of time? Do they secure jobs in the fields for which they have prepared? In short, are students and taxpayers receiving their money's worth? With these questions heard more and more frequently, student aid policy debates in the 1990s are likely to focus as much on academic quality and cost effectiveness as on access.

A principal though not exclusive object of concern regarding quality and standards has been the proprietary trade schools. As noted earlier, a substantial share of the government's student aid commitment now goes to finance training offered by proprietary schools. And much of that financing has focused on very low-income students who lack basic academic skills and enroll in short-term job training programs that may result (at best) in minimum-wage employment. The default rate on student loans in the proprietary sector has averaged over 40 percent—four times that of four-year collegiate institutions.

What kinds of education and training should be fostered through the mechanism of student aid? In the 1970s Congress substituted the term "postsecondary" for "higher" in the student aid statutes, and eligibility was broadened to include short-term vocational training provided by for-profit schools, as well as the traditional programs of public and non-profit private institutions. Congress embraced a marketplace philosophy: students would "Vote with their feet," taking their federal aid to institutions that met their needs. But the marketplace rationale begged important questions of institutional effectiveness and accountability. Few foresaw the burgeoning of the trade school industry that would be stimulated by the new federal incentives. Many for-profit programs came to be subsidized almost entirely by tax dollars, basing their prices on the aid package available to students from the federal government.

The federal student aid programs have traditionally relied on a so-called triad of institutional accreditation, state review, and federal oversight to ensure quality control. The federal responsibility, as carried out by the Department of Education, has included certifying accreditation agencies as well as ultimately approving institutions to participate in the federal aid programs. Over time, however, the triad arrangement has proven increasingly inadequate to the task. Federal certification of accrediting agencies and final approval of institutions have been largely pro forma. In many states, the state role has been weakened because a number of state agencies are responsible for reviewing different groups of institutions, with the result that the overall impact of state review is often uncoordinated and diluted. In addition, many states view proprietary schools as small businesses and therefore minimize regulation of them. But the weakest link of the triad has been the accrediting agencies themselves. Concentrating as they should on the academic attributes of institutions, these agencies are typically ill-equipped to make critical judgments about the financial soundness and suitability of institutions to participate in federal programs. Moreover, the fact that the institutions themselves provide the bulk of revenues of the accrediting agencies may create a less than arms-length relationship.

Restoring "integrity" to the student aid process was a principal theme of the 1992 reauthorization of the Higher Education Act. Congressional sponsors recognized that these issues had to be addressed if the programs under Title IV of the Act are to be viable in the intense competition for federal appropriations in the years ahead. The principal new thrust in the 1992 legislation is to place more reliance on state agencies as gatekeepers to help determine which postsecondary institutions should be eligible to participate in the federal Title IV programs. But how effective such an approach will be remains to be seen. The states' responsibility is activated only to the extent that federal funds are provided to support states in carrying out this function. Moreover, states may be reluctant partners in such an endeavor, state officials responsible for licensing and reviewing postsecondary programs have long complained they should not bear the brunt of regulatory problems that the federal government itself created by subsidizing the proprietary sector so substantially.

Meanwhile, the Department of Education has sought to tighten the system by prohibiting institutions with excessively high default rates from continuing to participate in the programs, and these efforts *have* had some impact in reducing the overall level of defaults and eliminating schools that were clearly abusing the system. But establishing the default rate cutoffs is arbitrary and problematic in many respects, and institutions have great incentives to manipulate their numbers to stay below the cutoff level. In addition, the due process entailed in withdrawing federal approval has proved to be so cumbersome that many institutions manage to participate for many years after being targeted as problem schools. In summary, the fundamental issues of institutional eligibility and quality control in the federal aid programs remain to be effectively addressed in the 1990s. The Clinton administration is considering fresh approaches in this area, including new performance and compliance standards that would condition institutional eligibility to participate in the aid programs.

## Issues of Affordability: Quality at What Price?

Concerns about quality ultimately are linked to concerns about cost. The rapid rise in tuition and other costs of attendance over the past decade has stimulated worries about whether college will continue to be affordable for a broad range of Americans and whether it will be worth the price. A number of important works on higher education finance in recent years have echoed this theme of affordability. Michael McPherson and Morton Schapiro wrote a book for the Brookings Institution entitled *Keeping College Affordable*,[9] and the bipartisan National Commission on Responsibilities for Financing Postsecondary Education received widespread publicity over its report, *Making College Affordable Again*.[10] Both studies call for an increased national commitment to need-based student aid to pay rising tuitions. The principal recommendation by the national commission is to make the level of federal aid more predictable and understandable for students and families by establishing a total amount of federal assistance for which any full-time undergraduate might be eligible each year.

Missing in these discussions, however, has been attention to the other side of the affordability equation, namely, how to reduce growth in the costs of a college education. In the final analysis, making college affordable again will depend on controlling the tuition spiral, and policy makers in the 1990s will be looking for ways to promote cost containment in higher education. An overall federal aid maximum, such as proposed by the national commission cited above, might eliminate possible incentives for some institutions to raise tuitions. Increases in the costs of attendance above the maximum would play no role in determining a student's eligibility for federal aid.

A more comprehensive approach to cost containment would be for the Secretary of Education to issue a schedule of "reasonable costs" for different types of postsecondary education and training—perhaps one standard for four-year academic training, one standard for two-year academic programs, and a variety of standards for different kinds of vocational training (based on what it should reasonably cost to provide training in automobile mechanics, cosmetology, computer programming, etc.). In some ways, such reasonable cost standards would be similar to the cost containment provisions in Medicare and Medicaid in which fees for a wide variety of services are prescribed in federal law or regulation. But in one important respect, higher education cost standards as sketched above would differ from those governing health care: namely, institutions would not be required to charge the standard amounts. They could charge students whatever they wanted, but would be reimbursed (through federal student aid) only up to the federal standard.

## Research Support

Federal spending on R&D and other aspects of science at colleges and universities antedates the federal commitment to student aid, going back to an 1883 law to support agricultural experiment stations. But the investment in academic science was fairly small until the needs of World War II caused federal spending for campus-based research to skyrocket. The boom in federally-sponsored research continued through the 1950s and early 1960s. Though such support has not continued to grow at anything like the rates of the early postwar decades, the federal government remains the largest source of financing for campus-based research, supplying roughly $10 billion in 1991. R&D expenditures at colleges and universities are summarized in Table 5. In constant dollars the federal contribution increased by more than 40 percent in the 1980s. Contributions from industry and all other sources grew much more. Overall, the 1980s was a very healthy decade for investment in university-based science. One observer has said, "If the 1960s were the golden age of research, then the 1980s were the gilded age."[11]

Unlike student aid, federal research funding is highly concentrated on a relatively small number of institutions, most of them major research universities. According to the National Science Foundation (NSF), the top 100 doctorate-granting institutions receive more than 80 percent of all federal R&D obligations to academia, a proportion that has remained quite stable over the years.[12] This support flows from multiple federal agencies and policy objectives. When NSF was created in 1950, Vannevar Bush envisioned an agency having broad purview over federal funding of research in the physical sciences, medicine, and defense, with a separate science advisory board to evaluate and integrate technical research sponsored by other government departments.[13] This vision is far from today's diffuse reality, with more than a dozen mission-oriented agencies separately deploying federal R&D resources to academic institutions for a variety of purposes.

While the nation's investment in science during the past half century has been repaid many times over in the form of thousands of pathbreaking discoveries and practical applications, political controversy and skepticism beset the academic research enterprise in the late 1980s and early 1990s. Ethical issues such as the protocols used in animal research have led to shrill campus protests. Publicized cases of research fraud have cast doubts about the conduct of scientific research that could threaten levels of financial support in the future.

Another sensitive issue is the growing practice of congressional earmarks to fund construction of research facilities on particular campuses around the country. More than $700 million was provided to colleges and universities in the form of earmarked appropriations in fiscal year 1992, and nearly $2.5 billion has been provided since 1980 when annual earmarks were roughly $10 million. Traditionally, federal campus-based research funds have been distributed on the basis of a peer review system in which individuals who are familiar with a field of research are asked to grade proposals for funding in that field. These peer reviews, along with considerations of cost effectiveness, largely determine which proposals receive funding. Proponents of peer review argue it ensures that the best research is supported. Opponents argue it is a vintage old boys network that precludes many worthwhile projects because the researchers are not tied into the network.

In part, the earmark phenomenon is a reaction to the heavy concentration of federal R&D spending on a relatively few institutions. Institutions outside this group go to their elected representatives and plead their case, often hiring expensive lobbyists in the process. Earmarking is also a response to a long-term problem affecting virtually all research universities—the deterioration

**Table 5. R & D Expenditures at Universities and Colleges by Source of Funds Fiscal Years 1981 and 1991 (dollars in millions)**

| Source | Fiscal Years 1981 | 1991 | Percentage Increase (in constant dollars) |
|---|---|---|---|
| Federal government | 4,565 | 9,650 | 43.1 |
| State and local governments | 546 | 1,553 | 92.5 |
| Industry | 291 | 1,250 | 191.0 |
| Institutional funds | 1,008 | 3,397 | 128.0 |
| All other sources | 436 | 1,350 | 109.6 |
| Total | 6,846 | 17,200 | 70.1 |

*Source:* National Science Board, *Science and Engineering Indicators—1991* (Washington, D.C.: National Science Board, 1991).

*Note:* Federal government dollars do not include amounts for federal funded research and development centers (FFRDCs).

and obsolescence of scientific equipment and facilities. Despite the substantial and growing federal investment in campus-based research over time, the inadequacy of the research infrastructure has been the subject of many studies and reports over the past decade. Only a small proportion of federal funds for research have been invested in facilities construction, maintenance, and renovation. In the 1950s and 1960s, separate appropriations were made for facilities, but in recent decades the bulk of funds for infrastructure has come through indirect cost recovery, an inefficient way of financing a crucial aspect of the research enterprise.

Indirect cost recovery itself has created the darkest cloud on the horizon for federal support of research. Stanford University was the catalyst for the emergence of this issue when it was revealed that expenses for a number of questionable items, including fancy provisions for the President's home and a donated yacht, had been submitted to the government over the years as part of Stanford's indirect costs on research grants and contracts. Adverse publicity and congressional hearings led to investigations of other research universities. Several institutions were required to return millions of dollars in questionable billings, and some institutions renegotiated their indirect cost recovery rates.

The issues underlying the system of indirect cost recovery, however, stretch far beyond the practices of Stanford and the other institutions that have been investigated. The existing system, which dates back over 30 years to the development of Office of Management and Budget (OMB) Circular A-21, is based on the principle that an institution's indirect cost recovery should be tied to the share of research-related costs in its total budget. But such a system gives institutions great incentive to categorize spending items as part of their pool of research-related costs. While Stanford was one of the most aggressive institutions in seeking indirect cost recovery, it and other universities correctly point out that they were playing according to the rules as they understood them. What complicated matters was the fact that the federal government was never very clear about what those rules were. Untangling this issue, therefore, will require reexamining the fundamental principles of the System itself.[14]

All of these issues take on particular significance in light of the dependence of universities on federal research dollars. While federal grants and contracts constitute less than 10 percent of total revenues of all colleges and universities, at some major research institutions federal dollars represent one-quarter or more of total revenues, and indirect cost reimbursements sometimes exceed 10 percent of a university's budget. Such federal dependence could become highly problematic under various future scenarios, including any radical change in the method of indirect cost recovery or drastic deficit-reduction initiatives such as a balanced budget amendment. Also, the end of the Cold War and the resulting decline in defense spending will likely have a disproportionate impact on institutions that are especially dependent on defense research dollars. The Clinton administration has announced its intention to equalize spending on defense and civilian R&D by 1998. The Clinton plan for R&D investment also assigns high priority to projects with clear potential for commercial applications, job creation, and economic competitiveness. And it calls for a series of multi-agency, inter-disciplinary initiatives emphasizing applied research as well as science, math, engineering, and technology education.

In sum, the tight federal budgetary outlook and questions about past practices will stir continued debate on the federal responsibility for research in the 1990s and beyond. What should be the role of university research in the post-Cold War world? Are universities still the best vehicle for federal investment in research, or should the emphasis shift to a more commercial, industrially-based strategy? Should federal research dollars be focused on the best researchers at a small set of universities, or would spreading the funds more widely produce better results? Whatever the answer to these questions, it is clear that universities will be challenged to do more with less, to identify their comparative advantages, to consolidate efforts with other research institutions, and to articulate more clearly to the public how research contributes to societal goals.

## Tax Policies

In addition to direct funding of students and institutions, the government indirectly assists higher education through a variety of tax policies. A number of exclusions, exemptions, and deductions in the federal tax code over the years have benefited education at all levels. Some of these provisions—for example, the personal exemptions parents may claim for students age 19 and over, and the recent tax break on proceeds from U.S. savings bonds that are used for higher education—affect individuals and families in their ability to save for and pay college costs. Other provisions affect the revenue and financing arrangements of colleges and universities; for example, their not-for-profit status allows them to receive tax-deductible contributions. The monetary benefits to institutions and students of these tax provisions, so-called tax expenditures in federal budgetary parlance, are measured by the estimated amount of federal revenue that would be collected in the absence of such provisions. Prior to the passage of the Tax Reform Act of 1986, estimated annual "tax expenditures" for higher education totalled over $4 billion.

Corporate investment in university-based research was promoted by the tax legislation of 1981, which gave tax credits to industry for investment in cooperative, applied research projects with universities and permitted enhanced deductions for gifts of research and research training equipment. The 1986 tax bill amended these provisions to balance the tax incentives for corporate investment in basic and applied research. But overall the reform legislation of 1986, a watershed in federal tax policy, had adverse implications for higher education. For colleges and universities, particularly private non-profit institutions, the principal setback came in the form of limitations on charitable giving. The legislation both tightened tax deductions for gifts of stock, land, works of art, and other appreciated property and terminated the deductibility of gifts by non-itemizing taxpayers. Since these changes went into effect, their impact has not been conclusively demonstrated, but many colleges have reported a drop in donations. Another factor that may have reduced the level of giving is that high-income taxpayers have less incentive to give as a result of lower marginal tax rates on income that were instituted as part of the 1986 reform. The 1986 law also changed the rules for tax-exempt bond financing, thus placing particular constraints on large private universities.

Other changes legislated in 1986 have affected students and parents:

- The elimination of tax-deductible Clifford Trusts designed for very high-income families and changes in taxation of unearned income of children under the age of 14 have reduced the advantage of transferring income income from parent to child as a means of saving for educational purposes. For the great majority of families, however, a transfer of income remains a viable college savings technique with a tax benefit.
- An individual may not take a personal exemption on his or her own tax return if he or she is eligible to be claimed as a dependent on another's return. Thus students under the age of 23 who up to 1986 were allowed to benefit from such an exemption are no longer able to claim it.
- The deduction for consumer interest, including interest on education loans to students and parents, was phased out. However, home mortgage interest remains deductible, and taxpayers are able to deduct interest payments on home equity loans used to meet educational expenses.

- Scholarships, fellowships, and federal grants to graduate and undergraduate students are counted as taxable income to the extent these awards, either individually or together, exceed the cost of tuition and related expenses. For most students, the increase in the standard deduction has mitigated the impact of this change, producing little or no tax liability. Those potentially affected are married students with spouses earning income, athletes receiving full scholarships, and, paradoxically, some of the neediest students (those with large grants).

Almost as soon as the Tax Reform Act of 1986 was signed into law, bills were introduced in Congress to restore the exclusion of scholarships and fellowships from taxable income, the deductibility of interest on student loans, the full deduction for gifts of appreciated property, and other provisions that had just been repealed or scaled back. But recovery of losses in the 1986 law has not come easily for higher education or any other constituency. Other than correcting technical errors, the congressional tax-writing committees in the late 1980s were determined to let the new law take effect, holding the line on the 1986 reform.

Moreover, higher education experienced something of a political backlash in the tax reform debate, with a perception in some quarters that well-endowed institutions had abused their tax-exempt status through creative financing schemes that took advantage of tax loopholes. At one point in the late 1980s the House Ways and Means Committee floated a proposal for a five percent tax on endowment income of colleges and universities. Also under scrutiny has been the question of taxing the unrelated business income of non-profit organizations, money gained from activities not directly tied to the organizations' purpose. Small businesses have complained that tax-exempt status gives non-profits an unfair competitive edge, and have singled out college and university travel services, bookstores, and research programs as examples.

With the relentless pressure for deficit reduction, the outlook for higher education in the tax policy arena has not substantially improved in the early 1990s. In 1993, however, higher education did win at least one significant concession as part of the five-year Clinton budget package. As passed by Congress, the legislation restores the full tax deductibility of gifts of appreciated property. The 1993 legislation also retroactively restores two tax provisions that had expired in 1992: the tax break for corporate spending on university research mentioned above, and the exemption from personal income tax of employer-provided educational benefits to employees.

Apart from the recent tax reform movement, higher education continues to absorb the impact of long-term growth in Social Security taxes and unemployment insurance contributions required by employers. Because college and university budgets are made up disproportionately of personnel costs, higher education is more heavily affected by the rapid rise in payroll taxes than are some other sectors.

## Federal Regulation and Its Impact

Concern about the impact of federal regulation on the internal affairs of universities was one of the most controversial issues in government-university relations in the late 1970s. One analyst wrote in dramatic tones:

> Not only legislatures and federal agencies but the courts as well are willing to scrutinize every exercise of discretion on the basis of a complaint. This is the twilight of autonomy and authority. The prevailing tides of opinion currently are egalitarian and legalistic and they are joined to a simplistic view of society and the likelihood of its improvement.[15]

Federal regulation of higher education derives from two principal sources: the requirements of accountability that accompany the receipt of federal funds; and the dictates of social legislation, as well as executive orders and judicial decisions stemming from such legislation.[16] To the degree that government officials insist on accountability for the proper expenditure of funds, and congressional mandates addressing a range of social problems remain in force, there will be complexity and strain in the relationship of government and higher education. Tensions are inherent, given the traditions of academic autonomy, the mandates of Congress, the missions of federal agencies, and the responsibilities of those agencies for the stewardship of taxpayer dollars.

The federal government influences higher education through scores of statutes and regulations administered by diverse federal agencies. Some mandates, such as the Americans with Disabilities Act, or regulations of the Environmental Protection Agency and the Occupational Safety and Health Administration, affect all types of organizations equally. Others, such as the Buckley Amendment on privacy rights of students and Title IX of the Education Amendments of 1972 barring sex bias, are specific to educational institutions. Colleges have long argued that such regulatory burdens contribute to their spiralling costs. But there is no documentation of the extent to which higher education is disproportionately affected by federal requirements, thereby justifying the more rapid increases in college charges during the past decade relative to prices of other goods and services in the economy.

The academic community has long been wary of entanglement with government, but only a few, mainly independent, religiously affiliated institutions, have consistently refused funds from Washington. The great majority of colleges have accepted federal patronage, even though it exacts a price in the expenses of compliance and in the distraction and intrusion of external controls. During the 1980s higher education's concerns on this front receded to some degree. The Reagan administration's widely publicized support for regulatory relief altered the climate of regulation. Enforcement eased in some areas, and over the years colleges learned to accommodate to the bureaucratic requirements of the government, tempering previous conflicts. Some institutions actually bargained with the federal government to lessen their regulatory burden. Prior to the highly publicized controversy over indirect costs in the early 1990s, for example, Yale and Stanford had accepted lowered indirect cost reimbursement on research contracts in exchange for reduced federal reporting requirements. But in many respects regulatory burdens have mounted not only for colleges but for all sectors of society in recent years. Higher education, along with other constituencies, has complained about the proliferation of "unfunded mandates" from Washington—legislative and regulatory requirements imposed by the federal government without federal funding to help pay the costs of compliance.

The balance of the 1990s will no doubt be replete with regulatory challenges for higher education. The indirect cost issue remains highly charged and problematic for the research universities. IRS scrutiny of colleges appears to be intensifying as tax regulations and compliance procedures grow more complex for non-profit institutions. An arena of ongoing debate and litigation will be civil rights enforcement and the desegregation of public systems of higher education.[17] While the Supreme Court's 1954 decision in *Brown* v. *Board of Education* applied to collegiate as well as to elementary and secondary education, it was not until 1992 that the Court handed down a decision providing guidance for ending patterns of racial segregation in state postsecondary systems. In *U.S.* v. *Fordice*, the Supreme Court ordered a lower court to review all policies that "Contribute to the racial identifiability" of Mississippi's public colleges and universities, and to eliminate those policies that cannot be justified. Interpreting and applying *Fordice* will take years, both in the federal courts and in the enforcement activities of the Office of Civil Rights of the U.S. Department of Education. A great deal is at stake not only for Mississippi, but for as many as 15 other states that have faced legal challenges to their higher education systems on grounds of alleged discrimination. Finally, a major challenge of the Clinton years will be in the student aid arena where, as suggested earlier in this chapter, the continuing high loan default rates and concerns about program abuse will demand policy solutions for the sake of both taxpayer and consumer protection.

The unique regulatory dilemma in student aid is the sheer number and diversity of schools and kinds of training supported by programs under Title IV of the Higher Education Act. Applying the same rules and simultaneously regulating the use of student aid subsidies by some 5,000 proprietary schools and 3,000 collegiate institutions simply does not work. So far Congress has been unwilling to consider disaggregating federal student aid policy and differentiating delivery mechanisms by postsecondary sector or length and nature of training. But the Clinton administration appears ready to take another look at this issue. Under consideration are proposals to split off vocational training from current student aid programs, possibly transferring responsibility for such training to the Labor Department where it would be supported through federal contract authority.

For collegiate institutions such a shift would have the effect of lifting some of the current burden of default prevention and related measures that are designed primarily to address trade school problems but must be applied across the board. But the colleges would not necessarily be let off the regulatory hook under the Clinton scenario. Traditional institutions of higher education have become increasingly vocational in their offerings, and many, especially two-year colleges, enroll large numbers of students who lack basic skills and enter college requiring remedial training that now is often supported by federal aid programs. If federal policymakers decide to treat postsecondary vocational training separately, many distinctions are going to have to be sorted out as to what constitutes "vocational" as well as "postsecondary."

Moreover, new federal cost and performance standards may be aimed at all types of schools. Clinton administration officials note that K-12 education policy debates are now centered on developing national standards, raising expectations of students and schools, systemic reform, and outcomes-based performance. They hope to spark a similar focus and movement in the postsecondary policy arena. Specific plans have yet to unfold, but lively debate on such proposals can be expected both in Washington and in the postsecondary community during the mid-1990s.

## Prospects for the Federal Role in Higher Education

To recap, among key issues that will shape the federal role in higher education in the 1990s and beyond are the following:

- Student aid reforms will continue to focus on improving the delivery of federal dollars to intended beneficiaries. Debates will focus on whether to establish an overall federal aid maximum per student, target Pell Grants to allow for increases in award levels, and strengthen cost and academic standards conditioning institutional eligibility for federal student aid. There may also be consideration of whether student aid is the most appropriate mechanism for funding all postsecondary activities, including short term vocational training and remediation for students unprepared to do college-level work.
- A principal question looming over the future federal role in research is whether federal funding will continue to increase in real terms given persistent concerns about existing research practices in academia and unrelenting pressure to reduce federal budget deficits. Specific issues will include finding means to upgrade the physical infrastructure of scientific research and reforming the indirect cost recovery process.
- Tax policy debates affecting higher education will center on continued efforts to restore or make permanent provisions that were deleted or made temporary by the 1986 and subsequent tax laws. These issues, however, will be considered in the much broader context of tax policy changes intended to stimulate economic growth and reduce the federal budget deficit.
- The chief regulatory issue for higher education in the 1990s is whether the trend toward unfunded mandates continues under the Clinton administration's campaign to reinvent government. Colleges should also be prepared for regulatory efforts specific to postsecondary student aid, including federal initiatives to promote both cost containment and greater quality control in higher education.

The federal government will undoubtedly continue to make important contributions to enhancing the academic enterprise and equalizing educational opportunities in America. As in the past, federal support will supplement the basic funding provided from state and private sources, and it will spring from objectives such as economic competitiveness rather than from an interest in education for its own sake. And funds, along with regulations, will continue to flow from a variety of agencies in Washington. Such support is untidy, piecemeal and not without headaches for institutions, students, and states. But the pattern serves a variety of national purposes and, in fact, ultimately may better serve to protect institutional diversity, students' freedom of choice, and independent thought in American education than would an overarching federal policy.

## Notes

1. For the historical development of the federal role in higher education, see George N. Rainsford, *Congress and Higher Education in the Nineteenth Century* (Knoxville, Tenn.: University of Tennessee Press, 1972). The two private universities benefitting from the Morrill Land-Grant College Act are MIT (established in 1861) and Cornell University (1865).

2. Terry Sanford, *Storm Over the States* (New York: McGraw Hill, 1967), p. 63.

3. Lawrence E. Gladieux and Thomas R. Wolanin, *Congress and the Colleges: The National Politics of Higher Education* (Lexington, Mass.: Lexington Books, 1976), p. 226.

4. An approach to assessing the indirect effects of student aid has been outlined by Michael S. McPherson in "Silver Linings: Student Aid's Unintended Good Deeds," paper presented at the Annual Meeting of the American Educational Research Association, April 1987.

5. Chester E. Finn, Jr., "A Federal Policy for Higher Education?" *Alternative*, May 1975, 18–19.

6. Washington Office of the College Board, *Trends in Student Aid: 1983 to 1993* (Washington, D.C.: College Entrance Examination Board, 1993).

7. Ibid.

8. For greater depth analysis on graduate student assistance, see Council of Graduate Schools, *Graduate Student Financial Support: A Handbook for Graduate Deans, Faculty, and Administrators* (Washington, D.C.: Council of Graduate Schools, 1990).

9. Michael S. McPherson and Morton Owen Schapiro, *Keeping College Affordable. Government and Educational Opportunity* (Washington, D.C.: The Brookings Institution, 1991).

10. National Commission on Responsibilities for Financing Postsecondary Education, *Making College Affordable Again* (Washington, D.C.: National Commission on Responsibilities for Financing Postsecondary Education, 1993).

11. Representative Rick Boucher, chairman of the Subcommittee on Science of the U.S. House of Representatives Committee on Science, Space, and Technology, "Science Policy for the 21st Century," *Chronicle of Higher Education*, September 1, 1993.

12. National Science Foundation, Division of Science Resources Studies, *Early Release of Summary Statistics on Academic Science/Engineering Resources* (Washington, D.C.: National Science Foundation, 1986).

13. Deborah H. Shapley and Roy Rustum, *Lost at the Frontier* (Philadelphia Institute for Scientific Information Press, 1985), p. 39.

14. Robert Rosenzweig, "The Debate Over Indirect Costs Raises Fundamental Policy Issues," *The Chronicle of Higher Education*, March 6, 1991; and U.S. General Accounting Office, *Federal Research System for Reimbursing Universities' Indirect Costs Should Be Reevaluated* (Washington, D.C., August 1992).

15. Robert A. Scott, "More Than Greenbacks and Red Tape: The Hidden Costs of Government Regulations," *Change*, April 1978, 16.

16. John T. Wilson, *Academic Science, Higher Education, and the Federal Government: 1950–1983* (Chicago: University of Chicago Press, 1983), pp. 104–106.

17. For more on the impact of civil rights enforcement and other litigation on colleges and universities, see the subsequent chapter in this volume by Walter C. Hobbs on the involvement of the courts in higher education.

# Policy Environments and System Design: Understanding State Governance Structures

KATHY REEVES BRACCO, RICHARD C. RICHARDSON, JR., PATRICK M. CALLAN, AND JONI E. FINNEY

As we approach the 21st century, many states face economic, political, technological, and demographic changes of enormous magnitude. Demand for access to higher education from an increasingly diverse student clientele continues to increase as changes in the economy demand greater skills. Technological developments have created entirely new mechanisms for the delivery of education and have introduced new providers into the market. Global competition threatens historical patterns of economic activity. Can state higher education systems designed to manage enrollment growth under conditions of expanding prosperity meet these and other challenges of a new century?

Elected leaders have responded to change by showing new interest in the performance of their higher education systems, approaching similar problems with widely differing solutions. Some have called for restructuring systems with proposals ranging from the discontinuance of statewide coordinating or system governing boards to the creation of new ones. The absence of trends or patterns in state restructuring efforts convinced us of the need to develop a better understanding of how performance and system design are related.

The research we report here is based on a national, three-year comparative study of state higher education governance structures, conducted with support from The Pew Charitable Trusts and The James Irvine Foundation. Our purpose was to improve understanding of how differences in the design of state governance structures affect performance. We also wanted to explore how structure affects the leadership strategies that state policy makers use to encourage institutions to respond to contextual change and new state priorities. Our study defined a state system of higher education to include public and private postsecondary institutions as well as the arrangements for regulating, coordinating, and funding them.

The broader research study looks at the impact of structure, leadership, and context on system performance, measured in a number of different ways. This paper will focus on one aspect of this study: the development of a new way of looking at state higher education governing structures, one that draws on, but also expands, existing typologies. For illustrative purposes, this paper will focus on three of the seven states included in the larger study. These three states–Illinois, Georgia, and Michigan–represent the major variations that we found in governance structures, based on our new framework.

We do not suggest that the explanations presented here are the only ones possible. A major purpose of this study (and of qualitative designs in general) is to challenge others to improve upon our explanation and thus contribute to the continuing scholarly dialogue on governance issues (Bogdan & Bicklen, 1992, p. 49). This explanation fits the data we collected for the seven states that participated in our larger study. The explanation must now be tested for its applicability to other states.

The paper begins with a brief description of our study methodology, followed by a review of the relevant literature. A second section explains the conceptual framework developed for this study, including the new framework for characterizing higher education governing structures. We then discuss the ways in which Michigan, Georgia, and Illinois illustrate the different characteristics of this new framework and conclude with some observations about the policy implications of this research.

## Study Procedures

We designed our selection criteria for selecting the study states to minimize differences among participants in terms of size and diversity of student populations, and to maximize differences in structure. This selection enhanced the probability that observable differences in outcomes could be related to variations in structure. The states selected were among the top twenty in the nation by both the size and diversity of their student populations. The research team also examined available data on inputs and outcomes for higher education systems. None of the data we examined suggested a more compelling basis for selecting states than the criteria of size, diversity, and differences in governance structures. Using these criteria, we selected seven states: California, Florida, Georgia, Illinois, Michigan, New York, and Texas.

We conducted undisguised comparative case studies in study states between September 1994 and September 1996. For each, researchers collected documents, examined archival data, and conducted interviews to obtain multiple sources of information about context, system design, governance structures, and performance.

We selected Illinois as the pilot case because of the long-term stability of its governance structure. While the study sought the cooperation of the higher education governing/coordinating board in each state, we did not require agreement to participate from the State Higher Education Executive Officer (SHEEO). We chose this approach to avoid biasing the study by limiting its purposeful sample only to states that wanted to participate.

We interviewed over 200 individuals during the study, using a common protocol for all interviews. Case study teams interviewed members of governors' staffs; state legislators; members of higher education coordinating or governing boards or commissions; current and former state higher education agency officials; legislative budget analysts; campus-, subsystem-, and system-level trustees, presidents, and staff; and representatives of faculty organizations. We also reviewed published articles on higher education and talked with education writers for major newspapers in several states. Additional documents reviewed in each state included budgets, master plans, statistical reports, board agendas, and system histories. Finally, we commissioned Kent Halstead of Research Associates of Washington to prepare a report that identified the principal operating variables for state-level public higher education systems and provided special commentary for the seven study states based on data available in the National Center for Education Statistics' Integrated Postsecondary Education Data System (IPEDS) and his own survey of state higher education financial officers.

A case report integrated all sources of data for each state in a format that preserved the interviewees' anonymity. Knowledgeable insiders from each participating state reviewed the case reports for accuracy. Following this check on the accuracy of individual case studies, we wrote an interpretive synthesis as a first step in the cross-case analysis, using a single case study (Illinois) to develop a draft model that explained the relationships among variables relevant to the research questions. Following a critique by a national advisory panel, we tested the model against each of the remaining six case studies and successively modified it until it represented the best explanation the research team could devise for all seven of the study states. This paper reflects further attempts to clarify and apply the model in states beyond the seven original participants.[1]

For the purposes of this article, we illustrate the components of the conceptual model with three of the original states–Michigan, Illinois, and Georgia–because they represent the major variations in the traditional taxonomy of state governing structures and illustrate what we found to be some of the most significant variations among our seven study states with regard to our framework. We use other states from our larger study, as well as from subsequent work, for contrast where this is helpful in explaining the conceptual model.

## Traditional Examinations of State Higher Education Governance Structures

The state's role in governing higher education has been the subject of debate in the higher education literature for the last forty years. The question has typically been framed as one of institutional autonomy versus state authority, or centralization versus decentralization. Moos and Rourke (1959) argued that institutions required autonomy and that only strong independent lay boards would insulate public institutions from political intrusion and inappropriate budgetary controls. Glenny (1959) called for greater state-level planning and coordination in higher education. He argued that voluntary coordination would lead to domination by the oldest and largest institutions while failing to provide for adequate representation of the public interest or for effective coordination of a large and increasing number of institutions. Berdahl (1971) suggested that state agencies were preferable to politicians in resolving such issues as approval of new campuses and new degree programs. Kerr and Gade (1989) warned of a "drift" in public sector higher education towards consolidation and control that ran counter to the competition and autonomy characterizing trends in American economic policy.

States vary considerably in the approaches they take to organizing their higher education systems. Concern about institutional autonomy after World War II focused on the state agencies that were established primarily to manage enrollment growth. Because of this concern, generally accepted taxonomies distinguish three basic types of state structures: consolidated governing boards, coordinating boards and planning agencies (Berdahl, 1971; Education Commission of the States, 1997).

*Consolidated governing board states.* A governing board has legal management and control responsibilities for a single institution or a cluster of institutions (Novak, 1993). Twenty-four states have consolidated governing boards that have such responsibilities for all public, four-year institutions in the state. Nine consolidated governing board states have a single board responsible for all higher education as in Georgia, South Dakota, and Utah. Fifteen consolidated governing board states, including Arizona and Florida, have a separate board for community colleges.

*Coordinating board states.* Twenty-four coordinating board states assign responsibility for some or all of nine functions (planning, policy leadership, policy analysis, mission definition, academic program review, budgetary processes, student financial assistance, accountability systems, and institutional authorization) to a single agency other than a governing board. Of these, twenty-one, including Illinois, Texas, and New York, have regulatory authority, while the remainder, including California, have advisory authority. A separate community college coordinating board may operate under the auspices of the statewide board as in Illinois or as an independent state agency as in California.

*Planning agency states.* The two planning agency states, Michigan and Delaware, have no organization with authority that extends much beyond voluntary planning and convening. Some states with consolidated governing boards may also have some form of planning agency.

No fewer than eleven footnotes are required to explain hybrid variations of the three basic structural arrangements in the most recent edition of the Education Commission of the States, *State Postsecondary Education Structures Handbook* (1997). The three states highlighted in this article represent the major variations in the traditional taxonomy of state governing structures.

Beyond these distinctions, some states, including Pennsylvania and New York, have a state board or agency with some responsibilities for all levels of education. Coordinating or governing boards may oversee subsystems of institutions with homogeneous missions as in California or multi-campus subsystems with heterogeneous missions as in New York. They may also coordinate primarily small subsystems or single campuses, as in Illinois or New Jersey, or mixed single campus and multi-campus institutions, as in Texas. In addition, states vary in the extent to which their formally structured higher education governance includes the private sector (Zumeta, 1992). Coordinating board and planning agency states are more likely than those with consolidated governing boards to recognize and incorporate private higher education in their policy and planning processes. Additional differences in the approaches states take to governing their higher education systems include variations in history, political culture, and demographics (McGuinness, 1994).

## Building a New Conceptual Framework

Even the most comprehensive efforts to classify differences fall short of capturing the full complexity of state structures present in some of the more populous states. Our model attempts to address this complexity by considering such factors as the constitutional powers of the governor (Burns, Peltason, & Cronin, 1990), the various roles of the legislatures and state higher education agencies, and the public and private, two- and four-year institutions in the state. In addition, we consider the historical, economic, political, and demographic context of each state.

Traditional classifications of higher education structures define systems along a single dimension–that of centralization versus decentralization. Most of the focus is on the state agency and the powers exhibited by that agency. While this dimension is important, we have come to believe that many more aspects need to be addressed. Our study suggests that state governance structures include two dimensions: first, the policy environment, which determines the role that state government plays in balancing the often competing influences of professional values on the one hand and the market on the other; and second, the structural environment, or system design, which includes the decisions that states make about how to design their higher education systems. (We further define these two environments below.) While we acknowledge the importance of leadership in our framework, it is not treated as a key variable in this paper.

### Policy Environment

The first dimension of our conceptual framework is the policy environment, or the role taken on by the state with regard to higher education. The distribution of authority between the state and higher education ultimately reflects the interests articulated by groups inside and outside of government as these interests are realized in the implementation of public policies and policy priorities. In other words, the higher education system in each state operates in a policy environment that is the result of balancing, or altering the balance between the sometimes conflicting interests of academic professionals and, as we define it, the market. Each state–and each state is unique–balances these influences according to its own policies and priorities; there is no ideal or permanent balance.

Academic interests are familiar influences. Our use of "market" forces is not. The "market," for our purposes, is the broad array of interests and influences that are external to the formal structures of both state government and higher education. Our concept of the market is broader than that of economists. It does include economic influences, such as competitive pressures, user satisfaction, and cost and price. But it also includes quantifiable factors, such as demographic characteristics and projections, and less quantifiable ones, such as political pressures, public confidence, and the availability of new technologies. Moreover, states can respond to market influences through a wide range of strategies, including promoting institutions (such as building community colleges), promulgating regulations (such as restricting the freedom of institutions to sell items in their bookstores that compete with those offered by the private sector), or encouraging competition (such as establishing performance-based budgeting or increasing student aid, thereby enhancing student choice).

Our view of the state policy environment is best understood as the progressive drawing of the triangle of tensions illustrated in Figure 1. The first line represents the tension between "Higher Education" and "State Authority." It incorporates the structural dimension and reflects what we have called the traditional approach to the study of higher education governance (Berdahl, 1970; Shattock, 1994). The second line between "Higher Education" and "Market" represents the tension between producer domination and consumer sovereignty and is the basis for the human capital literature and rate of return analysis (Johnstone, 1992; Psacharopoulis, 1992). The triangle was closed when Clark added the line between "State Authority" and "Market," foreshadowing the possibility of states "steering" rather than providing services directly through public bureaucracies (Clark, 1993).

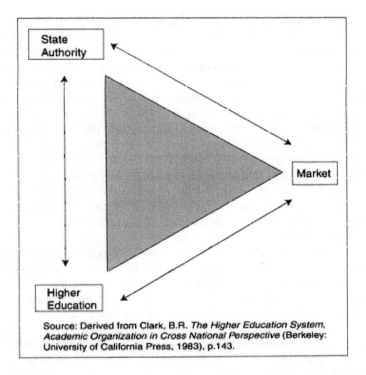

Source: Derived from Clark, B.R. *The Higher Education System, Academic Organization in Cross National Perspective* (Berkeley: University of California Press, 1983), p.143.

Williams (1995) argued that the Clark triangle was static and, therefore, best suited for description. In its place, he proposed a dynamic alternative that allowed consideration of government's variable roles in shaping the relative influence of the market and professional values on the types of services provided and their costs. In Williams's model, the role of the state changes as the force of the competing claims shifts among state, market, and academic interests. Among the state roles Williams described are promoter, referee, and consumer supporter. As promoter the state provides the facilities and sets the rules to achieve a given purpose that is seen as more important than the market. As referee, the state mediates between consumers and providers, ensuring fair play. As consumer supporter, the state throws its weight behind users. Our adaptation of Williams's model, shown in Figure 2, identifies four policy roles that lie along the continuum from state-provided higher education to the state as consumer role described by some advocates of privatization.

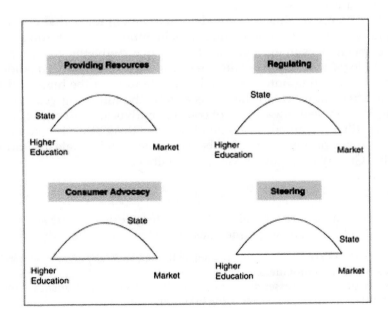

Like Williams's promoter, the state as provider in our scheme subsidizes higher education services with little regard for the market. As regulator, our second role, the state specifies the relationship between institutions and the market by controlling user charges, constraining administrative discretion in using resources, and eliminating or attenuating the incentives for efficient operation. As consumer advocate, the state redirects some allocations for higher education to students, increasing the influence of their market choices on institutional behavior. Our fourth role, steering, has no exact parallel in Williams's model but was popularized as a concept by Osborne and Gaebler in their book *Reinventing Government* (1992). States steer by structuring the market for higher education services to produce outcomes consistent with governmental priorities. The inclusion of private higher education institutions in the design of state systems is one example of steering, as is the use of vouchers that students may use to purchase approved services from any provider.

Low-tuition, low-aid strategies fall on the provider/regulator end of the scale. High-tuition, high-aid strategies are a good example of the consumer advocacy/steering end of the policy environment continuum. Examples of policies that move beyond consumer advocacy to approach steering include the aggressive inclusion of private institutions in planning to meet public needs, the use of contracts to take advantage of private capacity in lieu of creating or expanding public capacity, the use of targeted vouchers that enable students to purchase approved services from any providers, and the appropriation of different levels of funding for some degree programs based on state manpower needs. The key distinction between roles involves the use that a state makes of the market. In a market-dominated environment, price is a function of demand. In the consumer advocacy role, the state concentrates on supporting demand. In the regulating role, the state controls price.

All states exhibit some characteristics of each of the four policy roles. While one role will typically be more dominant than the others (the state may tend to lean more towards the market than it does towards institutions), this model represents a continuum, not simply four distinct roles.

States in our study that exhibited patterns of deference to professional values or relied heavily on regulation (Michigan, California, New York, and Texas) reported less satisfaction with higher education system performance than those that found a more dynamic balance between professional values and market forces (Florida, Georgia, and Illinois). Ignoring the market in favor of state-planned systems of public higher education increases costs and limits responsiveness to emerging state needs and priorities. Excessive state regulation removes institutional incentives for efficiency and quality. Too-heavy reliance on consumer choice substitutes what people are willing to buy at present for longer term investment strategies. Too-zealous market structuring can leave the most expensive tasks to public institutions while stripping them of critical mass and flexibility. Each of these influences can contribute to effective system balance, but each can also be detrimental if unchecked by governance structures and policies that balance all three in a way that is appropriate to a state's context and priorities.

Michigan exhibits a predominantly provider environment for higher education. Institutions expect and generally receive incremental increases in annual appropriations without regard to performance or even changes in enrollments. During our study, the governor was able for one year to persuade the legislature to reward the three institutions that followed guidelines for limiting tuition increases. The resulting outcry and political fallout from the higher education lobbying community led to a reinstatement of the status quo by the following year. Georgia has moved from a regulating environment toward one of consumer advocacy as a result of its widely known HOPE Scholarships. Illinois maintains a predominantly steering environment through such strategies as the careful management of competition between public and private institutions and its highly regarded Priorities, Quality and Productivity (PQP) initiative.

## System Design

The second dimension of our conceptual model is system design, or the structural environment. States make four sets of decisions when they design systems of higher education:

- Decisions about governance structures establish lines of authority and accountability between state government and providers.
- Decisions about work processes define responsibility for and characteristics of the major work processes: (a) collecting and disseminating information about performance, (b) prescribing the

framework for budgeting, (c) allocating responsibilities for monitoring program quality and redundancy, and (d) providing arrangements for encouraging higher education institutions to see themselves as a system and to work together on such tasks as school-to-college transitions and student transfer.

- Decisions about mission divide responsibilities for achieving higher education goals among types of institutions.
- Decisions about capacity determine the availability, quality.

In our model, we characterize state governance structures for higher education systems as segmented, unified, or federal. In the most segmented systems, multiple governing boards are each responsible for one or more institutions. There is no effective state agency with substantial responsibility for all higher education. State government reserves only the power to determine the appropriation each institution receives each year. Each governing board and its appointed executive represent institutional interests directly to state government through the budgeting process. Four-year institutions and community colleges may each have their own separate arrangements for voluntary coordination to identify issues on which they are willing to cooperate in dealing with state government and with each other.

Michigan is the most segmented design in our study. Each of its four-year institutions (with the exception of the University of Michigan campuses at Dearborn and Flint) have their own governing boards. There are no arrangements for statewide planning. No statewide agency provides information about higher education performance, and four-year institutions have worked actively to preserve this situation. Articulation between two- and four-year institutions is handled under a voluntary agreement that has never been signed by all of the public four-year institutions. Program review is also voluntary; and if an institution disagrees with the outcome, it may decide to offer the program anyway.

In unified systems, a single governing board manages all degree-granting higher education institutions and represents them in discussions with governors and legislators. Unified systems are characterized by Handy's (1992) principles of twin citizenship, interdependence, common rules, and common ways of communicating and measuring. Twin citizenship is determined by the degree to which participants feel themselves a part of both the larger system and the institution to which they have their primary allegiance.[2]

Georgia is the most unified system in our study. All of its degree-granting two- and four-year institutions are governed by a single board of regents. The system uses strategic planning and its program approval authority to address statewide need and to prevent mission creep. Its chancellor offers a single point of contact for state government. While this arrangement might encourage excessive intervention from the governor and legislators, Georgia seems to avoid these problems as a result of constitutional status for the entire system conferred by vote of the electorate in 1942.

Federal systems have a statewide board responsible for collecting and distributing information, advising on the budget, planning programs from a statewide perspective, and encouraging articulation. Federal systems, like their unified counterparts, emphasize interdependence, common rules, and common ways of communicating and measuring. To these characteristics, they add separation of powers and subsidiarity. Separation of powers divides responsibilities for representing the public interest (monitoring inputs, performance, and institutional accountability) from responsibilities for governing institutions (strategic direction, management accountability and institutional advocacy). The former are carried out by the coordinating board and the latter by institutional or system governing boards. Subsidiarity safeguards the legitimate roles of institutions by limiting the size and influence of central system agencies.

Illinois has a federal system. A strong coordinating board (that is neither higher education nor state government) negotiates a consolidated budget each year for all of higher education with the governor. The board also provides credible and comprehensive information about institutional performance to state officials who describe the board as "the institutional memory of higher education." The board uses its planning and program approval authority to maintain a viable private sector and to ensure that institutions focus on centrality to mission, quality, and productivity in making program decisions. The legislature keeps a watchful eye on the board to keep it from infringing on institutional prerogatives.

It is important to note that these categories of system design represent a continuum rather than discrete categories. Design characteristics tend to lean more toward one type of structure than another, but there are no absolutes. And, as we noted above, some states exhibit hybrid characteristics, combining an advisory agency with a consolidated governing board as in Oregon, or with segmented systems as in California.

## Policy Environment and System Design: Three Cases

The relationship between the policy environment and system design is critical to our conceptual framework. The role of the state as regulator, for example, works at cross-purposes with the deference to professional values that characterizes the most segmented systems. The regulator role is consistent with more centralized bureaucratic models, including the unified model. A federal system may work well in a steering environment but does not work well in an environment dominated by the state in a provider role. To perform effectively, systems must be compatible with the policy environments in which they function.

Our case studies suggest that system design, policy environment, and the degree of compatibility between design and environment all influence the kinds of performance systems achieve and the kinds of leadership that will be effective in each. As Table 1 indicates, Michigan, Georgia, and Illinois represent the three main categories of the traditional taxonomy. They also illustrate significant variations in the two dimensions of our new conceptual framework.

### Illinois

In 1961, Illinois established a "system of systems" for higher education that was specifically designed as a federal model. Responsibility for coordinating the system was given to the Illinois Board of Higher Education (IBHE). Until 1995, this system of systems included four public university governing boards with responsibility for 12 public universities and a system of community colleges coordinated by a state level board that worked closely with IBHE. The four-year systems included the Board of Regents, Board of Governors, the University of Illinois (U of I), and Southern Illinois University (SIU). The system of systems was created partly to bring together and thereby improve the capacity of several smaller four-year institutions to compete with the U of I and SIU, which remained as separate subsystems.

Private, nonprofit institutions, historically strong in urban areas, were defined as an integral part of the system in the late 1960s. Private institutions asked the state for need-based financial aid programs as well as capitation grants to subsidize Illinois residents attending private institutions, and asked that the state use the capacity in the private sector rather than starting new programs in public institutions. In return, private higher education agreed to be involved in the state's master planning process.

In the spring of 1995, legislation was passed that abolished the Board of Regents and Board of Governors, replacing them with individual governing boards for seven of the eight institutions they governed. The eighth institution was designated as a campus of the University of Illinois. While significant, these changes did not change the federal character of the Illinois system.

The IBHE has responsibility for all four of the work processes. Illinois has the most sophisticated information system of any of the states we studied, and state and institutional leaders rely on that information for policy decisions related to the budget and program planning. While the IBHE has authority only to recommend budgets, not to mandate them, the budget process is central to IBHE strategies. The board enhances the informal authority derived from its trust relationships with the governor and, to a lesser degree with the legislature, by concentrating on rational, responsible budget recommendations, and by reducing conflict among institutions and sectors.

Illinois exhibits all of the key characteristics of Handy's federal model. In terms of subsidiarity, we have evidence of a legislature that does not want an IBHE that is too strong. An attempt to strengthen IBHE powers was easily defeated during our study, despite support from a strong governor. The system also provides evidence of substantial interdependence. The reserved powers implicit in the budget process and the program review and approval processes prevent institutions from ignoring the concerns of the center. A high quality information system links all system participants in both the public and private sectors. This information is key to the common rules and language, another characteristic of the federal system. Twin citizenship is evident in the emphasis on consensus inherent in the Illinois system. Finally, there is a clear separation of powers, with various players having responsibility for monitoring (IBHE), management (institutions) and for strategy, policy, and direction (the governor and other elected leaders).

The policy role in Illinois can best be described as steering. The state has the capacity to identify and set priorities, and to monitor institutions' ability to address those priorities. The Priorities, Quality and Productivity (PQP) project evolved out of a call from the governor and board chair for institutions to set priorities, improve quality, and increase productivity. Each college and university was expected to focus its mission and consolidate or eliminate lower-priority and lower-quality programs and services. Resources saved were to be reinvested in higher-priority, higher-quality programs and services. The state "steers" the environment in this case by setting the direction (high priorities and high quality) but allowing institutions to come up with the specific solutions.

A second example of the steering role in Illinois is the extensive use of the private sector. A large student financial aid program, categorical grants to private institutions, and involvement of the private institutions in statewide planning activities are examples of ways in which the state uses the market to help meet priorities.

The steering role is well matched to the federal design in Illinois. The incentives in both are focused on responding to the environment and to market forces. The match between the structural and policy environments leads to high satisfaction among elected officials about the performance of the Illinois system.

Not all states match federal designs with steering or consumer advocacy policy environments. Texas uses a federal design within a predominantly regulatory policy environment. State officials are less confident about system performance. The coordinating board is not infrequently used as a scapegoat by both the legislature and higher education leadership producing a significantly more contentious environment than we observed in Illinois. Tennessee uses a federal design in a predominantly "providing" policy environment. After significant dissatisfaction with coordinating board performance by several successive leaders, the governor in 1997 appointed a blue-ribbon committee on excellence to propose changes to its system of governance.

## Georgia

The Georgia system has the simplest design of our study states and represents the unified model in our framework. A 1931 decision placed all degree-granting institutions under the supervision of a single governing board. Following a 1941 attempt by the governor to intervene in the hiring and firing of administrators, the electorate ratified an amendment that gave the board constitutional status to govern, control, and manage the system. Currently, the University System of Georgia includes 15 two-year and 19 four-year institutions.

The Board of Regents of the University System of Georgia has responsibility for the four main work processes. The board has the power to define institutional missions, to determine the array and size of institutions in the system, to allocate funds to institutions, and to determine how much higher education will cost. The effectiveness of board management of the work processes depends heavily on executive leadership. The system makes strong use of strategic planning but provides less information on performance than federal systems. Limiting information helps reduce the ability of external actors to intrude into system decisions.

As a unified structure, most decisions are made between the chancellor, the board, and elected officials. The system does not present the separation of powers inherent in the federal system. There are, however, examples of twin citizenship, interdependence, and common rules and ways of communicating. The institutional representatives we spoke with agreed that they identified with the University System of Georgia but also had loyalties to their own institutions, examples of twin citizenship. For the most part, they believed that they gained something from being a part of the larger system even if it meant that they also gave up some individual flexibility. There is interdependence; institutions cannot ignore concerns of the center because the governing board controls the budget process. As for common rules and language, a protocol in the university system guides how individual institutions (represented by their presidents) deal with the legislature. Typically, the university system does the lobbying; but if presidents are called upon to work with the legislature, it is as representatives of the university system. A "common law" provides an understanding that the system will work as a system. The formula funding process is another example of a common law of sorts in the Georgia system. While the formulas are not used for budget allocation to institutions, they are used for funding approximately 90-95 percent of the university system's budget. As a result, there is little discussion or negotiation over the major portion of the budget with the legislature or governor.

The unified structure is closely overseen by the governor through the Board of Regents, whom he appoints, and through his influence in the budget process. The governor can set priorities for higher education; but because of constitutional autonomy, these must often be addressed through nontraditional mechanisms. For example, to raise what have been relatively poor college-going rates, the current governor instituted a scholarship program in 1993 funded by the lottery. The program, Helping Outstanding Pupils Educationally (HOPE), provides full tuition and fees to students who maintain a B average in high school and attend a public college in Georgia. Those who maintain that B average in college continue to receive the award. Although critics of the program point out that it does not provide additional money to the poorest students if they are already receiving federal grants, it is generally seen as a model that helps to encourage access in a state that had not previously placed a high priority on higher education. The HOPE scholarships have helped to move the Georgia policy environment from regulatory toward consumer advocacy.

While Georgia's unified system design and policy environment seemed compatible during our study, the emphasis on central planning could become more problematic if elected officials further strengthen the market emphasis represented by the HOPE scholarships. Present strong leadership, along with constitutional status for the entire system may give Georgia more latitude for coping with any potential mismatch than other states confronting this issue.

The Florida system is similar to the Georgia design in the sense that all four-year institutions are governed by a single board. However, community colleges in Florida each have their own governing boards, while a statewide coordinating board serves as the interface between these institutions and state government. The policy environment in Florida is strongly regulatory. Significantly, the Florida legislature in this "weak governor state" is also moving toward a policy environment that places greater emphasis on consumer advocacy. New York groups all of its degree-granting institutions into two heterogeneous (two- and four-year institutions reporting to the same board) systems and has a predominantly regulatory policy environment. Efforts by the current governor to make the system more responsive to market forces have been largely thwarted by legislative refusal to relax regulations that prevent institutions from responding effectively.

## Michigan

Michigan represents the most segmented model in our system design framework. There is no statewide agency with significant responsibilities for higher education, and all four-year institutions have constitutional status. Thirteen of the fifteen four-year public institutions in the state have their own governing boards; the exceptions are the two branch campuses of the University of Michigan. Universities are seen as the "fourth branch of government" by many legislators.

While the 1963 constitution charged the state Board of Education with serving as the general planning and coordinating body for all of higher education, a 1975 court decision found that the University of Michigan did not need the board's approval to expand or establish programs, effectively limiting the authority of the state board to advising the legislature on requests for funds. Universities have refused to cooperate with the state board on several occasions, and resist any information-gathering or -coordinating activities as an encroachment on their constitutional autonomy.

In the absence of formal coordination, the four-year public institutions in the state established a voluntary Presidents Council in 1952. The council's activities include developing positions on the state budget for higher education, reviewing and monitoring legislation affecting higher education, collecting and disseminating data, reviewing academic programs, and interacting with state agencies and organizations (Presidents Council, 1992, p. 1). The policy community believes that institutions use the council for issues that benefit them but primarily stand by themselves when there is nothing to gain individually from collaborating.

The 30 community colleges (one tribally controlled) in the state are linked together through the voluntary Michigan Community College Association and a Community College Board that advises the State Board of Education. The Community College Board is not seen as a major player in the Michigan system, as might be inferred from the governor's actions in cutting its budget significantly and in eliminating board member per-diem expenses for meetings.

The private sector is included in state policy decisions to the extent that the state provides reimbursements for degrees awarded to Michigan residents. There is also a small need-based tuition grant program for students attending private institutions.

Because of the segmented nature of the structure, no one agency or institution has responsibility for the work processes in Michigan. Individual institutions define and modify their own missions. There is a voluntary program approval process under the auspices of the Presidents Council, but the process does not limit program duplication. Most articulation efforts are the result of local agreements. There is little statewide information on performance.

The only way for state government to influence higher education in Michigan is through the budget process. Funding is based primarily on historical funding patterns over the past 30 years. While the legislature is attentive to the priorities of the governor, it typically provides a lump sum to each institution at a common rate of increase. Institutions can spend their appropriation as they see fit.

The state uses the budget primarily to reinforce a carefully negotiated pecking order among institutions, based more on prestige than on state priorities. As a result, the state role is primarily that of provider—supporting institutions with across-the-board increases with few restrictions on how the money is spent. While many refer to Michigan as a "market model" because it has no statewide or systemwide boards, it was described to us as more of a "public monopoly." There is little competition from the private sector, and across-the-board increases in funding allow institutions to offer pretty much what they want.

There have been some attempts by Michigan governors to implement regulatory policies to encourage certain institutional actions, but these attempts have not always been successful. After tuition increased dramatically over a four-year period in the early 1990s, Governor John Engler developed a tuition tax credit plan designed to hold down tuition. Students attending institutions where tuition increases were held below the rate of inflation for the previous year received a tax credit. The incentive plan was not popular with most four-year institutions, whose leaders argued that the state should have provided more money to institutions to help keep tuition increases down. Others viewed the program as a violation of constitutional status which grants individual boards the right to set tuition. The tax credit was discontinued after one year, an example of how difficult it is for a state clearly in the provider role to use regulatory policies on its institutions.

The state-as-provider role is well aligned with the segmented design of the state system. The incentives in both environments emphasize deference to professional values. While some elected officials acknowledged that the system may not be as efficient as it should be, there was general satisfaction among those in Michigan with the structural and policy environments. For now, there is a general assumption that what universities provide equals the public interest.

California also uses a segmented design in a policy environment that, for the constitutionally autonomous University of California, is predominantly providing. Interestingly, the environment for the California State University and the California Community Colleges has historically been highly regulatory. The California Postsecondary Education Commission, an advisory agency, has many of the same credibility and effectiveness problems as the Tennessee Higher Education Commission. In both states, the providing policy environment for the major university makes opposition an extraordinarily high-risk activity. In California, there is the additional problem of having all key understandings about higher education enshrined in a master plan that no one seems able to alter even in the face of external changes that threaten the integrity of the promises on which it is based.

## Policy Implications

As these three descriptions make apparent, state systems of higher education are structured in a variety of ways. Each state system offers different tools and opportunities to those charged with leading it, and some of these tools are more useful than others in adapting to conditions that are likely to dominate the future. Less obvious, but equally real, are the different incentives–implicit and explicit–that are inherent within the state policy environment and that can prompt or even prevent states from achieving their policy priorities.

We suggest that each state has the responsibility to its citizens to assess the capacity of its higher education system to respond to the substantial changes that the next several decades are likely to bring. If this assessment suggests a lack in capacity (as reflected in unmet state needs or insufficient information), deeper probing becomes essential.

We propose two areas for such probing: the incentives and disincentives fostered by the state policy environment, and the allocation of responsibilities as determined by system design. For purposes of policy analysis in a particular state, it is also helpful to consider the most pragmatic effects of these in day-to-day governance and administrative practices, i.e. in the work processes (defined above as part of the system design). We can thus distinguish the tools available through the key work processes as a distinct and third level of inquiry. If a higher education system is to accomplish more than its aggregated campuses could do individually, it is in these three areas that solutions can be developed. In examining higher education's performance relative to present and future state needs, problems and solutions appear at one or more of these three levels of analysis and also in the interactions among elements of all three.

As state policy makers attempt to strike an appropriate balance between institutional interests and market forces, they have a wide array of options to achieve their objectives, as outlined by the four policy roles we have identified: providing resources, regulating, consumer advocacy, and steering. For instance, states can restrict or encourage competition; they can create new providers, such as the Western Governors' University; they can offer incentives to new or existing private or nonprofit programs of higher education; or they can seek to protect the student markets of existing institutions by impeding the entry of new providers. States can fund students directly on the basis of merit or need or both, or they can fund institutions. They can support institutions on a "maintain the asset" basis, on the basis of performance, or on the basis of performance and competition. They can act as the principal owner and operator of institutions (the maintenance approach). Or they can act as a consumer in the marketplace, purchasing instruction and research from the public and private institutions that meet state access, quality, and cost requirements. They can create centralized or federal governance structures, or they can leave each college and university to the exclusive guidance of its own board. They can regulate or create systems and agencies to manage and administer colleges and universities; they can have procedural accountability through extensive rules and control mechanisms; or they can hold institutions accountable for results and outcomes.

While all of these policy-affecting options are exercised in some form somewhere, most states employ a particular combination of options that has resulted from ad hoc responses to economic conditions or political problems that appeared at an earlier time in the state's history. Few states explicitly use policy to balance market and institutional interests to assure the right combination for their current priorities. We hold that greater awareness of options at all three levels of policy direction will lead to more intentional use of public policy to pursue specific priorities, as well as to more systematic and useful policy analysis.

One of the most difficult problems for state public policy is inconsistency or misalignment of the three policy levels. Misalignment may arise from state attempts to solve a problem at one policy level by measures more appropriate to another. Tools appropriate at the operational policy level–for example, tinkering at the margins of budgetary formulas–would not achieve the desired result if the problem were at the system-design level. Nor would they be effective in the presence of constitutional constraints that perpetuate inadequate funding. Misalignment may also result when state government adapts policy incentives aimed at enhancing the influence of market forces without altering the design of a higher education system that has grown accustomed to heavy regulation.

States that fail to address their systemic alignment will approach higher education reform through a series or package of discrete endeavors. Such approaches run the risks of misalignment and inconsistency. And, of most practical importance, they are unlikely to achieve the desired system performance.

## Conclusion

The conceptual framework described in this article suggests that statewide governance of higher education is best understood as the result of interaction between a policy environment shaped by government strategies to achieve balance among professional values and the use of market forces; and a system design which determines provider responsibilities, capacities, and linkages to each other and to elected leaders. Traditional examinations of state governance focus primarily on the relationship between the state agency and institutions of higher education. This new framework allows for a more complex understanding of the overall system structure.

It is the relationship between the two dimensions that becomes critical when trying to understand a state system. States may design or restructure governance arrangements without considering the degree to which effective operation depends on the incentives and disincentives of the policy environment. Conversely, policy environments can change over time to the point where governance structures designed for a different era no longer work very well. Outcomes are influenced both by design limitations and by the compatibility of the design with a policy environment. States where the policy environment and structural design are mismatched create unnecessarily contentious circumstances that make leadership extremely difficult. Systems with good leadership can at times overcome many of the constraints of poor design or incompatible policy environments, and systems with poor leadership are likely to fall short of their potential under the best of circumstances. Of course it follows that well-designed systems operating in compatible policy environments with good leadership have the best chance of performing in ways that satisfy policy priorities.

Kathy Reeves Bracco is Senior Policy Analyst at the National Center for Public Policy and Higher Education, San Jose, California. Richard C. Richardson, Jr., is a Professor of Educational Leadership and Policy Studies at Arizona State University, Tempe. Patrick M. Callan is President of the National Center for Public Policy and Higher Education, and Joni E. Finney is its Vice President. This article is based on R. C. Richardson, K. R. Bracco, P. M. Callan, and J. E. Finney, *Designing State Higher Education Systems for a New Century* (Phoenix, AZ: Oryx Press, 1998). An earlier version of this article was presented at the American Educational Research Association (AERA) annual meeting, April 1998, in San Diego. Address inquiries to Kathy Reeves Bracco, 152 N. Third Street, Suite 705, San Jose, CA 95112; e-mail: kbracco@highereducation.org

## Notes

1. Additional states that have contributed data used to test the model include Oregon, New Jersey, Tennessee, Washington, and Oklahoma.
2. We draw here upon a modified version of concepts that C. Handy (1992) uses to describe the integrated system and to distinguish federal from unified systems.

## References

Berdahl, R. O. (1971). *Statewide coordination of higher education.* Washington, D.C.: American Council on Education.

Bogdan R. C., & Bicklen, S. K. (1992). *Qualitative research for education: An introduction to theory and methods.* Boston: Allyn and Bacon.

Burns, J. M., Peltason, J. W., & Cronin, T. E. (1990). *State and local politics: Government by the people.* Englewood Cliffs, NJ: Prentice-Hall.

Clark, B. R. (1993). *The higher education system: Academic organization in cross-national perspective.* Berkeley, CA: University of California Press.

Education Commission of the States (1997). *State postsecondary education structures sourcebook*. Denver, CO: Education Commission of the States.

Glenny, L. A. (1959). *Autonomy of public colleges: The challenge of coordination*. New York: McGraw-Hill.

Handy, C. (1992, November-December) Balancing corporate power: A new federalist paper. *Harvard Business Review*, 59–72.

Johnstone, B. (1992). Tuition fees. In B. R. Clark & G. Neave (Eds.), *The Encyclopedia of Higher Education* (Vol. 2, pp. 1501–09). Oxford: Pergamon Press.

Kerr, C., & Gade, M. (1989). *The guardians: Boards of trustees of American colleges and universities, what they do and how well they do it*. Washington, D.C.: Association of Governing Boards.

McGuinness, A. C. (1994). The changing structure of state higher education leadership. In A.C. McGuinness, R. M. Epper, & S. Arredondo (Eds.), *Postsecondary education structures handbook*. Denver, CO: Education Commission of the States.

Moos, M., & Rourke, F. (1959). *The Campus and the State*. Baltimore: John Hopkins Press.

Novak, R. (1993, March/April). Statewide governance: Autonomy or accountability revisited. *Trusteeship*, 10–14.

Osborne, D., & Gaebler, T. (1992). *Reinventing government: How the entrepreneurial spirit is transforming the public sector*. Reading, MA: Addison-Wesley.

Presidents Council. (1992). *State Universities of Michigan 1992–93 Directory*. Lansing, MI: Presidents Council.

Psacharopoulis, G. (1992). Rate of return studies. In B. R. Clark & G. Neave (Eds.), *The Encyclopedia of Higher Education* (Vol. 2, pp. 999–1003). Oxford: Pergamon Press.

Shattock, M. (1994). *The UGC and the management of British universities*. Buckingham, UK: Open University Press.

Williams, G. L. (1995). The 'marketization' of higher education: Reforms and potential reforms in higher education finance. In D. D. Dill & B. Sporn (Eds)., *Emerging patterns of social demand and university reform: Through a glass darkly* (pp. 170–93). Tarrytown, NY: Elsevier Science.

Zumeta, W. (1992, July/August). State policies and private higher education. *Journal of Higher Education*, 63(4), 363–417.

# Are the States and Public Higher Education Striking a New Bargain?

## by DAVID W. BRENEMAN

A representative sample of recent newspaper and magazine headlines about higher education includes the following: "Higher Education at the Crossroads," "Pay or Decay," "A Revolt of the Flagships," "Colleges Ask for Spending Freedom," "Three Schools Seeking Charter Status," and "William & Mary Seeks Control Over Its Own Assets."

A casual reader might conclude that higher education was in the throes of some kind of revolution, and indeed would be largely correct. Clearly, the relationship between public higher education and state government is in flux in ways not been seen for decades. The general pattern is one of reduced state support followed by sharply rising tuitions and arguments for less state regulation. Those who are inclined to jump ahead to the seemingly inevitable destination for these trends talk of "privatization" or of "privately financed public universities."

Such talk, however, is exaggerated and unrealistic. State appropriations for operating expenses at public colleges and universities in fiscal 2004 totaled more than $60 billion, and it is inconceivable that institutions could replace those funds with either their collective endowments ($1.2 trillion would be required to generate the needed income at 5 percent payout) or increased tuition revenues (net of the increase in need-based financial aid that would be necessary to maintain enrollments). Admittedly, several major public universities have seen their state shares of institutional revenues decline over time to well below 20 percent, with some approaching single digits. Regional universities in several states also have seen declines in state revenues to below half of all revenues.

## Executive Summary

Shrinking state appropriations for public colleges and universities over the past two decades have prompted leaders at many institutions and systems to actively pursue alternative sources of revenue. Observers disagree as to whether the funding cuts are inevitable and permanent. Some have suggested they might gradually be reversed through political advocacy, while others say colleges and universities have attracted a backlash by overspending on luxurious facilities.

Most in the higher education and public-policy fields, however, have accepted the fact that with student enrollment swelling, modern public institutions have had to respond to the cuts by hiking tuition rates and relying more on the ability of their affiliated foundations to raise private funds to preserve quality and maintain financial health. The result has been the development of new definitions of the "compact" or "partnership" between public campuses and state government.

This paper examines experiments and proposed changes already underway in the public higher education systems in seven states: Colorado, Florida, Oregon, South Carolina, Texas, Virginia, and Washington. These separate efforts include allowing universities to set their own tuition, granting them greater regulatory flexibility, encouraging them to pursue greater efficiencies through performance contracting, and introducing a form of market-based vouchers in which state funds are given to students to use at the in-state college or university of their choice.

Such experimental programs in turn can prompt changes in governance structures, and in some cases will necessitate a more aggressive monitoring role for governing boards. For this reason, trustees and state leaders are advised to follow the ongoing debates as public higher education struggles to redefine its long-standing relationship with the states and as the nation strives to educate growing numbers of citizens.

Serious discussion, however, needs to focus not at the extremes of full state support or zero state support, but in the murky middle, where even the stories one tells to describe the "facts" are contested. Political scientist Michael Mumper recently conducted interviews with education and political leaders in 11 states and identified five distinct stories characterizing the current financing scene:

- The state made prices (tuition) rise.
- Medicaid and prisons made prices rise.
- High-quality programs cost money.
- Those unaccountable public colleges made prices rise.
- It only looks like a problem.

The purpose of this essay is to discuss the main ideas surfacing in several states that redefine the relationship of states to their public colleges and universities, to shed light on the current financing situation, and to examine the pros and cons of various approaches. Given that the history, culture, and circumstances of each state are distinct, it is difficult to assert meaningful generalizations. The stakes, however, are high, and it is worth our time to consider the issues carefully and act on an informed basis. It will be especially important that state policymakers and higher education leaders think through new financing or governance alternatives and have meaningful policy discussions about the effects on students, institutional missions and purposes, and state needs and priorities. To arrive at new definitions simply by default or inaction is to shortchange the interests of institutions, states, and students.

## Shrinking Funds

The dominant stories from the field are concentrated around the themes that states are short of money. National data clearly document the declining share of college and university budgets provided by the states. The share dropped from a peak of about 50 percent in 1979 to about 36 percent by 2000. Related measures also show that state appropriations for higher education, measured either as a share of total state outlays or per $1,000 of personal income, have dropped steadily since the late 1970s. The cuts in state support have been particularly sharp in recent years: In fiscal 2002, total state appropriations for higher education were $63.3 billion; in fiscal 2004, $60.5 billion, or a drop of 4.4 percent.

The National Conference of State Legislatures reports that between fiscal 2002 and 2004, higher education was the only major function of state government that took such large cuts in state funding. Some observe that these trends are cyclical, a result of a segment of the economy that is underperforming at any given time, and that the economy eventually will recover and boost state appropriations.

Others argue that long-term structural deficits are just beginning to emerge in the states and pose permanent problems for higher education—in other words, the dollars being taken away are never coming back.

What's worse, these most recent cuts have coincided with a demographic upturn in high school graduates, so that colleges and universities are under pressure to increase enrollments just as state support is dropping sharply. The severity of current cuts, coming after more than two decades of slow but steady relative decline in state support, has forced many education leaders to conclude that the old, often implicit, compacts between states and their universities—such as ensured access to affordable public colleges and universities for the state's high school graduates—have been abandoned. Hence it is understandable that we are seeing efforts to establish a new relationship that gives the institutions control over setting tuition and freedom from specific state regulations.

A few words should be added to address the views Mumper identified concerning the behavior of institutions. The arguments here are partly over data, and partly over interpretation. For example, some note that while the state share of support for higher education has been declining, the actual dollars have generally been going up, just not as fast as other revenue sources such as tuition, income from auxiliary enterprises, private gifts and endowment earnings, and research support, all of which at many institutions have grown rapidly and dramatically. In fact, state support per student has been relatively stable since the early 1990s, according to the State Higher Education Executive Officers.

Against this backdrop, some question the priorities communicated by institutions that spend lavishly on elaborate dormitories and dining halls, swimming and exercise facilities, athletic complexes, superstar faculty who do little teaching, and proliferating administrative staff. They recommend a fundamental restructuring of higher education to clarify priorities and reduce costs, similar to what the private sector goes through periodically.

Critics argue that competition in higher education leads to higher—rather than the expected lower—costs, which are then passed on either to the state or federal governments or to students and families. Meanwhile, those who argue that there really isn't much of a problem (Mumper's fifth story) point to rising enrollment rates in higher education in spite of cuts in state support and higher tuition. The reason for mentioning these stories is to suggest that there is more than a grain of truth to them, a reality that complicates the process of redefining the state-institutional partnership.

## Recent Reform Proposals

To demonstrate the range of proposals being developed, consider the ideas being advanced in Colorado, Florida, Oregon, South Carolina, Texas, Virginia, and Washington. (Fuller descriptions of actions in these seven states can be found in the *State Governance Action Annual 2004*, produced by AGB's Center for Public Trusteeship and Governance.) While not encompassing every conceivable change, the proposals from these states are worth discussing because they are concrete and are currently either being reviewed or implemented.

- *Colorado*: Much of the debate in Colorado has been framed in response to the TABOR (Taxpayer Bill of Rights) amendment, which is a tax, spending, and fee-limitation measure voters approved in 1992. In effect, this measure limits tuition and fee increases to an amount calculated on the basis of inflation plus population growth. Under TABOR, entities (including universities) that receive less than 10 percent of their total annual revenues from the state and local governments qualify for "enterprise" status. That means two things: It removes that university from the limits on tuition and fee increases, and allows it to issue bonds to finance new instructional facilities. Because the University of Colorado System already receives less than 10 percent of its support from state and local governments, the university actively campaigned on behalf of enterprise status. In 2003, however, the governor vetoed legislation that would have achieved that end, arguing that a case-by-case review of colleges and universities was necessary before such legislation should pass.

The governor's other objection was expressed in his State of the State address on January 8, 2004, in which he said, "I will not give unlimited authority to colleges and universities to raise tuition." As one reviews the various plans put forward to alter the relation of universities with state government, the authority to set tuition seems the one most important to institutions and the most troubling to governors and legislators. Freedom to set prices without state intervention appears to be the gold standard of this broad reform effort. While reduced state regulations promise efficiency gains, one has the sense that the core issue is control over price.

Still, Colorado lawmakers again tackled the enterprise issue in early 2004, allowing institutions new latitude in setting tuition (the exact amount is open to interpretation in that the legislature reserves some tuition-setting powers). And in the same bill, they acted to replace state appropriations to institutions for student enrollment with student stipends—essentially a voucher plan for allocating subsidies—drawn from a statewide "College Opportunity Fund." Each admitted student will receive an amount from the state toward college costs to be carried to the institution the student chooses. These educational vouchers would be supplemented not only by increased need-based financial aid to help meet costs above the voucher amount but also by "role and mission block grants" to institutions, in recognition of activities not directly related to instruction, such as research.

The final bill—signed into law by Gov. Bill Owens in May 2004—includes a provision that each public university governing board shall negotiate a performance contract with the coordinating board focused on student access and success, institutional efficiency, and state needs.

It should also be noted that in 2001 the Colorado legislature passed a bill to allow the state commission on higher education to enter into a performance compact with the Colorado School of Mines (CSM), a specialized engineering institution. The agreement provides CSM with tuition-setting authority at a higher rate than at other public institutions, and funding via a block grant. Negotiations also determined the mix of in-state versus out-of-state students. Central to this agreement is the ability of CSM to specify certain outcomes, such as graduation and employment rates that provide meaningful accountability.

Colorado's changes have taken the form they have largely in response to TABOR, legislation that is unique to that state. In the absence of TABOR, it is unclear what form proposals in this state might have taken; nonetheless, the key issue of tuition control is found in many states, and thus our discussion of that topic in the next section is broadly applicable.

- *Florida.* Governance of higher education in the Sunshine State has been changing rapidly. Within the past two years alone, three new governance structures have been approved. The statewide board of regents was abolished by legislative action, in part over disputes between the board and key legislators over the need for and location of new professional schools of law and medicine. Much of the political dynamic in Florida occurs because its fastest growing areas are home to relatively new and developing universities, while the older, established research universities—the University of Florida and Florida State University—are located away from major population centers. The result is intensely political competition for resources and programs.

During the 2003 legislative session, the University of Florida and Florida State proposed a new method of funding based on five-year performance contracts. Under this proposal, these two universities would receive lump-sum funding for agreeing to meet certain specified performance measures, as well as authority to set tuition. The legislature responded by directing its Council for Education Policy, Research and Improvement (CEPRI) to study the feasibility of such contracts among five Florida universities—Florida and Florida State plus Florida International University, the University of South Florida, and the University of Central Florida.

CEPRI responded by supporting such a plan in concept while proposing to extend it to all public colleges and universities in the state. The council's officials argued that the performance expectations should address state priorities, including reducing students' time-to-degree, ensuring access and graduation, containing tuition costs, responding appropriately to student and employer feedback, and maintaining accreditation with the Southern Association of Colleges and Schools. CEPRI officials further argued that if any of the key performance measures were not met in a given year, the university should lose its authority to increase tuition until the benchmarks had been met. Thus far, no formal action has been taken on this proposal.

Apart from tuition control, the Florida proposal focuses on performance contracting, hardly a new idea but one that is found in several states attempting to redefine the relationship of universities to state government.

- *Oregon.* The Beaver State has undergone severe budgetary problems in recent years, all of them complicating the relationship between the universities and the state. The universities and governor were working toward an agreement for incremental funding increases and increased flexibility in exchange for meeting enrollment targets and other performance goals, including limits to tuition increases. But plummeting state revenues in 2003 knocked much of this agreement off the table. Still, the universities have gained freedom from having to contract for services through state agencies and are allowed to retain interest earnings from private donations for new buildings or maintenance. The legislature, however, retained its authority to cap tuition increases.
- *South Carolina.* The Palmetto State has been at the forefront of performance funding for years. Whereas most states have used performance measures to allocate modest parts of the state higher education budget (usually 5 percent or less), South Carolina has attempted to allocate the entire higher education budget on a performance basis. Reports indicate that the state's effort may have been overly ambitious.

In the 2003 legislative session, the state's major research universities—Clemson, the University of South Carolina, and the Medical University of South Carolina—sought greater regulatory relief from the state's coordinating agency, the Commission on Higher Education, as well as from other state cabinet-level agencies. A bill in the legislature to grant such relief failed to pass, spawning new and sometimes divisive debates about governance, state coordination, and funding.

More recently, Gov. Mark Sanford sought two major governance changes: (1) a fundamental transformation of the commission from a relatively weak coordinating board to a strong governing board that "can implement a true statewide vision for higher education that gets at the waste and duplication currently in the system"; and (2) a radical privatization plan under which each public college or university would be given the option to become an independent nonprofit institution, forgoing any direct appropriation from the state. Each institution that chose this route would receive title to all buildings, real estate, and capital improvements on its campus and would agree to a "preferred tuition rate" for qualified South Carolina residents, a permanent covenant.

In the midst of this confusion, the Commission on Higher Education engaged outside consultants (including AGB) to examine the educational, social, and economic needs and priorities of the state and to recommend appropriate governance and finance systems that would engage college and universities on an agenda for action. After identifying the major needs and priorities, the consultants reported that finance mechanisms for higher education were "dysfunctional" and that the current commission lacked the capacity and credibility to provide statewide strategic leadership. Their advice: Abolish the commission and replace it with a new statewide public corporation organized as a public-private cooperative venture.

The new board would have members appointed by state government and the private sector and would be financed by public and private revenues. Its overall mission would be to link higher education to a sustained, long-term agenda of raising South Carolina's educational attainment, human resources, and intellectual capital. One of its first tasks would be to overhaul the financing mechanisms to bring them more in line with state needs and priorities. Whether the consultants' recommendations will be followed is unclear at this writing. And thus far, no public institution has taken up the governor's offer of independence, nor has any support been generated to convert the commission into a single statewide governing board.

Although the state has two of the most radical proposals in the nation still on the table (the governor's privatization plan and the consultants' proposed state entity public corporation), one sees in South Carolina the problems that can be created when radical approaches are introduced into a state with weak central coordinating mechanisms. At this point it is too early to determine what positive lessons can be drawn.

- *Texas.* In 2003, with an assist from Gov. Rick Perry and active support by the University of Texas, legislation was enacted that shifted authority to set tuition from the legislature to local governing boards. As a quid pro quo, Texas institutions must meet several standards in the areas of access, excellence, community service and support, and organizational efficiency and productivity. Institutions also are required to set aside a portion of increased tuition revenues for allocation to student financial aid, and the state has called for a study of the effects of these changes on student enrollment and persistence. In November 2003, the University of Texas Board of Regents approved tuition increases for 2004 ranging from 4 percent to 15 percent. It also set aside 20 percent of the increase for financial aid.

Efforts also are underway to establish a new accountability system that will reduce the regulatory burden on the state's colleges and universities. It should be noted, however, that the legislative budget board recently announced an audit of the University of Texas and of Texas A&M, suggesting that increased tuition authority may be accompanied by much closer financial scrutiny and accountability. The University of Texas System recently submitted its first report under a new accountability system intended to increase transparency of operations and reduce the regulatory burden on its universities and health-related institutions.

- *Virginia.* In late 2003, word leaked to the press that the University of Virginia, Virginia Tech, and the College of William & Mary were preparing materials that could be introduced into legislation to create Commonwealth Chartered Colleges and Universities. The proposal notes that Virginia spent 17 percent of its general-fund budget on higher education in 1985 but that by 2004, this figure had dropped to 10 percent; it is assumed that the state will be unable to return to earlier levels of support. Under the proposal, the state would limit its financial contributions to the universities to less than traditionally would have been expected (though no precise figures are supplied), and in exchange, the universities no longer would be subject to some state regulations concerning personnel, procurement, and capital projects.

In addition, the proposal envisions chartered universities having full control over tuition levels, accompanied by a pledge to devote substantial resources to need-based student financial aid. No governance changes are proposed; each institution would remain a public university, with boards appointed by the governor, just as they are now.

According to materials provided by the University of Virginia, the proposal would create a restructured relationship with the commonwealth that includes (1) a more stable funding model that allows participating institutions to take advantage of their respective market position as it relates to tuition and other charges, (2) a commitment to educate Virginians and to provide financial aid to ensure access, and (3) flexibility in day-to-day operations that focuses on post-audit rather than pre-audit oversight. A chartered university under this proposal would cease to be a state agency and instead would become a public corporation under Title 23 of the Code of Virginia. Although the proposal was introduced in the 2004 legislative session, it was not acted on and will likely be reintroduced in 2005.

- *Washington.* The Evergreen State has concentrated on performance contracting as a response to fiscal difficulties. A legislative working group has met several times to determine the feasibility and potential value of pursuing this approach. One should not confuse performance contracting with the performance budgeting discussed in the section on South Carolina. In the former, the emphasis is on the contract—an agreement binding on both parties and specifying what the institution will do in exchange for a given level of support from the state. Such an approach is consistent with an altered view of the public university as no longer a state agency but rather an independent contractor. Among the alleged benefits of this new approach are predictability, improved management, clarity of expectations, and recognition of varying missions.

In Washington, the working group was formed with the intent that "the state's primary interest would lie not in the management and operations of an institution but in the institution's contribution to achieving agreed-upon statewide goals and objectives for higher education," according to legislation that established one panel. The group explored a variety of performance measures that could be used to ensure contract compliance and debated whether pilot projects should be tried before considering wholesale adoption of this approach. As of this writing, no legislative proposal has been forthcoming.

## Alternatives to Restored Funding

Arching over all these specific state proposals remains the broad issue of whether it is correct that traditional state support is a withering asset and whether we indeed are stuck with an irreversible demise of the high-appropriation/low-tuition model.

Critics of those who have been busily advocating new models of finance and regulation argue that institutional leaders have been too quick to let the states off the hook and have become enablers of diminished state support by their enthusiasm for higher tuition, performance contracting, and the like. Perhaps a better approach, these critics say, would have been to argue more persuasively for efficient and effective state tax and revenue systems. This would have prevented the fiscal mess many states now are experiencing that has led to the sharp cuts to higher education. Under this view, it is not too late to make that case and move the state back to a position of enhanced support for college and university budgets. Many observers believe that there is no more effective way to ensure access to higher education than through uniformly low tuition, made possible by strong budgetary support for institutions.

If one subscribes to this view, then one regrets all the energy understandably being devoted to new mechanisms for coping with diminished state support. It would be far better, say these advocates, to have invested political capital in seeking to reestablish a world in which states acknowledge and honor their responsibility for providing low-tuition opportunities for those seeking postsecondary education. Concentrating energy and ingenuity on new models threatens to make continued decline in state support a self-fulfilling prophecy, as legislators conclude that higher education is willing and able to live with reduced public funding.

It is beyond the scope of this paper to argue the wisdom or political salience of this view, but this is a discussion that each governing board and administration should pursue, even at this late stage of the drama. The tradition of low-tuition higher education has a long history and has contributed enormously to the country's time-honored goal of creating an educated citizenry. Leaders of higher education should think carefully before giving up on a proven method of finance if there appears to be any hope politically of maintaining adequate state support. Nonetheless, it is clear that several states have reached the point where alternatives are clearly being sought or implemented, and thus it behooves all governing boards to evaluate the applicability of these new ideas in light of their own situations.

The astute reader will have realized that the ideas under discussion in the seven states are linked to a central metaphor—the market. Colleges and universities are being redefined as independent (or quasi-independent) entities, no longer as state agencies. As such, they are able to enter into contracts with the state, set their own prices, and be free of much of the regulatory apparatus that pertains to state agencies. In return, these newly independent entities forgo the basis of their prior claim on state support, with new terms and conditions to be negotiated. What follows are discussions of four key tools in the brave new world under discussion.

> • *Tuition Control*. The single most important issue to the institutions engaged in these conversations is the power to set tuition. What higher education leaders are trying to avoid can be seen in Figures 1 and 2 showing data from the University of Virginia. State support declined sharply from 1989–90 to 1995–96 and then began a steady increase to 2000–01. But it had not reached the 1989 level of support when it plummeted again a striking 34.1 percent. Figure 2 displays the effects of tuition caps, tuition freezes, and tuition rollbacks imposed by two governors during the 1990s. Had the 1995–96 tuition simply been allowed to increase at the Consumer Price Index, the university would have reached current tuition levels in a much smoother, more predictable fashion and without the huge loss of revenue indicated by the gap between the two lines. The value of tuition control for an institution, particularly a selective institution facing excess enrollment demand, is clear and undeniable.

There appear to be two economic downsides and one political downside to giving institutions control over their own prices. The political downside is that governors and legislators achieve significant political benefits from being able to step in and freeze (or reduce) tuition when circumstances temporarily permit it. Such actions play well among middle-class parents worried about the rising price of college, making this a form of control that politicians may be reluctant to give up. And even if one governor or legislature adopts such a policy, successors may seek to reverse it. Thus, institutions cannot simply rely on handshake agreements but must have this authority enshrined in statute—hence, the Virginia proposal to create the Commonwealth Chartered Colleges and Universities. Whether the institutions can make a strong enough case to political bodies to cede them tuition-setting authority in perpetuity remains (as in most states) to be seen.

It should be noted that a number of public universities, particularly flagship universities or their parent university systems, enjoy constitutional autonomy. This provides the tuition control that others, such as Virginia, seek. Examples include the universities of California and Michigan. Even in such cases, however, a governor or legislature can respond to rapid increases in tuition by imposing an effective 100 percent tax rate on the state appropriation, thereby threatening to offset tuition increases with state budget cuts. This fiscal game of poker suggests that tuition control will always remain hostage to political leaders to some degree so long as state appropriations continue. Rather than see this as a problem, however, some might view it as a reasonable form of check and balance that prompts institutions to be moderate in setting tuition increases.

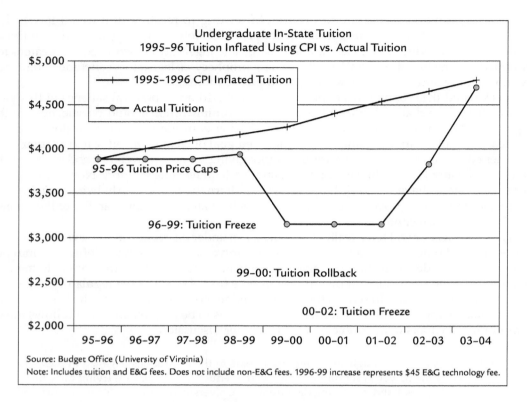

**Figure 1**

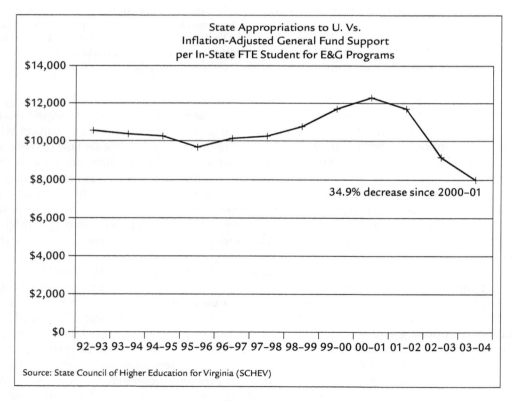

**Figure 2**

The economic downsides are the potential loss of access to higher education, particularly for students from low-income families, and the limited ability that less-selective public universities (which are in the majority) are likely to have in raising tuition without driving away students. These two issues obviously are connected, and they reflect the difficulty of implementing this quasi-market model for all students and colleges rather than just the select few. The ability to function like a private university, which is at the core of this approach, is simply not widespread.

The Virginia proposal acknowledges this fact in that only three universities initially proposed charter status—the University of Virginia, Virginia Tech, and William & Mary. All three are selective and face excess demand for enrollment, including substantial out-of-state demand. The number of similarly positioned public universities nationally is not large, being generally limited to the flagship campuses in each state or to other special-purpose institutions. Consequently, governing boards of less selective institutions may not find much relief in this approach. States that are seriously considering this model will have to deal with the differing market power of their institutions and respond accordingly. Any attempt at uniform treatment statewide is bound to fail, and that will pose political difficulties in some jurisdictions.

Implicit in the Virginia proposal is the notion that if the three universities are granted charter status, they will reduce their expectations for state support, thereby releasing funds that may flow to public institutions with less market power. This approach is a systemwide application of a change that the University of Virginia initiated in the 1990s in that two of the university's professional schools—the law school and the business school—relinquished most of their shares of the state appropriation in return for tuition control and other administrative flexibilities. Their ability to finance themselves with tuition and private support allowed the other schools of the university to benefit.

It seems certain that each state will have to adopt some form of the Virginia approach systemwide if this model is to achieve its goals without damaging either student access or institutional quality.

The second downside is the need to provide sufficient need-based financial aid so that low-income students are not priced out by higher tuition. Ideally, any state that moves to this market model (also called high tuition/high aid) should see increased funding for its state financial-aid agency as a major responsibility, requiring that agency to disburse funds solely on the basis of financial need. In that way, a given state outlay will ensure the maximum potential enrollment, a move most economists would celebrate as an efficient use of public resources.

One obstacle is that in the 1990s roughly a dozen states enacted merit-based financial-aid programs, loosely modeled on the Georgia HOPE Scholarship. Most of these programs have since been criticized as an inefficient use of public funds. If the state can afford to meet both the need of low-income students and fund a merit-based program, no one would quibble, but most states will not have the resources to do both. Hence, considerations of equity and efficiency would call for full state funding of the need-based program, which may prove difficult politically.

Again, the University of Virginia recently announced a $16 million program for need-based aid, designed to ensure that no low-income student who is admitted will be denied the opportunity to enroll for financial reasons. The dilemma is that only a handful of public universities are in a position to make this financial commitment. For those that cannot, the temptation will be to try to enroll higher income students and to use institutional financial aid in the way many private colleges do: to discount tuition selectively for students on a basis other than financial need.

- *Regulatory Flexibility.* Relief from some of the strictures that apply to state agencies is a second feature being considered in several states. It is hard to make strong arguments against these proposed changes, even if there were no fiscal crisis. Historically derided by some as "bureaucratic intrusion," state controls have been a periodic target for public institution leaders, who express frustration at rules and regulations that do not recognize higher education's differences from other state government agencies or its need for greater flexibility to pursue its public mission. Institutions that are created by state constitutions usually enjoy freedom from most of these controls.

The key concern would seem to be the administrative and organizational strength of each institution, and thus its ability to handle procurement, construction planning and oversight, investment management, financial processing, and other activities effectively. If an institution is proposing to move from state agency status to independent or quasi-independent status, governing boards should ensure that necessary management capacities are in place. The promise of such reform lies in potential savings to the institution, as activities are moved from pre-audit to post-audit status.

Several public colleges and universities without constitutional status have achieved progress in regulatory flexibility over the last decades. Many others have tried unsuccessfully or have made only incremental gains. Notable progress was achieved in the 1980s for the public colleges in Pennsylvania through the formation of the State System of Higher Education and for New Jersey's colleges and universities through the enactment of autonomy legislation. Successful deregulation also was achieved for the central offices and institutions of the Oregon University System and the University System of Maryland in the 1990s. All such efforts have required special legislation or language, including moves by institutions such as St. Mary's College of Maryland, the Oregon School for Health Sciences, and the Colorado School of Mines to quasi-independent or 501 (c) 3 status. Commonly, such efforts require new assurances of institutional performance and fiscal accountability. Rarely has flexibility legislation granted full tuition—setting autonomy—at least not before today's more broadly defined and ambitious proposals.

> • *Performance Contracting.* As noted earlier, this is not a new idea, though no model project has been implemented widely. Conceptually, the traditional way of funding universities through formula budgets can be seen as a type of performance contracting, in that the state agrees to provide a specific resource level for each student enrolled. The difference is that the formula usually was developed—often in cooperation with the institutions—and used as the guide to fund the university, which was seen as a state agency. Thus, the term "funding formula," as opposed to contract. What the new approach suggests is that the university no longer is a state agency but rather an independent or quasi-independent entity openly engaging in a contract discussion with a client—the state.

What is unclear is under what circumstances either party would be free to walk away from the contract negotiation, which should be possible if this model truly fits the definition of a contract. The fact is that there is one and only one client—the state—and thus the model appears to break down. The university has nowhere else to turn, nor does the state realistically have other options, particularly if large numbers of students are involved. Nonetheless, such an approach may have the advantage of changing the context for discussion about state support, and in principle it might work well. It is hard to see, however, in what way this mechanism can significantly increase the funding of American higher education.

The contract approaches being discussed would exist between institutions (as represented by their governing boards) and legislatures, and between institutions and states or higher education coordinating agencies—in Florida, for example, between the statewide board of governors and each institution. They are all multiyear and subject to renewal. Ideally for institutions, contracts could allow maximum tuition flexibility and autonomy; provide a guaranteed funding floor through a block grant, perhaps tied to inflation; and provide a high degree of administrative and fiscal freedom. For the state, they could assure a level of performance in areas tied to institutional mission, including contributions to the state's educational and economic priorities, and tie such performance to future funding levels; ensure fiscal and academic accountability in other desired areas; and require predictable tuition increases with dollars to be dedicated for need-based financial aid to help ensure access.

> • *Vouchers.* A variation on this idea was recently signed into law in Colorado, and a theoretical literature exists in economics and public policy describing it, but the idea has not generated as much discussion in higher education as it has in K-12. The differences are revealing, in that K-12 is mandatory and provided at taxpayer expense for all children; higher education is optional and has rarely been provided in this country at full taxpayer expense. The voucher concept in higher education has generally been conceived as a variation on the high-tuition/high-aid proposals, in which institutions would charge full-cost tuition and state subsidies would be allocated on the basis of financial need. The voucher model makes the current subsidy to all students in the public sector visible in the form of an explicit grant, which the student could carry to the institution of choice. Tuition would have to increase close to

full cost as the institutional subsidy is removed. Need-based financial aid would be required over and above the voucher for some students.

The question is, what has been gained through all this effort? What immediately would be exposed is that high school graduates who currently do not go on to college do not receive the subsidy for further education that their college-going peers receive. Having this fact thrust in one's face no doubt would give rise to pressure for a comparable payment to non-college-going young adults, perhaps in the form of an educational savings account for future use. While that is a reasonable proposition that has its advocates, states may want to think carefully before they make visible and explicit the subsidy that currently is embedded in institutional appropriations. The reason for the subsidy, however, lies in the public benefits to a well-educated populace that go beyond the private benefits captured by the individual graduate.

## Implications for Boards

Many of the proposals discussed in this paper would have direct ramifications on governance. First, it is important that trustees be integrally involved in new institutional or system models for independence or tuition authority so that they may advocate to elected leaders and other stakeholders the advantages to be attained and provide assurances that public missions will not be abandoned. It has been said that trustees have a foot in both camps—one in that of the state and the other in that of higher education. That being the case, it behooves board members to determine the advantages such proposals hold for both groups. Trustees must be able to articulate publicly the benefits that will accrue not only to institutions, but to states, citizens, students, businesses, and other stakeholders if the public asset they hold in trust—the university—is to evolve in a healthy manner.

Second, just as institutions must have the management capacity to handle increased administrative burdens if certain functions devolve from the state to campus officers, so too must governing boards have the capacity to ensure good and consistent policymaking. For example, the granting of greater independence will require boards to be more vigilant about monitoring and ensuring institutional accountability. If states grant full tuition autonomy, some process for public input when deciding tuition increases (such as public hearings and student testimony) may be necessary for boards to demonstrate they possess the political and financial acumen to oversee the new authority.

Third, though it is not spelled out in any of the proposed models that seek charter or quasi-independent status, a redefined relationship with the state suggests a reconfigured governing board—one whose members may not all be appointed by the governor or legislature, but rather one with a portion of members who are self-selected or self-perpetuating. Such configuration is not unheard of. For example, the Board of Governors for Pennsylvania State University, by statute a "state-related institution," has members appointed by multiple sources, including the governor, legislature, and alumni.

## Conclusion

Despite declines in public funding for colleges and universities, states still are prominent players in higher education and probably always will be. State dollars, whether directly appropriated or distributed through student aid or vouchers, will remain essential to public institutions and their pursuit of public missions. When one cuts to the heart of the various proposals in development, they all basically reduce to (1) considerable tuition increases, (2) greater independence for institutions from the state, and (3) state subsidies increasingly directed to students rather than to institutions.

If federal, state, and institutional financial aid is concentrated largely on students with financial need, it is possible (but not guaranteed) that a reduced amount of subsidy will result in no loss of access or of institutional quality. If subsidies are redirected competitively to higher income students as part of enrollment management strategies, substantial numbers of young people could be priced out of higher education. In the best outcome, we would have moved to the economist's nirvana of high tuition/high aid; in the worst, we would have higher tuition, poorly allocated aid, and diminished enrollment prospects for many students.

Public universities with the most to gain from such proposals are those that are highly selective, have good fund-raising efforts in place, and have the management skills necessary for reduced regulation. Less-selective colleges with limited fund-raising potential and weaker management structures have little to gain and much to lose. The blunt fact is that there are many more of the latter than of the former. A major cost of these new plans is that the more prestigious public universities may devote fewer resources to the broad effort to increase state support for public higher education, thereby leaving their less-prestigious brethren with diminished political support. A likely result of these market-driven policies will be increased social and economic stratification among students attending highly selective public colleges and their less-selective counterparts, a further blow to the policy objective of equal educational opportunity.

Each state and each governing board and administration must take a hard look at the strengths and weaknesses of all state institutions before deciding whether to endorse one of the new models. States also must decide whether selective application of these new proposals to the subset of institutions where they will work generates enough social gain to offset the clear losses that will occur for some students and institutions.

## Questions for Boards

- What are the projections for future funding in the state? Which components of this are within our board's control or influence, and which are not?
- What shares of institutional revenues are made up of tuition and state appropriations at our institution(s)? Do we want these shares to change? If so, to what new percentages?
- If we are free to set and raise tuition, how will we ensure that low-income and middle-income students will not be adversely affected? In a university system, would the board support differential tuition at constituent institutions, with resulting shifts in the allocation of state and student-aid dollars?
- Has the institution or system made a strong case for deregulating some state controls in exchange for specific performance goals? What new performance goals and accountability assurances might the institution or system provide that are acceptable to all stakeholders? Are board members willing to advocate the merits of deregulation to external stakeholders?
- Does our institution (or system institutions) have the management capacity to immediately handle greater responsibilities if the state no longer handles several of our current functions?
- What advantages would independent status bring not only to our institution(s), but also to the state? What disadvantages would it bring?
- How well are we meeting the needs and priorities of our state or community, including economic development and the economic well-being of our citizens?
- Does the board have the oversight capacity in place to assure our many stakeholders that newly granted autonomy to the institution(s) will not mean an end to public accountability?
- How will the board ensure that newly granted freedoms will not lead to an abdication of our public purposes?

## Questions for State Policymakers

- What are the prospects for state support of public colleges and universities? Has the state established a clear policy of reducing state appropriations, or have reductions resulted from a series of short-run decisions that call for review?
- What is the state's policy regarding access to and persistence in higher education for its citizens? How critical is low public tuition to the success of that policy? Does the state supply adequate need-based financial aid to offset rising public tuitions?
- Three critical financial variables influence access to higher education: the size of the state appropriation to each institution (which in turn influences tuition), the level of tuition, and the availability of need-based state financial aid. Does the state have policies that ensure that these variables are not set in isolation from one another, but rather are coordinated to meet state objectives?

- Does your state face rising numbers of potential college students as part of the "echo" baby boom? If so, are policies sufficiently flexible to create near-term capacity to serve these students (including partnering with independent institutions or other providers in targeted disciplines)? If public institutions gain more autonomy, what will ensure an adequate supply of places?
- Does the state have the capacity to establish and enforce performance expectations as a trade-off for granting colleges and universities regulatory relief?
- Does your state governing or coordinating board have the capacity to provide objective policy analysis on these proposals and to help broker the elements of a new bargain between the state and its colleges and universities?
- Is the state prepared to relinquish control over tuition levels in recognition of the changing financial circumstances of public higher education? Will the state be able to sustain policies that treat institutions differently—some with high tuition and high aid and others with low tuition and high state support—with a consequent shift in state subsidies?
- Will the types of changes discussed in this paper work for all of the public colleges and universities in the state, or will they have to be limited to the most selective institutions? What are the implications of these new approaches for community colleges and open-enrollment regional state universities?
- Is the state willing to broaden the basis for trustee selection to permit a portion of the trustees to be self-selecting?

## Resources

*Access Denied.* Washington, D.C.: Advisory Committee on Student Financial Assistance, 2001.

"Balancing Act: Public Higher Education in Transition." *State Governance Action Annual 2004.* Washington, D.C.: AGB, 2004.

Callan, Patrick M., *Coping with Recession: Public Policy, Economic Downturns, and Higher Education.* San Jose, Calif: National Center for Public Policy and Higher Education, 2002.

Heller, Donald E. (ed.), *The States and Public Higher Education Policy.* Baltimore: The Johns Hopkins University Press, 2001.

Hovey, Harold A., *State Spending for Higher Education in the Next Decade: The Battle to Sustain Current Support.* San Jose, Calif.: National Center for Public Policy and Higher Education, 1999.

Ikenberry, Stanley O., "The Dangers of Public Higher Education's Unplanned Future." *Trusteeship,* July/August, 2004.

*Losing Ground, A National Status Report on the Affordability of American Higher Education.* San Jose, Calif: National Center for Public Policy and Higher Education, 2002.

MacTaggart, Terrence J. and Associates, *Restructuring Higher Education, What Works and What Doesn't in Reorganizing Governing Systems.* San Francisco: Jossey-Bass Publishers, 1996.

*Measuring Up 2002: The State-by-State Report Card for Higher Education,* San Jose, Calif.: National Center for Public Policy and Higher Education, 2002.

Mumper, Michael, "The Paradox of College Prices: Five Stories With No Clear Lesson" (in Heller, op. cit., pp. 39–63).

*Overview of Findings: State Higher Education Finance (SHEF) Project, Fiscal 1991–2003 (draft).* State Higher Education Executive Officers. Denver: 2004.

*Policies in Sync: Appropriations, Tuition, and Financial Aid for Higher Education.* Boulder, Colo.: Western Interstate Commission for Higher Education, 2003.

Wellman, Jane V. *Weathering the Double Whammy: How Governing Boards Can Negotiate a Volatile Economy and Shifting Enrollments.* Washington, D.C.: AGB, 2002.

*David W. Breneman is university professor and dean of the Curry School of Education at the University of Virginia.*

# Effects of Key State Policies on Private Colleges and Universities: Sustaining Private-Sector Capacity in the Face of the Higher Education Access Challenge

FRED THOMPSON

*Atkinson Graduate School of Management,*
*Willamette University*

WILLIAM ZUMETA

*Evans School of Public Affairs and College of Education,*
*University of Washington*

## Abstract

The relationship between key state policy variables—(1) relative (private-public) tuition prices, (2) state student-aid funding, and (3) public institution density—and the competitive position of private colleges and universities is examined. Elite private schools are found to be nearly impervious to state policy. Large and moderately selective private institutions are adversely affected by public institution density and low public prices. Such prices divert students who would otherwise prefer these private institutions to similar public schools. State student aid funding most affects the enrollment market shares of the small, low-selectivity private colleges enrolling the greatest proportions of minority and modest-income students. The findings suggest state policies in this era of strong demand for higher education and constrained public sector capacity should use price signals (student aid and public institution pricing) to encourage students to consider seriously whether private higher education might serve their needs as well as or better than public institutions. © 2001 Elsevier Science Ltd. All rights reserved.

*JEL classification: 128*

**Keywords:** Educational finance; Privatization; Student financial aid

## Introduction

The conventional wisdom in economics is that the pattern of state support of higher education is often both inequitable and inefficient. W. Lee Hansen and Burton Weisbrod (Hansen & Weisbrod, 1969; Hansen, 1972; see also Baum & Sjogren, 1996) adumbrated the inequity argument. They argued that the beneficiaries of low public tuition prices will on average earn higher incomes than the taxpayers subsidizing their education; that the majority of students attending low-tuition public institutions are from high-income families and would have gone to college anyway; and that direct subsidies are highest on a per-student basis at selective public colleges and universities enrolling the lowest percentages of students from low- and moderate-income families.[1]

The efficiency argument comes originally from Sam Peltzman (1973)[2] who argued that government subsidization of higher education by means of low tuition at public institutions could actually reduce total consumption of higher education services. The best evidence on this point is provided by Ganderton (1992) (see also Kroncke & Ressler, 1993). Ganderton found that students substitute substantially lower quality public colleges for the schools they would have chosen in the private sector, which tends to confirm Peltzman's speculations about the possible effect of in-kind subsidies on student demand. This finding was based on extensive individual and college data and "a switching regression model that corrected for the joint decisions to apply to college and to choose the public or private sector" (Ganderton, 1992, p. 269).

Regardless of the validity of this specific finding, it is reasonable to presume that in-kind subsidies lead some students to substitute public college or university attendance for a private college or university education they would have preferred had they faced the true (unsubsidized) costs of their decisions. Recognition of this logic led Blaydon (1978) to propose a federal-state student-aid program to increase interstate student-aid portability so that students' choices would be less distorted by state-imposed constraints on their access to subsidies. This proposal has been endorsed by the Education Commission of the States (1990), among others, but faces political obstacles.

Economists and policy analysts have generally endorsed more even-handed state policies toward public and private colleges and universities—either by treating private institutions more like public institutions or by treating public institutions more like those in the private sector (Hansen & Weisbrod, 1969; Hansen, 1972; Spence & Weathersby, 1981; Zumeta, 1996). This would mean gradually raising tuition prices at public institutions to approach those of their private counterparts, increasing portable[3] student aid to help financially needy students bridge the remaining tuition-price gap, and, subject to a ceiling, replacing loans with grants for students from low- and moderate-income circumstances.

The evidence is that states with more even-handed policies—relatively high tuition at public institutions, greater reliance on need-based student aid, etc.—have higher rates of student participation and more graduates. And, they achieve these desirable outcomes at a lower cost to taxpayers than states giving more single-minded support to public institutions (Porter, 1990; Zumeta 1992, 1996). Zumeta (1992, 1996) also observed that more even-handed state policies were associated with a strong private sector, whether measured in terms of market share or enrollment growth, or expenditures on state relations. What he could not determine was whether even-handed polices produced strong private institutions or a strong private sector led to more even-handed policies.

The direction of causation is important. If causation runs from private-sector strength to even-handed policies rather than vice versa, it is unlikely that increases in public sector tuition rates will result in commensurate, complementary increases in portable state aid in jurisdictions with weak private institutions. Instead, higher tuition would merely shift more of the burden of support for public higher education from taxpayers to students and their families. The predictable result of such a shift would be decreased access, especially for students from low- and moderate-income families. Indeed, several scholars have observed that access and choice have already been impaired by the failure of need-based aid programs, especially grants, to keep pace with real increases in tuition during the last two decades (Wetzel, O'Toole, & Peterson, 1998; McPherson & Schapiro, 1991a, 1991b; McPherson & Schapiro, 1997; Kane, 1994; Savoca, 1991). This seems to be especially true for students from low-income families (McPherson & Schapiro, 1991b). Blacks and low-income whites are more likely to delay college entry in high-tuition states (Kane, 1996) and minority access by some measures actually diminished during the late 1970s and the 1980s as real tuition climbed (Paul, 1990).

It has also been argued that higher tuition at public institutions, greater state reliance on need-based student aid, and reduced expansion of the public higher education sector would not, in fact, cause private colleges and universities to accommodate substantially larger numbers of students. This assertion rests on the presumption that private colleges and universities are part of a complex competitive ecology whose history has forced each school to position itself toward a unique market segment or niche—a strategy imposed by the need to overcome rugged competition from tax-supported institutions (Birnbaum, 1983; Zumeta, 1999a). Carried to its ultimate conclusion, this line of reasoning implies that only those institutions that have successfully differentiated their products from those of their public counterparts—so that each now exploits an inelastic residual demand schedule (see Appendix B)—have survived. In this view, more even-handed policies would merely rotate the survivors' demand schedules up and to the right. Consequently, instead of accommodating substantially more students, the privates would respond to higher tuition at public institutions and increased state student aid by raising their prices even faster than would otherwise be the case and shifting a greater portion of their financial aid burden to the public fisc (McGuire, 1976; Clotfelter, 1996).[4]

These issues have important policy implications in the current context. Many states face sharp increases in demand for places in higher education due to population and demographic pressures—the maturing of the "baby boom echo" generation (Western Interstate Commission on Higher Education, 1998)—and to the incentives created by recent gains in the college wage premium (Marshall & Tucker, 1992). Yet, at the same time they also confront pressures for tax cuts and hard-to-control, caseload-driven spending demands in elementary/secondary education, health and long-term care, and criminal justice (Hovey, 1999). If states can divert significant numbers of students to private colleges and universities by means of public sector tuition increases and adjustments in need-based aid that make private institutions relatively more attractive, costly pressures to expand public higher education capacity could be reduced or averted. Thus it is crucial to know whether such policies are likely to be effective or not and which groups of private institutions are likely to be most responsive in terms of enrollment. In this paper, we offer a theoretical framework and empirical analysis designed to assess the effects of the types of state policies described.

## Effects of State Policies on Private Institution Enrollments and Enrollment Demographics: Astin and Inouye's Results

The only study relevant to the direction of causation issue identified here was published in this journal by Astin and Inouye (1988). Astin and Inouye took the *institution* as their basic unit of analysis (rather than the individual student or the state) and focused directly on the relationship between state policy variables and institutional enrollments and enrollment demographics (i.e., proportion of low-income and middle-income students, proportion of students from various ethnic groups), stratified by market segment (four such groups, ranging from highly selective to nonselective plus an "all institutions" group, were examined), for the period 1969–82. The primary explanatory variables examined were:

- The statewide private–public *tuition gap*, measured as the difference between the average tuition charged by the private institutions in a state and the average tuition charged by its public institutions, adjusted to 1983 dollars using the Higher Education Price Index (HEPI).
- Various measures of *state spending on student aid* per FTE student, including state grant aid dollars provided to private sector students per private sector FTE, and total state grant awards; data on state student aid were obtained from an annual survey by the National Association of State Scholarship and Grant Programs.
- Per-student dollar amounts of state funds going to private institutions via *direct appropriations or contracts*; data came from the Education Commission of the States.

Wherever possible, Astin and Inouye used data from the federal Higher Education General Information Survey (HEGIS) to construct their variables. This permitted them to analyze the behavior of nearly 1100 private institutions in all 50 states in their investigation of enrollment changes (defined in terms of undergraduate full-time-equivalent students [FTE] and, in separate but parallel analyses, using first-time, full-time freshman students enrolled). Due to limitations in the HEGIS data, their analysis of changes in ethnic and income distributions of students had to be performed using data from the Cooperative Institutional Research Program (CIRP) annual freshman surveys, which meant a much smaller sample of institutions (<150), but the analysis was designed to be nationally representative of all first-time, full-time freshmen students.[5]

The analytic approach used by Astin and Inouye was stepwise multiple regression, seeking to account for the values of the dependent variables (such as each private school's enrollment) at the end of the period by means of the values of the primary explanatory variables and several controls. These controls included, for the analyses of state student aid spending effects, such variables as institutional enrollment (or enrollments of students of various income or ethnic backgrounds for the analyses of these types of enrollment) at the beginning of the period; institutional type (university, 4-year college, 2-year college); institutional selectivity (using a measure based on the institution's average freshman SAT or ACT score in a base year); size of the higher education system (total enrollment) in the state; and the private sector's share of enrollments in the subject institution's state. These variables were entered into the regression equations in an institutional characteristics block, followed by a state characteristics block, prior to allowing the state policy variables to enter. For the analyses of the effects of the private-public tuition gap and of public tuition change over time, only initial institutional enrollment and change in statewide higher education enrollments over the period under examination were controlled (i.e., entered into the multiple regression model).

Astin and Inouye found:

- A significant positive relationship between change in public tuition and private institutions' enrollment change (FTE undergraduates), for all private institutions combined and for nonselective private schools. A similar, but less significant, relationship was found for moderate selectivity and low selectivity private institutions.
- Overall, a significant positive relationship between change in state student aid spending (on private sector students per private FTE) and enrollment change, although the relationship was inconsistent for low selectivity and nonselective institutions and nonexistent for high selectivity institutions.
- A positive relationship between change in per-student student aid spending and the proportion of private colleges' students from low-income and middle-income families, i.e., more aid was associated with a higher proportion of low- and middle-income enrollments.
- A significant *positive* relationship between the private–public tuition differential and private enrollments for all institutions and for several of the institutional selectivity groups examined;
- No relationship between state funds going to private institutions via direct appropriations or contracts and their enrollments.

Thus, Astin and Inouye found some evidence that increases in public sector tuition in a state may have increased private enrollments and evidence that increases in state spending on student aid were associated with gains in private enrollments, especially enrollments of targeted populations. These findings are, of course, consistent with *both* possible answers to the direction of causation question but suggest that state policies may have an effect. Astin and Inouye's finding that the private–public price differential is *positively* related to private institution enrollments, is a different matter. It appears to contradict the notion that higher tuition at public institutions, greater state reliance on student aid, and reduced investment in the expansion of public institutions would cause private colleges and universities to increase enrollments substantially or would influence public institutions to become more like private ones. It suggests instead that more even-handed state policies would lead primarily to higher private tuition prices. Reconciling these apparently anomalous findings thus has important implications for the selection of appropriate state policies.

## Moving Forward

The analysis that follows is intended to deal with the issue more conclusively through a more formal investigation of the segmentation and ~cross-price-elasticity questions. It was carried out in three stages. First, we replicated the Astin–Inouye study using somewhat more recent data.[6] Second, we reanalyzed the data explicitly using standard market and market-segmentation models. Third, we submitted our specifications and results in stage two to systematic sensitivity analysis to determine the robustness of our findings.

## Replicating Astin–Inouye

In the first stage (and successive stages) of this analysis, we made the following changes in Astin–Inouye's data and methodology (see also Appendix A):

- We used HEGIS enrollment and related data for the 1980–85 period.
- We replaced CIRP with HEGIS data in the analyses of the ethnic distribution of enrollments for the 1980–85 period, thus expanding by a factor of approximately seven the overall sample size for these analyses and permitting for the first time separate analyses by institutional selectivity grouping; also Hispanic enrollments were added to the analysis of the ethnic distribution of enrollments for this period, something Astin and Inouye could not do for the period they examined.
- On the assumption that state student aid spending and public sector tuition are likely to have effects on private institution enrollments in the same year, we dropped the 1-year lags between these variables and the dependent variables that had been used by Astin and Inouye.
- To create finer-grained public sector comparison groups for the analyses of public tuition impacts on private institution enrollments, we defined the private-public tuition gap and public tuition change variables based on the averages for the public institutions in the same state *and selectivity class* as the subject private institution (instead of the statewide public average used by Astin and Inouye).[7]
- We defined the state student aid award variable as dollars of aid to private sector students per private FTE.
- We made several minor changes in the controls utilized in particular analyses, mostly in the direction of using all the institutional and state-level controls in each of the analyses. Notable exceptions to this were that, in the analyses of changes in the proportions of black, Hispanic, and Asian enrollments, we dropped the income controls so that the effects of the explanatory variables on the ethnic mix of enrollments could be discerned more clearly; and in the analyses of changes in the percentages of low-income and middle-income students using the CIRP data (since this data was not collected by HEGIS), we used a minimum of controls, i.e., initial year proportions of such students only, due to the small sample size.
- We also changed the definition of the proportion of low-income and middle-income students. Astin–Inouye defined low-income students simply as the bottom fourth of the reported family income distribution of a particular year's CIRP freshmen and middle-income students as the middle half. Here, low-income students are defined as those reporting family-of-origin incomes in the lowest quartile of *all US family incomes* for that year (according to federal statistics), and middle-income students as those from families in the middle half of US family incomes in the relevant year. This gives a more accurate picture of low- and middle-income groups since we compare them to the general population rather than only to those who make it to college.
- We omitted data on state spending on direct appropriations to and contracts with private institutions because the data series was discontinued in 1981 (Astin–Inouye had found no significant relationships for this variable).
- We used the Higher Education Price Index (HEPI) to adjust all nominal dollar figures to 1990 dollars.

With these changes, we replicated the Astin–Inouye study. With one exception, we ran all the analyses on all four selectivity groupings of private institutions as well as on each state's subset of the entire HEGIS sample of over 1000 private schools.[8] We repeated the analyses twice, once using institutional undergraduate FTE enrollment (UG FTE) as the dependent variable, and then substituting first-time, full-time freshman enrollments (FTFT) as the dependent variable. For the analyses of ethnic and income distributions of private sector enrollments, data availability permitted only the use of the FTFT dependent variable. We ran all the analyses separately using first the state student aid *awards* to private sector students per-private-FTE variable, followed by change in this variable over the period under study, as the last variables entered in the stepwise regression; then,

**Table 1.  Summary of Regression Results: Effect of Public Sector Tuition and
State Student Aid on Private College and University Enrollment**

| Time period | Data source | Dependent variable | Selectivity group | N | Significant (0.05) variables[a] | b | B | Significance |
|---|---|---|---|---|---|---|---|---|
| 1969–80 | HEGIS | UG FTE | All | 1093 | Pub.TUT69 | −0.061 | −0.026 | 0.012 |
| | | | Nonsel. | 163 | Pub.TUTΔ | 2.10 | 0.080 | 0.048 |
| | | | Low sel. | 330 | Pub.TUTΔ | 1.06 | 0.088 | 0.018 |
| | | | Med. sel. | 390 | Pub.TUT69 | −0.154 | −0.049 | 0.001 |
| 1980–85 | HEGIS | UG FTE | All | 1032 | STAID$80 | 0.093 | 0.015 | 0.013 |
| | | | Nonsel. | 318 | STAID$80 | 0.184 | 0.059 | 0.001 |
| 1980–85 | HEGIS | % BlkFTFT | High sel. | 113 | STAIDAW80 | 0.672 | 0.100 | 0.045 |
| 1980–85 | HEGIS | %HispFTFT | All | 1032 | Pub.TUTΔ | 0.009 | 0.042 | 0.007 |
| | | | Nonsel. | 163 | Pub.TUTΔ | 0.016 | 0.062 | 0.011 |
| | | | Low sel. | 334 | Pub.TUT80 | −4E−4 | −0.065 | 0.035 |
| | | | High sel. | 113 | Pub.TUTΔ | 0.029 | 0.200 | 0.016 |
| 1980–85 | HEGIS | %AsianFTFT | All | 1032 | Pub. TUT80 | −3E−4 | 0.058 | 0.005 |
| | | | Med. sel. | 390 | Pub. TUTΔ | 0.010 | 0.075 | 0.018 |
| 1980–85 | CIRP | %LowIncome FTFT | All | 144 | ΔSTAID80–5 | 0.009 | 0.085 | 0.043 |
| 1980–85 | CIRP | %MiddleIncome FTFT | All | 144 | ΔSTAID80–5 | 0.015 | 0.097 | 0.043 |

[a] Variable definitions: PubTUT 69/PubTUT 80: average tuition level (constant dollars) in the indicated year for each independent institution's public sector comparison group (see text for detailed explanation of comparison groups); PubTUTΔ: percentage change in inflation-adjusted average tuition level for each independent institution's public sector comparison group (see text for detailed explanation of comparison groups); STAID$ 80: state need-based student aid grant dollars (constant dollars) to private sector undergraduate students FTE in 1980; STAID80: state need-based student aid grant awards to private sector undergraduates per private undergraduate FTE in 1980; ΔSTAID80–5: change in ratio of state need-based student aid grant awards to private sector undergraduates per private undergraduate FTE, 1980–85.

in the alternative, we substituted state aid *dollars* per-private-FTE and change in this value over the period for the awards variables.

Our results are summarized in Table 1. Given the above discussion, the first three columns in the table should be self-explanatory. The fourth column indicates the private institution selectivity groupings for which *significant* correlates of enrollment at the end of the period were found, and the fifth column shows the number of private schools in that selectivity class at both ends of the period. The next column gives an abbreviated name for each of the primary explanatory variables that reached statistical significance. (The variables are defined fully in a footnote to the table.) The last three columns are presented in order of the significant explanatory variables: the regression coefficient (b), the standardized regression coefficient (B), and the significance level of the t-statistic for the regression coefficient.

As expected, our results were similar to those reported by Astin–Inouye: public tuition change (Δ) is positively associated with private institution enrollments (i.e., greater increases in tuition at a private institution's competitive public institutions over the period were systematically associated with larger enrollments at that private school at the end of the period), significantly so for nonselective and low-selectivity privates (see first four rows in Table 1). State spending on private college student aid (STAID$80) was significantly associated with private institution enrollments. This relationship is strongly significant statistically for all private institutions combined and for the nonselective private institutions, but is considerably stronger for the latter group.[9] Also, similar to Astin–Inouye's surprising earlier findings, public tuition levels at the beginning of the period (Pub.TUT69, first and fourth rows of Table 1) were *negatively* associated with private enrollment shares at the end for all private institutions and the medium-selectivity segment.

State aid funding to private-sector students at the beginning of the period was not significantly related to the proportions of minority students in private institutions, with the single exception that state aid *awards* to private sector students in 1980 was positively associated with the percentage of black students enrolled at high-selectivity private institutions in 1985 (see %BlkFTFT in Table 1). On the other hand, increasing public sector tuition rates seems to increase enrollments of certain groups of minorities in private institutions appreciably (see %HispFTFT). The coefficient on the public tuition change variable is positive and significant at better than the 0.01 level in the analysis of percentage of Hispanic enrollments at all private institutions, and the results were almost as clear (and the coefficients larger) for Hispanic enrollments at both nonselective and highly selective private schools. A significant positive relationship between public tuition change and percentage of Asian enrollments in medium selectivity private institutions is also apparent (see %Asian FTFT). Finally, Table 1 shows that changes in state aid over the 1980–85 period were positively associated with the share of low-income and middle-income students among private institutions' first-time, full-time (FTFT) freshmen.

This stage of our research confirms the "accuracy" of the Astin–Inouye study. It does not confirm the validity of their findings. This is because the empirical specifications tested are entirely ad hoc, i.e., they are not derived from a formal model of market processes. Consequently, these findings could well be the result of misspecification or omitted variables.

## Market Segmentation Models

We approached the problem of determining the effect of state policies on private college enrollments from a theoretical perspective using two competitive models drawn from the marketing literature. The first is a static model derived from the Dorfman–Steiner theorem[10] by Lambin (1969, 1972). The second is essentially a dynamic version of the first designed to test direction of causation.

Demand for an organization's services is usually presumed to reflect the price and attributes of the service, given the prices and attributes of its competitors. It is reasonable to presume that the demand for the services produced by private (independent) educational institutions is like the demand for other services, which implies that:

$$m_i = f(N, \pi_i, \sum a_{ij})$$

where $m_i = q_i/Q_k$ is a private institution's market share, defined in terms of its enrollment [$q_i$=full-time equivalent undergraduates (FTE) enrolled in institution $i$ (variable names=UGFTE80; UGFTE85)] divided by total market demand [$Q_k$ = FTE in state $k$ (variable names=SWFTE80, SWFTE85)]; this variable can also be defined by market segment (i.e., selectivity group).[11] $N$ represents the competitors in the market ($N$=private institutions in state $k$ divided by total market demand=$N_k/Q_k$), this variable can also be defined by market segment.[12] $\pi_i = p_k/P_k$ is an institution's relative price, defined in terms of its price ($p_i$=tuition charged by institution $i$) divided by market price [$P_k$=tuition price charged by similar public institutions in state $k$ (variable names=TUIT80, TUIT85)].[13] $a_{ij} = a_{ij}/A_{kj}$ is an institution's relative attributes, defined in terms of $j$ characteristics, such as:

> *Institutional type* of the $i$th institution (variable names=4YR {coded 0,1}; 2YR {coded 0,1}) and the average institution in state $k$; this variable can also be defined by market segment (selectivity group) in state $k$.
> *Quality* of the $i$th institution (variable name=SAT82) and the average institution in state $k$; this variable can also be defined by market segment in state $k$.
> *Socioeconomic characteristics* of the $i$th institution (variable names=PBLKFT85, PHISFT85, PASFT85, LOWIN85, MEDIN85) and the average institution in state $k$, these variables can also be defined by market segment in state $k$.

We further presume that a private institution's market share is likely to be a function of the subsidies it receives from the state, either indirectly in the form of student aid or directly in the form of institutional subventions, and proximity to competitors—especially public sector competitors. Hence, it follows that:

$$M_i = f(N, \pi_i, \sum a_{ij}, s_i, c_i)$$

where $s_i$ is the subsidy provided by state $k$ to institution $i$, and $c_i$ is the distance from institution $i$ to the nearest public competitor.

Unfortunately, data on direct institutional subsidies and the location of competitors are missing. Consequently, we use the following proxies for the variables of concern. For purposes of this research we define $S$ as the sum of state student aid in state $k$ times the percentage of aid going to students attending private institutions in state $k$, divided by FTE undergraduate enrollment in all private institutions in state $k$ (variable names PRAIDD80, PRAIDD85); $C$ represents the public institutions per capita, defined as the number of public institutions in state $k$ divided by the state population (variable names PSC80, PSC85); this variable can also be defined by market segment (selectivity group).

The general form of the empirical model tested is:

$$m_i = b_0 + b_1 N + b_2 \pi_i + b_3 a_{1i} + .. b_n a_{mi} + b_{n+1} S + b_{n+2} C + e$$

where the terms are as previously defined, e.g., $\pi_i$ is relative price. In addition, where the variables in the empirical demand equation are expressed in logarithms, the $b$ coefficients can be interpreted as elasticities, i.e., the $b_1$ ($\ln m_i$, $\ln \pi_i$) coefficient is an estimate of institutional market share elasticity with respect to relative price. We used the same analytic approach as Astin and Inouye, stepwise multiple regression. However, in testing the static version of the model, we used the log formulation throughout for ease of interpretation[14] and, after omitting competitors in the market ($N$), entered variables into the regression equations in the same order as shown in the model above. This decision is important in the interpretation of our results owing to collinearity between several of the critical variables in the basic model—competitors in the market ($N$), relative tuition prices ($\pi$), state student-aid funding ($S$), and institutional density ($C$ or PSC). In some instances the order in which variables are entered affects the signs and significance levels of the coefficients, a point on which we comment further below.

Looking first at the results for the static models for all institutions (selectivity group "All" in Table 2(a, b)), the effect of both the relative tuition-price variable and the state student-aid funding variable on institutional market share seem anomalous. The coefficient of the relative tuition-price variable (*LTUIT*) is *positive*, although not nearly significant, using 1980 data. The relationship is positive and significant using 1985 data [Table 2(b)], implying that a larger private-public price ratio ("tuition gap") is associated with a *larger* institutional share of the market for private schools. The coefficient of the state student-aid funding variable (*LPRAID*) is *negative* and moderately significant using 1980 data (Table 2a); and just barely positive using 1985 data. Only the coefficient of institutional density variable (*PSC*) has both the expected sign (negative) and consistent significance and strength.

As would be expected given the probable competitive ecology, our results are better behaved when we look at the individual market segments. As expected, the relative tuition-price variable is consistently nonsignificant for the highly selective group. This finding tends to confirm the presumption that, as a general rule, in-state public institutions are not close substitutes for highly selective private colleges and universities, an inference that we will reinforce below. In contrast, the consistent significance and negative signs of both the relative tuition price and institutional density variables for the moderate selectivity group suggests that in-state public institutions are a close substitute for moderately selective private colleges and universities, a plausible conclusion.

Relative price and institutional density also matter to the less selective and nonselective institutions in our sample, but student aid matters most consistently. We would suggest that many public institutions are targeted mainly at roughly the same market niche as are the moderately selective private colleges and universities in our sample. They are also roughly comparable in size and scope to their private counterparts.

In contrast, public institutions are probably not satisfactory substitutes for most of the less-selective and nonselective private institutions in our sample, which tend to be much smaller. It is likely that these private schools are more parochial in their appeal, both in terms of catchment area and curricular scope. Indeed, some are religious institutions and many maintain religious affiliations, attributes that cannot be matched in the public sector. These institutions are evidently especially attractive to low-income and minority students. This is suggested by the inverse relationship evident in the data between the percentage of low-income students enrolled and institutional market share (i.e., enrollment size) and the direct relationship between institutional selectivity and market share. It seems likely that many of such students attending these small, less-selective private institutions would not have been enrolled in college but for state financial aid (see Hoenack, 1971; Tuckman, 1973).

**Table 2. Summary of Regression Results: Effect of Tuition, State Student Aid, and Institutional Density on Market Share of Private Colleges and Universities**

| Selectivity group | $N$ | $R^2$ | $F$ | Significant (0.05) variables | $b$ | $t$-ratio |
|---|---|---|---|---|---|---|
| *(a) Static models 1980* | | | | | | |
| All | 1026 | 0.754 | 56.6 | 4YR | −0.971 | −7.24 |
| | | | | 2YR | −0.148 | −7.14 |
| | | | | LPRAID80 | −0.099 | −8.47 |
| | | | | PSC80 | −0.859 | −18.9 |
| High | 116 | 0.103 | 37.3 | SAT82 | 0.191 | 4.74 |
| | | | | 4YR | −0.672 | −9.46 |
| Moderate | 404 | 0.248 | 41.9 | LTUIT80 | −0.070 | −6.62 |
| | | | | 4YR | −0.320 | −11.4 |
| | | | | 2YR | −0.104 | −9.26 |
| | | | | LPRAID80 | 0.008 | 6.62 |
| | | | | PSC80 | −0.340 | −5.17 |
| Low | 358 | 0.242 | 39.2 | LTUIT80 | −0.074 | −6.62 |
| | | | | 2YR | −0.320 | −9.27 |
| | | | | LPRAID80 | 0.022 | 7.76 |
| | | | | PSC80 | −0.342 | 4.96 |
| Non-selective | 117 | 0.128 | 24.2 | LTUIT80 | −0.703 | −6.46 |
| | | | | LPRAID80 | 0.089 | 3.17 |
| *(b) Static models 1985* | | | | | | |
| All | 1067 | 0.696 | 33.9 | LTUIT85 | 0.043 | 3.97 |
| | | | | 4YR | −0.661 | −5.57 |
| | | | | 2YR | −1.30 | −7.45 |
| | | | | SAT82 | 0.168 | 2.38 |
| | | | | LOWIN85 | −0.300 | −3.14 |
| | | | | LPRAID85 | 0.000 | 2.64 |
| | | | | PSC85 | −0.424 | −6.71 |
| High | 119 | 0.198 | 51.5 | SAT82 | 0.140 | 2.47 |
| | | | | 4YR | −0.340 | −20.76 |
| Moderate | 404 | 0.312 | 65.9 | LTUIT85 | −0.210 | −3.28 |
| | | | | 4YR | −1.28 | −9.42 |
| | | | | 2YR | −1.71 | −9.99 |
| | | | | SAT82 | 0.060 | 2.16 |
| | | | | LPRAID85 | 0.186 | 4.52 |
| | | | | PSC85 | −3.27 | −15.9 |
| Low | 358 | 0.204 | 37.3 | 2YR | −0.350 | −20.99 |
| | | | | LPRAID85 | 0.017 | 8.91 |
| Non-selective | 111 | 0.146 | 36.1 | 2YR | −0.030 | 9.77 |
| | | | | LPRAID85 | 0.070 | 3.06 |

These institutions also help to explain the unexpected relationship noted above between the relative price variable (private–public tuition ratio) and the market shares of private colleges (see selectivity group "All" in Table 2(b), where the relationship reaches statistical significance, and similar results in our replication of Astin–Inouye). The data show that states with high public tuition (thus a relatively low private–public tuition ratio) and high levels of state student aid tend to have high concentrations of low-selectivity and nonselective private colleges. Because these institutions are almost invariably small, high public tuition, which should theoretically be favorable to private institutions, appears in some of the multivariate analyses as associated with low private market shares, an apparent anomaly. Note that, *within the individual market segments* shown in Table 2(a, b), the relative tuition-price variable assumes the expected negative sign.

Table 3 shows the results of a series of regressions using 1985 data in which the density of *private* colleges and universities in the state is the dependent variable. These results are consistent with expectations and with the results for private institutions' enrollment market shares shown in the previous tables. The coefficients on all three state policy variables are significant in the expected

**Table 3. Summary of Regression Results: Effect of Tuition, State Student Aid, and Institutional Density on the Number of Private Colleges and Universities per Student ($N$): 1985 Data**

| Selectivity group | $N$ | $R^2$ | $F$ | Significant (0.05) variables | $b$ | $t$-ratio |
|---|---|---|---|---|---|---|
| All | 1026 | 0.245 | 28.7 | LTUIT85 | −0.400 | −2.77 |
| | | | | LPRAID85 | 0.240 | 4.90 |
| | | | | PSC85 | −0.284 | −9.85 |
| High | 116 | 0.064 | | LPRAID85 | 0.86 | 4.09 |
| Moderate | 404 | 0.289 | 44.3 | LTUIT85 | −0.960 | −2.74 |
| | | | | LPRAID85 | 0.468 | 15.2 |
| | | | | PSC85 | −0.236 | −6.98 |
| Low | 358 | 0.294 | 46.4 | LPRAID85 | 0.420 | 15.5 |
| | | | | PSC85 | −2.69 | −7.98 |
| Non-selective | 116 | 0.307 | 33.0 | LTUIT85 | −0.210 | −3.28 |
| | | | | LPRAID85 | 0.426 | 15.9 |

direction for all institutions combined and the student aid variable is significant for all four subgroups. The relative tuition-price variable is significant for two of the four subgroups (moderately selective and nonselective institutions), and public institution density is significant for two (moderate- and low-selectivity institutions).

The final stage in the analysis is intended to deal with the crucial direction of causation question. While it is unlikely that we would observe the pattern of relationships reported in the preceding section if a stronger private higher education sector caused even-handed state policies rather than vice versa, it could happen. Indeed, we would be surprised if there was not some simultaneity in these relationships (Hearn et al., 1996; see also Appendix B). However, the key question is whether more even-handed state policies would lead private institutions to enroll more students. To shed light on that question, we examine the relationship between policy changes and enrollment changes for the 1980–85 period. That is, the model: $\Delta m_i = f(\Delta \pi_i, \Delta S_i)$ which implies the following empirical specification: $m85_i / m80_i = b_0 + b_1(\pi 85_i) + b_2(S85 / S80) + e$.

Estimating this model produces the results shown in Table 4. Here is solid evidence that more even-handed policies would lead private colleges and universities to enroll more students.[15] The results suggest that a 1 percent reduction in relative tuition prices (presumably induced by a policy of higher public sector prices) would lead to 0.07 percent increase in the market share of the average private college or university in a state; and that a 1 percent increase in the state student aid growth ratio (1985/1980) would increase private institution market shares on average by 0.035 percent. Increased public tuition prices would most strongly benefit moderately selective private institutions and lead to the greatest increases in their enrollments. Increased state student aid would be of greatest benefit to nonselective schools, followed by those of low- and moderate-selectivity, according to these results. Thus, judging from the results shown earlier and what we know about the distribution of these enrollments, more generous state student aid policies would likely lead

**Table 4. Summary of Regression Results: Effect of Changes in Tuition and State Student Aid on Changes in Market Share ($m$)**

| Selectivity group | $N$ | $R^2$ | $F$ | Variables | $b$ | $t$-ratio |
|---|---|---|---|---|---|---|
| All | 1174 | 0.202 | 20.5 | L(TUIT85/TUIT80) | −0.072 | −2.42 |
| | | | | L(PRAID85/PRAID80) | 0.035 | 2.21 |
| High | 115 | 0.025 | 8.04 | L(TUIT85/TUIT80) | 0.0004 | 0.380 |
| | | | | L(PRAID85/PRAID80) | 0.0001 | 3.03 |
| Moderate | 394 | 0.307 | 65.9 | L(TUIT85/TUIT80) | −0.210 | −4.52 |
| | | | | L(PRAID85/PRAID80) | 0.042 | 15.9 |
| Low | 344 | 0.294 | 86.4 | L(TUIT85/TUIT80) | −0.064 | −1.21 |
| | | | | L(PRAID85/PRAID80) | 0.042 | 15.5 |
| Non-selective | 118 | 0.146 | 36.1 | L(TUIT85/TUIT80) | −0.003 | −1.87 |
| | | | | L(PRAID85/PRAID80) | 0.070 | 3.06 |

to greater increases in student enrollments from low-income and minority families in private colleges and universities.

### Sensitivity testing

We tested dozens of alternative formulations of the basic model. At the aggregate level, many of the coefficient values, signs and significance levels reported here tend to be unstable. By adding or omitting variables or changing the order in which they are entered, values and even signs change. However, this conclusion does not apply to our models for the individual market segments, which produce more consistent and robust estimators, consistent with the notion that these models better represent the competitive circumstances of private institutions. The estimators for our dynamic models (Table 4), which are most policy-relevant, are also the most consistent and robust. Of course, the validity of these models hinges on the validity of our market segmentation strategy. Ultimately, the empirical results reported here are no better than the theorizing that provides the foundation for our procedures (see Appendix B), but both the theory and the empirical results are quite plausible.

## Conclusions and policy implications

America's mixed system of competitive independent and public institutions is generally seen around the world as exemplary. Private (nonprofit) colleges and universities enroll about 30 percent of all baccalaureate students in the US and graduate their students at a higher rate than public institutions. Their capacity should be especially valuable during the coming decade when, in most states, the number of students graduating from high school will continue to increase (Western Interstate Commission on Higher Education, 1998). In many of those states, public systems are nearly full and it would be costly to expand them. Moreover, investments in the expansion of public systems could not be easily—let alone, costlessly—undone were new technology to render much of current higher education delivery systems obsolete.

Despite the benefits of relying more heavily on private colleges and universities, some public policies continue to threaten their health: large private-public tuition-price differentials and the low level of public funding for student aid in many states. The results reported here suggest that these policies could reduce enrollments in private colleges and universities at the same time that this capacity is most needed.

The basic policy idea underlying this paper is that, facing an era when demands for higher education are likely to strain public sector capacity and create pressures for costly expansion thereof, it is desirable for policymakers to have access to empirical analysis that sheds light on the relationship between state policies and enrollments in private higher education. Private-sector capacity might be employed as a partial substitute for costly additional public-sector capacity if it could be shown that private institutions respond discernibly and desirably to state policies. For example, as our empirical analysis suggests, states might seek purposively to redirect some enrollment demand from the public to the private sector by simultaneously increasing public institution prices (tuition) substantially while also expanding need-based student aid. The former step could generate additional revenue to help fund the latter one and, if additional aid were need-based and sufficient, students of modest incomes could theoretically be "held harmless".[16]

Table 4 in particular shows that private enrollments at the institution level did respond in predictable ways and at significant levels to plausible state policy variables in analyses using well-specified models of the enrollment market in higher education during a relatively recent period. This argues that the approach merits at least further state-specific study in jurisdictions with both strong growth in demand for higher education and an ample private academic sector.

## Acknowledgements

The authors gratefully acknowledge the assistance of Ronald D. Camp III, who executed most of the statistical analyses reported herein and aided in their interpretation, and of Sergio Trevino. The authors are grateful to the Lilly Endowment, the Pew Charitable Trusts, and the TIAA-CREF Strategic

Research Fund for financial support that made this research possible. The authors bear sole responsibility for the contents.

# Appendix A. Data Sources and Variables

The data for the analyses reported here were compiled from several sources. The description of the data sources is organized by variable. After editing files and eliminating institutions with missing or unusable data, the usable HEGIS file encompassed from 1026 to 1173 private colleges and universities for 1980 and 1985, depending upon the variables included in the model or models tested.

*Institutional market share.* This variable was constructed by dividing each private institution's (full-time equivalent undergraduate) enrollment in the year of interest (1980 or 1985) by the total public and private enrollment in the state in that year. The enrollment data came from institutions' responses to the US Department of Education's Higher Education General Information Survey (HEGIS) for fall 1980 and fall 1985, specifically from HEGIS data files maintained by the Higher Education Research Institute at the University of California, Los Angeles.

*Proportions of black/Hispanic/Asian students.* These proportions were derived from the HEGIS data by institution. Because HEGIS did not collect data on student ethnicity in 1985, but data were available for 1984 and 1986, the 1985 data were imputed by averaging the figures for the two adjacent years.

*Proportions of low/middle/high income students.* HEGIS did not collect data on students' family income. Thus, for analyses using this variable we were limited to institutions participating in the Higher Education Research Institute's Cooperative Institutional Research Program (CIRP) surveys in the two years. (The CIRP sample is designed to be nationally representative of the nation's first-time full-time freshmen in each year.) These surveys did contain questions on students' family income, although there is a 10–15 percent nonresponse rate on this question and no doubt some error in the students' estimates. To adjust for changes over time in income levels, we defined low-income students as those reporting family incomes in the lowest quartile of US family incomes for the year, middle-income students as those in the middle two quartiles of family incomes, and high-income students as those in the upper quartile nationally. These analyses were limited to the institutions that participated in the CIRP in these years.

*Institution selectivity.* This was determined by using an institution-level score on average SAT/ACT scores of entering freshmen in 1982 supplied by the Higher Education Research Institute, following a procedure developed by Astin and Henson (1977).

*Relative price and private/public tuition differential.* The institutional tuition data for these variables came from the HEGIS survey. For each private institution, the ratio (private tuition divided by public) and differential (private tuition minus public) were computed relative to the mean of public institutions of comparable selectivity in the state. Where no such comparable public institutions existed, the statewide public sector mean tuition was used to compute the ratio or differential. An adjustment for general price inflation was made using the Higher Education Price Index.

*Density of institutions within each state.* This variable was computed by dividing the number of public and private collegiate institutions in each state in each of the relevant years by the state's population as reported by the Census (or estimated for 1985). Public institution density and private institution density were also computed.

*State student aid spending on private sector students.* State spending on student aid grants to undergraduates was compiled from annual state survey reports compiled by the National Association of State Scholarship and Grant Programs (Reeher & Davis, annual publication). The data on the private sector share of these funds are in some cases only rough estimates since all the necessary data to make a precise computation for these years were not available. The estimated total state spending on grants to undergraduates in private institutions in each year was divided by the full-time equivalent enrollment in the private sector to provide an indication of the relative scale of the state's efforts. The Higher Education Price Index was used to adjust all dollar figures to 1990 dollars.

*Size of state's higher education system.* This variable was defined as the total enrollment in the state's public and private institutions in the relevant year. It was included to control for the possible influence of overall market size on the relationships of interest.

*Institution type.* This variable categorized each institution as a university, 4-year college, or 2-year college.

# Appendix B. The Effect of Differentiation on an Institution's Residual Demand Curve

An institution would be a price-taker if it faced a horizontal demand curve. A horizontal demand curve implies an infinite absolute price elasticity of demand. If an institution facing infinite price elasticity raised its price even slightly, it would lose all its enrollments. Such an institution cannot cause its price to rise by lowering its admissions. In contrast, an institution facing a downward-sloping demand curve could raise its price by decreasing admissions.

If the number of institutions in a market (made up of all the potential customers demanding products or services with similar attributes) is large, the demand curve facing any one of them will be nearly horizontal (elasticity of demand nearly infinite), even though the demand curve facing the market is downward sloping (absolute elasticity is relatively small). Indeed, for most market demand curves, there do not have to be very many institutions in a market for the elasticity of demand facing a particular institution to be large, implying that even modest tuition changes will result in large shifts in student demand in favor of the institution's competitors.

This result is shown by the demand curve facing a particular institution: the residual demand curve. An institution enrolls students whose demands are not met by the other institutions in the market. For positive quantities of residual demand, the residual demand, $D_r(p)$ is the market demand, $D(p)$, minus the supply of other institutions, $S_o(p)$: $D_r(p)=D(p)-S_o(p)$. If $S_o(p)$ is greater than $D(p)$, $D_r(p)$ is zero. The residual demand curve facing the individual institution is much flatter than the market demand curve.

Similarly, the single institution's demand elasticity is much higher than the market elasticity. The inverse residual demand function facing a single institution can be written as: $p_i = p = D(q_1+q_2+ \ldots +q_n) = D(Q)$. For example, if $n = 2$, $p = a-bQ = a-b(q_1+q_2) = a-bq_1-bq_2$. More generally, if there are $n$ identical institutions in the market, then the elasticity of demand facing any one institution $i$ is: $\varepsilon_i = \varepsilon n-\eta_o(n-1)$, where $\varepsilon$ is the market elasticity of demand (a negative value), $\eta_o$ is the elasticity of supply of the other institutions (a positive value), and $(n - 1)$ is the number of other institutions. Thus for a given market elasticity, as the number of institutions in a market, $n$, increases, the absolute elasticity facing a single institution $i$, $\varepsilon_i$, grows large in absolute value (more negative).

Similarly, the larger the elasticity of supply of the other institutions, or the more of these other institutions, the larger in absolute value (more negative) is the elasticity of demand facing institution $i$. In contrast, if potential student customers are not indifferent between institutions, institution 1's demand function will be subtly different insofar as $p_i \neq p$: $p_1 = a-b_1q_1-b_2q_2$, where $a>0$ and $b_1b_2>0$, which means that an increase in institution 1's output has a greater effect on its price than a similar increase in that of institution 2. Hence, the more an institution differentiates its product, the more insulated demand for its product is from the behavior of other institutions, the steeper the slope of its demand curves, and the greater its market power.

There is no doubt that private colleges and universities seek to differentiate themselves from their public counterparts. In the Pacific Northwest, for example, several small, private, regional comprehensive universities—Lewis and Clark College, University of Puget Sound, and Willamette University—have sought to reposition themselves as national liberal arts colleges in the last two decades (see also Breneman, 1996). Many have succeeded. According to Hoxby (1997), this has produced dramatic changes in both the price and quality of a college education. Based on panel data on 1121 baccalaureate-granting colleges, she concludes that changes in market structure explain tuition increases of 50 percent or more in real terms since 1950 for highly selective private colleges competing in national markets, and tuition increases of about 15 percent in real terms for public colleges and less selective private colleges. Hoxby argues, as we do here, that competitive markets have driven colleges to differentiate their products, thereby increasing their costs, quality, and tuition prices.

Regardless of whether potential students are indifferent or not between alternative institutions, the number of institutions serving a market or closely related markets will have a powerful effect on the number of student customers who choose a particular school.

## Notes

1. Some scholars also argue that indirect subsidies in the form of tax expenditures—income and property tax exemptions—are perhaps even more inequitable, because they disproportionately benefit a tiny number of elite public and private institutions (Clotfelter 1992, 1996; Clotfelter & Rothschild, 1991). These tax expenditures could amount to more than US$15 billion annually, although they are probably less than US$10 billion.

2. The logic outlined in Peltzman's article presents a special case of the general problem of subsidies-in-kind outlined in Alchian and Allen's popular introductory economics text (1969, pp. 168–174).

3. That is, tenable at the college or university of the student's choice—either public or private.

4. We would acknowledge at the outset that this conclusion is not easy to reconcile with the best econometric evidence (see Becker, 1990; Bishop, 1977; Chang & Hsing, 1996a, b; Doyle & Cicarelli, 1980; Fuller, Manski, & Wise, 1982; Galper & Dunn, 1969; Heller, 1997; Hight, 1975; Hoenack & Weiler, 1979; Hoenack, 1971; Hopkins, 1974; Knudsen & Servelle, 1978: Kohn, Manski, & Mundel, 1976; Lehr & Newton, 1978; Leslie & Brinkman, 1987; Psacharopoulos, 1973; Rives & Cassidy, 1982; Savoca, 1990; Schwartz 1985, 1986; Tuckman, 1973; Wetzel et al., 1998), which consistently shows substantially higher (absolute) price elasticities of demand for private higher education than for the higher education sector as a whole, or even with the most compelling anecdotal evidence (see Breneman, 1994). Even Clotfelter (1996) carefully restricts his argument to a handful of elite institutions. However, none of the better econometric analyses explicitly tests the hypotheses about institutional behavior laid out here and anecdotal evidence, no matter how plausible, remains anecdotal.

5. For a description of the Cooperative Institutional Research Program's annual freshman surveys during this period, see Dey, Astin, and Korn (1991).

6. Our data are for 1980–85. This period provides certain analytic benefits. First, it offers some overlap with the Astin–Inouye analysis. Second, this was a period in which states pursued a broad array of policies toward higher education. State policy initiatives in this field during the next 10 years were far more uniform and thus do not offer much opportunity to explain variance. Also, it is axiomatic that firm (institutional) behavior is driven by market (student) demand and costs, which are in turn a function of technology and relative factor costs. The studies reported in note 4 depict considerable underlying stability on the demand side. In the absence of any significant changes in technology or underlying factor prices, it is reasonable to presume that the period examined is irrelevant to our conclusions.

7. Our variables represent nominal tuition prices charged to undergraduate students. As an anonymous referee pointed out, it would be preferable to have a measure of actual price paid by the average student (average discounted tuition or net revenue per student). However, HEGIS survey data for the periods under study were not considered adequate to construct such a variable. In any case, "tuition discounting" was considerably less prevalent in the early 1980s and before than is the case today.

8. The exception was the analyses involving the percentages of low- and middle-income students in private colleges and universities since these had to use the small CIRP sample of private institutions. Here we had to limit the analysis to the entire private sector in each state.

9. The magnitude of the regression coefficient for the all-private-institutions set implies that, based upon the average state student aid level (aid dollars to private sector students divided by private sector FTE enrollment), an additional US$100 per FTE (1990 dollars) of such state aid to private sector students would be associated with an increase in enrollment in the typical private institution of 9.3 FTE undergraduates. For the nonselective private institutions, the analysis indicates that the effect is about twice as large.

10. We presume that most institutions are revenue (and cost) maximizers and that in the vast majority of cases their marginal costs are effectively zero, in which case both nominal tuition prices and enrollment levels are driven solely by residual demand (see Appendix B). That would also be the case under constant or decreasing costs (Panzar & Willig, 1977). It follows that a single-equation formulation would be appropriate to estimate the effects of price-related variables.

Nevertheless, there is one formulation under which increasing costs could be obtained, thereby giving rise to the possibility that our findings are an artifact of simultaneous equations bias: where marginal cost reflects the cost to *attract* the incremental student (see Thompson & Zumeta, 1981). Given that definition of cost, however, the Dorfman–Steiner theorem (Dorfman & Steiner, 1954) shows that a single equation can be used to estimate cost, holding price constant, or demand, holding institutional attributes constant.

11. See Appendix A.

12. See Appendix B.

13. Note that the coefficients of this variable are our counterparts to cross-price elasticities. Cross-price elasticities are defined as the change in the quantity of a target good, in this case private higher education, resulting from a change in the price of a rival good, here comparable public higher education. Cross-price elasticities are often used to identify close substitutes: the higher the value of the coefficient, the closer the substitute. That is true of the absolute values of our relative-price coefficients as well. However, because the public tuition price is in the denominator of this variable, its value will decrease when public tuition prices increase. This means that coefficients should have negative signs, taking values from zero to negative infinity.

14. Such variables are denominated: $L$ (variable name). Comparisons of alternative specifications showed that they had no appreciable effect on explained variance, $F$ values, or, where variables were included in the same order, the coefficient signs (the intercept excepted).

15. Regressing the change in public tuitions on the change in private tuitions suggests that a 1 percent increase in public tuition results in a 0.2 percent increase in private tuition. Of course, this response is subject to a great deal of variation. Once again there is no evident relationship between in-state public tuition growth and tuition at highly selective private colleges and universities—further proof that the latter compete in a national market. And, once again, the empirical relationship is strongest for our moderately selective group.

16. For an analysis of the challenges in designing such a policy regime to be both cost-effective and politically robust, see Zumeta (1999b).

# References

Alchian, A. A., & Allen, W. R. (1969). *Exchange and production: theory in use*. Belmont, CA: Wadsworth Publishing Company.

Astin, A. W., & Henson, J. W. (1977). New measures of college selectivity. *Research in Higher Education, 7* (September), 1–9.

Astin, A. W., & Inouye, C. J. (1988). How public policy at the state level affects private higher education institutions. *Economics of Education Review, 7*(1), 47–63.

Baum, S., & Sjogren, J. (1996). The distribution of subsidies to postsecondary students. *Eastern Economic Journal, 22*(2), 195–204.

Becker, W. E. (1990). The demand for higher education. In S. A. Hoenack, & E. L. Collins, *The economics of American universities: management, operations, and fiscal environment* (pp. 155–188). Albany: State University of New York Press.

Birnbaum, R. (1983). *Maintaining diversity in higher education*. San Francisco: Jossey-Bass.

Bishop, J. (1977). The effect of public policies on the demand for higher education. *Journal of Human Resources, 12*(3), 285–307.

Blaydon, C. C. (1978). State policy options. In D. W. Breneman, & C. E. Finn Jr, *Public policy and private higher education* (pp. 353–388). Washington: The Brookings Institution.

Breneman, D. W. (1994). *Liberal arts colleges: thriving, surviving, or endangered?* Washington: The Brookings Institution.

Breneman, D. W. (1996). Affordability and the private institution. *Educational Record, 66*(4), 14–27.

Chang, H. S., & Hsing, Y. (1996a). A study of demand for higher education at private institutions in the U.S.: a dynamic and general specification. *Education Economics, 4*(3), 267–278.

Chang, H. S., & Hsing, Y. (1996b). Testing increasing sensitivity of enrolment at private institutions to tuition and other costs. *American Economist, 40*(1), 40–45.

Clotfelter, C. T. (1992). *Who benefits from the nonprofit sector?*. Chicago: University of Chicago Press.

Clotfelter, C. T. (1996). *Buying the best: cost escalation in elite higher education*. Princeton, NJ: Princeton University Press.

Clotfelter, C. T., & Rothschild, M. (1991). *Studies of supply and demand in higher education*. Chicago: University of Chicago Press.

Dey, E. L., Astin, A. W., & Korn, W. S. (1991). *The American freshman: 25 year trends*. Los Angeles: Cooperative Institutional Research Program, University of California.

Dorfman, R., & Steiner, P. O. (1954). Optimal advertising and optimal quality. *American Economic Review, 64*(5), 28–36.

Doyle, C., & Cicarelli, J. (1980). The demand for higher education: a disaggregate approach. *American Economist, 24*(2), 53–55.

Education Commission of the States (1990). The preservation of excellence in American higher education: the essential role of private colleges and universities. Report of the Task Force on State Policy and Independent Higher Education. Denver, CO: author (July).

Fuller, W. C., Manski, C. F., & Wise, D. A. (1982). New evidence on the economic determinants of postsecondary schooling choices. *Journal of Human Resources, 17*(4), 477–498.

Galper, H., & Dunn, R. M. Jr. (1969). A short run demand function for higher education in the United States. *Journal of Political Economy, 77*(5), 765–777.

Ganderton, P. T. (1992). The effect of subsidies in kind on the choice of a college. *Journal of Public Economics, 48*(3), 269–292.

Hansen, W. L. (1972). Equity and the finance of higher education. *Journal of Political Economy, 80*(3), 60–73 (part II).

Hansen, W. L., & Weisbrod, B. A. (1969). The distribution of costs and direct benefits of public higher education: the case of California. *Journal of Human Resources, 4*(2), 176–191.

Hearn, J. C. et al. (1996). Resources and reason: a contextual analysis of state tuition and student aid policies. *Research in Higher Education, 37*(3), 241–278.

Heller, D. E. (1997). Price response in higher education: an update to Leslie and Brinkman. *Journal of Higher Education, 68*(6), 624–659.

Hight, J. E. (1975). The demand for higher education in the U.S., 1927–72: the public and private institutions. *Journal of Human Resources, 10*(4), 512–520.

Hoenack, S. A. (1971). The efficient allocation of subsidies to college students. *American Economic Review, 61*(3), 302–311 (part 1).

Hoenack, S. A., & Weiler, W. C. (1979). The demand for higher education and institutional enrolment forecasting. *Economic Inquiry, 17*(1), 89–113.

Hopkins, T. D. (1974). Higher education enrollment demand. *Economic Inquiry, 12*(1), 53–65.

Hovey, H. A. (1999). State spending for higher education in the next decade. Prepared by State Policy Research, Inc. for the National Center on Public Policy and Higher Education, San Jose, CA.

Hoxby, C. M. (1997). How the changing market structure of U.S. higher education explains college tuition. NBER working paper no. 6323.

Kane, T. J. (1994). College entry by blacks since 1970: the role of college costs, family background, and the returns to education. *Journal of Political Economy, 102*(5), 878–911.

Kane, T. J. (1996). College cost, borrowing constraints, and the timing of college entry. *Eastern Economic Journal, 22*(2), 181–194.

Knudsen, O. K., & Servelle, P. J. (1978). The demand for higher education at private institutions of moderate selectivity. *American Economist, 22*(2), 30–34.

Kohn, M. G., Manski, C. F., & Mundel, D. S. (1976). An empirical investigation of factors which influence college going behavior. *Annals of Economic and Social Measurement, 5*(4), 391–419.

Kroncke, C. O. Jr., & Ressler, R. W. (1993). The Alchian–Allen effect in higher education: public versus private enrolment. *Economics of Education Review, 12*(4), 345–349.

Lambin, J. J. (1969). Optimal allocation of competitive marketing efforts: an empirical study. *Journal of Business, 43*(4), 46–84.

Lambin, J. J. (1972). A computer on-line marketing mix model. *Journal of Marketing Research, 9*(2), 119–126.

Lehr, D. K., & Newton, J. M. (1978). Time series and cross sectional investigations of the demand for higher education. *Economic Inquiry, 16*(3), 411–422.

Leslie, L. L., & Brinkman, P. T. (1987). Student price response in higher education: the student demand studies. *Journal of Higher Education, 58*(2), 181–204.

Marshall, R., & Tucker, M. (1992). *Thinking for a living: education and the wealth of nations*. New York: Basic Books.

McGuire, J. W. (1976). The distribution of subsidy to students in California public higher education. *Journal of Human Resources, 11*(3), 343–353.

McPherson, M. S., & Schapiro, M. O. (1991a). *Keeping college affordable: government and educational opportunity.* Washington: The Brookings Institution.

McPherson, M. S., & Schapiro, M. O. (1991b). Does student aid affect college enrolment? New evidence on a persistent controversy. *American Economic Review, 81*(1), 309–318.

McPherson, M. S., & Schapiro, M. O. (1997). Financing undergraduate education: designing national policies. *National Tax Journal, 50*(3), 557–571.

Panzar, J. C., & Willig, R. D. (1977). Free entry and the sustainability of natural monopoly. *Bell Journal of Economics, 8*(1), 1–22.

Paul, F. G. (1990). Access to college in a public policy environment supporting both opportunity and selectivity. *American Journal of Education, 98*(4), 351–388.

Peltzman, S. (1973). The effect of government subsidies-in-kind on private expenditures: the case of higher education. *Journal of Political Economy, 81*(1), 1–27.

Porter, O. F. (1990). *Undergraduate completion and persistence at four year colleges and universities.* Washington: National Institute of Independent Colleges and Universities.

Psacharopoulos, G. (1973). A note on the demand for enrolment in higher education. *De Economist, 121*(5), 521–525.

Reeher, K. R., & Davis, J. S. (annual publication). National Association of State Scholarship and Grant Programs annual survey report. Harrisburg: Pennsylvania Higher Education Assistance Agency.

Rives, J. M., & Cassidy, G. W. (1982). Factors affecting the demand for higher education at public institutions. *American Economist, 26*(2), 17–24.

Savoca, E. (1990). Another look at the demand for higher education: measuring the price sensitivity of the decision to apply to college. *Economics of Education Review, 9*(2), 123–134.

Savoca, E. (1991). The effect of changes in the composition of financial aid on college enrolments. *Eastern Economic Journal, 17*(1), 109–121.

Schwartz, J. B. (1985). Student financial aid and the college enrolment decision: the effects of public and private grants and interest subsidies. *Economics of Education Review, 4*(2), 129–144.

Schwartz, J. B. (1986). Wealth neutrality in higher education: the effects of student grants. *Economics of Education Review, 5*(2), 107–117.

Spence, D. S., & Weathersby, G. B. (1981). Changing patterns of state funding. In J. R. Mingle et al., *Challenges of retrenchment* (pp. 226–242). San Francisco: Jossey-Bass.

Thompson, F., & Zumeta, W. (1981). A regulatory model of governmental coordinating activities in the higher education sector. *Economics of Education Review, 1*(1), 27–52.

Tuckman, H. P. (1973). Local colleges and the demand for higher education: the enrollment-inducing effects of location. *American Journal of Economics and Sociology, 32*(3), 257–268.

Western Interstate Commission on Higher Education and The College Board (1998). *Knocking at the college door: projections of high-school graduates by state and race/ethnicity, 1996–2012.* Boulder, CO: Author.

Wetzel, J., O'Toole, D., & Peterson, S. (1998). An analysis of student enrolment demand. *Economics of Education Review, 17*(1), 47–54.

Zumeta, W. (1992). State policies and private higher education: policies, correlates, and linkages. *Journal of Higher Education, 63*(4), 363–417.

Zumeta, W. (1996). Meeting the demand for higher education without breaking the bank: a framework for the design of state higher education policies for an era of increasing demand. *Journal of Higher Education, 67*(4), 367–425.

Zumeta, W. (1999a). How did they do it? The surprising enrolment success of private, nonprofit higher education from 1980 to 1995. Paper presented at the Association for the Study of Higher Education, San Antonio, TX, 19 November 1999.

Zumeta, W. (1999b). Utilizing private higher education for public purposes: design challenges facing efforts to help meet higher education access demands through the private sector. In S. S. Nagel, *The substance of public policy.* Commack, NY: Nova Science Publishers.

# Higher Education Policies and Representation

## C. E. COOK

*"You often hear that higher education doesn't lobby. Victorian phrases crop up in the debate about government relations. There is the use of words like* tainted.*"*

A lobbyist from one of the "Big Six"
higher education associations in Washington

It is not unusual to encounter a book on lobbying. What is unusual about this particular book is that the policy community that is under examination, higher education, is one that prided itself for decades on how little lobbying it did and how little it knew about the craft of advocacy. Higher education has always thought of itself as a national treasure, a public good whose value should not be questioned. Historically, its leaders believed that politics is a dirty business, one unworthy of a lofty enterprise like higher education. Observers agree that, as a result, the Washington representatives of colleges and universities remained on the sidelines during the early congressional debates on federal aid to higher education. For most of their history, the Washington higher education associations did not even want their representatives to be called "lobbyists" (Hawkins 1992, 124).

There are still vestiges of that attitude, and there are many reasons for it. Twenty years ago those who chronicled higher education's federal relations commented on the prevailing view of politics in the higher education community. One said, "Distaste for the art and practice of politics is mixed with a genuine concern that aggressive political action would somehow be inappropriate to the academic enterprise and might even be counterproductive" (Gladieux 1977, 272). Another commented that higher education associations tried to "ride above the waves" so as to avoid the "demeaning and lowly" political process. He said higher education lobbying was often "passive" because, "To enter the game of partisan politics as a traditional lobby would strip academia of its privileged status in society" (Murray 1976, 90–92).

Given the impact of federal funding and regulations, it is vital for colleges and universities to be well-represented in Washington. Simply put, higher education representatives are faced with a difficult paradox: On the one hand, higher education's image as a public good garners it the support of many public policy makers. If it lobbies just the same way other "special interests" do, it can look just like the others and risk a loss of support from those who consider it high-minded, above the fray.[1] On the other hand, if higher education does not lobby the same way as others, its gentility can lead to an absence of public attention and a low priority on the public agenda. To complicate the issue further, higher education institutions and associations have legal restrictions on their lobbying as a result of their nonprofit tax status.[2]

For all these reasons and others, a Washington policy analyst noted, "Higher education lobbying is treated by higher ed folks as if it is a different kind of undertaking. . . . They think this is a genteel endeavor, not an industry." A university lobbyist agreed, saying, "Those in higher ed are gun-shy about lobbying. They don't like combative situations." As a result, the higher education community historically lobbied in a somewhat half-hearted manner, if at all.

In the course of the 104th Congress, during 1995–96, a paradigm shift occurred in higher education advocacy. While the quantity and quality of higher education lobbying had been growing for a long time, it was not until the so-called Republican revolution that the community decided it was more important to keep higher education issues on the public agenda than to worry about losing support from those who thought colleges and universities should avoid political involvement. As one lobbyist put it, "We decided to stop looking like a 'country bumpkin promoting the public good'." Another commented, "During the 104th Congress we tried new tactics. . . . What a novel approach! Higher ed meekly stuck their toes in the water of modern lobbying. This is a timid crowd." For the first time, the higher education community focused full attention on advocacy and, without apology, engaged in vigorous lobbying activity.

This chapter gives an overview of the federal role in higher education, which shows how much is at stake. It then describes the Washington higher education community, especially the six major associations, and explains the diverse types of colleges and universities in the United States. Finally, it discusses the proliferation of federal access points which, in turn, has encouraged the proliferation of higher education actors in Washington.

## The Federal Role in Higher Education

What makes higher education and its federal relations worthy of special study is the sheer importance of American colleges and universities. They are considered the finest in the world. Historically, national policy has contributed to their excellence and value, so the higher education community seeks to ensure that the government continues to be a positive force.

There is much at stake in higher education policy making, especially because higher education has such an impact on the U.S. economy. College graduates command higher salaries and provide higher tax revenues than those who do not attend or graduate from college, and the higher education enterprise constitutes a $100 billion industry, accounting for 3.1 percent of the gross domestic product (Horton and Andersen 1994). As of 1996, there were 3,688 American colleges and universities, enrolling 14.3 million students either part-time or full-time (*Chronicle of Higher Education*, 2 September 1996).[3] Additionally, there are 800,000 instructional and research staff and one million administrative and support staff employed by these institutions (American Council on Education 1993). The American economy, prosperous by comparison with others, prospers in part because of the knowledge and skills taught by colleges and universities and the research done by their faculty. Both basic and applied university research contribute to American economic competitiveness in the global market.

Apart from its direct impact on the economy, higher education is important because it enriches the lives of the citizenry. Americans believe in upward mobility and typically consider education the key to mobility. In the contemporary era, it is a college degree or, increasingly, a graduate school degree that best promotes upward mobility. Furthermore, during their college years young people develop skills necessary for informed involvement in a participatory democracy, and policies promoting access serve to blur societal divisions, especially since more than half of high school graduates now attend college. Communities are enriched by the arts, sports, cultural events, and other resources of their local educational institutions, and millions of people benefit from various public service programs undertaken by colleges and universities. In short, it is difficult to imagine the quality of life experienced by Americans without the quality and quantity of higher education available to them.

In spite of the significance of the higher education enterprise, there is no comprehensive federal policy regarding colleges and universities. Federal involvement in higher education policy making has always been piecemeal, and the role of the national government is ambiguous. The U.S. Constitution is silent on the subject of all education, not just higher education, and although George Washington championed the establishment of a national university, the founding fathers ultimately decided against it. The Tenth Amendment of the Bill of Rights says that all power not specifically delegated by the Constitution to the federal government is reserved for the states, so the states have primary responsibility for higher education. As a result, it has been the state governments that have established and funded public institutions, and they continue to provide the largest share of institutional funding.

Before public institutions developed in this country, there were already private (independent) colleges and universities. Their autonomy was ensured by the Supreme Court's decision in the Dartmouth College case in 1819, which said the incorporation of an institution under government charter did not bring it under government control. Eventually an extensive system of public state-funded education began to appear side by side with private higher education, but neither the public institutions nor the privates developed under the aegis of the federal government. Nonetheless, the federal policy making role has not been insignificant.

The federal government first involved itself in higher education in 1787 when Congress passed the Northwest Ordinance requiring that each newly formed state should receive two townships dedicated toward support of a university. Although a few states appropriated the proceeds from this land to existing private institutions, most created new state universities. Nearly a century later, the Morrill Act of 1862 provided federal land in each state, from which the proceeds were to be used to support a college offering agricultural and mechanical education, and not excluding more traditional disciplines. Today, the institutions funded by the Morrill Act are those most commonly considered *land-grant* universities.

The federal government then passed the Hatch Act (1887) and the second Morrill Act (1890) to fund certain types of institutional research. Additionally, the federal government founded the service academies and has chartered institutions such as Howard University. The Reserve Officers' Training Corps, established on university campuses in 1916, was another form of federal support, and during the 1930s the federal government enacted a variety of other forms of financial aid.

It was not until after World War II that federal funding for higher education became quite substantial, based on national needs. For example, the GI Bill of 1944 (called the Servicemen's Readjustment Act) provided federal support for veterans' education, which served as a reward for their military service. In the 1950s the federal government also financed education for specific careers, and with the goal of contributions to global understanding.

Sponsorship of vital research became a major federal initiative in the postwar era. In 1945 President Truman's science advisor, Vannevar Bush, issued a report in which he argued that the federal government should develop a partnership with the nation's research universities and fund them to train young scientists and develop new scientific knowledge through basic research. His proposal was adopted, and the result was a large number of federal research initiatives, many of which were tied to strategic national defense objectives. The 1945 Fulbright Act, which financed the international exchange of scholars, was followed by the 1958 National Defense Education Act (NDEA). That Act, passed after the Russian launch of Sputnik, was one of many examples of higher education funding resulting from the Cold War mentality and competition with the Soviet Union. The NDEA encouraged students to study science and mathematics in return for federal financial aid.

Next came a series of agencies created to bolster American research capacity. The creation, in 1949, of the National Institutes of Health (NIH), which supports university-based medical research and is a division of the Department of Health and Human Services, was followed in 1950 by the establishment of the National Science Foundation (NSF), which funds other university-based scientific research. Then came the National Endowment for the Arts (NEA) and the National Endowment for the Humanities (NEH), both of which were created in 1965 to extend federal funding to non-scientific research and programs. (While the NEA has a very small budget, with little linkage to higher education institutions, faculty artists, poets, and creative writers occasionally receive NEA grants. The NEA is included in this list not because of its budget but because those faculty members in the arts and humanities so value its work.) Additional federal departments have provided large amounts of research funding to higher education, especially the Departments of Defense, Agriculture, Energy, and Health and Human Services, and the amounts grew especially when the Cold War was at its height. (By far the largest share of federal dollars fund scientific and medical research, as opposed to other types of university-based research. Although science policy issues are addressed only peripherally in this book, since they affect a relatively small number of colleges and universities, the observations and conclusions made here are broadly applicable to lobbying for the scientific realm as well.)

The federal government has been especially instrumental in regard to affirmative action in higher education. Affirmative action involves measures to correct or compensate for past discrimination or to prevent discrimination from recurring in the future, and it especially affects higher education employment, admissions, retention, and student financial aid. The principal piece of affirmative action legislation is the Civil Rights Act of 1964 (amended in 1972, 1978, and 1991), which was the cornerstone of President Lyndon Johnson's Great Society programs. The Act prohibits all forms of discrimination on the basis of race, color, gender, religion, or national origin. Title VII of the Act specifically applies to public and private employers with fifteen or more employees and, therefore, includes colleges and universities. Other employment-related federal statutes concern discrimination on the basis of age, physical or mental disability, veteran status, citizenship status, and disabilities.

Policies concerning student admission and retention in selective higher education programs have also been shaped by federal affirmative action goals. While landmark judicial decisions like the 1978 *Bakke* case have altered the way that institutions implement affirmative action legislation, the federal government has in fact acted for decades as a force for nondiscrimination in higher education.

Affirmative action legislation has also shaped institutional policies toward student aid, especially because the Civil Rights Act of 1964 was interpreted to allow institutions to take race into account in financial awards. The Higher Education Act (HEA) of 1965, developed during the early civil rights movement, differed not only in the magnitude of federal assistance, which was substantial, but also in its objective. It sought to remove barriers to educational opportunity by initiating a variety of types of federal grants, loans, and fellowships to both undergraduate and graduate students. In addition, the Act provided institutional funding for certain purposes. The 1965 Act thus constituted a far-reaching federal effort on behalf of higher education, and it has been amended and reauthorized five times since 1965—in 1972, 1976, 1980, 1986, and 1992 (and is scheduled for renewal in fiscal year 1998). (The federal *fiscal year* means the period from October 1 of each calendar year through September 30 of the following year.[4]) Along with the carrot has come the stick: Washington has used its financial aid, as provided in the Higher Education Act and its amendments, to enforce affirmative action objectives by threatening to cut off student financial aid at institutions that do not comply with federal mandates. One such mandate is Title IX of the 1972 HEA which prohibits discrimination on the basis of sex and is best known for its provision of better athletic opportunities for women students.

The magnitude of the federal role in higher education funding has grown substantially over the years. While states continue to supply about twice as much money, the federal share now constitutes nearly 15 percent of all college and university revenues. Unlike state aid, most federal funding goes directly to individuals (typically to students or professors), rather than to the institutions themselves. By 1996, federal student financial aid, both grants and loans, reached a high of $35.1 billion, and about a third of the students in postsecondary education were receiving some form of federal aid. As for federal grants and contracts for university-based research, they totaled $11.8 billion in 1996 (*Chronicle of Higher Education*, 2 September 1996) and were the major source of faculty members' research dollars. In addition to student aid and research money, there are other forms of federal funding (e.g., funding for critical foreign languages, or library support, or teaching improvement projects) that provide some of the *extras* that the higher education community counts on to fill in the gaps. However, federal funds remain largely uncoordinated and come from a wide variety of agencies and programs to serve a wide variety of purposes.

Along with the massive federal funding for higher education has come a proliferation of regulations. For example, the federal tax code has a substantial impact on higher education funding and institutional policies. While American institutions have an unusual amount of independence and autonomy by comparison with institutions in most other countries, it is increasingly difficult to find a single aspect of college or university activity that remains unaffected by the federal government in one way or another. Besides student aid, research, and affirmative action, Washington affects higher education policies on such diverse topics as, for example, campus safety, accreditation, faculty retirement age, graduation rates, substance abuse, telecommunications, and assessment of student learning. The variety of topics means that advocacy on behalf of higher education is a complex task.

## The Higher Education Community

The task of advocacy for the American higher education community is further complicated by its diversity. There are more than 3,600 colleges and universities, and they are located in every part of the country, including every state and city, and many towns. They vary from two-year community colleges granting associate degrees to research universities granting doctoral degrees. Of these institutions, 55 percent are private (i.e., independent) institutions whose budgets come largely from student tuition and private donations. Some state dollars go to private institutions, especially in the form of student aid, but the amount of state funding for private institutions is minuscule by comparison with the amount for public ones. About 22 percent of the 14.3 million students in American higher education are enrolled in private institutions (*Chronicle of Higher Education*, 2 September 1996).

The remaining 78 percent of American students, both undergraduate and graduate students, are enrolled in public institutions. Public colleges and universities, which are funded largely by state governments, are also dependent on student tuitions and private donations, but to a lesser extent than private institutions. State governments typically pay for most of the operating expenses and new buildings at public institutions. The fifty stare governments have fifty different systems for interacting with their own higher education institutions, and there is tremendous variation in the degree and types of controls they exercise. To monitor and influence policy making, colleges and universities send staff members both to their state capitals and also to Washington.

There is as much variation in institutional representation in Washington as there is in every other aspect of higher education. Large numbers of institutions have staff whose job descriptions include federal relations in whole or in part, and many of them commute regularly to the nation's capital. Beginning in the early 1970s, a few individual institutions began establishing their own Washington offices, and now there are more than a dozen of them. In addition, most of the large state systems of higher education have offices in the capital to represent the interests of all their member institutions.

Also in Washington are hundreds of associations representing higher education. For example, there are regional and state coalitions of colleges and universities and consortia of institutions of the same general type (e.g., church-related institutions, or historically black institutions). There are associations of people in the sane roles in their institutions (e.g., chief financial officers, or members of governing boards, or professors within each discipline), associations of people with the same general concerns (e.g., about the quality of graduate education, or the nature of international education), and associations of personnel with the same type of tasks to perform for the higher education community (e.g., accreditation). In fact, *The Encyclopedia of Associations* now lists several hundred groups whose customary work concerns various aspects of higher education, more than two hundred of which are located in the Washington area. Many of these groups do no federal relations at all, but some are engaged in educational or lobbying activities of one sort or another. Additionally, law, lobbying, and consulting firms are sometimes retained by individual institutions to advance their interests with the federal government, and ad hoc groups often spring up to work on a specific policy issue and then disband when the issue has been resolved.

To create order in the jumbled Washington landscape, a set of major associations serve as the principal voices of higher education. Like the organizations representing many other policy domains (see, for example, Heinz et al. 1993, 57), the major higher education associations have been the important players in the domain for several decades and are viewed as permanent fixtures. These six major associations differ from most other Washington higher education associations in that they are presidentially based. In other words, the presidents of colleges and universities are designated as the principal institutional representatives. It is customarily the presidents who make the final decisions about whether to join or renew membership, and it is the presidents who most often attend the association meetings. Nonetheless, the real members of these six associations, known as the *Big Six*, are the institutions themselves.[5]

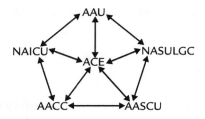

**Figure 1.  Relationship of the Big Six Associations**

The heads of the Big Six associations spend much of their time on federal relations and consider that activity to be their personal priority. As one of the major association presidents noted, "Federal relations is the reason we are in Washington instead of Jackson, Wyoming, where I would rather be." While all have some staff assigned to governmental affairs, with the number growing in recent years, the staff size and the proportion of the association budgets devoted to federal relations are usually quite modest, though they vary by association. Nonetheless, these groups stay in regular contact with members of Congress and the executive branch.

One of the Big Six associations, the American Council on Education (ACE), is the national coordinating body for American higher education. ACE represents all accredited colleges and universities, both public and private. ACE's membership is composed of individual institutions as well as national and regional higher education associations, including the other five major associations. Thus, ACE is, in part, an association of associations.

While the other five major associations have some association members as well, their main function is representation of a specific type of institution. Most American colleges and universities have memberships in one or more associations. Nonetheless, most institutions think of one of the five specialized associations as their *primary* association because it is the only one to which they belong, or the one they consider primary for federal relations. Because the jurisdictions of the five associations overlap to some extent, some institutions choose to belong to two of the five. These overlapping memberships will be explained further in chapter 5.[6] However, the majority of institutions are members of the single association that best represents their own type of institution, and then they usually join ACE as well (see Figure 1).

The five major associations are the American Association of Community Colleges (AACC), the Association of American Universities (AAU), the American Association of State Colleges and Universities (AASCU), the National Association of Independent Colleges and Universities (NAICU), and the National Association of State Universities and Land-Grant Colleges (NASULGC). The overlap among them occurs because AACC represents two-year institutions, both public and private; AASCU represents public master's (comprehensive) universities, most of which are four or more years, but a few of which have two-year degree programs as well; NASULGC represents mostly public universities that range from research and doctoral to master's; AAU represents the elite research universities, both public and private; and NAICU represents private institutions, ranging from research universities to two-year colleges. ACE represents all these major presidentially based associations, as well as other more specialized higher education associations, and also every type of college and university. (See chapter 5 for more discussion of this organizational structure.)

With the exception of AAU, which has the same dues for all its member institutions, the Big Six associations' annual charges are based either on size of enrollment or on a combination of enrollment and general expenditure data. The 1995 dues of the Big Six ranged from a low of $600 for the smallest NAICU college to a high of $38,200 for the largest NASULGC university.[7] The University of Michigan, for example, which has both a large enrollment and a large budget, paid about $90,000 in 1995 for its memberships in three Big Six associations (i.e., AAU, NASULGC, and ACE).

The memberships of the Big Six range from 60 to 1,800 institutions and associations. After ACE, AACC is the largest. Its members are public and private two-year degree-granting colleges.

AAU has the smallest membership because it is the voice of the elite research institutions and is the only one of the Big Six whose membership is by invitation only. AASCU's members are master's institutions and state systems of public higher education, and the degree programs of its institutions range from the associate degree to the doctorate. NAICU's members are independent (or private) institutions, plus organizations that coordinate private higher education within the states and some other smaller associations of private institutions. NASULGC's members are almost entirely public colleges and universities, especially land-grant institutions and the state flagship universities, as well as public higher education systems. It is smaller than all of the Big Six except AAU. (See chapter 5 for more detailed information about the membership of the Big Six.)

The principal differences among higher education institutions are those of control (i.e., public and private), length of program (two-year and four-year), and research institutions as compared to others. By virtue of its control, program, and emphasis or lack of emphasis on research, each higher education institution develops some basic attitudes on federal relations that are shared with others of the same type. Additional factors such as size and location also play a role in institutional attitudes. Through analysis of survey results, this book shows which of the differences seem especially important in setting an institutional approach to federal relations. (See chapter 7 for an analysis of the different attitudes of different types of institutions.)

The Carnegie classification system is often used to differentiate among various types of colleges and universities, so its terminology appears throughout this book and bears explanation. First developed in 1970, the classifications have been modified and updated periodically, including as recently as 1994. The current system uses the following descriptions:[8]

*Research Universities.* These institutions give high priority to research, have a minimum of $15.5 million in annual federal support for research, and award fifty or more doctoral degrees each year, as well as having a full range of baccalaureate programs. In 1994 there were 125 institutions classified as Research Universities by the Carnegie system. Those with the most federal funding and the largest numbers of doctoral degrees are members of AAU, and some of these elites are also members of NASULGC. The other Research Universities are often members of NASULGC or, less frequently, AASCU. Examples of Research Universities are the University of California at Berkeley and Yale University.

*Doctoral Universities.* These institutions are committed to graduate education through the doctorate, and they also offer a full range of baccalaureate programs. The Doctoral Universities award a minimum of ten doctoral degrees in three or more disciplines or twenty or more doctoral degrees in one or more disciplines. In 1994, 111 institutions qualified as Doctoral Universities. These institutions are primarily members of NAICU if they are private institutions, and either NASULGC or AASCU, or both, if public. Boston College and Western Michigan University are both examples of Doctoral Universities.

*Master's (or Comprehensive) Colleges and Universities.* These institutions also offer a full range of baccalaureate programs, plus graduate education through the master's degree. They award a minimum of twenty or more master's degrees annually in one or more disciplines. There were 529 Master's Colleges and Universities in 1994, about half of which are public and are likely to be members of AASCU; the other half, the privates, are likely to be members of NAICU. Examples of Master's Colleges and Universities are Mankato State University in Minnesota and Elon College in North Carolina.

*Baccalaureate (Liberal Arts) Colleges.* These institutions are primarily undergraduate colleges and emphasize their baccalaureate degree programs. Many of them award large percentages of their baccalaureate degrees in liberal arts fields. There were 637 Baccalaureate Colleges in 1994, and since most of them are private institutions, most are members of NAICU. The few public baccalaureate institutions are most likely to be members of AASCU. Williams College in Massachusetts and York College of the City University of New York are both examples of Baccalaureate Colleges.

*Associate of Arts Colleges.* These institutions offer associate of arts certificate or degree programs and usually do not offer baccalaureate degrees. There were 1,471 of these colleges in 1994. About one-third are private institutions which may be members of NAICU, and all of them, both public and private, may be members of AACC. Miami Dade Community College in Florida and Schoolcraft College in Michigan are both Associate of Arts Colleges.

*Specialized Institutions.*[9] These institutions offer degrees ranging from the bachelor's to the doctorate, and at least half of the degrees are in a specialized field, such as medicine, and the allied health fields, including pharmacy and chiropractic medicine; religion or theology; art, music, and design; business and management; engineering and technology; teachers colleges; and law. Other types of specialized institutions are military institutes, graduate centers, maritime academies, and tribal colleges. These specialized institutions may be members of ACE but are not ordinarily members of the other five major associations, except for some in NAICU.

The Carnegie classification system does not include proprietary (for-profit) schools. The 6,500 proprietary schools in the U.S. are mostly two-year or less-than-two-year technical and vocational schools, and they often differ from community colleges in the duration and breadth of their degree and certificate programs. However, the most important difference between the proprietaries and the community colleges is the locus of control. While community colleges are publicly funded and chartered, proprietary schools usually have a single owner or a board without external community accountability. The difference in profit motive and control mechanisms translate into differences of policy and operation, and most proprietary schools have the characteristics of small businesses. The 1,200 largest proprietary schools are members of the Career College Association (CCA), their umbrella organization. Although CCA is a member of ACE, most of its member institutions are not in ACE because most are not accredited.

For the purposes of this book, discussion of the higher education community is limited to the nonprofit institutions and does not include the vocational, proprietary schools because they differ so substantially from other types of postsecondary institutions. However, even with the exclusion of the proprietaries, higher education remains a diverse sector because of the substantial differences among nonprofit colleges and universities.

The higher education community overcomes some of the communication problems inherent in its diversity by having a common vehicle for information sharing, i.e., the *Chronicle of Higher Education.* The *Chronicle* is a weekly news magazine with subscribers in government, in associations, and, of course, in colleges and universities. Its news stories deal with legislative, judicial, and executive branch issues in the federal and state governments, as well as association news and issues of interest and concern on the campuses. While there are many other journals and magazines in higher education, the popularity of the *Chronicle* means that it provides a common base of knowledge for the higher education community and, therefore, contributes in Washington and elsewhere to cooperation and collaboration among its many players.

In spite of this common base of information, however, the higher education community's diversity makes consensus building difficult. Nonetheless, consensus is highly prized by academia since a collegial consensus building process defines college and university decision making and operates in faculty meetings on most campuses. Many of the community's Washington representatives, especially the major associations, operate through a similarly slow and deliberate consensus building process.

## Proliferation of Washington Lobbyists

Jonathan Rauch called the American interest group sector "a classic growth industry" (1994, 58), and that characterization applies to higher education as much as to other communities. As early as 1960 an ACE publication worried publicly about the Washington "babble of many voices speaking for higher education" (Gladieux and Wolanin 1976, 44), and the growth had only begun at that point. Of the new players in the Washington higher education community, some are newly hired federal relations personnel commuting to Washington from their college or university offices elsewhere. Still others are new staff in already well-established Washington associations who have been hired to accommodate the increased level of federal relations activity. The majority, however, are the staff of associations that have newly established Washington offices. In fact, the volumes of the *Encyclopedia of Associations* show an increase of about 400 percent from 1956 to 1996 in the number of associations in the Washington, D.C., area that include higher education as a significant component of their activities (see table 1).

**Table 1. Higher Education Associations in the Washington. D.C., Area**

| Year | Number of Associations |
|------|------------------------|
| 1956 | 44 |
| 1968 | 86 |
| 1976 | 102 |
| 1986 | 180 |
| 1996 | 221 |

**Source:** *Encyclopedia of Associations* (1956, 1968, 1976, 1986, & 1996).
**Note:** Data were derived from the *Encyclopedia of Associations* because that publication includes all types of associations, including those that do not feature higher education as their primary focus but do include it as a major concern. Given the difficulties of counting across categories in the *Encyclopedia of Associations* and determining association focus from textual description, the figures reported here may be slightly higher or lower than the actual number of associations. (The *Higher Education Directory* is also a good source of information about associations, but it includes only those that feature higher education as the primary focus, so the numbers in the Directory are lower than those in the *Encyclopedia*.)

The explosion in the number of higher education lobbyists has resulted from a variety of factors, many of which pertain to other communities as well. The increasing numbers of governmental actors is a major reason for the increasing numbers of groups (Gray and Lowery 1996b) because more federal access points have led to more people seeking access.

All three branches of the federal government make higher education policy,[10] and the relevant executive branch departments and agencies are numerous. College and university representatives maintain regular contact with them concerning budget requests, implementation of higher education legislation, and promulgation and implementation of regulations. For most of the higher education community, the most important executive branch agency is the Department of Education. It was established in 1979 as the successor, along with the Department of Health and Human Services, to the Department of Health, Education, and Welfare. The Department of Education houses a large number of higher education programs, including student financial aid (e.g., student loans, Pell grants, and a variety of graduate student fellowships), TRIO programs for at-risk students (Talent Search, Upward Bound, and Student Special Services, as well as the newer Equal Opportunity Centers and McNair Incentive Scholars Program), programs for developing institutions, international programs, and grants competitions of various kinds, especially the well-regarded Fund for the Improvement of Postsecondary Education (FIPSE). They are all administered by the assistant secretary for postsecondary education. Other executive branch departments and independent agencies are also critical to the higher education community, especially the Departments of Defense, Agriculture, Energy, the National Aeronautics and Space Administration (NASA), NSF, NEH, and NEA, and the Department of Health and Human Services, especially NIH.

The representatives of policy communities typically prefer interactions with one branch of government or another (Salisbury 1992, 97), and higher education representatives are like many others in devoting the largest share of their efforts to the legislative branch (Heinz et al. 1993, 215; Browne 1988, 209) because it is the part of government that the higher education community has historically influenced most successfully. Almost every congressional committee and subcommittee deals with topic(s) of interest to colleges and universities from time to time. However, there are certain committees (see table 2) that handle higher education issues most frequently, and the list is long enough to show why higher education lobbyists have their hands full.

It once was the case that lobbyists could carry the day if they could convince two or three Senate and House leaders to support their positions. That era is over. Although the congressional leadership has regained authority it lost in the 1970s and 1980s, the weakening of the congressional seniority system has allowed every member of Congress, not just the committee chairs, to introduce and affect legislation, including killing it. Each member of Congress has more staff than previously, and the staff have substantial influence. In addition, congressional reorganization has led to more committees and subcommittees, each of which has a burgeoning portfolio. Thus, it is necessary

**Table 2. Congressional Committees with Which Colleges and Universities Deal Most Often**

| Senate | House |
|---|---|
| Labor and Human Resources Committee and its Subcommittee on Education, Arts and Humanities | Economic and Educational Opportunities Committee[a] and its Subcommittee on Postsecondary Education, Training and Lifelong Learning |
| Appropriations Subcommittee for VA-HUD-Independent Agencies (NSF and National Service) | Science Committee[b] |
| Senate Appropriations Committee Subcommittee on Labor, Health and Human Services, and Education | Appropriations Subcommittee on Labor, Health and Human Services, and Education (Education Department and NIH) |

[a] Prior to the 104th Congress, this was called the Education and Labor Committee, with its Subcommittee on Postsecondary Education.
[b] Prior to the 104th Congress, this was called the Space, Science & Technology Committee.

for lobbyists to stay in contact with large numbers of members of Congress, as well as with their staff members.

Another factor affecting the number of lobbyists is the increase in congressional activity, both appropriations and regulations. The federal government is simply doing more than it used to, so policy communities think they need more representation simply to deal with the increase in activity. Additionally, the policy issues themselves are technical and complex, which in turn calls for more people to develop the necessary expertise to address them. As a result, the division of labor among lobbyists has grown, with more expert consultants and more for-profit, specialized firms. The costs of organizing have declined in this high-tech era, so organizing and mobilizing political activists gets easier all the time, which means that it is done more frequently. Finally, because there are so many more interests competing in Washington, each group thinks it has to mount more and more political activity to keep up with the interest group equivalent of the Joneses. Each group competes with others to get its concerns on the Washington radar screen or to protect what they have already achieved. The bottom line is that Washington representatives are much busier than they used to be.

Other factors leading to the proliferation of Washington representatives are more particular to higher education itself. For example, the increasing availability in the 1980s and early 1990s of *earmarked funds* (i.e., those funds that members of Congress designate for a specific use without an open competition or traditional review process) often have given the institutions that hired more lobbyists a good return on their investment in terms of new buildings or funded projects. Therefore, many institutions increased their Washington presence to respond to the opportunity. Additionally, the institutional missions of colleges and, especially, universities have expanded as they have engaged in more and more activities—from business development to nuclear waste disposal. Thus, institutions themselves have created more potential points of intersection with the federal government as their own portfolios have expanded.

## Conclusions

The higher education community is an especially interesting subject for study, in part because of the significance of the higher education enterprise to the future of the country. Additionally, it is interesting because there are so many federal higher education policy issues. A third aspect of the community is the variation in needs and preferences of the many different types of colleges and universities. The fact that the community has always had a very stable and structured set of associations and now finds itself with a multitude of new Washington higher education representatives adds to its challenges as well as its opportunities.

All of the factors cited above would make higher education lobbying an intriguing subject even without the arrival of the 104th (Gingrich) Congress. Yet that arrival tested the durability of the community's structures and the collegiality of its representatives as never before. The new Congress provided an unwelcome opportunity for the higher education community to examine the effectiveness of its lobbying skills. Those skills had been developing slowly, over a number of decades, as the following chapter will show.

# Policy Scholars Are from Venus; Policy Makers Are from Mars

## ROBERT BIRNBAUM

George Keller has used "trees without fruit" (1985, p. 7) as a metaphor to depict the sterility of the relationship between higher education scholarship and policy. I love metaphors. The best are simple, charming, and powerful, and this one is a classic. But simplifying complexity can be dangerous, and this linear perspective of a nonlinear world appears to suggest that the only purpose of trees is to bear fruit, and only fruit that is visible (preferably edible?) is of value. In reality, trees and fruit serve multiple and often conflicting purposes. Trees may provide shade, food, beauty, lumber, re-fuge, protection against erosion, and foundations for swings. Fruit serves different purposes for squirrels, worms, bees, trees themselves, and of course humans who may eat an apple, paint it, throw it, use it as a logo, or contemplate the nature of the universe as they watch it drop to the ground. Metaphors can obscure as much as they clarify. Is higher education scholarship useful only if it bears fruit, or might it instead serve as fertilizer, insecticide, or some other critical, if less visible, function?

Higher education is not alone in criticizing the presumed gap between policy scholars and policy makers. The disconnect appears to be a generalized feature of social research, and the attempt to use knowledge to improve policy has usually been disappointing (Cohen & Garet, 1975). The common complaint is that "many suppliers and users of social research are dissatisfied, the former because they are not listened to, the latter because they do not hear much they want to listen to" (Lindblom & Cohen, 1979, p. 1). Critics of the scholarship-practice chasm in higher education have been particularly caustic, characterizing research as "stale, irrelevant, . . . of little use to policy makers" (Layzell, 1990, p. B1) and also as "lifeless and pedestrian, inward looking and parochial, the product of assembly-line research that has generated few new findings and challenging ideas" (Conrad, 1989, p. 202). It is claimed that "college and university presidents do not consult the literature or use it. . . . If the research in higher education ended, it would scarcely be missed" (Keller, 1985, p. 7).

These critiques of higher education research are misdirected. They are based more on opinion than data and are uninformed by significant scholarship on social research and social policy. They appear to accept the myth of a one-to-one correspondence between a problem and its solution (Schon, 1971). Nevertheless, the arguments are widely repeated and enjoy some currency in the field. For example, an ad hoc group of higher education policy scholars (ASHE, 1996) reported that research lags behind policy needs, recommended that research agendas focus more attention on the questions being asked by policy makers so that policy-relevant research can be produced, and urged that research results be disseminated in formats congenial to policy makers and specify implications for policy.

## Misleading Assumptions

These critical views rest on four implicit but misleading assumptions about higher education policy scholarship and policy making:

- It is possible for policy makers to agree on the nature of policy problems and therefore on the kinds of research they would find most helpful.
- Policy scholars are not now engaged in policy-relevant research.
- Policy makers are not now influenced by policy scholarship.
- Increased attention by policy scholars to producing and disseminating policy-relevant research would improve policy making.

I believe that each of these assumptions is flawed and that higher education policy would be weakened rather than strengthened by asking researchers to define their agendas based on the current interests of policy makers.

*Misleading Assumption 1: Potential agreement on the nature of policy problems.* It is not easy to decide *a priori* whether any specific research program is, or is not, policy relevant. The number of policy questions is essentially unbounded, there is no agreement on which data are relevant to which problems, interest groups differ on what the major issues are, and preferences change over time. Three examples can illustrate the problem. First, I reviewed the listing of the top ten policy areas noted by the Association of Governing Boards in each year from 1994 to 1997 (*Ten public policy issues . . . ,* 1994, 1995, 1996, 1997) and identified 22 different items over the four-year period. Only one item appeared in each of the four years, and twelve appeared in only one of the four years. Of the ten items listed for 1994, four were not listed in any of the following years. Second, the 1997 policy initiatives or agendas of a group of higher education professional associations included 305 individual items (Komives, Endress, Kiely, & LaVoy, 1997). Third, an analysis of almost 800 references in the 1970 to 1994 literature of higher education identifying a "crisis" found that, while 60% were in 10 broad categories, over 300 referred to issues that, while policy relevant, were transient, localized, or idiosyncratic (Birnbaum & Shushok, 1998).

As these examples show, one person's critical policy issue is another person's irrelevancy, policy issues change over time, and many problems that will occupy the attention of policy makers in the future cannot be predicted in advance. These are all important issues for policy scholars. It takes time and preparation for policy scholars to develop the knowledge base of theory and practice and also the cultural understandings required to do research in any specific area (El-Khawas, 1995, p. 113). How can scholars focus on policy-relevant research if there is no way of predicting what future policy needs may be? We can be fairly certain that some, but not all, of the issues we study today will be *generally* relevant at some time over the next twenty years, even if we cannot predict the specific kind of knowledge necessary to respond to them. But there is no way to prepare scholars who can respond to *each* important policy issue of the next twenty years; the number of potential issues and their myriad subtleties dwarf the number of potential scholars and their specializations. Even with unlimited resources, policy scholars could not respond to all the policy issues in search of scholarly attention (see, e.g., Terenzini, 1996). Any list of current policy issues can contain only a fraction of the issues that could be developed, and solutions to specific and context-dependent problems today may provide little direction when we face an ostensibly similar problem in a different context tomorrow. As Schon (1971) has observed, "An idea that has come into good currency is no longer appropriate to its situation [and is almost never] pertinent to the problems on which one has to work" (p. 47).

*Misleading Assumption 2: Higher education scholars don't do policy-relevant research.* The suggestion that scholars don't do *any* policy-relevant research, don't do *enough* policy relevant research, or don't do enough policy-relevant research in the most *important* policy areas, is at best curious as two simple indicators will suggest. First, I analyzed (by title) 117 research and symposium panels listed in the 1995 and 1996 ASHE programs and found almost none that some important interest group would not find policy relevant. Second, over the past 26 years ASHE/ERIC has published ten volumes a year of its Higher Education Reports. I believe that most of these 260 essays are policy relevant and that the extensive higher education literature which they cite, by definition, must be policy relevant as well. A claim of inadequate attention to policy-relevant research would be unsupportable if *most*

ASHE presentations and *most* ASHE/ERIC Higher Education Reports are policy relevant. My analyses are informal at best, and I do not argue that they are reliable or valid. I would willingly recant upon the presentation of countervailing evidence drawn from some repository of recent higher education scholarship (for example, listings in ERIC for any period of a year or longer).

Perhaps a stronger argument is that policy scholars may not always focus on the problems as defined by the policy makers. However, the ways in which policy makers define a problem is often part of the problem. Scholars who respond to these problems as defined may therefore limit the alternatives considered and focus on immediate realities which may quickly change, thus making results obsolete and leaving the situation worse instead of better. Policy makers often frame their problems in politically charged ways; if scholars accept these frames as the basis for their own work "they probably will be, willingly or not, drawn into ideological battles based on those assumptions" (Griswold, 1999, p. 160).

*Misleading Assumption 3: Policy makers do not use higher education research.* Higher education research, like other forms of social research, may have a major effect on how policy makers think and on what they do "but not necessarily on discrete provisions nor in the linear sequence that social scientists expected" (Weiss, 1982, p. 620). Critics of social research appear to assume that the only social research that "counts" as useful is that which is produced by contemporary researchers and focused directly on a policy maker's contemporary problem. They give no attention to policy research that influences social problem solving more generally or to scholarship of the past that has informed the thinking of the present. Even when policy makers cannot identify a specific study they find useful in their work, they agree that "they had assimilated generalizations, concepts, and perspectives from the social sciences that inevitably colored their understandings and shaped their actions" (Weiss, 1991a, p. 186). This "knowledge creep" occurs as the accumulation of the findings of many studies eventually permeates the policy environment (Lindblom & Cohen, 1979).

Expectations that policy scholarship should have immediate and dramatic effects on policy makers are unrealistic. Complex social systems are resistant to most intended policy changes, and it takes time for knowledge to circulate. New programs or policies are often marginal "weak treatments." They provide only a small increment of knowledge over the huge body of ordinary knowledge possessed by policy makers, which it can modestly reshape but cannot displace (Lindblom & Cohen, 1979). Social research is only one of the many sources of knowledge that effective policy makers must consider; as higher education research knowledge is integrated into a policy maker's more general knowledge, "research information and ideas filter into their awareness, whether or not they label it as research as they absorb it" (Weiss, 1982, p. 635). The effects of research may be seen over an extended period of time "and after numbers of studies have yielded convergent results." Perceptions change as evidence accumulates, and policy decisions "often accrete through multiple disjointed stages [so that] looking for blockbuster impact from research studies represents a misreading of the nature of policy making" (Weiss, 1982, pp. 621, 633).

The concept of "usefulness" itself is problematic. Weiss has pointed out that there are at least three types—intrinsic usefulness, intellectual usefulness, and political usefulness (Tangri & Strasburg, 1979)—and that each type is based on different factors and logics. There is no agreement on exactly what constitutes "use" of research nor on the ways in which it might be assessed. In the absence of such agreement, "there is a serious question about whether it can be determined when use has occurred" (Shapiro, 1986, p. 176). Although it may be difficult to trace the specific effects of specific contemporary research on the development of specific contemporary policies, policy scholars provide policy makers with background data, conceptualizations, and ideas. We incorrectly assume that policy scholarship has no effect if it cannot be demonstrated that today's research is made part of the decision process for today's problems. This assumption confuses the effects of scholarship on specific educational decisions with the effect of scholarship on educational policy. While "individual studies typically affect no particular decisions, research traditions sometimes shape policy" (Cohen & Garet, 1975, p. 24) through their effect on policy climates.

*Misleading Assumption 4: Disseminating policy-relevant research would improve policy practice.* The belief that wider dissemination of research would lead to a greater impact on policy makers appears eminently reasonable. After all, as Knott and Wildavsky (1991) ask, "What could be wrong about transferring knowledge about public policy from those who have it to those who do not?" (p. 214). Their answer is that *plenty* could be wrong. The interests of the senders and receivers of information may not be identical. Policy makers do not suffer from a lack of information but rather from overload caused by too much information. Furthermore, simplification of information by the transmitter may reduce its usefulness for the receiver. "How likely is it that policy makers want knowledge but cannot get it? What evidence there is, at the very least, casts doubt on the proposition" (p. 217).

Even if *all* higher education research was explicitly policy relevant, it would be unlikely to have any greater influence on policy. This is because research rationality, like managerial rationality, is bounded; different scholars, with different ideologies, research paradigms, and disciplinary emphases frame questions in different ways and report contradictory findings (Hatch, 1998). Scholars whose disciplines have different research styles may reach different conclusions from the same data based on the *statistics* they traditionally employ (Cohen & Garet, 1975). "If even the very best empirical research can only provide an incomplete picture of reality, how can we expect researchers who view reality from different vantage points to reach sufficient agreement to take a collective stand?" (Donmoyer, 1997, p. 2). And if different researchers endorse different policy options and make antithetical recommendations (Donmoyer, 1996, p. 2), how should we expect policy makers to choose between them?

Trying to improve research methods is not a solution. Improving methodology does not reconcile differences in interpretation, and making issues "seem increasingly technical and arcane" (Cohen & Garet, 1975, p. 26) may move the arguments further away from the substantive problems themselves. Better research by scientific standards may be "no more authoritative by any political standard and often more mystifying by any reasonable public standard" (Cohen & Garet, 1975, p. 33). To further complicate the issue, differences in perceptions, beliefs and assumptions are characteristic of policy makers as well as policy scholars. The structures, histories, and cultures of the organizations and organizational systems within which policy makers function may also influence how they interpret the implications of research.

Differences in scholars' recommendations or policy makers' interpretations would not be reconciled by having scholars write in the direct and jargon-free style presumed to be preferred by policy makers. It would just make the disagreements more obvious, without giving policy makers the information required for them to understand *why* the recommendations were different. Cliff Notes versions of research findings will not help policy makers understand the nuances of difficult problems. If scholars use an op-ed style of communication, how can policy makers distinguish their products from those of political columnists? And what are the consequences when poor, less comprehensive, ideologically based research becomes influential, not because of its quality but because of its rhetoric?

## The Two Cultures

The intrinsic differences in the processes of educational policy making and the processes of educational policy scholarship lead to "two cultures" (Levin, 1991, p. 77) or two communities (Shapiro, 1986), of necessity separate and only loosely coupled. Policy scholars do by thinking; policy makers think by doing as they develop greater insights into system behavior, problems, and potential solutions through their activities. Scholars read, write, and try intellectually to optimize even as they deal in probabilities; policy makers talk, listen, and try in practical ways to satisfice even as they act to create certainty. Scholars value quiet contemplation, policy makers chaotic activity. Scholarship is static, policy making dynamic. Scholars weigh the evidence, are sensitive to nuance, consider things first on one hand and then on the other, and view their conclusions as tentative and conditional. Policy makers "have to decide. You have to come down on one hand or the other" (Resnick, 1997, p. 15). Scholars try to create knowledge that can be used in an indefinite future. Policy makers have "limited patience for academic critique. . . . They generally want to know 'what do I do . . . Monday'" (Donmoyer, 1996, p. 2).

Policy makers cannot be, and should not be, rational analysts who rely solely on intellectual arguments and data to make decisions. Policy scholars, in turn, also have nonrational agendas. By virtue of what they study, and how they study it, they are not merely engaged in a "disinterested attempt to improve policy, but rather a broad-aim social intervention designed to change the basis for decision making" (Cohen & Garet, 1975, p. 40). Policy research can thus be as political as policy making. But at the same time, policy makers can be as scientific as policy scholars. As Chandler observed, both good scholars and effective policy makers base their judgments in part on scientific observation defined as "deliberate search, carried out with care and forethought, as contrasted with the casual and largely passive perceptions of everyday life. It is this deliberateness and control of the process of observation that is distinctive of science" (Lindblom & Cohen, 1979, pp. 15–16). But while both scholars and policy makers may be scientific observers, their perspectives are much different. The soft data which policy makers consider relevant (Mintzberg, 1994) may be considered by scholars as fragmentary, anecdotal, impressionistic, and therefore invalid. The valid data towards which policy scholars strive may lead to findings that policy makers find irrelevant. Each has different ways of knowing. The scholars may believe that their more structured way of considering problems could improve policy making, but there are "reasons to doubt that relevance and methodological sophistication lead in any regular or consistent way to knowledge which is more relevant for policy purposes" (Cohen & Garet, 1975, p. 26).

The differences between policy makers and policy scholars are in many ways similar to those of managers and planners, as can be seen by substituting the roles in Mintzberg's (1994) analysis:

> The nature of [policy making] favors action over reflection, the short run over the long run, soft data over hard, the oral over the written, getting information rapidly over getting it right. . . . The result of all of this is that the [policy maker] understands the need to adapt to what does go on, while the [policy scholar] feels the need to analyze what should go on. The [policy maker] tends to chase opportunities when not being chased by crises, produces plans that exist only vaguely in his or her head, and exhibits an "occupational hazard" to be superficial in his or her work. . . . But the [policy scholar] promotes a process that seems overly simplified and sterile when compared to the complexities of strategy making. (p. 324)

Policy scholars are from Venus; policy makers are from Mars. Policy scholars don't know *better* than policy makers; they just know *different* than policy makers. Policy scholars may reject propositions that deny the ground assumptions of their field; policy makers may reject propositions that deny their common sense. What is unusual and interesting to one group may be considered common and obvious to the other. The strength of scholars is that they are detached from the problems they study; they know that they must not be distracted by irrelevant details if they are to develop basic principles. The strength of policy makers is that they are completely absorbed by the problems with which they deal; they know that only those embedded in the daily chaos of seemingly irrelevant details can make sound judgments in a dynamic environment.

Policy makers who act contrary to the recommendations of policy scholars may not be wrong. Practitioners and researchers interpret the world using different perspectives and logics, and policy scholars should recognize that policy makers may often know things that they do not. When scholars bemoan policy behavior that appears uninformed or irrational, they may be ignoring the possibility that policy behavior may be more sensible than policy precepts (March, 1984). Schon and Rein (1994) have suggested that policy scholars

> should seek first to understand policy practice . . . to describe and explain the kinds of inquiry in which policy makers engage. . . . If they disregard what practitioners already know or are already trying to discover, they are unlikely either to grasp what is really going on or to succeed in getting practitioners to listen to them. (p. 193)

Studying sensible action may be more useful for policy scholars than understanding research is for policy makers.

## Conclusions

Policy scholarship and policy making are, and ought to be, two distinct knowledge-producing activities whose insights may inform each other but are not dependent on each other. The notion that "the value of applied research lies in its ability to clarify policy goals and provide objective evidence concerning the appropriateness of alternative means for achieving chosen ends" is intuitively appealing but, as Cohen and Garet have pointed out (1975, p. 37), incorrect. Policy scholarship is more likely to lead to intensified conflict in the short term, even if it may transform the nature of the issues over the long term by setting the value and factual constraints within which policy makers construct plausible programs.

One reason that policy scholarship appears to have little influence on policy makers is our belief in a "'simple' model for research impact which has it that social research generates facts . . . and that such facts enable users to make unfettered decisions which will improve social life" (Biddle & Anderson, 1991, p. 6). This naive view posits policy scholarship as an independent variable and policy making as a dependent variable. A more realistic view is to consider them both as independent, collateral variables. "Like policy, social science research responds to the currents of thought, the fads and fancies of the period. Social science and policy interact, influencing each other and being influenced by the larger fashions of social thought" (Weiss, 1991b, p. 180). In the final analysis, policy scholarship is only one of the many forces that do, and should, affect policy decisions. "Information and analysis provide only one route because . . . a great deal of the world's problem solving is and ought to be accomplished through various forms of social interaction that substitute action for thought, understanding or analysis"; even when analysis is the process of choice, it can be provided through means other than professional social inquiry, such as the use of ordinary knowledge and casual analysis (Lindblom & Cohen, 1979, p. 10).

What is important is not that individual studies affect individual decisions, but that scholarly work over time influences the systems of knowledge and belief that give meaning to policy. The lengthy period of time needed before new ideas and concepts become generally accepted and influential means that today's problems are being influenced by *yesterday's* ideas. Today's ideas, after they have gone through a process of filtering and questioning, will in turn influence policy makers tomorrow. This suggests to faculty the critical importance of how and what we teach, because the values and concepts through which students are socialized today are likely to influence the beliefs of the policy makers of the future.

I believe that there is little scholars can do to make higher education policy scholarship more immediately useful to policy makers. Many proposals to bridge the presumed scholarship-policy gap appear plausible but are not supported either by theory or research evidence. For example, would scholarship offer more effective ideas for policy makers if it emphasized generalized rather than specialized knowledge, used qualitative research methods such as symbolic interactionism and hermeneutics (Conrad, 1989), moved toward dense, multifaceted interpretations of what is going on in higher education (Keller, 1985), or developed integrated research agendas? (Zemsky & Tierney, 1986). These are sensible proposals for scholars, but that is not what policy makers say they want or need. When the critics complain that we give too much attention to little questions, should we be studying bigger questions? There is no agreement on what the big questions are and no money to study them. Proposals for integrated research agendas cannot be implemented as stated and would not have the imagined influence on policy even if they could be accomplished. Is a "clear statement of why higher education does the kind of research it does, what the current research approach hopes to achieve, and how researchers expect to attain their goals" (Keller, 1986, p. 130) the answer? How can there be a statement of the purposes of higher education research clearer than a statement of the purposes of higher education itself? Should we try to reach consensus on scholarly findings to negate the criticism that we aren't heeded because we contradict each other and disagree on everything? (Resnick, 1997). To do so would deny the essential nature of scholarship.

So we are left with a series of paradoxes and conundrums, based on immutable truths that I immodestly refer to as Birnbaum's Laws of Policy Scholarship (BLOPS).

> BLOP 1. Any scholarly product of any kind may be used to inform some policy decision at some time.

> Corollary: No scholarly product of any kind can be assured of influencing any specific policy decision at any specific time.

> BLOP 2. For every scholarly product that suggests one course of policy action, there will be another scholarly product that suggests the opposite course of action.

> Corollary: The effects of scholarly study on any policy decision cannot be predicted.

BLOP 3. The specific variables that will be important to the policy maker at the time of a policy decision cannot be known before the decision is actually made.

Corollary: Even if policy makers were able to articulate the exact nature of the research they would find useful at time X, it is unlikely that the same information will be found useful at time X+1.

BLOP 4. By the time policy scholars respond to the interests of policy makers, the nature of the policy problem is likely to have changed.

Corollary: Since policy takes place in a policy environment which is constantly changing, previous research on a seemingly identical topic will be of limited relevance.

BLOP 5. Every policy-relevant scholarly product will be found by the policy maker to be lacking at least one key variable, thus compromising its usefulness.

Corollary: Policy makers will always find the procedures, methods and variables of studies whose findings are consistent with their own ideologies to be inherently more reasonable and rational than those whose findings are inconsistent with their ideologies.

BLOP 6: In the *absence* of scholarly analysis of relevant data, the effects of a proposed policy cannot be reliably predicted.

Corollary: In the *presence* of scholarly analysis of relevant data, the effects of a proposed policy cannot be reliably predicted.

## A Modest Proposal

We cannot define a higher education agenda for policy scholarship because we cannot know what knowledge will be policy relevant in the future. Instead, scholarship should continue to be driven by personal and professional interests developed in the intellectual marketplace of ideas rather than in a planned marketplace of current problems. I place my faith in what Veblen called the "idle curiosity" of scholars, because I know that their curiosity is usually driven by their desire to make sense out of things that do matter—or should matter—in the real world. Their individual agendas may be small, but this "cumulative piling up of many small pieces of data on many facets of higher education" later permits others confidently to make sweeping statements such as "higher education, taken as a whole, is enormously effective" and provide the evidence to support it (Bowen, 1977, p. 14). Even though small studies do not resolve the debate, they help to frame it. And *having* a debate informed by (although not resolved by) data is a value which is an educational good in itself.

Perhaps a change of metaphors would be useful. To replace the linear notion of trees and fruit, we might consider as metaphors for higher education policy scholarship the concepts of enlightenment and discourse. Weiss's concept of "enlightenment" (1982, p. 623) implies that "research modifies the definitions of problems that policy makers address, how they think about them, which options they discard and which they pursue, and how they conceptualize their purposes." Cohen and Garet's notion of "discourse" (1975, p. 42) recognizes that both policy scholars and policy makers are concerned with defining social reality. Policy scholars try to "interpret and structure the social world by establishing languages and symbolic universes used in comprehending and carrying on social life." Policy makers influence such languages and symbols through their actions. Language creates reality. Continuous discourse between those who do by thinking and those who think by doing cannot and should not lead them to interpret reality in the same way, but may help them to understand and appreciate each other's language.

The notions of enlightenment and discourse recognize that policy scholarship may be only loosely connected to policy making. "For those who had hoped for a greater direct influence on policy, it is a limited victory" (Weiss, 1982, p. 623). Limited, perhaps, but a worthwhile trade-off of short-term and ephemeral influence on specific decisions for long-term and pervasive influence on the policy climate in which future problems are considered.

*Robert Birnbaum* is Professor of Higher Education at the University of Maryland, College Park. This article is revised from a paper originally presented at the Annual Conference of the Association for the Study of Higher Education, 5–8 November 1998, Miami, Florida.

# References

Anderson, D. S., & Biddle, B. J. (Eds.). (1991). *Knowledge for policy: Improving education through research*. London, ENG: Falmer Press.

ASHE Research and Policy Group Meeting. (1996, 2 November). Minutes. Memphis, TN.

Biddle, B. J., & Anderson, D. S. (1991). Social research and educational change. In Anderson & Biddle, pp. 1–20.

Birnbaum, R., & Shushok, F. J. (1998, 5–8 November). *The crisis in higher education*. Paper presented at the Annual Meeting of the Association for the Study of Higher Education. Miami, Florida.

Bowen, H. R. (1977). *Investment in learning: The individual and social value of American higher education*. San Francisco: Jossey-Bass.

Cohen, D. K., & Garet, M. S. (1975, February). Reforming educational policy with applied social research. *Harvard Educational Review, 45*(1), 17–43.

Conrad, C. F. (1989, Spring). Meditations on the ideology of inquiry in higher education: Exposition, critique, and conjecture. *The Review of Higher Education, 12*(3), 199–220.

Donmoyer, R. (1996, November). This issue: Talking "truth" to power. *Educational Researcher, 25*(8), 2, 9.

Donmoyer, R. (1997, April). Introduction: Revisiting the "talking truth to power" problem. *Educational Researcher, 26*(3), 2.

El-Khawas, E. (1995, Winter). Searching for campus trends: Ambiguities in the study of higher education. *The Review of Higher Education, 19*(2), 111–120.

Griswold, C. P. (1999, Winter). Political turbulence and policy research: The National Commission on Student Financial Assistance. *The Review of Higher Education, 22*(2), 143–164.

Hatch, T. (1998, Spring). The differences in theory that matter in the practice of school improvement. *American Educational Research Journal, 35*(1), 3–31.

Keller, G. (1985, January/February). Trees without fruit: The problem with research about higher education. *Change*, pp. 7–10.

Keller, G. (1986, Winter). Free at last? Breaking the chains that bind educational research. *The Review of Higher Education, 10*(2), 129–134.

Knott, J., & Wildavsky, A. (1991). If dissemination is the solution, what's the problem? In Anderson & Biddle, pp. 214–224.

Komives, S. R., Endress, W. L. K., Kiely, L. J., & LaVoy, S. A. (1997, 27 June). *Toward a common agenda: Themes in policy initiatives among higher education associations 1997*. College Park: University of Maryland.

Layzell, D. T. (1990, 24 October). Most research on higher education is stale, irrelevant, and of little use to policy makers. *Chronicle of Higher Education, 37*(8), B1, B3.

Levin, H. M. (1991). Why isn't educational research more useful? In Anderson & Biddle, pp. 70–78.

Lindblom, C. E., & Cohen, D. K. (1979). *Usable knowledge: Social science and social problem solving*. New Haven, CT: Yale University Press.

March, J. G. (1984). How we talk and how we act: Administrative theory and administrative life. In T. J. Sergiovanni & J. E. Corbally (Eds.), *Leadership and organizational culture: New perspectives on administrative theory and practice* (pp. 18–35). Urbana: University of Illinois Press.

Mintzberg, H. (1994). *The rise and fall of strategic planning: Reconceiving roles for planning, plans, planners*. New York: Free Press.

Resnick, L. B. (1997, June/July). Competing visions for enhancing the impact of educational research. *Educational Researcher, 26*(5), 12, 15–16.

Schon, D. A. (1971, February). Implementing programs of social and technological change. *Technology Review*, pp. 47–51.

Schon, D. A., & Rein, M. (1994). *Frame reflection: Toward the resolution of intractable policy controversies*. New York: Basic Books.

Shapiro, J. Z. (1986). Evaluation research and educational decision-making: A review of the literature. In J. C. Smart (Ed.), *Higher Education Handbook of Theory and Research* (Vol. 2, pp. 163–206). New York: Agathon Press.

Tangri, S. S., & Strasburg, G. L. (1979, Summer). Can research on women be more effective in shaping policy? *Psychology of Women Quarterly, 3*(4), 321–341.

*Ten public policy issues for higher education in 1994*. (1994). Washington, D.C.: Association of Governing Boards.

*Ten public policy issues for higher education in 1995*. (1995). Washington, D.C.: Association of Governing Boards.

*Ten public policy issues for higher education in 1996*. (1996). Washington, D.C.: Association of Governing Boards.

*Ten public policy issues for higher education in 1997 and 1998*. (1997). Washington, D.C.: Association of Governing Boards.

Terenzini, P. T. (1996, Fall). Rediscovering roots: Public policy and higher education research. *The Review of Higher Education, 20*(1), 5–13.

Weiss, C. H. (1982). Policy research in the context of diffuse decision making. *Journal of Higher Education, 53*(6), 619–639.

Weiss, C. H. (1991a). Knowledge creep and decision accretion. In Anderson & Biddle, pp. 183–192.

Weiss, C. H. (1991b). The many meanings of research utilization. In Anderson & Biddle, pp. 173–182.

Zemsky, R., & Tierney, M. (1986, Winter). Toward an integrated research agenda. *The Review of Higher Education, 10*(2), 165–182.

# CHAPTER 3:
# POLICY INQUIRY/ANALYSIS

# The Study of Public Policy

## JAMES E. ANDERSON

As a consequence of American military intervention in Southeast Asia during the 1960s and early 1970s, more than 45,000 American soldiers lost their lives, many thousands more were wounded, and tens of billions of dollars were expended on the Indochina war effort. Protests and demonstrations against the war occurred, many young men went to prison or to Canada to avoid being drafted, and cynicism and distrust toward government increased. It is really difficult to estimate the impact that American Southeast Asia policy has had on the United States, let alone Southeast Asia and the rest of the world.

As a consequence of the Nixon Administration's policies following the development of the energy crisis, gasoline prices rose sharply and many motorists spent hours waiting in lines to purchase fuel. Whether rationing and price controls would have produced more satisfactory results is certainly open to argument. The point is, however, that what happened was not "natural," was not simply a matter of events following their normal course; public policy gave shape to the events that occurred.

In our daily lives and in our academic activities, such as political science courses, we make many references to public policy. The term may be used quite broadly, as in "American foreign policy," "Soviet economic policy," or "agricultural policy in Western Europe." It may also be employed with more specific referents, as when we speak of the national government's policy toward conglomerate mergers, the state policy of Texas on farm-to-market roads, or the policy of New York City on snow removal. Although public policy may seem rather abstract or we may think of it as something that "happens" to someone else, this is clearly not the case, as the preceding two examples should indicate. All of us are profoundly affected by a myriad of public policies in our daily lives.

Generally, the term "policy" is used to designate the behavior of some actor (e.g., an official, a group, a government agency) or set of actors in a given area of activity. Such usage may be adequate for ordinary speech, but, since the concern in this book is with the systematic analysis of public policy and its formation, we need a more precise definition, or concept, of public policy in order to communicate more effectively with one another.

## What Is Public Policy?

The literature of political science is full of definitions of public policy. Sooner or later, it seems, almost everyone gives in to the urge to define public policy and does so with greater or lesser success in the eyes of his critics. A few such definitions will be noted and their utility for analysis remarked upon. To be really useful and to facilitate communication, an operational definition (or concept, as I am using the two words somewhat interchangeably) should indicate the essential characteristics of the concept under discussion.

One definition of public policy holds that, "broadly defined," it is "the relationship of a government unit to its environment."[1] Such a definition is so broad as to leave most students uncertain of its meaning; it could encompass almost anything. Another definition states that "public policy is whatever governments choose to do or not to do."[2] There is a rough accuracy to this definition, but it does not adequately recognize that there may be a divergence between what governments decide to do and what they actually do. Moreover, it could be taken to include such actions as personnel appointments or grants of licenses, which are usually not thought of as policy matters. Richard Rose has suggested that policy be considered "a long series of more-or-less related activities" and their consequences for those concerned rather than as a discrete decision.[3] Though somewhat ambiguous, Rose's definition nonetheless embodies the useful notion that policy is a course or pattern of activity and not simply a decision to do something. Finally, let us note Carl Friedrich's definition. He regards policy as

> ... a proposed course of action of a person, group, or government within a given environment providing obstacles and opportunities which the policy was proposed to utilize and overcome in an effort to reach a goal or realize an objective or a purpose.[4]

To the notion of policy as a course of action, Friedrich adds the requirement that policy is directed toward the accomplishment of some purpose or goal. Although the purpose or goal of government actions may not always be easy to discern, the idea that policy involves purposive behavior seems a necessary part of a policy definition. Policy, however, should designate what is actually done rather than what is proposed in the way of action on some matter.

Taking into account the problems raised by these definitions, we offer the following as a useful concept of policy: *A purposive course of action followed by an actor or set of actors in dealing with a problem or matter of concern.* This concept of policy focuses attention on what is actually done as against what is proposed or intended, and it differentiates a policy from a decision, which is a choice among competing alternatives.

*Public policies* are those policies developed by governmental bodies and officials. (Nongovernmental actors and factors may, of course, influence policy development.) The special characteristics of public policies stem from the fact that they are formulated by what David Easton has called the "authorities" in a political system, namely, "elders, paramount chiefs, executives, legislators, judges, administrators, councilors, monarchs, and the like." These are, he says, the persons who "engage in the daily affairs of a political system," are "recognized by most members of the system as having responsibility for these matters," and take actions that are "accepted as binding most of the time by most of the members so long as they act within the limits of their roles."[5]

At this point it would be well to spell out some of the implications of our concept of public policy. First of all, purposive or goal-oriented action rather than random or chance behavior is our concern. Public policies in modern political systems are not, by and large, things that just happen. Second, policy consists of courses or patterns of action by governmental officials rather than their separate discrete decisions. For example, policy involves not only the decision to enact a law on some topic but also subsequent decisions relating to its implementation and enforcement. Third, policy is what governments actually do in regulating trade, controlling inflation, or promoting public housing, not what they intend to do or say they are going to do. If a legislature enacts a law requiring employers to pay no less than the stated minimum wage but nothing is done to enforce the law, and consequently no change occurs in economic behavior, then it is fair to contend that public policy in this instance is really one of nonregulation of wages. It seems nonsensical to regard an intention as policy without regard for what subsequently happens. Fourth, public policy may be either positive or negative in form. Positively, it may involve some form of government action to affect a particular problem; negatively, it involves a decision by government officials not to take action, to do nothing, on some matter on which governmental involvement is sought. Governments, in other words, can follow a policy of *laissez faire*, or hands off, either generally or in particular areas. Such inaction may have major consequences for a society or some of its groups. Lastly, public policy, at least in its positive form, is based on law and is authoritative. Members of a society accept as legitimate that taxes must be paid, import controls obeyed, and antitrust laws complied with unless one wants to run the risk of fines, jail sentences, or other legally imposed sanctions or disabilities. Public policy thus has an authoritative, potentially legally coercive quality that the policies of private organizations do not have.

The nature of public policy as a course of action can be better or more fully understood if it is broken down into a number of categories, these being policy demands, decisions, statements, outputs, and outcomes. In practice they will not necessarily occur in neat sequential order.

*Policy demands* are those demands or claims made upon public officials by other actors, private or official, in the political system for action or inaction on some perceived problem. Such demands may range from a general insistence that government ought to "do something" to a proposal for specific action on the matter. For instance, prior to the passage of the Landrum-Griffin Act of 1959 (formerly, the Labor-Management Reporting and Disclosure Act), some groups merely voiced a general desire for curbs on the power of labor unions; others called for the prohibition of particular union practices they found objectionable.[6] The demands that help give rise to public policy, and which it is designed to satisfy, at least in part, are important items for consideration in the study of public policy formation.

*Policy decisions* are decisions made by public officials that authorize or give direction and content to public policy actions. Included are decisions to enact statutes, issue executive orders or edicts, promulgate administrative rules, or make important judicial interpretations of laws. Thus, the decision by Congress to enact the Sherman Antitrust Act in 1890 was a policy decision; so was the ruling of the Supreme Court in 1911 that the Act prohibited only unreasonable restraints of trade rather than all restraints of trade. Each was of major importance in shaping that course of action called antitrust policy. Such decisions may be contrasted with the large numbers of relatively routine decisions made by officials in the day-to-day application of public policy. The Veterans Administration makes hundreds of thousands of decisions every year on veterans' benefits; most, however, fall within the bounds of settled policy.

*Policy statements* are the formal expressions or articulations of public policy. Included are legislative statutes, executive orders and decrees, administrative rules and regulations, and court opinions, as well as statements and speeches by public officials indicating the intentions and goals of government and what will be done to realize them. Policy statements are sometimes ambiguous. Witness the conflicts that arise over the meaning of statutory provisions or judicial holdings, or the time and effort expended analyzing and trying to divine the meaning of policy statements made by national political leaders such as the President of the United States or France or the rulers of the Soviet Union. Also, different levels, branches, or units of government may issue conflicting policy statements, as on environmental pollution controls or energy usage.

*Policy outputs* are the "tangible manifestations" of public policies, the things actually done in pursuance of policy decisions and statements. Simply stated, policy outputs are what a government does, as distinguished from what it says it is going to do. Here our attention is focused on such matters as taxes collected, highways built, welfare benefits paid, restraints of trade eliminated, ports blockaded, or foreign-aid projects undertaken. An examination of policy outputs may indicate that policy in actuality is somewhat or greatly different from what policy statements indicate it should be. Many laws on the statute books, such as local "blue laws" regulating work and amusements on Sundays, go entirely unenforced and thus policy is clearly not what the law states in such instances.

*Policy outcomes* are the consequences for society, intended or unintended, that flow from action or inaction by government. Welfare policies in the United States can be used to illustrate this concept. It is fairly easy to measure welfare policy outputs—amount of benefits paid, average level of benefits, number of people aided, and the like. But what are the outcomes (or consequences) of these actions? Do they increase personal security and contentment? Do they reduce individual initiative? In the case of aid to families with dependent children (AFDC), do they have the effect of encouraging promiscuity and illegitimacy, as some allege? Questions such as these may be quite difficult to answer, but they direct our attention to the impact of public policies, an item that should be of central concern to us as policy analysts. Among other things, we want to know whether policies accomplish what they are intended to accomplish. This is the task of policy evaluation that will be discussed in a later chapter.

## Why Study Public Policy?

Political scientists, in their teaching and research, have customarily been most concerned with political processes, such as the legislative or electoral process, or with elements of the political system, such as interest groups or public opinion. This is not to say, however, that political scientists have been unconcerned with policy. Foreign policy and policy relating to civil rights and liberties have attracted much attention. So has what Robert Salisbury calls constitutional policy, that is, "decisional rules by which subsequent policy actions are to be determined."[7] Illustrative of the procedural and structural "givens" that make up constitutional policy are legislative apportionment, the use of the city-manager form of government, and federalism. Each helps to shape decisions or substantive policy. Also, some political scientists with a normative bent manifest concern with what governments *should* do, with "proper" or "correct" public policy. Their value-oriented approach, however, has placed them outside the mainstream of political science in recent decades because political science as a "science" is supposed to be value-free. We will return to this particular matter a little later on.

Currently, political scientists are giving increased attention to the study of public policy—to the description, analysis, and explanation of the causes and effects of governmental activity. As Thomas Dye aptly states:

> This involves a description of the content of public policy; an assessment of the impact of environmental forces on the content of public policy; an analysis of the effect of various institutional arrangements and political processes on public policy; an inquiry into the consequences of various public policies for the political system; and an evaluation of the impact of public policies on society, both in terms of expected and unexpected consequences.

One is thus directed to seek answers to such questions as: What is the actual content of antitrust policy? What effects do urbanization and industrialization have on welfare policies? How does the organization of Congress help shape agricultural policy? Do elections affect the direction of public policies? Do welfare programs contribute to political quiescence or stability? Who is benefited and who is not by current tax policies or urban renewal programs?[8]

This leads us to the question posed in the heading of this section: Why study public policy? Or to put it another way: Why engage in policy analysis? It has been suggested that policy can be studied for scientific, professional, or political reasons.[9]

*Scientific Reasons.* Public policy can be studied in order to gain greater knowledge about its origins, the processes by which it is developed, and its consequences for society. This, in turn, will increase our understanding of the political system and society generally. Policy may be regarded as either a dependent or an independent variable for purposes of this kind of analysis. When it is viewed as a *dependent variable,* our attention is placed on the political and environmental factors that help determine the content of policy. For example, how is policy affected by the distribution of power among pressure groups and governmental agencies? How do urbanization and national income help shape the content of policy? If public policy is viewed as an *independent variable,* our focus shifts to the impact of policy on the political system and environment, How does policy affect support for the political system or future policy choices? What effect does policy have on social well-being?

*Professional Reasons.* Don K. Price makes a distinction between the "Scientific estate," which seeks only to discover knowledge, and the "professional estate," which strives to apply scientific knowledge to the solution of practical social problems.[10] We will not concern ourselves here with the issue of whether political scientists should help prescribe the goals of public policy. Although by no means all political scientists would agree, many argue that political scientists as political scientists have no particular skills beyond those of laymen for this endeavor. Whatever the answer here may be, it is quite correct to contend that if we know something about the factors that help shape public policy, or the consequences of given policies, then we are in position to say something useful concerning how individuals, groups, or governments can act to attain their policy goals. Such advice can be directed toward indicating either what policies can be used to achieve particular goals or what political and environmental factors are conducive to the development of a given policy. It puts us in the position of saying, for example, *if* you want to prevent economic monopoly, *then* you should do such and such. Questions of this sort are factual in nature and are open to, indeed require, scientific study. Certainly factual knowledge is a prerequisite for prescribing on, and dealing with, the problems of society.

*Political Reasons.* As was noted above, at least some political scientists do not believe that political scientists should refrain from helping to prescribe policy goals. Rather, they say that the study of public policy should be directed toward ensuring that governments adopt appropriate policies to attain the "right" goals. They reject the notion that policy analysts should strive to be value-free, contending that political science cannot be silent or impotent on current political and social problems. They want to improve the quality of public policy in ways they deem desirable, notwithstanding that substantial disagreement exists in society over what constitute "correct" policies or the "right" goals of policy. The efforts of these political scientists usually generate both heat and light in some proportion.

We should now explicitly distinguish between *policy analysis* and *policy advocacy*. Policy analysis is concerned with the examination and description of the causes and consequences of public policy. We can analyze the formation, content, and impact of particular policies, such as on civil rights or international trade, without either approving or disapproving of them. *Policy advocacy*, on the other hand, is concerned especially with what governments *should* do, with the promotion of particular policies through discussion, persuasion, and political activism. The candidate for public office serves as a good prototype of the policy advocate. Richard Nixon and George McGovern as Presidential candidates in 1972 each had his notions of what the government should do in foreign and domestic policy. In this book the focus will be on policy analysis.

To conclude this discussion we shall again call on Professor Dye, who states that policy analysis encompasses three basic considerations:

1. A primary concern with explanation rather than prescription.
2. A rigorous search for the causes and consequences of public policies [through] the use of scientific standards of inference.
3. An effort to develop and test general propositions about the causes and consequences of public policy and to accumulate reliable research findings of general significance. The object is to develop general theories about public policy which are reliable and which apply to different governmental agencies and different policy areas.[11]

So conceived, policy analysis can be both scientific and "relevant" to current political and social problems. Analysts with normative orientations do not have a corner on relevance.

## Theories of Decision Making

Political and social scientists have developed many models, theories, approaches, concepts, and schemes for the analysis of policymaking and its component, decision making. Indeed, political scientists have often shown much more facility and verve for theorizing about public policy than for actually studying policy. Nonetheless, concepts and models are necessary and useful to guide policy analysis, as they help clarify and direct our inquiry on policymaking, facilitate communication, and suggest possible explanations for policy actions. Clearly, when we set out to study policy we need some guidelines, some criteria of relevance, to focus our efforts and to prevent aimless meandering through the fields of political data. What we find depends partly upon what we are looking for; policy concepts and theories give direction to our inquiry.

In this and the subsequent section, we will examine a number of concepts and models for the study of public policy, without trying to determine which is "best." Before doing this we need to distinguish between decision making and policymaking, something that is not always done with clarity, if at all, by students of public policy. Decision making involves the choice of an alternative from among a series of competing alternatives. Theories of decision making are concerned with how such choices are made. A policy, to recall our earlier definition, is "a purposive course of action followed by an actor or set of actors in dealing with a problem or matter of concern." Policymaking typically involves a pattern of action, extending over time and involving many decisions, some routine and some not so routine. Rarely will a policy be synonymous with a single decision. To use a mundane example: A person is not accurate in saying it is his policy to bathe on Saturday night when, in fact, he bathes only with great infrequency, however elegant the decision-making process that results in his doing so on a particular Saturday. It is the course of action that defines policy, not the isolated event, and in this example the policy involved is essentially one of not bathing.

Three theories of decision making that focus on the steps or activities involved in making a decision will be discussed here. To the extent that they describe how decisions are made by individuals and groups, they are empirical. Viewed as statements of how decisions should be made, they are normative. It is not always easy to separate these two qualities in decision theories, as one will discover.

## The Rational-Comprehensive Theory

Perhaps the best-known theory of decision making, and also perhaps the most widely accepted, is the rational-comprehensive theory. It usually includes the following elements:

1.  The decision maker is confronted with a given problem that can be separated from other problems or at least considered meaningfully in comparison with them.
2.  The goals, values, or objectives that guide the decision maker are clarified and ranked according to their importance.
3.  The various alternatives for dealing with the problem are examined.
4.  The consequences (costs and benefits) that would follow from the selection of each alternative are investigated.
5.  Each alternative, and its attendant consequences, can be compared with the other alternatives.
6.  The decision maker will choose that alternative, and its consequences, that maximizes the attainment of his goals, values, or objectives.

The result of this process is a rational decision, that is, one that most effectively achieves a given end.

The rational-comprehensive theory has had substantial criticism directed at it. Charles Lindblom contends that decision makers are not faced with concrete, clearly defined problems. Rather, they have first of all to identify and formulate the problems on which they make decisions. For example, when prices are rising rapidly and people are saying "we must do something about the problem of inflation," what is the problem? Excessive demand? Inadequate production of goods and services? Administered prices by powerful corporations and unions? Inflationary psychology? Some combination of these? One does not, willy-nilly, attack inflation but the causes of inflation, and these may be difficult to determine. Defining the problem is, in short, often a major problem for the decision maker.

A second criticism holds that rational-comprehensive theory is unrealistic in the demands it makes on the decision maker. It assumes that he will have enough information on the alternatives for dealing with a problem, that he will be able to predict their consequences with some accuracy, and that he will be capable of making correct cost-benefit comparisons of the alternatives. A moment's reflection on the informational and intellectual resources needed for acting rationally on the problem of inflation posed above should indicate the barriers to rational action implied in these assumptions—lack of time, difficulty in collecting information and predicting the future, complexity of calculations. Even use of that modern miracle, the computer, cannot fully alleviate these problems.

The value aspect of the rational theory also receives some knocks. Thus it is said that the public decision maker is usually confronted with a situation in which value conflict rather than agreement exists, and the conflicting values do not permit comparison or weighing. Moreover, the decision maker might confuse his personal values with those of the public. And, finally, the rationalistic assumption that facts and values can be readily separated does not hold up in practice. Note how facts and values become intermingled in the following situation:

> Public controversy . . . has surrounded the proposal to construct a branch of the Cook County Hospital on the South Side in or near the Negro area. Several questions of policy are involved in

the matter but the ones which have caused one of the few public debates of an issue in the Negro community concern whether, or to what extent, building such a branch would result in an all-Negro or "Jim Crow" hospital and whether such a hospital is desirable as a means of providing added medical facilities for Negro patients. Involved are both an issue of *fact* (whether the hospital would be segregated, intentionally or unintentionally, as a result of the character of the neighborhood in which it would be located) and an issue of *value* (whether even an all-Negro hospital would be preferable to no hospital at all in the area). In reality, however, the factions have aligned themselves in such a manner that the fact issue and the value issue have been collapsed into the single issue of whether to build or not to build. Those in favor of the proposal will argue that the facts do not bear out the charge of "Jim Crowism"—"the proposed site . . . is not considered to be placed in a segregated area for the exclusive use of one racial or minority group"; or "no responsible officials would try to develop a new hospital to further segregation"; or "establishing a branch hospital for the . . . more adequate care of the indigent patient load . . . does not represent Jim Crowism." At the same time these proponents argue that, whatever the facts, the factual issue is secondary to the overriding consideration that "there is a here-and-now need for more hospital beds. . . . Integration may be the long-run goal, but in the short-run we need more facilities."[12]

Finally, there is the problem of "sunk costs." Previous decisions and commitments, investments in existing policies and programs, may foreclose many alternatives from consideration on either a short-run or a long-run basis. A decision to institute a system of socialized medicine represents a commitment to a particular mode of medical care that is not easily reversed or significantly altered in the future. An airport, once constructed, cannot be easily moved to the other side of town.

## The Incremental Theory

The incremental theory of decision making, or, more simply, incrementalism, is presented as a decision theory that avoids many of the problems of the rational-comprehensive theory and, at the same time, is more descriptive of the way in which public officials actually make decisions.[13] Incrementalism can be summarized in the following manner:

1. The selection of goals or objectives and the empirical analysis of the action needed to attain them are closely intertwined with, rather than distinct from, one another.
2. The decision maker considers only some of the alternatives for dealing with a problem, and these will differ only incrementally (i.e., marginally) from existing policies.
3. For each alternative only a limited number of "important" consequences are evaluated.
4. The problem confronting the decision maker is continually redefined. Incrementalism allows for countless ends-means and means-ends adjustments that have the effect of making the problem more manageable.
5. There is no single decision or "right" solution for a problem. The test of a good decision is that various analysts find themselves directly agreeing on it, without agreeing that the decision is the most appropriate means to an agreed objective.
6. Incremental decision making is essentially remedial and is geared more to the amelioration of present, concrete social imperfections than to the promotion of future social goals.[14]

Lindblom contends that incrementalism represents the typical decision-making process in pluralist societies such as the United States. Decisions and policies are the product of "give and take" and mutual consent among numerous participants ("partisans") in the decision process. Incrementalism is politically expedient because it is easier to reach agreement when the matters in dispute among various groups are only modifications of existing programs rather than policy issues of great magnitude or an "all or nothing" character. Since decision makers operate under conditions of uncertainty with regard to the future consequences of their actions, incremental decisions reduce the risks and costs of uncertainty. Incrementalism is also realistic because it recognizes that decision makers lack the time, intelligence, and other resources needed to engage in comprehensive analysis of all alternative solutions to existing problems. Moreover, people are essentially pragmatic, seeking not always the single best way to deal with a problem but, more modestly, "something that will work." Incrementalism, in short, yields limited, practicable, acceptable decisions.

## Mixed-Scanning

Sociologist Amatai Etzioni agrees with the criticism of the rational theory but also suggests there are some shortcomings in the incremental theory of decision making.[15] For instance, decisions made by incrementalists would reflect the interests of the most powerful and organized interests in society, while the interests of the underprivileged and politically unorganized would be neglected. Moreover, by focusing on the short-run and seeking only limited variations in current policies, incrementalism would neglect basic social innovation. Great or fundamental decisions, such as declaration of war, do not come within the ambit of incrementalism. Although limited in number, fundamental decisions are highly significant and often provide the context for numerous incremental decisions.

Etzioni presents mixed-scanning as an approach to decision making, which takes into account both fundamental and incremental decisions and provides for "high-order, fundamental policy-making processes which set basic directions and . . . incremental processes which prepare for fundamental decisions and work them out after they have been reached." He provides the following illustration of mixed-scanning:

> Assume we are about to set up a worldwide weather observation system using weather satellites. The rationalistic approach would seek an exhaustive survey of weather conditions by using cameras capable of detailed observations and by scheduling reviews of the entire sky is often as possible. This would yield an avalanche of details, costly to analyze and likely to overwhelm our action capacities (e.g., "seeding" cloud formations that could develop into hurricanes or bring rain to arid areas). Incrementalism would focus on those areas in which similar patterns developed in the recent past and, perhaps, on a few nearby regions; it would thus ignore all formations which might deserve attention if they arose in unexpected areas.
>
> A mixed scanning strategy would include elements of both approaches by employing two cameras: a broad-angle camera that would cover all parts of the sky but not in great detail, and a second one which would zero in on those areas revealed by the first camera to require a more in-depth examination. While mixed-scanning might miss areas in which only a detailed camera could reveal trouble, it is less likely than incrementalism to miss obvious trouble spots in unfamiliar areas.[16]

Mixed-scanning permits decision makers to utilize both the rational-comprehensive and incremental theories in different situations. In some instances, incrementalism will be adequate; in others, a more thorough approach along rational-comprehensive lines will be needed. Mixed-scanning also takes into account differing capacities of decision makers. Generally speaking, the greater the capacity of decision makers to mobilize power to implement their decisions, the more scanning they can realistically engage in; and the more encompassing is scanning, the more effective is decision making.

Mixed-scanning is thus a kind of "compromise" approach that combines use of incrementalism and rationalism. It is not really clear from Etzioni's discussion, however, just how it would operate in practice. This is something on which the reader can ponder and speculate. Certainly, though, Etzioni does help alert us to the significant facts that decisions vary in their magnitude (e.g., scope, impact) and that different decision processes may be appropriate as the nature of decisions varies.

## A Note on Decision Criteria

Whether the decision process they select is rational-comprehensive, incremental, or mixed-scanning in nature, those who make choices among alternatives must have some basis for doing so. While some "decisions" may be the product of chance, inadvertence, random selection, or inaction that permits particular actions to prevail, most decisions will involve conscious choice. The question then becomes: What kinds of criteria (values or standards) influence the actions of decision makers? Of course, many factors appear to impinge upon political decision makers—political and social pressures, economic conditions, procedural requirements (e.g., due process), previous commitments, the pressure of time, and so on. In our concern with these, however, we should be careful not to neglect the values of the decision maker himself, notwithstanding that they may be difficult to determine and impossible to isolate in many instances.

Most of the values that may serve to guide the behavior of decision makers may be summarized in four categories.

*Political Values.* The decision maker may evaluate policy alternatives in terms of their import for his political party or the clientele groups of his agency. Decisions are made on the basis of political advantage, with policies being viewed as means for the advancement or achievement of political party or interest group goals. Political scientists have often studied and evaluated policymaking from this perspective. Particular decisions will be "explained" as being made for the benefit, say, of organized labor, wheat farmers, or a given political party. The decision of the Eisenhower Administration to raise farm-price supports just prior to the 1956 Presidential election did appear to have a partisan hue. So did the enthusiasm of many congressional Democrats for campaign finance reform, including expenditure limits, prior to the 1972 election campaigns.

*Organization Values.* Decision makers, especially bureaucrats, may also be influenced by organizational values. Organizations, such as administrative agencies, utilize many rewards and sanctions in an effort to induce their members to accept, and act on the basis of, organizationally determined values. To the extent this occurs, the individual's decisions may be guided by such considerations as the desire to see his organization survive, to enhance or expand its programs and activities, or to maintain its power and prerogatives. Many bureaucratic struggles between rival agencies, such as the Army Corps of Engineers and the Bureau of Reclamation in the water-resource policy area, stem from their desire to protect or expand their programs and activities.

*Personal Values.* The urge to protect or promote one's physical or financial well-being, reputation, or historical position may also serve as a decision criterion. The politician who accepts a bribe to make a particular decision, such as the award of a license or contract, obviously has personal benefit in mind. On a different plane, the President who says he is not going to be "the first President to lose a war," and who acts accordingly, is also being influenced by personal considerations, such as concern for his "place in history."

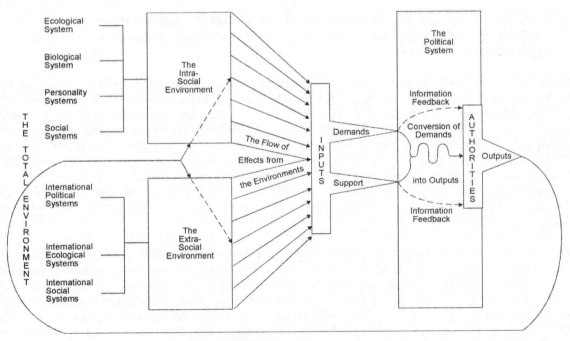

**Figure 1. Easton's "Dynamic Response" Model of a Political System. From *A Framework for Political Analysis* (Englewood Cliffs, N.J.: Prentice-Hall, 1965), p. 110.**

*Policy Values.* Neither the discussion to this point nor cynicism should lead us to conclude that political decision makers are influenced only by considerations of political, organizational, or personal benefit. Decision makers may well act on the basis of their perceptions of the public interest or beliefs concerning what is proper or morally correct public policy. A legislator who votes in favor of civil rights legislation may well do so because he believes it is morally correct and that equality is a desirable goal of public policy, notwithstanding that his vote may cause him some political risk. Studies of the Supreme Court indicate that the justices are influenced by policy values in deciding Cases.[17]

*Ideological Values.* Ideologies are sets of logically related values and beliefs which present simplified pictures of the world and serve as guides to action for people. In the Soviet Union, Marxist-Leninist ideology has served at least in part as a set of prescriptions for social and economic change. Although the Soviets have sometimes departed from Marxist-Leninist ideology, as in the use of economic incentives to increase production, it still serves as a means for rationalizing and legitimizing policy actions by the regime. In many of the developing countries in Asia, Africa, and the Middle East, nationalism—the desire of a people or nation for autonomy and deep concern with their own characteristics, needs and problems—has been an important factor shaping both foreign and domestic policies. Nationalism has become particularly important in world politics in the twentieth century, because it fueled the desire of colonial peoples for independence and created and intensified conflicts among both old and new nations.

## Some Approaches to Policy Analysis

Just as political scientists have created theories and models to help them understand and explain the decision making process, so have they also developed a variety of theoretical approaches to assist them in the study of the political behavior of entire political systems. Although most of these approaches have not been developed specifically for the analysis of policy formation, they can readily be converted to that purpose. The theoretical approaches that will come under brief examination here include systems theory, group theory, elite theory, functional process theory, and institutionalism. Such theoretical approaches are useful in, and to the extent, that they direct our attention to important political phenomena help clarify and simplify our thinking, and suggest possible explanations for political activity or, in our particular case, public policy.

### Political Systems Theory

Public policy may be viewed as the response of a political system to demands arising from its environment. The *political system,* as defined by Easton, is composed of those identifiable and interrelated institutions and activities in a society that make authoritative decisions (or allocations of values) that are binding on society.[18] *Inputs* into the political system from the environment consist of demands and supports. The *environment* consists of all those conditions and events external to the boundaries of the political system. *Demands* are the claims made by individuals and groups on the political system for action to satisfy their interests. *Support* is rendered when groups and individuals abide by election results, pay taxes, obey laws, and otherwise accept the decisions and actions of the authoritative political system made in response to demands. These authoritative allocations of values constitute public policy. The concept of *feedback* indicates that public policies (or outputs) may subsequently alter the environment and the demands generated therein, as well as the character of the political system itself. Policy outputs may produce new demands, which lead to further policy outputs, and so on in a continuing, never ending flow of public policy.

   The usefulness of systems theory for the study of public policy is limited by its highly general nature. It does not, moreover, say much concerning how decisions are made and policy is developed within the "black box" called the political system. Nonetheless, systems theory is a useful aid in organizing our inquiry into policy formation. It also alerts us to some significant aspects of the political process, such as: How do environmental inputs affect the content of public policy and the nature of the political system? How does public policy affect the environment and subsequent demands for action? What forces or factors in the environment act to generate demands upon the political system? How is the political system able to convert demands into public policy and preserve itself over time?

## Group Theory

According to the group theory of politics, public policy is the product of the group struggle. As one writer states: "What may be called public policy is the equilibrium reached in this [group] struggle at any given moment, and it represents a balance which the contending factions or groups constantly strive to weight in their favor."[19]

Group theory rests on the contention that interaction and struggle among groups is the central fact of political life. A group is a collection of individuals that may, on the basis of shared attitudes or interests, make claims upon other groups in society. It becomes a political interest group "when it makes a claim through or upon any of the institutions of government."[20] And, of course, many groups do just that. The individual is significant in politics only as he is a participant in, or a representative of, groups. It is through groups that individuals seek to secure their political preferences.

Public policy, at any given time, will reflect the interests of dominant groups. As groups gain and lose power and influence, public policy will be altered in favor of the interests of those gaining influence against the interests of those losing influence.

The role of government ("official groups") in policy formation has been described in the following manner by one proponent of group theory:

> The legislature referees the group struggle, ratifies the victories of the successful coalitions, and records the terms of the surrenders, compromises, and conquests in the form of statutes. Every statute tends to represent compromises because the process of accommodating conflicts of group interests is one of deliberation and consent. The legislative vote on any issue tends to represent the composition of strength, i.e., the balance of power, among the contending groups at the moment of voting. . . . Administrative agencies of the regulatory kind are established to carry out the terms of the treaties that the legislators have negotiated and ratified. . . . The judiciary, like the civilian bureaucracy, is one of the instrumentalities for the administration of the agreed rules.[21]

Group theory, while focusing attention on one of the major dynamic elements in policy formation, especially in pluralist societies such as the United States, seems both to overstate the importance of groups and to understate the independent and creative role that public officials play in the policy process. Indeed, many groups have been generated by public policy. The American Farm Bureau Federation, which developed around the agricultural extension program, is a notable example, as is the National Welfare Rights Organization. Public officials also may acquire a stake in particular programs and act as an interest group in support of their continuance. In the United States some welfare agency employees, including social workers, prefer current programs, with their emphasis on supervision and services (as well as benefits), to a guaranteed annual income, which would probably eliminate some of their jobs. In the Soviet Union, the bureaucracy has even been depicted as a "new class" that benefits from and supports the current system of state planning and controls.

Finally, we should note that it is rather misleading and inefficient to try to explain politics or policy formation in terms of group struggle without giving attention to the many other factors—for example, ideas and institutions that abound. This sort of reductionism, or unicausal explanation, should be avoided.

## Elite Theory

Approached from the perspective of elite theory, public policy can be regarded as the values and preferences of a governing elite. The essential argument of elite theory is that it is not the people or the "masses" who determine public policy through their demands and action; rather, public policy is decided by a ruling elite and carried into effect by public officials and agencies.

Thomas Dye and Harmon Zeigler, in *The Irony of Democracy*, provide a summary of elite theory:

1. Society is divided into the few who have power and the many who do not. Only a small number of persons allocate values for society; the masses do not decide public policy.
2. The few who govern are not typical of the masses who are governed. Elites are drawn disproportionately from the upper socioeconomic strata of society.
3. The movement of non-elites to elite positions must be slow and continuous to maintain stability and avoid revolution. Only non-elites who have accepted the basic elite consensus can be admitted to governing circles.
4. Elites share a consensus on the basic values of the social system and the preservation of the system. [In the United States, the elite consensus includes private enterprise, private property, limited government, and individual liberty.]
5. Public policy does not reflect demands of the masses but rather the prevailing values of the elite. Changes in public policy will be incremental rather than revolutionary. [Incremental changes permit responses to events that threaten a social system with a minimum of alteration or dislocation of the system.]
6. Active elites are subject to relatively little direct influence from apathetic masses. Elites influence masses more than masses influence elites.[22]

So stated elite theory is a rather provocative theory of policy formation. Policy is the product of elites, reflecting their values and serving their ends, one of which may be a desire to provide for the welfare of the masses. Thomas Dye has argued that development of civil rights policies in the United States during the 1960s can be suitably explained through the use of elite theory. These policies were "a response of a national elite to conditions affecting a small minority of Americans rather than a response of national leaders to majority sentiments." Thus, for example, the "elimination of legal discrimination and the guarantee of equality of opportunity in the Civil Rights Act of 1964 was achieved largely through the dramatic appeals of middle-class black leaders to the conscience of white elites."[23]

Elite theory does focus our attention on the role of leadership in policy formation and on the fact that, in any political system, a few govern the many. Whether the elites rule, and determine policy, with little influence by the masses is a difficult proposition to handle. It cannot be proved merely by assertions that the "establishment runs things," which has been a familiar plaint in recent years. Political scientist Robert Dahl argues that to defend the proposition successfully one must identify "a controlling group, less than a majority in size, that is not a pure artifact of democratic rules . . . a minority of individuals whose preferences regularly prevail in cases of differences of preferences on key political issues."[24] It may be that elite theory has more utility for the analysis and explanation of policy formation in some political systems, such as developing or Communist-bloc countries, than in others, such as the pluralist democracies of the United States and Canada.

## Functional Process Theory

Another way to approach the study of policy formation is to focus on the various functional activities that occur in the policy process. Harold Lasswell has presented a scheme involving seven categories of functional analysis that will serve as the basis for discussion here.[25]

1. *Intelligence:* How is the information on policy matters that comes to the attention of policymakers gathered and processed?
2. *Recommendation:* How are recommendations (or alternatives) for dealing with a given issue made and promoted?
3. *Prescription:* How are general rules adopted or enacted, and by whom?
4. *Invocation:* Who determines whether given behavior contravenes rules or laws and demands application of rules or laws thereto?
5. *Application:* How are laws or rules actually applied or enforced?
6. *Appraisal:* How is the operation of policies, their success or failure, appraised?
7. *Termination:* How are the original rules or laws terminated or continued in modified or changed form?

Although Lasswell refers to this as the "decision process," it goes beyond the making of a particular choice and really involves "the course of action on some matter" definition of policy that was presented earlier in the chapter. In the later stages of the process, policymakers may seek and utilize new information in order to change the original policy process.

This scheme of analysis is not tied to particular institutions or political arrangements and lends itself readily to comparative analysis of policy formation. One can inquire how these different functions are performed, to what effect, and by whom in different political systems or government units, for that matter. Its emphasis on functional categories, however, may lead to neglect of the politics of policy formation and the effect of environmental variables on the process. Obviously, policy formation is more than an intellectual process.

## Institutionalism

The study of government institutions is one of the oldest concerns of political science. Political life generally revolves around governmental institutions such as legislatures, executives, courts, and political parties; public policy, moreover, is initially authoritatively determined and implemented by governmental institutions. It is not surprising, then, that political scientists would devote much attention to them.

Traditionally, the institutional approach concentrated on describing the more formal and legal aspects of governmental institutions—their formal organization, legal powers, procedural rules, and functions or activities. Formal relationships with other institutions might also be considered. Usually little was done to explain how institutions actually operated, as apart from how they were supposed to operate, to analyze public policies produced by institutions, or to try to discover the relationships between institutional structure and public politics.

Subsequently, we should note, political scientists turned their attention in teaching and research to the political processes within governmental or political institutions, concentrating on the behavior of participants in the process and on political realities rather than formalism. To use the legislature as an example, concern shifted from simply describing the legislature as an institution to analyzing and explaining its operation over time, from its static to its dynamic aspects. In the curriculum the course on the "legislature" often became one on the "legislative process."

Institutionalism, with its emphasis on the formal or structural aspects of institutions, can nonetheless be usefully employed in policy analysis. An institution is a set of regularized patterns of human behavior that persist over time. (Some people, unsophisticated of course, seem to equate institutions with the physical structures in which they exist.) It is their differing sets of behavior patterns that really distinguish courts from legislatures, from administrative agencies, and so on. These regularized patterns of behavior, which we often call rules, structures, and the like, can affect decision making and the content of public policy. Rules and structural arrangements are usually not neutral in their impact; rather, they tend to favor some interests in society over others, some policy results rather than others. For example, it is contended that some of the rules (and traditions, which often have the effect of rules) of the Senate, such as those relating to unlimited debate and action by unanimous consent, favor the interests of minorities over majorities. In a federal system, which disperses power among different levels of government, some groups may have more influence if policy is made at the national level, other groups may benefit more if policy is made at the state or provincial level. Civil rights groups in the United States during the 1960s received a better response in Washington, D.C., than they did in Montgomery, Alabama, or Columbia, South Carolina, for example.

In summary, institutional structures, arrangements, and procedures can have a significant impact on public policy and should not be ignored in policy analysis. Neither should analysis of them, without concern for the dynamic aspects of politics, be considered adequate.

Although individual political scientists often manifest a preference for one or another of these or other theoretical approaches, it is not really possible to say which is the "best" or most satisfactory. Each focuses attention on different aspects of politics and policymaking and seems more useful for some purposes or some situations than others. Generally, one should not permit oneself to be bound too rigidly or dogmatically to a particular model or theoretical approach. A good rule is to be eclectic and flexible and use those theories as organizing concepts that seem most useful for the satisfactory analysis and explanation of a particular public policy or political action. It is my belief that the explanation of political behavior, rather than the validation of a given theoretical approach, should be the main purpose of political inquiry and analysis. Each of the theoretical approaches discussed in this section can contribute to our understanding of policymaking.

## The Plan of this Book

At this point it seems fair to give the reader some idea of what to expect in the remainder of the book. Our central concern will be with the policy process, which is a shorthand way of designating the various processes by which public policy is actually formed.[26] There is, it should be stressed, no one single process by which policy is made. Variations in the subject of policy will produce variations in the manner of policymaking. Foreign policy, taxation, railroad regulation, aid to private schools, professional licensing, and reform of local government are each characterized by distinguishable policy process. Furthermore, it makes a difference whether the primary institutional location of policymaking is the legislature, executive, judiciary, or administrative agencies. And certainly the process of forming, for instance, tax policy differs in the United States, the Soviet Union, and, say, Ethiopia.

All of this should not be taken to mean that each policymaking situation is unique and that it is impossible to develop generalizations on policy formation. Given the complexity and diversity in policy processes, it is not now possible to develop a "grand theory" of policy formation. But a useful start can be made toward what political scientists call "theory building" by seeking to generalize on such matters as who is involved in policy formation, on what kinds of issues, under what conditions, in what ways, and to what effect. Nor should we neglect the question of how policy problems develop. Such questions are really not as simple as they may first appear.

To provide a conceptual framework to guide our discussion, the policy process will be viewed as a sequential pattern of action involving a number of functional categories of activity that can be analytically distinguished, although in various instances this distinction may be difficult to make empirically. The categories will be presented briefly here.[27]

1. *Problem formation:* What is a policy problem? What makes it a public problem? How does it get on the agenda of government?
2. *Formulation:* How are alternatives for dealing with the problem developed? Who participates in policy formulation?
3. *Adoption:* How is a policy alternative adopted or enacted? What requirements must be met? Who adopts policy?
4. *Implementation:* What is done, if anything, to carry a policy into effect? What impact does this have on policy content?
5. *Evaluation:* How is the effectiveness or impact of a policy measured? Who evaluates policy? What are the consequences of policy evaluation? Are there demands for change or repeal?

Within this framework policy formation and implementation are perceived as political in that they involve conflict and struggle among individuals and groups having conflicting desires on issues of public policy. Policymaking is "political," it involves "politics," and there is no reason either to resist or to denigrate this conclusion, or to imitate those who dismiss policies they do not like with such phrases as "It's just a matter of politics."

This framework has a number of advantages. In actuality, policymaking often does chronologically follow the sequence of activities listed above. The sequential approach thus helps capture the flow of action in the policy process. Second, the sequential approach is open to change.[28] Additional steps can be introduced if experience indicates they are needed. Various forms of data collection and analysis—whether quantitative, legal, normative, or whatever—are compatible with it. Third, it yields a dynamic and developmental rather than cross-sectional or static view of the policy process. Moreover, it emphasizes the relationships among political phenomena rather than simply listing factors or developing classification schemes. Fourth, the sequential approach is not "culture-bound," and it can be readily utilized to study policymaking in foreign policymaking systems. Also, it lends itself to manageable comparisons, as of how problems get on the policy agenda in various countries or of the ways in which policies are adopted.

In presenting this framework for the analysis of policymaking, I will concentrate upon national domestic policies in the United States, though not to the total exclusion of foreign policy or other political systems. The discussion that follows is intended to provide the reader both with an understanding of the policy process and with some tools for his own analysis of policymaking.

## Notes

1. Robert Eyestone, *The Threads of Public Policy: A Study in Policy Leadership* (Indianapolis: Hobbs-Merrill. 1971), p. 18.

2. Thomas R. Dye, *Understanding Public Policy* (Englewood Cliffs, N.J.: Prentice-Hall, 1972), p. 18.

3. Richard Rose (ed.), *Policymaking in Great Britain* (London: Macmillan, 1969), p. x.

4. Carl J. Friedrich, *Man and His Government* (New York: McGraw-Hill, 1963), p. 79.

5. David Easton, *A Systems Analysis of Political Life* (New York: Wiley, 1965), p. 212.

6. Alan K. McAdam, *Power and Politics in Labor Legislation* (New York: Columbia University Press, 1964).

7. Robert H. Salisbury, "The Analysis of Public Policy: A Search for Theories and Roles," in Austin Ranney (ed.), *Political Science and Public Policy* (Chicago: Markham, 1968), p. 159.

8. Dye, *op. cit.*, p. 3.

9. The following discussion is based on Austin Ranney, "The Study of Political Policy Content: A Framework for Choice," in Ranney (ed.), *Science and Public Policy* (Chicago: 1968), pp. 13–19.

10. Don K. Price, *The Scientific Estate* (Cambridge, Mass.: Harvard University Press, 1965), pp. 122–35.

11. Dye, *op. cit.*, italics in original have been deleted.

12. James O. Wilson, *Negro Politics* (New York: Free Press, 1960), p. 89, as quoted in Amitai Etzioni, "Mixed-Scanning: A 'Third' Approach to Decision Making," *Public Administration Review*, XXVII (December, 1967), pp. 385–92.

13. The leading proponent of incrementalism undoubtedly is Charles Lindblom. See his "The Science of 'Muddling Through,'" *Public Administration Review*, XIX (1959), pp. 79–88; *The Intelligence of Democracy* (New York, Macmillan, 1964); *The Policymaking Process* (Englewood Cliffs, N.J.: Prentice-Hall, 1968); and, with David Braybrooke, *The Strategy of Decision* (New York: Free Press, 1963).

14. This summary draws primarily on Lindblom's "The Science of 'Muddling Through,'" *op, cit.*, and *The Intelligence of Democracy*, op. cit., pp. 144–48.

15. Amitai Etzioni, "Mixed-Scanning: A 'Third' Approach to Decision Making," *Public Administration Review*, XXVII (December, 1967), pp. 385–92.

16. *Ibid.*, p. 389.

17. Glendon Schubert, *Judicial Policymaking* (Chicago., Foresman, 1965).

18. David Easton, "An Approach to the Analysis of Political Systems," *World Politics*, IX (April, 1957), pp. 383–400. Cf. Easton, *A Framework for Political Analysis* (Englewood Cliffs, N.Y.: Prentice-Hall, 1965) and *A Systems Analysis of Political Life* (New York: Wiley, 1965). Those wishing to explore systems theory in depth should consult these works.

19. Earl Latham, *The Group Basis of Politics* (New York: Octagon Books, 1965), p. 36.

20. David Truman, *The Governmental Process* (New York: Knopf, 1951.), p. 37.

21. Latham, *op. cit.*, pp. 35–36, 38–39.

22. Thomas R. Dye and L. Harmon Zeigler, *The Irony of Democracy* (Belmont, Calif: Wadsworth, 1970), p. 6. This book examines American politics from the perspective of elite theory.

23. Dye *op. cit.*, pp. 39, 66.

24. Robert A. Dahl, "Critique of the Ruling Elite Model," *American Political Science Review*, LII (June, 1958), p. 464.

25. Harold D. Lasswell, *The Decision Process* (College Park, Md.: Bureau of Governmental Research, University of Maryland, 1956).

26. Here it is useful to distinguish an *Institutional Process*, such as the legislative process, from the policy process. Cf. Charles O. Jones, *An Introduction to the Study of Public Policy* (Belmont, Calif: Wadsworth, 1970), pp. 4–5.

27. This framework obviously draws on Lasswell's scheme, discussed earlier in the chapter. It also benefits from Jones, *op. cit.*

28. See, generally, Richard Rose, "Concepts for Comparison," *Policy Studies Journal*, I (Spring, 1973), pp. 122–27.

# The Science of "Muddling Through"

## Charles E. Lindblom

Suppose an administrator is given responsibility for formulating policy with respect to inflation. He might start by trying to list all related values in order of importance, e.g., full employment, reasonable business profit, protection of small savings, prevention of a stock market crash. Then all possible policy outcomes could be rated as more or less efficient in attaining a maximum of these values. This would of course require a prodigious inquiry into values held by members of society and an equally prodigious set of calculations on how much of each value is equal to how much of each other value. He could then proceed to outline all possible policy alternatives. In a third step, he would undertake systematic comparison of his multitude of alternatives to determine which attains the greatest amount of values.

In comparing policies, he would take advantage of any theory available that generalized about classes of policies. In considering inflation, for example, he would compare all policies in the light of the theory of prices. Since no alternatives are beyond his investigation, he would consider strict central control and the abolition of all prices and markets on the one hand and elimination of all public controls with reliance completely on the free market on the other, both in the light of whatever theoretical generalizations he could find on such hypothetical economies.

Finally, he would try to make the choice that would in fact maximize his values.

An alternative line of attack would be to set as his principal objective, either explicitly or without conscious thought, the relatively simple goal of keeping prices level. This objective might be compromised or complicated by only a few other goals, such as full employment. He would in fact disregard most other social values as beyond his present interest, and he would for the moment not even attempt to rank the few values that he regarded as immediately relevant. Were he pressed, he would quickly admit that he was ignoring many related values and many possible important consequences of his policies.

As a second step, he would outline those relatively few policy alternatives that occurred to him. He would then compare them. In comparing his limited number of alternatives, most of them familiar from past controversies, he would not ordinarily find a body of theory precise enough to carry him through a comparison of their respective consequences. Instead he would rely heavily on the record of past experience with small policy steps to predict the consequences of similar steps extended into the future.

Moreover, he would find that the policy alternatives combined objectives or values in different ways. For example, one policy might offer price level stability at the cost of some risk of unemployment; another might offer less price stability but also less risk of unemployment. Hence, the next step in his approach—the final selection—would combine into one the choice among values and the choice among instruments for reaching values. It would not, as in the first method of policymaking, approximate a more mechanical process of choosing the means that best satisfied goals that were previously clarified and ranked. Because practitioners of the second approach expect to achieve their goals only partially, they would expect to repeat endlessly the sequence just described, as conditions and aspirations changed and as accuracy of prediction improved.

## By Root or by Branch

For complex problems, the first of these two approaches is of course impossible. Although such an approach can be described, it cannot be practiced except for relatively simple problems and even then only in a somewhat modified form. It assumes intellectual capacities and sources of information that men simply do not possess, and it is even more absurd as an approach to policy when the time and money that can be allocated to a policy problem is limited, as is always the case. Of particular importance to public administrators is the fact that public agencies are in effect usually instructed not to practice the first method. That is to say, their prescribed functions and constraints—the politically or legally possible—restrict their attention to relatively few values and relatively few alternative policies among the countless alternatives that might be imagined. It is the second method that is practiced.

Curiously, however, the literatures of decision making, policy formulation, planning, and public administration formalize the first approach rather than the second, leaving public administrators who handle complex decisions in the position of practicing what few preach. For emphasis I run some risk of over-statement. True enough, the literature is well aware of limits on man's capacities and of the inevitability that policies will be approached in some such style as the second. But attempts to formalize rational policy formulation—to lay out explicitly the necessary steps in the process—usually describe the first approach and not the second.[1]

The common tendency to describe policy formulation even for complex problems as though it followed the first approach has been strengthened by the attention given to, and successes enjoyed by, operations research, statistical decision theory, and systems analysis. The hallmarks of these procedures, typical of the first approach, are clarity of objective, explicitness of evaluation, a high degree of comprehensiveness of overview, and, wherever possible, quantification of values for mathematical analysis. But these advanced procedures remain largely the appropriate techniques of relatively small-scale problem-solving where the total number of variables to be considered is small and value problems restricted. Charles Hitch, head of the Economics Division of RAND Corporation, one of the leading centers for application of these techniques, has written:

> I would make the empirical generalization from my experience at RAND and elsewhere that operations research is the art of sub-optimizing, i.e., of solving some lower-level problems, and that difficulties increase and our special competence diminishes by an order of magnitude with every level of decision making we attempt to ascend. The sort of simple explicit model which operations researchers are so proficient in using can certainly reflect most of the significant factors influencing traffic control on the George Washington Bridge, but the proportion of the relevant reality which we can represent by any such model or models in studying, say, a major foreign-policy decision, appears to be almost trivial.[2]

Accordingly, I propose in this paper to clarify and formalize the second method, much neglected in the literature. This might be described as the method of *successive limited comparisons*. I will contrast it with the first approach, which might be called the rational-comprehensive method.[3] More impressionistically and briefly—and therefore generally used in this article—they could be characterized as the branch method and root method, the former continually building out from the current situation, step-by-step and by small degrees; the latter starting from fundamentals anew each time, building on the past only as experience is embodied in a theory, and always prepared to start completely from the ground up.

Let us put the characteristics of the two methods side by side in simplest terms.

Rational-Comprehensive (Root)

1a. Clarification of values or objectives distinct from and usually prerequisite to empirical analysis of alternative policies.
2a. Policy-formulation is therefore approached through means-end analysis: First the ends are isolated, then the means to achieve them are sought.

3a. The test of a "good" policy is that it can be shown to be the most appropriate means to desired ends.

4a. Analysis is comprehensive; every important relevant factor is taken into account.

5a. Theory is often heavily relied upon.

Assuming that the root method is familiar and understandable, we proceed directly to clarification of its alternative by contrast. In explaining the second, we shall be describing how most administrators do in fact approach complex questions, for the root method, the "best" way as a blueprint or model, is in fact not workable for complex policy questions, and administrators are forced to use the method of successive limited comparisons.

## Intertwining Evaluation and Empirical Analysis (1b)

The quickest way to understand how values are handled in the method of successive limited comparisons is to see how the root method often breaks down in *its* handling of values or objectives. The idea that values should be clarified, and in advance of the examination of alternative policies, is appealing. But what happens when we attempt it for complex social problems? The first difficulty is that on many critical values or objectives, citizens disagree, congressmen disagree and public administrators disagree. Even where a fairly specific objective is prescribed for the administrator, there remains considerable room for disagreement on sub-objectives. Consider, for example, the conflict with respect to locating public housing, described in Meyerson and Banfield's study of the Chicago Housing Authority[4]—disagreement which occurred despite the clear objective of providing a certain number of public housing units in the city. Similarly conflicting are objectives in highway location, traffic control, minimum wage administration, development of tourist facilities in nation parks, or insect control.

Successive Limited Comparisons. (Branch)

1b. Selection of value goals and empirical analysis of the needed action are not distinct from one another but are closely intertwined.

2b. Since means and ends are not distinct, means-end analysis is often inappropriate or limited.

3b. The test of a "good" policy is typically that various analysts find themselves directly agreeing on a policy (without their agreeing that it is the most appropriate means to an agreed objective).

4b. Analysis is drastically limited:
   i. Important possible outcomes are neglected.
   ii. Important alternative potential policies are neglected.
   iii. Important affected values are neglected.

5b. A succession of comparisons greatly reduces or eliminates reliance on theory.

Administrators cannot escape these conflicts by ascertaining the majority's preference, for preferences have not been registered on most issues; indeed, there often *are* no preferences in the absence of public discussion sufficient to bring an issue to the attention of the electorate. Furthermore, there is a question of whether intensity of feeling should be considered as well as the number of persons preferring each alternative. By the impossibility of doing otherwise, administrators often are reduced to deciding policy without clarifying objectives first.

Even when an administrator resolves to follow his own values as a criterion for decisions, he often will not know how to rank them when they conflict with one another, as they usually do. Suppose, for example, that an administrator must relocate tenants living in tenements scheduled for destruction. One objective is to empty the buildings fairly promptly, another is to find suitable accommodation for persons displaced, another is to avoid friction with residents in other areas in which a large influx would be unwelcome, another is to deal with all concerned through persuasion if possible, and so on.

How does one state even to himself the relative importance of these partially conflicting values? A simple ranking of them is not enough; one needs ideally to know how much of one value is worth sacrificing for some of another value. The answer is that typically the administrator chooses—and must choose—directly among policies in which these values are combined in different ways. He cannot first clarify his values and then choose among policies.

A more subtle third point underlies both the first two. Social objectives do not always have the same relative values. One objective may be highly prized in one circumstance, another in another circumstance. If, for example, an administrator values highly both the dispatch with which his agency can carry through its projects *and* good public relations, it matters little which of the two possibly conflicting values he favors in some abstract or general sense. Policy questions arise in forms which put to administrators such a question as: Given the degree to which we are or are not already achieving the values of dispatch and the values of good public relations, is it worth sacrificing a little speed for a happier clientele, or is it better to risk offending the clientele so that we can get on with our work? The answer to such a question varies with circumstances.

The value problem is, as the example shows, always a problem of adjustments at a margin. But there is no practicable way to state marginal objectives or values except in terms of particular policies. That one value is preferred to another in one decision situation does not mean that it will be preferred in another decision situation in which it can be had only at great sacrifice of another value. Attempts to rank or order values in general and abstract terms so that they do not shift from decision to decision end up by ignoring the relevant marginal preferences. The significance of this third point thus goes very far. Even if all administrators had at hand an agreed set of values, objectives, and constraints, and an agreed ranking of these values, objectives, and constraints, their marginal values in actual choice situations would be impossible to formulate.

Unable consequently to formulate the relevant values first and then choose among policies to achieve them, administrators must choose directly among alternative policies that offer different marginal combinations of values. Somewhat paradoxically, the only practicable way to disclose one's relevant marginal values even to oneself is to describe the policy one chooses to achieve them. Except roughly and vaguely, I know of no way to describe—or even to understand—what my relative evaluations are for, say, freedom and security, speed and accuracy in governmental decisions, or low taxes and better schools than to describe my preferences among specific policy choices that might be made between the alternatives in each of the pairs.

In summary, two aspects of the process by which values are actually handled can be distinguished. The first is clear: evaluation and empirical analysis are intertwined; that is, one chooses among values and among policies at one and the same time. Put a little more elaborately, one simultaneously chooses a policy to attain certain objectives and chooses the objectives themselves. The second aspect is related but distinct: the administrator focuses his attention on marginal or incremental values. Whether he is aware of it or not, he does not find general formulations of objectives very helpful and in fact makes specific marginal or incremental comparisons. Two policies, X and Y, confront him. Both promise the same degree of attainment of objectives $a, b, c, d,$ and $e$. But X promises him somewhat more of $f$ than does Y, while Y promises him somewhat more of $g$ than does X. In choosing between them, he is in fact offered the alternative of a marginal or incremental amount of $f$ at the expense of a marginal or incremental amount of $g$. The only values that are relevant to his choice are these increments by which the two policies differ; and, when he finally chooses between the two marginal values, he does so by making a choice between policies.[5]

As to whether the attempt to clarify objectives in advance of policy selection is more or less rational than the close intertwining of marginal evaluation and empirical analysis, the principal difference established is that for complex problems the first is impossible and irrelevant, and the second is both possible and relevant. The second is possible because the administrator need not try to analyze any values except the values by which alternative policies differ and need not be concerned with them except as they differ marginally. His need for information on values or objectives is drastically reduced as compared with the root method; and his capacity for grasping, comprehending, and relating values to one another is not strained beyond the breaking point.

## Relations between Means and Ends (2b)

Decision making is ordinarily formalized as a means-ends relationship: means are conceived to be evaluated and chosen in the light of ends finally selected independently of and prior to the choice of means. This is the means-ends relationship of the root method. But it follows from all that has just been said that such a means-ends relationship is possible only to the extent that values are agreed upon, are reconcilable, and are stable at the margin. Typically, therefore, such a means-ends relationship is absent from the branch method, where means and ends are simultaneously chosen.

Yet any departure from the means-ends relationship of the root method will strike some readers as inconceivable. For it will appear to them that only in such a relationship is it possible to determine whether one policy choice is better or worse than another. How can an administrator know whether he has made a wise or foolish decision if he is without prior values or objectives by which to judge his decisions? The answer to this question calls up the third distinctive difference between root and branch methods: how to decide the best policy.

## The Test of "Good" Policy (3b)

In the root method, a decision is "correct," "good," or "rational" if it can be shown to attain some specified objective, where the objective can be specified without simply describing the decision itself. Where objectives are defined only through the marginal or incremental approach to values described above, it is still sometimes possible to test whether a policy does in fact attain the desired objectives; but a precise statement of the objectives takes the form of a description of the policy chosen or some alternative to it. To show that a policy is mistaken one cannot offer an abstract argument that important objectives are not achieved; one must instead argue that another policy is more to be preferred.

So far, the departure from customary ways of looking at problem-solving is not troublesome, for many administrators will be quick to agree that the most effective discussion of the correctness of policy does take the form of comparison with other policies that might have been chosen. But what of the situation in which administrators cannot agree on values or objectives, either abstractly or in marginal terms? What then is the test of "good" policy? For the root method, there is not test. Agreement on objectives failing, there is no standard of "correctness." For the method of successive limited comparisons, the test is agreement on policy itself, which remains possible even when agreement on values is not.

It has been suggested that continuing agreement in Congress on the desirability of extending old age insurance stems from liberal desires to strengthen the welfare programs of the federal government and from conservative desires to reduce union demands for private pension plans. If so, this is an excellent demonstration of the ease with which individuals of different ideologies often can agree on concrete policy. Labor mediators report a similar phenomenon: the contestants cannot agree on criteria for settling their disputes but can agree on specific proposals. Similarly, when one administrator's objective turns out to be another's means, they often can agree on policy.

Agreement on policy thus becomes the only practicable test of the policy's correctness. And for one administrator to seek to win the other over to agreement on ends as well would accomplish nothing and create quite unnecessary controversy.

If agreement directly on policy as a test for "best" policy seems a poor substitute for testing the policy against its objectives, it ought to be remembered that objectives themselves have no ultimate validity other than they are agreed upon. Hence agreement is the test of "best" policy in both methods. But where the root method requires agreement on what elements in the decision constitute objectives and on which of these objectives should be sought, the branch method falls back on agreement wherever it can be found.

In an important sense, therefore, it is not irrational for an administrator to defend a policy as good without being able to specify what it is good for.

## Non-Comprehensive Analysis (b)

Ideally, rational-comprehensive analysis leaves out nothing important. But it is impossible to take everything important into consideration unless "important" is so narrowly defined that analysis is in fact quite limited. Limits on human intellectual capacities and on available information set definite limits to man's capacity to be comprehensive. In actual fact, therefore, no one can practice the rational-comprehensive method for really complex problems, and every administrator faced with a sufficiently complex problem must find ways drastically to simplify.

An administrator assisting in the formulation of agricultural economic policy cannot in the first place be competent on all possible policies. He cannot even comprehend one policy entirely. In planning a soil bank program, he cannot successfully anticipate the impact of higher or lower farm income on, say, urbanization—the possible consequent loosening of family ties, possible consequent eventual need for revisions in social security and further implications for tax problems arising out of new federal responsibilities for social security and municipal responsibilities for urban services. Nor, to follow another line of repercussions, can he work through the soil bank program's effects on prices for agricultural products in foreign markets and consequent implications for foreign relations, including those arising out of economic rivalry between the United States and the U.S.S.R.

In the method of successive limited comparisons, simplification is systematically achieved in two principal ways. First, it is achieved through limitation of policy comparisons to those policies that differ in relatively small degree from policies presently in effect. Such a limitation immediately reduces the number of alternatives to be investigated and also drastically simplifies the character of the investigation of each. For it is not necessary to undertake fundamental inquiry into an alternative and its consequences; it is necessary only to study those respects in which the proposed alternative and its consequences differ from the status quo. The empirical comparison of marginal differences among alternative policies that differ only marginally is, of course, a counterpart to the incremental or marginal comparison of values discussed above.[6]

## Relevance as Well as Realism

It is a matter of common observation that in Western democracies public administrators and policy analysts in general do largely limit their analyses to incremental or marginal differences in policies that are chosen to differ only incrementally. They do not do so, however, solely because they desperately need some way to simplify their problems; they also do so in order to be relevant. Democracies change their policies almost entirely through incremental adjustments. Policy does not move in leaps and bounds.

The incremental character of political change in the United States has often been remarked. The two major political parties agree on fundamentals; they offer alternative policies to the voters only on relatively small points of difference. Both parties favor full employment, but they define it somewhat differently; both favor the development of water power resources, but in slightly different ways; and both favor unemployment compensation, but not the same level of benefits. Similarly, shifts of policy within a party take place largely through a series of relatively small changes, as can be seen in their only gradual acceptance of the idea of governmental responsibility for support of the unemployed, a change in party positions beginning in the early 30s and culminating in a sense in the Employment Act of 1946.

Party behavior is in turn rooted in public attitudes, and political theorists cannot conceive of democracy's surviving in the United States in the absence of fundamental agreement on potentially disruptive issues, with consequent limitation of policy debates in relatively small differences in policy.

Since the policies ignored by the administrator are politically impossible and so irrelevant, the simplification of analysis achieved by concentrating on policies that differ only incrementally is not a capricious kind of simplification. In addition, it can be argued that, given the limits on knowledge within which policymakers are confined, simplifying by limiting the focus to small variations from present policy makes the most of available knowledge. Because policies being considered are like present and past policies, the administrator can obtain information and claim some insight. Non-incremental policy proposals are therefore typically not only politically irrelevant but also unpredictable in their consequences.

The second method of simplification of analysis is the practice of ignoring important possible consequences of possible policies, as well as the values attached to the neglected consequences. If this appears to disclose a shocking shortcoming of successive limited comparisons, it can be replied that, even if the exclusions are random, policies may nevertheless be more intelligently formulated than through futile attempts to achieve a comprehensiveness beyond human capacity. Actually, however, the exclusions, seeming arbitrary or random from one point of view, need be neither.

## Achieving a Degree of Comprehensiveness

Suppose that each value neglected by one policymaking agency were a major concern of at least one other agency. In that case, a helpful division of labor would be achieved, and no agency need find its task beyond its capacities. The shortcomings of such a system would be that one agency might destroy a value either before another agency could be activated to safeguard it or in spite of another agency's efforts. But the possibility that important values may be lost is present in any form of organization, even where agencies attempt to comprehend in planning more than is humanly possible.

The virtue of such a hypothetical division of labor is that every important interest or value has its watchdog. And these watchdogs can protect the interests in their jurisdiction in two quite different ways: first, by redressing damages done by other agencies; and, second, by anticipating and heading off injury before it occurs.

In a society like that of the United States in which individuals are free to combine to pursue almost any possible common interest they might have and in which government agencies are sensitive to the pressures of these groups, the system described is approximated. Almost every interest has its watchdog. Without claiming that every interest has a sufficiently powerful watchdog, it can be argued that our system often can assure a more comprehensive regard for the values of the whole society than any attempt at intellectual comprehensiveness.

In the United States, for example, no part of government attempts a comprehensive overview of policy on income distribution. A policy nevertheless evolves, and one responding to a wide variety of interests. A process of mutual adjustment among farm groups, labor unions, municipalities and school boards, tax authorities, and government agencies with responsibilities in the fields of housing, health, highways, national parks, fire, and police accomplishes a distribution of income in which particular income problems neglected at one point in the decision processes become central at another point.

Mutual adjustment is more pervasive than the explicit forms it takes in negotiation between groups; it persists through the mutual impacts of groups upon each other even where they are not in communication. For all the imperfections and latent dangers in this ubiquitous process of mutual adjustment, it will often accomplish an adaptation of policies to a wider range of interest than could be done by one group centrally.

Note, too, how the incremental pattern of policy making fits with the multiple pressure pattern. For when decisions are only incremental—closely related to known policies, it is easier for one group to anticipate the kind of moves another might make and easier too for it to make correction for injury already accomplished.[7]

Even partisanship and narrowness, to use pejorative terms, will sometimes be assets to rational decision making, for they can doubly insure that what one agency neglects, another will not; they specialize personnel to distinct points of view. The claim is valid that effective rational coordination of the federal administration, if possible to achieve at all, would require an agreed set of values[8]—if "rational" is defined as the practice of the root method of decision making. But a high degree of administrative coordination occurs as each agency adjusts its policies to the concerns of the other agencies in the process of fragmented decision making I have just described.

For all the apparent shortcomings of the incremental approach to policy alternatives with its arbitrary exclusion coupled with fragmentation, when compared to the root method, the branch method often looks far superior. In the root method, the inevitable exclusion of factors is accidental, unsystematic, and not defensible by any argument so far developed, while in the branch method the exclusions are deliberate, systematic, and defensible. Ideally, of course, the root method does not exclude; in practice it must.

Nor does the branch method necessarily neglect long-term considerations and objectives. It is clear that important values must be omitted in considering policy, and sometimes the only way long-run objectives can be given adequate attention is through the neglect of short-run considerations. But the values omitted can be either long-run or short-run.

## Succession of Comparisons (5b)

The final distinctive element in the branch method is that the comparisons, together with the policy choice, proceed in a chronological series. Policy is not made once and for all; it is made and re-made endlessly. Policymaking is a process of successive approximation to some desired objectives in which what is desired itself continues to change under reconsideration.

Making policy is at best a very rough process. Neither social scientists, nor politicians, nor public administrators yet know enough about the social world to avoid repeated error in predicting the consequences of policy moves. A wise policymaker consequently expects that his policies will achieve only part of what he hopes and at the same time will produce unanticipated consequences he would have preferred to avoid. If he proceeds through a *succession* of incremental changes, he avoids serious lasting mistakes in several ways.

In the first place, past sequences of policy steps have given him knowledge about the probable consequences of further similar steps. Second, he need not attempt big jumps toward his goals that would require predictions beyond his or anyone else's knowledge, because he never expects his policy to be a final resolution of a problem. His decision is only one step, one that if successful can quickly be followed by another. Third, he is in effect able to test his previous predictions as he moves on to each further step. Lastly, he often can remedy a past error fairly quickly—more quickly than if policy proceeded through more distinct steps widely spaced in time.

Compare this comparative analysis of incremental changes with the aspiration to employ theory in the root method. Man cannot think without classifying, without subsuming one experience under a more general category of experiences. The attempt to push categorization as far as possible and to find general propositions which can be applied to specific situations is what I refer to with the word "theory." Where root analysis often leans heavily on theory in this sense, the branch method does not.

The assumption of root analysts is that theory is the most systematic and economical way to bring relevant knowledge to bear on a specific problem. Granting the assumption, an unhappy fact is that we do not have adequate theory to apply to problems in any policy area, although theory is more adequate in some areas—monetary policy, for example—than in others. Comparative analysis, as in the branch method, is sometimes a systematic alternative to theory.

Suppose an administrator must choose among a small group of policies that differ only incrementally from each other and from present policy. He might aspire to "understand" each of the alternatives—for example, to know all the consequences of each aspect of each policy. If so, he would indeed require theory. In fact, however, he would usually decide that, for *policymaking purposes*, he need know, as explained above, only the consequences of each of those aspects of the policies in which they differed from one another. For this much more modest aspiration, he requires no theory (although it might be helpful, if available), for he can proceed to isolate probable differences by examining the differences in consequences associated with past differences in policies, a feasible program because he can take his observations from a long sequence of incremental changes.

For example, without a more comprehensive social theory about juvenile delinquency than scholars have yet produced, one cannot possibly understand the ways in which a variety of public policies—say on education, housing, recreation, employment, race relations, and policing—might encourage or discourage delinquency. And one needs such an understanding if he undertakes the comprehensive overview of the problem prescribed in the models of the root method. If, however, one merely wants to mobilize knowledge sufficient to assist in a choice among a small group of similar policies—alternative policies on juvenile court procedures, for example—he can do so by comparative analysis of the results of similar past policy moves.

## Theorists and Practitioners

This difference explains—in some cases at least—why the administrator often feels that the outside expert or academic problem-solver is sometimes not helpful and why they in turn often urge more theory on him. And it explains why an administrator often feels more confident when "flying by the seat of his pants" than when following the advice of theorists. Theorists often ask the administrator to go the long way round to the solution of his problems, in effect ask him to follow the best canons of the scientific method, when the administrator knows that the best available theory will work less well than more modest incremental comparisons. Theorists do not realize that the administrator is often in fact practicing a systematic method. It would be foolish to push this explanation too far, for sometimes practical decision makers are pursuing neither a theoretical approach nor successive comparisons, nor any other systematic method.

It may be worth emphasizing that theory is sometimes of extremely limited helpfulness in policymaking for at least two rather different reasons. It is greedy for facts; it can be constructed only through a great collection of observations. And it is typically insufficiently precise for application to a policy process that moves through small changes. In contrast, the comparative method both economizes on the need for facts and directs the analyst's attention to just those facts that are relevant to the fine choices faced by the decision maker.

With respect to precision of theory, economic theory serves as an example. It predicts that an economy without money or prices would in certain specified ways misallocate resources, but this finding pertains to an alternative far removed from the kind of policies on which administrators need help. On the other hand, it is not precise enough to predict the consequences of policies restricting business mergers, and this is the kind of issue on which the administrators need help. Only in relatively restricted areas does economic theory achieve sufficient precision to go far in resolving policy questions; its helpfulness in policymaking is always so limited that it requires supplementation through comparative analysis.

## Successive Comparison as a System

Successive limited comparisons is, then, indeed a method or system; it is not a failure of method for which administrators ought to apologize. None the less, its imperfections, which have not been explored in this paper, are many. For example, the method is without a built-in safeguard for all relevant values, and it also may lead the decision maker to overlook excellent policies for no other reason than that they are not suggested by the chain of successive policy steps leading up to the present. Hence, it ought to be said that under this method, as well as under some of the most sophisticated variants of the root method—operations research, for example—policies will continue to be as foolish as they are wise.

Why then bother to describe the method in all the above detail? Because it is in fact a common method of policy formulation, and is, for complex problems, the principal reliance of administrators as well as of other policy analysts.[9] And because it will be superior to any other decision making method available for complex problems in many circumstances, certainly superior to a futile attempt at superhuman comprehensiveness. The reaction of the public administrator to the exposition of method doubtless will be less a discovery of a new method than a better acquaintance with an old. But by becoming more conscious of their practice of this method, administrators might practice it with more skill and know when to extend or constrict its use. (That they sometimes practice it effectively and sometimes not may explain the extremes of opinion on "muddling through," which is both praised as a highly sophisticated form of problem-solving and denounced as no method at all. For I suspect that in so far as there is a system in what is known as "muddling through," this method is it.)

One of the noteworthy incidental consequences of clarification of the method is the light it throws on the suspicion an administrator sometimes entertains that a consultant or adviser is not speaking relevantly and responsibly when in fact by all ordinary objective evidence he is. The trouble lies in the fact that most of us approach policy problems within a framework given by our view of a chain of successive policy choices made up to the present. One's thinking about appropriate policies with respect, say, to urban traffic control is greatly influenced by one's knowledge of the incremental steps taken up to the present. An administrator enjoys an intimate knowledge of his past sequences that "outsiders" do not share, and his thinking and that of the "outsider" will consequently be different in ways that may puzzle both. Both may appear to be talking intelligently, yet each may find the other unsatisfactory. The relevance of the policy chain of succession is even more clear when an American tries to discuss, say, antitrust policy with a Swiss, for the chains of policy in the two countries are strikingly different and the two individuals consequently have organized their knowledge in quite different ways.

If this phenomenon is a barrier to communication, an understanding of it promises an enrichment of intellectual interaction in policy formulation. Once the source of difference is understood, it will sometimes be stimulating for an administrator to seek out a policy analyst whose recent experience is with a policy chain different from his own.

This raises again a question only briefly discussed above on the merits of like-mindedness among government administrators. While much of organization theory argues the virtues of common values and agreed organizational objectives, for complex problems in which the root method is inapplicable, agencies will want among their own personnel two types of diversification: administrators whose thinking is organized by reference to policy chains other than those familiar to most members of the organization and, even more commonly, administrators whose professional or personal values or interests create diversity of view (perhaps coming from different specialties, social classes, geographical areas) so that, even within a single agency, decision making can be fragmented and parts of the agency can serve as watchdogs for other parts.

## Notes

1. James G. March and Herbert A. Simon similarly characterize the literature. They also take some important steps, as have Simon's recent articles, to describe a less heroic model of policymaking. See *Organizations* (John Wiley and Sons, 1958), p. 137.

2. "Operations Research and National Planning—A Dissent," 5 *Operations Research* 718 (October, 1957) Hitch's dissent is from particular points made in the article to which his paper is a reply; his claim that operations research is for low-level problems is widely accepted.

   For examples of the kind of problems to which operations research is applied, see C. W. Churchman, R. L. Ackoff and E. L. Arnoff, *Introduction to Operations Research* (John Wiley and Sons, 1957); and J. F. McCloskey and J. M. Coppinger (eds.), *Operations Research for Management*, Vol. II, (The Johns Hopkins Press, 1956).

3. I am assuming that administrators often make policy and advise in the making of policy and am treating decision making and policymaking as synonymous for purposes of this paper.

4. Martin Meyerson and Edward C. Banfield, *Politics, Planning and the Public Interest* (The Free Press, 1955).

5. The line of argument is, of course, an extension of the theory of market choice, especially the theory of consumer choice, to public policy choices.

6. A more precise definition of incremental policies and a discussion of whether a change that appears "small" to one observer might be seen differently by another is to be found in my "Policy Analysis," 48 *American Economic Review* 298 (June, 1958).

7. The link between the practice of the method of successive limited comparisons and mutual adjustment of interest in a highly fragmented decision making process adds a new facet to pluralist theories of government and administration.

8. Herbert Simon, Donald W. Smithburg, and Victor A. Thompson, *Public Administration* (Alfred A. Knopf, 1950), p. 434.

9. Elsewhere I have explored this same method of policy formulation as practiced by academic analysts of policy ("Policy Analysis," 48 *American Economic Preview* 298 [June, 1958]). Although it has been here presented as a method for public administrators, it is no less necessary to analysis more removed from immediate policy questions, despite their tendencies to describe their own analytical efforts as though they were the rational-comprehensive method with an especially heavy use of theory. Similarly, this same method is inevitably resorted to in personal problem-solving, where means and ends are sometimes impossible to separate, where aspirations or objectives undergo constant development, and where drastic simplification of the complexity of the real world is urgent if problems are to be solved in the time that can be given to them. To an economist accustomed to dealing with the marginal or incremental concept in market processes, the central idea in the method is that both evaluation and empirical analysis are incremental. Accordingly I have referred to the method elsewhere as "the incremental method."

# The Scientific Method, Social Science, and Policy Analysis

## Lewis G. Irwin

## Nested Challenges

Effective policy analysts are effective because they understand the various challenges inherent in the analytic task itself. In an ideal world, analysts would be able to arrive at rational answers to rational questions through a rational process of deliberation and analysis, since *rationality*, or the systematic consideration and selection of logical alternatives in light of carefully applied evaluative criteria, is the policy analyst's major objective. Unfortunately, however, policy analysis almost never plays out in this way. We live in a human and political world, and with it comes a variety of subjective concerns and uncertain conditions that prevent us from ever completely reaching that ideal standard. So although we continually strive as policy analysts to achieve or at least approximate this ideal of objective rationality, human and methodological factors invariably get in the way of at least one of the steps toward that goal. From this perspective, the analytic task can be summarized as three sequential and nested processes, each containing a distinct set of methodological and contextual challenges. Effective policy analysts actively manage these challenges from the outset of their analysis.

The first of the three processes that confront the analyst is the challenge of the *scientific method*. When we speak of the scientific method, we are merely speaking of the goal of identifying important questions, theorizing answers to those questions, and then seeking confirmation of our theories through logical reasoning and objective observation. The basic goal of the scientific method is *empirical analysis,* or the establishment of facts determined by the gathering of information through one or more of the five senses. Because policy analysts, like professionals in other fields, view the world through the lenses of preconceived notions about how the world works, they find the scientific method to be particularly challenging.

Put another way, we all carry preconceived beliefs, ideological and otherwise, that tend to shape the ways in which we perceive the world. In some cases and for some analysts, maybe more often than not, preconceptions about "right" and "wrong" turn out to be the correct answers to our important questions as we make policy decisions. But when we fail to subject our assumptions about the world to the scrutiny afforded by a rigorous application of the scientific method, we run the risk of carrying faulty logic or misconceptions throughout our whole problem-solving effort. This failure results in incorrect or incomplete policy recommendations, often with dire and far-reaching consequences. In France during World War II, the failure of the Maginot Line, which led to the occupation of France by Germany, serves as an extreme example of the potentially catastrophic effect of untested and faulty assumptions. Based on outdated data, the French leadership's assumptions regarding German intentions and capabilities caused a misallocation of resources and led to disastrous failure when intelligent and well-intentioned people assumed that things would work as they always had. For policy analysts, the application of the scientific method means always examining and reassessing your basic assumptions and basing one's analysis on empirical evidence whenever possible.

The second process that makes the task of policy analysis challenging is the application of the scientific method to social science questions. When we speak of the *social sciences,* we are speaking of all fields of scholarship and policy that deal with human behavior and human interactions in society. Almost every policy question includes one or more human elements, and thus the special challenges associated with social scientific inquiry almost invariably apply to policy analyses. The basic goals of social science include empirical analysis and the establishment of facts and the validation of theories, but social scientists also often engage in *normative analysis* as part of their research efforts. Normative analysis is value-laden analysis that seeks to assess whether some phenomenon is "good" or "bad." This variety of analysis comes with its own inherent challenges, a topic discussed elsewhere in this book. In general, the special challenge of the application of the scientific method to questions of social science is that human factors, behaviors, and responses are inherently complex and often difficult to measure accurately. Our efforts at wholly rational analysis are almost always bounded by the characteristics of *uncertainty* of measurement and the complexity of human phenomena, meaning that even in the best case we can never hope to get it right all of the time.

As if these challenges were not enough, the policy analyst faces one more set of challenges in his or her bid to achieve objective rationality. Nested within the application of the scientific method to social science is the third process of policy analysis itself. Policy analysis is a special case of social science in that this endeavor comes with its own distinctive methodological and contextual constraints. Every policy analyst operates within a context of practical and political challenges that further limit him in the pursuit of objective and rational solutions to policy problems. These challenges include a wide range of considerations such as decision makers' boundaries, time and resource constraints, prior policy commitments, and other aspects of the policy environment and the context in which decisions will be made. We will address the particulars of these and other constraints in more detail in subsequent sections of the book. To make the task of policy analysis even more challenging, these constraints and the decision-making context frequently change at least once, even after the analyst has begun the analytic process.

Nevertheless, effective policy analysts are effective because they understand and confront these inherent and nested challenges at the outset of the analytic task. Policy analysis is hard to do well because to be successful, the analyst has to deal squarely with all three of these sequential sets of challenges, each step of which can prove fatal if ignored. When things go wrong or if the recommendation proves faulty, analytical shortcomings can usually be traced back to one of these three potential problem areas. The challenge is to anticipate and account for potential problems before beginning each successive step of the problem-solving methodology.

In sum, the policy analyst has to confront the challenges posed by the scientific method, the additional hazards of that method as it is applied to social scientific questions, and the final and critical constraints and challenges specific to policy analysis itself. In order to perform effective policy analysis, we have to understand these challenges and likely limitations of our analytic task from the beginning. Therefore, effective policy analysis must be grounded in an understanding of all three distinctive sets of challenges that face the problem solver. They are considerations that the effective policy analyst always keeps in the back of his or her mind while working through a problem. These distinctive challenges are a large part of the reason that the process of policy analysis is often iterative rather than simply sequential in its application. In the next few sections, we will examine in detail each one of the three nested processes and the related challenges that each process poses for the analyst.

## The Scientific Method

As noted previously, when we speak of the scientific method we are referring to the goal of identifying important questions and then answering those questions as best we can through careful theorizing and objective observation. The effective policy analyst understands that this process is best described as a method that proceeds logically from the characterization of the problem at hand to the identification and collection of information needed to evaluate the problem. The analyst also understands that the scientific method, applied correctly, provides for the crafting of a problem-solving plan of action that will allow him to gather the data needed to analyze the problem at hand efficiently and effectively. There are always time constraints in the world of policy analysis.

Figure 1 captures the scientific method in greater detail, and the research pyramid that it contains offers an easy way to visualize the scientific method as a six-step process. Each level of the pyramid represents a level of the process, and we work our way down those levels for the first three steps of the operation, then work our way back to the top of the pyramid for the last three steps. In order, the steps are as follows:

## Step 1: Formulate Your Theory

In the first of the six steps of the scientific method, we formulate our theory, in essence defining the nature of our research question or policy problem. In this initial and consequential step of the process, we draw upon our own reason, experience, and judgment as well as other research in formulating a statement of our expectations. Our *theory* can be a relatively abstract statement about how some aspect of the world works, a hunch about a relationship between various phenomena that occur in nature or society, or even merely a statement of our area of analytical interest. It is during this step of the process that we draw upon any previous work done by others to find out what is and is not known about our particular question or hunch. In the research process viewed generally, it is during this step that we decide whether we will aim to extend or challenge the findings of the previous scholarship. The policy analyst uses this preliminary examination of the evidence to begin to structure the problem and to begin to identify the existing empirical evidence that will shape our eventual policy alternatives and the evaluative criteria that we will use to assess them.

## Step 2: Operationalize the Theory

Once we have formulated our theory, the next step in the scientific method is to *operationalize* it. We operationalize our relatively abstract theory when we turn it into a set of concrete, measurable, and testable *hypotheses*. As Figure 1 shows, ideally we aim to create a set of hypotheses rather than only one hypothesis, as the usual problems with uncertainty make it better to have multiple tests of our theory's validity rather than only one. During the process of operationalization, we also identify our *independent* and *dependent* variables. As these names suggest, if we believe that two variables are related in some way, we are also likely to believe that we can use one variable to predict changes in the other; the dependent variable is the one whose value depends upon the value of the other variable. We call that other variable the independent variable because we believe it to be varying freely, at least in the sense that its value is independent of the dependent variable's value.

When we hypothesize these types of relationships between variables, it is usually helpful to graph the relationship. Figure 2 shows an example of such a relationship. As we can see in Figure 2, this analyst has a theory that there is a relationship between a person's level of education and his overall wealth. The analyst has operationalized that theory into a set of testable hypotheses. One of those hypotheses is described graphically in Figure 2, as the analyst believes that we will find a *positive correlation* between the variables "years of education" (the independent variable) and "yearly income" (the dependent variable). That is, this analyst expects that if we were to plot various people's educational attainment measured in years versus their respective amounts of annual income, we would find that as the education increased, the income would increase at the same time. This means that on the graph, $X4$ is greater than $X2$, and we expect that $Y4$ is also greater than $Y2$ in a positive correlation. Conversely, in a *negative correlation* the value of the dependent variable decreases as the value of the independent variable increases.

It is also important to note that we may or may not believe that the changes in our independent variable actually cause the corresponding changes in the dependent variable. In some cases, we may theorize *causality*, or a cause and effect relationship, but in other cases we may merely see a *correlation*, or a statistical relationship. In *spurious relationships* there is a statistical relationship between two variables but that relationship is purely coincidental.

During this second step of the six-step research process, it is critical that we carefully sort out these issues while defining our key terms and translating our theory into concrete, measurable, and

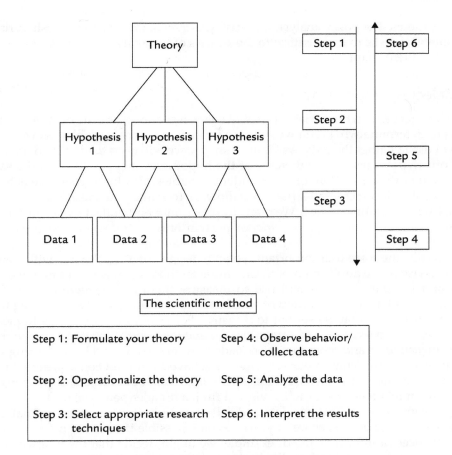

The scientific method

Step 1: Formulate your theory    Step 4: Observe behavior/
                                          collect data

Step 2: Operationalize the theory    Step 5: Analyze the data

Step 3: Select appropriate research    Step 6: Interpret the results
        techniques

**Figure 1.  The Research Pyramid**

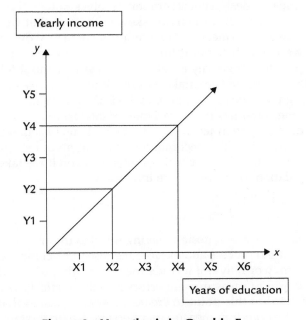

**Figure 2.  Hypothesis in Graphic Form**

testable hypotheses. The policy analyst has a distinctive set of tasks to accomplish during this phase of policy analysis, tasks that are critical to the success of the analysis. These tasks are described in detail in subsequent chapters.

## Step 3: Select Appropriate Research Techniques

Once we have decided on the variables we will use to test our theory, the next step of the scientific method is to determine what data we will use to measure those variables, as well as the means that we will use to gather the data. As Figure 1 shows, we will need to identify data to be collected for all of our hypotheses, although some of the hypotheses might rely upon the same data for measuring either the dependent or independent variables. Our basic goal here is to select types of data and collection techniques that will allow us to make *generalizations* about the broader theory that we are aiming to test. We want to select data and collection techniques that avoid giving us results that are *sample specific,* or pertain only to the particular data that we have collected.

Additionally, there are four important research design concerns that we will need to consider during this phase of the application of the scientific method. First, we want to make sure that our variables and the data that we will use to measure them are *appropriate* to our hypothesis. Appropriateness refers to the question of whether or not we are actually measuring the characteristic, quality, or feature that we set out to measure. For example, if we aimed to measure yearly income, but selected a technique of data collection that ignored the income a person received from interest on investments and other income outside of wages, we would be measuring wages rather than yearly income. This shift in our variable might have significant consequences for the validity of the generalizations that we would make after completing our analysis, even though the difference might seem relatively minor when viewed from a broader perspective.

We also want to ensure that our data and collection techniques are *feasible.* That is, it does not help us to identify the best measure of yearly income possible if there are no means of accurately gathering the needed information. For example, we might decide that the best way of measuring yearly income would be to examine the income tax returns of all of the residents of a particular town. Even though the income tax returns would provide us with a solid (though not perfect) measurement of yearly income, this measure is not a feasible one. It is not feasible because we are unlikely to gain access to that personal information, and even if we did have that access, it is unlikely that we would have the time to look at every person's return in even a modest sized town.

A third important research design consideration involves potential *biases* in our data and data collection methods. *Bias* refers to any systematic skew in the way that we measure our variable of interest. For example, if we were to measure the average income in a town through questions asked in a telephone survey, we would bias our estimate of average income upward due to the fact that we would be excluding from our survey all of those citizens without telephones. The term bias refers to any non-random errors that we make as a result of our choice of data collection methods. The fourth aspect of design that we are concerned with is the possibility of other *measurement errors,* or random errors in our measurement of the variables of interest to our study. In general, we would like to select data and data collection techniques that enable us to achieve *efficient estimates* of our variable values. An efficient estimating technique is one that gives us a good chance of achieving estimates close to the true value of the variable of interest, even if we take a relatively small sample from the whole population in which we are interested.

## Step 4: Observe Behavior/Collect Data

After we have completed our research design, having selected the appropriate research techniques, we begin the fourth step of the process and execute the research action plan. As we begin our data collection efforts, which may or may not include the observation of specific behaviors, we aim to avoid introducing any biases or measurement errors into those efforts. It is important to note that while we have worked hard to this point to create a research design that precludes or manages potential sources of bias and random measurement errors, we understand that we cannot foresee everything that will take place once we actually begin our data collection. With this in mind, we have to remain vigilant even as we execute the plan, identifying and managing unanticipated sources of bias or measurement error and adapting our collection strategies as necessary as the plan unfolds.

## Step 5: Analyze the Data

Once we have gathered our data, we begin to work our way back up the research pyramid, evaluating each of our hypotheses in light of the data that we have collected. During this step in the process, we also ask ourselves whether or not we believe in the data that we have collected, now that we have it. In other words, now that we have gathered the information that we thought we needed, we ask ourselves whether we find those data to be compelling and persuasive. What do the data tell us?

## Step 6: Interpret the Results

Once we are convinced of the validity of our data and the implications of those data for our hypotheses, we return to the top of our research pyramid by interpreting our results. In this sixth and final step we use our data and hypotheses to comment on the validity of our theory. Did we confirm what we thought in the first place? Or did we discover that the evidence does not support our theory? Did we accomplish what we set out to do? At this stage in our research effort, we also consider how we might use the knowledge we have gained, and we ask ourselves what the implications of our findings might be. As we will see later in our examination of this process applied specifically to the task of policy analysis, it is also important that we now ask ourselves exactly how we will articulate our results.

# Social Science and the Challenge of Uncertainty

While the application of the scientific method presents its own challenges to the policy analyst seeking to achieve objective and rational analytic results, the fact that we generally operate in the realm of social science adds additional challenges to that mix. The application of the scientific method to the social sciences is often more difficult than the application of that method to the physical sciences owing to the challenge of uncertainty. *Uncertainty* is a general term that refers to all of the potential difficulties that social scientists experience in defining and measuring variables of interest to our various research endeavors. For example, if a chemist decides to measure a quantity of some substance, such as the metal iron, he can do so with relative ease. He selects an arbitrarily defined unit such as a gram, specifies the conditions of temperature and pressure under which the measurement will take place, and measures the amount of the substance that he is examining. This measurement is uncontroversial, as other chemists would agree that this chemist had measured so many units of the substance and that the substance was iron.

On the other hand, consider the task that faces the political scientist aiming to measure a person's political partisanship. What unit of measurement does she use? How does she gather the data or take the measurement? She can define a "Democrat" in any number of ways including party registration, voting behaviors, other forms of political participation, and public policy attitudes. Furthermore, if she decides to use voting behaviors as the means through which she will measure political partisanship, how will she get access to that information? If she decides to conduct a sample survey to gather information on people's voting histories, there are numerous ways that her data can be biased or measured incorrectly. For example, people might forget who they actually voted for some time ago, or they might misrepresent their voting records. Furthermore, some types of people might be more likely than others to respond to this kind of request for personal information, and this political scientist might find her results to be biased for that reason. Finally, after she had collected her data, it would be likely that other political scientists might want to challenge those findings, arguing that other methods of defining "political partisanship" or collecting the data were more appropriate than those she selected. These uncertainties all combine to make investigations in the social sciences harder to conduct well than those in the physical sciences in terms of basic research design, and this uncertainty also means that we are generally less confident of the universal applicability of our findings when we have finished our research effort.

To be more precise on this point, the social scientist faces the challenge of uncertainty at every step of the six-step research process. Social science is concerned with the study of human behaviors, interactions, and societies, and this focus on all things human has inherent complexity and a measure of arbitrariness that colors our research effort from the start. As we formulate our theory, we find that it is often difficult to isolate, even theoretically, the likely causes of some human event, reaction, or tendency. Human nature and human interactions are so complex that it is a distinct challenge to sort through the logic we use to establish our basis for investigation. This challenge of uncertainty becomes even more pronounced as we begin to operationalize our rather abstract theory into workable hypotheses.

Returning to the example of the theorized relationship between "education" and "wealth" that we considered earlier, we find that the challenges of uncertainty inherent in the application of the scientific method to social scientific questions are readily apparent. First, while a social scientist might believe that education does in fact help to determine a person's wealth, no social scientist would claim that education was the only factor determining that wealth. So from the outset of our research, into the relatively broad and abstract notion that there is a relationship between a person's education and his or her overall wealth, the social scientist must admit from the start that there are numerous other variables at work that will influence the relationship that we seek to assess.

Furthermore, the process does not get any easier as we operationalize the theory. As we seek to turn the abstract notions of "education" and "wealth" into more concrete and measurable variables that we can use to create testable hypotheses, we run into more sources of uncertainty as we go along. For example, we might use years of education to measure education and yearly income to measure overall wealth, as suggested in Figure 2. However, we would quickly find inadequacies in those measures that might cause problems for us later on when we sought to make generalizations about our findings after gathering the necessary data.

One such potential problem would be found in the use of years of education to measure education in general. While it would be a relatively easy matter to measure a person's number of years of education on a numeric scale, we must also acknowledge that not all years of education are comparable. Some schools are better than others, some students work harder than others during a calendar year, and some types of postsecondary educational experiences could be expected to have a greater impact upon earning potential than others. So while the variable "years of education" could be expected to capture certain aspects of the larger concept "education," we can also see that this measure falls short in several other respects at the same time. Again, this shortcoming falls under the umbrella of the larger idea of uncertainty, and the task that confronts us as social scientists (and policy analysts) is to manage the sources of uncertainty as best we can, understanding that we will never be able to eliminate the potential problem completely. In fact, after carefully considering the alternatives, the researcher might conclude that despite the measure's shortcomings, "years of education" is the most appropriate, feasible, unbiased, and best-measured variable that can be used to get at the larger concept of "education" given the constraints at hand.

As we can see, the same kinds of argument would probably surround the use of yearly income as a measure of overall wealth as well, though we might have even more misgivings about that particular variable. Furthermore, other similar challenges would await us as we next selected the mechanisms through which we would gather our data. Typical methods of data collection in the social sciences include personal and telephonic interviewing, surveys, direct (or participant) observation, primary and secondary document or dataset analysis, and other related means. Each of these methods of data collection comes with its own set of methodological advantages and disadvantages in terms of potential biases, measurement errors, and other plausible sources of uncertainty. The social science researcher is well advised to spend a considerable amount of time in thinking through these and other methodological challenges in advance of any serious data collection or even in advance of a preliminary gathering of relevant evidence. Time spent thinking through these challenges at the outset is usually repaid handsomely in time saved later on in the project and leads to greater validity in the results. Careful research design is the key source of efficiency in any research endeavor, and this is unquestionably true in social science research, given the particular challenges of uncertainty that the social scientist must confront and manage.

# Empirical Analysis and Normative Concerns

Before we turn our attention fully to the specific task of policy analysis, it is appropriate to elaborate a bit upon the distinction between *empirical* and *normative analysis.* Simply put, empirical analysis deals with questions of "is," while normative analysis addresses questions of "ought." In a very real sense, normative concerns add to the nested challenges of the task facing the policy analyst. While physical scientists certainly do not wholly disregard normative concerns or questions of "right" and "wrong" in applying the scientific method in their research endeavors, these normative considerations are frequently secondary at best. That is, one major goal of the scientific method is to separate opinions, hunches, and personal beliefs from the pursuit of substantive truths about the ways that nature works. Therefore, while normative concerns clearly have a place in the physical scientist's endeavors, these concerns are generally relegated to the position of second-order questions. Physical scientists search for "truth," and the normative implications of that truth are considered after its empirical revelations.

Social scientists, however, and the policy analyst as one of those social scientists, even if they share the physical scientists' goal of separating normative concerns from the scientific enterprise, find that normative concerns are inextricably mixed up in the questions they investigate. In fact, it is difficult to think of any public policy question debated in the public sphere today that does not have a significant human component. Similarly, most business concerns have incorporated a respect for the human and social consequences of their business activities into their standard operating practices and decision making, whether out of pragmatism, necessity, or a simple desire to do the right thing.

In any event, normative considerations shape the social scientists' application of the scientific method to social science questions in a number of ways. First, normative considerations in policy analysis add a layer of subjectivity to our analysis that is difficult to avoid, if it can be avoided at all. This subjectivity comes from the basic premise that values are exactly that—subjective interpretations of what is an acceptable behavior or attitude, and what is not, Therefore, not only will the policy analyst almost necessarily bring to bear his or her own values to any policy analysis, but that analyst is also likely to run into at least modest differences in values among the other participants in the analytic task. The normative components of the policy analysis that serve as the basis for a policy recommendation may be agreed upon by members of one organization, only to be rejected or seriously questioned by members of another. This subjectivity inherent in normative considerations can also take the form of constraints upon potential courses of action that will prevent us from approaching the objective rationality that we strive to achieve.

Likewise, normative concerns almost always include additional sources of uncertainty (for example, additional issue complexity and difficulty of qualification or quantification) that can obscure the analytic task. By their very nature, normative concerns are difficult to define and measure, a characteristic that has significant consequences when we try to impose a rational and ordered method of criterion assessment upon competing potential courses of action. As we look further into the specific techniques of policy analysis, it will be apparent that the additional challenges that the normative components of our analysis present should not be underestimated and that they are challenges that must be confronted squarely by the policy analyst throughout the analysis.

None of these points regarding the role of normative analysis should be construed as aiming at diminishing the role or importance or of normative considerations in policy analysis and other social scientific research endeavors. On the contrary, it is these normative concerns that make the analytic task as critical as it is. There are human consequences to the choices and recommendations that we make in the course of our analysis. The inevitability of these consequences makes it especially important that we understand the nature of the challenges that the social scientist must confront, so that we take the proper steps to give ourselves the best chance possible of arriving at the "right" answers. More often than not, the normative considerations asserted or implied by the social scientist's theory formulation are in fact the first-order questions of most importance to us all.

# The Goals of Policy Analysis

The ultimate goal of the policy analyst is to achieve objective rationality in the consideration of important issues, but in a sense this goal represents the Holy Grail of the analytical world. That is, effective policy analysts continually strive to achieve this standard, even as they know full well that they can never quite get there given the limits inherent in the analytic task. Nevertheless, *objective rationality* is the goal, and this term refers to analysis based upon careful reasoning, logic, and empirical observation that is uninfluenced by emotion, predispositions, and personal preferences. This is not to say that hunches, experience, and intuition cannot be right on occasion or that they contribute nothing to the analysis, but rather that no assumption should remain untested, or at least unconsidered, during the process of objective rational analysis. The point here is that we strive to approximate objective rationality, even when we know that we can never wholly eliminate those considerations that divert us from that standard.

In addition to this overarching goal, which shapes the effective analyst's approach to problem solving in the first place, the analyst also usually has another related objective in mind from the outset of the analytical effort. Generally speaking, policy analysts are either interested in finding the most efficient solution to their problems, one that maximizes a particular criterion value, or they are alternately intent upon finding a solution that achieves the optimal combination of a number of specified criteria of interest to them. To put this in practical terms, analysts concerned with *efficiency* are usually interested in finding a solution to their issue that maximizes the net benefit to be realized from a policy change, with this net benefit most often measured in dollars. In the second case, the analyst concerned with achieving *optimality* is interested in identifying the solution that offers the most desirable mix of values among a set of criteria. These criteria can include anything of importance to the analyst, including normative considerations, and the various criteria can be weighted in importance in any way deemed appropriate by the analyst.

These alternative objectives correspond to the two most prevalent methods of policy analysis. *Cost-benefit analysis* (CBA) allows the analyst concerned with achieving efficiency in terms of net costs and benefits to consider alternatives in light of this criterion in a structured way. CBA involves the careful identification and quantification of all of the costs and benefits associated with potential policy changes. Competing potential courses of action, including the status quo, are then compared with one another on the basis of projected net costs or benefits. The alternative that offers the greatest likely net benefit is the option that is recommended to the decision maker.

For those analysts interested in identifying the optimal mix among a set of utilitarian and normative criteria, *multi-attribute analysis* (MAA) is the appropriate analytical technique. MAA allows the analyst to identify the policy alternative in a set of potential courses of action that will offer the most attractive combination or best balance among a set of consequential criteria. In the application of this technique, competing potential courses of action, again including the status quo, are evaluated in accordance with the various selected criteria. The criteria values for each course of action are then translated to a common scale, with the various criteria weighted in terms of their relative importance. Each potential course of action receives an overall score, and the alternative with the best overall score becomes the recommended alternative.

Given the usual uncertainties associated with many issues, the calculated net benefits and the multi-attribute scores may in fact be represented as the expected values of a set of probabilities. Furthermore, in the application of each of the methods of policy analysis, the critical assumptions that shape the analytical logic are examined carefully to determine whether the results are sensitive to change. These methods of analysis, each examined in detail in later chapters, represent the formal ways in which policy analysts seek to solve policy problems by approximating objective rationality as well as possible.

# The Limits of Rationality

A number of factors inherent in the process of policy analysis prevent us from attaining the objective rationality that we set out to achieve. As noted in previous sections, the scientific method itself comes with distinct challenges in terms of our ability to carry out empirical analysis. Even in the best of situations, it is difficult to define our theories and hypotheses precisely, and it is similarly difficult to find data that are wholly appropriate to the variables and concepts that we seek to measure. Furthermore, the application of the scientific method to social science questions adds an additional layer of uncertainty and difficulty to our research efforts given the challenges of measurement and the arbitrariness and complexity of human behaviors in the first place. The research enterprise would be difficult enough if these were the only challenges that we faced in the pursuit of objective rationality.

However, our bid for this ideal standard is further limited by additional challenges inherent in the analytic task itself The two most important additional challenges that policy analysts face are those of *prediction* and *particularity*. In general, social scientists aim to accomplish three distinct goals at different times. Sometimes social scientists attempt to *explain* various human phenomena or human events, that is, they examine a mass of information pertaining to a phenomenon or event with the goal of identifying the most important facts regarding an aspect of that characteristic or event. An example of this goal is provided by the historian who attempts to explain the rationale behind a nation's decision to go to war. A second goal of the social scientist is to *describe* human characteristics or a human event. In this instance, the social scientist uses a limited amount of information, and extrapolates from the limited known information to tell us more than we knew before about a characteristic or event. An example of this research endeavor is the political scientist who conducts a limited exit poll during a state election but uses the information gathered to make broad generalizations about what it was that caused the entire electorate of the state to vote the way they did.

The third, and most challenging, goal of the social scientist, however, is to predict future human events or the implications of changes in the human condition, social relationships, or social arrangements. When the social scientist offers a *prediction,* this means that the social scientist is taking a limited amount of information and projecting future events and outcomes. The idea here is that regardless of the amount of information available to the social scientist, the uncertainty and complexity inherent in social science endeavors means that at best we can provide probabilities in our predictions, but not guarantees. Even worse, in the realm of policy analysis, it is probable that we will not be able to account for everything that is likely to occur once a policy change is implemented. Policy analysts call this usual unanticipated variance from predicted outcomes "the law of unintended consequences." Effective policy analysts understand the limits of rationality from this perspective. Things will never turn out exactly the way that we expect.

The second direct challenge to objective rationality that the policy analyst faces to a greater extent than other social scientists is the challenge presented by the *particularity* of the usual policy problem. *Particularity* refers to the fact that most policy problems and their potential solutions are specific to a particular context. More than most social science endeavors, policy analysis does not lend itself readily to out-of-sample generalization. As an example, if the city of Atlanta changes its policy of binding arbitration that defines its negotiating relationship with its firefighters and police officers, it does not necessarily follow that comparably sized Pittsburgh will realize the same effects if it makes a similar change. Some of the consequences of the change in Atlanta will be different from the implications of the change for Pittsburgh, owing to variations in political climate, citizen expectations, union reactions, negotiating tactics, and budgetary differences, among other differences. Prediction and particularity challenge the policy analyst in the pursuit of rationality, and they limit the rationality possible in both the process and the product.

## Other Challenges for the Policy Analyst

In addition to the challenges inherent in the social science task itself, there are a number of other contextual challenges that also conspire to prevent the analyst from approaching objective rationality. The first of these additional challenges is ordinary: lack of enough time to carry the analysis through to its logical completion. Deadlines, competing demands for time, and the scope of the analytic task itself limit the analyst's time, and it is unlikely that the analyst will have the luxury of unconstrained time to deliberate on a given policy question except for the most critical of analytic tasks. Analysts almost always end up making hard trade-offs between time and depth of analysis.

Likewise, analysts typically face other resource constraints in their efforts at thorough, rational, and unbiased analysis. They often have to choose methods of data collection that are less effective but also less resource intensive than others in order to get the baseline information upon which they will base their predictions. To explain this constraint another way, policy analysis is usually conducted within a budget, and analysts are frequently limited in the range of data collection methods available to them in their analysis given budgetary constraints. This constraint can involve limits on the purchase of relevant datasets, limits on money available for surveying or telephonic interviewing, or other similar restrictions.

The policy analyst is likely to encounter other roadblocks on the path to rationality as well. Many times, the range of feasible prospective policy changes is limited by prior policy commitments or decisions made in the past in the particular issue area. These prior commitments can limit the range of feasible change in two ways. First, the prior commitments can reduce the number of potential courses of action available to the analyst. Furthermore, the prior commitments can encourage *incrementalism,* or a tendency to implement only modest changes to the existing policies, in the overall approach to change. Decision makers' preferences, political considerations, and other factors serve to reinforce this tendency toward incrementalism in policy making in general and therefore serve as further constraints on the rational analyst's pursuit of objective and reasoned policy recommendations. With all of these caveats in mind, one might wonder why we should bother engaging in formal policy analysis in the first place. We bother because it is the process of formal policy analysis that gives us the best chance of "getting it right," even if our rationality exists only in segments within the boundaries of a political and uncertain world.

## The General Analytical Framework

Although this book outlines two distinct problem-solving methods aimed at two different sets of evaluative criteria, there is a basic analytical framework common to those and other rational approaches to policy analysis. This problem-solving framework proceeds sequentially but is also iterative. That is, even though this method of considering policy problems is intended to proceed in a logical and progressive step-by-step fashion, it is common for the analyst to repeat steps of the process as new information defines and redefines the problem, alternatives, and evaluative criteria. Even so, there is a beginning, middle, and end to the task. In essence, this analytical framework represents the scientific method applied to the particular case of policy analysis.

As Table 1 illustrates, there are nine steps in the process viewed generally. The first and possibly most crucial step of the problem-solving process is that of *defining the problem.* During this stage of the process of policy analysis, we conduct our preliminary investigation of the issue area, gather relevant evidence, and define the terms of the issue as precisely as we can. As the problem

### Table 1.  The Basic Analytical Framework

**The Basic Analytical Framework**

Step 1:   Define the problem

Step 2:   Generate potential courses of action (COA)

Step 3:   Identify the potential advantages and disadvantages of each COA

Step 4:   Select the evaluative criteria

Step 5:   Predict the consequences of each COA in terms of the evaluative criteria

Step 6:   Analyze the sensitivity of your critical assumptions and findings

Step 7:   Choose a recommended COA

Step 8:   Articulate your recommendation

Step 9:   Implement, supervise, and assess the results

of definition has critical implications for the shape of all activity that will follow, we will take a much closer look at this process in chapter 2. After we have defined the problem and in the process determined whether a problem actually exists, we turn our attention to *generating potential courses of action*, or COAs. It is important to note from the outset that this is a distinct step in itself, and it is the second rather than first step in the analytical process. More often than not, many analysts and decision makers begin their analysis as a "yes/no" proposition that revolves around one seemingly desirable potential COA. It is not uncommon for this kind of "analysis" to become an exercise in rationalization in which the "analyst" is instructed to find evidence that will support a particular recommendation. Check with any local legislator's staff if you doubt that this kind of analysis exists. This kind of analytical activity has given rise to the wry expression, "That's a solution in search of a problem."

But for the objective and rational analyst in search of an honest assessment of a policy problem, the generation of potential COAs involves brainstorming, interviewing, primary and secondary document analysis, and other activities. The analyst's goal is to take an open-minded approach to the consideration of potential solutions to a well-defined need. The analyst is careful to generate all of the potential COA prior to beginning to evaluate any of them. The effective analyst understands that COA generation and evaluation are distinct steps in the analytical process. Chapter 3 addresses this process in much more detail.

Once we have generated potential solutions to our well-defined policy problem, we then begin our assessments of each of these potential COAs. We accomplish this initial assessment through a somewhat freeform *identification of the advantages and disadvantages of each COA*. That is, we aim to identify every potential advantage and disadvantage that might be associated with a possible policy change, however large or small and whether empirical or normative in nature. In some cases, we may find that potential disadvantages associated with a COA might even preclude that COA's further consideration, and it is at this point that we would reject that COA as being unfeasible.

As we identify these potential advantages and disadvantages, we also begin to think about the characteristics of any solution to our problem that are likely to be most important to us. We then *select the evaluative criteria* that we will use to formally assess our alternative COAs. It is at this point that we also select an analytic technique, as we most often either focus on the sole criterion of efficiency or seek to achieve optimality among a set of criteria. In chapter 4 we carefully examine the application of cost-benefit analysis as it relates to the pursuit of efficiency, while in chapter 5 we detail the application of the technique of multi-attribute analysis, which enables us to achieve the rational optimality that we might seek. Using these techniques then, we *predict the consequences of each COA in terms of the evaluative criteria*.

These predictions are based on logic, empirical evidence, and probabilities, and we therefore take the additional precaution of *analyzing the sensitivity of our analysis in light of our critical assumptions and assessments*. After that careful analysis of the sensitivity of our assumptions and findings, we *choose a COA* that we will recommend, and we *articulate our findings and recommendation*. Finally, we *implement* our policy change, supervise that implementation to ensure that the decision maker's intent is met, and assess the consequences, both intended and otherwise, of the policy change. In some cases the analyst has a role in the implementation and in some cases not, but in all cases the analyst seeks to learn from that implementation as it certainly affects future policy analysis in that issue area. Chapters 6 and 7 examine some of these special considerations in the final stages of the analytical process.

## Notes and Supplementary Readings

Complete bibliographic entries for the sources listed in this section and in the notes for the succeeding chapters are contained in the bibliography at the end of the book. While this list of works is certainly not an exhaustive compilation of the fine literature in the fields of policy analysis and policy making, taken together these scholarly works are intended to provide insightful, focused, and comprehensive insights into key topics addressed in the associated chapters.

- Scholars and analysts have debated the desirability and feasibility of the pursuit of rationality in policy analysis for many years. S.I. Benn and G.W. Mortimore offer various definitions of "rationality" as commonly employed in the social sciences as well as a classic critique of those applications in their edited volume, *Rationality and the Social Sciences* (1978). The book is a collection of papers by various scholars in the social sciences dealing with the different aspects and implications of rationalism as it pertains to social scientific inquiry. Of particular note is S. I. Benn's chapter 10, "Rationality and Political Behaviour," in which the author gives an effective overview of Anthony Downs's concept of voter "role-rationality." Benn also describes "strong" versus "weak" rationality as they relate to public preferences and participation in political and policy-making events.

- In a parallel vein, Stuart Nagel describes alternative definitions of "rationality" in chapter 1 of *Policy Studies: Integration and Evaluation* (1988), and he addresses the criteria for evaluating the quality of policy studies research in chapter 2 of the book. Among these criteria, he includes usefulness, validity, and importance, and he analyzes the fundamental goals of the criteria selection.

- In *Public Policy Decision Making: Systems Analysis and Comparative Advantages Debate* (1973), Bernard L. Brock, James Chesebro, John Gragus, and James Klumpp, offer a critique of earlier attempts at rational, comprehensive policy analysis in describing the evolution of the decision-making process. In chapter 1, the authors focus on the limits inherent in the "comprehensive rational" approach and on the challenges posed by having policy participants and decision makers involved in the problem solving process. In chapter 2, the authors address the implications of the policy-making environment for the analytic process. The authors describe the characteristics of "closed" versus "open" policy systems and the impact of environmental interaction on the resulting decision-making processes. Subsequent chapters of the book relate these and other concepts to the broader process of policy analysis viewed from a "systems" perspective.

- Morris P. Fiorina and Ian Shapiro debated the validity of rational choice approaches to social science questions in a pair of articles in the *New York Times* on February 26, 2000. Fiorina argued that the rational choice approach has limitations, like other social science models, but that its benefits outweigh its shortcomings. He went on to argue that the model's validity is apparent in most analyses of political outcomes, and he saw the model as being particularly valuable in the high-stakes political choices and the key policy decisions that individual actors and governments make. Shapiro, on the other hand, saw shortfalls in the predictive capabilities of political science models based upon rational choice assumptions. These scholars' exchange is representative of an ongoing debate in much of social science regarding the validity and desirability of rational choice approaches to a variety of questions.

- Catherine Hakim elaborates upon the importance of research design considerations as they apply to social science research generally in chapter 1 of *Research Design: Successful Designs for Social and Economic Research* (2000). She also describes the respective advantages and disadvantages of the various methods of data collection in chapters 4 through 9 of the book, including a look at the challenges of sample surveying in chapter 6.

- Lavinia Mitton, Holly Sutherland, and Melvyn Weeks describe the benefits of "microsimulation models" in policy analysis in chapter 1 of their edited volume, *Microsimulation Modelling for Policy Analysis* (2000). This technique involves the use of micro-level data to glean insights into the effect of policy changes at the individual level. These insights can then be aggregated to offer estimates of the likely overall effect of a potential policy change. The book also addresses in detail the various and significant challenges of prediction that confront the policy analyst in the pursuit of valid estimates.

- Chapter 3 of William N. Dunn's edited volume, *Values, Ethics, and the Practice of Policy Analysis* (1983), examines the role of normative considerations in public policy analysis. In that chapter, Pamela Doty finds that normative concerns are prominent in the majority of policy products obtained from policy-oriented research institutes, regardless of the areas of policy interest. This finding suggests that the cost-benefit analyses and efficiency-based policy evaluations that predominate today may in fact be missing key policy concerns as a result of the reliance on this particular method.

- Stuart Nagel offers a description of rational choice theory and rational choice approaches to policy analysis in chapter 2 of his edited volume, *Improving Policy Analysis* (1980). In chapter 2, John E. Brandl also addresses the fine line between viewing rational choice theory as a descriptive theory and embracing it as a normative standard. Brandl then examines the implications of self-interested behaviors and motives as they relate to the interpretation of policy alternatives. Chapter 4 offers a critique of attempts at purely "rational" analysis, as Jack Byrd Jr. argues that these efforts risk losing the advantages conferred by the judgment, intuition, and experience of the analyst.

- Gary King, Robert O. Keohane, and Sidney Verba analyze the essential features of effective research design in their important book, *Designing Social Inquiry* (1994). The first chapter explores the implications of the application of the scientific method to the social sciences in rigorous detail, and their subsequent chapters examine the concepts of "uncertainty," "bias," "measurement errors," and other design considerations. Additionally, the authors describe the various trade-offs that researchers make in selecting their means of data collection, as well as the various interpretations of the relationships that we theorize in our analysis.
- Charles Lindblom explains the limits on rationality in executive decision making and policy analysis in his article, "The 'Science' of Muddling Through" (1959), as well as his book, *The Policymaking Process* (1980), He describes the "root" method, or a rational-comprehensive approach, as unrealistic, and contrasts this approach with "successive limited comparisons," or a "branch" method. In chapter 3 of the book, Lindblom offers his thoughts on the limits of rational analysis given the usual context of politics in which that analysis occurs.
- In chapter 4 of *Agendas, Alternatives, and Public Policies* (1994), an important book on the policy-making process, John W. Kingdon identifies the natural limits on rational decision making and other factors that shape policy analysis. Additionally, he offers insights into the challenges associated with interview and case-study methodologies in his "Appendix on Methods" in the book. Richard F. Fenno Jr. also provides an important perspective on these and other methodological challenges in his own "Notes on Method: Participant Observation" in *Home Style: House Members in Their Districts* (1978).
- Robert Formaini describes the challenges of uncertainty in the context of risk assessment and probabilities in chapter 1 of *The Myth of Scientific Public Policy* (1990).
- David R. Mayhew provides an excellent example of the rational application of theory leavened with empirical analysis in *Congress: The Electoral Connection* (1974).
- In chapter 1 of Frank Fischer and John Forester's edited volume, *Confronting Values in Policy Analysis* (1987), Charles W. Anderson describes the challenges inherent in reducing public issues from relatively abstract values to specific policy choices. In chapter 2, Douglas J. Amy offers thoughts on the incorporation of ethics into policy questions and policy administration. In chapter 5, Bruce Jennings highlights the difficulties that face the analyst in interpreting the actual effects of existing policies and offers some potential prescriptions for those difficulties. Timothy W. Luke critiques rational choice theory in chapter 7, while Rosemarie Tong describes the particular ethical and political challenges that routinely confront policy analysts and administrators in the execution of their public responsibilities in chapter 8. In chapter 9, Leonard A. Cole elaborates on the ethical limitations on experimentation in social scientific inquiry in his description of the U.S. Army's testing procedures of the 1950s.
- In chapter 2 of *Theoretical Issues in Policy Analysis* (1988), M.E. Hawkesworth critiques the reliance upon empirical methods and rationalism in policy analysis, asserting the existence of a "fact/value dichotomy" that limits the effectiveness and desirability of those methods.
- In chapter 6 of Frank P. Scioli Jr. and Thomas J. Cook's *Methodologies for Analyzing Public Policies* (1975), Donald S. Van Meter and Herbert B. Asher offer a cautionary note regarding the limitations on the specification of cause and effect relationships in public policy analyses. At the same time, the authors argue for the need for theorizing causality in order to generate meaningful analytic designs. Van Meter and Asher also offer examples of partial and complete models of student performance to illustrate the importance of this step in the analytical process.
- Chapter 1 of Duncan MacRae Jr. and James A. Wilde's *Policy Analysis for Public Decisions* (1985) provides an alternative perspective on the elements of a successful policy analysis. This chapter also includes a brief glossary in which the authors outline some of the terms commonly found in the field of policy analysis.
- Randall S. Clemons and Mark K. McBeth offer a critique of the "rational public policy method" in chapter 2 of *Public Policy Praxis* (2001), and they comment on the difficulties of prediction inherent in the task of policy analysis. The authors go on in chapter 4 to give an overview of Kingdon's model of the public agenda setting process, offering that process as an alternative to rational formalism. Clemons and McBeth offer a variety of mini cases in support of their perspectives on policy making and analysis.
- Michael Corbett provides an alternative perspective on social scientific research methods along with an introduction to the MicroCase statistical software package in *Research Methods in Political Science* (2001).
- In chapter 1 of Stella A. Theodoulou and Matthew A. Cain's *Public Policy: The Essential Readings* (1995), Theodoulou differentiates between the "politics" and "policy" of public policy analysis. She also introduces a variety of theoretical perspectives on the policy-making process,

including group theory, elite theory, corporatism, and the theory of subgovernments. In chapter 2 of the book, Paul Sabatier traces the development of public policy studies as a subset of American political science.

- Charles F. Bonser, Eugene B. McGregor Jr., and Clinton V. Oster Jr. outline the history of the development of regulatory policies in American government in chapter 4 of *American Public Policy Problems* (2000).

- B. Guy Peters elaborates upon the wide variety of issues and forms of regulations encompassed by the term "public policy" in chapter 1 of *American Public Policy: Promise and Performance* (2000).

- Frank Fischer elaborates upon the challenges of integrating empirical analysis and normative concerns in chapter 1 of his book, *Evaluating Public Policy* (1995). Fischer goes on to offer a framework with which the analyst can place the evaluative criteria selected into the context of the organizational situation. In chapter 9 of the book, Fischer provides insight into the particular constraints and challenges that correspond to the consideration of environmental policy changes.

- Deborah Stone describes the shortcomings of efficiency-based techniques of policy analysis as they relate to normative considerations in *Policy Paradox: The Art of Political Decision Making* (1997). In chapter 2 of her book, the author examines the often-conflicting policy goals of equity, efficiency, security, and liberty.

- J. Johnston's *Econometric Methods* (1984) provides a detailed explication of the mathematics underlying applied econometrics. Peter Kennedy's *A Guide to Econometrics* (1998) offers similar rigor in its treatment of the subject of econometrics, but this text approaches the subject in a manner that will be more accessible to those with less grounding in mathematics.

- Stephen Van Evera's *Guide to Methods for Students of Political Science* (1997) offers an alternative explanation of the fundamental principles of social science research methodology applied to political questions. Chapter 2 of his book outlines an effective approach to case study selection as well as guidelines for knowing when the case study approach is an appropriate research technique.

- Fritz W. Scharpf explains rational choice applications and game theory in the analysis of institutions in *Games Real Actors Play: Actor-Centered Institutionalism in Policy Research* (1997).

- Chapter 1 of Kenneth A. Shepsle and Mark S. Bonchek's *Analyzing Politics: Rationality, Behavior, and Institutions* (1997) describes the evolution of goals within the field of political science over the last century. This chapter also offers an alternative perspective on the use of models and the assumption of rationality as they are applied in the discipline today.

- Chava Frankfort-Nachmias and David Nachmias present a thorough treatment of the various steps of the scientific method applied to human questions in *Research Methods in the Social Sciences*, 6th edition (2000). The chapters of this book survey the scientific method, research design, various data collection techniques, and the interpretation of the results. The book also includes an introduction to the SPSS statistical software package (SPSS, Inc.).

# Innovation and Diffusion Models in Policy Research

## FRANCES STOKES BERRY AND WILLIAM D. BERRY

Although most actions by governments are incremental in that they marginally modify existing programs or practices, and much research about policymaking seeks to explain why it tends to be incremental, ultimately every government program can be traced back to some nonincremental *innovation*.[1] Thus, one cannot claim to understand policymaking unless one can explain the process through which governments adopt new programs. Recognizing this, public policy scholars have conducted extensive inquiry into policy innovation.

When people speak of innovation in common parlance, they usually refer to the introduction of something *new*. But when should a government program be termed "new?" The dominant practice in the policy innovation literature is to define an innovation as a program that is new to the government adopting it (Walker 1969, p. 881). This means that a governmental jurisdiction can innovate by adopting a program that numerous other jurisdictions established many years ago. By embracing this definition, students of policy innovation explicitly choose not to study policy *invention*—the process through which *original* policy ideas are conceived. To flesh out the distinction via illustration, a single policy *invention* can prompt numerous American states to *innovate*, some many years after the others.

This chapter will review the dominant theories of government innovation in the public policy literature. However, we will see that these theories borrow heavily from ones developed to explain innovative behavior by *individuals*: for example, teachers using a new method of instruction (studied by education scholars), farmers adopting hybrid seeds and fertilizers (studied by rural sociologists), and consumers purchasing new products (studied by marketing scholars).[2] We will also see that theories of government innovation share many commonalities with models that seek to explain *organizational* innovation.

Some studies of government innovation have been cross-national, investigating how nations develop new programs and how such programs have diffused across countries (Heclo 1974; Collier and Messick 1975; Brown et al. 1979; Tolbert and Zucker 1983; Kraemer, Gurbaxani, and King 1992; Simmons 2000; Simmons and Elkins 2004; Weyland 2004; Brooks 2005; Gilardi 2005; Meseguer 2005a, 2005b). Other studies have focused on innovation by local or regional governments within the United States (Aiken and Alford 1970; Crain 1966; Bingham 1977; Midlarsky 1978; Lubell et al. 2002) or regional governments in other nations (Ito 2001). But the vast majority of empirical research on government innovation has examined policymaking by the American states. Because of this, we will devote our primary attention to state-level research. Although most models of policy innovation we describe can be extended to national and local governments, some of these models hinge at least partially on the competitive nature of states within a federal system and thus must be modified when applied to local or regional governments within a unitary system, or to nations in an international system or an organization like the European Economic Community.

Despite the extensive number of studies of state government innovation, at a general level, there are two principal forms of explanation for the adoption of a new program by a state: *internal determinants* and *diffusion* models (Berry and Berry 1990). Internal determinants models posit that the factors leading a jurisdiction to innovate are political, economic, or social characteristics internal to the state. In these models, states are not conceived as being influenced by the actions of other states. In contrast, diffusion models are inherently intergovernmental; they view state adoptions of policies as emulations of previous adoptions by other states. Both types of models were introduced to political scientists in Walker's (1969) seminal study of state government innovation across a wide range of policy areas.[3]

This chapter begins with separate discussions of the central features of internal determinants and diffusion models. We then turn to the methodologies that have been used to test them. Although most scholars have acknowledged that few policy adoptions can be explained purely as a function of (1) internal determinants (with no diffusion effects) or (2) policy diffusion (with no impact by internal factors), most *empirical* research conducted before 1990 focused on one type of process or the other. At the time of their introduction during the late 1960s and early 1970s, the "single-explanation" methodologies developed were highly creative approaches using state-of-the-art quantitative techniques. However, more recent research has shown that these traditional methodologies are severely flawed (Berry 1994b). In 1990, Berry and Berry presented a model of state lottery adoptions reflecting the simultaneous effects of both internal determinants and policy diffusion on state adoption behavior and employed event history analysis to test their model. In the last decade and a half, this approach has been emulated and extended in dozens of studies (see the Appendix).

## Diffusion Models

Rogers (1983, p. 5) defines diffusion as "the process by which an innovation is communicated through certain channels over time among the members of a social system." Students of state policy innovation positing diffusion models conceive of the governments of the fifty American states as a social system and maintain that the pattern of adoption of state policy results from states emulating the behavior of other states. Various alternative diffusion models have been developed (each of which will be discussed below), with the primary difference being the "channels" of communication and influence assumed to exist. However, we would argue that all these models hypothesize that states emulate each other for one of three basic reasons.

First, states *learn* from one another as they borrow innovations perceived as successful elsewhere. Relying on the classic model of *incremental* decisionmaking (Lindblom 1965; Simon 1947), Walker (1969) hypothesizes that state policymakers faced with complex problems seek decision-making shortcuts (see also Glick and Hays 1991; Mooney and Lee 1995). Lindblom (1965) maintains that one critical method of simplification is to restrict consideration to only those alternatives that are marginally different from the status quo. Walker argues that another simplification method is to choose alternatives that, although not minor modifications of current policy, have been pursued and proven effective or promising in other states. In essence, by showing how emulation of other states' innovations can be an aid in simplifying complex decisions, policy diffusion theorists have demonstrated how the adoption of *non*incremental policies can be consistent with the logic underlying incrementalism.[4]

Second, states *compete* with each other: they emulate policies of other states to achieve an economic advantage over other states or avoid being disadvantaged. For instance, states may decrease welfare benefits to match the levels of their neighbors to prevent becoming a "welfare magnet" for the poor (Peterson and Rom 1990; Volden 2002; Berry, Fording, and Hanson 2003; Bailey and Rom 2004; Berry and Baybeck 2005). Similarly, a state may adopt a lottery to reduce the incentive for its own citizens living near a boundary to cross the border to play in another state's game (Berry and Berry 1990; Berry and Baybeck 2005). In a final example, states may adopt economic development incentive programs already present in other states to prevent an exodus of businesses from the state (Gray 1994).[5]

Third, Walker (1969, p. 891) argues that, despite the autonomy that states possess in a federal system, there is pressure on all states to conform to nationally or regionally accepted standards. Such pressure leads states to adopt programs that have already been widely adopted by other states. Sometimes the pressure is what DiMaggio arid Powell (1983) label "coercive" when federal mandates give state governments little choice. In other cases, there is "normative" pressure on state officials to adopt the best practices in other states. State officials tend to be socialized into shared norms by common professional training (such as the master's in public administration degree) and by interaction in professional associations (e.g., the National Emergency Management Association).

As we review the various diffusion models developed in the policy innovation literature, each focusing on a different channel of communication and influence across government jurisdictions, we will see that each model relies on one or more of these three reasons to justify why states emulate other states when making public policy. We begin with the two models most commonly proposed in the literature—the national interaction model and the regional diffusion model—and finish with several other models positing different channels of influence.

## The National Interaction Model

This model assumes a national communication network among state officials regarding public-sector programs in which officials learn about programs from their peers in other states. It presumes that officials from states that have already adopted a program interact freely and mix thoroughly with officials from states that have not yet adopted it, and that each contact by a not-yet-adopting state with a previous adopter provides an additional stimulus for the former to adopt. The probability that a state will adopt a program is thus proportional to the number of interactions its officials have had with officials of already-adopting states (Gray 1973a). There are, indeed, formal institutional arrangements that encourage the thorough mixing of states. Chief among these are various associations of state officials that allow individuals with similar positions across the fifty states to meet periodically in national conferences. These include associations of elected "generalist" officials such as the National Governors' Association and the National Conference of State Legislatures, each of which have numerous committees on specific policy areas, as well as organizations of functionalist officials such as the National Association of General Service Administrators.

This learning model was developed and formalized by communication theorists analyzing the diffusion of an innovation through a social system (assumed to be of fixed size) consisting of individuals. In equation form, the model can be expressed as

$$\Delta N_t = N_t - N_{t-1} = bN_{t-1}\,[L - N_{t-1}].\ \text{[Equation 1]}$$

In this model, $L$ is the proportion of individuals in the social system that are potential adopters (a value assumed to remain constant over time), and serves as a ceiling on possible adoptions. If every person in the system is unconstrained and may adopt, $L$ equals one. $N_t$ is the cumulative proportion of adopters in the social system at the end of time period $t$, $N_{t-1}$ is the cumulative proportion at the end of the previous period, and thus $\Delta N_{t-1}$ is the proportion of new adopters during period $t$.[6] With some algebraic manipulation, the terms in Equation 1 can be rearranged to yield

$$N_t = (bL + 1)\,N_{t-1} - bN^2_{t-1}.\ \text{[Equation 2]}$$

Then, since Equation 2 is linear, given data on the timing of adoptions by all potential adopters, the parameters $b$ and $L$ can be estimated by regressing $N_t$ on $N_{t-1}$ and $N^2_{t-1}$.[7]

When the cumulative proportion of adopters is graphed against time, Equation 1 yields an S-shaped curve, like that reflected in Figure 1. Early in the diffusion process, adoptions occur relatively infrequently. The rate of adoptions then increases dramatically but begins to taper off again as the pool of potential adopters becomes small.

In an important early effort to enhance the theoretical precision of state government innovation research and explain states' adoptions of new policies with a widely applicable general theory of innovation, Virginia Gray (1973a; see also Menzel and Feller 1977; Glick and Hays 1991) employs Equation 2, assuming that the social system is the community of American states. Setting the time period as the calendar year, her regression analyses show that adoptions of several state policies—including Aid to Families with Dependent Children, education policies, and civil rights

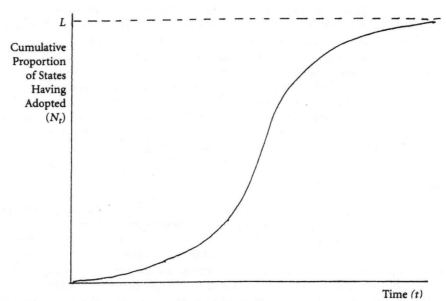

**Figure 1. S-Shaped Curve Consistent with National Interaction Model (Equation 1)**

laws—fit the equation very closely. But several factors limit the utility of the national interaction model—as traditionally conceived in Equations 1 and 2—for students of government innovation.

First, the model assumes that, during any time period, all potential adopters that have not yet adopted are equally likely to do so; the only variable influencing the probability that a potential adopter will adopt during any time period is the cumulative number of adopters prior to that period. Indeed, the model treats all potential adopters as totally undifferentiated actors who interact "randomly," that is, who are equally likely to have contact with all other members of the social system. Thus, the theory is well suited for when the social system is a large society of individuals and the scholarly interest is in a macro-level description of the diffusion process. While certainly in any society friendships and work and family relations guarantee that an individual's interactions with other members of the society are nonrandom, when studying the diffusion of a new consumer product through a large society, for instance, it may suffice to employ a model assuming random interaction. But when studying the diffusion of a policy through the fifty states, it seems less reasonable to treat the states as undifferentiated units; we know that Mississippi differs in many ways from New York, and our theory should probably take some of these differences into account. It is also likely that contacts between officials from different states are patterned rather than random.[8] It makes sense, for example, that politicians and bureaucrats in New York will have more contact with their counterparts in New Jersey than with officials in Mississippi.

Recently, the logic underlying the national interaction model has been modified to reflect a recognition that the professional associations encouraging interaction among state officials involve some states more than others, thereby prompting probabilities of policy adoption that vary across states. For example, Balla (2001) hypothesizes that states whose insurance commissioners sat on a committee of the National Association of Insurance Commissioners with jurisdiction over the regulation of HMOs were more likely than others to adopt model legislation proposed by the committee, due to the greater centrality of commissioners in the informational networks surrounding the proposed legislation.

## The Regional Diffusion Model

Whereas the national interaction model assumes that states interact with each other on a national basis, the regional diffusion model posits that states are influenced primarily by those states geographically proximate. Most of these models assume that states are influenced exclusively by those states with which they share a border; as such, we call them *neighbor* models. Specifically, these models hypothesize that the probability that a state will adopt a policy is positively related to the number (or proportion) of states bordering it that have already adopted it (e.g., Berry and Berry 1990; Mintrom 1997; Balla 2001). Other models, which we term *fixed-region* models, assume that the nation is divided into multiple regions (of contiguous states) and that states tend to emulate the policies of other states within the same region (e.g., Mooney and Lee 1995).

Both learning and competition can be the basis for assuming that diffusion channels are regional in nature. States are more likely to learn from nearby states than from those far away because states can more easily "analogize" to proximate states, which tend to share economic and social problems and have environments similar enough so that policy actions may have similar effects (Mooney and Lee 1995; Elazar 1972). However, it is when policy adoptions are attempts to compete with other states that the likelihood of regionally focused, rather than nationally based, diffusion seems greatest. Because of constraints on the mobility of most individuals and firms, states are more likely to compete with nearby states than with those far away. For example, states worried about losing revenue—especially those with large population centers near a border—are likely to be very concerned about whether their immediate neighbors have lotteries but unconcerned about remote states. Similarly, states fearful of becoming a welfare magnet may make immediate responses to policy changes by neighbors with large concentrations of poor people near their borders but may pay no attention to policy adjustments in far-away states (Berry and Baybeck 2005).

Although fixed-region and neighbor models are similar in that their emphasis is on the emulation of nearby states, the models are subtly different in their specified channels of influence. Fixed-region models presume (if only implicitly) that all states within the same region experience the same channels of influence. In contrast, neighbor models—by avoiding fixed regional groupings of states and instead pointing to the influence of all bordering states—assume that each state has a unique set of reference states for cues on public-sector innovations. Although one can discern policies where a neighbor model makes more sense than a fixed-region formulation (e.g., in the case of lottery adoptions), and vice versa, neither pure model is entirely realistic. Fixed-region models imply implausibly that some states—those bordering another region—are completely unaffected by some of their neighbors. Neighbor models assume that states that are close but share no border (e.g., Vermont and Maine) have no influence on one another. A more realistic regional diffusion model might assume that states are influenced most by their neighbors but also by other states that are nearby. One simple specification consistent with this assumption is that the level of influence of one state over another is proportional to the distance between the two states.

## Leader-Laggard Models

Leader-laggard models assume that certain states are pioneers in the adoption of a policy, and that other states emulate these leaders (Walker 1969, p. 893). Most often, scholars presume that leadership is regional, with states taking cues from one or more pioneer states within their geographical region (Walker 1969, 1973; Grupp and Richards 1975; Foster 1978). This model can be modified easily, however, to reflect the notion of national leaders: states that, when they adopt a new program, increase the likelihood that other states, regardless of their geographical location, will adopt. Leader-laggard models are consistent with the presumption that, in any policy area, some states' personnel are more highly regarded by their peers than other states' and that policymakers are more likely to turn to these states for cues.[9] As such, these models assume that states emulate other states in a *learning* process rather than because of interstate competition or a general pressure to conform.[10]

Although there are certainly strong reasons to expect leader states to emerge, thus forming the groundwork for leader-laggard diffusion, such models are often flawed by their failure to identify a priori (1) the states (or even types of states) that are expected to be pioneers, and (2) the predicted order of adoption of the states expected to follow. Indeed, without an a priori theoretical prediction of which state(s) will lead and the order in which the remaining states will follow, a leader-laggard model is virtually nontestable; any adoption pattern will involve some state (which ex-post-facto could be designated the pioneer) adopting a policy first and other states adopting afterward.

One leader-laggard model that clearly specifies the channels of diffusion is the *hierarchical* model developed by Collier and Messick (1975). Studying the pattern of social security adoptions by nations around the world, these authors hypothesize that the pioneers in social security were highly (economically) developed nations and that social security programs diffused down a hierarchy of nations from most developed to least developed.[11] Such an hypothesis specifies (in a testable fashion) the characteristics of leaders (high economic development) and a clear ordering of successive adoptions (from most-developed to least-developed countries). But note that, though the hierarchical model specifically posits diffusion of a policy across jurisdictions, its empirical prediction of a strong relationship between economic development and earliness of adoption is indistinguishable from that of an internal determinants model, which assumes no influence of states on one another and, instead, posits that the sole determinant of the propensity of a state to adopt is its level of development.

## Isomorphism Models

Some have argued that a state is most likely to take cues about adopting a new policy from other states that are similar, as these states provide the best information about the nature of the policy and the likely consequences of adopting it.[12] Sometimes this may lead to regional diffusion, as nearby states tend to be similar in a variety of ways. But states share similarities with states that are not geographically proximate. Grossback, Nicholson-Crotty, and Peterson (2004; see also Nicholson-Crotty 2004) stress especially the importance of ideological similarity, proposing that the effect of a policy adoption by a state will be greatest on states that are the most ideologically similar (on a liberal-conservative continuum). But Volden (2006) finds that policies diffuse based on a wide range of "political, demographic and budgetary similarities across states." Weyland (2004, p. 256) concludes that policies diffuse along "channels of cultural commonality and historic connection" among nations in Latin America, and Brooks (2005, p. 281) expects policies to diffuse within "peer groups [of nations], organized on the basis of shared geopolitical and economic characteristics."

## Vertical Influence Models

The vertical influence model sees states as emulating not the policies of other states—as part of a "horizontal" diffusion process—but, instead, the policies of the national government. One might view this model as conceptually similar to a leader-laggard model, which specifies that there is a single pioneer state; in effect, the national government serves the same role as a state-level pioneer. To the extent that states emulate the national government as a result of a learning process, the similarity between models is indeed quite strong; the national government is analogous to a widely respected leader state. But the reasons states are influenced by the national government to adopt policies extend beyond learning. In some cases, the national government can simply mandate certain activities by states (e.g., the National Voter Registration Act, which required states to allow people to register to vote at the same time they register their motor vehicles). Although one might label such a process diffusion, it is a highly uninteresting form of diffusion, as nearly all state discretion is eliminated by national-level fiat. A more interesting theoretical process results when states retain discretion but the national government provides incentives for the adoption of a policy by states. Typically, there are financial incentives resulting from a federal grant-in-aid program, as in the case of Medicaid and associated administration provisions. In another example, Derthick (1970) shows how the Social Security Act of 1935 shaped state welfare programs through the AFDC grant to the states. Moreover, Welch and Thompson (1980) find that policies for which the federal government offers incentives diffuse faster than "state preserve" policies (see also Brown 1975; Soss et al. 2001; Allen, Pettus and Haider-Markel 2004).[13]

## Internal Determinants Models

Internal determinants models presume that the factors causing a state to adopt a new program or policy are political, economic, and social characteristics of the state. Thus, in their pure form, these models preclude diffusion effects in which a state is influenced by the actions of other states or the national government. Certainly, once a policy is adopted by one state, it is extremely unlikely that another state's adoption would be *completely* independent from the previous one. Unless the two states arrived at the same (or very similar) policy via a highly improbable coincidence, at a minimum there must have been a diffusion from one state to the other of the *idea* for the policy. Thus, we believe that internal determinants models must acknowledge that, when a state adopts a policy new to the American states, media coverage and institutionalized channels of communication among state officials make it likely that knowledge of the policy spreads to other states.[14] However, such models assume that, once a state is aware of the policy, the internal characteristics of the state are what determine if and when an adoption will occur, rather than pressure created by other states' adoptions or explicit evaluations of the impacts of the policy in earlier-adopting states.

## The Choice of a Dependent Variable

One important theoretical issue in the construction of internal determinants models is how the dependent variable—the propensity of a state to adopt a policy or a set of policies—is defined. In research prior to the 1990s, most internal determinants models made the American state the unit of analysis and employed a dependent variable that assumes that, the earlier a state adopts, the greater its "innovativeness." Empirical analysis was cross-sectional, and the dependent variable was generally measured at the interval level by the year of adoption (or some linear transformation thereof) or at the ordinal level by the rank of a state when states are ordered by their time of adoption (Canon and Baum 1981; Glick 1981; Gray 1973a; Walker 1969). However, a dichotomous version of this variable, which indicates whether a state had adopted a policy by a specified date, was also used (Filer, Moak, and Uze 1988; Glick 1981; Regens 1980).

More recent research generally conceptualizes the propensity of a state to adopt a policy differently. The unit of analysis is still the American state but is now the state in a particular year. More precisely, the unit of analysis is the American state before it adopts the policy and, thus, still eligible to adopt in a particular year.[15] The dependent variable is the probability that a state eligible to adopt will do so during that year (e.g., Berry and Berry 1990, 1992; Hays and Glick 1997; Mintrom 1997). Empirical analysis is pooled (cross-sectional/time-series), where states are observed over multiple years.

One important distinction between the two dependent variables is that the *probability of adoption* is a concept that is (1) defined for each state at any point in time and (2) free to change over time, whereas the *earliness of adoption* takes on a single fixed value for each state, determined by the year it adopts. A second distinction is that, while the timing of a state's adoption relative to other states is fundamental to its score on the "earliness of adoption" variable, relative timing is not necessarily relevant to a determination of a state's propensity to adopt when a "probability of adoption" conception is utilized. A state adopting a policy decades later than most other states is not necessarily deemed as having had a (stable) low propensity to adopt; it is possible that the state had a low probability for many years but that changing conditions led to an increased probability of adoption.

Although we are reluctant to declare either of these dependent variables—earliness of adoption or probability of adoption—as unambiguously the best one for internal determinants models, we believe that greater advances have come from models using the latter dependent variable, a position on which we will elaborate below. Furthermore, our discussion of the theory underlying internal determinants models in this section will emphasize conceptualizations in which the dependent variable is the probability of adoption.

When propensity to adopt is conceived of as the probability of adoption, the focus of research must be a single policy.[16] However, when studying the innovativeness of states as reflected by their earliness of adoption, attention can focus on either one policy or a set of policies. At one extreme are studies designed to explain states' adoptions of a single policy or program (e.g., Berry and Berry's [1990] analysis of the lottery, and Hays and Glick's [1997] research on state living wills). Other internal determinants models have focused on multiple policy instruments in a single issue area (e.g., Sigelman and Smith's [1980] research on consumer protection, covering twenty-eight different kinds of consumer legislation). At the other extreme is Walker's (1969) analysis of a state's innovativeness index, reflecting the earliness of adoption of a set of eighty-eight policies spanning a wide range of economic and social issue areas, and Savage's (1978) innovativeness measure based on sixty-nine policies.

Implicit in the Walker and Savage measures of innovativeness is that it is reasonable to conceive of a *general proclivity* of a state to innovate across a wide range of issue areas. Some are skeptical of this claim; in a classic exchange with Walker, Gray (1973a, 1973b) claims that states can be highly innovative in one program area but less innovative in others, thereby rendering any general innovativeness score useless. Of course, whether states are innovative generally and across a range of policy areas is an empirical question, and if the evidence is supportive, it is useful to develop models explaining generic innovativeness.

But even the variation already documented in state innovativeness across issue areas makes it obvious that, for any individual policy, the propensity of states to adopt the policy cannot be explained fully by a general proclivity to innovate (Gray 1973a). For this reason, even if generic innovativeness is a useful concept, we still ought not treat it as the *ultimate* dependent variable. A good alternative is to take the course of Mooney and Lee (1995), Hays and Glick (1997), and Soule and Earl (2001), who conceive of a state's general proclivity to innovative as just one of a set of independent variables that influences the probability that a state will adopt a particular policy. The idea is that states vary in their general receptivity to new ideas, and that this is one factor that accounts for their differential probabilities of adopting any specific program. The strength of the role played by general receptivity relative to other specific determinants of the probability of adoption is assessed empirically.

## Hypotheses from Internal Determinants Models

Much of the theory underlying internal determinants models of state government innovation can be traced to research about the causes of innovativeness at the individual level. For example, a tremendous level of support has been generated for the proposition that persons with greater socioeconomic status—higher levels of education, income, and wealth—are more likely to innovate than persons with less status.[17] A high level of education provides individuals access to knowledge about innovative practices and an openness to new ideas. Many innovations cost money or involve financial risks for those who adopt them; greater income and wealth provide people the resources necessary to absorb these costs. Similar hypotheses have been developed about innovation in organizations. Organizations of greater size and with greater levels of "slack resources" are assumed to be more innovative than smaller organizations and those with fewer resources (Rogers 1983; Cyert and March 1963; Berry 1994a). In turn, Walker (1969, pp. 883–884) explicitly draws on these organizational-level propositions to support the hypothesis that larger, wealthier, and more economically developed states are more innovative.

Indeed, we can turn to the literature on organizational innovation for a framework useful for assessing the variety of internal determinants likely to influence the probability that states will innovate. Lawrence Mohr (1969, p. 114) proposes that the probability that an organization will innovate is inversely related to the strength of obstacles to innovation, and directly related to (1) the motivation to innovate, and (2) the availability of resources for overcoming the obstacles. This proposition suggests a valuable organizational device, since among the hypotheses frequently reflected in internal determinants models are those concerning the motivation to innovate, as well as the obstacles to innovation and the resources available to surmount them.

We will review these hypotheses, emphasizing those that seem to be applicable to a wide range of policies. However, we recognize that explaining the adoption of any specific policy is likely to require attention to a set of variables that are ad hoc from the point of view of innovation theory but critical given the character of the politics surrounding the issue area in question. For example, states with strong teacher unions are less likely to adopt school-choice reforms (Mintrom 1997), and states with large fundamentalist populations are less likely to adopt several policies considered immoral by many fundamentalists: state reforms (in the pre-Roe period) making abortions more accessible, and state lotteries (Mooney and Lee 1995; Berry and Berry 1990). A strong presence of religious fundamentalists in a state does not diminish the likelihood of adoptions of every policy, just those raising moral issues central to their religious beliefs.

An explanation of the adoption of any specific policy also is likely to require independent variables that are relevant not because they are determinants of the propensity of a state to adopt a *new* policy but because they influence the preferences of policymakers concerning the substantive issues raised by the new policy. For instance, a legislator's response to a proposal for a new welfare program should be driven partially by the same factors determining the legislator's reaction to a proposal for an incremental change in existing welfare programs, such as increasing benefit levels. In another example, research by Berry and Berry (1992, 1994) on state tax policy finds that the factors explaining states' adoptions of new tax instruments are virtually identical to the variables accounting for decisions to increase the rates in existing taxes—despite the fact that the imposition of a tax new to a state can unambiguously be termed a policy innovation whereas an increase in the rate for an existing tax would probably be viewed as an incremental policy choice. What seems to drive the politics of taxation in the American states is the unpopularity of taxes, and this unpopularity affects both tax adoptions and tax increases.[18]

Our review of hypotheses from internal determinants theories of government innovation will emphasize variables that seem especially relevant for explaining the adoption of *new* programs. This means that we will not discuss a wide range of factors widely believed to influence both innovative and routine policymaking.[19] For example, citizen and elite ideology are frequently hypothesized to influence the adoption of many programs that reflect traditional liberal-conservative cleavages (e.g., Mooney and Lee 1995; Berry and Berry 1992; Sapat 2004). But their influence is not relevant to an understanding of policy innovation per se, because ideology is widely perceived to influence routine or incremental policy choices as well (Hill, Leighly and Andersson 1995; Clingermayer and Wood 1995).[20]

### Factors Reflecting the Motivation to Innovate

Numerous scholars have hypothesized that problem severity is an important determinant of the motivation to innovate. Problem severity can influence the motivation of state officials to adopt a policy directly by clarifying the need for the policy, or indirectly by stimulating demand for the policy by societal groups. For instance, Allard (2004, p. 529) maintains that poor economic conditions contributed to the adoption of Mothers' Aid programs by increasing "demand and need for assistance." Similarly, Stream (1999) proposes that the rate of uninsurance among a state's population influences the likelihood that the state will adopt a set of health insurance reforms. Also, Mintrom and Vergari (1998, p. 135) argue that the greater the ratio of state education funding to local funding, the more likely that a state legislature will consider "systemic reform like school choice."

Social scientists often assume that the principal goal of elected officials is to win reelection (e.g., Mayhew 1974; Kiewiet and McCubbins 1985). Although this assumption suggests that elected officials should be responsive to public opinion when deciding whether to adopt a new policy, the response should vary with the level of electoral security of state officials: the more insecure they feel, (1) the more likely they are to adopt new policies that are popular with the electorate, and (2) the less likely they are to adopt new policies that are widely unpopular, or at least sufficiently unpopular with some segment of the electorate to be deemed controversial. Two corollaries of this proposition have frequently been introduced in the state innovation literature. One relates to interparty competition. Walker (1969) argues that politicians anticipating closely contested elections are especially likely to embrace new programs to try to broaden their electoral support. Implicit in this hypothesis is that the new programs are popular with the public. In the case of unpopular programs (like the imposition of a new tax), electoral competition is likely to reduce the probability that a state's politicians will support the program.

Politicians' levels of electoral security also vary with the amount of time until their next election. Reasoning similar to the above suggests that the closer it is to the next statewide election, the more likely a state is to adopt a new popular program and the less likely it is to adopt an unpopular new policy or one that is highly controversial. This proposition has received support in the case of highly popular state lotteries (Berry and Berry 1990), very unpopular mandatory taxes (Mikesell 1978; Berry and Berry 1992), and controversial school choice initiatives (Mintrom 1997).

### Obstacles to Innovation and the Resources Available to Overcome Them

Theories of individual and organizational innovation have stressed the importance of financial resources (i.e., wealth and income levels for individuals and "slack resources" for an organization) and other characteristics (e.g., a high level of education for an individual and large size for an organization) reflecting the capability of the potential adopter to innovate. Similar kinds of resources are often held to be critical for government innovation.

Some new government programs require major expenditures, and therefore the availability of financial resources is a prerequisite for adoption. Thus, one can hypothesize that the fiscal health of a state's government often has a positive impact on the propensity of a state to adopt a new policy (Allard 2004; Lowry 2005).[21] Analogous to the notion of highly capable individuals or organizations is the concept of states with strong governmental capacity. Walker (1969), Sigelman and Smith (1980), Andrews (2000), and McLendon, Heller and Young (2005) maintain that states having legislatures that give their members generous staff support and extensive research facilities should be more likely to adopt new policies than states with less professionalized legislatures, and Brooks (2005) posits that party fragmentation is inversely related to the likelihood of innovation.[22] Alternatively, it can be argued that the capacity of a state's economy to finance extensive public services is the ultimate determinant of the state's propensity to innovate (Daley and Garand 2005). Such capacity is reflected by several measures of economic development common in the literature, including per capita income, gross domestic product, and level of urbanization.

Walker (1969, p. 884) suggests that states with high levels of economic development have a greater probability of adopting even those policies which do not require large budgets (e.g., enabling legislation for zoning in cities or a state council on the arts), partly due to their greater adaptivity and tolerance for change. Furthermore, Wagner (1877; see also Mann 1980; Berry and Lowery 1987) hypothesizes that economic development prompts increased demand for government services. Greater personal income by a state's citizens leads them to demand governmental services that might be considered luxuries when personal income is low. Similarly, greater urbanization and industrialization lead to social problems that often require "collective" governmental solutions (Hofferbert 1966).

Others have argued that, although adequate financial resources are a prerequisite for government innovation, individuals who advocate policy ideas and are willing to devote their energies to pushing these ideas can be critical to the adoption of a new policy. Most of the scholarly attention to the importance of so-called policy entrepreneurs, both inside and outside of government, has focused on their role in agenda setting (Kingdon 1984; Baumgartner and Jones 1993; Schneider, Teske and Mintrom 1995). But recently, Mintrom (1997; see also Mintrom and Vergari 1996) offers evidence of the importance of policy entrepreneurs in facilitating the adoption of school choice initiatives in the states.[23] Similarly, Sabatier and Jenkins-Smith (2006) argue that *advocacy coalitions*—coordinated groups of governmental officials, activists, journalists, researchers, and policy analysts—can be crucial in paving the way for policy adoptions.[24]

Indeed, several theorists, recognizing the rarity of government innovation, have argued that innovation can be expected to occur only in the unusual case wherein various independent conditions happen to occur simultaneously. Kingdon (1984, chap. 8) speaks of policy windows—rare periods of opportunity for innovation—that are created when a new political executive takes office, an important congressional committee chair changes hands, and/or some event or crisis generates an unusual level of public attention to some problem. He argues that policy entrepreneurs consciously wait for such windows of opportunity to press their policy demands. In their study of tax adoptions, Berry and Berry (1992; see also Hansen 1983) argue that taxes tend to be adopted when several unrelated political and fiscal conditions converge to create a rare "political opportunity"; for example, the presence of a fiscal crisis in government occurring when the next election is not near and when one or more neighboring states has recently adopted a new tax.

## A Unified Model of State Government Innovation Reflecting Both Internal Determinants and Diffusion

We propose that models of state government innovation should take the following general form:

$$ADOPT_{i,t} = f(MOTIVATION_{i,t}, RESOURCES/OBSTACLES_{i,t}, OTHER\text{-}POLICIES_{i,t}, EXTERNAL_{i,t}) \text{ [Equation 3]}$$

The unit of analysis for this equation is the American state eligible to adopt a policy in a particular year ($t$). The dependent variable—$ADOPT_{i,t}$—is the probability that state $i$ will adopt the policy in year $t$. $EXTERNAL_{i,t}$ denotes variables reflecting diffusion effects on state $i$ at time $t$; thus, these variables would measure the behavior of other states (or the national or local governments) at time $t$, or in the recent past.

The remainder of the terms in the function $f$ are internal determinants. $MOTIVATION_{i,t}$ represents variables indicating the motivation of public officials in state $i$ at time $t$ to adopt the policy; these variables would include the severity of the problem motivating consideration of the policy, the character of public opinion and electoral competition in the state, and other ad hoc motivation factors. $RESOURCES/OBSTACLES_{i,t}$ denotes variables reflecting obstacles to innovation and the resources available for overcoming them. For many policies, the state's level of economic development and the professionalism of its legislature would be among the variables included. Factors indicating the presence (and skill) of interested policy entrepreneurs, or the strength of advocacy coalitions, in a state could also be included.[25] Finally, $OTHERPOLICIES_{i,t}$ is a set of dummy variables indicating the presence or absence in state $i$ of other policies that have implications for the likelihood that the state will adopt the new policy.

The impacts of previous policy choices on the probability of adopting a new policy have virtually been ignored in the empirical literature on state government innovation, but we contend that models of policy innovation must recognize the effects of one policy choice on another. Mahajan and Peterson (1985, pp. 39–40) identify four types of "innovation interrelationships": innovations may be (1) independent, (2) complementary, (3) contingent, or (4) substitutes. This typology has relevance for explaining state policy adoptions.

If we are seeking to explain the adoption of policy B, and policy A is largely independent of B (in the sense that a state's probability of adopting B is unaffected by whether it has already adopted A), obviously we need not concern ourselves at all with policy A. But policies of the other three types are not so safely ignored. Sometimes two policies are complementary: the adoption of policy A increases the probability that a state will adopt policy B. For example, a state that has previously chosen to license one type of auxiliary medical practitioner (such as physician assistants) may have created a precedent that would make it more likely that advocates of licensing other auxiliary personnel (such as nurse practitioners) will be successful. If so, a model designed to explain state licensing of one type of medical practitioner should include an explanatory variable indicating whether a state has previously adopted licensing of some other type of auxiliary medical personnel.

Note that a positive relationship between the probability of adoption of policy B and the presence of policy A can exist without A and B being complementary if the relationship is spurious—resulting from both policies' adoptions being influenced by a common set of variables. For example, if the probability that a state will adopt one type of welfare reform is positively related to the presence of another similar type of reform, yet that relationship is exclusively due to the fact that the same kinds of causal forces are at work in the adoption of both policies, the two welfare reforms should not be viewed as complementary. Only when the adoption of one policy changes conditions in a state so as to make the state more receptive to the other policy would we term the two policies complementary.

Another possibility is that policy B's adoption is contingent on the previous adoption of policy A, in which case the probability that a state will adopt B is zero until the state adopts A. Brace and Barrilleaux (1995) present a theory of state policy reform designed to explain changes in existing programs in a variety of policy areas. The adoption of many of these policy changes is contingent on a state's previous adoption of the program being reformed. In this case, the units of analysis must exclude each state in all years prior to its adoption of the initial legislation.[26]

A final alternative is that policy A is a substitute for policy B. When A is an *exact* substitute for B, completely precluding the possibility of adopting B, the solution is to exclude from the units of analysis those state-years in which A is present. However, exact policy substitutes are rare; partial substitutes are more likely. In this case, the adoption of A does not preclude the adoption of B; it only reduces its likelihood. For instance, it may be that different "school-choice" plans currently being considered by states are partial substitutes. One possibility is that states create charter schools in an attempt to diminish the prospects that a more "radical" program—such as school vouchers—will be adopted. In this case, a state's previous adoption of a charter school program would lower the probability that the state would establish a voucher program.[27]

A recognition that some policies are substitutes suggests that we should also entertain models that involve more complex dependent variables than the probability that an individual policy will be adopted (*ADOPT*, in Equation 3). Sometimes it might be best to assume that a state makes a choice between multiple alternatives. For example, Berry and Berry (1992) studied the adoption of sales and income taxes separately, assuming for each that states without the tax may choose to adopt or not in any year. But it may more accurately reflect the process of decisionmaking to conceptualize states that have neither tax in any year as having three choices: adopt a sales tax, adopt an income tax, or adopt neither.[28]

Another way in which a conceptualization of a dependent variable can oversimplify reality is by failing to distinguish between what Glick and Hays (1991, p. 836; see also Downs and Mohr 1976) refer to as "superficial" and "deep" adoption. For example, two states might adopt an anti-discrimination program (in housing or the workplace), one of which is largely symbolic, whereas the other involves an extensive commitment of resources through investigatory and enforcement actions. Calling them both anti-discrimination programs and treating them as functionally equivalent may mask variation essential for understanding the innovation process at work.

Some of the variation in the "depth" of a policy adoption may be due to what Glick and Hays (1991; see also Clark 1985) call policy *reinvention*. Implicit in the notion of reinvention is a diffusion model, which justifies the states' emulation of other states' policies by an assumption that states learn from each other. This learning model is more sophisticated than those discussed above, however, because it assumes that states use information about the impacts of a policy in other states not only to assist them in deciding whether to adopt the policy but to help them refine the policy in light of the other states' experiences. In turn, early adopters can reform their policies to take advantage of the experiences of late adopters who passed a modified version of the initial policy.[29]

# Early Approaches to Testing Internal Determinants and Diffusion Models

Prior to 1990, the literature on state government innovation was dominated by empirical research testing (1) internal determinants explanations that assume no diffusion occurs, or (2) diffusion models that assume no effects of internal determinants. Berry (1994b) argues that each of the three major models of government innovation—internal determinants, national interaction, and regional diffusion—is associated with a distinct methodology for empirical testing and explores the ability of these techniques to detect the true innovation process underlying policy adoptions. She does this by applying the methodologies to data generated from simulated innovation processes with known characteristics. Berry's results, which we summarize here, paint a very pessimistic picture of the ability of the traditional methodologies to help us understand state government innovation.[30]

## Testing Internal Determinants Models

Internal determinants models were traditionally tested with cross-sectional regression (or probit or discriminant) analysis (e.g., Regens 1980; Glick 1981; Canon and Baum 1981; Filer, Moak, and Uze 1988). The dependent variable was a measure of how early a state adopted one or more policies (or whether or not some policy had been adopted by a certain date), whereas the independent variables were political and socioeconomic characteristics of the states.

Several problems with this cross-sectional regression strategy are immediately apparent. The first pertains to the year for observing independent variables. If one measures the independent variables in a year that is later than some states' adoptions, one winds up attempting to account for the behaviors of these states with variables measured after the behavior has occurred. Thus, the only logical alternative is to measure the independent variables in the year that the *first* state adopts (or some earlier year). But when adoptions of the policy are spread over many years, this approach requires an implausible assumption that late-adopting states' behavior can be explained by the characteristics of those states many years prior. Moreover, the cross-sectional approach to testing an internal determinants model does not permit an assessment of the effects of variables that change substantially over time; each state is a single case in the analysis, having a fixed value for each independent variable. Finally, although the cross-sectional approach is suitable for testing an internal determinants model in which the propensity to adopt is defined as the "earliness of adoption," a cross-sectional model cannot be used if the dependent variable is conceptualized as the probability of adoption in a particular year.

In addition to these limitations, Berry finds that the cross-sectional approach to testing internal determinants models cannot be trusted to discern whether the adoptions of a policy by states are actually generated by internal determinants. She finds, for example, that simulated policy adoptions generated out of a *pure* regional diffusion process—with no impact at all by internal state characteristics—tend to exhibit evidence of internal determinants when a traditional cross-sectional model containing independent variables frequently used in the literature is estimated. The empirical problem is that states near each other tend to have similar values on many political and socioeconomic characteristics of states. Thus, policies that diffuse regionally—say by being passed to bordering states—tend to yield an order of adoption by states that correlates highly with these internal characteristics.

## Testing the National Interaction Model

As noted earlier, the national interaction model was traditionally tested using time-series regression to estimate a model in the form of Equation 2. However, Berry finds that this regression approach cannot reliably discern whether a policy's adoptions are the result of national interaction. In particular, when data for simulated policy adoptions generated either (1) by a pure regional diffusion process, or (2) solely as a result of internal determinants are used to estimate Equation 2, the results often support the hypothesis that the policies spread via a national interaction process.

The empirical problem here is that, for any policy for which a graph of the cumulative proportion of states having adopted against time approximates an S-shape similar to Figure 1, the regression approach will generate support for the national interaction model. Unfortunately, this S-shape will result from *any* process that produces a period of infrequent adoptions followed by a period of more frequent adoptions (which is inevitably followed by a tapering off in the rate of adoptions as the number of remaining potential adopters declines). Policies that diffuse regionally can produce this adoption pattern. Even policies that are adopted as independent responses to internal state conditions can. Consider, for example, a policy that is most likely to be adopted by states with healthy economies; if a national economic boom cycle lifts the economies of all states, adoptions by many states may be clumped together to produce a period of frequent adoptions sandwiched by periods with less frequent adoptions.

## Testing Regional Diffusion Models

The classic approach to testing regional diffusion models was Walker's (1969; see also Canon and Baum 1981) factor analytic technique. Walker used factor analysis to isolate groupings of states that have similar orders of adoption for eighty-eight policies. He then observed that the groupings coincide with regional clusters of states, which he interpreted as empirical evidence for regional diffusion.

Berry simulates state adoptions of 144 policies, each diffusing regionally based on a pure neighbor model. When the data for these 144 policies are factor analyzed according to Walker's procedure, there is strong support for the regional diffusion proposition. Thus, Berry finds evidence that Walker's methodology correctly identifies neighbor-to-neighbor diffusion when it exists. Our hunch is that the methodology also successfully shows support for the regional diffusion hypothesis when employed with policies that diffuse via fixed-region diffusion. If we are correct, the good news would be that factor analysis reliably detects diffusion when it exists in either of two prototypic forms: neighbor to neighbor, or in fixed regions. But the bad news would be that the technique is not able to distinguish the two similar—but still distinct—types of regional diffusion. Even more disconcerting is that Berry finds that Walker's methodology yields support for the regional diffusion hypothesis when applied to simulated policies known to diffuse via a pure national interaction model with no regional element whatsoever. She also finds evidence that policy adoptions generated purely as a result of internal determinants can indicate the presence of regional diffusion when an alternative single-explanation methodology is used.[31]

## Testing a Unified Model of State Government Innovation Reflecting Both Internal Determinants and Diffusion Using Event History Analysis

State politics scholars have developed a number of explanations for the adoptions of new policies by the American states. These include both internal determinants models and a range of diffusion models pointing to the influence of states on one another. Dating back to early path-breaking studies on policy innovation and diffusion by Walker (1969) and Gray (1973a), scholars have recognized that these various models are not mutually exclusive, that a state may adopt a new policy in response to both conditions internal to the state and the actions of other states. Prior to 1990, however, when conducting empirical analysis, these same scholars ignored the nonexclusive nature of these explanations by analyzing them in isolation. Of course analysts did not purposely misspecify their models; rather, the arsenal of methods commonly used by social scientists prior to the 1990s did not permit proper specification.

Unfortunately, Berry's (1994b) simulation results show that the discipline's pre-1990 compartmentalized approach to testing the various explanations of government innovation calls into question the empirical evidence about these explanations from this era. Berry finds no evidence of "false negatives," that is, no reason to believe that the early tests for the presence of regional diffusion, national interaction, and the impact of internal determinants fail to discern these processes when they are present. But she does find a disturbing pattern of "false positives"—a tendency for the methodologies to *find* regional diffusion, national interaction, or the effect of internal determinants when no such influence actually exists. In 1990, Berry and Berry developed a model of the adoption of state lotteries taking the form of Equation 3, positing that a state's propensity to adopt a lottery is influenced by forces both internal and external to the states, and they tested it using event history analysis. In the next section, we summarize Berry and Berry's event history analysis model. Then we examine a variety of important refinements that other scholars have introduced as the literature has developed. Since 1990—but especially since the turn of the century—event history analysis has been employed across a wide variety of policy arenas to test a model of state innovation reflecting both internal determinants and interstate diffusion; the Appendix lists some of these studies.[32]

### Berry and Berry's (1990) Event History Analysis Model

Event history analysis is an ideal methodology for estimating the coefficients of an innovation model taking the form of Equation 3 (Box-Steffensmeier and Jones 2004). In event history analysis, we conceive of a *risk set*, the states that (at any point in time) are at risk of adopting the policy in question. In a discrete-time model, the period of analysis is divided into a set of discrete time periods, typically years. The dependent variable—the probability that a state in the risk set will adopt during year *t*—is not directly observable. However, we can observe for each state in the risk set whether the state adopts the policy in the given year (typically coded 1) or not (scored 0). For policies that can be adopted by a state only once, states fall out of the risk set after they adopt the policy; thus, for each state that adopts during the period of analysis, the time-series for the dependent variable is a string of zeros followed by a single 1 in the year of adoption. Given data for the states in the risk set over a period of years, the event history model, having a dichotomous observed variable, can be estimated using logit or probit maximum likelihood techniques.[33]

The maximum likelihood estimates of the coefficients for the independent variables in the event history model offer information on the predicted impacts of these variables on the propensity of states in the risk set to adopt the policy. Using procedures common in the analysis of probit and logit results, the coefficient estimates can, in turn, be used to generate predictions of the probability that a state with any specified combination of values on the independent variables will adopt the policy in a given year. Furthermore, one can estimate the change in the probability of adoption associated with a specified increase in the value of any independent variable when the remaining independent variables are held constant (Tomz, Wittenberg, and King 2003). Such estimated changes in probability yield easily interpretable estimates of the magnitude of the effect of the independent variable.

Berry and Berry (1990) employ event history analysis to test a model of state lottery adoptions. Their model includes internal determinants reflecting the motivation of politicians to adopt a lottery (e.g., the proximity to elections), the obstacles to innovation (e.g., the presence of a sizable population of religious fundamentalists), and the presence of resources for overcoming obstacles (e.g., whether there is unified political party control of government), as well as a variable specifying interstate diffusion—the number of previously adopting neighboring states.

## Recent Refinements to Event History Modeling of State Policy Innovation

In event history studies of state policy innovation conducted since 1990, the inclusion among the independent variables of the number (or percentage) of contiguous states that have previously adopted a policy remains the most common specification of diffusion (e.g., Mintrom 1997; Hill 2000; Balla 2001; Allard 2004; Chamberlain and Haider-Markel 2005; Langer and Brace 2005; Allen 2005). But recent event history studies have specified several alternative forms of diffusion. Mooney and Lee (1995), Andrews (2000), and Allen, Pettus, and Haider-Markel (2004) have modeled fixed-region diffusion by defining regions of the country and including a measure of the percentage (or number) of states from a state's region that have previously adopted. Balla (2001) includes a measure of whether a state's insurance commissioner sat on a committee with jurisdiction over the regulation of HMOs in a model predicting the adoption of model legislation proposed by the committee. Allen, Pettus, and Haider-Markel's (2004) study of the adoption of truth-in-sentencing laws specifies vertical influence, with a variable indicating whether the national government had passed 1994 legislation creating financial incentives for states to adopt.

Event history analysis is flexible enough to model other forms of policy diffusion as well. Our earlier suggestion to allow for the greatest influence by $i$'s neighbors, yet some influence by other nearby states (an effect that diminishes with the distance from $i$), can be operationalized by constructing a dummy variable for each state (1 if a state has adopted the policy, 0 if not) and taking a weighted average of these dummies across states, where the weights are proportional to the distance from state $i$. Leader-laggard diffusion can be modeled with a dummy variable indicating whether state $i$'s presumed "leader" has already adopted the policy. Even the thorough mixing of states assumed by the national interaction model can be specified in an event history model; the independent variables would include the percentage of the fifty states that has previously adopted the policy. However, we do not recommend this approach, preferring that scholars develop more realistic formulations of national interaction.

Although the above event history specifications of diffusion reflect a variety of channels of intergovernmental influence, empirical support for these specifications fail to shed light on the reasons one government emulates the actions of another. Two recent papers have sought to overcome this weakness of previous research by designing models to determine whether interstate diffusion is due to policy learning or economic competition. In a study of Indian gaming innovation, Boehmke and Witmer (2004) claim that *learning* should influence the signing by a state of its first Indian gaming compact, but not the subsequent expansion of these compacts. In contrast, *competition* should influence both the initial signing of a compact and ensuing expansion. Boehmke and Witmer use generalized event count regression to estimate models of the number of compacts signed by a state in a year, and they find evidence of both learning and competition. Berry and Baybeck (2005) argue that, if a state adopts a lottery due to policy learning, its response to neighboring states' adoptions will be the same regardless of the location of the state's population within its borders. If, however, the state adopts a lottery to prevent a loss of revenues when its residents cross state borders to play other states' lotteries (i.e., competition), its response to neighboring states' adoptions will vary depending on the distance of its residents from other states with lotteries (and, thus, the ease with which residents can travel to the other states). Berry and Baybeck use geographic information systems (GIS) software to measure the concern of state officials about residents going to other states to play the lottery based on the location of the state's population, and employ this variable in a model of state lottery adoption to assess the presence of economic competition. Their empirical analysis shows that the diffusion of the lottery occurs due to competition rather than policy learning.

Our general model of state innovation—Equation 3—includes a set of variables ($OTHER$-$POLICIES_{i,t}$) indicating the presence or absence of other policies influencing the likelihood that a state will adopt the new policy, but early applications of event history analysis did not incorporate this aspect of Equation 3. Several recent studies have tested models incorporating the impacts of other policies. Balla's (2001) analysis of the adoption of the HMO Model Act includes a variable indicating whether a state had previously adopted another model act complementary to the HMO legislation. Soule and Earl (2001) test whether the propensity of a state to adopt a hate crime law is influenced by whether the state had adopted other hate crime legislation.

Berry and Berry's (1990, 1992, 1994) initial applications of event history analysis to the study of state policy innovation assumed that the probability of adoption is constant over time. Yet, it is unlikely that the true policy process occurring in states conforms to this assumption. For instance, the pressure to adopt a new policy—and hence the probability of adoption—can increase gradually over time as coalitions designed to promote the policy are built. Similarly, when intense efforts to secure adoption of a policy fail in a year, the probability of adoption may be reduced the year following as advocates of the policy tire of the battle and decide to marshal their resources for the future. More recent studies have allowed the probability of adoption to vary over time (i.e., have allowed for "duration dependence") using strategies suggested by Beck, Katz, and Tucker (1998) and Buckley and Westerland (2004); they include dummy variables for time periods, or a time counter (or some transformation of time—e.g., the natural logarithm or cubic smoothing splines) among the independent variables.

The vast majority of event history innovation studies have confined their attention to a non-repeatable event—the adoption of a policy or program that can occur only once—so that, after a state adopts, it is no longer at risk of adoption. Jones and Branton (2005) note that event history analysis is also applicable to modeling state innovation when multiple policies can be adopted, so that states remain at risk for adoption after their first adoption. Berry and Berry (1992) offer an example of this form of repeated-event event history analysis in their study of state tax innovation, in which the observed dependent variable is a dichotomous indicator of whether *any* new tax is adopted in a year. Boehmke and Witmer (2004) specify an innovation model in which multiple events (e.g., a state signing an Indian gaming compact) may occur in the same year and estimate it with generalized event count regression. This alternative to event history analysis is appropriate when it is reasonable to assume that variation in the number of adoptions in a year yields substantively meaningful information about the "extent" or "degree" of adoption.

Volden (2006) recently introduced directed-dyad event history analysis into the study of state policy innovation. In traditional event history analysis, the unit of analysis is the state-year, and each state is included in the dataset during each year it is at risk of adopting the policy. With directed-dyad event history analysis, the unit of analysis is the dyad-year—where a dyad refers to a pair of states—and the dependent variable measures whether one state in the pair emulates the policy of the other state. As a consequence, directed-dyad event history analysis can be enormously valuable in tracing the way a policy diffuses from one state to another.

## Conclusion

Over the last three decades, social scientists have proposed numerous theories to explain policy adoptions by the American states. These theories include internal determinants explanations and a variety of diffusion models that point to cross-state channels of influence. When cast in isolation, these theories are drastically oversimplified models of policy innovation. Prior to 1990 these models were tested individually, using techniques prone to result in deceptive conclusions (Berry 1994b). However, the logic of internal determinants models and the various diffusion explanations are not incompatible. In the last decade and a half, scholars have developed models that allow for the simultaneous impacts of internal political, economic, and social characteristics of states as well as multiple channels of regional and national cross-state influence—and then tested these models using event history analysis. (The Appendix lists numerous studies of policy adoptions by American states that have developed and tested such models.)

Furthermore, since the turn of the century, policy scholars have developed similar models to explain policy adoptions by other types of governments. Some have examined subnational governments in the United States and abroad (Lubell et al.'s [2002] study of local watershed partnerships; Hoyman and Weinberg's [2006] research on county governments in North Carolina; Ito's [2001] analysis of Japanese prefects). There have also been numerous applications by comparativists seeking to explain the diffusion of economic liberalization across nation states in Latin America (Meseguer 2004; Jordana and Levi-Faur 2005), western Europe (Gilardi 2005), or the world (Simmons 2000; Simmons and Elkins 2004; Brooks 2005; Way 2005). This recent work illustrates the wide applicability of a model taking the form of Equation 3. In this essay, we propose a framework for analysis to guide the further development and refinement of such models.

Nevertheless, even achieving the greatest imaginable success in the development and testing of innovation models taking the form of Equation 3 would not yield a satisfactory theory of the *overall* policymaking process. This may distinguish our proposed approach to policy innovation and diffusion research from some of the other theoretical approaches discussed in this volume, especially the Advocacy Coalition Framework (ACT) (Sabatier and Jenkins-Smith 2006). By proposing that innovation models take the form of Equation 3, we are recommending that scholars de-emphasize the global concept of innovativeness on a wide range of policies and focus attention on explaining the propensity of states to adopt *specific* policies and programs. Though we believe that explanations for adoptions must recognize the complexity of the policy process (the importance of intergovernmental influences and the key roles played by policy activists inside and outside of government), our focus is inherently more narrow than the ACF's focus on the comprehensive analysis of policy subsystems.

Is our narrow focus an advantage or disadvantage? The debate will only be settled as scholars conduct research about policymaking at varied levels of generality and we see what insights the different approaches yield. But we would note that the complexity faced by students of policymaking is not unique. For instance, there is no widely accepted general theory of the political behavior of individual citizens. It would be difficult to argue that an individual's vote choice in a single election (whether to vote and, if so, for whom) is a discrete event independent from a larger longitudinal process of attitude development in which ideology, partisan identification, candidate evaluations, and specific issue positions change. Yet this recognition does not prevent scholars from investigating the factors that influence vote choice by doing research on specific individual elections. Similarly, the fact that discrete policy adoption events by states are not independent from a larger longitudinal and intergovernmental process of policymaking should not deter us from studying discrete policy adoptions as a vehicle for understanding the broader process.

When models in the form of Equation 3 are tested, they are capable of answering important questions about the conditions that promote and impede the adoption of new government policies. For example, those interested in the impact of electoral security on the policymaking behavior of public officials learn from Berry and Berry's (1992) analysis of state tax innovation that, when other independent variables are held constant at central values within their distributions, the probability that a state will adopt a gasoline tax is only .03 during a gubernatorial election year but grows to .42 in the year immediately following an election.[34] When accompanied by similar findings regarding the adoption of other types of taxes, this is powerful evidence that elected officials establish their tax policies with an eye toward electoral security. Moreover, the specific empirical finding about probabilities of adoption offers an easily interpretable measure of the *strength* of the effect of politicians' electoral security on state tax policy.

We do recognize that the data requirements for our approach to innovation research are substantial. Testing a model in the form of Equation 3 requires pooled data; independent variables must be observed for each state in each year during the period of analysis. Data collection is especially challenging when the independent variables go beyond aggregate state characteristics to include the nature and behavior of policy entrepreneurs, interest groups, and advocacy coalitions. However, research by Mintrom (1997) shows that the collection costs are not insurmountable. Moreover, the Appendix shows that the hurdle imposed by the need for pooled data has been overcome by many scholars using event history analysis and analyzing dozens of different polices and programs.

When key concepts central to one's theory of government innovation cannot be observed for all states over a period of years, what should be done? Berry's simulation results show clearly that a return to the more traditional research strategies is unacceptable. Although the traditional methodologies (cross-sectional analysis to test internal determinants models, time-series regression to test national interaction models, and factor analysis to test regional diffusion models) are less demanding in their need for data, they yield untrustworthy empirical results. When it is not feasible to measure important variables for as many units as pooled state data analysis requires, the only reasonable alternative is to sacrifice the benefits available from large-sample quantitative research for the gains secured by intensive analysis of a small number of cases via case studies or small-sample comparative designs. The theories need not change—only the approach to empirical testing.

## Notes

1. For a review of the literature on incremental decisionmaking, see Berry (1990).
2. Rogers (1983, chap. 2) discusses numerous examples of research on innovation at the individual level.
3. Walker calls what we term his "internal determinants model" an analysis of the "correlates of innovation."
4. Richard Rose (1993) refers to learning as "lesson-drawing." For a provocative discussion of the role of learning in the diffusion of social policy across Western nations, see Heclo (1974).
5. Whether firms do indeed move in response to various financial incentives and poor people actually move in search of greater welfare benefits are empirical issues. But note that state officials may *perceive* that such behaviors occur and make policy choices for this reason, even if the behaviors do not occur.
6. Since $\Delta N_t$ denotes the proportion of new adopters during time period $t$ and $L - N_{t-1}$ is the proportion of potential adopters who have not adopted by the beginning of time period $t$, $bN_{t-1}$ must represent the proportion of remaining potential adopters that actually adopt in time period $t$. Alternatively, $bN_{t-1}$ can be viewed as the probability that an individual who has not yet adopted prior to time period $t$ will do so during $t$. Those familiar with calculus should note that Equation 1 can be cast in continuous terms by defining $N(t)$ as the cumulative number of adopters at time $t$, defining $L$ as the total number of potential adopters, and specifying (see Mahajan and Peterson 1985) that $dN(t)/dt = bN(t-1)\ [L-N(t)]$.
7. Since there is no "constant" term in Equation 2, the model predicts that the regression intercept is zero.
8. Gray (1973b) recognizes that the national interaction model's assumption of a thorough mixing of states is unrealistic, but she adopts a position of methodological nominalism (Friedman 1953), arguing that the essential issue is not whether the assumption is realistic but whether it sufficiently approximates reality to be useful for explanation.
9. This "inequality of esteem" across states was observed by Grupp and Richards (1975) in their survey of upper-level state administrators.
10. Volden (2006) posits that successful policies are more likely to diffuse across states than ones that have failed. This proposition relies on logic similar to the leader-laggard model. Presumably, highly esteemed states are perceived as the ones most likely to adopt successful policies.
11. Hierarchical models—based on population rather than economic development—originated in geographers' theories of the diffusion of product and cultural innovations among individuals. The models predicted that such innovations tend to flow from more populated cities to less populated rural areas (Hagerstrand 1967; Blaikie 1978).
12. This reasoning parallels individual-level diffusion models that assume people are most likely to emulate the innovations of persons who share common beliefs, education, and social status (Rogers 1983, pp. 274–275).

13. Implicitly presenting an alternative vertical influence model that reverses the standard direction of influence, Nathan (1989, pp. 16–17) points out that various national New Deal programs were copies of 1930s state-level programs. Rockefeller (1968) and Boeckelman (1992) also use historical evidence to support the claim that the federal government uses states as learning laboratories.

14. Rogers (1983, p. 20) views *knowledge* as the first stage in the "innovation decision-process."

15. Using the traditional terminology of event history analysis, the unit of analysis is the American state *at risk* of adopting.

16. This is also true of diffusion models, which by their very nature focus on the spread of a single policy.

17. For a review of the research on the determinants of individual innovativeness, see Rogers (1983, pp. 251–263).

18. Taxation may be unique in this regard. Adopting a new tax instrument may be closer to routine policy-making than adopting most other major new policies, since most proposals for new policies face the difficult task of finding a spot on a crowded governmental agenda; governments' need for revenue gives the issue of tax policy a permanent place on the agenda.

19. For a review of a variety of factors found to influence state public policy outputs in cross-sectional quantitative studies, see Blomquist's (2006) chapter in this volume.

20. Moreover, the effect of ideology on innovation varies across policies. For example, a high level of liberalism should promote the adoption of new social welfare initiatives but impede the adoption of conservative criminal justice programs inconsistent with liberal ideology.

21. Brooks (2005) advances a similar proposition in a cross-national study of pension privatization. Yet, for some policies, it is actually *poor* fiscal health that contributes to an increase in the likelihood of adoption. Such situations have occurred with state taxes (Berry and Berry 1992) and industrial policies designed to attract new business to a state (Gray and Lowery 1990). For conceptual and operational definitions of "fiscal health," see Reeves (1986), Ladd and Yinger (1989), and Berry and Berry (1990).

22. Similarly, Sapat (2004) hypothesizes that the level of administrative professionalism influences the probability of adoption of environmental policy innovations by state administrative agencies, and Kim and Gerber (2005) propose that the capacity of a state public utility commission—as reflected by the amount of discretion granted to the commission—influences its probability of adopting regulatory reforms.

23. Note also Allen's (2005) study of the impact of non-economically focused interest groups on the adoption of state animal cruelty felony laws, Soule and Earl's (2001) research on the impact of the presence of the Anti-Defamation League in a state on the prospects for adoption of hate crime legislation, and Allard's (2004) analysis of the impact of women's group activities on the adoption of state Mothers' Aid programs in the early 1900s.

24. The character and activities of advocacy coalitions—which are presumed to consist of numerous individuals across the American states—might be conceived as factors influencing state government innovation that are neither purely "internal" nor "external" to states.

25. Some might argue that it is not feasible to measure accurately the presence or strength of entrepreneurs and advocacy coalitions when doing a fifty-state analysis. But Mintrom (1997) develops such measures for school-choice entrepreneurs in the American states.

26. Mintrom (1997) exhibits similar reasoning by constructing an equation predicting the probability that a state will *consider* a school choice proposal, and then a second equation predicting the probability that a state considering the proposal will actually *adopt* it. In our terminology, Mintrom assumes that policy adoption is contingent on preliminary policy consideration.

27. An alternative proposition is that a charter school program and a school voucher policy are complementary: when a state adopts one type of school choice reform, the political environment is changed, and the state becomes more amenable to other school-choice initiatives. Presumably, empirical analysis could resolve these competing hypotheses.

28. Innovation processes that allow for a choice among three or more policies can be specified using a multinomial logit model (Greene 1993) or a variant of a Cox duration model (Jones and Branton 2005).

29. Models that allow for variation across states and over time, not only in the probability of adoption of a policy but also in the content of the policy, are beyond the bounds of the framework for research reflected in Equation 3.

30. The rest of this section draws extensively from Berry's (1994b) results.

31. The method is an event history model (like those described in the next section of this paper) with a single independent variable: the number of bordering states that have previously adopted.

32. The high level of recent activity in this subfield is reflected in the fact that thirty-three of the forty-two articles listed in the Appendix had not yet been published when we were preparing this paper for the first edition of this volume in 1997.

33. For a more detailed discussion of event history analysis, see Box-Steffensmeier and Jones (2004), Allison (1984), and Buckley and Westerland (2004).

34. The period of analysis is historical: 1919–1929.

# References

Aiken, Michael, and Robert R. Alford. 1970. "Community Structure and Innovation: The Case of Public Housing." *American Political Science Review, 64,* 843–864.

Allard, Scott W. 2004. "Competitive Pressures and the Emergence of Mothers' Aid Programs in the United States." *Policy Studies Journal, 32,* 521–544.

Allen, Mahalley D. 2005. "Laying Down the Law? Interest Group Influence on State Adoption of Animal Cruelty Felony Laws." *Policy Studies Journal, 33,* 443–457.

Allen, Mahalley D., Carrie Pettus, and Donald Haider-Markel. 2004. "Making the National Local: Specifying the Conditions for National Government Influence on State Policy-making." *State Politics and Policy Quarterly, 4,* 318–344.

Allison, Paul D. 1984. *Event History Analysis Data.* Beverly Hills: Sage Publications.

Alm, James, Michael McKee, and Mark Skidmore. 1993. "Fiscal Pressure, Tax Competition and the Introduction of State Lotteries." *National Tax Journal, 46,* 463–476.

Andrews, Clinton J. 2000. "Diffusion Pathways for Electricity Deregulation." *Publius, 30,* 17–34.

Bailey, Michael A., and Mark Carl Rom. 2004. "A Wider Race: Interstate Competition across Health and Welfare Programs." *Journal of Politics, 66,* 326–347.

Bali, Valentina A., and Brian D. Silver. 2006. "Politics, Race, and American State Electoral Reforms after Election 2000." *State Politics and Policy Quarterly, 6,* 21–48.

Balla, Steven J. 2001. "Interstate Professional Associations and the Diffusion of Policy Innovations." *American Politics Research, 29,* 221–245.

Baumgartner, Frank R., and Bryan D. Jones. 1993. *Agendas and Instability in American Politics.* Chicago: University of Chicago Press.

Beck, Nathaniel, Jonathan N. Katz, and Richard Tucker. 1998. "Taking Time Seriously: Time Series–Cross-Section Analysis with a Binary Dependent Variable." *American Journal of Political Science, 42,* 1260–1288.

Berry, Frances Stokes. 1994a. "Innovation in Public Management: The Adoption of State Strategic Planning" *Public Administration Review, 54,* 322–329.

_____. 1994b. "Sizing Up State Policy Innovation Research." *Policy Studies Journal, 22,* 442–456.

Berry, Frances Stokes, and William D. Berry. 1990. "State Lottery Adoptions as Policy Innovations: An Event History Analysis." *American Political Science Review, 84,* 395–415.

_____. 1992. "Tax Innovation in the States: Capitalizing on Political Opportunity." *American Journal of Political Science, 36,* 715–742.

_____. 1994. "The Politics of Tax Increases in the States." *American Journal of Political Science, 38,* 855–859.

Berry, William D. 1990. "The Confusing Case of Budgetary Incrementalism: Too Many Meanings for a Single Concept?" *Journal of Politics, 52,* 167–196.

Berry, William D., and Brady Baybeck. 2005. "Using Geographic Information Systems to Study Interstate Competition." *American Political Science Review, 99,* 505–519.

Berry, William D., Richard C. Fording, and Russell L. Hanson. 2003. "Reassessing the 'Race to the Bottom' in State Welfare Policy: Resolving the Conflict between Individual-Level and Aggregate Research." *Journal of Politics, 65,* 327–349.

Berry, William D., and David Lowery. 1987. *Understanding United States Government Growth: An Empirical Assessment of the Postwar Era.* New York: Praeger.

Bingham, Richard D. 1977. "The Diffusion of Innovation among Local Governments." *Urban Affairs Quarterly, 13,* 223–232.

Blaikie, P. 1978. "The Theory of the Spatial Diffusion of Innovativeness: A Spacious Cul de Sac." *Progress in Human Geography, 2,* 268–295.

Blomquist, William. 2006. "The Policy Process and Large-N Comparative Studies." In Paul A. Sabatier, ed., *Theories of the Policy Process.* Boulder, CO: Westview Press.

Boeckelman, Keith. 1992. "The Influence of States on Federal Policy Adoptions." *Policy Studies Journal, 20*, 365–375.

Boehmke, Frederick J., and Richard Witmer. 2004. "Disentangling Diffusion: The Effects of Social Learning and Economic Competition on State Policy Innovation and Expansion." *Political Research Quarterly, 57*, 39–51.

Box-Steffensmeier, Janet M., and Bradford S. Jones. 2004. *Event History Modeling: A Guide for Social Scientists.* Cambridge: Cambridge University Press.

Brace, Paul, and Charles Barrilleaux. 1995. "A Model of Policy Reform in the American States." Paper presented at the annual meeting of the American Political Science Association, Chicago, Illinois.

Brace, Paul, Melinda Gann Hall, and Laura Langer. 1999. "Judicial Choice and the Politics of Abortion: Institutions, Context, and the Autonomy of Courts." *Albany Law Review, 62*, 1265–1302.

Brooks, Sarah M. 2005. "Interdependent and Domestic Foundations of Policy Change: The Diffusion of Pension Privatization around the World." *International Studies Quarterly, 49*, 273–294.

Brown, L., R. Schneider, M. Harvey, and B. Ridell. 1979. "Innovation Diffusion and Development in a Third World Setting: The Cooperative Movement in Sierra Leone." *Social Science Quarterly, 60*, 249–268.

Brown, L. A. 1975. "The Market and Infrastructure Context of Adoption: A Spatial Perspective on the Diffusion of Innovations." *Economic Geography, 51*, 185–216.

Brown, L. A., and K. Cox. 1971. "Empirical Regularities in the Diffusion of Innovation." *Annuals of the Association of American Geographers, 61*, 551–559.

Buckley, Jack, and Chad Westerland. 2004. "Duration Dependence, Functional Form, and Correct Standard Errors: Improving EHA Models of State Policy Diffusion." *State Politics and Policy Quarterly, 4*, 94–114.

Canon, Bradley C, and Lawrence Baum. 1981. "Patterns of Adoption of Tort Law Innovations." *American Political Science Review, 75*, 975–987.

Caudill, Steven B., Jon M. Ford, Franklin G. Mixon Jr., and Ter Chao Peng. 1995. "A Discrete-Time Hazard Model of Lottery Adoption." *Applied Economics, 27*, 555–561.

Chamberlain, Robert, and Donald P. Haider-Markel. 2005. "'Lien on me': State Policy Innovation in Response to Paper Terrorism." *Political Research Quarterly, 58*, 449–460.

Clark, Jill. 1985. "Policy Diffusion and Program Scope: Research Directions." *Publius, 15*, 61–70.

Clingermayer, James, and B. Dan Wood. 1995. "Disentangling Patterns of State Debt Financing." *American Political Science Review, 89*, 108–120.

Collier, David, and Richard E. Messick. 1975. "Prerequisites Versus Diffusion: Testing Explanations of Social Security Adoption." *American Political Science Review, 69*, 1299–1315.

Crain, Robert L. 1966. "Fluoridation: The Diffusion of Innovation among Cities." *Social Forces, 44*, 467–476.

Cyert, Richard M., and James G. March. 1963. *A Behavioral Theory of the Firm.* Englewood Cliffs, New Jersey: Prentice-Hall.

Daley, Dorothy M., and James C. Garand. 2005. "Horizontal Diffusion, Vertical Diffusion, and Internal Pressure in State Environmental Policymaking, 1989–1998." *American Politics Research, 33*, 615–644.

Derthick, Martha. 1970. *The Influence of Federal Grants.* Cambridge, MA: Harvard University Press.

DiMaggio, Paul J., and W. W. Powell. 1983. "The Iron Cage Revisited: Institutionalism and Collective Rationality in Organizational Fields." *American Sociological Review, 48*, 147–160.

Downs, George W., Jr., and Lawrence B. Mohr. 1976. "Conceptual Issues in the Study of Innovation." *Administrative Science Quarterly, 21*, 700–713.

Elazar, Daniel. 1972. *American Federalism: A View from the States.* New York: Thomas Crowell.

Erekson, O. Homer, Glenn Platt, Christopher Whistler, and Andrea Ziegert. 1999. "Factors Influencing the Adoption of State Lotteries." *Applied Economics, 31*, 875–884.

Filer, John E., Donald L. Moak, and Barry Uze. 1988. "Why Some States Adopt Lotteries and Others Don't." *Public Finance Quarterly, 16*, 259–283.

Foster, John. 1978. "Regionalism and Innovation in the American States." *Journal of Politics, 40*, 179–187.

Friedman, Milton. 1953. *Essays in Positive Economics.* Chicago: University of Chicago Press.

Gilardi, Fabrizio. 2005. "The Institutional Foundations of Regulatory Capitalism: The Diffusion of Independent Regulatory Agencies in Western Europe." *Annals of the American Academy of Social and Political Sciences, 598*, 84–101.

Glick, Henry R. 1981. "Innovation in State Judicial Administration: Effects on Court Management and Organization." *American Politics Quarterly, 9*, 49–69.

Glick, Henry R, and Scott P. Hays. 1991. "Innovation and Reinvention in State Policymaking: Theory and the Evolution of Living Will Laws." *Journal of Politics, 53,* 835–850.

Grattet, Ryken, Valerie Jenness, and Theodore R. Curry. 1998. "The Homogenization and Differentiation of Hate Crime Law in the United States, 1978 to 1995: Innovation and Diffusion in the Criminalization of Bigotry." *American Sociological Review, 63,* 286–307.

Gray, Virginia. 1973a. "Innovation in the States: A Diffusion Study." *American Political Science Review, 67,* 1174–1185.

_____. 1973b. "Rejoinder to 'Comment' by Jack L.Walker." *American Political Science Review, 67,* 1192–1193.

_____. 1994. "Competition, Emulation and Policy Innovation:" In Lawrence Dodd and Calvin Jillson, eds., *New Perspectives in American Politics.* Washington D.C.: Congressional Quarterly Press.

Gray, Virginia, and David Lowery. 1990. "The Corporatist Foundations of State Industrial Policy." *Social Science Quarterly, 71,* 3–24.

Greene, William H. 1993. *Econometric Analysis.* 2nd ed. New York: Macmillan.

Grossback, Lawrence J., Sean Nicholson-Crotty, and David A. M. Peterson. 2004. "Ideology and Learning in Policy Diffusion." *American Politics Research, 32,* 521–545.

Grupp, Fred W., Jr., and Alan R. Richards. 1975. "Variations in Elite Perceptions of American States as Referents for Public Policy Making." *American Political Science Review, 69,* 850–858.

Hagerstrand, T. 1967. *Innovation Diffusion as a Spatial Process.* Chicago: University of Chicago Press.

Haider-Markel, Donald P. 2001. "Policy Diffusion as a Geographical Expansion of the Scope of Political Conflict: Same Sex Marriage Bans in the 1990s." *State: Politics and Policy Quarterly, 1,* 5–26.

Hansen, Susan. 1983. *The Politics of Taxation.* Westport, CT: Praeger.

Hays, Scott P., and Henry R. Glick. 1997. "The Role of Agenda Setting in Policy Innovation: An Event History Analysis of Living Will Laws." *American Politics Quarterly, 25,* 497–516.

Heclo, Hugh. 1974. *Modern Social Politics in Britain and Sweden.* New Haven, CT: Yale University Press.

Hill, Kim Quaile, and Carl Klarner. 2002. "The Many Faces of Elite Power in the 'System of 1896:'" *Journal of Politics, 64,* 115–136.

Hill, Kim Quaile, Jan Leighly, and Angela Hinton-Andersson. 1995. "Lower Class Mobilization and Policy Linkage in the United States." *American Journal of Political Science, 39,* 75–86.

Hill, Twyla J. 2000. "Legally Extending the Family: An Event History Analysis of Grandparent Visitation Rights Laws." *Journal of Family Issues, 21,* 246–261.

Hofferbert, Richard. 1966. "The Relation between Public Policy and Some Structural and Environmental Variables in the American States." *American Political Science Review, 60,* 83–92.

Hoyman, Michele, and Micah Weinberg. 2006. "The Process of Policy Innovation: Prison Sitings in Rural North Carolina." *Policy Studies Journal, 34,* 95–112.

Jones, Bradford S., and Regina P. Branton. 2005. "Beyond Logit and Probit: Cox Duration Models of Single, Repeating and Competing Events for State Policy Adoption." *State Politics and Policy Quarterly, 5,* 420–443.

Jordana, Jacinct, and David Levi-Faur. 2005. "The Diffusion of Regulatory Capitalism in Latin America." *Annals of the American Academy of Political and Social Science, 598,* 102–124.

Ito, Shuichiro. 2001. "Shaping Policy Diffusion: Event History Analyses of Regional Laws in Japanese Prefectures." *Japanese Journal of Political Science, 2,* 211–235.

Ka, Sangjoon, and Paul Teske. 2002. "Ideology and Professionalism: Electricity Regulation and Deregulation over Time in the American States." *American Politics Research, 30,* 323–343.

Kiewiet, D. Roderick, and Matthew D. McCubbins. 1985. "Congressional Appropriations and the Electoral Connection." *Journal of Politics, 47,* 59–82.

Kim, Junseok, and Brian Gerber. 2005. "Bureaucratic Leverage over Policy Choice: Explaining the Dynamics of State-Level Reforms in Telecommunications Regulation." *Policy Studies Journal, 33,* 613–633.

Kingdon, John W. 1984. *Agendas, Alternatives, and Public Policies.* Boston: Little, Brown and Company.

Kraemer, Kenneth I., Vijay Gurbaxani, and John Leslie King. 1992. "Economic Development, Government Policy, and the Diffusion of Computing in Asia-Pacific Countries." *Public Administration Review, 52,* 146–156.

Ladd, Helen F., and John L. Yinger. 1989. *America's Ailing Cities: Fiscal Health and the Design of Urban Policy.* Baltimore: Johns Hopkins University Press.

Langer, Laura, and Paul Brace. 2005. "The Preemptive Power of State Supreme Courts: Adoption of Abortion and Death Penalty Legislation." *Policy Studies Journal, 33,* 317–340.

Lindblom, Charles E. 1965. *The Intelligence of Democracy: Decision Making through Mutual Adjustment*. New York: Free Press.

Lowry, William R. 2005. "Policy Reversal and Changing Politics: State Governments and Dam Removals." *State Politics and Policy Quarterly, 5*, 394–419.

Lubell, Mark, Mark Schneider, John T. Scholz, and Mihriye Mete. 2002. "Watershed Partnerships and the Emergence of Collective Action Institutions." *American Journal of Political Science, 46*, 148–163.

Mahajan, V., and R. A. Peterson. 1985. *Models for Innovation Diffusion*. Beverly Hills, CA: Sage Publications, Inc.

Mann, Arthur J. 1980. "Wagner's Law: An Econometric Test for Mexico: 1925–1976." *National Tax Journal, 33*, 189–201.

Mayhew, David. 1974. *Congress: The Electoral Connection*. New Haven: Yale University Press.

McLendon, Michael K., Donald E. Heller, and Steven P. Young. 2005. "State Postsecondary Policy Innovation: Politics, Competition, and the Interstate Migration of Policy Ideas." *Journal of Higher Education, 76*, 363–382.

Menzel, Donald C., and Irwin Feller. 1977. "Leadership and Interaction Patterns in the Diffusion of Innovations among the American States." *Western Political Quarterly, 30*, 528–536.

Meseguer, Covadonga. 2004. "What Role for Learning? The Diffusion of Privatisation in OECD and Latin American Countries." *Journal of Public Policy, 24*, 299–325.

_____. 2005a. "Policy Learning, Policy Diffusion, and the Making of a New Order." *Annals of the American Academy of Political and Social Science, 598*, 67–81.

_____. 2005b. "Rational Learning and Bounded Learning in the Diffusion of Policy Innovation." University of Notre Dame Working Paper #316.

Midlarsky, Manus I. 1978. "Analyzing Diffusion and Contagion Effects: The Urban Disorders of the 1960s." *American Political Science Review, 72*, 996–1008.

Mikesell, John I. 1978. "Election Periods and State Tax Policy Cycles." *Public Choice, 33*, 99–105.

Miller, Edward Alan. 2006. "Bureaucratic Policy Making on Trial: Medicaid Nursing Facility Reimbursement, 1988–1998." *Medical Care Research and Review, 63*, 189–216.

Mintrom, Michael. 1977. "Policy Entrepreneurs and the Diffusion of Innovation." *American Journal of Political Sciences, 41*, 738–770.

Mintrom, Michael, and Sandra Vergari. 1996. "Advocacy Coalitions, Policy Entrepreneurs, and Policy Change." *Policy Studies Journal, 24*, 420–434.

_____. 1998. "Policy Networks and Innovation Diffusion: The Case of State Education Reforms." *Journal of Politics, 60*, 126–148.

Mohr, Lawrence. 1969. "Determinants of Innovation in Organizations." *American Political Science Review, 75*, 111–126.

Mooney, Christopher Z. 2001. "Modeling Regional Effects on State Policy Diffusion." *Political Research Quarterly, 54*, 103–124.

Mooney, Christopher Z., and Mei-Hsien Lee. 1995. "Legislating Morality in the American States: The Case of Pre-Roe Abortion Regulation Reform." *American Journal of Political Science, 39*, 599–627.

_____. 2000. "The Influence of Values on Consensus and Contentious Morality Policy: U.S. Death Penalty Reform, 1956–82." *Journal of Politics, 62*, 223–239.

Mossberger, Karen. 2000. *The Politics of Ideas and the Spread of Enterprise Zones*. Washington D.C.: Georgetown University Press.

Nathan, Richard P. 1989. "The Role of the States in American Federalism." In Carl Van Horn, ed., *The State of the States*. Washington D.C.: Congressional Quarterly Press.

Nicholson-Crotty, Sean. 2004. "The Politics and Administration of Privatizaiton: Contracting Out for Corrections Management in the United States." *Policy Studies Journal, 32*, 41–57.

Peterson, Paul E., and Mark C. Rom. 1990. *Welfare Magnets*. Washington D.C.: Brookings.

Pierce, Patrick A., and Donald E. Miller. 1999. "Variations in the Diffusion of State Lottery Adoptions: How Revenue Dedication Changes Morality Politics." *Policy Studies Journal, 27*, 696–706.

Preuhs, Robert R. 2005. "Descriptive Representation, Legislative Leadership, and Direct Democracy: Latino Influence on English-Only Laws in the States, 1984–2002." *State Politics and Policy Quarterly, 5*, 204–224.

Price, Byron E., and Norma M. Riccucci. 2005. "Exploring the Determinants of Decisions to Privatize State Prisons." *The American Review of Public Administration, 35*, 223–235.

Reeves, H. Clyde. 1986. *Measuring Fiscal Capacity*. Boston: Oelgeschlager, Gunn and Hain.

Regens, James L. 1980. "State Policy Responses to the Energy Issue." *Social Science Quarterly, 61*, 44–57.

Rockefeller, N. A. 1968. *The Future of Federalism*. New York: Atheneum.

Rogers, Everett M. 1983. *Diffusion of Innovations*. New York: The Free Press.

Rogers, Everett M., and F. Floyd Shoemaker. 1971. *Communication of Innovations: A Cross-Cultural Approach*. New York: The Free Press.

Rose, Richard. 1993. *Lesson-Drawing in Public Policy*. Chatham, NJ: Chatham House.

Rosenson, Beth A. 2003. "Against Their Apparent Self-Interest: The Authorization of Independent State Legislative Ethics Commissions, 1973–96." *State Politics and Policy Quarterly, 3*, 42–65.

Sabatier, Paul A., and Hank C. Jenkins-Smith. 2006. "The Advocacy Coalition Framework: An Assessment." In Paul A. Sabatier, ed., *Theories of the Policy Process*. Boulder, CO: Westview Press.

Sapat, Alka. 2004. "Devolution and Innovation: The Adoption of State Environmental Policy Innovations by Administrative Agencies." *Public Administration Review, 64*, 141–151.

Satterthwaite, Shad B. 2002. "Innovation and Diffusion of Managed Care in Medicaid Programs." *State and Local Government Review, 34*, 116–126.

Savage, Robert L. 1978. "Policy Innovativeness as a Trait of American States." *Journal of Politics, 40*, 212–224.

Schneider, Mark, Paul Teske, and Michael Mintrom. 1995. *Public Entrepreneurs*. Princeton: Princeton University Press.

Sigelman, Lee, and Roland E. Smith. 1980. "Consumer Legislation in the American States! An Attempt at Explanation." *Social Science Quarterly, 61*, 58–69.

Simmons, Beth A. 2000. "International Law and State Behavior: Commitment and Compliance in International Monetary Affairs." *American Political Science Review, 94*, 819–835.

Simmons, Beth A., and Zachary Elkins. 2004. "The Globalization of Liberalization: Policy Diffusion in the International Political Economy." *American Political Science Review, 98*, 171–189.

Simon, Herbert. 1947. *Administrative Behavior*. New York: Macmillan.

Soss, Joe, Sanford F. Schram, Thomas P. Vartanian, and Erin O'Brien. 2001. "Setting the Terms of Relief: Explaining State Policy Choices in the Devolution Revolution." *American Journal of Political Science, 45*, 378–395.

Soule, Sarah A., and Jennifer Earl. 2001. "The Enactment of State-Level Hate Crime Law in the United States: Intrastate and Interstate Factors." *Sociological Perspectives, 44*, 281–305.

Stream, Christopher. 1999. "Health Reform in the States: A Model of State Small Group Health Insurance Market Reform." *Political Research Quarterly, 52*, 499–525.

Tolbert, Pamela, and Lynne Zucker. 1983. "Institutional Sources of Change in the Formal Structure of Organizations: The Diffusion of Civil Service Reform, 1880–1935." *Administrative Science Quarterly, 28*, 22–39.

Tomz, Michael, Jason Wittenberg, and Gary King. 2003. "CLARIFY: Software for Interpreting and Presenting Statistical Results." Version 2.1. Stanford University, University of Wisconsin, and Harvard University. http://gking.harvard.edu (January 5, 2003).

Volden, Craig. 2002. "The Politics of Competitive Federalism: A Race to the Bottom in Welfare Benefits?" *American Journal of Political Science, 46*, 352–363.

_____. 2006. "States as Policy Laboratories: Emulating Success in the Children's Health Insurance Program." *American Journal of Political Science, 50*, 294–312.

Wagner, Adolph. 1877. *Finanzwissenshaft*, pt. 1. Leipzig: C. F. Winter.

Walker, Jack L. 1969. "The Diffusion of Innovations among the American States." *American Political Science Review, 63*, 880–899.

_____. 1973. "Comment." *American Political Science Review, 67*, 1186–1191.

Way, Christopher R. 2005. "Political Insecurity and the Diffusion of Financial Market Regulation." *Annals of the American Academy of Political and Social Science, 598*, 125–144.

Welch, Susan, and Kay Thompson. 1980. "The Impact of Federal Incentives on State Policy Innovations." *American Journal of Political Science, 24*, 715–729.

Weyland, Kurt, ed. 2004. *Learning from Foreign Models in Latin American Policy Reform*. Washington D.C.: Woodrow Wilson Center Press.

Wong, Kenneth K., and Francis X. Shen. 2002. "Politics of State-Led Reform in Education: Market Competition and Electoral Dynamics." *Educational Policy, 16*, 161–192.

# Appendix

Published Studies Using EHA to Test a Model of Innovation Reflecting Both Internal Determinants and Intergovernmental Diffusion

Berry and Berry (1990): lotteries
Berry and Berry (1992): taxes
Alm, McKee, and Skidmore (1993): lotteries
Berry (1994a): strategic planning by state agencies
Berry and Berry (1994): tax rate increases
Caudill et al. (1995): lotteries
Mooney and Lee (1995): abortion regulation reform
Hays and Glick (1997): living will laws
Mintrom (1997): school choice
Grattet, Jenness, and Curry (1998): state hate crime laws
Mintrom and Vergari (1998): school choice
Brace, Hall and Langer (1999): whether state supreme court hears a challenge to a state statute on abortion access or funding
Erekson et al. (1999): lotteries
Pierce and Miller (1999): lotteries
Andrews (2000): electricity sector regulatory reforms
Hill (2000): grandparent visitation rights statutes
Mooney and Lee (2000): death penalty reform
*Simmons (2000): acceptance of International Monetary Fund rules (Article VIII) by nations
Balla (2001): Health Maintenance Organization Model Act
Haider-Markel (2001): bans on same-sex marriage
*Ito (2001): various laws enacted by Japanese prefectural governments relating to the environment, freedom of information, and citizens with disabilities
Mooney (2001): lotteries, tax adoptions
Soule and Earl (2001): hate crime laws
Hill and Klarner (2002): direct democracy reforms
Ka and Teske (2002): electricity deregulation
*Lubell et al. (2002): local watershed partnerships
Satterthwaite (2002): managed care in Medicaid programs
Wong and Shen (2002): charter school legislation
Rosenson (2003): authorization of independent state legislative ethics commissions
Allard (2004): mothers' aid programs
Allen, Pettus, and Haider-Markel (2004): truth-in-sentencing laws
Boehmke and Witmer (2004): the signing of Indian gaming compacts
Buckley and Westerland (2004): lotteries
Grossback, Nicholson-Crotty, and Peterson (2004): lotteries, academic bankruptcy laws, sentencing guidelines
*Meseguer (2004): privatization in Latin American countries
Nicholson-Crotty (2004): corrections privatization
Sapat (2004): environmental policy innovations by state administrative agencies
*Simmons and Elkins (2004): adoption of economic liberalization policies by International Monetary Fund nations
Allen (2005): animal cruelty felony laws
Berry and Baybeck (2005): lotteries
*Brooks (2005): nations' adoptions of pension privatization
Chamberlain and Haider-Markel (2005): laws against the use of frivolous liens
*Gilardi (2005): creation of independent regulatory agencies in western European nations
Jones and Branton (2005): restrictive abortion laws, obscenity laws
*Jordana and Levi-Faur (2005): creation of regulatory agencies in Latin American nations
Kim and Gerber (2005): telephone regulation reform
Langer and Brace (2005): restrictive abortion laws; death penalty
McLendon, Heller, and Young (2005): higher education reforms
Preuhs (2005): English only laws
*Way (2005): financial system liberalization by nations

Bali and Silver (2006): electoral reform
*Hoyman and Weinberg (2006): prison sitings in rural North Carolina counties
Miller (2006): Medicaid nursing facility reimbursement reform
Volden (2006): Children's Health Insurance Program

*Note:* Unless otherwise indicated, a study analyzes the adoption of a policy or program by American states via legislation. Studies denoted with an asterisk (*) analyze adoptions of policies by governments other than American states (nations, local or regional governments in the United States, or subnational governments in other nations).

# Substance Versus Politics: Through the Dark Mirror of Governance Reform

DAVID W. LESLIE AND RICHARD J. NOVAK

*This article explores recent initiatives by the states to reform governance of public higher education. It synthesizes theoretical and empirical literature to suggest that richer understanding might result from "qualitative heuristic" treatment of multiple case studies. It proposes that data be analyzed to weigh the main and residual effects of political and instrumental goals of key actors in reform. Five exploratory case studies of state governance reform are summarized. Political factors were found to outweigh instrumental factors in most of the cases. The authors conclude with a discussion of fluidity in the political environment, noting that solutions seem to be continuously moving targets.*

***Keywords:*** *postsecondary policy; case studies; governance*

BETWEEN 1985 AND 2000, as McLendon (in press) has pointed out, state governments considered "in excess of 100 proposals to reform structural, functional, and authority patterns of their higher education systems." He further pointed out that "virtually nothing is known about how or why state governments undertake reforms of their higher education systems." His own analysis of these reforms suggested simultaneous trends toward centralization and decentralization with effects that appear to fit no consistent pattern. His analysis suggested, but did not affirmatively conclude, that the mix of factors affecting governance reforms may vary with time as well as from venue to venue. Tracing the effort to theorize about (and therefore to understand) governance change, McLendon went on to explore the more traditional "systems" and "incremental" models as well as to assess the usefulness of a group of "neoinstitutionalist" approaches.

We are struck by the extent to which several decades of work on public governance of higher education has yet to converge on any consistent explanatory framework. In effect, and despite what McLendon (in press) has reported as increasingly sophisticated analytical work, the field has moved very little beyond the definitive classifications developed by Berdahl (1971). Moreover, our own

EDUCATIONAL POLICY, Vol. 17 No. 1, January and March 2003 98–120
DOI: 10.1177/0895904802239288
© 2003 Corwin Press

analysis of proposed governance and finance reforms during the 1930s concluded that debates over state governance of higher education had already begun and that

> at the heart of the process lie continued efforts to strike a balance between the state's need for planning, oversight, and incentives on behalf of the greater social good, and institutions' interests in their maximizing their own freedom and autonomy. (Novak & Leslie, 2000, p. 74)

Although the balance clearly swung toward more oversight (if not outright control) during the succeeding decades, a broader debate over the role of government—whether in the direction of privatization or reinventing government—has influenced what we see as repeated experimentation, or tinkering, with varying models for coordination, control, and oversight of higher education.

McLendon's (2000) own research involved one of the rare empirical examinations of the political dynamics of governance reform. He conducted three in-depth case studies in different states and concluded that varied political contingencies had led to the reforms. Although his investigation was framed in concepts about political agenda setting, his results did not appear to fit neatly into a parsimonious explanatory template. To the contrary, he suggested that the fluidity and complexity of broad policy agendas and the simultaneous search by individual political actors for opportunities to achieve their own goals made for characteristically idiosyncratic outcomes in any particular situation.

Indeed, it may be difficult or impossible to predict governance reform because policy outcomes are essentially unpredictable. Smith (2002) has argued that explanatory precision may be unattainable in certain avenues of political inquiry because political behavior itself may be grossly irregular and unpredictable. Constitutionally, *policy* is whatever government says it is, and *government* is whoever happens to be in a position to decide at any given point in time. In an open democratic system, issues may be continuously in play, and even relatively new reforms may be continually subject to shifts in the salience of issues to the public, the ambient event context (or what people perceive or know to be happening contemporaneously), emergent or embedded ideologies, political dynamics, and other contingencies.

We also suspect that some higher education policy may be made in substantial part by default or displacement. In several states, higher education itself may or may not be central to any given political or institutional agenda but may, rather, be an obliquely collateral issue that is superficially or impulsively managed precisely because (a) its structure of governance is largely invisible to the public, and (b) it is a residual of bargaining over appropriations and other substantive legislation. In other words, in many states, higher education policy may not fit into templates of policy making that explain certain types of decision precisely because it is an ancillary matter to other decisions.

Because theorizing assumes a substantial base of valid observation and inference, and because efforts to transfer existing frameworks have so far yielded conflicting results, we think it is important to return to the foundations of inquiry. Greenberg, Miller, Mohr, and Vladeck (1977) reminded political scientists that collecting data is essential to building and testing theory.

Our article begins with some general observations from our work in the policy arena during the past two decades. We then briefly review some key theoretical work on policy development and change and agenda formation. We apply that work to recent studies of state-level higher education policy formation and argue that the existing empirical foundations for generalizing are insufficient to support any systematic template for understanding. We introduce the idea of heuristics as a starting point in our pursuit of a clearer understanding of higher education policy making and then report on five exploratory case studies and emergent ideas about patterns we have found. We conclude with suggestions for more inductive and case study research relying on methods of grounded theory.

## Theoretical Foundations

Although the constitutions of some states (e.g., Michigan) provide final, authoritative allocation of control over higher education, most public colleges and universities are simply statutory entities subject to whatever a working legislative majority wishes to do with them. McLendon and others have grappled with alternative explanations or theories about how and why the organization of public higher education rises to the level of legislative agenda and how and why varied solutions are adopted. But we think conceptualization should follow observation—we are at a fundamentally inductive stage of developing understanding because we have so little in the way of data to draw on. As David Hume warned, "A wise man . . . proportions his belief to the evidence" (p. 110). Evidence about governance reform is in fairly short supply in the published literature.

We suggest that certain basic realities characterize the political process, realities that both limit and suggest a range of conceptualizations that would fit the data. Drawing loosely on Greenberg et al. (1977), the overriding characteristics of policy making appear to be complexity and fluidity. In other words, all variables are in a state of more or less constant flux. Who decides, what they decide, what levers of power are used, and where benefits flow all change more or less continuously. In this conceptualization, there is no beginning or end and no static outcome. Even the law may not reflect actual behavior and practice on the ground. (Selective enforcement of speed limits is one example.)

Data on policy formation suggest that the process is also nonlinear and discontinuous (but not random, either). Baumgartner and Jones (1993) introduced the idea of "punctuated equilibrium" to describe widely observed "unpredictable surges and declines in agenda dynamics" (p. 270). We have no reason to believe that higher education policy is made in an arena that differs in any way from policy on other subjects. This means, of course, that explanations for governance reform should conceptualize complexity, fluidity, randomness, and unpredictability, as well as respect the patterns that have been observed in other decision arenas.

Whereas process may be difficult to pin down concretely, product may also be problematic. There is no obviously *best* or even *better* model for organizing and governing systems of public colleges and universities. Notwithstanding the work of Berdahl (1971), MacTaggart (1996), and commentaries too numerous to cite here, there appears to be little (nonideological) consensus on what would result in a particularly effective and efficient system of public higher education. Many states have altered their systems—some to more central control, some to less—in the past decade. Because there is no obvious best way, the motives and methods—not to say politics and preferences—of those who decide may be the most powerful variables in play.

This leads directly to the question of agenda. Why do legislatures and governors take up certain issues and not others? Why do they pass some bills and not others? Who decides and how? These questions are at the core of research initiated by Cobb and Elder (1983) and pursued by Kingdon (1987), Baumgartner and Jones (1993), and Gray and Lowery (2000). As Gray and Lowery synthesized this literature, they suggested that it typically focuses on three stages of policy development: problem identification, policy formulation, and enactment. Sources of influence on policy initiatives typically are found to converge on insiders to the legislative process: legislators, staff, and lobbyists. This is consistent with Marshall, Mitchell, and Wirt (1985), who also found that actual patterns of influence varied from state to state. And Gray and Lowery suggested that influence patterns also vary from issue to issue.

Although nowhere in this literature is it suggested that policy is made capriciously, several lines of thought about the process grapple with its variability and unpredictability. These newer lines of thought are represented by Kingdon's (1987) "policy streams" approach, Sabatier and Jenkins-Smith's (1993) advocacy coalition framework, and Baumgartner and Jones's (1993) notion of punctuated equilibrium. These conceptualizations draw on earlier foundational efforts to explain unconventional institutional and organizational behavior under conditions of "bounded rationality" (Birkland, 2001). Lindblom's (1959) now classic work on incremental decision making, Cohen and March's (1974) work on "organized anarchies," Weick's (1976) "loosely coupled systems," and the organizational metaphors proposed by Morgan (1986) all suggest variants on the same theme. They draw on assumptions about how decisions are made when neither rationality nor institutional structures explain the outcome.

*Neoinstitutionalism* (Meyer & Rowan, 1977) helps to frame ideas about behavior in institutions and organizations that is only partially understood. Neoinstitutional thought accepts the shaping and bounding qualities of institutions, such as governmental bodies that make policy. But it also accepts the variability of behavior and of outcomes within otherwise normed and norming conditions. Firestone (1989) described this variability in terms of games that are played in making policy.

Different groups may construct different rules for playing, depending on how they calculate their own interests in relation to the legitimacy of others' interests. The existence of different rules may lead to the appearance of impulsive and incoherent decisions, but only to observers who do not know what the rules are.

These ideas, particularly those of Firestone's (1989) games and Morgan's (1986) images, suggest to us that policy making might best be understood via a series of cases that illustrate how widely the processes and products of policy formation vary. Policy is likely the product of many different interests working independently (at least in part) on many different issues simultaneously. Varied ways of thinking, acting, and deciding may characterize the behavior of participants. We propose to explore the similarities and differences among cases employing a variant of the "qualitative heuristic" method suggested by Kleining and Witt (2000). This approach can help visualization of the variables in play, giving observers (and players) a set of alternative frames with which to interpret the course of events.

We suggest that deep, comparative case studies can form the basis for qualitative heuristic approaches to understanding policy. Although deep, comparative case studies are often used in a grounded theory effort to establish similar patterns and commonalities among the cases, an heuristic approach would focus on variability among them and on constructing alternative scenarios (Kleining & Witt, 2000). These alternative scenarios can serve in part as descriptive templates that help participants to strategize. They can also serve as rough explanatory frameworks that provide retrospective understanding of outcomes.

## Studies of State-Level Higher Education Restructuring

One reason we are attracted to the heuristic idea is because recent studies of higher education policy imply that the conceptual equivalent of dark matter remains to be discovered in explaining outcomes of many actions taken by states. Even the most sophisticated analyses appear to be looking for explanations from points of view that give too little leverage. Each of the authors cited below concluded by speculating that political variables may explain more than originally supposed.

Marcus's (1997) study noted a mix of factors affecting trends in governance reform. His survey of state higher education executives focused on rationales for recently enacted centralization and decentralization of state systems. Although the resulting explanations suggested that pragmatic reforms to solve specific problems were at least partly behind the changes, Marcus also noted that issues related to power and control emerged in significant ways. He concluded,

> The correlation between the existence of a power struggle and the effort to increase the role of the governor and legislature in higher education apparently confirms the observation that if the institutions and the state-level board are battling with each other or if the state-level board is not able to mediate power struggles occurring among institutions, then elected officials may seek to restore order by taking a strong hand themselves. (p. 410)

From a different analytical angle, Frost, Hearn, and Marine (1997) reviewed a case of policy making in North Carolina, assessing the degree to which the decision had benefited from the analysis of data. Concluding that analytical reasoning had been almost wholly absent from the decision, they acknowledged that "state-level decision making inevitably involves attention to political reasoning, bureaucratic structures, time constraints, and the nature of pressing public concerns" (pp. 388–389). This case study also suggests that how states deal with higher education may be governed more by concerns and issues that are only tangentially about higher education per se.

In her study of conflict between the University of California and the California legislature, Zusman (1986) framed the analysis in terms of power relations. She implied that outcomes in any particular decision event should be interpreted as part of "ebbs and flows" (p. 416) in continuing tests of political will among the parties.

These three studies point to a similar conclusion: Politics and power relations may explain more about decision events affecting higher education, governance reform included, than analytical frames based on the content of these decisions or on their outcomes. They also imply that multivariate frames of reference fit better than univariate frames of reference. The most powerful variables, however, may have little to do with higher education per se. (Zumeta [1996] did find that different forms of state-level higher education governance could be associated with differences in funding patterns, but it was not clear what was cause and what was effect.)

Conceptually, this means that higher education governance reforms—along with many other substantive issues decided by states—may be best understood as a direct (not indirect) product of political factors. Politics, in other words, is not the "residual" (Graham, 2000). Political factors may account for main effects. Substantive outcomes may be the residuals—what happens to higher education governance may well be more or less random fallout from a larger adjustment of political issues.

This is where we think comparative case studies can be most helpful. What variables most effectively predict that governance reform will reach the political agenda, and what variables most effectively predict how governance reform will turn out? Comparing outcomes statistically—which states centralized, which states decentralized, and which did neither, for example—might lead to conclusions about differences among states on selected variables, as in Marcus's (1997) study. But comparative case studies allow for any and all explanations to surface. The strategic difference lies in whether one selects variables to study a priori or whether the case study approach more readily allows any and all variables to emerge in whatever formulation might be inferred from the data. If the adjustment of a state's political dynamics to regime change or financial stringency or any other complex of issues is central, and if governance reform is ancillary, then the only way to find out is to let all the variables emerge. Comparative case studies give those variables a chance to emerge and provide data on which state-to-state analyses can be conducted.

## Main And Residual Effects

We have reconstructed five cases of state-level governance reform from a series of interviews, correspondence with knowledgeable informants, and document reviews. In general, we asked informed insiders in three of the states to report as complete reconstructions of reform in their states as possible. Given a reasonable level of consistency among reports and documents, we accepted the face validity of these accounts. For all five cases, we relied on state government reports; newspaper articles and online sources; and published books, articles, and studies. In four of the states, our own direct experiences as outside consultants and expert advisors served to further inform our data.

Throughout this article, we use the terms *governance reform, reorganization,* and *restructuring* interchangeably. The notion of governance reform, however, may mean different things to different people. In the eyes of its supporters, it may be seen as a necessary remedy to remove faults and defects in the current governance structure or process, but those who oppose the remedy may dispute the existence of such faults and defects. In addition, reform can also encompass more than rearranging governing boards or the reporting lines of institutions. For example, reform can mean an improved process to select trustees and make such appointments less a form of political patronage. Despite these distinctions, we use the three terms interchangeably in the following cases, all of which describe state policy initiatives to substantially alter higher education governance.

In analyzing the cases, we asked whether "instrumental" or "political" factors constituted the main (explanatory) effects in each case. If we could affirm that either was a main, or explanatory, effect, we next assessed whether the remaining factor could reasonably be termed a "residual" (Graham, 2000). It is possible that the two interact, however, meaning that both instrumental and political factors operate simultaneously to explain outcomes.

We define *instrumental* factors in reform as practical objectives for improving the effectiveness or efficiency of state-level governance. For example, governance reform may result from a calculation that a weak coordinating board has resulted in too much disparity in funding among institutions of higher education, so, politics aside, centralization may be an instrumental goal for reform—and therefore a main or explanatory effect.

On the other hand, *political* factors in reform may stem from some explicit or implicit need of political elites to consolidate power or thwart interests counter to their own. For example, a turnover in legislative control may motivate a governor enjoying a new partisan majority to implement governance reform so he or she can make patronage appointments to a new governing board. In that case, we would conclude that political factors were main effects. Instrumental results may well fall out as residuals and may even be cited as the rationale for change. But those results would be ancillary to the main political reasons reforms were undertaken.

As noted earlier, our method was the qualitative heuristic method described by Kleining and Witt (2000). We claim only to have compared five episodes of policy change, and mainly to illuminate what we think is a helpful way to present and compare cases. Our case reports should be seen as more useful for the data than for our classification of main effects—which, in the end, is judgmental.

## Higher Education's Political Environment

The five cases occurred in a political environment that has changed in dramatic ways. In 1974, Democrats controlled three quarters of all state legislatures. In 2000, Democrats controlled one third. In 1977, Democrats controlled three quarters of the nation's governorships. In 2000, they controlled just more than one third. In the 1994 elections, state governments underwent one of the most sweeping changes in party control in 40 years. Republicans captured a majority of legislatures and governorships, foretelling the prospect of major policy shifts. Coincident with these electoral outcomes, many states have instituted major changes in the governance of public universities and the systems of which they are a part.

Many changes in the political and economic environment for higher education are associated with these trends:

- a shift toward less government and lower taxes;
- reinvention of government by granting more discretion to the lower levels of government;
- increasing belief in the validity of market forces and a concomitant effort to privatize many government activities;
- a greater tendency to frame policy debates in ideological or partisan, rather than in pragmatic, terms;
- more use of "direct democracy" through the "initiative and referendum" process, including constitutional amendment;
- structural deficits resulting from spending and tax limitations, dedicated spending on certain government services (including federal mandates), and outmoded tax systems that fail to capture sufficient revenues when the economy grows (Hovey, 1999);
- the increasing importance of research, knowledge, and technologically sophisticated workers to the business community raises the competitive climate for higher education; and
- fragmentation and ambivalence of the higher education community about important policy issues in the face of an increasingly fractious political environment.

The outcomes of these policy trends have largely been in the direction of decentralization, local control, marketization of public policy, and increasingly fluid coalitions. Speaking to the effects on higher education, Yudof (2002) observed,

> [Contemporary) elected officials prefer market accountability—with institutions competing with each other for students—rather than traditional public oversight to ensure quality. And rather than provide operational support to universities, they encourage universities to charge higher tuition, then favor giving direct aid to students in the form of scholarships and tax benefits to help make that tuition affordable. (p. B24)

These indicators do not amount to a political science of higher education. They do not answer basic questions about why governance changes occur, who initiates these changes, with what calculations about who benefits, and with what levers of power changes are effected. Our cases are presented to illustrate specific answers to important political questions.

## Cases

In the five case reports that follow, we present the general story of the reform, identify both instrumental and political factors that surfaced, and present our estimate of the main and residual effects.

As noted earlier, we relied on interviews, correspondence with knowledgeable informants, documents, and our own experiences with the states to outline for each case: (a) The macro-politics of contexts in which reform has occurred—What changes or issues may have led to reform? (b) The institutional framework for reform—What was changed and how? and (c) The actions and motives of key players in reform—What changes emerged, and whose interests do those change serve (i.e., who benefits)?

## Minnesota

Restructuring legislation passed in the Minnesota legislature in 1991 and combined three separate and disparate systems, the six state universities, the community colleges, and the technical colleges, each with its own board, executive, and staff, into one integrated organization. The new merged system, called the Minnesota State Colleges and Universities, although not official and fully operational until July 1995, began with 160,000 students, 20,000 faculty, and 60 campuses. It was the eighth largest employer in Minnesota (MacTaggart, 1996).

There had been growing concern that the total higher education enterprise in the state had become diluted, too expansive, and too expensive. Even though participation rates were high, funding per student was in decline. The semblance of a middle-class taxpayer revolt was also appearing. A state blue ribbon commission in the mid-1980s tried to address the problem of overexpansion but failed. The state's coordinating board lacked sufficient authority over the state systems to enforce any degree of lasting fiscal discipline. And a legislative proposal to create a superboard, including the University of Minnesota, got nowhere, particularly because of the university's constitutional status and opposition to such a board.

The Senate majority leader was a true believer in education for the masses. He was a strong proponent of this populist belief and felt that it had not permeated deeply enough into those segments of the population requiring technical education and work skills. Higher education would be more welcoming and customer-friendly to this segment of the population. The majority leader's resolve won out. He refused to allow the 1991 legislature to adjourn until it agreed to his merger language for the new system, attached to the higher education appropriations bill. The house education committee chair, also a strong supporter of higher education, opposed the merger. He reluctantly agreed to approve the bill and believed that it could be overturned in subsequent legislative sessions. He later observed that the systems

> wouldn't need to worry about merger if they had learned to work together twenty years ago. Credit transfer, duplication of effort, lack of cooperation, and budget sharing all joined to frustrate the legislature and the governor to the point of merger. (MacTaggart, 1996, p. 138)

Higher education leaders also opposed the merger; some remained silent, at best. The technical colleges voiced the loudest opposition—they were partially controlled by local school districts in addition to a statewide board.

The bill passed because of a combination of political will (Senate majority leader) and political opportunity (growing legislative unease with higher education's rising costs, duplication of programs, and a sense that centralization would bring more rationality and efficiency to all of higher education).

We see Minnesota as a case of balanced effect by both instrumental (efficiency, rationality) and political factors (timing of the issue and the use of political capital by a single leading legislator). Whatever instrumental goals the higher education community may have had—especially in preserving the status quo—lost out to the sense of political leaders that change was needed.

## Kentucky

Restructuring legislation in Kentucky passed the legislature in 1997. It created a new and strengthened state coordinating agency, the Council on Postsecondary Education, and created a new 2-year Kentucky Community and Technical College System by combining most of the community colleges that had been part of the University of Kentucky system and the technical colleges operated by the Cabinet for Workforce Development. At the same time, more dollars were committed to the state colleges and universities, directly by the state and through a new public/private match (called Bucks for Brains) that was directed to building the Universities of Kentucky and Louisville into more prominent research campuses and to creating programs of distinction at the regional universities.

The impetus for these substantive changes were clearly the desire to align policies of control, finance, and accountability to pursue a new state agenda for higher education that would lead to a more competitive Kentucky, namely, a better educated workforce, increased access (including the initiation of a distance learning university), reduced adult illiteracy, and increased university research capacity tied to the state economy.

The champion of reform in Kentucky was Governor Paul Patton, who risked a great deal of political capital but won the reform battle with his larger goals intact. He campaigned tirelessly on the road, in the media, and with the legislature to enact his program. He relied on outside consultants to provide much of the needed research and comparative analysis to other states. He became convinced that a stronger coordinating agency could provide both incentives and statewide policy direction. He also felt that more direct and consistent involvement by the governor, top legislators, and key state council members was necessary.

The University of Kentucky and its legislative allies bitterly opposed the restructuring that removed all but two of the community colleges from the University of Kentucky system when the new 2-year system was approved. The legislation also created a unique statutory entity, called the Strategic Committee on Postsecondary Education (SCOPE), to ensure continued focus on the implementation and goals of the restructuring. It consists of the president (chief executive) of the Council of Postsecondary Education, five members of the Council selected by the chair, six persons designated by the governor, the president of the Senate, the Speaker of the House, the majority and minority floor leaders of both chambers, and other legislative leaders. A strong executive was considered essential to a successful new Council on Postsecondary Education. A veteran coordinating board executive was to take the position and implement the reform and restructuring.

As in Minnesota, the Kentucky reforms resulted from the investment of political capital by a state leader. Those universities that saw their own instrumental goal to keep the status quo were overridden.

## New Jersey

Restructuring of New Jersey higher education occurred over a 10-year span from 1985 to 1995. It was a difficult road for advocates of greater institutional independence from central state authority over this 10-year period, however. Change came at two different times, 1985–1986 and 1994–1995.

The first period of change affected the nine state colleges. Under the leadership of the state college presidents and then-Governor Tom Kean, the colleges were given a "fair hearing" about excessive state oversight. After a special blue ribbon commission studied how to achieve greater institutional improvement (and proposed a new University of New Jersey System—a proposal that was rejected by the state colleges after a vigorous debate), a package of three bills was devised in 1985 to grant the state colleges greater institutional autonomy and remove them from "state agency status" (Novak, 1989, pp. 9–11).

The bills were defeated in 1985 (due to substantial opposition from faculty and employee unions) but passed in the 1986 legislative session. The nine institutions were given greater autonomy from the Department and Board of Higher Education, a strong state coordinating agency and board, and from several state executive agencies that oversaw college business practices in operational areas like financial affairs, personnel management, purchasing, outside contracting, and managing investment income.

New Jersey higher education was highly regulated (and well funded), but Governor Kean and the presidents of the public institutions agreed that the institutions could be more efficient and productive if freed from excessive, paternalistic controls. It was agreed that the colleges had matured and evolved as comprehensive institutions to such an extent that they no longer needed such strong Board of Higher Education involvement in their internal affairs. Thus an "efficiency through de-centralization" argument was put forward and gained political support from Democrats as well as Republicans. The chancellor and the board assented to much of the autonomy bill as proposed by the presidents.

Governor Kean was a champion of educational improvement (he was one of several "education governors" from both political parties of the early and mid-1980s), and he saw autonomy as a key to the colleges' growth and success. He also instituted state incentive funding for higher education quality and improvement, making New Jersey one of the first states to provide such incentives. Kean made reform one of his three legislative priorities for 1985, highlighted it in his State of the State Address, and worked actively for its passage.

But in 1985, Democrats controlled both houses of the legislature and could not oppose the several union amendments that were proposed to the bills. Those amendments made the bills unacceptable to the governor and the colleges, and he vetoed two of the three reform bills. However, in the 1985 election, Governor Kean carried 70% of the vote and with it the General Assembly. Having the assembly in the Republican camp helped immensely in passing legislation in 1986. The popular press was generally supportive. The state college association of presidents and governing boards, created by the only bill that survived the governor's 1985 veto and newly operational in early 1986, also lobbied vigorously for passage. The presidents devoted considerable time to this and put much at risk in doing so. Also, in 1986, the chief sponsor of the bill in the Senate, a Democrat, stood up to the unions and opposed their amendments and led the fight for passage of the bills on the Senate floor. He was a higher education supporter and well respected by fellow Democrats. Leadership of the measures was thus bipartisan, supported by a Republican governor and a Democratic Senate leader (Novak, 1989, pp. 28–31).

Although the 1986 legislation significantly freed the state colleges from bureaucratic oversight and intrusion, they felt it had not been fully implemented under the succeeding 4 years of a Democratic governor. At the same time, a growing political fight was brewing between mainstay Democratic stalwarts (unions, Democratic legislators, civil rights activists, etc.) and newer, more free-market-oriented Republican leaders that would soon play itself out in higher education governance.

Christine Todd Whitman was elected governor in 1993. Governor Whitman campaigned on a promise to cut state income taxes by 30%, 15% during her first year of office. She proposed to reduce the size of state government and substitute local control and deregulation. Higher education was the first area of government for which she proposed deregulation. Her office began confidential negotiations with the state college association and some of its members. Governor Whitman then proposed in her March 1994 budget address to eliminate the Board and Department of Higher Education and to strengthen institutional governance and autonomy. Eventually, a legislative package was recommended based on the recommendations of a special governor's advisory panel on restructuring (Greer, 1998, p. 93).

Opposition was vigorous from the same groups that opposed the 1986 legislation. This time they voiced concern about unbridled institutional competition, the lack of state controls on college costs, the loss of state oversight to ensure access and diversity, and infringements on academic freedom. Private institutions also opposed the elimination of the Board of Higher Education, fearful that they would lose state protection from public sector competition. Some compromises were made along the way before the bill passed the Republican-controlled legislature. These compromises led to statewide and institutional accountability reporting, performance measures, and interim reports on implementation of the legislation.

The 1994 reforms can be attributed to a personal and political commitment by the governor, combined with her political commitment to deregulation. But it is also partly attributable to the opportune strategizing by state college presidents. They prepared a 10-page draft on specific steps that could be taken to grant greater policy autonomy to the state colleges, particularly to the governing boards of the state colleges—explaining it as a natural progression and continuity from the 1986 autonomy legislation. They gave it to the governor during her transition before she assumed office. She bought into their ideas. So their agenda and her agenda conformed, giving the governor an opportunity to achieve her first "reinventing government" initiative; it was deemed high profile and doable.

The decision to abolish the Board of Higher Education and the chancellor's office was entirely the governor's. Rather than wait and eventually appoint most of the members of the board and encourage them to choose a new chancellor to her liking, she chose to eliminate the agency instead. The governor had little reason to placate the unions and other Democratic allies that opposed her bill. She was willing to fight traditional Democratic coalitions and also willing to stand up to fellow Republicans who supported the Board of Higher Education (Greer, 1998, pp. 95–96).

The New Jersey case differs from Minnesota and Kentucky. The 1986 changes appeared to be a joint product of the higher education community's initiative and a sympathetic and effective governor's concurrence. The 1994 changes appear to us to have been more strongly political, but they also served the institutions' instrumental goals. Presidents managed the politics with opportunistic strategies. Instrumental goals of the institutions remained in focus and could be characterized as one of the main effects of reforms. But at the very least, New Jersey represents a case where both political and instrumental goals were achieved.

## Maryland

Maryland created the University System of Maryland in 1988, combining two existing university systems, the five-campus University of Maryland System, and the six-campus State Universities and Colleges. In 1998, the legislature and governor agreed to review the system 10 years after its creation and appointed a special task force to do so.

Higher education became a priority for Governor William Donald Schaefer when he took office in 1987. As he learned more, the governor felt that a single person or agency should be in charge of higher education (Berdahl & Schmidtlein, 1996, p. 165). Schaefer was characterized as very persuasive, punitive, somewhat impulsive, and persistent. He made clear that he wanted reorganization as a means of streamlining a complicated higher education bureaucracy, ensuring greater accountability, reducing duplication of effort, and enhancing efficiency and quality. It has long been reported that he wanted to have one person to speak to at the other end of the phone.

He initiated legislation, but alternatives soon surfaced from various quarters. Ultimately, a political split between the lieutenant governor and Schaefer (both Democrats) over the original bill allowed Senate leaders to craft a new compromise bill with the assent of the Senate majority leader. This bill called for a single board of regents yet significant campus autonomy including lay campus advisory boards, a coordinating agency with considerable powers (although less than the governor wanted), and designated flagship status for the University of Maryland at College Park. After a conference committee with the House, a bill emerged that created the 11-campus University of Maryland System (later renamed the University System of Maryland) and created a new coordinating agency, the Maryland Higher Education Commission, with authority to approve missions, develop an institutional accountability reporting process, administer state student aid, approve academic programs, and develop a state plan for higher education (Berdahl & Schmidtlein, 1996, pp. 172–175).

These two "500-pound gorillas," as noted by one prominent senator, were the result of political compromise (Berdahl & Schmidtlein, 1996, p. 181). The compromise, however, was rocky from the beginning. The two boards never worked smoothly together, and the considerable bureaucratic overlap led to friction and confusion among the institutions.

A melange of factors appeared responsible for passage of the 1988 reform. Governor Schaefer's interest and initiative was clearly the overriding factor. His desire to do something about higher education, coupled with a Democratic majority in both houses of the legislature, became too strong to resist. A second factor included support by legislators protective of the Maryland private colleges. The role of state coordination (which helped ensure the funding of the state funding formula for institutional aid) could have been significantly diminished if the private colleges had not argued for a new coordinating board, the Maryland Higher Education Commission, an agency to protect their interests.

Third, the Baltimore and suburban Washington legislative delegations played off of each other in every area of the budget and state politics, including higher education. The competition spilled over into defense of local institutions by legislators and was, in effect, a third force in the governance of higher education in Maryland.

Finally, public higher education's resistance was appeased by Schaefer with the promise of new money once a restructuring was completed, a promise that was kept.

A combination of events 10 years afterward led to a legislative resolution (with the assent of Governor Parris Glendening) to appoint a 23-member task force to study the "governance, coordination, and funding of the University System of Maryland" (House Joint Resolution 12, 1998). Members were jointly appointed by the Speaker, the Senate majority leader, and the governor.

The appointment of the task force came after the College Park president and members of his local advisory board were able to make a successful endrun around the University of Maryland System and attain a substantial multiyear budget commitment from the governor. The task force operated, sometimes openly, sometimes behind the scenes, as a constituent group for the various institutions and regions of the state. Five presidents were members, as were several key members of the legislature. This made it more difficult to recommend radical change. It concluded that the system, despite a shaky start, had found its bearings sufficiently to continue with some finetuning (Martini, 2000). It recognized that institutional successes were accumulating and so were system successes.

The task force recommended retaining the system with significant changes, including strengthened autonomy and authority for institutional presidents and the campus boards of visitors, including the freedom for institutional presidents to create new academic programs (for 3 years pending review) without system or coordinating agency approval; substantial changes in the system budget request and allocation process guaranteeing budget enhancements and per student spending floors; and creation of the system as a 501(c)(3) public corporation—allowing it greater freedom from state fiscal and bureaucratic control (*A Report of the Task Force*, 1999). These recommendations and others were put into legislation and passed in the spring of 1999.

Politics, more than instrumental factors, appears to have driven both the 1988 and 1998 reforms in Maryland. Advocacy for greater recognition of the flagship status of the University of Maryland at College Park was part of the reason for the changes, although in general the higher education community appeared to have no particular agenda beyond maintaining as much autonomy and funding for individual institutions as possible. Both were residual outcomes to the 1988 and 1998 restructurings. Political interests, on the other hand, were clear. A perceived need for tighter control and a reassertion of the state's interest in higher education—as well as a recognition of political territoriality—led to negotiated restructuring.

## Florida

From 1905 until 2001, Florida had a single board to govern its state colleges and universities. In 1965, the unified board was codified as the Board of Regents for the State University System of Florida. The board governed a system of 10 campuses. Community colleges were separately coordinated. Despite centralized governance structures, legislative intervention in higher education has been common since at least the 1950s (Trombley, 2001).

A constitutional amendment to create a new, governor-appointed state board of education and an appointed commissioner of education was passed by the legislature and then by the voters in November 1998. As a result, a blue ribbon commission was appointed and recommended legislation that passed the legislature, the Education Reorganization Act of 2000. In the act, all education governing boards for public schools, community colleges, and universities were merged into a seven-member Florida Board of Education. The state university campuses were each placed under a new gubernatorially appointed board of trustees with considerable authority.

Subsequent to its passage, the Education Governance Reorganization Transition Task Force was jointly appointed by Governor Bush and legislative leaders and charged with recommending additional legislation to implement provisions of the act. Chaired by a close friend of the governor, the task force made recommendations to implement the reorganization.

As the task force developed its legislative proposals, it recommended devolving responsibilities to new institutional boards, including authority to hire and fire presidents (with state board approval); approving new academic programs up to the master's degree; conducting collective bargaining individually; and setting their own tuition subject to legislative approval (*Recommendations to the Florida Legislature*, 2001). These provisions made it into law. Other provisions suggested by the college presidents, who initially and collectively urged retention of the Board of Regents but began to see advantages in a new decentralized structure, were left out of the act. These provisions included such things as exclusion of presidential searches from the freedom-of-information law. In the end, the legislature accelerated the transition to the new structure by a full year, hastening the demise of the regents.

Years of Democratic governors (Graham and Chiles) and a Democratic legislature resulted in a long-term majority of Democratic appointments to the old Board of Regents. A regime change to Republican majorities in the legislature and a Republican governor in 1998 represented a dramatic political sea change. Governor Bush appeared committed to shrinking state government. But residual issues provided hair-trigger incentives for change.

Unresolved controversies over many issues, such as location of new law and medical schools and presidential personnel issues, had set key legislators in opposition to positions taken by the board. Finally, the presidents abandoned the board as their collective support for the reorganization became clearer, because they felt it meant greater autonomy for them and their institutions. In the end, and for different reasons, the governor, the legislature, and the presidents had varied reasons to abolish the board—from ideological (on the part of the governor), to political (on the part of the legislature), to instrumental (on the part of the presidents).

Governance reform in Florida occurred in a highly charged political environment. Although autonomy and smaller, more efficient government appeared to be instrumental goals for some of the parties, the results of reform include a large bureaucracy but a small board with responsibility for K-20 education; probably even greater concentration of power in the legislature for campus budget allocation authority; and (although lessened with amendments in 2002) confusion over the roles, efficiency, and effectiveness of new institutional boards. It is clear that unresolved political issues between the old Board of Regents and key legislators played an overriding role in the change. The result was a perfect storm that swept the existing governance structure away (Trombley, 2001). Among our cases, Florida appears to be skewed the furthest along the continuum toward political motives for change.

## Conclusion

The cases presented here may be interpreted in a variety of ways. Obviously, each state has reached decisions about governance reform in unique ways, for unique reasons, with unique outcomes, even though in the majority of our cases, a discernable shift toward decentralization and a more reasoned balance of authority between central board control and institutional discretion is evidenced. This suggests how important politics can be in decisions about structuring higher education governance. In none of the cases did we find political factors to be merely residual. Instead, they were usually central to the story of reform (a finding that is consistent with those of other studies we reviewed earlier in the article). Instrumental goals of the higher education community were sometimes at least equally important (New Jersey is a good example) but were often secondary to those of political leaders.

The cases, however, are few, and the varied circumstances of each causes us concern about generalizing. The heuristic value of the cases, taken both individually and collectively, suggests ways of interpreting and understanding how states decide, especially how they allocate authority over significant state functions like higher education.

Each of these cases illustrates how governance remained a moving target for all of the parties involved. Both instrumental and political objectives shifted as contending economic and social forces, organizational tensions, political power balances, and personal agendas intersected and interacted. The context of specific events in each of the states provided a matrix in which higher education governance emerged and/or receded on the agenda.

Interactions between instrumental and political objectives does seem to us to constitute a useful framework for understanding governance reform. In all of our cases, some or all of the parties were motivated by interests in the efficiency and/or effectiveness of governance arrangements. At the same time, politics—the continued quest for power and control—entered decisions about how to govern higher education. Governors and legislative leaders (particularly governors in the majority of our cases) constantly play the levers available to them as they seek to achieve both control of governmental apparatus and their own policy objectives. Higher education is typically, give or take, 11% or 12% of a state's appropriations and a significant enough benefit to large numbers of voters to require continued attention. This requires assertion of enough control to ensure allocation of money and benefits in politically acceptable ways—the definition of which may vary with either the partisan majority or with the specific interests of individual political leaders.

We suggest that further study via the case method may help clarify both the interactive quality of instrumental and political factors and the circumstances under which governance reform emerges on states' agendas. Practically speaking, we also suggest that the higher education community needs to see how the fluidity of states' policies in this area may be used to advantage in achieving instrumental goals. Reform has to be approached strategically, with clear goals and rationales, with a period of consensus building, with persistence and opportunism, and with a deep understanding of the politics of reform at any given time under any given regime.

The merits alone will not carry the day unless politics are taken into account. But purely political decisions may serve the merits badly. So the interaction between the two is the ground where outcomes will be decided and where, in the final analysis, the public may be best served.

# References

Baumgartner, F. R., & Jones, B. D. (1993). *Agendas and instability in American politics.* Chicago: University of Chicago Press.

Berdahl, R. O. (1971). *Statewide coordination of higher education.* Washington, D.C.: American Council on Education.

Berdahl, R. O., & Schmidtlein, F. A. (1996). Restructuring and its aftermath: Maryland in restructuring higher education. In T. J. MacTaggart (Ed.), *Restructuring higher education: What works and what doesn't in reorganizing governing systems* (pp. 157–202). San Francisco: Jossey-Bass.

Birkland, T. A. (2001). *Introduction to the policy process: Theories, concepts, and models of public policy making.* Armonk, NY: M. E. Sharpe.

Cobb, R. W., & Elder, C. D. (1983). *Participation in American politics: The dynamics of agenda building* (2nd ed.). Baltimore: Johns Hopkins University Press.

Cohen, M. D., & March, J. G. (1974). *Leadership and ambiguity: The American college president*, New York: McGraw-Hill.

Firestone, W. (1989). Educational policy as an ecology of games. *Educational Researcher, 18*(7), 18–24.

Frost, S. H., Hear, J. C., & Marine, G. M. (1997). State policy and the public research university: A case study of manifest and latent tensions. *Journal of Higher Education, 68*, 363–397.

Graham, J. M. (2000). *Interaction effects: Their nature and some post hoc exploration strategies.* Paper presented at the annual meeting of the Southwest Educational Research Association, Dallas, TX. Retrieved from http://cricae.net/ft/tamu/interaction.pdf

Gray, V., & Lowery, D. (2000). Where do policy ideas come from? A study of Minnesota legislators and staffers. *Journal of Public Administration Research and Theory, 10*, 573–597.

Greenberg, G., Miller, J. A., Mohr, L. B., & Vladeck, B. C. (1977). Developing public policy theory: Perspectives from empirical research. *American Political Science Review, 71*, 1532–1544.

Greer, D. (1998). Defining the scope and limits of autonomy: New Jersey. In T. J. MacTaggart (Ed.), *Seeking excellence through independence*(pp. 84–106). San Francisco: Jossey-Bass.

House Joint Resolution 12. (1998). *Maryland charter for higher education governance, coordination, and funding of the university system of Maryland.* Retrieved from http://mlis.state.md.us/1998rs/billfile/hj0012.htm

Hovey, H. A. (1999). *State spending for higher education in the next decade: The battle to sustain current support.* San Jose, CA: National Center for Public Policy and Higher Education.

Hume, D. (1975.) *Enquiries concerning human understanding and concerning the principles of morals* (3rd ed.). Oxford: Clarendon.

Kingdon, J. W. (1987). *Agendas, alternatives, and public policies* (2nd ed.). New York: HarperCollins.

Kleining, G., & Witt, H. (2000). The qualitative heuristic approach: A methodology for discovery in psychology and the social sciences. *Forum: Qualitative Social Research.* Retrieved from http://www.qualitative-research.net/fqs-textc/1-00/1-00kleiningwitt-e.pdf

Lindblom, C. E. (1959). The science of "muddling through." *Public Administration Review, 19*(2), 79–88.

MacTaggart, T. J. (1996). The human side of restructuring. In T. J. MacTaggart (Ed.), *Restructuring higher education: What works and what doesn't in reorganizing governing systems* (pp. 132–156). San Francisco: Jossey-Bass.

Marcus, L. R. (1997). Restructuring state higher education governance patterns. *Review of Higher Education, 20*, 399–418.

Marshall, C., Mitchell, B., & Wirt, F. (1985). Influence, power and policy making. *Peabody Journal of Education, 62*(4), 61–89.

Martini, P. J. (2000). *The Larsen Commission and the development of university systems: Maryland's 21st century road map for higher education and governance.* Unpublished Ed.D. dissertation, George Washington University, Washington, D.C.

McLendon, M. K. (2000). *Setting the agenda for state decentralization of higher education: Analyzing the explanatory power of alternative agenda models.* Unpublished Ph.D. dissertation, University of Michigan, Ann Arbor.

McLendon, M. K. (in press). State governance reform of higher education: Patterns, trends, and theories of the public policy process. In J. Smart (Ed.), *Higher education: Handbook of theory and research* (Vol. 18). New York: Agathon.

Meyer, J. W., & Rowan, B. (1977). Institutionalized organizations: Formal structure as myth and ceremony. *American Journal of Sociology, 83,* 340–363.

Morgan, G. (1986). *Images of organization.* Newbury Park, CA: Sage.

Novak, R. (1989). *The New Jersey state colleges success in achieving operational autonomy: Accountability and the ability to govern fully.* Washington, D.C.: American Association of State Colleges and Universities.

Novak, R., & Leslie, D. W. (2000). A not so distant mirror: Great Depression writings on the governance and finance of public higher education. *History of Higher Education Annual, 20,* 59–78.

*Recommendations to the Florida Legislature.* (2001). Tallahassee, FL: Education Governance Reorganization Transition Task Force.

*A Report of the Task Force to Study the Governance, Coordination, and Funding of the University System of Maryland.* (1999). Annapolis, MD: Department of Legislative Services.

Sabatier, P., & Jenkins-Smith, H. C. (Eds.). (1993). *Policy change and learning: An advocacy coalition framework.* Boulder, CO: Westview.

Smith, R. M. (2002). Putting the substance back in political science. *Chronicle of Higher Education, 48*(30), B10–B11.

Trombley, W. (2001). Florida's new K-20 Model. *National Crosstalk, 9*(2), 1, 14–16.

Weick, K. E. (1976). Educational organizations as loosely coupled systems. *Administrative Science Quarterly, 21,* 4–19.

Yudof, M. (2002, January 11). Is the public research university dead? *Chronicle of Higher Education,* p. B24

Zumeta, W. (1996). Meeting the demand for higher education without breaking the bank: A framework for the design of state higher education policies for an era of increasing demand. *Journal of Higher Education, 67,* 367–425.

Zusman, A. (1986). Legislature and university conflict: The case of California. *Review of Higher Education, 9,* 397–418.

David W. Leslie is Chancellor Professor of Education at the College of William and Mary. His interests include state policy and public finance of higher education.

Richard J. Novak is executive director of the Center for Public Higher Education Trusteeship and Governance at the Association of Governing Boards. The center's mission is to strengthen relationships between public higher education leaders and state policy makers.

# Understanding the Relationship of Federal Policies and Community Colleges: A Proposed Analytical Policy Framework

CHERYL D. LOVELL

*University of Denver*

*The primary purpose of this study was to develop a policy framework that could be used to better understand the relationship to and influence of federal policies on community colleges. A thorough investigation and policy analysis was conducted to explore the relationships between the federal government and community colleges. Content analysis procedures were used to review federal legislation and related documents to identify the range of federal policies that affect community colleges. Interviews were conducted with community college leaders to determine the level of influence of these federal policies. Subsequently, a policy framework was developed that expands on previous research and provides a more comprehensive view of the federal influence on community colleges. The findings of this study are intended to assist those at the local level as they respond to the external pressures of the federal government. The results purport to be illustrative of the federal-community college relationship and are not intended to generalize to all community colleges.*

Community colleges are often considered "local" institutions; they have carried this label since their inception. While local in many aspects, the community college of today (and tomorrow) has more connections to the federal government than many realize. The level of federal influence is great for many community colleges and shows no signs of reversing anytime soon. As a result, community college leaders must understand the far-reaching arm of the federal government and understand the opportunities for "localizing" that influence.

Such "localizing" of influence can occur in a variety of ways. Federal funding can be utilized to increase the budget of the local college. For example, certain federal funds might help a community college provide more academic programs in a high need area such as engineering technology. As a result, the college experiencing budget declines can provide more academic opportunities for the students without increasing the tuition or fees. A community college might also "localize" the federal influence by hiring additional staff to provide specific support services for students with learning disabilities. The federal influence, consequently, can be an advantage for a campus if the community college administrators know about the federal opportunities and can use them to their advantage through leveraging the funds for programs, staff and faculty, or equipment that might not otherwise be available. A framework for assessing the impact of federal regulations may be a valuable tool for administrators who want to gain greater knowledge of the variety of federal policies and associated programs and the range of influence they can have on the local community college.

While the history of community colleges has been well documented (Brint & Karabel, 1989; Cohen & Brawer, 1989; Cohen, Brawer, & Associates, 1994; Goodchild & Wechsler, 1997; and Ratcliff, Schwarz, & Ebbers, 1994) little is known about the extent of the federal influence on local community colleges. Several thoughtful discussions about the general nature of federal influence on American postsecondary education have excluded specific attention to community colleges (Gladieux & King, 1998; Goodchild, Lovell, Hines, & Gill, 1997; and Lovell, 2000).

Gladieux and King (1998) present the best discussion to date on the range of federal activities related to higher education, even though their discussion does not fully account for the activities of the community college. The four major dimensions of their framework are federal tax laws, federal research support, federal student financial aid, and federal regulations. This framework provides a good introduction to understand the range of federal influence (Gladieux & King, 1998). Lovell (2000; 2001) provides a useful and comprehensive discussion of federal state policies and federal-community college policies. These discussions, however, are somewhat limited in terms of understanding the relationship to and influence on individual community colleges. An in-depth examination is needed to better understand the influence of the federal government on community college campus operations. How, for example, does federal support for research impact the community college? How do federal tax policies and laws relate to community colleges? To date, these questions have not been addressed in any comprehensive, practical, theoretical, or conceptual manner.

The purpose of this study was to better understand the relationship between community colleges and the federal government and how this relationship can influence, and in some cases, drive the activities and focus of the local community college. A policy framework was developed that expands on previous research by Gladieux and King (1998) and provides a potentially more comprehensive view of how to understand this federal influence on community colleges. The framework is intended to help campus administrators determine the level of response a particular federal policy might require since not all federal policies have the same level of local influence. Determining how much the policy will or might influence the local campus is critical if community college administrators are to anticipate what actions might be necessary to respond to the federal initiative.

Building on the Gladieux and King policy classification scheme I will discuss the methods used to develop the new framework and discuss the federal policies included in the analytical policy framework. This new analytical framework is intended to provide local administrators with a new way to classify and understand the potential level of federal influence on their institutions.

## Methods

Content analysis was used to identify the federal policies that affect community colleges. The investigation began with the classification of federal policies and enactments according to the four dimensions of federal support for research, federal tax laws, federal student financial aid, and federal regulations (Gladuiex & King, 1998). Modifications to the framework were made to expand the fourth dimension, federal regulations, to two categories: funded and unfunded mandates. Interviews were conducted with local and state level community college administrators to determine whether the federal policies had any influence on the local community college and if so, how much influence.

## Federal Policies

Major federal policies from Congress and the US Department of Education enacted during 1990–1998 were reviewed. A federal policy, by definition, was considered "major" when the American Association for Community College's (AACC) governmental relations office had issued a policy alert to its community college members. These policy alerts are a normal way of communicating important federal legislation to the members of AACC. Each time a significant legislative enactment is presented in Congress, AACC staff alert its members to the potential legislation and encourage the community college administrators to respond to their congressional representatives for support or rejection of the legislation. The AACC policy alerts are available to the public via their website at www.aacc.nche.edu and are updated daily. Other major federal policies were included that had been enacted prior to the online policy alerts and which were identified through the review of research literature on community colleges. Some of the federal policies included in this analysis are the Taxpayer Relief Act of 1998 (TRA), Pell Grants, the Workforce Investment Act (WIA), the Student Right to Know Act (SRK), the Integrated Postsecondary Education Data System (IPEDS), the Americans with Disabilities Act (ADA), and the Family Education Rights and Privacy Act (FERPA).

## Expanded Policy Framework

The expanded federal policy framework included five dimensions: federal research support, federal tax laws, federal student financial aid, federal funded mandates, and federal unfunded mandates. Merely classifying or categorizing federal policies has limited utility, so the next step then was to determine the "range of influence" the policies might have on community colleges. This range of influence scale in combination with the policy framework provided a multidimensional perspective in the influence of the federal policies on community colleges.

The proposed framework may be useful to local administrators early on in the policy formulation stage and throughout the policy making process until final implementation. An administrator may determine, based on the framework, that a proposed policy could have a high level of influence. As a result, federal representatives might be contacted to express views for or against the proposed legislation based on the expected level of influence on the local community college. Furthermore, if the legislation passed and was implemented, a community college administrator might decide not to participate in the federal program, assuming it is not mandatory, since it might require too much time and staff institutional resources with little or no return for the effort. Therefore, identifying and verifying the range of influence was an important and unique aspect to this study.

## Range of Influence Scale

The range of influence scale, as developed by the researcher, included a low, medium, or high influence on the instution in terms of its compliance with or response to the federal enactment.

**Low** influence was characterized as something for the community college administrators to know about and something to which they should pay attention, but the policy did not have operational influence on the campus. Some examples of a "low" level of influence included posting voter registration information as required by the voter Registration Act. The low level of influence required little on the part of the campus to comply with the federal requirement.

**Medium** influence was characterized as causing the community college to accommodate the federal exactment in some way, but not requiring a strategic change or operational change of the campus. Examples of a "medium" level of influence were changes in the federal workstudy program or receiving a National Science Foundation (NSF) grant. The influence was felt on the campus in a moderate way but did not require the institution to alter its fundamental focus or mission to comply with the new federal policy.

**High** influence was characterized as causing a commitment of significant campus resources or staff to comply with the federal policy or to receive the federal funding. A policy having a high level of federal influence might also have been responsible for a change in the strategic or operational goals of the campus. There are several examples of the "high" level of influence including many compliance requirements for the reporting of data through IPEDS, FERPA, or ADA. A major federal policy having a "high" influence on the community college might also have caused an institution to add an academic program that would make it eligible to receive the targeted federal funding. The addition of the academic area might also have caused the campus to change its strategic or operational goals.

Interviews were conducted to validate the utility of the new multidimensional policy framework, that is, to test the accuracy of the policy framework for classifying and categorizing the range of federal influence on community colleges. Those interviewed were asked to provide their perceptions of the level of influence of the legislation on their campus.

## Participants

Purposive sample techniques were utilized (Patton, 1980) and additional participants were identified to enlarge the base of information. Two community colleges in the west were selected: one located in a downtown urban setting, and the other in a suburban residential community. Individual community college administrators were selected based on their likely involvement and familiarity with federal policies (e.g., individuals who work with federal financial aid programs, individuals who administer federally funded grant programs in Title III, and a community college President). Emerging sampling design (Lincoln & Guba, 1985) allowed for the addition of other administrators as participants suggested. Furthermore, staff from the statewide community college system who coordinated and managed federal programs at the state level were also interviewed. A total of ten campus and/or statewide community college administrators comprised the sample for this study: eight (8) community college administrators, and two (2) statewide administrators. Since the purpose of this study was to be illustrative of the federal-community college relationship, purposive sample techniques provided the best means to identify key campus administrators who could share institutional perspectives on key federal policy initiatives.

## Limitations

More "testing" of the model should be conducted by other scholars to determine if it is indeed useful, comprehensive, and parsimonious. The small number of institutions included in the study should also be noted. The purpose of the study, however, was to illustrate this federal-community college relationship and not generalize beyond these institutions. Further, some of the federal policies are so recent that the influence might not yet be fully comprehended by the community college leaders. Interviews with administrators several years after policy enactment might prove useful to see if their initial views on the level of influence have changed. Finally, while the framework is proposed for community colleges, its use with all types of postsecondary institutions should be examined.

## Results and Discussion

The five dimensions of this new policy framework, shown in Figure 1, were found to be adequate to classify major federal policies. The range of influence scale was also found to be useful in reflecting the level of federal influence on community colleges. Each dimension of this new conceptual policy framework is further discussed.

## Federal Research Support

Figure 1 displays the recent legislation that has resulted in significant federal funding to support applied research activities in the community colleges. The National Science Foundation (NSF) has awarded 160 grants to community colleges to improve the quality of advanced technological education in science and engineering fields, basic math, and core science programs (AACC, 1999). These NSF grants are examples of new programs that have had a medium level effect on community colleges. Community college leaders interviewed for this study indicated they could participate or opt not to be involved. However, they said receipt of a grant might have required the institution to change or modify existing practices to comply with the grant stipulations or regulations. The community college administrators indicated that the research support could have a higher level of influence on their campus if more of their budget came from these research programs. At present, however, they considered the federal research to have a medium level of influence. Most of the administrators were both elated and concerned about these grants. The elation came from the infusion of new money into their campus budgets, but they thought the substantial increase in these federal revenues might cause the campus to lose local control of its academic programs.

## Federal Tax Laws

Tax laws and policies have had a very direct influence on all postsecondary institutions in a general way and have had very immediate and high effect on community colleges. The laws that have elicited the greatest concern among community colleges are those recently passed by Congress under the Taxpayer Relief Act (TRA). Two significant tax deductions were provided that would essentially allow the first two years of postsecondary education to be tax deductible. The HOPE Scholarship is a tax credit program that allows a student to deduct up to $1,500 over the first two years of college. This was hailed as a tremendous benefit to community colleges since the average cost of community college tuition on a national level is about $1,300. This is a clear example of a very high impact on community colleges. Community college leaders in this study viewed these new tax laws as important and of high priority and high influence on their campuses. Some administrators indicated that the Unrelated Business Income Tax (UBIT) laws were always important to be aware of, but all of the administrators shared that no tax laws are more important to the community colleges than the new personal income tax deductions provided for through TRA. It is essential to keep in mind that the TRA is directed to individual taxpayers and has no direct financial gain or loss to community colleges, or any other postsecondary institution, yet it provides individual taxpayers with significant federal income tax deductions that might be equal to the total tuition many community colleges charge. So, even though the new law is directed toward the individual, all administrators agreed this federal policy had a significant influence on their community colleges through potential increases in student enrollments.

## Federal Student Financial Aid

In this dimension the monies in almost all cases go directly to the student and not to the institution. While the influence seems indirect, the result of these federal appropriations very directly, and highly, concerns these community college administrators. The federal student financial aid programs cover three broad areas: grants, loans, and workstudy. The most beneficial to the student and the community college is grant funding. These funds do not have to be repaid, and the institution has no collection or default liability. Loans are available in two ways: subsidized and unsubsidized. With the subsidized loans the federal government defers the interest while the student is enrolled. Unsubsidized loans do not allow for the deferment of interest during enrollment. Other loans include the PLUS program where loans are obtained by and awarded to the parents of the student. Institutions are penalized for students who default, and if the community college is a direct lending institution, they have all the repayment and collection issues to manage.

Federal financial aid policies overall have a medium influence on community colleges, according to the administrators interviewed for this study, though some of the specific programs, such as grants, have a higher level of influence. These community college administrators indicated that they have to accommodate and modify campus policies in many ways to receive the federal funds, whether they come directly or indirectly to the institution. Remaining eligible for federal financial aid requires the institution to respond in a certain manner, and the community college administrators indicated they tended to pay close attention to these requirements since so many of their students receive federal financial aid. For example, many of the interviewed administrators stated that the Pell Grant Programs were of higher influence to the community colleges than the unsubsidized students loans since more of their students applied for grant funding than for loans. Some of the federal financial aid programs have a higher level of influence on the community colleges than some of the other federal aid programs. All administrators, however, were concerned that federal financial aid policies required tremendous commitment from the campus, and several indicated that they offer certain kinds of programs or alter their programs to make sure they comply with regulations for eligibility of federal aid.

## Funded Mandates

According to those interviewed, federal regulations are growing in the level of importance to their institutions. The increase in federal mandates required expanding this dimension to two categories: funded and unfunded mandates. The fourth dimension of the new framework, funded mandates, are those that have come with targeted funding to support the new laws. In reality, funding for these programs comes only if the community college decides to participate. Technically, then, participation is not mandated. Most administrators interviewed in this study, however, indicated a belief that such participation is often the only way for them to obtain additional funding for their campuses. Furthermore, many of these administrators shared that it is often not politically possible to reject the option to participate in these funded programs. Therefore, these programs come with such "weight" or pressure to participate they are perceived as required and thus mandated, according to those interviewed.

Many of the administrators indicated that federal funding and federal mandates change community colleges in very direct ways and can have a high level of influence on them. Some key examples of particular interest to these community college administrators included the Perkins Vocational Act III, Workforce Investment Act (WIA), and Fund for the Improvement of Postsecondary Education (FIPSE). The Perkins Act provides federal funding to enhance vocational-related programs. The program is specifically designed for pre-baccalaureate programs in community colleges and high schools where many of the occupational and vocational programs are offered. The administrators indicated that this program has a high influence on the community colleges that participate. Several of the administrators indicated that these federal programs resulted in new strategic efforts such as new academic programs or new administrative units in order to become eligible for the funding.

The WIA also has a high influence on community colleges in the form of funding to assist institutions to form partnerships with industry with a focus on workforce improvement. Again, this funding very directly and highly affects community colleges, according to the interviewed administrators. Funded mandates and regulations, by their very nature, would provide a high influence on community colleges. The administrators reported that money available through a competitive proposal process often causes changes for the community college. For example, one community college formed a new strategic partnership with businesses and high schools to receive the targeted funds available through a new federal policy.

Many of these federally funded programs also involve state policies and regulations. For example, many of the workforce programs are part of statewide programs that were created with the federal funds. Funding is awarded to the states that, in turn, set up statewide agencies and services to fulfill the federal requirements. This causes many community college administrators to deal with more state agencies and state policies for the federal money that "flows" through the states. This additional layer often requires more responses from the participating institutions and may contribute to a perception of a higher level of influence of the specific federal program. It may also contribute to the perception that the specific community college has to participate in the federal program since their state developed a statewide program.

## Unfunded Mandates

The fifth dimension of the new framework, unfunded mandates, has the greatest influence on the campus. Those interviewed indicated that many community colleges are not staffed at a level to provide adequate response to unfunded mandates, and this causes much consternation for the campus administrators. For example, more accountability regulations now exist, and community colleges are often struggling to collect, monitor, and report the necessary data. The recent Student Right to Know (SRK) legislation requires campuses to make graduation and crime data available to students, prospective students, employees, prospective employees, and parents. Community colleges often have limited staff to perform institutional research functions. As a result, these unfunded regulations burden these institutions.

The Americans with Disabilities Act (ADA) protects individuals who have need for accommodations that might be either (or both) physical or academic and requires accommodation. Community colleges have long been viewed as the "open door" to higher education. They might tend to have a higher proportion of students needing services under ADA. Legally, full compliance would require a great deal of financial support. This federal legislation, however, comes with no appropriations.

Like the ADA, the Occupational Safety and Health Administration (OSHA) regulations influence community colleges that offer vocational programs where use of chemicals and potentially hazardous situations are involved. Many technical and occupational programs offered by community colleges are subject to these regulations and have to comply with them, but without benefit of funds to make the accommodations.

In summary, overall, federal policies do influence community colleges in various ways. A majority of the federal policies included in this analysis were perceived to have a high level of influence on the community colleges. Most of the administrators interviewed indicated significant changes at the campus level were required to comply with the federal enactments. Campus infrastructures, in some cases, were altered to accommodate the federal policies relating to federal student financial aid. Equally influential were the federal mandates, especially the unfunded ones. Compliance with federal policies without the necessary financial support forced the community college administrators to add new staff positions specifically to deal with these unfunded mandates. Notably, of all five dimensions, unfunded mandates was perceived to have the highest level of influence. These unfunded mandates are also some of the more recent of the federal policies and are one area of public policy that previously has been excluded from research. Whether or not future mandates will come with funding remains unclear.

## Implications for Use of the Proposed Analytical Framework

This new policy framework is intended to provide a better understanding of how to characterize the federal-community college relationship. Local and state community college leaders should pay a great deal of attention to what happens on the national level. "Localizing" the federal influence should be at the top of the agenda for the local community college.

This framework might be helpful in localizing the federal influence in several ways. As noted earlier, a community college administrator might feel compelled to express his/her views of the potential impact of a federal policy if a high level of influence was expected. The campus might be able to provide specific examples of the potential impact of the federal policy that might alter the pending legislation. A campus might decide a policy is so important to their campus that they encourage their federal representatives to support the legislation. The framework can assist campus leaders to anticipate the necessary effort for compliance with the new federal legislation.

A campus may be able to plan resources around new federal funding to maximize the federal dollars. Some campus officials may want to alter their academic programs if substantial new resources are available. And some community colleges may need to hire additional staff to comply with a new federal initiative. The framework may help campus leaders look for new funding sources. The framework may enable community college leaders to take a proactive approach with the campus to maximize the federal role.

The policy framework also fills a gap in our conceptual understanding of the role of the federal government with community colleges. It gives us a new way to view directly the proximity of federal policies to institutions, in this case, community colleges. The model also provides the basis for future studies of federal policies and their relationship to and influence on postsecondary campuses. The level of influence of the federal policies was found to be high for many community colleges. The impact of federal policies should be monitored closely to see if the greater policy good was served by the specific congressional enactment. There may be other uses of the proposed framework beyond the intended scope of the present research. Hopefully this research will provide a foundation for others to explore and modify as necessary.

# References

Brint, S. & Karabel, J. (1989). *The diverted dream: Community colleges and the promise of educational opportunity in America, 1900–1985*. New York: Oxford University Press.

Cohen, A. & Brawer, F. (1989). *The American conmmunity college*. San Francisco: Jossey Bass.

Cohen, A., Brawer, F., & Associates. (1994). *Managing community colleges*. San Francisco: Jossey Bass.

Gladieux, L. & King, J. (1998). The federal government and higher education. In Altbach, P. Berdahl, R., & Gumport, P. (Eds.). *American higher education in the 21st century: Social, political, and economic challenges*. pps. 217–250. Boston, MA: Boston College Center for International Higher Education.

Goodchild, L., Lovell, C., Hines, Ed., & Gill, J. (1997). *Public policy and American higher education*. Needham Heights, MA: Simon & Schuster.

Goodchild, L., & Wechsler, H. (1997). *The history of higher education*. Needham Heights, MA: Simon & Schuster.

Lincoln, Y. & Guba, E. (1985). *Naturalistic inquiry*. Beverly Hills, CA: Sage Publications.

Lovell, C. D. (2000). Pressures and issues of postsecondary education: a stale perspective. In J. Losco & B. Fife (Eds.). *Higher education in transition. The challenges of the new millennium*. Westport, CT: Greenwood Press.

Lovell, C. D. (2001). Federal policies and community colleges: A mix of federal and local influences. In B. Townsend & S. Twombley (Eds). *Educational policy in the 21st century, Volume 2—Community colleges: Policy in future context*. Westport, CT: Ablex Publishing Corporation.

Patton, M. (1980). *Qualitative evaluation methods*. Beverly Hills, CA: Sage Publications.

Ratcliff, J., Schwarz, S. & Ebbers, L. (1994). *Comnmunily colleges*. Needham Heights, MA: Simon & Schuster.

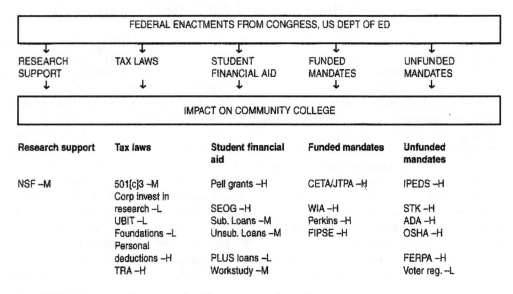

**L** = Low influence or compliance required from community college.
**M** = Medium influence or compliance required from community college.
**H** = High influence or compliance required from community college.

**Figure 1.  Proposed Policy Framework for Understanding the Relationship of Federal Policies on the Community College**

# Conducting Policy Analysis in Higher Education

## JUDITH I. GILL AND LAURA SAUNDERS*

Policy analysis is a real-world phenomenon and, as such, is subject to all of the ambiguity characteristic of real-world problems and issues. Policy analysis describes a type of applied research and analysis conducted for policymakers to assist them in the decision-making process. Policy analysis is broader than an analysis of a policy issue, or development of a policy statement. It can include an analysis of the impact of an existing policy, or an analysis of activities having a direct or indirect relationship to policy. For example, it can include an analysis of issues affecting enrollment policies, student rights issues, or issues influencing faculty hiring and promotion decisions.

Policy analysis in higher education requires an understanding of the issues, but, equally important, it requires an understanding of the higher education environment, including interrelationships of forces and structures within the environment. Any attempt to develop recommendations on faculty hiring, as Elms (this volume) explains, is meaningless without an understanding of the role of departments and colleges.

Policy analysis is not a discrete, self-contained activity. It is a process involving continuous review and evaluation of new information against existing information. It is a process that is sensitive to organizational culture and politics, and that continuously scans the environment looking for important interactions among people, resources, and organizations. It also requires a focused examination of factors affecting policy implementation. Policy analysis is a fascinating process, and because limited fiscal resources require tough decision making involving interdependent activities, it is critical to the development and maintenance of a quality system of higher education.

In this chapter, we lay out a road map for the policy analyst. However, the analyst's path is unlikely to be a straight line from beginning to end. Try to visualize a length of helix coil: The issues in the analysis are strung out along a spiral that cuts through a variety of environmental and structural issues, and many issues will be examined more than once in the course of the analysis. The road map for conducting policy analysis in higher education is diagrammed in Figure 1. The repetitive nature of policy analysis is highlighted by the interrelationships among the policy analysis stages, policy analysis tools and the outputs of analysis.

## Policy Analysis Tools

The policy analyst uses three basic tools: the iterative process, intuition and judgment, and the advice and opinions of others. The iterative process is a requirement because most decisions, especially those important enough to require policy analysis, will affect other policies and practices.

* *Note:* The authors would like to acknowledge the assistance of Dr. Ellen Wagner, professor of education, Northern Colorado University, for her assistance in developing Figure 1, Conducting Policy Analysis in Higher Education.

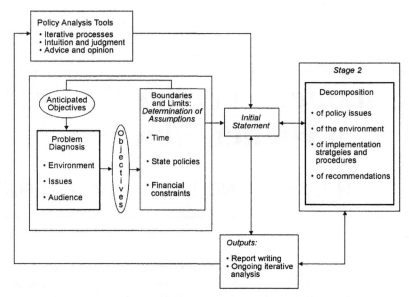

**Figure 1. Conducting Policy Analysis in Higher Education**

This spillover effect is widespread in higher education because colleges and universities have interdependent relationships with their environments; they do not exist as closed systems.

The iterative process of constant examination and reexamination may be frustrating and, to some, may appear redundant. However, if a combination of common sense and intuition are used to ensure that the objectives of the analysis are maintained and that the boundaries remain realistic, the iterative process ensures good analysis; and good analysis is analysis that can be used because it has been developed by continuous measurement against real-world factors.

While the rational higher education environment does not easily admit to the role of intuition in analysis, it is an important tool. Policy analysis requires an accurate reading of the politics of the organization and its people, and this is based as much on intuition as it is on rational and logical analysis of an issue. Intuition is honed by years of experience in the organization and an understanding of and sensitivity to the forces that affect change. Recommendations that are a logical outcome of good analysis, but deficient in the understanding of politics, will miss the mark. Mortimer (this volume) provides two excellent policy analysis examples that were analytically correct but politically wrong and thus significantly flawed.

Finally, the true test of policy analysis is in the real world, and the policy analyst is rare who has or who can gain, in isolation, a comprehensive understanding of all of the issues that should be considered. Therefore, field testing is an important analytical tool. There are several approaches that can be taken to field testing, but one of the more useful is to identify a panel of advisers and use these individuals to discuss the analysis as it proceeds.

Unlike an objective fact-finding panel, the policy analyst wants advisers who have vested interests or even biases in the policy area. Unbiased reactors do not provide crucial information on acceptability and implementation in the real world. This field-testing group should have a commitment to the issue and some area of expertise that expands the analyst's understanding.

Advisers are an invaluable source of information. They can save the analyst substantial time in researching the issues. They serve as reactors to the analytical work throughout its course. The sense of the experienced institutional observer or politician as to what will or will not work in a particular setting can save the analyst from embarrassing misstatements.

Field testing is conducted when there is new information to be examined, when there are significant changes in the environment, and when models and recommendations are being discussed. Field testing eliminates some of the surprises that frequently accompany the announcement of recommendations, surprises that may impede or kill the adoption of recommendations.

There are risks to field testing. Because the advisers have vested interests, they may lobby the analyst into a position that clouds objectivity. However, the benefits of an advisory panel outweigh the costs because the failure to consult with others limits the opportunity for comprehensive understanding of the issues.

## How to Do Policy Analysis

Writing about "how to do policy analysis" is difficult because the process is not linear; each step does not follow from the previous one. The following description of "how to do" is grouped by general features, but the order may vary in any given analysis.

There are two major stages of analysis. The first is a mini-analysis of the problem to be investigated. It requires an identification of the study's objectives, environment, and limitations. It concludes with the development of an initial statement of analysis. This statement is the foundation for the second stage of analysis where many interdependent components of the issue are investigated and recommendations tied to the objectives of the analysis are constructed.

**Stage 1: Diagnosing the Problem.** The policy analyst's work begins with a preliminary sketch or initial statement of the issues and factors to be included in the analysis. The statement may best be understood by thinking of it as the strategy for analysis. It should be written, because the writing process is an analytical tool. If possible, it also should be reviewed and approved by the person making the assignment; this usually is the policymaker who will use the analysis. Jordan (this volume) provides a good example of an initial statement of analysis that guided the enrollment planning analysis used by the Arizona University System.

Because university life and activities within its environment do not stop while analysis is conducted, the initial statement may require modification as work progresses. For example, Olswang (this volume) explains how the University of Washington's initial strategy for investigating a sexual harassment complaint was changed because of a newspaper advertisement.

Most analysts expect continuous modification of their analysis strategies. Unlike a controlled laboratory experiment with a predetermined protocol, policy analysis is analogous to investigatory laboratory work. The analyst starts with a general idea of what to expect and how to proceed but is open to new ideas that are formulated as data are collected and analyzed.

The policy analyst who is inflexible and unwilling to make changes to the initial strategy may end up with recommendations that are not useful because they are not applicable to an environment that changed while the analysis was being conducted. If the recommendations do not reflect new information as well as the changed environment, they may not be adopted. As in legal cases, the analysis may become moot.

*Defining the Objectives.* There are two kinds of objectives that must be understood and accounted for in the analysis: the assigned objective of the study and the objective of the policymaker. There may be several objectives within each category, and there may be conflicts among the objectives.

The analyst begins by clarifying the study's objectives. Answers to very basic questions are needed: Why should the analysis be conducted? And what are the intended outcomes of this analysis? The objectives are the reasons for conducting the analysis. They can include policy clarification, evaluation of the impact of policy, or identification and analysis of practices that have an impact on policy. The intended outcome of the analysis may be a recommendation for policy revision, adoption of new campus practices and procedures, or development of a model to predict certain outcomes based on given policies or environmental conditions.

In 1990, the Western Interstate Commission for Higher Education (WICHE) began an analysis of the relationship between higher education and the economy, the objective of which was to help state policymakers understand this relationship so that higher education's role in improving the state's economy would be considered during the budget development process. The intended outcomes of the study were policy recommendations promoting a strengthening of this relationship (Western Interstate Commission for Higher Education, 1992).

Higher education policy analysis is most frequently conducted to assist in the decision-making process of policymakers such as a university administrator, a governing board member, or a legislator. Therefore, the policymaker's objectives must be understood. However, the assigned objective of the analysis may not always be the policymaker's objective. For example, the objective of the analysis may be to demonstrate institutional accountability to a state higher education coordinating board, and the desired outcome may be no change in current campus practices and policies. The analyst needs to understand these circumstances and prepare accordingly. The naive analyst may arrive at loggerheads with institutional leaders if the objective is not understood and taken into account in the preparation of the analysis. Unless the real objective is understood, many hours of analytical effort may be spent in areas that do not meet the policymaker's objectives.

In the problem diagnosis stage, possible conflicts among objectives may also be identified. The objectives may inherently conflict with the interests of important constituencies as well as produce tension between the analyst and the policymaker. These conflicts in objectives need to be identified early in the analytical process so that they can be resolved or so that factors related to areas of conflict can be addressed as part of the analysis.

A final word about defining the objectives of analysis: The analyst must not expect the objectives to remain static and unchanging. The objectives of analysis, as well as the intended outcomes, may change over the course of the investigation as more information is learned, better data are gathered and examined, and a more complete understanding of the underlying factors is gained. Stubborn adherence to the original definition of the objectives may limit the analysis unduly and preclude a full examination of the issues.

*Understanding the Environment.* Policy analysis requires a comprehensive understanding of the environment and culture affected by the policy being examined. This includes an understanding of the organization's values, important current and historical issues, and the organizational structures and decision-making processes.

The environment makes higher education policy analysis different from public policy analysis focusing on federal, state, and local government issues. The higher education environment is dominated by a culture that includes faculty governance, autonomy, and academic freedom; the values of teaching, research, and public service; and, at public colleges and universities, accountability issues.

A basic list of environmental factors includes key individuals who are currently identified with the issue or who may become involved (for example, institutional administrators, staff, faculty, students, governing board members, community leaders, and elected officials) and the responsibilities and influence of these individuals in the operation and decision-making structure of the organization. An understanding of past organizational struggles of a similar nature may help in identifying these individuals.

Identification of important factors provides clues to the location of studies that may prove beneficial to the analysis. Institutional histories and discussions with other analysts who have studied similar issues may provide meaningful insights.

The higher education policy analysis environment includes everything and everyone that has an interdependent relationship with issues being analyzed. But time and resources limit the number of factors that can be included in the analysis. Therefore, the analyst has to identify those factors having the greatest influence on the issue.

The analyst understands that just as the objectives may change over the course of the study, so too does the environment. To adapt a term from computer science, policy analysis is conducted in "real" time, and the world of the institutional executive or state official does not stop while the analyst works. It is imperative that the analyst keep abreast of changes in the environment while work is in progress so that when the analysis is completed, the result fits the real world. For example, recommendations for tuition increases based on an analysis of the relationship between tuition and access policies that did not consider recent action to reduce student loan program funds would be unrealistic.

*Boundaries and Limits.* Identification of the assumptions that guide analysis is an important component in the diagnosis of the problem. Assumptions provide boundaries for analysis and are factors accepted as truth. Four primary assumptions guided WICHE's analysis of the relationship of higher education to the economy: (1) Higher education's role in the economy is far more comprehensive than is its contribution to economic development. Through teaching, research, and public service, higher education's role involves a wide range of activities from improving the quality of life to promoting economic growth. (2) State policies can serve to strengthen the relationship between higher education and the economy. (3) Financial constraints, in large part, will determine the feasibility of implementing policy recommendations. (4) Because of financial constraints, new models of cooperation and better differentiation among colleges and universities may be needed if higher education is to contribute more effectively to society and to the economy.

Boundaries also are provided by the seriousness of the issue, the environment, and the social forces at play. Policy analysis in a crisis is somewhat different, at least in degree, from policy analysis undertaken in a calm and dispassionate environment. For example, for many colleges and universities, the analysis of divestiture of institutional holdings in South African stocks needed to be done quickly, had significant implications for the institution's credibility with students and other constituent groups, and carried significant financial consequences. The urgency of the issue gave a far different feeling to the policy analysis than would have a long-range financial plan of desired investment yields.

The methodology used in analysis also provides a significant boundary, and it should be identified in the initial statement. It should include not only a brief description of the quantitative and qualitative approaches to be used but also an identification of who and/or what will be consulted for data, opinions, institutional history, and comparative information.

In the course of analysis, the boundaries of an issue almost always expand: therefore, it is important that the initial diagnosis be focused, and that the impact of time and resource limitations on the analysis be identified. Boundaries frequently are determined by the amount of time that can be devoted to the analysis. Deadlines are boundaries that have a particularly formative effect on policy analysis. Frequently, policy analysis work is time-dependent. Rough and timely, rather than exhaustively complete, are the watchwords of the policy analyst.

*Initial Statement.* The initial statement is the diagnosis of the issue. It identifies the objectives of the analysis, including intended outcomes, important environment factors, and the initial boundaries for analysis that will guide data collection and other research activities. The initial statement also defines the strategy for analysis. It may include the language of the initial request for analysis. It is, however, a far more comprehensive statement. It is the guidepost used throughout the process to judge whether the developing analysis is meeting its objectives.

The write-up of the initial statement provides the opportunity to identify clearly the problems, ambiguities, conflicts, scope, and resource costs. A written statement can serve as the document of agreement between the analyst and the person who made the assignment. Discussion of the written statement can highlight disagreements about or misunderstandings of terms and language.

Terms must be defined and agreed on. Assumed definitions, like assumed values, can be mine fields for the unwary analyst. "I didn't know that was what you meant by retention!" can be the death knell for a substantial piece of work. Language is the tool of the policy analyst, and nowhere is its care and precision more needed than in the initial statement.

**Stage 2: Unraveling the Policy Analysis Knot.** The initial statement is the analyst's framework for conducting policy analysis, and the analyst will continually refer back to this statement when examining new information.

*Four Basic Components.* The primary components of policy analysis are the policy issue, the environment, the factors affecting policy implementation, and the proposed alternatives or recommendations. The attention given to each component depends on its relative emphasis in the initial statement of analysis, as well as its importance in the analyst's growing understanding of the issue. If the initiative for policy analysis is a recommendation for developing assessment outcomes, the focus will be on understanding assessment issues. If the initiative is politically motivated, considerable attention will be focused on the environment promoting political concerns. If faculty behavior is being studied, the analysis may emphasize factors affecting the implementation of faculty policies. If the legislature is demanding change, the focus will be on the development of recommendations for new policies.

Of the four components, an understanding of the policy issue is typically the most straight forward. Information may come from available data sources, literature reviews, and surveys that the analyst designs and conducts. An understanding of the environment, identification of factors affecting policy implementation, and development of recommendations or models are more cumbersome. These components require comprehensive knowledge of the organizational structure its decision-making mode, its information networks, its culture and history, and its people and resources. As well as the individual elements, the analyst also must consider the interrelationships among these factors.

Complex interrelationships are involved in most policy analysts work. The following examples of policy questions illustrate this complexity. First, how will state revenue declines affect the recommendation for a small business development center at a land grant university? Long-range and short-term state and university needs must be examined. Although the center may contribute to state economic development, revenue declines may mean that it only can be funded at the expense of some other project. The federal government will support some of the program costs, thus bringing new dollars into the state, but these dollars will be lost if the state cannot provide its share of needed dollars. Extension programs are an important component of the land grant university's role and mission, and in the twenty-first century the definition of extension should include small business development centers.

Second, how do faculty tenure and promotion policies affect the board of trustees requirement that the college give more attention to teaching? Most tenure and promotion decisions are made by faculty committees in the discipline, and research, not teaching, is the valued activity. Standard criteria exist for evaluating outstanding research. What are the criteria for evaluating outstanding teaching?.The outstanding teacher is not the highly sought out faculty member, the outstanding researcher is. External funding is available for research activities, not teaching.

Third, how do accreditation requirements affect the development of telecommunications programs in the health sciences? The health sciences have very strong professional standards and accreditation associations. Many courses offered via telecommunications cannot be evaluated by the same standards as applied to traditionally offered courses. Most professional accreditation associations are dominated by faculty members. The number of faculty members who endorse the offering of telecommunications courses is limited, as is the number who have actually used telecommunications.

A policy analyst's greatest asset is his or her understanding of the higher education environment, and of the many different avenues that need to be explored to determine the potential impact of decisions on institutional policies and practices. However, most policy analysts are generalists, and they should not be expected to understand all of the details of complex problems. Their role is to know where to begin, how to develop the analysis, and how to wrap it up. A detailed understanding of issues can come from other resources and people.

*Policy Issue.* The process of gaining an understanding of the policy issue is frequently identified in the literature as policy research. Information on policy issues may come from literature reviews, a network of colleagues, campus surveys and data bases, and campus faculty. A literature review frequently provides useful initial insights and may identify methodological frameworks that can be used to array important factors. Examination of existing reviews of the literature (such as those produced in the ASHE-ERIC series), or recent topical articles such as those found in the New Directions for Institutional Research series, can help to identify critical factors. Colleagues can provide information on the development and implementation of similar issues on other campuses. And reviews of available data bases can provide clues to what information is known and what additional information may need to be collected.

Analytical tools are used throughout the investigation to gain a better understanding of the issue. The policy analyst should have a fairly broad acquaintance with the social science research literature since frameworks from a variety of disciplines can be helpful in identifying relevant factors. For example, economic factors are important in understanding issues related to student enrollment trends, while knowledge of small group behavior and organizations may be more helpful in looking at alternative organizational forms for faculty governance.

The seasoned analyst also knows that many higher education issues are recycled issues; not only do they reflect trends in the larger society that are cyclical in nature, but they reflect institutional dynamics of birth, growth and maturity, and decline. Issues related to economic factors are among the most common. The recessions of the mid-1970s and early 1990s brought to institutional attention many of the same issues: balancing of demand and resource constraints, quality and access, and faculty productivity. The fact that so many higher education issues are recycled highlights the importance of understanding their histories of analysis and policy implementation. Incorporation of the results of earlier studies ensures continuity and provides a more comprehensive overview of an issue.

*Environment.* In stage 1, diagnosing the problem, the analyst identifies the broad array of environmental factors important to the analysis. These factors include people and organizations; policies, practices, and laws; and histories, values, and trends. In stage 2, the interdependency of these factors is fully examined, and as greater understanding of these factors develops, the list may grow.

In assessing the policy environment, the policy analyst assumes the role of institutional politician and gives attention to significant groups within the college or university, as well as to groups external to the institution. Different groups have different interests in policy. Some policies may be of interest to a large number of groups, and others may affect only a small number of people. Understanding the formal and informal authority and prestige structure within an institution is important to understanding the connections among factors.

The analyst must understand the factors that will constrain the implementation of policies and practices and therefore limit the kinds of decisions that can be made. Constraints may be legal: state statutes, administrative procedures, or riders to appropriations acts. Or they may be matters of political and social custom. In the latter case, constraints are sometimes qualified: they may be more or less of a constraint depending on other factors. For example, funding for faculty merit increases may depend on the amount of dollars that are left in the salary pool after allocating cost-of-living increases for all faculty. Political constraints can be internal to the institutions and related to people or culture (for example, involvement of the faculty senate president at meetings of the board of trustees), or external and related to the roles or personalities of governing boards members, state legislators, other college or university administrators, or the general public (for example, unofficial presentation of the university budget request to the higher education coordinating board before it is formally submitted to the governor).

An understanding of the environment is the key to good analysis, and because higher education is a unique organization, the analyst must have a comprehensive understanding of the traditions, values, purposes, and operations of colleges and universities. One of the unique components of higher education as an organization is that although colleges and universities are formally organized along hierarchical lines, there are significant players who do not fit in a neat linear organizational chart and have no formal role in the decision-making process. If recommendations are developed without taking account of significant groups (such as members of the faculty or the student senate), they will have little or no chance of being successfully implemented. It makes no difference that some of these groups do not show up as a box on an organizational chart.

The environmental factors provide clues to the level and type of data and analysis that are needed and appropriate. Recently, several reports were released proclaiming a significant faculty shortage in the late 1990s. Many of these studies based their conclusions on nationally aggregated data. While these reports provided important information, their conclusions were not appropriate to individual colleges and universities. Higher education policy analysts know that institutional decisions related to future faculty supply and demand require institutional data on faculty retirement rates, faculty separation rates and reasons for faculty attrition, student enrollment trends and projections by college, national trends in the number of Ph.D. recipients, and national and local nonacademic employment markets for Ph.D. recipients. Some of these data are hard to collect, for example, national employment markets for Ph.D. recipients, and some of these data may be sensitive, for example, reasons for faculty attrition. Higher education policy analysts also know that if the state coordinating board and/or legislature wants a general idea of the state's faculty supply and demand picture, the required data collection activities will depend on the use of common definitions by colleges and universities. Development of common definitions will be institutionally sensitive.

*Implementation and Recommendations.* Intended outcomes of analysis are usually recommendations for policy changes, new policies, new practices and procedures, or models that provide a better understanding of the consequences of policy actions. While policy analysis usually does not include implementation activities, a comprehensive analysis needs to consider the factors affecting the implementation of the recommendations.

Intuition, field testing, and the iterative process of analysis provide significant clues to the likelihood of recommendations being implemented. From these policy analysis tools comes the ability to develop realistic recommendations. However, if time permits, the best approach to developing realistic recommendations is to discuss preliminary recommendations with individuals who will have a role in the implementation of "the real thing." The practice of trying out an idea on experienced players can eliminate the initially attractive but infeasible proposal. Presidents and chancellors may have a limited number of issues that they will champion at any one time. Effective presidents develop a strategic sense of what will and will not work on any policy issue.

In developing recommendations for the WICHE project on higher education and the economy, staff analysts discussed with state and higher education policymakers implementation issues relating to draft recommendations calling for greater campus accountability in the use of state funds. While state leaders supported the recommendations, campus leaders indicated frustration with the continual call for accountability in the wise use of state funds which are insufficient for meeting the state's demands. These conversations led to revisions in the recommendations.

The recommendations finally presented to the WICHE commissioners called for the adoption of a state strategic agenda for higher education that identifies both the funding needed for meeting state priority needs and the campus that will meet each need. Campuses are to be held accountable for meeting the specific needs that have been identified and funded. The revised recommendations were adopted.

Initial recommendations or models should be refined and revised after reviewing implementation possibilities. For each recommendation, the analyst must ask, Can it work? Is it likely? Is it reasonable? The goal is to develop the "win-win" recommendation. But policy changes often engender conflict. Given a relatively short time frame and a constrained and politicized environment, the win-win outcome may simply not be possible. In these cases, the analyst should consider discussing the results and recommendations of the analysis with groups that will be negatively affected by the proposed policy, prior to submitting the analysis. Except in political campaigns, the doctrine of no-surprises is almost always a good strategy to adopt and may enable, through minor revisions, the development of "win-almost win" outcomes.

The development of recommendations is shaped by everything that has gone before. The checklist for the final draft of recommendations should include answers to the following questions: Are the objectives addressed? Can they be implemented? Have constraints been addressed?

While policy analysis depends on and draws from research studies, the standards for developing alternatives and recommendations come more from the political arena than the methodological and quantitative arena. However, this does not preclude development of creative recommendations.

Recommendations and models that have been tried in other institutional settings should be included in the final report. Well-publicized solutions adopted at prominent institutions provide reference points for the decision maker and the analyst.

## Written Report

The development of recommendations is not the final stage of analysis. The writing process involves considerable analysis in itself. Because writing is an analytical tool, the analyst should not avoid writing until all of the variables are accounted for and the recommendations developed.

The analyst presents the work in a final written report. In addition to brief reviews of the literature and environmental and other factors influencing the study, the main body of the written report focuses on the recommendations and the implementation issues, including, as mentioned above, examples from other states or colleges and universities. A rationale is needed for each recommendation, but the methodology used in the analysis should be very brief or included in an appendix. As a rule, a policy analyst cannot expect the policymaker to read a detailed report. Therefore, the most salient issues must be presented concisely. The analyst must also remember the audiences for the report and provide information in a format and language appropriate to them.

## Reference

Western Interstate Commission for Higher Education (WICHE). *Meeting Economic and Social Challenges: A Strategic Agenda for Higher Education (Policy Recommendations)*. Boulder, Colo.: WICHE, 1992.

# PART II

## *Current Issues in Public Policy and Higher Education*

# Current Issues in Public Policy and Higher Education

## DIANE R. DEAN

Part II introduces the reader to selected current issues in postsecondary policy. While a few are new, most are familiar perennial issues. What changes, though, is how the problem is defined, the new elements of understanding brought to it, the policy options that are available, and the level of importance assigned to it in a world of competing agendas. For example, the issue of access has been addressed through the Morrill Land-Grant Acts of 1862 and 1890, the Serviceman's Readjustment Act of 1944, and the Higher Education Act of 1965 and its subsequent reauthorizations (1968, 1972, 1976, 1980, 1986, 1992, 1998, and 2008). In each, the problem definition differed: from promoting the liberal and practical education of the industrial classes (1862 and 1890) to providing college and vocational education to returning soldiers and diverting economic depression (1944) to addressing racial injustice and eliminating poverty by providing college access to low income and minority citizens (1965) and to expanding college affordability for the middle classes (1976, 1980, 1986, 1992, and 1998). In each, the policy options also changed: from funding institutions, in the case of the Morrill Acts, to funding individuals in the case of the Serviceman's Readjustment and Higher Education Acts, and finally to loaning individuals money to fund themselves, in the case of subsequent reauthorizations of the Higher Education Act.

Also changing are the actors or agents who claim authority for establishing the policy agenda for postsecondary education, those who lead the dialogue on policy issues and solutions, identify and direct public and government attention and resources to that agenda, and those who are held accountable for meeting policy goals. Federal and state legislators and agencies, nonprofit philanthropic foundations, think-tanks, lobbyists, and the media all lay claim to parts of the postsecondary education policy agenda, along with colleges, universities, and the associations and accrediting bodies that represent them. At times, authority and accountability blur. Such is the case with college affordability. Over the past several decades, the authority, accountability, and responsibility for assuring college affordability has slipped like quicksilver among individual institutions, the states, and the federal government. Recent federal legislation, however, positions the federal government as the authority for college affordability policy goals, with the federal government, state governments, and individual institutions as holding shared accountability and responsibility for making college affordability a reality. Through the College Cost Reduction and Access Act of 2007 and the Higher Education Opportunity Act of 2008, the federal government set out extensive college-cost reporting requirements, state appropriations regulations, and education-lending regulations, while ramping up its own contributions to student loans, need-based aid, and programs and institutions that support underserved student populations. Section II of this Reader not only introduces readers to this and other selected current issues in postsecondary education policy, but it also conveys the variety of participants in the current public policy arena and the variety of perspectives, problem definitions, and policy options they each propose.

This section was compiled using the same methodology developed for the first edition of the Reader. The editors selected more than a dozen higher education associations and organizations, purposefully seeking diversity in terms of perspectives represented, including those of colleges and universities, governing boards, scholars, policymakers, legislators, and the media. This included entities such as the American Association of State Colleges and Universities, the American Council on Education, the Association of Governing Boards, *The Chronicle of Higher Education*, the Council on Independent Colleges, the State Higher Education Executive Officers, the National Conference of State Legislators, and our own Association for the Study of Higher Education. Next, the editors sought records of what each entity had considered to be the most salient higher education policy issues since the first edition of this Reader 10 years ago. To do this, they sampled 10 years' of document data from each entity, spanning 1998 to 2008, including items such as periodicals, annual reports, conference and professional development programs, and special reports. The editors identified and catalogued what each entity presented as the important policy issues, based on each issue's frequency of appearance across entities. Finally, they distilled this collection into a single list of salient postsecondary education policy issues spanning the years 1998–2008, which were organized into four broad areas derived logically and sequentially: getting into college (College Access), paying for college (Postsecondary Finance), what happens in college (Outcomes & Assessment), and improving the preparation of those who will educate future generations (Teacher Education).

## Synopsis of Readings in Section II

The base collection of articles initially considered for inclusion in Section II numbered more than 150. These were selected and then winnowed through a process identical to that used for Section I. The resulting 27 articles cover a diverse selection of materials from policy briefs to peer-reviewed journal articles in addition to an array of foci, including federal, state, local, and institutional. They exemplify the current discourse in postsecondary education policy debates, and present a solid representation of several diverse definitions of changing understanding of and proposed solutions to the challenges facing American higher education today. What follows is a synopsis of the readings.

### College Access

#### College readiness

Callan and colleagues, in *Claiming Common Ground: State Policymaking for Improving College Readiness and Success* (2006), discuss the need to improve our nation's performance in preparing and graduating high school students that are either workforce or college ready. Achieving this goal relies upon P–16 coordination. Although the movement of young people between high school and college should be the common ground of both educational systems, it has become a "no man's land." Callan and colleagues offer four recommendations for state policy to reclaim that common ground. The primary action items involve aligning curricula and assessment, and implementing statewide data systems to track students throughout their P–16 education. Yet bringing about the necessary coordination will not be an easy task, as the authors point out, because U.S. elementary, secondary, and postsecondary education are a collection of systems that originated independently and have very different structures, goals, and cultures. Supporting action items to improve this endeavor involve providing fiscal incentives and requiring public-outcomes reporting to encourage collaboration and accountability.

Oliva, in *Reluctant partners, problem definition and legislative intent: K–16 policy for Latino college success* (2004), describes how the disconnect between K–12 and postsecondary education inhibits Latinos transitions between the two. Based on qualitative research, she illustrates the development of K–16 policies within the state of Texas. Her work provides a concrete example of practice to complement the broader conceptual work put forth in the preceding article.

#### Enrollment and Transfer

Unfortunately, evolving P–16 policies such as those Oliva and Callan et al. describe are few. What, then, have states done to increase college enrollment? Perna and colleagues, in *A typology of federal and state programs designed to promote college enrollment* (2008), ask this question. They categorize and analyze 103 federal and state programs designed to promote college enrollment in five states. The results yield a typology of government-sponsored access programs that reveal a daunting lack of coherent, systematic, and intentional policy development. The majority of programs (90%) the team studied addressed only the barrier of financial need and did not address other barriers critical to postsecondary access, such as academic preparation or providing college information. Furthermore, most programs sidestepped both the schools and the universities and were implemented directly from the government to the student. The authors' work demonstrates a clear need for a review and overhaul of government-sponsored enrollment programs to eliminate gaps and overlaps.

The movement of students into their first year of college forms only one part of the enrollment picture. Equally important is the movement of students between two-year and four-year colleges and universities. When two-year college students subsequently enroll in four-year institutions to continue their education (vertical transfer), they face nearly all of the same considerations that they did when they entered their first year, with the added concern of whether or not their two-year college course work will transfer and count towards a baccalaureate degree. In the 1990s, two-year and four-year colleges began addressing that concern by creating formal agreements to specify which courses would be accepted for transfer and how they would count towards degrees. Anderson, Sun, and Alfonso, in *Effectiveness of statewide articulation agreements on the probability of transfer: A preliminary policy analysis* (2006), review the history of such articulation transfer relationships and related policies. Using data from the "Beginning Postsecondary Student Longitudinal Study of 1989-1994," the authors examine whether the existence of articulation agreements increased the probability of student transfers from two-year to four-year institutions. Their findings show that the presence of such policies alone is not associated with increased transfer rates. Rather, the predictors of vertical transfer mirror those that predict first-year enrollment and college persistence: parents' education, reliance on parents' income, receipt of financial aid, and full-time enrollment.

### Mission Differentiation and Stratification

Is it enough to simply get into college? Or does it also matter where one enrolls? Bastedo and Gumport, in *Access to what? Mission differentiation and academic stratification in U.S. public higher education* (2003), explore the tensions between access, mission differentiation, and stratification of students across institutions by their race and socioeconomic background. Through comparative case studies of public higher education in Massachusetts and New York, they bring the reader's attention to three recent policy initiatives: program productivity policies that are designed to eliminate duplicate programs that have low graduation rates; initiatives to shift remedial education functions from the four-year colleges to the community colleges; and initiatives to create a public honors college in each state, or build a strong system-wide honors program. Bastedo and Gumport find that the initiatives increase selectivity within state systems and campus systems, and subsequently contribute to increased stratification of programs and student enrollment. The authors challenge policy analysts to include the stratification of student opportunity in their consideration and analyses of college access.

The authors of the next article undertake that challenge. In *Minority enrollment demand for higher education at historically black colleges and universities from 1976 to 1998: An empirical analysis* (2005), economists Sissoko and Shiau uncover the determinants of black student enrollment at historically black colleges and universities (HBCUs) versus predominately white institutions (PWIs), finding that the high retention rates at HBCUs predict continued strong enrollment of black students at these institutions. However, the rising cost of attendance at the nation's 103 HBCUs has triggered a decline in their share of enrollments among all blacks enrolled in postsecondary education and a migration to PWIs.

## Postsecondary Finance

Turning attention to postsecondary finance, the next section of articles covers government appropriations, college affordability, and student aid.

### Government Appropriations

Beginning with an overview of financing higher education, Johnstone, in *Patterns of finance: Revolution, evolution, or more of the same?* (1998), provides a framework for examining trends and effects of higher education finance. He suggests that patterns of finance can be described along three dimensions: total resources devoted to higher education; the share of costs borne by taxpayers, philanthropists, and students; and the cost per unit of the teaching and research functions. Johnstone walks the reader through several "what if" scenarios, suggesting what might result from various types of changes to the way American higher education is financed. He concludes that the U.S. enterprise of higher education is so vast and complex that any change will be slow and incremental. America is more likely, he concedes, to see little change in the funding of higher education. His predictions offer a sober counterpoint to the ambitious goals set forth in subsequent articles in this section.

Community colleges also struggle with maintaining affordability for their students (NCPPHE, 2006). Dowd and Grant isolate the reader's attention to public financing of two year colleges, in their (2005) article, *Equity and efficiency of community college appropriations: The role of local financing*. Their research demonstrates significant disparities in local appropriations to community colleges, exacerbated by institutional variations in size, location, and program offerings. Viewing their work through the lens provided by Johnstone, the reader might similarly conclude that patterns in community college finance—due to their wide variance—are also likely to remain the same in the coming decade.

### Affordability

Students and their families are concerned with what proportion of college expenses must be financed from their own fiscal resources (the net cost of college, or tuition minus student aid), whereas governments are concerned with their ability to provide revenue to support higher education along with other competing fiscal priorities, say Finney and Kelly, in *Affordability: Obtaining and making sense of information about how students, families, and states pay for higher education* (2004). The authors examine how tuition pricing, state appropriations and student aid combine to determine college affordability. State funding formulas, they point out, contribute to increased enrollment stratification by providing incentives for colleges to enroll the best academically prepared. Moreover, while tuition-setting policies unintentionally raise tuition ever and ever higher, states have not made significant investments in student aid. Their article issues a clear call for the redesign of state policies to improve and ensure the affordability of higher education.

The price of tuition affects college aspirations, access, choice, retention, and completion, as Mumper and Freeman argue, in their article, *The causes and consequences of public college tuition inflation* (2005). In the previous article, Finney and Kelly (2004) enumerated how tuition policies raise college costs, such as setting annual tuition prices based on peer institutions (ratcheting up), setting annual tuition to compensate for reduced or inadequate state appropriations (back-filling), or maintaining tuition as a fixed share of educational costs even when other funding sources for college operations are adequate or increasing (sand-bagging). Mumper and Freeman continue in this vein, delving into tuition-setting policies and other factors that increase tuition prices, providing the reader with greater content knowledge in this area.

Reindle, in *Hitting home: Quality, cost and access challenges confronting higher education today* (2007), discusses the fundamental changes in American higher education that will be required if we are to reach the enrollment, affordability, and attainment goals set forth for this nation. He offers calculations that suggest that America needs an additional 10.6 million more people of color earning postsecondary degrees in order to meet our national workforce needs, global competiveness, and national quality of life. His proposed agenda targets the ways in which the government funds higher education and in which colleges and universities operate and work together. He urges legislators, policymakers and college leaders to establish goals and assess performance on access, quality, and affordability; to focus government funding on academic priorities and program redesign; and to streamline student transfers and promote timely degree completion in order to reduce attrition and maintain a fluid enrollment capacity.

### Student Aid

Our section on student aid presents articles covering three major sources of aid: federal, state, and institutional. Turner (2001) covers the federal role, in *Federal financial aid: How well does it work?* She frames federal aid policies as a government investment decision and reviews research on the effectiveness of such policies. Proposing the use of postsecondary enrollment by student/family income levels as a primary way of evaluating effectiveness, she concludes by offering strategies for improving how we assess the impact of federal financial aid on student outcomes.

Titus (2006) covers the state role, in *No college student left behind: The influence of financial aspects of a state's higher education policy on college completion.* His analysis of data from multiple sources explores the extent to which state higher-education financing policies affect college completion rates. Using multi-level hierarchical modeling to isolate and control for both institutional and student variables, his findings demonstrate that many student-controlled variables predict college completion rates, as do institutional variables like academic selectivity, average SES of the freshman class, and per-student expenditures. State higher education policy, however, plays the major role. Specifically, Titus firmly connects college completion rates with state need-based student aid funding, both in terms of the proportion of need-based aid provided as a part of overall higher education appropriations, and the amount of such aid awarded per student. His work is vitally important in an era in which serious discussion is on the table that would link federal aid programs to student outcomes (USDoE, 2006), essentially penalizing colleges and universities for failing to meet outcome criteria that are influenced so heavily by agents and policies outside their control.

Perry's article, *Toward a theoretical framework for membership: The case of undocumented immigrants and financial aid for postsecondary education* (2006) highlights an emerging issue in state student aid funding: the eligibility of undocumented immigrant students. He uses interviews with policymakers, legislators, staff members, and undocumented immigrants in Texas to develop principles for determining state residency and student aid eligibility. He concludes, as did Texas legislators, that undocumented immigrants should have access to such state resources for postsecondary education. Perry's article introduces the reader to an important policy debate that is likely to increase in years to come, one that pits social justice arguments against a consumer culture that has driven higher education policy to respond primarily to taxpayer-consumers. Infused in the dialogue are deep-seated opposing values concerning whether non-citizen residents are "illegal" or "undocumented," and contention concerning what should be their resulting status and the government's response. Perry's article provides a social justice point of view, one that is sorely absent in the prevailing taxpayer-centric policy conversations.

Returning to an observation posed earlier by Finney and Kelly, an accurate state-by-state picture of college affordability is hindered by the absence of information on the amount and adequacy of institutional financial aid awarded to students. In the final article on postsecondary finance, Ehrenberg, Zhang, and Levin examine that very issue. *Crafting a class: The trade-off between merit scholarships and enrolling lower-income students* (2006) uses data from 100 colleges and universities to demonstrate how increases in institutional selectivity (as measured by the number of National Merit Scholars among the student body), correlate with decreases in enrollments of lower income students (as measured by number of Pell Grant recipients among the student body). The authors are careful to point out that the shift is not a mere matter of seat displacement. It results from institutional financial aid policies. Merit aid increases institutional selectivity and contributes to stratified college enrollment by student SES, whereas need-based aid increases opportunity, but decreases an institution's performance ranking on measures such as student precollege achievements.

## Outcomes and Accountability

Graduation rates are only one measure of college outcomes. The policy arena has heightened its attention to what those degrees mean and what students actually learn. This next section deals with college learning, assessment, and accountability for postsecondary outcomes.

### College-level Learning

*Measuring up on college-level learning* (Miller & Ewell, 2006) reports on the findings and recommendations of the National Forum on College Level Learning, which evaluated college-level learning in Illinois, Kentucky, Nevada, Oklahoma, and South Carolina. The Forum drew upon results from the National Adult Literacy Survey and existing assessment data, adding specially designed tests to assess both the knowledge and skills among the state's college-educated residents and how well the state's colleges and universities were collectively increasing the knowledge and skills of their graduates. The Forum's work provides a more lucid picture of "educational capital" beyond numbers of degree holders. The difference is akin to giving a person a complete health checkup, rather than making a determination by eyeballing the outside appearance. Additionally, using the state as the level of analysis (rather than specific institutions) gives policymakers and legislators the data they need to make informed decisions intended to improve the educational capacity of the state.

Merisotis and Phipps direct our attention to the other end of the continuum: Those who are in college but are at risk, unready to complete college-level curricula. In *Remedial education in colleges and universities: What's really going on?* (2000), they address the lack of consensus about what remedial education is, whom it serves, and whether it's worth the cost. The current trend has been towards transferring the locus of remedial education from the four-year to the two-year college level. In a thorough review of the college remediation function, however, including its history, purposes, programs, and participation, Merisotis and Phipps conclude that remedial education is and has always been a core function of the academy and should remain so. Their analysis of program performance and costs/benefits concludes that remedial education's value to society outweighs all costs. Nevertheless, they recommend reducing the need for it by focusing on improving college readiness and improving remedial education's cost efficiency and performance by expanding it into comprehensive programs that rely upon institutional collaboration and technology.

### Assessment

Despite the public policy discourse on skill development and knowledge acquisition manifested through degree attainment, there remains very little consensus about how and what should be assessed. Kuh, Kinzie, Buckley, Bridges, and Hayek (2008), in an exhaustive review of the most salient literature on student success noted, "Although cognitive development and direct measures of student learning are of great value, relatively few studies provide conclusive evidence about the performance of large numbers of students at individual institutions." We have included one such study in this Reader (Miller & Ewell, 2005). For a thorough review of trends and perspectives on assessment, we direct readers to the ASHE Reader on Assessment & Program Evaluation, 2nd Ed. (Lee, 2004). In this section, we consider an essential policy implication of the assessment movement: tracking student data.

Statewide student data systems hold the potential to monitor individual and institutional performance, enabling states, schools, and colleges to target their efforts for increasing college readiness, access, and outcomes attest Hearn, McLendon and Mokher (2008) in *Accounting for student success: An empirical analysis of the origins and spread of state student unit-record systems*; but not everyone is in favor of such systems. Privacy issues, data integrity, and increased regulation pose several areas of strong concern. The authors report that states that have adopted such systems are more likely to have liberal political climates, large populations, and federal civil-rights monitoring. Such conditions are not readily found in a majority of states. While gaining the necessary support to adopt such systems may be difficult to achieve at the state level, particularly in states that lack these conditions, the momentum for their adoption has already begun at the federal level (USDoE, 2006).

Next, Renn and Lunceford tackle a critical issue in the mechanics of student data tracking: identifying students by race and ethnicity. Over a decade ago, the federal government revised guidelines and mandated changes in all federal data collection. Yet most current practices for collecting education-related data lump together many distinct races into mega-ethnic categories and do not allow for multi-racial identification. This practice blurs the variances in educational performance and attainment that occur among groups, thereby potentially masking problem areas. Additionally, education data no longer articulate with federal census data, which allows for racial specificity and multiracial designation, and which considers Hispanic or Latino identity as a cultural designation across racial categories and not a distinct racial category. Renn and Lunceford, in *Because the numbers matter: Transforming postsecondary education data on student race and ethnicity to meet the challenges of a changing nation* (2004), survey the current status of education data tracking by race and ethnicity, addressing these and other considerations, and making recommendations for policy and practice.

### Accountability

Improving educational opportunity and capacity in this nation is a shared responsibility of the federal and state government, K–12, postsecondary education systems, and individual families. Yet accountability for college readiness, access, and outcomes may not be equally shared. In this section, we turn the reader's attention to accountability and accreditation.

The history and tradition of American higher education is based in self governance and self regulation, says Eaton, in *Institutions, accreditors, and the federal government: Redefining their "appropriate relationship"* (2007), as she explicates what she sees as encroaching federalism on the accreditation system.

Proposed changes in the locus of authority and action for monitoring and regulating academic quality (USDoE, 2006), would diminish the peer-review and self-governing traditions that have ushered American higher education through its rise to greatness. Eaton does not dispute the need to establish new standards, strategies, and measures for tracking student achievement and institutional performance. However, she champions the accreditation system as rigorous and able to achieve these objectives without federal intrusion. She puts forth a collection of suggestions that would strengthen the current accreditation function and redefine the relationship between the federal government and postsecondary education, precluding encroaching federalism. The recent 2008 reauthorization of the Higher Education Act echoes Eaton's principles, forbidding the U.S. Department of Education from dictating accreditation standards (ACE, 2008). The situation echoes the enactment of SPRE (the State Postsecondary Review Entities), created in the 1993 Higher Education Act to provide centralized oversight of postsecondary institutions receiving federal funds, but averted through combined lobbying efforts of higher education institutions and associations (Cook, 1998).

Turning attention to the state level, in *Called to account* (2006), McLendon, Hearn, and Deaton analyze the origins and spread of three types of state postsecondary education accountability policies: performance reporting, which requires colleges to collect and publicly report performance information across agreed upon institutional and state-wide measures; performance funding, in which state appropriations are consistently and directly linked to college performance; and performance budgeting, in which state appropriations are variably and only partially linked to college performance. Using event history analysis (EHA) techniques on a 47-state longitudinal database spanning 23 years and incorporating a variety of secondary sources, the authors determine that the adoption of performance-funding and performance-budgeting policies are primarily influenced by the characteristics of the legislative party in office coupled with the structure and control of higher education governance in that state. Specifically, a Republican-majority legislature coupled with decentralized campus governance predicts a greater likelihood of adopting performance-funding policies (consistent and direct linkages between appropriations and performance). Whereas a Republican-minority legislature coupled with centralized campus governance predicts a greater likelihood of adopting performance-budgeting policies (variable and partial linkages between appropriations and performance). Interestingly, the state's educational attainment levels, economic climate, and growth in undergraduate tuition levels have no significant linkage to the adoption of performance funding or performance budgeting policies, nor do variables such as gubernatorial power and party affiliation, the professionalization of the state legislature, and the presence of postsecondary education performance policies in neighboring states. Furthermore, the adoption of performance-reporting policies has no statistically significant influence at all. McLendon, Hearn, and Deaton's work contributes a new understanding for examining state-higher education accountability relationships, suggesting that politics and organizational structures drive the adoption of such policies, not necessarily actual outcomes in terms of postsecondary education attainment or affordability.

Moving from theory to practice, the next article provides a ground-level examination of state accountability policy in action. Martinez and Nilson, in *Assessing the connection between higher education policy and performance* (2006), use South Dakota as a case study to evaluate the effectiveness of state-sponsored incentive programs for improving public higher education performance. Their case study uncovers strong evidence that public postsecondary education performance can be affected by state policy goals when the policy agenda is clear, the goals are measurable, and performance is incentivized through performance-funding. In the case of South Dakota, the authors report that the policy goals included: increasing enrollments, P–16, inter-university collaboration, external funding, and improving student learning outcomes. Martinez and Nilson suggest that the goals for increasing enrollments and collaboration were easier to meet because the targets were clear and easier to measure through indicators such as state resident enrollment, increased enrollments in targeted programs, and the sharing of faculty and facilities. In contrast, the authors suggest that the goals for improving student learning outcomes and increasing external funding proved to be more difficult to meet because clear targets were not established (in the case of external funding) or were difficult to measure (in the case of student learning). Their case study offers much to be learned by states that would seek to implement incentivized performance policies, or for those who study the formation and effectiveness of such policies.

Huisman and Currie, in *Accountability in higher education: Bridge over troubled water. Higher Education* (2004), bring these two conversations together (how policy is formed and whether it works) in their study of the accountability movement in Europe and the United States. As with McLendon and colleagues, they consider the origins and spread of such policies. However, they look to changing relationships among governments, universities, and society as the momentum behind accountability policies. In particular, they attribute such policies to the way in which increased costs of postsecondary education has led the government and taxpayers to be more critical of its products and services. They support the need to make those products and services more visible, as postsecondary education evolves into colleges and systems that are international, digital, and amorphous. As with Martinez and Nilson, they consider why some performance and accountability mechanisms have not yet yielded the intended results. Examining four universities, they observed that the trend has been to use soft mechanisms (which involve monitoring and reporting only) rather than hard mechanisms (which would involve justification, rewards, and sanctions). In the absence of hard mechanisms, academics and managers in the institutions they studied tended to use or repurpose the existing data tracking mechanisms that were already in place, rather than creating and implementing new instruments and measures. Their findings suggest that the accountability movement, at least in the institutions and locations they studied, was more akin to policy rhetoric rather than true reform.

Adelman offers another U.S.-European comparative view in *The Bologna club: What U.S. higher education can learn from a decade of european reconstruction* (2008). Through the Bologna Process, 46 countries are creating the European Higher Education Area (EHEA) to improve access to higher education and lift the educational capital of the continent. The required underlying reforms entail creating articulation agreements and mechanisms for assuring quality, accountability, and equal opportunity in postsecondary participation across national borders; reforms that, as Adelman points out, are highly relevant to the challenges faced by U.S. postsecondary education. He recommends seven actions that U.S. policymakers, legislators, and colleges and universities should consider. Four of these are familiar, such as improving access to higher education; improving our treatment of part-time students; going beyond articulation agreements between two-year and four-year colleges and building dual-admissions programs in their place; and developing detailed qualifications frameworks for state higher education systems that describe what skills and knowledge students should obtain from various degree levels and programs of study. Three, however, are new, including revising our college credit system; introducing a new class of intermediate credentials; and developing diploma supplements similar to learning portfolios which would summarize individual student achievement.

## Teacher Preparation

Higher education is not alone with pressures for improved quality and outcomes. K–12 education faces the same demands. At the nexus of the two lies the function of teacher preparation, which bears the full brunt of the challenges faced by both postsecondary and the K–12 education. The nation needs more and better prepared teachers in order to improve K–12 education and facilitate the attainment of college and workforce readiness goals for high school graduates. In order to do so, colleges and universities need to do a better and broader job of educating future teachers. Nearly all of the teacher preparation function is under contention, right down to the basic strategies for preparing, inducting, and assessing teachers. This reader, however, deals only with the policy issue of where the responsibility and authority for teacher preparation lies.

First, Coble, Edelfelt, and Kettlewell take on this issue directly in *Who's in charge here? The changing landscape of teacher preparation in America* (2004). Their article describes new ways of thinking about teacher preparation, as well as various models emerging across the nation. Their conclusions point to school-university partnerships as an appropriate and effective locus for teacher preparation. Next, Coulter and Vandal describe the emerging role of two-year colleges in the teacher preparation function. In *Community colleges and teacher preparation: Roles, issues, and opportunities* (2007), the authors describe how two-year colleges can build upon their missions and legacies in workforce preparation and service to local communities in order to increase their role in teacher preparation, particularly in high demand areas. Finally, Cohen-Vogel gives us the *Federal role in teacher quality: "Redefinition" or policy alignment?* (2005), in which she traces the history of the federal government's role in teacher preparation. Although the federal government seemed to redefine its role in teacher education with the implementation of the No Child Left Behind Act (2001), Cohen-Vogel sees current federal activity not so much as a role redefinition, but rather as an attempt to bring greater alignment to K–12 educational reform policies, teacher preparation, and ongoing teacher professional development.

## Final Thoughts

Section II builds upon the foundation laid in the first section, introducing four selected perennial issues in postsecondary education policy: getting into college (College Access), paying for college (Postsecondary Finance), what happens in college (Outcomes and Assessment), and improving the preparation of those who will educate future generations (Teacher Education). It provides exposure to federal, state, and local or institutional perspectives on these issues through readings that call for policy development, explain the policy adoption process, and debate how we assess policies' effects. As the reader will discern, there are serious disconnects among the components of problems, where the accountability and authority lie, what policy levers are used to address these problems, and how improvements are measured. What clearly emerges from the readings is an understanding that the problems facing American higher education are converging. Each cascades into another. What also emerges is an understanding that further improvements in P–16 educational production and performance will require coordinated efforts between P–16 education providers, states, and the federal government. Each has become interdependent on the other. Through this collection of articles, the editors' intent is that the reader will gain an appreciation that crafting public policy is a political process of compromise that demands an understanding of complex issues, competing arrays of potential solutions, the multiple actors or agents involved both inside and outside of higher education, and the ways in which various policy options would impact stakeholders.

Although the United States has made tremendous gains in higher education participation and degree attainment, as Perna, Rowan-Kenyon, Bell, Thomas, and Li (2008) point out persistent gaps indicate that existing policies and programs are not adequate for accomplishing their underlying goals. The policies implemented over the years were intended to address definitions and understandings of the problems at that time, and are inadequate for addressing those problems as they have evolved and are defined and understood today. Unfortunately, once policies are in place, efforts to revisit, revise, reduce, and realign them are arduous. Such efforts are not, however, impossible. Readings in this section offered pathways and examples of how states and institutions might navigate this quandary. The nation has economic and ethical imperatives to do so.

## References

Cook, C. E. (1998). *Lobbying for higher education: How colleges and universities influence federal policy.* Nashville, TN: Vanderbilt University Press.

Kuh, G. D., Kinzie, J., Buckley, J. A., Bridges, B. D., and Hayek, J. C. (2008). *Piecing together the student success puzzle: Research, prepositions, and recommendations.* ASHE Higher Education Report 32(5). San Francisco: Jossey Bass.

Lee, W. Y. (2004). *ASHE Reader on assessment & program evaluation*, 2nd Ed. Boston: Pearson Custom Publishing.

National Center for Education Statistics (2005). *The Condition of Education.* Washington, D.C.: US Department of Education.

National Center for Public Policy and Higher Education (2006). *Measuring Up: 2006.* Palo Alto, CA: Author.

Perna, L. W., Rowan-Kenyon, H., Bell, A., Thomas, S. L. & Li, C. (2008). A typology of federal and state programs designed to promote college enrollment. *Journal of Higher Education, 79*(3), 243–267.

United States Department of Education. (2006). *A test of leadership: Charting the future of US Higher Education.* Washington, D.C.: Author.

# CHAPTER 4:
# COLLEGE ACCESS

# Claiming Common Ground

## State Policymaking for Improving College Readiness and Success

PATRICK M. CALLAN, JONI E. FINNEY, MICHAEL W. KIRST, MICHAEL D. USDAN AND ANDREA VENEZIA

## Foreword

There is widespread agreement among policymakers, the business community, and educational leaders that the United States needs to raise the educational achievement of its young population. Many states have sought to meet this challenge by developing policies to advance and support student achievement in K–12 schools, including standards-based reforms, state assessments, and high school redesigns. Some states have also sought to expand access to postsecondary education in order to increase the numbers of students completing education or training beyond high school. Yet the reforms of K–12 schools have not improved the college readiness of high school graduates, as measured by the percentage of college students who take remedial education, or by college completion rates. Likewise, state policies to expand access to higher education, which have been limited by setbacks in the affordability of college, have not led to higher percentages of the young population obtaining a college degree. Reforming K–12 schools and broadening access to college are necessary but not sufficient conditions for advancing educational opportunity.

In earlier times, when only a small proportion of high school students attended college, it made sense for states to develop and maintain educational policies and governance structures that divided K–12 and postsecondary education into separate entities. Today, however, when the vast majority of high school students aspire to attend college, states need policies that require K–12 and postsecondary education to collaborate to improve the college readiness of all high school students. This report identifies four state policy dimensions for improving college readiness and success: the alignment of coursework and assessments; state finance; statewide data systems; and accountability.

The recommendations in this report build from previous collaborative work among the National Center for Public Policy and Higher Education, the Institute for Educational Leadership, and the Stanford Institute for Higher Education Research.[1] The research began in 2003 with Partnerships for Student Success, a project funded by the Ewing Marion Kauffman Foundation. For Partnerships for Student Success, researchers analyzed state-level policies, programs, and governance structures that connect K–12 and postsecondary education in Florida, Georgia, New York, and Oregon. The National Center published the final report of that project, *The Governance Divide: A Report on a Four-State Study on Improving College Readiness and Success,* in September 2005.

National Center Report #06-1

## State Policy Dimensions for K-16 Reform
Wingspread Conference Center *September 12–13, 2005*

### Participants

**Linda Beene**
*Director*
Arkansas Department of
Higher Education

**Julie Davis Bell**
*Program Director, Education
Program*
National Conference of State
Legislatures

**Patrick M. Callan**
*President*
National Center for Public
Policy and Higher
Education

**Sally Clausen**
*President*
University of Louisiana
System

**Michael Cohen**
*President*
Achieve, Inc.

**Richard Lee Colvin**
*Director*
Hechinger Institute on
Education and the Media

**Ronald Cowell**
*President*
Education Policy and
Leadership Center

**Ann Daley**
*Executive Director*
Washington Learns

**Virginia Edwards**
*Editor and Publisher*
Education Week

**Peter T. Ewell**
*Vice President*
National Center for Higher
Education Management
Systems

**Joni E. Finney**
*Vice President*
National Center for Public
Policy and Higher Education

**Marlene Garcia**
*Principal Consultant*
Senate Office of Research
California Legislature

**Boyd H. Gibbons III**
*President*
The Johnson Foundation

**Susan Heegaard**
*Director*
Minnesota Office of Higher
Education

**Carole Johnson**
*Program Officer for
Education*
The Johnson Foundation

**Christine Johnson**
*President*
Community College of
Denver

**Stanley Jones**
*Commissioner*
Indiana Commission for Higher
Education

**Jan Kettlewell**
*Associate Vice Chancellor for
P–16 Initiatives*
Board of Regents of the
University System of Georgia

**Michael W. Kirst**
*Professor of Education*
Stanford University

**Dewayne Matthews**
*Senior Research Director*
Lumina Foundation for
Education

**Peter McWalters**
*Commissioner*
Department of Elementary and
Secondary Education
State of Rhode Island

**Jennifer Muskovin**
*Wingspread Fellow Student*
Benedictine University

**Rogéair Purnell**
*Program Officer, Youth*
The James Irvine Foundation

**Margo Quiriconi**
*Director of Research and
Policy, Education*
Ewing Marion Kauffman
Foundation

**Piedad Robertson**
*President*
Education Commission of the
States

**Drew Scheberle**
*Vice President for
Education and Workforce
Development*
Greater Austin Chamber
of Commerce

**Janis Somerville**
*Senior Associate*
National Association of
System Heads

**David Spence**
*President*
Southern Regional Education
Board

**Michael D. Usdan**
*Senior Fellow*
Institute for Educational
Leadership

**Joel Vargas**
*Senior Project Manager*
Jobs for the Future

**Andrea Venezia**
*Senior Policy Analyst*
National Center for Public
Policy and Higher Education

**Duncan Wyse**
*President*
Oregon Business Council

In completing the governance study, we learned a great deal about the range of policy options available to states to connect K–12 and postsecondary education, and we learned that changes in governance structures alone cannot significantly improve the percentage of students who prepare for, enroll in, and succeed in postsecondary education or training. After we completed that project, we broadened our understanding of these issues by examining information about related policy changes in other states. As part of this process, we convened policy and education leaders from across the United States to participate in "State Policy Dimensions for K-16 Reform," a two-day conference held in September 2005 at The Johnson Foundation's Wingspread Conference Center in Racine, Wisconsin (see list of participants). The suggestions of this group helped us clarify our thoughts and expand our understanding of state policy directions. The quotations in the margins of this report represent only a fraction of the insights we gained at the conference.

We are grateful to Achieve, Inc., The James B. Hunt, Jr. Institute for Educational Leadership and Policy, and The Johnson Foundation for partnering with us at Wingspread, and to the Ewing Marion Kauffman Foundation for its financial support of the meeting and the research. In addition, we would like to thank Boyd H. Gibbons III, President of The Johnson Foundation, and his staff, particularly Carole M. Johnson, Program Officer for Education, Theresa Oland, Director of Communications, and Wendy S. Butler, Program Assistant.

As always, responsibility for errors and misinterpretations remains with the authors. We welcome the responses of readers.

*Patrick M. Callan*
*Joni E. Finney*
*Michael W. Kirst*
*Michael D. Usdan*
*Andrea Venezia*

# Introduction

Major demographic shifts in the population of the United States, combined with persistent gaps in educational achievement by ethnic group, could decrease the portion of the workforce with college-level skills over the next 15 years, with a consequent decline in per capita personal income in the United States.[2] Meanwhile, the competitive edge of the U.S. workforce is slipping; several other developed countries now surpass the United States in the percentage of their young working-age population enrolling in college and attaining a bachelor's degree.[3] At a time when the knowledge-based, global economy requires more Americans with education and training beyond high school, the nation confronts the prospect of a sustained drop in the average educational levels of the U.S. workforce.[4] This challenge places the United States at a crossroads: we can improve college readiness and completion rates and thereby prepare the workforce for the economic and civic challenges of the next generation, or we can allow gaps in educational achievement to undermine our competitive edge and our communities' economic prosperity.

Leaders from throughout the country—in public and private schools, charter schools, foundations, educational and policy organizations, businesses, states, and the federal government—have taken up this challenge. For example, reforming high schools has become a major focus in an overall drive to raise student achievement. Many of these efforts to improve our secondary schools have targeted student readiness for both college and work as a single key objective: the skills and knowledge required for middle-income jobs closely mirror those required for college success. As research has documented, reforms that focus either on K–12 schools or on colleges and universities are likely to perpetuate some of the key barriers to improving educational achievement for students.[5] Yet the focus of most state educational reforms has been limited to K–12 school systems. Some of the most robust challenges in raising student achievement can be found at the juncture—or more accurately the disjuncture—between our K–12 systems and our colleges and universities.

In the United States, secondary and postsecondary education have developed divergent histories, governance structures, policies, and institutional boundaries. As a result, there are few widespread practices or traditions for these two systems of education to communicate with each other, much less to collaborate to improve student achievement across institutions. Advocacy organizations are working on behalf of K–12 schools on the one hand or colleges and universities on the other, but there are no lobbying groups in state capitals seeking to improve college readiness by bridging the divide between K–12 and higher education. There are few accountability systems that track college readiness from secondary to postsecondary education. And no one is held responsible for the students who drop between the cracks of the two systems.

Gaining admission to college is not the most daunting challenge facing high school graduates—although many students think that it is and most college preparation efforts focus on admissions. The more difficult challenge for students is becoming prepared academically for college coursework. Once students enter college, about half of them learn that they are not prepared for college-level courses. Forty percent of students at four-year institutions and 63% at two-year colleges take remedial education.[6] According to *Measuring Up 2004*, the state-by-state report card on higher education, the timely completion of certificates and degrees remains one of the weakest aspects of performance in higher education.[7]

This report identifies four state policy dimensions for improving college-readiness opportunities for all high school students:

- **Alignment of coursework and assessments:** States should require K–12 and postsecondary education to align their courses and assessments. Currently, the K–12 standards movement and efforts to improve access and success in higher education are not connected.

- **State finance:** States should develop financial incentives and support to stimulate K–12 and postsecondary education to collaborate to improve college readiness and success. Most existing state finance systems perpetuate the divide between K–12 and postsecondary education.

- **Statewide data systems:** States should develop the capacity to track students across educational institutions statewide. Currently, most states do not collect adequate data to address the effectiveness of K–12 reforms in improving student readiness for college.

- **Accountability:** States should publicly report on student progress and success from high school through postsecondary education. Schools, colleges, and universities should be held accountable for improving student performance from high school to college completion.

Through these policy levers, states can create the conditions for claiming common ground between our systems of K–12 and postsecondary education.

## Context and Findings

Many forces are converging to create a pressing need for state policies to improve college readiness and success. For example, the fastest growing job sectors in our economy require workers to have at least some education or training beyond high school.[8] Yet completion rates for associate's and bachelor's degree programs have stalled over the past decade, and wide gaps remain in college completion by ethnic and income group.[9] Whereas the United States was once the world leader in offering college opportunity to its residents, several countries have now overtaken the U.S. in this area. The educational attainment of the young workforce in the United States (ages 24 to 34) currently ranks fifth among industrialized nations.[10]

Unless the educational achievement of the young population improves, the competitiveness of the U.S. workforce is projected to decline over the next decades. Economists Anthony Carnevale and Donna Desrochers have estimated that by 2020 the United States could face a shortfall of 14 million workers who have the knowledge and skills needed to compete for middle-income jobs in a global economy.[11] In addition, recent population studies have found that unless states can improve the education of all students, the percentage of the U.S. workforce with a bachelor's degree will decrease over the next 15 years, with a corresponding drop in personal income per capita. Minority groups with the lowest average levels of education will grow rapidly, while the baby boomers—the most highly educated generation in U.S. history, are expected to retire in record numbers. From 1980 to 2020, the minority portion of the workforce is projected to double from 18% to 37%, and the Hispanic/Latino portion will almost triple, from 6% to 17%. During the same period, the white working-age population is projected to decline from 82% to 63%.[12]

Educators and policymakers have known since the 1980s that this country would need a more highly educated workforce. For the past several decades, they have broadcast a consistent message urging high school students to attend college—and students have responded. Today's high school students have higher academic aspirations than ever before; almost 90% of high school students of all racial and ethnic groups aspire to attend college. Almost 60% of high school graduates enroll in college right after high school,[13] and many additional students enroll in college within a few years of high school graduation. But educators and policymakers have not fulfilled their side of the bargain; they have not developed coherent state systems of education that adequately prepare high school students for the academic expectations of college. High school students who seek to enroll in college must navigate a maze of disconnected curricula and assessments that are reinforced by state policies that are themselves unconnected and often at cross purposes with each other.[14] These fractured and fragmented systems waste taxpayer money on duplicated and inefficient uses of resources, they create barriers for high school students who seek to prepare for college, and they undermine efforts to improve college completion rates. The K–12 and postsecondary education systems in the United States should be working together to improve college readiness and success, yet our nation's educational systems remain sharply divided.

## Leaks in the Pipeline

Despite the high educational aspirations of high school students, the United States has low and inequitable high school graduation and college completion rates. About two-thirds of ninth graders (68%) graduate from high school within four years. And less than one-fifth of ninth graders (18%) finish high school within four years, go on to college right after graduation, and then complete either an associate's degree within three years of enrolling or a bachelor's degree within six years.[15] In examining student progress from high school to college, there are also large gaps between ethnic groups (see figure 1). Almost a quarter (23%) of white students receive an associate's degree within three years or a bachelor's degree within six years of enrolling in college. In contrast, only 9% of African-Americans and 10% of Hispanic/Latinos do so.[16]

There is also an increasing educational divide by income in the United States. For those high school graduates from the wealthiest quartile (25%) of the overall population, about two of every three enroll in a four-year college or university. In contrast, only about one in five from the lowest socioeconomic quartile enrolls in a four-year institution. At the nation's most selective colleges and universities, about three-quarters of the student body are from the top socioeconomic quartile and only three percent are from the poorest quartile.[17]

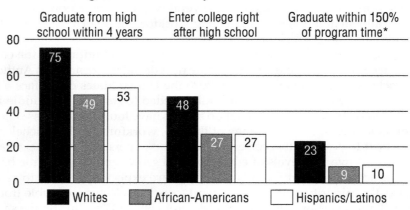

Of 100 ninth graders, how many …

*150% of program time is three years for those seeking an associate's degree, and six years for those seeking a bachelor's degree.

Notes: These "educational pipeline" data are from 2001. The analysis is not a longitudinal study that tracks a sample of students over time. It is developed based on a combination of several national data sources that measure student success rates at each transition point. Due to data limitations, it does not account for transfer students.

Sources: Analysis by National Center for Higher Education Management Systems (www.higheredinfo.org), based on data from NCES Common Core Data; IPEDS 2002 Fall Enrollment Survey; IPEDS 2002 Graduation Rate Survey.

**Figure 1. U.S. Educational Pipeline by Race/Ethnicity**

## Standards for College Readiness Are Confusing

From the students' perspective, the divide between high school and college is very real, even for those who plan to attend a community college. Community colleges, which enroll about 44% of undergraduate students,[18] have multiple missions and most admit any student over age 18 who applies and who can benefit from instruction. Since these and other broad-access institutions do not have stringent admission requirements, many high school students assume that they do not need rigorous academic preparation. They do not understand that, as with four-year colleges and universities, community colleges have academic standards for taking college-level courses and completing a certificate or degree program.[19] After students enroll in college, they learn that they must take placement exams to determine if they qualify for college-level work or if they must take remedial courses first. About half the college students in the United States are required to enroll in remedial education.[20] This percentage could be reduced dramatically if high schools and colleges were to connect their standards, assessments, policies, and coursework.

The disjunctures between high schools and postsecondary education manifest themselves in many ways. For example, high school assessments often emphasize different knowledge and skills than do college entrance and placement requirements. College placement tests for math often include Algebra II, while the assessments required for admission rarely exceed Algebra I.[21] In addition, much of the coursework in high school does not build toward college readiness. For example, a recent ACT study found that high school teachers consider grammar and usage skills to be the least important writing skills, and only 69% of high school teachers reported that they teach grammar and usage.[22] In contrast, the study also found that college instructors consider these skills to be the most important writing skills for incoming students. Given the need to improve student achievement in high school and college, it would make sense for college and university systems to communicate extensively with high schools about what students need to know and be able to do to succeed in college. But the vast majority of high school teachers receive no information from colleges about their admissions and placement standards and policies.[23]

## Few Reforms Address College Readiness

Traditionally, states have viewed high schools as performing two primary tasks: preparing some students for postsecondary education and preparing most students for work. Although that division may have been appropriate decades ago, it is no longer relevant today, primarily because of the increasing technological and educational demands of the contemporary workplace. The knowledge and skills that students need to succeed in postsecondary education are equivalent to the ones they need in the workforce. As a result, some high schools are aiming for a new primary goal: to create an educational environment that provides all students with the knowledge and skills they need to succeed in education and training beyond high school.

Improving student readiness for college does not mean that every student will want or need to complete four years of a traditional liberal arts education. Some will become employed or join the military directly after high school, and many will qualify, based on their skills, for training on the job. Many high school graduates will enroll in and complete certificate or other training programs. And many will finish several years of postsecondary education, completing an associate's or bachelor's degree. No matter which career paths students choose, the completion of a high school diploma should prepare them for existing opportunities for education and training beyond high school. The diploma should also provide their prospective employers and college admissions officers with the assurance that students have attained college-ready knowledge and skills. This can only occur if public policies for K–12 and postsecondary education converge upon a common set of goals.

Since the 1980s, states have concentrated substantial resources on the reform of K–12 schools. Many of these reforms have focused on the development of statewide standards and the assessment of student achievement based on those standards. Yet most standards-setting activities—such as high school exit exams—end at the 10th grade level, which does not represent adequate preparation for college. For example, states that have a high school graduation assessment based on minimum standards may be undermining their college-readiness efforts by sending mixed signals to students about what it takes to graduate from high school and succeed in college.

Recently, several national reforms focusing on college readiness have been underway, including the American Diploma Project and initiatives springing from the policy discussions at the 2005 National Education Summit sponsored by the National Governors Association and Achieve. A consensus is emerging around a central goal: to prepare all high school graduates to engage successfully in college-level academic work.

# Recommendations

The federal government, local school districts, and colleges and universities have important roles to serve in developing educational policy and practice. College-readiness reform, however, is primarily a state-level policy responsibility. As the entities that perform the major funding and policy-setting functions for public K–12 and higher education, states are in a unique position to create and adopt policies that require the systems of education to collaborate to improve college readiness and success. Currently, most collaborations between schools and colleges can be described as voluntary, localized efforts that are dependent upon ad hoc leadership commitments. States that are seeking to improve college readiness and success must move their educational systems beyond localized collaborations by taking action in four key areas of statewide policy: alignment of coursework and assessments, state finance, statewide data systems, and accountability. If states are not using their policy levers in at least these four areas to align K–12 and postsecondary education, they cannot expect significant improvements in college readiness and success.

## Alignment of Coursework and Assessments

**States should require K–12 and postsecondary education to align their coursework and assessments.**

Requiring K–12 and postsecondary education to work together to align their coursework and assessments is a key step to improving college readiness.

Currently, the K–12 standards movement and efforts to improve access and success in higher education are operating on different tracks. For example, a widespread K–12 reform strategy has been to increase enrollments in college preparatory courses. Yet despite some successes in this area, remediation rates in college remain high and college completion rates remain low. As a nation, we are learning that the number of courses that high school students take, and the units and names assigned to them, are often inadequate proxies for whether or not high school graduates are prepared to succeed in college-level work. The quality and level of the coursework and instruction, and their level of alignment with postsecondary expectations, are the key elements of reform. Making improvements in these areas requires that colleges and universities participate in the new wave of high school reforms, so that new standards and curricula in high school are linked to what students need to know and be able to do in college.

High school assessments provide another example of the multiple ways students receive mixed messages about the skills they need to develop for college. High school graduation tests in most states are benchmarked at the 8th, 9th, or 10th grade levels. There are few standards developed for the 11th or 12th grades or connected to the academic expectations of college. Recently, the *Boston Globe* reported that in Massachusetts "37% of incoming freshmen from public high schools had to take a remedial course in reading, writing, or math last year, down only two percentage points from 2002, the year before the MCAS English and math tests [the statewide 10th grade assessments] became a graduation requirement."[24]

High school students should receive diagnostic information through assessments at key intervals in high school—well before entering college—concerning their preparation for college-level academic work, so that they can change their course-taking patterns and improve their college readiness. In order for this to take place, states must require K–12 and postsecondary education to align their assessments—for example, by aligning high school assessments with college placement tests. By taking courses and assessments that build toward college-level academic work, high school students can become better informed about and better prepared for the requirements of college.

The Early Assessment Program at California State University

As an example of promising collaborative work between K–12 and postsecondary systems, California State University (CSU) has partnered with the State Board of Education and the California Department of Education to develop the Early Assessment Program. The program was established by CSU to provide high school juniors with opportunities to measure their readiness for college-level math and English, and to help them improve their knowledge and skills during their senior year. The program's goal is to ensure that high school graduates who attend CSU are prepared to enroll and succeed in college-level courses.

The impetus for the program was the high remediation rate within CSU. To be admitted to CSU, all high school students must complete a college preparatory curriculum and earn a grade point average of B or higher. Yet even with these requirements, about half of first-time freshmen at CSU must take remedial education in English, math, or both.[25] Based on this and other information, it became clear to CSU that the college preparatory curriculum and grade-point-average requirements were not effective in developing college readiness.

The Early Assessment Program includes three components: an 11th grade testing program, preparation opportunities for high school students, and professional development for high school teachers. The 11th grade assessment is part of the state's testing and accountability system, is criterion-referenced, and includes items associated with 12th grade standards.[26] School teachers worked with university faculty to augment the California Standards Tests (which are end-of-course exams all students must take) with math and English items that measure college-readiness knowledge and skills. In math, the items assess student knowledge of advanced algebra and geometry. Similarly, the English proficiency standards are aligned with the state standards in English-language arts, yet require additional demonstration of advanced reading and writing skills. For example, there is a 45-minute essay requirement.

High school students volunteer in the spring of their junior year to take the augmented sections of the California Standards Tests. The scoring of college readiness involves a combination of performance on selected items from the core tests and on the augmented items. High schools and students receive scores by early August, prior to the students' senior year. Students who meet the readiness standards are exempt from additional placement testing after they are admitted to CSU. Students who do not meet the standards are guided to further instructional and diagnostic assistance in the 12th grade. For example, the diagnostic assistance includes courses and online tutorials; students can access the CSU Diagnostic Writing service online and use materials from the Mathematics Diagnostic Testing Project.[27] In addition, K–12 and postsecondary educators have developed a 12th grade expository reading and writing course that high schools may pilot and adopt to help students advance their skills in English. The course is aligned with California's content standards; it is geared toward preparing students for college-level English; and it focuses on analytical, expository, and argumentative reading and writing.[28]

**Early Assessment Program Key Principles**

There is a shared view of college readiness standards across higher education.

There is a substantial core of K–12 standards and assessments that can be aligned with collegiate readiness standards.

Postsecondary education should lead in connecting its readiness standards to K–12 standards.

K–12 standards and postsecondary education readiness standards need to be aligned.

There needs to be direct assessment of college-readiness standards.

Additional tests and testing time should be minimized.

The timing of tests should be early enough to help students improve their preparation for college.

The work should be cost-effective.

Source: David Spence, "Early, Assessment Academic Preparation Initiative," presentation at "State Policy Dimensions for K–16 Reform," Wingspread Conference Center, September 12, 2005.

In spring 2004, testing for the Early Assessment Program was available in all California high schools. Out of approximately 386,000 elligible students, about 153,000 took the language arts test. Based on the results, 22% of these students were exempted from taking placement tests at CSU. In math, out of approximately 157,000 eligible students, 115,000 took the test and 55% of these students were exempted.[29]

There are many anticipated benefits to the Early Assessment Program. For the first rime, a large-scale, statewide program is providing students with information about their level of preparedness for college. If the program succeeds, students who participate will have the information and support to improve their academic readiness during their senior year in high school, and CSU will in turn have enrollees who will need fewer remedial classes and will graduate more quickly. The data generated will enable educators from both K–12 and postsecondary education to track student progress from high school through the CSU system—and thereby be in a better position to improve the alignment of coursework and assessments between high school and college.[30]

Even though the statewide scope of this work is promising, its impact on California's public schools will be limited because the state's community college system, which enrolls about two-thirds of the college students in the state, has not participated in its development or implementation. Community colleges in Los Angeles, however, have decided to pilot the use of the Early Assessment Program for their campuses.

## State Finance

**States should develop financial incentives and support to stimulate K–12 and postsecondary education to collaborate to improve college readiness and success.**

As well as requiring public educational systems to align their assessments and coursework, states need to create budget and finance incentives that can stimulate increased collaboration between K–12 and postsecondary education to improve student achievement across the systems. Creating

---

**CSU "Lessons Learned" from the Early Assessment Program**

State-level leadership and policy direction is needed to ensure that the same college-readiness signals are given to all high schools in a state and that college-readiness standards and assessments are aligned with K–12 standards and assessments.

Public postsecondary and K–12 education systems must adopt the college-readiness standards.

Include all open door and broad-access postsecondary institutions, since they have the potent to send the strongest, clearest signals about college readiness.

Emphasize policies and standards for placement into college-level courses, not admission to college.

Focus college-readiness standards on skills, such as reading, writing, and mathematics.

Define threshold performance levels and focus on a workable set of core skills.

Align the college-readiness standards and assessments with statewide high school standards and assessments, and evaluate the match between the sets, re-aligning if necessary. Do not rely on surrogate tests.

State high school assessments should include all of the college-readiness standards and range high enough in difficulty to indicate whether or not students have mastered the standards. High stakes tests are probably not suitable because the performance levels are too low and the tests might contribute to high school dropout rates. Comprehensive tests or end-of-course tests are better candidates.

Embed the college-readiness standards into curricula and assessments for grades 8 to 12. This includes teacher pre-service and in-service opportunities.

Source: David Spence, "Development of State College Readiness: School-Based Standards and Assessments," presentation at "State Policy Dimensions for K–16 Reform," Wingspread Conference Center, September 12, 2005.

such incentives will require state legislative committees that oversee the budget processes for K–12 and higher education to work more closely together to find common goals in advancing college readiness and success. Currently, most states maintain separate legislative committee structures governing K–12 and postsecondary education. To the extent that these legislative oversight functions remain isolated from each other, they can and often do perpetuate the divide between schools and college systems.

No state has fully aligned state budget, financial aid, and other policies to provide incentives for K–12 and postsecondary education to support college readiness. However, several states have taken steps to provide such incentives in some areas, ranging from redesigning state budget processes for public education systems to, on a much smaller scale, providing incentives for dual enrollment. Two promising, ambitious examples are summarized below: Oregon is exploring the development of an integrated K–20 finance model; Indiana is using a financial aid program to increase and broaden access to college preparatory classes.

## Oregon's K–20 Finance Model

In Oregon, the state political leadership has established expectations for improvement in how K–12 and postsecondary education collaborate to advance student success. For example, the governor has set concrete goals in the areas of high school graduation, college completion, and system delivery. In addition, the Joint Boards—comprised of members from the State Board of Education and the State Board of Higher Education—has recommended the following three infrastructure redesigns:

- a unified education delivery system with curriculum aligned so that exit standards from one sector equal entrance standards to the next;
- a unified data system that can track students across the continuum and by institution; and
- a unified, transparent budget that connects all education sectors.[31]

The Oregon Business Council has taken the lead in developing an integrated statewide budget and finance model that would span from preschool to graduate school. According to Duncan Wyse, president of the Oregon Business Council, the state's public education system, as in most states, "is composed of distinct sectors, budgeted and governed separately. There are no consistent [high school] exit and [postsecondary] entrance standards for students. Student movement through the system is organized by time rather than by achievement."[32]

In developing the model, the Business Council analyzed the 2002–03 expenditures by K–12 and postsecondary education as though they derived from one budget. The council found that the level of state investment per student varied by grade and degree, with community colleges receiving the least state funding and special education in K–12 schools receiving the most.[33] In addition, since the 1990 passage of Oregon's ballot measure establishing limits on property taxes, state investment in pre-K programs, middle school education, K–12 special education, and community college developmental education has increased. State investment in all other educational areas—elementary and high school education, community college lower-division education and professional training, and Oregon University System lower-division, upper-division, graduate, and professional education—decreased.[34]

The Business Council consequently recommended that Oregon adopt a reform plan to coordinate governance, budgeting, and management of education from preschool to graduate school. The council proposed that budgets would be based on per-student costs per service; outcomes would be established for every educational level and service; school spending would be more transparent; and aggregate student performance for every program and at every institution would be publicly reported. The governor, the Legislature, and the Joint Boards would set performance expectations and priorities for the budget, create teams to work on efficiencies and delivery improvements in high-impact areas, and set forth a two- or three-biennium plan to accomplish the work. Through the Joint Boards, the governor would lead policy discussions and assign teams to address improvements in areas such as high school redesign, high school and lower-division alignment, policies for tuition and need-based aid for public and private institutions, K–12 transportation, special education, and English as a second language.[35]

The Oregon Business Council has acknowledged that there are many hurdles to overcome in implementing this reform plan. For example, the state's budget and accounting systems are not adequate to collect and report comparable per-student costs by service across institutions, and developing this capacity would require significant legislative and public support. In addition, these transformations would take longer than any single governor's term; sustaining reforms across administrations is difficult. Finally, since some stakeholders are likely to perceive the changes as threatening, there could be political setbacks along the way as people resist the reforms.[36]

According to the Business Council, if Oregon succeeds in implementing this model (for example, see appendix), the state should be able to reduce financial inefficiencies, target resources more strategically, improve student achievement across every educational level, and provide a more transparent and unified system of financing. The council has suggested that the benefits would also include more informed decisions for policy and educational leaders; transparency of tax dollar use; the creation of opportunities for broad redesign and reinvention; and increases in program effectiveness by focusing on service quality and continuous improvement.[37]

## Indiana's Twenty-first Century Scholars Program

State financial aid, a traditional means for broadening access to college, can also be used to leverage college-readiness reforms. Indiana's Twenty-first Century Scholars Program is a national model in both broadening access to college and improving college readiness. Initiated in 1990, the program was the first state financial aid program to promise the future payment of college tuition for middle school students who qualify for the federal free and reduced lunch program. The Scholar's Program targets low-income students in the eighth grade and requires each participating student to complete a pledge to finish high school, maintain at least a C grade point average, remain drug- and alcohol-free, apply for college and financial aid, and enroll in an Indiana postsecondary institution within two years of completing high school. In return, Indiana (1) encourages the Scholars to pursue a college preparatory curriculum; (2) provides support services to them and for those who fulfill the pledge (3) pays their tuition and fees (after other financial aid awards) at a public institution in Indiana (or contributes a similar portion for tuition at an independent college).[38] The program pays for 80% of the approved tuition and fees for students completing a regular high school diploma; 90% of tuition and fees for students completing a more rigorous high school diploma, called a core 40 diploma; and 100% of tuition and fees for students completing the most rigorous diploma, the academic honors diploma. Through these incentives, the program sends clear signals to students regarding academic preparation for college.[39]

Since the Scholars Program targets low-income students, the majority of students who receive the awards already qualify for some level of state financial aid. As a result, the program's award amounts are relatively modest.[40] In contrast, the Georgia HOPE Scholarship provides financial aid to students who earn a B or better in the college preparatory track, regardless of financial need. As with Indiana's Scholars Program, the HOPE Scholarship provides clear signals to students about the importance of college readiness. Because HOPE is not tied to financial need, however, it is expensive for the state and has been criticized for its failure to target low-income students.

The Scholars Program is increasing enrollment in rigorous preparatory curricula in high school and enrollment in colleges and universities. The percentage of traditionally underserved students taking college preparatory curricula in high school has increased, as has the percentage of all students taking such courses. In 1993–94, 12% of Indiana's high school graduates earned an academic honors diploma, 87% earned a regular diploma, and 1% were in the "other" category. In 2003–04, 29% earned an academic honors diploma, 36% earned a core 40 diploma, and 35% earned a regular diploma. Although gaps in educational attainment by race and ethnicity persist, they are narrowing, and the performance of each racial and ethnic group is improving. For example, in 1998, 23% of African-American, 29% of Hispanic, 45% of white, and 36% of multiracial high school graduates earned a core 40 diploma. In 2004, those percentages increased to 47%, 51%, 67%, and 66%, respectively.[41]

In addition, the percentage of students enrolling in postsecondary education has risen. From 1994 to 2002, the percentage of Indiana's high school graduates who enrolled in college right after high school increased from 50% to 62%, raising the state's rank on this measure from 34th to 10th in the nation. In terms of raw numbers, in 1988 Indiana had 69,004 high school graduates and 30,905 college freshmen. In 2002, it had 60,943 high school graduates and 38,023 college freshmen.[42]

A report from the Lumina Foundation found that the Scholars Program is encouraging more low-income students to enroll in postsecondary education. The report also found that the program is improving persistence and completion rates for students earning two-year college degrees. The Lumina report concludes that "state policy can affect the curricula that students actually complete, which, in turn, can influence their college success."[43]

As states seek to develop their own budget or financial incentives to improve college readiness and success, they need to be mindful of unintended effects of such efforts. For example, many state legislators, concerned about the high costs of college, may be interested in creating incentives to improve certificate- or degree-completion rates at state colleges or universities. Some states, for example, have provided postsecondary institutions with additional funds for each student who graduates. Such incentives do not always succeed, however, because many institutions can improve their graduation rates by raising their admission requirements in ways that have the effect of reducing access to college statewide. States might consider developing programs similar to Indiana's Scholars Program, which addresses financial need and college readiness, thereby broadening access to college while also improving students' abilities to perform at higher levels.

## Statewide Data Systems

**States should develop the capacity to track students across educational institutions statewide.**

A third important element in college-readiness reform is the development of statewide databases that can track student progress across educational institutions. A robust statewide data system is needed to determine the effectiveness of programs and reforms in improving student achievement.

Currently, the data derived from state information systems are generally more useful for supporting budget allocations to institutions than for examining student progress across multiple institutions. At the K–12 level, most state databases cannot track students who leave one school district and enroll in another. Many cannot accurately determine the percentage of students graduating from high school each year. State databases are even more deficient in examining student transitions from high school to college; most states have data systems that stop at grade 12 and others that begin anew at grade 13, with little or no connection between them. As a consequence, these states do not have adequate information to address the effectiveness of K–12 reforms in improving student performance in college.

As states seek to align and expand their information systems across K–12 and postsecondary education, they need to better understand the relationship between student readiness in high school and student success in college. Currently, 18 states do not even collect data on the courses taken by high school students. In most states, it is not currently possible to identify and analyze completion rates for students who enter college from the workforce, for students who attend part-time, and for students who attend multiple institutions. In short, without databases that connect educational institutions, it is difficult—if not impossible—to assess needs accurately, identify where the most substantial problems are, and design appropriate interventions.

In tracking student progress across educational institutions and systems, state information systems need to standardize and report data on high school academic courses and assessments; high school graduation; college and work readiness; transitions between high school and college; transfers between colleges; student progress while in college; and completion of postsecondary education and training programs. For example, the databases should be designed to answer questions related to college readiness:

- How do students who take college preparatory courses in high school perform in postsecondary education?
- How do students who pass (or earn a proficient score on) state assessments perform in college?
- Considering those students who require remediation in college, what percentage took a college preparatory curriculum in high school?
- Given their students' performance in college, how can high schools strengthen their curricula and instruction to improve student readiness for college?

Most states have been developing better ways to track student achievement, and a few have been working to connect their information systems for K–12 and postsecondary education. Florida's linked data systems represent one of the more ambitious efforts to connect the two education systems through better data gathering.

## Florida's Linked Data Systems

Florida has linked two data collection systems in order to track student progress through the state's education systems, their participation in other public systems, and their later status in the workforce: the Data Warehouse and the Florida Education and Training Placement Information Program. In integrating the data systems, Florida is developing common standards, procedures, and quality assurance; eliminating duplicated functions and services; providing for improved accountability and public reporting; and establishing longitudinal reporting about the status and performance of students and other public program participants.

The Data Warehouse combines longitudinal student data from public schools, community colleges and technical centers, and the university system. Florida has had a history of gathering data across educational institutions on an ad hoc basis, but over the past several years the State Department of Education has worked to formally connect all public databases using common student identifiers. The Data Warehouse is managed by the Information and Accountability Division of the Office of K–20 Education. The warehouse includes data on K–12 students; adult, vocational, and associate's programs in community and technical colleges; public university, baccalaureate, master's, doctorate, and professional programs in four-year in-state universities; assessment systems, financial aid, teacher certification, and facilities across the K–20 spectrum; and employment and continuing education outcomes. The warehouse includes the following data categories: individual students (demographics, enrollment, courses, test scores, financial aid, awards, and employment); educational curricula; staff information; program costs; and workforce information.[44]

The Florida Education and Training Placement Information Program follows students when they leave any level of schooling (at the high school level or above), whether they continue their education, participate in a training program (for example, vocational rehabilitation), receive public assistance, enter a correctional facility, or earn an occupational licensure. The program also contains data about whether a former student is employed or unemployed. The program integrates data from a variety of state and federal agencies, including Florida's Agency for Workforce Innovation, Department of Children and Families, Department of Corrections, and Department of Education; and the federal government's Department of Defense, Office of Personnel Management, and United States Postal Service.[45]

Because of its integrated data systems, Florida can track students over time and across educational institutions, enabling state staff, researchers, and others to answer many questions about the effectiveness of education at various levels (see Box).

---

**Florida's Linked Data Systems Enable the State to:**

Track students across K–12 schools and districts.

Analyze the impact of specific policies (for example, the participation of students in the Bright Futures Scholarship Program or their completion of Algebra I) to understand the policies' impact on students' future educational attainment and earnings.

Examine student performance on the high stakes test and determine the test's validity in relation to student activities in the ensuing years.

Track students beyond the K–12 system, including students who drop out, to see the overall impact of their experiences in school.

Track students who were successful on state exams—and those who were not—in order to examine the characteristics of teachers who appear to be successful (at the aggregate level).

Examine longitudinal data for students who complete high school in various ways (for example, through obtaining a standard diploma, a special certificate, or a certificate of completion), their success in postsecondary education, and their employment status.

Determine former high school students' earnings based on their highest level of education attained: high school dropout, high school diploma, adult diploma, vocational, college credit vocational, associate's degree, bachelor's degree, or more than a bachelor's degree.

Compare how different student groups exited high school. In 1996, for example, 89,461 students earned a standard diploma; 2,329 earned a special diploma; 247 earned a special certificate; and 31,775 dropped out. For students with disabilities, those figures were 4,653; 2,262; 224; and 5,166, respectively.

Source: Jay J. Pleitter, Assistant Deputy Commissioner of Accountability, Research, and Measurement, Florida Department of Education, "Florida's Education Pipeline: ESE Students with Standard High School Diplomas," presentation to the Florida Legislature, January 16, 2006.

## Accountability

**States should publicly report on student progress and success from high school through postsecondary education.**

To be effective in improving college readiness, states should establish student achievement objectives that require the educational systems to collaborate to achieve them. Schools, colleges, and universities should be held accountable for improving student performance from high school to college completion.

The public reporting of student progress and achievement across educational levels is crucial to the development of collaborative efforts to advance student-readiness reforms. Requiring educational institutions to report data to state departments of education, however, will not suffice in making the systems more accountable for student achievement. States need to work with educational leaders to develop clear student achievement targets that will require K–12 and postsecondary systems to achieve them jointly. Ultimately, the primary outcomes for state accountability systems should become the percentage of the young population completing high school prepared for college (college readiness); the percentage enrolling in college (participation and access); the percentage staying in college (persistence), and the percentage graduating (completion). In addition, key indicators at various stages can include, for example, high school graduation and transfers from community colleges to four-year institutions.

Although no state has instituted a comprehensive accountability system focused on improving college readiness and success, several states have developed accountability elements linking K–12 and higher education. Kentucky's accountability system for postsecondary education offers a promising example.

## Kentucky's Accountability System for Postsecondary Education

In 1997, the Kentucky Legislature passed the Postsecondary Education Improvement Act of 1997 (House Bill 1). In addition to establishing goals for the state's system of postsecondary education (see sidebar), the legislation charged the Council on Postsecondary Education with developing an accountability system to "ensure institutions' compliance with the strategic plan and to measure educational quality and student progress in the postsecondary education system; research and service opportunities; and use of resources by institutions."[46] To address this charge, the council developed a public agenda focusing on accountability, degree completion, and affordability of postsecondary and adult education through 2010.

The state's accountability system was developed around the following key questions:

- Are more Kentuckians ready for postsecondary education?
- Is Kentucky postsecondary education affordable to its citizens?
- Do more Kentuckians have certificates and degrees?
- Are college graduates prepared for life and work in Kentucky?
- Are Kentucky's people, communities, and economy benefiting?[47]

The council developed state-level indicators for each question and outlined related benefits. For example, to answer the first question regarding college readiness, the council has required that the following data be collected:

- K–12 student achievement (average ACT);
- the percentage of high school students scoring a three or higher on Advanced Placement exams;
- the percentage of incoming Kentucky high school graduates not requiring remediation in math and English; and
- the number of Kentuckians earning general equivalency diplomas (GEDs).[48]

By including indicators for college readiness in its accountability system for postsecondary education, Kentucky has set high expectations for collaborative work between K–12 schools and colleges and universities to improve student achievement. There is evidence that the reform efforts may be improving student success in college (see sidebar).

## The Challenges Ahead

The policies recommended in this report do not exhaust the range of steps that states may need to consider. For example, K–16 governance commissions can assist in initiating and maintaining state action in the four policy areas. Creating these entities, however, is not sufficient in itself. In some cases, statewide K–16 bodies have become little more than discussion forums—deflecting energy from policy changes and sometimes even exacerbating tensions between K–12 and postsecondary leaders. To be effective, K–16 commissions should be charged with substantive responsibilities in such areas as alignment and coordinating the development of data and accountability systems; they

| Kentucky's Goals for Postsecondary Education | Indicators of Kentucky's Improvement in Postsecondary Education |
|---|---|
| Provide an integrated system of postsecondary education to enhance job opportunities and the quality of life for Kentucky's residents. | Undergraduate students enrollment increased from 160,926 In 1998 to 205,882 in 2005. |
| Raise the level of national recognition for state's flagship universities. | By 2004, 82% of adults ages 25 or order had a high school diploma or a GED, up from 78% in 1998. |
| Promote cooperation among postsecondary institutions in order to increase access. | At public universities in 2004, 44% of students gradated within six years of enrolling in college up from 37% in 1998. |
| Design a community and technical college system to improve access. | After the development of the Kentucky Community and Technical College System, enrollment grew from 52,201 in 2000 to 81,990 in 2004. |
| Increase the efficiency, responsiveness, quality, and quantity of postsecondary education services. | The Research Challengers Trust Fund spent $350 million on postsecondary education from 1997 to 2003, enabling the University of Kentucky and the University of Louisville to hire dozens of new professors. |
| Source: http://cpe.ky.gov/NR/rdonlyres/ 04F25118-4FBB-4C8A-8D1B-4197EA4CEAEA/ 0/SummaryHB1_20050401.pdf | Source: http://www.highereducation.org/ crosstalk/ct0405/news0405-kentucky.shtml. |

should be provided the requisite resources; they should have sufficient influence and authority to make real change; and they should be held accountable for their own performance.

Improving collaboration among state agencies and among state legislative committees can also be important in developing effective state policies for K–16, particularly since most states have created regulatory and governing frameworks that perpetuate the divide between K–12 and postsecondary education. In addition, adopting legislation that outlines elements of K–16 reform appears to be useful in creating the conditions for change, but is not sufficient in itself.*

Engaging in reforms suggested by this report necessarily involves political as well as educational challenges. States may struggle with how to involve the governor or the appropriate legislative committees, and how to sustain the reforms after leaders leave office. Each state's responses to these challenges will be unique, tempered by historical context, political culture, and the educational and other resources that are available. Nonetheless, no state's political or educational context creates insurmountable hurdles to this agenda. Challenges await, but the appropriate policy levers are available to each state, and each state must determine how best to implement them.

## Conclusion

In many ways, the United States produces the college outcomes that its systems of education were designed to produce. Its K–12 system was developed to provide education to everyone; its college and university system was developed when only a few were expected to attend college. Today, the vast majority of high school students aspire to attend college, but only about half of the students who enroll in college are prepared for college-level academic work. And less than 40% of the young workforce (ages 25 to 34) has a postsecondary degree.[49] The era of providing postsecondary education for only a small group of students is over; yet our state educational policies remain locked in a former era.

As the entities that perform the major funding and policy-setting functions for education, states are in the unique position to claim common ground between K–12 and postsecondary education. This report identifies four state policy dimensions to advance college readiness and success: the alignment of coursework and assessments; state finance; statewide data systems; and accountability. By developing and coordinating their policies in each of these areas, states can require and assist schools, colleges, and universities in working together toward a common goal—to significantly increase the number of students graduating from high school and completing college-level education and training—and thereby advance the educational achievement of millions of young Americans.

---

\* For example, Georgia passed legislation mandating that a statewide P–16 council meet on a regular basis. The council made progress under former Governor Roy Barnes, but has not met under Governor Sonny Perdue.

# Appendix

## A Sample Unified Performance-Based Budget for Preschool to Grade 20

### Developed for Oregon by the Oregon Business Council Based on the 2002–03 School Year

## A Sample Unified Performance-Based

### Developed for Oregon by the Oregon

| Program | # of FTE* Students Served | Estimated Expenditures Per FTE* Student Served | | | | |
|---|---|---|---|---|---|---|
| | | State | Local | Federal and Other Grants | Tuition and Fees | Total |
| **K–20 Stand-Alone Programs** | | | | | | |
| Pre-Kindergarten/Head Start | 10,026 | $3,287 | $0 | $4,683 | $1 | $7,971 |
| Early Intervention for Children Ages 0 to 5 Years Old | 7,158 | $4,196 | $2,171 | $1,030 | $10 | $7,407 |
| Grades K–5 Regular Instruction, Administration, and Support | 241,344 | $3,341 | $1,729 | $696 | $254 | $6,020 |
| Grades 6–8 Regular Instruction, Administration, and Support | 131,443 | $3,162 | $1,636 | $665 | $287 | $5,751 |
| Grades 9–12 Regular Instruction, Administration, and Support | 166,162 | $3,429 | $1,774 | $762 | $493 | $6,459 |
| Alternative Education Programs | 7,363 | $3,747 | $1,939 | $1,510 | $80 | $7,276 |
| Special Education Outside the Regular Education Setting for Students with Severe Disabilities | 8,862 | $10,635 | $5,503 | $4,663 | $289 | $21,090 |
| Remedial Programs / Developmental Education | 18,613 | $1,697 | $704 | $530 | $901 | $3,831 |
| Community College: Lower Division and Professional Training | 74,084 | $1,951 | $809 | $628 | $1,036 | $4,424 |
| OUS: Lower-Division Baccalaureate | 23,058 | $2,923 | $0 | $306 | $3,560 | $6,789 |
| OUS: Upper-Division Baccalaureate | 33,072 | $4,080 | $0 | $468 | $4,776 | $9,324 |
| OUS: Graduate Programs | 13,413 | $6,319 | $0 | $783 | $7,131 | $14,233 |
| OUS: Professional Programs | 1,136 | $9,377 | $0 | $1,212 | $10,347 | $20,936 |
| **K–20 Supplements to Regular Education** (Students included below are enrolled in a stand-alone program listed above) | | | | | | |
| Special Education within the Regular Education Settings for Students with Mental and Physical Disabilities | 63,010 | $2,745 | $1,420 | $929 | $62 | $5,157 |
| English as a Second Language | 49,580 | $860 | $445 | $120 | $16 | $1,440 |
| K–12 Student Transportation: Regular Students | 467,077 | $194 | $100 | $13 | $6 | $313 |
| K–12 Student Transportation: Special Education Students | 71,872 | $366 | $189 | $22 | $4 | $580 |
| Student Assistance Commission Undergraduate Need Grant** | 17,340 | $960 | $0 | $0 | $0 | $960 |
| **GRAND TOTAL** | | | | | | |

\* FTE = Full-time-equivalent.

\*\* Figures for this row are based on the 2000–01 school year.

Note: This table was developed by the Oregon Business Council based on the educational expenditures by K–12 and postsecondary education for the 2002–03

Source: Duncan Wyse, President, Oregon Business Council, "Thinking K–16 for State Budgets," presentation at "State Policy Dimensions for K–16 Reform," Wing

# Budget for Preschool to Grade 20

## Business Council (Based on 2002-03)

| Total State and Local Government Investment | Examples of Performance Expectations |
|---|---|
| $32,951,819 | XX% of students show learning gains in literacy, language, mathematics, science, creative arts |
| $45,574,948 | XX percentage point reduction in the proportion of K–12 students identified as needing special education |
| $1,223,620,032 | XX% of students with math and reading learning gains in grades 3–5; XX% of students proficient in reading, math, and writing in grades 3 and 5 |
| $630,757,207 | XX% of students with math, reading, and writing learning gains in grades 5–8; XX% of students proficient in reading, math, and writing in grade 8 |
| $864,494,052 | XX% of students with math, reading, and writing learning gains in grades 9–10; XX% of students proficient in reading, math, and writing in grade 10; XX% graduation rate among incoming 9th graders |
| 41,865,695 | Alternative schools held to grade-specific outcomes described above |
| $143,017,714 | Reduce achievement gap between students with and without severe disabilities by XX% while raising achievement of both groups |
| $44,678,297 | XX% of students complete remediation and take lower-division courses or professional training; XX% of Adult Basic Education students earn literacy completion points |
| $204,497,342 | XX% of entering AA students complete degree; XX% of AA graduates earn greater than $XX/hour; XX% of students graduate within 2 years and transfer to university or enter workforce |
| $67,402,920 | XX% 2nd year retention of incoming freshmen |
| $134,919,418 | XX% 4th year retention of incoming freshman; XX% graduate on time; XX% of graduates with employment earning greater than $XX/hour |
| $84,754,666 | XX = number of masters and doctoral degrees within 4 years |
| $10,652,286 | XX% of first-time entrants graduate; XX% of graduates obtain professional licenses |
| $262,465,097 | Reduce achievement gap between students with and without disabilities by XX% while raising achievement of both groups; graduate XX% of students from special education status |
| $64,698,630 | XX% make progress on ACTFL; XX% of Level XX students exiting from ESL within XX months |
| $137,288,868 | Provide safe and reliable access to school while improving student attendance |
| $39,876,441 | Provide safe and reliable access to school while improving student attendance |
| $16,646,400 | Share of low-income students attending OUS institutions equals XX percent |
| $4,050,161,832 | |

school year
spread Conference Center, September 13, 2005.

## Endnotes

1. Additional joint publications include *The Learning Connection: New Partnerships Between Schools and Colleges* (2001); *Gathering Momentum: Building the Learning Connection Between Schools and Colleges* (2002); *Betraying the College Dream: How Disconnected Systems Undermine Student Aspirations* (2003); and *From High School to College: Improving Opportunities for Success in Postsecondary Education* (2004).

2. National Center for Public Policy and Higher Education, "Income of U.S. Workforce Projected to Decline if Education Doesn't Improve," in *Policy Alert* (San Jose, CA: Nov. 2005).

3. Organisation for Economic Co-operation and Development (OECD), *Education at a Glance* (Paris, France: 2004).

4. Patrick Kelly, *As America Becomes More Diverse: The Impact of State Higher Education Inequality* (Boulder, CO: National Center for Higher Education Management Systems, 2005).

5. Andrea Venezia, Michael Kirst, and Anthony Antonio, *Betraying the College Dream: How Disconnected K–12 and Postsecondary Education Systems Undermine Student Aspirations* (Stanford, CA: Bridge Project, Stanford Institute for Higher Education Research, 2003).

6. National Center for Education Statistics, *The Condition of Education* (Washington, D.C.: U.S. Department of Education, 2001), p. 148.

7. National Center for Public Policy and Higher Education, *Measuring Up 2004* (San Jose, CA: 2004), www.highereducation.org.

8. Anthony Carnevale and Donna Desrochers, *Standards for What? The Economic Roots of K–16 Reform* (Princeton, NJ: Educational Testing Service, 2003), http://www.ets.org/research/dload/standards_for_what.pdf.

9. National Center for Public Policy and Higher Education, *Measuring Up 2000, Measuring Up* 2002, and *Measuring Up 2004* (San Jose, CA: 2000, 2002, 2004), www.highereducation.org.

10. OECD, *Education at a Glance.*

11. Carnevale and Desrochers, *Standards for What?*

12. National Center for Public Policy and Higher Education, "Income of U.S. Workforce Projected to Decline."

13. Tom Mortenson, "Postsecondary Education Opportunity," Nov. 2004, No. 149, p. 10.

14. Michael Kirst and Andrea Venezia (eds.), *From High School to College: Improving Opportunities for Success in Postsecondary Education* (San Francisco: Jossey Bass, 2004).

15. National Center for Public Policy and Higher Education, "The Educational Pipeline: Big Investment, Big Returns," in *Policy Alert* (San Jose, CA: April 2004).

16. National Center for Education Statistics, Common Core Data, "IPEDS 2002 Fall Enrollment Survey" and "IPEDS 2002 Graduation Rate Survey," Early Release Data (Washington, D.C.: U.S. Department of Education, 2002).

17. R. D. Kahlenberg, *America's Untapped Resource; Low Income Students in Higher Education* (New York: Twentieth Century Fund, 2004).

18. National Center for Education Statistics, "Enrollment in Postsecondary Institutions" and "Financial Statistics Fiscal Year 2002" (Washington, D.C.: U.S. Department of Education, Fall 2002).

19. Kirst and Venezia (eds.), *From High School to College.*

20. National Center for Education Statistics, *The Condition of Education,* p. 148.

21. The Education Trust, "Ticket to Nowhere. The Gap Between Leaving High School and Entering College and High Performance Jobs," in *Thinking K–16,* Vol. 3, Issue 2 (Washington, D.C.: Fall 1999).

22. http://www.act.org/news/releases/2003/pdf/english.pdf.

23. Venezia, Kirst, and Antonio, *Betraying the College Dream.*

24. Maria Sacchetti, "Colleges Question MCAS Success: Many in State Schools Still Need Remedial Help," *Boston Globe,* June 26, 2005.

25. http://www.calstate.edu/eap/.

26. David Spence, Executive Vice Chancellor Emeritus, California State University, "Early Assessment Academic Preparation Initiative," presentation at "State Policy Dimensions for K–16 Reform," Wingspread Conference Center, September 12, 2005.

27. Ibid.

28. http://www.calstate.edu/eap/.

29. Spence, "Early Assessment Academic Preparation Initiative."

30. Ibid.

31. Duncan Wyse, President, Oregon Business Council, "Oregon Public Education: A 'System' in Need of Direction (And Why the Budget is the Key Tool)," presentation at "State Policy Dimensions for K–16 Reform," Wingspread Conference Center, September 13, 2005.

32. Duncan Wyse, President, Oregon Business Council, "Governing the Enterprise Pre-K–20: Oregon Is Poised to Adopt a New Vision and a New Structure to Meet 21st Century Demands for More and Better Education," presentation to the Oregon Business Council, Portland, Oregon, 2005.

33. Ibid.

34. Wyse, "Oregon Public Education: A 'System' in Need of Direction."

35. Ibid.

36. Ibid.

37. Ibid.

38. Edward St. John, Jacob Gross, Glenda Musoba, and Anna Chung, *A Step Toward College Success: Assessing Attainment among Indiana's Twenty-first Century Scholars* (Indianapolis: Lumina Foundation for Education, 2005), http://www.luminafoundation.org/publications/CollegeSuccess.pdf.

39. Phone conversation with Dennis Obergfell, State Student Assistance Commission, Aug. 2, 2005.

40. St. John, Gross, Musoba, and Chung, *A Step Toward College Success.*

41. Stanley Jones, Commissioner of Higher Education, State of Indiana, "Access to Higher Education in Indiana," presentation at "State Policy Dimensions for K–16 Reform," Wingspread Conference Center, September 12, 2005.

42. Ibid.

43. St. John, Gross, Musoba, and Chung, *A Step Toward College Success.*

44. http://edwapp.doe.state.fl.us/doe/EDW_Facts.htm.

45. Phone conversation with Jay J. Pfeiffer, Assistant Deputy Commissioner of Accountability, Research, and Measurement, Florida Department of Education, January 27, 2006.

46. http://cpe.ky.gov/NR/rdonlyres/04F25118-4FBB-4C8A-8DlB-4197EA4CEAEA/0/Summary HBl_20050401.pdf.

47. http://cpe.ky.gov/planning/5Qs/default.htm.

48. http://cpe.ky.gov/NR/rdonlyres/E88C6729-09CA-4DF4-BB34-CD6C34CBDD37/0/StateKI_Summary.pdf.

49. Kelly, *As America Becomes More Diverse.*

# Reluctant Partners, Problem Definition, and Legislative Intent: K-16 Policy for Latino College Success

MARICELA OLIVA

**Abstract:** *Improving access to college for Latinos and other underrepresented minorities is a serious policy dilemma, particularly in states where they constitute large and growing numbers of the college-age population. Latinos as a group face numerous obstacles to college attendance, including a lack of knowledge about college and how to get there, inadequate financial resources, and the absence of adequate adult guidance for navigating the college choice and enrollment process. This article describes the separation between K–12 and postsecondary education that contributes to Latino students' transition problems between levels. School-university collaboration and partnerships and early interventions activities have helped to mitigate such problems since the 1960s. A new form of interaction between levels, K-16 educational coordination, is described as a recent and increasingly popular policy strategy for addressing the problem. Texas is used to illustrate the development of such policy over five state legislative sessions and within the state's race-neutral context.*

**Resumen:** *Mejorar acceso a la universidad para Latinos y otras minorías con representación mínima es un dilema político serio, particularmente en estados donde aquellos constituyen un número creciente y grande de la población en edad universitaria. Como grupo, Latinos encaran obstáculos numerosos, incluyendo la falta de conocimiento universitario y de cómo llegar ahí, recursos financieros inadecuados, y la ausencia de guía adulta adecuada para navegar la selección universitaria y el proceso de admisión. Este manuscrito describe la separación entre la educación desde Jardín de Niños hasta Preparatoria y la educación universitaria, la cual contribuye a los problemas entre los niveles de transición de estudiantes Latinos. Colaboraciones entre escuelas y universidades, asociaciones, y actividades de intervención temprana han ayudado a mitigar dichos problemas desde los 60s. Aquí se describe una nueva forma de interacción entre los niveles, la coordinación educacional desde Jardín de Niños hasta universidad como estrategia política popular reciente la cual atiende al problema. Texas es usado para iluminar el desarrollo de tal política a través de cinco sesiones legislativas del estado y en el contexto estatal de raza neutral.*

**Keywords:** *policy; K-16 coordination; school-university collaboration*

*Journal of Hispanic Higher Education*, Vol.3, No.2, April 2004, 209-230
DOI: 10.1177/1538192704263574
© Sage Publications 2004

# The Problem

One of the most serious higher education policy dilemmas of the current era is how to improve access to college for underrepresented minority students (Attinasi, 1989; Center for Higher Education Policy Analysis [CHEPA], 2003; Fry, 2002; Immerwahr, 2003; Kezar, 2000a, 2000b; Rendón, Jalomo, & Nora, 2000). Studies (see, e.g., Texas Higher Education Coordinating Board [THECB], 2000a) reveal that not only is the total higher education participation rate for the growing number of Latino and African American students inadequate and disproportionately low, but the gap in the participation rate between Anglos and minorities is growing (THECB, 2000a). In Texas, for example, demographic data for years have pointed to explosive population growth within those student groups, particularly in the Latino community, that make the policy dilemma a difficult one. The growing gap in Texas resulted recently in part from a post-Hopwood policy context that prohibited the consideration of race for college admissions and scholarships (Hurtado & Cade, 2001; Tienda, Leicht, Sullivan, Maltese, & Lloyd, 2003). Before the 1996 Hopwood ruling and during the 1980s and early 1990s, steps had been taken to improve minority student access to college. However, Texas policy interventions, even before Hopwood, were attempting to redress prior segregation within the Texas higher education system that had historically worked against equitable access to postsecondary education (for more, see Oliva, 2002).

Other states with large and growing Latino populations—like California—did not have the same history of official and accepted segregation in the higher education sector that had been in effect in Texas, yet that does not mean they were immune from the discriminatory practices that had derived from and been institutionalized within universities due to mid-20th century social values and norms.[1] Before the *Brown v. Board of Education* ruling and the Civil Rights Act of 1964, admissions policies, curricular practices, and social norms had made overt discrimination in higher education against non-Anglos possible throughout the country (Olivas, 1989). Since those landmark rulings, California educators have attempted to respond to Latino and minority student underrepresentation in college. As in Texas, however, they have been hamstrung in recent years by policies (e.g., Proposition 204) that prohibit the use of race for college admissions.

Moreover, the shrinking size of the Anglo population, coupled with the persistent underrepresentation of minority and particularly Latino students in higher education, does not bode well for state higher education systems such as those in Texas, California, and Florida that depend on academically prepared, highly motivated, and well-supported high school graduates to fill college classrooms. The explosively growing minority college-age population across states foreshadows and portends seriously negative social and economic consequences (Murdoch et al., 2002) if participation rates among those groups do not increase. It is clear that if interventions are not developed that will increase the numbers of underrepresented, particularly Latino, students who are adequately prepared for college, attend, and graduate with a degree, the Latino college access problem in Texas and affected states threatens to become a state and potentially a national economic crisis.

In the sections that follow, I briefly discuss the emergence of K-16 educational coordination as an important strategy for addressing this problem, the development of K-16 educational coordination policy in Texas as one example of an effort to implement this strategy, and the implications of this policy innovation for the problem of Latino underrepresentation in college. Particular attention is given in each of these sections to the specific Texas context as an illustrative example.

# Related Factors From the Research Literature

A monograph of the CHEPA at the University of Southern California identifies nine "propositions for enabling students to get into a college or university" (Tierney, Corwin, & Colyar, in press, p. 1) that can be found in the research literature on college access and success. Those propositions to promote positive college outcomes include a rigorous academic curriculum; co-curricular activities; academic, college, and career counseling; mentoring; family and community engagement; peer support; incorporating students' cultures into early intervention efforts; the timing of interventions; and funding priorities. Although largely self-explanatory, these propositions nevertheless also make clear that not all are about what happens once a student arrives at and matriculates in college. Some of them are about incorporating the experiences and cultural/background attributes that students bring from home into the college preparation and attendance experience rather than asking them to separate from home communities to better integrate to the academic environment (Rendón et al., 2000; Tierney, 1992; Tinto, 1988). Furthermore, as Attinasi (1989) documented in his research with lst-year Mexican American college students, some of these categories have to do with the "getting ready" behavior of the students and their families. Getting ready activities occur before students attend college and can include anticipatory socializalion about what it means to attend and succeed in college as well as fraternal and mentor modeling, among other activities. Attinasi distinguished these activities from the "getting in" behaviors that have to do with succeeding in college once a student is admitted and matriculated. Getting in activities are further broken down as getting to know the campus social, academic, and physical geographies and as scaling down the institutional expanse of geographies to a more manageable size for effectively navigating the institution.

For Attinasi (1989), Rendón et al. (2000), and Tierney (1992) as for Tierney, Corwin, and Colyar (2003), student collegiate success can only be understood as the outcome of a series of events and actions that span a continuum on both sides of a college matriculation boundary. In this sense, collegiate success is as much about what happens with students from Kindergarten through high school as it is about what happens from the 1st year of college to baccalaureate graduation. This is no less true—indeed, I contend that it is especially true—for first-generation students such as the Mexican American students who are underrepresented in Texas institutions of higher education and nationally.

Nevertheless, college student access and success has only recently been explicitly articulated in terms of the continuum of activities from Kindergarten through college (see, e.g., Callan, 1998, and Haycock, 1998). In the research literature, for example, although attention had been given to students' academic preparation in high school, the emphasis was on explaining or understanding variable postsecondary student success. Rarely did such a review of precollegiate events contend with the question of how K–12 and higher education can better support student collegiate success or how they might be reconceptualized to do so. Instead, the division between levels and the commensurate focus by practitioners and researchers on what happens with students within rather than across them is a socially and historically constructed practice and taken for granted belief about how education is done in the United States (Brubacher & Rudy, 1976). Furthermore, the fact that traditional activities at the K–12 and postsecondary levels were informed by distinct values, assumptions, and cultures compelled both scholars and educational practitioners to attend to one or the other but not to both levels.

## Texas Education Context

In Texas, as in most states, this bifurcated K–12 and postsecondary orientation to education has been enacted within the state organizational structure for education. Separate organizations are in charge of K–12 education (Texas Education Agency [TEA]) and of higher education (THECB).[2] Because each has its separate executive, board, and legislatively assigned functions, the work of these educational sectors often do not connect and sometimes even result in uncoordinated policies or approaches to the same problem, sometimes even aimed at different ends. Thus, rather than identify joint educational problems and solutions for them and align policy approaches, more time can be spent by the different sectors in blaming each other for educational outcomes.[3]

During the 1990s, several events occurred that highlighted the growing salience of the K–16 orientation within education agency and policy circles. The THECB created a whole new division, the Division of Educational Partnerships, to foster and support higher education and public school collaboration activity. Furthermore, the university systems of both the University of Texas and Texas A & M created administrative vice chancellorships for K-16 partnerships to promote the development of similar activity within their member institutions.

Since these early efforts, the THECB has established policy objectives to (a) increase the numbers of students prepared for and attending college in Texas by a total of 300,000 by the year 2015 and (b) increase the numbers of underrepresented (Mexican American and African American) students going to college to a level at parity with the college-going rate of Anglo students (THECB, 2000a). Through the policy initiative and master plan, titled *Closing the Gaps*, policy makers and practitioners seek to close the gaps in participation, success, excellence, and research among student groups and institutions in the state.

# Emergence of K-16 Coordination in Scholarship and Policy

A student-centered K-16 policy agenda responds to the first *Closing the Gaps* objective, that of increasing Latino and other underrepresented minority student access to and success in college. Depending on how one defines and understands interaction across the K–12 and higher education levels, such activity has been ongoing to varying degrees since the late 1960s. Haycock (1998), CHEPA (2002), and McLendon and Heller (2002) offered useful frameworks for thinking about K-16 interaction as both collaboration across education and social institutions and as related policy. The first of these, Haycock (1998) provides a historical scheme for understanding the existence and development of K-16 interaction that helps us to think of it in terms of changing social and organizational priorities. The second, CHEPA (2002), helps us to understand the scholarship and programmatic activity as early intervention on college-going that can take many forms. Finally, the third of these, McLendon and Heller, helps us to move from a traditional disciplinary understanding of educational practice (Wolverton, Kinser, Coaxum, Hyle, & Rusch, 2002) to our current focus on how such activity is reflected in, encouraged by, and increasingly mandated through policy.

Haycock (1998) contended that there have been three waves of "school-university collaboration" (her term for K-16 interaction) and that each of these has been characterized in particular ways. She situated the waves of partnership as occurring from 1965 to the present,[4] from 1980 to the present, and from 1990 to the present. Although the waves exist in a particular time frame and chronology, they are not sequential in that subsequent waves coexist with rather than supersede earlier ones. In this way, they can be thought of as discursive orientations to school-university partnerships that change as educators and policy makers prioritize such interactions in new ways.

The first wave, driven by higher education, was largely informational in nature and focused on activities that would help high school students to become more knowledgeable about college going and college attendance in order to improve student outcomes. The second wave shifts the focus from students to teachers, including the ways in which schools and universities can work to improve teacher preparation and, indirectly, student outcomes. A significant component of this second wave is attention to school and university reform to remove impediments to successful teacher preparation and student learning. In the third wave, Haycock contended that attention shifts to workforce preparation, such as that required by the reauthorization of the Carl Perkins Vocational and Applied Technology Education Act of 1990. This wave also adds business to the K-16 partnership, thus extending partnership activity beyond educational institutions (Haycock, 1998) for the direct benefit of targeted students and, indirectly, for the benefit of the private sector and broader social communities.

Articulated technical and vocational programs such as 2+2 and 2+2+2 degree programs that were funded in the Perkins Act brought schools into partnership with community colleges and sometimes also with universities (American Vocational Association, 1990). These partnerships were an innovation on liberal arts-oriented interactions of earlier "waves" in that the focus was no longer on traditional academic programs and activities. The technical/vocational programs of this legislation were designed to enhance academic preparation of students destined primarily for the workforce, most of whom did not aspire to achieve baccalaureate degrees. The legislation asked institutions to develop programs specifically for targeted student groups of the legislation—those who were handicapped, had limited English proficiency, were educationally and economically disadvantaged, or were seeking occupational training that was nontraditional for their gender. Within this context and to that end, the federal policy makers encouraged and financially supported new interaction and dialogue across educational levels. The Perkins Act also funded research on how to improve outcomes for targeted students, which encouraged even research-oriented university faculty to become engaged by involving themselves with technical and vocational programming. Thus, educators in high schools, community colleges, and universities became engaged on common programmatic, student performance, and student outcomes issues beyond the traditional academic college preparation venues.

# Early Intervention Programs as K-16 Partnerships

Like others who focus on first-wave activities to help students better prepare for college (Kezar, 2000a, 2000b, 2000c; King, 2000; Perna, 2000a; Perna, Fenske, & Swail, 2000), CHEPA (2002) conceptualized K-16 interactions as early intervention for college. *Early intervention* is a term that is used to describe either ad hoc or systemic, organized or informal, primarily student-oriented activities designed as interventions to improve college outcomes while students are still enrolled in K–12 institutions. Although not exclusively, early interventions often focus on students who are not attending college in numbers proportional to their percentage of the college-age population. Early intervention programs can be funded at local, state, and/or federal levels, and a partial list includes Upward Bound, Upward Bound Mathematics and Science, National Early Intervention Scholarship Program, Gaining Early Awareness and Readiness for Undergraduate Programs (GEAR-UP), the Puente Project, the Futures Project, Early Academic Outreach, the University of Texas and Texas A & M University Outreach Program, the Eisenhower Mathematics and Science Program, and numerous other systemic partnerships that may not be as well known because they involve less well-known institutions or because they are limited to a particular state or region (see Timar, Ogawa, & Orillion, 2003).

Early intervention programs occur primarily at high school and sometimes at middle school levels. What makes them early is that from the perspective of college-level educators, they have to do with activities that occur before students actually enroll in college. Traditionally, college student service and student affairs support activities and interventions have been constructed as occurring once a student arrives on a college campus. This traditional approach has not tended to concern itself with whether or which students actually walk through the college gates. Implicitly, then, higher education administrators, faculty, and other practitioners working with early intervention programs focus on increasing and otherwise positively affecting the number and diversity of students who are prepared to enter college.

CHEPA (2002) contributed to our understanding of early intervention by presenting a model of such programs that makes evident necessary key components as well as the variety of options that are possible within each. In their model, key components of early intervention programs (i.e., the issues that program participants, designers, and evaluators should keep in mind) are the following:

- program characteristics, such as role and mission, service delivery process, the targeted population, the organizational infrastructure, primary funding sources, types of programs (whether dropout prevention, early identification of prospects, etc.), and program size and location;
- instructional components, such as academic services (preparatory or supplemental), nonacademic services (trips and cultural activities, social and motivation skills development, career guidance), and modes of delivery (in-school, afterschool or weekend, summer bridge); and
- desired outcomes, such as short-term outcomes (persistence, higher grade point average, improved study skills, college attendance, dropout prevention) and long-term outcomes (college graduation, academic preparation, development of self-regulated learning, and sociocultural development) to name a few (p. 11).

This model gives us a sense of how early intervention programs have been and can be organized. Furthermore, the variety of options evident in the model reflects the diversity of possibilities within the large number of such activities (see Haycock, 1998).

Unfortunately, there is not space here for a thorough description of second- and third-wave K-16 interactions within this article; however, a few brief comments on those will provide a rationale for deferring a discussion of those until another time. Second-wave partnerships are often discussed as reforms in teacher preparation that enabled the evolution of primarily classroom-centered teacher training at universities to school-centered and field-based training to improve preservice teacher candidate learning and to minimize attrition during the induction year. Training at field sites in this second wave was conducted not only by university faculty, some of whom had have been professionally removed from school teaching for several years, but also by master teachers from the schools. Because school-based teachers were addressing, on a day-to-day basis, the problems and dilemmas of teacher practice, teacher preparation was strengthened and aligned better in this phase to the requirements of practice.

Third-wave partnerships, as described by Haycock (1998), have multiplied, and not simply with technical-vocational programs. Across the board, the participation of business and industry in educational work at both K–12 and higher education levels has increased and intensified. Business and corporate values are increasingly influential (Wallenfeldt, 1983) in higher education as stakeholders attempt to make higher education more cost efficient and subject to the organizational and management practices of business (Lucas, 1994; Nelson, 1997; Zumeta, 2001). This is often attractive to a lay public and to policy makers but has been less of a priority for educators in higher education than the more traditional democracy, liberal arts, and faculty governance "narratives" (Birnbaum, 2001). In summary, a more extensive discussion of second- and third-wave K-16 partnerships, although potentially enlightening and fruitful, would take us away from the purpose here, which is to explore how K-16 partnerships and policies affect Latino student success in college academic programs.

## K-16 Education Coordination and High School to College Transition

Recent college access research has more closely investigated the interconnections between schools and universities with respect to its impact on college going. A key example of this research is that of the Bridge Project (Merchant, 2002; Venezia, Kirst, & antonio, 2001) at Stanford University and the discussion of school-university early intervention partnership programs, such as those lauded in a recent issue of the *ERIC Review*. The Stanford cross-state policy research investigated not only student preparation for college but also student and family knowledge of what it takes academically and financially to attend college as well as the college-going and success patterns of students from different demographic groups. These examples of K-16 research and scholarship make evident that the "seamless pipeline" is increasingly replacing a bifurcated and disjointed view of K–12 and higher education practice and policy as the most compelling image for educational policy and practice.

Situating their discussion of this image as one of both K-16 reform and of high school-to-college transition, McLendon and Heller (2002) explicitly connected the development of K-16 partnerships with emerging policy to support underrepresented student access and success in college, primarily through K-16 education reform. Like other authors, these scholars are increasingly concerned with the "gaping disjuncture between education reform efforts in the K–12 sector and the policies and practices of higher education systems" (McLendon & Heller, 2002, p. 2). For more on this, see also Haycock (1998), Merchant (2002), Timar et al. (2003), Venezia et al. (2003), and Wirthlin Worldwide (2002). Although McLendon and Heller (2002) agreed with scholars who view cross-level reform as a new and emergent policy strategy (see Usdan & Podmostko, 2001), they described policy developments throughout the country that are designed to facilitate students' transition from public to postsecondary education levels. Two of these policies— affordability policy and academic preparation and standards policy—reflect traditional access and early intervention activities that have been discussed and researched since the first wave of K-16 interactions. However, these authors also spent considerable time discussing a policy innovation—P-16 coordination and accountability measures—because it is emerging among policy makers as a favored mechanism for promulgating both education reform and improved student outcomes. They specifically discussed formal manifestations of P-16 educational coordination, including policies that, as of 2002, had institutionalized P-16 Councils in 18 states, not including Texas.

P-16 Councils are viewed as valuable in promoting reform and increased college access for several reasons. Organizations such as the P-16 Councils focus on educational issues that are not characterized by level but by timely and successful student movement from lower to higher grades, including college and graduate or professional schools. As such, they are not focused on the discrete issues and problems of K-12 or higher education systems and their contexts. Rather, the goal of P-16 Councils is to improve "student transitions between the primary, secondary, and higher education systems within a state" (McLendon & Heller, p. 14). Furthermore, once in place, they serve as structured organizations through which P-16 ideas, practices, programs, and policies are generated (for a rationale, see also Venezia et al., 2003). They become incubators and sustainers of

P-16 knowledge and serve as "another mechanism by which state governments . . . achieve comprehensive, systemic, and structural integration of the K–12 and higher education sectors" (McLendon & Heller, 2002, p. 15).

Four factors have been found to influence whether states develop policy around P-16 educational coordination and around formalized P-16 Councils. These include sociodemographic factors, political factors, intrastate policy diffusion, and specific state contexts. State contexts, however, have been found to be particularly important for the development of P-16 coordination mechanisms. Indeed, these scholars encourage other researchers to study "how state context influences the policy behavior of state governments and, more importantly for purposes of discussion, how context influences the probability and patterns of state involvement in the college transition policy arena" (McLendon & Heller, 2002, p. 18). From the perspective of these policy researchers, the state context is inextricably a factor in how students transition to college but also in the extent to which policy makers see P-16 policies and mechanisms as necessary to support it.

Besides McLendon and Heller (2002), other scholars and organizations view P-16 mechanisms as important strategies to address the student college access problem. Higher education policy makers contend that such mechanisms could encourage more academically prepared students who graduate from high school and apply to college but never enroll (Terenzini, et al., 2003) to actually attend college. In fact, estimates are that 20% of academically prepared students who apply to college never actually enroll (Terenzini, et al., 2003, p. 5). As a result, Callan (2001), Perna et al. (2000), the THECB (2000a, 2000b, 2000c) and Timar et al. (2003) promoted such mechanisms for improved minority student outcomes. However, the most compelling case for the implementation of P-16 policy strategies is in research by the Bridge Project at Stanford University.

In *Betraying the College Dream: How Disconnected K–12 and Postsecondary Education Systems Undermine Student Aspirations* (Venezia et al., 2003), the authors contended,

> Most states implicitly discourage K-16 policymakers by having separate K-16 and higher education legislative committees and state agencies. These structural barriers inhibit joint policymaking and communication for issues such as funding, data sharing, student learning (curriculum, standards, and assessment), matriculation and transfer, teacher training and professional development, and accountability. (p. 49)

The authors of this report contended that this discouragement contributes, in turn, to the development of college access and success problems and to poor outcomes that can only be remedied by greater educational coordination. Moreover, the lack of educational coordination across levels contributes to the existence of serious obstacles for students (and their families) as they attempt to enroll in college—problems such as multiple and confusing educational testing and assessment, disconnected curricula, and an overall lack of P-16 governance that results in no one being held accountable for poor outcomes.

Based on their research in six U.S. states, these researchers found that students, parents, and K–12 educators do not know enough about or understand higher education and its requirements. Stakeholders seriously miscalculate what it costs for college attendance, what it takes to prepare for and be admitted to college, and even where to go for authoritative and legitimate information about college. Most important, low socioeconomic status (SES), minority, and first-generation students are especially at risk from these problems given that they are already underrepresented in college and so are not likely to benefit from the college knowledge of parents or peers who have attended.

The authors made concrete recommendations to remedy the identified problems stemming from the disjuncture between education levels. Recommendations involve three main strategies, including (a) providing all stakeholders with good information about college and college expectations, (b) shifting the focus and attention of decision makers from elite colleges to broad access colleges attended by the majority of students, and (c) expanding the policy focus from college access to college retention.[5] They recommended that states create K-16 databases of student records so that policy makers can monitor progress and enhance accountability and that states create resource pools or grant programs as funding incentives for K-16 activity in schools and colleges. As in the research described above, researchers with the Bridge Project make apparent the emergence of K-16 coordination as a recognized strategy for improving educational outcomes, particularly for minority and low-SES students, and the extent to which the strategy has already been legitimated through enactment in numerous states.

The section that follows describes the development of P-16 educational coordination in Texas, particularly after the *Hopwood v. Texas* ruling. Sources of information for this legislative history and analysis include the Texas Legislature Online, which can be accessed at http://www.capitol.state.tx.us/, as well as THECB-produced analyses (THECB, 1997, 1999, 2001, 2003) highlighting the outcomes of 75th, 76th, 77th, and 78th Texas Legislatures. THECB reports are regularly produced by the agency immediately after completion of the biennial spring Texas legislative sessions.

Not surprisingly given the *Hopwood v. Texas* ruling in 1996, developing race-neutral strategies to improve minority student outcomes is evident as an especially compelling objective in Texas during several of these past sessions. Because such strategic policy interventions are race-neutral initiatives, they remain in force despite a repeal of the Hopwood ruling that was effected by the Supreme Court decision in *Grutter v. Bollinger* unless modified by new legislative action. School-university collaborations like these link educational institutions throughout the K-16 sector for improved student outcomes (Braskamp & Wergin, 1998; Corrigan, 2002; Kirst & Venezia, 2001; Venezia et al., 2003).

## 74th Texas Legislature (1995)

The 74th Texas legislative session took place 1 year before the *Hopwood v. Texas* ruling of 1996. Still able to do so, policy makers took race into account as they considered ways to improve and support minority student access to and retention in college. Proposed legislative interventions included studies of the number of women and minority administrators in higher education. However, the work on minority and underrepresented person involvement in higher education was occurring along traditional venues and pathways, that is, framed in the bifurcated K–12 or higher education agency and institution activity. Except for the modest preexisting venues for cross-level policy coordination that were already in place,[6] no mention was found of an innovative policy to promote active collaboration across institutional or agency education levels.

## 75th Texas Legislature (1997)

A key intervening event, the *Hopwood v. Texas* ruling of 1996, fundamentally altered the policy context by prohibiting the use of race in college admissions and in the awarding of scholarships. Partly for this reason, the 75th Texas Legislature expended considerable time and effort on the issue of minority student access to and degree completion in college and produced three educational coordination statutes. House Bill (HB) 588 for the first time mandated uniform undergraduate admissions criteria for colleges and universities in the state to guarantee that the top 10% of students graduating from high schools across the state were automatically admitted to public institutions of higher education. Because Texas is a demographically segregated state, this protected a baseline of minority participation in college during the race-neutral admissions and financial aid era. HB 2146 directed the THECB to study minority participation in higher education as well as the impact of the recent court rulings on enrollment targets by student group. Finally, Senate Bill (SB) 148 enacted a process to handle transfer disputes that occur when students move between institutions and is included on this list because it was about facilitating higher education participation and baccalaureate degree attainment for students.

## 76th Texas Legislature (1999)

During this session, a primary focus of the legislature regarding higher education continued to be how to respond to the changed policy environment in which race could no longer be used as a criterion for college admissions and for publicly funded financial aid. In contrast to the pre-Hopwood context in which many race-based access and success programs had been developed (see Oliva, 2002), policy makers were challenged to find effective race-neutral policy vehicles for increasing

Latino and minority college participation. Their efforts to do so were reflected in legislative highlights (THECB, 1999) regarding higher education.

Specifically, test-driven admissions criteria were viewed as negatively affecting minority student college admissions and enrollment. In the race-neutral environment, race could no longer be used as a criterion to balance this effect. Rider 18 of that year's state appropriations bill (SB 1) directed the THECB to report on alternative admissions criteria, their possible use, and their impact. HB 510 required school districts and their high schools to post information on automatic admissions to state colleges and universities provided for by HB 588 so that more students could learn about their, in some cases, new eligibility for access to public higher education institutions, including flagship institutions. HB 1678 required the THECB to develop a uniform strategy to identify, attract, retain, and enroll students that reflect the population of the state (THECB, 1999). Rider 37 of the state budget (SB 1) created the Economically Disadvantaged Student Retention Performance Fund to encourage institutions to achieve better outcomes with low-SES students. Because financial and other factors contribute to lower attendance, retention, and graduation of low-SES minority students—a large proportion of the overall minority student population (Murdoch et al., 2002)—these measures were designed to have an impact on minority student college outcomes without explicitly focusing on race. HB 713 created a new major grant program with two components to assist economically disadvantaged (and presumably minority) college students. The Texas Grant Program Toward Excellence, Access, and Success provided financial aid to students who graduated from a public or accredited private Texas high school and enrolled at a college in the state. Students with the greatest financial need were given priority for these funds. Eligibility was limited to students with the recommended or advanced high school curriculum. The Teach for Texas Conditional Grant Program provided grants to college juniors and seniors who agreed to enter the teaching profession in critical shortage fields. Beginning in the fall of 2001, only Texas grant recipients would be eligible for the Conditional Grant Program.

Between the 76th and 77th Texas legislative sessions, the THECB's (2000a) new master plan for Texas higher education, *Closing the Gaps by 2015*, was published and distributed statewide. The plan focused on and prioritized higher education efforts to address gaps in student participation in college, student retention in colleges and universities, higher education institutional excellence, and higher education research funds generated and expended by public colleges and universities in the state. This master plan documented national benchmarks for each of the objectives to make the case that improvement across these indicators was needed. The rationale for improvement on participation objectives was largely economic, with the state's changing demographics and the low higher education participation rate of minority students forecasting future economic hardship. Policy goals in the report were intended to avert the future economic problem for the state as a whole and were generally framed within predictions of state economic, business, and income stagnation and decline if minority student underrepresentation in college was not remedied through aggressive intervention and action.

## 77th Texas Legislature (2001)

The coordination of educational activities across THECB and TEA agencies gathered momentum during this legislative session, so much so that a section on P-16 initiatives was included in the Summary of Higher Education Legislation prepared by the THECB (2001). Furthermore, although the THECB identifies legislation that was filed in each session but did not pass, no P-16 legislation was reported as "failing to pass." The absence of failed legislation in this section indicates that strong legislative support for this policy innovation[7] was in place during 2001.

Under the P-16 rubric, five bills were developed and passed by the 77th Texas Legislature to formalize and prioritize K-16 educational coordination involving educational institutions subject to both the THECB and TEA. HB 400 mandated that high schools in the lowest decile of schools sending graduates to college work with local postsecondary education institutions to increase the number of their students who attend college. HB 1144 made the Recommended High School Curriculum the default curriculum to minimize misinformation about how to adequately prepare for college. The same bill also mandated that THECB and TEA create a P-16 record database to facilitate accountability across the K-16 and K-20 educational pipeline. SB 82 extended the dual enrollment option through which high school students get both college and high school credit for the same class. Limited to high school and university partnerships in prior years, the option was extended to community colleges by the statute. SB 158 required school counselors at elementary, middle, and high school levels to provide students and their families with information about college and the way to get there. SB 573 required the THECB to initiate a statewide public awareness campaign about college, the benefits of attending, and the ways to apply for admissions and financial aid.

Between the 77th and 78th legislative sessions, the Texas Sunset Advisory Commission reviewed the THECB as a state agency to determine whether there was an ongoing functional need for the agency within Texas state government. Staff of the commission also analyzed THECB agency operations to determine where activities could be eliminated, modified, and/or improved. A key recommendation of the commission was to formalize a P-16 Council that had recently begun operating informally at the staff level. Staff of the commission had learned that the purpose of the informal council was to bring staff members from the THECB and TEA together to discuss problems and issues spanning agency boundaries, to develop proposed action plans, to disseminate proposals for action to respective boards, and to promote sustained and collaborative action on joint issues. The commission report correctly pointed out that activities of the council seemed to duplicate some functions of the Joint Advisory Committee (JAC), a unit that had been in statute since 1985. However, in contrast to the evidence about the informal P-16 Council, evidence indicated to commission staff that the JAC was not operating as effectively. They proposed eliminating the JAC and creating a formal charge in statute for the P-16 Council to ensure its long-term effectiveness. In making their recommendation to create a P-16 Council, the commission noted the existence of functioning P-16 Councils in approximately half of the states.[8] They argued that the continued existence of the informal Texas P-16 Council would be threatened by changes in agency leadership until the council was institutionalized. They further recommended that board-to-board communication among THECB, TEA, and other agency board members—which had been facilitated by JAC when it was operating effectively—be continued through biennial governing conferences of board members.

## 78th Texas Legislature (2003)

During the 78th Texas Legislature, the Supreme Court of the United States was considering the *Gratz v. Bollinger* and *Grutter v. Bollinger* cases regarding the use of race as a criterion for higher education admissions. Notwithstanding this, Texas had been operating in a race-neutral environment since the 1996 Hopwood ruling, and legislative activity regarding access to higher education continued in a race-neutral vein.

The THECB (2003) report highlighting legislative activity from this session again included a P-16 Initiatives section on its contents page. Several P-16 initiatives were found in SB 286, a bill centered on THECB agency operations that responded to the Sunset Advisory Commission recommendations for the agency. Specifically, THECB governance was streamlined by cutting the number of board members in half; in addition, staff members were charged to closely monitor the *Closing the Gaps* plan, institutional performance data (including enrollment by ethnicity) were required to be made publicly available beginning in 2003, the agency was instructed to "approve" and oversee a common course numbering process that had been voluntarily in place to facilitate transfer, the sale of promotional items for the College for Texans campaign was authorized, and the P-16 Council was formalized in statute. After transferring JAC responsibilities to the new staff-level P-16 Council, the board-level JAC was repealed in the Texas Education Code. A key achievement of this session is that informal K-16 educational coordination was institutionalized in statute, thus formalizing and legitimating the strategy as a viable and appropriate (for the Texas context) race-neutral mechanism for addressing state higher education access and retention goals that had been prioritized in *Closing the Gaps*.

## Discussion and Conclusion

This review of K-16 educational coordination policy development in Texas through the five most recent Texas legislative sessions foregrounds the significance for the state of several policy influencers over time. Those include vestiges of the state's history of segregation, the state's growing Latino and other minority student populations, state population demographic changes that make minority student populations increasingly important to the health of the higher education system and state economy, and the 1996 *Hopwood v. State of Texas* ruling that created a policy context prohibiting the use of race in higher education admissions and financial aid processes from 1996 to 2003. The post-Hopwood context was not a positive one for policy makers attempting to meet state policy goals given that the constraints against the use of race made it difficult to directly address the state's priorities and objectives regarding racially defined groups. For example, with respect to student higher education participation rates, the THECB goal was to increase the overall state participation rate from 5% to 5.7% by 2015. This overall goal was benchmarked to participation levels of peer states, several of which had higher state-level participation rates than the participation rate in Texas. However, notwithstanding the state's race-neutral context after Hopwood, to accomplish the overall 5.7% participation goal, state policy makers knew that they had to not only increase the participation rate of Latino students in higher education but do so at dramatically higher numbers than the numbers for African American and Anglo students. The reason for this was that population growth estimates already projected that Latinos would make up approximately 40% of the population by 2015 and that together, the Latino and African American populations would be a majority of the state by that time. When higher education enrollment increases across groups were projected in the *Closing the Gaps* plan (THECB, 2000a), participation targets were considerably different for each group. That plan estimated that to achieve state participation goals by 2015, college enrollment would have to increase by 35,000 Anglo-American students, 19,300 African American students, and 120,000 Latino students (THECB, 2000a). Thus, the growth in the Latino college enrollment would have to almost quadruple the growth for the largest current college participation group, Anglo students, for participation rates of each to reach 5.7%. Provocatively, this enrollment increase for Latino students alone implies an increased enrollment capacity need at colleges and universities equivalent in size to four flagship universities.

Despite the clear need to make progress on state goals to improve college going for Latinos and African Americans, the Hopwood ruling of 1996 razed existing race-based programming and policy that had been in place and prohibited the development of new race-based policy. This compelled Texas policy makers from the 75th through 78th Legislatures (1997-2003) to become creative in constructing race-neutral interventions to address state objectives. In a number of cases, they were inventive by creating a percent plan (HB 588) for admission that was intended to protect a baseline of minority enrollment in the state's colleges and universities. Despite its innovativeness and its diffusion into other states, the percent plans were inadequate without other race-based criteria to meeting Texas participation and diversification goals. For example, whereas the state's percent plan for enrollment protected a baseline enrollment given the state's geographic population segregation, it was not flexible enough to account for growth in the minority student population reflected in the differential enrollment participation targets by group (for more on percent plans, see American Council of Education, 2001; Stern, 2003; Tienda et al., 2003).

In the post-Hopwood race-neutral policy environment, Texas higher education policy makers seem to have settled on K-16 education coordination as a race-neutral means for achieving Latino and minority student participation goals. As we have seen, scholars have identified a lack of college information, parent and adult guidance, misinformation, and the lack of K-16 accountability for outcomes as obstacles to Latino higher education participation. Policy diffusion and earlier waves of school-university collaboration had made K-16 educational coordination available as an established strategy for addressing these problems, and Texas policy makers increasingly focused on the development of such policies as a remedy. Evidence indicates that because this strategy is also race neutral, it became the key means through which joint dialogue, concrete action, and accountability to meet state minority participation goals was increasingly organized in Texas.

Now that the *Hopwood v. State of Texas* ruling has been superseded by the Supreme Court ruling in *Grutter v. Bollinger* (Chemerinsky et al., 2003), the policy and higher education context for the state is no longer race neutral. State universities and policy makers are currently debating whether to use race in admissions, and the public dialogue has already resulted in the elimination of a legacy program at one state institution. Namely, Texas A & M University, the state's land grant university, in 2003 was the only Texas public institution with a legacy admissions program. Despite the fact that the University of Texas–Austin and Rice University announced a return to affirmative action in college admissions, Texas A & M University executives determined and publicly announced that they would not use race as a factor for admissions. The decision to nonetheless keep the legacy admissions program that primarily benefited Anglo students produced a public outcry from legislators and stakeholder groups throughout the state. The legacy program was eliminated shortly afterwards to remain consistent with the "merit" rationale given for not using race in admissions. Texas institutions and policy makers will continue to adjust local policy in light of the Supreme Court ruling, and discussions about how best to respond while addressing state objectives are bound to generate a frenzy of new legislative and policy action to improve Latino and minority participation in college. It remains to be seen whether the growing interest in P-16 accountability such as that supported by the development of a K-16 records database in Texas will be enough to sustain P-16 educational coordination as a key strategy for meeting state minority higher education participation goals.

## Notes

1. For more on how this was shaped by Plessy vs. Ferguson (163 US 538 [1896]) legal doctrine, see Teddlie and Freeman (2002).

2. Until the mid-1960s, there was only one agency for both K–12 and higher education. However, because there were vastly more school districts than postsecondary institutions in the state, policy makers concluded that higher education was not being given the attention that it deserved to support state objectives. Under the gubernatorial administration of John Connolly, the unified agency was separated into two entities during 1965.

3. I was Texas Higher Education Coordinating Board staff liaison from 1991 to 1994 to an early educational coordination entity, the Joint Advisory Committee. In that capacity, I facilitated the development of strong interagency and personal relationships among members so that they could move from their or constituents' defensive postures to addressing cross-level outcomes. Defining and addressing joint problems for action was a task to which Joint Advisory Committee members were strongly committed.

4. Perna, Fenske, and Swail (2000) also described K-16 collaborations as existing since the 1960s.

5. Fry (2002). Immerwahr (2003), Wirthlin Worldwide (2002), and others have pointed out that both Latino students and parents value higher education as the means for social advancement and so aspire at high levels to attend. However, financial and other obstacles cause Latinos to leave college at disproportionately high levels.

6. In 1985, the Joint Advisory Committee of the Texas Higher Education Coordinating Board and the State Board of Education was enacted by legislation. The primary function of this committee of board members from the two educational agencies was to determine the distribution of federal technical and vocational education funds. Shortly thereafter, in 1989, the legislature enacted Section 61.076 of the Texas Education Code. That section mandated coordination and cooperation between the two education agencies to "ensure that long-range plans and educational programs established by the boards complement the functioning of the entire system of public education." Over time, the responsibilities and membership of the Joint Advisory Committee changed. It was eliminated by statute during the 78th Texas Legislature (Texas Higher Education Coordinating Board, 2003); key responsibilities were assigned to a staff-level P-16 Council.

7. McLendon and Heller (2002) distinguished between policy innovations and policy inventions, with innovations being policy initiatives that are new to a particular context although they are in use elsewhere. Because P-16 initiatives were already in place in at least 18 states, implementation of a similar initiative in Texas is only an innovation.

8. This awareness of the existence of P-16 Councils elsewhere reflects "policy diffusion," which McLendon and Heller (2002) described as the tendency of states to implement policies that have been created or implemented elsewhere. In this case, the process resulted in the creation of a formal P-16 Council for Texas. In

other cases, such as with Texas's invention of percent plans for admission, the states of California and Florida implemented similar policy innovations.

# References

American Council of Education. (2001). *"Percent plans" for college admissions*. Washington, D.C.: Author.

American Vocational Association. (1990). *The AVA guide to the Carl D. Perkins Vocational and Applied Technology Education Act of 1990*. Alexandria, VA: Author.

Attinasi, L. C., Jr. (1989). Getting in: Mexican Americans' perceptions of university attendance and the implications for freshman year persistence. In C. Turner, M. Garcia, A. Nora, & L. Rendón (Eds.), *Racial and ethnic diversity in higher education* (pp. 189–209). New York: Simon & Schuster.

Birnbaum, R. (2001). *Management fads in higher education: Where they come from, what they do, why they fail*. San Francisco: Jossey-Bass.

Braskamp, L. A., & Wergin, J. F. (1998). Forming new social partnerships. In W. G. Tierney (Ed.), *The responsive university* (pp. 62–91). Baltimore: Johns Hopkins University Press.

Brubacher, J. S., & Rudy, W. (1976). Articulation of secondary and higher education. In J. S. Brubacher & W. Rudy (Eds.), *Higher education in transition: A history of American colleges and universities, 1636–1976* (pp. 241–263). New York: Harper & Row.

Callan, P. (1998). The role of state policy systems in fostering separation or collaboration. In P. M. Timpane & L. S. White (Eds.), *Higher education and school reform* (pp. 41–56). San Francisco: Jossey-Bass.

Callan, P. (2001). Reframing access and opportunity: Problematic state and federal higher education policy in the 1990s. In D. E. Heller (Ed.), *The states and public higher education policy* (pp. 83–99). Baltimore: Johns Hopkins University Press.

Center for Higher Education Policy Analysis. (2002). *Making the grade in college prep: A guide for improving college preparation programs*. Los Angeles: Author.

Center for Higher Education Policy Analysis. (2003). Asking questions of college preparation: Nine propositions. *The Navigator: Directions and Trends in Higher Education Policy, 2*(2), 1–2.

Chemerinsky, E., Days, D., Fallon, R., Karlan, P., Karst, K., Michelman, F., et al. (2003). *Reaffirming diversity: A legal analysis of the University of Michigan affirmative action cases*. Boston: Civil Rights Project at Harvard University.

Corrigan, D. (2002). The role of the university in community building. In Center for Higher Education Leadership, *Higher education as a field of inquiry: Informing the future* (pp. 128–141). College Station: Texas A & M University Center for Leadership in Higher Education.

Fry, R. (2002). *Latinos in higher education: Many enroll, too few graduate*. Washington, D.C.: Pew Hispanic Center.

Haycock, K. (1998). School-college partnerships. In P. M. Timpane & L. S. White (Eds.), *Higher education and school reform* (pp. 57–82). San Francisco: Jossey-Bass.

Hurtado, S., & Cade, H. W. (2001). Time for retreat or renewal? Perspectives on the effects of Hopwood on campus. In D. E. Heller (Ed.), *The states and public higher education policy* (pp. 100–120). Baltimore: Johns Hopkins University Press.

Immerwahr, J. (2003). *With diploma in hand: Hispanic high school seniors talk about their future*. San Jose, CA: National Center for Public Policy and Higher Education/Public Agenda.

Kezar, A. (2000a). Does it work? Research on early intervention. *ERIC Review, 8*(1), 9–12.

Kezar, A. (2000b). Putting it all together: An action plan. *ERIC Review, 8*(1), 39–40.

Kezar, A. (2000c). *Higher education trends (1997–1999): Administration*. Washington, D.C.: Office of Educational Research & Improvement.

King, J. E. (2000). Helping your child prepare for college. *ERIC Review, 8*(1), 24–31.

Kirst, M., & Venezia, A. (2001). Bridging the great divide between secondary schools and postsecondary education. *Phi Delta Kappan, 83*(1), 92–97.

Lucas, C. J. (1994). *American higher education: A history*. New York: St. Martin's Griffin.

McLendon, M. K., & Heller, D. E. (2002, May). *High school to college transition policy: Barriers to conducting cross-state comparative studies*. Paper presented at the Spencer Foundation-sponsored symposium, "Building Capacity for Educational Policy: Barriers to Conducting Cross-State Comparative Studies," Atlanta, GA.

Merchant, B. (2002). *The Bridge Project: Strengthening K-16 transition policies in Illinois*. Paper presented at the meeting of the University Council for Educational Administration, Pittsburg, PA.

Murdoch, S., White, S., Hoque, M. N., Pecotte, B., You, X., & Balkan, J. (2002). *A summary of the Texas challenge in the twenty-first century: Implications of population change for the future of Texas.* College Station: TAMU Center for Demographic and Socioeconomic Research and Education.

Nelson, C. (Ed.). (1997). *Will teach for food: Academic labor in crisis.* Minneapolis: University of Minnesota Press.

Oliva, M. (2002). Access to doctoral study for Hispanic students: The pragmatics of "race" in (recent) Texas history and policy. *Journal of Hispanic Higher Education, 1*(2), 158–173.

Olivas, M. (1989). *The law and higher education: Cases and materials on colleges in court.* Durham, NC: Carolina Academic Press.

Perna, L. (2000). Promoting college enrollment through early intervention. *ERIC Review, 8*(1), 4–9.

Perna, L. W., Fenske, R. H., & Swail, W. S. (2000). Sponsors of early intervention programs. *ERIC Review, 8*(1), 15–18.

Rendón, L., Jalomo, R. E., & Nora, A. (2000). Theoretical considerations in the study of minority student retention in higher education. In J. M. Braxton (Ed.), *Reworking the student departure puzzle* (pp. 127–156). Nashville, TN: Vanderbilt University Press.

Stern, G. M. (2003, May 14). Percent plans: Affirmative action mirage? *Hispanic Outlook in Higher Education, 13*(20), 13–15.

Teddlie, C., & Freeman, J. A. (2002). Twentieth-century desegregation in U.S. higher education: A review of five distinct historical eras. In W. A. Smith, P. G. Altbach, & K. Lomotey (Eds.), *The racial crisis in American higher education: Continuing challenges for the twenty-first century* (Rev. ed., pp. 77–99). Albany: State University of New York Press.

Terenzini, P., Strauss, L., Heller, D., Caffrey, H. S., Reason, R., & Reindl, T. (2003). *What works: Policy seminar on student success, accreditation and quality assurance.* University Park, PA: American Association of State Colleges & Universities and Pennsylvania State University Center for the Study of Higher Education.

Texas Higher Education Coordinating Board. (1997). *Summary of significant higher education legislation.* Austin, TX: Author.

Texas Higher Education Coordinating Board. (1999). *Summary of significant higher education legislation: 76th legislature.* Austin, TX: Author.

Texas Higher Education Coordinating Board. (2000a). *Closing the gaps: The Texas higher education plan.* Austin, TX: Author.

Texas Higher Education Coordinating Board. (2000b). *Report on alternative admissions criteria.* Austin, TX: Author.

Texas Higher Education Coordinating Board. (2000c). *Agency strategic plan for the fiscal years.* Austin, TX: Author.

Texas Higher Education Coordinating Board. (2001). *Summary of higher education legislation: 77th legislature.* Austin, TX: Author.

Texas Higher Education Coordinating Board. (2002). *Responses to staff report, Sunset Advisory Commission.* Austin, TX: Author.

Texas Higher Education Coordinating Board. (2003). *Summary of higher education legislation: 78th Texas legislature.* Austin, TX: Author.

Tienda, M., Leicht, K. T., Sullivan, T., Maltese, M., & Lloyd, K. (2003). *Closing the gap? Admissions & enrollments at the Texas public flagships before and after affirmative action.* Retrieved January 21, 2003, from http://www.texastop10.princeton.edu/publications/tienda012103.pdf

Tierney, W. G. (1992). An anthropological analysis of student participation in college. *Journal of Higher Education, 63*(6), 603–618.

Tierney, W. G., Corwin, Z. B., & Colyar, J. E. (Eds.). (in press). *From high school to college: Evaluating access.* Albany, NY: SUNY Press.

Timar, T. B., Ogawa, R., & Orillion, M. (2003). Expanding the University of California's outreach mission. *Review of Higher Education, 27*(2), 187–209.

Tinto, V. (1988). Stages of student departure: Reflections on the longitudinal character of student leaving. *Journal of Higher Education, 59*(4), 438–455.

Usdan, M. D., & Podmostko, M. (2001). *The legislative status of K–12 and higher education relationships.* Washington, D.C.: Institute for Educational Leadership.

Venezia, V., Kirst, M. W., & antonio, a. l. (2003). *Betraying the college dream: How disconnected K–12 and postsecondary education systems undermine student aspirations.* Palo Alto, CA: Stanford Institute for Higher Education Research.

Wallenfeldt, E. C. (1983). *American higher education: Servant of the people or protector of special interests?* Westport, CT: Greenwood Press.

Wirthlin Worldwide. (2002). *Texas higher education coordinating board literature review* (for the College for Texans Campaign). South Jordan, UT: Wirthlin.

Wolverton, M., Kinser, K., Coaxum, J., Hyle, A., & Rusch, E. (2002). *Navigating borders: Intentional talk between higher education and educational administration faculty.* Paper presented at the Association for the Study of Higher Education, Sacramento, CA.

Zumeta, W. (2001). Public policy and accountability in higher education: Lessons from the past and present for a new millennium. In D. E. Heller (Ed.), *The states and public higher education policy* (pp. 155–197). Baltimore: Johns Hopkins University Press.

*Maricela Oliva, Ph.D., is an assistant professor of higher education at Texas A & M University. A native of Texas, she has more than 18 years of administration and policy experience in the state, including with the Texas Higher Education Coordinating Board.*

# A Typology of Federal and State Programs Designed to Promote College Enrollment

## Laura W. Perna, Heather Rowan-Kenyon, Angela Bell, Scott L. Thomas and Chunyan Li

Over the past four decades, policymakers have developed numerous policies and programs with the goal of increasing college enrollment. A simple Google search of the phrase "college access program" generates 226,000,000 hits. Entering the same terms into the search engine on the U.S. Department of Education's Web site generates 500 hits.

Despite the apparent plentitude of policies and programs, however, college access and choice for recent high school graduates remain stratified by socioeconomic status and race/ethnicity (Thomas & Perna, 2004). Young people from low-income families and whose parents have not attended college, as well as those of African American and Hispanic descent, are less likely than other young people to enroll in college. When they do enroll, these students find themselves concentrated in lower-priced institutions, such as public two-year colleges and less-selective four-year colleges and universities (Baum & Payea, 2004; Ellwood & Kane, 2000; National Center for Education Statistics [NCES], 2003, 2004; Thomas & Perna, 2004).

Despite a dramatic expansion of higher education enrollments over the past three decades (NCES, 2004), persisting gaps in participation suggest that existing policies and programs are not accomplishing their underlying goals. Efforts to understand why policies and programs are not working are hampered by the absence of a framework for organizing the myriad efforts designed to reduce participation gaps and, by extension, for demonstrating policy blind spots and redundancies. Such a framework is necessary to assist in organizing, and thus simplifying, the complexity of the policy domain for college participation—a complexity defined in part by multiple policies and programs sponsored by multiple entities at different levels of government. By characterizing

An earlier version of this paper was presented at the annual meeting of the American Educational Research Association in April 2006. This research was funded in part by the Lumina Foundation for Education. The opinions expressed in this paper are those of the authors and do not necessarily represent the views of the Lumina Foundation or its employees.

*Laura W. Perna is Associate Professor in the Graduate School of Education at the University of Pennsylvania. Heather Rowan-Kenyon is Assistant Professor in the Curry School of Education at the University of Virginia. Angela Bell is a doctoral candidate in the higher education program at the University of Georgia. Scott L. Thomas is Associate Professor in the Institute of Higher Education at the University of Georgia. Chunyan Li is a doctoral candidate in the higher education program at the University of Pennsylvania.*

*The Journal of Higher Education,* Vol. 79, No. 3 (May/June 2008). Copyright © 2008 by The Ohio State University.

the ways that particular programs are intended to encourage enrollment, a typology provides a necessary first step in an empirical examination of the ways that programs separately and together shape higher education opportunity for different groups of students.

Hearn's (2001) assessment of federal student aid policies and programs offers three conclusions that are useful for understanding the nature of college-enrollment policies and programs more generally.[1] First, Hearn shows that federal financial aid policies and programs lack "philosophical coherence," as reflected by the wide array of distinct goals, including promoting access for low-income students, improving college affordability for middle-income students, rewarding achievement, advancing economic development, and encouraging human capital investment. Second, Hearn notes that federal student aid programs lack "well-considered patterns of policy development." In other words, over the years there has been "no systematic 'housecleaning' to reduce the policy and program contradictions, inefficiencies, and illogics accumulated in the years since the Great Society era" (p. 269). Periodic amendments to the Higher Education Act have altered only "operational details" of the programs. Third, Hearn observes that, taken together, federal student aid policies lack "programmatic clarity and distinctiveness." In other words, based on his review of the literature, Hearn concludes that, "instead of an array of clearly discrete programmatic efforts addressing in distinctive fashion a set of overarching policy objectives, constituents for the programs . . . confront an array of overlapping efforts with rather vaguely differentiated objectives" (p. 270).

The absence of philosophical coherence, systematic and intentional policy development, and program clarity and distinctiveness in federal financial aid policies and programs and, by extension, college-enrollment policies and programs more generally, necessarily complicates attempts to assess the effectiveness of these efforts and identify required improvements. As a way to inform policy, practice, and research relating to college enrollment, this study develops a typology of college-enrollment programs to sort out the tangled web of governmental efforts in this area. Our focus is on government-sponsored programs that are designed to encourage college-going behavior and to reduce enrollment gaps among racial-ethnic and socioeconomic groups. Developed from an examination of federal and state programs in five states, the typology categorizes the approaches that policymakers are using to promote college enrollment. The typology also offers guidance for subsequent analyses that examine the ways in which policies and programs at multiple levels separately and together promote college enrollment for different groups of students. Through the development and application of this typology, we conclude that Hearn's (2001) observations about federal student aid policies and programs are generalizable to state enrollment programs. This article offers a framework for bringing order to the complexity of the college-enrollment policy domain.

## Importance of the Study

Other researchers have developed typologies to organize policies and programs. These typologies focus on policies and programs related to such topics as teacher staffing (Rice, Roellke, & Sparks, 2005; Timar, 1989), educational monitoring systems (Richards, 1998), and state welfare policies (McKernan, Bernstein, & Fender, 2005). Most substantively relevant to this study, Gándara (2001) developed a typology for describing early-intervention programs, a subset of the population of policies and programs that are designed to promote college enrollment. Based on a review of relevant research and documents, Gándara's typology categorizes early-intervention programs along two dimensions: barriers to college enrollment and program sponsor. The ten-by-five matrix identifies ten barriers and five sponsors. The barriers are inequalities of familial cultural and social capital; inequality of resources in neighborhoods and communities; lack of peer support for academic achievement; racism; inequalities in K–12 schools including unequal distribution of well-qualified teachers; segregation of Black and Hispanic students; poor high school counseling; low expectations and aspirations; high dropout rates; and, limited financial resources. The sponsors are private nonprofit organizations; university-based or K–16 partnerships; state or federal governments; community organizations; and K–12 schools.

This study extends Gándara's (2001) work in at least two ways. First, this study examines a broader range of programs that are designed to increase college access, including not only early-intervention programs but also programs that use other approaches. Second, this study locates programs within particular domains, focusing not on the sponsor but on the specific contexts in which programs are implemented (e.g., states, higher education institutions, schools). Framed in this way, the analysis provides a "map" of the potential influence of specific programs, as well as the combined effects of portfolios of programs, on students and families in particular school and state settings. Third, recognizing the key role of states in education policy development and implementation (Murphy, 1980), this study focuses on differences and similarities in approaches to college enrollment within and across five states.

## Conceptual Framework

The conceptual model for this study draws on the multilevel model of college enrollment developed by Perna (2006) and the balanced access model developed by St. John (2003). Based on a review and synthesis of prior research, Perna's conceptual model is designed, in part, to illustrate the multiple ways in which policymakers may intervene to promote college enrollment. Drawing on an economic approach to decision making, Perna's model assumes that students make decisions about college enrollment based on an assessment of the benefits and costs of enrollment relative to their preferences, tastes, and uncertainty. Reflecting sociological theoretical perspectives, the model also assumes that students' decisions are made within multiple levels of context. The four levels of the model are students and their families; K–12 schools; higher education institutions; and the broader societal, economic, and policy context.

Perna's (2006) model assumes that public policies and programs shape students' college-enrollment decisions directly and indirectly through these levels of context. For example, with the federal Pell Grant program, the federal government aims to influence college enrollment directly by providing grants to students that reduce college prices. The federal GEAR-UP program is designed to influence college enrollment indirectly by providing grants to states and partnerships of schools and other entities for programs that improve schools in ways that raise students' academic preparation and achievement, thereby promoting their college enrollment.

This multilevel model, and the review of research on which the model is based, suggests that the most important student-level predictors of college enrollment are academic preparation and achievement, financial resources, knowledge and information about college, and family support (Perna, 2006). The small number of studies that examine linkages among particular contextual levels and student behavior suggest that student-level college-enrollment behavior is also influenced by these various levels of context. For example, research shows that students' college-enrollment decisions are influenced by the quality and quantity of counseling and other resources at the high schools they attend (McDonough, 1997; Perna & Titus, 2005), passive and active efforts by higher education institutions to transmit college-related information to students (Chapman, 1981; McDonough, antonio, & Trent, 1997), and state policies pertaining to K–12 education, higher education appropriations, and need-based financial aid (Perna & Titus, 2004).

While Perna's model (2006) provides a framework for understanding the role of multiple levels of context in shaping college-enrollment behavior and the forces that shape an individual's college-enrollment decisions, St. John's (2003) work sheds light on the ways that public policy interventions shape college-enrollment behavior. In his framework for assessing the influence of policy on educational opportunity, St. John identifies several key steps in the educational attainment process: K–12 attainment and achievement, postsecondary transitions and access, undergraduate and graduate student outcomes, and individual development and educational attainment. St. John's framework posits that K–12 policies pertaining to schooling and school reform (e.g., standards and testing) shape K–12 attainment and achievement; that policy interventions (e.g., financial aid policy, postsecondary information, and affirmative action) shape postsecondary transitions and access; and that college and university policies (e.g., financial and academic strategies) shape undergraduate and graduate student outcomes.

Figure 1 shows the ways that Perna (2006) and St. John (2003) may be used together. Drawing from Perna, Figure 1 depicts the multiple layers of context that shape students' college-enrollment decisions. Drawing from St. John, Figure 1 specifies the connections between particular policies and students' college-enrollment behaviors.

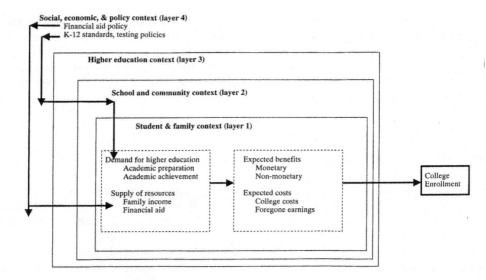

**Figure 1. Conceptual Model of Student College Enrollment with Policy Linkages**

SOURCE: Adapted from Perna (2006) and St. John (2003).

## Research Method

Drawing on Perna's (2006) multilevel conceptual model and St. John's (2003) specification of the linkages between policies and college-related outcomes, this study uses descriptive statistics to generate a typology of programs that are designed to promote college enrollment. The study addresses the following two sets of research questions:

1. What types of programs have the federal government and selected states adopted to encourage college enrollment? What are the similarities and differences among five states in the types of college-enrollment programs adopted?
2. What are the relationships among various dimensions of college-enrollment programs, including level of implementation, barriers addressed, populations targeted, and grade levels targeted?

We developed the typology based on an examination of 103 programs that are sponsored by the federal government and state government agencies in five states. The five states are California, Florida, Georgia, Maryland, and Pennsylvania.

## Sample

We used a two-stage strategy to select programs for this study. First, we purposively selected the five states based on their variation in demographic, economic, political, and educational characteristics. For example, Table 1 shows that, although the five states are among the nation's most populous, each will experience a different level of growth in the college-eligible population, with projected changes in the number of high school graduates between 2001–02 and 2017–18 ranging from a 6% decline in Pennsylvania to a 30% increase in Florida and a 45% increase in Georgia (Western Interstate Commission for Higher Education [WICHE], 2003). The racial/ethnic composition of the states' college-eligible populations also varies, with Blacks representing a higher share of high school graduates in 2001–02 in Georgia (33%) and Maryland (33%) than in Florida (20%), Pennsylvania (10%), and California (7%) (WICHE, 2003). Hispanics represent a substantially higher share of high school graduates in California (33%) and Florida (17%) than in Georgia (2%), Maryland (4%), and Pennsylvania (3%) (WICHE, 2003). Table 1 shows variations in economic conditions, as measured by both poverty rates and per-capita incomes. The political environment also varies across the five states, as suggested by differences in the strength of the governor (weak in Georgia, moderate in California and Florida, and strong in Maryland and Pennsylvania) (Gray & Hanson, 2003).

## Table 1. Demographic, Economic, and Educational Characteristics of Study States

| Characteristics | California | Florida | Georgia | Maryland | Pennsylvania |
|---|---|---|---|---|---|
| Population rank, 2006[a] | 1 | 4 | 9 | 19 | 6 |
| Population, 2006[a] | 36,132,147 | 17,798,864 | 9,072,576 | 5,600,388 | 12,429,616 |
| % population up to age 4[a] | 7% | 6% | 8% | 7% | 6% |
| % population age 5–17[a] | 19% | 17% | 18% | 18% | 17% |
| % population age 65 and older[a] | 11% | 17% | 10% | 12% | 15% |
| % high school graduates from public schools[b] | 91% | 86% | 89% | 88% | 87% |
| Projected change high school graduates, 2001–02 to 2017–18[b] | 10% | 30% | 45% | 13% | –6% |
| % public high school grads who are Black, 2001–02[b] | 7% | 20% | 33% | 33% | 10% |
| % public high school grads who are Hispanic, 2001–02[b] | 33% | 17% | 2% | 4% | 3% |
| % speak language other than English at home [a] | 41% | 24% | 11% | 13% | 8% |
| % eligible for free- and reduced-lunch, 2003[c] | 39% | 37% | 38% | 24% | 22% |
| Poverty rate, 2002–03[a] | 13.1% | 12.6% | 11.5% | 8.0% | 10.0% |
| Per capital income, 2004[a] | $35,019 | $31,455 | $30,051 | $39,247 | $33,348 |
| Strength of governor (range 2.7 to 4.1), 2005[d] | 3.2 (moderate) | 3.6 (moderate) | 3.2 (weak) | 3.8 (strong) | 3.7 (strong) |
| % 35–44 with BA or higher, 2003[a] | 29% | 25% | 26% | 35% | 24% |
| % total state expenditure to K–12, 2004[e] | 23% | 21% | 26% | 18% | 19% |
| % of total state expenditure to higher ed, 2004[c] | 11% | 8% | 14% | 15% | 5% |
| High school dropout rate, 2003[a] | 7% | 8% | 11% | 6% | 8% |
| % high school graduates enrolling in college, 2002[f] | 51% | 55% | 59% | 57% | 60% |
| Postsecondary governance structure[h] | Coordinating Board | Governing Board | Governing Board | Coordinating Board | Coordinating Board |
| # degree-granting Title IV-eligible institutions, 2003–04[a] | 401 | 169 | 126 | 63 | 262 |
| % total institutions that are private four-year [a] | 36% | 31% | 26% | 33% | 37% |
| % total institutions that are public four-year [a] | 8% | 9% | 17% | 22% | 17% |
| % total institutions that are public two-year [a] | 27% | 15% | 41% | 25% | 8% |
| % state grant aid based only on merit, 2003–04 [g] | 8% | 59% | 68% | 6% | 0% |
| Total state grant $ per 18–24 population, and state rank, 2003–04[g] | $182 (19) | $214 (16) | $479 (3) | $115 (30) | $305 (9) |

[a] SOURCE: Chronicle of Higher Education (2005).
[b] SOURCE: Western Interstate Commission for Higher Education (2003).
[c] SOURCE: National Center for Education Statistics (2006).
[d] SOURCE: Gray & Hanson (2003).
[e] SOURCE: National Association of State Budget Officers (2004).
[f] SOURCE: National Center for Higher Education Management Systems (2006).
[g] SOURCE: National Association of State Student Grant and Aid Programs (2005).
[h] SOURCE: State Higher Education Executive Officers (2007).

The data in Table 1 also suggest variations across the five states in terms of the K–12 and higher education contexts. The postsecondary education governance structure varies, with coordinating boards in three states (California, Maryland, and Pennsylvania) and governing boards in two states (Florida and Georgia). Maryland is relatively low in the share of state expenditures to K–12 education (18% versus 26% in Georgia) but relatively high in the share of expenditures to higher education (15%). Following a different pattern, Pennsylvania is relatively low in the share of expenditures to both K–12 (19%) and higher education (5%) (National Association of State Budget Officers, 2004). College-enrollment rates for high school graduates range from 51% in California to 60% in Pennsylvania (National Center for Higher Education Management Systems, 2006). The composition of the states' higher education systems also varies. For example, public two-year institutions represent a substantially higher share of the total number of higher education institutions in Georgia (41%) than in Pennsylvania (8%) and Florida (15%).

The five states also vary in terms of their orientation to student financial aid. In Florida and Georgia, about two thirds of all state grant aid are awarded based only on merit, compared with none of the state grant aid awarded in Pennsylvania, 8% of the grant aid in California, and 6% of the grant aid in Maryland (National Association of State Student Grant and Aid Programs [NASSGAP], 2005). State grant aid is relatively more plentiful in Georgia (third highest among the 50 states in state grants per 18–24-year-old population) and relatively less plentiful in Maryland (30th of 50 states) (NASSGAP, 2005).

The second step in the sampling process involved selecting programs to review. To reduce the complexity, improve the manageability of the analyses, and maintain the focus on state government interventions, we limited the sample to programs that are funded by the federal government and selected state governments. As suggested by an insightful anonymous reviewer, we view "programs as formalized and funded extensions of policies, which are more abstract, and can even be unwritten." In addition to programs that are sponsored by the U.S. Department of Education, we include programs that are sponsored by state departments of elementary and secondary education, state departments or commissions of postsecondary or higher education, state financial aid commissions, and state systems of higher education. We identified programs through a search and review of documents available on the Internet. In addition to reviewing readily available information on government-sponsored Web sites, we also conducted Web searches of programs that included "college" or "higher education" in the title or description. We also contacted a small number of state education officials (e.g., officials at the Board of Regents of the University System of Georgia) to learn more about some programs. The focus on "college" reflects our interest in examining efforts designed to promote greater equity in college-enrollment opportunities.

Despite their prevalence and likely impact, we do not examine the numerous nongovernmental policies and programs that are operating to increase college access. Although some of the programs are large and well recognized (e.g., Gates Millennium Scholarship Program), others are small in terms of dollars spent and numbers of students served. We also do not include attention to programs that operate within a state with the support of federal grants (e.g., from the National Science Foundation, Byrd Scholarships). Identifying the population of all programs operating in each state is beyond the scope of this study, which focuses on government approaches to college enrollment.

## Analysis

Following the example of others who have conducted policy reviews to develop typologies (e.g., McKernan et al., 2005; Richards, 1998), we used the following procedures to analyze the programs. First, we created a database that classifies each program in terms of multiple variables. These variables include measures of such characteristics as purpose, components, requirements for participation, funding level, and implementation history, as well as characteristics identified from the college-enrollment literature. More specifically, the database identifies the barrier to college enrollment that each program is designed to address, as well as the level(s) of context in which the program is implemented (e.g., states, schools, students), the demographic and academic characteristics of the population to which the program is targeted, and the grade level of students targeted. The database also includes financial support for the program in the most recent available year (i.e.,

2005–06 or 2006–07). Funding information for state programs includes funding from multiple state sources (e.g., state appropriations, lottery) but not from nonstate entities (e.g., federal government, matching grants).

We then used the information in this database to develop a typology of state college-enrollment programs. A typology is "a simplification, a heuristic device, which helps us to organize important points of comparison" (Richards, 1998, p. 107). This typology, grounded in the conceptual model (Figure 1), has two dimensions: level of implementation and barrier addressed by program components. In all cases, we assumed that the program was sponsored by the federal or state government (level 4 of the model) and (ultimately) intended to shape students' college-enrollment behavior (level 1 of the model). The level of implementation dimension specifies the extent to which programs operate directly on a student or indirectly through other layers of context, particularly higher education institutions and K–12 schools. The barriers addressed by the components describe the focus of the program (e.g., academic preparation, financial resources, knowledge about college). Next, we describe the programs in terms of other ways that the barriers to college enrollment may be addressed, including characteristics of the targeted population and the grade level at which the program is implemented. Finally, we use the typology to compare similarities and differences across the federal government and the five states in approaches to increasing college enrollment.

The analyses reflect a weighting of programs based on their relative funding level. The weight is the percentage of the total funding for college-enrollment programs that is allocated to a particular program, multiplied by the number of programs sponsored by that government.

## Limitations

The analyses have several limitations. First, in addition to excluding nongovernment programs, the analyses also exclude some state programs that may indirectly shape college enrollment. Federal and state policymakers shape college enrollment through policies and programs other than those with college-enrollment-related labels. For example, federal and state efforts to improve K–12 teacher quality and state efforts to reduce tuition through appropriations to public colleges and universities impact college enrollment. Nonetheless, as these efforts are designed to achieve multiple goals, we do not include these programs in this analysis. We also exclude programs that are sponsored by public colleges and universities even though these efforts are likely supported in part by state funds (e.g., University of California Regents Scholarship).

Second, weighting programs by relative financial support has several implications for this consideration of programs. For example, although the federal or state government may offer several variations of a particular program (e.g., Cal-Grant A, B, C, T), funding data are often available only for the program in the aggregate. Other programs, like Florida's Talented Twenty, which gives priority for Florida Student Assistance Grants to public high school graduates in the top 20% of their class but provides no additional financial award, are also not reflected in the analyses. A second implication is that state budgets and other documents do not specify funding levels for a small number of particular programs (e.g., some P–16 initiatives) or for various information-related activities (e.g., publications, financial aid workshops, counselor training, websites). In addition, funding levels for some college-enrollment programs are not available in state appropriations documents because the programs are funded through other sources or are unfunded mandates. For example, the Maryland Tuition Waiver for Foster Care Recipients is funded not through appropriations but through a reduction in higher education revenues. Federal and state funds for college tax credits are not included in appropriations documents, although in some instances (e.g., Maryland and Pennsylvania) state appropriations cover administrative and advertising/promotional costs. California requires school districts to notify students about coursework required to be admitted to a California public university, but the state provides no funds specifically for these efforts.

Third, while the weighting of programs by relative funding provides an indicator of program reach, this indicator is imperfect. For example, weighting by funding level ignores potential differences in numbers of students served by different programs. This procedure also does not recognize that some federal and state programs are not equally available to all students but are limited to entities that successfully compete for participation in these programs (e.g., Project 720 serves up to 80 of the state's 501 school districts).

Finally, the analyses reflect the programs that were in place at one point in time in only five states. Although varying in multiple dimensions, the five states are not representative of all 50 states. Therefore, the generalizability of the findings to other times and states may be limited.

## Findings

### Types of College-Enrollment Programs Adopted

The majority of college-enrollment policies and programs are implemented directly from the government to the student. Table 2 shows that, after weighting the programs by their relative level of funding, 88% of the 103 college programs in the analyses emanate from state or federal governments and are designed to benefit students directly, 8% are delivered to students through schools, 3% are designed to benefit students indirectly through colleges and universities, and 2% reach students through colleges and universities as well as schools.

The pattern of implementation varies somewhat across the five states and the federal government. Table 2 shows the emphasis on programs that are implemented directly from the government to students in all five states and the federal government. However, California and Florida also have notable shares of programs that are implemented from the government through schools to students (20% and 17%, respectively). In California, 7% of all programs (weighted by funding) involve a state government agency, higher education institutions, schools, and students. The federal government places a greater emphasis on the role of higher education institutions than the states, as 15% of federal programs but only 3% all programs reviewed for this study are implemented from the government to higher education institutions to students.

The most common component of these college-enrollment programs is financial. About 90% of the 103 programs reviewed offer participating students (only) some type of financial award. About 6% of the programs focus only on academic preparation, 3% on academic preparation and knowledge about college, and 1% on knowledge about college only. Less than 1% of all programs include both academic preparation and financial resources or both financial resources and knowledge about college; no program included all three components (academic preparation, financial resources, and knowledge about college).

Program components vary somewhat across the states and federal government. Table 2 shows that, when weighted by their relative level of funding, all of the programs sponsored by the federal government and the state of Maryland include only a financial component. In Georgia and Pennsylvania, more than 90% of programs include only a financial component, with the remainder (4% in Georgia and 8% in Pennsylvania) including only an academic preparation component. While also emphasizing finances, Florida and California have a somewhat more diverse set of programs. In Florida, 83% of programs include only a financial component, 11% include only an academic component, and 6% include an academic and knowledge component. In California, 73% of programs include only a financial component, 13% include only an academic component, 7% include an academic and knowledge component, and 7% include only a knowledge component.

Table 2 reveals that a range of criteria are used to target college-enrollment programs. About two fifths (41%) of the programs are targeted toward students with low financial resources and one fourth (26%) are targeted toward students with high academic abilities. About 13% are targeted toward students with high academic achievement and low financial resources, 9% are targeted toward students attending a particular type of institution, and 7% are not limited to particular groups of students. Table 2 shows that very small shares of programs target students with other characteristics, including low academic achievement, underrepresented minorities, low college-participation rates, particular career fields, or other finite populations (e.g., dependents of law enforcement personnel, youth in foster care, etc.).

In terms of variations across government sponsors, Table 2 shows that, compared with those in other states, programs in California are more likely to be targeted at students with high academic achievement and low financial resources (79% versus 13% overall). Programs in Florida and Georgia tend to place greater emphasis on serving students with high academic achievement

## Table 2. Characteristics of College-enrollment Policies in Five States

| Characteristic | Total Number Unweighted | Weighted | % | CA | FL | GA | MD | PA | Federal |
|---|---|---|---|---|---|---|---|---|---|
| **Total** | | | | | | | | | |
| Number | 103 | 103 | 103 | 15 | 18 | 24 | 19 | 13 | 14 |
| **Level of model** | | | | | | | | | |
| Total | 103 | 103 | 100 | 100 | 100 | 100 | 100 | 100 | 100 |
| Gov't – student | 59 | 90 | 87.9 | 73.3 | 83.3 | 95.7 | 100 | 92.3 | 84.6 |
| Gov't – school – student | 19 | 8 | 7.8 | 20.0 | 16.7 | 4.3 | — | 7.7 | — |
| Gov't – HE – student | 12 | 3 | 2.6 | — | — | — | — | — | 15.4 |
| Gov't – HE – school – student | 13 | 2 | 1.7 | 6.7 | — | — | — | — | — |
| **Component** | | | | | | | | | |
| Total | 103 | 103 | 100 | 100 | 100 | 100 | 100 | 100 | 100 |
| Academics | 10 | 6 | 5.6 | 13.3 | 11.1 | 4.2 | — | 7.7 | — |
| Finances | 66 | 93 | 90.1 | 73.3 | 83.3 | 95.8 | 100 | 92.3 | 100.0 |
| Knowledge | 3 | 1 | 1.1 | 6.7 | — | — | — | — | — |
| Academics & finances | 5 | 0 | 0.3 | 6.7 | — | — | — | — | — |
| Academics & knowledge | 17 | 3 | 2.6 | — | 5.6 | — | — | — | — |
| Finances & knowledge | 2 | 0 | 0.2 | — | — | — | — | — | — |
| Academics, finances, & knowledge | 0 | 0 | — | — | — | — | — | — | — |
| **Target Population** | | | | | | | | | |
| Total | 103 | 103 | 100 | 100 | 100 | 100 | 100 | 100 | 100 |
| High academic | 14 | 26 | 25.6 | — | 50.0 | 66.7 | 10.0 | — | — |
| Low academic | 4 | 0 | 0.4 | — | — | — | — | — | — |
| Low finances | 15 | 42 | 40.8 | 78.6 | 16.7 | — | 70.0 | 91.7 | 100.0 |
| High academic – low finances | 7 | 13 | 12.8 | — | — | — | 10.0 | — | — |
| Low academic – low finances | 2 | 0 | 0.2 | — | — | — | — | — | — |

*(Continued)*

**Table 2. Characteristics of College-enrollment Policies in Five States (Continued)**

| Characteristic | Total Number | | % | CA | FL | GA | MD | PA | Federal |
|---|---|---|---|---|---|---|---|---|---|
| | Unweighted | Weighted | | | | | | | |
| Underrepresented minorities | 4 | 1 | 0.7 | — | 5.6 | — | — | — | — |
| Low college participation | 6 | 1 | 0.9 | — | — | — | — | — | — |
| Particular career field | 17 | 2 | 1.8 | — | — | 4.2 | 5.0 | — | — |
| Particular type institution | 9 | 9 | 9.1 | — | 16.7 | 24.3 | — | — | — |
| Other finite populations | 8 | 1 | 0.7 | — | — | — | 5.0 | — | — |
| Competitive grant | 1 | 0 | 0.1 | — | — | — | — | — | — |
| Not limited | 16 | 7 | 7.0 | 21.4 | 11.1 | 4.2 | — | 8.3 | — |
| **Grade level** | | | | | | | | | |
| Total | 103 | 103 | 100 | 100 | 100 | 100 | 100 | 100 | 100 |
| Grades 6–12 | 5 | 1 | 0.6 | — | — | — | — | — | — |
| Grades 9–12 | 24 | 6 | 5.4 | 21.4 | — | 4.2 | — | 7.7 | — |
| Freshmen/Undergraduates | 64 | 93 | 89.9 | 78.6 | 83.3 | 95.8 | 100.0 | 92.3 | 100 |
| Grades 9–12 – Undergraduates | 1 | 0 | 0.3 | — | — | — | — | — | — |
| Grades K–12 | 3 | 3 | 3.0 | — | 16.7 | — | — | — | — |
| Grades K – Graduate | 6 | 1 | 0.6 | — | — | — | — | — | — |

NOTE: Analyses are weighted by the relative funding level for a given level of government.

(50% in Florida, 67% in Georgia, 26% overall). Maryland, Pennsylvania, and federal programs place relatively greater emphasis on serving students with low financial resources: 70% in Maryland, 92% in Pennsylvania, and 100% of federal programs. Programs that target students attending particular types of institutions are most common in Georgia (25% of all programs).

The most common time of intervention for these programs is at college enrollment. Table 2 shows that 90% of the programs are available to entering freshmen and continuing college students. About 5% of the programs are available to high school students, and 3% of the programs are available to students in grades K–12. Very few programs are available to students in grades 6–12 (0.6%), grades 9 through undergraduate (0.3%), or grades K–16 (0.6%).

The grade level of implementation varies somewhat based on the sponsoring government. The vast majority of programs in all states are directed toward entering freshmen and continuing college students: 79% in California, 83% in Florida, 96% in Georgia, 100% in Maryland, 92% in Pennsylvania, and 100% of federal programs. One fifth (21%) of programs in California are directed toward high school students, and 17% of programs in Florida are directed toward students in grades K–12.

## Relationships among Various Dimensions of College-Enrollment Programs

The most common type of program is implemented directly from the government to the student and includes components that address the financial barriers to college. Table 3 shows that, when weighted by relative funding level, 89% of all programs in this review are implemented by the government directly to students and include only a financial component. This type of program is typified by the need and non-need-based financial aid programs that are sponsored by the federal and state governments. This type of program is the most common in all five states examined: California (73% of all programs), Florida (83%), Georgia (96%), Maryland (100%), Pennsylvania (92%), and federal government (85%). Examples of this type are the Cal-Grant in California, the HOPE Grant and the HOPE Scholarship in Georgia, the Bright Futures Scholarship Program in Florida, Educational Assistance Grants in Maryland, PHEAA State Grants in Pennsylvania, and the Federal Pell Grant program.

The second most common type of program, but representing only 6% of all programs, involves government, schools, and students and focuses on academic preparation. This program type is

### Table 3. Percentage Distribution of Policies by Level of Implementation and Program component (weighted)

| Component | Total | Gov't – Student | Gov't – School – Student | Gov't – Higher ed – Student | Gov't – Higher ed – School – Student |
|---|---|---|---|---|---|
| **Total** | | | | | |
| Total | 100.0 | 89.1 | 7.9 | 2.0 | 1.0 |
| Academics | 5.9 | — | 5.9 | — | — |
| Finances | 91.1 | 89.1 | — | 2.0 | — |
| Knowledge | 1.0 | — | 1.0 | — | — |
| Academics & finances | 0.0 | — | — | — | — |
| Academics & knowledge | 2.0 | — | 1.0 | — | 1.0 |
| Finances & knowledge | 0.0 | — | — | — | — |
| **California** | | | | | |
| Total | 100.0 | 73.3 | 20.0 | 0.0 | 6.7 |
| Academics | 13.3 | — | 13.3 | — | — |
| Finances | 73.3 | 73.3 | — | — | — |
| Knowledge | 6.7 | — | 6.7 | — | — |
| Academics & finances | 0.0 | — | — | — | — |
| Academics & knowledge | 6.7 | — | — | — | 6.7 |
| Finances & knowledge | — | — | — | — | — |

*(Continued)*

**Table 3. Percentage Distribution of Policies by Level of Implementation and Program component (weighted)  (Continued)**

| Component | Total | Gov't – Student | Gov't – School – Student | Gov't – Higher ed – Student | Gov't – Higher ed – School – Student |
|---|---|---|---|---|---|
| **Florida** | | | | | |
| Total | 100.0 | 83.3 | 16.7 | — | — |
| Academics | 11.1 | — | 11.1 | — | — |
| Finances | 83.3 | 83.3 | — | — | — |
| Knowledge | — | — | — | — | — |
| Academics & finances | — | — | — | — | — |
| Academics & knowledge | 5.6 | — | 5.6 | — | — |
| Finances & knowledge | — | — | — | — | — |
| **Georgia** | | | | | |
| Total | 100.0 | 95.7 | 4.3 | — | — |
| Academics | 4.3 | — | 4.3 | — | — |
| Finances | 95.7 | 95.7 | — | — | — |
| Knowledge | — | — | — | — | — |
| Academics & finances | — | — | — | — | — |
| Academics & knowledge | — | — | — | — | — |
| Finances & knowledge | — | — | — | — | — |
| **Maryland** | | | | | |
| Total | 100.0 | 100.0 | — | — | — |
| Academics | — | — | — | — | — |
| Finances | 100.0 | 100.0 | — | — | — |
| Knowledge | — | — | — | — | — |
| Academics & finances | — | — | — | — | — |
| Academics & knowledge | — | — | — | — | — |
| Finances & knowledge | — | — | — | — | — |
| **Pennsylvania** | | | | | |
| Total | 100.0 | 92.3 | 7.7 | — | — |
| Academics | 7.7 | — | 7.7 | — | — |
| Finances | 92.3 | 92.3 | — | — | — |
| Knowledge | — | — | — | — | — |
| Academics & finances | — | — | — | — | — |
| Academics & knowledge | — | — | — | — | — |
| Finances & knowledge | — | — | — | — | — |
| **Federal** | | | | | |
| Total | 100.0 | 84.6 | — | 15.4 | — |
| Academics | — | — | — | — | — |
| Finances | 100.0 | 84.6 | — | 15.4 | — |
| Knowledge | — | — | — | — | — |
| Academics & finances | — | — | — | — | — |
| Academics & knowledge | — | — | — | — | — |
| Finances & knowledge | — | — | — | — | — |

NOTE: Analyses are weighted by the relative funding level for a given level of government.

relatively more common in California (13% of all programs), Florida (11%), and Pennsylvania (8%). This program type includes California's College Readiness Program, College Preparation Program, and the California High School Exit Examination, as well as Florida's state assessment programs and Pennsylvania's Project 720.

In California, 7% of all programs are implemented from the government through schools to students and involve provision of college knowledge. Examples of this type of program include the appropriation of $75 million in 2006–07 for additional counselors for grades 9–12. An additional 7% of the programs in California involve the government, schools, higher education institutions, and students and involve both academic preparation and college-related knowledge. Examples of this type are the Student Opportunity and Access Program (Cal-SOAP), Puente, and Mathematics Engineering Science Achievement (MESA) programs.

In Florida, 6% of all programs are implemented by the government through schools to students and involve both academic preparation and college-related knowledge. This program type is exemplified by Florida's Centers of Excellence program, a program designed to encourage elementary and secondary school students from historically disadvantaged groups to attend college.

While programs that are implemented by the government to students and that provide only financial resources are the most common type of federal program, programs that are implemented by the government through higher education institutions to students and that provide financial resources are the second most common type of federal program (15% of all federal programs). Examples of this latter type of program include the Federal Work-Study Program and the Perkins Loan Program.

## Characteristics of a Particular Type of Policy

In an effort to more completely understand government approaches to college enrollment, we examined additional characteristics of the most common type of program: programs that involve government and students and that provide students with financial resources to attend college. Even within this type, governments offer differing approaches.

Table 4 shows variations in this type in terms of the targeted population. All federal and Pennsylvania government programs of this type are targeted toward students with low financial resources. Examples of programs that are sponsored by the federal government, implemented directly to students, include only financial resources, and are available only to students with low financial resources are the Federal Pell Grant program, the Federal Family Education Loan Program, and the Leveraging Educational Assistance Program. In Pennsylvania, this program type is exemplified by the PHEAA State Grant.

About 70% of Maryland programs of this type also target students with low financial resources, but smaller percentages of policies in other states have this target population: 20% in Florida, 0% in California, and 0% in Georgia. In California, all of the programs of this type are targeted toward

### Table 4. Government-Student Policies that Focus on Finances by Target Population and State

| Target | Total | CA | FL | GA | MD | PA | Federal |
|---|---|---|---|---|---|---|---|
| Total (weighted) | 100.0 | 100.0 | 100.0 | 100.0 | 100.0 | 100.0 | 100.0 |
| High academic | 28.9 | — | 60.0 | 68.2 | 10.0 | — | — |
| Low finances | 43.3 | — | 20.0 | — | 70.0 | 100.0 | 100.0 |
| High academic - low finances | 14.4 | 100.0 | — | — | 10.0 | — | — |
| Underrepresented minorities | — | — | — | — | — | — | — |
| Particular career field | 2.2 | — | — | 4.5 | 5.0 | — | — |
| Attend particular type institution | 10.0 | — | 20.0 | 27.3 | — | — | — |
| Other finite populations | 1.1 | — | — | — | 5.0 | — | — |
| Not limited | — | — | — | — | — | — | — |

NOTE: Analyses are weighted by the relative funding level for a given level of government.

### Table 5. Government-Student Policies that Focus on Finances by Grade Level and State

| Grade | Total | CA | FL | GA | MD | PA | Federal |
|---|---|---|---|---|---|---|---|
| Total (weighted) | 100.0 | 100.0 | 100.0 | 100.0 | 100.0 | 100.0 | 100.0 |
| Grades 9–12 | — | — | — | — | — | — | — |
| Freshmen/Undergraduates | 100.0 | 100.0 | 100.0 | 100.0 | 100.0 | 100.0 | 100.0 |
| K-Graduate | — | — | — | — | — | — | — |

NOTE: Analyses are weighted by the relative funding level for a given level of government.

students with high academic achievement and low financial resources (e.g., Cal Grant program). In Florida and Georgia, about two thirds of this program type are targeted toward students with high academic achievement (60% of all Florida programs of this type and 68% of all Georgia programs of this type). Examples of these programs are the merit-based student aid programs in these states (i.e., Florida Bright Futures Scholarship, Georgia HOPE Scholarship). In Florida and Georgia, a notable share of programs of this type is also targeted toward students who attend a particular type of institution: 20% in Florida and 27% in Georgia. Examples of this program type are the William L. Boyd IV Florida Resident Access Grant (FRAG), which provides tuition assistance to undergraduates attending eligible in-state private, nonprofit colleges and universities, and the Georgia HOPE Grant program, which is available to students attending eligible certificate and diploma programs.

Table 5 shows no variation across governments in programs of this type in terms of the grade level of participating students. Not surprisingly, all programs of this type target entering and continuing college students regardless of government sponsor.

## Conclusions

Several conclusions may be drawn from this study. First, the analyses reveal distinctive state approaches to improving college enrollment. At one end of the continuum, Maryland focuses almost exclusively on providing financial resources directly from the government to low-income students at the point of college entry. Pennsylvania's approach is similar, although with a small share of initiatives that attempt to encourage college enrollment through high schools and promoting academic achievement. Like Maryland and Pennsylvania, the federal government also emphasizes direct aid to low-income students at the point of college entry. But, unlike other states, the federal government implements a notable (15%) share of programs through higher education institutions. Florida and Georgia also emphasize the provision of financial resources directly to students at the point of college entry, but unlike the federal, Maryland, and Pennsylvania governments, they target these resources to students with high academic achievement. Unlike Georgia, Florida also sponsors a small number of programs that are implemented through schools and that are designed to address nonfinancial barriers to college enrollment, particularly barriers related to academic achievement and knowledge. Of the government programs examined in this study, California has the smallest share of programs that are implemented directly from the government to the student and that include only financial resources. Also unlike other states, California targets most resources toward students based on both academic achievement and financial need. California also has a relatively higher share of programs that are implemented through high schools and that target nonfinancial barriers to college enrollment.

Second, the patterns revealed through our data are remarkably consistent with Hearn's (2001) observations about federal student financial aid policies and programs, suggesting that his observations may be applied to college-enrollment programs more generally. The number of different program types (as shown in Table 3) and variations in the pattern of program types across the five states and the federal government suggest that college-enrollment programs lack philosophical coherence, systematic and intentional policy development, and program clarity and distinctiveness. The lack of programmatic clarity is also suggested by the range of populations that college-enrollment programs target. Only about 41% of all programs are specifically directed to students with low financial resources. Examining the populations targeted by college-enrollment programs suggests other goals include rewarding students who have high academic performance and encouraging students to attend particular types of institutions.

Third, while illustrating that multiple program types exist, the typology offers a framework for bringing order to the complexity of the college-enrollment policy domain. Multiple entities will likely continue to sponsor multiple programs, all with goals that are related to college enrollment. Although programs are generally developed and implemented in isolation, the typology reveals both overlap and distinctiveness among policy objectives. The most common program type is one that involves the government and the student and that provides financial resources to offset college prices.

## Implications for Policy and Practice

The typology developed in this study has several implications for policy and practice. First, for policymakers and practitioners, the typology helps to situate the goals and objectives of individual programs within the broader context of existing efforts. This typology may serve as a tool for policymakers and practitioners who are not satisfied with the current approach of incremental and discrete approaches to policy but who are interested in working toward "more reflective policymaking, policy delivery, and policy evaluation" (Hearn, 2001, p. 308). By mapping current approaches to college enrollment, this typology may encourage policymakers to adopt approaches that are characterized by philosophical coherence, well-considered patterns of policy development, and programmatic clarity and distinctiveness (Hearn, 2001). For example, state and local officials might use the results of this study to identify gaps when designing or modifying programs. The typology gives specific information about which students are and are not targeted, at which levels, and with what interventions. Coupled with information about local and/or regional college-enrollment policies and programs, the typology provides a tool for understanding where interventions are most needed and least redundant.

Second, policymakers and practitioners should consider the strengths and disadvantages of the most common type of college-enrollment programs. The typology suggests that the most common approach to increasing college enrollment is to provide resources directly from the government to the student. While 88% of all programs are implemented from the government to the student, only 2% involve government, higher education institutions, schools, and the students. The analyses also suggest that the most common point of intervention is when students are entering or continuing college. But intervening at this point necessarily excludes students who have already "leaked out" of the pipeline to college enrollment. These patterns raise questions about the relative effectiveness of programs that involve different levels of context and different components and that target different populations of students at different points in time.

## Implications for Research

Knowledge of the effectiveness of existing college-enrollment programs is informed largely by quantitative analyses that focus on discrete programs (e.g., student financial aid, Upward Bound). While illuminating understanding of the impact of these programs on students' college-going behaviors, most existing research focuses on the independent influence of particular programs, ignoring the wider range of efforts that exist at the federal, state, and local levels. As a result, little is known about the ways in which programs at multiple levels (e.g., federal government, state government, K–12 schools) with distinct and uncoordinated purposes (e.g., K–12 academic preparation, higher education affordability) interact to shape higher education opportunity for young people of different demographic backgrounds.

Therefore, as mentioned above, future research should address questions about the relative effectiveness of different program types. The typology developed in this study may be a tool for understanding the extent to which multiple programs separately and together influence college enrollment among different groups of students. Such research should be designed to inform policymakers and practitioners about the most effective types of programs for improving college enrollment for all students.

Future research should use the typology to assess the consistency between stated aims and characteristics of college-enrollment programs and actual implementation of the programs. We developed the typology based on a review of documents describing the programs rather than an evaluation of the programs as implemented. Such research should also consider the extent to which policies are achieving stated college-enrollment-related goals.

Finally, when conducting these and other future analyses, researchers must recognize the variation in programs across states, even among programs with the same or similar name. For example, "dual enrollment" programs exist in Florida, Georgia, and Pennsylvania. However, the program characteristics vary. In Florida, both the community college system and state university system offer dual enrollment; high school students who participate are not responsible for registration, matriculation, or laboratory fees. In Georgia, students in the dual enrollment program may opt to use some of their HOPE credit hours to support the costs of participating in the program. In Pennsylvania, the state provides grants to school districts to offset the costs of dual enrollment programs, including tuition, fees, books, and transportation (Pennsylvania Department of Education, 2007).

## Note

1. A corpus of work on policy formation, adoption, and dissemination suggests that these processes are incremental, haphazard, and highly dependent on political context and the power of the actors involved (e.g., Gladieux & Wolanin, 1976; Hannah, 1996; Hearn & Griswold, 1994; McLendon, 2003).

## References

Baum, S., & Payea, K. (2004). *Education pays 2004: The benefits of higher education for individuals and society.* Washington, D.C.: The College Board.

Chapman, D. W. (1981). A model of student college choice. *Journal of Higher Education, 52*(5), 490–505.

Chronicle of Higher Education. (2005). *Almanac Issue: 2005–06, 52*(1).

Ellwood, D. T., & Kane, T. J. (2000). Who is getting a college education? Family background and the growing gaps in enrollment. In S. Danziger & J. Waldfogel (Eds.), *Securing the future: Investing in children from birth to college* (pp. 283–324). New York: Russell Sage Foundation.

Gándara, P. (2001). *Paving the way to postsecondary education: K–12 intervention programs for underrepresented youth.* Washington, D.C.: National Postsecondary Education Cooperative Working Group on Access to Postsecondary Education.

Gladieux, L. E., & Wolanin, T. (1976). *Congress and the colleges: The national politics of higher education.* Lexington, MA: Lexington Books.

Gray, V. & Hanson, R. L. (2003). *Politics in the American states: A comparative analysis* (8th ed.). Washington, D.C.: CQ Press.

Hannah, S. B. (1996). The higher education act of 1992: Skills, constraints and the politics of higher education, *Journal of Higher Education, 67,* 498–527.

Hearn, J. C. (2001). The paradox of growth in federal aid for college students, 1960–1990. In M. B. Paulsen & J. C. Smart (Eds.), *The finance of higher education: Theory, research, policy, and practice* (pp. 267–320). New York: Agathon Press.

Hearn, J. C., & Griswold, C. P. (1994). State-level centralization and policy innovation in U.S. postsecondary education. *Educational Evaluation and Policy Analysis, 16*(2), 161–190.

McDonough, P. M. (1997). *Choosing colleges: How social class and schools structure opportunity.* Albany: State University of New York Press.

McDonough, P. M., antonio, A. L., & Trent, J. W. (1997). Black students, Black colleges: An African American college choice model. *Journal for a Just and Caring Education, 3,* 9–36.

McKernan, S., Bernstein, J., & Fender, L. (2005). Taming the beast: Categorizing state welfare policies: A typology of welfare policies affecting recipient job entry. *Journal of Policy Analysis and Management, 24,* 443–460.

McLendon, M. K. (2003). State governance reform of higher education: Patterns, trends, and theories of the public policy process. In J. M. Smart (Ed.), *Higher education: Handbook of theory and research* (Vol. 18, pp. 57–144). London: Kluwer.

Murphy, J. T. (1980). The state role in education: Past research and future directions, *Educational Evaluation and Policy Analysis, 2*(4), 39–51.

National Association of State Budget Officers. (2004). *State expenditure report, 2003.* Washington, D.C.: Author.

National Association of State Student Grant and Aid Programs. (2005). *35th annual survey report on state-sponsored student financial aid: 2003–04 academic year.* Retrieved February 27, 2006, from www.nassgap.org

National Center for Education Statistics. (2003). *Enrollment in postsecondary institutions, fall 2001 and financial statistics, fiscal year 2001* (NCES 2004-155). Washington, D.C.: Author.

National Center for Education Statistics. (2004). *Digest of education statistics 2003* (NCES 2005-025). Washington, D.C.: Author.

National Center for Education Statistics. (2006). *State education data profiles*. Retrieved March 5, 2006 from http://nces.ed.gov/programs/stateprofiles/

National Center for Higher Education Management Systems. (2006). *Participation; College-going rates of high school graduates*. Retrieved March 5, 2006, from http://www.higheredinfo.org

Pennsylvania Department of Education. (2007). Dual enrollment grant program. Retrieved May 17, 2007, from www.project720.org

Perna, L. W. (2006). Studying college choice: A proposed conceptual model. In J. C. Smart (Ed.), *Higher education: Handbook of theory and research* (Vol. 21, pp. 99–157). Springer.

Perna, L. W., & Titus, M. (2004). Understanding differences in the choice of college attended: The role of state public policies. *Review of Higher Education, 27*, 501–525.

Perna, L. W., & Titus, M. (2005). The relationship between parental involvement as social capital and college enrollment: An examination of racial/ethnic group differences. *Journal of Higher Education, 76*, 485–518.

Rice, J. K., Roellke, C., & Sparks, D. (2005, March). *Piecing together the teacher policy landscape: A multi-level case study linking policies to problems*. Paper presented at the annual meeting of the American Education Finance Association, Louisville, KY.

Richards, C. E. (1998). A typology of educational monitoring systems. *Educational Evaluation and Policy Analysis, 10*, 106–116.

St. John, E. P. (2003). *Refinancing the college dream: Access, equal opportunity, and justice for taxpayers*, Baltimore, MD: Johns Hopkins University Press.

State Higher Education Executive Officers. (2007). *SHEEO agencies*. Retrieved May 7, 2007, from www.sheeo.org/agencies.asp

Thomas, S. L., & Perna, L. W. (2004). The opportunity agenda: A reexamination of postsecondary reward and opportunity. In J. C. Smart (Ed.), *Higher education: Handbook of theory and research* (Vol. 19, pp. 43–84). Dordrecht, The Netherlands: Kluwer Academic Publishers.

Timar, T. B. (1989). A theoretical framework for local responses to state policy: Implementing Utah's career ladder program. *Educational Evaluation and Policy Analysis, 11*, 329–341.

Western Interstate Commission for Higher Education. (2003). *Knocking at the college door: Projections of high school graduates by state, income, and race/ethnicity: 1988 to 2018*. Boulder, CO: Author.

# Effectiveness of Statewide Articulation Agreements on the Probability of Transfer: A Preliminary Policy Analysis

GREGORY M. ANDERSON, JEFFREY C. SUN, AND MARIANA ALFONSO

## Introduction: Framing the Issue

Two-year colleges have long been known for their affordability, location, and open admissions policies, as well as traditionally serving as an alternative educational avenue toward completion of the first two years of a baccalaureate degree (Barry & Barry, 1992; Bauer, 1994; Bernstein, 1986; Fields, 1962; Kintzer, 1970, 1973, 1996; Kintzer & Wattenbarger, 1985; Knoell, 1966; Knoell & Medsker, 1965; Rifkin, 1996; Witt, Wattenbarger, Gollanttscheck, & Suppiger, 1994). Emerging from the original purpose of community colleges is the transfer function which furnishes a portion of those students with an opportunity to continue toward a baccalaureate degree by transferring from two-year to four-year colleges—also referred to as vertical transfers (Barry & Barry, 1992; Bogart & Murphey, 1985; Cohen & Brawer, 1987, 2003; Cuseo, 2001; Hungar & Liberman, 2001; Karabel, 1986; Kintzer, 1970, 1973, 1996; Kintzer & Wattenbarger, 1985; Lombardi, 1979; Palmer, 1987; Witt, Wattenbarger, Gollanttscheck, & Suppiger, 1994). Thus, for many, community colleges seemingly serve as the gateway to the road toward the baccalaureate because of their low cost and open admission policies.

Unfortunately, during the 1970s and 1980s, empirical data and other reports indicated sharp declines on transfer rates from two-year to four-year colleges which inevitably result in fewer students achieving the baccalaureate degree when commencing postsecondary studies at community colleges (Brint & Karabel, 1989; California Community Colleges, 1994; Dougherty, 1992, 1994; Fields, 1962; Grubb, 1991; Koltai, 1981; Lombardi, 1979; Pascarella & Terenzini, 1991; Pincus, 1980; Pincus & Archer, 1989; Shaw & London, 2001). The effects are even worse for minority students for whom community colleges serve a disproportionate percentage (Nora & Rendon, 1990; Pincus & Archer, 1989). Roger Barry and Phyllis Barry (1992) highlight the decline in transfer rates from "57 percent in 1970–1971 to 28 percent in 1984–1985" (p. 37). Although the transfer rates have been relatively stable for the past 20 years, they have been far from impressive; and such data call into question the characterization of community colleges as accessible paths toward the baccalaureate degree. Most recently, the U.S. Department of Education (2003) calculated the national average for transfer rates from two-year to four-year institutions to be 28.9%.[1]

In an effort to facilitate the transfer process, institutions as well as state coordinating boards and legislatures have opened discussions about the possibility of adopting state-mandated articulation policies (Florida Post-secondary Education Planning Commission, 1999; Kintzer, 1970, 1973, 1996; Knoell, 1966, 1990; Knoell & Medsker, 1965). By 1991, according to our calculations, 12 states had adopted mandated articulation agreements; in less than a decade, more than half of the states had them (Ignash & Townsend, 2000).

Articulation agreements are the principal instruments to facilitate the transfer process. Specifically, articulation agreements serve to negotiate the requirements for students' movement from institution to institution and support the transfer intent. Initially, these agreements were limited to negotiations between two-year and four-year colleges at the academic program or institutional level. However, in 1971, Florida became the first state to legislatively mandate a statewide articulation policy. The underlying belief was that this policy would enhance the state transfer rate between two-year and four-year colleges and that these gains would ultimately outperform the transfer rates of other states (Florida Postsecondary Education Planning Commission, 1999; Kintzer & Wattenbarger, 1985). Expecting similar results, other states mimicked Florida, adopting statewide articulation agreements as policy instruments.

The heuristic that articulation agreements are synonymous with actual improved transfer of students from two-year to four-year institutions became an accepted (or heavily relied on) proposition (Barry & Barry, 1992; Ignash & Townsend, 2000, 2001; Kintzer, 1970, 1973, 1996; Kintzer & Wattenbarger, 1985). Given this belief, a state-mandated articulation policy should further enhance a state's transfer rate relative to states without such a policy. Yet in the absence of follow-up data and clearly defined goals, states relied on publications of best practices which had not been empirically tested for their effectiveness as articulation models (Ignash & Townsend, 2000, 2001; Welsh, 2002). Similarly, policy briefs on articulation were equally unreliable as they left unanswered questions about efficiency, goals, and measurements (California Postsecondary Education Commission, 1990; Wright et al., 1996). To be sure, numerous data-driven reports were generated; but either they lacked sufficient recommendations on implementation, or policymakers opted to ignore the findings (Banks, 1992, 1994; Kintzer & Wattenbarger, 1985; Palmer, Ludwig, & Stapleton, 1994; Wellman, 2002). As a result, the effectiveness of statewide articulation agreements as a policy instrument to enhance states' transfer rates relative to those of referent states without such policies has not been analyzed at the national level. The presumption has been that, for purposes of increasing transfer rates, compulsory policy instruments such as statewide articulation agreements would likely yield better outcomes when compared to states without statewide mandates (Banks, 1992, 1994; Ignash, 1992), yet the reality may counter this intuition (see, e.g., Knoell, 1990).

Because access to higher education is currently at a premium in the United States due to rising tuition, a consistently shrinking percentage of higher education relative to other state expenditures, and changes in both demographics and patterns of employment and job growth (Commission on National Investment in Higher Education, 1996; Kane, Orszag, & Gunter, 2003; Zusman, 1999), the possibility of enhancing transfer between two-year and four-year institutions through statewide articulation agreements is an important development to analyze and assess. Surprisingly, very little research focuses specifically on the relationship between state policy and the effectiveness of transfer between two- and four-year institutions. This study, as a result, provides an essential starting point for more comprehensive research in the areas of state policy and the transfer function of community colleges.

## Research Question

We begin by posing the following research question: Does the existence of statewide articulation agreements increase the probability of vertical transfers from two-year to four-year colleges? Stated differently, is there a difference in transfer rates between states with articulation mandates versus those without such policies? Additionally, this paper culls from data on student characteristics to identify other factors impacting the probability of transferring. These individual student characteristics can inform policymakers of alternative or supplemental initiatives, which will likely increase or decrease transfer rates. In short, this paper addresses the effectiveness of state-mandated articulation policies and suggests the consideration of additional policies that will likely increase student transfers from two-year to four-year institutions. This analysis of the effectiveness of statewide articulation agreements as a policy instrument contributes to the literature and policy research on whether community colleges may, over the long run, be reconstituted as an alternative to the first two years of a university education.

## General Overview of the Study

Before discussing the literature, we supply meaningful definitions of transfer and vertical articulation—an important step since the interactive nature of transfer and articulation also explains these terms' significance. After providing working definitions for our study of statewide articulation agreements and the probability of transfer, we explore the articulation-transfer relationship in the context of the evolution of community colleges. Finally, we evaluate the extent to which statewide agreements—as an alternative to transfer arrangements between two- and four-year institutions—can be viewed as a new, effective policy instrument.

In our empirical analysis, we rely on the Beginning Postsecondary Student Longitudinal Study of 1989–1994 (BPS89) to estimate the effect of statewide articulation agreements on the probability of transfer of (a) *all* community college students, and (b) community college students *with baccalaureate aspirations*. To estimate the effect on transfer rates of students enrolling at public community colleges in states with statewide articulation agreements by holding constant other factors that could also affect transfers, we apply a logistic regression analysis. Our analyses of both the full and restricted samples indicate that students who enroll in states with mandatory articulation agreements do not experience an increased probability of transferring. We conclude by discussing the limitations of the study, especially the need for research using more recent data before reaching definitive conclusions on the probability of transfer. In short, we adopt a wait-and-see approach on the long-term impact of statewide articulation agreements.

## Definitions

According to Arthur Cohen and Florence Brawer (1987), "transfer is an *intention* expressed by some students who take community college classes and a behavior manifested by those who eventually matriculate at a four-year college or university" (p. 89). Frederick Kintzer (1999) refers to a transfer as the mechanics of the movement process. The ultimate concern is determination through some consistent, systematic method of the transfer rate of students from two-year to four-year higher education institutions.

Articulation supports the transfer intent. "Articulation refers to the range of processes and relationships involved in the systematic movement of students between and among post-secondary institutions. The goal of articulation is to promote [the] problem-free transfer of courses from one institution to another" (Wright et al., 1996, p. 6). Cohen and Brawer (2003) define articulation as "the movement of students—or, more precisely, the students' academic credits—from one point to another" (p. 205). Similarly, Leland Medsker (1960) "finds the essence of articulation in joint efforts of individuals and institutions across a wide spectrum of activities. . . . Their endeavors facilitate the transfer of students from one school to another" (pp. 1–2). Viewed another way, Jan Ignash and Barbara Townsend (2001) refer to articulation as the "what" process to student transfers.

## Literature Review: The Articulation-Transfer Relationship

### The Evolving Role of Community Colleges

Since their inception, community college enrollments increased. They became the obvious choice of many students seeking access to higher education. The attraction of community colleges as accessible institutions for the first two years of higher education has led to their expansion in terms of number of schools, enrollment figures, and range of offerings (Phillippe & Patton, 2000;

U.S. Department of Education, 2003). For instance, in 1965, the student enrollment ratio between two-year and four-year institutions was approximately 1:2, but by 1995, that ratio became 1:1.1, with community college enrollments increasing 173% from 1965 to 1995. In addition, the American Association of Community Colleges reports that by 1998 there were 1,132 community colleges in the United States (Phillippe & Patton, 2000). To manage increases in numbers of college students, the growth became so sharp at one point that "between 1960 and 1970, the number of community colleges increased two and half times, opening at a rate of nearly one per week" (Phillippe & Patton, 2000, p. 9). Given this growth of community colleges, it is easy to see that they manage larger shares of the postsecondary student population and serve an increasingly larger role in higher education.

For many, community colleges function as an educational alternative for the first two years of college, and the expectation is that transferring to a four-year college would occur after the successful completion of two years of coursework (Cohen & Brawer, 1987, 2003; Medsker, 1960; Menacker, 1975; Witt, Wattenbarger, Gollanttscheck, & Suppiger, 1994). Unfortunately, when compared to figures in the 1970s and 1980s (Grubb, 1991), the reality of this transfer possibility has gradually become bleaker. Today, the national transfer rate hovers around 28.9% (U.S. Department of Education, 2003).

## Articulation Agreements as Policies

To combat the poor rates of transfer, states formulated policies to ease the transfer process (Bender, 1990; Knoell, 1990; Wellman, 2002). At the state level, mechanisms to support the transfer process included raising standards in community college courses (Wright et al., 1996); recommending open discussions between two-year and four-year colleges, particularly through faculty involvement (Barry & Barry, 1992; Berman, Curry, Nelson, & Weiler, 1990; Ignash & Townsend, 2000, 2001); improving advisement and distributing information about the transfer process to two-year students (Banks, 1994; Berman et al., 1990; California Postsecondary Education Commission, 1990; Council for Higher Education Accreditation, 2000; Dougherty, 1994; Wright et al., 1996); collecting more data to assess the barriers (Berman et al., 1990; Robertson & Frier, 1996; Welsh, 2002; Welsh & Kjorlien, 2001); determining students' remedial and developmental course needs (California Postsecondary Education Commission, 1990; Knoell, 1990); offering financial incentives to improve transfer rates (Burke, 1997; Hayward et al., 2004; Robertson & Frier, 1996); creating special programs to support the increasing presence of minority and low-income students (Knoell, 1990; Zamani, 2001); and adopting state-mandated articulation agreements (Barry & Barry, 1992; Bender, 1990; Kintzer, 1970, 1973; Kinzter & Wattenbarger, 1985; Ignash & Townsend, 2000, 2001; Robertson & Frier, 1996; Wellman, 2002).

Few effective alternatives have existed at the state level to address the problems of transfer rates (Kintzer, 1973, 1996; Kintzer & Wattenbarger, 1985; Knoell, 1990; Robertson & Frier, 1996; Wellman, 2002). According to published reports and research articles, articulation agreements contribute to improved transfer rates (Bender, 1990; California Postsecondary Education Commission, 1990; Donovan, Schaier-Peleg, & Forer, 1987; Kintzer, 1970, 1973; Knoell, 1990; Medsker, 1960; Townsend, 2002). With the same expectations, a number of states adopted mandatory articulation agreements as the preferred policy instrument (Banks, 1992, 1994; Education Commission of the States, 2001; Kintzer & Wattenbarger, 1985; Wellman, 2002). As these agreements have become more popular, Louis Bender (1990) has observed that state legislatures and higher education coordinating boards have become increasingly involved in creating and adopting them.

## Earlier Studies on Articulation Agreements

Studies on the articulation-transfer relationship began as early as 1924 when Leonard Koos (1924) initially influenced researchers to delve into the transfer phenomenon. His study provided success stories on the transfer process and the mechanisms in place to help move the student to a baccalaureate institution. Indeed, these mechanisms were the beginnings of the articulation concept. In 1965, Dorothy Knoell and Leland Medsker (1965) conducted the first-large scale study on articulation and the transfer function. Their sample consisted of 7,243 junior college students who transferred in 1960 to one of 43 colleges and universities in 10 states (California, Florida, Georgia, Illinois, Kansas, Michigan, New York, Pennsylvania, Texas, and Washington). The authors found increased articulation and coordination between institutions and, by the end of the study, began to notice "a number of proposals for coordination being readied for introduction during the 1965 sessions of various state legislatures" (Knoell & Medsker, 1965, p. 73).

Other national studies also summarized the status of statewide articulation policies (Bender, 1990; Education Commission of the States, 2001; Ignash & Townsend, 2000, 2001; Kintzer, 1973; Kintzer & Wattenbarger, 1985). For instance, Kintzer (1970) surveyed the 50 states and reported his findings state by state. Similarly, the Education Commission of the States (2001) listed its findings on articulation and transfer measures by indicating the existence (and, if so, the policy language) of legislation, cooperative agreements, transfer data reporting, incentives and rewards to help the transfer process, statewide articulation guide, a common core of courses, and/or a common course numbering system. Working from Kintzer's (1970, 1973) research, Frederick Kintzer and James Wattenbarger (1985) categorized the states based on their articulation policies: (a) formally and legally based policies, (b) state system policies, and (c) voluntary agreements between individual institutions or systems. At the time of their study, Kintzer and Wattenbarger placed eight states in the first category (Florida, Georgia, Illinois, Massachusetts, Nevada, Rhode Island, South Carolina, and Texas). Smaller scale studies representing a select number of states also examined articulation policies but, like many national studies, simply offered descriptive analyses of practices and policies (California Postsecondary Education Commission, 1990; Knoell, 1990; Wellman, 2002). Although these studies contributed to the overall body of knowledge about state-mandated articulation policies, they did not evaluate those policies' effectiveness as determined by their effects on transfer rates.

Some studies offer insights on state policies and the significance of articulation agreements. For example, Jan Ignash and Barbara Townsend (2000, 2001; see also Townsend & Ignash, 2000) expanded the study of articulation agreements by developing their own analyses of state policies. They surveyed the 50 states of which, 43 states responded. Based on these results, Ignash and Townsend identified items which they thought contributed to the overall strength of statewide articulation policies. One example was faculty involvement, rated as "very involved," "somewhat involved," "not very involved," and "not at all involved." Other items included degree of sophistication of the transfer direction (i.e., vertical, horizontal, and reverse), and the presence of general education requirements, general education core, program majors, and a common course numbering system. From these elements, Ignash and Townsend formed their own assessment on the strength of articulation agreements in each state. The final outcome was their evaluating statewide articulation agreements as "strong," "fairly strong," "moderate," "fairly weak," and "weak or no articulation." These findings did indeed provide information to state policymakers about the aspects of the policy's success that Ignash and Townsend found important; however, they did not specficially examine the articulation-transfer relationship.

In contrast, Debra Banks (1992, 1994), examined the effect of environmental factors (e.g., economic conditions, proximity to four-year colleges, tuition rates, student demographics, etc.) on the transfer rate at 78 community colleges in 15 states. With a substantial percentage of her sample from California and Texas, Banks found no statistical significance in transfer rates between Texas, which has a formal statewide articulation policy, and California, which does not. However, based on institutional-level data, Banks identifies other factors which appear to influence individual transfer rates at particular institutions. For instance, two-year colleges located in high-income communities and in a state with a formalized articulation agreement yielded better transfer rates.

## Empirical Strategy

### Dataset

To obtain a nationally representative sample, we relied on BPS89. This survey, conducted by the National Center of Education Statistics (NCES), is comprised of individuals who first entered postsecondary education in the 1989–1990 academic year.[2] The uniqueness of BPS89 is that it contains only first-time beginners and thus captures both students who enroll in post-secondary education right after high school and students who enroll after a considerable delay. We restricted our sample to students who responded to all three waves (1990, 1992, and 1994) and who reported the same primary institution for both the BPS89 and the NPSAS90 studies. We needed to deal with a single institution to correct for BP589's complex survey design.

For the purpose of this study, we further restrict the dataset to only the 680 first-time beginners who were initially enrolled at a public two-year college. The reason for such restriction is that most state-level articulation agreements involve transfers only from public community colleges. For example, Ignash and Townsend (2001) indicate that, out of 33 existing articulation agreements in 1999, 23 covered only public institutions. In addition, students at public two-year colleges represented 43.2% of all first-time beginners in 1989, while only 5.5% were enrolled at private two-year institutions. (See Table 1.) Furthermore, those enrolled in public and private less-than-two-year colleges are generally vocational/trade schools that do not offer transfer programs.[3]

## The Dependent Variable

Our dependent variable is a dichotomous variable: "transfer to a four-year college or university." Consequently, our study considers students to have transferred if they begin their postsecondary schooling at a public community college and enroll after the first year at any four-year college or university—whether public, private, or proprietary (for-profit). We assigned students who meet this criterion within the five years of data coverage of BPS89 a "1." Thus, we do not restrict the sample to students who earn an associate degree prior to transferring or who accumulate a certain number of credits. We coded students who did not transfer to a four-year college, whether they graduated from the community college or not, as not having transferred and assigned them a "0."

We now briefly comment on the two components of the transfer variable. The first involves the numerator, or the ratio of students who transfer. While we restrict the sample to students who initially enrolled at public community colleges, we have not restricted this ratio to involve only upward movements to public four-year institutions. If we restrict transfers only to those occurring within the public system, we would be unfairly penalizing states with more comprehensive articulation agreements.

The second component of the definition of transfer is the denominator or "base," or what constitutes the potential transfer student. Transfer rates vary considerably depending on the group of community college students we consider as "transferable" (Bradburn, Hurst, & Peng, 2001; Hungar & Lieberman, 2001; Laanan & Sanchez, 1996; Townsend, 2002; Wellman, 2002). The most inclusive definition of "transferable students" would be total community college enrollment. However, such a definition perforce yields low transfer rates; transfer rates increase as we restrict the sample to community college students who are enrolled in a transfer program or who aspire to a baccalaureate degree (Grubb, 1991; Spicer & Armstrong, 1996; Wellman, 2002).

## Table 1. Composition of BPS89 by Type of College Attended in 1989

| Type of College | Percentage of Total | Unweighted Size |
|---|---|---|
| Public, less than two-year | 1.78 | 170 |
| Public, two-three year | 43.17 | 684 |
| Public, four-year | 28.96 | 1612 |
| Private, not for profit, less than two-year | 0.24 | 42 |
| Private, not for profit, two-three year | 1.68 | 286 |
| Private, not for profit, four years | 13.97 | 2151 |
| Private, for profit, less than two years | 6.33 | 616 |
| Private, for profit, two years or more | 3.86 | 379 |

Source: Authors' computations based on BPS89.

**Table 2. Transfer Rates from Public Community Colleges to Any Four-Year College**

| | Transfer Rate | |
| --- | --- | --- |
| Type of Articulation Agreements | All Community College Students | Baccalaureate Aspirants |
| No system-wide agreement | 20.5% | 29.6% |
| | 108 | 102 |
| System-wide articulation agreement | 22.0% | 31.6% |
| | 42 | 39 |
| Total | 20.9% | 30.1% |
| | 150 | 141 |

Key: Row proportions, unweighted cell sizes
Source: Authors' computations based on BPS89.

In our empirical analysis, we estimate the effect of statewide articulation agreements on the probability of transfer of (a) *all* community college students, and (b) community college students *with baccalaureate aspirations*. We use the entire sample of first-time beginners at community colleges because we hypothesize that a strong articulation agreement should enhance the chances of transfer for all students, regardless of whether they are in a transferable program or whether they aspire to a bachelor's degree. That is, we assume that any student at a community college has the theoretical possibility of transferring. In BPS89, the overall transfer rate is 20.9%. (See Table 2.)

To further investigate whether statewide articulation agreements affect the transfer probabilities of students who aspire to a bachelor's degree, we also restrict the sample to community college students with baccalaureate aspirations. BPS89 has two variables that allow us to identify the degree intentions of community college students. The first asks the students for their highest degree aspiration, given all practical constraints. The other asks students which degree they are working toward in their first year of postsecondary studies. We used the first variable to identify student intentions of attaining a baccalaureate degree because the sample size using the second variable is very small. Second, we can argue that statewide articulation agreements will be more effective if they enhance the transfer probabilities of all students with baccalaureate aspirations, regardless of whether they are working toward that degree during their first year of college. Restricting the sample to baccalaureate aspirants at community colleges increases the transfer rate to 30.1%.

## Main Independent Variable: Classifying States by Their Articulation Agreements

To empirically estimate the impact of statewide articulation agreements on the transfer rate, we created a dichotomous category indicating whether the state where the student is enrolled has a statewide articulation policy. Although Kintzer (1973) and Kintzer and Wattenbarger (1985) provide useful classifications for determining the type of policy a state maintains, those categories are not mutually exclusive and allow a state to be situated in more than one category. Ignash and Townsend (2001) also offer a well-crafted and complex typology but do not focus on legal state mandates, instead choosing to assess the relative strength or weakness of individual state articulation agreements. Our approach is more like Bender's (1990), since we are interested in differentiating between compulsory statewide agreements and other arrangements (voluntary or localized) or instances in which articulation agreements do not exist. The reason for our focus is that we are concerned most with how state policy affects the probability of transfer.[4]

Townsend and Ignash (2000) adopted a distinction at the state level and acknowledged the presence or absence of a formal, statewide agreement. The following year, Ignash and Townsend (2001) proposed a multi-dimensional typology, rating state policies as "strong," "fairly strong," "moderate," "fairly weak," and "weak or no articulation" according to five dimensions with multiple components within each category. Similarly, a subsequent study of articulation agreements and state policies is reported by the Education Commission of the States (2001) with a state-by-state breakdown of transfer and articulation policies in place immediately prior to February 2001. Finally,

Bender (1990) notes some of the complications with coding statewide articulation agreements. Searching for consistency in items to evaluate, Bender proposes an anlysis of articulation agreements based on voluntary-localized versus mandated/statewide.

To properly measure the effect of compulsory policy instruments in the context of the BPS89 dataset, states with statewide articulation agreements in effect by 1991 must have had formalized mandates in place stipulating that the completion of a defined program or set of courses would be transferable to a public four-year institution within the state. (See Appendix.) If statutes, regulations, and/or policies contained descriptions of the process (as opposed to a merely normative approach with aspirational language), we classified the agreement as statewide. Thus, a state statute simply identifying the transfer function as a mission for all public two-year colleges does not constitute the existence of a statewide articulation agreement. Frequently, we classified states that mandated transferability upon completion of common core requirements and/or a defined number of credits as examples of a statewide agreement. We also included policies or laws applying to nearly all majors or areas of study offered at the two-year and four-year institutions.

We found that several states had limited policies or mandates—for example, policies that covered only program-to-program transfers. When the agreements were restricted to only a few academic programs, we did not categorize the policy as statewide. Moreover, if the adopted policy permitted waivers or voluntary participation, we did not classify it as having a mandated statewide articulation policy. As a result, our findings differ somewhat from those of other researchers comparing state-level mandates with other forms of transfer policy instruments since we are concerned not only with promoting transfer policies but also with explicit mandates at the statewide level (Kintzer, 1973; Kintzer & Watterbarger, 1985; Knoell, 1990). (See Table 3.)

In summary, the main independent variable is an indicator of whether the student was enrolled at a community college in a state that had a statewide articulation agreement by 1991. We coded

### Table 3. States with and without System-Wide Articulation

| States with Systemwide Articulation [a] | States with No Systemwide Articulation | |
|---|---|---|
| Alaska [b] | Alabama | Montana |
| Arkansas | Arizona | Nebraska |
| Colorado | California | Nevada |
| Florida | Connecticut | New Hampshire |
| Kansas | Delaware | New Jersey |
| Ohio | Georgia | New Mexico |
| Rhode Island | Hawaii | New York |
| Texas | Idaho | North Carolina |
| Utah | Illinois | North Dakota |
| Virginia | Indiana | Oklahoma |
| Washington | Iowa | Oregon |
| West Virginia | Kentucky | Pennsylvania |
| | Louisiana | South Carolina |
| | Maine [c] | South Dakota |
| | Maryland | Tennessee |
| | Massachusetts | Vermont |
| | Michigan | Wisconsin |
| | Minnesota | Wyoming |
| | Mississippi | |
| | Missouri | |

[a] Based on the data collection and use of our narrow definition of statewide articulation agreements, these states had laws or policies that applied. Some of the literature as well as representatives from several of the states such as Colorado, Rhode Island, and Texas questioned the enforcement of these agreements. We did not evaluate enforceability. Instead, our focus was only to identify the presence or absence of a statewide mandate.
[b] Although a statewide articulation agreement existed, BPS89 had no students enrolled at public two-year institutions in Alaska.
[c] Maine does not have a community college system.

this variable "1" for such states (12 states did) and "0" for students in states with only institution-by-institution or program-by-program articulation agreements, or states without an articulation agreement of any type by 1991. We excluded Alaska since no community college students in Alaska appeared in our BPS89 sample.

## Statistical Approach

To estimate the effect on transfer rates of students enrolling at public community colleges in states with statewide articulation agreements by holding constant other factors that could also affect transfers, we applied a logistic regression analysis. In this model, the dependent variable is the dichotomous indicator previously described, signifying whether a student does or does not transfer within the period covered by the survey. The independent variable of interest is, as described earlier, a dummy that indicates the existence of a statewide articulation agreement. What this means is: We estimate the probability of transferring to a four-year college or university, which we assume is a function of the student's observable characteristics and the type of articulation agreement that the state maintains. We can therefore formulate the probability of transfer as follows:

$$\text{Prob}\ (Y_i = 1\ ) = \Lambda\ (\alpha X_i + \beta A_{ij})$$

where

$$\Lambda\ (\alpha X_i + \beta A_{ij})\ = \frac{e^{(\alpha X_i + \beta A_{ij})}}{1 + e^{(\alpha X_i + \beta A_{ij})}}$$

and where $Y_i = 1$ indicates that student $i$ transferred and 0 that the student did not; $X_i$ is a vector of the student's demographic, socioeconomic (SES) and educational characteristics, and enrollment pattern variables (all variables described below); and $A_{ij}$ is a vector that contains the indicator for the type of articulation agreement that exists in state $j$ where individual $i$ attends college.[5]

This logistic model allows us then to indicate which variables contribute significantly to the probability of transfer and whether having a statewide articulation agreement makes a significant difference in the transfer rate. The parameter of interest is $\beta$, which can be interpreted as the effect that a statewide articulation agreement has on the probability of transferring from a community college to a four-year institution. However, the reader should note that the parameters of a logistic model are not the marginal effects—defined as the effect on the dependent variable of an increase of one unit in the independent variable. Therefore, we compute also the marginal effects, which provide us with a more straightforward interpretation of the effect of a change in one of the independent variables—in our case, the indicator for a statewide articulation agreement—while holding the other variables constant.

As stated earlier, other controls—based on existing empirical literature on transfers (Lee & Frank, 1990; Surette, 2001; Velez, 1985)—include demographics, SES and educational background variables, and variables that indicate enrollment patterns. The demographic controls are in a dummy format, indicating whether the student is female (male is reference), whether the student is from a racial/ethnic minority (White is reference), and whether the student was age 22 or older when he or she first enrolled in postsecondary education. The SES and educational background variables include the logarithm of household income in 1988, an indicator of whether the student was dependent on his or her parents' income in 1989 (independent students are the reference), two dummies indicating parental education (with high school or less as reference), a dummy for having received financial aid in AY1989–1990 (no aid is reference), a dummy for whether the student has a General Education Development (GED) diploma (high school diploma is the reference), and a dummy for having taken at least one remedial course in college (no remedial course is the reference). Lastly, we include two variables that control for enrollment patterns. The first controls for the cumulative percentage of full-time enrollments in 1989–1990 and the other for the number of months working while enrolled in the academic year 1989–1990.

The descriptive statistics of our two samples are shown in Table 4. As expected, students with baccalaureate aspirations come from households of higher SES, and they have a educational background and a more traditional enrollment pattern. Finally, 27% of the students, in both the full and restricted sample, are enrolled at community colleges in states with statewide articulation agreements.

## Discussion of Findings

What is the effect of enrolling at a community college in a state with a state-mandated articulation agreement? Our analyses of both the full and restricted samples indicate that students in such states do not experience an increased probability of transferring. (See Table 5.) In other words, after holding constant the students' demographic, educational, SES, and enrollment characteristics, they have, statistically speaking, the same probability of transferring from a community college to any four-year college or university as a student who enrolls in a state without such an articulation agreement.

### Table 4. Descriptive Statistics

| Variables | All Community College Students | Baccalaureate Aspirants |
|---|---|---|
| Transfer rate (dependent variable) | 24.49% (.0216) | 34.64% (.0283) |
| In state with statewide agreement by 1991 | 26.86% (.0431) | 26.55% (.0454) |
| Students with baccalaureate aspirations | 67.73% (.0237) | 100.0% (.000) |
| Female | 50.46% (.0232) | 48.79% (.0287) |
| White | 75.80% (.0271) | 73.17% (.0309) |
| Black | 8.45% (.0163) | 10.28% (.0205) |
| Hispanic | 11.52% (.0202) | 11.80% (.0215) |
| Other race | 4.22% (.0103) | 4.76% (.0136) |
| 22 years old or older | 24.03% (.0237) | 16.78% (.0232) |
| Household income in 1988 (in natural log) | 10.087 (.0493) | 10.139 (.0579) |
| Dependent in 1989 | 52.34% (.0246) | 59.72% (.0298) |
| Parents' education: high school or less | 49.67% (.0237) | 42.12% (.0278) |
| Parents' education: some college | 21.49% (.0196) | 23.38% (.0241) |
| Parents' education: BA degree or higher | 28.84% (.0211) | 34.50% (.0264) |
| Received financial aid in 1989 | 28.16% (.0232) | 26.50% (.0255) |
| Received a GED | 6.24% (.0129) | 5.65% (.0164) |
| Took at least one remedial course | 17.86% (.0183) | 18.52% (.0214) |
| Percentage of full-time enrollments in 1989 | 59.788 (2.752) | 66.526 (2.875) |
| Months working while enrolled in 1989 | 6.339 (.1708) | 6.808 (.2038) |
| Unweighted sample size | 517 | 351 |

Note: Standard errors in parenthesis
Source: Authors' computations based on BPS89

# Table 5. Estimation Results

| Variables | All Community College Students | | All Community College Students, with BA/BS Aspirations Dummy | | Baccalaureate Aspirants | |
|---|---|---|---|---|---|---|
| | Coefficient | Marg. Effect | Coefficient | Marg. Effect | Coefficient | Marg. Effect |
| *In state with statewide agreement by 1991* | *0.0227* | *0.0035* | *-0.0072* | *-0.0009* | *-0.0334* | *-0.0067* |
| | (.2730) | (.0422) | (.2826) | (.0344) | (.2939) | (.0589) |
| Student with baccalaureate aspirations | (—) | (—) | 2.5240** | 0.2432** | (—) | (—) |
| | | | (.4625) | (.0357) | | |
| Female | 0.1296 | 0.0199 | 0.1832 | 0.0223 | 0.1415 | 0.0286 |
| | (.2453) | (.0375) | (.2637) | (.0324) | (.2749) | (.0554) |
| Black | -0.4880 | -0.0657 | -0.6263 | -0.0633 | -1.1143** | -0.1769** |
| | (.4311) | (.0517) | (.5054) | (.0411) | (.4991) | (.0618) |
| Hispanic | 0.3464 | 0.0575 | 0.2902 | 0.0383 | 0.1677 | 0.0348 |
| | (.4211) | (.0763) | (.4747) | (.0682) | (.4969) | (.1062) |
| Other race | 0.9182* | 0.1765 | 0.8303 | 0.1306 | 0.8231 | 0.1882 |
| | (.5230) | (.1195) | (.5362) | (.1043) | (.5527) | (.1370) |
| Age 22 or older | -0.6536 | -0.0900 | -0.5490 | -0.0606 | -0.5362 | -0.1013 |
| | (.5039) | (.0597) | (.5074) | (.0495) | (.5266) | (.0900) |
| Household income in 1988 (in natural log) | 0.1653 | 0.0253 | 0.1408 | 0.0172 | 0.1153 | 0.0233 |
| | (.1500) | (.0225) | (.1509) | (.0184) | (.1609) | (.0323) |
| Dependent in 1989 | 0.5069* | 0.0772* | 0.4742 | 0.0575 | 0.5082 | 0.1019 |
| | (.2989) | (.0460) | (.2997) | (.0363) | (.3190) | (.0634) |
| Parents' education: some college | 0.4107 | 0.0676 | 0.2790 | 0.0360 | 0.1287 | 0.0264 |
| | (.3185) | (.0565) | (.3452) | (.0477) | (.3606) | (.0752) |
| Parents' education: BA degree or higher | 0.4945* | 0.0808 | 0.2979 | 0.0380 | 0.1163 | 0.0237 |
| | (.2888) | (.0509) | (.3147) | (.0428) | (.3301) | (.0682) |

| Variables | All Community College Students | | All Community College Students, with BA/BS Aspirations Dummy | | Baccalaureate Aspirants | |
|---|---|---|---|---|---|---|
| | Coefficient | Marg. Effect | Coefficient | Marg. Effect | Coefficient | Marg. Effect |
| Received financial aid in 1989 | 0.7319** | 0.1234** | 0.8291** | 0.1152** | 0.8429** | 0.1816** |
| | (.2529) | (.0456) | (.2761) | (.0428) | (.2932) | (.0655) |
| GED | -1.5729** | -0.1539** | -1.7076** | -0.1233** | -1.7175** | -0.2306** |
| | (.7751) | (.0438) | (.7796) | (.0326) | (.7717) | (.0612) |
| Took at least one remedial course | 0.1131 | 0.0177 | 0.1177 | 0.0147 | 0.1453 | 0.0299 |
| | (.2684) | (.0428) | (.2821) | (.0361) | (.2946) | (.0614) |
| Percentage of full-time enrollments in 1989 | 0.0085** | 0.0013** | 0.0069* | 0.0008* | 0.0056 | 0.0011 |
| | (.0037) | (.0006) | (.0038) | (.0005) | (.0039) | (.0008) |
| Months working while enrolled in 1989 | 0.0975** | 0.0149** | 0.0794** | 0.0097** | 0.0665* | 0.0134* |
| | (.0353) | (.0053) | (.0371) | (.0046) | (.0361) | (.0071) |
| Constant | -4.8256** | — | -6.3585** | — | -3.2341* | — |
| | (1.524) | | (1.542) | | (1.653) | |
| Unweighted sample size | 517 | | 517 | | 351 | |
| Pseudo R-squared | 0.1575 | | 0.2445 | | 0.1254 | |

*Note:* standard errors in parenthesis
* Significant at the 0.1 level.
** Significant at the 0.05 level.
*Source:* Authors' computations based on BPS89.

Despite Banks's (1992, 1994) findings, these results were surprising particularly since policymakers from many states argued that statewide policies would ease the transfer process through systematic change and uniformity. Reaffirming this belief, Kintzer (1970) wrote: "It is abundantly clear that the community college will remain in a difficult if not untenable position if systematic statewide plans are not quickly developed" (p. 3). Since compulsory policies to address articulation processes increased significantly after this period, we expected to find statistically significant differences between states with agreements and those without, because these mandates presumably eliminated serious obstacles to transfer. For instance, commentators on the vertical transfer process have asserted as significant barriers the unequal power dynamics between two-year and four-year institutions (Cuseo, 1998; Ignash, 1992, 1993; Wright et al., 1996), the four-year college's acceptance of courses (Bender, 1990; California Postsecondary Education Commission, 1990; Wright et al., 1996), and students' awareness about transfer procedures (Council for Higher Education Accreditation, 2000; Wellman, 2002; Welsh, 2002; Welsh & Kjorlien, 2001). Although few alternative policy models have been presented, the belief is widely held that state-mandated articulation policies eliminate these concerns and enhance transfer rates. Nonetheless, comparing states with such policies to those without them, we find no significant differences—and certainly not an improvement—in the transfer rates.

Jane Wellman (2002) called "the 2/4 community college-baccalaureate function . . . one of the most important state policy issues in higher education because its success (or failure) is central to many dimensions of state higher education performance, including access, equity, affordability, cost effectiveness, degree productivity, and quality" (p. 3). Yet given our findings, perhaps these policies are driven by concerns over managing reductions in state appropriations for higher education and dealing with the growing college student population. Thus, the goal of enhancing transfer rates may be less significant than advertised (Anderson, Alfonso, & Sun, forthcoming).

Examples of these conflicting and often ambiguous goals involving state-mandated policies include attempts to balance the multiple missions of community colleges and their commitment to the transfer function (Bailey & Averianova, 1999; Kissler, 1982; Lombardi, 1979; Townsend, 2001); a lack of state incentives (as opposed to penalties) linked to transfer performance (Hungar & Lieberman, 2001; Wellman, 2002); and the poor information and data control infrastructure to fully inform students, college advisors, and policymakers about the transfer function (Wellman, 2002; Welsh, 2002; Welsh & Kjorlien, 2001). In the end, these policies do not improve the probability of students transferring from two-year to four-year colleges. Additionally, based on our findings, the prescriptive approach (i.e., state-mandated articulation policies) that 12 states have adopted to deal with the transfer dilemma does not currently support the view that articulation agreements represent an effective policy choice.

The estimation results of individual characteristics which contribute to the probability of student transfers are also presented in Table 5. For the unrestricted sample of all community college students, we find that students who depend on their parents' income, students with highly educated parents, students who receive financial aid in their first year of college, students with higher percentages of full-time enrollment, and students who work while enrolled have higher estimated probabilities of transferring. Similarly, students who have a GED, rather than a regular high school diploma, have a lower estimated probability of transferring from a community college to a four-year college or university. These findings are consistent with the literature as these factors also contribute to college persistence (Astin, 1975, 1977, 1993; McCormick, 1997; Pascarella & Terenzini, 1991; Tinto, 1987).

Next, we re-estimate the model for the unrestricted sample, but this time include a dummy variable that indicates whether the student had a baccalaureate aspiration when first enrolled at a community college. We find that students who aspire to a bachelor's degree have a significantly higher estimated probability of transferring. The inclusion of the control for aspirations erases the effects of the SES variables, suggesting that the student's SES has an effect that varies with his or her degree aspiration.

For the restricted sample of community college students who aspire to a bachelor's degree, we found that Black students and students with a GED have a lower estimated probability of transferring. In contrast, receiving financial aid, working while enrolled, and depending on parental income increases that probability. In contrast to Blacks, we found that the probability of Hispanic students transferring is statistically similar to that of Whites. Another interesting finding in light of their increased enrollments in higher education is that female students are as likely as males to transfer to a four-year institution, suggesting that gender discrimination is probably less a matter of access to higher education than women's experiences in the labor market (Jacobs, 1996).

Our findings also suggest that students wishing to obtain a higher degree would be wise to avoid deviating from traditional high school patterns of graduation, as GED holders transfer at lower rates than regular high school diploma earners. Financial aid is also an important consideration, as we find that students receiving financial assistance are more likely to transfer. From a policy perspective, this finding implies that, if statewide articulation agreements include financial aid packages at both two- and four-year levels, it is probable that transfer rates will increase. In addition, our findings involving the variable "working while enrolled" seems counter-intuitive. However, it should be noted that this variable includes on-campus employment, which has been found to increase educational attainment.

Although we have identified in our analysis the importance of key characteristics that increase probability of transfer, we are acutely aware of the overall importance of community colleges' long-standing open-door policies and the role—albeit at times a contradictory one—that these institutions have played by providing access especially for students from low SES and minority backgrounds and GED recipients. We therefore assert the importance of assessing the probability of transfer from multiple perspectives to avoid misidentifying one aspect of the articulation-transfer dilemma as solely determining outcomes. We elaborate on some of the individual characteristics, but the BPS89 data do not allow us to identify political or additional social factors which are likely connected to increases in transfer probabilities. This uncertainty raises the question of whether statewide articulation agreements by themselves carry sufficient policy strength to enhance transfer rates for states. Perhaps, policymakers should consider the multiple policy approaches as suggested by Ignash and Townsend (2000) and Education Commission of the States (2001).

## Recommended Future Studies and Conclusion

In 1970, Kintzer cautioned: "It is abundantly clear that the community college will remain in a difficult if not untenable position if systematic statewide plans are not quickly developed" (p. 3). In an effort to increase transfer rates, a number of states adopted statewide-mandated articulation agreements as compulsory policy instruments. The overall consensus was that these policies would aid in the transfer process and enhance transfer rates, but such assumptions were for the most part untested, especially on a national scale.

In attempting to address these matters, it is important to highlight that our study has focused on a relatively small number (12) of states with comprehensive articulation agreements in place by 1991. An upsurge in state-mandated articulation agreements has followed since that date, so this study represents a preliminary analysis during a period when adopting such policies grew. Based on an empirical approach, our analysis has relied solely on BPS89 and has been limited by the dataset's five-year span (1989–1994). Consequently, we have carefully selected only those states with statewide articulation agreements by 1991, thus providing the maximum allotted time for these agreements to take effect on student transfers.

Although our findings seem disparaging to state legislatures and higher education coordinating boards, the fact that statewide articulation agreements do not result in an increased probability of transferring must be contextualized before making sweeping generalizations. Certainly, the use of compulsory policy instruments did not yield the intuitively expected results for the reference period of this dataset, but these policies were in their infancy in many of these states. We suspect that, as the presence of additional statewide agreement post-1991 become more prevalent, the understandings of their role and significance would eventually heighten awareness among community college students of their options regarding the possibility of transfer. In other words, statewide articulation agreements as policy instruments may actually enhance transfer rates, given sufficient time since their promulgation into law.

In the meantime, and consistent with other commentaries (Bogart & Murphey, 1985; Wright et al., 1996), we also suggest that more active measures from state legislatures are needed and, to that end, highlight individual characteristics that contribute to increased transfer rates. Because recipients of financial aid and holders of a traditional high school diploma are more likely to transfer, programs targeting those who are less likely to transfer may increase the overall rates.

Equally important, some recent efforts seem to contribute to improved transfer performance. Perhaps, as Ignash and Townsend (2001) suggest, these activities, when combined with statewide articulation agreements, would enhance transfer rates at the state level. Such policy initiatives include faculty engagement in the transfer discussion (Townsend & Ignash, 2000),[6] better counseling and advisement (Bogart & Murphey, 1985; Hungar & Lieberman, 2001; Robertson & Frier, 1996), dissemination of new sources of transfer information such as handbooks and informal knowledge being passed to students (Barkley, 1993; Cuseo, 2001; Timmerman & Associates, 1995), establishment of more course equivalencies (Education Commission of the States, 2001; Florida Postsecondary Education Planning Commission, 1999; Ignash, 1993; Timmerman & Associates, 1995; Wright et al., 1996), and improved coordination and data collection systems (Hungar & Lieberman, 2001; Robertson & Frier, 1996; Welsh, 2002; Welsh & Kjorlien, 2001), and increased funding (Knoell, 1990).

Now that statewide articulation policies have been in place for more than a decade in many states, newer data may indicate rate improvements in those states associated with general knowledge about the transfer process from students and others. Moreover, our sense is that states with supporting services augmenting the statewide articulation policy might actually demonstrate statistically higher transfer rates. For instance, with more course equivalencies in place, the data may indicate improved rates in a given state with a mandated articulation plus a course equivalency guide. Again, this assertion would be consistent with Ignash and Townsend's (2001) typology of articulation agreements ranging from "strong" to "weak or no articulation." Their typology also includes in a number of items besides the articulation agreement itself. Additionally, information about the course equivalencies and other transfer information may be better disseminated today. Technological advancements such as websites and blogs probably help inform students about transfer qualifications.

Another consideration also related to time involves the need to compare the results of this study with more up-to-date datasets, since most of the statewide articulation agreements became fully operational only by the mid-1990s. We recommend a study using BPS96 data and encourage states to more actively participate in data collection and monitoring while continuing efforts toward a seamless transfer process. If Congress decides to weigh in on the credit transfer discussion, a third study may be helpful to assess the impacts of federal involvement (Bursh, 2005; College Credit Mobility, 2005a, 2005b, 2005c, 2005d).

As an additional consideration, demographic changes have occurred throughout this decade, and our findings involving minority and low SES students transferring at lower rates may not necessarily have the same effect when utilizing more current data. Finally, we suggest broader and more intensive dialogue on the issue. Perhaps a roundtable to identify best practices at the state level would be useful as well as a discussion on programs to target groups with lower transfer rates.

Despite the study's limitations, the initial results regarding the effect of compulsory policy instruments on the probability of transfer nevertheless raise important concerns about the capacity of state policy alone to generate desired outcomes in higher education. Indeed, as our study reveals, state policy is not a panacea for what ails postsecondary education unless other factors contributing to student success (such as financial aid, effective compensatory and counseling programs, and improvement in K–12 public schools leading to higher rates of retention and high school graduation) are also built into a multidimensional approach to enhance the probability of transfer.

## Appendix: Data Collection and Operationalizing the Research

To determine the presence of statewide articulation agreements, we organized a three-phase data collection process. For the first phase, conducted in September and October 2002, we searched current state statutes and regulations governing articulation agreements and student transfer processes between two-year to four-year colleges using WESTLAW and official publications for each state's statutes and regulations. If a law existed for a particular state, it usually pertained only to public institutions; however, a few states such as Florida, Illinois, and Washington include language covering private institutions as well. Even today, not all states have statutes or regulations governing articulation agreements (e.g., Idaho, Louisiana, Maine, Michigan, New

Hampshire); however, there have been substantial increases in the promulgation of these laws—aiding in the development of a more seamless transfer system within a given state.

Based on the annotations of the current state statues and regulations, we were able to trace the history of the laws back to 1989. In some cases, these histories provided some perspectives on the process such as the shift in legislative or state agency foci on state articulation agreements. We performed additional legal searches covering the critical period of 1989 to 1991. Using traditional methods of legal research, we reviewed statutes and regulations pertaining to two-year colleges. For the most part, each state had maintained the same chapter or numbered sequence for laws pertaining to higher education. In addition to the bound state laws, we also reviewed the supplements sometimes referred to as "pocket-parts." These searches yielded five states with a state statute or regulation that ostensibly established the existence of a state articulation agreement.

For the second phase, we electronically mailed queries to each State Higher Education Executive Officer (SHEEO) inquiring about the existence of statewide articulation agreements from 1989 to 1994, emphasizing our interest in agreements in place by 1991 since the students in the dataset began college in 1989. Several state directors responded immediately with information, but most forwarded the question to the person responsible for coordinating matters related to articulation agreements. That initial email yielded a 44% response rate (22 states) from an officer or coordinator of the state office.

To address the remaining 56% and to follow up on the responses provided by electronic mail, from October to December 2002 we telephoned each of the SHEEO offices or an equivalent state office to inquire about articulation agreements in 1989–1991 or to ask follow-up questions. When SHEEO representatives were not absolutely certain, we investigated further by contacting other SHEEO staff members and academic affairs' officials at several institutions within the state. Pennsylvania was the only state whose officers were unable to respond to our question; however, we located an article by Leland Myers (1999) from the Pennsylvania Commission for Community Colleges, which confirmed what our other research had already indicated, namely, that Pennsylvania did not have a statewide agreement.

A vast majority of the states did not have a statewide articulation agreement in place during the relevant period; however, many of these states had adopted a policy or some mechanism to assist with transfer of credits such as common course numbering systems, scholarships that encourage transferring from a two-year to four-year institution, and a clear statement of general education requirements qualifying one to transfer.

Our third phase consisted of gathering articles from our initial literature review that specifically addressed the existence or nonexistence of laws or policies on statewide agreements. As a measure of reliability, we crosschecked our findings with a number of articles that also collected data on state articulation agreements. For instance, a few reports and publications consisted of listings of state statutes and regulations, some of which spelled out the language pertaining to state articulation laws in effect from 1989 to 1993 (Education Commission of the States, 2001). Others included fairly comprehensive listings of state policies and their analyses of the policy's content (Ignash & Townsend, 2001; Townsend & Ignash, 2000; Welsh, 2002). Finally, a few reports provided a general analysis or summary of policies or laws from selected states (California Postsecondary Education Commission, 1990; Florida Postsecondary Education Planning Commission, 1999).

## Notes

1. This figure represents the percentage of first-time students who began at a public two-year college in 1995–1996 but who had transferred to a four-year college by June 2001. The data are from the Beginning Postsecondary Student Longitudinal Study of 1996–2001 (BPS96). Although this percentage is higher than that obtained from the Beginning Postsecondary Student Longitudinal Study of 1989–1994 (BPS89), some of the increases from BPS89 to BPS96 may be accounted for by the fact that BPS89 is a five-year study while BPS96 is a six-year study.

2. These students were part of the National Postsecondary Student Aid Study (NPSAS90), which included everyone in postsecondary education, regardless of age or level of postsecondary enrollment. For BPS89, students included in NPSAS90 who had just started their postsecondary education were interviewed twice more during their education and entry into the work force.

3. The percentages presented and discussed in this and the remaining sections are weighted to represent the total U.S. student population.

4. Several authors have presented sets of categories to distinguish these agreements. For example, Menacker (1975) notes the existence of informal versus formal articulation processes. Informal arrangements may be phone calls and discussions that lead to a student's transfer into a four-year college. In contrast, a formal arrangement may entail the publication of curriculum guides and course requirements that qualify students to transfer.

Elizabeth King (1988) offers two types of categories. First, she suggests that articulation agreements may be viewed in terms of courses. She distinguishes between block transfer agreements which qualify completion of educational sequences into the receiving institution's baccalaureate program versus course-specific transfer agreements which evaluate transfers course by course. Second, she takes an institutional perspective by acknowledging that articulation may be vetted through system-wide agreements. Such an arrangement simplifies the transfer process under a single agreement for a state's university system or all the public institutions in a given state as opposed to arrangements based on an individual program or institution-specific agreements that require more negotiation at a more micro-level.

Other researchers classify articulation agreements by degree of state involvement. Kintzer (1973) poses the most cited typology of articulation agreements and transfer policies (Barry & Barry, 1992; Kintzer, 1996; Kintzer & Wattenbarger, 1985). Recognizing the increasing presence of state involvement, Kintzer identifies three general categories as formally and legally based policies, state system policies, and voluntary agreements between individual institutions or systems.

5. It is important to note that the particular survey stratification of BPS89 is being considered when conducting this empirical analysis. Stated differently, the results are corrected for survey design, allowing us to compute the right standard errors and assign significance correctly.

6. Wright et al. (1996) suggest that many of the problems related to the unsuccessful transfers of students from two-year to four-year colleges result from poor faculty attitudes at the university level.

# References

Anderson, G. A., Alfonso, M., Sun, J. C. (forthcoming). Rethinking cooling out at public community colleges: An examination of fiscal and demographic trends in higher education and the rise of statewide articulation agreements. *Teachers College Record*.

Astin, A. W. (1975). *Preventing students from dropping out*. San Francisco: Jossey-Bass.

Astin, A. W. (1977). *Four critical years: Effects of college on beliefs, attitudes, and knowledge*. San Francisco: Jossey-Bass.

Astin, A. W. (1993). *What matters in college: Four critical years revisited*. San Francisco: Jossey-Bass.

Bailey, T. R., & Averianova, I. E. (1999). *Multiple missions of community colleges: Conflicting or complementary?* Community College Research Center Brief, No. 1. New York: Teachers College, Columbia University.

Barkley, S. M. (1993). A synthesis of recent literature on articulation and transfer. *Community College Review, 20*(4), 38–50.

Banks, D. L. (1992). *External and institutional factors affecting community college student-transfer activity*. Phoenix, AZ: Paper presented at the annual conference of the Council of Universities and Colleges. (ERIC Document Reproduction Service No. ED343630)

Banks, D. L. (1994). Effects of environmental conditions on student-transfer activity. *Community College Journal of Research and Practice, 18*(3), 245–259.

Barry, R., & Barry, P. (1992). Establishing equality in the articulation process. In B. W. Dziech & W. R. Vilter (Eds.), *Prisoners of elitism: The community college's struggle for stature*. New Directions for Community Colleges, No. 78, No. 2, pp. 35–44. San Francisco: Jossey-Bass.

Bauer, P. F. (1994). The community college as an academic bridge. *College and University, 69*(3), 116–122.

Berman, P., Curry, J., Nelson, B., & Weiler, D. (1990). *Enhancing transfer effectiveness: A model for the 1990s*. Washington, D.C.: American Association of Community and Junior Colleges.

Bender, L. W. (1990). *Spotlight on the transfer function: A national study of state policies and practices report*. Washington, D.C.: American Association of Community and Junior Colleges. (ERIC Document Reproduction Service No. ED142020)

Bernstein, A. (1986). The devaluation of transfer: Current explanations and possible causes. In S. Zwerling (Ed.), *The community colleges and its critics*. New Directions for Community Colleges, No. 54 (pp. 31–40). San Francisco: Jossey-Bass.

Bogart, Q. J., & Murphey, S. I. (1985). Articulation in a changing higher education environment. *Community College Review, 13*(Fall), 17–22.

Bradburn, E. M., Hurst, D. G., & Peng, S. (2001). *Community college transfer rates to four-year institutions using alternative definitions of transfer*. Washington, D.C.: National Center for Education Statistics, U.S. Department of Education.

Brint, S., & Karabel, J. (1989). *The diverted dream: Community colleges and the promise of educational opportunity in America, 1900–1985.* New York: Oxford University Press.

Bursh, S. (2005, May 20). Credit-transfer rules weighed in Congress. *Chronicle of Higher Education, 51*(37), A22.

Burke, J. C. (1997). *Performance-funding indicators: Concerns, values, and models for two- and four-year colleges and universities.* Albany, NY: Nelson A. Rockefeller Institute of Government, State University of New York.

California Community Colleges (1994). *Transfer: Preparing for the year 2000.* Sacramento: California Community Colleges. (ERIC Document Reproduction Service No. ED371810)

California Postsecondary Education Commission. (1990). *Transfer and articulation in the 1990's: California in the larger picture* (CPEC Report 90–30). Sacramento, CA: Author. (ERIC Document Reproduction Service No. ED338200)

Cohen, A. M., & Brawer, F. B. (1987). *The collegiate function of community colleges: Fostering higher learning through curriculum and student transfer.* San Francisco: Jossey-Bass.

Cohen, A. M., & Brawer, F. B. (2003). *The American community college.* San Francisco: Jossey-Bass.

*College Credit Mobility: Congressional Testimony before the House Committee on Education and the Workforce.* (2005a, May 6). 2005 WLNR7121500. Statement of Theresa Klebacha, Director, Florida Department of Education.

*College Credit Mobility: Congressional Testimony before the House Committee on Education and the Workforce.* (2005b, May 6). 2005 WLNR7121475. Statement of Philip Day, President, National Articulation and Transfer Network.

*College Credit Mobility: Congressional Testimony before the House Committee on Education and the Workforce.* (2005c, May 6). 2005 WLNR7121509. Statement of Jerome Sullivan, Executive Director, American Association of Collegiate Registrars and Admissions.

*College Credit Mobility: Congressional Testimony before the House Committee on Education and the Workforce.* (2005d, May 6). 2005 WLNR7121486. Statement of Dr. Nancy Zimpher, President, University of Cincinnati.

Commission on National Investment in Higher Education. (1996). *Breaking the social contract: The fiscal crisis in higher education.* Santa Monica, CA: Rand.

Council for Higher Education Accreditation (2000). *A statement to the community: Transfer and the public interest.* Washington, D.C.: Author. (ERIC Document Reproduction Service No. ED448812)

Cuseo, J. B. (1998). *The transfer transition: A summary of key issues, target areas, and tactics for reform.* Rancho Palos Verde, CA: Marymount College. (ERIC Document Reproduction Service No. ED425771)

Cuseo, J. B. (2001). *The transfer transition: Student advancement from two-year to four-year institutions.* Rancho Palos Verde, CA: Marymount College. (ERIC Document Reproduction Service No. ED462130)

Donovan, R. A., Forer, B., & Schaier-Peleg, B. (Eds.). (1987). *Transfer: Making it work. A community college report.* Washington, D.C.: American Association of Community and Junior Colleges.

Dougherty, K. (1992). Community colleges and baccalaureate attainment. *Journal of Higher Education, 63*(2), 188–214.

Dougherty, K. (1994). *The contradictory college: The conflicting origins, impacts, and futures of the community college.* Albany: State University of New York Press.

Education Commission of the States. (2001). *State notes: Transfer and articulation policies.* Denver, CO: Author.

Fields, R. R. (1962). *The community college movement.* New York: McGraw-Hill.

Florida Postsecondary Education Planning Commission. (1999). *Evaluation of Florida's two-plus-two articulation system.* Tallahassee, FL: Author.

Grubb, W. N. (1991). The decline of community college transfer rates: Evidence from national longitudinal surveys. *Journal of Higher Education, 62*(2), 194–222.

Hayward, G., Jones, D., McGuinness, A., Jr., Timar, A., & Schulock, N. (2004). *Ensuring access with quality to California's community colleges: Prepared for the William and Flora Hewlett Foundation.* San Jose, CA: National Center for Public Policy and Higher Education. (National Center Report No. 04–3)

Hungar, J. Y., & Liberman, J. (2001). *The road to equality: Report on transfer for the Ford Foundation.* New York: Ford Foundation. (ERIC Document Reproduction Service ED455856)

Ignash, J. (1992). *In the shadow of baccalaureate institutions.* Washington, D.C.: ERIC Clearinghouse for Junior Colleges. (ERIC Document Reproduction Service No. ED348129)

Ignash, J. (1993). *Community college non-liberal arts: Implications for transferability.* Paper presented at the annual meeting of the Association for the Study of Higher Education, Sacramento, CA. (ERIC Document Reproduction Service No. ED358900)

Ignash, J. M., & Townsend, B. K. (2000). Evaluating state-level articulation agreements according to good practice. *Community College Review, 28*(3), 1–21.

Ignash, J. M., & Townsend, B. K. (2001). Statewide transfer and articulation policies: Current practices and emerging issues. In B. K. Townsend & S. B. Twombly (Eds.), *Community colleges: Policy in the future context.* Westport, CT: Ablex Publishing.

Jacobs, J. A. (1996). Gender inequality and higher education. *Annual Review of Sociology, 22,* 153–185.

Karabel, J. (1986). Community colleges and social stratification in the 1980s. In S. Swerling (Ed)., *The community college and its critics.* New Directions for Community Colleges, No. 54 (pp. 31–40). San Francisco: Jossey-Bass.

Kane, T. J., Orszag, P. R., & Gunter, D. L. (2003). *State fiscal constraints and higher education spending: The role of Medicaid and the business cycle.* Washington, D.C.: Brookings Institution. Retrieved on May 1, 2003, from http://www.sppsr.ucla.edu/faculty/kane/KOGWorkingPaper042103.doc.

King, E. C. (1988). Winning together: Negotiating transfer agreements in allied health. In C. Prager (Ed.), *Enhancing articulation and transfer.* New Directions for Community Colleges, No. 61 (pp. 63–71). San Francisco: Jossey-Bass.

Kintzer, F. C. (1970). *Nationwide pilot study on articulation.* Los Angeles, CA: University of California. (ERIC Document Reproduction Service No. ED045065)

Kintzer, F. C. (1973). *Middleman in higher education.* San Francisco: Jossey-Bass.

Kintzer, F. C. (1996). *An historical and futuristic perspective of articulation and transfer in the United States.* Los Angeles: University of California. (ERIC Document Reproduction Service No. ED389380)

Kintzer, F. C. (1999). Articulation and transfer: A symbiotic relationship with lifelong learning. *International Journal of Lifelong Education, 18*(3), 147–154.

Kintzer, F. C., & Wattenbarger, J. L. (1985). *The articulation/transfer phenomenon: Patterns and directions.* Washington, D.C.: American Association of Community and Junior Colleges.

Kissler, G. R. (1982). The decline of the transfer function: Threats or challenges? In F. C. Kintzer (Ed.), *Improving articulation and transfer relationship.* New Directions for Community Colleges, No. 10 (pp. 19–29). San Francisco: Jossey-Bass.

Knoell, D. M. (1966). *Toward educational opportunity for all.* Albany: State University of New York.

Knoell, D. (1990). *Transfer, articulation, and collaboration: Twenty-five years later.* Washington, D.C.: American Association of Community and Junior Colleges.

Knoell, D. M., & Medsker, L. L. (1965). *From junior to senior college: A national study of the transfer student.* Washington, D.C.: American Council on Education.

Koltai, L. (1981). *The state of the district, 1981.* Los Angeles: Los Angeles Community College District. (ERIC Document Reproduction Service No. ED207654)

Koos, L. V. (1924). *The junior college.* Minneapolis: University of Minnesota Press.

Laanan, F. & Sanchez, J. R. (1996). New ways of conceptualizing transfer rate definitions. In T. Rifkin (Ed.), *Transfer and articulation: Improving policies to meet new needs.* New Directions for Community Colleges, No. 96 (pp. 35–43). San Francisco: Jossey-Bass.

Lee, V. E., & Frank, K. A. (1990). Students' characteristics that facilitate the transfer from two-year to four-year colleges. *Sociology of Education, 63*(3), 178–193.

Lombardi, J. (1979). *The decline of transfer education.* Washington, D.C.: National Institute of Education. (ERIC Document Reproduction Service No. ED179273)

McCormick, A. C. (1997). *Changes in educational aspirations after high school: The role of postsecondary attendance and context.* Paper presented at the annual meeting of the Association for the Study of Higher Education, Albuquerque, NM, November 6–9.

Medsker, L. L. (1960). *The junior college: Progress and prospect.* New York: McGraw-Hill.

Menacker. (1975). Inequality: Implications for career guidance. *Vocational Guidance Quarterly, 23*(3), 243–249.

Myers, L. (1999). Pennsylvania community colleges: Troubled past, bright future? *Community College Journal of Research and Practice, 23*(3), 283–302.

Nora, A., & Rendon, L. (1990). Determinants of predisposition to transfer among community college students: A structural model. *Research in Higher Education, 31,* 235–255.

Palmer, J. (1987). Bolstering the community college transfer function: An ERIC review. *Community College Review, 14*(3), 53–63.

Palmer, J. C., Ludwig, M., & Stapleton, L. (1994). *At what point do community college students transfer to baccalaureate-granting institutions? Evidence from a 13-state study.* Washington, D.C.: American Council on Education. (ERIC Document Reproduction Service No. ED373844)

Pascarella, E., & Terenzini, P. T. (1991) *How college affects students.* San Francisco: Jossey-Bass.

Phillippe, K. A., & Patton, M. (2000). *National profile of community colleges: Trends and statistics* (3rd ed.). Washington, D.C.: American Association of Community Colleges.

Pincus, F. L. (1980). The false promises of community colleges: Class conflict and vocational education. *Harvard Educational Review, 50,* 332–361.

Pincus, F. L., & Archer, E. (1989). *Bridges to opportunity? Are community colleges meeting the transfer needs of minority students?* New York: College Board.

Rifkin, T. (Ed.). (1996). Transfer and articulation policies: Implications for practice. In T. Rifkin (Ed.), *Transfer and articulation: Improving policies to meet new needs.* New Directions for Community Colleges, No. 96 (pp. 35–43). San Francisco: Jossey-Bass.

Robertson, P. F., & Frier, T. (1996). The role of the state in transfer and articulation. In T. Rifkin (Ed.), *Transfer and articulation: Improving policies to meet new needs.* New Directions for Community Colleges, No. 96 (pp. 19–29). San Francisco: Jossey-Bass.

Shaw, K. M., & London, H. B. (2001). Culture and ideology in keeping transfer commitment: Three community colleges. *Review of Higher Education, 25*(1), 91–114.

Spicer, S. L., & Armstrong, W. B. (1996). Transfer: The elusive denominator. In T. Rifkin (Ed.), *Transfer and articulation: Improving policies to meet new needs.* New Directions for Community Colleges, No. 96 (pp. 45–54). San Francisco: Jossey-Bass.

Surette, B. J. (2001). Transfer from two-year to four-year college: An analysis of gender differences. *Economics of Education Review, 20*(2), 151–163.

Timmerman, L., & Associates (1995). *Transfer success work group report.* Austin: Texas Association of Junior and Community College Instructional Administrators.

Tinto, V. (1987). *Leaving College: Rethinking the causes and cures and attrition.* Chicago: University of Chicago Press.

Townsend, B. K. (2001). Redefining the community college mission. *Community College Review, 29*(2), 29–42.

Townsend, B. K. (2002). Transfer rates: A problematic criterion for measuring the community college. In T. H. Bers & H. D. Calhoun (Eds.), *Next steps for the community college.* New Directions for Community Colleges, No. 117 (pp. 13–23). San Francisco: Jossey-Bass.

Townsend, B. K., & Ignash, J. M. (2000). *Assumptions about transfer behavior in statelevel articulation agreements: Realistic or reactionary?* Paper presented at the Association for the Study of Higher Education, Sacramento, CA, November 17–20. (ERIC Document Reproduction Service No. ED143150)

U.S. Department of Education (2003). *The condition of education, 2003* (NCES 2003–067). Washington, D.C.: Author.

Velez, W. (1985). Finishing college: The effects of college type. *Sociology of Education, 58*(3), 191–200.

Wellman, J. V. (2002). *State policy and community college-baccalaureate* (National Center Report, No. 02–6). Washington, D.C.: National Center for Public Policy and Higher Education and the Institute for Higher Education Policy.

Welsh, J. F. (2002). Assessing the transfer function: Benchmarking best practices from state higher education agencies. *Assessment & Evaluation in Higher Education, 27*(3), 257–268.

Welsh, J. F., & Kjorlien, C. (2001). State support for interinstitutional transfer and articulation: The impact of databases and information systems. *Community College Journal of Research and Practice, 25*(4), 313–332.

Witt, A. A., Wattenbarger, J. L., Gollanttscheck, J. F., & Suppiger, J. E. (1994). *America's community colleges: The first century.* Washington, D.C.: American Association of Community Colleges.

Wright, M. I., Briden, M., Inman, A. H., & Richardson, D. (1996). *Articulation and transfer: Definitions, problems, and solutions.* Tempe, AZ: Maricopa County Community College District. (ERIC Document Reproduction Service No. ED390512)

Zamani, E. M. (2001). Institutional responses to barriers to the transfer process. In F. S. Laanan (Ed.), *Transfer students: Trends and issues.* New Directions for Community Colleges, No. 114 (pp. 15–24). San Francisco: Jossey-Bass.

Zusman, A. (1999). Issues facing higher education in the twenty-first century. In P. G. Altbach, R. O. Berdahl, & P. J. Gumport (Eds.), *American higher education in the twenty-first century: Social, political, and economic challenges* (pp. 109–148). Baltimore, MD: The Johns Hopkins University Press.

GREGORY M. ANDERSON is an Associate Professor of Higher Education, Teachers College, Columbia University, New York City. JEFFREY C. SUN is a Ph.D. student at Teachers College, Columbia University, and an Assistant Professor of Educational Leadership and Affiliate Professor of Law at the University of North Dakota in Grand Forks. MARIANA ALFONSO is a Postdoctoral Research Associate in Public Policy at the A. Alfred Taubman Center for Public Policy and American Institutions, Brown University, Providence, Rhode Island.

# Access to What? Mission Differentiation and Academic Stratification in U.S. Public Higher Education

MICHAEL N. BASTEDO AND PATRICIA J. GUMPORT

*University of Illinois at Urbana—Champaign*

**Abstract.** *Academic policy initiatives have long been a powerful lever for mission differentiation within U.S. public higher education. Although the higher education literature has examined basic issues in the design of public systems, the tension between access and differentiation has not been explored. Drawing upon comparative case studies of public higher education in Massachusetts and New York, this article examines recent policy initiatives to terminate academic programs, eliminate remedial education, and promote honors colleges within each state system. The analysis depicts how these policies contribute to increased stratification of programs and students within a state system as well as within particular campuses in a system. The authors argue that policy analysis in higher education should develop a more refined conceptualization of access that examines the cumulative impact of contemporary policies on the stratification of student opportunity.*

*Keywords: access, differentiation, diversity, policy, public colleges, stratification, system*

It has become a cliché among higher education researchers that when someone broadly refers to "accountability," someone else retorts, "Accountability to whom? For what?" The reply is for good reason, for without specifying the relationship between the "to whom" and "for what" questions, accountability fails to be meaningful. Policy analysis in higher education has not yet reached this level of scrutiny with regard to student access. Although researchers have been intensely interested in the rates at which minority and low-income students attend higher education, and their initial enrollment into two- and four-year colleges, there has been far less attention to the academic programs that are available to students once they have been admitted (Eaton 1995).

Equality of opportunity for all students to attend public higher education in their state, without regard to their background or preparation, is a foundational principle of higher education policymaking in the United States. Opportunities to attend open-admissions institutions, usually community colleges, exist in nearly every state, and transfer and articulation policies in principle provide the opportunity to earn a baccalaureate degree. Since the GI Bill, financial aid mechanisms have been developed to provide grants, loans, tax credits, and savings incentives to encourage college attendance. In addition to providing access, a second tenet of policymaking is that state systems of public higher education can concentrate resources on various campuses to achieve different missions. Particularly in times of resource constraint, mission differentiation has gained momentum in the name of avoiding unnecessary program duplication. The consequences of policies that promote differentiation warrant scrutiny, however, especially for the ways in which they limit access. Indeed, an ongoing tension exists between the twin principles of access and differentiation in the design of public systems. As Marian Gade has observed, "Citizens need a choice of educational opportunities, institutions and programs with minimal geographic and demographic gaps, or access becomes a hollow promise" (Gade 1993, p. 1).

Against the backdrop of this policy climate, this article aims to move the access discourse forward by posing the question, "Access to what?" While ensuring affordable access to some form of higher education will always be a cornerstone of state policymaking, we want to extend the analytical focus to the array of academic programs available to students once they have been admitted. We illustrate this proposed focus by examining a series of contemporary academic restructuring initiatives within state systems, bringing to light how policies that differentiate academic programs and students by level contribute to the stratification of student opportunity within state systems.

## Conceptual Background

State policymakers in the U.S. have engaged in ongoing redesign of their public higher education systems. During the 1990s, accountability, efficiency, and effectiveness were at the forefront of their agenda (MacTaggart 1996; Gumport and Pusser 1999; Richardson et al. 1999). There were visible attempts to accelerate mission differentiation in various states (Davies 1986; Benjamin and Carroll 1997), and more specifically, to develop academic policies that increase the stratification of students and academic programs (Gumport and Bastedo 2001). States increased the differentiation of systems by targeting resources to "strong" academic programs (Barrow 1996) and by consolidating and terminating "weak" academic programs in the name of reducing duplication (Gumport 1993; Morphew 2000a; Slaughter 1993).

In historical perspective, mission differentiation became prominent in the 1950s and 1960s, when state coordinating boards developed and enrollments expanded. Over the past four decades, statewide coordinators, planners and governing boards have considered various structural alternatives for achieving excellence and affordable access for diverse student populations. These alternatives included diversifying campus missions, facilitating transfer and articulation agreements, and providing mechanisms to demonstrate accountability. But even in states with master plans specifying a division of labor and responsibilities, colleges and universities at the same segmental level were able to develop an array of academic programs that were virtually identical from one campus to the next.

During the 1990s, new approaches to policy making in general strongly influenced the state policy environment for public higher education. On the forefront of these new approaches was the movement to "reinvent government," which encouraged mission differentiation to increase efficiency (Osbourne and Gaebler 1997; Moore 1995). Advocates of reinventing government urged government agencies to move from being rule-driven, which increases regulation and bureaucracy, to being mission-driven. Indeed, they have criticized government agencies for being driven by managers who increase bureaucracy and dysfunction in the system to maintain their own prerogatives. As a corrective, proponents wanted government agencies to become goal-oriented by pursuing specific missions that will make them more effective, efficient, innovative, and adaptive. Becoming mission-driven requires moving the focus from process to product, and using agency goals as the criteria for evaluating effectiveness. As applied to higher education systems, this mandate encourages the redesign of public system structures and processes, and has prompted initiatives for academic program review and termination, assessment, and administrative restructuring. Further, the reinventing government movement has provided an opportunity for campus leaders to depart from established routines, even as they are subjected to increased scrutiny of institutional performance.

Mission differentiation has also been a key issue in the international arena, where much of the focus has been on examining the diversity of institutional types within national systems of higher education (Meek et al. 1996; Meek, Huisman and Goedegebuure 2000). Increased mission differentiation has become an imperative for national systems in Europe, despite a number of governmental and policy forces that serve to constrain it, most recently through the development of the

European Union (Neave 1996). This has led to a higher degree of convergence than is presently seen in the U.S.; indeed, the U.S. has long been positively regarded for the wide variety of institutional types that are contained within its system, even as convergence pressures persist (Birnbaum 1983; Clark 1983; Rhoades 1990). It remains to be seen, however, whether differentiation pressures at a policy level will result in substantial increases in system diversity, which are a separate dynamic from institutional-level forces towards specialization carried by new faculty and the disciplines (Clark 1983; Morphew 2000b).

In addition to having momentum in the contemporary policy climate, mission differentiation can also be substantiated in theory. Mission differentiation, either planned or ad hoc, is consistent with a functionalist approach to organizations and system design. Functionalist theorists in higher education have viewed differentiation as a necessary accompaniment to growth, yielding greater structural heterogeneity across campuses in a system (Birnbaum 1983; Clark 1983; Trow 1987). In the face of complexity, differentiation has been used as a solution to wider value conflicts, mediating normative tensions between egalitarianism and competitive excellence (Smelser 1974). The prototype for this type of structural redesign is undoubtedly the California Master Plan of 1960 (Kerr 1963; Smelser 1974).

Although this functionalist model is simple and transparent, observers of higher education have critiqued the way in which it obscures dysfunction in the system (Rhoades 1990; Slaughter 1990). One problem is with the principle of concentrating talent and resources: the most capable undergraduate students are encouraged to attend research universities that rarely make their education a priority, while underprepared students end up in community colleges, which have fewer resources for each student. Ironically, research has found that attending highly selective universities in the U.S. adds little if any value to the subsequent earnings of most graduates (Brewer et al. 1999; Dale and Krueger 1999), but it provides substantial gains to minority students and their communities (Bowen and Bok 1998). In addition to questioning the principle of concentration of talent, there is an increasing consensus among researchers that the sorting criteria are problematic (Crouse and Trusheim 1988; Jencks and Phillips 1998). Furthermore, the possibilities for ascending this hierarchy are rarely realized, as research has shown that students who begin their postsecondary education at community colleges are 13% less likely to attain the baccalaureate degree than students who begin at four-year colleges, *ceteris paribus* (Whitaker and Pascarella 1994).

As a second line of critique, this functionalist model understates conflict within a system, particularly frustration from students who have been excluded from access to the upper levels of higher education. An awareness of persistent stratification has fueled the contested arena in which students compete for access to a stratified array of institutions that offer different educational opportunities and prestige. Although the educational and direct economic benefits of elite education for the majority of students may be minimal, a degree from one of these institutions continues to serve as a status marker of high achievement (Collins 1979). Students are also increasingly aware that the sorting of students into different levels of higher education is the culmination of prior sorting practices, including tracking in elementary and secondary education. Indeed, some scholars have proposed that the entire process of schooling reproduces stratification in the wider society by allocating students to their respective roles in the division of labor (Bowles and Gintis 1976).

Pulling together the conceptual threads from these scholarly literatures, we can see how mission differentiation has been proposed as a viable solution to value conflicts, even as it, in turn, contributes to conflict within state systems of higher education. Among the many tensions that exist in system design between centralization and decentralization, it is the tension between access and differentiation that we believe warrants immediate attention.

## Research Design and State Contexts

The authors conducted two case studies of public higher education systems in Massachusetts and New York, from 1990–2001. The comparative case study approach was chosen to permit a richness of detail in the sites and to enable analysis of cross-site differences (Yin 1994). Following Yin's dicta on purposive sampling, the cases of New York and Massachusetts were selected as critical cases to explore the nature of contemporary policy dynamics in public higher education. For each case we collected systemwide data and archival documents (reports, policy briefings, academic plans), as well as media coverage (newspaper articles and editorials). Content analyses were conducted and data were examined for the rationales underlying policy initiatives, evidence of stratification effects, as well as emergent themes. We also examined the rationales of system officers, trustees, and elected officials, to determine if their perspectives differed from the campuses in the system. In addition, we scoured the data for evidence of sorting of students into lower-level institutions or stratification of access to knowledge areas.

The Massachusetts system consists of 29 campuses coordinated by a Board of Higher Education, whose members are appointed by the state governor. There are three segments of public higher education: the 15 community colleges, the 9 state (comprehensive) colleges, and the five campuses of the University of Massachusetts, with a total Full-Time Equivalent (FTE) enrollment of about 120,000. The system is led by a chancellor who reports to the Board of Higher Education. There are campus boards of trustees, appointed by the governor, at the University of Massachusetts and each community and state college campus. The Board of Higher Education has varying levels of statutory authority over the segments, having governing-level authority over the state and community colleges and coordinating-level authority over the University of Massachusetts (Crosson 1996).

James F. Carlin, an insurance magnate and former trustee of the University of Massachusetts, led the Board of Higher Education from 1995 to 1999. During the 1980s, he was well known as the Secretary of Transportation and state-appointed receiver for the troubled city of Chelsea. Carlin's appointment by Governor Weld was, in part, due to Carlin's leadership of the "Democrats for Weld" during his first campaign for governor against Boston University president John Silber. Carlin joined the Board with a clear agenda to reform public higher education: increasing admissions standards, lowering tuition and fees, eliminating duplicative academic programs, and reforming the system of faculty tenure (Carlin 1997; Massachusetts Board of Higher Education 1998). He was highly successful at implementing his agenda, to the ire of the state's relatively weak faculty unions. After some health problems, he resigned the post in 1999 and has vowed to take his agenda for higher education reform to the national level. The Board's chancellor during the Carlin years, Stanley Z. Koplik, died in January 2000 and was replaced with his vice chancellor, Judith I. Gill, marking the end of a turbulent era.

In contrast to Massachusetts, public higher education in New York is divided between two large systems, organized geographically, with the City University of New York (CUNY) serving New York City and the State University of New York (SUNY) serving upstate New York and Long Island. Each system is distinct and heterogeneous and managed by its own chancellor and governing board. A Board of Regents governs all education in the state, but its influence is relatively weak in higher education, because its priority tends to be K–12 education. We focus our New York case study on CUNY. A wide range of political actors in New York have substantive and political authority over CUNY, including its chancellor and Board of Trustees, the state Board of Regents, the Mayor of New York City, the Governor, and the Legislature. The relationship between CUNY and its multiple levels of governance is probably the most complex in the country. It is no surprise that observers and policy analysts alike see the CUNY system as more over-governed and politicized than is healthy for a public higher education system (Gill 1999). Turnover of key leaders was salient here as well.

Enrolling over 200,000 students, CUNY is a system of 18 campuses, constituted by 6 community colleges, 11 senior colleges that grant the baccalaureate and master's degrees, and a graduate center as the only doctoral-granting university. Along with the segmented structure, CUNY is known to have a fragmented political structure dominated by "regional biases and political divisions" that hampers statewide planning and information gathering (Richardson et al. 1999, p. 73). Within CUNY, City College is the oldest and most well-known campus, but it has never been officially identified as the system's flagship. Indeed, in recent years other senior colleges, such as Brooklyn, Hunter, and Baruch, have often had better academic reputations. The CUNY faculty union, called the Professional Staff Congress (PSC), is active in promoting faculty and student interests within the CUNY system.

In both Massachusetts and New York, policymakers launched visible and at times controversial academic policy initiatives during the 1990s. Our analysis focuses on three initiatives that occurred simultaneously in the two cases. Our objectives were to explore the rationales of state policymakers, the potential impact of these policies on mission differentiation, and the implications for academic stratification. In the first section, we examine academic program review, consolidation, and termination policies. The second section on remedial education analyzes the implementation of limits on the number of students who may take remedial courses and the mandate to move students with remedial education needs to community colleges. The final section looks at initiatives that foster elite functions, including the creation of specialized honors programs and to attract the highest-performing students.

## Data and Interpretation

### Academic Program Termination

In September 1996, Massachusetts began implementing its Program Productivity policy, designed to eliminate programs that graduated few students each year and were offered at other campuses within the system. All programs with five graduates or less per year averaged over the prior three years were targeted for review. The policy quickly sparked debate on campuses about what it means to be a college at all. As one state college philosophy major put it, "Aren't state colleges supposed to provide a well-rounded education at an affordable price?" (Dembner 1997, p. B1). System chancellor Stanley Z. Koplik, however, responded that eliminating programs did not cause any serious harm to the state. "Sure, there's some dislocation for the student," he said, "but we have to look at the public system as a whole. It's a question of priorities. For programs in low demand, it's fine if they're offered only in one public college in the state" (Dembner 1997, p. B1).

In 1997 and 1998, 52 programs were eliminated across the 29 campuses (Massachusetts Board of Higher Education 1998). According to campus presidents, however, the cost savings have been minimal (Van Voorhis 1998). Some of the terminated programs were taught primarily by part-time faculty, while others were taught primarily by faculty from other programs in the college. At the same time, the potential for program closure enabled many presidents to retool an existing program into a new one. For example, the Massachusetts College of Liberal Arts eliminated its chemistry major, only to move all of its existing courses into a new program in environmental sciences, leaving the Board open to the charge that nothing substantively has changed, since all of the courses and faculty continue to exist.

Nevertheless, the Board considered the program to be a success, and to a large extent, the state's newspapers have agreed. "It has caused all the campuses to look very, very hard at their programs and if that is all it did, it would be worth the effort," according to Board Chairman Carlin (Van Voorhis 1998, p. 41). In addition, although short-term savings are minimal, Carlin argued that there will be substantial long-term savings are advanced courses and the faculty who teach them are discontinued. The editorial board at the *Worcester Telegram and Gazette* agreed, saying, "With funding for mainstream courses of study at a premium, it makes little sense for public colleges and universities to dabble in frippery, duplication and academic arcana" (Editorial Board 1998, p. A6). Plans are going forward to target more programs during 2002, and other states such as Illinois and Virginia have continued to target programs as well.

Academic program termination was launched in New York even earlier than in Massachusetts. In 1992, new CUNY chancellor W. Ann Reynolds initiated a systemwide review of academic programs, due to a fiscal crisis in the university. A committee chaired by Leon Goldstein, the president of Kingsborough Community College, developed a plan to eliminate programs throughout the system, in a bid to centralize authority at the system office. The faculty reacted angrily, seeing the report as a bureaucratic infringement upon their traditional rights to evaluate and maintain academic programs. The president of the faculty union said, "If the purpose is to give more authority to the Chancellor, then it won't work. That would amount to an academic dictator, an academic Führer. I don't believe the Chancellor would want such a designation" (Newman 1992, p. A1).

The faculty was unified in its opposition to this program. "It's been an amazing sort of thing, because it's a proposal that has unified faculties in a way that I haven't seen in a long time. The traditional left-right divisions or whatever just don't exist on this. There is a very intense sense of outrage about this," Hunter College's faculty senate chair said (Newman 1993). Faculty opposition turned out to be very effective, and Reynolds dropped the plan within six months (Weiss 1993a). The attempt was not entirely a failure, however: Forty-five programs were eliminated voluntarily by the campuses, and the CUNY Board voted to institute academic program reviews throughout the system and to give the chancellor more authority in evaluating their results (McFadden 1993).

Reynolds later used her power of the purse to distribute an extra $15 million to colleges that backed the new proposal by terminating additional academic programs (Weiss 1993b).

The new CUNY administration, headed by Chancellor Matthew Goldstein, has encouraged the development of elite functions within CUNY. The *CUNY Master Plan for 2000–2004* articulates a vision for the future that entails creating a "flagship environment" within highly selective colleges and a university-wide honors college. There will not be a single flagship campus; instead, academic programs of strength will be identified throughout the system and receive a special infusion of resources. One strategy has been cluster hiring, where new full-time faculty have been hired to enhance the identified programs. Since 1999, 20% of all new faculty have been senior professors hired for identified programs of strength, including photonics, structural biology, and art history (Arenson 2000b). The program has been very well received by the government and local media, and is the core effort of a comprehensive strategy of institutional renewal for CUNY, tied with the goals of high standards and accountability.

Nevertheless, we are concerned that restructuring will create greater stratification of academic programs, ultimately depriving low-income students of broad access to fields of knowledge. Although the flagship environment proposals in New York have been more palatable, mostly because they have not required the reallocation of existing resources, the impact will be similar to earlier program review processes. Research has shown that academic restructuring tends to occur in fields that are low-status, often because they are dominated by women or minority interests (Slaughter 1993). In addition, low-income and female students are more likely to be affected, since they are less likely to select the high-paying fields of study that are supported by the state (Davies and Guppy 1997; Jacobs 1995). So although academic program review is often a necessary, if painful, process for public universities, the inadvertent impact of these policies will be to increase the stratification of academic programs within these public universities in a way that disproportionately affects certain student populations.

## Remedial Education

Massachusetts made remediation issues a priority with the ascension of Board Chairman James Carlin in September 1995. When he was appointed, 24% of entering freshman at state comprehensive colleges needed remediation, as did 22% at the University of Massachusetts (Massachusetts Board of Higher Education 1998). A series of articles in *The Boston Globe* focused attention on high remedial enrollments in the state's selective public colleges (Dembner 1996a, b; Mazzeo 2000). In response, the Board of Higher Education set strict policies in September 1996 to reduce remedial education and to increase admissions standards simultaneously.

By fall 1997, only 10% of first-time freshmen at four-year colleges were permitted to enroll in remedial education courses, and by fall 1998 that was reduced to 5%. Community colleges were identified in the segment's mission statement as the site of remedial education in Massachusetts, and the four-year colleges were encouraged to create partnerships with local community colleges to eliminate remedial education at the four-year campuses altogether. Summer academies were developed to help students meet the new standards prior to fall enrollment. Incentive funds to develop these partnerships were provided through Campus Performance Improvement Program grants, a $6 million fund set aside by the legislature for the Board to use at its discretion.

At this point, no extensive analysis of the impact of the remedial education in Massachusetts has been conducted. Examination of IPEDS data, however, reveals no consistent pattern of impact on the proportion of minority students in Massachusetts public higher education. Since fall 1996, the proportion of minority students at the University of Massachusetts Amherst, as well as all campuses of the University, has increased slightly (NCES 2001). This is true at seven of the nine comprehensive colleges as well. These results are good news for the BHE staff, who have worked with a multi-segment advisory group to develop appropriate placement standards and to establish collaborative arrangements between two- and four-year colleges (Shaw 2001).

Compared to Massachusetts, CUNY's remedial education initiatives were developed in an even more politicized environment.[1] The CUNY remediation controversy began in 1995 when the planning committee of the CUNY board recommended moving students who needed more than a year of remediation from its senior colleges to community college or night school. At that time, two-thirds of all entering freshmen at senior colleges needed at least one remedial course, and 15,000 students were enrolled in remedial courses in fall 1994 at a cost of $17 million per year (Hevesi 1995). The planning committee's proposal to reduce remediation was not driven by a call for academic standards, but by the need to reduce costs during the financial exigency declared by Chancellor Reynolds in 1995. It was estimated that the committee's proposal would save $2 million per year, and the plan passed the CUNY board with relatively little debate in June 1995.

The topic was revisited in January 1998, when New York City Mayor Rudolph Giuliani, supported by Governor George Pataki, called for an end to open admissions at CUNY. Giuliani and Pataki lacked the authority to move on the issue themselves, however, so they used the power of appointment and budget to force the CUNY board to meet their demands. The CUNY board, after a great deal of discussion and compromise, approved a plan in June 1998 to eliminate remedial education at four-year colleges and to establish transition programs for students to meet the new standard (Healy 1998). The New York State Board of Regents demanded to review the policy in 1998. They approved it in November 1999 after a favorable review by an outside panel (Zemsky et al. 1999) and a number of controversial compromises negotiated by members of the Friends of CUNY, who had previously opposed any change in remedial policy (Arenson 1999).

At the same time, Mayor Giuliani established a Task Force to investigate CUNY from top to bottom. The Task Force was chaired by Benno C. Schmidt, former president of Yale University and the current president of the Edison Group, a corporation that provides private sector alternatives to public school problems. Other members of the committee included Manhattan Institute fellow Heather Mac Donald, who previously called for the end of open admissions and the termination of all remedial programs in the CUNY system, and Herman Badillo, chairman of the CUNY Board of Trustees and a principal architect of the new policy on remedial education.

The Schmidt report claimed to be "shocked by both the scale and depth of CUNY students' remediation needs" (Schmidt et al. 1999, p. 21), the result of being "inundated by NYCPS graduates who lack basic academic skills" (p. 5). The Schmidt report, if implemented, would allow some of the CUNY community colleges to offer remedial education, but only under certain conditions. The primary condition was that, "CUNY must recognize remediation for what it is: an unfortunate necessity, thrust upon CUNY by the failure of the schools, and a distraction from the main business of the University" (p. 35).

The immediate effects of the new remediation policy have been unclear, although there seems to be greater differentiation and stratification within the CUNY system, but also increasing enrollment and legitimacy for the system. Increasing standards for transfer students has forced CUNY to reject 2,000 applications for intra-CUNY transfers from community to senior colleges (Renfro and Armour-Garb 1999). In spring 2000, approximately 250 students were barred from enrolling in the senior college that admitted them (Arenson 2000a). Clearly, the long-term effect of the remediation policy will be to increase the stratification of students among institutions within the CUNY system, which may well be the express intent of the policy (Gumport and Bastedo 2001).

At the same time, growing evidence suggests that the overall minority profile of the senior colleges has remained relatively stable. In 2000, when remedial education was eliminated at seven senior colleges, minority student enrollments remained within one percent of the previous year. In 2001, when the remaining four senior colleges implemented the new policy, only City College saw a reduction in its freshman enrollment, by a substantial 17% (Arenson 2001). This was seen as a result of a reduction in the number of students admitted to City's SEEK program, which is intended for underprepared students with potential. Although, because of demographics, colleges across the country have seen recent increases in enrollment, it is also notable that the CUNY colleges have implemented a number of summer immersion and dual enrollment programs that have softened the blow of the new policy while maintaining the new standards. Enrollment in summer immersion courses is up 17% from 1999 (Hebel 2002). Minority enrollments seem not to have decreased in the four senior colleges, but there has been a staggering reduction in ESL (English as a Second Language) students, down 7% from 1999–2000 and 46% since 1995–96 (Arenson 2002; Hebel 2002).

## Honors Programs

In September 1996, Massachusetts Board of Higher Education member Aaron Spencer proposed to create an elite public college to attract honors students from around the state to the public higher education system (Dembner 1996). A concept paper for "Commonwealth College" was circulated by the Board in December, advocating a college that would support 1500 to 2500 students, have tough admissions criteria, enforce a strict honor code, and require a thesis from all graduating seniors (Massachusetts Board of Higher Education 1996). The original idea was to transform one of the state's comprehensive colleges into the new Commonwealth College, and thus to make it a specialty college much like the state's College of Art and Maritime Academy. In turn, it was expected that there would be a "halo effect" for the rest of the campuses in the system, increasing resources, attention, and legitimacy from state policymakers and the public.

In March 1997, campuses from throughout the state presented proposals for the new college in one of the legislature's committee rooms, with Spencer chairing the effort. After considering the proposals, the Board supported renaming the honors program at University of Massachusetts Amherst, the system's acknowledged flagship, as Commonwealth College. The Board also supported directing additional funds at the program, and providing it with additional facilities, faculty, and administrative resources, including $15 million for a new complex on the campus's highest point to house the entire operation. (The state legislature refused to fund the project.) Today, the project is controversial: some students and faculty see the program as elitist, stealing resources from the mainstream students, while others believe it has increased the standards at the flagship campus (Healy 2000). The minority profile for Commonwealth College is not encouraging—black and Latino students are enrolled at less than half of their rates in the general undergraduate population (University of Massachusetts Amherst Office of Institutional Research 2001).

CUNY has also embraced the development of its systemwide honors college, pouring funds into the program and earning accolades from local media and politicians. Students in the honors college get a full scholarship, a laptop computer, a cultural passport that offers free admission to museums and events in the city, and a $7500 academic spending account for research or study abroad. There are currently about 200 students in the program (accepted from over 1400 applicants), with an average SAT score of 1300 (Goldstein 2001). According to Executive Vice Chancellor Louise Mirrer (CUNY Matters 2001), these students

> " . . . will be taught by a pool of the most talented, most creative faculty from our undergraduate, graduate, and professional schools if an upper division student wants to study with, say, a scientist working on huge magnets at City College's Structural Biology Center, that could be done. If an Honors College student wants to study with a leading scholar anywhere in the University, we'll facilitate that".

This level of special treatment sparked early criticism from CUNY trustee John Morning, who called the program "an example of the gentrification of the university . . . We have to find a way to make sure that we're not turning away from our traditional mission" (Shin 2000). In general, however, the initiative has been warmly welcomed as a way to restore CUNY's reputation while maintaining access. In July 2001, the Mellon Foundation awarded $1.5 million to the systemwide honors college, and the Muehlstein Foundation did the same for City College's program. In addition, a grant for $500,000 was developed to fund scholarships for minority students. As another indicator of success, applications for fall 2002 are up a staggering 91% (Hebel 2002).

## Conclusion and Implications: Reframing the Access Debate

The internal dynamics of establishing these academic policy initiatives in each state system are noteworthy for the differences in the degree of conflict that was evident. In Massachusetts, all three sets of policies were approved with little public debate and were barely opposed. Yet in New York, the entire CUNY system has been under intensive public scrutiny since at least the 1970s. Differences in the environmental context of each state may account for these vastly different outcomes. In New York, there was weak administrative leadership, a long history of protest movements related to higher education since the advent of open admissions in 1970, a highly organized faculty union, and geographic proximity among institutions and actors that facilitated communication and contact. In Massachusetts, on the other hand, there was strong administrative leadership from the system's coordinating board, a weakly organized faculty union that was split among the three major segments of higher education, and a lack of geographic proximity that made coordination of protest more difficult than in New York.

There were notable differences in political resources between the leaders of the two systems. In New York, there was a great deal of personnel turnover at the campus, chancellor, and trustee levels within CUNY, due to the low level of financial resources and the high-pressure environment of an urban university. In addition, due to the large number of political actors who have substantive or process authority over the university – including the governor, legislature, board of regents, mayor of New York City, board of trustees, and campus presidents – there was a severe fragmentation of leadership for the system. In Massachusetts, a single leader, Board Chairman James F. Carlin, had the political, financial, and personal resources needed to impose his will upon public higher education. Facilitating this was a unified and coherent hierarchy of authority within the system that allows decisions to be enforced through accountability to only one authority. The shared values among Board members, the legislature, and the executive office ensured that Carlin's plans would not be derailed.

In both case studies, the policy changes in public higher education were mission-driven and the objective was to promote differentiation both across and within institutions. The underlying rationales were clear and often explicit: to increase the legitimacy of the system, to reduce duplication and concentrate resources in programmatic areas of identified strength, and to provide more academic opportunities for high performing students. These policies have unexamined consequences for the stratification of students and programs within the system as well as within particular college and university campuses. In our view, those who promote mission differentiation are trying to manage the competing demands of egalitarianism and competitive excellence. Yet there may be substantially negative effects on students, academic programs, and even the faculty who are left out. Ironically, without anticipating and attempting to mitigate these effects, policymakers will face continued–if not heightened–conflict over access, not only to the system as a whole, but also to those campuses and programs with the most resources within that system.

Successive initiatives for mission differentiation by state policymakers make it even more imperative to reframe the access debate in higher education to consider the question, "Access to what?" In the case of academic program termination, the question is what programs and knowledge areas will be available to which students within a public system. Well-prepared students at research universities have access to a wide variety of academic programs and disciplines, while students at state colleges may face a situation where comprehensive coverage of the disciplines is no longer a priority. Students who cannot travel outside of their local area may find that they have limited access to areas of study and thus potential careers, and these place-bound students are more likely to be from low-income families and members of ethnic and racial minorities. Similarly, resource concentration may sustain high-status programs, while lower status programs are allowed to falter. Selective excellence may satisfy some policy objectives but it does not serve all students well.

With regard to remedial education, the question becomes whether equitable access is provided when those who are underprepared for college are encouraged, and even mandated, to attend community colleges. There is no evidence that community colleges provide a better education in remedial courses than four-year colleges. And as stated earlier, students who begin their education at community colleges are less likely to ultimately attain the bachelor's degree. Nevertheless, state policymakers have relegated remedial education to community colleges, as part of their strategy to promote a concentration of talent in the highest levels of the higher education system. A concern for the impact of these policies on minority students is obvious as both states in these two states are now monitoring this situation; preliminary data show no substantial decline in minority enrollment. It remains to be seen, however, what the long-term impacts will be not only for minority enrollment, but also for student transfer to four-year campuses. As the proportion of minority and low-income college students increases in both Massachusetts and New York, the public will not be served if a disproportionate number of them are "cooled out" into community colleges, or fail to graduate because they cannot escape remedial status.

Serving the needs of an increasingly diverse student population should not be eclipsed by efforts to create opportunities for high-performing students. Honors students have been purposefully separated from their less-prepared counterparts into specialized programs and colleges to encourage academic excellence and provide a "halo effect" for the rest of the public system. The availability of community colleges and financial aid programs for all students obscures the fact that minority and low-income students are less likely to be admitted into the highest-prestige programs in the system. If minority and low-income students are disproportionately represented in lower-level programs and schools, it remains questionable whether equitable access has truly been provided. Conversely, a credential from these honors programs will undoubtedly provide the most opportunities for future wealth and prestige. Although these programs will provide an opportunity for high-level education for a small number of students, they may simultaneously devalue standard degrees from the university system.

Clearly, student access to the system as a whole does not mean access to the whole system. Access to public systems of higher education must be treated far less monolithically than has been done in the past, by examining access to specific segmental levels, academic programs, and honors colleges. Asking the question, "Access to what?" can advance the research agenda within higher education to address shifts in the stratification of student opportunity. Further research on the effects of heightened mission differentiation within public systems and institutions is needed to more fully understand the effect of state policy on the stratification of opportunity. Data on the differential impact of academic program termination policies and the characteristics of academic programs "of strength" should be collected by state boards of higher education to analyze the differential impact across academic programs and the availability of quality academic programs more generally. In addition, states should collect data on the demographics of students enrolled in honors programs on public campuses. Finally, at the national level, there is a need for better data on remedial education to identify effective practices and programs. These data collection efforts will be vital to informing policymakers and higher education leaders about the cumulative impact of mission differentiation on the stratification of students and academic programs.

## Notes

1. A draft of this article was presented at the annual meeting of the Association for the Study of Higher Education, Sacramento, CA, November 16–19, 2000.
2. For expanded analysis of the data on remedial education at CUNY, see Gumport and Bastedo (2001).

## References

Arenson, K. W. (1999, November 24). 'Opponents of a change in CUNY admissions policy helped pass a compromise plan', *New York Times*, B3.

Arenson, K. W. (2000a, February 6). 'CUNY tests, a last hurdle, stump many', *New York Times*, A29.

Arenson, K. W. (2000b, October 31). 'Vision of CUNY as a contender in select fields', *New York Times*, B1.

Arenson, K. W. (2001, September 10). 'Enrollment and standards rise at CUNY', *New York Times*, B1.

Arenson, K. W. (2002, February 2). 'City College, the faded jewel of CUNY, is recovering its luster and its achievers,' *New York Times*, B1.

Barrow, C. W. (1996). 'The strategy of selective excellence: Redesigning higher education for global competition in a postindustrial society', *Higher Education, 31*, 447–469.

Benjamin, R. and Carroll, S. J. (1997). *Breaking the Social Contract: The Fiscal Crisis in California Higher Education.* Santa Monica, CA: RAND.

Birnbaum, R. (1983). *Maintaining Diversity in Higher Education.* San Francisco: Jossey-Bass.

Bowen, W. G. and Bok, D. (1998). *The Shape of the River: Long-Term Consequences of Considering Race in College and University Admissions.* Princeton, NJ: Princeton University Press.

Bowles, S. and Gintis, H. (1976). *Schooling in Capitalist America: Educational Reform and the Contradictions of Economic Life.* New York: Basic Books.

Brewer, D., Eide, E. and Ehrenberg, R. (1999). 'Does it pay to attend an elite college? Cross cohort evidence on the effects of college type on earnings', *Journal of Human Resources, 34*, 104–123.

Carlin, J. F. (1997). 'I know my campus is broken, but if I try to fix it I'll lose my job'. *Presented at the Greater Boston Chamber of Commerce* Boston, November 4, 1997.

Carlin, J. F. (1998). *Taking Massachusetts Public Higher Education to the Head of the Class.* Boston: Massachusetts Board of Higher Education.

Clark, B. R. (1983). *The Higher Education System: Academic Organization in Cross-National Perspective*. Berkeley, CA: University of California Press.

Collins, R. (1979). *The Credential Society: An Historical Sociology of Education and Stratification*. New York: Academic Press.

Crosson, P. H. (1996). 'Where all politics is local: Massachusetts', in MacTaggart, T. J. (ed.), *Restructuring Higher Education: What Works and What Doesn't in Reorganizing Governing Systems*. San Francisco, CA: Jossey-Bass, pp. 74–102.

Crouse, J. and Trusheim, D. (1988). *The Case against the SAT*. Chicago, IL: University of Chicago Press.

CUNY Matters (2001). 'Louise Mirrer on the honors college, standards, resources, and Medieval Spain', *CUNY Matters* Winter 2001.

Dale, S. B. and Krueger, A. B. (1999). *Estimating the Payoff to Attending a More Selective College*. Cambridge, MA: National Bureau of Economic Research.

Davies, G. K. (1986). 'The importance of being general: Philosophy, politics, and institutional mission statements', in Smart, J. C. (ed.), *Higher Education: Handbook of Theory and Research* (Volume II). New York: Agathon Press, pp. 85–102.

Davies, S. and Guppy, N. (1997). 'Fields of study, college selectivity, and student inequalities in higher education', *Social Forces, 75*, 1417–38.

Dembner, A. (1996a, March 17). 'Remedial ed: Playing catch-up in college', *Boston Globe*, B1.

Dembner, A. (1996b, March 18). 'State sifting strategies for remedial education', *Boston Globe*, B1.

Dembner, A. (1997, January 18). 'Major debate hitting campuses: State cracking down on less popular degrees', *Boston Globe*, B1.

Eaton, J. S. (1995). *Investing in American Higher Education: An Argument for Restructuring*. New York: Council for Aid to Education.

Editorial Board (1998, October 1). 'Cutting 'crust': State colleges, universities get a needed trim', *Worcester Telegram & Gazette*, A6.

Gade, M. (1993). *Four Multicampus Systems: Some Policies and Practices That Work*. Washington, D.C.: Association of Governing Boards of Colleges and Universities.

Gill, B. P. (1999). *The Governance of the City University of New York: A System at Odds with Itself*. Santa Monica, CA: RAND.

Goldstein, M. (2001). *CUNY and the City*. New York: CUNY.

Gumport, P. J. (1993). 'The contested terrain of academic program reduction', *Journal of Higher Education, 64*, 283–311.

Gumport, P. J. and Bastedo, M. N. (2001). 'Academic stratification and endemic conflict: Remedial education policy at CUNY', *Review of Higher Education, 24*, 333–349.

Gumport, P. J. and Pusser, B. (1999). 'University restructuring: The role of economic and political contexts', in Smart, J. (ed.), *Higher Education: Handbook of Theory and Research* (Volume XIV). Bronx, New York: Agathon Press, pp. 146–200.

Healy, P. (1998, June 5). 'CUNY's 4-year colleges ordered to phase out remedial education', *Chronicle of Higher Education*, A36.

Healy, P. (2000, September 24). 'For some, honors college is no honor: Charges of elitism greet new school on UMass campus', *Boston Globe*, A1.

Hebel, S. (2002, March 1). 'A new look for CUNY: Tough admissions policies have drawn good students, but turned some immigrants away', *Chronicle of Higher Education*, A35.

Jacobs, J. A. (1995). 'Gender and academic specialities: Trends among recipients of college degrees in the 1980s', *Sociology of Education, 68*, 81–98.

Jencks, C. and Phillips, M. (Eds.) (1998). *The Black-White Test Score Gap*. Washington, D.C.: Brookings Institution Press.

Kerr, C. (1963). *The Uses of the University*. Cambridge: Harvard University Press.

MacTaggart, T. J. (ed.) (1996). *Restructuring Higher Education: What Works and What Doesn't in Reorganizing Governing Systems*. San Francisco, CA: Jossey-Bass.

McFadden, R. D. (1993, June 29). 'CUNY board gives backing to a redesign', *New York Times*, B1.

Massachusetts Board of Higher Education (1996). *Commonwealth College*. Boston, MA: BHE.

Massachusetts Board of Higher Education (1998). *An Agenda for Performance and Improvement: A Mid-Point Assessment*. Boston, MA: BHE.

Massachusetts Community College Developmental Education Committee (1998). *Access and Quality: Improving the Performance of Massachusetts Community College Developmental Education Programs*. Boston, MA: MCCDEC.

Mazzeo, C. (2000). 'Stakes for students: Agenda-setting and remedial education'. *Paper presented at the annual meeting of the American Educational Research Association.* New Orleans, LA, April 24–28, 2000.

Meek, V. L., Goedegebuure, L., Kivinen, O. and Rinne, R. (eds.) (1996). *The Mockers and the Mocked: Comparative Perspectives on Differentiation, Convergence and Diversity in Higher Education.* Oxford: Pergamon.

Meek, V. L., Huisman, J. and Goedegebuure, L. (eds.) (2000). *Diversity, Differentiation, and Markets. Special issue of Higher Education Policy, 13*(1).

Moore, M. H. (1995). *Creating Public Value: Strategic Management in Government.* Cambridge, MA: Harvard University Press.

Morphew, C. C. (2000a). 'The realities of strategic planning: Program termination at East Central University', *Review of Higher Education, 23,* 257–280.

Morphew, C. C. (2000b). 'Institutional diversity, program acquisition and faculty members: Examining academic drift at a new level', *Higher Education Policy, 13,* 55–77.

National Center for Education Statistics. (2001). *Integrated Postsecondary Education Data System* [IPEDS]. Washington, D.C.: U.S. Department of Education.

Neave, G. (1996). 'Homogenization, integration, and convergence: The Cheshire cats of higher education analysis', in Meek, V. L. et al. (eds.), *The Mockers and the Mocked: Comparative Perspectives on Differentiation, Convergence and Diversity in Higher Education.* Oxford: Pergamon.

Newman, M. (1992, December 9). 'CUNY plan is questioned by faculty', *New York Times,* B1.

Newman, M. (1993, February 28). 'CUNY reorganization unites students and faculty in anger', *New York Times* A33.

Osborne, D. and Gaebler, T. (1993). *Reinventing Government: How the Entrepreneurial Spirit Is Transforming the Public Sector.* New York: Plume.

Renfro, S. and Armour-Garb, A. (1999). *Open Admissions and Remedial Education at the City University of New York.* New York: Mayor's Advisory Task Force on the City University of New York.

Rhoades, G. (1990). 'Political competition and differentiation in higher education', in Alexander, J. C. and Colomy, P. (eds.), *Differentiation Theory and Social Change.* New York: Columbia University Press.

Richardson, R., Bracco, K., Callan, P. and Finney, J. (1999). *Designing State Higher Education Systems for a New Century.* Phoenix: Oryx Press.

Schmidt, B. C., et al. (1999). *The City University of New York: An Institution Adrift.* New York: Mayor's Advisory Task Force on the City University of New York.

Shaw, K. M. (2001). 'Reframing remediation as a systemic phenomenon: A comparative analysis of remediation in two states', in Townsend, B. K. and Twombly, S. B. (eds.), *Community Colleges: Policy in the Future Context.* Westport, Conn.: Ablex, pp. 193–221.

Shin, P. H. B. (2000, October 26). 'CUNY going first class: Wooing top students with plenty of perks', *New York Daily News,* 2.

Slaughter, S. (1990). *The Higher Learning and High Technology: Dynamics of Higher Education Policy Formation.* Albany, NY: SUNY Press.

Slaughter, S. (1993). 'Retrenchment in the 1980s: The politics of prestige and gender', *Journal of Higher Education, 64,* 250–82.

Smelser, N. (1974). 'Growth, structural change, and conflict in California public higher education', in Smelser, N. and Almond, G. A. (eds.), *Public Higher Education in California.* Berkeley, CA: University of California Press, pp. 9–141.

Trow, M. (1987). 'Academic standards and mass higher education', *Higher Education Quarterly, 41,* 268–92.

University of Massachusetts Amherst, Office of Institutional Research (2001). 'Race/ Ethnicity of undergraduates and Commonwealth College students (U.S. citizens), Fall 2001', unpublished data. Available upon request.

Van Voorhis, S. (1998, May 29). 'Program cuts not too painful for colleges', *Boston Business Journal,* 3–4.

Weiss, S. (1993a, June 5). 'Head of CUNY drops plan to cut course offerings', *New York Times,* A1.

Weiss, S. (1993b, July 17). 'Rewards for colleges backing CUNY reorganization', *New York Times,* A23.

Whitaker, D. G. and Pascarella, E. T. (1994). 'Two-year college attendance and socioeconomic attainment: Some additional evidence', *Journal of Higher Education, 65,* 194–210.

Yin, R. K. (1991). *Case Study Research: Design and Methods.* Thousand Oaks, CA: Sage.

Zemsky, R., et al. (1999). *New York State Education Department Review of CUNY's Proposed Master Plan Amendment.* Albany, NY: New York State Board of Regents.

# Minority Enrollment Demand for Higher Education at Historically Black Colleges and Universities from 1976 to 1998: An Empirical Analysis

MACKI SISSOKO, LIANG-RONG SHIAU

## Introduction

Historically black colleges and universities (HBCUs) were established during the segregation period of U.S. history in response to the demand for education by Blacks who did not have access to White educational institutions. As a group, Blacks share a common historical experience of segregation that was characterized by relatively limited educational resources to meet the demand of the black population for higher education. Currently there are 103 HBCUs (53 private and 50 public institutions), representing approximately 3% of the total U.S. institutions of higher education and about 2% of the total U.S. college enrollment (National Center for Education Statistics, 1996). Collectively, these institutions have also been undergoing, over the past three decades, a declining share of black high graduates' enrollment in higher educational institutions. Despite federal desegregation policies, such a relative decline has not been compensated by a corresponding increase in HBCUs' relative share of the total population of non-Black high school graduates' enrollment in higher education.

Although most HBCUs experienced enrollment growth during the periods of educational expansion in the U.S., overall their share of national enrollment has declined because of two factors: the increase in community colleges and the Adams court decisions desegregating higher education in the south (Hauptman & Smith, 1994). Table 1 shows that the total enrollment in HBCUs expanded by about 18.69% from 222,613 students in 1976 to 273,472 in 1998. Despite the modest increase in the number of non-Black students attending HBCUs, the level of diversity in terms of race and ethnicity has remained almost unchanged. Hence, Black students have consistently represented about 81% of the total annual enrollment at HBCUs during that period.

Table 2 indicates that the total U.S. enrollment of Blacks 14 to 34 years of age in postsecondary educational institutional institutions increased significantly by 66% from 996,000 in 1980 to 1,640,000 in 1998. Consequently, the total Black enrollment in all colleges and universities rose from 9.78% in 1980 to 12.75% in 1998. However, as a group, HBCUs' relative share of the total Black enrollment in higher educational institutions declined from 18.18% in 1980 to 13.70% in 1998. In contrast, Black students' enrollment in other institutions of higher education, as a percentage of the total Black enrollment in the U.S., rose from 80.82% in 1980 to 86.3% in 1998. While Black students' enrollment in other colleges and universities rose by 76% from 805,011 in 1980 to 1,415,255 students in 1998, the enrollment of non-Black students in HBCUs rose only by 16.82% (from 42,568 to 49,727) during the same period.

Several factors may have contributed to the decline of HBCUs' relative share of total Black student enrollment in postsecondary educational institutions, and there is no empirical evidence about their effects in the literature. The survival and growth of many HBCUs depend on their ability to maintain or improve their relative share of Black students, who traditionally represented their major source of enrollment. The purpose of this paper is to provide an empirical analysis of the determinants of Black student enrollment in HBCUs. Such information may be useful for policy decisions. An overview of the factors influencing Black enrollment in higher education and a description of the methodological framework as well as the data used in this study are provided in the next section.

## Methodology and Data Collection

### The Determinants of Enrollment Demand

The literature provides a large body of information on the various factors that have been influencing the demand for higher education by Black high school graduates in the U.S. Demographic trends affect the demand for higher education as well as the supply of high school graduates who attend the various postsecondary institutions. The number of high school graduates who are willing and financially capable of pursuing college education is perhaps viewed as the most obvious determinant of enrollment demand for higher education. The post-World War II period has been characterized by an unprecedented increase in the demand for higher education due to the baby boom the U.S. experienced between 1946 and 1964. Enrollment rose sharply during the 1960–1975 period and then remained relatively constant in the late 1970s. Unlike their parents, baby boomers chose either to have fewer children or to postpone child bearing. Consequently, the size of the 18-year-old population, which ceased to grow rapidly in the mid-1970s, began to decline sharply after 1982, a trend that was projected to continue until the late 1990s (Solmon & Wingard, 1989). Although the post-baby boom period was characterized by an overall decline of the U.S. birth rate, many minority groups, Hispanics in particular, experienced both birth rate and immigration increases. As a result, the potential number of minority students attending higher educational institutions is expected to rise for these groups.

The decision to attend college is influenced by the cultural and social capital on which individuals and families rely in order to meet a certain set of established values in society. Coleman (1988) described social capital as the networks that provide information, social norms, and achievement support. Bourdieu and Passeron (1977) described cultural capital as the system of factors individuals derived from their parents that defines their class status. Social and cultural capital are resources people may invest in order to enhance profitability (Bourdieu & Passeron, 1977), increase productivity (Coleman, 1988), and facilitate upward mobility (DiMaggio & Mohr, 1985). Although social and cultural capital affect high school graduates' demand for college education, the process of deciding to invest in a 4-year college varies among Blacks, Hispanics, and Whites (Jackson, 1990; Perna, 2000; St. John, 1991).

It is well documented that economic and financial factors have a significant impact on high school graduates' demand for college education in the U.S. (Coleman, 1990, 1988; DiMaggio & Mohr, 1985; Hearn, 1991; Hossler, Braxton, & Coopersmith, 1989; Litten, Sullivan, & Brodigan, 1983). The demand for college education is influenced by the expected stream of benefits, including the additional lifetime income resulting from higher education and the additional social and intellectual amenities an individual might expect to gain from attending college. Schultz (1961) developed the investment approach to the theory of demand for education, and Becker (1964) suggests that an individual will purchase a college education if the present value of the expected stream of benefits gained from the education exceeds the present costs of the education. Earning a degree from college has been viewed as a symbol of achievement in American society because it provides the recipients with employment opportunities associated with higher incomes and enhances the chance of assuming important leadership positions. Such a view is, perhaps, widely shared among members of the different minority ethnic and racial groups who had limited educational and employment opportunities in the past. On average, college graduates earn more money and experience less unemployment than high school graduates do in the labor force. Several studies provided evidence that earning differentials and lower probabilities of unemployment exert an important influence on college enrollment (Bishop, 1977; Campbell & Siegel, 1971; Florito & Dauffenbach,

1982; Freeman, 1986; Leslie & Brinkman, 1988; Willis & Rosen, 1979). A study by James et al. (1988) also found that higher financial returns are associated with attendance at selective institutions.

Family income can be viewed as part of a student's investment capital available for education. Thus, as evidenced in many studies (Bishop, 1977; Corman, 1983; Glaper & Dunn, 1969; Schwartz, 1986; Sples, 1978), there is a positive association between income and college enrollment. Other studies showed that the average expenditure on college rises with family income (Astin, 1985; Hearn, 1988). Moreover, it is well documented that White students gain higher returns on their investment in higher education than Black students do; however, Blacks who graduate from higher educational institutions do better than those who do not (Becker, 1975; Cohen, 1979; Freeman, 1976; Schultz, 1961; Thurow, 1972).

As one of the major factors of demand for higher education, the cost of college education has experienced a remarkable increase over the past three decades. The average cost of tuition, fees, and room and board paid by a full-time undergraduate rose from $2,275 in 1976–1977 to $9,536 in 1996–1997 for all types of institutions. However, the level of increase varies quite significantly among the different types of educational institutions. Four-year institutions experienced a much greater cost increase than 2-year institutions did. Thus, the average level of these costs rose from $2,577 to $11,227 for all 4-year institutions, and from $1,598 to $5,075 for all 2-year institutions (U.S. Department of Education, National Center for Education Statistics [NCES], 1998). Similarly, private institutions experienced a much higher cost increase than public institutions did. Hence, on the average, these costs rose from $1,935 to $7,334 for all 4-year public institutions, and from $1,491 to $4,404 for all 2-year public institutions. In contrast, they increased from $3,977 to $19,143 for all 4-year private institutions, and from $2,971 to $12,481 for all 2-year private institutions (NCES, 1998).

According to Becker (1964) and Nerlove (1972), a major reason for the high cost of higher education is imperfection in the capital market arising from the ignorance, risk, and lack of collateral that are inherent to a capital market. However, this problem relates more to low-income families who have limited access to capital than to high-income families. Differences in tuition and other costs among the various types of institutions will undoubtedly affect individual students' choice of college for education. Cost-sensitive Black students may shift their enrollment demand to low-cost competing institutions, such as 2-year community junior colleges or vocational and technical institutions that an conveniently located near their residences.

Changes in tuition rates and financial aid affect students from various socioeconomic groups differently. Many studies reviewed by Heller (1997) documented that lower-income students are more sensitive to changes in tuition and aid than are students from middle- and upper-income families. Moreover, Heller (1997) also found that Black students are more sensitive to changes in tuition and financial aid than other groups are; consequently, their enrollment demand is relatively higher for 2-year institutions than for 4-year institutions. It should be pointed out that the sensitivity of minority students to changes in tuition and financial aid is related more to their financial status than to their cultural differences with the dominant group in the U.S.

The gap in college participation rates between low-income and high-income students, on the one hand, and between minorities and Whites, on the other, has widened significantly over the past 20 years, thus contributing to a new inequality in college access. Upon reviewing trends related to financial access, St. John (2002) developed a conceptual model for analyzing the enrollment behavior of college-qualified students. His model, which incorporates both academic and economic variables for explaining college access, showed that finances exerted a much more substantial influence on creating the new inequality.

Several empirical studies conducted on the effect of changes in tuition, fees, and other explicit costs on college enrollment ascertained the expected negative sign. Campbell and Siegel (1971) found a negative relation between college tuition and the demand for college education, and they obtained a price elasticity of demand of –0.44. This negative relationship between college enrollment and tuition price is also reported by Radner and Miller (1975), Funk (1984), Ehrenberg and Sherman (1984), and Schwartz (1986). McPherson (1978) obtained a median coefficient of price elasticity of about –0.7 from the estimates of 10 studies he reviewed. In their study, Fuller, Manski, and Wise (1982) measured the effect of a $100 tuition rise on enrollment, finding a general student price response coefficient of –0.23 for all students whose application to college was accepted.

Leslie and Brinkman (1987) reviewed 25 studies and used a three-step process for standardizing each study in order to compare their results. For each study, Leslie and Brinkman calculated a student price response coefficient (SPRC), which is the change in the college participation rate of 18–24-year-olds for every $100 increase in tuition price based on 1982–1983 dollars for each study. They found that the mean price response is about 0.7%. Thus, given the 1982–1983 average higher education price of $3,420, a $100 increase in tuition would contribute to a drop in the 18–24-year-old participation rate by about three fourths of a percentage point. Leslie and Brinkman's estimated SPRCs from the 25 studies ranged from –0.2 to –2.4. Similar findings were obtained by Jackson and Weathersby (1975), whose estimated SPRCs from seven studies ranged between –0.05 and –1.46, and by McPherson (1978), who reviewed 11 studies and found SPRCs ranging between –0.05 and –1.53.

Savoca (1990) argued that treating the decision to apply to college as an exogenous variable may have underestimated the tuition sensitivity coefficients of the college enrollment decisions of most previous studies. Analyzing the same subset of the National Longitudinal Survey of 1972 used by Fuller, Manski, and Wise (1982), Savoca obtained a coefficient of tuition sensitivity of the decision to apply to college of –0.26. However, Heller (1997) indicated that Savoca's analysis was weakened by her assumption that the institution's tuition-setting behavior is independent of its admission policies. St. John (1990) conducted an update of the 1987 study by Leslie and Brinkman, using a cross-sectional analysis of the sophomore cohort of all types of institutions from the High School and Beyond Survey. He found that a $1,000 tuition increase resulted in a 2.8% decrease in enrollment, which is lower than Leslie and Brinkman's range of –0.50 to –0.8 for a $100 tuition increase.

Rouse (1994) used data from the National Longitudinal Survey of Youth (NLSY) to conduct a comparative analysis of enrollments at 2-year versus 4-year institutions. Using the tuition price at public comprehensive colleges and community colleges from various states and holding a wide range of background characteristics unchanged, Rouse obtained an estimated SPRC of –1.0 when both 2-year and 4-year tuition prices are increased simultaneously. Her model predicted that community colleges would experience more than two thirds of the decline in enrollments. Moreover, she conducted a cross-sector SPRCs analysis that showed community colleges are viewed as substitutes for 4-year comprehensive institutions. In other words, a change in the price of one type of institution affects enrollment in the other type.

Using data from current students, Bryan and Whipple (1995) developed a computer-based model that examined the relationship between tuition elasticity and projected earnings, including the substitution effects of a tuition increase on the choice of institution. The elasticity estimates of enrollment demand with respect to tuition price allow university administrators to determine the appropriate rate of tuition change in order to achieve a desired level of enrollment and retention. They found that the target institution is not pursuing a pricing policy that maximizes its net earnings; rather, its nonprofit goals may have a higher priority. Their model also showed that many students substituted lower-tuition institutions for higher-tuition institutions.

Heller (1997) used a combination of state cross-sectional and time-series data from the Integrated Postsecondary Education Statistics (IPEDS) to calculate fixed-effects models of public college enrollment rates. Controlling for state unemployment levels and grant awards, his analysis of the relationship between tuition and enrollment rates showed an estimated SPRC of –0.36 for a $100 tuition increase at community colleges, using 1993 as a base year. Heller's estimate is lower than Leslie and Brinkman's 1987 finding because, as he pointed out, his study analyzed the enrollment response of all students, not just those enrolled for the first time. There is a consensus among the 20 studies Heller (1997) reviewed: Every $100 increase in tuition results in a decline in enrollments of 0.5 to 1.0 percentage points, a result that is quite consistent with the findings reported by Leslie and Brinkman (1987).

The consensus in the literature that college costs have a negative effect on enrollment is not shared by all sectors in higher education. Clotfelter, Ehrenberg, Getz, and Siegfrid (1991) found no indication that tuition increases exerted a negative influence on the number of applications for a sample of 24 selective colleges and universities for the years 1981–1988. The sample used by Clotfelter et al. consisted of the nation's most prestigious colleges and institutions, including Harvard, whose applications increased at the same time as tuition.

The opportunity cost of pursuing higher education may also involve implicit costs such as income a college student would have earned from jobs available to high school graduates. However, forgone income does not predict consistently the direction of enrollment demand because college students who work often earn their incomes by competing for the same jobs available to high school graduates.

Federal policies and programs intended to either desegregate higher education or increase the demand for college education may have affected enrollment at HBCUs. The landmark Supreme Court decision, Brown v. Board of Education, 347 U.S. 483 (1954), found that state policies to segregate students on the basis of race were unconstitutional and required all school systems to take affirmative steps to remove the vestiges of past discrimination "with all deliberate speed." The Court also ruled in Florida ex rel. Hawkins v. Board of Control, 350 U.S. 413 (1956), that Brown also applied to higher education. Despite these rulings, which were followed by a disruptive and violent transitional period (1955–1965), significant desegregation did not occur until after the passage of the 1964 Civil Rights Act. That act empowered the U.S. attorney general to bring lawsuits on behalf of Black plaintiffs and prohibited the distribution of federal funds to colleges and universities that discriminate based on race, color, or national origin.

Following his election, President Nixon adopted a new policy of non-enforcement of desegregation laws and policies. In 1970, the Legal Defense and Educational Fund of the National Association for the Advancement of Colored People (NAACP) brought a lawsuit, Adams v. Richardson, against the Department of Health, Education, and Welfare (DHEW). It accused DHEW for not enforcing Title VI of the 1964 Civil Right Act against states that operated dual segregated public systems of higher education. The U.S. district court for the District of Columbia, presided by Judge John H. Pratt, mandated enforcement of desegregation laws. It also stipulated that states must achieve a better racial mix of students, faculty, and staff in public colleges, and increase the access and retention of minorities at all levels of higher education. Furthermore, the court acknowledged the role of HBCUs in promoting access and higher retention rates for Black students, and pointed out that desegregation and equity efforts should be achieved at the expense of these institutions.

Federal courts' civil rights decisions, Black marches and demonstrations, federal troop actions, the threat of withdrawing federal educational grants to southern institutions, and the tying of federal educational funding to nondiscriminatory practices contributed to the extensive desegregation of many southern school districts and colleges and universities (Roebuck & Murty, 1993). Predominantly White Institutions with low Black enrollment records are trying to increase diversity in their enrollment programs by appealing to Black high school graduates whose performance is comparable to the average performance of White high school students.

Efforts to desegregate higher education suffered major drawbacks during the 1980s and early 1990s under the Reagan and Bush administrations. President Reagan ran for office on a platform opposing desegregation and affirmative action, and with more ideological consistency than his predecessors, he proceeded to either dismantle or neglect initiatives intended to empower minorities and women (Hauptman & Smith, 1994). Efforts to eliminate or overturn civil rights and affirmative action rulings under the Reagan and Bush administrations contributed to the deterioration of educational opportunity (Conclatore, 1989). In 1987, the Reagan administration, opposed the district court's jurisdiction of higher education, persuaded Judge Pratt to dismiss the Adams case on the ground that the plaintiffs no longer had a legal standing. However, this ruling was overturned in 1989 (Hauptman & Smith, 1994). Moreover, President Reagan attempted to seek tax-exempt status for segregated schools, opposed busing, and decreased the amount of financial aid available in grants while increasing the burden of student loans (Hauptman & Smith, 1994).

Many southern states responded to the dismissal of the Adams case by indicating that the desegregation plan was long overdue, contending that they were better equipped than the federal government to develop plans aimed at attracting minority students and faculty to higher education. In contrast, HBCUs asked the federal court to reverse the dismissal of the Adams case and to shift its focus on their needs. In general, desegregation has been more successful in White colleges and universities than it has been in HBCUs because the percentage of Black students attending White institutions is much higher than the percentage of Black students enrolled in HBCUs (Roebuck & Murty, 1993). As a result, the HBCUs experienced a decline in enrollment during this period (Roebuck & Murty, 1993).

A number of federal programs may have affected HBCUs over the past 35 years. The Higher Education Act (HEA) was initially passed in 1965 under a White House and a Congress dominated by Democrats as an omnibus bill that authorized a variety of institutional, student, and programmatic aid programs for higher education. Hannah (1996) described the historical evolution of HEA under various administrations, including the skills, constraints, and politics that shaped the federal policy-making process. HEA made work-study a permanent part of federal higher education policy, established a federally subsidized Guaranteed Student Loan program for families with moderate incomes, and incorporated Upward Bound from the Poverty Program to recruit and support needy minority students (Gladieu & Wolanin, 1976).

HEA underwent several changes under successive federal administrations. The 1972 amendment strengthened the initial act by creating a system of federally funded Basic Educational Opportunity Grants (BEOG) that would be supplemented by matching State Educational Opportunity Grants (SEOG) to assure every able and needy student a set amount of aid to help meet college costs (Hannah, 1996). Along with the signing of the Middle Income Assistance Act of 1978 by President Carter, which essentially removed income as an eligibility requirement for federally subsidized loans for postsecondary education, these enhancements contributed to the expansion of the eligibility and participation in federal student aid programs (McAdam, 1989). However, a divided Congress along party lines and an increased federal budget deficit under the Reagan administration adversely affected federal policies toward higher education throughout the 1980s. The 1986 HEA Re-authorization and the 1988 and 1990 Budget Reconciliation Acts increased loan limits and interest rates, reinstituted income caps, and added restrictions on students, lenders, and institutions in order to deal with the alarming growth of defaults (Hannah, 1996).

President Reagan signed Executive Order 12320, targeting HBCUs for special attention. Congress passed the 1986 Higher Education Act authorizing $100 million exclusively for HBCUs. Following his election, President Bush signed Executive Order 1267 of April 1989, mandating several actions designed to advance the development of human potential, strengthen the capacity of HBCUs to provide quality education, and increase opportunities to participate in federal programs. Executive Order 1267 established the President's Board of Advisors on HBCUs to supervise the annual development of a federal program designed to increase the participation of HBCUs in federally sponsored programs, and to provide advice on how to increase the role of the private sector in strengthening HBCUs. However, critics argued that neither of these two executive orders was successful because the federal departments involved failed to assist their implementation (Blumenstyle, 1989). The Bush administration also initiated a controversial plan in 1991 allowing federal agencies to work with HBCUs based on their missions and programs. Critics pointed out that such a plan would allow federal agencies and private organizations to focus their attention more on the small number of rich HBCUs and less on the large number of poorer ones (Blumenstyle, 1989).

The 1992 HEA Re-authorization, signed by President Bush, provided funding for five years for $20 billion per year for student grant, loan, and scholarship programs, and for all students eligible for federal loans regardless of income. Besides providing more than three quarters of all financial aid available to students enrolled in postsecondary education (College Board, 1992, 1994), the 1992 HEA Re-authorization represented a major shift in federal policy toward higher education. It shifted from an historic commitment to promote access to postsecondary education through grants based on need to a broader strategy of insured loans regardless of family income (Hannah, 1996). Other provisions of the 1992 HEA Re-authorization included the establishment of a pilot direct loan program, the eligibility of less-than-half-time students for aid, the adoption of a single federal aid application form, and the elimination of the value of a family home or farm from students' aid-need analysis.

The Advisory Committee on Student Financial Assistance (2002) reported that shifts in policies and priorities at the federal, state, and institutional levels have contributed to raising the financial barriers to a college education sharply, thus resulting in a shortage of student aid, particularly need-based grant, as well as rising college tuition. The purchasing power of the Pell Grant maximum, the nation's largest need-based grant program designed to insure that students have access to college education, has eroded significantly from a high of 84% of public college tuition in the mid-1970s to a low of 34% in the mid-1994s. Moreover, budget shortfalls caused by recessionary conditions have contributed to the reduction in state appropriations, thus causing substantial increases in public sector tuition as high as 21% in some states and 7.7% nationwide, even in states that experienced tuition reduction in the 1990s.

The literature provides evidence on differences in the responsiveness to financial aid among racial groups. St. John and Noell (1989) measured the effects of financial aid on the enrollment of

White, Black, and Hispanic students from the sophomore and senior cohorts of the High School Beyond (HSB) survey of 1980, including controls for socioeconomic status, family income, and ability. They reported that Black students were the most responsive to financial offers, followed by Hispanics and Whites, respectively. Using the senior cohort of the HSB survey, Jackson (1989) also analyzed the sensitivity of Black, White, and Hispanic students to financial aid offers, controlling for socioeconomic status, family income, and ability. Similar to St. John and Noell's (1989) finding, Jackson concluded that Black students' enrollment demand was more sensitive to financial offers than the other two groups' demands were.

Heller (1997) used a cross-sectional analysis to compare the responsiveness of White and minority (Black and Hispanic) students to changes in public college tuition, state need-based grants per capita, and unemployment rates. The results from the different models indicated that minority students were more sensitive to tuition increases than their counterpart White students were, and the gap between the two groups increased when grants and unemployment were used as controlled variables. As pointed out earlier, Heller (1997) reported that Black students are more sensitive to changes in tuition and financial aid than White students are. Further, another key observation from his review of studies is that students from community colleges, which have a disproportionately high percentage of Black students, are more sensitive to tuition and aid changes than are students attending 4-year public colleges and universities. Heller (1997) also indicated that financial aids have varying effects on college access and choice, and thus policymakers need to understand how students from different races, incomes, and college sectors respond to these changes differently.

High school graduates applying for college education are affected by their perceptions of barriers to participation in higher education, including the level of congruence between the academic environment of a college and their needs and goals. In her survey of Black students, Freeman (1997) analyzed the economic, psychological, and social barriers affecting their participation in higher education and provided a better understanding of the issues affecting minority students. Black students' perceptions about quality differences among educational institutions—based on criteria such as quality of teaching, availability of learning-enhancing technology, and records of job placement after graduation—may have affected their preference over time. However, as pointed out by Clotfelter et al. (1991), the process by which consumers formulate their perception of quality from their evaluations is not at all self-evident. High-ability students most often saw as indicators of quality a large variety of courses, small classes, and well-equipped laboratories and libraries, while their parents placed greatest interest on the faculty with good teaching and research records (Litten & Hall, 1989). Using average SAT score as an institution's measure of perceived quality, Manski and Wise (1983) found that the probability of choosing a particular institution rose with the student's SAT score up to a certain point, and it then declined when the institution's average score exceeded the student's own score by more than 100 points.

Besides the cost and quality of education factors, the choice of a college or university by Black high school graduates may be influenced by their perception of an institution's academic and social environment in terms of racial tolerance, degree of adjustment, requirements, and support systems. A good fit between students (their needs, attitudes, goals, and expectations) and the environment (its pressure, demands, supports, and the characteristics of its inhabitants) has a positive impact and promotes satisfaction, achievement, and personal growth, whereas a poor fit causes stress (Huebner, 1980). The literature documents that Black students who attend predominantly White colleges and universities experience greater difficulty in adjusting to these academic environments than their White counterparts do. The difficulties facing them include the perception of greater racial tension and hostility in their environments (Wright, 1981), greater levels of isolation (Fleming, 1984), and lower levels of satisfaction (Allen, 1981). Other studies reported that Black students identified less with the institution (Allen, Bobo, & Fleuranges, 1982) and experienced feelings of alienation related to attrition (Suen, 1983). Moreover, Fleming (1984) indicated that Black graduates from predominantly White colleges and universities derived lower levels of intellectual and psychological development than their counterparts who graduated from predominantly Black higher educational institutions. Despite these negative perceptions, the number of Black students attending predominantly White institutions has been rising since the desegregation laws and policies went into effect. Although Black high school graduates' demand for higher education in predominantly White colleges and universities is beyond the scope of this research, it is important to point out a study done by Thompson and Fretz (1991). The study concluded that black students' academic and social adjustment is likely associated with greater acceptance of different learning situations and greater responsiveness to the demand of the traditionally White environment.

Fleming (1984) pointed out the importance of strong, supportive campus interpersonal relations and social networking for cognitive, intellectual, and career-related functioning of Black students on Black campuses. In her comparative analysis of the intellectual development of Black students in Black and White colleges, Fleming's result showed that the patterns of intellectual development are consistently more positive for students in Black schools. She pointed out that Black students attending predominantly Black institutions experience better social adjustment, whereas Black students attending predominantly White institutions experience a crisis in social adjustment. Allen (1992) also reported similar findings, indicating that unlike White institutions, HBCUs provide Black students benefits that are manifested in positive psychological adjustments, more significant academic gains, and greater cultural awareness and commitment than Black students on White campuses.

From the late 1950s through the 1970s, the U.S. experienced a significant expansion of 2-year community junior colleges and state-supported urban universities, whose number increased from approximately 200 at the turn of the twentieth century to nearly 1,100 institutions by 1975. As a result, there has been a significant increase in the availability of higher education institutions to millions of students who wanted to attend college close to their homes. Lower costs, proximity to students' homes, flexible programs making it relatively easier for students to acquire part-time jobs, and reduced risks of not completing schooling increased the demand for education at 2-year junior community colleges (Rogers & Ruchlin, 1971). However, studies (Anderson, Bowman, & Tinto, 1972; Bishop, 1977; Weiler, 1986) found that the effect of proximity on enrollment growth is positive but very small.

Finally, college admission policy affects enrollment. Two major activities designed by educators to affect the size of enrollment are the selection of candidates for admission and for recruitment. The former is a form of non-price rationing while the latter represents one attempt to influence the demand curve (Clotfelter et al., 1991). Student affirmative action programs designed under the federal policies discussed earlier contributed to an increase in the number of minority students in predominantly White institutions. However, the effects that rationing places on the demand for college education are not well known yet, due to the limited empirical research on this issue.

## Empirical Model and Data Collection

Taking into consideration the various factors described above, the enrollment demand function of undergraduates in 4-year HBCUs can be expressed as follows:

$$\text{ENR}[O.\text{sub}.t] = f([Y.\text{sub}.t], [P.\text{sub}.t], P[G.\text{sub}.t], \text{FHE}[D.\text{sub}.t], Q[P.\text{sub}.t])(1)$$

$\text{ENR}[O.\text{sub}.t]$ represents the annual enrollment of Black students in all types of HBCUs in year t. Changes in the annual enrollment level represent the net gains or losses from new freshmen and transfer students after the number of students that either graduate, transfer, or drop out from HBCUs has been taken into account in the reported total enrollment. It should be pointed out that, despite the federal desegregation laws, non-Black high school graduates represent less than 5% of the total enrollment at HBCUs. $[Y.\text{sub}.t]$ is real median income of Black households. $[P.\text{sub}.t]$ represents the real average tuition and fees for all types of institutions of higher education used as a proxy for all HBCUs' average real tuition and fees in year t. The federal government's effort to increase Black high school students' participation in higher education and to desegregate higher educational institutions is represented in the model by two variables: $P[G.\text{sub}.t]$ and $\text{FHE}[D.\text{sub}.t]$. $P[G.\text{sub}.t]$ represents the real average Pell Grant per student under HEA need-based support programs, while $\text{FHE}[D.\text{sub}.t]$ represents the federal desegregation effort under different administrations on Black student enrollment in HBCUs. $Q[P.\text{sub}.t]$ represents the perception of quality by students and their parents based on the average real HBCU expenditure (teaching, administration, research, laboratory, library, hospitalization, etc.) per student during year t.

A rise in the real average cost of tuition and fees of HBCUs, $[P.\text{sub}.t]$, while holding the other explanatory variables (the enrollment demand shifters) constant, would cause the quantity demanded of enrollment to decrease. On the other hand, a change in one or more of the demand shifters, holding [P.sub.t] constant, would cause the demand for enrollment at HBCUs to either increase or decrease. Thus, an increase in the real median income of Blacks can cause enrollment at HBCUs to rise (all other variables held constant) if Black high school graduates consider education from HBCUs to be good. Otherwise, enrollment at HBCUs would decline as real median income increases. An increase in the average expenditure per student, used as a proxy for quality perception, can cause an increase in enrollment at HBCUs. Conversely, when the average expenditure per student decreases, the demand for education at HBCUs would decline.

An increase in the real average Pell Grant (P[G.sub.t]) per student will undoubtedly result in an increase in the number of Black students' participating in higher education, without necessarily contributing to a significant increase in HBCUs' enrollment. Since the program does not restrict the recipients of need-based support grants to any particular type of institution, they may well choose to enroll in non-HBCUs. The effects of federal laws and policies (FHE[D.sub.t]) on Black students' enrollment at HBCUs could be either positive or negative, depending on the level of law enforcement and the educational policies by the existing administration at the White House as well as the relative influence of Democrats and Republicans in Congress. Thus, an increase in federal efforts to desegregate higher educational institutions by a Democratic or Republican administration would lower Black high school students' enrollment and increase non-Black students' enrollment in HBCUs. On the other hand, a decrease in federal need-based financial aid for higher education would reduce Black students' enrollment in post-secondary educational institutions, including HBCUs.

The enrollment demand function in Equation 1 is homogeneous of degree 0 in all prices and incomes. In addition, eligible high school graduates' expectations, preferences, or tastes for higher education are assumed to remain unchanged, an assumption that approximates reality given the value this society places on education. For the empirical analysis, an autoregressive model of Equation 1 is specified in the following mathematical form:

ENR[O.sub.t] + [a.sub.O] + [a.sub.1][P.sub.t] + [a.sub.2][Y.sub.t] + [a.sub.3]P[G.sub.t] + [a.sub.4]Q[P.sub.t] + [a.sub.4]ENR[O.sub.t-1][a.sub.6]FHE[D.sub.t] + [a.sub.7]E[T.sub.t] − [[epsllon].sub.t](2)

where, ENR[O.sub.t], [P.sub.t], [Y.sub.t], P[G.sub.t], Q[P.sub.t], and FHE[D.sub.t] are as defined above. The dependent variable, ENR[O.sub.t], lagged one year (ENR[O.sub.t − 1]), was included in the specified model to capture the effect of retention.

The implementation difference between Democrats and Republicans of federal educational laws and policies is a qualitative determining factor that may result in enrollment level differences at HBCUs between periods of Democratic and Republican administrations. Explanatory variables that are qualitative in nature such as male versus female (in classical studies of differences in earnings based on gender discrimination) are generally constructed in econometric modeling using a dummy variable (Gujurati, 2002; Ramanathan, 2002; Theil, 1971). Thus, FHE[D.sub.t] is included in the model as a dummy variable to measure the impact of Republican and Democratic administrations on enrollment at HBCUs. Since it is difficult to quantify the implementation effort of federal laws and the overall educational policy achievement of a particular administration, FHE[D.sub.t] is used in the model as a binary variable that takes the value of 1 if the federal administration is Republican and 0 if it is Democrat.

The values of 0 for Democrats and 1 for Republicans were assigned according to their term years in office. Given the time it takes for a newly elected president to have his administration fully in place and to have his first fiscal budget passed by Congress, the values assigned to his term years are lagged one year to account for the delayed effect of policy changes. Although the choice of value assigned to either administration is arbitrary, the value 0 for Democrats implies that their administration terms are considered in the regression analysis as control periods. Thus, for

FHE[D.sub.t] − 1, [a.sub.6] represents the coefficient of the dummy variable for republican administrations; and for FHE[D.sub.t] = 0, [a.sub.0] represents the coefficient for democratic administrations.

It is common practice to introduce the time or trend variable in an econometric model for several reasons: (1) to find out how the dependent variable behaves over time; (2) to use the trend variable such as a surrogate for a basic variable affecting the dependent variable such as population increases; and (3) to avoid the problem of spurious correlation associated with time series data (Gujarati, 2002). Thus, $E[T_t]$ was included in Equation 2 to represent the effects of demographic shifts of the Black population on Black enrollment at HBCUs. Chronologically, $E[T_t]$ takes 1 as value for 1976, 2 for 1977, 3 for 1978, and so on, in accordance with the years covered by the study period. Since enrollment at HBCUs increases as the Black population increases, the relationship between population and time may be linear. Therefore, $E[T_t]$ is used as a proxy to measure the effect of the growing trend of the Black population on enrollment at HBCUs. $[\epsilon]_t$ is an error term that follows a random normal distribution with zero mean and constant variance. The intercept parameter $[a_0]$ shows the value of $ENR[O_t]$ when the value of the all other explanatory variables are equal to zero. The other parameters ($[a_1]$, $[a_2]$, $[a_3]$, $[a_4]$, $[a_5]$, $[a_6]$, and $[a_7]$) are slope parameters, each one reflecting the effect on enrollment demand of a unit change of the corresponding explanatory variable. The expected sign of each slope parameter reflects the economic relationship between the explanatory variable and the dependent variable. Thus, the slope parameter $[a_1]$, which measures the change in quantity of enrollment demanded per real dollar change in college costs, is expected to have a negative coefficient based on logic and findings from previous studies. The sign of the slope parameter $[a_2]$, measuring the change in enrollment at HBCUs per unit change in real median income, may be positive or negative depending on whether an increase in Black household real median income would cause an increase or a decrease in the demand for enrollment at HBCUs. The sign of the slope parameter $[a_3]$, measuring the effect of change in the real average Pell Grant per student on enrollment, is expected to be positive. The sign of the parameter $[a_4]$, measuring the effect of a change in average spending per full-time student, is expected to carry a positive sign. The parameter $[a_5]$, which represents the effect of a change retention in $ENR[O_{t-1}]$ on HBCUs' enrollment, may be positive or negative depending on HBCUs' record on retention rate. The sign of parameter $[a_6]$, which measures the effects of Republican administrations' implementation of federal laws and policies on enrollment at HBCUs, may be either positive or negative. An increase in federal effort to desegregate higher educational institutions would have a negative effect on the demand for enrollment at HBCUs. Conversely, a decrease in federal desegregation effort would have a positive effect on the demand for enrollment at HBCUs by Black high school graduates. Finally, the sign of the parameter $[a_7]$ may be either positive or negative depending on Black graduates' population size and decision to enroll at HBCUs. Thus, a growing population of Black high school graduates with a high preference level for enrollment at HBCUs would have a positive trend coefficient. In contrast, either a declining number of Black high school graduates or a rising population of Black high school graduates with a lower preference level for HBCUs' academic programs would result in a negative coefficient of enrollment. Data on enrollment, average tuition and fees, average Pell Grant, and average HBCU expenditure per student for the 1976–1998 period were obtained from the 2001 Digest of Education Statistics published by the National Center for Education Statistics (NCES). Black median income data and the consumer price index (CPI) were collected from the Statistical Abstract of the U.S. Department of Commerce and the Bureau of Labor Statistics, respectively. All variables with nominal incomes, costs, and financial aid were measured in real terms using 1982–1984 as the base period.

## Results

The parameters of the factors that influence annual Black enrollment at HBCUs—namely, the average tuition, the median income, the average Pell Grant, the average expenditure per student (used as a proxy for quality perception), the lagged dependent variable used as a proxy for retention, the federal desegregation policies, and the trend variable—were estimated using ordinary least squares (OLS) procedures. The estimates of two variant models of Equation 2 are reported in Table 3.

The average expenditure per student makes up the difference between the two models. However, its inclusion in model 2 did not contribute to a major improvement of the regression analysis in terms of the statistical significance of the coefficients nor did it explain the variations observed in the dependent variable. Based on the overall statistics of the two models, model 1 appeared to be the best fit for the data used, and its regression equation is given by Table 3.

The Durban-h statistic indicated no evidence of the presence of first-order serial autocorrelation. Moreover, no presence of spurious regression was detected in the estimated regression. With the exception of the coefficients of the real median Black income, the estimated parameters of the other variables in model 1 were, as indicated in the P-Value column, statistically significant. In addition, the coefficient of determination (adjusted [R.sup.2]) is quite high, 0.9697, which implies that approximately 97% of the variation in enrollment at HBCUs is explained by the model.

As expected, the coefficient of tuition and fees ([P.sub.t]) is negative and statistically significant at the 3% level, which suggests that the cost of education is a major factor in explaining the variation observed in Black students' enrollment at HBCUs. The negative relationship between enrollment and education costs was reported by previous studies (e.g., Campbell & Siegel, 1971; Ehrenberg & Sherman, 1984; Fuller, Manski, & Wise, 1988; Funk, 1984; McPherson, 1978; Radner & Miller, 1975; Schwartz, 1986) on the enrollment of Whites and other socioeconomic groups at non-HBCUs. The coefficient of the slope shows that a rise in the real average cost of tuition and fees by $100 would result in a decrease in Black enrollment at HBCUs by about 4,250 students, which represents approximately 2% of the average Black enrollment. This result is consistent with earlier studies (Heller, 1997; St. John, 1989, 1991) that reported that Black students are more sensitive to tuition increase than other socioeconomic groups.

The coefficient of real median income of Black households ([Y.sub.t]) is positive but statistically insignificant. The decline in the real Black median income throughout the 1980s and early 1990s may have contributed to the non-significance level of this variable in determining Black students enrollment at HBCUs. It should also be pointed out that the growing number of Black households with higher earnings is a trend that may have resulted in a growing number of Black students attending other institutions whose academic programs may be perceived as superior to those of HBCUs. Consequently, this trend may have undermined the significance of the median income, as a measure of central tendency, in determining Black enrollment at HBCUs. The affordable tuition policy and lower academic requirements that most HBCUs maintained in the past provided Black students, especially those from low-income households, access to higher education. However, as the educational gap between White and Black high school students narrows and the number of Black households with higher earnings continues to rise, Black enrollment in relatively more expensive and more academically challenging universities and colleges will continue to increase.

The coefficient of the real average Pell Grant, P[G.sub.t], is positive and statistically significant at the 9% level, an indication that need-based financial aid plays an important role in determining the level of Black student enrollment at HBCUs. This result supports previous studies (Heller, 1991; Jackson, 1989; St. John & Noell, 1989) that found Black students to be more sensitive to changes in financial aid than White and Hispanic students. As reported by the Advisory Committee on Student Financial Assistance (2002), the real average Pell Grant per student has eroded significantly, thus making the access to college education by low-income students more difficult. The erosion of the purchasing power of the Pell Grant maximum, along with the decrease in state appropriations caused by budget shortfalls and the tuition increase most universities and colleges have experienced over the past 20 years, contributed to the decline of Black student enrollment at HBCUs. The coefficient of the real average Pell Grant indicates that a $100 increase would result in an increase in Black enrollment at HBCUs by approximately 2,755 students.

As pointed out earlier, the perception of quality was positive but insignificant, suggesting that it did not account notably for the changes observed in enrollment at HBCUs. Such a result is not surprising given the revenue and expenditure disparities that exist among the various types of HBCUs on the one hand, and between HBCUs and all higher educational institutions in the U.S. on the other. According to the NCES July 1996 Report on Historically Black Colleges and Universities, the gap between HBCUs and all public colleges and universities on educational and general expenditure per student has widened since the late 1970s. From 1976–1977 to 1993–1994, the real educational and general expenditure per student rose by 4% for HBCUs as compared to 11% for all public institutions (NCES, 1996). Moreover, the significant erosion of the real average expenditure per student contributed in part to the reduction of the real purchasing power of HBCUs, thus limiting their ability to hire highly qualified faculty and to maintain or improve the quantity as well as the quality of their equipment for teaching and research and their library materials.

The coefficient of the lagged dependent variable (ENR[O.sub.t-1]), representing student retention at HBCUs was positive and quite highly significant at the 0% level. This result indicates that the level of enrollment in any given year is significantly determined by the retention rate from the previous year's enrollment. Because of the costs associated with transferring to predominantly White colleges and universities, most Black students who enroll at HBCUs stay until completion of their academic programs. As reported by Fleming (1984) and Allen (1992), Black institutions are perceived as providing Black students an environment that has positive impact and promotes satisfaction, achievement, and personal growth.

The dummy variable representing federal laws and policies on higher education (FHE[D.sub.t]) under Republican administrations exhibited a positive and statistically significant coefficient. The sign of the coefficient suggests a positive relationship between Black student enrollment at HBCUs and the enforcement of federal laws and policies on higher education under Republican administrations. Historically, Republican administrations have not been strong in their implementation of federal desegregation laws regarding higher educational institutions. On the other hand, both Presidents Reagan and Bush (whose administrations were in office for more than half of the study period) signed executive orders that provided HBCUs funding for the development of human potential and the strengthening of their capacity to provide quality education. Overall, Republican enforcement of federal laws, as well as their implementation of programs on higher education, may have contributed to the increase in Black enrollment at HBCUs by approximately 7,366 students. Any effort to desegregate higher education would be unsuccessful unless it is based on sound federal policies primarily designed, on the one hand, to narrow the educational gap between White and minority high school students, and on the other hand, to provide HBCUs the additional resources they need in order to develop comparable quality academic programs.

The estimated coefficient of the trend variable is positive and statistically significant at the 2% level, which indicates that enrollment at HBCUs was in part determined by changes in the population. As the coefficient of the trend variable shows, over the period from 1976 to 1998, Black enrollment at HBCUs increased at the absolute rate of 2,777 students per year. However, this coefficient should be interpreted as the net increase in the level of total annual enrollment. The enrollment of freshmen and transfer students at HBCUs determines whether the total annual enrollment at HBCUs has increased or decreased following a decline caused by the number of students that drop out, transfer to other institutions, or graduate from HBCUs each year. In 1993–1994, more than 36,467 degrees were conferred by HBCUs (NCES, 1996). A total of 39,244 new students enrolled at HBCUs in 1993–1994, a total that is approximately 3% of all black students enrolled in all institutions of higher education during that year. Thus, the enrollment of new students at HBCUs in 1993–1994 exceeded the number of students who graduated by 2,777.

## Conclusion

This study provides empirical evidence of the determinants of enrollment at HBCUs from 1976 to 1998 by Black students using OLS techniques. The results show that Black student enrollment at HBCUs is essentially determined by the average cost of tuition and fees, the average Pell Grant per student, the retention rate, federal policies, and Black population trend. The coefficient of tuition and fees cost was negative and statistically significant, a result that further supports previous studies on higher education that also reported a negative relationship between enrollment and education cost. Thus, a rise in the real average cost of tuition would result in a decline in Black student enrollment at HBCUs. In contrast, the coefficient of the real median Black Income was positive but insignificant in the determining some of the changes observed in Black student enrollment at HBCUs. Such a result was probably attributed to the fact that the real median Black Income experienced several years of decline during the study period.

The coefficient of the average Pell Grant per student was positive and statistically significant. This finding provides additional empirical evidence that Black students are more sensitive to changes in need-based financial aid than White students are. Therefore, in light of the recent report by the Advisory Committee on Student Financial Assistance (2002), an increase in the need-based grant by the federal administration would make access to college education possible to a significant percentage of Black high school graduates. The access to colleges and universities by Blacks would become increasingly difficult without periodic increases in financial aid to offset the erosion of the

TABLE 1

>Enrollment of Black and Non-Black Students in Historically Black
>Colleges and Universities for Selected Years

| >Years | Total Enrollment | Black Enrollment | | Non-Black Enrollment | |
|---|---|---|---|---|---|
| | | Number | Percent | Number | Percent |
| >1980 | 233,577 | 190,989 | 81.77 | 42,568 | 18.23 |
| >1990 | 257,152 | 208,682 | 81.15 | 48,470 | 18.85 |
| >1998 | 273,472 | 223,745 | 81.81 | 49,727 | 18.19 |

>SOURCE: Enrollment numbers were collected from Tables 184 and 223 of the
>National Center for Educational Statistics, U.S. Department of Education
>(1998).

>TABLE 2

>Enrollment of Black Students 14 to 34 Years of Age in Black and
>Non-Black Colleges and Universities for Selected Years

| >Years | Enrollment in All U.S. Colleges and Universities | | | Black Enrollment in HBCUs | |
|---|---|---|---|---|---|
| | Total | Black | Percent | Number | Percent |
| >1980 | 10.181,000 | 996,000 | 9.78 | 190,989 | 19.18 |
| >1990 | 11,303,000 | 1,167,000 | 10.32 | 208,682 | 17.88 |
| >1998 | 12,860,000 | 1,640,000 | 12.75 | 223,745 | 13.7 |

| >Years | Black Enrollment in Non-HBCUs | |
|---|---|---|
| | Number | Percent |
| >1980 | 805,011 | 80.82 |
| >1990 | 958,318 | 82.12 |
| >1998 | 1,415,255 | 86.3 |

>SOURCE: Enrollment numbers were collected from Tables 184, 213, and 223
>of the National Center for Educational Statistics, U.S. Department of
>Education (1998).

>TABLE 3

>Results of the Regression Analysis

### Model 1

| >Variable | Coefficient | t-Statistics | P-value |
|---|---|---|---|
| >Constant | -62298.3 | -1.9776 | 0.067 |
| >[P.sub.t] | -42.5746 | -2.3551 | 0.033 |
| >[Y.sub.t] | 2.7873 | 1.1838 | 0.255 |
| >PGt | 27.5469 | 1.7944 | 0.093 |
| >Q[P.sub.t] | | | |
| >ENR[O.sub.t-1] | 1.2196 | 10.4165 | 0.000 |
| >FHE[D.sub.t] | 7366.28 | 2.2212 | 0.042 |
| >E[T.sub.t-1] | 2777.18 | 2.4657 | 0.026 |
| >Adjusted [R.sup.2] | 0.9697 | | |
| >F-statistic | 113.054 | | |
| >Durbin-h | -0.0395 | | |

### Model 2

| >Variable | Coefficient | t-Statistic | P-value |
|---|---|---|---|
| >Constant | -136686 | -1.8500 | 0.086 |
| >[P.sub.t] | -55.0300 | -2.6015 | 0.021 |
| >[Y.sub.t] | 3.2535 | -1.8500 | 0.192 |
| >PGt | 12.6954 | 0.6264 | 0.541 |
| >Q[P.sub.t] | 8.3343 | 1.1111 | 0.285 |
| >ENR[O.sub.t-1] | 1.2756 | 10.0708 | 0.000 |
| >FHE[D.sub.t] | 8489.30 | 2.4661 | 0.027 |
| >E[T.sub.t-1] | 1681.55 | 1.1282 | 0.278 |
| >Adjusted [R.sup.2] | 0.9701 | | |
| >F-statistic | 98.5962 | | |
| >Durbin-h | -0.5586 | | |

>ENR[O.sub.t] = -62298.3 -42.5746[P.sub.t] + 2.7873[Y.sub.t] +
>27.5469P[G.sub.t] + 1.2195ENR[O.sub.t-1] (31501.4) (18.0780) (2.3545)
>(15.3511) (0.1170) 7366.28FHE[D.sub.t] + 2777.18E[T.sub.t]
>(3316.30) (1126.31)

>The numbers in parenthesis represent standard errors.

>APPENDIX A

>Descriptive Statistics of the Regression Variables

|  | FHED | ENRO | PG | QP | P | Y |
|---|---|---|---|---|---|---|
| >Mean | 0.61 | 201,970.10 | 1,115.57 | 13,419.92 | 2,189.70 | 15,968.09 |
| >Median | 1.00 | 192,242.00 | 1,109.00 | 13,719.37 | 2,164.00 | 16,062.00 |
| >Maximum | 1.00 | 231,198.00 | 1,334.00 | 15,846.75 | 3,055.00 | 18,039.00 |
| >Minimum | 0.00 | 178,628.00 | 934.00 | 11,109.60 | 1,602.00 | 14,091.00 |
| >Std. Dev. | 0.50 | 19,271.05 | 104.03 | 1,468.22 | 495.51 | 1,010.49 |
| >Skewness | (0.45) | 0.38 | 0.30 | 0.02 | 0.29 | 0.12 |
| >Kurtosis | 1.20 | 1.51 | 2.30 | 1.70 | 1.75 | 2.57 |
| ># of Obs | 23.00 | 23.00 | 23.00 | 23.00 | 23.00 | 23.00 |

|  | ET |
|---|---|
| >Mean | 12.00 |
| >Median | 12.00 |
| >Maximum | 23.00 |
| >Minimum | 1.00 |
| >Std. Dev. | 6.78 |
| >Skewness | 0.00 |
| >Kurtosis | 1.80 |
| ># of Obs | 23.00 |

>APPENDIX B

>HBCU Data set.

| >Years | ENR[O.sub.t] | ENR[O.sub.t-1] | P[G.sub.t] | Q[P.sub.t] | [P.sub.t] |
|---|---|---|---|---|---|
| >1976 | 190,500 |  | 1,334 | 11,110 | 1,624 |
| >1977 | 191,274 | 190,500 | 1,251 | 11,466 | 1,624 |
| >1978 | 192,242 | 191,274 | 1,248 | 11,833 | 1,646 |
| >1979 | 191,666 | 192,242 | 1,280 | 11,935 | 1,602 |
| >1980 | 190,989 | 191,666 | 1,070 | 11,837 | 1,664 |
| >1981 | 186,814 | 190,989 | 934 | 11,712 | 1,603 |
| >1982 | 182,639 | 186,814 | 994 | 11,878 | 1,685 |
| >1983 | 181,721 | 182,639 | 1,018 | 12,118 | 1,790 |
| >1984 | 180,803 | 181,721 | 1,069 | 12,656 | 1,910 |
| >1985 | 179,716 | 180,803 | 1,189 | 13,097 | 2,027 |
| >1986 | 178,628 | 179,716 | 1,187 | 13,551 | 2,109 |
| >1987 | 186,390 | 178,628 | 1,147 | 13,719 | 2,164 |
| >1988 | 194,151 | 186,390 | 1,183 | 13,820 | 2,247 |
| >1989 | 201,417 | 194,151 | 1,160 | 13,851 | 2,290 |
| >1990 | 208,682 | 201,417 | 1,109 | 13,955 | 2,308 |
| >1991 | 218,366 | 208,682 | 1,123 | 14,180 | 2,413 |
| >1992 | 228,963 | 218,366 | 1,100 | 14,455 | 2,507 |
| >1993 | 231,198 | 228,963 | 1,042 | 14,663 | 2,648 |
| >1994 | 230,162 | 231,198 | 1,013 | 15,009 | 2,729 |
| >1995 | 229,418 | 230,162 | 994 | 15,059 | 2,846 |
| >1996 | 223,498 | 229,418 | 1,005 | 15,293 | 2,909 |
| >1997 | 222,331 | 223,498 | 1,057 | 15,616 | 2,963 |
| >1998 | 223,745 | 222,331 | 1,151 | 15,847 | 3,055 |

| >Years | [Y.sub.t] | [E.sub.t] | FHE[D.sub.t] |
|---|---|---|---|
| >1976 | 16,243 | 1 | 1 |
| >1977 | 15,781 | 2 | 1 |
| >1978 | 16,686 | 3 | 0 |
| >1979 | 15,942 | 4 | 0 |
| >1980 | 15,381 | 5 | 0 |
| >1981 | 14,594 | 6 | 0 |
| >1982 | 14,091 | 7 | 1 |
| >1983 | 14,564 | 8 | 1 |
| >1984 | 14,852 | 9 | 1 |
| >1985 | 15,600 | 10 | 1 |
| >1986 | 16,062 | 11 | 1 |
| >1987 | 16,202 | 12 | 1 |
| >1988 | 16,339 | 13 | 1 |
| >1989 | 16,298 | 14 | 1 |
| >1990 | 16,391 | 15 | 1 |
| >1991 | 15,821 | 16 | 1 |
| >1992 | 15,041 | 17 | 1 |
| >1993 | 14,908 | 18 | 1 |
| >1994 | 16,665 | 19 | 0 |
| >1995 | 17,041 | 20 | 0 |
| >1996 | 16,904 | 21 | 0 |
| >1997 | 17,821 | 22 | 0 |
| >1998 | 18,039 | 23 | 0 |
| > |

real purchasing power due to inflation and the changes in demand for enrollment by high school graduates due to demographic shifts.

As implied by the positive and highly significant coefficient of the lagged dependent variable used as a proxy for retention, current enrollment is significantly determined by past enrollment levels. The high retention rate of HBCUs is perhaps due to the suitable environment they provide to

Black students, as Hucbner (1980) pointed out, for the achievement of their growth without any fear of racial tension or academic stress.

The quality perception displayed a positive but insignificant coefficient, implying that it was not a major factor in determining black student enrollment at HBCUs. The decline of the real average expenditure per student HBCUs experienced during the period under consideration may be attributed for the relative insignificance of this variable in explaining the enrollment changes observed at HBCUs.

The coefficient of the dummy variable representing Republican administrations indicates that their level of enforcement of federal laws regarding higher education and the changes observed in Black students enrollment at HBCUs were positively and significantly associated. Historically, Republicans have maintained weaker federal desegregation law enforcement policies than Democrats have. Since most of the study period was essentially predominated by Republican administrations, the country's gradual shift to the right may have contributed to an increase in Black students' enrollment at HBCUs.

Finally, the coefficient of the trend variable is positive and statistically significant, perhaps indicating that the demographic changes the Black population has experienced during the 1976–1998 period contributed to an increase in Black student enrollment at HBCUs.

# References

Advisory Committee on Student Financial Assistance. (June 2002). Empty promises: The myth of college access in America, a report of the Advisory Committee on Student Financial Assistance.

Allen, W. R. (1992). The color of success: African-American college student outcomes at predominantly White and historically Black public colleges and universities. *Harvard Educational Review, 62*(1), 26–44.

Allen, W. R., Bobo, L., & P. Fleuranges (1984). Preliminary report: 1982 undergraduate students attending predominantly White-supported universities. Ann Arbor, MI: Center for Afro-American and African Studies.

Anderson, C. J., Bowman, M. J., & Tinto, V. (1972). *Where colleges are and who attends: Effects of accessibility on college attendance.* New York: McGraw-Hill.

Astin, A. W. (1985). The American freshman: National norms. Los Angeles: Cooperative Institutional Research Program.

Becker, G. S. (1975). *Human capital* (2d ed.). New York: Columbia University Press.

Bishop, J. (1977). The effects of public policies on the demand for higher education. *Journal of Human Resources, 12*, 285–307.

Bordieu, P., & Passeron, J. C. (1977). *Reproduction in education, society, and culture.* Beverly Hills, CA: Sage.

Brown v. Board of Education, 347 U.S. 483 (1954).

Bryan, G. A., & Whipple, T. W. (1985). Tuition elasticity of the demand for higher education among current students: A pricing model. *Journal of Higher Education, 66*, 560–574.

Campbell, R., & Siegel, B. N. (1971). *The demand for higher education in the United States, 1919–1964.* In D. C. Rogers & H. S. Ruchlin (Eds.), *Economics and Education.* New York: The Free Press.

Clotfelter, C. T., Ehrenberg, R. G., Getz, M., & Slegfrid, J. J. (1991) *Economic challenges in higher education.* Chicago: The University of Chicago Press.

Cohen, E. (1979). *The economics of education.* Cambridge, MA: Harper & Row.

Coleman, J. S. (1988). Social capital in the creation of human capital. *American Journal of Sociology, 94*, 95–120.

College Board. (1992). *Trends in student aid: 1980 to 1990.* New York: College Board Publications.

College Board. (1994). *Trends in student aid: 1984 to 1994.* New York: College Board Publications.

Conclatore. (1989, August). Appeals court breathes life into Adams desegregation suit, Black Issues in Higher Education.

Corman, H. (1983). Postsecondary education enrollment responses by recent high school graduates and older adults. *Journal of Human Resources, 17*(2), 247–267.

DiMaggio, P., & Mohr, J. (1985). Cultural capital, educational attainment, and marital selection. *American Journal of Sociology, 94*, 1231–1261.

Ehrenberg, R. G. & Sherman, D. R. (1984). Optimal financial aid policies for a selective university. *Journal of Human Resources, 19*, 202–230.

Fiorito, J. & Dauffenbach, R. C. (1982, October). Market and nonmarket influences on curriculum choice by college students. *Industrial and Labor Relations Review*, 88–101.

Fleming, J. (1984). *Blacks in college: A comparative study of students' success in Black and White institutions*. San Francisco: Jossey-Bass.

Florida ex rel. Hawkins v. Board of Control, 350 U.S. 413 (1956).

Freeman, R. B. (1976). *The overeducated American*. New York: Academic Press.

Freeman, R. B. (1986). Demand for education. In O. Ashenfelter & R. Layard (Eds.), *Handbook of Labor Economics*. Amsterdam; North-Holland.

Freeman, K. (1997, September/October). Increasing African Americans' participation in higher education. *Journal of Higher Education, 68*, 523–550.

Fuller, W., Manski, C., & Wise, D. (1982). New evidence on economic determinants of postsecondary schooling choices. *Journal of Human Resources, 12*, 477–495.

Funk, H. J. (1972, November). Price elasticity of demand for education at a private university. *Journal of Educational Research, 66*, 130–134.

Gladieu, L. E., & Wolanin, T. R. (1976). *Congress and the colleges: The national politics of higher education*. Lexington, MA: D.C. Health.

Gujarati, D. N. (2002). *Basic econometrics* (4th ed.). New York: McGraw-Hill, Inc.

Hannah, S. B. (1996). The Higher Education Act of 1992: Skills, constraints, and the politics of higher education. *Journal of Higher Education, 67*, 498–527.

Hauptman, A., & Smith, P. (1994). Financial aid strategies for improving minority student participation in higher education. In M. J. Justiz, R. Wilson, & L. G. Bjork (Eds.), *Minorities in higher education*. American Council on Education, Oryx Press.

Hearn, J. C. (1980). Academic and nonacademic influence in the college destinations of 1980 high school graduates. *Sociology of Education, 64*, 158–172.

Hearn, J. C. (1988). Attendance at high-cost colleges: Ascribed, socioeconomic, and academic influences on student enrollment patterns. *Economics of Education Review, 7*(1), 65–76.

Heller, D. E. (1997). Student price response in higher education: An update to Leslie and Brinkman. *Journal of Higher Education, 68*, 624–659.

Hossier, D., Braxton, J., & Coopersmith. G. (1989). Understanding student college choice. In J. C. Smart (Ed.), *Higher education: Handbook of theory and research* (Vol. 5, pp. 231–288). New York: Agathon Press.

Hucbner, L. A. (1980). Interaction of students and campus. In U. Delworth & G. R. Henson, (Ed.), *Student services: A handbook for the professor* (pp. 117–155). San Francisco: Jossey-Bass.

Jackson, G. A. (1989) *Responses of Black, Hispanic, and White Students to financial aid: College entry among recent high school graduates*. College Park, MD: National Center for Postsecondary Governance and Finance, University of Maryland.

Jackson, G. A. (1990). Financial aid, college entry, and affirmative action. *American Journal of Education, 98*, 523–550.

Jackson, G. A., & Weathersby, G. B. (1975). Individual demand for higher education. *Journal of Higher Education, 46*, 623–652.

James, E., et al. (1988). *College quality and future earnings: Where should you send your child to college?* Washington, D.C.: U.S. Department of Education, Office of Research.

Karen, D. (1991). The politics of class, race, and gender: Access to higher education in the United States, 1960–1986. *American Journal of Education, 99*(2), 208–237.

Lamont, M., & Lareau, A. (1988). Cultural capital: Allusions, gaps, and glissados in recent theoretical developments. *Sociological Theory, 6*, 153–168.

Leslie, L. L., & Brinkman, P. T. (1987). Student price response in higher education: The student demand studies. *Journal of Higher Education, 58*, 181–204.

Leslie, L. L., & Brinkman, P. T. (1988). *The economic value of higher education*. New York: American Council on Education, MacMillan.

Litten, L. H., & Hall, A. E. (1989). In the eyes of our beholders: Some evidence oh how high school students and their parents view quality in colleges. *Journal of Higher Education, 60*, 302–324.

Litten, L. H., Sulllvan, D., & Brodigan, D. (1983). *Applying market research in college admissions*. New York: The College Board.

Manski, C. F., & Wise, D. A. (1983). *College choice in America*. Cambridge, MA: Harvard University Press.

McAdam, J. (1992). *Summary of Title IV provisions of the Conference Agreement on Higher Education Amendments Act of 1992*. Washington, D.C.: The McAdam Group.

McPherson, M. S. (1978). The demand for higher education. In D. W. Breneman & C. E. Finn (Eds.), *Public policy and private higher education*. Washington, D.C.: Brookings.

National Center for Education Statistics. (1996). *Historically black colleges and universities: 1976 to 1994*. Washington, D.C.: Author.

Nerlove, M. (1972). On tuition and the costs of higher education: Prolegomena to a conceptual framework. *Journal of Political Economy, 80*, 5178–5218.

Perna, L. W. (2000). Differences in the decision to attend college among African Americans, Hispanics, and Whites. *Journal of Higher Education, 71*, 117–141.

Radner, R., & Miller, L. S. (1975). *Demand and supply in U.S. higher education*. New York: McGraw-Hill.

Ramanathan, R. (2002). *Introductory econometrics with applications* (5th ed.). United States: South-Western

Roebuck, J. B., & Murty, K. S. (1993). *Historically black colleges and universities*. Westport, CT: Praeger.

Rouse, C. E. (1994). What to do after high school: The two-year versus four-year college enrollment decision. In R. G. Ehrenberg (Ed.), *Choices and consequences: Contemporary policy Issues In education* (pp. 59–88). Ithaca, NY: ILR Press.

Schultz, T. W. (1961). Investment in human capital. *American Economic Review, 51*, 1–17.

Schwartz, J. B. (1986). Wealth neutrality in higher education: The effects of student grants. *Economics of Education Review, 5*(2), 107–117.

Solmon, L. C., & Wingard, T. (1989). The changing demographics: Problems and opportunities. In P. G. Altbach & K. Lomotey (Eds.), *The racial crisis in American higher education*. Albany, NY: State University of New York Press.

Spies, R. R. (1978). *The effects of rising costs on college choice: A study of the application decisions of high-ability students*. New York: College Entrance Examination Board.

St. John, E. P. (1990). Price response in enrollment Decisions: An analysis of the High School and Beyond sophomore cohort. *Research in Higher Education, 31*, 161–176.

St. John, E. P. (1991). What really influences minority attendance? Sequential analysis of the High School and Beyond sophomore cohort. *Research in Higher Education, 32*, 141–158.

St. John, E. P. (2002). *The access challenge: Rethinking the causes of the new inequality*. Policy Issue Report #2002–01. Bloomington, IN: Indiana Education Policy Center, Indiana University.

St. John, E. P., & Noell, J. (1989). The effects of student financial aid on access to higher education: An analysis of progress with special consideration of minority enrollment. *Research in Higher Education, 30*, 563–581.

Suen, H. (1983). Alienation and attrition of black college students on a predominantly white campus. *Journal of Student Personnel, 24*, 117–21.

Thell, H. (1971). *Principles of econometrics*. New York: John Wlley & Sons.

Thompson, C. E., & Fretz, B. R. (1991). Predicting the adjustment of black students at predominantly white institutions. *Journal of Higher Education, 62*, 437–450.

Thurow, L. C. (1972). Education and economic equality. Public Interest, *28*, 66–81.

U.S. Department of Education (1998). *National center for education statistics: Higher education general information survey (HEGIS)*. Washington, D.C.: Author.

Weiler, W. C. (1986). A sequential logit model of the access effects of higher education institutions. *Economics of Education Review, 5*(1), 49–55.

William, J. B, III (Ed.) (1988). *Desegregating America's colleges and universities: Title VI regulation of higher education*. New York: Teachers College Press.

Willis, R. J., & Rosen, S. (1979). Education and self-selection. *Journal of Political Economy, 87*(5), 7–36.

Macki Sissoko is assistant professor of Economics at Norfolk State University. Liang-Rong Shiau is professor of Economics at Norfolk State University.

**Publication Information:** Article Title: *Minority Enrollment Demand for Higher Education at Historically Black Colleges and Universities from 1976 to 1998: An Empirical Analysis*. Contributors: Macki Sissoko — author, Liang-Rong Shiau - author. Journal Title: *Journal of Higher Education*. Volume: 76. Issue: 2. Publication Year: 2005. Page Number: 181 +. COPYRIGHT 2005 Ohio State University Press; COPYRIGHT 2005 Gale Group

# CHAPTER 5:
# POSTSECONDARY FINANCE

# Patterns of Finance: Revolution, Evolution, or More of the Same?

## D. BRUCE JOHNSTONE

This examination of the prospect of revolutionary change in patterns of financing American higher education in the next decade begins with a consideration of current patterns of financing along three dimensions: total resources, cost per unit, and apportionment of costs (Johnstone, 1993a, forthcoming). I pose several questions for each dimension, describing ways in which current patterns might change and suggesting the likelihood of such changes being revolutionary or evolutionary. My personal conclusion is that the next decade will consist largely of struggling in the same ways with the difficulties all too familiar from the current decade.

## Current Patterns and Major Issues

The patterns and discernible trajectories of higher education finance in any country may be described along three dimensions:

1. *The total resources devoted to higher education and to its traditional products of teaching, research or scholarship, and service. The most important part of this sum is the total of public, or taxpayer-provided, resources.*

Currently, measured by the scale of resources, American higher education must be characterized as enormous, even controlling for our great population and great wealth. This observation is true whether "scale" is measured by the proportion of the traditional college-age population matriculating, enrolling, or completing college, or by the percentage of adults currently enrolled or having some tertiary degree, or by the percentage of total gross domestic product or of total public expenditures devoted to higher education (Johnstone, 1991). On the dimension of total financial resources devoted to higher education, or the scale of the aggregate enterprise, speculations about radical changes in the near-term future would include these questions:

- Is higher education likely in the next decade to claim an appreciably greater or lesser amount either of the nation's total resources, or more narrowly, of our public (taxpayer-originated) resources?
- If there is to be some "revolutionary change" in scale, and if that change is to involve that which institutions of higher education mainly do—which is to teach—would such a change entail more or fewer students entering into the system, thereby changing what we have come to describe as participation, or access? Or might it more likely entail more (or less) higher education for the average student enrolled, thus changing persistence or completion or the prevalence of post-baccalaureate education, or perhaps the amount of continuing or lifelong education, but without radically changing the proportion of any age cohort ultimately accessing higher education?
- Or might the change in scale have to do more with the total time and resources that the nation's more than 500,000 full-time and nearly 300,000 part-time faculty presently devote to research

and the dissemination of knowledge (and the volume of articles and books published and the number of scholarly conferences) as opposed to teaching? This change might yield considerably more teaching and commensurably less scholarship for little or no change in the total resources devoted to the nation's higher education enterprise.

2.  *The productivity, or efficiency, or cost per unit of the higher educational enterprise, whether these "units" be numbers of students taught, units of actual learning, or new knowledge generated.*

Because teaching (actually, learning) is the main, although by no means the only, product of American higher education, and because we still have no reliable, affordable measure of the learning added by the college or university, the dominant measure of efficiency in higher education is the cost per student credit hour, or cost per full-time equivalent student. This cost, in turn, is a function of: (a) the average faculty and staff costs, which are determined mainly by the level of salaries and whether the faculty and staff are full-time, with benefits, or part-time, with low wages and no benefits; (b) the prevailing faculty/staff-to-student ratio, which, given the traditional teaching paradigm, is mainly a function of class size and teaching loads; and (c) expenditures for items other than teaching, whether technology, facilities, student affairs, marketing and public relations, or general administration. In the near term, speculations of "revolutionary changes" in the productivity or efficiency of American higher education would ask, for example, these questions:

- Are average teaching loads or class sizes likely to be enlarged substantially, and thus more students taught per faculty member, with or without the benefit of new instructional technologies?
- Can and will the cost of faculty and staff be otherwise substantially lowered, most likely through the further hiring of low-paid, part-time faculty instead of moderately paid, full-time faculty and staff and/or through contracting out more of the university's noninstructional activities?
- Can and will the prevailing instructional paradigm of "courses" and "classes" meeting for fixed periods of time (e.g., semesters or terms), each with a number of students and an instructor, change in the direction of more independent study or other modes of self-paced learning? More importantly, can such changes significantly lower the cost per student or per graduate or per some other realistic measure of student learning?
- Can the seemingly irreversible trend toward more administrative and professional (non-teaching) staff be turned around so that more of the resources go directly toward teaching, or at least toward teaching and scholarship?

3.  *Finally, how the burdens of meeting these costs, whatever they may be, are apportioned among parents (from current income, savings, or debt), students (from part-time earning and debt), taxpayers (directly, through support of institutional expenditures or indirectly, through student grants and loan subsidies), and philanthropists (through endowments and current gifts).*

The current pattern of financing American higher education along this dimension is characterized by a substantial and increasing reliance on revenues from sources other than the government or taxpayer—particularly from parents and students through tuition, and from philanthropists or donors. This pattern (less reliance on taxpayers) is seen especially in the public sector and particularly in the more costly (and generally the more selective) public research universities. Speculations about "revolutionary change" along this dimension focus mainly on the degree to which, and the form by which, public tuitions may rise at even greater rates than in the recent past, displacing even more taxpayer resources. Such increases may possibly be accompanied by more need-based grants to preserve accessibility, but the outcome will essentially be the privatizing of the financing of public higher education (Hansen & Weisbrod, 1969; Carnegie Commission, 1973; McPherson & Winston, 1993). Consider these questions:

- Will "high tuition-high aid" become the dominant pattern of public higher education finance, with public-sector tuitions set at, or very near, full cost, accompanied by higher need-based grants from both federal and state government? Such a change would shift enrollment from the public to the private sector, possibly causing either the radical transformation or the closure of some public institutions.
- Will radically new forms of deferred payment plans–very long term loans, income-contingent repayments, or graduate taxes–be implemented to mask, if only cosmetically, the effects of even greater shifts of financial responsibility to students?

- If "high tuition-high aid" is to be a growing pattern, will the "high aid" part of the equation actually materialize as promised by its proponents? Or will the real result (and perhaps, for some, the real agenda) be high tuition, only modest aid, based on merit as well as need, greatly diminished access at the "low end" of the continuum of academic preparedness, and, as suggested above, an increasingly privatized public sector?
- Might "high tuition-high aid" occur only or mainly at the post-baccalaureate level, leaving the mix of enrollments and missions essentially unchanged (as between the current public and private sectors) at the undergraduate level, but greatly raising tuitions and creating the above-mentioned impacts at the graduate, advanced professional, and continuing education levels?

## Finance, Institutional Missions, and Prevailing Teaching-Learning Paradigms

Patterns of finance are inextricably connected with institutional missions and the prevailing teaching-learning paradigms in American higher education. It is difficult to contemplate radical changes in patterns of finance that do not either arise from, or cause, profound changes in the substance of the higher educational enterprise. For example, what if a decision were made to no longer award financial aid mainly on the basis of parental income, as now, but on the basis of academic promise and performance—i.e., to deny financial assistance to lower-achieving students in spite of financial need? Such a decision would almost certainly drive out of higher education hundreds of thousands and possibly millions of students who may be marginally prepared academically and who are often ambivalent about higher education. Many of these students now try for a college education, and sometimes succeed, because they feel that college can lead to a better life as long as the attempt is financially possible without the prospect of unmanageable debt. Debt can be made somewhat more manageable through longer repayment periods and by linking repayments to future earnings. But a debt is still a debt, even if it is dressed up as a "graduate tax" or an "advance on future income"; and a big debt, even in fancy dress, is still daunting, particularly to those who are ambivalent about higher education to begin with.

Greatly increasing the public sector tuition and providing financial aid based largely on merit would have profound financial consequences for the nation's higher educational enterprise, public and private. It would lead to the downsizing and even the closure of many less selective institutions. On the positive size, such a consequence would save significant public resources. On the negative side, it would have a major and almost certainly detrimental impact on the lives of those no longer accommodated. But these are not really so much revolutionary changes in the pattern of financing higher education as a revolutionary change in the peculiarly American *vision* of opportunity and social mobility, in which our colleges and universities, through their present patterns of finance, play such a significant role.

Similarly, a significant number of the nation's "regional" public doctoral-granting universities (as opposed to the nationally or internationally eminent public research universities) could teach students at a lower cost if they were to cease operating as research universities and if their faculty instead were given the high teaching loads characteristic of two- or four-year teaching colleges. But such a change, even if it were to be politically possible (which it almost certainly is not), would not lead to a *more productive* institution, but rather to a fundamentally different *kind* of institution: cheaper in per-student costs perhaps (although low-cost graduate teaching assistants would no longer be available), but not necessarily cheaper in per-student learning. Unquestionably it would be less productive in scholarship and probably in service to the community. Again, this change would be not so much a radical shift in a pattern of finance as a radical redefinition of the very missions of these dozens or hundreds of institutions.[1]

In fact, the only way to create revolutionary changes in the patterns of higher educational finance that would *not* require or cause radical change in the missions of the institutions or in the nature of the prevailing teaching-learning paradigm would require either of two circumstances or assumptions. The first is the assumption already held by many citizens and elected officials that there is substantial waste in colleges and universities that could be eradicated simply with better management, less diversion of resources into expensive nonteaching activities, and a rejuvenated work ethic, all of which, we assume, would lead to significantly lower per-student costs. The problem with this assumption is that it is almost certainly untrue of most or all of the nation's nearly 1,500 community colleges and most of the nearly 1,000 less-selective, regional, baccalaureate and comprehensive colleges, public and private alike.[2] In these institutions, teaching loads are already high, faculty and staff costs almost always low (due to very large numbers of part-time faculty and low-cost contract staff), and amenities lean. Fund raising and marketing, even at the public campuses, are already aggressive. Inflation-adjusted budgets have been cut for most of the past ten or fifteen years. The low-hanging fruit of productivity gains has long since been picked. In contrast, high-cost colleges and universities with well-paid faculty, low teaching loads, low student-faculty ratios, modern facilities, and other amenities almost certainly have not yet taken all possible efficiencies—or at least cost reductions. But these colleges and universities are expensive, not because the taxpayer is picking up higher costs, but because parents, students, and donors have paid handsomely, and continue to do so, for precisely the kinds of "extras" that such colleges feature. They may also have faculty who are paid near the top of the faculty pay scale and who teach fewer courses than faculty at other institutions. But most of these faculty are both hard-working and astonishingly productive in doing what they were hired (and ultimately promoted) to do: internationally recognized scholarship that brings prestige to their institution, their colleagues, and ultimately to their students (regardless of who actually teaches them). The Harvards, Stanfords, and Williamses may be expensive, at least relative to most other colleges and universities. But it is difficult to call them unproductive, when parents and students are lining up to be given the opportunity to buy what these and other high-cost institutions provide: a great learning ambiance, prestige, and future benefits that come from selectivity and a lifetime of rewarding associations. It would be foolish to predict any significant change—let alone a "revolutionary" change—in the financial patterns of such institutions.

This is not to say that there will not be changes in how colleges and universities are financed, even without dramatic change in the underlying teaching-learning paradigm. State governments can always withdraw even more money, forcing public colleges and universities to raise tuition even more sharply, to further reduce faculty costs (by having fewer and/or more part-time), to cut academic and support programs, to reduce enrollments, and possibly, in the most extreme cases, to close campuses. But however disaffected state politicians and even the electorates may be, at least in certain states, there is as yet no evidence that either the voters or the elected officials want either to limit access dramatically or to downgrade the scholarly missions of their research universities to the point of substantially diminishing their prestige, wherever they currently are in that fiercely competitive institutional pecking order. Although a few private colleges may go out of business, there are actually more private institutions of higher education in the mid-1990s than there were in the mid-1970s. Private colleges have shown themselves incredibly robust: more vulnerable, in the end, to adverse demographics than to finances per se. And if a few go out of business altogether, their demise will strengthen (slightly) those that remain, rather than signal any radically new financial pattern in the sector generally.

## Outside the Box: Alternative Teaching-Learning Paradigms

The analyses and speculations above have all been predicated on a continuation of the predominant teaching-learning paradigm: that is, degrees are awarded through an accumulation of course credits, and most course credits are awarded through traditional didactic instruction, in which an instructor teaches, by lecture, discussion, or combinations thereof, directly to a class of students at a set time of the day/week for a fixed period of weeks. Large classes with relatively inexpensive instructors who also teach several other large classes are very inexpensive. Very small classes with costly professors who teach few of them are relatively expensive. Some radically different paradigms exist, some of which may be less expensive per unit of learning but all of which, to be less expensive, must yield more student learning per dollar spent on faculty, probably with the aid of technology and/or self-paced learning. Many alternative paradigms—for example, teaching that is enriched with live (synchronous) distance learning via high-resolution, interactive fiber optic cable, or individualized self-paced distance instruction via video cassettes and e-mail—hold the prospect of substantially more powerful teaching and learning, and perhaps an extension of participation (already extremely high in the United States). But these technological changes will most likely bring greater, not lesser, per-student costs.

Clearly, new teaching-learning paradigms that feature technology-assisted, asynchronous instruction (e.g., videos and instructional software) and that assume a large volume of learners can be highly cost-effective, virtually by definition. The "virtual university," made theoretically possible by the Internet, generally proclaimed by proponents of the new Information Age, and endorsed in 1995 by some western governors, is such an example. And surely, some, perhaps many, who are "into the Internet," who are self-motivated, and who are unable or unwilling to partake of traditional higher education may take advantage of such technology-aided, cost-effective learning. The potential for changing the nature and the financing of graduate and other forms of post-baccalaureate education, including continuing professional education as well as strictly recreational and self-improvement learning, is enormous.

However, most traditional-age undergraduate students engage in higher education for purposes other than, or at least in addition to, learning: for the prestige of being admitted to a selective institution, for the fun of college life, or for the social learning that comes of interacting with fellow students, professors, and other adult professionals. Such students will achieve few if any of these life goals from the Internet or from other forms of self-paced learning.

By this reasoning, radical new patterns of higher education finance predicated on conceivable "out of the box" possibilities presented by the new learning technologies are likely to have a major cost-reducing impact more on firm-specific and continuing professional education, or on personal or recreational forms of postsecondary education, but not on mainstream undergraduate education nor on elite graduate higher education, except when such education is enriched—and made more expensive—as additional resources are brought to it.

## Radical Changes in "Who Pays?"

This resistance to change in the first two dimensions leaves the third dimension of higher education finance—the sharing of costs among parents, students, and taxpayers—in which there might be some revolutionary change in financial pattern, with or without fundamental change in institutional mission or in the dominant teaching-learning paradigm. Indeed, the core premise of the "high tuition-high aid" argument is that significant additional costs could be shifted from the taxpayer to the middle- and upper-middle-class parent without altering the accessibility of higher education, the missions of institutions, or the nature of the teaching-learning process.

The argument against high tuition-high aid is more political than economic. Suffice it to say for the purpose of this section that a full-scale adoption of "high tuition-high aid," even if it did not ultimately diminish access and participation, would profoundly alter the relative fortunes of the public and private sectors of higher education, dramatically shifting more academically prepared students to the private sector and relegating to many or even most of the nation's more than 1,600 public colleges and regional universities the task of educating those students that the private sector chooses not to accept.

The next decade is likely to see a continuation of the pressures on state treasuries. Businesses, entire industries, and affluent individuals have become increasingly mobile, seeking tax breaks as well as cheap labor, sunshine, and social amenities. These factors all put great strain on the taxing capacity of states. Furthermore, the federal government is trying to extricate itself from spending obligations on health and human services, which will place additional pressure on already strained state budgets. With the theoretical logic of "high tuition-high aid" and the current (mid-1990s) ambivalence about such once-dominant social goals as "access" and "equal opportunity," the result is likely to be a continued shift of costs from the state taxpayer to the family and particularly to the student.

At the same time, a truly profound further shift in the direction of "high tuition-high aid" is unlikely for two reasons. First, affordable public higher education has broad political appeal. Welfare and other transfer payments as well as many forms of governmental regulation (and the offending public sector bureaucrats) may be vulnerable to the social and economic conservatism that emerged in the mid-1990s. But affordable public higher education is something that conservative middle-class voters get for their taxes, and there is no evidence that either voters or elected officials are ready to eliminate relatively low tuitions at most public sector institutions.

Second, the major shift in the direction of higher public-sector tuition may already have occurred in most states by the mid-1990s. Although stipulating the real costs of undergraduate education is difficult and a bit subjective, it is likely that public-sector tuition in many states is already covering between one-third and one-half of the real costs of undergraduate instruction. Clearly, this fraction could increase still more, particularly in some states of the South and West that continue the tradition of very low public tuition. But there is no evidence to suggest any imminent, profound, national shift toward the elimination of a significantly subsidized public sector tuition.

## Financing Higher Education in the Coming Decade: More of the Same

Predicting future patterns in something so large, complex, and politically robust as higher education finance is simultaneously difficult and simple. It is difficult because the effects of two critical determinants—politics and technology—are, for different reasons, very difficult to predict. At the same time, it is simple because this very vastness—together with the enormous variation already in the system, both in the per-student expenses and in the sharing of these costs, plus the existence of powerful parties with stakes in the status quo—all make revolutionary change unlikely. That there are problems or dissatisfactions with the current patterns of higher education finance, or that radical alternatives are conceivable and technically feasible, does not make them likely. My best prediction is that there will be no revolutionary change in the financial patterns of mainstream American higher education, although there may well be radical changes on the peripheries, such as continuing professional education, or learning for strictly recreational purposes. But the most likely changes in financial patterns in the coming decade are the following:

- *Scale:* Higher education will continue to expand slightly in scale and, therefore, in the percentage it takes of the nation's gross domestic product. The proportion of high school graduates going on to higher education will remain about constant, but the numbers of the traditional college-age cohort will increase slightly. The rates of those achieving completion and post-baccalaureate continuation will also increase slightly.

- *Financial assistance:* Financial assistance will be increasingly "managed" in the form of individualized price discounting for cost-effective enrollment management, or the meeting of net tuition revenue goals. Less aid will be available to the very needy high-risk student.

- *"Access"* in the traditional meaning of the term will actually diminish, with less financial aid available to those least prepared and/or academically ambivalent about college.

- *Productivity:* The resources consumed per student—a rough measure of productivity or efficiency—will continue to decline slightly in real terms in most institutions in response to tightening public (mainly state) revenues and to increasing family resistance to tuition and other cost increases. Well-endowed, selective institutions will be the exception, but they will maintain this selectivity by scholarships, or price discounting, which both their wealth and their market power make possible. Most institutions will control costs mainly as they have for the past decade: by trimming full-time faculty and staff and deferring maintenance. Dramatic changes in financial patterns via "restructuring" or "reengineering" will not be the norm.

- *Technology:* The use of instructional technology will continue to increase, although unevenly among institutions, faculties, and individual professors, and mainly as add-ons or enrichment, rather than as a change in the prevailing undergraduate instructional production function.

- *Learning productivity:* Other forms of learning productivity will increase—particularly college-level learning in high school and greater use of the full academic year—but the proportion of students completing a baccalaureate in less than the traditional four years will not increase appreciably nor will the underlying per-student instructional costs.

- *Cost-sharing:* The portions of instructional cost borne by the parent in the form of higher public tuition and by the student in the form of term-time or "stop out" earnings or loans will continue to creep upward. Still they will fall considerably short of the full or near-full cost advocated by the proponents of "high tuition-high aid."

- *"Special programs" to obscure the shift of the burden from taxpayer to the student and family.* Government, both federal and state, will continue to propose, and occasionally to implement, programs or devices that cost the taxpayer nothing and do nothing to alter the underlying cost of instruction but which will make rising debt burdens more manageable, at least for some students, or otherwise lower the cost to the middle- and upper-middle income families who are financially able to prepay tuition.

- *Financing on higher education's periphery.* Far more dramatic changes in finance, both in underlying instructional costs and in who pays for these costs will be seen on the periphery of higher education: in firm-specific and other forms of continuing professional education, in the extension of higher education to place-bound students or to the elderly, and to technologically oriented individuals pursuing post-baccalaureate learning for recreation or self-improvement.

In summary, the decade will see continued pain, turbulence, and dissatisfaction with the financing of higher education—in short, more of the same.

*Bruce D. Johnstone* is University Professor of Higher and Comparative Education at State University of New York at Buffalo and former Chancellor of the SUNY system.

# References

Carnegie Commission on Higher Education. (1973). *Higher Education: Who Pays/Who Benefits? Who Should Pay?* New York: McGraw-Hill.

Carnegie Foundation for the Advancement of Teaching. (1994). *A classification of institutions of higher education*. Princeton, NJ: Carnegie Foundation.

Hansen, W. L., & Weisbrod, B. (1969). *Benefits, Costs, and Finances of Public Higher Education*. Chicago: Markham Publishing.

Johnstone, D. B. (forthcoming). Financial issues in American higher education. In P. G. Altbach, R. O. Berdahl, and P. J. Gumport (Eds.), *American higher education in the twentieth century: Social, political, and economic challenges*. Baltimore: Johns Hopkins University Press.

Johnstone, D. B. (1991). Higher education in the United States in the year 2000. *Prospects, 31*(3), 430–422; reprinted in Z. Morsy & P. Altbach (Eds.), *Higher education in international perspective* (pp. 178–90). New York: Garland Press.

Johnstone, D. B. (1992). *Learning productivity: A new imperative for American higher education*. Albany: State University of New York.

Johnstone, D. B. (1993a). The costs of higher education: Worldwide issues and trends for the 1990s. In P. Altbach and D. B. Johnstone (Eds.), *The funding of higher education: International perspectives* (pp. 3–24). New York: Garland Press.

Johnstone, D. B. (1993b). *The high tuition-high aid model of public higher education finance: The case against*. Albany: State University of New York.

Massy, W. F., & Zemsky, R. (1996). Information technology and academic productivity. *EDUCOM Review, 31*, 12–15.

McPherson, M. S., Schapiro, M. O., & Winston, G. C. (1993). *Paying the piper: Productivity, incentives, and financing in U.S. higher education*. Ann Arbor: University of Michigan Press.

Twigg, C. A. (1996). *Academic productivity: The case for instructional software*. Washington, D.C.: EDUCOM.

# Equity and Efficiency of Community College Appropriations:

## The Role of Local Financing

### ALICIA C. DOWD, JOHN L. GRANT

More than two decades ago, David Breneman and Susan Nelson posed the question, "Should Serrano Go to College?" (1981). The authors of *Financing Community Colleges* were referring to the landmark case of *Serrano v. Priest,* which was decided in the California State Supreme Court in 1971. The *Serrano* decision found the California school financing system unconstitutional under the equal protection provision of the state constitution. The educational resources provided to students depended on the wealth of the neighborhoods in which they lived, a fundamentally unjust arrangement stemming from the tradition of local control and local financing. Breneman and Nelson concluded that, similarly, the local finance role for community college systems likely creates resource disparities that disadvantage students in less affluent communities (p. 126).

As in primary and secondary school (K–12) finance, approximately half the states in the United States have a local government finance role for funding community colleges. Colleges serving areas with a weak economic base that rely on local property or other taxes for a share of their revenues will receive lower revenues than peer colleges located in wealthier areas of their state, creating an inequitable finance system.

Three decades after *Serrano,* which set off waves of school finance litigation and reform across the United States (Verstegen, 1998), the effect of local control on school finance equity is still a matter of contentious debate and legal action. (The Web site of the Campaign for Fiscal Equity *http://www.schoolfunding.info/* summarizes recent legal actions and court decisions.) In contrast, since Breneman and Nelson's consideration of community college finance equity, and a similar study at that time by Walter Garms (1981), the role of local control in community college finance systems and its effect on equity have received comparatively little attention.

This comparative inattention may result from the authors' conclusion that community college finance equity is a less pressing issue than school finance equity because a college education is not compulsory, nor "essential for functioning or succeeding in life" (p. 124). In addition, Breneman and Nelson (1980, p. 174) argued the efficiency benefits of local control: Those who are most likely to take advantage of a community college have the opportunity to express their educational preferences through the local governance and tax system. Furthermore, the task of disentangling geographic and program cost differentials across colleges in a state, economies of scale on large and small campuses, and the impact of student college choice and their effects on measures of resource equity presents a daunting challenge that may have inhibited study of this topic. With funding coming from state, local, and federal governments and from the private sector in the form of tuition, fees, and philanthropic donations, community college finance systems are relatively more complex than K–12 finance systems.

Nevertheless, even in an era when efficiency rhetoric dominates the politics of public finance (Alexander, 2000; Dowd, 2003), the issue of community college finance equity has not entirely faded. Several state-level reports provide evidence that wide variations do exist in the level of resources allocated to community colleges and that finance equity is a concern of state policy analysts (*Budget Development*, 2000; *Community Colleges and SUNY*, 1999; *Iowa Community College*, 1998). The Education Commission of the States (*State Funding*, 2000) issued a comprehensive state-by-state portrait of community college finance systems and highlighted policy questions that arise from the local finance role, including the issue of equal access to postsecondary education within states (p. 10). In a paper updating the application of the economic tenets of equity and efficiency to an analysis of community college finance, Richard Romano (2003) highlights local taxes as more regressive than state and federal taxes, because they rely on property taxes, rather than more progressive income taxes. Flores (2003) analyzed state community college finance data from Texas and found inequities in the funding of Hispanic-serving institutions (HSIs) located on the U.S.-Mexican border. Most recently, in a case with arguments echoing K–12 finance litigation, three community colleges in Oregon challenged the state's equalization formula, arguing that it was unfair to penalize colleges that received relatively high, local property-tax revenues. In November 2003, a circuit court judge ruled against the plaintiffs, upholding the right of the Board of Education to determine the funding formula. The decision did not directly rule on the equity of the finance system (Gomstyn, 2003).

In a trend perceived as equity enhancing, the local share of income for community colleges has declined over time (Breneman & Nelson, 1981; *State Funding*, 2000). From 1950 to 1997, it decreased on average from 49% to 19%, while the average share of state revenue increased from 26% to a high of 60% in 1980, before declining to 44% in 1997 (Romano, 2003, *Table 3*). The view that financing systems are more equitable under state control is consistent with the direction of court-ordered school finance reforms, which have often mandated "power-equalizing" roles for state governments to redistribute resources among school districts of disparate wealth.

While a community college education is not compulsory and states do not have a legal obligation to provide equitable postsecondary schooling resources, as they do for primary and secondary schooling, there is, perhaps, a growing sense that an associate's degree is today the minimal credential necessary to attain social and economic security. This view is reflected in the rhetoric that surrounded Bill Clinton's initial proposal for the federal "Hope Scholarship." In his acceptance speech at the Democratic National Convention in 1996, Clinton proposed a tax credit for the first two years of college to "make at least two years of college as universal as four years of a high school education is today" (Bill Clinton, 1996).

That the implementation of the "scholarship" as a tax credit provided a boon for the middle class more than it helped low-income students enter college (*Study*, 2003) demonstrates the tension between the rhetoric of access and the politics of resource distribution. The growing importance of a college education and heightened conflicts over financial resources suggest that the equity of community college financing systems deserves greater national consideration. This study contributes to that goal by analyzing the local role, which is generally viewed as an equity-reducing component of finance systems, in resource distribution to community colleges within state systems.

## Conceptual Framework

Based on national data, this study characterizes current intrastate variation in revenues from state and local sources to community colleges and analyzes differences and similarities in distribution patterns in states with and without local-share financing. We consider the fairness of these funding variations from the perspective of equity and efficiency. The conceptualization of equitable and efficient funding strategies is based on the scholarship of school finance (Monk, 1990; Odden & Picus, 2004; Verstegen, 1998; Wong, 1994) and community college finance (Breneman & Nelson, 1981; DesJardins, 2002; Garms, 1981). Equal funding for students with equal needs is understood as creating "horizontal equity," while the provision of greater resources for students with greater need contributes to "vertical equity."

Under the principles of horizontal and vertical equity, equal funding does not necessarily represent equitable funding. Equal funding is considered just when students have equal needs but unjust when students have disparate needs. Providing more public resources to less affluent communities is understood as promoting vertical equity, while providing more resources to affluent communities undermines it.

Disparities in funding can be created by rational and political factors. Rational funding strategies such as cost adjustments for urbanization, economies of scale, and program type may create funding disparities as a matter of efficiency. These factors generate disparities in per capita student funding that are not viewed as inequitable, as, for example, when a state provides greater resources to colleges to rent facilities in high-cost urban areas. A plan to locate high-cost facilities for technical programs at just one campus in a system may be argued from the perspective of investment efficiency, even though it would provide greater resources to one college in comparison to the others. The investment benefits of initiating such a program might well be outweighed by the costs if the state undertook to build the necessary facilities on each campus. A college's capacity to convert resources to outputs presents another efficiency consideration, that of productive or "technical" efficiency. For example, some states award funding premiums to rural schools and colleges to offset inefficiencies in the "production" of educated students due to smaller class sizes in comparison to more populated urban areas.

However, these rational systems may be undermined by "politically mobilized and well-connected groups," who garner a greater share of resources through political means (Timar, 1994, p. 144). These political forces can have equitable effects (as when their efforts result in creating categorical aid for students with high educational needs) or inequitable effects (as in the flow of funds to wealthy suburbs). Recent research by Caroline Hoxby (2001), Jeffrey Metzler (2003), and Thomas Timar (2003) shows that court-ordered finance reform is often an ineffective tool to counter finance inequities. Their studies indicate that rational resource allocation systems are undermined by political lobbying and individual choices in educational markets. Therefore, rational policies can be counteracted by political systems operating at both the local and state levels.

Within this conceptual framework, we addressed the following questions:

1.  How much do college revenues per student vary within state systems?
2.  Is local-share funding associated with higher or lower revenues per student?
3.  Is local-share funding associated with higher intrastate variation in tuition and fees?
4.  Is local-share funding associated with higher intrastate variation in revenues per student?

To establish the context of revenue disparities, Questions 1 and 2 provide descriptive information. Question 3 evaluates the relationship between local funding and variation in tuition and fees to test a conclusion presented in the Education Commission of the States community college financing report, where the authors observed: "Dramatic differences in property tax valuations across a state can lead to large disparities in tuition rates between wealthier communities and poorer districts, because poorer districts may be forced to raise tuition and fees to meet their basic budgets" (*State Funding*, 2000, p. 10). We would therefore expect greater variation in tuition and fees in states with local financing.

Question 4 builds on the assumption that states relying strictly on state funding will have lower variation in revenues than states with local shares, due to the equalizing effects of the state role. As high variation in state-funded states may be created by power-equalizing formulas, which are intended to direct greater than average funds to colleges with high-need students, we also examine the relationship between funding disparities and community wealth.

This study focuses on local and state appropriations and tuition and fees, which are the largest sources of revenues for community colleges. Other sources of funding may well have an impact on finance equity, but we do not address these effects here. Our purpose is to document revenue disparities and present descriptive statistics and graphs that facilitate comparisons of revenue distribution patterns in local-share and state-funded states. The study serves as a starting point for future state-level analyses by supporting purposeful sampling of states with similar and dissimilar funding patterns. It fills a gap in the literature by providing a systematic national analysis of contemporary community college funding patterns with a focus on the role of local financing.

## Data and Methods

We analyzed a subsample of data from the national 2000–2001 Integrated Postsecondary Education Data System (IPEDS) Finance survey. IPEDS is a census survey of higher education institutions in the United States. Because IPEDS is a census and the analyses are descriptive, we treat the data as population rather than sample data and do not present tests of statistical significance for observed differences in values. We limit the sample to institutions that IPEDS classifies as two-year public colleges in U.S. states (not territories) and that did not contain the word "technical" in their names. Our reason for omitting technical colleges was that technical programs often carry greater costs for equipment and materials. While this step restricts the institutional type, it does not completely omit technical programs, which are also offered in community colleges.

Since we focused on variation in revenues to colleges within a state, we excluded those reporting financial data on fewer than five community colleges. This step excluded 15 states: Alaska (2), Delaware (3), Idaho (3), Indiana (13 of 14 technical colleges), Kentucky (which reported financial data for Lexington Community College only), Maine (7 of 7 technical colleges), Montana (5 of 8 technical colleges), Nevada (3), New Hampshire (5 of 7 technical colleges), Rhode Island (1), South Dakota (4), Utah (3), Vermont (1), West Virginia (3) and Wisconsin (16 of 17 technical colleges). The remaining sample includes 705 community colleges with nonmissing data in 35 states.

Our primary focus is on appropriations from state and local governments. To compare revenue across colleges with different enrollments, we analyzed appropriations per full-time equivalent student (FTE).[1] We group colleges in five local funding-share categories based on the ratio of local appropriations to state appropriations. Based on the distribution of colleges in these five categories, we designate states as primarily local-share funded or as state-funded.

Our measure of variation in local and state appropriations is the deviation from the median value for each state. We used median values as the measure of central tendency because the means are affected by outliers that may be colleges with a special mission or unusual funding. Similarly, we measure dispersion by statistics that are not affected by extreme values, including the interquartile range (*IQR*) and the ratio of 90th to 10th percentile values. The mean of absolute revenue deviations for each state provides a summary statistic of variation for comparison across states. A college's position above or below the median of state and local appropriations within the state is also represented by an index of the college's revenue divided by the state median. The index is an expression of revenue deviations that is not sensitive to the differing magnitudes of spending in states. To test the direction of revenue deviations as flowing toward relatively wealthy or poor communities, we used the proportion of full-time students at each college who receive federal grant aid as a measure of community wealth. A college's geographic locale is indicated with an ordinal variable with seven categories ranging from "large city" to "rural."

## Limitations

The research design has several important limitations. First, the study does not directly account for state-level differences in community college history, mission, status, governance, and finance structure. We treat local funding as evidence of a local political role but do not investigate the nature of state and local political structures. For this reason, we measure revenue disparities at the state level and present descriptive statistics summarizing revenue deviations by state. This step facilitates the review of the findings by knowledgeable analysts at the state level.

Second, while all surveys are subject to measurement error, with hundreds of institutional researchers and administrators across the country entering complex financial data, IPEDS may suffer from this problem even more greatly than usual. We acknowledge this limitation but emphasize that IPEDS is the primary national collection of college financial data. Analyses of the type reported here that may reveal significant measurement error may strengthen this major data source.

We use the percentage of full-time students receiving federal financial aid as a proxy for community wealth for each community college. Variation in tuition and fees, which occurs both across and within states, partially determines who qualifies for financial aid. Both financially needy students and students attending more expensive colleges are more likely to be eligible for aid. Therefore, we restrict our analysis to intrastate differences in the proportion of students receiving grant aid and to states where the correlation between tuition and aid is weak.

We evaluated the accuracy of using this financial aid variable as a measure of community wealth by using census data from New York State and Massachusetts, matching colleges to the county or counties in which they are located. Using logarithmic transformations to correct for skewed distributions, we found that the Pearson correlation between aid and the percentage of children in poverty was moderately strong at $r = .766$ and $r = .614$ in New York State ($n = 32$) and Massachusetts ($n = 15$), respectively.

Finally, the study uses the NCES's FTE measure, in which three part-time students are treated as equivalent to one full-time student, to compare per capita funding. This measure is not sensitive to potential differences in the resource needs of campuses with high and low proportions of part-time students and may not be equally appropriate to campuses serving different populations of students. Alternative measures of student enrollment may produce different results concerning resource disparities among campuses.

## Results

In this sample of U.S. community colleges, state appropriations are the largest source of all revenues with a mean share of 38%. Tuition and fees contribute 20% and federal grants and contracts add another 13%. Including colleges with zero local share, local appropriations average 13%. The local share contingent on non-zero local funding increases to 20%, reducing the state share to 34%. Auxiliary revenues contribute 6%, and state grants contribute 5%. Other sources of revenue such as private gifts and local grants contribute 3% or less, on average.

The mean value of total revenues from all sources except tuition and fees per FTE is $8,230, with a standard deviation ($SD$) of $3,800. The mean value of state and local appropriations per FTE is $5,180 ($SD = $2,440$). The median of this skewed variable is $4,740. Average tuition and fees are $1,400 ($SD = $717$). Table 1, which presents the median and interquartile range of state and local appropriations per FTE by state, reveals a great deal of variation both within and across states. In 16 states in the sample, the median value is zero local appropriations. A review of the full range of values indicates that in ten states no colleges received local funding.

We created five categories of local funding share based on the ratio of local appropriations to state appropriations. These categories, which were created based on the overall distribution of ratios as shown by a histogram, encompass local-share funding ratios of 0.0–0.01 ($n = 268$), 0.02–0.50 ($n = 199$), 0.51–1.0 ($n = 121$), 1.01–2.0 ($n = 70$), 2.1 and above ($n = 47$). Colleges within the same state may appear in different local funding share categories, because the ratios differ by college. Table 2 shows the distribution of colleges within the local-share categories by state, divided into 17 "local-share" and 17 "state-funded" states (n = 256 and 368 colleges respectively). We designated states as funded by local share when at least 75% of the colleges reported ratios greater than 0.02. All local-share states also have state funding.

In some states, such as Connecticut, Florida, and Georgia, colleges consistently report no local funding. Five states—Alabama, Arkansas, Colorado, Ohio, and Oklahoma—are dominantly state funded, but have two or more cases reporting local funding. In two of these states, Arkansas and Ohio, local taxes may be raised and used to fund community colleges in 2000. In Colorado, two junior colleges previously funded by their local districts were recently incorporated into the state system and uniquely continued to receive local funding (*State Funding*, 2000, pp. 12–13).

We apply the "local-share" designation to states where local funding is a regular component of the funding system. In states with a local funding role, such as Illinois, Kansas, and Maryland, colleges are distributed across the funding share categories. California colleges report local funding share across the five categories. However, we analyze California separately due to the large number of colleges and the state's unique funding system in the state. Here "districts receive a portion of the 1% countywide property tax based on their proportional share of property tax revenue received from their county prior to tax control (Prop. 13, 1978)" (*State Funding*, 2000, p. 12).

Table 3 presents the mean and standard deviation of tuition and fees and the percentage of students receiving federal grant aid, by local funding category and by state. The tuition burden

## Table 1. State and Local Appropriations ($s) per FTE

| State | n | State | | Local | |
|---|---|---|---|---|---|
| | | MDN | IQR | MDN | IQR |
| AL | 21 | 4187 | 1669 | 0 | 27 |
| AR | 15 | 5361 | 2368 | 0 | 416 |
| AZ | 19 | 1396 | 1344 | 3188 | 1243 |
| CA | 77 | 3044 | 1073 | 1824 | 1046 |
| CO | 15 | 3243 | 1771 | 0 | 0 |
| CT | 12 | 7197 | 1109 | 0 | 0 |
| FL | 28 | 4617 | 1513 | 0 | 0 |
| GA | 14 | 6211 | 2203 | 0 | 0 |
| HI | 7 | 4609 | 886 | 0 | 0 |
| IA | 14 | 3439 | 853 | 675 | 355 |
| IL | 45 | 1560 | 869 | 2302 | 1388 |
| KS | 19 | 1856 | 664 | 3773 | 2927 |
| LA | 6 | 3363 | 757 | 0 | 0 |
| MA | 14 | 5840 | 1554 | 0 | 0 |
| MD | 15 | 2307 | 988 | 2844 | 1307 |
| MI | 28 | 3129 | 1058 | 2484 | 3505 |
| MN | 12 | 4618 | 2237 | 0 | 0 |
| MO | 10 | 2727 | 1169 | 940 | 1335 |
| MS | 15 | 4348 | 955 | 722 | 377 |
| NC | 49 | 6142 | 1561 | 1008 | 426 |
| ND | 5 | 5057 | 1882 | 0 | 0 |
| NE | 5 | 4000 | 182 | 1147 | 117 |
| NJ | 19 | 1662 | 350 | 2037 | 712 |
| NM | 15 | 4693 | 1714 | 658 | 990 |
| NY | 33 | 2359 | 229 | 1786 | 914 |
| OH | 28 | 3750 | 743 | 0 | 0 |
| OK | 14 | 3569 | 1003 | 0 | 0 |
| OR | 13 | 4222 | 1148 | 2209 | 688 |
| PA | 14 | 2495 | 312 | 1462 | 885 |
| SC | 5 | 5401 | 737 | 0 | 0 |
| TN | 10 | 3691 | 316 | 0 | 0 |
| TX | 58 | 3432 | 1103 | 1194 | 1569 |
| VA | 24 | 4055 | 850 | 23 | 22 |
| WA | 27 | 3928 | 657 | 0 | 0 |
| WY | 7 | 4414 | 897 | 1365 | 1964 |

Source: NCES IPEDS 2000-2001
Number of colleges in state based on n reporting financial data.

placed on students varies considerably, from a low of $314 in California to a high of $2,650 in Ohio. As the standard deviations indicate, tuition and fee charges vary considerably within states.[2] State-funded states have higher mean tuition, $1700 (SD = $555), than local-funded states, which have a mean tuition of $1,479 and higher variation (SD = $638). Whether assessed by the range or IQR of the distribution, local-share states have greater variation in tuition and fees. The median range and IQR in local-share states are $1,412 and $300, both more than double the respective values of $713 and $138 in state-funded states.

The mean proportion of students receiving grant aid ranges from a quarter to half, with the lowest standard deviation at 8% and typical values ranging between 10 to 19%. This indicates that in all states the dispersion of the grant aid variable is sufficient to distinguish the relative wealth of the college's local community. The mean and standard deviation of grant aid receipt is similar in state- and local-funded states, at 35% (SD = 16%) and 38% (SD = 18%), respectively. The value in California where tuition is low is also relatively low at a mean of 29% (SD = 15%).

The upper panels of Table 4 and Figure 1 illustrate that colleges in the zero local-share category have the lowest median appropriations, which at $4,259 is roughly $400 to $1,000 less per FTE than the median value of any of the local-share categories. With an inter-quartile range only

## Table 2. Distribution of Colleges by Funding Type by State

| State | State-Funded State | | | | | | Local-Share State | | | | |
|---|---|---|---|---|---|---|---|---|---|---|---|
|  | 0.0- | 0.02- | 0.51- | 1.1- | >2.0 |  | 0- | 0.02- | 0.51- | 1.1- | >2.0 |
| AL | 19 | 2 |  |  |  |  |  |  |  |  |  |
| AR | 11 | 4 |  |  |  |  |  |  |  |  |  |
| AZ |  |  |  |  |  |  |  | 1 | 1 | 5 | 12 |
| CO | 13 |  |  | 1 | 1 |  |  |  |  |  |  |
| CT | 12 |  |  |  |  |  |  |  |  |  |  |
| FL | 28 |  |  |  |  |  |  |  |  |  |  |
| GA | 14 |  |  |  |  |  |  |  |  |  |  |
| HI | 7 |  |  |  |  |  |  |  |  |  |  |
| IA |  |  |  |  |  |  | 1 | 13 |  |  |  |
| IL |  |  |  |  |  |  |  | 6 | 9 | 13 | 13 |
| KS |  |  |  |  |  |  |  | 2 | 5 | 4 | 8 |
| LA | 6 |  |  |  |  |  |  |  |  |  |  |
| MA | 14 |  |  |  |  |  |  |  |  |  |  |
| MD |  |  |  |  |  |  | 1 |  | 5 | 8 | 1 |
| MI |  |  |  |  |  |  | 6 | 5 | 5 | 9 | 3 |
| MN | 12 |  |  |  |  |  |  |  |  |  |  |
| MO |  |  |  |  |  |  | 1 | 6 | 3 |  |  |
| MS |  |  |  |  |  |  |  | 15 |  |  |  |
| NC |  |  |  |  |  |  |  | 46 |  |  |  |
| ND | 5 |  |  |  |  |  |  |  |  |  |  |
| NE |  |  |  |  |  |  |  | 5 |  |  |  |
| NJ |  |  |  |  |  |  |  |  | 7 | 11 | 1 |
| NM |  |  |  |  |  |  | 2 | 9 | 4 |  |  |
| NY |  |  |  |  |  |  |  | 4 | 20 | 8 | 1 |
| OH | 22 | 3 | 2 | 1 |  |  |  |  |  |  |  |
| OK | 12 | 1 | 1 |  |  |  |  |  |  |  |  |
| OR |  |  |  |  |  |  |  | 7 | 5 | 1 |  |
| PA |  |  |  |  |  |  |  | 7 | 7 |  |  |
| SC | 5 |  |  |  |  |  |  |  |  |  |  |
| TN | 10 |  |  |  |  |  |  |  |  |  |  |
| TX |  |  |  |  |  |  | 7 | 34 | 13 | 3 | 1 |
| VA | 24 |  |  |  |  |  |  |  |  |  |  |
| WA | 27 |  |  |  |  |  |  |  |  |  |  |
| WY |  |  |  |  |  |  |  | 5 | 1 | 1 |  |
| *CA |  |  |  |  |  |  | 9 | 24 | 33 | 5 | 6 |
| Total | 241 | 10 | 3 | 2 | 1 |  | 18 | 165 | 85 | 63 | 40 |

*Source:* NCES IPEDS 2000-2001

Number of colleges in state based on n reporting financial data. Local-share categories represent a ratio of local-to-state appropriations of 0.0-0.01, 0.02-0.50, .51-1.0, 1.1-2.0, > 2.0.

Local-share states include those with at least 75% of colleges reporting a ratio of local-to-state appropriations > = 0.02

*California colleges report local shares; but we examine that state, which includes a large proportion of U.S. community colleges, separately.

slightly higher or less than the other categories, the 75th percentile value for zero local-share colleges is always less than the 75th percentile in the other categories and, in some comparisons, is closer to the median value for colleges receiving local appropriations. Only one college with local funding has per FTE appropriations less than the lowest values in the zero-share category. Typically, then, colleges that receive local funding have higher levels of appropriations per FTE from state and local sources than colleges that receive state-level appropriations only.

The lower panel of Table 4 and Figure 1 illustrate these analyses using a measure of revenues per FTE from all sources, excluding tuition and fees. Colleges in the zero local-share category no longer have the lowest median value. At a median of $7,454 and *IQR* of $3,132, the distribution is very similar to that for colleges in the local-to-state appropriations ratio categories of 0.51–1.0 and

**Table 3. Tuition/Fees and Federal Grant Aid by Funding Type and State**

| State-Funded | Tuition/Fees($s) | | Grant Aid(%) | |
|---|---|---|---|---|
| | M | SD | M | SD |
| AL | 1681 | 158 | 48 | 17 |
| AR | 1042 | 218 | 48 | 17 |
| CO | 1739 | 284 | 34 | 15 |
| CT | 1870 | 34 | 26 | 12 |
| FL | 1438 | 149 | 30 | 11 |
| GA | 1646 | 505 | 40 | 14 |
| HI | 1061 | 19 | 30 | 8 |
| LA | 1178 | 338 | 39 | 10 |
| MA | 1822 | 190 | 30 | 15 |
| MN | 2621 | 155 | 34 | 14 |
| ND | 1948 | 88 | 56 | 19 |
| OH | 2650 | 568 | 32 | 15 |
| OK | 1296 | 451 | 34 | 17 |
| SC | 2200 | 0 | 36 | 12 |
| TN | 1437 | 6 | 27 | 22 |
| VA | 1181 | 167 | 42 | 16 |
| WA | 1725 | 56 | 23 | 10 |

| Local-Funded | Tuition/Fees($s) | | Grant Aid(%) | |
|---|---|---|---|---|
| | M | SD | M | SD |
| AZ | 910 | 105 | 38 | 19 |
| IA | 2208 | 220 | 36 | 14 |
| IL | 1522 | 190 | 29 | 19 |
| KS | 1387 | 119 | 34 | 10 |
| MD | 2165 | 436 | 33 | 19 |
| MI | 1754 | 378 | 32 | 15 |
| MO | 1504 | 271 | 38 | 15 |
| MS | 1144 | 358 | 54 | 12 |
| NC | 897 | 64 | 42 | 18 |
| NE | 1429 | 95 | 42 | 27 |
| NJ | 2284 | 448 | 36 | 18 |
| NM | 808 | 392 | 52 | 16 |
| NY | 2560 | 248 | 49 | 14 |
| OR | 1726 | 230 | 36 | 18 |
| PA | 2156 | 294 | 26 | 12 |
| TX | 874 | 275 | 37 | 21 |
| WY | 1469 | 109 | 34 | 11 |
| CA | 314 | 61 | 28 | 17 |

*Source:* NCES IPEDS 2000–2001

1.1–2.0. Colleges reporting a local-share ratio of 0.02–0.50 have the highest distribution of revenues from all sources per FTE, with a median value $1000 greater than that for colleges with no local share. The colleges with a local share greater than 2.0 have a high median, but also have a high *IQR*, which makes the overall distribution similar to the zero-share category. Typically, then, colleges with no local appropriations have levels of total revenue similar to those of colleges with local appropriations, with the exception of colleges in the smallest local-share category.

Table 5 reports, by state within the local- and state-share funding categories, the extent to which the FTE funding received by colleges from local and state appropriations varies within states. Five states each have one case reporting revenues more than double the 95th percentile value in the state. These have been treated as extreme, unique values and omitted from the estimates of average revenue deviations.[3] The mean (absolute value) deviation of revenues from the state median is $973

### Table 4. Variation in Revenue per FTE ($s) by Local-Share Categories

#### Local and State Appropriations

| Local-Share Funding Ratio | n | Min | Mdn | IQR | Max |
|---|---|---|---|---|---|
| 0.0–.01 | 259 | 2007 | 4259 | 1984 | 32373 |
| 0.02–0.50 | 175 | 2574 | 5207 | 2656 | 34652 |
| 0.51–1.0 | 88 | 2586 | 4636 | 2036 | 9677 |
| 1.1–2.0 | 65 | 3175 | 4979 | 2290 | 10853 |
| >2.00 | 41 | 1283 | 5389 | 1954 | 11208 |
| Total | 628 | 1283 | 4676 | 2276 | 34652 |

#### Total Revenues, Minus Tuition and Fees ($s)

| Local-Share Funding Ratio | n | Min | Mdn | IQR | Max |
|---|---|---|---|---|---|
| 0.0–0.01 | 259 | 3182 | 7454 | 3132 | 58690 |
| 0.02–0.50 | 175 | 3840 | 8459 | 2839 | 47286 |
| 0.51–1.0 | 88 | 4444 | 7390 | 2791 | 14054 |
| 1.1–2.0 | 65 | 4720 | 7347 | 3181 | 13931 |
| >2.00 | 41 | 3373 | 8059 | 3246 | 15550 |
| Total | 628 | 3182 | 7715 | 3121 | 58690 |

Source: NCES IPEDS 2000-2001

($SD$ = $314) per FTE, excluding California, which has a mean deviation of $1,330. The ratio of appropriations at the 90th percentile to the 10th percentile is equal to or greater than 2.0 in 13 of the 26 states. The majority of states exceed an $IQR$ of $1,000 per FTE and 15 states have an $IQR$ greater than $1,500.

Local-share funding is associated with a slightly higher intrastate variation of local and state appropriations per FTE. The upper panel of Table 6 and Figure 3 compare the distribution of average absolute deviations per FTE measured in dollars by local-share and state-funded states.[4] At $904, the median deviation in local-share states is $100 more than the median value of $807 in state-funded states. The 25th percentile in local-share states ($846) is also higher than the median value in state-funded states. One hundred dollars is 2% of the mean value of $5,000 of state and local appropriations per FTE. Thus, while variation is typically larger in local- than in state-funded states, the revenue disparities at the center of the distribution are not great. Above the median, local-funded states cluster near a 75th percentile value of $1,350, while state-funded states fall around a lower 75th percentile value of $1,081. This difference in variation, nearing $300, is greater, but still a relatively small proportion of typical state and local appropriations.

The larger variation in revenues in local-share states is in part due to higher levels of spending in those states. When revenue deviations are indexed by college as a proportion of the state median (Table 6, lower panel), the distribution is quite similar under both funding types, with the exception that the index for local-share states has a higher maximum value. In addition, as shown in Figure 2, the local-share category includes 6 of 17 states with an average deviation lower than the median in the state-funded category, which indicates that variation in local-share states is not uniformly high. Similarly, six states without a local role have an average deviation greater than $900, the midpoint of deviations in local-share states, which indicates that high-revenue deviations are found in states with no local role.

To assess the hypothesis that revenue deviations in state-funded states promote vertical equity by providing higher levels of funding to communities with greater need, while deviations in local-funded states are regressive, we selected an average funding deviation of $1,000 as a threshold for

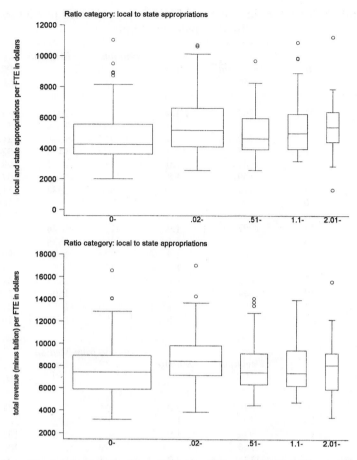

**Figure 1.** *Local and state appropriations (top panel) and revenues from all sources excluding tuition (lower panel) per FTE by college ratio of local appropriations to state appropriations. The width of the boxes corresponds to the proportion of cases in each category. The lower and upper bounds of the box represent the 25th and 75th percentile, the center line is the median, and the circles beyond the whiskers are outliers. Five extreme values are omitted, excluding one case in 0.0–0.01 and 4 in 0.02–0.50 categories*

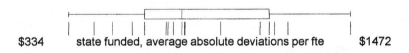

**Figure 2.** *Average absolute deviations per FTE by state and local funding. The lower and upper bounds of the box represent the 25th and 75th percentiles nd the center line is the median. Each vertical line under the boxes represents he location of a state in the distribution of values*

**Table 5. Variation in Local and State Appropriations per fte by Funding Type and State**

| State Funded | n | Mean Deviation ($s) | 90P/10P | Deviations from Median | | |
|---|---|---|---|---|---|---|
| | | | | IQR ($s) | min ($s) | 90P ($s) |
| AL | 21 | 763 | 1.6 | 1713 | -1045 | 1543 |
| AR | 15 | 1334 | 2.5 | 2368 | -2778 | 3764 |
| CO | 15 | 1052 | 2.4 | 1945 | -1814 | 2242 |
| CT | 12 | 757 | 1.5 | 1109 | -1478 | 1524 |
| FL | 28 | 1081 | 2.0 | 1513 | -1551 | 2987 |
| GA | 14 | 1139 | 1.8 | 2203 | -3804 | 1070 |
| HI | 7 | 929 | 2.4 | 886 | -942 | 4313 |
| LA | 6 | 590 | 2.0 | 757 | -885 | 1569 |
| MA | 14 | 815 | 1.5 | 1554 | -1217 | 1288 |
| MN | 12 | 1097 | 1.9 | 2237 | -1674 | 1487 |
| ND | 5 | 780 | 1.6 | 1882 | -1878 | 142 |
| OH | 28 | 807 | 1.9 | 1223 | -1025 | 1898 |
| OK | 14 | 817 | 1.8 | 1431 | -767 | 1997 |
| SC | 5 | 651 | 1.7 | 737 | -1679 | 841 |
| TN | 10 | 454 | 1.8 | 316 | -1504 | 665 |
| VA | 24 | 690 | 2.0 | 840 | -1014 | 2248 |
| WA | 27 | 533 | 1.8 | 657 | -1142 | 1163 |

| State Funded | n | Mean Deviation ($s) | 90P/10P | Deviations from Median | | |
|---|---|---|---|---|---|---|
| | | | | IQR ($s) | min ($s) | 90P ($s) |
| AZ | 19 | 846 | 2.0 | 1796 | -1441 | 1749 |
| IA | 14 | 792 | 1.8 | 769 | -1026 | 2866 |
| IL | 45 | 904 | 1.9 | 1303 | -2781 | 1925 |
| KS | 19 | 1266 | 2.1 | 2549 | -2025 | 2003 |
| MD | 15 | 1128 | 2.2 | 1425 | -1485 | 4077 |
| MI | 28 | 1467 | 2.8 | 2788 | -3558 | 2555 |
| MO | 10 | 334 | 1.4 | 705 | -523 | 671 |
| MS | 15 | 517 | 1.4 | 1052 | -1503 | 1327 |
| NC | 49 | 1472 | 2.0 | 1827 | -2598 | 2381 |
| NE | 5 | 753 | 1.8 | 299 | -686 | 2778 |
| NJ | 19 | 633 | 1.6 | 755 | -1270 | 1571 |
| NM | 15 | 1360 | 2.1 | 1800 | -3623 | 1955 |
| NY | 33 | 872 | 1.7 | 1103 | -1435 | 1471 |
| OR | 13 | 856 | 1.4 | 1132 | -1564 | 970 |
| PA | 14 | 551 | 1.6 | 1088 | -733 | 1250 |
| TX | 58 | 1350 | 2.4 | 2341 | -2241 | 2792 |
| WY | 7 | 697 | 1.4 | 1912 | -603 | 1698 |
| CA | 77 | 1330 | 2.5 | 1488 | -4748 | 2036 |

Source: NCES IPEDS 2000–2001
Mean deviation equals the sum of the absolute value of deviations from the state median divided by the number of colleges with non-missing data in the state. 90P/10P is the 90th percentile/10th percentile ratio.

designating high-disparity states. This designation encompasses five state-funded states (Arkansas, Colorado, Florida, Georgia, and Minnesota) and six local-funded states (Kansas, Maryland, Michigan, North Carolina, New Mexico, and Texas). The use of an *IQR* exceeding $1,500 as a selection criterion would add Alabama, Massachusetts, and North Dakota as state-funded, high-disparity states and Arizona, Illinois, New Mexico, and Wyoming as high-disparity local-funded states. We graphed revenue deviations against the proportion of full-time, first-time students at each college receiving federal grant aid. Since the grant aid proportion serves as a proxy for community wealth, we first

### Table 6. Variation in Revenue Deviations by Funding Type

| In Dollars | n | Min | 25P | Mdn | 75P | 90P | Max |
|---|---|---|---|---|---|---|---|
| State funded | 256 | 454 | 690 | 807 | 1081 | 1139 | 1334 |
| Local funded | 368 | 334 | 846 | 904 | 1350 | 1472 | 1472 |
| Total | 624 | 334 | 763 | 872 | 1334 | 1467 | 1472 |

| Revenue Index | n | Min | 25P | Mdn | 75P | 90P | Max |
|---|---|---|---|---|---|---|---|
| State funded | 256.00 | 0.39 | 0.86 | 1.00 | 1.14 | 1.37 | 2.15 |
| Local funded | 368.00 | 0.32 | 0.89 | 1.00 | 1.19 | 1.38 | 2.60 |
| Total | 624.00 | 0.32 | 0.74 | 1.00 | 1.16 | 1.38 | 2.60 |

Source: NCES IPEDS 2000–2001
n is based on sample with non-missing data, excluding California.
The revenue index is the absolute value of college revenue deviations as a proportion of the state median.

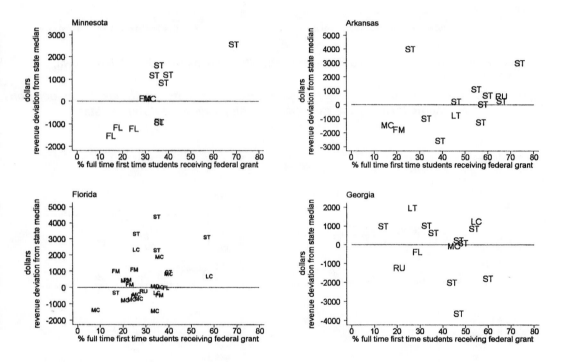

LC large city, MC midsize city, FL fringe large city, FM fringe midsize city, LT large town, ST small town, R rural

**Figure 3. *Revenue deviations by grant receipt in state-funded states, with geographic locale as case marker. The y-axis scale differs by state.***

obtained the Pearson's correlation between tuition/fees and grant aid. The correlation between these two variables was relatively weak, ranging from $r = .11$ to $r = .23$, with the exception of Arkansas and Colorado, where the values were $r = .28$ and $r = .47$, respectively. We excluded Colorado from the analysis to eliminate variation in tuition as a strong alternative explanation for differences in the proportion of students receiving financial aid.

Scatterplots graphing revenue deviations by the proportion of students receiving grant aid are presented for state-funded states in Figure 3 and local-share states in Figures 4 and 5. The case markers indicate the geographic locale of the college to assess simultaneously if revenue deviations may be attributed to geographic cost differences or economies of scale. Revenue deviations in Minnesota are strongly correlated with grant aid receipt ($r = .80$). In addition, all colleges with positive revenue deviations are located in small towns, while most with negative deviations are located on the fringe of large cities, suggesting economies of scale for larger campuses. Deviations are more weakly, but positively, correlated in Florida ($r = .35$) and Arkansas ($r = .12$), where, in the latter case, the low value does not provide a good summary. The graph for Arkansas shows a stronger

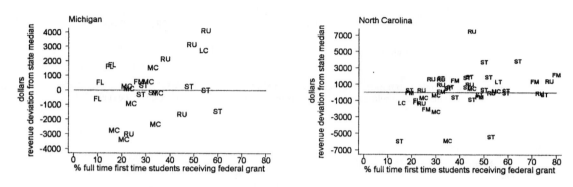

LC large city, MC midsize city, FL fringe large city, FM fringe midsize city, LT large town, ST small town, R rural

**Figure 4.** *Revenue deviations by grant receipt in local-share states, with positive associations. Geographic locale is the case marker. The y-axis scale differs by state.*

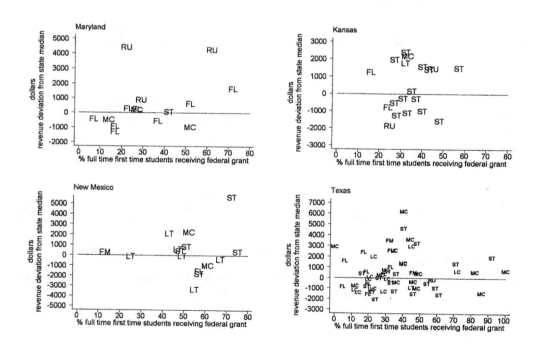

LC large city, MC midsize city, FL fringe large city, FM fringe midsize city, LT large town, ST small town, R rural

**Figure 5.** *Revenue deviations by grant receipt in local-share states, with no association. Geographic locale is the case marker. The y-axis scale differs by state.*

linear relationship with the exception of an unusual case with high positive revenue deviations and a relatively small proportion of grant recipients. In both these states, small towns tend to have positive deviations. In contrast, the correlation in Georgia is negative ($r = -.26$). Colleges with lower proportions of grant recipients have positive revenue deviations. Small towns appear both above and below the median line.

In local-share states, Michigan and North Carolina (Figure 4) have positive correlations with grant receipt ($r = .31$ and $.19$, respectively). Rural and small towns appear both above and below the median line in both states. Maryland (Fig. 5) has a positive correlation of $r = .39$, but this high value is strongly affected by one rural college with high positive deviations and high grant receipt. The association between funding and need in Maryland is much weaker among the remaining cases. Similarly, Kansas, New Mexico, and Texas have weak correlations, at $r = .13$, $.10$, and $.08$, respectively. In Texas, all but one of six colleges with more than 70% of students receiving grant aid have positive revenue deviations, but many colleges with lower proportions of grant recipients show equivalent or higher positive deviations. In California (not shown), where the average absolute revenue deviation is $1,330, there is no correlation between revenue deviations and grant receipt ($r = .01$) In summary, while deviations in three of four state-funded colleges are positively associated with grant aid, this relationship is found in only two of six local-share colleges. Positive revenue deviations in state-funded states are also more consistently associated with smaller geographic locales, suggesting that economies of scale are at play in these states.

## Discussion

This study examines several questions about the impact of local funding on community college finance equity. Community college systems in half of the United States have a structure similar to K–12 finance systems in that they rely on local governments for funding. By analogy between community college and K–12 finance structures, we hypothesized that local funding in community colleges creates revenue disparities that disadvantage the least affluent communities in a state.

Analyzing the federal IPEDS 2000–2001 finance data in 35 states, the study demonstrates that significant intrastate revenue disparities do exist. The average amount of appropriations from local and state governments for community colleges is $5,000 per FTE. The average of the absolute value of college revenue deviations from the state median is close to $1,000, approximately 20% of typical appropriations. The majority of the 35 states analyzed have an inter-quartile range of revenue disparities greater than $1,500 per FTE. In half of the states analyzed, the ratio of appropriations at the 90th and 10th percentiles falls in the range of 2.0 to 2.8. In comparison, Kenneth Wong (1994) characterizes spending disparities between high and low revenue K–12 districts of 2.6 in New York, 3.1 in Illinois, and 2.8 in Texas as among the "most severe" (p. 277), based on a 1990 report by the Congressional Research Service.

Though not as pronounced as these K–12 disparities, the size of community college revenue disparities in many states may nevertheless be considered quite substantial. Further analysis is required to determine where these disparities may be attributed to different combinations of general education, vocational, remedial, and other programs across campuses in a state. Several states employ weighting schemes in their funding formulas, based on cost studies of different fields of instruction, in which technical and remedial courses receive 1.5 to 2.0 times the funding of general education courses (*State Funding*, 2000).

Revenue variations tend to be larger in states with a local finance role, but the difference is a small proportion of total funding and is due in part to higher levels of appropriations in those states. Taking into account this broader context, state- and local-funded states have quite similar levels of revenue variation. However, some resource disparities are progressive, or equity enhancing, while others are regressive. To assess the equity of resource differences, we examined a subsample of 10 states with average absolute deviations exceeding $1,000 per FTE. We observed revenue deviations in these high-disparity states as equity enhancing in three of four state-funded states and in two of six local-share states, suggesting that local funding is more often, though not always, regressive. Since all local-share states also have state funding, these differences in funding patterns cannot be attributed exclusively to the local role but may be understood as resulting when local funding is commingled with state funding. Thus, the direction of revenue disparities, not the overall level, presents a cause for concern.

The results support theoretically based equity and efficiency arguments about the effects of a local role on community college finance. The local finance role appears to create revenue disparities that do not promote vertical equity. On the other hand, local-share states tend to have lower tuition and higher levels of funding from within-state sources, which may reflect the "efficient" nature of local voters supporting their local colleges. Colleges with a ratio of local appropriations to state appropriations of less than one-half also have the highest levels of revenues from all sources, excluding tuition and fees. This correlation suggests that, when local governments have responsibility for funding community colleges in collaboration with state governments, students benefit from a broader revenue stream. With government officials at both the state and local level having a stake in the success of the local college, lobbying on behalf of the college and support for entrepreneurial activities may well increase.

These findings have implications for community college finance systems. States with a local finance share subordinate to the state share appear to receive higher revenues. It appears that intrastate variation in the resources available to a college in these states is also less likely to be determined by "rational" planning objectives, such as budget adjustments for low-income students or economies of scale. This situation may be socially beneficial if local financing contributes to a "leveling up" of resources, where all colleges benefit from higher public funding than they would in the absence of the local contribution. If this is the case, states with an existing local finance role should maintain them, while adopting policies that tax relatively high local revenue districts to provide additional funds to low-revenue districts. As Hoxby (2001) has shown in her analysis of the "leveling up" and "leveling down" effects of K–12 finance reforms, the tax price on high wealth districts should not be so high that it provides a disincentive for local funding in those districts; otherwise, the equalization policy may depress funding.

As state funding decreases, even states without a traditional local-finance role are placing greater expectations on individual colleges to generate additional funds, whether through academic entrepreneurship, auxiliary business activities, or fund raising (Burke & Serban, 1998). These efficiency initiatives have the potential of raising additional revenues but also create equity concerns as the state role in allocating resources diminishes. These states should also incorporate resource-sharing policies into incentive plans.

It is important to note that several factors for which controls have not been included due to data limitations may affect the interpretation of the findings. Most important, the observed correlation between positive revenue deviations and the proportion of students receiving grant aid may have meanings other than the equity-enhancing effect ascribed to it in this analysis. The proportion of students receiving grant aid may be affected by access to information and counseling regarding financial aid or by clarity of purpose among first-time students. If such factors are decisive in determining the proportion of grant recipients at a college, the positive correlation between higher levels of local and state appropriation and grant receipt may indicate revenue disparities in favor of more affluent communities with higher levels of college-related information and networking, or "social capital" (Coleman, 1988). In future analyses, the use of the IPEDS federal grant receipt variable should be supplemented with census income and poverty data to provide a better control for community wealth.

The higher levels of funding going to small-town colleges in some states have been interpreted here as compensating for diseconomies of scale. However, determining whether observed revenue disparities are appropriate for that purpose requires more information about fixed and variable costs and controls for geographic price differences among urban, suburban, and rural areas. Higher costs in urban areas are likely to diminish the purchasing power of each dollar in revenue. This means that, for more accurate comparison revenue, differences must be adjusted by a cost index similar to those developed for studies of K–12 finance equity. Generally, we would expect that the use of a geographic index will shift state funding from rural to urban areas (Carey, 2003; Odden & Picus, 2004). With significantly greater appropriations per FTE awarded to rural and small colleges in several of the high-disparity states, it is important to evaluate whether the appropriation premiums for small size are based on actual cost differences. Such estimates are clearly politically sensitive, as they have the potential to significantly shift funding among institutions. In states where white residents are disproportionately located in small towns and students of color in urban areas, the higher funding for small towns may be due to racial group politics and disparities in legislative power. Complex interactions may also be at play. Stella Flores (2003) shows that Texas's funding formula and reliance on local-share funding results in both higher and lower funding for Hispanic Serving Institutions (HSIs) in communities providing a threshold tax rate. The majority of the HSIs receiving the short end of the deal are located on the U.S.-Mexican border.

As discussed above, some portion of the revenue disparities may be due to the location of high-cost programs, but there may also be differences in the geographic accessibility of students to those programs. States may locate specialized programs requiring technical facilities at a small number of campuses and expect mobile adults to travel to them, but this may not be a realistic option for students constrained by work and family commitments. Thus, while high-cost programs may explain some portion of the funding disparities, their location may also raise equity issues in regard to program access.

K–12 finance equity cases initially focused on inputs, but over time the judicial focus has shifted to promoting equitable student outcomes. This approach is termed "adequacy," and it holds states accountable for providing resources to schools sufficient to enable students to meet educational standards and become successful competitors in a global economy (Verstegen, 1998). The incorporation of adequacy standards into community college finance analyses would be consistent with the recent policy focus on higher education performance accountability (Dowd, 2003). An adequacy, or "outcome equity," approach shifts the question from "Is equitable funding being provided to colleges in the state?" to "Are equitable program completion rates being achieved?" The answer to the latter question implies disparate funding because students with greater educational needs will require greater resources. For example, a college enrolling a relatively high proportion of immigrants in a nursing degree program may well require resources to provide language tutoring to attain graduation rates equal to those of a program enrolling native English speakers. This example underscores the significance of such funding decisions when we consider the shortage of bilingual and ethnically diverse nurses in the United States (Butters, 2003). Similarly, as community colleges take on an increasing role in remedial education, it is important to ask what levels of resources are needed to successfully educate students to desired standards of achievement.

This study has focused on states with high-revenue deviations. However, it should also be noted that states with low funding disparities may have inequitable systems if students with unequal needs are being treated as equals by the financing system. In addition, without state-by-state information about unique programs and institutional missions, the analysis has focused on conservative measures of variation that were not determined by extreme values. This approach may have minimized the characterization of funding inequities in some states.

Half of the states in the sample have 90th percentile revenue deviation values greater than $1,900, which may deserve greater attention. Does the high funding for these institutions stem from unique institutional histories, unusual levels of political clout, data-reporting error, or rational planning decisions to efficiently locate high-costs programs? This study provides a foundation for future multivariate analyses and purposeful sampling for case studies. State analysts and institutional researchers may wish to replicate the results for their state using IPEDS and state data. The following factors should be considered when evaluating the equity of revenue disparities: economies and diseconomies of scale, geographic price differences, mix of program types, community and student racial and demographic characteristics, and program completion rates.

Notwithstanding the recent community college finance litigation in Oregon (Gomstyn, 2003), determination of what constitutes "fair" intrastate community college resource allocations will most likely depend on political processes, rather than on legal decisions like those that have so significantly shaped K–12 financing. While primary and secondary schooling are a constitutional right mandated by state law, postsecondary education is not. Today, however, many would argue that a community college education now sets the contemporary standard for full participation in the economic and democratic institutions of our country. If this rhetorical claim gains political support, then it could also be argued that states have a responsibility to fund community colleges according to adequacy or "outcome equity" standards. Many community college students have limited options about where they attend college, constrained as they often are by family responsibilities, employment obligations, and financial hardship. In these conditions, the funding disparities documented in this paper certainly deserve greater understanding through academic analysis, action research by community college practitioners, and political debate within states.

# References

Alexander, F. K. (2000). The changing face of accountability. *Journal of Higher Education, 71*(4), 411.

Bill Clinton's view on education: From acceptance speech. *Chronicle of Higher Education* (1996, September 16). Retrieved December 19, 2003, from *http://www.chronicle.com*.

Breneman, D. W., & Nelson, S. C. (1981). *Financing community colleges: An economic perspective*. Washington, D.C.: Brookings Institution.

*Budget development approach/options and impact of formula/fair share funding*. (2000). (Budget Request Framework Proposal). Boston: Board of Higher Education.

Burke, J. C., & Serban, A. M. (Eds.). (1998). *Performance funding for public higher education: Fad or trend?* San Francisco: Jossey-Bass.

Butters, C. (2003). *Associate degree nursing students: A study of retention in the nursing education program*. Unpublished dissertation, University of Massachusetts Boston.

Carey, K. (2003). *The funding gap: Low-income and minority students still receive fewer dollars in many states*. Retrieved December 15, 2003, from *http://www2.edtrust.org/EdTrust/Product+Catalog/special+reports.htm#2003*.

Coleman, J. S. (1988). Social capital in the creation of human capital. *American Journal of Sociology, 94* (Supplement), S95–S120.

*Community colleges and the State University of New York*. (1999). Boulder, CO: National Center for Higher Education Management Systems.

DesJardins, S. L. (2003). Understanding and using efficiency and equity criteria in the study of higher education policy. In J. C. Smart & W. G. Tierney (Eds.), *Higher education: Handbook of theory and research* (pp. 173–219). New York: Agathon Press.

Dowd, A. C. (2003, March). From access to outcome equity: Revitalizing the democratic mission of the community college. *Annals of the American Academy of Political and Social Science, 586*, 92–119.

Flores, S. (2003, November). *Disproportionate policies: Latino access to community colleges in Texas*. Paper presented at the Association for the Study of Higher Education, Portland, Oregon.

Garms, W. I. (1981). On measuring the equity of community college finance. *Educational Administration Quarterly, 17*(2), 1–20.

Gomstyn, A. (2003). Oregon judge rejects community-colleges' lawsuit seeking more state money. *Chronicle of Higher Education*. Retrieved November 17, 2003, from *http://chronicle.com*.

Hoxby, C. M. (2001, November). All school finance equalizations are not created equal. *Quarterly Journal of Economics*, 1189–1231.

*Iowa Community College funding formula task force report*. (1998). N.p.: Iowa Department of Education.

Metzler, J. (2003, Spring). Inequitable equilibrium: School finance in the United States. *Indiana Law Review, 36*, 561–608.

Monk, D. H. (1990). *Educational finance: An economic approach*. New York: McGraw Hill.

Odden, A. R., & Picus, L. O. (2004). *School finance: A policy perspective* (3rd ed.). Boston: McGraw-Hill.

Romano, R. M. (2003, October). *Financing community colleges across the states: An economic perspective*. Paper presented at the "Complex Community College" Conference, Cornell Higher Education Research Institute, Cornell University, Ithaca, NY.

*State funding for community colleges: A fifty-state survey*. (2000). Denver, CO: Center for Community College Policy, Education Commission of the States.

*Study: Hope and Lifetime Learning are middle-class tax benefits, not financial aid*. (2003, March 14, 2003). Retrieved December 19, 2003, from www.NASFAA.org.

Timar, T. B. (1994). Politics, policy, and categorical aid: New inequities in California school finance. *Educational Evaluation and Policy Analysis, 16*(2), 143–160.

Timar, T. B. (2003). *School governance in California: You can't always get what you want*. Retrieved April 30, 2003, from www.ucla-idea.org.

Verstegen, D. A. (1998, Summer). Judicial analysis during the new wave of school finance litigation: The new adequacy in education. *Journal of Education Finance, 24*, 51–68.

Wong, K. K. (1994). Governance structure, resource allocation, and equity policy. *Review of Research in Education, 20*, 257–289.

# Footnotes

1. The FTE calculation is based on the same ratio used to publish enrollment statistics in the annual *Digest of Education Statistics*. For the public two-year sector, the FTE equals full-time enrollment plus part-time enrollment multiplied by one-third.

2. To some extent, such variations in tuition and fees are due to mismeasurement at the college level. A review of reported tuition charges in Massachusetts, where the Board of Higher Education sets a uniform tuition, showed that individual colleges reported different tuition rates, in some cases due to different approaches to calculating full-time enrollment status. In Massachusetts, fees are set by the individual colleges and therefore create valid variation in the total of tuition and fees.

3. The cases and values are Mid-South Community College, Arizona ($26,648 per FTE above the state median of local and state appropriations), South Piedmont Community College, North Carolina ($27,547), Coahoma Community College, Minnesota (($15,516), Illinois Eastern Community Colleges—Olney Central College, ($13,491), and Foothill College, California ($9,114).

4. The five extreme cases are excluded from the calculation of average deviations.

*Alicia C. Dowd is Assistant Professor, Department of Leadership in Education, University of Massachusetts Boston.*

*John I. Grant is Director, Office of Institutional Research and Development, Cape Cod Community College. Sections of this paper were presented in earlier drafts at the Cornell Higher Education Research Institute's (CHERI) "Complex Community College" Conference (October 2003) and at the Association for Institutional Research's Annual Forum (May 2003). The authors thank Jeff Groen and Jane Wellman for their review of the CHERI draft.*

# Affordability

## Obtaining and Making Sense of Information about How Students, Families, and States Pay for Higher Education

### Joni E. Finney and Patrick J. Kelly

*Affordability*—the ability of students and other funders to contribute to the support of colleges and universities—is a topic of increasing salience. In this Resource Review, we examine the affordability of college from two perspectives: from that of students and their families, and from that of the state. We also identify many references to up-to-date databases, analyses, and policy perspectives relevant to issues of affordability in higher education.

## Understanding Affordability

For students and families, *affordability* is best defined as the proportion of annual family income required to pay for educational expenses (tuition, room/board), after deducting financial aid from all sources (federal and state governments, and institutions), often called "net price." Affordability for state government consists of its willingness and ability to provide revenue to support goals related to higher education. Adopting a framework based on *both* these perspectives assumes that all critical finance policies—tuition, state appropriations and student financial aid—play interdependent roles in providing affordable higher education for students, families, and the state.

We believe that such a policy framework represents a significant departure from the finance policies at the state and federal levels that guided higher education for the 50 years after World War II. These historic policies successfully established the basic higher education infrastructure in the United States and enormously expanded its capacity.

New campuses were constructed in every state, and clear mission and role distinctions were established (for example, research universities, public colleges and universities, and community colleges). National and economic interests were well served because these actions yielded steadily increasing numbers of students graduating from high school and enrolling in additional postsecondary education or training, which in turn generated a quarter of the total population with a baccalaureate degree.

Under current conditions, though, we believe a new policy framework is needed based on ensuring affordable education for students/families and the states. Underlying this framework is a broad premise that the demand for a highly educated population will increase substantially in the emerging century.

This demand will be fueled by the needs of a globally competitive economy and a democracy that faces increasing complexity on many domestic issues. The state finance policies that so successfully guided the country since World War II must undergo major changes to meet this challenge. To understand this new framework, we must examine each of its basic elements more closely.

## State Appropriations

State appropriations made by far the greatest contribution to post-World War II expansion and diversification of higher education. And state appropriations continue to provide the most money per student to subsidize and develop research universities, somewhat fewer dollars per student for state colleges and universities to develop a professionally trained work force, and still fewer dollars per student for the development of junior and community colleges to focus on transfer and career preparation. Appropriated state dollars, together with a large federal investment in research, worked brilliantly in the United States to expand higher education capacity—from research to career preparation—compared to other systems throughout the world.

In spite of the current fiscal climate, states currently spend about $60 billion annually for higher education (James Palmer, *Grapevine*, Illinois State University, Fiscal Year 2004). Although the overall share of state support for higher education has declined over the past 20 years, overall dollar amounts have increased. From 1980 to 2000, state support per student for public institutions increased 24 percent in inflation-adjusted dollars from $6,467 to $8,044 (*Losing Ground: A National Status Report on the Affordability of American Higher Education*, Data Updates, May 2003, The National Center for Public Policy and Higher Education [NCPPHE], San Jose, CA). How best to utilize these dollars in assuring affordability for students and the state is *the* critical policy question.

State appropriation processes and resource allocation mechanisms are called into play when the need to better utilize and target resources is imperative. Indeed, properly *targeting* resources directed toward higher education may be at least as important as their amount. For example, funding formulas that routinely provide significantly more dollars per student to those colleges and universities that enroll the best prepared (and thus most easily educable) portion of the population are an artifact of a funding system designed when only a small portion of the population required education or training beyond high school. New funding policies must be used to target those most in need if the country is to substantially increase overall educational attainment levels.

## Tuition

Tuition policies directly affect affordability for students. In combination with institutional appropriations from the state, they also provide the necessary capacity to address public educational needs and goals. Typically, however, the policies that establish tuition are narrowly framed in one of the following ways—all of which tend to raise tuition levels:

1. Tuition based on selected "peer" institutions. This method generally ratchets tuition upward because the selection of peers is frequently based on institutional aspirations and mission-specific characteristics instead of the ability of students and families to pay for higher education.
2. Tuition defined as a fixed share of total educational costs. This method results in tuition increases when other shares of revenues (like institutional operating funds) are increasing and rarely results in tuition rollbacks when these other sources of revenue decline.
3. Tuition rates established to "back-fill" revenue losses when state appropriations decline. Once again this causes an immediate rise in tuition, which is rarely reduced when state budgets recover.

As shown in the NCPPHE report, these three predominant approaches to establishing tuition levels were largely responsible for a 117 percent increase in tuition and fee revenue for higher education between 1980 to 2000. The results of these policies have been detrimental, especially to low-income students. In 2000, all but the wealthiest families (defined as the top income quintile) paid more of their income to go to college than they did in 1980. According to the report, the poorest Americans (defined as the bottom income quintile) paid 13 percent of their annual family income to attend a public four-year college in 1980; in 2000 they paid 27 percent of their annual income to attend.

All three of the historic ways to establish tuition levels tend to underemphasize or completely overlook one important factor: family ability to pay for higher education. Historic tuition policies were designed primarily to ensure a steady or increased base of revenue to support college and university operations, regardless of whether state appropriations were increasing or declining. These policies ratcheted up the costs of higher education to the state in good times when state appropriations increased. But they made it more difficult for the state to continue to fund at these higher base funding levels when the economy turned down.

Given these options, the only ways to keep higher education affordable to students and families—absent major changes in institutional appropriations—are to a) greatly increase student financial aid to offset tuition increases, b) significantly reduce enrollment in highly subsidized institutions, or c) reduce enrollment at all colleges and universities. None of these options, however, are good choices if the nation wants to increase educational attainment at all levels.

## Student Financial Aid

Most states have not made significant investments in state financial aid. In fact, only six states account for about 60 percent of all of the state need-based aid that was awarded in 2003-04 (National Center for Higher Education Management Systems, *State Student Financial Aid Survey*, 2003–04, Boulder, CO). Many states, especially in the West, have relied on low tuition instead of financial aid to ensure broad access.

Some states with large private sectors (for example, New York and Pennsylvania) have invested heavily in financial aid programs to offset tuition at both public and private colleges and universities. During the 1990s, substantial growth in state merit-based student aid programs (for example, in Georgia and Florida) had the effect of distributing dollars to students who were the most likely to attend college anyway—and who could afford to pay—and to institutions that already receive the largest public subsidy.

Growth in institutional aid jumped dramatically in the 1990s, mostly as a result of "recycling" a portion of tuition revenue. Growing evidence is available that institutional aid dollars are used primarily to attract meritorious students rather than financially needy, but still qualified, students. Institutions with the greatest public subsidies—and those able to charge the highest tuitions—are usually the most successful in garnering tuition from one student and converting it into financial aid for another.

This approach to financial aid cannot, and does not, work very effectively for less well-to-do colleges and universities serving middle- and lower-income students. It therefore has significant limitations for helping the country significantly increase educational attainment.

Making higher education affordable to low- and middle-income students and families requires state governments to significantly increase their support for state-level student aid programs. Moreover, these programs can operate most efficiently by targeting dollars toward students and families with high financial need, regardless of the institution in which they enroll.

Decisions about how much state aid is needed to meet such policy goals, how aid dollars are distributed (for example, need vs. merit or some combination) and the appropriate level of distribution (for example, institutional vs. state) are rarely systematically considered by state policymakers—especially as they relate to tuition policies and policies that guide institutional appropriations.

With vast differences in levels of state support for higher education and tuition and fees across the nation, it is not surprising that the ability of students and families to pay for college can vary dramatically from state to state. But like nearly all statistics, any measure created for ability to pay is likely to vary just as much *within* states as across states.

Chart 1 provides one example. It shows the total annual cost of attendance (not accounting for student aid) at public two-year institutions in one state—Missouri—as a percentage of personal income for the counties in which the state's two-year institutions are located.

Like most states, the gross costs of attending public institutions within the same sector in Missouri are fairly similar. But these costs as a percentage of the *average personal income* of the area served differ dramatically. This doesn't necessarily call for differential tuition pricing, but it certainly can help further policymakers' understanding of the need for *well-targeted* state financial aid.

**Chart 1. Total Expenses (Annual Tuition, Required Fees, and Book Supplies) at Missouri Two-Year College as a Percentage of Personal Income in the Counties in which the Institutions are Located**

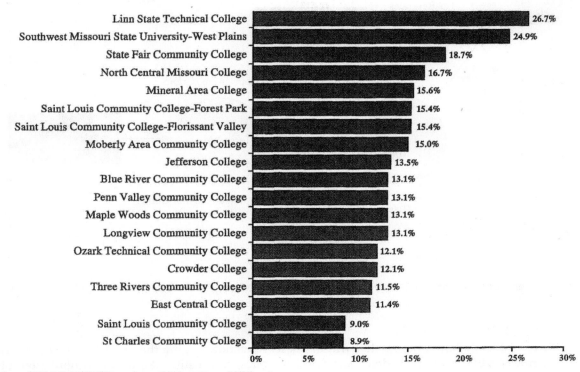

Source: NCES, IPEDS 2002-03 Finance Survey, U.S. Census Bureau (2000 Census)

## Looking at Resources for Affordability

How does the combination of established finance policies for higher education in a given state—including tuition, institutional appropriations, and financial aid—affect the provision of affordable higher education to students and families in a manner that states can also afford? We don't pretend to know all the answers to this question, but we can identify relevant resources—policy ideas, analysis, and useful up-to-date databases—to begin to address these issues within the framework we have proposed. But to put all of these resources in their proper context, we first need to look at the big picture.

Chart 2 shows the interrelated components of state higher education finance policy—the combination of factors that address affordability for both students and for the state. In order for a state to make informed policy, it needs to have basic information about each of the key elements noted:

- *The overall economy*, which has an impact on all facets of higher education finance.
- *Affordability to students*, which addresses the ability of students to pay their share of the costs of higher education, and under what conditions they can do so.
- *The state's ability to pay*, which includes the state's tax effort, its tax capacity, and its likely fiscal future.
- *The adequacy of institutional finance*, which reflects the extent to which postsecondary education institutions, individually and collectively, have sufficient revenues from *all* sources to fulfill the missions assigned to them.

The last factor is especially important because it raises a final critical policy question: Can institutions themselves carry some of the shared responsibility for ensuring affordability when state appropriations are diminished?

**Chart 2. Understanding Higher Education Finance**

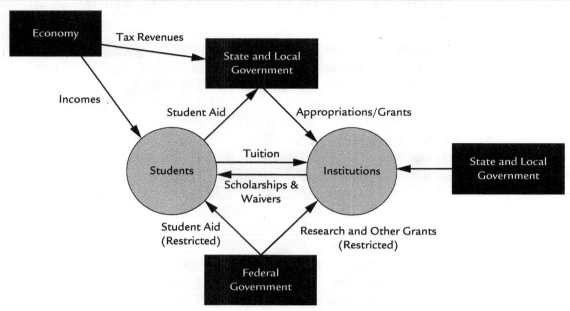

*Source:* Dennis Jones, National Center for Higher Education Management Systems (NCHEMS)

## The Economy

Little can be said about affordability without at least acknowledging the impact of the economy. Economic conditions affect students and families, states, and institutions alike. Without attempting to point to all available measures of economic conditions, it is useful to highlight a few. At the heart of affordability from the state perspective are two factors: its underlying ability to raise revenues that can be allocated to higher education and other public purposes, and the extent to which the state has any additional capacity to generate tax revenue should it choose to do so.

- The State Higher Education Executive Officers (SHEEO) annually collects data that measure relative tax capacity per capita for each state and their actual tax revenues as a percent of tax capacity. These data are very useful in gauging a given state's tax capacity and effort. They are available at www.sheeo.org and at www.higheredinfo.org

Equally important issues are a) the ability of each state to maintain a constant level of support to eligible recipients of state services within the level of revenues that will likely be generated by their current tax structures, and b) whether or not funding for higher education will have to grow faster than funding for the rest of state government in order to maintain current service levels.

- *State Spending for Higher Education in the Coming Decade* (Donald Boyd, the Rockefeller Institute of Government, New York State University at Albany, 2002) provides projections to 2010 for state and local budget surpluses and shortfalls, as well as the changes in spending for higher education and other programs that would be needed to maintain current services. The study was conducted for the National Center for Higher Education Management Systems (NCHEMS) and is available at www.nchems.org

## Affordability from the Student Perspective

Recent declines in state support for colleges and universities—combined with unprecedented tuition and fee hikes and the inability of state and federal financial aid to keep pace with them—have stimulated many efforts to understand how these trends are affecting the ability of students from low- and middle-income families to go to college. Calculating the cost of college attendance is far more difficult than it may seem.

Radical changes in college tuition and fees from year to year (particularly in the last few years)—combined with the need to account for federal, state, and institutional financial aid—complicate this calculation and make the need for current data imperative. In spite of these difficulties, useful data are available about a) student and family ability to pay for college, b) federal grants and loans, c) state need- and merit–based aid, and d) levels of unmet need facing low- and middle-income students. When combined, these data can help one assemble a fairly clear picture of current conditions within each state regarding college affordability for students and families. These sources include:

- The Advisory Committee on Student Financial Assistance, *Access Denied: Restoring the Nation's Commitment to Equal Educational Opportunity, 2001* and *Empty Promises: The Myth of College Access in America, 2002.* Washington, D.C., (www.ed.gov/ACSFA). These congressional committee reports address broad issues of educational opportunity, including access and affordability. Contents include data on financial aid, student borrowing, levels of unmet need for low- and middle-income students, and the consequent impact on access to postsecondary education.
- American Council on Education (ACE), *Putting College Costs Into Context, 2004* and the *2003 Status Report on Federal Education Loan Programs,* Washington, D.C., (www.acenet.edu). These reports authored by Jacqueline E. King of ACE are published regularly and are available online. They contain information on the rising costs of postsecondary education for students relative to other investments, student borrowing, data on important trends in the largest federal education loan programs, as well as the characteristics of student borrowers and the role borrowing plays in students' higher education financing schemes.
- *The National Association for State Student Grant and Aid Programs (NASSGAP) Annual Survey,* (www.nassgap.org/researchsurveys/default.htm). This source contains historical state data on federal grants and loans, and state need- and merit-based aid—as well as the volume of loans as a percentage of the state's population, the student population, and total state support for higher education. The results of the annual surveys are available online.
- The College Board, *Trends in Student Aid* and *Trends in College Pricing,* New York, NY: College Board Publications (available at $15 each or online at www.collegeboard.com/research/home). These two reports, produced annually from 1983 to 2003, provide trend data on state, federal, and institutional grants and loans and cost of attendance. Unlike federal databases, the College Board tuition data are based on estimates of tuition for the following year, but they are released sooner than federal data.
- King, Tracey and Bannon, Ellynne, *The Burden of Borrowing: A Report on the Rising Rates of Student Loan Debt,* The State Public Interest Research Group (PIRG) Higher Education Project. March 2002, Washington, D.C., (available at www.pirg.org/highered/BurdenofBorrowing.pdf). This report provides an analysis of student loan debt since the early 1990s, including breakdowns of borrowers by income and race or ethnicity.
- McPherson, Michael S. and Morton O. Shapiro, "The Blurring Line Between Merit and Need in Financial Aid," *Change,* Vol. 34, Number 2, March/April 2002, pp. 39–46. This article confronts the use of institutional aid dollars, showing that even those dollars specifically targeted for financially needy students are distributed primarily on the basis of merit, thereby understating the total amount of merit aid that institutions distribute.
- Mortenson, Tom, *Postsecondary Education Opportunity,* Oskaloosa, IA (available at $148 for 12 issues; see www.postsecondary.org). This monthly newsletter presents data on all aspects of financing higher education. With regard to affordability, the publications and Web site contain particularly useful data on federal Pell Grant recipients, relative to state need-based grants and the undergraduate population.
- The National Center for Higher Education Management Systems (NCHEMS) in Boulder, Colorado, on behalf of the National Center for Public Policy and Higher Education (NCPPHE) in San Jose, CA, has conducted a state-level survey for the past two years that captures the most up-to-date state allocations for need- and merit-based aid programs. These data are available at www.higheredinfo.org.
- The National Center for Public Policy and Higher Education, *Measuring Up: The State-by-State Report Card for Higher Education,* San Jose, CA, 2000 and 2002 (available online at www.measuringup.highereducation.org). Affordability is one of six areas in which states are graded in this national report card. The grade is based on a) family ability to pay—the percentage of income needed to pay for college by sector, state grant aid targeted to low-income families as

a percentage of federal Pell Grant aid, b) the percentage of income that the poorest families need to pay for tuition at the lowest priced colleges in the state, and c) the average loan amount under graduate students borrow to pay for college each year.

- The National Center for Public Policy and Higher Education, *Losing Ground: A National Status Report on the Affordability of American Higher Education*, San Jose, CA, 2003 (available at www.measuringup.highereducation.org). This report highlights trends in finance related to affordability for students and the state. It contains trend data on tuition and fees, family income, state and local support for higher education, student borrowing, and state and federal grant aid to students.

- Price, Derek V., *Borrowing Inequality: Race, Class, and Student Loans*, Lynne Rienner Pub., Boulder, CO, 2004 (61 pages available at $45). This book provides trends related to student financial aid over the past two decades and describes the transition from a financial aid system based on grants to one based on loans, providing evidence to suggest that increasing over-reliance on loans is contributing to education attainment gaps.

## Affordability from the State Perspective

The notion of "ability to pay" is as applicable to states as it is to students and families. Here, several useful barometers for measuring the levels of state funding for higher education are available, both in terms of direct support to institutions of higher education and the provision of student financial aid. The most useful metrics for institutional support are those that look at state support for higher education relative to support for other state programs, the size of the state's population, and the number of students being served. Some helpful measures and data sources are:

- Palmer, James, *Grapevine: A National Database of State Tax Support for Higher Education*, Illinois State University (published annually and available at www.coe.ilstu.edu/grapevine). Measures that show changes in state revenues and general expenditures relative to higher education expenditures in this report can provide insights into each state's revenue capacity, willingness, and higher education effort. Measures that show the burden borne by state tax-payers to support higher education include state tax appropriations for higher education per capita and per $1,000 of personal income.

- The National Center for Public Policy and Higher Education (NCPPHE), *Losing Ground: A National Status Report on the Affordability of American Higher Education*, 2003 (available at measuringup.highereducation.org). This report provides data on total revenues for public colleges and universities from all sources, the growth of all sources of revenue for higher education, and the growing dependence on tuition to pay for higher education.

- State Higher Education Executive Officers (SHEEO), *State Higher Education Finance*. Denver, CO (available at www.sheeo.org). Indicators of state appropriations for higher education per full-time equivalent student and total funding (including tuition and fees) per full-time equivalent student contained in this report reveal overall levels of state support for higher education and whether this support is being sustained over time, as well as the overall resources available to the state's higher education system.

The report also contains information on the percentage of collected tax revenues appropriated for higher education. Finally, the report provides an indicator that calculates tuition and fees as a percentage of total funding for higher education. When combined with data about state support, this measure indicates the relative dependence of institutions on contributions from students and families.

- The Western Interstate Commission for Higher Education (WICHE), *Changing Direction* (available at www.wiche.edu/Policy/Changing_Direction/index.htm). With support from the Lumina Foundation for Education, WICHE has commissioned nationally recognized leaders in higher education policy to publish a series of articles about the alignment of state financial aid and finance policies to maximize participation, access, and success for all students. This multiyear project also involves a number of state case studies intended to provide in-depth documentation of particular tuition, financial aid, and appropriations policies and practices.

Finally, an important source of state support for higher education is provided directly to students in the form of financial aid awards. And the combined dollar amount of these awards often accounts for a sizable part of a state's budget allocation for higher education. So the information on state-based aid described in the previous section on affordability from the student perspective is equally useful for examining affordability from the state perspective.

## Conclusion

The ability to piece together an accurate state-by-state picture of affordability is complicated by the absence of information in two critical areas: the amount of institutional aid granted to undergraduate students within state systems of higher education and some understanding of the adequacy of institutional support. In the absence of accurate and timely data on institutional aid, it is difficult to reach a solid conclusion about the net cost of college attendance. In many states, the total amount of institutional aid granted to undergraduates may exceed that awarded by the state. Unlike federal and state financial aid, there is no national data repository that contains data about the amount of aid awarded to students by institutions with their own dollars.

Current discussions about affordability and finance in most states are also typically conducted in the absence of any evidence about the overall *adequacy* of institutional funding. As a result, in times of decreasing state appropriations, public institutions often attempt to offset revenue shortfalls by simply raising tuition. This begs the question of how many resources institutions really need to do their jobs. Using Chart 2 as a guide, it is important that we are able to simultaneously answer questions about the ability of students and families to pay, the ability of states to pay, and the adequacy of institutional funding.

Finally, simply having information about higher education finance available in a timely manner does not ensure that the country will create new public policies aimed at providing affordable higher education—but it is certainly unlikely that we can develop or assess appropriate public policies in the absence of such information. Redesigning state policies to ensure that higher education remains an affordable public good to both students and the state will require a lot of thought and analysis. Identifying sound information, data, and other resources is an important first step.

*Joni E. Finney is vice president of the National Center for Public Policy and Higher Education (NCPPHE). Patrick J. Kelly is senior associate at the National Center for Higher Education Management Systems (NCHEMS) and director of its higher education information Web site. Much of the information reviewed in this article can be accessed at www.higheredinfo.org, a Web site created by NCHEMS.*

# The Causes and Consequences of Public College Tuition Inflation

MICHAEL MUMPER AND MELISSA L. FREEMAN

*Ohio University*

Everyone in America knows that college prices have been going up at an alarming rate. For nearly three decades, tuition inflation has been the subject of continuing family concerns, student anxiety, gubernatorial proclamations, and congressional investigations. In spite of this, there is no end in sight. In the last three years, tuition inflation has accelerated to its fastest level yet. In 2002–03, tuition and fees at four-year and two-year public institutions rose, often startlingly so, in every state. In Massachusetts, for example, tuition jumped from $3,295 to $4,075, an increase of 24 percent in one year. Iowa, Missouri, and Texas increased tuition by 20 percent. In Ohio, the increase was 17 percent. Sixteen other states increased tuition by more than 10 percent (Trombley, 2003, p. 1). There is no reason to believe that this acceleration of tuition inflation rate was a one-year phenomenon. Rather, it seems likely to be simply the next wave in a steadily accelerating price spiral that has been going on for nearly 25 years.

In spite of this, it is important to note that rising prices do not seem to be driving down the demand for higher education. The number of students enrolled in college seems to increase every year. The portion of high school graduates attending college increases as well. In 2002–03, for example, more than 15 million students were enrolled in degree granting institutions of higher education. Twelve million of these students, about 65 percent, attended public institutions. By almost any measure, more students are entering college in spite of the rising prices. One study put it this way, "To enhance their opportunities and realize their educational aspirations, Americans work more hours than in the past, incur greater debt, and devote larger portions of their incomes to paying for college" (National Center for Public Policy and Higher Education, 2002b, p. 1).

This chapter explores both the causes and consequences of public college tuition inflation. We have chosen to focus on public colleges for several reasons. The vast majority of students in the United States attend public colleges. In addition, public colleges have traditionally served as a way for lower-income and disadvantaged students to earn the skills necessary to get a get a good job and to obtain entry into the middle class. As prices rise, there is some reason to believe that public colleges may no longer be able to perform this important role. Public and private institutions of higher education are constructed on quite different financial foundations. There have been two outstanding books focusing on the reasons for the price inflation at the nation's elite private colleges (Ehrenberg, 2000; Clotfelter, 1996). Yet, the best studies of public college tuition inflation are now more than a decade old and predate the rapid tuition inflation of the early 2000s. Finally, we limit our focus to the period after 1980. This is the point at which real public college prices began their current upward trajectory.

J.C. Smart (ed.), *Higher Education: Handbook of Theory and Research, Vol. XX,* 307–361. © 2005 *Springer Printed in Great Britain.*

In addressing these important questions, we begin by looking closely at the patterns of tuition inflation. In the first part of this analysis, we look at recent patterns in tuition and fees at two- and four-year colleges. Next we turn to the factors that seem to be driving prices upward. We examine the different ways in which public colleges set tuition. Then we look at the factors that have contributed to the rising prices. To do this, we take a careful look at the recent changes in the sources of revenue available to public colleges and the spending levels and patterns of these institutions. We will also examine how changes in the level of support provided by state governments have altered the financial basis on which public institutions operate. Here, we consider the particular impact of the recession of the early 21st Century and the rapid increases in Medicaid spending on the ability of state governments to continue to support higher education at traditional levels.

In the second part of the chapter, we examine the consequences of tuition inflation on students, families, and institutions. Here, we seek to determine if citizens and policymakers should be concerned about the short- and long-term impact of rising prices. The answer to this is not as straightforward as some people assume. In this section, we show the impact that rising prices have on enrollment, particularly among students from lower income or disadvantaged backgrounds. We do this by looking at the research on the role price plays in determining student aspirations for col-

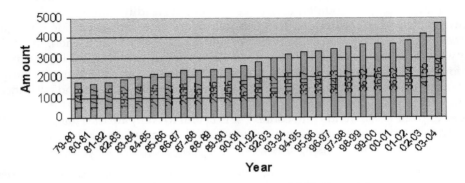

**Figure 1. Average Tuition and Fees at Four-Year Colleges Enrollment Weighted**

lege, their choice of institution, their likelihood of graduation, and their post-graduation debt levels. We will show how rising prices have a disproportionate impact on the lowest income families at each stage. Finally, we consider the troubling impact that the same changes in the fiscal environment that are driving college costs upward are having for public universities.

## The Twenty-Five Year Trends in College Prices

While public college prices have increased at a remarkable rate over the last two decades, a closer look at those increases over time and across sector reveals complex and variable patterns. During the 1970s, constant dollar tuition and fees at public colleges actually declined slightly. When this drop in prices is coupled with the dramatic increases in federal grant aid, access to public colleges improved markedly for all income groups (Mumper, 1993).

But beginning in about 1980, prices at four-year public colleges began a relentless upward spiral in which average prices increased every year for the next 24 consecutive years. Figure 1 shows that, in constant dollars, tuition at a public four-year institution increased by more than 168 percent between 1980–81 and 2003–04. However, those increases have not happened at a steady pace. During the 1980s and early 1990s, as measured in real terms, four-year public college tuition inflation was about 5 percent per year. Then in the mid-1990s, it suddenly slowed down. From 1995–96 to 2000–01 the real rate of increase was less than 2 percent per year. Unfortunately, as the new century began, the price spiral returned with even more intensity. Between 2000–01 and 2003–04, public college tuition increased by a remarkable 28 percent.

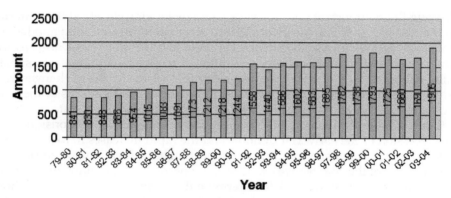

**Figure 2. Average Tuition and Fees Public Two Year Colleges Enrollment Weighted**

The pattern of price increases at two-year colleges has been slightly less severe, but much more volatile. Figure 2 shows that between 1980 and 2003, real prices in this sector increased by 126 percent. As with their four-year counterparts, prices increased steadily throughout the 1980s and then slowed toward the end of the decade. This was followed by a rollercoaster ride through the 1990s, where prices alternated between large increases and modest reductions. Then, in 2003–04, prices spiked upward again, increasing by more than 11 percent in one year. While the trend lines for two- and four-year colleges were different, the eventual outcome was the same. By the early part of the 21st Century, prices in both sectors were higher than they had ever been, and price increases were accelerating at unprecedented rates.

In order to place these trends into context, it is useful to compare the changes in college prices with the trends in family income over the same period. A recent report by a congressional subcommittee described the relationship this way:

> If tuition had doubled over the past decade, but incomes tripled during that same time, the general public may not be nearly as concerned about the affordability of higher education. However, the fact is that by two common measures of income — median household income and per capita disposable income — college tuition increased faster than income (Boehner and McKeon, 2003, p. 2).

Indeed, this has been the case since 1980. Table 1 shows the relationship between family income and public college prices between 1980 and 2001. A family earning the mean income at the top fifth of the distribution would spend less than 3 percent of their annual income to cover one year at a four-year public college. A family earning the mean income of the middle fifth of the distribution would spend 8.5 percent. The family at the mean of the lowest fifth of the distribution would pay 36 percent

**Table 1. Portion of Annual Household Income Required to Pay for One Year of Tuition and Fees at a Public Four-Year Institution by Income Quintile**

| Income Quintile | 1980 | 1985 | 1990 | 1995 | 2001 |
|---|---|---|---|---|---|
| Highest Fifth | 1.8% | 2.2% | 2.3% | 2.6% | 2.5% |
| Second Fifth | 4.7% | 4.0% | 4.5% | 5.5% | 5.5% |
| Middle Fifth | 4.0% | 6.0% | 6.7% | 8.5% | 8.5% |
| Fourth Fifth | 7.8% | 9.9% | 11.1% | 14.2% | 14.3% |
| Lowest Fifth | 18.7% | 24.5% | 27.7% | 34.8% | 36.0% |

Source: Author's calculations. Income data from: US Census Bureau 2004, www.census.gov/hhes/income/histinc/f03.html, tuition data from College Board (2003).

of their annual income to cover the costs of one year at a four-year college. As a consequence, from the point of view of American families, the impact of the post-1980 public college tuition inflation was quite uneven. For those families near the top of the distribution, incomes increased enough to nearly keep pace with public college tuition inflation. Put another way, the share of their income needed to cover the cost of a public higher education remained relatively stable. But for families in all the other income quintiles, the cost of a public college education took an ever larger portion of their income. Those 20 percent of families at the bottom of the distribution now find one year at a four-year college equal to more than one-third of their annual pre-tax income. It is no wonder why these rising prices have received so much attention in the media and have created so much anxiety for American families.

## Tuition Setting at Public Colleges

Before we turn our attention to why prices have increased, it is important to understand the philosophies which guide tuition setting and the different ways by which public institutions set their tuition. In this section we review the different views on the proper level of public college tuition, we describe the processes through which institutions set tuition, and then discuss some of the problems that these differences have for establishing responsibility, or accountability, for the current round of tuition inflation.

There are two schools of thought on the appropriate level of public college tuition. In one view, states ought to keep public college tuition as low as is reasonably possible. Low tuition is said to encourage increased participation and open the doors of higher education to the widest possible number of citizens. Moreover, increasing the number of people going to college benefits the whole community economically and socially. It was based on this view that most states kept tuition low throughout the 1950s and 1960s.

But in the 1960s, as baby boomers began to enter college in record numbers, many states could no longer afford to provide the generous subsidies necessary to maintain low tuition. As prices began to edge upward, a number of scholars and policy analysts began to argue that the philosophy of low tuition pricing was misguided. In this view, when states keep tuition low, they provide a subsidized education for all students. But many of those students could afford to pay for most, or all, of their higher education from personal or family funds. This was seen as an inefficient use of public funds. Instead, they argued that the states should pursue a high tuition/high aid policy in which they raise public college tuition for everyone and then use the extra funds to provide need-based grants to those with financial need. By doing this, states could develop a pricing pattern that followed a sliding-scale in which families see their price increase as their family income increases.

While high tuition/high aid pricing became popular at some private colleges in the 1980s, it has played a very small part in the price increases at public colleges. Few states have embraced the high tuition approach. In a survey conducted by the State Higher Education Executive Officers, 20 states reported embracing a philosophy of keeping tuition at a low or moderate level. Only six states described their present philosophy as high tuition/high aid. The remaining states reported that their state has no statewide tuition philosophy, that tuition policy is guided by institutional levels philosophies, or that there is no statewide philosophy at all (Rasmussen, 2003, p. 9).

### The Process of Tuition-Setting

States vary widely in where they vest the authority to set public college tuition. That authority may be exercised by the legislature, the state governing/coordinating agency, individual system boards and/or individual institutions. In several states, that authority is shared by more than one entity. In some states, a governing board holds authority for setting tuition for its member institutions while selected other institutions are individually responsible for determining tuition rates (Pennsylvania and Mississippi). In Kentucky, the authority to set tuition was transferred from the state-level Council on Postsecondary Education to individual institutions beginning in 2000. North Dakota, Oklahoma, and Virginia have also recently decentralized tuition making authority to institutions.

However, state governments have important direct and indirect ways in which they can control tuition even when they do not have tuition setting authority. Most directly, state governments

**Table 2. Primary Authority for Establishing Tuition**

| Legislature (4) | State Coordinating/ Governing Agency (18) | System Board (12) | Individual Institutions (16) |
|---|---|---|---|
| Florida | Arizona | Connecticut | Alabama |
| Louisiana | Georgia | Illinois | Arkansas |
| Oklahoma | Hawaii | Minnesota | Delaware |
| Texas | Idaho | Nebraska | Florida |
| | Iowa | New Jersey | Illinois |
| | Kansas | New Hampshire | Indiana |
| | Louisiana | New York | Kentucky |
| | Maine | Pennsylvania | Maryland |
| | Massachusetts | Tennessee | Mississippi |
| | Missouri | Vermont | Missouri |
| | Nevada | Washington | Ohio |
| | New Mexico | Wisconsin | Pennsylvania |
| | North Carolina | | South Carolina |
| | North Dakota | | Virginia |
| | Rhode Island | | Washington |
| | South Dakota | | West Virginia |
| | Utah | | |
| | Wyoming | | |

Source: Rasmussen (2003, p. 10)

can impose caps on tuition inflation. Between 1999 and 2002, 19 states imposed a "curb, cap, freeze or other limitation" on the ability of its institutions or a state board to set tuition. In Connecticut and Washington, for example, the legislature appropriated replacement revenue that allowed institutions to freeze or maintain tuition increases below a certain level. In New Jersey, the Governor advised institutions to limit their tuition increases to 10 percent or face a special audit from the Commission on Higher Education. Missouri experimented with indexing tuition to the Consumer Price Index. Maryland fixed tuition increases at 4 percent per year. In Ohio, the state lifted tuition caps in 2002 after several years with a 6 percent cap. The resulting 12 percent increase across the state that year led the state to re-impose the cap following the year (Rasmussen, 2003, p. 13).

States also have less direct, but equally effective ways to control price setting at public colleges. Since the state legislature determines the appropriation to higher education each year, they are in a position to punish campuses that attempt to raise tuition beyond accepted limits. They can also reward campuses who hold the line on price increases. Similarly, governors often appoint the members of the campus Boards of Trustees or the state governing board. These appointees, in turn, oversee campus budget decisions. Governors can thus indirectly influence pricing through the type of person they appoint and through their interaction with those appointees.

## Public Accountability and Public College Tuition Inflation

Despite the seemingly straightforward divisions of authority between campus and state leaders, the situation in practice is much more ambiguous. In most states tuition levels are actually the result of a negotiation, often implicit, between campus leaders and the state government. Public colleges rely on the states for a substantial portion of their revenue. States often try to use the leverage that this gives them to try to force colleges to hold their prices down. Similarly, colleges use threats of price increases as a tactic to leverage additional dollars from state policymakers. When tuition inflation is high, colleges place the blame on reductions in state support. State policymakers, in turn, blame campuses for uncontrolled spending. Conversely, during times of lower tuition inflation, campuses take credit for their attention to the bottom-line and their careful institutional planning. States also claim credit for the achievement, arguing that it was the result of their more generous support of campuses or to the careful exercise of their oversight responsibilities.

The result of this ambiguity is that the public can never be clear on who is accountable for rising public college prices. One report described it this way

> The authority to set tuition is generally shared among the legislature, governor, governing boards, and sometimes the campuses in multicampus systems. As such, decisions about tuition changes occur where there is a broad based shared responsibility between government and higher education, rather than the authority to act unilaterally, which is clearly held by one side or the other. This means that tuition decisions are political, and that a number of interest groups try to influence the process (Institute for Higher Education Policy, 1999, p. 24).

This lack of a clear chain of accountability also makes it less likely that any one side will take the initiative to bring the problem fully under control. Since tuition is generally negotiated by several interested parties and over time, no single institution is clearly responsible for the rising prices. Moreover, since no one seems to be clearly to blame, as tuition increases, no one is likely to receive the credit for slowing its growth. That same report made this point.

> Because tuition increases are a political hot potato and because responsibility for approving them is shared between the academy and state government, the result is a form of tuition "chicken" where each waits for the other to take the initiative (Institute for Higher Education Policy, 1999, p. 25).

One important response to this ambiguous accountability has been that the U.S. Congress has occasionally felt compelled to address the issue of tuition inflation. This occurred first in 1997 with the creation of the National Commission on the Cost of Higher Education. While the Commission was in operation less than a year, its final report, *Straight Talk About College Costs and Prices* (1998), represented the most comprehensive work on the subject to date. More recently, in preparation for the reauthorization of the Higher Education Act, Representatives John Boehner and Howard McKeon issued a follow-up report entitled, *The College Cost Crisis: A Congressional Analysis of College Costs and Their Implications for America's Higher Education System* (2003). This report proposed legislation that would penalize all institutions of higher education for raising tuition by making them ineligible for participation in some of the Title IV student aid programs. While it would not cut Pell subsidies or federal student loans, students would be at risk of loosing support from other programs such as College Work Study and Supplemental Educational Opportunity Grant Programs. Proponents of the legislation claim that higher education consumers—parents and students—are worried that they will not be able to afford college if campuses continue to raise tuition at twice the rate of inflation.

Opponents believe that any attempt to control higher education prices will lead to a decline in quality and access. As Jamie P. Merisotis, president of the Institute for Higher Education Policy states, "A federal foray into controlling the prices charged by institutions would be unwise and potentially destabilizing" (Burd, 2003). Regardless of their ultimate effectiveness, such reports illustrate the great concern tuition inflation creates for national policy makers.

## The Multiple Causes of Public College Tuition Inflation

The causes of the public college price spiral have been the source of substantial study of the past few years. While each of these studies identifies a slightly different configuration of factors, all of them agree that the phenomenon is not the result of a simple cause. Indeed, the best explanation of the causes of tuition inflation remains the one presented by Arthur Hauptman in *The College Tuition Spiral* (1990):

> What is the bottom line reason for the college price spiral? This report identifies a number of hypotheses, each of which is found by the subsequent analysis to have something to contribute to the argument. But the bottom line is that there is *no* overarching explanation (p. vii).

Certainly the most highly publicized study of the causes of tuition inflation was conducted by the National Commission on the Cost of Higher Education. It brought together a wide range of opinions, and it made use of extensive quantitative analysis as well as expert testimony. Yet, the Commission was unable to reach agreement over the causes of the price increases. It did agree on five "convictions," including such non-controversial positions as, "The concern about rising college prices is real" and "The public and its leaders are concerned about where higher education places its priorities" (1998, p. 13).

The National Commission report set out to identify the causes of rising college prices. Yet, after reviewing pages of statistical and testimonial data regarding each potential cause, it hedged in its conclusions. After posing the question, "Have increases in college and university administrative costs affected tuition increases?" the answer was a definitive "Possibly" (p. 248). In response to the question, "Have costs to construct and renovate campus facilities affected tuition increases?" the answer was "Probably" (p. 266). And, the answer to "Have technology costs driven tuition up?" was "Possibly" (p. 266). Such answers, of course, are less than satisfying. Yet, the fault does not lie with the Commission or its staff. These tentative conclusions reflect the substantial and heated disagreement among the experts on these issues (Mumper, 2001).

## The Elements of the Public Campus Budget

The search for the causes of tuition inflation begins with an examination of the public college budget. On its face, that budget is not a complex document. Campuses receive their revenue from subsidies provided by state governments; tuition and fees paid by students; private gifts; and from auxiliaries such as dormitories, food services, and research commercialization. A few generate revenue from endowment income. They spend those dollars on instruction, administration, research, student services, libraries, and the operation of those auxiliaries. It is noteworthy that many of these functions are very labor intensive. As such, public colleges devote substantial portions of their budgets to the salaries and benefits of their employees.

Since 1980, public colleges have experienced changes in both their revenue and expenditure patterns that have driven much of the tuition inflation. In the following section, we will consider the ways in which campus revenues have changed and the ways in which expenditures have changed. Finally, we consider how demographic and economic forces have altered the demand for higher education which, in turn, has also created pressures for institutions to raise prices.

## Changes in Campus Revenue

Public colleges generate revenue from a combination of public and private sources. As shown in Table 3, public colleges today receive the largest portion of their income, 35.8 percent, from state governments. They receive an additional 10.8 percent from the federal government and 3.8 percent from local government. This represents just over 50 percent of public college revenue that is generated from government sources. However, as recently as 1980, governments supplied 66.2 percent of all public college revenue. Clearly, public colleges are relying less on these public funds than at any time in the recent past.

**Table 3. Percentage Distribution of Current Fund Revenue of Public Degree Granting Institutions by Source**

| Type of Revenue | 1980 | 1985 | 1990 | 1995 | 2000 |
|---|---|---|---|---|---|
| Tuition and Fees | 12.9% | 14.5% | 16.1% | 18.8% | 18.9% |
| Federal Government | 12.8% | 10.5% | 10.3% | 11.1% | 10.6% |
| State Government | 45.6% | 45.0% | 40.3% | 35.8% | 35.7% |
| Local Government | 3.8% | 3.6% | 3.7% | 4.1% | 3.8% |
| Private Gifts | 2.5% | 3.2% | 3.8% | 4.1% | 4.5% |
| Endowment Income | 0.5% | 0.6% | 0.5% | 0.6% | 0.6% |
| Sales and Services | 19.6% | 20.0% | 22.7% | 22.2% | 22.3% |
| Other | 2.4% | 2.6% | 2.6% | 3.3% | 3.7% |

Source: U.S. Department of Education (2002, p. 372).

A closer look at these figures reveals that the decline in government support occurred primarily at the state level. The portion of revenue from the federal government declined during the early 1980s. But since 1985, it has remained largely stable. Moreover, this measure significantly underestimates the overall level of federal support. This is because the majority of federal aid to higher education is appropriated in the form of grants and loans to students. Students, in turn, use these funds to pay for their tuition, fees, room, and board. As such, institutions receive these grant and loan dollars from students, and they are thus classified as tuition income rather than federal support. Still, in many cases those tuition dollars would not be there without the federal grant or loan.

It is the state portion of public college revenue that has declined over time. In 1980, state governments provided public colleges with 45.6 percent of their revenue. By 2000, that had declined to 35.8 percent. The decline occurred primarily during the recession of the late 1980s and early 1990s. These may seem like relatively small changes, especially considering that the trends occurred over nearly 25 years. But even small changes in state support can produce a dramatic impact on public college tuition. A report by the National Education Association Research Center (2003) illustrates the point

> If a college receives an average of $5000 per student in support from the state and each student pays $1000 in tuition, a total of $6000 is spent on the student's education. However, if the state support is eroded by 10 percent, or $500, tuition must go up 50 percent to compensate. Small cuts in state support thus result in large relative increases in tuition (p. 3).

In order to replace the revenue that was no longer supplied by state government, public colleges have increasingly turned to private revenue sources. The largest of these is revenue from tuition and fees. In 1980, public colleges received 12.9 percent of their revenue from tuition and fees. By 2000, that had increased to 18.5 percent. This shift is a central reason for the tuition inflation of the past 25 years (Mortenson, 2003b, pp. 1–10).

Other changes in campus revenue patterns reveal a similar substitution of private for public funds. Sales and services increased from 19.6 percent of public college revenue in 1980 to 21.6 percent in 2000. Private gifts, grants, and contracts increased from 2.5 percent to 4.8 percent. In combination, tuition, fees, sales, services, grants, contracts, and gifts, largely private sources of revenue has increased from 35 to 45 percent (National Center for Education Statistics 2004a). It represents a clear substitution of public support for public colleges with private support.

A study examining the relationship between tuition, campus revenue, and campus expenditures reached the following conclusion

> For public four year institutions, revenue from state appropriations remains the largest source of revenue and is the single most important factor associated with changes in tuition. Over the period of time examined, state appropriations revenue decreased relative to other sources of revenue for all types of public four year institutions and, in fact, experienced real annual decreases for research/doctoral and comprehensive institutions. Decreasing revenue from government appropriations was the most important factor associated with tuition increases at public four year institutions over the period of the analysis (Cunningham, Wellman, Clinedinst, and Merisotis 2001, p. 8).

Similarly, in an examination of public college tuition inflation between 1974 and 2004, Thomas Mortenson (2003b) places the blame for tuition inflation at public college squarely on the back of state government. He finds that tuition rates are strongly negatively related to state funding effort.

These broad aggregate relationships should not obscure the significant differences that exist among the states in the ways in which they support public higher education. As shown in Table 4, some states like California and North Carolina continue to receive relatively low portions of their revenue from tuition. These states have been able to maintain low tuition. Conversely, states like Vermont rely to a much larger extent on tuition and much less on state appropriations.

## State Budgets and Tuition Inflation

The fact that colleges now receive a smaller portion of their revenue from state subsidies is, at least in part, a result of decisions by the states to provide less generous support to public colleges.

**Table 4. Percentage of Current Fund Revenue of Public Degree Granting Institutions by Source of Funds Selected States: 1998–99**

| State | Tuition and Fee Revenue | State and Local Appropriations | All Other Revenue Sources |
|---|---|---|---|
| California | 12.3% | 46.4% | 41.3% |
| Georgia | 15.2% | 51.7% | 33.1% |
| Illinois | 18.1% | 44.9% | 37.0% |
| North Carolina | 10.8% | 51.9% | 37.3% |
| Ohio | 27.5% | 34.3% | 38.2% |
| New York | 23.5% | 44.1% | 32.4% |
| Virginia | 22.8% | 31.5% | 45.7% |
| Vermont | 43.0% | 13.4% | 43.6% |

Source: U.S. Department of Education (2002, p. 379).

In a widely cited analysis, Harold Hovey (1999) describes the role that higher education plays in state budgets as a "balance wheel." He argues that when state finances are strong, appropriations for higher education have risen disproportionately to appropriations for other functions. But appropriations for higher education are cut disproportionately when state fiscal circumstances are weak. He describes it this way:

> Selection as a balance wheel results from some perceived characteristics of higher education relative to other objects of state spending. First, higher education institutions have separate budgets with reserves of their own and perceived fiscal flexibility to absorb temporary fiscal adversity, unlike state agencies which do not have those features. Second, higher education is perceived as having more flexibility to translate budget changes into employee pay than state agencies which are bound by statewide pay scales, and local education agencies which are subject to collective bargaining and multi-year employee contracts. Third, higher education is seen as having more flexibility to vary spending levels (e.g. through changes in courses offered and class sizes) than most programs, which have spending levels that are more fixed. Fourth, in most states, higher education has the ability to maintain and increase spending levels by shifting proportions of costs to users by tuition and fee increases (Hovey, 1999, p. 19).

A survey of the chairs of state education committees found that a strong majority believe that "The ability of colleges to raise their own money through tuition, research grants, and gifts" was a significant factor in determining how much money the legislature will appropriate to higher education (Ruppert, 1996, p. 9).

## The Changing Shape of State Budgets

The last two decades have been a period of extreme stress for state budgets. The 1990s began with a recession, was followed by a period of sustained growth, and ended with another recession. Along the way, the states were whipped-sawed between increasing demands of citizens for greater services, the ebbs and flows of state revenue from all sources, and the on-going pressure to reduce state tax burdens. Citizens in many states were unwilling to support tax increases during lean budget years and then demanded tax rate reductions when state budgets were healthy. The federal government passed on an endless stream of mandates that required new expenditures, yet they were increasingly less willing to provide the states with financial relief for those mandates. Finally, state sales tax revenues were hurt by the substantial growth of untaxed internet sales (National Association of State Budget Officers, 2003, p. 10).

Table 5 shows how state expenditures have changed since 1989. The most striking development is the steady decline in the share of state budgets devoted to education at all levels, public assistance and transportation. Conversely, corrections and Medicaid spending increased. There was

**Table 5. Comparison of Shares of State Spending Fiscal 1987–2003**

|  | Elementary/ Secondary Education | Higher Education | Public Assistance | Medicaid | Corrections | All Other |
|---|---|---|---|---|---|---|
| 2003 | 36.0% | 12.4% | 2.3% | 16.5% | 7.0% | 25.8% |
| 2002 | 35.4% | 12.6% | 2.3% | 16.0% | 6.9% | 26.8% |
| 2001 | 35.2% | 12.7% | 2.3% | 15.2% | 6.9% | 27.8% |
| 2000 | 35.7% | 12.8% | 2.7% | 14.4% | 7.0% | 27.6% |
| 1999 | 35.7% | 12.4% | 2.7% | 14.4% | 7.0% | 27.6% |
| 1998 | 35.2% | 13.1% | 3.0% | 14.8% | 6.9% | 27.1% |
| 1997 | 34.5% | 13.0% | 3.6% | 14.6% | 6.8% | 27.5% |
| 1996 | 34.4% | 12.9% | 3.9% | 14.7% | 6.9% | 26.8% |
| 1995 | 33.3% | 12.9% | 4.4% | 14.4% | 6.7% | 28.1% |
| 1994 | 33.9% | 13.0% | 4.9% | 14.2% | 6.2% | 27.9% |
| 1993 | 34.8% | 13.1% | 5.1% | 13.3% | 5.7% | 28.1% |
| 1992 | 34.0% | 13.5% | 5.1% | 12.1% | 5.6% | 29.6% |
| 1991 | 33.4% | 14.1% | 5.3% | 10.5% | 5.7% | 31.0% |
| 1990 | 33.5% | 14.6% | 4.9% | 9.5% | 5.5% | 32.1% |
| 1989 | 34.6% | 15.2% | 5.0% | 9.0% | 5.3% | 31.0% |
| 1987 | 34.5% | 15.5% | 5.1% | 8.7% | 5.2% | 31.0% |

Source: National Association of State Budget Officers (2003)

substantial growth in corrections spending during the decade, peaking in 1999 and then falling back to the early 1990s level. But the most striking development is the rapid growth in state spending for Medicaid. In 1990, state spending on Medicaid surpassed higher education as the second largest expenditure item and by 2003, seemed poised to pass elementary and secondary education as the largest expenditure item. Mortenson (1997) describes the trends this way

> Clearly, the funding priorities of state and local governments have shifted and continue to do so. Presumably, these priorities reflect the will of the voters and the changing priorities of the voters over the last 45 years. Between the mid-1950s and 1982, voters appear to have supported increased expenditure shares for higher education in state and local government budgeting. Since 1982, however, that has reversed with resources shifted from higher education to new budget priorities of medical care and corrections—and tax cuts (p. 10).

Between 1989 and the present, state spending for higher education declined from 12.0 to 10.7 percent of total state spending. This may seem like a relatively small decline. But total state expenditures were in excess of $1 trillion in 2003. That 10.7 percent share represents $107 billion in annual spending. To increase that to the 1989 level of 12 percent, states would need to increase their overall spending by $13 billion.

One measure commonly used to examine trends in state support for higher education is state appropriations for higher education as a percent of $1,000 in personal income. Figure 3 shows state appropriations for higher education per $1,000 of personal income between 1980 and 2004. Appropriations increase when state economies are good and state budgets are growing. They decline as state economies worsen. But the overall downward trend is unmistakable. As recently as 1980, states appropriated $10.56 of state tax funds to higher education for every $1,000 in personal income. In 2002, that level had dropped to $7.35. This was the weakest level of state investment since 1967 and represents a continuation of a trend that began in the late 1970s. Today, this steady state decline represents an almost insurmountable problem for public college budgets. Kane and Orszag (2003) estimate that since personal income is now more than $14 trillion, it would take an increase of $14 billion in additional state appropriations to higher education simply to return to the level of state support experienced in 1977. Yet, all evidence points to further decreases in state support rather than increases of any level, let alone those in the multi-billion dollar range.

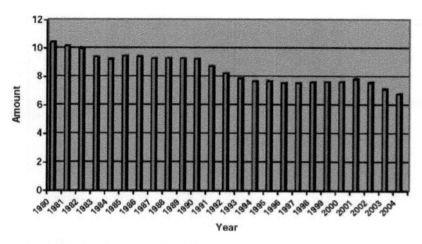

**Figure 3. Appropriations of State Tax Funds for Operating Expenses of Higher Education per $1000 of Personal Income FY 1980 to FY 2004**

## Why Have States Reduced Support to Higher Education

As states experience growing budget problems, the appropriation to higher education stands out as the logical place to cut. This was often not because of dissatisfaction with the performance of the colleges. Many policymakers were well aware that the cuts would be painful to campus budgets and require them to raise tuition. But public colleges had a mechanism to raise new revenue to replace the funds lost to state cuts. A member of the Ohio House of Representatives explained that, "It was easier to cut something that could be replaced. When we made the budget cuts, we really felt that we were not hurting higher education" (Mathesian, 1995, p. 23). Thus, from the perspective of a state, higher education could be cut, without being forced to eliminate programs, or even reduce staff. Indeed, cutting the appropriations to public colleges and universities was seen as quite different from cuts to corrections, transportation, or other agencies that had nowhere else to turn to secure replacement revenues (Mumper, 2001).

Clearly, as states experience revenue shortfalls, higher education seems an especially appealing target for spending reductions. But why have states been so aggressive in seeking such cuts? The answer is that during the last two decades, state governments have found themselves in a kind of perpetual fiscal squeeze. Two factors seem most directly responsible for driving the state budget problems and in turn, force states to reduce their support for higher education. The first is the ups and downs of the business cycle. The second is the dramatic increase in state spending for Medicaid.

All states except Vermont are required by law to balance their budget each year. These requirements force state policymakers to reduce expenditures and reduce taxes during an economic turndown. Typically states cut back on programs during a downturn and then expand them during the subsequent recovery. Higher education has historically been among the most cyclical of state expenditures. As the economy entered a recession in the early 1980s, for example, appropriations declined in real terms. Then, during the recovery of the mid-1980s, appropriations recovered to pre-recession levels. This cyclical pattern is similar to the one that had been evident in previous business cycles (Callan, 2002)

That trend appears to have changed during the business cycle of the 1990s. As the economy entered the recession in the early 1990s, real appropriations per capita declined, just as it had in previous recessions. But then during the boom of the 1990s, appropriations for higher education recovered only very slowly, and higher education spending did not exceed pre-recession levels until 1999. Indeed, as the state economies grew in the 1990s, policymakers in many states chose to cut taxes and undertake new spending in other areas (Boyd, 2002). As a result, state support for higher education failed to recover as state economies recovered. This created an especially severe problem as the next decade began. Public higher education had only recently recovered from the previous downturn when the new one began.

One of the most important factors driving the state budget problems of recent years is the escalating costs of Medicaid. Medicaid provides medical assistance to the low-income elderly and disabled, as well as to low-income families and pregnant women. Medicaid costs to the states rose rapidly in the late 1980s and early 1990s, reflecting both expanded program eligibility and increases in costs per enrollee (Kane and Orszag, 2003, p. 2). Medicaid is a means tested entitlement program funded jointly by the states and the federal government. It provides medical insurance for about 47 million low-income Americans. Of all Medicaid beneficiaries, about 25 percent are elderly and disabled. The remaining 75 percent are children and non-disabled adults. Yet, the elderly receive nearly 75 percent of all Medicaid spending while children and the nondisabled account for only 25 percent (National Association of State Budget Officers 2003, p. 1).

As recently as 1980, when measured in 2003 dollars, states spent only about $25 billion on Medicaid. This represented only less than 10 percent of total state spending. By 1990, state Medicaid spending had increased to $45 billion or 12.5 percent of total spending. By 2000, spending had more than doubled to $95 billion—nearly 20 percent of total state spending. By 2003, spending had accelerated to $122 billion and the rate of increase in clearly accelerating (National Association of State Budget Officers 2003, pp. 4–5). The increasing costs of Medicaid are driven primarily by two factors: increases in the number of Medicaid recipients and the increased costs of prescription drugs. Between 2000 and 2003, the number of Medicaid recipients increased by nearly 15 percent. The cost of outpatient prescription drugs increased an average of 18 percent a year during those three years (National Association of State Budget Officers, 2003).

The relationship between these increases in Medicaid spending and public college tuition inflation is clear. In a recent examination of the link between the two, Kane and Orszag (2003) find that

> Econometric analysis based on variations in Medicaid and higher education spending across the states and time suggests that each new dollar in Medicaid spending crowds out higher education appropriations by about six to seven cents. To put these figures in perspective, note that real state Medicaid spending per capita increased from roughly $125 in 1988 to roughly $245 in 1998. Over the same period of time, real higher education appropriations per capita declined from $185 to $175. According to our estimates, the predicted effect of the increase in Medicare spending would be a reduction in higher education appropriations per capita of about $8. Therefore, Medicaid spending appears to explain the vast majority of the $10 decline in higher education appropriations per capita (p. 3).

They conclude that

> The bottom line is that there is a strong negative relationship between higher education appropriations and Medicaid spending. The substantial increases in Medicaid spending during the 1980s and early 1990s, appear to have played an important role in the failure of higher education appropriations to rise significantly during the 1990s boom (p. 4).

These trends make clear that whenever states have budget difficulties, it is bad news for public higher education. Whether it is the short-term impact of the business cycle, or the emergence of acute problems like Medicaid spending, states pass on their revenue shortages to their public colleges. In previous periods, state support tended to bounce back quickly after a recession, and states were able to address their acute problems in reasonable time periods. But the current experience calls into question the longer pattern of state support. In the most recent recession, state support took many years to rebound. Similarly, the Medicaid problem is even more severe today than it was a decade ago and no solution is in sight. If states are no longer willing to finance higher education at current service levels, further tuition inflation seems inevitable.

## The Future of State Support: Long Term Structural Imbalance

What we have described so far are a series of external forces that caused state governments to reduce their support for public higher education. This declining support forced colleges to shift a larger portion of the costs of higher education from taxpayers to students and families. A number of analysts have examined whether this pattern of declining state support is likely to continue in the years ahead (Hovey, 1999; Boyd, 2002; Callan, 2002). These studies paint a chilling picture of the future of state support for public higher education. This is because they conclude that states will continue to experience rapid growth in other areas such as Medicaid and corrections, and that enrollment in public higher education are almost certain to grow in the next decade. This combination means that

> The percentage of state funding devoted to higher education will need to increase annually in order for higher education just to maintain current services. Since the percentage of the state budget dedicated to higher education has actually declined over the past decade, continuing to fund current service levels for higher education would represent a significant shift in state budget trends (Hovey 1999, p. vii).

Every indication is that the severe fiscal problems states face in funding higher education are only partially related to the current economic situation. States are also facing long-term structural problems that will make it increasingly difficult to maintain present levels of support for higher education. There are two primary reasons for this difficulty. First, in the 1990s, state revenue growth was fueled by dramatic increases in tax revenue from capital gains. The growth in the stock market that drove these revenue increases is unlikely to continue. Second, the increased volume of internet sales is likely to drive down state sales tax revenues. A 2002 study by Don Boyd of the National Center for Higher Education Management Systems estimates that within eight years, state governments are likely to face budget shortfalls of 3.4 percent of total revenue. A total of 44 states face revenue shortfalls, and 12 others face gaps in excess of 5 percent of total revenue. In combination, these factors will hold down state revenue. At the same time, programs like Medicaid will demand a larger share of available revenue. This is almost certain to crowd out spending for higher education.

In addition to these revenue difficulties, enrollments are likely to grow in ways that will require new spending in order for states to maintain sufficient access to public colleges for their citizens. In the 1960s and 1970s, the baby-boom generation attended college in remarkably large numbers. In order to accommodate this enrollment growth, new campuses were opened and expansions took place at virtually all existing campuses. Today, another tidal wave of college enrollment is on the way. In 1988, there were more than 4 million births in the United States. That was the highest number since 1964. This baby-boom echo generation is crowding elementary and secondary schools, and they are now on the verge of going to college (Carnevale and Fry, 2002). Between 2002 and 2012, college enrollment is projected to increase by 15.6 percent (National Center for Educational Statistics, 2003a).

Some of the reasons for this increase are obvious. The National Center for Education Statistics projects that public high school graduates will increase by more than 10 percent between now and 2012 (National Center for Educational Statistics, 2003b). The college continuation rates of recent high school graduates are now 64 percent, up 59 percent from a decade ago. That means more students are graduating from high school, and a higher percentage of them are going on to college.

But this is by no means the only factor driving the enrollment surge. A recent report identifies three other factors that seem destined to crowd our colleges in the next decades (Carnevale and Fry, 2002). The first is immigration. Since the 1980s, 800,000 immigrants have come to the U.S. every year. This has already changed the character of elementary and secondary education. As recently as 1990, about 15 percent of all school-age children will be the children of immigrants. By 2010, it will have increased to 22 percent. Second, the changing labor market will force many workers to return to school to add to their skills. These new college students might be looking for mid-career advancement, education, preparing for a career change, or retooling after a lay-off. The federal Hope and Lifelong Learning tax credits will make returning to college even more affordable to many Americans. Finally, better academic preparation among high school graduates will mean that more of them are prepared for college than at any time in the past. Comparing academic readiness is always difficult. But most empirical evidence suggests that student achievement levels have been rising over the last 30 years. In explaining this trend, Carnevale and Fry (2000) point out

> Rising scores do not necessarily imply that our schools are performing better, however. The apparent rise in cognitive skills could reflect improvements in other areas such as better preparation or higher family income (p. 15).

Regardless of the reason for the improvement, better prepared students will head to college in larger numbers and move toward graduation at higher rates.

These factors leave little doubt that the next decade will bring an influx of new students hoping to enroll in public colleges that are already operating close to capacity. Exacerbating these trends is the fact that states will not have, or are not willing to spend, the funds to build or expand the physical capacity of their public colleges. The enrollment surges brought on by the G.I. Bill and the baby-boom each produced an enormous expansion in the number of campuses in the country and the capacity of those campuses. In the decades ahead, however, states are simply not going to be able to add capacity in that way.

As a consequence, many states face a long-term structural problem with regard to higher education. In the years ahead, it is unlikely that there will be sufficient revenue to fund all programs at current service levels. Especially during recession years, there will be constant pressures for spending reductions and few available resources for new initiatives. Demands for more state Medicaid spending will further reduce available funds. As the ongoing fiscal crisis unfolds, an ever larger number of citizens seek to enter public colleges. To maintain present tuition and fee levels, states will need to locate substantial new revenue. A more likely consequence is that states will continue to reduce their support for higher education, to shift a larger share of those dollars on programs to aid middle income students, and fuel an acceleration of public college tuition inflation lasting well into the next decade.

## Changes in Campus Expenditures

There is much more to the story of public college tuition inflation than simply changes in campus revenues and state budgets. Colleges are also spending those revenues in different ways than they did two decades ago. Table 6 shows the overall per student expenditures by public colleges from 1980–81 to 1999–00. In real terms, public four-year institutions spend more than $25,000 per student each year. This is an increase of about 50 percent since 1980–81. At public two-year colleges, annual per student spending was just under $9,000. This was a 27 percent increase over 20 years (National Center for Education Statistics 2004b). While these spending increases are well below the rate of tuition inflation, they represent a substantial increase in the amount that institutions are paying to provide a college education.

Campuses are not only spending more per student, they are spending those dollars in different ways. Table 7 shows the changes in the percent distribution of educational and general expenditures. Public institutions reduced the share of these expenditures devoted to instruction from 38.5 percent to 34.0 percent of their educational and general expenditures. This represents a substantial redirection of campus spending away from instruction and toward other areas. Seen another way, in 1999–00, public institutions would need to spend an additional $4 billion on instruction simply to return to the 1980–81 spending share. The share of total spending directed to the operation and maintenance of the physical plant also declined by a substantial amount.

**Table 6. Current Fund Expenditures per FTE Equivalent Student in Degree Granting Institution Public Institutions by Type (in constant 1999–00 Dollars)**

|  | Four Year Institutions | Two Year Institutions |
|---|---|---|
| 1980–81 | $19,138 | $7,023 |
| 1985–86 | $20,839 | $7,676 |
| 1990–91 | $21,505 | $7,656 |
| 1995–96 | $23,432 | $8,217 |
| 1999–00 | $25,256 | $8,924 |
| Source: U.S. Department of Education (2002, p. 388). | | |

**Table 7. Percent Distribution of Current Fund Expenditures on Educational and General Expenditures of Public Degree Granting Institutions by Purpose 1980–2000**

|  | 1980–81 | 1985–86 | 1990–91 | 1995–96 | 1999–00 |
|---|---|---|---|---|---|
| Instruction | 38.5% | 37.7% | 36.6% | 35.3% | 34.0% |
| Research | 19.7% | 19.7% | 21.7% | 21.8% | 22.4% |
| Public Service | 8.3% | 8.0% | 8.2% | 8.2% | 8.4% |
| Administration | 12.9% | 13.9% | 13.7% | 13.7% | 14.1% |
| Student Services | 3.8% | 3.7% | 3.6% | 3.8% | 3.8% |
| Operation of Plant | 9.1% | 8.8% | 8.2% | 8.2% | 6.5% |
| Scholarships | 3.5% | 3.8% | 4.5% | 5.9% | 6.5% |
| All Other | 4.2% | 4.4% | 2.2% | 1.6% | 4.3% |

Source: U.S. Department of Education (2002, p. 393).

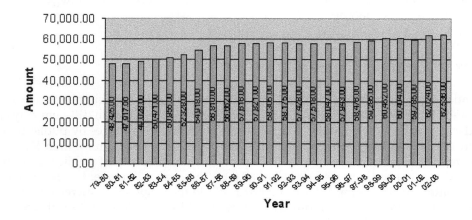

**Figure 4. Average Salary at Public Institutions 2002 Constant Dollars**

At the same time, the share of expenditures on research, public service, student services, institutional support, and scholarships all increased steadily over the 20-year period. In real terms, the amount spent on research doubled, from $8 billion to $16 billion. Spending on scholarships, in real terms, increased even more rapidly. In 1980, real spending by public institutions on scholarships and fellowships was $2.4 billion. In 2000, it had increased to $6.8 billion.

Not all changes in campus spending patterns can be seen in these tables. One area where spending has increased is faculty salaries and benefits. Figure 4 traces the increase in average faculty salaries at public colleges since 1980. It shows that, for all ranks and types of institutions, these salaries have increased by 30 percent in real dollars. Interestingly, these increases occurred disproportionately in the mid-1980s and the late 1990s and early 21st Century. When state economies are poor, increases in faculty salaries are low. But as those economies improve, salaries spike upward. Later, as state economies slide into the next recession, they must continue to pay those higher salaries.

When the full costs of faculty compensation are considered, the impact on public college expenditures is brought into even greater focus. Figure 5 shows that in 1980–81, the average faculty salary at a public institution was $47,917. Institutions paid an additional $8,750 per person in benefits—including health insurance and pension payments. By 2002–03, the average faculty salary had increased to $62,536. But institutions paid an additional $15,868 per person in benefits. Much of this increase is accounted for by the spiraling costs associated with providing health insurance

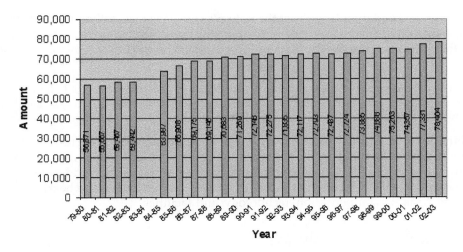

**Figure 5. Average Compensation at Public Institutions in Constant 2002 Dollars**

for faculties and their families. Thus, the rapid rise in health care costs has had a double impact on tuition inflation. Rising Medicaid expenditures significantly reduced the dollars that states have available to support higher education. Then campuses were forced to direct a larger portion of their already reduced funds to pay for the increased health care costs.

An additional area of spending growth for public colleges is technology. There is no doubt that colleges are now spending more on technology and that at least a portion of these costs are passed on to students in the form of higher tuition. Since this spending has occurred across all campus activities and by virtually every unit on campus, its full impact is difficult to isolate. In describing his experiences at Cornell, Ronald Ehrenberg (2000) observes:

> If the price of computer power is falling, why are information technology costs at the university rising so rapidly? One reason is that the shift to networks, the Web, and a client/server computing system based heavily on personal computers and individual work sites has multiplied the number of staff needed to support the use of information technology at the university. When I came to Cornell in 1974, my college had one computer/statistical consultant on its staff to support all academic and administrative computing. Now, with a student body and faculty unchanged in size, the college has ten professionals and many part-time student employees in the information technology area. The functions they perform include maintaining and supervising networks, networked computer labs, creating and maintaining web pages for the college, responding to problems that individual faculty members have with their computers and printers, helping professors prepare on-line material for classes, and answering students' question (p. 189).

While this observation was made about an elite private institution, the very same developments are evident at every public four-year college in the nation and in the vast majority of public two-year colleges.

When considering the impact of increased technology spending on tuition inflation, the National Commission on the Cost of Higher Education (1998) concluded

> Institutions must provide equipment for faculty and students as well as the infrastructure to accommodate it. Given the age of many campus buildings, and the state of the infrastructure to support this equipment, this expense is substantial (p. 11).

They go on to say that those "increasing costs for technology almost certainly translate into higher prices charged to students" (p. 11).

Still another area of increased campus spending is in improving the decaying physical plant. These problems, no doubt exacerbated by years of deferred maintenance and repairs, have presented colleges with an increasing cost simply to keep their programs operating. A National Science Foundation (1996) survey of scientific and engineering research facilities estimated the deferred maintenance costs to replace or repair these facilities at $9.3 billion. Another recent report placed the total cost of deferred maintenance at the nation's colleges at $26 billion (Kaiser, 1996). In addition to these on-going repairs and renovations, institutions face the extra costs of improving the quality of that infrastructure. As the National Commission on the Cost of Higher Education (1998) put it

> Thus, not only are many college and university buildings and laboratories old and outdated in terms of computer wiring and other infrastructure needs, but they are also struggling to maintain quality information access within the walls of these buildings on our nation's campuses (p. 265).

In sum, campus expenditures certainly play a role in fueling public college tuition inflation. These institutions are spending more per student than they ever have and are passing that increase along in the form of higher tuition. Campuses are spending more on research and public service. They are also spending a smaller portion of their budgets on instruction. At the heart of these changes are increasing costs for compensation, technology, and facilities.

## Is all this New Spending Necessary?

There is no doubt that public colleges are spending more per student than they ever have, and that they are passing a portion of the costs of these increases on to their students in the form of higher tuition. Whether or not these expenditures are justified remains a source of great dispute. State policymakers often urge campuses to limit spending and focus their attention on instruction and economic development activities. A recent Congressional committee concluded its deliberations with this concern

> This Commission finds itself in the discomforting position of acknowledging that the nation's academic institutions, justly renowned for their ability to analyze practically every other major economic activity in the United States, have not devoted similar analytic resources to their own internal financial structures. Blessed, until recently, with sufficient resources that allowed questions costs and internal crosssubsidies to be avoided, academic institutions now find themselves confronting hard questions about whether their spending patterns match their priorities and about how to communicate the choices they have made to the public (Boehner and McKeon, 2003, p. 5).

Discussions over the real costs associated with providing a public higher education often becomes bogged down in disagreements about terminology. Specifically, there is no agreement on what constitutes a price and a cost. The National Commission on the Cost of Higher Education (1998) described the relationship between the two terms as "opaque" (p. 12), and goes on to complain that

> The terms of analysis used by different parties are not always consistently defined; institutional costs and student costs are two different things, prices and costs are not the same, and prices charged and prices paid often bear very little relationship to each other. The persistent blurring of terms (both within and beyond higher education) contributes to system-wide difficulties in clarifying the relationship between cost and quality; defining the difference between price and cost; distinguishing between what institutions charge and what students pay; and ultimately to systemic difficulties in controlling costs and prices (pp. 14–15).

These differences in terminology reflect the different viewpoints of the policymakers. When a campus invests in new technology or adds an expensive new program, it sees the resulting expenditures as a necessary part of the costs of their operation. Similarly, when the price of health insurance for faculty and staff increases, campus leaders see this as an uncontrollable cost to the campus. They absorb these expenses as costs of operations and often pass them on to their students indirectly as higher prices.

Decisions about where and when to make new expenditures can seem quite arbitrary to state policy makers. They wonder if the new programs were necessary, if the expensive new technology is really necessary at every campus, and if the current faculty could not be made more productive rather than requiring that new faculty members be hired. Indeed, looked at in one way, tuition inflation may simply reflect the rising prices of the goods and services purchased by campus leaders. But looked at in another way, increased campus expenditures are not really a cause at all. Simply because college leaders chose to increase their spending does not mean that those increases are necessary or justified. Sowell (1992) makes the point that when "a college expends its range of resources first, and then calls it 'increased costs' later, this tends to . . . erode the very concept of living within one's means" (p. 24). He goes on

> When parents are being asked to draw on the equity in their home to pay rising tuition, it is not simply to cover the increased costs of educating their children, but also to underwrite the many new boondoggles thought up by faculty and administration, operating with little sense of financial constraints (p. 24).

The view that colleges do not always spend their money in appropriate ways is not restricted to conservative political commentators. A survey of state legislators revealed that "many believe that higher education does not spend its money wisely, and that tuition increases could be avoided if colleges realigned their spending with those areas the public most cares about, especially undergraduate education and job preparation" (Ruppert, 1996). Similarly, in a survey by the Education Commission of the States (1998), 68 percent of the Chairs of Education Committees in State Legislatures, "feel strongly that colleges and universities should focus more of their attention on undergraduate education as the core of their enterprise" (p. 14). This report quotes one committee chair who summed up this view, "In times of decreased financial support, we should put the money where it serves the greatest number of people, and that is basic core education" (p. 14).

Public colleges have been quick to respond that these spending increases are essential to maintaining the quality of these programs and institutions. These were not frivolous new expenditures, but necessary investments required to hire and retain the top faculty, to provide students with the newest facilities, and to keep pace with the private colleges. The view that rising college costs are driven primarily by the high costs associated with providing a high quality education was clearly laid out in the *New York Times* by Charles Kiesler (1993). He argued that policies to control college prices are based on a misunderstanding of the problem of college costs. Indeed, "most law makers and policymakers are misled by standards of measure that betray an inadequate grasp of the financial challenges we face, especially at major research universities" (p. A19). This is because the Consumer Price Index and the Higher Education Price Index, the most common measures of the costs facing colleges, present a distorted picture. In his view, both of these measures "dramatically underestimate the institutions true cost of doing business—costs over which the institutions often have no control" (p. A19). Seen this way, the causes of the problem are simple, even if they are often misunderstood. It was the increasing costs of a quality higher education that have caused college prices to rise. As operating expenditures for colleges increased, tuition was increased as those higher costs were passed along to students. The quality of higher education can only be maintained at the expense of higher college prices. In this view, what good is gaining access to a public college if the quality of that institution has been significantly compromised in order to expand that access?

## The Consequences of Public College Tuition Inflation

The fact that college prices have increased is beyond dispute. But whether these increases have produced serious negative consequences is less obvious. The U.S. is now well into its third decade in which public college tuition has increased faster than overall inflation and family incomes. In fact, rising college prices have been a source of Congressional concerns since at least 1978. Yet, through this entire period, public college enrollment has continued to grow. When tuition inflation is slow, public college enrollments increase. As tuition inflation accelerates, enrollments seem to accelerate as well. This has led some to conclude that rising prices may not be having the widely assumed negative impact on college access.

In this section, we consider several of the consequences of rising public college prices. The focus is particularly on the consequences for low-income students. First, we examine changes in the federal and state student financial aid programs that are designed to help low-income families pay the costs of college. Recent changes in these programs have reduced their value to the neediest students and left them even more vulnerable to the effects of tuition inflation. Second, we examine the link between college prices and college participation. We do this by looking at the impact that price seems to have at each stage of the college-going process. Finally, we consider the impact that rising prices have had on the institutions themselves. As we will show, state and institutional efforts to control prices have led to revenue shortages that have made it difficult for public colleges to compete with private institutions.

## Tuition Inflation, Financial AID and Public College Affordability

The fact that public college prices are increasing rapidly is not the same as saying that college is becoming less affordable. Affordability also considers the resources that potential consumers have to purchase the product. In an earlier section we showed that family income has increased at widely differential rates across the distribution. The slow rates of growth among the families at the bottom have raised special concerns about tuition inflation. But income is not the only resource available to families to pay for college. The federal and state governments have long operated need-based financial aid systems to insure that low-income and disadvantaged families are able to afford higher education. If these programs had increased sufficiently, the impact of rising prices and stable incomes on college access for the disadvantaged might have been mitigated. Unfortunately, at precisely the time when there has been the greatest need for redistributive financial aid programs, they have been changed in ways that make them less valuable to needy families (Spencer, 2002).

## The Declining Value of the Pell Grant

Since 1965, what is now the Pell Grant program has been the primary policy mechanism to reduce the price barriers to college facing lower-income students. The Pell grant is a means tested federal program that, in 2002, awarded more than $11 billion to low-income students to cover the cost of higher education. Unfortunately, over the past 25 years, the purchasing power of the Pell Grant has not kept up with public college tuition inflation. The maximum Pell Grant is awarded to the student with the greatest financial need. As shown in Table 8, such a student in 1980 would be eligible to receive a grant equal to 67 percent of the annual price of attending a four year public institution. By 1995, the value of the grant had declined to less than 35 percent of the annual cost of attendance. During the late 1990s, as tuition inflation moderated and federal Pell grant spending increased, the value of the maximum grant was restored to 45 percent. But the recession of the early 2000s drove the value downward again.

The declining purchasing power of the Pell grant has left low-income students with a difficult choice (King, 2003). Federal grant aid now regularly leaves this student with substantial unmet need as they consider how to pay for college. They can choose not to attend and thus fail to reap the economic benefits of a college degree. They can attend part-time and put off those benefits. They can attend a less expensive two-year institution and, as we will discuss later, reduce their chances of earning a bachelor's degree. Or they can borrow the money and risk the resulting post-graduation debt.

**Table 8. Maximum Pell Grant as Percent of Average Cost of Attendance at a Four Year Public Institution Selected Years 1980–2002 (in constant 2002 dollars)**

| Year | Maximum Pell Grant | Average Pell Grant | Maximum Pell Grant as Percent of Average Cost of Attendance at a Four Year Public Institution |
|------|--------------------|--------------------|----------------------------------------------------------------------------------------------|
| 1980 | $3,634 | $1,831 | 67.1% |
| 1985 | $3,471 | $2,114 | 54.2% |
| 1990 | $3,089 | $1,946 | 44.3% |
| 1995 | $2,724 | $1,764 | 34.7% |
| 2000 | $3,785 | $2,096 | 45.0% |
| 2002 | $4,000 | $2,415 | 40.3% |

Source: King (2003, p. 28).

## A New Generation of Student Assistance Programs

During the 1990s, in the face of rising tuition and the Pell Grant and other need-based financial aid, state and federal policymakers under-took a major effort to overhaul the way the government provides financial aid to college students. They did not eliminate or restructure the existing need-based aid programs. Rather, they constructed a new, parallel system of student support based on very different principles. Over the next several decades, these new programs are poised to grow much faster than the need-based student aid programs. This will not happen through a direct replacement, but a slower process in which all new funds are directed to the new programs as the value of the need-based aid programs continues to erode (Gladieux, 2002). The result is that student aid will no longer serve to offset the impact of tuition inflation on low-income and disadvantaged students as it has in the past.

These new programs are designed to make college more affordable to middle and upper-income students. This is a noble goal, but realizing it seems likely to come at the cost of access for the low-income. The programs that best exemplify this new approach to college finance are the federal HOPE scholarship and Lifelong Learning tax credit and the various state-level merit scholarship programs modeled after Georgia's HOPE scholarship. The Federal HOPE Scholarship was loosely based on the Georgia program. While the federal program operates differently, it retains the same name given to Georgia's program by then Governor Zell Miller.

The Taxpayer Relief Act of 1997 created a number of new programs designed to help families pay for college. These included the federal HOPE Scholarship, the Lifelong Learning credit, a student loan interest deduction, and an expansion of education IRAs (Wolanin, 2001). The HOPE Scholarship and Lifelong Learning credit, by far the largest of the initiatives, allow students to obtain credits that reduce their federal tax liability. They are designed to provide relief for those students who are already going to college rather than providing an incentive for others to attend. Also, unlike the need-based federal programs, the HOPE scholarship and Lifelong Learning credit were not designed to target benefits to the most needy. Instead

> These two new programs are targeted toward students and families who generally are not eligible for need based grants but still need financial assistance to meet all of their expenses. The tax credit programs include income caps to prevent upper income students from qualifying for benefits while providing relief to middle income students. But they do relatively little to aid low-income students, most of whom have no tax liability, and, therefore will not be eligible for the credit (Hoblitzell and Smith, 2001, pp. 1–2).

These programs carry a substantial cost, but it must be measured in foregone revenues rather than direct expenditures. The estimated cost of these new higher education tax credit programs is $41 billion over their first five years (Kane, 1999). This is roughly the same size as the Pell grant program, and it is almost certain to grow during the next decade as more eligible students use the tax credit and institutions begin to set prices so that students can take full advantage of the program benefits.

The vast majority of these tax credits go to middle- and upper middle-income students. Disadvantaged families, who pay little or no tax, are less likely to be aware of the tax credit and are more likely to attend lower-priced community colleges. The benefits of the tax credit are directed toward families with annual incomes between $80,000 and $160,000 (Kane, 1999). This is far above the eligibility for the Pell grant that usually is awarded to only those with taxable incomes below $40,000. Thus the HOPE credit represents a new type of targeting in which the most-needy are left out entirely and awards are carefully targeted to the politically powerful middle- and upper-income families (Wolanin, 2001). The result is a not so subtle redistribution of benefits to families higher up the income ladder. In annual appropriations battles the funds for Pell grants must come out of federal revenues that have already been reduced by revenues lost to the HOPE credits. Given these patterns, it seems certain that the federal government will continue to spend more on these tax expenditure programs (as well as the various student loan programs), and it will have little positive impact on the college access available to disadvantaged students and their families.

State governments also made policy changes in the 1990s to address the problem of tuition inflation (Heller, 2002). The fastest growing state initiatives in this regard are merit scholarships modeled on the popular HOPE Scholarship program in Georgia. These merit programs offer full or partial scholarships to all graduates of a state high school who earn a specified GPA and attend an in-state public college or university. On its face, such programs seem like an ideal way for states to encourage and reward academic achievement without regard for the student's racial or economic status. In practice, however, the early evidence is that, like the federal tax credits, these merit aid programs direct a large portion of funds to middle- and upper-income students. Lower-income students are less likely to meet the minimum GPA, less likely to maintain it through college, and more likely to attend less expensive institutions.

Since 1990, thirteen states have established new merit scholarship programs and eight more operate programs that have a merit component (National Association of State Student Grant & Aid Programs, 2001). While these programs vary in their structure, funding source, and eligibility criteria, all ignore the student's family income. The dollar growth of these merit programs is especially noteworthy.

> At the state level, new grant aid has shifted steadily in favor of merit based aid and against need based aid. Since 1993, funding of merit programs has increased by 336 percent in real dollars. During the same time period, funding for need-based financial aid programs had increased only 88 percent, which reflects the broad political appeal and support for these programs (Advisory Committee on Student Financial Assistance, 2001, p. 8).

Today, more than $900 million, or 23 percent of total state grants, are awarded as merit scholarships, up from 10 percent in 1991 (National Association of State Student Grant & Aid Programs, 1991; 2001). While these merit scholarship programs seem to be designed to appeal to all families, only those students who meet the requisite grade or test requirements earn the award. In most programs, the student must also maintain a predetermined GPA to keep the scholarship. In practice this has meant that a far higher percent of upper- and middle-income students receive the award. Lower-income and minority students, who often come from lower performing high schools, receive these scholarships in much smaller percentages.

In his testimony before the Advisory Committee on Student Financial Assistance, Heller (2003) lamented this trend.

> There is no question that the focus of state scholarship programs is moving away from serving needy students. While the bulk of the state dollars spent for financial aid is still in need-based programs, virtually all of the new initiatives have been geared towards merit scholarship programs. And evidence is becoming available that merit scholarship programs do little to serve needy students, but rather, are addressed at the political interests of middle and upper income students and their families (p. 3).

The emergence of this new generation of federal and state student aid programs has helped to undermine the goal of equal opportunity that characterized the Title IV student aid programs. These are explicitly not need-based programs. Instead, they are designed to make higher education more affordable to middle- and even upper-income families. There is substantial evidence that these programs are creating a future in which government spending on student aid is unlikely to help low-income and disadvantaged students compensate for the rapid tuition inflation.

Despite these design problems, the politics of these new generation programs almost guarantees that they will expand. As tuition inflation increases, there will be enormous pressure on policymakers to insure that the value of the tax credits keeps pace with those increases. Similarly, state merit scholarship programs will cost states more each year as tuition increases and this will bring enormous pressure to maintain the program in their present structure. One commentator described it this way

> The biggest problem with the scholarships may be simply that the public loves them too much. College officials and lawmakers alike complain that the merit programs have become so popular that they are impossible to change. For some state policy makers, the scholarships are becoming to middle-class parents what Social Security is to an older generation (Selingo, 2001, p. A20).

The Executive Director of the New Mexico Commission on Higher Education echoed these concerns with their merit program when he said, "If it isn't an entitlement yet, in folks' minds then it is getting pretty close." A Georgia State Representative put it this way, "It's less painful to jump off a cliff than to change HOPE" (in Selingo, 2001, p. A20).

As the tax credit programs are more widely understood and institutionalized, and the merit scholarship model migrates to other states, their cost will mushroom. It is almost inevitable that they will attract a larger and larger portion of the government spending on higher education which will, in turn, accelerate public college tuition inflation. Attempts to restrain the growth of these new programs are likely to mobilize their vast numbers of middle-income supporters. Redistributing state funds out of these popular programs and back to the kind of institutional support that will slow tuition inflation will not be easy. And, it will only become more difficult as a generation of middle- and upper-income families build their children's college funds on the assumption that these benefits will always be there.

## The Consequences of Public College Tuition Inflation For Low-Income and Disadvantaged Students

As public college tuition increases, household income remains stable, and the value of student financial aid is diminished, families often struggle to figure out ways to pay these higher prices. This is a problem for all families, but especially those with the fewest resources. Low-income and disadvantaged families are less likely to have sufficient savings for college than their higher-income counterparts. They are also often less willing to take out loans for college. This is only reasonable since their chances of success in college are uncertain and the economic rewards of graduation difficult to predict. Consequently, there is reason for concern that rising college prices will diminish the opportunities available to low-income students to attend a public college.

Talented young people from low-income families often choose not to go on to higher education. According to the Advisory Committee on Student Financial Assistance (2002), during the first decade of the 21st Century, nearly 2 million low-income students, who are qualified to attend college, will not. One factor underlying this troubling situation is public college tuition inflation. Indeed, there is strong evidence that rising prices have a chilling impact on the enrollment of low-income students in many different ways. In the following section, we review recent research examining the impact that college prices have on the aspirations of students from low-income families to attend college, on the type of college they choose to attend, on their chances to graduate, and on their level of post-graduation debt. Finally, we will review the financial nexus model developed by Edward St John and Michael Paulsen. This model reveals the central role that price plays in the decision of whether or not to attend college.

### Price and College Participation

Nearly everyone agrees that price is an important factor in determining whether a student will enroll and persist in college. Its impact is especially powerful on students from low-income families. Research on this relationship has focused on determining the responsiveness of different students to changes in tuition or subsidy patterns (Paulsen, 1998). Leslie and Brinkman (1988) conducted a groundbreaking meta-analysis to provide an integrative review of the literature. Using statistical procedures to transform findings into a common metric, they standardized the results to a student price response coefficient (SPRC) per $100 of price change. Looking specifically at 18–24-year-old potential, first-time students, they found that students do respond to prices. As tuition increases, enrollments decrease and vice versa. The average SPRC was −.7, or for every $100 increase in price. In other words, for every $100 increase in tuition, there was a drop of .7 percentage points in the first-time enrollment rate among this cohort. The relationship was especially strong for low-income students.

In a follow-up study to Leslie and Brinkman, Heller (1997) confirmed the tuition sensitivity of low-income students. He found that for every $100 tuition increase, enrollments dropped in the range of .5 to 1.0 percentage points across all types of institutions. One word of caution he provided was that this range was based on data and tuition prices from the 1970s and early 1980s. With current tuition levels, the effect would probably be even greater. Additionally, as financial aid declined so did enrollment, depending upon the type of aid awarded. Generally, enrollment was more sensitive to grant aid than to loan or work aid. Second, black students were more sensitive to tuition and aid changes than white students, while the evidence for Hispanic students was inconsistent. Finally, students in community colleges were more sensitive to tuition and aid changes than students in four-year public colleges and universities.

These studies focused on the aggregate impact of price changes on the college participation of different students. One approach conceptualizes the decision to attend college as a series of steps: aspiring to college, selecting the proper courses in high school, selecting an institution, persisting at that institution, and finally graduating. Seen this way, price has a depressing effect on the participation of low-income students at each stage of the process. A second set of studies have sought to identify the "financial nexus" underlying college participation. We explore each of these approaches below.

## Price and College Aspirations

The first place where researchers have identified the effect of price on participation is in determining the aspirations of high school students. If students perceive that college will be beyond their financial reach, they may see little need to prepare for college. They may not select the necessary college preparatory classes, pay insufficient attention to their high school grades, and fail to gather information about college requirements or deadlines. As a result, they shut the door to college even if they later find that they were able to cover the costs through grants or scholarships. Thus, reports of public college tuition inflation may cause fewer low-income students to aspire to college years down the road.

Hossler, Schmidt, and Vesper (1999) studied this problem by developing a model of college aspirations. Although grounded in sociological theory, there are financial considerations made by students within the aspiration model. The model has three stages. They are predisposition, search, and choice. Predisposition refers to student plans for either higher education or employment following high school graduation. The search stage happens when the students discover and evaluate the various collegiate options available to them. Here, students evaluate the characteristics and options offered by colleges and determine which are most important to them. Finally, the choice stage occurs when students choose the school from among those that were considered during the search stage. During all stages, factors such as family background, academic performance, peers, and other high school experiences influence the development of post-high school plans.

One of the most important findings of their study was the difference between the factors that influence student aspirations and those that influence student achievement. What influences a ninth-grade student's decision is quite different from what influences a senior's decision about college attendance. As students come closer to high school graduation, they learn more about higher education options and issues. Students are not interested in college costs until the senior year. At that point, the reality of the costs significantly impacts students' decisions about, not only where they will attend, but will they attend. Additionally, parental support, especially financial, was an important indicator of student responsiveness.

Similarly, a study conducted by Somers, Cofer, and VanderPutten (2002) indicated that the decision to attend any postsecondary institution was most influenced by socioeconomic status (SES) and college expense. Those students from the lowest income quartile were much less likely to attend any postsecondary education than their highest income quartile counterparts. In fact SES seems to have a cumulative effect on college enrollment that begins during the preschool years and continues throughout the secondary years. It is estimated that high SES students are four times as likely to enroll in college as low SES students. This is in part determined by parental encouragement (Hossler and Gallagher, 1987). The intersection of all these factors significantly curtails low-income student aspirations to college when the costs continue to rise. Inaccurate information about the true cost of college and financial aid options coupled with a lack of parental encouragement or support often create a barrier to those aspiring to attend. And, there was a clear bifurcation between those who attend four-year schools versus two-year schools.

This conclusion is supported by research conducted by Advisory Committee on Student Financial Assistance (2002). They find that because of the combination of rising prices and changes in the financial aid programs, families of low-income, college qualified high school graduates face an annual unmet need of $3,800. This requires these families to spend $7,500 to cover the full cost of attendance at a public four-year institution. This represents two-thirds of college expenses and one third of annual family income (2002, p. v). The committee also estimated that financial barriers now prevent 48 percent of college qualified low-income high school graduates from attending a four-year college and 22 percent from attending any college at all within two years of graduation. Similarly, 43 percent of students from moderate income families are unable to attend a four-year college and 16 percent attend no college at all. The cumulative impact of all this is that each year 400,000 college qualified students will be unable to attend a four-year college and 170,000 will attend no college at all.

## College Price and Institutional Choice

College prices also have an important impact on the type of institution a student attends. Low-income students are far more likely to attend a two-year college as opposed to a four-year college (Advisory Committee on Student Financial Assistance, 2002). The primary reasons for this are rising public college prices and the shift from need-based, or grant aid, to merit-based aid by the states and loan aid by the feds. Leslie and Brinkman (1988) and Heller (1997) confirmed that college cost increases were directly related to a decline in low-income enrollment in four-year institutions, while enrollment increased at two-year community colleges. Kane (1995) and Rouse (1994) had a similar finding that increasing low-income student enrollment at two-year public colleges was a direct reaction to the rising tuition and state appropriation reductions during the 1980s and 1990s. Clearly, lower-income students have the greatest difficulty with increasing tuition. When looking at tuition as a percentage of household income, average annual tuition at a four- year college is now twice as expensive as it is at a two-year college. It is no surprise that low-income enrollment at public two-year colleges is growing while it is declining at public four-year institutions. Similarly, students from the most affluent families are increasing their enrollment in the most selective undergraduate institutions (National Center for Postsecondary Improvement, 1998).

There is also growing racial segregation among types of public institutions. Carter (1999), found that African-American students reported that they attend their first choice institution less often, attend institutions closer to home, and chose their institution based on lower cost than what their white counterparts reported. Finally, while there was no significant difference in the rate at which white and African-American students attend two-year versus four-year institutions, there was a significant difference between private versus public schools, higher cost versus lower cost, and larger versus smaller institutions. For all three, African-American students were on the short end of the receiving line.

It may be comforting to think that even as prices at four-year institutions increase, low-income students can always attend low-priced community colleges. Indeed, many states have consciously pursued policies to encourage low-income students to enter two-year colleges with the hope that they will then transfer to four-year institutions after earning their an associates degree. There are two problems with this approach. First, tuition and fees at these institutions are rising as well and, in many states, have already reached the point that they are unaffordable to many needy residents. Second, many potential four-year graduates stop after they complete their two-year degree.

> Among traditional college age students, only 29 percent of Whites and 27 percent of Hispanics, and 20 percent of African American transfer to four year schools after completing two-year programs. This has an important impact on future earnings. While a worker with an associates degree earns 21 percent more than a high school graduate, a bachelors degree commands 31 percent more and a masters degree 35 percent more (Carnevale and Fry, 2000, p. 32).

Forcing low-income students into community colleges rather than beginning at a four-year campus, thus dramatically reduces their chances of earning a four-year degree and unnecessarily limits their life chances.

## Price and College Persistence

Persistence, grounded in sociological theory, is the likelihood that students will reenroll in college. Historically, research has been dubious as to the link between cost and/or financial aid and persistence (St. John, Paulsen, and Starkey, 1996). Tinto (1993) explains that finances are more likely an excuse to drop out, rather than the reason for dropping out. He states, "though departing students very often cite financial problems as reasons for their leaving, such statements are frequently ex post facto forms of rationalization which mask primary reasons for their withdrawal" (Tinto, 1993, p. 66). Similarly, Leslie and Brinkman (1988) noted that upperclassmen were less responsive to the price changes. They attribute this to the notion that upperclassmen have already invested in the institution and because these students would not be subject to the higher prices for as many years as first-time students.

Recently, the persistence model has been viewed through an economic lens. As such, the notion that there is no correlation between cost and persistence has been called into question. In fact, St. John, Paulsen, and Starkey (1996) note that national studies demonstrate a clear link between persistence and tuition, subsidies, financial aid, and living costs. Similarly, Heller (2000) compared different racial groups and institutional types. His findings demonstrated that for most racial groups there was a correlation between continuing students and tuition price responsiveness. For every $1,000 increase in tuition prices, there were large decreases in enrollment.

## Post Graduation Debt

As tuition at public institutions increases, low-income families must find a way to pay those costs. Either more of the family budget must be being directed toward higher education or they must borrow money to cover the costs (Cavanagh, 2002; College Board, 2003b). With household income stable, an increasing number of low-income students have chosen to borrow, either through the many federal loan programs or through alternative loans.

There are several reasons for the increased reliance on loans. First, federal grant aid has not kept pace with tuition inflation. Second, financial need has increased even more rapidly than educational costs. Third, increases in loan limits and the ease to obtain loans have led to more students who receive loans. As a result of this, students at all income levels are borrowing more. From 1994–95 to 1999–2000, the amount students borrowed to attend a postsecondary institution increased from $24 billion to $33.7 billion. Most of the growth in loan aid has been through the Stafford Unsubsidized Loan program. From 1992–93 to 2002–2003, the amount of loans rose dramatically from $1.019 billion to $16.5 billion. During the same time, the amount of Stafford Subsidized loans grew from $12.5 billion to $17.8 billion (U.S. Department of Education, 2003). This is in large part due to the increase in tuition coupled with the decrease in Pell subsidies, which has resulted in an over-reliance on loan aid (Redd, 2001).

Students from all income levels are borrowing more than ever before. McPherson and Shapiro (1999) note that even though the majority of loans have probably gone to middle- and upper-income students, there is little evidence that this form of aid is essential to enabling them to attend college. Yet, there is considerable evidence that federal dollars targeted to low-income students do influence college enrollment decisions. Low-income students are more likely to enroll in higher education with grant aid than with loan aid (Paulsen, 1998). And, borrowing is a much greater burden for low-income students than their wealthy counterparts.

Loan debt of low-income students raises two issues. First, low-income students are more likely to be inhibited from enrolling for fear of debt. Families cannot help to repay loan debt and there is a higher likelihood of dropout by low-income students. Thus, the lack of a bachelor's degree and the good paying job that goes with it means that there is an even greater struggle for paying off the debt. Additionally, many low-income students help to support the family unit while attending college. Second, the financial consequences of post graduation debt impacts students' lives long after graduation. It impacts their ability to purchase a home, start a family, or save for retirement. In addition, low-income students may be making choices driven by economic factors such as what career path they will follow. Efforts to attract quality graduates into important, but low-paying jobs, such as teaching, may well be undermined by substantial debt burdens. This not only is harmful to the individual, but to society as well (National Center for Public Policy and Higher Education, 2002).

## The Financial Nexus

In a series of articles, Edward St. John and Michael Paulson develop an integrative model that explains the complex interactions between finance and academic preparation in influencing college choice. In doing so, they examine how financial concerns present barriers at every stage of the college selection process. In this view, finances can be seen to have both direct and indirect influence on enrollment behavior. Some potential students simply cannot afford the high cost of college. But finances also shape the expectations and condition the choices of students and families well before they are thinking about college. In particular, St. John shows how students respond differently to changes in subsidies (grants, loans, and work) than to changes in price (tuition, fees and living expenses). The effects of changes in prices and subsidies on student persistence are different than their effect on students' first enrollment. Moreover, students' responses change over time as a result of changes in government financing strategies and the labor market.

The financial nexus model is the intersection of aspirations, student choice, and persistence (St. John, Paulsen, and Starkey, 1996). In their 1996 study, St. John, Paulsen, and Starkey found that students made mental calculations about the costs and benefits of their college experiences. Financial and academic factors influenced the enrollment and persistence decisions of students. Similarly, when students made decisions about re-enrollment they also made mental calculations about whether or not the quality of their education was worth the cost. In a follow up study, Paulsen and St. John (1997) looked at the difference between public and private institutions. An interesting finding was that financial aid in private colleges was sufficient, while financial aid in public colleges was insufficient. This is likely due to investments that private colleges make to help offset the loss of student financial aid. However, the nexus analysis did find a negative correlation between choosing a private college because of financial aid and persistence. Thus, finances appear to be more important to those students who enrolled in public institutions. This is likely due to the fact that those attending private colleges are from higher socioeconomic backgrounds. Here the authors note that in the early prematriculation stages, financial aid administrators must supply students and parents with accurate information about the actual costs of college and financial aid options (Paulsen and St. John, 1997).

Further studies by Paulsen and St. John (2002) and St. John (2003) refined the financial nexus model to examine persistence by undergraduates in four distinct income groups. The analyses looked at the differences among social class and income group in regard to perceptions and expectations of costs and the effect of cost on choice and persistence decisions. Their findings confirmed earlier studies. Not only do low-income student perceptions about the cost of college influence the decisions they make, but so too does the actual cost. Among poor and working-class students, tuition had an alarmingly high negative influence on persistence. Each $1000 of tuition differential decreased the probability that the otherwise-average student would persist by about 16 and 19 percentage points, respectively (p. 223). This study also found that financial aid was not adequate enough for many low-income students to persist in college. Both grants and loans had a direct negative effect on persistence decisions made by low-income students.

St. John (2003) sums up the role of finances on low-income decisions.

> Finances have both direct and indirect influences on enrollment behavior. The most substantial effects of finances are indirect. Low-income families—parents and children—are concerned about college costs. In eighth grade, many of these students expect that they will not be able to afford college, yet they take the steps to prepare. In twelfth grade, 20 percent do not expect to go to college. Those students who do go to college face costs that are in excess of 20 percent of their families' total income (p. 170).

# The Cumulative Consequences for Low-Income Students

While increasing tuition impacts all economic sectors, there are especially troubling trends for low-income students. They are college participation rates, economic segregation and type, and degree attainment.

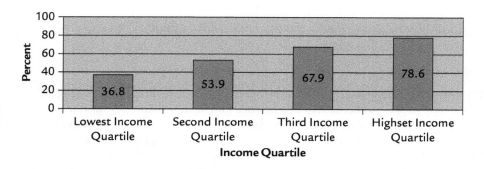

**Figure 6. College Participation Rates by Income Quartile for Dependent 18 to 24 Year Olds**

## College Participation Rates

College participation rate is defined as the percentage of those students who graduate from high school and continue on to college. In other words, they are the proportion of dependent, 18- to 24-year olds who reach college by overcoming admissions and price barriers. For low-income students, who face a myriad of obstacles to obtaining admission to higher education, college participation is often an unrealized dream. In fact, in 2001, college participation for dependent, 18- to 24-year olds in each of the family income quartiles were 36.8 percent for the bottom quartile; 53.9 percent for the second quartile; 67.9 percent for the third quartile; and 78.6 percent for the top quartile (see Figure 6). Thus, students in the top income quartile were more than twice as likely to attend college as their counterparts in the bottom income quartile. And, this has been consistent since the 1980s (Mortenson, 2003c).

When examined through a racial lens, participation among minorities is not much better. According to St. John (2003), in 1975, participation rates among Whites and Blacks were nearly equal, 32.3 percent and 31.5 percent, respectively. Hispanics had a slightly higher participation rate of 35.5 percent. But by 1999, a large disparity had arisen with Whites accounting for 45.3 percent, Blacks accounting for 39.2 percent, and Hispanics accounting for 31.6 percent of college participants. Blacks and Hispanics did increase their participation rates during this time, but not at the level in which their White counterparts did. White participation had increased 12 percent. Yet Blacks and Hispanics lost ground with their participation rates being 6.1 percent and 13.7 percent lower, respectively.

## Economic Segregation by Institutional Type

Beginning in the 1980s, segregation of American higher education has accelerated at an alarming rate. Low-income students, as measured by Pell grant eligibility are increasingly pushed toward two-year public colleges. Of those low-income students who opt for a four-year public college, they are usually segregated into open-door, four-year institutions. The reverse is true for upper-income and wealthy students, who disproportionately attend the most selective four-year institutions in the U.S. In fact, in 1980, 60 percent of Pell grant recipients attended a public, four-year institution, while 40 percent attended a two-year institution. In 2002, however, only 44.7 percent of Pell grant recipients attended a public, four-year institution, while 55.3 percent attended a two-year institution (Mortenson, 2003b). This growing economic segregation of American higher education has been the direct result of federal, state, and institutional policies. The cumulative effect of these policies has resulted in the sorting and redistribution of higher education according to economic class (Mortenson, 2003b).

At the federal level, policies have been such that financial aid based on need has been greatly restricted, while aid based on merit has been greatly expanded. At the state level, as states have reduced their support of higher education, they have forced institutions to increase tuition and fees charged to students. Finally, four-year institutions have become increasing selective in their admissions policies and process. They recruit more affluent students and package financial aid in such a manner as to attract students from wealthier backgrounds. This in turn, again, disadvantages low-income students, who are often entering higher education less academically prepared and thus, less likely to be awarded these financial aid packages.

## Degree Attainment

Over a 20-year period, degree attainment rates have varied considerably among low-income and high-income students. In 2001, the estimated bachelor's degree completion rate by 24-year olds by each of the family income quartiles were 12.2 percent for the bottom quartile; 22.9 percent for the second quartile; 36.2 percent for the third quartile; and 65.5 percent for the top quartile. Here, the problems faced by low-income students are even more pronounced as those in the top income quartile are more than *five times as likely* to complete a bachelor's degree by the age of 24 as their bottom income quartile counterparts. This has been the trend since the early 1980s where college completion rates for low-income students has declined by 13.6 percent from 1983 to 2001. Despite any successes low-income students may have garnered on the road to enrollment, government and institutional policies have been such that a hostile environment now appears to exist for low-income higher education access and success (Mortenson, 2003c).

For Blacks and Hispanics, the problems are even more pronounced. The overall population of dependent, black 18- to 24-year olds was 16.1 percent in 2001. Yet, they represented 27.9 percent of the bottom family income quartile, 15.5 percent of the second, 9.2 percent of the third, and only 6.2 percent of the top quartile. Hispanics have not faired much better, representing 17.7 percent of the dependent 18 to 24 year olds in 2001. Hispanic income distribution was 28.9 percent of the bottom quartile. 19.7 percent of the second, 11.0 percent of the third and 6.9 percent of the top income quartile (Mortenson, 2003c). Given the larger percentage of low-income minorities—Blacks and Hispanics, specifically—at the bottom income quartile, clearly degree attainment is especially elusive for these populations.

# The Impact of Revenue Shortages on Public College Quality

Low-income students are not the only ones who are harmed by the spiral of public college tuition inflation. Public colleges are also harmed in important ways. The most obvious is the increasing economic segregation among institutions that has resulted from the price increases. As tuition rises much faster than income and grant resources, some students who might have preferred a four-year institution now choose a two-year institution instead. Students who might have attended full time, may now only attend part time. And others who might have attended a low price institution may now choose not to attend at all.

In a study focusing on the period 1980 to 1994, Michael McPherson and Morton Owen Shapiro (1999) found that lower-income students were enrolling in community colleges in much higher proportions and upper income students in much lower proportions. Similarly, a study by the Institute for Higher Education Policy (2000) found that between 1990 and 2000, the proportion of low-income freshman decreased at most types of four-year colleges, but increased at two-year colleges. The proportion of higher income students decreased at less selective four-year institutions and increased at more selective four-year institutions. Jacqueline King (2003) found that only 29 percent of low-income students attended four-year institutions as compared to more than 50 percent of middle and upper-income students. She also found that low-income students were less likely to attend full time than middle and upper-income students and thus were less likely to complete their degree.

The result of these trends has been to reinforce the economic segregation among public institutions. As college choice becomes more closely linked to family income, institutions find themselves facing more homogeneous enrollments. The resulting loss of diversity in the student population hinders everyone's learning and diminishes the richness of student interactions. As a consequence, public higher education may be providing an increasing number of students with the same kind of uni-ethnic, uni-cultural, uni-income environment that has now become the norm in many American secondary schools.

There is a second problem that faces institutions as prices rise. Even at their current levels of tuition inflation, these institutions have not been able to generate revenue at a rate sufficient to compensate for the loss of state funds. This has created revenue crunches on many public campuses that hold down spending per student and risk harming the quality of the educational experience they offer. Kane and Orszag (2003) describe it this way:

> Fearful of the political consequences, state governors and legislators have been reluctant to allow the higher tuition increases that would be necessary to fully offset the state cuts to higher education and to allow public institutions to keep pace with private ones. As result, educational spending per full-time equivalent student has declined at public institutions relative to private institutions: the ratio fell from 70 percent in 1977 to about 58 percent in 1996. These differential spending trends have begun to manifest themselves in indirect measures of quality in public higher education (p. 4).

This concern is most clearly seen in the declining salaries of faculty members at public institutions relative to their private counterparts. As discussed earlier, faculty salaries and compensation have increased steadily at public colleges. During that same period, however, faculty salaries at private institutions increased even more rapidly. In 1980, average faculty salaries at public institutions were higher than they were at private institutions. By 1990, faculty salaries at private institutions had surpassed their public counterparts. During the 1990s, faculty salaries at public institutions, as measured in constant 2000 dollars, increased by only three percent. Faculty salaries at private colleges have increased by 8 percent. Moreover, the trends driving these differentials seem to be accelerating.

Several observers have speculated that these salary trends are making it difficult for public colleges to recruit and retain the best faculty. There is no national data series on turnover rates among faculty members. However in 1990, one study used AAUP data to estimate the turnover rates of faculty at different types of institutions. Reflecting on their findings more recently, the author of the study anticipated the impact on public institutions if the trends in turnover continued.

> We found that other factors held constant, institutions with higher average salaries tended to have higher continuation rates (that is lower voluntary turnover rates) than their competitors. Moreover, the magnitude of the relationship was largest at doctoral universities. Given the pattern of public-private salary differentials in recent years, one would expect that private institutions of higher education would have higher average continuation rates among associate professors than their public sector counterparts (American Association of University Professors, 2003, http://www.aaup.org/surveys/zrep.htm).

While the impact that rising public college prices have on students is clear, its impact on the institutions themselves is no less a concern. The segregation of the student body as a result of rising prices has forced public colleges to engage in new spending initiatives. Targeted institutional scholarships, increased tuition discounting, and expanding recruitment staffs have all undertaken to compensate for the impact of rising prices. These initiatives all require additional spending that can further fuel tuition inflation. Additionally, pressure to hold down prices and maintain enrollments serves to limit the revenue available to campus leaders. They have responded by holding salary increases well below those paid by private institutions. This risks losing the best faculty to competitor institutions and diminishing the overall quality of the campus and its programs. Thus, as low-income students are losing access to more expensive institutions, revenue pressures are reducing the quality of those lower priced institutions that are still within their reach.

## Conclusion

Since 1980, the real price of attending a public two-year or four-year college has increased 168 and 126 percent, respectively. While the rate of increase has not been consistent over time, or from state to state, there is an unmistakable upward trend everywhere. There are multiple reasons for these price increases and substantial disagreement over which were the most important. The ongoing budget troubles of the states certainly played a part. As states faced severe revenue shortfalls resulting from economic downturns, and were forced to spend each year more on Medicaid, they reduced support for higher education as a portion of their total expenditures. Public colleges responded to these cuts by substituting tuition and fee revenue for the lost state dollars. Public colleges have also increased their spending per student and are increasing their spending on research, salaries, benefits, technology, and facilities. These increases have also been financed by the revenue generated by tuition increases.

These tuition increases have had important consequences for students, and to a lesser extent, the institutions themselves. Tuition inflation, coupled with important changes in federal and state student aid, have threatened to move public higher education out of the reach of many lower income students. The impact of price increases can be seen in several ways. Low-income students are less likely to aspire to college, more likely to choose a two-year institution, and less likely to graduate. These factors have lead to a widening gap between the college participation rates of low-income students and their higher-income counterparts. It has also left a growing number of college-prepared, low-income students from entering college at all.

Public colleges have also experienced problems resulting from tuition inflation. As prices rise, many campuses are becoming less economically and racially diverse. This is most evident at four-year institutions and at those campuses that have selective admissions requirements. Some institutions have attempted to address this problem by developing institutional scholarship programs to encourage or maintain diversity. But these are expensive and risk further driving up the price for everyone else. Finally, there is some preliminary evidence that public colleges may be experiencing revenue shortages that are having a negative impact on program quality. If public colleges are unable to pay faculty salaries equal to their private competitors, they run the risk of losing their best faculty. Over time, this will diminish the ability of these institutions to offer programs of comparable quality to their private competitors.

Students, their families, the general public, and state and federal policymakers all view public college tuition inflation as a cause for great concern. This analysis concludes that these concerns are justified. Rising prices do matter. But it also shows that holding down tuition is no easy matter. The causes of tuition inflation are complex and disputed. Congressional efforts to sort out their fundamental causes have proven unsuccessful. The approach most likely to succeed is to significantly increase state support to public higher education. But this is beyond the financial reach of most states. Moreover, increases in the number of students seeking to enter higher education in the next decade will force states to increase their level of support simply to maintain current levels of service. Policymakers are, thus, left with a difficult choice. If they take no action, the result will almost surely be higher prices, reduced access for low-income students, and less diverse and lower quality public campuses. Improving access, however, will require state and federal policymakers to spend more on higher education. These additional expenditures will strain state budgets even further and require either higher taxes or the redistribution of funds from other state programs.

# References

Advisory Committee on Student Financial Assistance (2001). *Access Denied: Restoring the Nation's Commitment to Equal Educational Opportunity*. Washington, D.C.: author

Advisory Committee on Student Financial Assistance (2002). *Empty Promises: The Myth of College Access in America*. Washington, D.C.: Author.

American Association of University Professors (2003). *Unequal Progress: the Annual Report on the Economic Status of the Profession, 2002–03*. Washington, D.C.: author.

Arenson, K. W. (2003, July 25). Illinois enacts plan to freeze tuition rates at its colleges. *New York Times*. Retrieved February 2, 2004, from http://query.nytimes.com

Boehner, J. A., and McKeon, H. P. (2003). *The College Cost Crisis: A Congressional Analysis of College Costs and Implications for America's Higher Education System*. Washington, D.C.: U.S. Congress.

Boyd, D. (2002). *State Spending for Higher Education in the Coming Decade*. Boulder CO: National Center for Public Policy and Higher Education.

Burd, S. (2003, September 23). Rep. McKeon's plan to penalize colleges for steep tuition increases is criticized in House hearing [Electronic version]. *The Chronicle of Higher* Education. Retrieved September 24, 2003, from http://chronicle.com/prm/daily/2003/09/2003092401n.htm

Callan, P. M. (2002). *Coping with Recession: Public Policy, Economic Downturns, and Higher Education*. Washington, D.C.: The National Center for Public Policy and Higher Education.

Carnevale, A., and Fry, R. (2000). *Crossing the Great Divide: Can we Achieve Equity When Generation Y Goes to College?* Princeton NJ; Educational Testing Service.

Carnevale, A. P., and Fry, R. A. (2002). The demographic window of opportunity: College access and diversity in the new century. In D. E. Heller (ed.), *Condition of Access: Higher Education for Lower Income Students* (pp. 137–152). Washington, D.C.: American Council on Education/Praeger.

Carter, D. E. (1999). The impact of institutional choice and environments on African-American and white students' degree expectations. *Research in Higher Education, 40*(1): 17–41.

Cavanagh, S. (2002, May 29). College students straining to cover rising tuition at public institutions. *Education Week*, 6–7.

Clotfelter, C. T. (1996). *Buying the Best: Cost Escalation in Elite Higher Education.* Princeton, NJ: Princeton University Press.

College Board (2003a). *Trends in College Pricing 2003.* Retrieved October 31, 2003, from http://www.collegeboard.com/prod_downloads/press/cost03/cb_trends_pricing_2003.pdf

College Board (2003b). *Trends in Student Aid 2003.* Retrieved October 31, 2003, from http://www.collegeboard.com/press/cost02/html/CBTrendsAid02.pdf

Cunningham, A. F., Wellman, J. V, Clinedinst, M. E., and Merisotis, J. P. (2001). *Study of College Costs and Prices, 1988–89 to 1997–98* (National Center for Education Statistics Rep. No. 2002–157). Washington, D.C.: U.S. Department of Education.

Education Commission of the States. (1998). *Survey of Perceptions State Leaders.* Denver, CO: Author.

Ehrenberg, R. G. (2000). *Tuition Rising: Why College Costs so Much.* Cambridge, MA: Harvard University Press.

Gladieux, L. E. (2002). Federal student aid in historical perspective. In D. E. Heller (ed.), *Condition of Access: Higher Education for Lower Income Students* (pp. 45–58). Washington, D.C.: American Council on Education/Praeger.

Hauptman, A. M. (1990). *The College Tuition Spiral: An Examination of Why Charges Are Increasing.* Washington, D.C.: The College Board and American Council on Education.

Heller, D. E. (1997). Student price response in higher education. *Journal of Higher Education, 68*(6): 624–659.

Heller, D. E. (2000). Are first-time college enrollees more price sensitive than continuing students? *Journal of Staff, Program, and Organizational Development, 17*(2): 95–107.

Heller, D. E. (2002). *Condition of Access: Higher Education for Lower Income Students.* Washington, D.C.: American Council on Education/Praeger.

Heller, D. E. (2003, September 11). *Hearing On HR 3039, The Expanding Opportunities in Higher Education Act.* Testimony given to House Education and Workforce Committee, Subcommittee on 21st Century Competitiveness, U.S. Congress. Testimony retrieved December 12, 2003, from http://edworkforce.house.gov/hearings/108th/21st/hr3039091103/heller.htm

Hoblitzell, B. A., and Smith, T. L. (2001). *Hope Works: Student Use of Education Tax Credits.* Indianapolis, IN: Lumina Foundation.

Hossler, D., and Gallagher, K. (1987). Studying student college choice: A three-phase model and the implications for policymakers. *College and University, 62*(3): 207–221.

Hossler, D., Schmit, J., and Vesper, N. (1999). *Going to College: How Social, Economic, and Educational Factors Influence the Decisions Students Make.* Baltimore, MD: The Johns Hopkins University Press.

Hovey, H. (1999). *State Spending for Higher Education in the Next Decade: The Battle to Sustain Current Support.* San Jose, CA: National Center for Public Policy and Higher Education.

Institute for Higher Education Policy. (1999). *The Tuition Puzzle: Putting the Pieces Together.* Washington D.C.: author.

Kaiser, H. (1996). *A Foundation to Uphold: A Study of Facilities Conditions at U.S. Colleges and Universities.* Alexandria, VA: Association of Higher Education Facilities Officers.

Kane, T. J. (1995, April). *Rising Public College Tuition and College Entry: How Well do Public Subsidies Promote Access to College?* Cambridge, MA: National Bureau of Economic Research Working Paper No. 5164.

Kane, T. J. (1999). *The Price of Admission.* Washington, D.C.: Brookings Institution Press.

Kane, T. J., and Orszag, P. R. (2003, September). *Higher Education Spending: The Role of Medicaid and the Business Cycle* (Policy Brief No. 124). Washington, D.C.: The Brookings Institution.

Kiesler, C. (1993, July 28). Why college costs rise and rise and rise. *New York Times*, p. A19.

King, J. (2003). *2003 Status Report on the Pell Grant Program.* Retrieved September 29, 2003, from http://acenet.edu/bookstore/pdf/2003_pell_grant.pdf

Leslie, L. L., and Brinkman, P. (1988). *The Economic Value of Higher Education.* New York, NY: Macmillan.

Mathesian, C. (1995, March). Higher ed.: The no longer sacred cow. *Governing*, 20–24.

McPherson, M. S., and Schapiro, M. O. (1999). *Reinforcing Stratification in American Higher Education: Some Disturbing Trends.* Standford, CA: National Center for Postsecondary Improvement.

Mortenson, T. (1997). FY 1997 state budget actions. *Postsecondary Education Opportunity, 55*: 10.

Mortenson, T. (2003a, December). Pell grant students in undergraduate enrollments by institutional type and control 1992–93 to 2000–01. *Postsecondary Education Opportunity, 138*: 1–16.

Mortenson, T. (2003b, October). Economic segregation of higher education opportunity 1973 to 2001. *Postsecondary Education Opportunity, 136*: 1–16.

Mortenson, T. (2003c, September). Family income and higher educational opportunity 1970 to 2001. *Postsecondary Education Opportunity, 135*: 1–16.

Mumper, M. (1993, Winter). The affordability of public higher education: 1970–1990. *The Review of Higher Education, 16*(2): 157–180.

Mumper, M. (1996). *Removing College Price Barriers: What the Government has Done and Why it Hasn't Worked.* Albany, NY: SUNY.

Mumper, M. (2001). The paradox of college prices: Five stories with no clear lessons. In D. E. Heller (ed.), *The States and Public Higher Education Policy: Affordability, Access, and Accountability* (pp. 39–63). Baltimore, MD: The Johns Hopkins University Press.

National Association of State Budget Officers (2003). *State Expenditure Report 2002.* Washington, D.C.: author.

National Association of State Student Grant and Aid Programs (1991, April). *21st Annual Survey Report.* Albany, NJ: author.

National Association of State Student Grant and Aid Programs (2001, April). *31st Annual Survey Report.* Albany, NJ: author.

National Center for Education Statistics (2003a). Total Enrollment in all degree granting institutions, by sex, attendance, and control of institutions, with alternative projections: Fall 1988 to fall 2013. *Projections of Education Statistics.* Washington, D.C.: National Center for Education Statistics.

National Center for Education Statistics (2003b). High school graduates by control of institution with projections: 1987–88 to fall 2012–13. *Projections of Education Statistics.* Washington, D.C.: National Center for Education Statistics.

National Center for Education Statistics (2004a). Current fund revenue of public degree granting institutions by source: 1980–81 to 1999–2000. *Digest of Educational Statistics.* Washington, D.C.: National Center for Educational Statistics.

National Center for Educational Statistics (2004b). Current fund expenditures and general expenditures per full-time equivalent student in degree-granting institutions, by type and control of institution: 1970–71 to 1999–2000. *Digest of Educational Statistics.* Washington, D.C.: National Center for Educational Statistics.

National Center for Postsecondary Improvement (1998, September/October). *The Choice-income Squeeze: How do Costs and Discounts Affect Institutional Choice?* Stanford, CA: author.

National Center for Public Policy and Higher Education (2002a, October). *State Spending for Higher Education in the Coming Decade.* San Jose, CA: author.

National Center for Public Policy and Higher Education (2002b). *Losing Ground: A National Status Report on the Affordability of American Higher Education.* San Jose, CA: author.

National Commission on the Cost of Higher Education (1998). *Straight Talk About College Costs and Prices: A Report of the National Commission on the Cost of Higher Education.* Washington, D.C.: author.

National Education Association (2003, December). Why are college prices increasing and what should we do about it? *Update, 9*(5).

National Science Foundation (1996). *Scientific and Engineering Research Facilities at Colleges and Universities.* Washington, D.C.: author.

Nelson A. Rockefeller Institute of Government (2003, July). State budgetary assumptions in 2003: States cautiously projecting recovery. *State Fiscal Brief, 68.* Retrieved February 2, 2004, from http://www.rockinst.org/publications/state_fiscal_briefs.html

Paulsen, M. B. (1998). Recent research on the economics of attending college: Returns on investment and responsiveness to price. *Research in Higher Education, 39*(4): 471–489.

Paulsen, M. B., and St. John, E. P. (1997). The financial nexus between college choice and persistence. *New Directions for Institutional Research, 35*: 65–82.

Paulsen, M. B., and St. John, E. P. (2002). Social class and college costs: Examining the financial nexus between college choice and persistence. *The Journal of Higher Education, 73*(2): 189–236.

Rasmussen, C. J. (2003). *Student Tuition, Fees, and Financial Aid Assistance Policies, 2002–2003.* Retrieved January 30, 2004, from http://www.ecs.org/html/offsite.-asp?document = http%3A%2F%2Fwww%2Esheeo%2Eorg%2F

Redd, K. E. (2001). *Why do Students Borrow so Much? Recent National Trends in Student Loan Debt.* ERIC Digest. Retrieved February 11, 2004, from http:www.ericdigests.org/2001–4/loans.html

Rouse, C. (1994). What to do after high school? The two-year vs. four-year college enrollment decision. In R. Ehrenberg (ed.), *Contemporary Policy Issues in Education* (pp. 59–88). Ithaca, NY: School of Industrial and Labor Relations.

Ruppert, S. (1996). *The Politics of Remedy: State Legislative Views on Higher Education.* Washington D.C.: National Education Association.

Selingo, J. (2001, January 19). Questioning the merit of merit scholarships. *Chronicle of Higher Education,* A20–A22.

Somers, P., Cofer, J., and VanderPutten, J. (2002). The early bird goes to college: The link between early college aspirations and postsecondary matriculation. *Journal of College Student Development, 43*(1): 93–107.

Sowell, T. (1992). The scandal of college tuition. *Commentary, 95*: 24.

Spencer, A. C. (2002). Policy priorities and political realities. In D. E. Heller (ed.), *Condition of Access: Higher Education for Lower Income Students* (pp. 153–172), Washington, D.C.: ACE/Praeger.

St. John, E. P. (2003). *Refinancing the College Dream: Access, Equal Opportunity, and Justice for Taxpayers.* Baltimore, MD: The Johns Hopkins University Press.

St. John, E. P., Paulsen, M. B., and Starkey, J. B. (1996). The nexus between college choice and persistence. *Research in Higher Education, 73*(2): 175–221.

State Higher Education Executive Officers (SHEEO). (2003). *Appropriations of State Tax Funds for Operating Expenses of Higher Education.* Retrieved February 2, 2004, from http://www.ecs.org/html/offsite.asp

Tinto, V. (1993). *Leaving College: Rethinking the Causes and Cures of Student Attrition* (2nd ed.). Chicago, IL: University of Chicago Press.

Trombley, W. (2003, Winter). The rising price of higher education. *National Crosstalk,* 1–5.

U.S. Department of Education (2000). Loan Volume Update. Retrieved February 27, 2004, from http://www.ed.gov/finaid/prof/resources/data/opeloanvol.html

U.S. Department of Education (2003). Loan Volume Update. Retrieved February 27, 2004, from http://www.ed.gov/finaid/prof/resources/data/opeloanvol.html

U.S. Department of Education (2002). *Digest of Education Statistics, 2002.* Retrieved January 30, 2004, from http://nces.ed.gov/programs/digest/d02/tables/dtl72.asp

Wolanin, T. R. (2001). *Rhetoric and Reality: Effects and Consequences of the HOPE Scholarship.* Washington, D.C.: The Institute for Higher Education Policy.

# Hitting Home

## TRAVIS REINDL

The United States needs to increase its production of postsecondary education degrees *and* reduce gaps in achievement among racial and socioeconomic groups. Otherwise, the country will not be able to meet workforce needs, maintain international economic competitiveness, and improve the quality of life for all Americans.

If current production patterns in postsecondary education persist, the nation will face a significant "degree gap" that puts it at a disadvantage relative to other leading developed nations. In fact, the size of this gap—the difference between degrees produced in the United States and those produced by nations who are among our top competitors—could reach almost 16 million degrees by 2025, according to new data prepared for the *Making Opportunity Affordable* initiative.

To close the gap, the nation's colleges and universities will need to increase the annual rate of degree production by more than 37 percent. This estimate—prepared by the National Center for Higher Education Management Systems—focuses on top degree producing nations who are members of the Organisation for Economic Cooperation and Development and does not include India and China, whose degree production is also rising rapidly.

According to the new data, closing the gap will require the nation's colleges and universities to ensure that minority groups, non-traditional-age college students, and students from low-income backgrounds achieve the same levels of attainment that we see today among white and Asian Americans, traditional-age college students, and wealthier students. Simply reaching the current attainment levels of white students will depend on about 10.6 million more people of color earning postsecondary degrees by 2025 than do so today. Paying for this level of expansion in postsecondary education will demand implementation of a two-fold agenda:

- Introducing a new public investment strategy that includes growth in funding and a much sharper focus on expanding capacity and bolstering productivity in the delivery of higher education;
- Encouraging higher education systems and institutions to be more cost-effective and collaborative with K-12 education in order to enhance student access and success, further contain costs, and introduce additional productivity improvements.

This will require states and institutions to set goals for quality, cost, and access, and to establish metrics for measuring progress. States and institutions also must institute multi-tiered strategies to address these challenges. These strategies include: strengthening inter-institutional collaboration through comprehensive approaches to articulation and transfer; focusing resources on core academic priorities; streamlining student transitions from K-12 to postsecondary education; promoting timely degree completion; and redesigning academic programs to improve student results while reducing cost. While there have been some examples of state and institutional action in these areas, this action has not been comprehensive, coordinated, or sustained. But those states and institutions that have moved forward to adopt these changes have seen promising results.

The multi-year *Making Opportunity Affordable* initiative aims to provide research, tools, and support to help states and institutions transform how they deliver postsecondary education to serve more students without reducing quality. By introducing more cost-effective approaches, states and their higher education systems can reinvest in access and quality improvements. Support for the initiative has been provided by Lumina Foundation for Education.

## Changing Workforce Demands

A recent study by the Bureau of Labor Statistics indicates that high-skill jobs that require advanced learning will make up almost half of all job growth in the United States. While low-skill jobs will continue to grow, the rapid expansion of high-skill work is an indication of the nation's shift from manufacturing and farming toward a more service- and information-based economy. In fact, jobs requiring an Associate's degree or beyond will increase at faster rates than jobs requiring less than an Associate's degree between now and 2014 (see Figure 1). The minimum level of education required in high-growth fields is also likely to increase in the years ahead, which could widen the gap.

High educational attainment correlates with state economic strength and high income. A dozen states (California, Connecticut, Colorado, Delaware, Illinois, Maryland, Minnesota, New Hampshire, New Jersey, New York, Virginia, and Washington) have both high levels of personal income per capita and high percentages of working-age adults with four-year degrees. Only three states have high per-capita income and low educational attainment: Alaska, Michigan, and Nevada, all with economies tilted toward high-wage industries requiring lower levels of education.

## Underlying Problems

In many ways the United States is doing better *and* worse when it comes to higher education. The nation's higher education system has historically been the strongest in the world, and by some measures still is. The number of students pursuing degrees is at an all-time high. Academic preparation for college-level work is improving. College-going rates are holding steady despite double-digit tuition increases.

But these signs of success mask deeper problems. The percentage of our population earning college degrees is stagnating, because a larger proportion of young people are not entering or not progressing through postsecondary education. Low-income and minority students—the segments of the population growing most rapidly—are not succeeding at rates equivalent to their growth.

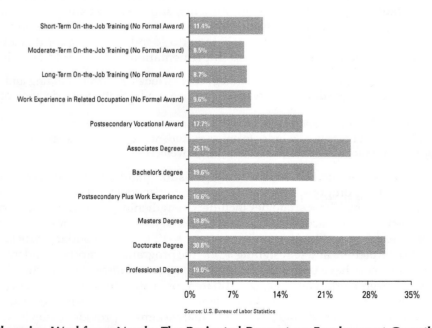

Source: U.S. Bureau of Labor Statistics

**Figure 1. Changing Workforce Needs: The Projected Percentage Employment Growth in the U.S. from 2004 to 2014 by Level of Education Required**

Meanwhile, rising expenditures by students and taxpayers are not resulting in better learning, which points to a dangerous "productivity gap."

## Changing Demographics

The number of students attending higher education institutions has grown dramatically recently, but the composition of that population is changing along with that of the population as a whole. According to the U.S. Census Bureau, the percentages of African Americans and Latinos from 18 to 44 years old will rise by about 30 percent between 2000 and 2025, an increase of about 10 million people. Meanwhile, as the white population ages, the percentage of white adults from 18 to 44 will decline by 6.1 percent, a drop of 4.4 million. Among 18- to 24-year-old white young adults, the population will drop 9.6 percent. So the United States must dramatically increase degree production while more effectively serving groups who typically have not succeeded at the same rates as whites.

## Rising Costs and Prices

The costs of providing higher education and the prices paid by students and their families have increased substantially. Even when adjusted for inflation, tuition and fees have risen 24 percent at four-year public universities over the past five years and 32 percent over the past decade, according to *Trends in College Pricing 2006,* a study conducted by the College Board. The report reveals that tuition and fees at private institutions have risen 11 percent in the past five years and 25 percent in the past decade in inflation-adjusted dollars. Meanwhile, public two-year institutions have done a better job limiting price increases, but even their tuition and fees have risen 22 percent in the past decade when adjusted for inflation (see Figure 2).

The result has been that lower- and middle-class families are having a harder time paying for college. More poor students are staying away, and large percentages of students face heavy debt as they enter the workforce. According to the American Association of State Colleges and Universities, today two out of three students who attend public colleges and universities graduate with debt, and the average borrower owes $17,250 in student loans. Ten years ago, the average student borrower attending a public college or university graduated owing $8,000 in student loans after adjusting for inflation.

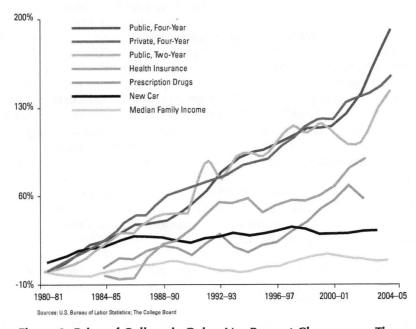

Sources: U.S. Bureau of Labor Statistics; The College Board

**Figure 2. Price of College is Going Up, Percent Change over Time**

Rising prices are the tip of the iceberg. The amount of money that colleges and universities spend to provide education to their students is rising faster than consumer prices and health care costs. Over the past decade, the Higher Education Price Index has increased significantly faster than the nation's Consumer Price Index, which measures the relative cost of a typical basket of goods and responds to changes in the economy as a whole. According to data from the Commonfund Institute, the past decade has seen the HEPI rise 31 percent, including an 18 percent increase in the last five years alone. Meanwhile, the CPI has risen 22 percent and 12 percent, respectively.

There are disagreements about the causes of these cost increases, and some experts argue that universities cannot control spending growth because funding is always needed to improve quality. The *Making Opportunity Affordable* initiative is investigating the real patterns of spending in higher education and has found evidence that cost increases are *not* inevitable. Institutions can control costs and maintain access and quality if they do a better job of targeting resources to programs that benefit students. A new study to be released by the initiative later this year will provide new information on what is driving up costs.

In the past, colleges have avoided coming to terms with cost management by seeking new revenues—in the form of private fundraising and student tuition increases—rather than changing practices. This promotes what Charles Miller, chairman of the U.S. Secretary of Education's Commission on the Future of Higher Education, has called "a top-line structure with no real bottom line." The revenue chase cannot continue. State appropriations for higher education are failing to keep pace with enrollment increases and inflation. Legislatures have increased funding for higher education by an average of 3 percent annually in recent years, but have many competing priorities. States also are facing large structural deficits—service demands in excess of available revenues—that could limit resources available to address these challenges. Private giving is highly variable and cannot be relied on by higher education as a budget balancer.

The public is beginning to push back against constant tuition hikes, raising questions about whether college is worth it and whether colleges are doing the best they can to enable students to attend. More than two-thirds of Americans (68 percent) believe that colleges and universities could reduce their costs without hurting the quality of the institutions, according to a 2004 *Chronicle of Higher Education* poll.

## Quality

How well are students doing? Our understanding of student knowledge and skills comes from national studies, which indicate that the mathematical proficiency and document/prose literacy of college graduates have not improved and, in some cases, actually have declined over the past decade. Adults with college degrees dropped 11 points in prose literacy and 14 points in document literacy between 1992 and 2003, according to the National Assessment of Adult Literacy. A 2005 study by American Institutes for Research revealed that 20 percent of U.S. college students completing four-year degrees—and 30 percent of students earning two-year degrees—have only basic quantitative literacy skills. According to the study, more than 75 percent of students at two-year colleges and more than 50 percent of students at four-year colleges score below the literacy proficiency level. They lack the skills to perform complex literacy tasks, such as comparing credit card offers with different interest rates or summarizing the arguments of newspaper editorials.

In addition, structural forces make it difficult for states and institutions to focus on these issues in a sustained way. State funding cycles promote reactivity and crisis management rather than thoughtful planning. Also, many states and institutions do not fully understand why costs are rising, in what areas they are rising, and what tools or knowledge will help them determine what to do.

As a result of changing demographics, rising costs and prices, the erosion of quality, and these structural forces, we are losing ground in helping to ensure that all Americans can attend college at a cost the nation and its families can afford.

## The Degree Gap

According to the analysis of OECD data, the U.S. deficit in degree attainment poses a serious threat to the nation's economic well-being. Other highly competitive nations are improving the quality of the education they provide their young people, while also radically increasing the capacity of the systems that serve them. These nations have overtaken the United States' long-time position as the world leader in degree production relative to population as a whole.

Today seven nations (Belgium, Canada, Ireland, Japan, Norway, South Korea, and Sweden) lead the United States in degree attainment (see Figure 3). More than half of Japanese and Canadian 25- to 34-year-olds, for example, have a Bachelor's or Associate's degree, while only 4 in 10 Americans in this age group have earned postsecondary degrees.

We are losing ground to other nations largely because of relatively low college completion rates. Although the United States still ranks in the top five in the proportion of young people who attend college, it ranks 16th in the proportion who actually finish, according to the National Center on Public Policy and Higher Education's *Measuring Up 2006* report. While estimates vary, American universities award about 18 degrees for every 100 full-time students enrolled. The leading nations (Japan, Portugal, and the United Kingdom) award about 25 degrees. So these nations are experiencing more positive returns on their investments in higher education.

As other countries ratchet up access and attainment, American Baby Boomers, the best-educated workers in history, are retiring and being replaced in the workforce by young people who possess less knowledge and weaker skills than the current generation. In fact, the United States and Germany are alone among OECD nations in this respect: The percentage of their workers ages 25–34 who

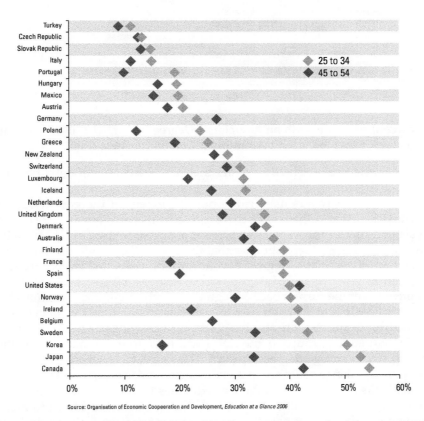

Source: Organisation of Economic Coopeeration and Development, *Education at a Glance 2006*

**Figure 3. Differences in College Attainment (Associate's Degree and Higher) Between the OECD Countries and the U.S. and Between Young and Older Adults, 2004**

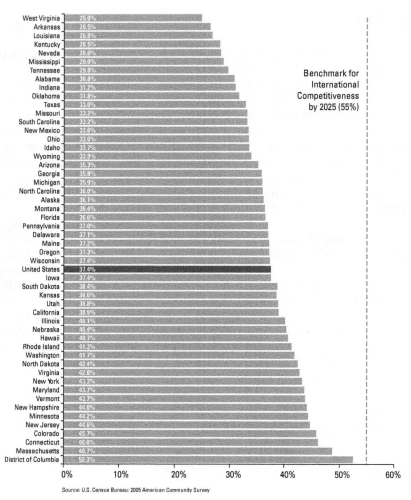

**Figure 4. Percent of Adults with an Associate's Degree or Higher (2005) Compared with Benchmark for International Competitiveness (2025)**

have a postsecondary degree is actually smaller than the percentage of Baby Boom workers ages 45–54 with such a degree.

For the first time, researchers have examined the extent of the gap in degree attainment between the United States and the rest of the world and its consequences. A new report, based on data analysis conducted for *Making Opportunity Affordable* by NCHEMS, will be released in May. This report, *The Degree Gap*, estimates that the United States will need to produce 15.6 million more Bachelor's and Associate's degrees beyond currently expected levels if the nation is to keep up with its best-performing peers—781,000 additional degrees per year between now and 2025, an increase of 37 percent over the current pace of degree production. According to the report, only eight states and the District of Columbia are on pace to meet this ambitious goal. But even states on course to close the gap will do so only by more effectively serving a growing population of historically under-represented racial and ethnic groups. Some states will have to more than double the numbers of young people who obtain college degrees by 2025. This could have severe fiscal consequences, but states that take on the challenge could see tremendous economic benefit (see Figure 4).

However one looks at the problem, the United States has miles to go to eliminate racial and ethnic disparities in degree production, strengthen the domestic workforce to meet demand for higher skills and knowledge, and remain internationally competitive. Colleges and universities will have to ensure that minority groups achieve at the same levels as white and Asian Americans, and earn about 10.6 million more postsecondary degrees by 2025 than would be the case given current circumstances (see Figure 5).

Minorities = African Americans, Hispanics/Latinos, and Native Americans

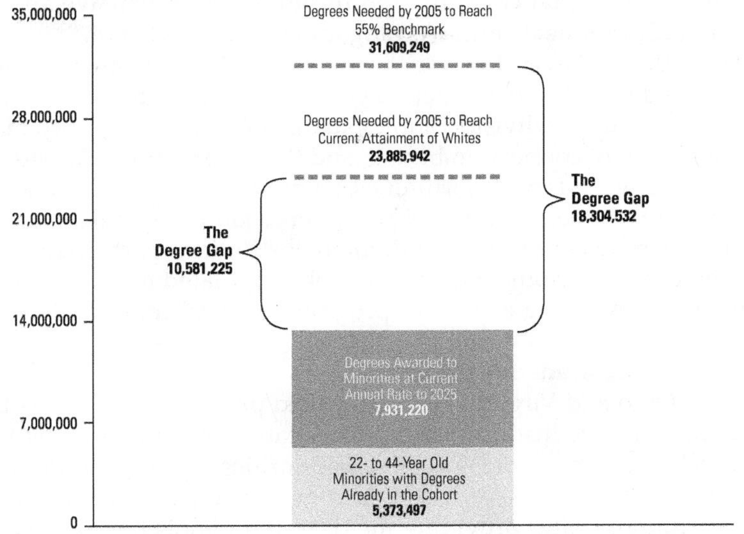

Source: U.S. Census Bureau 2005 ACS, Population Projections, NCES, IPEDS Completions Survey (2004–05)

**How We Measured the Degree Gap**

NCHEMS estimates that by 2025, the proportion of the population with an Associate's or Bachelor's degree will be 55 percent in the three top-performing countries (Canada, Japan, and South Korea) compared to 40 percent in the United States today.

To stay even with these countries, the United States will need to have a total of 94 million working-age adults with Associate's or Bachelor's degrees. Of those, about 31 million current degree-holders will still be in the workforce in 2025, leaving the United States about 63 million degrees short.

At the current pace of production, the United States will produce about 41 million degrees by 2025, leaving a gap of 22 million. When adjusted for net gains from immigrants with degrees (i.e., those entering the United States with postsecondary degrees minus degree-holders leaving the United States), the "degree gap" will amount to about 15.6 million degrees.

**Figure 5. Achieving Racial/Ethnic Parity Relative to Current Attainment Rates for Whites and Benchmark for International Competitiveness**

# What Needs to be Done

The magnitude of the challenge indicates that business as usual is unacceptable. The solution combines two approaches: a) sustained investment in higher education; and b) redesigned institutional practice and public policy to promote greater cost-effectiveness, informed by new knowledge and metrics.

A national agenda for redesigning the higher education system should include several crucial elements. Consumers and the federal government must continue to advocate broader access, improved productivity, and better quality in postsecondary education. Much of the heavy lifting, however, needs to come from state policymakers and higher education decision-makers to:

## Set goals for quality, cost, and access, and establish metrics for measuring progress.

Development of strategic plans and public agendas at the campus, system, and state levels demands goals and metrics that address resource use in relation to student results. Because much of the data and information essential to this work are not currently available or widely used, the *Making Opportunity Affordable* initiative will make significant investments in creating and testing these tools.

## Pursue multiple strategies for meeting these goals, including:

**Strengthening inter-institutional collaboration through comprehensive approaches to articulation and transfer to reduce repeat course-taking and student attrition.**

Florida has taken the lead in addressing these concerns by ensuring that most community college graduates will be deemed to have met all general education requirements and will be guaranteed admission into the upper division (junior status) of a state university. State institutions also abide by a uniform system of course numbering, and the state offers a Web site that provides unbiased advising about postsecondary opportunities. Some states have initiated joint degree programs to fully utilize existing investments. North Dakota offers a joint program in nursing in which course delivery moves from campus to campus, with many institutions participating, allowing a needed program to be offered on a periodic basis in sparsely populated areas without the typical inefficiencies associated with providing expensive programs in rural communities.

**Focusing resources on core academic priorities.**

A few states, such as Ohio and Virginia, have instituted productivity reviews that identify undersubscribed majors at all public institutions and reallocate public funds away from those majors if they fall below a designated threshold. The Illinois Priorities Quality and Productivity initiative in the mid-1990s pursued this goal by providing a common set of data about individual program-performance to institutions. After providing the data, the Illinois Board of Higher Education left the decision about which programs to eliminate up to the institutions so long as they improved institutional performance within established guidelines.

**Streamlining student transitions to reduce rework and attrition.**

This includes offering accelerated learning options (e.g., Advanced Placement/International Baccalaureate, dual/concurrent enrollment, Early College High Schools) and early intervention programs to boost student preparation. In California, the 11th grade standards test serves as a barometer of readiness for courses in the California State University system, giving students early warning about their college preparation. Washington's Running Start program reaches about 10 percent of high school juniors and seniors in the state. Running Start students who transfer their credits to four-year institutions complete Bachelor's degrees with an average of 33 fewer state-supported credits than other students, resulting in lower net costs for both the student and the state. Once in college, Running Start students also appear to perform as well as, and in some cases better than, their peers.

**Promoting timely degree completion to create increased capacity for new enrollment.**

New York's Bundy Aid program, for example, rewards private institutions for graduating New York State residents, providing strong incentives for ensuring degree completion. Western Governors University uses test-out provisions and other institutions use College Level Examination Program scores to allow qualified students to advance faster.

**Redesigning academic programs to improve student results while reducing cost.**

Institutions don't need to tie up several faculty members to teach introductory courses in high-demand subject areas. A recent pilot study by the National Center for Academic Transformation found that 25 of 30 institutions that redesigned a popular course by making smart use of technology and engaging professors as tutors, rather than lecturers, improved learning outcomes, while reducing cost by an average of 37 percent.

Later in 2007, the National Center for Public Policy and Higher Education will release a detailed report for the initiative on effective practices to promote lower cost, equitable access, and higher quality and productivity among states and institutions.

We are at a crucial turning point. The U.S. economy is still strong, and has the potential to remain strong into the future. The nation's workforce is one of the most highly skilled and productive in the world, and can stay that way. But this will happen only if the country makes strategic choices about how we prepare today's workforce—and the workforce of 20 years from today.

The structural changes necessary to put the system on track to meet the attainment benchmark will require breaking with tradition, on many levels, and recentering institutions on their core missions.

Higher education in the United States successfully addressed the economic, demographic, and technological challenges of the 19th and 20th centuries, educating new Americans in the Industrial Age, educating the "greatest generation" in the post-WWII era, and opening doors to women and minorities in more recent times. The development of land grant colleges, the expansion of higher education made possible by the GI Bill, and the establishment of community colleges reduced disparities in opportunity, created a workforce able to satisfy the demands of the state and local economies, and they drove innovation that resulted in continuous economic growth and improvements in the quality of life and standard of living for almost all Americans. States, institutions, and the nation must make no less a commitment to confront the new global challenges of the 21st century, acting boldly to expand opportunity and produce the talent the nation needs at a cost taxpayers and students can afford.

## About Making Opportunity Affordable

Lumina Foundation for Education's multi-year *Making Opportunity Affordable* initiative seeks to help states and institutions move forward with the best information, significant support, and new tools and strategies to address key problems. The initiative will:

- **Spark a national dialogue about cost, quality, and access.**
- **Mobilize and support leaders eager to take action.**
- **Unite courageous innovators in a national network to share ideas and strategies.**
- **Produce research** to answer key questions in the field, including the magnitude of the challenge, the causes of skyrocketing costs, and the changes in policy and practice likely to be most potent.
- **Develop tools and information** to help colleges, policymakers, and the public understand what is at stake and how to evaluate the productivity of their postsecondary systems.
- **Fund model programs in states and institutions.** The initiative will award multi-year Opportunity Grants to up to five states and their higher education systems. These grants will help states audit current campus practices and system/state policies related to quality, cost, and access to identify priority areas that need redesign. The process will yield ways to strengthen core academic functions, streamline student transitions into college, promote accelerated degree completion, and encourage systemic approaches that carefully integrate long-term efforts to lower cost, increase quality, and bolster access.
- **Identify, document, and disseminate** analyses of existing models and new ideas to encourage broader implementation. The conclusions the initiative reaches can serve as the basis for engaging additional states, their higher education systems, and public and private institutions in the quest.

www.makingopportunityaffordable.org

**Lumina Foundation for Education,** an Indianapolis-based, private, independent foundation, strives to help people achieve their potential by expanding access and success in education beyond high school. Through grants for research, innovation, communication, and evaluation, as well as policy education and leadership development, Lumina Foundation addresses issues that affect access and educational attainment among all students, particularly underserved student groups, including adult learners. The Foundation bases its mission on the belief that postsecondary education remains one of the most beneficial investments that individuals can make in themselves and that society can make in its people.
www.luminafoundation.org

**Jobs for the Future** believes that all young people should have a quality high school and postsecondary education, and that all adults should have the skills needed to hold jobs that pay enough to support a family. As a nonprofit research, consulting, and advocacy organization, JFF works to strengthen our society by creating educational and economic opportunity for those who need it most.
www.jff.org

# Federal Financial Aid: How Well Does It Work?

## SARAH E. TURNER
### *University of Virginia*

Much of the national policy debate during the 1990s in higher education has focused on the relationship between the cost of college and access to higher education. Yet, despite the marked federal investments in student financial aid—in terms of both loans and grants—surprisingly little is known about the effectiveness of these programs. Federal financial aid policy is often motivated by the argument that the existence of credit constraints prevents students, particularly those from the most economically disadvantaged backgrounds, from making optimal investments in higher education. Yet both researchers and policy makers have an incomplete picture of the prevailing magnitude of credit constraints, the responsiveness of students to changes in demand, and the effectiveness of federal policy in alleviating this problem.

The first section of this paper sets forth the public policy problem: Why is there a potential role for the government in financing higher education? In practice, we observe a substantial role of the federal government in financing higher education through grants, loans, and direct subsidies to universities. [Table 1 presents some basic figures on the magnitude of the federal investment in direct aid to college students.] Perhaps the most persuasive argument for government intervention in this market is that the provision of financial aid can help resolve credit constraints for individuals facing a positive return to higher education but unable to finance college costs out of pocket. Other arguments for a federal role in the provision of financial aid include the generation of some externalities—both nonmarket and fiscal—from individual investments in postsecondary education and the potential reduction of intergenerational inequality.

Empirical research on the relationship among family circumstances, postsecondary outcomes and federal financial aid falls into two broad categories: descriptive analysis and causal inference.[1] A number of important descriptive questions include the relationship between family income and educational attainment, trends in the educational attainment and choices of different demographic groups, or differences across geographic areas in educational outcomes. Measuring educational outcomes is certainly more difficult in practice than in theory and the importance of "getting the facts right" should not be underestimated in research discussions. Research focusing on causal inferences aims to understand the effects of interventions or policies on an outcome such as college attendance. The bulk of this chapter then focuses on the discussion of two broad questions:

The author would like to thank Neil Seftor and Kara Olson for excellent research assistance. In addition, Mike McPherson and Jim Heam raised important and interesting questions in response to an earlier draft.

444

## Table 1. Aid Awarded to Students by Source of Aid
### (millions of 1997-98 academic year dollars)

| | 1970-71 | | 1980-81 | | 1990-91 | | 1997-98(p) | |
|---|---|---|---|---|---|---|---|---|
| | $ | % of Aid | $ | % of Aid | $ | % of Aid | $ | % of Aid |
| **Federal Programs** | | | | | | | | |
| *Generally available aid* | | | | | | | | |
| Pell grants | 0 | 0.0% | 4,457 | 14.8% | 5,961 | 17.1% | 6,256 | 10.3% |
| SEOG Grants | 670 | 3.7% | 689 | 2.3% | 553 | 1.6% | 583 | 1.0% |
| State student inc. grants | 0 | 0.0% | 135 | 0.4% | 71 | 0.2% | 46 | 0.1% |
| Work-study | 816 | 4.5% | 1,233 | 4.1% | 879 | 2.5% | 1,007 | 1.7% |
| Perkins loan | 979 | 5.4% | 1,295 | 4.3% | 1,051 | 3.0% | 1,058 | 1.7% |
| GSL, PLUS, and SLS | 4,133 | 22.9% | 11,581 | 38.5% | 15,308 | 44.0% | 32,714 | 54.0% |
| | 6,598 | 36.5% | 19,389 | 64.4% | 23,823 | 68.3% | 41,663 | 69.8% |
| *Specially directed aid* | | | | | | | | |
| Social Security | 2,032 | 11.3% | 3,516 | 11.7% | 0 | 0.0% | 0 | 0.0% |
| Veterans benefits | 4,564 | 25.3% | 3,201 | 10.6% | 820 | 2.4% | 1,354 | 2.2% |
| Other | 499 | 2.8% | 718 | 2.4% | 1,004 | 2.9% | 969 | 1.6% |
| Total federal aid | 13,691 | 75.8% | 26,824 | 89.2% | 25,647 | 73.6% | 43,986 | 72.6% |
| State grant programs | 961 | 5.3% | 1,496 | 5.0% | 2,246 | 6.5% | 3,349 | 5.5% |
| Institutionally awarded aid | 3,407 | 18.9% | 3,033 | 10.1% | 6,958 | 20.0% | 13,196 | 21.8% |
| Total | 18,059 | 100.0% | 31,353 | 100.0% | 34,852 | 100.0% | 60,532 | 100.0% |

Notes:Table is from The College Board, *Trends in Student Aid*, 1998.
(p) Preliminary data.
GSL: Guaranteed Student Loans, PLUS: Parent Loans for Undergraduate Students,
and SLS: Supplemental Loans for Students.

1. What is the observed relationship between the financial resources available to a potential student and his or her investment in college training?
2. How does the availability of federal financial aid alter student behavior?

The second section of this paper turns to the empirical evidence on college enrollment and college completion by family income. The measurement of college enrollment and persistence by the resources of a young person's family is often used as a gauge of the extent to which public policies such as the Pell grant initiative help to facilitate economic opportunity. Yet, commonly used data do not provide clear answers to the most basic questions of how differences in financial resources at the time of college entry affect postsecondary educational attainment of students from different backgrounds. Difficulties associated with the measurement of family resources, the distinction between permanent and transitory income, and unobserved variation in student characteristics affecting the return to college all complicate attempts to bound the most basic question of the extent to which differences in family economic circumstances create barriers to postsecondary educational attainment. This section reviews the available estimates from traditional microdata and discusses new estimates from Fry and Turner (1999).[2]

The third section presents an analysis of the broad range of estimates of the change in behavior brought about by changes in college costs through federal financial aid programs. The largest piece of this puzzle concerns the question of how individuals respond to changes in college costs. In short, by how much do we expect the behavior of individuals to change with increases in tuition prices or additional financial aid? Essentially, this involves measuring the price elasticity of demand. Beyond the behavior of individuals, changes in the availability of federal financial aid may also affect the pricing strategies for colleges and universities and their allocation of financial aid resources. The analysis in this section concentrates on the trade-offs implicit in using different analytic strategies to identify responsiveness to changes in aid policy (e.g., cross-sectional variation versus changes over time). In addition to reviewing the range of estimates for the traditional college-age population, this section presents evidence on the relationship between federal aid policy and the enrollment behavior of non-traditional students. At issue is whether there are other research strategies and information collection initiatives to be considered which would help policy makers to choose how to target scarce financial aid resources.

The final section connects the statutory changes in policy to the observed changes in behavior and concludes with an eye to the future. In many respects, research in economics and higher education has not delivered precise point estimates that measure the effect of federal financial aid policy over the last three decades. At the same time, much progress has been made in better focusing the problem and structuring clear tests to measure the effects of variations in resources on student outcomes. This evidence has clear implications for how recently instituted programs such as the Hope credits may change access and choice. In this respect, refining the questions and narrowing the bounds are key objectives for researchers concerned with the impact of public policy in higher education into the next century.

## Section I: Why Federal Financial Aid?

While it has become increasingly common to take the federal role in financing college education for granted, it is worth reconsidering the motivation for a positive role for government intervention in this market. As a starting point, consider the individual decision to invest in education and the choices that follow given the opportunities and constraints in the market. To begin, defining education as an investment (rather than a consumption expenditure)[3] implies that individuals make choices based on the relative costs and benefits. Costs include forgone earnings, as well as direct college costs. Benefits include the expected increase in earnings, as well as any changes in non-monetary compensation. Education is thus seen to be a "good" investment if the benefits, at the margin, exceed the costs. Of course, the relative magnitude of costs and benefits is likely to depend on a myriad of characteristics including the extent to which the individual is "present oriented," individual ability, and the state of the labor market.

Thus, individuals considering the pursuit of a four-year college program compare the value of the discounted streams of payments afforded to them by college attendance and the alternative, which might be immediate participation in the labor market. Each individual would expect to face wage offers $Y_{it}^H$ and $Y_{it}^C$ where $Y_{it}^H$ is the annual earnings that an individual would expect without further training in year t, and $Y_{it}^C$ is the earnings level the individual would expect with college level training.[4] Given both a rate of return present for other investments in the market and an expected length of participation in the labor force, workers implicitly calculate whether "education pays" by comparing the present value of the stream of payments associated with a college education to the present value of the stream of payments associated with the alternative (terminating formal education after high school). If, while individuals are in school, they are not able to work (they must forgo wages and experience) and must also pay tuition (F), the value of each option then takes the following form with four years of college:

$$PDV^H = \sum_{t=1}^{R} \frac{Y_{it}^H}{(1+r)^t} = \frac{Y_{it}^H}{(1+r)} + \frac{Y_{it}^H}{(1+r)^2} + \cdots + \frac{Y_{it}^H}{(1+r)^R}$$

$$PDV^C = \sum_{t=1}^{4} \frac{-F_t}{(1+r)^t} + \sum_{t=5}^{R} \frac{Y_{it}^C}{(1+r)^t} = \frac{-F_t}{(1+r)^1} + \cdots + \frac{Y_{it}^C}{(1+r)^5} + \frac{Y_{it}^C}{(1+r)^6} + \cdots + \frac{Y_{it}^C}{(1+r)^R}$$

Thus, college can be said to be a good investment when $PDV^C - PDV^H > 0$. Or, rearranging terms and presenting the expression more fully,

$$\sum_{t=1}^{4} \frac{-F_t}{(1+r)^t} + \sum_{t=1}^{4} \frac{Y_{it}^H}{(1+r)^t} < \sum_{t=5}^{T} \frac{Y_{it}^C - Y_{it}^H}{(1+r)^t}$$

This expression can be viewed in terms of the costs (direct tuition payment and forgone earnings on the left hand side) and the benefits (higher wages on the right hand side of the inequality).

From these characteristics, we are able to derive a demand curve which specifies the amount—or type—of education that an individual will consume at any price. It follows that changes in any of the parameters in this expression affect individual propensities to attend college. Perhaps the most pivotal piece is the earnings increment associated with college attendance. A decrease in the college premium leads to both a decline in the benefits associated with college and an increase in the (relative) cost of time spent in school through forgone earnings. Increases in tuition price surely affect the decision at the margin and increases in financial aid reduce direct college costs from F to F-A, where A is the amount of financial aid.

The ability of individuals to borrow to make investments with positive expected values is key. Perhaps the most commonly cited motivation for federal intervention in higher education is that credit constraints prevent individuals from borrowing the optimal amount to finance college education. Credit constraints arise because education, unlike cars or coffee, is embodied and cannot be effectively collateralized. As such—and without indentured servitude—individuals can only rent their skills in the labor market. It follows that lenders in this market face a large unsecured risks and may well refuse to provide any funding, even when expected outcomes are likely to be quite positive.

Since potential students from the most economically disadvantaged families have fewer resources within the family unit to draw from, these students are likely to be disproportionately affected by credit constraints. Such a circumstance is inefficient and will exacerbate intergenerational inequality in outcomes. Not only will credit constrained students be less likely to enroll in college, but it may also be that they are unable to make the best matches between institutional characteristics and their own attributes if they are unable to finance the cost of the most preferred alternative.

While credit constraints are among the most-widely referenced justifications for federal intervention in the education market, the magnitude of this problem is considerably less clear as an empirical matter. Consideration of differences in education by family income provides one metric of the potential magnitude of this problem, though this is something less than a complete measure. One issue is that differences in family income may be correlated with other differences across families in resources that affect collegiate attainment. Closing the credit gap may leave a substantial resource gap if families living in poverty have lower investments in pre-collegiate education or in the information available about collegiate resources. [The next section provides some evidence about the limited information that is available on the relationship between family income and student out-comes.]

Heckman (1999) suggests a useful thought experiment to frame the difference between short-term credit constraints and other factors associated with family resources that affect student achievement. Consider the award of a million dollar lottery to a random sample of families with children of different ages. For those with older children near the completion of high school, there will be little opportunity to change long-run decisions that affect college preparedness. Lottery winners with young children may have the opportunity to invest in better primary and secondary schooling, as well as saving for college. If short-term credit constraints are substantial, we would expect to see large changes in college enrollment irrespective of the age of the children at the time the lottery was won (Heckman, 1999, pp. 95–96). While credit constraints and pre-collegiate preparedness are by no means mutually exclusive explanations, a better sense of the importance of these factors would help to sharpen the public policy alternatives.

Perhaps credit constraints are so widely cited by economists in discussing the motivation for federal financial aid because they have a relatively clear policy solution: provide students with the opportunity to borrow for higher education expenditures. Guaranteed student loans provide one solution to this type of market failure. Society as a whole may face much less risk than individuals as it is able to diversify across a wide range of students. As such, a related opportunity for federal intervention may be to reduce individual uncertainty associated with investments in education. One widely discussed—if not commonly implemented—solution to the problem is the introduction of income contingent loans in which the repayment level is based upon after college income.[5]

Other "market failures" which may merit federal intervention are both more difficult to identify and may not yield clear policy solutions. While economists have long focused on the question of investments in college assuming that students have full information about the costs and benefits of college, neither piece of information may be well-understood by students in their late teens, and those from the most disadvantaged backgrounds may have the greatest deficiencies in information. Information on college costs may be particularly difficult to obtain for students who are aid eligible, as benefit determination is likely to be a complex function of parental assets, parental income, tax rates, tuition levels, and family composition.

A second, more broadly based argument for direct federal subsidies in higher education is that spending on education beyond the level that individuals would choose at the market level may yield additional benefits in terms of both higher aggregate income and other gains in quality of life. In terms of the economic model, the basic picture is one in which the social benefits from education exceed the private benefits. Haveman and Wolfe (1984) provide a listing of these factors though it is inherently difficult to quantify the magnitude of such nonmarket effects. There remains considerable debate—and little empirical evidence—about the extent to which these externalities are quantitatively important. Plainly, measuring the externalities generated by higher education even as outputs—much less valuing them, is quite difficult. Yet, a proposition that has been widely repeated is that the social benefits to education may be concentrated in the pre-collegiate grades.

## Section II: Measuring Access and Attainment

Measures of college enrollment and collegiate attainment are among the most widely referenced numbers in any policy discussion about financial aid. Unfortunately, such reference measures—particularly when combined with measures of family resources—are among the most widely misunderstood and misused numbers in the policy debate. Perhaps because so few understand the pitfalls inherent in trying to measure collegiate enrollment and collegiate attainment by family income, few realize the potential errors that force a distortionary wedge between the empirical concept and the available measures.

Assertions like "in 1979, a student from the top income quartile was four times more likely to obtain a college degree by age 24 than a student coming from the bottom quartile; by 1994, he or she was 10 times more likely to get a degree" have been repeated so many times in the popular press, including citations in the *New York Times* and the *Chronicle of Higher Education,* that policymakers and researchers alike often fail to question the methods underlying such calculations.[6] That such statements have not drawn more skeptical responses is evidence of the near data vacuum faced by policy makers concerned with the empirical relationship between family resources and postsecondary educational outcomes. Bad data may actually contribute to bad policy and the presentation of alternative calculations on college participation and completion serves to underscore what is known (and unknown) about these important relationships.

Before pressing forward, some definitions and distinctions are in order. College enrollment specifies a flow variable, which is defined as enrollment at a fixed point in time or over a fixed interval of time. Other measures capture stock variables and quantify the amount of postsecondary education during any period in an interval. Among the stock variables most often considered are:

- *Participation*: Did the individual attend college for any period during the year in question?
- *Years of attainment*: How many years of college credit did the individual complete?[7]
- *Degree completion*: Did the student complete a BA degree, an Associate's degree, or another widely recognized postsecondary credential?

While there is an unambiguous relationship between the flow measures of enrollment at a point in time and the stock measures of attainment, the measures of attainment by family resources are, in principle, the telling indicators of the long-term social and economic significance of differences in educational attainment. From a policy perspective, understanding the link between the change in the availability of federal financial aid and collegiate attainment is crucial. If the student at the margin of enrolling in college is likely to complete a modest number of credit hours, the expected return may be much smaller than if the availability of aid changes both enrollment and persistence.

Beyond considering measures of enrollment and attainment, there is a qualitative dimension of the collegiate experience that is rarely mentioned in the national dialogue. The external margin—whether or not one attends—seems to dominate the internal margin of college quality in most policy discussions. This is particularly unfortunate if some of the largest social gains follow from a better matching of students, particularly those from disadvantaged backgrounds, with institutions. Recognizing that there is an implicit trade-off between increasing access and improving college quality among economically disadvantaged students is sorely lacking from policy discussions. Yet, the ability of researchers to quantify this trade-off is severely constrained by lack of data.

Consider the pieces of information that are necessary to calculate the enrollment rate by family resources before turning to the discussion of the nationally available data.

1. Individual age and educational attainment
2. Parental earnings and, ideally, assets

Given the proliferation of micro-data analysis over the last three decades, there has been a growth in the availability of survey data with information on adult earnings and educational attainment. The remaining gap in the data is in the link between parents and their children. Surveys that focus on the educational choices and outcomes of young adults often have sparse or limited information on parental resources. In many cases, information on parental income will be reported by the children. Such measures are likely to be error ridden, perhaps indications of consumption rather than financial resources. Moreover, it may be that "permanent" resources are more telling, as it has long been recognized that the measurement of the effects of parental income on the outcomes of children may be clouded by the mismeasurement of parental income.[8] Even if fuller parental records were available for these surveys, the infrequency of observation and relatively small sample size impose substantial limitations on researchers' ability to make direct calculations of educational attainment by parental income.

The current population survey (CPS) is, perhaps, the most frequently referenced source for data on enrollment rates for recent college graduates. Unambiguously, these data show the overall rise in the college enrollment rate of recent high school graduates, from about 49 percent in 1980 to 67 percent in 1997 (*Digest of Education Statistics*, 1999, Table 184). Unfortunately, the ability to link young people and their parents is limited immediately after high school graduation and nearly impossible when individuals are in their early twenties. The problem is that individuals who are no longer residing with their parents are not a random slice of the population. Potential students who come from families with few financial resources are more likely to strike out on their own, leaving disproportionately wealthy students in the pool of records with viable parental income.

Moreover, sample sizes become excessively small and even statistically unreliable, particularly when estimating the enrollment of minorities or the college entry of recent high school graduates. Furthermore, it is difficult to distinguish between those attending college part-time and those attending full-time. As a result, college participation rates seem higher than they otherwise would be. Moreover, if minorities or low-income students are more likely to attend college part-time, this failure understates the differences in participation rates among various groups (Hauser, 1991). Finally, other attributes that may impact college participation are not measured at all, such as academic ability.

Adding a time series dimension to the problem makes the measurement even more complicated for several reasons. First, secular changes in educational options and labor market opportunities affect the relative merits of continued residence with one's parents or living independently. Secondly, changes over time in the distribution of income make the measurement of family income in the tails of the distribution particularly important. While interquartile ranges are often points of consideration in the literature (e.g., comparing the attainment of students in the bottom fourth to students in the top fourth), the precipitous widening of the variance in earnings over the last 15 years underscores the importance of asking whether an individual or family in the bottom quartile of the income distribution is likely to have more or less real income than a family at the same point in the distribution in an earlier period. The significance of this point for public policy in the context of the measurement of participation in higher education merits discussion by example. Suppose the college enrollment rate of students from the bottom quartile of the income distribution drops from 30 percent to 15 percent. What does it mean? Well, one hypothesis is that college costs or some other determinant of college enrollment shifted, thereby affecting the behavior and options of all students in this interval. An alternative explanation is that the distribution of income shifted such that students in this segment of the income distribution were from families that were less well off than in the previous period. Increasing poverty and increasing college costs surely both affect investments in education; however, appropriate policy remedies to address these issues are simply quite different.

In summary, a rapidly growing literature has examined the role of family origins in college success using longitudinal data on youth. Most of it has concentrated on entry and enrollment in college, not the attainment of postsecondary credentials. While few would disagree that secondary achievement is a key determinant of postsecondary attainment, there is solid empirical evidence suggesting that the income gap in educational attainment remains sizable after controlling for achievement at the secondary level. The recent analysis by Ellwood and Kane (1998) uses the U.S. Department of Education longitudinal studies of recent high school graduating classes to examine time trends in entry into postsecondary education. Classifying high school seniors by their contemporaneous family income quartile, they find that entry into postsecondary education has risen over time for all seniors, but more so for seniors from the richest income quartile of families than seniors from the poorest quartile. That is, the "income gap" in postsecondary entry may have widened over time.

Recent analysis with my colleague Rick Fry of ETS using the Panel Study of Income Dynamics (PSID) helps to narrow the range of estimates of the magnitude of the gap in college completion by family income and the extent to which this gap has changed over time. The PSID is unique among longitudinal micro datasets in that it includes panel data from a range of age cohorts, beginning in the late 1960s. Records from "parents" and the linked information on their children yields measures that are less subject to reporting error than in many of the longitudinal surveys. However, the largest potential drawback to using the PSID is that at the level of any single birth cohort, sample sizes are relatively small, necessitating some aggregation and somewhat larger confidence intervals than optimal.

In short, we do not find that the relationship between real income and educational outcomes has changed over this interval, though the confidence intervals are quite large. We have considered a range of alternative specification of the period effects and the characterization of family income, as shown in Table 2 for the outcome variable of baccalaureate completion. For example, we have specified real income as a quadratic function, as a logarithmic series, and as a set of discrete categories; we have considered both an interval and a continuous specification of the time effects as well. Without question, measured family income is strongly associated with college completion.[9] However, in no case do we find a significant interaction between period and family resources.

#### Table 2. Logit Estimates of the Effect of Family Income on College Completion

|  | (1) | | | (2) | |
| --- | --- | --- | --- | --- | --- |
|  | Coefficient | Std Err |  | Coefficient | Std Err |
| Female | -0.1566 | (0.1441) | Female | -0.2078 | (0.1468) |
| Yrg 74-78 | 0.1649 | (0.2583) | Time | 0.0802 | (0.3826) |
| Yrg 79-83 | 0.3583 | (0.2751) | Time-Squared | 0.0122 | (0.0049) |
| Real Fam Y < 30 k | -2.2761 | (0.4972) | Ln Real Family Y | 1.6871 | (0.2837) |
| Real Fam Y 30-45 | -1.3302 | (0.3368) | Time*Ln Real Fam Y | -0.0203 | (0.0346) |
| Real Fam Y 45-60 | -0.7634 | (0.3059) | Constant | -19.5314 | (3.0934) |
| Yrg 74-78*Real Fam Y < 30 k | 0.0937 | (0.7492) |  |  |  |
| Yrg 74-78*Real Fam Y 30-45 | 0.1836 | (0.4799) |  |  |  |
| Yrg 74-78*Real Fam Y 45-60 | -0.5507 | (0.4162) |  |  |  |
| Yrg 79-83*Real Fam Y < 30 k | 0.2369 | (0.6808) |  |  |  |
| Yrg 79-83*Real Fam Y 30-45 | -0.4429 | (0.5196) |  |  |  |
| Yrg 79-83*Real Fam Y 45-60 | 0.1647 | (0.4223) |  |  |  |
| Constant | -0.6679 | (0.2128) |  |  |  |
|  |  |  |  |  |  |
| N= | 1381 | | | 1381 | |
| Chi-Sq | 100.08 | | | 95.48 | |
| Log L | -625.36 | | | -616.67 | |

Yrg = Year group
Source: Observations include PSID individuals age 16 between 1969 and 1983. In model (1), those age 16 between 1969 and 1973. In model (2), "Time" is a continuous variable beginning with 0 in 1969. Estimates are from Turner and Fry (1999).

Thus, neither the effects of increasing college tuition costs nor other changes in the behavioral relationship between family income and postsecondary educational attainment are compelling explanations for the rise in the absolute difference in educational attainment between those in the top and bottom quartiles of the income distribution. This analysis points to increased income inequality as the explanation for the rise in interquartile measures of educational attainment by family income.

The addition of other measures of family resources, including parental education, moderates but does not eliminate the link between individual educational attainment and family income. The addition of a measure of mother's education reduces the magnitude of the income effects quite markedly, relative to those in the prior table. The addition of other covariates for family structure and state fixed effects has little additional effect on the magnitude of the family income effects or the maternal education effects.

As an empirical matter, there are a number of points of agreement and a number of unresolved questions with regard to the relationship between the income of a potential student's family and his or her outcomes later in life. First, students from relatively low income families are less likely to enroll in college and less likely to complete college than students from relatively affluent families. This difference narrows once measures of student achievement are considered, but persists all the same.

Second, gaps are apparent in both initial enrollment and measures of educational attainment such as years of schooling and baccalaureate degree attainment. This empirical regularity raises the policy question of whether the individual and public returns would be better placed in efforts promoting persistence rather than those emphasizing the margin of college enrollment.

A third question concerns the issue of whether gaps in collegiate attainment between individuals from more or less affluent families widen or narrow over the life course. (Perhaps only the PSID would provide answers to this question.) The answer would appear to be of significance because a persistent widening of the gap would underscore concerns about intergenerational transmission of educational and earnings inequality. A narrowing of the gap would fulfill a necessary—though not sufficient—condition for the explanation of differences in attainment based on credit constraints.

If analysis of the magnitude of the difference in educational gaps by family resources appears unsettled, the literature on how public policy initiatives change postsecondary outcomes must be regarded as decidedly chaotic. In the next section, we focus on the measurement of the behavioral effects of means-tested federal financial aid on student outcomes.

# Section III: Federal Financial Aid and Access

In brief, the era of federal support to individuals to cover the costs of college was initiated with the G.I. Bill (the Serviceman's Readjustment Act) in 1944. But, it was not until the introduction of the Pell Grant program (formerly known as the BEOG) through the Higher Education Act of 1972 that fully portable financial aid became available to Americans passing only a means test. Table 1 (page 440) illustrates the dramatic rise in the pool of resources devoted to portable grant aid for low income students, with expenditures on the Pell program rising to over $4 billion in 1980 and reaching $6.25 billion in the late 1990s. In the last decade, the growth in the availability of loan funds has created a marked change in the distribution of federal financial aid dollars. To be sure, a range of more narrowly targeted federal programs also provide aid to potential students. Examples include veterans and G.I. benefits, Social Security Student Benefits to the children of deceased beneficiaries, and the recently introduced Hope credits.

## Empirical Methods

Assessing the impact of changes in federal financial aid programs requires consideration of two related questions. First, how do institutions—colleges and universities—adjust to changes in the availability of federal financial aid?[10] Second, what type of behavioral adjustment would we expect from individuals in response to changes in the availability of federal financial aid? In particular, are additional aid dollars going to students who would have attended college in the absence of the federal programs? An additional question is whether these resources affect the college choices of potential students?

Focusing on the individual's investment decision, federal financial aid unambiguously reduces the direct cost of college. Still, even if federal aid paid the full tuition cost of college, individuals would still "give up" some opportunities in the labor market in order to attend college. To measure the effect of federal financial aid, it is useful to frame the problem in terms of an experiment and then discuss why direct observation presents additional challenges.

First, suppose we observed a group of individuals with different levels of income (high and low). The low income students attain, on average, two years of college. The high income students achieve, on average, four years of college. The research question would be to discern whether increasing financial aid to low income individuals would change their educational investments. The open question is whether there are other differences—beyond resources—between high and low income potential students that affect both the enrollment decisions and the likelihood of receiving aid. Ideally, one might set up an experiment and offer aid awards to some of the low income students (the treatment group) and to compare their choices to the decisions of those who did not receive aid (the control group).

Yet, in a world without experimental evidence, the researcher faces substantial challenges in trying to infer the causal effect of a change in aid (or college cost more generally) on educational attainment from observed outcomes. The first problem, alluded to above, is that aid recipients may differ from those who don't receive aid in ways that are also associated with decisions to invest in education. If the objective is to estimate the causal impact of aid on educational attainment in a nonexperimental setting, the researcher may attempt to measure these other factors such as individual ability, family assets, and tastes for education directly. Inclusion of such factors in the regression equation would thus resolve the bias caused by omitted variables. However, it is rarely the case that all such differences are observed by the researcher and can be included in the estimation.

Consider a simple example across states. We certainly observe wide differences across states in tuition prices and we also observe that some states provide means-tested aid to residents. Yet, comparisons of educational investments across states with lower tuition (or higher aid) will not provide unbiased indicators of the effects of college costs. States with the lower college costs may also differ systematically in other dimensions that affect postsecondary investments such as resources expended at the secondary level or parental educational attainment.

In principle, we might think of including a range of controls. However, even the most thorough cross-sectional approaches are unlikely to allay concerns that unobserved differences across individuals or geographic regions are affecting results. Thus, adding changes over time as another dimension of variation often provides considerable leverage on this problem.

The most straightforward specification is known in the econometrics and treatment literature as "differences in differences." Meyer (1995) discusses this approach in detail, though the intuition is straightforward. Consider the case where low income individuals are eligible for financial aid in period 1, but not in period 0 and we observe similar populations of individuals and their educational investments in period 1 and period 0. Examining the change in the enrollment behavior of the low income population between period 0 and period 1 may yield spurious estimates if there are other changes that affect enrollment over time.[11] "Differences in differences" estimates focus on the extent to which the change in the behavior over an interval for the treatment group differs from the change observed for the control group. In a regression context:

$$ED_j = \alpha + \beta_1 Period1_j + \beta_2 IncGroup_j + \beta_3 Period1_j \times IncGroup_j + \varepsilon_j$$

The estimated parameter $\beta_3$ measures the program effect. When changes in the availability of aid are large and there is a sharp break between periods, the differences in differences approach will be particularly powerful (Angrist and Krueger, 1998). The transparency of this approach is certainly appealing. Note, however, that the difference in difference estimator is not immune to potential bias. The key identifying assumption is that $\beta_3$ would be equal to zero in the absence of the change in the availability of aid. Difference estimators may be viewed as a special case of a more general set of panel data methods, including fixed effects.

Two important caveats merit note when considering the application of these approaches to answering the question of how will a change in federal financial aid affect investments in education of the intended beneficiaries. First, to make a meaningful statement about the impact of any intervention we need to be able to quantify the size of the program effect. Considering the price elasticity of demand—the percentage change in educational attainment associated with a percentage change in college costs—is a preferred metric, though the higher education literature is often inclined to present the change in levels. For example, if college costs decreased by $1,000, what would be the expected change in years of educational attainment. It is often—and likely—the case that statutory changes in the availability of financial aid differ markedly from the actual change in college costs. Colleges and universities are likely to adjust their aid allocations and their prices—in some cases quite markedly—to changes in the availability of federal financial aid (see Turner, 1998, for a full discussion of these effects). In this regard, researchers may face some difficulty in quantifying the program effect. Yet, even when the net change in college costs is directly observed, some caution is in order in making comparisons across programs. By and large, each program is a bundle of information and aid, and understanding the separate effects is not easy. More importantly, the marginal changes and average changes may be quite different.

Secondly, the techniques discussed above are inherently partial equilibrium measures. They do not account for how the return to skill or other factors affecting the individual's investment decision will adjust in the face of large-scale changes in the cost of college. In brief, increases in federal financial aid may increase the supply of college-educated workers which in turn reduces the wages that they will be offered in the labor market. Heckman, Lochner, and Taber (1998) model such general equilibrium adjustments to a change in the subsidy for higher education and find an appreciably smaller impact of aid on collegiate attainment than would be predicted assuming that wages and tuition prices remained fixed.

## Empirical Results

Cross-sectional estimates of enrollment sensitivity to changes in student aid estimated by Manski and Wise in their 1983 monograph *College Choice in America* produced estimates of the effect of the Pell program on the enrollment rates of low income students in the range of an increase of between 20 and 40 percent. Manski and Wise used data from the National Longitudinal Survey of the Class of 1972 (NLS 72) and presented a carefully specified model that accounted for the application decision, the student aid amount, and other achievement and family factors that might be thought to affect outcomes.

Yet such estimates are appreciably larger than corresponding evidence that also includes changes over time. A straightforward differences in differences strategy, employed by Lee Hansen in 1983, failed to support these early estimates and instead indicated that the likely enrollment effect of the introduction of the Pell grant was not appreciably different from zero. Kane (1994, 1995) revisits Hansen's analysis and addresses some initial concerns by focusing on the results for women (who were less likely to have been unaffected by distortions associated with Vietnam) and using slightly longer intervals before and after the introduction of the Pell program.

In the same analysis, Kane also uses a panel data estimation strategy of a longer time horizon in which he estimates the aid eligibility for each individual and then uses this variable as a regressor. In these estimates, the effect of the Pell grant program is positive in sign but appreciably smaller in magnitude than the corresponding estimates of individual responsiveness to changes in tuition prices.

While it is often the case that those involved in the public dialogue find it convenient to discuss enrollment behavior in terms of an expected "percentage point change in response to a $1,000 change in price," analysts should be particularly wary of cross-study comparisons in this metric. First, it is important to convert to constant dollars as $1,000 in 1976 would buy far more "college" than it does today. Moreover, increasing the enrollment rate from, say, 40 percent to 45 percent, is not necessarily equivalent to changing the enrollment rate from 80 percent to 85 percent. Given the more general confusion about the amount of educational attainment corresponding to any change in enrollment, it would be far preferable if policy analysts resolved to present the elasticities associated with years of educational attainment. Given the dependent variables used in many early studies, it is simply not possible to make such conversions from the data at hand.

By comparing implied elasticities across studies, we begin to bound the expected impact of any change in federal aid on collegiate attainment. Table 3 presents elasticities of enrollment demand from a number of well-regarded studies on the impact of changes in the net cost of attending college, whether through increases in tuition rates or changes in financial aid programs, on enrollment rates. Although each study uses different data sources, reference time periods, and methods of analysis, they all estimate a percentage point change in participation rates due to a change in the net cost of college. In order to compare these studies, a common elasticity of demand for college is reported in the final column of the table. The net cost (tuition and fee) elasticity of demand is based on average in-state tuition and fees in 2-year and 4-year public institutions, as well as the college enrollment rate of 18- to 24-year-olds, in the year in which the study estimated its percentage

**Table 3. Comparison of estimated behavioral responses to changes in college costs**

| Paper | Data | Estimation Strategy | Elasticity of Demand | |
|---|---|---|---|---|
| Dynarski (1999) | National Longitudinal Survey of Youth (NLSY) | Difference in differences approach comparing students before and after the elimination of the Social Security Student Benefit Program | 2-yr total cost: -0.62 | 4-yr total cost: -0.68 |
| White 1Q (lowest) | Current Population Survey (CPS) | Pooled times series | -1.21 | -1.31 |
| 2Q | | | -.82 | -.89 |
| 3Q | | | -.56 | -.61 |
| 4Q (highest) | | | -.18 | -.19 |
| Black 1Q (lowest) | | | -2.45 | -2.66 |
| 2Q | | | -2.05 | -2.22 |
| 3Q | | | -1.83 | -1.99 |
| 4Q (highest) | | | -1.41 | -1.53 |
| McPherson and Schapiro (1991) | Current Population Survey and American Freshman Survey | Regressed participation rate on income and net cost | -0.88 | -.93 |
| Leslie and Brinkman (1987) | | Standardized 25 studies on the effect of net costs on college enrollment | -1.89 | -1.77 |
| Manski and Wise (1983) | National Longitudinal Survey of the Class of 1972 | Structural cross-sectional model of college application, admission and enrollment | -2.01 | 0.14 |

Notes: The above arc elasticities are calculated using the enrollment rates and change in college costs estimated in the noted paper. However, to standardize these elasticities, a common cost measure is used throughout the elasticity calculation. Specifically, average tuition and required fees paid by full-time equivalent students in both 4-year or 2-year public institutions were obtained from the U.S. Department of Education, National Center for Education Statistics' Institutional Surveys (HEGIS/IPEDS). The opportunity cost of attending college (forgone earnings) is calculated from data in the U.S. Census Bureau's Historical Income Tables (the P-28 Series). We assume that students could have earned the average income of 18- to 24-year-olds with a high school education during the nine months of the school year if they didn't attend school. We used nominal cost data for the year specified in the paper.

point decline. The total cost elasticity adds to the tuition and fees to the average earnings of 18- to 24-year-olds with only a high school education, reflecting the fact that the full cost of college enrollment includes both the direct cost and the opportunity cost.

The analysis of enrollment responses to within state changes in college costs by Tom Kane is one of the most convincing analyses of the behavioral responses to changes in college costs. The results suggest an average total cost elasticity of about .6 for whites and about 2 for blacks, with much larger elasticities for low income youth than those from more affluent backgrounds. Using a very different source of variation, the recent evaluation of the effect of the Social Security Student Benefit Program by Susan Dynarski also suggests a quite large impact of grant aid on educational investments. Before 1982, this program provided about $6,400 in tuition and living expenses for the children of deceased Social Security recipients. Dynarski compares the educational attainment of potential beneficiaries before and after the termination of the program and finds that the educational attainment of this group declined much more than for the population in general after the program was eliminated.[12] The implied total cost elasticity from these estimates is about .7. The McPherson-Schapiro estimates are also in this range, if a bit larger, with an implied total cost elasticity associated of about 0.9.

The widely cited consensus estimates from Leslie and Brinkman (1987) are much larger, with an implied total cost elasticity on the order of 1.8. Plainly, this number is much closer to the cross-sectional estimates from the Manski and Wise study than it is to any of the estimates that derive

## Table 4. Changes in College Enrollment Rates of Females With the Establishment of the Pell Grant Program

| | (1) | (2) | | (3) | (4) |
|---|---|---|---|---|---|
| Black | -0.027 | 0.044 | Black | 0.020 | 0.022 |
| | (0.023) | (0.020) | | (0.005) | (0.006) |
| Post | 0.025 | -0.008 | Post | 0.018 | 0.018 |
| | (0.010) | (0.010) | | (0.002) | (0.002) |
| Black * Post | 0.027 | -0.015 | Black * Post | 0.019 | 0.017 |
| | (0.028) | (0.025) | | (0.007) | (0.007) |
| Lowest Income Quartile * Post | -0.026 | 0.005 | Lowest Income Quartile * Post | 0.011 | |
| | (0.023) | (0.022) | | (0.005) | |
| | | | Pell Eligible * Post | | 0.011 |
| | | | | | (0.004) |
| Family Background Included? | No | Yes | | | |
| Number of Observations | 12,163 | 12,163 | Number of Observations | 62,405 | 62,405 |

Notes. Columns (1) and (2) are from Kane (1995), Table 5, and consist of changes in college enrollment of dependent 18-19 year old females using data from 1970-72 and 1973-77; each equation included dummy variables for income quartiles, region, and a constant. Columns (3) and (4) are from Seftor and Turner (2000), and consist of changes in college enrollment of independent 22-34 year old females using data from 1969-72 and 1974-77; each equation included dummy variables for region, age ranges, and a constant.

their identification from variation over time. While there is certainly room for further discussion in this arena, the difficulty in capturing the causal effect of aid in cross-sectional estimation points to the likelihood of overestimation of the behavioral effect of aid on enrollment in these analyses.

In a very recent monograph that synthesizes much of this work, Kane (1999) puts forward the hypothesis that the small behavioral response to the Pell grant program may reflect the high information costs associated with determining program eligibility. This type of explanation is a compelling and intriguing counterbalance to policy debates focusing only on the level of aid awards rather than the full set of program design parameters. It is my understanding that Kane is now spearheading a modest experimental design in the Boston area to test this hypothesis more rigorously.

Still, one view of the research on the behavioral response to the program is that it has focused nearly exclusively on only a modest fraction of the total pool of potential beneficiaries. While dependent students—those who are in their late teens and still residing with their parents—may have been the "typical" college student in 1960, this is far from true today.[13] Consideration of how the introduction of the Pell program changed the behavior of older students—those well-beyond the expectation of receiving college financing from their parents—has been largely ignored in the literature. A recent analysis with my colleague Neil Seftor does suggest some new insight to this point.

We find that, particularly for women, the introduction of the Pell program had a substantial effect on the educational attainment of those in their twenties and thirties. While Kane finds that college enrollment rates grew by 2.6 percentage points more slowly for dependent 18- to 19-year-old women in the lowest income quartile during the period around the inception of the Pell program, we find that the enrollment rates of older, independent women grew by 1.1 percentage points or a relative increase of about 13 percent in college enrollment for this age group. Using the average Pell grant, this implies an elasticity of about −.8 asssociated with an increase in student aid for this population.

We also find that changes in program parameters in the late 1980s that essentially eliminated eligibility for those without dependents who were younger than 24 also had a substantial and negative impact on enrollment. For independent women in their early 20s (21 to 23), college enrollment rates grew by more than 3 percentage points more slowly, when the treatment group is defined as those who are single without children. Using a more detailed estimate of those who would have been eligible for a Pell grant were it not for the change in 1987 shows an even greater effect, over 5 percent, on enrollment rates. Furthermore, when the analysis is confined to those most likely to be affected, the 23-year-olds, the impact is a 10 percent reduction in enrollment rates.

## Section IV: The Evidence and Public Policy: Questions for the Future

As stated at the outset, economists and education analysts have been considering the question of how the demand for higher education changes with adjustments in financial aid for more than three decades. Despite hundreds of research efforts, the range of empirical estimates is wide and there is a decided lack of consensus about how the evidence informs public policy.

In attempting to narrow the range of estimates, several points are unambiguously clear. First, far more precision is necessary in defining the research question(s) in terms of the target population and the outcome variables. The underlying investment decision, as well as the financing options, is fundamentally different for an 18-year-old and a 28-year-old. Simple-minded extrapolation of the results from one group to another will not suffice. The population considering investments in education is no longer comprised mainly of students in their late teens who reside with Mom and Dad. Just as the same empirical estimates are unlikely to apply to both groups, it is certainly also the case that a 'one size fits all' approach to student aid policy may be inappropriate.

In terms of outcome variables, the research community needs to move beyond the beltway fascination with "access" defined as enrollment rates. Whether someone enrolled in—perhaps not even completing—a course or two in October has little economic resonance. A result in which "enrollment" devoid of attainment affects later life outcomes suggests a serious hole in models ascribing human capital or the generation of productive skills to postsecondary experiences.

To "do better" as researchers in capturing outcome measures and the behavior of a demographically diverse population probably requires more data—and more creative use of existing resources. While the longitudinal micro surveys such as NLS 72, High School and Beyond, NLSY, and NELS have provided a number of insights they are also limited in some marked ways:

- Information on family resources is often poorly reported if available at all. Since the question of the magnitude of credit constraints is at the heart of many policy debates, such omissions are particularly regrettable.
- Many microdata sets focus on experiences of people in their young adult years. While educational investments at this stage are certainly important, it is increasingly necessary to also examine the choices made by students in mid-life.
- Finally, few national data sets are large enough to provide the capacity to test hypotheses across states or across institutional types. Both economies of scale and recent advancements in computer aided survey techniques suggest that increasing sample sizes would be a most worthwhile endeavor.

Turning to empirical techniques, the research literature has moved far past the point where cross-sectional estimates with little truly exogenous variation in financial aid availability add much beyond recyclables. Ending—or failing to publish—papers and "policy reports" that rely on such strategies would be an enormous public service. Students, faculty and policy makers need to be relentless in convincing themselves that the variation in financial aid eligibility used to identify educational attainment effects is truly exogenous. Since there are only a limited number of cases of national variation in aid policies, it may be that some of the most fruitful unexplored natural experiments occur at the state level. A recent example is Susan Dynarski's work on the Hope program in Georgia (Dynarski, 2000).

Finally, much more effort needs to be devoted to the analysis of how program design—not just aid amounts—affects student decisions. A particular problem discussed by Tom Kane is whether the complexity of federal programs and the difficulty in calculating the aid awards ex ante may substantially dilute the impact of many policies. We do not, at present, have many clear tests of how differences in the timing and reporting requirements affect student decisions. This is an area of tremendous importance since it may be that modest reforms will yield large improvements in the effectiveness of federal financial aid.

At the end of the day, researchers and policy analysts concerned with higher education are fortunate to operate in a climate where educational attainment is high on the national agenda. The time is now to rise to the challenge and to push the research frontier forward to provide policy makers with the information necessary to improve the efficiency and effectiveness of the full range of federal financial aid programs.

# References

Adelman, C. (1999). *Answers in the toolbox: Academic intensity, attendance patterns, and bachelor's degree attainment.* Available: http://www.ed.gov/pubs/Toolbox/Title.html

Angrist, J., and Krueger, A. (1998). Empirical strategies in labor economics. Princeton University Industrial Relations Working Paper #401.

Barton, P. (1997). *Toward Inequality.* Princeton, NJ.: Educational Testing Service.

Bound, J., and Turner, S. (2000). Going to war and going to college: Did World War II and the G.I. Bill increase educational attainment for returning veterans? PSC Research Report 00-453. September.

Cameron, S., and Heckman, J. (1999). Can tuition policy combat rising wage inequality? In M. Kosters (ed.), *Financing College Tuition.* Washington, D.C.: AEI Press.

Dynarski, S. (2000). Hope for Whom? Financial aid for the middle class and its impact on College Attendance. NBER Working Paper 7756

Ellwood, D., and Kane, T. (1998). Who is getting a college education: Family background and the growing gaps in enrollment. Kennedy School of Government Mimeo.

Friedman, M., and Kuznets, S. (1945). *Income from Individual Professional Practice.* New York: NBER.

Fry, R., and Turner, S. (1999). Growing college inequality? Evidence on family income background and college completion and college access. Mimeo for presentation at American Educational Research Association, Montreal, April, 1999.

Hansen, W. L. (1983). Impact of student financial aid on access. In J. Fromkin (ed.), *The Crisis in Higher Education.* New York: Academy of Sciences.

Hauser, R. (1991). What happens to youth after high school? *Focus, 13*(3): Institute for Research on Poverty, University of Wisconsin, Madison.

Haveman, R., and Wolfe, B. (1984). Schooling and economic well-being: The role of non-market effects. *Journal of Human Resources, XIX*(3).

Heckman, J. (1999). Doing it right: Job training and education. *The Public Interest, 135*(2):86.

Heckman, J. L., Lochner, and Taber, C. (1998). Explaining rising wage inequality: Explorations with a dynamic general equilibrium model of earnings with heterogeneous agents. *Review of Economic Dynamics, 1*(1): 1–54.

Kane, T. (1994). College entry by blacks since 1970: The role of college costs, family background, and the returns to education. *Journal of Political Economy, 102*(5).

Kane, T. (1995). *Rising Public College Tuition and College Entry: How Well do Public Subsidies Promote Access to College?* NBER Working Paper No. 5164.

Kane, T. (1999). *The Price of Admission.* Washington, D.C.: The Brookings Institution.

Kane, T., and Rouse, C. (1999). The community college: training students at the margin between education and work. *Journal of Economic Perspectives.*

Leslie, L., and Brinkman, P. (1987). Student price response in higher education: the student demand studies. *Journal of Higher Education, 58*(2).

Manski, C. F., and Wise, D. (1983). *College Choice in America.* Cambridge: Harvard University Press.

Manski, C. F. (1992). *Parental Income and College Opportunity.* Institute for Research on Poverty.

McPherson, M., and Schapiro, M. 1991. Does student aid affect college enrollment? New evidence on a persistent controversy. *American Economic Review, 81*(March): 309–318.

McPherson, M., and Schapiro, M. (1993). Measuring the effects of federal student aid. In M. McPherson et al. (eds), *Paying the Piper: Productivity, Incentives, and Financing in U.S. Higher Education.* Ann Arbor: University of Michigan Press.

Meyer, B. (1995). Natural and quasi-experiments in economics. *Journal of Business and Economic Statistics, 13*(2): 151–61.

Mortenson, T. G. (1988). Pell grant program changes and their effects on applicant eligibility, 1973–1974 to 1988–89. *ACT Student Financial Aid Research Report Series,* 88-1.

Nerlove, M. (1975). Some problems in the use of income-contingent loans for the finance of higher education. *The Journal of Political Economy, 83*(1): 157–184.

Seftor, N., and Turner, S. (2000). Back to school: federal student aid policy and adult college enrollment. Virginia Project on the Economics of Higher Education working paper.

Stanley, M. (1999). College education and the mid-century G.I. bills: Effects on access and educational attainment. Mimeo.

Turner, S. (1998). Does federal aid affect the price students pay for college? Evidence from the Pell program. Mimeo.

## Notes

1. This distinction can also be applied to empirical studies more generally. See Angrist and Krueger (1998) for a full discussion.

2. An innovation of this analysis is the use of full and complete data on both parental resources and student outcomes. The long history of the Panel Study of Income Dynamics facilitates examination of complete educational trajectories (as opposed to just initial college enrollment in the year subsequent to high school completion). Moreover, the observation of different cohorts from the 1970s through the 1990s provides an opportunity to examine the extent to which the relationship between family resources and access and persistence has changed over time.

3. The consumption dimension of education is a complication to the basic framework that needs to be taken seriously and considered in more depth. One implication is that the income elasticity of demand for college education will be positive, implying that potential students from relatively affluent families will invest in more education in the absence of credit constraints. As such, it may be that without further government intervention, this factor exacerbates of intergenerational inequality.

4. This setup is very typical in the labor economics literature. [See Ehrenberg and Smith, *Modern Labor Economics,* for one textbook treatment.] Note that the expected earnings levels need not be constant across individuals. Moreover, we might expect earnings differences to increase over time.

5. Milton Friedman and Simon Kuznets introduced this idea in 1945. Yale University provided a limited test of the program; see Nerlove (1975) for full analysis. While the idea of an income contingent loan solves some market imperfections, it also represents potential "costs" as the structure of the program may generate some adverse selection (students with low expected incomes would be most likely to enroll) as well as moral hazard in the sense that securitization reduces incentives to "work hard" after college.

6. Such estimates were initially reported by Thomas Mortenson in a publication titled *Postsecondary Educational Opportunity*, and are repeated in Barton (1997).

7. Note that "years" as a unit of measure may have become increasingly anachronistic over time as individuals are less likely to attend school full-time. Increasingly, students accumulate college credits on a part-time basis.

8. In the classical case, mismeasurement of permanent income in a regression model of enrollment on income will produce a downward biased estimate of the effect of changes in income on educational outcomes. In this regard, transitory variation in parental earnings yields a situation in which a long horizon of earnings data may be a more informative measure of the effect of resources on educational attainment because it is an indicator of ability to pay. This explanation differs from the Cameron and Heckman (1999) hypothesis that parental earnings early in the life cycle contribute to precollegiate investments in human capital.

9. Recent research efforts have focused more carefully on the degree completion outcome. For example, Adelman (1999) finds that a measure of the academic content and performance from secondary schools and continuous participation once enrolled in higher education have considerable explanatory power beyond family income and other measures of socioeconomic status. Of course, the correlation among these variables is likely to be high and family resources may well affect the quality of education a student receives at the secondary level.

10. This topic is pursued at length in Turner (1998).

11. If the return to education increased between period 0 and period 1, the direct comparison would overestimate the change due to an increase in the availability of financial aid. Both the low income, as well as high income, individuals would have increased their educational investments.

12. Another set of behavioral estimates follows from review of the enrollment response to the educational benefits provided to returning servicemen under the G.I. Bills. Bound and Turner (2000) use changes in military manpower requirements to identify changes in educational attainment and present estimates placing the elasticity associated with an additional year of collegiate attainment between 0.4 and 0.6 at a public institution. Stanley (1999) obtains estimates of similar magnitudes using a quite different empirical strategy.

13. Under Title IV of the Higher Education Act, federal financial aid policy makes a statutory distinction between "dependent" and "independent" students in the determination of program eligibility. For "dependent" students, needs analysis is based on the ability to pay of both the student and his or her parents. Eligibility for independent students rests only on the financial position of the applicant and his or her spouse, relative to direct college costs and other demands on resources including the number of children in the family. To be eligible for aid as an independent student, an individual must not be claimed as a dependent in the prior or current year for tax purposes and may only receive limited cash and in-kind contributions from parents. While the parameters of the formula for determining aid eligibility differ for independent and dependent students, the underlying mechanics are quite similar.

# No College Student Left Behind:
## The Influence of Financial Aspects of a State's Higher Education Policy on College Completion

## Marvin A. Titus

Using the No Child Left Behind Act of 2001 as a frame of reference, federal policymakers are considering policy options associated with the reauthorization of the Higher Education Act which link institutional eligibility for federal student financial aid programs to college student completion rates (Burd, 2003; Institute for Higher Education Policy, F2003). Some campus leaders contend that college completion rates are influenced by student and institutional characteristics and are related to the higher education policy context of a state (American Association of State Colleges and Universities, 2002).

Although some studies have investigated the association between college student persistence and institutional variables (Astin, 1993; Dey, 1990; Kamens, 1971; Marcus, 1989; Saupe, Smith, & Xin, 1999; Titus, in press-a, in-press-b), no known research has systematically made an effort to understand the relationship between college completion rates and a state's higher education policy context. Sarah Turner (2004) alludes to the need to understand how such higher education policies as state funding of colleges and universities influence college completion rates. Using national datasets and employing multilevel modeling techniques, this study examines the influence of financial aspects of a state's higher educations policy context on college completion.

## College Completion and the State Higher Education Policy Context

Although federal policymakers are endeavoring to link federal funding to college student completion rates, state governments are the largest source of funds for public higher education (Burd, 2003). In 2000, states provided 31% of all funds to public four-year institutions (National Center for Education Statistics, 2002). Between 1996 and 2001, state awards for undergraduate need-based grant programs grew by 41% to $3.5 billion (NASSGAP, 2002).

In addition to providing financial support for higher education, states develop and implement policies with regard to communicating statewide goals and objectives to the public. Financial aspects of higher education policy have the potential of being flexible tools to achieve such statewide objectives as maintaining a comparative economic advantage through increasing the flow of college educated human capital (Western Interstate Commission for Higher Education, 2003). States view the enhancement of human capital as an investment in the public good, reflected in part as increasing economic development and sustaining economic growth in a competitive market (Longanecker, 2005). Because the market fails to achieve the socially optimal level of college-educated human capital investment (Paulsen, 2000) which may be necessary for economic growth and development, states are taking a more active role in providing financial incentives to higher education institutions to achieve state-wide goals such as increasing college completion rates (Massey, 2004).

The extent to which a state is able to positively influence college completion rates may be dependent on statewide fiscal conditions, the specific mix of finance-related higher education policies, the characteristics of higher education institutions, and the characteristics and experiences of students attending colleges and universities in a state. This characterization of the context in which higher education policy operates is congruent with the conceptual framework that focuses on stakeholders in the higher education market (Martinez & Richardson, 2003), rather than on the unique characteristics of the higher education market (Winston, 1999) or external forces that influence it (Richardson et al., 1998). These stakeholders—which include the state, institutions, and students—interact and may influence outcomes such as college completion. College completion may be also be influenced, albeit indirectly, by the competition for state funds. State support for higher education is influenced by competing interests within a state's political economy in such sectors as the prison system, primary and secondary education, health, and welfare (Okunade, 2004). Partly because of increased competition between these sectors for funding, states have rationed scarce financial resources using market-based policies. For higher education, these policies include reduced government appropriations to colleges and universities and an increased reliance on tuition as a source of institutional revenue (Massey, 2004). As a result of the rise in college tuition, states have called for increased institutional accountability in such areas as the number of degrees awarded and college completion rates. Additionally, a majority of states, through state statues, legislative mandates, and state higher education governing or coordinating boards, require higher education institutions to provide accountability reports and engage in performance funding, based on such indicators of institutional performance as graduation rates (Burke, Minassians, & Yang, 2002).

In addition to state governments, in the past, the federal government has attempted to hold higher education institutions accountable for college student graduation rates. Through the 1992 Higher Education Act, the federal government authorized the creation of State Postsecondary Review Entities (SPREs) and charged them with developing quantified performance standards in, among other areas, graduation rates. It was only after the higher education community opposed attempts to "federalize" academic accreditation in higher education that federal funding for SPREs ended.

Recently, the issue of college completion rates at the state level, which in 2001, ranged from 31% to 87% (National Center for Education Statistics, 2004), has been highlighted in such reports as *Measuring Up 2004: The National Report Card on Higher Education* (National Center for Public Policy and Higher Education, 2004). Other documents such as *Cracks in the Education Pipeline* (Committee for Economic Development, 2005) have called for systemic change while others such as *Policies in Sync: Appropriations, Tuition, and Financial Aid for Higher Education* (Western Interstate Commission for Higher Education, 2003) have called for better coordination of state higher education policies to improve college student graduation rates.

The increased discourse on state responsibility for improving college completion rates is also evident in such reports as *A Matter of Degrees: improving Graduation Rates in Four-Year Colleges and Universities* (Carey, 2004), *Correcting Course: How We Can Restore the Ideals of Public Higher Education in a Market-Driven Era* (Futures Project, 2005), and *One Step from the Finish Line* (Carey, 2005). Other documents, such as *Accountability for Better Results: A National Imperative for Higher Education* (National Commission on Accountability in Higher Education, 2005), call for state-level higher education budgeting strategies to improve institutional performance, including graduation rates.

With regard to college student completion and the state policy context, higher education analysts (Jones & Paulson, 2001) ask: What factors might influence college completion? Evaluations of the statewide higher education performance reported in *Measuring Up 2000* (National Center for Public Policy and Higher Education, 2001), suggest a relationship between college completion rates and such statewide variables as state expenditures on higher education (Martinez, 2001), unemployment, and overall fiscal conditions (Ewell, 2001). Those preliminary evaluations, however, ignored student- and institution-level predictors of college completion and lacked a conceptual framework. Although researchers (Hearn & Holdsworth, 2002) have investigated the context in which financial aspects of state higher education policies are being implemented to influence college student learning outcomes, no known study has explored the extent to which financial aspects of higher education policy influence college student degree completion.

## Theoretical Framework

This study uses the Berger-Milem (2000) organizational behavior/student outcomes college impact model. Drawing on organizational behavior theory (Bolman & Deal, 1991), the research literature on peer group effects (Weidman, 1989), student involvement (Astin, 1984), and utilizing an organizational perspective of college impact on student outcomes, Berger and Milem posited that both institutional and student characteristics influence affective and cognitive student outcomes, including college persistence. Berger and Milem characterize organizational behavior as, among other things, having a systemic dimension. Drawing on open-systems theories (Birnbaum, 1988), they explore the systemic dimension of organizational behavior from several perspectives, including resource dependency. This theory explains an organization's internal adjustment to changes in the availability of such external resources (e.g., finances that an organization must have to function) as a form of organizational behavior (Pfeffer, 1997; Scott, 1995). In addition to organizational behavior, the Berger-Milem (2000) model hypothesizes that student entry characteristics (e.g., gender, race/ethnicity, socioeconomic status, and previous academic achievement), institutional structural-demographic features (e.g., size, control, mission, and student diversity), and student peer group climate (e.g., aggregate behavior and perceptions) influence student outcomes, including persistence.

On the topic of college student persistence, Berger and Milem urge using retention literature as a guide for selecting student-level variables. Although Vincent Tinto's (1987, 1993) student interactionalist model, which focused on student-level variables internal to the institution, has been used extensively in college retention studies, Alberto Cabrera et al. (1992) suggests that constructs from John Bean's (1980, 1983) student attrition model appear to be more robust than the interactionalist model in explaining the student departure process. Cabrera et al. concluded that the superior performance of the student attrition model is due to the inclusion of student-level variables which are external to the institution. Building on his earlier work (Bean, 1980, 1983), and incorporating Alexander Astin's (1984) framework of student involvement, Bean (1990) enhanced the student attrition model to include student background, integration, and the external environment as influences on student departure.

Drawing from Bean's (1990) student attrition model and using constructs from the Berger-Milem (2000) college impact model, my conceptual model (2004) investigates the influence of student- and institution-level variables on persistence. It also demonstrates that college student persistence is positively related to such institutional characteristics as selectivity as an aspect of student peer climate and institutional size, after controlling for student-level variables. Prior research (Kim, Rhoades, & Woodward, 2003; Ryan, 2004; Titus, in press-b) also showed that aspects of an institution's financial context help to further explain student persistence. However, these studies did not take into account the influence of financial aspects of a state's higher education policy context on college completion rates.

Dennis Jones and Peter Ewell (1993) contend that, in addition to institutional resources, administrative procedures, and organizational culture, state policy influences undergraduate student outcomes. This argument suggests that, in addition to institution-level variables, state-level variables may also influence college completion. Consequently, in an effort to examine the influence of state level-variables on college completion, this study extends the Berger-Milem (2000) college impact model to include variables which reflect aspects of higher education policy.

Building on earlier studies (Titus, in press-a, in press-b), and addressing the limitations of past research, this research explores the extent to which college completion is influenced by financial aspects of a state's higher education policy context after taking student- and institution-level variables into account and while controlling for a state's demographic and economic characteristics.

# Research Method

This study uses student-, institution-, and state-level data, and a multilevel modeling statistical technique to address the following research questions:

1. What student-level variables influence college completion within a four-year institution?
2. After taking into account student-level predictors of college completion, what institution-level variables explain differences between four-year institutions in college completion rates?
3. After taking into account student-level and institution-level predictors of college completion, what state-level variables explain differences between states in college completion rates?

## Sample

I drew student-level data from the 1996-2001 Beginning Postsecondary Students (BPS:96/01) survey, a longitudinal database sponsored by the U.S. Department of Education's National Center for Education Statistics (NCES). Institution-level data are drawn from the NCES's Integrated Postsecondary Education Data System (IPEDS) Fiscal Year 1996 Financial Survey and Fall 1995 Enrollment Survey.

State-level data come from the 27th annual National Association of State Student Grant and Aid Programs (NASSGAP) Survey and various Current Population Surveys (CPS). The analytic sample for this study is limited to fall 1995 first-time, full-time, degree-seeking undergraduates attending four-year colleges and universities and is comprised of 5,776 students attending 400 four-year institutions in 48 states. I excluded Nevada, because it was not covered in the BPS:96/01 survey, and New Mexico, because there were insufficient data from its college students.

## Variables

The dependent variable in this study is "having completed a bachelor's degree program within six years after first enrolling in the same four-year institution." The independent student-level variables include measures of student background characteristics, college experiences, attitudes, and environmental pull variables (e.g., financial need and work responsibilities). Environmental pull variables reflect aspects of Bean's (1990) student attrition model.

Student background characteristics include pre-college academic performance, gender, race/ethnicity, and socioeconomic status (SES). I measure precollege academic performance by standardized SAT scores. Gender is coded "1" if the student is female and "0" if male. I include four racial/ethnic groups in the analyses—African American, Hispanic, Asian, and White—with White serving as the reference group. Socioeconomic status is measured by a composite sum of standardized parental income and standardized parental educational attainment.

Four components measure student experiences: college academic performance, declaring a major, living on campus, and student involvement (defined below) during the freshmen year. The measure for college academic performance is GPA at the end of the freshman year. The BPS:96/01 survey item—whether the student declared a degree major in his or her first year—measures declaring a major (1 = yes, 0 = no). Living on campus during the freshman year is coded 1 = yes, 0 = no. Student involvement is a factor composed of eight items measuring how often (0 = "never," to 2 = "often") students reported participating in school clubs; participating in fine arts activities; attending lectures, conventions, or field trips; going places with friends; having social contact with faculty; attending study groups; meeting with one's advisor about plans; and talking with faculty outside of class. I rotated the factors using oblique and orthogonal (quartimax) rotation methods and principal axis factoring (Pedhazur & Schmelkin, 1991). Because the alpha reliability coefficient (.65) of the student involvement factor composite is below that recommended by Liora Pedhazur and Elazar Schmelkin (1991), it should be interpreted with caution. Student attitudes are measured by whether they are satisfied with the campus climate (1 = yes, 0 = no).

I coded the number of hours worked per week into four categories: 0 hours, 1–10 hours, 11–20 hours, and more than 20 hours, with "0" as the reference category.

Reflecting several constructs from the Berger-Milem (2000) college impact model, the independent institution-level variables include measures of student peer characteristics and experiences, structural-demographic characteristics of a four-year institution, and financial aspects of a four-year institution. Student peer group characteristics are measured by the percentage of female, racial/ethnic diversity, and socioeconomic status (SES) of full-time freshmen attending the same institution. I used data from the IPEDS Fall 1995 Enrollment Survey to calculate the percentage of full-time women first-year students at each institution. This study uses an index of racial/ethnic diversity based on a formula developed by Mitchell Chang (1999). According to Chang, the institutional diversity index should be measured by the reciprocal of the following formula:

$$\sqrt{\frac{(\% \ Asians - \mu)^2 + (\% \ Hispanics - \mu)^2 + (\% \ African \ Americans - \mu)^2 + (\% \ Whites - \mu)^2}{4}}$$

where, $\mu$ = the sum of the percentages for Asians, Hispanics, African Americans, and Whites at each institution divided by four. The reciprocal of this formula reflects an institution's heterogeneity with respect to the racial/ethnic composition of undergraduate student enrollment. In this study, this index measures the variance in the racial/ethnic composition of full-time freshmen enrollment at an institution. Using the student-level composite, institutional-level peer group SES is derived by computing the average SES for full-time freshmen attending the same institution.

The analyses include variables reflecting such structural characteristics as whether an institution is private, whether an institution is a historically black college or university (HBCU), enrollment size, and its selectivity (measured by the average academic ability of its full-time first-year students). To minimize the effects of a skewed distribution of institutional enrollment (skewness value = 1.215, standard error of skewness value = .122), I recoded size into three groups: small (less than 4,000); large (more than 15,000); and medium (4,000 to 15,000), with medium as the reference group. Following the recommendation of Paul Kingston and John Smart (1990), I organized institutional selectivity into three groups: high selectivity (the average pre-college college academic performance index for students in the highest quartile); low selectivity (the average SAT score for students in the lowest quartile); and middle selectivity (the average SAT score for students in the second and third quartiles). Middle selectivity is the reference group.

Reflecting resource dependency theory, the financial context of a four-year institution is measured by revenue and expenditure variables. The revenue variables include percentage of revenue from (a) state appropriations, (b) tuition, and (c) competitive grants and contracts. This study also includes the percentage of revenue from endowment income. Expenditure variables include percentage of expenditures on (a) instruction, (b) student services, (c) grants and scholarships, (d) research, (e) administration, and (f) total educational and general (E&G) expenditures per full-time equivalent student.

The independent state-level variables include several variables reflecting a state's demographic, economic, and higher education characteristics and the financial aspects of its higher education policy context. The variables measuring state characteristics include the percentage of adult state residents who have attained at least a bachelor's degree and the unemployment rate. These analyses also include the number of private higher education institutions per capita.

According to Art Hauptman (2001) financial aspects of a state's higher education policy context appear in three broad areas: appropriations to higher education institutions, tuition policy for public institutions, and student financial aid funding levels and rules. In this study, I measure the financial aspects of state higher education policies per full-time equivalent student by (a) state appropriations to four-year public institutions (b) state appropriations to four-year private institutions, (c) tuition revenue at four-year public institutions, (d) tuition revenue at four-year private institutions, (e) percentage of total state grants as a percentage of appropriations of state tax funds for operating expenses of higher education; and (f) state need-based financial aid awards for individuals in the traditional college-age (18–24) cohort.

Although not shown, correlation analyses reveal that the percentage of total state grants as a percentage of appropriations of state tax funds for operating expenses of higher education and state need-based financial aid awards for individuals in the traditional college-age (18–24) cohort are positively and strongly related ($r = .0.861, p < .001$). Consequently, state tax funds for higher education operating expenses and state need-based financial aid awards per traditional college-age individual may be jointly determined.

Because Durbin-Wu-Hausman tests (Davidson & MacKinnon, 1993) revealed that OLS regression analyses did not produce consistent estimates of state need-based awards for traditional college-age individuals and total state grants as a percentage of appropriations of state tax funds for operating expenses of higher education, I used simultaneous equations to jointly estimate state need-based awards for individuals age 18–24 and total state grants as a percentage of appropriations of state tax funds for the operating expenses of higher education.[1] I used tuition revenue and state appropriations to higher education to estimate total state grants as a percentage of appropriations of state tax funds for operating expenses of higher education. I then used total state grants as a percentage of appropriations of state tax funds for operating expenses of higher education, tuition revenue, and state appropriations to higher education to estimate state need-based awards per traditional college-age (18–24) individual. The estimated state need-based award for these individuals and total state grants as a percentage of appropriations of state tax funds for operating expenses of higher education were then used in the HLM analyses. All continuous variables are standardized.

I included six geographic regions as a proxy for differences in a region's tradition and philosophy toward higher education, grouping states as Midwest, Southeast, Southwest, Rockies/Plains, Northwest, and Northeast regions. The Northeast serves as the reference region.

## Analyses

This study uses a three-level hierarchical generalized linear modeling (HGLM) technique to address the research questions. This multilevel statistical technique allows for a comprehensive analysis of how state-level variables influence college completion after taking student- and institution-level variables into account (Raudenbush & Bryk, 2002). Additionally, using HGLM techniques results in more efficient parameter estimates through full maximum likelihood techniques compared to generalized or ordinary least squares techniques (Bryk & Raudenbush, 1996). This multilevel estimation method combines maximum likelihood techniques with empirical Bayes techniques (Bryk & Raudenbush, 1992; Goldstein, 1995; Longford, 1993; Raudenbush & Bryk, 2002).

An empirical Bayes approach to parameter estimation combines information from both the sample data for a group and estimates of the true values of parameters from the population based on a distribution of those values. This approach allows for inferences about population value errors that are not dependent on specific estimates of the standard error. Multilevel methods that include the use of empirical Bayes estimation techniques result in weighted estimates and allow for the estimation of individual-level random varying coefficients based on data from all groups and an estimate of data from similar groups (Bryk & Raudenbush, 1992; Raudenbush & Bryk, 2002). For these reasons, this study uses a multilevel method based on HGLM techniques.

In HGLM, a sampling model has to be developed and estimated. Because the outcome variable is binary, the sampling model is Bernoulli:

$$\text{Prob } (Y_{ijk} = | \beta_{jk}) = \phi_{ijk} \tag{1}$$

The study proceeds with the use of within-institution, between-institution, and between-states models in an effort to address the research questions. Following the notation from Raudenbush and Bryk (2002), the within-institution model with student-level predictors is expressed as follows:

$$\eta_{ijk} = \log\left[\frac{\phi_{ijk}}{1 - \phi_{ijk}}\right] = \pi_{0jk} + \pi_{1jk}* (\text{STUDENT CHARACTERISTICS})_{ij}$$
$$+ \pi_{2jk} * (\text{STUDENT EXPERIENCES})_{ij}$$
$$+ \pi_{3jk} * (\text{STUDENT ATTITUDES})_{ij} \tag{2}$$
$$+ \pi_{4jk} * (\text{EXTERNAL PULL})_{ij}$$
$$+ \pi_{5jk}\text{missing\_data}_{ijk} + \varepsilon_{ijk}$$

where $\eta_{ijk}$ denotes the log odds of college completion within six years of enrollment, $i$ denotes the student, $j$ denotes the institution, $k$ denotes the state, and $\varphi_{ijk}$ denotes the predicted probability ranging from 0 to 1. STUDENT CHARACTERISTICS, STUDENT EXPERIENCES, and EXTERNAL PULL are the vectors of student-level variables described above.

The student-level coefficients in equation (2) reflect the distribution of college persistence in institution $j$ given observable student characteristics, experiences, and external pull variables. In this study, with the exception of the intercept, the analyses constrain the coefficients for all within-institution predictors to be the same for all institutions (Bryk & Raudenbush, 1992). The chi-square tests revealed that none of the coefficients varied systematically across institutions.

The between-institution model takes into account the variance in the intercept across institutions and is expressed by equation (3):

$$\pi_{0jk} = \beta_{00jk} + _{01}*(\text{INSTITUTIONAL CHARACTERISTICS})_{jk}$$
$$+ \beta_{02jk}*(\text{INSTITUTIONAL REVENUE PATTERNS}_{jk}$$
$$+ \beta_{03jk}*(\text{INSTITUTIONAL EXPENDITURE PATTERNS})_{jk} \tag{3}$$
$$+ r_{0jk}$$

where $j$ denotes the institution, $k$ denotes the state, and INSTITUTIONAL CHARACTERISTICS, INSTITUTIONAL REVENUE PATTERNS, and INSTITUTIONAL EXPENDITURE PATTERNS are vectors of the institution-level variables as described above. In this study, with the exception of the intercept, the analyses constrain the coefficients for all within-state predictors to be the same for all states (Bryk and Raudenbush, 1992). The chi-square tests revealed that none of the institution-level coefficients varied systematically across states.

The between-state model takes into account the variance in the intercept across states and is expressed by equation (4):

$$\beta_{00k} = \gamma_{000} + \gamma_{001k}*(\text{STATE CHARACTERISTICS})_k$$
$$+ \gamma_{002k}*(\text{STATE HIGHER ED APPROPRIATIONS})_k$$
$$+ \gamma_{003k}*(\text{STATE TUITION REVENUE})_k$$
$$+ \gamma_{004k}*(\text{STATE NEED - BASED FINANCIAL AID})_k \tag{4}$$
$$+ \gamma_{005k}*(\text{REGION})_k$$
$$+ \mu_{00k}$$

where $k$ denotes the state and STATE CHARACTERISTICS, STATE HIGHER EDUCATION APPROPRIATIONS, STATE TUITION REVENUE, STATE NEED-BASED FINANCIAL AID, and REGION are vectors of the state-level variables as described above.

To control for differences in student and institutional characteristics between states, with the exception of variables aggregated at a higher level, all student-level and institution-level variables are centered around their grand means.[2] According to Raudenbush and Bryk (2002), grand-mean centering results in an interpretation of the intercept as an adjusted mean for each state, or as a statewide six-year college completion rate.

According to Raudenbush and Bryk (2000), in HGLM analyses, the intraclass correlation is not useful as a measure of the proportion of variation explained by state-level variables. Following Russell Rumberger and Scott Thomas (2000), I used empirical Bayes (EB) estimates of the residuals from the multilevel model to calculate "adjusted" state-level college graduation rates. Before taking institution- and state-level variables into account, the interquartile range of "adjusted" graduation rates was 14%, revealing considerable variation across states.[3]

I used the population-average estimates with robust standard errors, as Rumberger and Thomas (2000) recommend. With the population-average estimates, I explored the average effect across students and institutions in the sample of a one-unit change in a given state-level predictor on the odds of completing a bachelor's degree within six years of enrolling in college (Raudenbush & Bryk, 2002; Raudenbush et al., 2000).

The variables are entered sequentially in the HGLM analyses in conceptually related blocks, with only the statistically significant variables from the preceding step retained in the subsequent step (Raudenbush & Bryk, 2002). Because the number of state-level variables that may be included in the HGLM analyses is limited by the number of states (n = 48), I tested a series of state-level models to distinguish the most important state-level predictors of college completion.[4]

This study uses odds-ratios to facilitate the interpretation of results. The odds-ratio represents the change in the odds of college completion relative to not completing that is associated with a one-unit change in a specific independent variable while holding all other variables constant (Peng et al., 2002). An odds-ratio greater than one represents an increase in the likelihood of completing college relative to not completing. An odds-ratio of less than one represents a decrease in the likelihood of completion. Odd-ratios are presented only for the statistically significantly parameters.

**Table 1. Student-Level Predictors of College Completion within Six Years at a Four-Year Institution after First Enrolling at the Same Institution Among Fall 1995 First-Time Full-Time Degree-Seeking Freshmen**

| Variables | Coefficients (log-odds) | S.E. | Odds-ratios |
|---|---|---|---|
| *Student-level fixed effects* | | | |
| SAT score | 0.119 | 0.037 | 1.126** |
| Female | 0.103 | 0.062 | |
| *Male (reference)* | | | |
| African American | -0.269 | 0.125 | 0.764* |
| Asian | -0.054 | 0.112 | |
| Hispanic | -0.163 | 0.126 | |
| *White (reference)* | | | |
| SES | 0.152 | 0.033 | 1.164*** |
| College GPA | 0.742 | 0.038 | 2.100*** |
| Declared a major | 0.057 | 0.073 | |
| *Did not declare a major (reference)* | | | |
| Lived on campus | 0.359 | 0.094 | 1.432*** |
| *Lived off campus (reference)* | | | |
| Involvement | 0.240 | 0.032 | 1.271*** |
| Satisfied with campus climate | 0.176 | 0.069 | 1.192* |
| *Not satisfied with the campus climate (reference)* | | | |
| Unmet financial need | -0.073 | 0.030 | 0.930* |
| *Worked zero hours (reference)* | | | |
| Worked 1 to 10 hours | 0.009 | 0.090 | |
| Worked 11 to 20 hours | -0.176 | 0.075 | 0.839* |
| Worked more than 20 hours | -0.418 | 0.084 | 0.658*** |
| Worked off campus | -0.074 | 0.059 | |
| *Did not work off campus (reference)* | | | |
| Missing data items | -0.155 | 0.108 | |
| *Random effects (variance components)* | | | |
| Student and institution | 0.076*** | | |
| Reliability | 0.254 | | |

* p < .05, ** p < .01, *** p < .001
*Note:* Sample includes 5,776 students attending 400 four-year institutions in 48 states.
*Source:* Analysis of BPS:96/01 survey data

## Limitations

This study is limited in at least four ways. First, like all analyses of secondary data, it is limited by the availability of variables in the datasets. In this study, the indicators of the financial aspects of a state's higher education policy context are represented as surrogates for a set of interrelated policies.

Second, the analysis is limited by missing data at the student level. To avoid listwise deletion and the associated reduction in sample size at the student level, the student-level model includes a single independent variable that reflects the "tendency to have missing data" (Cohen & Cohen, 1983). Following the recommendation by Jacob Cohen and Patricia Cohen (1983), I calculate a single independent variable at the student level that reflects the "tendency to have missing data" (p. 296) as the number of independent variables on which data are missing.

Stephen DesJardins and associates (2002) explain that college persistence research can produce biased results if self-selection is not addressed. Third, like most other higher educational research, this study does not adjust for the possibility of self-selection at the student level in such areas as on-campus housing and on-campus jobs, at the institution level in such areas as enrollment in private institutions, and at the state level in enrollment in particular states. In an effort to address selection bias, Bellio and Gori (2003) have begun to explore the combined use of such statistical methods as two-stage procedures, propensity scores, and matching with multilevel models. Because the combined use of such methods (e.g., multiprocess models) is in the first stages of development, this study employs only HGLM techniques to address the research questions. Finally, the HGLM analysis is limited by the inability to apply weights at the student level.

## Results

Table 1 shows which student-level variables influence college completion. Taking into account the student-level predictors of college completion, Table 2 displays the effects of institution-level variables on college completion. Table 3 shows the effects of state-level variables on college completion, after both student-level and institution-level predictors are taken into account.

## Student-Level and Institution-Level Predictors of College Completion

Table 1 shows that college completion within six years at a four-year institution after first enrolling at the same institution is positively influenced by two measures of student background. College completion is positively associated with SAT score (odds-ratio = 1.126, $p < .01$), and socioeconomic status (odds-ratio = 1.164, $p < .001$). The results of this study also show that college completion is positively influenced by certain aspects of the college experience. Table 1 reveals that college completion is positively related to college GPA (odds-ratio = 2.100, $p < .001$), living on campus (odds-ratio = 1.432, $p < .001$), and involvement during the freshmen year (odds-ratio = 1.192, $p < .05$). Being satisfied with the campus climate in the freshmen year also has a positive influence on college completion (odds-ratio = 1.192, $p < .001$).

In contrast to satisfaction and the college experience variables, certain student characteristics and environmental pull variables have a negative effect on college completion. Table 1 shows that the likelihood of completing college is negatively related to being an African American (odds-ratio = 0.764, $p < .05$). The chance of completing a college degree is negatively associated with unmet financial need (odds-ratio = 0.930, $p < .05$), working 11 to 20 hours per week (odds-ratio = 0.839, $p < .05$) and more than 20 hours per week (odds-ratio = 0.658, $p < .001$). These findings validate the influence of environmental pull variables in Bean's (1990) student attrition model.

This research reveals that, even after controlling for student-level variables, the likelihood of completing a college degree varies across institutions and states. Table 2 shows that student- and institution-level random effects (variance component = 0.076, $p < .001$) are statistically significant. These results further warranted taking institution- and state-level variables into account when examining college completion.

The results of this study indicate that certain institutional student peer group characteristics influence college completion. Table 2 reveals that after taking student- and other institution-level variables into account, the chance of college completion is positively related to the average SES of the freshmen class (odds-ratio = 1.281, p < .001). The results also illustrate that the chance of college completion is positively related to being enrolled at a high-selectivity institution (odds-ratio = 1.334,

**Table 2. Institution-Level Predictors of College Completion within Six Years at a Four-Year Institution after First Enrolling at the Same Institution among Fall 1995 First-Time Full Time Degree-Seeking Freshmen, Taking Student-Level Predictors in Account (See Table 1)**

| Variables | Coefficients (log-odds) | S.E. | Odds-Ratios |
|---|---|---|---|
| *Institution-level fixed effects* | | | |
| *Institutional student (freshmen) peer characteristics* | | | |
| Female percent | -0.025 | 0.042 | |
| Racial/ethnic diversity | 0.056 | | 0.029 |
| Average SES | 0.248 | 0.055 | 1.281*** |
| *Institutional structural-demographic characteristics* | | | |
| Private | 0.262 | 0.080 | 1.300** |
| *Public (reference)* | | | |
| HBCU | 0.055 | 0.162 | |
| *Other (reference)* | | | |
| Small size: enrollment less than 4,000 | -0.156 | 0.102 | |
| Large size: enrollment more than 15,000 | 0.005 | 0.091 | |
| *Medium size - enrollment 4,000 – 15,000 (reference)* | | | |
| Average SAT | | | |
| High selectivity - 4th quartile | 0.288 | 0.109 | 1.334** |
| Low selectivity - 1st quartile | -0.181 | 0.080 | 0.834* |
| *Mid selectivity - 2nd and 3rd quartiles (reference)* | | | |
| *Institutional revenues* | | | |
| Percent from tuition | 0.002 | 0.001 | 1.002*** |
| Percent from grants and contracts | 0.006 | 0.007 | |
| Percent from state appropriations | 0.033 | 0.096 | |
| Percent from endowment income | 0.004 | 0.014 | |
| *Institutional expenditures* | | | |
| Percent on administration | -0.638 | 0.754 | |
| Percent on instruction | -0.846 | 0.960 | |
| Percent on student services | -0.600 | 1.383 | |
| Percent on grants and scholarships | -0.613 | 0.742 | |
| Percent on research | -0.949 | 0.889 | |
| E&G expenditures per FTE student (x 1,000) | 0.139 | 0.053 | 1.149** |
| | | | |
| *Random effects (variance components)* | | | |
| Institution-level intercept | 0.079*** | | |
| Reliability of intercept | 0.198 | | |

\* p < .05, \*\* p < .01, \*\*\* p < .001
*Note:* Sample includes 5,776 students attending 400 four-year institutions in 48 states.
Source: Analysis of BPS:96/01, Fall 1995 IPEDS, and FY 96 IPEDS survey data

$p < .01$) and negatively associated with being enrolled at a low-selectivity institution (odds-ratio = 0.834, $p < .05$).

Consistent with previous research (Titus, in press-b), this study also demonstrates that a student's probability of completion is related to certain financial aspects of a four-year institution. Table 3 shows that college completion is positively associated with the percentage of revenue derived from tuition (odds-ratio = 1.002, $p < .001$) and the level of educational and general (E&G) expenditures per FTE student (odds-ratio = 1.149, $p < .01$). The non-significance of the coefficients reflecting institutional expenditure patterns is the result of collinearity among the variables.

## State-Level Predictors of College Completion

The results of this study reveal that college completion is influenced by financial aspects of a state's higher education policy context. Table 3 shows that, after controlling for student- and institution-level predictors, college completion is positively associated with the percentage of total state grants as a percentage of appropriations of state tax funds for the operating expenses of higher education (odds-ratio = 1.086, $p < .05$) and state need-based grant dollars per individual in the traditional college-age (18–24) population (odds-ratio = 1.055, $p < .05$).

**Table 3. State-Level Predictors of College Completion within Six Years at a Four-Year Institution after First Enrolling at the Same Institution among Fall 1995 First-Time Full-Time Degree-Seeking Freshmen, Taking Student-Level and Institution-Level Predictors into Account (See Tables 1 and 2)**

| Variables | Coefficients (log-odds) | S.E. | Odds-Ratios |
|---|---|---|---|
| *State-level fixed effects* | | | |
| *Economic and demographic context* | | | |
| Percent of population with a bachelor's degree | 0.031 | 0.041 | |
| Unemployment rate | 0.028 | 0.048 | |
| *Higher education policy context* | | | |
| Number of private higher ed. institutions per student | 0.001 | 0.001 | |
| State appropriations to 4-year public HE per FTE student | -0.031 | 0.035 | |
| State appropriations to 4-year private HE per FTE student | 0.010 | 0.022 | |
| Tuition revenue to 4-year public HE per FTE student | 0.084 | 0.048 | |
| Tuition revenue to 4-year private HE per FTE student | 0.046 | 0.038 | |
| Pct. of state appropriations to HE – financial aid | 0.083 | 0.037 | 1.086* |
| State need-based financial aid per 18-24 yr. old | 0.054 | 0.026 | 1.055* |
| *Region* | | | |
| Northwest | -0.372 | 0.073 | 0.689*** |
| Midwest | -0.098 | 0.085 | |
| Southeast | -0.013 | 0.088 | |
| Southwest | -0.262 | 0.145 | |
| Rockies/Plains | -0.547 | 0.121 | 0.579*** |
| *Northeast (reference group)* | | | |
| | | | |
| *Random effects (variance components)* | | | |
| State-level intercept | 0.001 | | |
| Reliability of intercept | 0.002 | | |

* p < .05, ** p < .01, *** p < .001
Note: Sample includes 5,776 students attending 400 four-year institutions in 48 states.
Source: Analysis of BPS:96/01, Fall 1995 IPEDS, FY 96 IPEDS, NASSGAP survey, and CPS.

Table 3 also reveals that after controlling for other state-level variables, institution-level variables, and student-level variables, the chance of college completion is lower in certain regions of the nation. The odds of college completion is negatively associated with being in the Northwest (odds-ratio = 0.689, $p < .001$) and the Rockies/Plains (odds-ratio = 0.579, $p < .001$) regions.

As shown in Table 3, the chance of college completion is not related to such state demographic and economic characteristics as the percentage of the population with a bachelor's degree and unemployment rate, respectively. This study also reveals that the chance of college completion is not related to: state appropriations to four-year public, state appropriations to private institutions, tuition revenue from private institutions, tuition revenue from public institutions, and the number of private higher education institutions per FTE student. The statistical non-significance of the relationship between college completion as of academic year 2001 and state appropriations to or tuition revenue from institutions as of fiscal year 1996 could be the result of a temporal misalignment between state appropriations in the freshmen year and odds of having graduated six years later. In other words, between 1996 and 2001, the relationship between college completion and state appropriations to and tuition revenue from four-year higher education institutions per FTE student may better be captured by dynamic than by static data analyses. More research, using alternative statistic techniques such as dynamic panel (Blundell & Bond, 1998) or multilevel event history (Barber et al., 2000) analysis may reveal how changes in college completion rates or time to degree completion are influenced by changes in state appropriations to and tuition revenue of four-year higher education institutions.

## Conclusions and Implications

At least seven conclusions may be drawn from this study. First, at least two aspects of student background characteristics, pre-college academic performance and SES, are useful for explaining college completion within a four-year institution. This result is consistent with prior research that explored how college completion is influenced by SES and pre-college academic performance (Astin, 1993).

Second, consistent with prior research, the results of the study underscore how college completion is positively influenced by such aspects of the college freshmen experience as performing academically while in college, living on campus, and being involved on campus. The chance of college completion is also positively influenced by the extent to which a student is satisfied with the campus climate. Colleges and universities should be able to reshape campus environments to make them more conducive to positive student experiences, thus contributing to persistence to degree.

Third, this study demonstrates that such variables as unmet financial need and the number of hours spent working have a negative effect on college completion. This finding is consistent with Bean's (1990) observation that institutions are probably less able to influence variables external to the campus compared to those that reflect student experiences on campus.

Fourth, this study demonstrates that, even after taking student-level variables into account, college completion is positively associated with the percentage of institutional revenue derived from tuition. This finding is consistent with prior research (Titus, in press-a) and survey results (Anderson, 1985) suggesting that, as institutions increase their reliance on tuition as a source of revenue, they will increasingly focus on retaining students.

Fifth, this study demonstrates that a state's effort with respect to funding for financial aid as a percentage of total spending for higher education (odds-ratio = 1.086, $p < .05$) positively influences the chance of college completion. This study provides further empirical evidence that, to improve college student completion rates, states should increase the share of higher education funding allocated to student financial aid. Given states' increased reliance on market-based approaches to financing higher education (such as increases in tuition) and the relative decline in federal grants as a share of financial aid, in the future, the role of state financial aid becomes even more influential on students' chances of completing their degrees.

Sixth, this research shows that a state's expenditures with regard to providing need-based undergraduate financial aid (odds-ratio = 1.055, $p < .05$) helps to further explain differences between states in college six-year completion rates at four-year institutions. The results of the analyses are also consistent with prior research (Perna & Titus, 2004), which suggests that state need-based financial aid positively influences student access and college choice within a state. This study provides evidence that state need-based financial aid also contributes to students' success even after entering college, highlighting the importance of need-based aid in college attainment. This finding is also consistent with at least one state-specific descriptive study (Maryland Higher Education Commission, 2004), which suggests that students enrolled at public four-year institutions and who receive state need-based aid complete college at the same rate or higher than students who do not receive state need-based aid. More state-specific research in this area for specific groups of students within different types of higher education institutions is needed.

Seventh, states in the Northwest and Rockies/Plains regions have lower college completion rates than those in other regions. This finding suggests that college completion rates may be shaped by other aspects of the higher education policy context that are apparently unique to states in the Northwest and the Rockies/Plains regions. Future research should explore this point.

## Implications for Policy

This study's results have implications for policy, particularly with respect to the options associated with the reauthorization of the Higher Education Act, which link institutional eligibility for federal student financial aid programs to college student completion rates (Burd, 2003; Institute for Higher Education Policy, 2003) and state strategies for financing higher education. The results of this research show that, even after taking student- and other institution-level predictors of college completion into account, rates of college completion are influenced by financial aspects of the state higher education policy, more specifically, the availability of need-based financial aid within a state. Consequently, rather than linking federal aid for colleges and universities to institutional graduation rates, federal policymakers should consider how college completion rates are influenced by student characteristics and financial aspects of a state's higher education policy context which are beyond the control of campus leaders. Although this study's findings suggest that campus leaders can increase graduation rates by increasing institutional selectivity (i.e., from Table 2: high selectivity odds-ratio = 1.334, $p < .01$) and because pre-college academic performance is positively related to SES (Astin, 1993), such efforts may result in more social stratification of colleges and universities. Therefore, federal policies seeking to link financial rewards to institutional graduation rates may result in unintended outcomes with regard to college access and choice.

Although these findings show how campus leaders may shape such aspects of the campus environment as student residence on campus and student involvement in campus activities to improve college completion at four-year institutions, this study also underscored the importance of the state's financial aid as part of its overall financial support of higher education. College completion is positively related to the percentage of state appropriations to higher education allocated to financial aid (i.e., Table 3: odds-ratio = 1.086, $p < .05$) and per capita level of state need-based aid (i.e., Table 3: odds-ratio = 1.055, $p < .05$) provided to undergraduates. Both are dimensions of higher education policy that state policymakers, not campus leaders, control.

As state strategies to finance higher education converge toward more market-based approaches, policymakers should consider using state financial aid to help avoid the divergence between states in college completion rates. Policymakers at the federal level should consider funding state need-based financial aid programs that are designed to help students persist to degree completion. For example, such state programs as Massachusetts's Performance Grant Program, which provides incentives to low-income college students to complete a degree, should be federally funded (Institute for Higher Education Policy, 2003).

Additionally, as state leaders continue to increasingly utilize higher education financing policies with incentives to promote such statewide objectives as raising the level of educational attainment (Burke, Minassians, & Yang, 2002; Conklin & Wellner, 2004) by increasing college completion rates, state higher education policymakers should consider the type of state support necessary to help colleges and universities meet those statewide objectives. This study shows that the chance for college completion is positively related to the relative importance of student financial aid in a state's overall financial support for higher education. This research also provides evidence of a direct correlation between the amount of need-based financial per capita in a state and the rates of four-year college degree completion in that state.

This finding supports the case made by Newman, Couturier, and Scurry (2004) that, in addition to making need-based aid available to help students gain access to higher education, it should also be provided to increase their chances of completing college. Such a development would enable state higher education policy to move beyond addressing access issues toward the more important issue of degree attainment.

Finally, this paper illustrates how exploring the relationship between college completion and financial aspects of a state's higher education policy context furthers our understanding of the differences between states in college completion rates. This understanding of the complexities of college completion, as related to the higher education policy context, is facilitated through the use of the extended Berger-Milem (2000) model, a comprehensive framework. This comprehensive framework allowed for an examination of how college completion is influenced by the financial aspects of state higher education policy, while taking into account student characteristics and experiences as well as institutional behavior. This multilayered perspective helps to better inform higher education policymakers at the institution, state, and federal level.

*Marvin A. Titus* is an Assistant Professor of Higher Education in the Department of Adult and Community College Education at North Carolina State University, in Raleigh. He presented an earlier version of this paper at the annual meeting of the American Educational Research Association in San Diego in April 2004. He thanks the participants in the 2004 Higher Education Finance Roundtable at the University of Houston and Ronald Ehrenberg, in particular, for valuable feedback on an earlier draft of this paper. He also thanks anonymous reviewers and participants in the 2004–2005 Stanford Institute for Higher Education Research Seminar Series for their comments and feedback.

# References

American Association of State Colleges and Universities. (2002). *Accountability and graduation rates: Seeing the forest and the trees.* Washington, D.C.: Author.

Anderson, C. J. (1985). *Conditions affecting college and university financial strength.* Washington, D.C.: American Council on Education.

Astin, A. W. (1984). Student involvement: A developmental theory for higher education. *Journal of College Student Personnel, 25,* 297–308.

Astin, A. W. (1993). *What matters in college? Four critical years revisited.* San Francisco, CA: Jossey-Bass.

Barber, J. S., Murphy, S. A., Axim, W. G., & Maples, J. (2000). Discrete-time multilevel hazard analysis. *Sociological Methodology, 30*(1), 201–235.

Bean, J. P. (1980). Dropouts and turnover: The synthesis and test of a causal model of student retention. *Research in Higher Education, 12*(2), 155–187.

Bean, J. P. (1983). The application of a model of turnover in work organizations. *The Review of Higher Education, 6*(2), 129–148.

Bean, J. P. (1990). Why students leave: Insights from research. In D. Hossler, & J. P. Bean (Eds.), *The strategic management of college enrollments* (pp. 147–169). San Francisco, CA: Jossey-Bass.

Bellio, R., & Gori, E. (2003). Impact of evaluation of job training programmes: Selection bias in multilevel models. *Journal of Applied Statistics, 30,* 893–907.

Berger, J. B., & Milem, J. F. (2000). Organizational behavior in higher education and student outcomes. In J. C. Smart (Ed.), *Higher Education: Handbook of theory and research* (Vol. 15, pp. 268–338). New York: Agathon Press.

Birnbaum, R. *How colleges work: The cybernetics of academic organization and leadership.* San Francisco: Jossey-Bass.

Blundell, R., & Bond S. (1998). Initial condition and moment restrictions in dynamic panel data models. *Journal of Econometrics, 87*(1), 115–143.

Bolman, L. G., & Deal, T. E. (1991). *Reframing organizations: Artistry, choice, and leadership.* San Francisco, CA: Jossey-Bass.

Bryk, A. S., & Raudenbush, S. W. (1992). *Hierarchical linear models.* Newbury Park, CA: Sage.

Burd, S. (2003, January 3). Education department wants to create grant program linked to graduation rates. *Chronicle of Higher Education,* Retrieved January 15, 2003, from http://chronicle.com.

Burke, J. C., Minassians, H., & Yang, P. (2002). State performance reporting indicators: What do they indicate? *Planning for Higher Education, 31*(1), 15–29.

Cabrera, A. F., Castañeda, M. B. Nora, A., & Hengstler, D. (1992). The convergence between two theories of college persistence. *The Journal of Higher Education, 63*(2), 143–161.

Carey, K. (2004). *A matter of degrees: Improving graduation rates in four-year colleges and universities.* Washington, D.C.: The Education Trust.

Carey, K. (2005). *One step from the finish line: Higher college graduation rates are within our reach.* Washington, D.C.: The Education Trust.

Chang, M. J. (1999). Does racial diversity matter?: The educational impact of a racially diverse undergraduate population. *Journal of College Student Development, 40*(4), 377–95.

Cohen, J., & Cohen, P. (1983). *Applied multiple regression for the behavioral sciences.* Hillsdale, NJ: Erlbaum. Committee for Economic Development. (2005). *Cracks in the education pipeline: A business leader's guide to higher education reform.* Washington, D.C.: Author.

Conklin, K., & Wellner, J. (2004). *Linking tuition and financial aid policy: The gubernatorial perspective.* Boulder, CO: Western Interstate Commission for Higher Education

Davidson, R., & MacKinnon, J. G. (1993). *Estimation and inference in econometrics.* New York: Oxford University Press.

DesJardins, S. L., McCall, B. P., Ahlburg, D. A., & Moye, M. J. (2002). Adding a timing light to the "tool box." *Research in Higher Education, 43*(1), 83–114.

Dey, E. L. (1990, April). *Evaluating college student retention: Comparative national data from the 1981–1984 entering freshmen classes.* Paper presented at the annual meeting of the American Educational Research Association, Boston, MA.

Ewell, P. (2001). *A review of tests performed on the data in Measuring Up 2000.* San Jose, CA: National Center for Public Policy and Higher Education.

The Futures Project. (2005). *Correcting course: How we can restore the ideals of public higher education in a market-driven era.* Providence, RI: A. Alfred Taubman Center for Public Policy and American Institutions.

Goldstein, H. (1995). *Multilevel statistical models.* London: Arnold.

Hauptman, A. M. (2000). Reforming the ways in which states finance higher education. In D. E. Heller (Ed.), *The states and public higher education policy* (pp. 64–80). Baltimore: The John Hopkins University Press.

Hearn, J. C., & Holdsworth, J. M. (2002). Influences of state-level policies and practices on college students' learning, *Peabody Journal of Education, 77*(3), 6–39.

The Institute for Higher Education Policy. (2003). *Reauthorizing the Higher Education Act: Issues and options.* Washington, D.C.: Author.

The Institute for Higher Education Policy. (2003). *Protecting access and affordability: New opportunities for Massachusetts public higher education in times of rising student charges.* Washington, D.C.: Author.

Jones, D. P., & Paulson, K. (2001). *Some next steps for states: A follow-up to Measuring Up 2000.* National Center for Public Policy and Higher Education. Retrieved June 20, 2003, from http://www.highereducation.org.

Kamens, D. H. (1971, Summer). The college "charter" and college size: Effects on occupational choice and college attrition. *Sociology of Education, 44,* 270–296.

Kim, M. M., Rhoades, G., and Woodard, D. B. Sponsored research versus graduating students? Intervening variables and unanticipated findings in public research universities. *Research in Higher Education, 44*(1), 51–81.

Kingston, P., & Smart, J. (1990). The economic payoff to prestigious colleges. In P. Kingston & L. Lewis (Eds.), *The high status track: Studies of elite private schools and stratification* (pp. 147–174). Albany, NY: SUNY Press.

Longanecker, D. (2005). State governance and the public good. In A. J. Kezar, T. C. Chambers, J. C. Burkhardt, & Associates (Eds.), *Higher education for the public good* (pp. 57–70). San Francisco, CA: Jossey-Bass.

Longford, N. (1993). *Random coefficient models.* Oxford: Clarendon Press.

Marcus, R. D. (1989). Freshmen retention rates at U.S. private colleges: Results from aggregated data. *Journal of Economic and Social Measurement, 15*(1), 37–55.

Maryland Higher Education Commission. (2004). *A comparison of retention, transfer, and graduation rates of need-based financial aid recipients at Maryland public colleges and universities with the performance of non-recipients.* Annapolis, MD: Author.

Martinez, M. (2001). *Supplementary analysis for measuring up 2000: An exploratory report.* National Center for Public Policy and Higher Education. Retrieved June 20, 2003, from http://www.highereducation.org.

Martinez, M., & Richardson, R. C. (2003). A view of the market through studies of policy and governance. *American Behavioral Scientist, 46*(6), 883–901.

Massey, W. F. (2004). Markets in higher education: Do they promote internal efficiency? In P. Teixeira, B. Jongbloed, D. Dill, and A. Amaral (Eds.), *Markets in higher education* (pp. 13–34). Amsterdam, The Netherlands: Kluwer Academic Publishers.

NASSGP. National Association of State Scholarships & Grant Programs (2002). *32nd NASSGAP annual survey report, 2000–2001 academic year.* Retrieved June 20, 2003 from www.nassgap.org.

National Center for Education Statistics (2002). *Enrollment in postsecondary institutions, fall 2000, and financial statistics, fiscal year 2000.* Washington, D.C.: Author.

National Center for Public Policy and Higher Education (2000). *Measuring up 2000.* San Jose, CA: Author.

National Center for Public Policy and Higher Education (2002). *Measuring up 2002.* San Jose, CA: Author.

National Center for Public Policy and Higher Education (2002). *Measuring up 2004.* San Jose, CA: Author.

National Commission on Accountability in Higher Education. (2005). *Accountability for better results: A national imperative for higher education.* Denver, CO: State Higher Education Executive Officers.

Newman, F., Couturier, L., & Scurry, J. (2004). *The future of higher education: Rhetoric, reality, and the risks of the market.* San Francisco: Jossey-Bass.

Okunade, A. A. (2004). What factors influence state appropriations for public higher education in the United States? *Journal of Education Finance, 30*(2), 123–138.

Paulsen, M. B. (2000). The economics of human capital and investment in higher education. In M. B. Paulsen & J. C. Smart (Eds.), *The finance of higher education: Theory, research, policy, and practice* (pp. 55–82). New York: Agathon Press.

Pedhazur, E. J., & Schmelkin, L. P. (1991). *Measurement design and analysis: An integrated approach.* Hillsdale, NJ: Lawrence Erlbaum Associates.

Peng, C. J., So, T.-S. H., Stage, F. K., & St. John, E. P. (2002). The use and interpretation of logistic regression in higher education journals. *Research in Higher Education, 43*(3), 259–294.

Perna, L. W., & Titus, M. A. (2004). Understanding differences in the choice of college attended: The role of state public policies. *The Review of Higher Education, 27*(1), 501–526.

Pfeffer, J. (1997). *New directions for organization theory: Problems and prospects.* New York: Oxford University Press.

Raudenbush, S. W., & Bryk, A. S. (2002). *Hierarchical linear models.* Newbury Park, CA: Sage.

Raudenbush, S. W., Bryk, A. S., Cheong, Y. F., & Congdon, R. (2000). *HLM 5: Hierarchical linear and nonlinear modeling.* Lincolnwood, IL: Scientific Software International.

Richardson, R. C., Jr., Bracco, K. R., Callan, P. M., & Finney, J. E. (1998). *Higher education governance: Balancing institutional and market influences.* San Jose, CA: National Center for Public Policy and Higher Education.

Rumberger, R. R., & Thomas, S. L. (2000, January). The distribution of dropout and turnover rates among urban and suburban high schools. *Sociology of Education, 73,* 39–67.

Ryan, J. F. (2004). The relationship between institutional expenditures and degree attainment at baccalaureate colleges. *Research in Higher Education, 45*(2), 97–114.

Saupe, J. L., Smith, T. Y., & Xin, W. (1999, May). *Institutional and student characteristics in student success: First-term GPA, one-year retention and six-year graduation.* Paper presented at the annual Association for Institutional Research Forum, Seattle, WA.

Scott, W. R. (1995). *Institutions and organizations.* Thousand Oaks, CA: Sage.

Tinto, V. (1987). *Leaving college: Rethinking the causes and cures of student attrition.* Chicago: University of Chicago Press.

Tinto, V. (1993). *Leaving college: Rethinking the causes and cures of student attrition* (2nd ed.) Chicago: University of Chicago Press.

Titus, M. A. (2004). An examination of the influence of institutional context on student persistence at four-year colleges and universities: A multilevel approach. *Research in Higher Education, 45*(7), 673–699.

Titus, M. A. (in press-a). Understanding the influence of the financial context of institutions on student persistence at four-year colleges and universities. *Journal of Higher Education.*

Titus, M. A. (in press-b). Understanding college degree completion of students with low socioeconomic status: The influence of institutional financial context. *Research in Higher Education.*

Turner, S. E. (2004). Going to college and finishing college: Explaining different educational outcomes. In C. M. Hoxby (Ed.), *College choices: The economics of which college, when college, and how to pay for it* (pp. 15–61). Chicago: University of Chicago Press.

Weidman, J. C. (1989). Undergraduate socialization: A conceptual approach. In J. C. Smart (Ed.), *Higher education: Handbook of theory and practice* (Vol. 5, pp. 289–322). New York: Agathon.

Western Interstate Commission for Higher Education. (2003). *Policies in sync: Appropriations, tuition, and financial aid for higher education.* Boulder, CO: Author.

Winston, G. C. (1999). Subsidies, hierarchy, and peers: The awkward economics of higher education. *Journal of Economic Perspectives, 13*(1), 13–36.

## Footnotes

1. Following recommendations by Blundell and Bond (1998), I used first-differenced values of the independent variables as instruments in the simultaneous equations.

2. Variables, such as SES, which are aggregated at a higher unit, were group-mean centered. This approach allows for the appropriate testing and interpretation of whether the estimated coefficient varies systematically across units at a higher level.

3. After taking institution-level variables into account, the interquartile range of "adjusted" graduation rates was 11%, revealing moderate variation across states.

4. Following Raudenbush and Bryk (2000), I conducted hypothesis testing in the state-level (level-3) models through univariate tests for the fixed effects. I excluded predictors with $t$ ratios of less than 2 from the model.

# Toward a Theoretical Framework for Membership: The Case of Undocumented Immigrants and Financial Aid for Postsecondary Education

## ANDRE M. PERRY

## Purpose of the Study

Whom we deem as members determines with "whom we make those choices, from whom we require obedience and collect taxes, [and] to whom we allocate goods and services" (Walzer, 1983, p. 31). "Membership" and "members" refer to the group of people in a political community who are "committed to dividing, exchanging, and sharing social goods, first of all among themselves" (Walzer, 1983, p. 31). In general, society is amenable and/or morally obligated to providing resources to those it deems as members. However, what specific factors constitute the commitment that Walzer identifies in his definition?

Several conceptualizations of membership exist within proposed and enacted policies that limit or expand educational benefits to undocumented students. Two policies in particular—that enunciated in *Plyler, Superintendent, Tyler Independent School District, et al. v. Doe, Guargian, et al.* (1982; hereafter *Plyler v. Doe*) and the Illegal Immigration Reform and Immigrant Responsibility Act of 1996 (IIRIRA)—offer juxtaposing positions on who should (in principle) be eligible for in-state tuition benefits. These differences in principles reflect dissimilar ideas among stakeholders regarding what type of membership status (i.e., citizens, residents) should make one eligible for financial aid. In this study, I seek to identify and analyze stakeholders' basic beliefs on the topic of membership that can be considered in normative arguments on whether to allocate in-state tuition benefits to undocumented immigrants. If we can assume that a political community is generally obligated to distribute resources to its members, then a framework that captures our expectations for membership can be helpful. The study responds to the primary research question, "Should undocumented immigrants receive financial aid?", by pursuing a conception and framework of membership. The study aims to answer the sub-question, "What does it mean to be a member of society?", by examining individual stakeholders' beliefs of why they consider themselves a member (or not) of the United States.

This study categorizes these beliefs into essential factors that lead to the commitment of potential members (as an individual or as a group) to divide, share, and exchange among official citizens. From this framework, stakeholders should be better equipped to understand the concept of membership in moral and ethical disputes of whether undocumented immigrants should receive financial aid.

476

Methodologically, the study is a philosophical analysis/case study that uses (a) empirical evidence from stakeholders of a policy-relevant issue and (b) theoretical writings on membership to make a logical response to the primary research question. The analysis incorporates case study techniques to help filter the enormous amount of data from stakeholders and policies connected to the issue. I also examine the beliefs and policies of stakeholders involved in Texas House Bill 1403 (2001).

## Literature Review

To help accomplish the study's aims, I review and analyze membership within working models of membership and benefit distribution. Two models in particular, *Plyler v. Doe* and IIRIRA, offer juxtaposing moral positions on who should be eligible for in-state tuition benefits. The following literature review summarizes how these two highly influential policies present membership, thus shaping the debate. These conflicting policies offer differing ideas about the type of membership status (i.e., citizens, residents) that warrants financial aid. Not surprisingly the immigration rights and distributive justice literatures, which I also summarize, reflect a similar tension.

The 1982 U.S. Supreme Court decision held in *Plyler v. Doe* prevents public elementary and secondary schools from considering immigration status when a student is seeking to enroll. In a five-to-four decision, the Court held that a Texas law blocking the use of state funds to educate undocumented citizens was unconstitutional. The ruling was based on the equal protection provisions of the Fourteenth Amendment. Of particular concern to the Court was the fact that children—rather than their parents—were involved. The Court believed that denying undocumented children access to education punished children for their parents' behavior. Such an action, the Court noted, did not square with basic ideas of justice (Hunter & Howley, 1990; Yachnin, 2001). In addition, the court acknowledged that residency, time spent in the country, and the unlikelihood of deportation are factors to be considered in the allocation of education benefits *(Plyler v. Doe)*. The court noted that children of undocumented parents should be taken as future members of society and granted benefits befitting such a status.

As a result of this act, thousands of undocumented school-age children attend public primary and secondary institutions. While graduation rates of this population are difficult to assess, the Urban Institute calculates that, in 2001, there were probably 60,000 to 80,000 undocumented high school graduates who have lived in the United States for at least five years and that an additional 65,000 are apparently currently enrolled in college (Passel, 2001). However many of those attending college do not receive the benefit of in-state tuition, partly because of the Illegal Immigration Reform and Immigrant Responsibility Act of 1996 (IIRIRA).

Because of a common interpretation of section 505 of IIRIRA, undocumented students are ineligible for in-state tuition. IIRIRA amended the Immigration and Nationality Act, which served as the primary law that regulated border control and immigration. IIRIRA provisions have five aims: (a) to improve border control and facilitate legal entry; (b) enhance enforcement and penalties against alien smuggling; (c) advance the inspection, apprehension, detention, and removal of inadmissible and deportable aliens; (d) bolster the enforcement of restrictions against alien employment; and (e) place restrictions on benefits for aliens, including higher education benefits. Section 505 provides that if a state offers in-state tuition or any other higher education benefit to undocumented students, the state must provide the same benefit to out-of-state U.S. citizens.

This ruling is grounded in the belief that, if states are going to provide undocumented immigrants with benefits typically reserved for citizens, then the same benefit must be provided equally to all members, namely, U.S. citizens. Unlike the *Plyler* decision, the act does not take into consideration residency, amount of time spent in the country, or unlikelihood of deportation as factors to be considered in allocating education benefits. In other words, IIRIRA does not conceptualize undocumented immigrants as being resident members who are eligible for in-state tuition. While the legitimacy of section 505 is questionable—Congress does not have the ability to regulate state benefits—many states consider this statute binding (Olivas, 1995, 2002). Because citizens and permanent residents are the only categories of students eligible for federal financial aid, a state's adoption of IIRIRA effectively eliminates all forms of financial aid for undocumented students.

Subsequently, many undocumented graduates lack the financial aid which may make it possible for them to attend college (King, 1999).

Literature on post-national membership analyzes relationships among a nation, its citizens, and their rights (Y. N. Soysal, 1994). Post-national theorists—most notably Yasmin Nuhoglu Soysal—critique national membership models that assume rights and privileges must be strictly allocated among compatriots (Hammar, 1986, 1989, 1990; Marshall, 1998; Y. N. Soysal, 1994, 1998). Soysal (1998) describes a transition from an old model of citizenship that is defined by a particular nation-state to one that is universal: "The post war era [World War II] is characterized by a reconfiguration of citizenship from a more particularistic one based on nationhood to a more universalistic one based on personhood" (p. 189). The literature claims that the rights of men, women, and children were historically defined by their membership status in a nation-state. Rights differed between citizens and aliens (Marshall, 1998).

Because rights differed, attitudes toward non-citizens were governed by their legal standing or designation, rather than their membership standing. However, in the post-war era, "an intensified discourse of personhood and human rights has bent the bounded universality of national citizenship, generating contiguities beyond the limits of national citizenry" (Soysal, 1998, p. 191). The human rights discourse that occurred globally during the World War II period forced countries to provide basic security and welfare for all residents. Theorists in this camp consequently argue for the distribution of rights based on personhood, human rights, and residency.

Delanty (1998) notes that many discussions on post-national citizenship lack accuracy in their conceptualizations of citizenship and benefit distribution. He suggests that the rights and responsibilities associated with citizenship are also bound to membership, which is developed more locally and substantively. In this regard, membership and rights associated with it cannot be governed outside the context of the political community. In addition, post-national theorists argue that nation-states are not currently distributing benefits based on human rights nor do they acknowledge other membership statuses. However, as we have seen, some K-12 benefits are granted to various residents in the United States based on criteria other than citizenship. Joppke (1998) writes:

> Postnational membership argument is premised on a colossus of "national citizenship" that never was. Yasmin Soysal thinks that in the old nation-states "national belonging constitutes the source of rights and duties of individual." This is a fiction. . . . Civil and social rights have never been dependent on citizenship. Instead, modern constitutions . . . have conceived of civil and social rights as rights of the person residing in the territory of the state, irrespective of her citizenship status. (p. 271)

However, does the United States facilitate a type of membership that unduly precludes those members from rights that society expects members to have? Does the nature of the community facilitate a type of membership that warrants higher education benefits? If Delanty is correct that our day-to-day exchanges stir the membership stew, then an examination of our beliefs should reflect how our behaviors construct our membership realities. The study takes the perspective that the distribution of rights to non-citizens can be more easily dealt with if we know what it means to be a member of society.

## Methodology and Data Collection

The goal of this analysis is not to discover new facts. I do not create a definition of "membership" per se. Rather, I systematically arrange a sample of stakeholders' experiential beliefs about membership to inductively reach some conclusions of its meaning. This case study draws upon Rawls's (1971) methodology of forming a conception from which can be induced principles with which to organize a reasonable conception of membership (1993).

Rawls had a practical goal of achieving "reasonably reliable agreement in judgment to provide a common conception of justice." In *Theory of Justice,* he posits that differing conceptualizations of a supposedly comparable idea make it difficult to adjudicate claims of distributive justice. Rawls (1971) adds that we do not know our sense of justice until "we know in some systematic way covering a wide range of cases what these principles are" (p. 46) Instead of justice, this study seeks to conceptualize membership by its principles and hence to achieve a better understanding of membership.

In the tradition of Hobbes, Locke, and Rousseau, Rawls conducts a "device of representation" (or thought experiment) to achieve social agreement or an overarching consensus of what the basis for social order should be. Rawls posits that the only way people can be fair in creating this foundation for justice in society is to place them in the "original position" behind a "veil of ignorance." He argues that, if people are unaware of their potential position in society, they will choose rational principles of justice.

Rawls knew that many of our conceptualizations of justice are tinted with culture, politics, religion, and other doctrines that often are irreconcilable in the same political space. Therefore, Rawls attempted to disarm these sociopolitical/cultural biases in his method of achieving a rational conceptualization of justice. Methodologically speaking, Rawls sought to get at people's rational, intuitive beliefs about a just means of distributing communally determined goods. Rawls's methodological device for achieving this aim was his "original position" and "veil of ignorance." If people were placed in a hypothetical situation of otherness (original position) in which they could not have access to their personal sociopolitical, cultural, and economic backgrounds (behind a veil of ignorance), they would make rational choices about justice.

Similarly, subjects in this study are burdened by ideological, political, and economic agendas, as well as by their personal biases. In a community filled with members and non-members, Republicans and Democrats, rich and poor, etc., how can a study get at people's basic ideas about membership? My methodological goals differ significantly from those of Rawls in that I wanted to garner information from actual stakeholders. Rawls's thought experiment was just that—purely esoteric. I could not place a stake-holder in an original position behind a veil of ignorance without creating methodological problems. For example, I could have asked stakeholders a Rawlsian "original position" question like: "What type of law would you create if you were an immigrant?" However, I doubt that I would receive unbiased responses in the same sense that Rawls sought. Nonetheless, the study benefited from his thinking about how to determine basic beliefs and attitudes about membership.

I used semi-structured interviews and qualitative approaches associated with case studies as an appropriate method of eliciting stakeholders' beliefs about membership. In an attempt to get fair and intuitive beliefs about membership, I developed two questions: "Do you feel as if you're a part of an American community? Why do you think that?" I believe that these membership questions get at what people feel membership is without removing their moral convictions of that belief. Also, these questions minimize the inherent conflict between different aspects of the interviewee's belief systems. Affirmative and negative responses to the questions identified people's basic ideas concerning membership. From these responses, various themes of membership emerged, which I used to form a conception or framework.

In addition to the two primary questions, the interview protocol consisted of other semi-structured interview items that addressed persistent issues that crop up repeatedly in the debate on undocumented immigrant educational rights. Broadly these questions examined the distribution of individual and citizen rights, membership development, immigrant resource usage, and conflicts between state and federal law.

I adapted interview protocols to the stakeholder. For instance, questions to the students included: "When and how did your parents [guardian or family member] emigrate to the United States?" "When did you realize that you were undocumented?" "Did you or your parents attempt to stabilize your citizenship status?" "If so, when and what happened?" "If not, why?" Questions to legislative and national stakeholders included: "What criteria should determine postsecondary educational benefits?" "What should determine the receipt of postsecondary benefits and why?" "Does the denial of higher education benefits interfere with federal immigration laws?" Still, the primary membership questions led the procedures for all subjects.

## The Texas Case

Stake's (1995) approach to case studies sees two primary roles for the researcher: (a) interpreting meaning locally (at the subject's level), and (b) identifying and articulating overarching constructs that catalog the behaviors being studied. To filter the enormous amounts of information which constitute the knowledge needed to properly analyze, clarify, and organize principles of membership, I placed my exploration within the "bounded system" of Texas House Bill 1403 (Creswell, 1998). This case study develops conceptual categories to illustrate, support, or challenge theoretical assumption held prior to data gathering (Merriam, 1998, p. 38).

Because of its demographics, political influence in the union, laws, and openness to talking about the issue of undocumented immigrant benefits, Texas made an ideal place to situate my study. In addition, pressing legal and ethical considerations about student selection contributed to my decision to conceptualize membership in the context of Texas.

The student respondents in this study are vulnerable to deportation. To reduce the risks involved in identifying undocumented students, I narrowed my case selection to states that have current legislation permitting some level of aid to undocumented students. Texas makes its undocumented students eligible for in-state tuition through House Bill 1403. In Texas, students who attend college and receive some form of aid are already located and identified by postsecondary institutions. These students acknowledge their status, and these acknowledgements are recognized by official agencies in their respective states. These undocumented students do not have deportation immunity. State legislation does not supersede federal immigration laws. However, I did not put students in further jeopardy by locating undocumented students currently in postsecondary institutions.

I used a combination of purposeful and convenient sampling techniques. Of the many types of undocumented students, I interviewed students whose parents had entered the country illegally without any formal documentation. I did not consider students whose parents had entered legally but whose documentation had expired. I developed a pool of students from various public agencies that interact with undocumented immigrants. I made verbal contacts with these organizations and presented my human subjects approval form; the organizations subsequently directed students to contact me by phone or email. I relied on staff members within these organizations for subject recruitment because I did not think undocumented students would have agreed to attend a research interview session if I, a stranger, had contacted them without an intermediary.

I also interviewed state and national stakeholders who displayed an interest in the Texas case. I gathered names from correspondence on House Bill 1403, including legislators and interests groups. All of the national stakeholders work as staff members at various associations or think tanks in the D.C. metropolitan area. These interest groups have produced position papers on this particular policy and topic.

The human subjects involved in this study included 21 undocumented students from four-year and community colleges in the Houston area; 17 legislators, policymakers, and staff members in Texas state government including members of its House of Representatives and staff members, members of the Texas Higher Education Coordinating Board, a former judiciary officer, and a high school principal, and seven representatives of various interest groups in Washington, D.C.

## Data Analysis

"Interpretational analysis is the process of examining case study data closely in order to find constructs, themes, and patterns that can be used to describe and explain the phenomenon being studied" (Gall, Borg, & Gall, 1996, p. 453). Researchers can use cases to locate abstract constructs, which can lead to theory building, or the researcher can use cases to test theoretical constructs.

For data collection, I used the coding strategies for case study analysis described by Stake (1995), including the "direct interpretation of the individual instance and aggregation of instances until something can be said about them as a class" (p. 74). Direct interpretation involves pulling an idea or instance apart and putting it together again more meaningfully (p. 75). Collecting instances generates issue-relevant meanings. Stake's techniques interfaced well with my goal of conceptualizing membership from emerging patterns or consistencies within certain conditions. Stake calls such pattern consistencies "correspondence."

For this analysis, I used preexisting categories, which were identified by Galston (1991) and the U.S. Immigration and Naturalization Service (2003).

- time or physical presence in the United States (residency)
- allegiance to the country (allegiance)
- belief in core community values (Constitution)
- economic and social investments (investments)
- moral character (law abidingness)
- cultural awareness.

I analyzed interview transcripts with the intent of extracting instances pertinent to these preexisting categories. After identifying such instances, I looked for patterns or consistencies that emerged from the categories and formed new ones. When such dominant themes surfaced, I termed them principles. Together the principles form a construction of membership.

I took considerable pains to assure the trustworthiness of both the data and their interpretation. Triangulation is the substantiation of interpretations through tertiary sources (Stake, 1995). This study incorporates Stake's system, which demands the validation of data sources and the researcher's interpretations of those sources. When possible, I used alternative accounts of data source information. For instance, interviews of teachers, parents, lawyers, school officials, and politicians associated with the case, as well as meetings with my research team, helped verify data sources and interpretations. In addition, I employed the services of philosophers who examined membership, community, citizenship, and immigration to help check the clarity of the membership framework constructs.

# Findings

What are the principles that make up our conceptualizations of membership? My chief goal in this section is to identify and analyze principles that make up stakeholders' conceptions of membership. Rawls (1993) suggested that differing conceptualizations of a supposedly comparable idea make it difficult to adjudicate claims of distributive justice. Therefore, an imperative of the analysis was to examine the heterogeneity of stakeholders' intuitions about membership—the extent to which beliefs of membership are shared.

The analysis generally found that stakeholders share the same beliefs regarding membership. Citizens and non-citizens, Republicans and Democrats, students and non-students all mentioned similar views of what it means to be a member. I attribute this commonness to the ability of the primary questions to eliminate bias associated with sociopolitical status. The general findings corroborate Rawls's (1993) ideas that the original position and veil of ignorance in an "unbiased" account may lead to some "universal" principles.

The remainder of this section is organized by the principles that emerged from the philosophical analysis/case study. The study found that the principles of residency, social awareness, reciprocation, investment, identification, patriotism, destiny, and law abidingness form a philosophical framework of membership that explains what it means to be a member of a political community/nation-state.

## Residency

In response to the two primary questions, all but two of the respondents reported residency as a reason why they feel or do not feel part of the American community. More specifically, the subjects made statements such as: "I lived here all my life," "I'm a Texas resident," "I live here," "This is my home," "I live in America," and "My family has been here since about the depression." Terms involving residency were the most consistently reported factor among the range of stakeholders. For instance, Todd, a forty-five-year-old immigration lawyer, stated:

> It depends on what you're talking about, but this [America] is my home. My great grandfather emigrated from Germany . . . my family has been here [in America] ever since. . . . I've lived in [the same city] all my life.

Similarly, Leticia, a nineteen-year-old undocumented college student, stated:

> I lived here [America] all my life. . . . We represent the colors [Mexican flag], but this is the only place I know. . . . Most of my friends can't remember the last time they were in Mexico.

I did not find any differences on the basis of race/ethnicity, place of birth, citizenship status, education, or political affiliation. Respondents repeatedly used the root terms "live" and "resident" without further prodding. Other synonyms included "grew up," "brought up," and "raised." Because so many subjects saw living or not living in a space as a rationale for feeling part of the American community, I created a principle based upon those finding. The emergence of residency as a principle from the data suggests that stakeholders believe that sustained residence in a particular space is relevant in defining membership.

## Social Awareness

In response to the primary interview questions, all of the respondents mentioned specific types of knowledge that facilitated their sense of membership in the American community. Some of the responses were broad and ambiguous. For instance, one student stated, "I know America more than I know Mexico." Another commented, "You have to understand everything." A legislative stakeholder reported, "I should feel a part of the community because this is all I know. You are what you know. . . . I only know American stuff." An interest-group respondent observed, "I'm American because I know how to be one."

In response to the follow-up question, "How does 'knowing America' make you feel a part of its community?", a legislative stakeholder said, "If I skydived in[to] Russia . . . I wouldn't know where to go. I wouldn't even know how to ask for help." Subjects' responses reinforced the concept that contextualized information facilitated their feelings of membership. Luis, a 19-year-old undocumented immigrant, stated:

> I feel like I'm in the American community now, but when I was young I didn't. . . . When I first came, the hardest part of being here was understanding everything. It was hard, you know? See, I didn't understand anything. I couldn't speak English but that wasn't the hard part. It took me a couple weeks to get home. . . . [laughing] I kept getting lost. I went to a White school. . . . She [Carla] had somebody to help her [learn]. All the immigrants went to [Johnson High]. Nobody helped me [learn]. I just went to class and went home every day. . . . I just waited for my family to get home [from work].

Respondents further reported specific types of knowledge that made them feel part of the American community: language, history, and civic awareness. A student respondent stated, "You have to know English." Another student commented, "I know English." A legislative stakeholder reported, "I know the language. I participate in American traditions." A respondent from a D.C. association mused, "I feel a part 'cause I know customs, laws, and traditions. . . . There are basic things everyone needs to know in America."

For respondents who did *not* feel part of the American community, I asked a two-part follow-up question: "What community do you feel part of and why?" The same themes emerged from the only two negative responses garnered from the study. For instance, an interest-group respondent reported, "I'm a part of a Black American community. . . . You need to know our sense of struggle . . . history." In general, responses suggested a need for broad as well as specific types of knowledge as necessary for feeling part of a community.

## Reciprocation

As the principle of social awareness quickly emerged from the interviews, I began to search for the places where and mechanisms by which citizens or potential citizens gained membership information. I asked follow-up questions such as: "Where did you learn English? How did you learn about your American community? How did you learn to communicate with other Americans?" In response to these questions, as well as to the primary research questions, respondents reported specific situations in which transfers of knowledge took place: school, places of employment, and interactions with family. Such transactions were significant factors in feeling part of an American community.

Leticia stated, "I learned English in school." Another student said, "The reason why I know English and my family don't is because we have to speak English in school. . . . They don't have to speak English on the farm." Luis commented, "I learned it [how to understand American culture] in school. I watched TV and then I would see how it was said in school." Students commonly reported school as the primary institution in which they acquired needed information about the community. Students also mentioned specific American family members who helped them acculturate. Joseph stated, "I have a cousin who help[ed] us come in. . . . They took care of us. . . . They showed us how to get along."

Similarly, many legislative and interest-group respondents mentioned school and family as significant sources of information about the community. Arlene commented, "My family taught me everything." Dorian said, "I learned [about] being an American through my family." Anton stated, "College is the place where you can learn about your specific community."

Other citizen respondents identified employment as contributing knowledge about the American community. Frank said, "I spend so much time at work. . . . This is where I learn." In general, citizen respondents mentioned work more often than students as where they learned knowledge that helped them feel like members of the American community. Jaber, an immigration lawyer, reported how significantly participation in professional settings influences learning and membership:

> This is the place [Texas/America] where I work and live. . . . Working is important. I learned more about the Constitution and the law at work than at law school . . . I'm ashamed to say I spend more time at work than at home.

The data suggest that social exchanges between individuals and various institutions help shape their commitment and sense of belonging to a community. Jaber's commitment to his employer and the community of which it is part seems contingent upon his learning and participation. Likewise, the more Jaber learned, the more valuable he became to his employer, which thus led to his increased participation. Subjects who responded positively to the primary research questions acquired knowledge through their participation in various institutions, which in turn facilitated membership and institutional growth. I assumed, as did the respondents, that without such participation, the same level of information and growth could not have been achieved.

## Investment

Especially among the citizen respondents, people said they felt a part of the community because they paid taxes. Legislative stakeholder Todd stated, "I pay taxes." Greg reported, "I pay taxes, vote, and everything else that's required of me." William states, "I vote . . . pay taxes." Likewise, undocumented immigrants frequently mention taxes when asked the primary interview questions. When asked the follow-up question, "So you paid taxes?", undocumented student Luis explained, "Yeah, they took taxes out of my check." Carlos reported, "When they took taxes out of my check I was, like, cool. . . . I thought everything was okay. . . . I thought I was finally good . . . with [the] government." In general, undocumented students and citizen responses suggested that paying taxes contributed to a sense of membership. However, they also mentioned other types of investments.

Paying taxes meant more than just an involuntary requirement. One legislative stakeholder stated, "My taxes are an investment in American citizens." Another observed, "I pay taxes with the expectation that it will help people . . . [and] the country." The theme of investment seemed important to the students as well. Undocumented student Erica stated:

> I want to go to grad school after I graduate. . . . I want to be a professor like my favorite teacher Dr. [Smith]. . . . I would like to teach at a school like [State University]. . . . I can't wait till it's over [being naturalized]. Then I can just let my worries go.

Erica clarified that she wanted to invest in graduate school for the future return of becoming a professor in the United States. Similarly, Zack saw his education as an investment in membership: "Yeah, I want to stay here. Why do you think I'm going to college? . . . I want to take care of my family . . . here in America."

Students frequently mentioned that they went to school to gain future employment. Citizen respondents also reported making an outlay of some resource in hopes of a future return. Interest-group respondent Frank stated, "My grandparents sacrificed everything so that I could live a comfortable life here in the country. . . . But they did it the right way." In response to the follow-up question, "How does paying taxes make you feel that you're a member of the American community?", interest-group respondent Anton stated, "I give a lot of myself for this country. . . . I deserve everything I get."

Stemming primarily from interview data, the membership principle of investment leads to a greater sense of inclusion in the political community and, hence, a stronger sense of membership. The principle of investment is defined similarly to our everyday understanding. However, I borrow Amitai Etzioni's (1998) definition, which he used in the essay, "A Communitarian Note on Stakeholder Theory." He defines investment as "the outlay of money, time, or other resources, in something that offers (promises) a profitable return" (p. 682). Resources are anything that can be seen as being exchanged for some type of gain or benefit. As with any investment, the returns can "rise or fall, or even be wholly lost, depending on the ways the investment is used" (p. 682).

## Identification

When asked the follow-up question, "In terms of nationality how do you identify?", undocumented respondents generally claimed some form of American identity. Two respondents said, "Chicano." Four said, "Mexican American." Twelve undocumented immigrants' self-definitions included being an American although they were not officially so. In response to the follow-up question, "You are not a U.S. citizen. Why do you claim an American identity?", one student stated, "I feel American. . . . I tell people that I'm American, but I know that I'm not." All but one of the legislative and national stakeholders claimed an American national identity.

I will spend more time discussing identification in the responses of undocumented students because American identification among citizens is predictable. Still, responses among all stakeholders to the primary questions yielded similar beliefs. For instance, legislative stakeholder stated, "It's my identity. I consider myself American before anything else."

Although many undocumented respondents saw themselves as having an immigrant background, they did not differentiate themselves from other Americans. These beliefs generally tended to be based upon cultural notions of membership. They saw their day-to-day behaviors and beliefs as similar to those of American students. Students typically acknowledged their immigrant background, but still saw themselves as American. Carla stated, "I feel a part of the American community . . . Being an immigrant is American. . . . I belong because I fit in. . . . I love America because everybody is an immigrant." When asked the follow-up question, "Why do you consider yourself American?", Carla said, "This is what I am. I don't know why people question who I am."

The general findings suggest that self-concept contributes to the general sense of a commitment to exchange resources with others who have the same commitment. The identity that a person gives herself impacts whether one develops that commitment. Plainly, undocumented immigrants are more likely to exchange resources with American citizens if they see themselves as American.

## Patriotism

When asked the follow-up question, "How do you identify?", most of the respondents reported multiple identities including an American character. For instance, undocumented immigrant Leticia stated, "We live in a multicultural community. . . . I hang out in different communities all the time. . . . You just can't hang with people in your race." Luis remarked, "I have to be a part of the Guatemalan community, Mexican community, and American community." In response to the follow-up question, "What does it mean to be Latino?", Gretchen commented, "We [friends] do American things. We're Chicano. I do salsa and meringue . . . Latino American stuff."

The legislative stakeholders and interest-group respondents also mentioned multiple identities when responding to the follow-up question, "How do you identify or what other communities do you belong to?" Todd stated, "I am very active in my fraternity . . . [and] my political party." Yvonna described: "I am in several communities . . . I'm a Texan . . . Republican . . . PTA . . . There is no one American community." Lincoln remarked, "We have our own country in Texas." Juliaine said, "I belong to several communities. . . . We are a tossed salad. . . . That's what makes America great." Despite the multiple identities, most respondents claimed an American national identity.

Shabini (2002) asks, "Who's afraid of patriotism?" in his article on the subject's binding force on citizenship. In a country swarming with cultural, ethnic, and political diversity, calls for patriotism in a post-September 11 era have often been poorly disguised allegiance checks. These checks of allegiance remind us of a time when nationalistic educational tools were used to exclude some members or force others to stake essentialist beachheads on either American or enemy soil (Gottlieb, 1989).[1]

Despite its flawed historic uses, "[n]ationalism . . . is a powerful indication of a desire and need to belong to a politico-cultural entity that determines one's identity" (Shabini, 2002, p. 419). The respondents in this study communicated this same need, but patriotism in the proposed membership framework is not the ethno-nationalistic brand that liberals have criticized as being steeped in tribal or familial notions of national belonging (Taylor, 1985; Walzer, 1983, 1990). Rather, the principle of patriotism reflects an apparent need for civic belonging in a political community that is diverse and pluralistic. Shabini captures the essence of this theme: "Civic patriotism . . . [is] what promises to replace nationalism by providing the civic bond of citizenship necessary for one's sense of belonging and identity while avoiding nationalism's damaging features" (p. 420). From the respondents' answers, it became clear that patriotism was a need inherent to their commitment to share and exchange resources with likeminded beings.

## Destiny

Responses to the primary interview questions included references to the interviewees' future relationship with the country. Undocumented students related how their educational aspirations involved future employment in the United States. Erica stated, "I want to go to grad school after I graduate. . . . I want to be a professor like my favorite teacher Dr. [Smith]." Undocumented students' responses also suggested that parents planned for their child to stay in the country. Lolita said, "My parents worked so I could have a future."

Citizen subjects also reported references to the future. Clifford stated, "This is where I'm going to stay. I'm going to be here. . . . This is my home and my children's home." Eben said, "I live in the same house [where] my grandparents lived. . . . My kids will probably stay here." Jaber, interest-group participant, stated, "I work so that my family can live comfortably. . . . Yes, here in America." The sense that one belongs in his or her future community was a subtle but distinct finding. Many of the remarks that led to this category stemmed from the primary or follow-up question: "Where do you see yourself in five years? In 10 years?" Respondents consistently reported participation in family, school, and work in the country in which they identified. Therefore, I wanted to encapsulate feelings about future participation relevant to why someone feels like a member of a country.

The term *destiny* captures the future vision of where someone sees himself or herself inside or outside of a particular political community. It is the extent to which a person links himself or herself to the fate of the community. This construct seems to be a subcomponent of identity. However, the frequency with which the concept of destiny was mentioned warranted the construction of a principle that emphasized its importance.

## Law-Abidingness

This principle was not derived from the two primary membership questions. When I asked students, "Have you ever been arrested for any crime?", all of the respondents said no. I did not expect to hear otherwise, and I did not have access to criminal or disciplinary data to validate responses. However, student responses did align themselves with the spirit of state policies that permit the distribution of financial aid to qualified undocumented high school graduates.

Many of the proposed policies that would or do grant undocumented immigrants some form of financial aid require that residents have demonstrated "good moral character" upon applying for the subsidy (U.S. House of Representatives, 2001; U.S. Senate, 2001). Typically this requirement is interpreted as not having an arrest record for a certain class of crimes. Many of the non-student stakeholders generally saw law-abidingness as an indication that the person can be a *good* future citizen. Galston's (1991) citizenship virtues and U.S. naturalization policy also require law abidingness as a virtue or condition of membership (U.S. Department of Justice, 2000).

Students who responded that they have not been arrested of any crime also reported that they resided in the country for a significant period of time, participated in many institutions, knew critical information about the state, identified with an American community and connected their fates with that of the nation-state. Assuming that there are virtues that make for a good member of a community, this principle assumes that moral behaviors facilitate membership. The analytic question underlying this principle asks, "What basic moral standards facilitate membership in a political community?"

Without codifying a list of ethical behaviors that should be explored in membership, what basic, assessable behaviors can policymakers pull from to consider moral/ethical behavior in membership formation? Law observance seems to be a pragmatic and sensible way to examine basic moral behaviors. I make the obvious assumption that public policy and law generally comport with basic notions of justice that are considered morally sound. There are certainly instances where good people break laws for just reasons. However, ignoring aberrant circumstances, the principle assumes that breaking laws is, in part, a reflection of a person's aversion to the moral doctrine of the state, which is negatively correlated with being a member (or at least a good member). The negative responses to "Have you ever been arrested for any crime?", supports the presence of normative behaviors associated with feelings of membership.

## Conclusion: Substantive Membership

Empirically, the study posits a moral based upon stakeholders' common intuitions of membership. In other words, the study generally establishes an evidence-driven account of what we believe membership *should* be. More specifically, it responds to the question: "What makes me (stakeholder) a member of society?" Separately, the principles do not define membership. (Many of the enacted policies that give benefits to the undocumented are based on one, or at most a few, of the principles). The principles derived from the multiple data sources make a logical map of political membership. These principles make up *substantive membership*.

Substantive membership entails living in particular spatial boundaries; attaining community knowledge, skills, and resources; receiving communal provisions through exchange with significant community institutions; investing in communal provisions for membership; accepting the community's identity and fate; and accepting the political community's basic moral philosophy. Substantive membership answers the question, "What makes a person a member?" It assumes that not all substantive members are citizens and that not all citizens are substantive members. Still, citizenship matters, and the rights associated with citizenship should be carefully guarded. The question then becomes, "Should higher education benefits be a right or benefit exclusive to citizens?"

The Supreme Court's decision in *Plyler v. Doe* reflects the need for democratic societies to ensure that its substantive members receive the political and social attributes necessary to maintain a healthy democracy. Why does this need exist? We can get to the root of this need by asking why citizens generally commit to the goals of the country.

Not only do countries protect the rights of its members, but citizens also participate, exchange, and deliberate in the country *because* they have developed into substantive members. As noted by Walzer (1983), membership is a sense of commitment to exchanging and sharing with likeminded beings. That commitment is facilitated and encouraged by other members. Citizens are born (or naturalized) and members are made. The danger of not allocating rights to members can result in a legalized second-class citizenry, which can cause dissention among substantive members in a political community. Marshall (1998) suggests that "citizenship has itself become, in certain respects, the architect of legitimate social inequality" (p. 93).

Therefore, countries have a moral obligation and practical need not to deny rights and privileges to those who are doing everything required of them as members. In this regard, citizenship and its rights must recalibrate themselves periodically to capture its substantive members. This study offers a guide toward making such changes. However, some of the principles are hard to acquire through some type of administrative process. For instance, how does one know if a person has reached a reasonable degree of patriotism? Policymakers have an easier time operationalizing residency (current residency laws), social awareness (high school completion), and law abidance (no criminal record).

If we have similar beliefs about membership, then why do we have such stark differences in policy? If differing conceptualizations of membership are not the problem, then what is? The interviewees commented that differing policy positions occur because of differing views on naturalization rules, conflicts on the amount of resources needed to ensure citizens' postsecondary benefits, differing beliefs about how members are developed, beliefs about how distributing postsecondary benefits to undocumented residents may affect national goals, and, of course, simple discrimination. These problem areas may be "intellectual detours" that move policymakers away from enacting policies that reflect our basic beliefs. Upcoming research will help reconcile these differences. In addition, future studies may warrant political analyses if the pursuit of power can account for the differences in policy.

# References

Creswell, J. W. (1998). *Qualitative inquiry and research design: Choosing among five traditions.* Thousand Oaks, CA: Sage.

Delanty, G. (1998). Reinventing community and citizenship in the global era: A critique of the communitarian concept of community. In E. A. Christodoulidis (Ed.), *Communitarianism and citizenship* (pp. 33–52). Aldershot, Hants, Eng.: Ashgate.

Etzioni, A. (1998). A communitarian note on stakeholder theory. *Business Ethics Quarterly, 8*(4), 51–66.

Gall, M. D., Borg, W. R., & Gall, J. P. (1996). *Educational research: An introduction* (6th ed.). White Plains, NY: Longman.

Galston, W. A. (1991). *Liberal purposes: Goods, virtues, and diversity in the liberal state.* New York: Cambridge University Press.

Gottlieb, S. (1989). In the name of patriotism: The constitutionality of "bending" history in public secondary schools. *History Teacher, 22*(4), 411–495.

Hammar, T. (1986). Citizenship: Membership of a nation and of a state. *International Migration, 24,* 735–747.

Hammar, T. (1989). State, nation, and dual citizenship. In W. R. Brubaker & German Marshall Fund of the United States (Eds.), *Immigration and the politics of citizenship in Europe and North America* (pp. 81–96). Lanham, MD: University Press of America/Washington, D.C.: German Marshall Fund of the United States.

Hammar, T. (1990). *Democracy and the nation state: Aliens, denizens, and citizens in a world of international migration.* Aldershot, Hants, Eng.: Ashgate.

Hunter, J., & Howley, C. (1990). Undocumented children in the schools: Successful strategies and policies. *ERIC Digest.* 1990-09-00 (ED321962).

Immigration and Naturalization SErvice. (2003). *Form I-485: Application to Register Permanent Residence or Adjust Status.* Retrieved December 26, 2003, from http://uscis.gov/graphics/formsfee/forms/files/i-485.pdf.

Joppke, C. (1998). *Challenge to the nation-state: Immigration in Western Europe and the United States.* New York: Oxford University Press.

King, J. E. (1999). *Financing a college education: How it works, how it's changing.* Phoenix, AZ: Oryx Press.

Marshall, T. H. (1998). Citizenship and social class. In G. Shafir (Ed.), *The citizenship debates: A reader.* Minneapolis: University of Minnesota Press.

Merriam, S. B. (1998). *Qualitative research and case study applications in education* (2nd ed.). San Francisco: Jossey-Bass.

Olivas, M. (1995). Storytelling out of school: Undocumented college residency, race, and reaction. *Hastings Constitutional Law Quarterly, 22,* 1019–1086.

Olivas, M. (2002, June). A rebuttal to FAIR. *University Business,* p. 72.

Passel, J. S. (2001). *Demographic information relating to H.R. 1918: The Student Adjustment Act.* Washington, D.C.: Urban Institute.

*Plyler, Superintendent, Tyler Independent School District, et al. v. Doe, Guargian, et al.,* 457 202 (U.S. Supreme Court 1982).

Rawls, J. (1971). *A theory of justice.* Cambridge, MA: Belknap Press of Harvard University Press.

Rawls, J. (1993). *Political liberalism.* New York: Columbia University Press.

Shabini, O. A. (2002). Who's afraid of constitutional patriotism? The binding source of citizenship in constitutional states. *Social Theory and Practice, 28*(3), 419–443.

Soysal, Y. N. (1994). *Limits of citizenship: Migrants and postnational membership in Europe.* Chicago: University of Chicago.

Soysal, Y. (1998). Toward a Postnational Model of Membership. In G. Shafir (Ed.), *The citizenship debates: A reader.* Minneapolis: University of Minnesota Press.

Stake, R. E. (1995). *The art of case study research.* Thousand Oaks, CA: Sage.

Taylor, C. (1985). *Philosophy and the human sciences.* New York: Cambridge University Press.

U.S. Department of Justice, Immigration and Naturalization Service. (2000). *A guide to naturalization* (Form No. M-476). Washington, D.C.: Immigration and Naturalization Service.

U.S. House of Representatives (2001). 107th Cong., 1st Sess. *Student Adjustment Act of 2001.*

U.S. Senate. (2001). 107th Congress, 2nd Sess. *Development, relief, and education for alien minors act (DREAM).*

Walzer, M. (1983). *Spheres of justice: A defense of pluralism and equality.* New York: Basic Books.

Walzer, M. (1990). What does it mean to be an "American"? *Social Research, 57,* 591–614.

Yachnin, J. (2001, April 11). Bills in 2 states would cut college costs for some illegal immigrants. *Chronicle of Higher Education,* p. A36.

## Note

1. The Gottlieb article examines how the treatment of Reconstruction, McCarthyism, and the Vietnam War in high school textbooks were one-sided, nationalistic views on the topics.

*ANDRE M. PERRY is Assistant Professor of Educational Leadership, Counseling, and Foundations at the University of New Orleans. He presented an earlier version of this paper at the 30th Annual Conference of the Association for the Study of Higher Education, November 16–19, 2005, at Philadelphia.*

# Crafting a Class:
## The Trade-Off between Merit Scholarships and Enrolling Lower-Income Students

RONALD G. EHRENBERG, LIANG ZHANG, JARED M. LEVIN

## Introduction

One of the strengths of the American higher education system is its competitive nature. Colleges and universities compete for faculty, for students, for external research funding and on the athletic fields. Given the wide publicity that the *U.S. News & World Reports* annual rankings of colleges and universities receive and the importance of student selectivity in these rankings, American colleges and universities are increasingly using merit aid as a vehicle to attract students with higher test scores and thus to improve their rankings (McPherson & Schapiro, 1998, 2002; Duffy & Goldberg, 1998; Ehrenberg, forthcoming).

It is well known that test scores are correlated with students' socio-economic backgrounds. Hence, to the extent that colleges are successful in "buying" higher test-score students, one should expect that their enrollment of students from families in the lower tails of the family income distribution should decline. However, somewhat surprisingly, there have been no efforts to test if this is occurring.

Our paper presents such a test. While institutional-level data on the dollar amounts of merit scholarships offered by colleges and universities are not available, data are available on the number of National Merit Scholarship (NMS) winners attending an institution on scholarships that have been funded by the institution itself, rather than the National Merit Scholarship Corporation (NMSC). These institutional scholarships are awarded to high-test-score students only if they attend the institution. Our research strategy was to estimate whether an increase in the number of recipients of these scholarships at an institution is associated with a decline in the number of students from lower- and lower-middle-income families attending the institution, while holding other factors constant. We measured the number of these students by the number of Pell Grant recipients attending the institution.

The second section of our paper briefly describes the National Merit Scholarship and the federal Pell Grant programs. Next, we describe our analytical approach, followed by our empirical findings and some brief concluding remarks.

## The National Merit Scholarship and Pell Grant Programs

The National Merit Scholarship Program (www.nationalmerit.org) began in 1955. High school students qualify for awards based on their scores on the PSAT examination, high school records, letters of recommendation, information about the students' activities and leadership, and personal essays.

Three types of NMS awards exist. The first is a set of scholarships awarded to top students independent of family financial circumstances by the NMSC itself; these awards currently are $2,500 scholarships for one year of college at only institutions to which the winner has been admitted. The second is a set of scholarships awarded by corporations to top students who are employees of the corporations, children of employees, residents of a community in which the corporations have operations, or students pursuing college majors or careers in which the corporations have a special interest. These scholarships may either be for one year of study or can be renewable for four years. Again there is no restriction on the college or university that the student may attend.

The final type, and the focus of our attention, is the NMS awards funded by colleges and universities. Finalists in the NMS competition notify the NMSC of their first-choice college or university, and the NSMC in turn notifies the institution. Each institution that offers this type of award makes awards to a subset of the finalists who have indicated that they wish to attend the institution. Crucially, an award is cancelled if the student decides not to attend the institution. Hence, these awards are contingent on attending the institution.

These college- and university-funded awards are renewable for up to four years of undergraduate study and provide stipends that range from $500 to $2,000 a year. Awards of this amount pale when compared to the $30,000 tuition and fee levels that are now common at the nation's most selective private colleges and universities. However, previous research has indicated that offering a top student a named scholarship enhances the likelihood that a student will attend an institution (Avery & Hoxby, 2004). In addition, it is likely that institutions offering NMS awards will also offer additional merit aid to students; hence, the dollar amount of the NMS awards likely understates the amount of merit aid that the recipients receive from the institution.

Table 1 provides information on the total number of NMS awards and the number of these awards funded by colleges and universities, provided to us by NMSC for selected academic years between 1983 and 2003. The total number of NMS awards grew from 5,566 in 1983 to 8,244 in 2003. As the third column indicates, the percentage of these awards funded by colleges and universities increased from 42.8% in 1983 to 56.5% in 1995 and has remained at about that percentage since then.

NMS awards are heavily concentrated among a small number of our nation's 3,500-plus colleges and universities. Our econometric research analyzes panel data for the 100 colleges and universities with the most new NMS winners attending them in 2003. The names of the institutions and their number of NMS winners in 2003 appear in the appendix. (The sample actually contains 103 institutions because of a tie for 100th place.)

### Table 1. Number of Total and Institution-Funded *National Merit Scholarship* Students[a]

| Year | All Institutions | | | Top 100 Institutions[b] | | |
|------|-------|---------------------|------------------------------|-------|---------------------|------------------------------|
|      | Total | Institution Funded | Percent Institution Funded | Total | Institution Funded | Percent Institution Funded |
| 1983 | 5566 | 2,382 | 42.8 | 4330 | 1796 | 41.5 |
| 1987 | 6127 | 2,976 | 48.6 | 4844 | 2214 | 45.7 |
| 1991 | 6552 | 3,463 | 52.9 | 4982 | 2489 | 50.0 |
| 1995 | 7030 | 3,975 | 56.5 | 5496 | 2951 | 53.7 |
| 1999 | 8081 | 4,582 | 56.7 | 6594 | 3660 | 55.5 |
| 2003 | 8254 | 4,670 | 56.6 | 6965 | 3856 | 55.4 |

[a] The National Merit Scholarship Corporation provided data on the number of National Merit Scholarship students by institution for 1983, 1984, 1985, 1986, 1987, 1991, 1995, 1999, and 2003. The *Chronicle of Higher Education* publishes the top X institutions (where X varies across years from 30 to 100) that enroll the most National Merit Scholarship students in many years. Because of the changing coverage, we have not used the *Chronicle's* data. [b] We determined the top 100 institutions by the total number of merit *NMS* students in an institution in 2003; these institutions are not necessarily the top 100 in earlier years. These institutions enroll about 80% of all *NMS* (ranging from 78% in 1983 to 84% in 2003).

These top 100 institutions enrolled about 84% of all of the NMS winners in 2003 with somewhat lower percentages in the earlier years.[1] Many of these institutions are among the small number of colleges and universities that still employ need-blind admissions and need-based financial aid policies. A number of them accordingly offer *no* college- and university-funded NMS awards. However, even in this group of 100 institutions, the percentage of NMS awards funded by the institutions themselves rose from 41.5% in 1983 to about 55.5% at the turn of the 21st century.

Table 2 provides information for each year during our sample period on the numbers of institution-funded and noninstitution-funded NMS students at these institutions at the 25th percentile, 50th percentile (median), 75th percentile, and mean institution in our top 100 sample. The total number of NMS students increases at each point in the distribution; this increase is at least partially due to the way the institutions were selected (top 100 in 2003). What stands out, however, is that virtually all of the growth in the number of NMS winners occurred in the institution-funded category. For example, the mean number of institutional funded awards in the sample rose from 17 in 1983 to 37 in 2003. As late as 1995–1996, the 25th percentile institution (in terms of total number of NMS awards in 2003) offered *no* institution-funded NMS awards. By 2003–2004, however, the 25th percentile institution in the group offered 12 institutionally funded NMS awards.

Our interest is in how the growth of merit scholarships has influenced the proportion of students from lower- and lower-middle-income families attending selective institutions. While the U.S. Department of Education does not collect institution-level data on the family income distribution of students, data on the number of Pell Grant recipients at each institution are collected annually.

The Pell Grant program is the largest need-based financial aid program in the United States; it provided about $12.6 billion dollars in funding to 5.1 million undergraduate students in 2003–2004 (*Trends,* 2004, tables 1, 3). Eligibility for Pell Grants for a dependent student is based on a dependent student's family income and wealth, the number of siblings in college, and the expected costs of attending the institution; for independent students, eligibility is based on the income of the student and his or her spouse. According to Neil Seftor and Sarah Turner (2002), throughout the 1990s, half of Pell Grant recipients were independent students, although this fraction is likely to be much lower in the selective institutions that are in our sample where most students are full-time students. Prior to 1993, awards were also constrained to be less than 60% of the costs of attending an institution. Some students who attended low-cost institutions were excluded from participating in the Pell Grant program for this reason.

Data from the *2002–2003 Title IV/Federal Pell Grant Program End-of-Year Report* indicate that in that academic year, 87% of all Pell Grant recipients at four-year public institutions came from families with family incomes of $40,000 or less; the comparable figure at four-year private institutions was 86.6% (*2002–2003 Title IV,* Table 2A). Hence, the share of Pell Grant recipients among an institution's undergraduate student body is a good proxy for the share of its students coming from lower- and lower-middle-income families. Jeffrey Tebbs and Sarah Turner (2005) caution that the Pell Grant recipient data refer to students attending an institution anytime during a year, while IPEDs enrollment data refer to a point of time in the fall. Hence, other factors held constant, if turnover of students is high at an institution during the year, the "share" of Pell Grant recipients at the institution will appear artificially high. We control for this problem in the empirical work that follows by including institutional fixed effects in our estimation models.

Table 3 presents information, by year, on the mean ratio of the number of Pell Grant recipients at an institution to the number of full-time undergraduates attending the institution for the 100 institutions in our sample during the 1983 to 2000 period. The column headed "unweighted" presents information on the average percentage across institution, while the column headed "weighted" is a weighted average, with the enrollments used as weights. These data suggest that the percentage of Pell Grant recipients among the undergraduate students at these institutions fluctuated but gradually increased during the period.[2]

This increase tells us little about the impact of the growth of institutionally funded NMS at these institutions on the number of Pell Grant recipients at the institutions during the period; the share of Pell Grant recipients at these institutions will vary over time as the income distribution of the populations changes, as eligibility rules change, as maximum award levels change and as tuition levels at the institutions change. Hence, to analyze the impact of changes in the number of NMS recipients on the number of Pell Grant recipients, we must control for these other factors in our analyses.

**Table 2. Distribution of National Merit Scholarship Students at the Top 100 Institutions: By Source of Sponsorship**

| Year | All | | | | Institution Funded | | | | Non-Institution Funded | | | |
|---|---|---|---|---|---|---|---|---|---|---|---|---|
| | 25th | 50th | 75th | mean | 25th | 50th | 75th | mean | 25th | 50th | 75th | mean |
| 1983–84 | 12 | 24 | 47 | 42 | 0 | 5 | 20 | 17 | 5 | 10 | 29 | 25 |
| 1987–88 | 20 | 30 | 52 | 47 | 0 | 14 | 26 | 21 | 5 | 9 | 29 | 26 |
| 1991–92 | 20 | 32 | 55 | 48 | 0 | 16 | 34 | 24 | 6 | 12 | 24 | 24 |
| 1995–96 | 23 | 36 | 57 | 53 | 0 | 20 | 36 | 29 | 5 | 12 | 23 | 25 |
| 1999–00 | 28 | 41 | 85 | 64 | 6 | 25 | 41 | 36 | 6 | 15 | 31 | 28 |
| 2003–04 | 29 | 44 | 77 | 68 | 12 | 26 | 40 | 37 | 7 | 14 | 33 | 30 |

**Table 3. Percentage of Full-Time Undergraduate Students That are Pell Grant Recipients at the Top 100 Institutions (as defined in Table 1)**

| Year | Unweighted | Weighted |
|------|-----------|----------|
| 1983 | 18.60 | 21.16 |
| 1984 | 18.32 | 21.02 |
| 1985 | 18.23 | 21.12 |
| 1986 | 15.94 | 18.67 |
| 1987 | 16.58 | 19.77 |
| 1988 | 19.50 | 23.14 |
| 1989 | 19.75 | 23.42 |
| 1990 | 19.34 | 23.21 |
| 1991 | 21.30 | 25.56 |
| 1992 | 22.64 | 27.32 |
| 1993 | 21.98 | 25.89 |
| 1994 | 22.05 | 26.01 |
| 1995 | 21.71 | 25.60 |
| 1996 | 21.72 | 25.75 |
| 1997 | 21.72 | 25.79 |
| 1998 | 21.95 | 26.24 |
| 1999[b] | 20.05 | 23.97 |
| 2000 | 19.22 | 23.19 |

[a] The Pell Grant data are from the Federal Pell Grant Program administered by the Department of Education. We received data from the Department of Education for academic years 1983–1984 to 2003–2004 on the number of students receiving Pell Grants and total amount of Pell Grants received at each Title IV institution each year during the period. Data on the number of full-time undergraduates enrolled at each institution and the number of full-time first-time freshman at each institution are from Webcaspar (http:// caspar.nsf.gov). The percentage of Pell Grant recipients at an institution in a year is 100 times the number of Pell Grant recipients at the institution in the year divided by the number of full-time undergraduates enrolled at the institution in a year.
[b] Webcaspar did not provide 1999 enrollment data, so we used the average of the 1998 and 2000 figures for that year.

## Analytic Approach

Our goal is to see how the number of institutionally financed new NMS winners ($M_t$) at an institution influence the number of Pell Grant recipients ($P_t$) at the institution, other factors being held constant. A problem that immediately presents itself is that the number of NMS winners refers to entering first-year students, while the number of Pell Grant recipients refers to all enrolled undergraduates. If we had data on the number of Pell Grant recipients who were first-year students at an institution, we would use this information and information on the number of new first-year students at the institution to construct the fraction of first-year students who were Pell Grant recipients at the institution and then estimate how changes in the number of NMS winners affected that ratio. However, Pell Grant data are not available at the institutional level by the year that the student is enrolled in college.

A solution to this problem is possible if we make some very strong and admittedly unrealistic assumptions. Specifically, if one is willing to assume for simplicity that all students at the institution enter as first-year students, that no students drop out before graduation, that students' Pell Grant eligibility does not change during the years they are enrolled in college, and that all students who graduate do so in four years, then the following relationship holds

(1) $P_{it} = P_{it} + P_{it-1} + P_{it-2} + P_{it-3}.$

Here $p_{it}$ is the number of new first-year Pell Grant recipients who enroll at the institution in year t. Put simply, the total number of Pell Grant recipients at the institution in year t is the sum of the number of new first-year Pell grant recipients that enrolled at the institution in year t and in each of the three preceding years. If one writes down the equivalent expression for $P_{it-1}$ and then subtracts it from $P_{it}$, one finds that

$$(2)\ P_{it} - P_{it-1} = P_{it} - P_{it-4}.$$

Given the assumptions that we have made, the difference between the number of Pell Grant recipients at an institution in year t and year t−1 is the difference between the numbers of first-year Pell Grant recipients in year t and year t−4. Hence, if we want to estimate how changes in the number of NMS influence changes in the number of Pell Grant recipients at the institution between years t and t−1, the correct change in the number of NMS winners to use is the difference between $M_t$ and $M_{t-4}$. So the dependent variable in our econometric analyses is based on one-year changes in the numbers of Pell Grant recipients, while our explanatory variable is based on four-year changes in the number of institutionally funded NMS winners.

Our empirical approach is to use our institutional-level panel data to estimate equations in which the one-year change in the ratio of the number of Pell Grant recipients to the number of full-time undergraduate students at an institution is specified as a linear function of the four-year change in the share of first-year full-time undergraduate students who receive institutionally financed NMS awards at the institution, institutional fixed effects, year fixed effects, and a random error term.

$$(3)\ (P_{it}/F_{it}) - (P_{it-1}/F_{it-1}) = a_0 + a_1\ ((M_{it}/N_{it}) - (M_{it-4}/N_{it-4})) + u_i + v_t + e_{it}$$

Here $F_{it}$ is the number of full-time enrolled undergraduates at institution i in year t, $N_{it}$ is the number of full-time first-year students enrolled at institution i in year t, the $a_0$ and $a_1$ are parameters, the $u_i$ are the institutional fixed effects, the $v_t$ are the year fixed effects, and the $e_{it}$ is a random error term. We include the institutional fixed effects in the model to control for institution-specific factors other than changes in the number of NMS award winners that might affect the change in the share of Pell Grant recipients at an institution. The year fixed effects are included to control for changes in national factors that might affect the share of Pell Grant recipients over time; these factors include changes in the distribution of family income of college-age students, changes in Pell Grant eligibility and generosity rules, and changes in Pell Grant funding levels.

The Pell Grant and NMS variables have each been deflated by a relevant size variable (total full-time undergraduate students or total full-time first year students) to control for changes in the size of each institution over time. Because part-time students enrolled for at least one-half of a normal full-time load are eligible to receive Pell Grants, in the empirical work in the next section, we also experiment with deflating the Pell grant and NMS variables by the total number of undergraduate students and the total number of first-year students at the institution.

Finally, we should note that our use of the one-year change in the number of Pell Grant recipients at an institution to measure the four-year change in the number of freshman Pell Grant recipients at an institution will probably be subject to substantial measurement error because of the set of strict assumptions that we had to make to derive this equivalence. However, if the measurement error is random, it will only increase the imprecision of our estimates; it will not bias the coefficient of the NMS variable.

## Empirical Findings

Table 4 summarizes our initial estimates of equation (3). The coefficients in the table are estimates of the parameter $a_1$ that come from four different model specifications. The first is based on the total number of new NMS recipients at an institution, regardless of the source of funding. The second is based on the number of institutionally funded NMS recipients. The third is based on the number of NMS recipients at the institution who are not funded by the institution. The final specification includes both the number of institutionally funded NMS and the number of NMS recipients funded in other ways as explanatory variables. For each specification, we present estimated coefficients for models that excluded and included year fixed effects; the estimates are not very sensitive

**Table 4. Estimates of the Impact of a Change in the Share of Freshmen at an Institution Who are National Merit Scholarship Winners on the Change in the Share of Undergraduates at the Institution Who Receive Pell Grants: Fixed Effects Models (t Statistics)**

| | Share of Pell Grant Recipients $Pell_t - Pell_{t-1}$ | |
|---|---|---|
| (1) Share of Total $Merit_t - Merit_{t-4}$ | -0.200 (-2.35) | -0.171 (-2.16) |
| (2) Share of Inst. $Merit_t - Merit_{t-4}$ | -0.415 (-3.16) | -0.409 (-3.38) |
| (3) Share of Non-inst. $Merit_t - Merit_{t-4}$ | -0.070 (-0.52) | -0.004 (-0.03) |
| (4) Share of Inst. $Merit_t - Merit_{t-4}$ | -0.418 (-3.12) | -0.427 (-3.44) |
| Share of Non-inst. $Merit_t - Merit_{t-4}$ | 0.018 (0.14) | 0.086 (0.69) |
| Year Fixed Effects Included | No | Yes |

to these variables. The panel used in this estimation uses four years of NMS recipient data (1983, 1987, 1991, and 1995) so we have three change observations for each institution in the sample.[3]

The coefficients in row 1 suggest that increasing the ratio of new NMS award winners, irrespective of source of funding, at an institution to the size of the institution's first-year full-time student body reduces the ratio of the institution's number of Pell Grant recipients to its full-time undergraduate enrollments. If the sizes of the institution's first-year full-time student body and its full-time undergraduate enrollments remain constant, the interpretation of the coefficients are that an increase in NMS awards of 10 at an institution is associated with a reduction in the number of Pell Grant recipients at the institution of about two.

When we restrict our attention to the number of institutional funded NMS, the magnitude of the reduction is doubled to a reduction of four Pell Grant recipients for every 10 additional institutionally funded NMS award winners, again holding constant full-time freshman and full-time total undergraduate enrollment levels. Indeed, when we restrict our attention to NMS winners not funded by the institution in row 3, an increase in the number of these winners at an institution has *no* statistically significant effect on the number of Pell Grant recipients at the institution. This finding is confirmed in the coefficients from the last model (row 4). When we included both the number of institutionally financed and other NMS award recipients as explanatory variables, only increases in the former have a negative effect on the number of Pell Grant recipients at the institution. Put simply, in our sample of institutions, other factors held constant, including the total full-time undergraduate and first-year enrollment levels, offering more institutionally funded NMS awards is associated with fewer Pell Grant recipients attending the institution; and the magnitude of the reduction is roughly four fewer Pell Grant recipients for each 10 additional institutional NMS recipients enrolled at the institution.

Table 5 presents estimates of coefficients from the models in Table 4 that included year fixed effects, in which the models were estimated for various subgroups of our sample. In particular, we present estimates for the entire sample (the same as in table 4), for the top 80 institutions in terms of the number of Pell Grant recipients in 2003, for the top 60 institutions, for the top 40 institutions, for the top 20 institutions, and for the top 10 institutions. These analyses confirm that only the institutionally financed and awarded NMS adversely influence the number of Pell Grant recipients at an institution. However, the magnitude of this displacement effect varies by institution. In particular, the magnitude of the displacement effect increases as we move from the top 100 institutions, to the top 80, down to the top 10 (in terms of total number of Pell Grant recipients in 2003). It is at institutions with the largest number of Pell Grant recipients that the displacement of Pell Grant recipients by institutionally funded NMS recipients is the largest. Indeed, we cannot reject the hypothesis that, other factors held constant, at the top 10 institutions, every additional institutionally financed NMS recipient who attends the institution is associated with one fewer one Pell Grant recipient attending the institution. Four of the top 10 institutions are selective private universities that have no institutionally financed NMS recipients. Four of the other six are flagship public universities. (See Appendix.)

**Table 5. Estimates of the Impact of a Change in the Share of Freshman at an Institution that are National Merit Scholarship Winners on the Change in the Share of Undergraduates at the Institution that Receive Pell Grants: Fixed Effects Models Estimated Separately For Different Samples[a]**

| | Share of Pell Grant Recipients $Pell_t - Pell_{t-1}$ | | |
|---|---|---|---|
| | Top 100 | Top 80 | Top 60 |
| (1) Share of Total Merit$_t$ - Merit$_{t-4}$ | -0.171 (-2.16) | -0.176 (-1.91) | -0.172 (-1.63) |
| (2) Share of Inst. Merit$_t$ - Merit$_{t-4}$ | -0.409 (-3.38) | -0.420 (-3.00) | -0.436 (-2.69) |
| (3) Share of Non-inst. Merit$_t$ - Merit$_{t-4}$ | -0.004 (-0.03) | -0.001 (-0.01) | 0.012 (0.07) |
| (4) Share of Inst. Merit$_t$ - Merit$_{t-4}$ | -0.427 (-3.44) | -0.442 (-3.08) | -0.465 (-2.78) |
| Share of Non-inst. Merit$_t$ - Merit$_{t-4}$ | 0.086 (0.69) | 0.102 (0.69) | 0.122 (0.73) |
| | | | |
| Year Fixed Effects | Yes | Yes | Yes |

| | Share of Pell Grant Recipients $Pell_t - Pell_{t-1}$ | | |
|---|---|---|---|
| | Top 40 | Top 20 | Top 10 |
| (1) Share of Total Merit$_t$ - Merit$_{t-4}$ | -0.288 (-2.50) | -0.397 (-2.14) | -0.699 (-2.74) |
| (2) Share of Inst. Merit$_t$ - Merit$_{t-4}$ | -0.551 (-3.25) | -0.824 (-2.93) | -1.471 (-4.06) |
| (3) Share of Non-inst. Merit$_t$ - Merit$_{t-4}$ | -0.130 (-0.65) | -0.209 (-0.62) | -0.392 (-0.85) |
| (4) Share of Inst. Merit$_t$ - Merit$_{t-4}$ | -0.558 (-3.16) | -0.867 (-2.84) | -1.465 (-3.77) |
| Share of Non-inst. Merit$_t$ - Merit$_{t-4}$ | 0.031 (0.16) | 0.129 (0.39) | -0.020 (-0.06) |
| | | | |
| Year Fixed Effects | Yes | Yes | Yes |

[a] Using panel data for 1983, 1987, 1991 and 1995

Several extensions of our analyses warrant brief mention. First, we replicated the analyses found in Table 5 separately for public and private institutions. The pattern of displacement effects for the private institutions was very similar to those for the entire sample; the coefficients of the institutional NMS variable were indistinguishable for each subgroup between private institutions and for the overall sample (reported in Table 5). In contrast, the displacement effects of increasing institutional NMS awards at public institutions were not significantly different from zero when we used the top 80 and top 100 samples. This finding suggests that, at public institutions that are not in the top institutions in 2005 in terms of total NMS recipients, we find no evidence that Pell Grant recipients are displaced by institutionally funded NMS recipients.

Second, we replicated the analyses found in Table 5, adding data for 1999 to the sample. Because IPEDS did not collect 1999 enrollment data, we estimated the 1999 number of full-time, first-year students for each institution by the average of the 1998 and 2000 values of this variable for each institution. We found that, even with the measurement error induced by this method, our estimates of the displacement effects of increasing the number of institutionally sponsored NMS recipients at an institution on the number of Pell Grant recipients at the institution were roughly of the same order of magnitude as those found in Table 5.

Third, part-time students attending an institution at least half-time are eligible to receive Pell Grants. While we do not know the number of part-time students at each institution each year who meet this criteria, we experimented with either including part-time students in the total enrollment figures that make up the denominator of the dependent variable in equation (3), including part-time, first-year students in the total first-year enrollment figure that make up the denominator of the explanatory variables in equation (3), or doing both simultaneously. None of these changes substantially affected the findings that we have reported so far.

Finally, we divided our sample into institutions that experienced increases in total full-time enrollments during both the 1987–1991 and 1991–1995 periods and all other institutions. We estimated variants of the models that underlie Table 4 for both groups. We found that a strong statistically significant negative relationship exists between the change in the ratio of institutionally funded NMS to the number of full-time, first-year students and the change in the ratio of the number of Pell Grant recipients to the total full-time undergraduates enrolled at the institution only at the "growing" ones. Thus, the displacement of Pell Grant recipients by institutionally awarded NMS recipients in our sample appears to occur only at institutions with growing enrollments and largely reflects a change in the share of Pell Grant recipients in the student body, not always an absolute decline in the number of Pell grant recipients.

## Conclusion

Our study has provided the evidence that, with other factors being held constant, an increase in the share of institutionally funded NMS students in a college or university's first-year class is associated with a reduction in the share of Pell Grant recipients among the undergraduate student body at the institution. The magnitude of this displacement effect is largest at the institutions in our sample that enroll the greatest number of NMS students, and it occurs primarily in institutions whose enrollment is growing. We stress that we have observed this displacement effect, as we expected, only for institutionally sponsored NMS; we do not observe any displacement of Pell Grant recipients if an institution is able to increase the number of NMSC- or company-sponsored recipients that it enrolls. Those NMS winners who receive their awards regardless of their choice of institution do not appear to displace any student from lower-income families when they enroll at an institution.

While our research has focused only on NMS awards, it highlights the trade-off that may exist more broadly between using institutional grant aid to craft a more selective student body than would otherwise occur and using institutional grant aid to attract more students from families from the lower tail of the family income distribution. If selective institutions, especially public ones, are committed to serving students from all socioeconomic backgrounds, these institutions must track the share of their students who receive Pell grants and have as goals both socioeconomic diversity and student selectivity. Without concerted efforts by these institutions to increase the representation of students from lower- and lower-middle-income families in their student ranks, current inequalities in the distribution of students attending these institutions by family income class are likely to persist or worsen over time (Bowen, Kurzweil, & Tobin, 2005).

*Ronald G. Ehrenberg* is the Irving M. Ives Professor of Industrial and Labor Relations and Economics at Cornell University, Director of the Cornell Higher Education Research Institute (CHERI) and a research associate at the National Bureau of Economic Research.

*Liang Zhang* is an Assistant Professor of Higher Education at the University of Minnesota and a faculty associate at CHERI.

*Jared M. Levin* is an undergraduate research assistant at CHERI. CHERI is financially supported by the Andrew W. Mellon Foundation, the Atlantic Philanthropies (USA), Inc., and the TIAA-CREF Institute, and the authors express gratitude for their support. However, the views expressed in this paper are entirely the authors' own.

## Appendix

### Appendix Colleges and Universities with the Most Freshman NMS in 2003

| Rank | Institution | Total NMS | Sponsored by Institution |
| --- | --- | --- | --- |
| 1 | Harvard University | 37 | 80 |
| 2 | University of Texas at Austin | 258 | 201 |
| 3 | Yale University | 22 | 80 |
| 4 | University of Florida | 224 | 185 |
| 5 | Stanford University | 21 | 70 |
| 6 | University of Chicago | 182 | 148 |
| 7 | Arizona State University | 176 | 153 |
| 8 | Rice University | 173 | 102 |
| 9 | University of Oklahoma | 170 | 146 |
| 10 | Princeton University | 165 | 0 |
| 11 | Washington University in St. Louis | 162 | 125 |
| 12 | University of Southern California | 161 | 132 |
| 13 | Massachusetts Institute of Technology | 15 | 10 |
| 14 | University of North Carolina at Chapel Hill | 143 | 117 |
| 14 | Vanderbilt University | 143 | 103 |
| 16 | Brigham Young University | 140 | 97 |
| 17 | Texas A&M University | 137 | 103 |
| 18 | New York University | 136 | 115 |
| 19 | University of California at Los Angeles | 125 | 94 |
| 20 | Duke University | 10 | 30 |
| 21 | University of Pennsylvania | 10 | 10 |
| 22 | Northwestern University | 96 | 53 |
| 23 | Ohio State University | 93 | 77 |
| 23 | Purdue University | 93 | 75 |
| 25 | Carleton College | 79 | 62 |
| 26 | Georgia Institute of Technology | 77 | 62 |
| 27 | University of Georgia | 75 | 59 |
| 28 | Iowa State University | 69 | 55 |
| 29 | University of California at Berkeley | 67 | 0 |
| 30 | Michigan State University | 60 | 46 |
| 31 | University of Arizona | 59 | 47 |
| 31 | University of Michigan at Ann Arbor | 59 | 0 |
| 33 | University of California at San Diego | 56 | 38 |
| 34 | Boston University | 54 | 39 |
| 35 | Case Western Reserve University | 53 | 28 |
| 36 | University of Nebraska at Lincoln | 52 | 40 |
| 37 | Macalaster College | 51 | 48 |
| 38 | California Institute of Technology | 50 | 0 |
| 38 | University of Kansas | 50 | 40 |
| 40 | Johns Hopkins University | 49 | 32 |
| 40 | University of Tulsa | 49 | 38 |
| 40 | University of Maryland at College Park | 49 | 34 |
| 43 | Brown University | 47 | 0 |

**Appendix Colleges and Universities with the Most
Freshman NMS in 2003  (Continued)**

| Rank | Institution | Total NMS | Sponsored by Institution |
|---|---|---|---|
| 43 | Columbia University | 47 | 0 |
| 45 | Oberlin College | 46 | 38 |
| 45 | Tulane University | 46 | 36 |
| 47 | Dartmouth College | 45 | 0 |
| 47 | University of Kentucky | 45 | 33 |
| 47 | University of South Carolina at Columbia | 45 | 34 |
| 47 | Wheaton College (Ill.) | 45 | 40 |
| 51 | University of Notre Dame | 44 | 0 |
| 51 | University of Washington | 44 | 26 |
| 53 | Harvey Mudd College | 43 | 32 |
| 54 | Kenyon College | 41 | 33 |
| 54 | Tufts University | 41 | 37 |
| 56 | Baylor University | 40 | 31 |
| 56 | Grinnell College | 40 | 35 |
| 56 | University of Arkansas at Fayetteville | 40 | 33 |
| 56 | University of Minnesota-Twin Cities | 40 | 26 |
| 60 | Cornell University | 38 | 0 |
| 60 | Emory University | 38 | 27 |
| 62 | George Washington University | 37 | 32 |
| 62 | Georgetown University | 37 | 0 |
| 62 | St. Olaf College | 37 | 31 |
| 65 | University of Alabama at Tuscaloosa | 35 | 28 |
| 66 | Rose-Hulman Institute of Technology | 34 | 24 |
| 67 | Clemson University | 33 | 26 |
| 67 | Miami University (Ohio) | 33 | 26 |
| 67 | University of Central Florida | 33 | 28 |
| 67 | University of Illinois at Urbana-Champaign | 33 | 0 |
| 67 | University of Virginia | 33 | 0 |
| 72 | Louisiana State University at Baton Rouge | 32 | 25 |
| 72 | University of Mississippi | 32 | 24 |
| 74 | Brandeis University | 31 | 24 |
| 74 | Furman University | 31 | 29 |
| 74 | University of Miami | 31 | 22 |
| 74 | University of Texas at Dallas | 31 | 28 |
| 78 | Carnegie Mellon University | 29 | 0 |
| 78 | North Carolina State University | 29 | 21 |
| 80 | Auburn University | 28 | 20 |
| 80 | University of Wisconsin at Madison | 28 | 4 |
| 82 | University of Houston | 27 | 25 |
| 83 | Williams College | 26 | 0 |
| 84 | Amherst College | 25 | 0 |
| 84 | University of California at Irvine | 25 | 20 |
| 86 | Mississippi State University | 24 | 21 |
| 86 | University of Tennessee at Knoxville | 24 | 20 |
| 88 | Bowdoin College | 23 | 21 |
| 88 | Pomona College | 23 | 6 |
| 88 | University of Iowa | 23 | 19 |
| 88 | University of Utah | 23 | 17 |
| 88 | Washington and Lee University | 23 | 13 |
| 93 | Swarthmore College | 21 | 0 |
| 93 | University of Rochester | 21 | 18 |
| 93 | University of South Florida | 21 | 17 |
| 93 | Virginia Tech | 21 | 15 |
| 97 | Bowling Green State University | 20 | 18 |
| 97 | Calvin College | 20 | 17 |
| 97 | Kansas State University | 20 | 12 |
| 97 | Pennsylvania State University at University Park | 20 | 5 |
| 97 | Trinity University (Tex.) | 20 | 17 |
| 97 | University of Richmond | 20 | 12 |
| 97 | Whitman College | 20 | 16 |

# References

Avery, C., & Hoxby, C. M. (2004). Do and should financial aid decisions affect students' college choices? In C. Hoxby (Ed.), *College choices: The new economics of choosing, attending, and completing college.* Chicago: University of Chicago Press, 2004.

Bowen, W. G., Kurzweil, M. A., & Eugene M. Tobin. (2005). *Equity and excellence in American higher education.* Charlottesville: University Press of Virginia.

Duffy, E. A., & Goldberg, I. (1998). *Crafting a class: College admissions and financial aid, 1955–1994.* Princeton, NJ: Princeton University Press.

Ehrenberg, R. G. (2005, September). Method or madness? Inside the *USNWR* college rankings. *Journal of College Admissions.*

McPherson, M. S., & Schapiro, M. O. (1998). *The student aid game.* Princeton, NJ: Princeton University Press.

McPherson, M. S., & Schapiro, M. O. (2002, March/April). The blurring line between merit and need in financial aid. *Change, 34,* 38–46.

Seftor, N. S., & Turner, S. E. (2002, Spring). Back to school: Federal student aid policy and adult college enrollment. *Journal of Human Resources, 37,* 336–352.

Tebbs, J., & Turner, S. (2004, July/August). College education for low income students: A caution about using of data on Pell Grant recipients. *Change, 37,* 34–43.

*Trends in Student Aid 2004.* (2004). Washington D.C.: College Board.

*2002–2003 Title IV/Federal Pell Grant Program End-of-Year Report* [Web Page.] http://www.ed.gov/finaid/prof/resources/data/pe110203/ope.html.

# Footnotes

1. The lower enrollment shares in earlier years are an artifact of how the panel was constructed. This occurs because there is some variation in the institutions that appear in the top 100 list from year to year.

2. We caution the reader that part-time students attending at least half-time are eligible for Pell Grants. However, the 2002–2003 *Title IV/Federal Pell Grant Program End-of-Year Report* (Table 13) indicates that 86.9% of the Pell Grant recipients attending public four-year institutions and 87.8% of the Pell Grant recipients attending private four-year institutions were full-time students that year. For the institutions in our sample, part-time students represent only 12.6% of all students, and using total undergraduate students in the denominator of our ratio does not change the trends reported above or any of the econometric results that follow. We also caution that only U.S. citizens and permanent residents are eligible for Pell Grants. Thus, if an institution enrolls a high fraction of foreign students, its Pell Grant ratio will, other factors held constant, appear low.

3. The 2003 data could not be used because IPEDs data are not yet available for full-time, first-year students and total full-time undergraduate enrollment for 2002 or 2003. We exclude the 1999 data because IPED enrollment data were not collected for that year. However, we report below our efforts to include data for 1999 by using the average of the institution's enrollment in 1998 and 2000 as a proxy for its 1999 enrollment level.

# CHAPTER 6:
## OUTCOMES AND ACCOUNTABILITY

# Measuring Up on College-Level Learning

## MARGARET A. MILLER, PETER T. EWELL

## Foreword

*Measuring Up 2000,* the first state-by-state report card on higher education performance, gave all 50 states an Incomplete in the category of learning. Although *Measuring Up* evaluated, compared, and graded the states in other key categories of higher education performance (including preparation for college, participation, completion, and affordability), the report card found that "there is no information available to make state-by-state comparisons" of higher education's most important outcome, learning. The primary purpose of the Incomplete was to stimulate a more robust discussion and debate about what states should know about college-level learning.

Shortly after the release of *Measuring Up 2000,* an invitational forum of public policy, business, and education leaders was convened by James B. Hunt Jr., governor of North Carolina, and hosted by Roger Enrico, vice chairman of PepsiCo, at the PepsiCo corporate headquarters in Purchase, New York. The purpose of the forum was to advise the National Center on next steps to address the issue of student learning at the state level. The forum recommended that the National Center begin by using information already available on college outcomes as the building blocks of a model to collect comparative state-by-state information on learning. Forum participants urged the National Center to move ahead with a "demonstration project" to determine whether or not it was feasible to collect information on learning at the state level that would be useful to state policy leaders.

The National Center was fortunate to enlist the help of Margaret Miller, professor at the Curry School of Education, to lead the National Forum on College-Level Learning, a five-state demonstration project to develop a model of college-level learning for the states. Peter Ewell, vice president of the National Center for Higher Education Management Systems (NCHEMS), was the senior consultant to the project. The Pew Charitable Trusts supported the project through a grant to the Institute for Educational Leadership (IEL).

The most recent edition of the report card, *Measuring Up 2004,* included a brief summary of the results of the demonstration project. This report provides a more comprehensive account of the project, its findings, and conclusions, as well as information that will be useful to states that may wish to replicate the model. The report concludes that providing comparative state-by-state information about learning outcomes is not only feasible, but also important and useful for policy.

The model described in this report enables states to gather information that addresses two critical questions:

1. What is the "educational capital," or the knowledge and skills of the population, that states have available to them for developing or sustaining a competitive economy and vital civic life?
2. How do all the colleges and universities in the state (that is, public, private, not-for-profit, and for-profit) contribute to the development of the state's educational capital?

This approach is different from asking or requiring individual colleges and universities to assess or evaluate student learning. Colleges and universities can and should be accountable for assessing student learning and reporting results, but the measures used by individual institutions may not add up to a comprehensive assessment of educational capital for the state as a whole. The statewide approach, as shown by the demonstration project, allows comparisons among states, providing information about a state's relative standing to the rest of the nation in developing the knowledge and skills of its population.

In a knowledge-based global economy, the fortunes of states depend on the knowledge and skills of their residents. The demonstration project has shown that states can assess their educational capital feasibly and effectively to provide useful information for policymakers and educators in identifying problems and stimulating and targeting improvement. State leaders are urged to participate in similar efforts to expand their state's understanding of the knowledge and skills of their residents in order to enhance the economic and civic vitality of their state.

*Patrick M. Callan*
President
National Center for Public Policy and Higher Education

## Introduction

At the symposium of policy leaders marking the release of *Measuring Up 2000*,[1] which was the first 50-state report card on higher education, one of the most dramatic moments was the unveiling of a U.S. map representing each state's performance in learning—the sixth and final graded category in the report card. In contrast to the brightly colored patchworks portraying grades for each of the states in the other five categories, the learning map was a uniform gray (see figure 1). A large question mark superimposed upon it represented the Incomplete that all states had earned in that category. The conversation among those at the symposium ended without a satisfactory answer to the sharply posed question: "Why can't we grade the states on learning, if that is the most important result colleges and universities produce?"

At one level, institutions and states actually know a good deal about what their college students know and can do. Apart from the many times students' work is evaluated in class, every institution must determine its success in educating students in order to meet the requirements of regional accreditors. Moreover, most states have some kind of statewide assessment requirement in place to improve performance, to give state officials a sense of what their investment in higher education has yielded, or both. But unlike the information collected in the other categories of *Measuring Up*, there are no comprehensive national data on college-level learning that could be used to compare state performance in this area.

The information states do have on collegiate learning is incomplete for their own purposes as well. When every campus within a state assesses its students' learning differently, the state has no

**Figure 1. In *Measuring Up 2000* and *2002,* all states received an Incomplete in learning**

effective method for interpreting the resulting information because there are no external benchmarks against which to measure a given program's or institution's performance. Even those states that employ common measures statewide for public colleges and universities know virtually nothing about the learning results of their private institutions. Nor do they know how the learning of their college-educated residents or current college attendees compares to the learning of those in other states.

Subsequent to the release of *Measuring Up 2000*, the National Center's Board of Directors considered eliminating the learning category. The board concluded, however, that the category—and the idea behind it—was too important to abandon. Subsequently, The Pew Charitable Trusts decided to sponsor an investigation into how to generate grades in that category. As a result of that decision, the National Forum on College-Level Learning was born.

## The National Forum, Phase One

The National Forum on College-Level Learning began with interviews of higher education and policy leaders around the country, during which three questions were posed:

1. Should the National Forum attempt to assess student learning in comparable ways at the state level?
2. If so, what questions should be answered by whatever information the National Forum collects?
3. How should the National Forum go about collecting the information?

In November 2001, a group of higher education, policy, and business leaders considered the same set of questions at a meeting in Purchase, New York (see list of participants below). Their answers echoed those of the leaders interviewed earlier:

- **Should the National Forum attempt to assess student learning in comparable ways at the state level?** The answer to this question was a resounding "yes." Meeting participants observed that national pressures to assess collegiate learning, dating back to before the congressional ratification of the National Education Goals in 1994, were not dissipating. In fact, they were increasing. Moreover, it was "outrageous," as one participant put it, not to know more about higher education's most important product. Finally, without information about learning results, *Measuring Up*—as a state-by-state report card on higher education—would always present an incomplete picture of the success of higher education policy in the states.

**Participants
National Forum on
College-Level
Learning**
*November 27–28, 2001*
Purchase, New York

**The Honorable Garrey
Carruthers**
*President and Chief
Executive Officer*
Cimarron HMO, Inc.

**Gordon K. Davies**
*President*
Kentucky Council on
Postsecondary
Education

**Thomas Ehrlich**
*Senior Scholar*
Carnegie Foundation
for the Advancement of Teaching

**Roger A. Enrico**
*Vice Chairman*
PepsiCo., Inc.

**The Honorable Jim
Geringer**
*Governor of Wyoming*

**Milton Goldberg**
*Executive Vice President*
National Alliance of
Business

**The Honorable James
B. Hunt Jr.**
Womble, Carlyle,
Sandridge & Rice

**Glenn R. Jones**
*President and Chief
Executive Officer*
Jones International,
Ltd.

**Ann Kirschner**
*President and Chief
Executive Officer*
Fathom

**The Honorable John
R. McKernan, Jr.**
*Vice Chairman*
Education Management Corporation

**Charles Miller**
*Chairman*
Meridian National, Inc.

- **What questions should be answered by whatever information the National Forum collects?** Participants formulated two state policy questions that any information gathered about learning should answer:

  1. "What do the state's college-educated residents know and what can they do that contributes to the social good?" This question became known as the "educational capital" question, because it sought to measure the level of educational capital within each state.
  2. "How well do the state's public and private colleges and universities collectively increase the intellectual skills of their students? What do those whom they educate know, and what can they do?" This second set of questions was directed toward finding out how the higher education system in each state (including public and private institutions) was performing as a whole.

- **How should the National Forum go about collecting the information?** To answer this question, participants adopted a model proposed by the project's advisory committee, developed with the assistance of a panel of assessment experts convened prior to the meeting (see sidebar for National Forum staff and advisory committee members). The model's key components included:

  1. information drawn from existing licensure and graduate-admission tests that many students take when they graduate,
  2. results from the National Adult Literacy Survey (NALS), and
  3. results of specially administered tests of general intellectual skills.

The State of Kentucky, as it turned out, already had access to information on student learning that fit into the first two categories of the proposed model. That is, the state had assembled scores

---

**Participants National Forum on College-Level Learning, con't.**

**Lillian Montoya-Rael**
*Executive Director*
Regional Development Corporation

**Michael Nettles**
*Professor of Education and Public Policy*
University of Michigan

**Steffen E. Palko**
*Vice Chair and President*
XTO Energy, Inc.

**The Honorable Paul E. Patton**
*Governor of Kentucky*

**Charles B. Reed**
*Chancellor*
California State University

**Sean C. Rush**
*General Manager*
Global Education Industries
IBM Corporation

**Edward B. Rust, Jr.**
*Chairman and Chief Executive Officer*
State Farm Insurance Companies

**Ted Sanders**
*President*
Education Commission of the States

**The Honorable Jack Scott**
*State Senator*
California State Senate

**Kala M. Stroup**
*Commissioner of Higher Education*
State of Missouri

**National Forum Staff and Advisory Committe**
*Staff*

*Project Director*
**Margaret A. Miller**
Professor, Curry School of Education
University of Virginia

*Project Manager*
**Margaret Peak**
Curry School of Education University of Virginia

*Intern*
**Melinda Vann**
Virginia Polytechnic Institute and State University

*Advisory Committee*

**David W. Breneman**
*Dean, Curry School of Education*
University of Virginia

**Patrick M. Callan**
*President*
National Center for Public Policy and Higher Education

**Emerson J. Elliott**
*Retired Commissioner*
National Center for Education Statistics

on some licensure and graduate-admission tests and was willing to collect more. Secondly, it had administered the Kentucky Adult Literacy Survey in 1996, a replica of the NALS. With the generous cooperation of the state, the model was applied to Kentucky as an illustration in *Measuring Up 2002*, using the partial information that was available. Results were encouraging enough for The Pew Charitable Trusts to fund the next phase of the National Forum's work, in which five states would undertake a demonstration project to implement the model in full.

## The National Forum, Phase Two

The states that joined Kentucky in the demonstration project were Illinois, Oklahoma, Nevada, and South Carolina—several small and one large state from various regions of the country. Between 2002 and 2004 the project team assembled information on the NALS and on graduate-admission and licensure tests for each demonstration state. Meanwhile, the states administered general intellectual skills tests to a random sample of students at a representative sample of public and private two- and four-year institutions within their borders. The four-year institutions also attempted (unsuccessfully as it turned out) to collect information about their alumni's perceptions of their own intellectual skills. Also, both two- and four-year institutions in each state administered surveys aimed at gauging students' engagement with their collegiate experience, since research suggests that engagement is associated with learning. The engagement measures were subsequently dropped from the model, since they are not direct measures of learning.

The results of the demonstration project were published in *Measuring Up 2004*. All five participating states were awarded a "Plus" in the learning category in acknowledgment of their successful implementation of the model. They had demonstrated that college-level learning could be assessed in a way that makes interstate comparison possible, that these assessments were consistent with other information that *Measuring Up* had revealed about these states, and that the information could be useful to policymakers in each state.

Experience with the demonstration project suggests that it is feasible to extend this approach to other states and eventually to create a nationwide benchmark for learning. While the project encountered difficulties in the logistics of administering tests, institutional commitment and preparation, and student motivation to participate, these challenges are typical of a first effort of this kind. With increased preparation and resources, these barriers can be overcome. To facilitate this process, detailed explanations of the logistics and costs associated with implementing the National Forum's learning model are contained in the appendix. The next edition of the report card on higher education, *Measuring Up 2006*, will report results for additional states in this category.

## Why Measure Learning at the State Level?

Even with generous support from The Pew Charitable Trusts, the implementation of the demonstration project was challenging, and it required serious commitment and leadership from the participating states. Contributing to the purposes of a nationwide report card on higher education would not have been sufficient motivation for these states to make an effort of this magnitude, without an accompanying belief that the project would be useful to them.

Fortunately, they did believe in its usefulness. In Kentucky and Oklahoma, the project supplemented or completed existing statewide accountability systems. In South Carolina, it dovetailed with work being done on an accountability project supported by the Fund for the Improvement of Postsecondary Education (FIPSE). Leaders in Illinois and Nevada believed that the project would produce information that could be used to improve their higher education systems.

But what does this approach to assessing college-level learning tell states that their existing assessment approaches do not?

First, it tells states how much educational capital they have—an asset that every state needs to advance its economic, civic, and social welfare. It is virtually a truism now that education and training beyond high school is necessary for individuals and states to be players in the global economy. In addition, the pressing, complex challenges of our political life and the sophistication of attempts to influence the electorate, so vividly demonstrated in the 2004 national elections, require critical thinking skills that are increasingly essential to the workings of a democracy. Finally, the decisions individuals must face in everyday life—ranging from how to ensure the best schooling for their children, to planning for retirement, to completing the myriad forms that control access to services—have become so challenging that education increasingly differentiates those who are able to negotiate them successfully from those who are not. Certificates and degrees are increasingly inadequate proxies for educational capital. It is the *skills* and *knowledge* behind the degrees that matter.

Secondly, this approach to assessing college-level learning tells a state the extent to which its institutions are collectively effective in contributing to its store of educational capital. Until now, when states have raised the question of learning, the unit of analysis has always been the institution. The model's focus on the state as a whole permits states to ask broader questions that are quite different from how well individual institutions are performing. Among these questions are:

- How well are we doing in serving the various regions of the state?
- Are there achievement gaps among population groups that we should be concerned about and address collectively?
- How well are our workforce-development efforts working?
- Are we producing enough well-trained professionals in areas that are critical to the state's welfare?
- What economic development options are available to our state—or are denied to us—because of the educational capital resources we have?

### Kentucky's Experience with the Demonstration Project

Upon initiating a major reform of postsecondary education in 1997, Kentucky developed an accountability system focused on a public agenda and organized around five key questions:

1. Are more Kentuckians prepared for college?
2. Are more students enrolling in college?
3. Are more students advancing through the system?
4. Are college graduates prepared for life and work?
5. Are Kentucky's communities and economy benefiting?

For each of these questions, the Council on Postsecondary Education developed specific outcome measures called "key indicators" of progress. Valid measures allowing comparisons across states were available for the first three questions, and Kentucky has demonstrated progress on most of these measures. But the fourth and fifth questions were more challenging. Kentucky's participation in the demonstration project assisted the state in developing indicators to address question four. The state's results are also helping to answer questions frequently posed by stakeholders who are external to higher education about the quality of the education being provided to the dramatically increased number of students now enrolled in postsecondary institutions in the state.

The results of the demonstration project for Kentucky suggest that the state's two-year institutions (where most of the recent enrollment increase has occurred) are doing a comparatively good job in preparing graduates for life and work. Students at the universities are faring less well on the direct assessments administered through the project, and the state as a whole remains challenged by low literacy levels in its general population.

Kentucky plans to seek $600,000 in recurring state funding to expand the application of these measures of student learning, in order to further investigate these conclusions and to develop baseline data that will allow the state to set the same kinds of improvement goals for learning that it created to measure progress in other areas. Discussions to refine and develop the measures are already underway with postsecondary institutions. These discussions are focused on integrating the National Forum's efforts with a parallel initiative to develop a competency-based assessment of general education outcomes based on the Greater Expectations project administered by the Association of American Colleges and Universities. In the final analysis, efforts to increase participation in postsecondary education must be judged in terms of the extent to which these increases prepare graduates to be successful citizens and workers who contribute to the quality of life of their communities, the state, and the nation.

- Do we have the range of college preparation programs or graduate opportunities needed for the economy and lifestyles that our residents want?
- How does the mobility of the graduating college population—coming here to work and live, or leaving our institutions to go elsewhere—affect our responsibilities to our residents or our ability to create the community life and employment opportunities we want?

A collective examination also enables cost-benefit analyses to be performed concerning the learning that the state's system of higher education is producing in relation to the state's investment. Armed with answers to these kinds of questions, a state can undertake further analyses, target resources where they are most needed to address urgent state priorities, and promote collective solutions to collective problems.

Third, as is true for all the *Measuring Up* categories, a state can benchmark its performance against that of other states and against itself over time, to chart progress and identify good practice. Given sample sizes that are large and representative, institutions too can see how well they perform relative to their peers on a few key assessment measures. These external benchmarks can serve to anchor their more extensive campus-based assessment methods, which continue to be essential to improvement.

Finally, this model represents a way to address the growing national mandate for accountability without creating a federal program. The No Child Left Behind (NCLB) Act has demonstrated the urgency with which the public is demanding a commitment to standards and educational equity through evidence of learning—an urgency that is beginning to be felt in higher education as well as in K–12 schools. The implementation of NCLB has highlighted the dangers of adopting federal solutions to national, state, and local problems. Because much of the information used in the National Forum's model derives from existing databases—and because the tests that are administered are voluntary and sample-based, and are not high stakes—the National Forum's approach is cost effective, minimally intrusive, and nonpunitive for students and institutions.

## A Model for Measuring College-Level Learning

For the National Forum's demonstration project, the learning category was constructed much as the other five performance categories in *Measuring Up* had been created. Indicators that reflected various dimensions of state performance were grouped under several overall themes, or clusters, and each was weighted:

- **Literacy Levels of the State Population** (25%). This cluster of indicators reflects the proportion of residents who achieve high levels of literacy. It directly addresses the question, "What are the abilities of the state population?"

> **Oklahoma's Experience with the Demonstration Project**
> Oklahoma welcomed the opportunity to participate in the National Forum's demonstration project because it dovetailed well with the existing assessment and accountability initiatives of the Oklahoma State System for Higher Education. These initiatives include:
> - a mandated, system-wide, college student assessment policy that has been in place since 1991 and that includes assessment of general education and program-level outcomes;
> - the Educational Planning and Assessment System (EPAS), which links 8th and 10th grade assessments to the ACT and other information about college preparation;
> - the federally sponsored Gaining Early Awareness and Readiness for Undergraduate Programs (GEAR UP), which focuses on school interventions down to the 5th grade and features an information campaign targeted to families to encourage college attendance;
> - the Report Card on Oklahoma Higher Education, which includes many of the same measures as *Measuring Up*; and
> - a partnership with the Oklahoma Business and Education Coalition (OBEC), the Oklahoma State Department of Education, and Achieve, Inc., which is leading to a comprehensive standards and benchmarking study.

For the demonstration project, the data used were the same as those included in the benefits category of *Measuring Up* and were based on the 1992 National Adult Literacy Survey (NALS) for residents ages 25 to 64, updated using the 2000 census. The NALS assessment poses real-world tasks or problems that respondents must perform or solve in the following areas:

1. *Prose literacy:* reading and interpreting texts;
2. *Document literacy:* obtaining or acting on information contained in tabular or graphic displays; and
3. *Quantitative literacy:* understanding numbers or graphs and performing calculations.

With new data available from the National Assessment of Adult Literacy (NAAL) in 2004, it will be possible to sharpen this cluster of indicators to capture the literacy levels of the college-educated population rather than of the state population as a whole. Due to limitations in the statistical procedure used to update the 1992 NALS, however, this was not possible for this analysis.

- **Graduates Ready for Advanced Practice** (25%). The measures in this area reflect the contributions of colleges and universities to a state's stock of educational capital. This cluster of indicators examines the proportion of the state's college graduates (from both two- and four-year institutions) who are ready for advanced practice in the form of vocational/professional licensure or graduate study. It addresses the policy question, "To what extent do colleges and universities educate students to be capable of contributing to the workforce?"

For the demonstration project, the measures were based on the proportion of college graduates (that is, associate's or bachelor's degree holders) within each state who have demonstrated their readiness for advanced practice through:

1. *Licensure examinations:* taking and passing a national examination required to enter a licensed vocation/profession such as nursing or physical therapy;
2. *Competitive admissions exams:* taking a nationally recognized graduate-admission exam such as the Graduate Record Examination (GRE) or the Medical College Admissions Test (MCAT) and earning a nationally competitive score; or

Participation in the National Forum benefited Oklahoma in several ways. First, the project provided institutions with an opportunity to experiment with state-of-the-art assessment measures like the Collegiate Learning Assessment (CLA) during tight budget times and to expand their use of the ACT WorkKeys, which had been piloted in Oklahoma already. The project also reinvigorated statewide conversations about: (1) using common assessments to help align courses and learning goals throughout the system, and (2) establishing common general education competencies. Institutions were also encouraged to use learning assessment data in a recently established performance-funding approach.

Findings from the demonstration project were shared with numerous groups, including the presidents of the 25 public institutions, the vice presidents for academic and student affairs, the faculty advisory councils, the chairmen of all governing boards, and business leaders. All results were also provided to campus assessment coordinators for further analysis or local use. The findings indicated a possible writing deficiency among Oklahomans that has since been confirmed in discussions with the academic officers. Recently, much emphasis has been placed on improving math preparation, followed by reading; as a result, writing may have been overlooked. Another finding that Oklahoma took note of was the relatively low number of students prepared for graduate school: few seek advanced education, and many of those who do so do not achieve competitive test scores.

A number of initiatives in Oklahoma are planned as a result of the state's participation. First, the state plans to build on the work of the National Forum in collecting licensure and graduate examination scores, which has been a difficult task in the past. The state also hopes to explore other ways to compare teacher certification information. Finally, by hosting a follow-up meeting to the National Forum project in Oklahoma next year, assessment coordinators plan to consider other national measures that were not included in the demonstration project and hope to expand collection of these measures beyond the five pilot states.

3. *Teacher preparation measures:* taking and passing a teacher licensure exam in the state in which they graduated.

- **Performance of the College Educated** (50%). This cluster of indicators focuses on the quality of the state's higher education "product" by addressing the all-important question, "How effectively can students who are about to graduate from two- and four-year colleges and universities communicate and solve problems?"

For the demonstration project, the measures consisted of two general intellectual skills assessments:

1. *At two-year institutions:* the WorkKeys assessments administered by the American College Testing (ACT) Service. These assessments examine what students can do with what they know. Items on reading comprehension and locating information, for instance, might require students to extract information from documents and instructions; questions in applied math might test their abilities in using mathematical concepts such as probability or estimation in real-world settings. The business writing assessment requires students to prepare an original essay in a business setting.
2. *At four-year institutions:* the Collegiate Learning Assessment (CLA). The CLA is an innovative examination that goes beyond multiple-choice testing by posing real-world tasks that a student is asked to understand and solve. For example, students could be asked to draw scientific conclusions from a body of evidence in biology or examine historical conclusions based on original documents. Or they might be asked to write a persuasive essay, and analyze and then refute a written argument with logic and evidence.

Measures included under the first two clusters above—"literacy levels of the state population" and "graduates ready for advanced practice"—are available nationally and can potentially be calculated for all 50 states, although the smaller size of the national samples and the reduced number of state over-samples between the NALS in 1992 and the NAAL in 2004 make this difficult to do for the smaller states. The National Forum therefore endorses the recommendation made in the report of the National Commission on Accountability in Higher Education, sponsored by the State Higher Education Executive Officers (SHEEO), that the size of the next adult literacy survey be increased (see http://www.sheeo.org/account/accountability.pdf). Measures included in the third cluster above—"performance of the college educated"—will require special data-collection efforts similar to those undertaken by the five demonstration project states in 2004.

As with any data used to determine a grade in *Measuring Up,* values for each of the indicators within each cluster must be compared with a common standard. For the calculations in the five other categories in the report card, this standard is set by the best-performing states. Because the demonstration project involved only five states, however, the standard chosen was the national average on each measure. For those cases in which national data were unavailable, the five-state average was used.

## Results for Participating States

The set of measures collected according to the National Forum's model can be used to create a "learning profile" that communicates graphically each state's strengths and challenges with respect to collegiate learning. Each state's performance on this profile is reflected by how many percentage points *above* or *below* the national or state benchmark its own performance lies. Horizontal bars on each state profile correspond to each of the measures and portray an overall pattern of performance for each state in relation to other states (see figure 2, page 507). Bars to the left of the vertical line in the center of the display indicate how far below the national benchmark the state falls on a comparable scale for these measures. Bars to the right of the vertical line indicate how many percentage points above this benchmark the state performs. For example, 26% of Illinois residents achieved high scores on the National Adult Literacy Survey (NALS) in prose literacy, compared with 24% nationally who did so—a difference of 8.3% in favor of Illinois ($26 - 24 = 2$; $2 \div 24 = .083$), as shown in the top bar of figure 2. Deviations of only a few percentage points on a given measure indicate that the state's performance is not markedly different from that of other states, while larger deviations (that is, about ten points or more) suggest that the state is above or below most others on this dimension of performance.

It is important to emphasize that the evaluation of learning results presented for each state should be confined to raising issues for discussion and making broad comparisons. Because relatively small numbers of students were tested on the direct measures of student learning, and because the extent to which this test-taker population is representative of all graduates of two- and four-year colleges in each state is unknown, results should be treated with caution. Readers should look primarily at the overall *pattern* of such results without making too much of the individual values for each measure.

## Illinois

Illinois has historically had a strong and well-funded higher education system and enjoys a diverse economy and relatively high levels of educational attainment. These strengths are reflected in its above-average performance with respect to literacy in all three areas: prose, document, and quantitative literacy (see figure 2, page 507). For example, 26% of Illinois residents who took the NALS earned the highest scores in prose literacy, compared with a national average of 24%. The other four demonstration states scored a high of 22% and a low of 18% on this measure. Results on the other two literacy measures show equivalent performance differences between Illinois and other states.

But higher education institutions in Illinois also tend to emphasize traditional over vocational fields of study. The state's community colleges, for instance, are all comprehensive community colleges rather than technical colleges. This emphasis is reflected in the cluster of indicators reflected in "graduates ready for advanced practice." For example, about ten percent fewer of the state's two- and four-year college graduates take and pass vocational or professional licensing examinations than is the case nationally. But four-year college graduates in Illinois take graduate-admission examinations at just above the national average, and they perform well on them. Fifty-two percent of Illinois graduates who take such exams achieve nationally competitive scores, compared with only 31% in other states.

Illinois students also perform at above-average levels on all direct measures of student learning with the exception of the applied math skills of students at two-year colleges. For instance, 26% of the state's test-takers at two-year colleges achieved top scores on the WorkKeys business writing test, compared with only 18% across the five states. And 61% of Illinois' test-takers at four-year institutions achieved top scores on the CLA problem-solving measure, while only 53% did so across all five states. While not as dramatic, score differences between Illinois and other states on the other assessments administered for the project within this cluster of indicators were similar. This favorable outcome probably reflects the strong high school backgrounds typical of Illinois high school graduates: Illinois received an A in preparation in *Measuring Up 2002* and a B+ in *Measuring Up 2004*.

But Illinois does face a challenge with respect to the performance of its minority students in higher education. African-American and Hispanic students in Illinois score not only below white students, but also at significantly lower levels than their counterparts in other states. Across all six assessments, white students in Illinois were more than twice as likely as their nonwhite counterparts to achieve high scores. For example, 55% of Illinois' white test-takers at two-year colleges achieved top scores on the WorkKeys reading for information test, while only 21% of the state's nonwhite counterparts achieved this level of performance.

## Kentucky

Kentucky has recently made major investments in both K–12 and postsecondary education, in large part because it faces substantial challenges with respect to literacy and educational attainment. These challenges are reflected in literacy performances significantly lower than those of other states (see figure 3). For example, only 18% of Kentucky's residents scored in the top performance categories in prose literacy, while 24% did so nationwide. The state also lags the nation, but not as severely, in document and quantitative literacy.

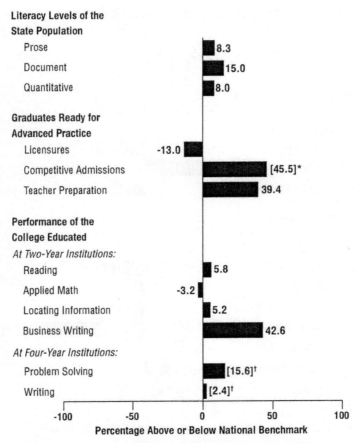

**Literacy Levels of the State Population**
Prose — 8.3
Document — 15.0
Quantitative — 8.0

**Graduates Ready for Advanced Practice**
Licensures — -13.0
Competitive Admissions — [45.5]*
Teacher Preparation — 39.4

**Performance of the College Educated**
*At Two-Year Institutions:*
Reading — 5.8
Applied Math — -3.2
Locating Information — 5.2
Business Writing — 42.6

*At Four-Year Institutions:*
Problem Solving — [15.6]†
Writing — [2.4]†

Percentage Above or Below National Benchmark

\* GRE scores used as part of the calculation of "competitive admissions" for Illinois were based on the national average because of missing data for key institutions. All other test score data are specific to Illinois.

† These scores must be qualified because of the limited number of institutions participating.

**Figure 2. Illinois Learning Measures**

Kentucky has recently made a significant investment in its community and technical college system, allowing these institutions to play a much stronger role in workforce development. These investments appear to have paid off with higher-than-average proportions of graduates taking and passing licensing examinations in fields like nursing or physical therapy. For example, about half again as many Kentucky graduates of two-year colleges take licensing exams as do their counterparts in other states, and 86% of the Kentucky test-takers achieve passing scores, compared with 84% of those taking such examinations elsewhere. However, the state remains less competitive with respect to the proportion of four-year college graduates taking and performing well on examinations governing admission to graduate schools. Only about three-fourths as many Kentucky graduates of four-year institutions take exams like the GRE as do their counterparts in other states. The proportion of test-takers achieving nationally competitive scores on such tests is 23% in Kentucky, compared with a national average of 31%.

Kentucky's two-year college students perform at high levels on the WorkKeys exams, especially business writing. More than a third (37%) of the state's test-takers achieved top scores on this measure, while only about 18% did so in other states. The performance of four-year college students in Kentucky is less competitive and constitutes a challenge for the state. For example, 44% of Kentucky's test-takers at four-year colleges and universities achieved top scores on the task-based CLA problem-solving assessment, compared with a five-state average of 53%. There are also notable performance gaps between white and African-American students on all these examinations in Kentucky, although the state's African-American students do perform better than their counterparts in other states.

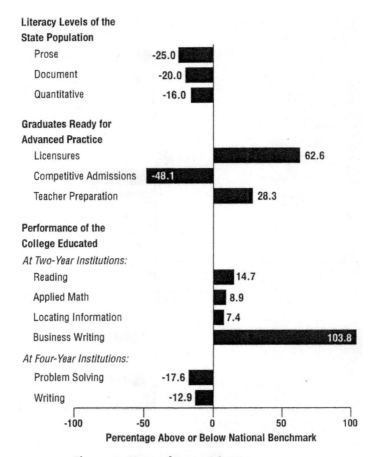

**Figure 3. Kentucky Learning Measures**

## Nevada

Nevada has a unique economy and a small, nonselective, higher education system composed entirely of public institutions. The state has performed at the lower end of most *Measuring Up* scales with respect to preparation (receiving a D in *Measuring Up 2004*) and educational attainment. The state's below-average results on the literacy measures reflect this standing (see figure 4), as the state's residents consistently score about ten percentage points below the national average across all three indicators.

Meanwhile, Nevada faces an unprecedented teacher shortage as its K–12 system tries to keep up with an expanding population. The state appears to be meeting this challenge, as shown by an unusually high proportion of graduates taking and passing teacher licensure examinations: almost twice as many college graduates do so in Nevada as across the nation. But the state is far less competitive in the other two indicators of "graduates ready for advanced practice." About 20% fewer Nevada students take licensing examinations as compared with other states, though the pass rates of Nevada students are competitive nationally. At the same time, graduates of four-year institutions in other states take graduate-admission exams at about one and a half times the rate of Nevada's graduates, and only 22% of Nevada graduates who take these exams earn competitive scores, while 31% of their counterparts elsewhere do so. These results probably reflect lower levels of student preparation upon entering college and the fact that fewer students graduate from college in Nevada; the state received an F in completion in *Measuring Up 2004*.

Because of problems encountered in the testing process beyond the state's control, direct evidence of the quality of outcomes is unavailable for four-year college students in Nevada. The performance of the state's two-year college students is below the five-state averages on all four of the skill areas tested. This was especially the case on the WorkKeys business writing exam, where only about 11% of Nevada test-takers scored at the highest level, while more than 18% did so across the five states.

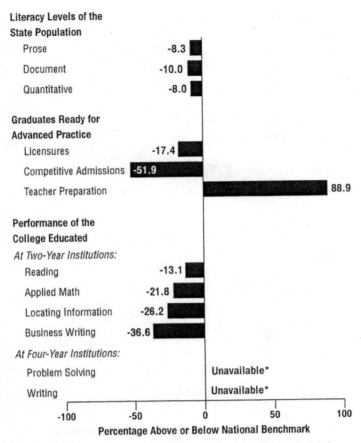

**Literacy Levels of the State Population**

Prose          -8.3

Document       -10.0

Quantitative   -8.0

**Graduates Ready for Advanced Practice**

Licensures              -17.4

Competitive Admissions  -51.9

Teacher Preparation     88.9

**Performance of the College Educated**

*At Two-Year Institutions:*

Reading               -13.1

Applied Math          -21.8

Locating Information  -26.2

Business Writing      -36.6

*At Four-Year Institutions:*

Problem Solving   Unavailable*

Writing           Unavailable*

-100   -50   0   50   100

**Percentage Above or Below National Benchmark**

\* These data were unavailable due to insufficient numbers of test-takers and logistical problems with test administration.

**Figure 4. Nevada Learning Measures**

## Oklahoma

Oklahoma has recently been active in attempting to improve the quality of its higher education system. The state faces substantial educational challenges with respect to baccalaureate attainment (it is in the bottom half of the 50 states) and the quality of its preparation of students in K–12 schools (the state earned a C–in preparation in *Measuring Up 2004*). The literacy levels of Oklahoma's residents reflect these challenges (see figure 5). The state lags behind national averages in the proportions of its residents achieving top scores by about five to ten percent across all three measures.

Oklahoma's higher education system is heavily and deliberately oriented toward workforce preparation, and this emphasis is reflected in its performances on measures of the readiness of graduates for advanced practice. The proportion of its graduates taking professional and vocational licensure examinations is well above the national average, with almost two-thirds more two-year college students in Oklahoma taking such examinations than in other states. Furthermore, the pass rates of Oklahoma's two-year college students on such exams are also competitive, matching national averages on such tests. But about 60% fewer four-year college graduates take graduate-admission examinations in Oklahoma than in other states, and only 23% of these test-takers achieve top scores in Oklahoma, compared with 31% elsewhere.

Students at two- and four-year institutions perform at or just below national averages on direct measures of student learning. While Oklahoma's minority students perform at lower levels than white students in the state on all six measures, the performance levels of Oklahoma's nonwhite students are about the same as those in other states. Written communication skills, though, constitute a particular policy challenge for Oklahoma across all population groups. This is reflected in below-average performances on the WorkKeys business writing exam taken by the state's two-year college

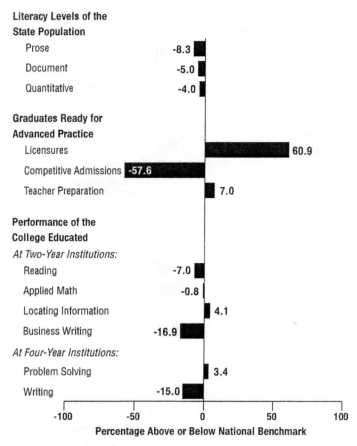

**Figure 5. Oklahoma Learning Measures**

students (15% achieved top scores in Oklahoma, compared with more than 18% across the five states), on the CLA writing assessment taken by the state's four-year college students (just under 32% achieved top scores in Oklahoma, compared with more than 37% across the five states), and in prose literacy for the general population (22% of Oklahoma residents achieved top scores on the NALS, compared with more than 24% for the U.S. population as a whole).

## South Carolina

South Carolina's "educational pipeline" loses many students early, with almost half of the state's ninth graders failing to graduate from high school within four years. However, those who do make it to college are comparatively well prepared, and the state's colleges and universities have very good rates of college completion (earning the state a B in completion in *Measuring Up 2004*).

This bifurcated pattern is also reflected in the learning measures assembled for South Carolina by the demonstration project (see figure 6). Literacy levels are well below national averages, with the proportions scoring in the top categories on the NALS lagging on all three measures. For example, 19% of South Carolina residents achieved top scores in quantitative literacy compared with 25% for the nation as a whole. But the performance of South Carolina students on direct measures of student learning is mostly above average. For example, on the WorkKeys reading for information test taken by the state's two-year college students, 65% achieved top scores while only about 57% did so across the five states. Similarly, over 56% of the state's test-takers at four-year institutions achieved top scores on the task-based CLA problem-solving assessment, while only 53% did so across the five states. This above-average performance, however, is not reflected in writing. At the two-year level, about half as many of the state's test-takers achieved top scores on the WorkKeys

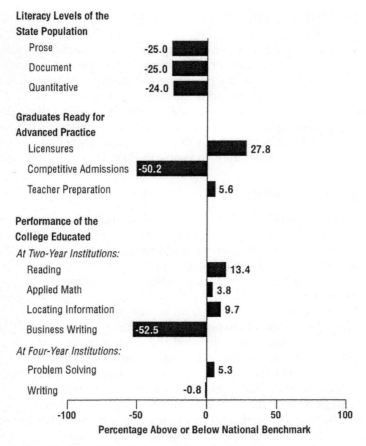

**Figure 6. South Carolina Learning Measures**

business writing assessment as did test-takers across the five states (9% vs. 18%). At the four-year level, South Carolina test-takers were about as likely as their counterparts elsewhere to achieve top scores in writing (both at about 37%).

Much of the policy challenge for South Carolina lies with the state's African-American student population, which constitutes more than a quarter of all students enrolled. South Carolina's African-American students not only perform at levels below those typical of the state's white students, but also frequently score lower than their counterparts in other states. To take an extreme case, 62% of South Carolina's white test-takers at two-year colleges achieved top scores on the WorkKeys applied math exam while only 13% of the state's nonwhite test-takers did so. Both of these statistics can be compared with 25% of nonwhite test-takers achieving top performances across the five states. While performance gaps on the other five measures between white and nonwhite students in South Carolina are not as large as those in applied math, the pattern of results is similar.

In the realm of graduates ready for advanced practice, the proportion of South Carolina graduates who take and pass licensing examinations governing entry to vocational and technical professions is above average. Two- and four-year college students take such examinations at a rate about 20% higher than is typical nationally, and their pass rate is 88% in South Carolina, compared with a national rate of 84%. This probably reflects South Carolina's historic commitment to two-year technical colleges and the many applied programs (especially in health-related fields) offered by the state's four-year colleges. On the other hand, only about two-thirds as many four-year college graduates take graduate-admission examinations in South Carolina as do so across the country. The proportion achieving nationally competitive scores on such examinations in South Carolina is 25%, compared with 31% nationally.

## Two Challenges for Learning

The five-state demonstration project provided the National Forum on College-Level Learning with an opportunity to examine two important challenges the nation faces in the realm of collegiate learning. The first is a notable gap in the performance of white students and students of color on the direct measures of learning. The second is the uneven performance of states in preparing future teachers. Because both topics were incidental to the main purpose of the demonstration project—to generate and interpret comparable information on student learning across states—the results reported here represent only a beginning of this discussion. Nonetheless, the results do suggest the magnitude of the task the nation may be facing in these two important areas.

### Performance Gaps by Race/Ethnicity

*Measuring Up 2004*, like its predecessors, reported several areas of performance in individual states where differences in outcomes or experiences for students of color had a substantial bearing on overall state performance. If such differences could be narrowed or eliminated, the report argued, the state in question would be substantially better off. Not surprisingly, the National Forum's demonstration project revealed parallel differences in college-level learning across racial/ethnic groups in all five participating states.

Figures 7 and 8 present standardized mean scores[2] for all six of the examinations used: the four WorkKeys exams administered to two-year college students (see figure 7) and the two Collegiate Learning Assessment (CLA) tasks administered to four-year college students (see figure 8). The results are broken down by four major racial/ethnic groups across all five participating states. Although individual patterns vary by examination and the performance gaps are in some cases small, white students consistently do better than their counterparts from other racial/ethnic groups. These performance gaps are particularly wide for African-American students at two-year colleges in applied math and business writing, and for African-American students at four-year institutions in task-based problem solving. Equally notable is the fact that Asian students did not outperform white students in applied math in two-year colleges or in problem solving at four-year colleges and universities, despite the fact that other studies show that they tend to do so consistently on more conventional algorithm-based math exams. In contrast, the examinations employed in the demonstration project emphasized the use of mathematical tools and concepts in more complex problem-based settings where language skills are important.

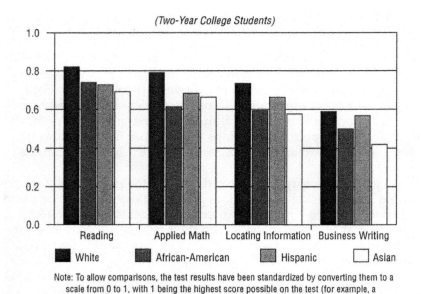

Note: To allow comparisons, the test results have been standardized by converting them to a scale from 0 to 1, with 1 being the highest score possible on the test (for example, a score of 4 with a maximum of 7 yields a standardized score of 0.571).

**Figure 7. WorkKeys Examinations: Mean Scores**

The numbers of students tested in the demonstration project were insufficient to confidently explore patterns of performance across all racial/ethnic populations within individual states. But enough cases were available to examine performance gaps between white students and students from all other racial/ethnic groups on a state-by-state basis. Figures 9 to 14 present standardized mean scores for each of the six examinations for white and nonwhite test-takers in each of the five participating states, and in the nation as a whole.

As is apparent in these figures, a performance gap between white and nonwhite students is present for virtually every examination in every state, suggesting a widespread and systematic pattern of adverse impact. Such differential patterns of performance for these two groups may significantly affect the overall results for individual states. In Illinois, for example, nonwhite students frequently perform at lower levels than their nonwhite counterparts in other states. Yet overall, Illinois is one of the strongest-performing states on these measures because the impact of nonwhite

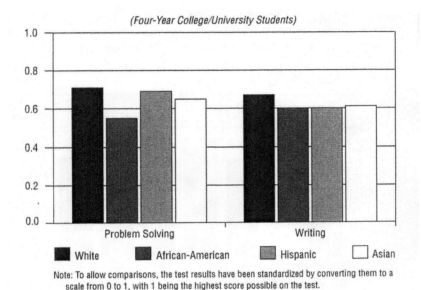

Note: To allow comparisons, the test results have been standardized by converting them to a scale from 0 to 1, with 1 being the highest score possible on the test.

**Figure 8. Collegiate Learning Assessment: Mean Scores**

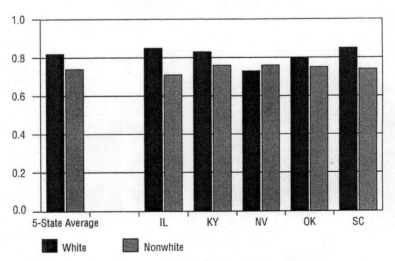

Note: To allow comparisons, the test results have been standardized by converting them to a scale from 0 to 1, with 1 being the highest score possible on the test.

**Figure 9. WorkKeys, Reading: Mean Scores**

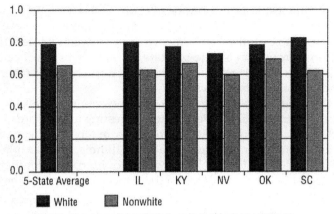

Note: To allow comparisons, the test results have been standardized by
converting them to a scale from 0 to 1, with 1 being the highest score
possible on the test.

**Figure 10. WorkKeys, Applied Math: Mean Scores**

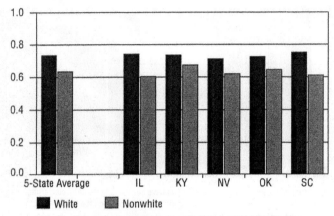

Note: To allow comparisons, the test results have been standardized by
converting them to a scale from 0 to 1, with 1 being the highest score
possible on the test.

**Figure 11. WorkKeys, Locating Information: Mean Scores**

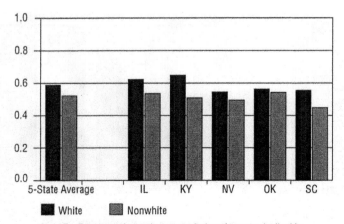

Note: To allow comparisons, the test results have been standardized by
converting them to a scale from 0 to 1, with 1 being the highest score
possible on the test.

**Figure 12. WorkKeys, Business Writing: Mean Scores**

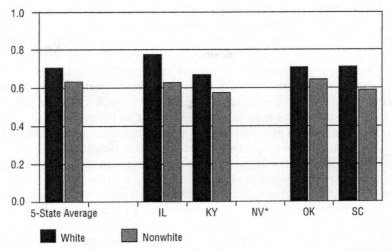

* Data for Nevada were unavailable due to insufficient numbers of test-takers and logistical problems with test administration.

Note: To allow comparisons, the test results have been standardized by converting them to a scale from 0 to 1, with 1 being the highest score possible on the test.

**Figure 13. CLA, Problem Solving: Mean Scores**

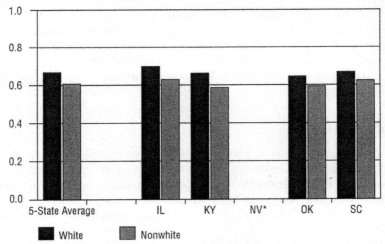

* Data for Nevada were unavailable due to insufficient numbers of test-takers and logistical problems with test administration.

Note: To allow comparisons, the test results have been standardized by converting them to a scale from 0 to 1, with 1 being the highest score possible on the test.

**Figure 14. CLA, Writing: Mean Scores**

performance is masked by their limited numbers. The state's overall performance would have been even higher had these substantial performance gaps not been present. Similarly, nonwhite students in South Carolina also perform at relatively low levels compared with whites across all of these examinations. But the impact of this performance gap on overall state performance is far higher than in other states because nonwhite students constitute a substantial proportion of the South Carolina student population.

The demonstration project is certainly not the first learning assessment initiative to discover such performance gaps. Indeed, virtually every published report of a large-scale testing program in the United States at a national or state level shows similar gaps in performance. Calling particular attention to this issue in the context of *Measuring Up* and the National Forum, however, is compelling for at least two reasons. First, performance gaps based on race/ethnicity and income are already a persistent theme across many of the dimensions examined by *Measuring Up*, ranging from college preparation to collegiate access and persistence. For example, Oklahoma has made progress in narrowing the gaps in college completion between white and minority students over the last decade, but African-American students are still only three-quarters as likely to complete a degree as their white counterparts. In Illinois over the same period, the proportion of Hispanic students receiving certificates and degrees has increased from 8 to 11 per 100 enrolled; nevertheless, Hispanic students in Illinois remain only about half as likely as white students to complete certificates and degrees. Parallel performance gaps in learning measures only serve to further confirm that this is a national problem worth significant policy attention.

Second, the notion of educational capital that forms the conceptual foundation of the National Forum's work emphasizes the need to educate *everybody* in order to sustain economic and civic vitality. Performance gaps in learning, if they continue, will seriously erode state and national competitiveness—especially as the diversity of young adults in many states increases. This threat has already been documented for many states through data on inequities in educational attainment. A recent report by the National Center for Higher Education Management Systems (NCHEMS) concluded that total personal income (and associated state tax revenue) for Nevada, for example, would be $2.2 billion higher than its projected base of $43.9 billion by 2020 if Hispanics, African-Americans, and Native Americans achieved the same levels of education as whites.

This is occurring at a time when other nations are rapidly overtaking the United States in the proportion of young residents earning a baccalaureate degree, and they are doing so largely *because of* such performance gaps with respect to income and race/ethnicity. According to data provided by the Organisation for Economic Co-operation and Development (OECD), for example, overall baccalaureate attainment rates among young American adults (ages 25 to 34) are now lower than their counterparts in four other countries. Disaggregating these data reveals the fact that attainment rates for young white males in the United States approximately match the overall attainment rates achieved by residents in these other countries. Our growing underperformance internationally is a direct result of this nation's inability to increase the attainment levels of its nonwhite young adult population.

## Educating Future Teachers

Since the publication of *A Nation at Risk* more than 20 years ago, states and the federal government have been engaged in substantial efforts to improve the quality of America's elementary and secondary schools. Higher education's critical responsibility in this effort is centered on preparing future teachers who are masters of their subject areas and are ready to take on the challenges of increasingly crowded and diverse classrooms. Yet our knowledge of how well the nation's colleges and universities are fulfilling this crucial responsibility remains limited. As reported in *Measuring Up 2004*, we know that most states have made progress in "teacher quality," as measured by the proportion of teachers in their K–12 classrooms who are teaching in the field in which they majored in college. But how much do prospective teachers actually know about the subjects they are preparing to teach? Title II of the Higher Education Act, whose reporting requirements went into effect in fall 2002, was designed to provide answers to that question by requiring publicly available reports on the pass rates of teacher candidates in each subject—with data available by institution and by state. Each state, however, can choose its own examinations. Even if states use the same exam, each can establish its own standards for licensure. As a result, published Title II reports do not provide consistent information to compare performance across states.

The demonstration project provided a limited opportunity to address this condition because three participating states—Kentucky, Nevada, and South Carolina—use many of the same examinations to certify teachers. These tests are provided by the Educational Testing Service (ETS) as part of the Praxis examination series and are used to assess both subject-area knowledge and basic skills in these three states. Teacher candidates first are tested in the basic skills of reading, writing, and mathematics using the Praxis I battery—either as an exit standard for certification or to enter many institutions' teacher education programs and become a candidate for certification. They then must pass a combination of other subject-area examinations in the Praxis II battery, depending on the

**Table 1. Pass Rates for Praxis II: Subject Knowledge**
**Percentage of Students Passing**

|  | Reported Pass Rate Based on State's Own Standards | Recalculation of Pass Rate Based on Highest State Standard for Passing |
|---|---|---|
| Kentucky | 81.3% | 57.4% |
| South Carolina | 77.4% | 59.1% |
| Nevada | 89.9% | 71.9% |

**Table 2. Praxis I: Basic Skills**
**Percentage of Students Passing**

|  | Reported Pass Rate Based on State's Own Standards | Recalculation of Pass Rate Based on Highest State Standard for Passing |
|---|---|---|
| Kentucky | 100.0% | 31.1% |
| South Carolina | 69.1% | 37.8% |
| Nevada | 82.8% | 52.7% |

particular certification they are seeking. A total of 66 different Praxis examinations were used by these three states from 2001 to 2003: 9 in basic skills and the remaining 57 in subject areas ranging from agriculture to teaching visually handicapped children. By obtaining actual test results from these three states instead of publicly reported pass rates, the states' performances could be directly compared. The two remaining demonstration project states—Illinois and Oklahoma—both employ their own, noncomparable teacher examinations and therefore could not be included in this analysis.

Following *Measuring Up's* established procedure of benchmarking each state's performance to that of the best-performing states, the highest standard for passing each Praxis examination in any of the 50 states was identified using published Title II reports. This score was then established as the standard and was applied to actual student scores in the three demonstration project states. The results show for each state: (1) the reported pass rate at the level actually used for teacher certification within the state and (2) what the state's pass rate would have been if the highest state standard in the nation had been applied (see table 1). If the highest national standards had been applied to each of these states, the percentage of students passing the teacher licensure exams would have been noticeably lower in all three states.

The situation is more complex with respect to Praxis I, the basic skills examinations administered to future teachers, because of differences among the states in the way these tests are used. In Kentucky, for example, Praxis I exams are used by many (but not all) institutions to govern entrance to teacher education programs. As a result, that state's published Title II reports accurately show 100% pass rates on these exams, because all certified teachers would have had to attain the state's designated passing score in order to enter a teacher education program in the first place. In South Carolina and Nevada, on the other hand, many individual institutions establish additional entrance standards in basic skills. Teacher candidates in those two states must meet state-established basic skills standards in order to be certified—just as they must meet such standards with respect to subject-area knowledge. As a result of these differences, the actual pass rates within these two states are lower than in Kentucky (see table 2). As a final note, these examinations truly do test basic skills, reflecting levels of functioning in reading, writing, and mathematics that are typical of the ninth-grade level—which may be a relatively low standard for prospective teachers, regardless of where they are in the teacher-preparation pipeline.

As is evident from table 2, overall state performance is strikingly different for these three states when the nation's highest performance standards are applied. Only about a third of test-takers in Kentucky and South Carolina, and about half in Nevada, performed at the levels expected in the state with the highest standard for passing (Virginia). Supporting some of the test results reported earlier, these differences were particularly apparent in mathematics for Kentucky and in writing for Nevada and South Carolina. For example, South Carolina test-takers achieved a mean score of 174.1 on the Praxis I in writing—above the state's standard for passing of 173 but below the standard of 178 established in Virginia.

Are these differences important? States have long maintained that local conditions vary and that standards for licensing teachers should be set to match them. And it could be argued that current standards are adequate for practicing teachers and that states such as Virginia and Maryland may simply have set standards that are inappropriately high. In addition, many states are facing unprecedented teacher shortages (among them, most strikingly, Nevada), and it is questionable whether establishing higher standards for licensure would really help them to educate more children better under these conditions. Each state must make its own determination of what such differences, if they are detected, really mean. The key point is that current Title II data reporting, which is confined to local pass rates, does not enable states to detect such differences in the first place. Results of the National Forum's demonstration project show that many states can in fact benchmark their performances in teacher education against external standards if they choose to do so, which would in turn make such a policy conversation possible.

These two analyses—concerning performance gaps by race/ethnicity and educating future teachers—are examples of the kinds of issues that can be addressed when comparable statewide information about collegiate learning is available. With larger sample sizes, states would be able to perform other, more thorough analyses and comparisons with the information this model produces.

## Conclusion

### Modest Investment, Collective Benefit

Despite substantial challenges, the National Forum's five-state demonstration project achieved its principal objective of showing the feasibility of assembling indicators of collegiate learning on a comparable basis across multiple states. The resulting information about educational capital is consistent with what we already know about higher education in the five participating states, and the costs of obtaining this information are modest (see appendix for information about those costs). But in today's climate of constrained resources, why should a state support such an investment at all?

One answer is accountability. States spend millions, and sometimes billions, of dollars each year on higher education but have in the past been able to produce little information that can demonstrate to residents and taxpayers the effectiveness of these investments. Learning represents the inescapable bottom line for the nation's colleges and universities. On these grounds alone, not having information about learning presented in succinct and comparable form is increasingly hard to justify—just as participants in the National Forum's initial meeting at Purchase, New York, concluded more than three years ago.

But if accountability were the only reason to pursue this agenda, states might legitimately pause. Even more importantly, information about educational capital can complement other state-specific information on the strengths, challenges, and benefits of higher education to help forge a powerful public agenda for action. For example, a state's leadership can use information that has been broken down by geographic area or by population group to identify concrete problems and thereby begin to mobilize public action. These steps have already been taken in some states that have disaggregated data from *Measuring Up* by population or region in areas such as participation and affordability. Although the vignettes presented in the previous section of this report, "Two Challenges for Learning," remain preliminary, they illustrate how a useful disaggregation of information about learning can be accomplished.

Using consistent statewide information about learning outcomes in this way—to identify the specifics of a collective policy challenge that *all* institutions can help address—is far more attractive than the customary (and feared) use of performance information to reward and punish individual institutions. At the same time, having comparable information across states can help policymakers identify best practices and track progress. These are essential conditions for improving performance, and the demonstration project shows they can be purchased at an affordable price.

The National Forum on College-Level Learning has put to rest the question of whether assessment can be done in a way that allows for meaningful state comparisons. It can. The implementation of the model described here requires leadership, hard work, and resources. But the principal recommendation from the National Forum's work is that states should adopt the model because the information it produces:

- is valid and useful for state policy;
- supplements existing accountability approaches and campus-based assessment efforts;
- leads to informed discussions about a public agenda for higher education; and
- can help provide motivation toward achieving that public agenda.

In its report, the National Commission on Accountability, convened by the State Higher Education Executive Officers (SHEEO), has called for all states to adopt the National Forum's model for assessing learning at the state level. In an era of heightened accountability, with not only states but also the federal government interested in determining what value they get for the investment they make in higher education, it is time for the higher education community to take the lead in determining how that value should be assessed. The model presented here is not perfect, and it was not perfectly implemented in the demonstration project. But it is as promising a place to begin as any yet seen in this country.

# Appendix: How to Implement the Model for College-Level Learning

If state policymakers choose to adopt the model presented by the National Forum on College-Level Learning for assessing student learning, they need to address several issues, including:

- the roles of officials at the state and campus levels;
- the logistics of survey and test administration, and analysis of the resulting information; and
- the resources that will be required.

This appendix addresses each of these issues, based on the experiences of states that participated in the pilot project.

## State- and Campus-level Leadership

Assessment at the state level cannot be accomplished without strong and consistent leadership at both the state and campus levels. Since governing or coordinating boards generally assume strategic leadership for state higher education systems, this generally is the logical place for state-level responsibility for such an initiative to be lodged. The unwavering and clear commitment of the board and its chief executive (generically known as the State Higher Education Executive Officer, or SHEEO) is a necessary condition for obtaining the campus cooperation that is crucial to implementing the model.

Active involvement of the SHEEO is particularly important, especially in the early stages of implementing such an effort. He or she is in the best position to generate the political impetus and board support needed to move the initiative forward. The SHEEO is also best able to create buy-in from the campuses by convincing them of the value of this kind of assessment for various stakeholders, reducing the threat of inter-institutional comparison that cross-campus assessment might seem to pose, encouraging and supporting campus leadership, and using the results to help create a public agenda for higher education and enrich the state's accountability system.

In the five-state demonstration project, a senior-level governing or coordinating board staff person was assigned to lead the effort in each state. That state leader worked with the campuses to move the project forward by consulting with senior campus leadership, channeling resources to the institutions, keeping campus personnel informed through the various phases of implementation, and consulting with them about the strategies and protocols for testing.

Through periodic meetings and regular email communication, the state project directors provided campus leaders with crucial administrative and moral support. In a survey administered at the end of the pilot project, campus coordinators stressed the importance of such lines of communication between themselves and the state project leader. Especially important to them was timely information about the purposes and value of the project, the psychometric properties of the assessments to be used, and effective implementation strategies. The coordinators suggested in particular that the state director involve them early in the design of sampling and testing procedures, since they knew best how to recruit students for local assessment efforts.

Campus leadership is as important as state leadership. The president's role is to communicate the purposes of the project—as well as the value and uses of the information that it produces—to faculty, staff, and students. He or she also needs to ensure that the campus coordinators are provided with the resources of time and money required to do the job and that the results are disseminated and used to benchmark the results of campus-based assessments of student learning.

Campus coordinators are the people most directly responsible for the success or failure of the effort. In the demonstration project, they explained the sampling and testing protocols established by the project team to the personnel who recruited the students and administered the assessments, and they worked with them to develop incentive strategies. (Since the biggest difficulty the pilot ran into was enlisting students to take the tests, the budget for this work now includes a payment to students for participating.) Campus coordinators at four-year institutions also collected other needed information, including GRE scores (available from ETS at a nominal fee), information from the Integrated Postsecondary Educational Data System (IPEDS), and SAT scores for students taking the Collegiate Learning Assessment. Campus leaders need to ensure that the people administering the tests are consulted early in the project and have sufficient time for implementation, adequate staffing and resources, and an understanding of how the information will be used at both the campus and state levels.

Campus leaders also need to motivate students to show up (and do their best) and to coordinate this project with other campus activities so that it becomes a useful supplement to campus assessment efforts, not simply a data collection "add-on." The logistical challenges of this approach also include those associated with administering online surveys and tests, including scheduling rooms and computers for testing, dealing with software problems, and accessing technical support.

## Logistics

Overall, states should allow about a year and a half from the beginning of the project to the point at which they will have usable data. This allows sufficient time to assemble the measures needed in the first two clusters—"literacy levels of the state population" and "graduates ready for advanced practice"—which must be obtained directly from testing companies and other agencies. It also allows sufficient time for the detailed planning that is needed to administer the direct measures of student learning on selected college and university campuses.

## Literacy Levels of the State Population: National Assessment of Adult Literacy (NAAL)

The National Assessment of Adult Literacy (NAAL) has replaced the National Adult Literacy Survey (NALS) as the nation's most direct measure of educational capital. Like the NALS, the NAAL is a household survey that assesses the prose, document, and quantitative literacy of a representative sample of the nation's adults, both the college-educated and those with a high-school diploma or less. In 1992, when the NALS was administered, a number of states over-sampled their residents in order to get results that were also representative at the state level, but only six did so when the NAAL was administered in 2003. Even without the over-sample, however, it is possible to approximate a representative state-level sample in the larger states by employing the methodology used for the adult literacy measure in the benefits category of *Measuring Up 2004*.[3]

The NALS was used in the demonstration project to determine the level of literacy of the state's residents, calculated as the proportion of its residents scoring at the highest levels (4 and 5) on all three tests. Given large enough sample sizes, it could also help states determine the value added by a college education with respect to the literacy levels of the population. The original plan in the demonstration project was to use information from the newer NAAL, which was due for release in 2003. Because of a delay in that release, however, the National Forum instead created a placeholder by using simulated literacy data, created by applying a regression procedure to adjust 1992 NALS results on the basis of population characteristics drawn from the 2000 census. For at least the next five years, actual NAAL results will be available as a ready source for states to calculate this measure. The NAAL results will enable states to sharpen this cluster of indicators to capture the literacy levels of the college-educated population rather than of the state population as a whole. Due to limitations in the statistical procedure used to update the 1992 NALS, however, this was not possible for this analysis.

States are strongly encouraged to over-sample their residents in any future administrations of the adult literacy survey. Unfortunately, it has been administered no more frequently than once a decade or longer. (SHEEO's National Commission on Accountability recommends in its report that the federal government administer it more often and to larger numbers of people.) In the meantime, states with over-samples on the NAAL or states that are large enough for the statistical approximation can use the information produced by the NAAL to calculate the required performance indices.

The budget in this appendix presumes that the National Center for Higher Education Management Systems (NCHEMS) will analyze state data from the NAAL to produce state-level statistics, from which it will then calculate index scores for the literacy levels of the college-educated population. States that choose to do this on their own will have to obtain detailed breakdowns of the performance of college-educated individuals on each of the three assessments for their states and for the nation as a whole.

## Graduates Ready for Advanced Practice: Licensure and Graduate-Admission Tests

The demonstration project used state-level results from those licensure and graduate-admission tests that satisfied three criteria:

1. national and state-level performance data are available;
2. the tests are required in order to practice a profession or enter graduate school; and
3. possession of a two- or four-year college degree is required to take the tests.

In addition, each state supplied data on the results of its teacher examinations.

Measures in the "graduates ready for advanced practice" cluster were computed for the demonstration project using the same methodology applied to Kentucky in *Measuring Up* 2002. This consisted of defining a particular level of performance on each test that could be used as a benchmark, above which a particular test-taker could be deemed "ready for advanced practice." In the case of licensure examinations with established national standards, this level of performance was passing the examination and being licensed. In the case of graduate-admission examinations, a criterion score was set at a level generally accepted as "competitive" with respect to gaining admission to a graduate program. The number of individuals achieving this level or higher was then counted. This number was divided by the total number of applicable degrees (baccalaureate or associate) associated with the credential and separately reported for nine licensure examinations and five graduate-admission tests. Fields included in the licensures list included nursing, clinical pathology, physical therapy, respiratory therapy, radiology, and physician's assistant. Admissions examinations included Graduate Record Examination (GRE), the Graduate Management Admissions Test (GMAT), the Medical College Admissions Test (MCAT), the Law School Admissions Test (LSAT), and the Pharmacy College Admissions Test (PCAT).

All test scores except GREs can be obtained directly from national sources. GRE scores were compiled by asking participating institutions in each state to request their scores from ETS, which can be done via a standard report for a small fee. This meant that the number of degrees used in the denominator of the calculation had to be adjusted to include only those institutions reporting GRE scores.

Comparing performances across states is problematic for teacher education because of differing standards in each state, as well as the use of different test batteries. The measure for teacher education used for the demonstration project was the number of individuals passing licensure examinations in the state (obtained from Title II reports) divided by the number of applicable degrees for individuals entering teaching obtained from the Integrated Postsecondary Educational Data System (IPEDS). "Applicable degrees" were defined as "education" plus all fields of study recognized in secondary education when counting teachers teaching "in field" for the teacher quality indicator included in the preparation category of *Measuring Up 2004*.

The budget presented later in this appendix assumes that a third-party organization like NCHEMS (which played this role in the demonstration project) will contact the testing companies and assemble and analyze licensing and graduate-admission testing data. If states choose to undertake this task themselves, another responsibility that the state coordinator must assume is communication with the testing companies and collecting and analyzing the data they provide. For states that pursue this avenue, the following description of the procedures may be helpful.

Several months prior to the final assembly of information, the state-level coordinator should collect from those sites the pass rates for regular, first-time examinees on each examination at the state and national levels for the three most recent years for which data are available. State-level results for some tests are posted by state on the Web sites of the administering organization. This is the case, for example, for the MCAT, the GMAT, and the two nursing exams: the National Council Licensure Examination for Registered Nurses (NCLEX-RN) and the National Council Licensure Examination for Practical Nurses (NCLEX-PN). The state coordinator will need to directly contact the organizations that conduct the other examinations to solicit state-level results because they do not provide the information publicly (some may charge a small fee for this service). The GRE board has refused thus far to release state-level information for its test. But scores can be obtained and aggregated if the state coordinator asks each four-year institution to request from ETS the standard institutional report for the most recent three years.

Scores on all available professional licensure and graduate-admission examinations for all three years must be aggregated to create a single index score for each type of examination. The basic method for doing so involves determining the number of eligible students in the state who pass their licensure tests or achieve a competitive score (that is, one that will gain them admission to graduate school) on a graduate-admission test. The resulting number of "graduates ready for advanced practice" is then divided by the total number of applicable degrees associated with the credential, separately aggregated for licensure examinations, graduate-admission tests, and teacher licensure examinations.

Before using these data to construct index scores, a number of initial calculations are required to make them comparable:

- **Subscore Aggregation**. For tests with multiple subscores but no total score, subscores must be aggregated to create a single indicator of performance, weighting each subscore equally. The same procedure is used to average the number of individuals passing or scoring at or above a particular level where multiple subscores are present.
- **Standardizing Scores**. To adjust for differences in test-score scaling, summary test-score performance data should be indexed to a standardized value range of 0 to 1, depending upon the top score possible on a given test (for example, a GRE score of 450 with a maximum of 800 yields a standardized score of 0.5625).
- **Time Period Aggregation**. Up to three years of the most recent data should be used in these calculations to create an "average year." This approach allows more data to be used in cases where the number of test-takers in a given state is small. In cases where three years of data are available, data from all three should be aggregated and divided by three. In cases where two years are available, these two should be combined and divided by two.

After these initial adjustments, the resulting data consist of comparable summary performance statistics for each test, including number of test-takers, mean and median scores, standard deviation, and number passing or achieving at or above a designated score. From these data, the "graduates ready for advanced practice" indicator can be calculated. The following steps are used to create this indicator:

1. Determine the number of individuals ready for advanced practice. For licensure tests, this is the number of individuals passing the examination. For admissions examinations, it is the number of individuals achieving at or above a given nationally competitive score (GRE=600, GMAT=600, LSAT=155, MCAT=10, PCAT=215).
2. Determine the appropriate number of graduates associated with each potential test-taking population using IPEDS data. In most cases, these are baccalaureate degrees, but in some cases they are associate degrees and in others, both. For teacher examinations, the denominator used was the total number of baccalaureate degrees in education plus all other fields of study listed as providing a "qualified" teacher in the teacher quality measure used in the preparation category of *Measuring Up*. If multiple testing years were available, degree data were similarly aggregated by year to create an "average year."
3. Create a ratio between these two numbers. This is the fraction of educational capital within a state that is represented by this test.
4. Add the resulting fractional contributions to educational capital for each of the states under consideration and for the nation.

Pass rates and raw or composite scores of students taking the teacher licensure tests can generally be obtained from the state's department of education. Pass rates and the numbers taking each test are also posted on the Title II Web site at www.title2.org. The measure for teacher education used in the demonstration project was calculated by taking the number of individuals passing licensure examinations in the state and dividing it by the number of applicable degrees as defined under item #2 above. If raw or composite scores can be obtained, however, the state can perform the kinds of comparative analyses illustrated in this report (see tables 1 and 2, page 517) by applying the highest passing standard among the states on each test as reported on the Title II Web site.

## Performance of the College Educated: General Intellectual Skills Tests

The demonstration project used two test batteries to assess the general intellectual skills of students. The two-year institutions administered four American College Testing Service (ACT) WorkKeys tests.

The four-year institutions used the Collegiate Learning Assessment (CLA), which is administered by the Council on Aid to Education (CAE), a subsidiary of the RAND Corporation.

The ACT WorkKeys assessments principally examine what students can do with what they know. Items on reading comprehension and locating information, for instance, are focused on how well test-takers can extract information from complex documents and instructions, while items on applied mathematics test students' ability to use mathematical concepts like probability or estimation in real-world settings. The WorkKeys writing assessment also requires students to complete an extended essay. The WorkKeys battery used in *Measuring Up 2004* included four tests—reading for information, applied mathematics, locating information, and business writing—and the results of each test are reported separately. Additional information about the WorkKeys examinations is available at www.act.org/workkeys/.

The CLA goes beyond typical multiple-choice testing by posing multifaceted tasks—anchored in an academic discipline—that a student is asked to understand and solve. The CLA battery used in the demonstration project consisted of two types of assessments—a set of four authentic tasks and a set of two writing prompts drawn from the Graduate Record Examination (GRE). Because they are different kinds of assessments examining essentially different skills, performance on them was reported separately—problem solving for the tasks and writing for the GRE prompts. Additional information on the CLA assessment is available at www.cae.org/content/pdf/CLA-Opportunity ToParticipate.pdf.

Administering the WorkKeys and CLA examinations constitutes the greatest challenge to implementing the National Forum's model. The subsections below describe: (1) the sampling procedures used in the demonstration project to select potential students to participate; (2) the administration of the tests; and (3) the analysis of results.

### Sampling Procedures

The design for collecting testing data requires a total sample of some 1,200 test-takers for each of the two test batteries in a given state. This necessitates a cluster-sampling approach: first, a sample of institutions is drawn, and second, the sample of students to participate from each institution is selected. This sampling approach represents a compromise, based on the conflicting need to attain some degree of statewide representativeness and the desire to include enough test-takers at participating institutions to enable them to use the resulting data for local purposes. The basic sampling plan thus envisions about 75 to 100 test-takers at 12 to 15 four-year institutions and at an equivalent number of two-year institutions in a given state. However, many states may wish to select more institutions, or more students at each institution, to participate. Indeed, several states in the National Forum's demonstration project chose to do so. In Nevada, where there are only two four-year institutions and four two-year institutions, all were chosen, and the numbers of students targeted for testing at each was higher. In Kentucky and Oklahoma, all public institutions were invited to participate, with the institutional sampling frame used only to select private institutions.

In each case where a selection of institutions must be made, the universe of applicable institutions (four-year public, four-year private, and two-year) should be divided into groups of roughly comparable institutions. Variables used to construct these groups should at minimum include institutional size, type, disciplinary mix, selectivity, urban/rural location, full-time/part-time ratio, and racial/ethnic distribution. The resulting sampling groups can then be checked by running statistics for various combinations of potential selections within them to ensure that they produce samples that closely resemble known statewide distributions on such variables as full-time/part-time breakdown, gender, race/ethnicity, and disciplinary emphasis. The typical result for a state will be five to seven distinct groups of institutions within each category of institutions (public four-year, private four-year, and two-year). The first group in each cluster will consist of institutions that are required to participate because they are large, unusually selective, or otherwise distinctive. But given the need for flexibility in recruiting institutions, each state has the discretion to select a given number of institutions within the remaining sampling groups.

Once participating institutions are identified, the next step is to randomly select a group of students to be invited to participate in the testing. Accordingly, a set of sample-selection guidelines have been developed for use by participating institutions. The target population for sampling includes all students officially enrolled in the most recent fall term who are expected to complete a two-year or a four-year degree the following spring (identified by numbers of credits or courses completed). Institutions should be directed to randomly select an initial sample of students who meet these criteria, together with two backup samples to be used to replace members of the initial group who decline to participate. Institutions in the demonstration project were provided with several methods for conducting the random selection procedure and for employing the backup sample (see http://measuringup.highereducation.org/docs/technicalguide_2004.pdf, pp. 80–83).

### Test Administration

The CLA and the WorkKeys batteries should be administered using protocols supplied by the vendors, customized for use in the demonstration project. The CLA assessments are typically completed in a Web-based format. Each CLA test-taker should be asked to complete either one task or two GRE prompts. Each CLA test-taker in the demonstration project also completed the National Survey of Student Engagement (NSSE), although results of this survey are not included in this report because they are not direct measures of student learning. The total testing time for the CLA battery administered in this way was just over two hours. Each WorkKeys test-taker should be asked to complete: (a) the applied mathematics and the reading for information examinations, or (b) the locating information and the business writing examinations. The tests were completed in a paper-and-pencil format in the demonstration project but will soon be available from ACT in a computer-based format. Each test-taker in the demonstration project also completed the Community College Survey of Student Engagement (CCSSE), although results of this survey are not included in this report. The total testing time for the WorkKeys battery administered in this way was about one and a half hours.

Additional testing materials should be supplied to each campus in case more students than expected show up for testing. Members of the initial sample should be invited to participate by means of a letter from the college president accompanied by recruitment materials (samples of both that can be adapted by each institution are available on the National Forum Web site at http://collegele vellearning.org). Members of this initial targeted group who decline participation or do not reply should be re-contacted in a week. If the response is still negative, the institution should recruit replacements from the pre-selected backup samples, selecting students with the same or similar majors and, ideally, the same full-time/part-time attendance status.

Encouraging students to participate was the largest single challenge of the demonstration project and will likely be a challenge for any state trying to implement the National Forum's model. Campus coordinators reported that the length of the tests (up to two hours) was a problem, especially for working students and for seniors, who are the most difficult students to recruit. For that reason the budget below includes a $75 payment for each test-taker. Some states may prefer to give students academic credit instead, but this may require individual score reports for each of the students. With individual score reports, the WorkKeys can be used as a work certificate and the CLA can be noted on the student transcript. This would require students to take three WorkKeys tests or two tasks from the CLA, thus increasing the investment of student time and state money. Whichever incentive is chosen, it needs to be of significant value to the students.

Once the student samples are selected, campuses must schedule a number of dates near the end of the fall semester for testing. The exams need to be proctored, which means that rooms must be reserved if a paper-and-pencil format is used. If a Web- or computer-based format is used, campus coordinators must find a sufficient number of available computers. This was not an easy task in the demonstration project: increasingly, students are bringing their own computers to campus, and campus computer laboratories are in many cases getting smaller instead of larger (CAE is currently exploring the possibility of letting students use their own computers). Campus coordinators should begin room scheduling as soon as the institutions have agreed to participate. In the demonstration project, some four-year institutions determined that they needed to take the CLA to their Institutional Review Boards (IRBs), a process that also should be started early if it is required. The RAND Corporation (whose Council on Aid to Education oversees the CLA) has its own IRB, which has reviewed the exam. As a consequence of that review, the Council on Aid to Education requires students to fill out privacy and consent forms.

### Analyzing and Reporting Results

The completed exams are sent to ACT and CAE respectively, where the results are analyzed and reports created for the institutions and the state. Campuses that have adequate numbers of test-takers and that can supply IPEDS data and SAT or ACT scores for the participating students can also request from CAE an analysis of how well their students test compared with what might be predicted based on the performance of similar test-takers who have taken the exam before.

Results described in this report for these examinations are based on the proportions of test-takers scoring above a given level on each of the tests given. For CLA, this level was based on adjusted scores of 26 and above, calculated separately for task-based problem solving and the GRE-based writing sample. For the WorkKeys tests, the levels differed because the scales for each of the four tests differ—high scores are six and above for reading and for applied mathematics, five and above for locating information, and four and above for business writing. Finally, results for the demonstration project were weighted as needed by race and ethnicity, gender, and institutional size to make them more representative. Such a procedure should be followed by any state undertaking its own analyses if it finds substantial and consequential differences in response rates between men and women or across demographic groups. Test-takers from larger institutions should also count more in computing the state's aggregate score than those from smaller institutions, in proportion to how much of the state's total undergraduate full-time equivalent (FTE) enrollment that each represents. Results should then be compared with the available national or multi-state norms on each examination.

## Resource Requirements

Although the demonstration project has shown that the National Forum's approach to assessing college-level learning at the state level can be cost effective, it does require resources. The project team consulted the project budget and surveyed state and campus coordinators to determine both the time and money required to complete the tasks described above. Future implementations of this model will be done under different circumstances and will be affected by a host of variables that cannot be predicted, including increased charges for materials and services. Moreover, states may want to implement the most pared-down version of the model or a more robust one that generates more information but requires greater resources. Therefore, the cost estimations that follow are approximate.

## Time

The first variable is personnel time. The project team did not try to translate these time estimates into salary dollars, given the many variables that affect compensation levels, such as the locality and the seniority of the people working on the project. The best source of information for the time spent by state leaders on the project came from the surveys of the state coordinators. Since they did not keep timesheets, they could only estimate the hours they had worked. Estimates for state leaders averaged about 180 hours spent on the project over two years. Much of the model's groundwork has already been laid and will not have to be replicated. But if the states were to take on some of the responsibilities of the project team, such as negotiating with the testing companies or analyzing the data, then their time devoted to the project could increase to as much as 250 hours. Campus coordinators were also surveyed, and they reported an average of about 100 hours spent administering the project. These duties included selecting the sample, recruiting students, administering the tests, and providing the project team and testing companies with information.

## Administrative Costs: $25,500

The survey also asked for information about the costs to the coordinating or governing board and to the campuses of administering the project, and that information was pooled with the project budget. It appears that these costs were minimal: roughly and on average $1,500 at the state level and $1,000 at the campus level (multiplied by approximately 24 campuses). At the state level this would include expenses such as the cost of meetings, and at the campus level, the postage and telephone charges associated with the recruitment of students.

## Materials

In the pilot project, the costs of materials were covered by the grant from The Pew Charitable Trusts. In the future, these costs will be assumed by the state.

As table 3 reveals, the range of potential costs to the states is broad. For instance, a state would incur non-personnel costs of *less than $87,000* if it chooses: to implement the model as part of a five-state consortium (which would enable economies of scale in collecting and analyzing data); not to pay students but give them academic credit instead; to administer tests to only 100 students per institution; and not to administer the National Survey of Student Engagement (NSSE), the Community College Survey of Student Engagement (CCSSE), or the College Results Survey. By contrast, a state that pays students, implements the model by itself, administers 200 tests per institution, and uses the CCSSE, the NSSE, and the College Results Survey could spend *up to about $370,000*, including personnel costs for data collection and analysis.

**Table 3. Costs Per State**

| Item | Description | Cost Estimation | Minimum Cost | Maximum Cost |
|---|---|---|---|---|
| WorkKeys | $11 per student (the mean for two tests) x 1,200 | $13,200 | $13,200 | $13,200 |
| CLA for 200 students per institution — or — CLA for 100 students per institution | $6,500/institution x 12 — or — $4,500/institution x 12 | $78,000 — or — $54,000 | - - $54,000 | $78,000 - - |
| GRE reports (3 years) | $225/institution x 12 | $2,700 | $2,700 | $2,700 |
| Licensing exam analysis by testing companies | $250/exam x 3 | $750 | $750 | $750 |
| Data Analysis* | | | | |
| Cost to Set Up Data System | | $25,000 | - - | $25,000 |
| Fixed Cost for Data Analysis (NCHEMS) | | $50,000 | $15,600 for a five-state consortium | $50,000 |
| Marginal Cost for Data Analysis (NCHEMS) | | $7,000/state | | - - |
| Optional costs | | | | |
| Student payment | $75 x 2,400 | $180,000 | - - | $180,000 |
| NSSE/CCSSE | $1.50/student x 2,400 | $3,600 | - - | $3,600 |
| | $300/campus x 24 | $7,200 | - - | $7,200 |
| College Results Survey | Web site for 3 months | up to $4,400 | - - | $4,400 |
| | Survey, $2.00/graduate x 1,200 | $2,400 | - - | $2,400 |

* The cost to set up the data system is calculated based on the investment that the National Center for Higher Education Management Systems (NCHEMS) has already made to do so. If a state chose not to use NCHEMS for data analysis, it would need to replicate that work and would incur that cost. If the state did use NCHEMS, that investment would not need to be made again. The fixed and marginal costs for data analysis represent the costs associated with analytical work performed by NCHEMS. If only one state participated, that cost would be $50,000 (the fixed cost). If more than one state participated, the cost represented by each additional state would be $7,000 (the marginal cost). For example, if five states participated, the cost would total $78,000 ($50,000 + [$7,000 x 4]), and each state would pay $15,600.

Note: CLA stands for the Collegiate Learning Assessments. GRE stands for Graduate Record Examination. NSSE is the National Survey of Student Engagement. CCSSE is the Community College Survey of Student Engagement.

## About The Authors

**Margaret A. Miller**, project director of the National Forum on College-Level Learning, is a professor of higher education policy at the Curry School of Education, University of Virginia, and editor of *Change* magazine. Having begun her academic career as an English professor at the University of Massachusetts, Dartmouth, she went on to serve as the chief academic officer for the State Council of Higher Education for Virginia and then as president of the American Association for Higher Education. She has been a member of the *Measuring Up* advisory board since its inception. She currently also serves as a TIAA/CREF institute fellow and vice chair of the National Center for Higher Education Management System's board of directors.

**Peter T. Ewell** is vice president of the National Center for Higher Education Management Systems (NCHEMS). His work focuses on assessing institutional effectiveness and the outcomes of college, and involves both research and direct consulting with institutions and state systems on collecting and using assessment information in planning, evaluation, and budgeting. He has directed many projects on this topic, including initiatives funded by the W.K. Kellogg Foundation, the National Institute for Education, the Consortium for the Advancement of Private Higher Education, the Lumina Foundation, and the Pew Charitable Trusts. In addition, he has consulted with over 375 colleges and universities and 24 state systems of higher education on topics related to the assessment of student learning. He has authored six books and numerous articles on the topic of improving undergraduate instruction through the assessment of student outcomes. In addition, he has prepared commissioned papers for many agencies, including the Education Commission of the States, the National Governors Association, the National Conference of State Legislators, and the National Center for Public Policy and Higher Education. In 1998, he led the design team for the National Survey of Student Engagement (NSSE). A graduate of Haverford College, he received his Ph.D. in political science from Yale University in 1976 and was on the faculty of the University of Chicago.

## The National Center For Public Policy And Higher Education

The National Center for Public Policy and Higher Education promotes public policies that enhance Americans' opportunities to pursue and achieve high-quality education and training beyond high school. As an independent, nonprofit, nonpartisan organization, the National Center prepares action-oriented analyses of pressing policy issues facing the states and the nation regarding opportunity and achievement in higher education—including two- and four-year, public and private, for-profit and nonprofit institutions. The National Center communicates performance results and key findings to the public, to civic, business, and higher education leaders, and to state and federal leaders who are poised to improve higher education policy.

Established in 1998, the National Center is not affiliated with any institution of higher education, with any political party, or with any government agency; it receives continuing, core financial support from a consortium of national foundations that includes The Pew Charitable Trusts, The Atlantic Philanthropies, and The Ford Foundation.

152 North Third Street, Suite 705, San Jose, California 95112
Telephone: 408-271-2699 • FAX: 408-271-2697
www.highereducation.org

## National Center Publications

The National Center publishes:

- Reports and analyses commissioned by the National Center,
- Reports and analyses written by National Center staff,
- National Center Policy Reports that are approved by the National Center's Board of Directors, and
- *National CrossTalk*, a quarterly publication.

The following National Center publications—as well as a host of other information and links—are available at **www.highereducation.org.** Single copies of most of these reports are also available from the National Center. Please FAX requests to 408-271-2697 and ask for the report by publication number.

*Measuring Up on College-Level Learning,* by Margaret A. Miller and Peter T. Ewell (October 2005, #05-8). In this report, the National Forum on College-Level Learning proposes a model for evaluating and comparing college-level learning on a state-by-state basis, including assessing educational capital. As well as releasing the results for five participating states, the National Forum also explores the implications of its project findings in terms of performance gaps by race/ethnicity and educating future teachers.

*The Governance Divide: A Report on a Four-State Study on Improving College Readiness and Success,* by Andrea Venezia, Patrick M. Callan, Joni E. Finney, Michael W. Kirst, and Michael D. Usdan (September 2005, #05-3). This report identifies and examines four policy levers available to states that are interested in creating sustained K–16 reform: finance, assessments and curricula, accountability, and data systems. In addition, the report examines the importance of other factors—such as leadership and state history and culture—in initiating and sustaining K–16 reform.

*Borrowers Who Drop Out: A Neglected Aspect of the College Student Loan Trend,* by Lawrence Gladieux and Laura Perna (May 2005, #05-2). This report examines the experiences of students who borrow to finance their education but do not complete their postsecondary programs. Using the latest comprehensive data, this report compares borrowers who drop out with other groups of students, and provides recommendations on policies and programs that would better prepare, support, and guide students—especially low-income students—in completing their degrees.

*Case Study of Utah Higher Education,* by Kathy Reeves Bracco and Mario Martinez (April 2005, #05-1). This report examines state policies and performance in the areas of enrollment and affordability. Compared with other states, Utah has been able to maintain a system of higher education that is more affordable for students, while enrollments have almost doubled over the past 20 years.

*Measuring Up 2004: The National Report Card on Higher Education* (September 2004). *Measuring Up 2004* consists of a national report card for higher education (report #04-5) and 50 state report cards (#04-4) The purpose of *Measuring Up 2004* is to provide the public and policymakers with information to assess and improve postsecondary education in each state. For the first time, this edition of *Measuring Up* provides information about each state's improvement over the past decade. Visit www.highereducation.org to download *Measuring Up 2004* or to make your own comparisons of state performance in higher education.

*Technical Guide Documenting Methodology, Indicators, and Data Sources for* **Measuring Up 2004** (November 2004, #04-6).

*Ensuring Access with Quality to California's Community Colleges,* by Gerald C. Hayward, Dennis P. Jones, Aims C. McGuinness, Jr., and Allene Timar, with a postscript by Nancy Shulock (April 2004, #04-3). This report finds that enrollment growth pressures, fee increases, and recent budget cuts in the California Community Colleges are having significant detrimental effects on student access and program quality. The report also provides recommendations for creating improvements that build from the state policy context and from existing promising practices within the community colleges.

*Public Attitudes on Higher Education: A Trend Analysis, 1993 to 2003,* by John Immerwahr (February 2004, #04-2). This public opinion survey, prepared by Public Agenda for the National Center, reveals that public attitudes about the importance of higher education have remained stable during the recent economic downturn. The survey also finds that there are some growing public concerns about the costs of higher education, especially for those groups most affected, including parents of high school students, African-Americans, and Hispanics.

*Responding to the Crisis in College Opportunity* (January 2004, #04-1). This policy statement, developed by education policy experts at Lansdowne, Virginia, proposes short-term emergency measures and long-term priorities for governors and legislators to consider for funding higher education during the current lean budget years. *Responding to the Crisis* suggests that in 2004 the highest priority for state higher education budgets should be to protect college access and affordability for students and families.

*With Diploma in Hand: Hispanic High School Seniors Talk about their Future*, by John Immerwahr (June 2003, #03-2). This report by Public Agenda explores some of the primary obstacles that many Hispanic students face in seeking higher education, barriers which suggest opportunities for creative public policy to improve college attendance and completion rates among Hispanics.

*Purposes, Policies, Performance: Higher Education and the Fulfillment of a State's Public Agenda* (February 2003, #03-1). This essay is drawn from discussions of higher education leaders and policy officials at a roundtable convened in June 2002 at New Jersey City University on the relationship between public purposes, policies, and performance of American higher education.

*Measuring Up 2002: The State-by-State Report Card for Higher Education* (October 2002, #02-7). This report card, which updates the inaugural edition released in 2000, grades each state on its performance in five key areas of higher education. *Measuring Up 2002* also evaluates each state's progress in relation to its own results from 2000.

*Technical Guide Documenting Methodology, Indicators, and Data Sources for* **Measuring Up 2002** (October 2002, #02-8).

*State Policy and Community College-Baccalaureate Transfer*, by Jane V. Wellman (July 2002, #02-6). Recommends state policies to energize and improve higher education performance regarding transfers from community colleges to four-year institutions.

*Fund for the Improvement of Postsecondary Education: The Early Years* (June 2002, #02-5). The Fund for the Improvement of Postsecondary Education (FIPSE) attained remarkable success in funding innovative and enduring projects during its early years. This report, prepared by FIPSE's early program officers, describes how those results were achieved.

*Losing Ground: A National Status Report on the Affordability of American Higher Education* (May 2002, #02-3). This national status report documents the declining affordability of higher education for American families, and highlights public policies that support affordable higher education. Provides state-by-state summaries as well as national findings.

*The Affordability of Higher Education: A Review of Recent Survey Research*, by John Immerwahr (May 2002, #02-4). This review of recent surveys by Public Agenda confirms that Americans feel that rising college prices threaten to make higher education inaccessible for many people.

*Coping with Recession: Public Policy, Economic Downturns, and Higher Education*, by Patrick M. Callan (February 2002, #02-2). Outlines the major policy considerations that states and institutions of higher education face during economic downturns.

*Competition and Collaboration in California Higher Education*, by Kathy Reeves Bracco and Patrick M. Callan (January 2002, #02-1). Argues that the structure of California's state higher education system limits the system's capacity for collaboration.

*Measuring Up 2000: The State-by-State Report Card for Higher Education* (November 2000, #00-3). This first-of-its-kind report card grades each state on its performance in higher education. The report card also provides comprehensive profiles of each state and brief states-at-a-glance comparisons.

*Beneath the Surface: A Statistical Analysis of the Major Variables Associated with State Grades in* **Measuring Up 2000**, by Alisa F. Cunningham and Jane V. Wellman (November 2001, #01-4). Using statistical analysis, this report explores the "drivers" that predict overall performance in *Measuring Up 2000*.

*Supplementary Analysis for* **Measuring Up 2000**: *An Exploratory Report*, by Mario Martinez (November 2001, #01-3). Explores the relationships within and among the performance categories in *Measuring Up 2000*.

*Some Next Steps for States: A Follow-up to* **Measuring Up 2000**, by Dennis Jones and Karen Paulson (June 2001, #01-2). Suggests a range of actions that states can take to bridge the gap between state performance identified in *Measuring Up 2000* and the formulation of effective policy to improve performance in higher education.

*A Review of Tests Performed on the Data in* **Measuring Up 2000,** by Peter T. Ewell (June 2001, #01-1). Describes the statistical testing performed on the data in *Measuring Up 2000* by the National Center for Higher Education Management Systems.

*Recent State Policy Initiatives in Education: A Supplement to* **Measuring Up 2000,** by Aims C. McGuinness, Jr. (December 2000, #00-6). Highlights education initiatives that states have adopted since 1997–98.

*Assessing Student Learning Outcomes: A Supplement to* **Measuring Up 2000,** by Peter T. Ewell and Paula Ries (December 2000, #00-5). National survey of state efforts to assess student learning outcomes in higher education.

*Technical Guide Documenting Methodology, Indicators and Data Sources for* **Measuring Up 2000** (November 2000, #00-4).

*A State-by-State Report Card on Higher Education: Prospectus* (March 2000, #00-1). Summarizes the goals of the National Center's report card project.

*Great Expectations: How the Public and Parents—White, African-American and Hispanic— View Higher Education,* by John Immerwahr with Tony Foleno (May 2000, #00-2). This report by Public Agenda finds that Americans overwhelmingly see higher education as essential for success. Survey results are also available for the following states:

*Great Expectations: How Pennsylvanians View Higher Education (May 2000, #00-2b)*

*Great Expectations: How Floridians View Higher Education (August 2000, #00-2c)*

*Great Expectations: How Coloradans View Higher Education (August 2000, #00-2d)*

*Great Expectations: How Californians View Higher Education (August 2000, #00-2e)*

*Great Expectations: How New Yorkers View Higher Education (October 2000, #00-2f)*

*Great Expectations: How Illinois Residents View Higher Education (October 2000, #00-2h)*

*State Spending for Higher Education in the Next Decade: The Battle to Sustain Current Support,* by Harold A. Hovey (July 1999, #99-3). This fiscal forecast of state and local spending patterns finds that the vast majority of states will face significant fiscal deficits over the next eight years, which will in turn lead to increased scrutiny of higher education in almost all states, and to curtailed spending for public higher education in many states.

*South Dakota: Developing Policy-Driven Change in Higher Education,* by Mario Martinez (June 1999, #99-2). Describes the processes for change in higher education that government, business, and higher education leaders are creating and implementing in South Dakota.

*Taking Responsibility: Leaders' Expectations of Higher Education,* by John Immerwahr (January 1999, #99-1). Reports the views of those most involved with decision making about higher education, based on focus groups and a survey conducted by Public Agenda.

*The Challenges and Opportunities Facing Higher Education: An Agenda for Policy Research,* by Dennis Jones, Peter T. Ewell, and Aims C. McGuinness (December 1998, #98-8). Argues that due to substantial changes in the landscape of postsecondary education, new state-level policy frameworks must be developed and implemented.

*Higher Education Governance: Balancing Institutional and Market Influences,* by Richard C. Richardson, Jr., Kathy Reeves Bracco, Patrick M. Callan, and Joni E. Finney (November 1998, #98-7). Describes the structural relationships that affect institutional effectiveness in higher education, and argues that state policy should strive for a balance between institutional and market forces.

*Federal Tuition Tax Credits and State Higher Education Policy: A Guide for State Policy Makers,* by Kristin D. Conklin (December 1998, #98-6). Examines the implications of the federal income tax provisions for students and their families, and makes recommendations for state higher education policy.

*The Challenges Facing California Higher Education: A Memorandum to the Next Governor of California,* by David W. Breneman (September 1998, #98-5). Argues that California should develop a new Master Plan for Higher Education.

*Tidal Wave II Revisited: A Review of Earlier Enrollment Projections for California Higher Education,* by Gerald C. Hayward, David W. Breneman, and Leobardo F. Estrada (September 1998, #98-4). Finds that earlier forecasts of a surge in higher education enrollments were accurate.

*Organizing for Learning: The View from the Governor's Office,* by James B. Hunt Jr., chair of the National Center for Public Policy and Higher Education, and former governor of North Carolina (June 1998, #98-3). An address to the American Association for Higher Education concerning opportunity in higher education.

*The Price of Admission: The Growing Importance of Higher Education,* by John Immerwahr (Spring 1998, #98-2). A national survey of Americans' views on higher education, conducted and reported by Public Agenda.

*Concept Paper: A National Center to Address Higher Education Policy,* by Patrick M. Callan (March 1998, #98-1). Describes the purposes of the National Center for Public Policy and Higher Education.

## Notes

1. *Measuring Up 2000: The State-by-State Report Card for Higher Education* (San Jose: National Center for Public Policy and Higher Education, 2000). Subsequent editions of *Measuring Up* were published in 2002 and 2004, and the next edition is planned for 2006.

2. See note to figure 7 for an explanation of how scores are standardized.

3. *Technical Guide Documenting Methodology, Indicators, and Data Sources for Measuring Up 2004* (San Jose: National Center for Public Policy and Higher Education, 2004).

# Remedial Education in Colleges and Universities: What's Really Going On?

## JAMIE P. MERISOTIS AND RONALD A. PHIPPS

Offering coursework below college level in higher education institutions is coming under increased scrutiny. Variously referred to as "remedial education," "developmental education," "college prep," or "basic skills," it constitutes a field about which policy makers are asking: Why are so many students in institutions of higher learning taking basic reading, writing, and arithmetic—subjects that should have been learned in high school, if not junior high school?

Over the past several years, some states—including Arkansas, Louisiana, Oklahoma, Tennessee, and Virginia—are attempting to limit remedial education. In 1998, the trustees of the City University of New York (CUNY) voted to phase out most remedial education in the system's 11 four-year institutions, and the CUNY plan has moved ahead steadily since its implementation in September 1999. Following similar patterns, some states such as Florida have moved virtually all remediation to community colleges. Legislators in Texas and other states are expressing concern that tax dollars are being used in colleges to teach high school courses. In response, the legislatures in the states of New Jersey, Montana, Florida, and Oregon, among others, are considering proposals that would require public school systems to pay for any remedial work that a public school graduate must take in college.

A survey of state legislators showed that they were split three ways on the topic. In response to the statement that colleges and universities should give remedial education more attention, 34% disagreed, 32% agreed, and 32% were neutral. While state legislators agree that the problem is inherited from the K-12 sector, they are less clear about who to hold responsible (Ruppert, 1996). Educators mirror this ambivalence. Proponents and opponents alike point to the effects of remedial education on the quality, accountability, and efficiency of higher education institutions. The quality of discussions on the effect of remediation on diversity, educational opportunity, and enrollment is diminished by the lack of agreement on the nature of remediation. There is little consensus and understanding about what remedial education is, whom it serves, who should provide it, and how much it costs. Consequently, this lack of fundamental information and imprecision of language often renders public policy discussions ill informed at best.

This article, which is adapted from a recent publication on remediation by The Institute for Higher Education Policy (1998a), seeks to bring some clarity to the policy discussions. It includes an analysis of remediation's core function in the higher education enterprise, a review of the current status of remedial education at the college level, a discussion of financing remedial education, an argument about the costs of not providing remedial education, and a set of recommendations intended to reduce the need for remediation while also enhancing its effectiveness.

# Remediation's Core Function in Higher Education

Given the increased attention to remedial education, it may be easy to conclude that efforts providing compensatory education to underprepared students in colleges and universities are recent events that somehow reflect the present condition of U.S. postsecondary education. Although some individuals may argue that the quality of the higher educational enterprise has decreased over the years, the fact remains that remedial education has been part of higher education since early colonial days. Dating back to the 17th century, Harvard College provided tutors in Greek and Latin for those underprepared students who did not want to study for the ministry. The middle of the 18th century saw the establishment of land-grant colleges, which instituted preparatory programs or departments for students below average in reading, writing, and arithmetic skills (Payne & Lyman, 1998). In 1849, the first remedial education programs in reading, writing, and arithmetic were offered at the University of Wisconsin (Breneman & Haarlow, 1998). By the end of the 19th century, when only 238,000 students were enrolled in all of higher education, more than 40% of first-year students college participated in precollegiate programs (Ignash, 1997).

Due to increased competition for students among higher education institutions at the beginning of the 20th century, underprepared students continued to be accepted at growing rates. For instance, over half of the students enrolled in Harvard, Princeton, Yale, and Columbia did not meet entrance requirements and were placed in remedial courses. The vast influx of World War II veterans taking advantage of the G.I. Bill created another surge in the need for remedial education. Then thousands of underprepared students enrolled in colleges and universities from the 1960s to the 1980s in response to open admissions policies and government funding following the passage of the Civil Rights Act of 1964 and the Higher Education Act of 1965 (Payne & Lyman, 1998).

In short, those halcyon days when all students who enrolled in college were adequately prepared, all courses offered at higher education institutions were "college level," and students smoothly made the transition from high school and college simply never existed. And they do not exist now. A comprehensive survey of remediation in higher education, conducted by the National Center for Education Statistics (NCES) for fall 1995, provides evidence of this reality. Remedial courses were defined as courses in reading, writing, and mathematics for college students lacking skills necessary to perform college-level work at the level required by the institution. Thus, what constituted remedial courses varied from institution to institution. Here are NCES's major findings (U.S. Department of Education, 1996):

- Over three-quarters (78%) of higher education institutions that enrolled first-year students in fall 1995 offered at least one remedial reading, writing, or mathematics course. All public two-year institutions and almost all (94%) institutions with high minority enrollments offered remedial courses.
- Twenty-nine percent of first-time first-year students enrolled in at least one remedial reading, writing, or mathematics course in fall 1995. First-year students were more likely to enroll in a remedial mathematics course than in a remedial reading or writing course, irrespective of institution attended.
- At most institutions, students do not take remedial courses for extended periods of time. Two-thirds of the institutions indicated that the average time a student takes remedial courses was less than one year, 28% one year, and 5% more than one year.

Because NCES conducted similar surveys for the academic year 1983-1984 and for fall 1989, it is possible to compare the intensity of remedial education course offerings over the past decade. The consistency is striking. In 1983–1984, 82% of the institutions offered remedial education in all three areas (reading, writing, and mathematics), compared to 78% in fall 1995. Sixty-six percent provided remedial reading courses in 1983–1984 compared to 57% in fall 1995; for remedial writing, 73% and 71%; and remedial mathematics, 71% and 72%, respectively.

Statistics for first-year students enrolled in remedial courses were not estimated for the academic year 1983-1984; however, comparisons can be made between fall 1989 and fall 1995. Thirty percent of first-year students enrolled in all three remedial courses in fall 1989 compared to 29% in fall 1995. Thirteen percent of first-year students enrolled in remedial reading for both years. Remedial writing courses were taken by 16% of the first-year students in fall 1989 compared to 17% in fall

1995. In remedial mathematics, the percentages were 21% and 24%, respectively. Interestingly, although little change resulted in the percentage of students enrolling in remedial courses from fall 1989 to fall 1995, college and university enrollment increased by approximately a half million students.

## Institutions That Do Not Offer Remediation

Twenty-two percent of the institutions in the NCES survey indicated that they did not offer remedial education courses. Of that percentage, two-thirds noted that their students did not need remediation. Approximately a quarter reported that those students needing remediation take such courses at another institution and/or that institutional policy prohibits the offering of remedial courses on their campus.

There is some reason to believe that the percentage of institutions not offering remedial courses is much lower than reported and, conversely, that the percentage of students requiring remedial courses is higher. This conclusion, based on the nature of the higher education enterprise, is supported by anecdotal evidence. For example, many institutions do not find it in their best interests to acknowledge that they enroll students who require remediation. In a paper presented to the American Council on Education, Astin (1998) posits that an institution's "excellence" is defined primarily by resources and reputation. A major boost to an institution's reputation is the enrollment rates of students with the highest GPAs, the top test scores, and the strongest recommendations. Astin states:

> It goes without saying that the underprepared student is a kind of pariah in American higher education, and some of the reasons are obvious: since most of us believe that the excellence of our departments and of our institutions depends on enrolling the very best-prepared students that we can, to admit underprepared students would pose a real threat to our excellence. (1998, p. 11)

However, there is a disproportionate emphasis on the credentials and the abilities of the *applicants* compared to the knowledge and skills of the *graduates*–as evidenced by virtually every national ranking publication (Astin, 1998, p. 11).

Steinberg, as cited in Breneman and Haarlow, refers to the National Assessment of Educational Progress and the Third International Math and Science Study to suggest that more high school students than we would like to admit are unprepared for college-level work (Breneman & Haarlow, 1998). Even in high-performing states, only one-third of American high school students meet or exceed levels of grade-appropriate proficiency in mathematics, science, reading, and writing. The country's 12th graders perform as poorly on standardized math and science tests as their counterparts from the worst-performing industrialized countries in the world. Steinberg states:

> Even if we assume that none of these sub-proficient students graduating from American high schools goes on to postsecondary education (surely an untenable assumption), the fact that somewhere close to 60% of U.S. high school graduates do attend college suggests that a fairly significant number of college-bound young people cannot do, and do not know, the things that educators agree that high school graduates ought to know and be able to do. (Qtd. in Breneman & Haarlow, 1998, p. 46)

The purpose of this analysis is not to place blame or point fingers at the nation's K-12 system or the higher education community. It is merely to suggest that there is validity behind the hypothesis that more remedial activities are occurring than meet the eye. Therefore, it is reasonable to say that a portion of the 22% of institutions reporting that they do not offer remedial education courses enroll underprepared students and provide some sort of remedial service. Also, it is likely that *at least* 78% of higher education institutions enroll underprepared students and that, in all probability, more than 30% of the students require remediation.

## The Many Faces of Remedial Education

The discussion of remedial education evokes the image of courses in reading, writing, and mathematics whose content is below "college-level." The term "college-level" suggests that agreed-upon standards exist, or at least enjoy a consensus by educators. A reasonable assumption would be that the academic community has identified specific knowledge and skills that are required of students to be successful in a college or university. Conversely, if students do not possess the specified knowledge and skills, remedial education is needed for academic success.

The fact is that remedial education is in the eye of the beholder. Rather than being based on some immutable set of college-level standards, remedial education, more often than not, is determined by the admissions requirements of the particular institution. Obviously, remediation at a community college with open admissions is not the same as remediation at a doctoral research institution. As Astin points out: "Most remedial students turn out to be simply those who have the lowest scores on some sort of normative measurement–standardized tests, school grades, and the like. But where we draw the line is completely arbitrary: lowest quarter, lowest fifth, lowest 5%, or what? Nobody knows. Second, the 'norms' that define a 'low' score are highly variable from one setting to another" (Astin, 1998, p. 13). A case in point is the 21-campus California State University (CSU) System. Although state policy in California mandates that students entering CSU are supposed to be in the top third of their high school graduating class, the *Los Angeles Times* reported that 47% of the fall 1997 first-year class required remedial work in English and 54% needed remedial work in mathematics (National Center, 1998).

Furthermore, remediation standards vary even for institutions with similar missions. A 1996 study by the Maryland Higher Education Commission found that policies, instruments, and standards used by Maryland colleges and universities to identify and place remedial students differed, even within the community college sector. Institutions employ various approaches toward the particular subject areas of remediation, including locally developed norms, nationally developed norms, grade-level equivalences, and specific deficiencies and/or competencies.

Another study conducted in 1998 by the Maryland Higher Education Commission illuminates the relationship between high school preparation and the need for remediation in college. The conventional wisdom is that students who complete college preparatory courses in high school will not need remedial education in college, while students who have not taken a college preparatory curriculum in high school will probably need remediation. This particular study measured the college success rates of recent high school graduates. The basic findings of the report agree with common sense. Students who completed college-preparatory courses in high school performed better in college than students who did not complete college-preparatory courses in high school. College-preparatory students earned higher grades in their initial math and English courses and had higher grade point averages after their first year in college than students who did not complete the college-preparatory curriculum. Also, fewer college-preparatory students required assistance in math, English, and reading.

It is helpful, however, to examine these data further. First, a significant number of students who took college-preparatory courses in high school needed remediation in college. For students who completed college-preparatory courses in high school and immediately attended a community college, 40% needed math remediation, one out of five required English remediation, and one out of four needed remedial reading. At one community college, 73% of college-preparatory students needed math remediation, 79% English remediation, and 76% reading remediation. At the public four-year institutions, 14% of college-preparatory students needed math remediation, 7% English remediation, and 6% reading remediation.

Some disconnect exists between what high schools consider college-preparatory, particularly in mathematics and English, and what colleges are requiring of their entering students. But a more interesting question emerges from these data. The percentages of *college-preparatory* students requiring remediation at the community colleges is dramatically higher than the percentage of *college-preparatory* students at the public four-year institutions. How can that be? Conventional wisdom would suggest that the percentages would be approximately the same for both higher education sectors because all of the students have completed a state-mandated college preparatory curriculum. Or, for those who contend that community colleges are less academically rigorous than four-year institutions with selective admissions (a debatable argument), the expectation would be that the percentages would be reversed. That is, since all students have enjoyed the benefit of a college-preparatory curriculum, those enrolling in community colleges would be quite prepared for the easier curriculum compared to those enrolling in four-year institutions with the more academically rigorous curriculum.

There can be many explanations for this intriguing issue. One could argue that the college-preparatory students admitted by the four-year institutions are academically superior to the college-preparatory students admitted by the community colleges and therefore need less remediation. Also, it could be that community colleges, because of their open-door mission, have more structured procedures than four-year colleges for determining which students require remedial courses. Critics of the quality of high schools may posit that college preparatory students from high schools that lack academic rigor, in spite of the college preparatory label, choose to attend a community college because they are concerned about their academic preparation. Whatever the explanation, this example helps to affirm the essential point made by Astin and others: remedial education in colleges and universities is relative and arbitrary.

## Remedial Education's Diverse Client Population

The examination of remedial education is incomplete if it focuses only on recent high school graduates. According to several studies, a substantial proportion of postsecondary education students are 25 years of age or older, and many of these adult students are enrolled in remedial courses. The exact proportion or number of older students requiring remedial education, however, is difficult to discern and the data on age distribution of remedial students vary widely from state to state.

One important source of national data in the composition of students in remedial courses is provided by the National Center for Developmental Education (NCDE). NCDE data indicated that approximately 80% of remedial students in the country's colleges and universities are age 21 or younger (Breneman & Haarlow, 1998). However, other data suggest that a much higher proportion of older students is taking remedial courses and that the remediation population is bipolar in terms of age and time elapsed between secondary and postsecondary experiences. According to NCES, 31% of entering first-year students who took a remedial education class in 1992–1993 were 19 or younger. In contrast, 45% of the entering first-year students who took a remedial course were over twenty-two years of age, the traditional age of the baccalaureate degree graduate. Another study found that one-quarter (27%) of entering first-year students in remedial courses were 30 or older (Ignash, 1997).

Data from individual states support the NCES findings. For instance, Maryland found that more than three-fourths of remedial students in the community colleges in 1994–1995 were 20 years of age or older (Maryland Higher Education Commission, 1996). In Florida, a reported 80% of the students in remedial classes were not recent high school graduates but older students who needed to brush up their skills, usually in mathematics, before entering the higher education mainstream (National Center, 1998). First-year students also are not the only students who take remediation. NCES data show that 56% of students enrolled in remedial courses were first-year students, 24% were sophomores, 9% were juniors, and 9% were seniors (Ignash, 1997).

The policy debate about remediation in higher education must address not only first-year students who recently graduated from high school but also students of all ages and levels of undergraduate progress. In fact, it appears that, in the future, older students will attend colleges and universities in record numbers and will require remedial education. According to a recent report, between 1970 and 1993, the participation in higher education by students age 40 and over increased from 5.5% of total enrollment to 11.2%—the largest jump of any age cohort (Institute for Higher Education Policy, 1996). Policies addressing remediation must recognize that the demand for remedial education is being fueled in part by older students who need refresher courses in mathematics or writing.

## How Successful Is Remedial Education?

Research about the effectiveness of remedial education programs has typically been sporadic, underfunded, and inconclusive. For instance, a study of 116 two- and four-year colleges and universities revealed that only a small percentage conducted any systematic evaluation of their remedial education programs (Weissman, Bulakowski, & Jumisco, 1997). The Southern Regional Education Board has observed that, because few states have exit standards for remedial courses, it is unclear whether many states know whether their programs work (Crowe, 1998). Adelman (1998) examined college transcripts from the national high school class of 1982 and, not surprisingly, found an inverse relationship between the extent of students' need for remedial courses and their eventual completion of a degree. Of the 1982 high school graduates who had earned more than a semester of college credit by age 30, 60% of those who took no remedial courses, and 55% of those who took only one remedial course, had either earned a bachelor's or associate's degree. In contrast, only 35% of the students who participated in five or more remedial courses attained either a bachelor's or associate's degree.

Focusing upon reading remediation reveals another perspective. Sixty-six percent of students required to take remedial reading were in three or more other remedial courses, and only 12% of this group earned bachelor's degrees. Among students who were required to take more than one remedial reading course, nearly 80% were in two or more other remedial courses, and less than 9% earned bachelors' degree. When reading is at the core of the problem, the probability of success in college appears to be very low.

According to Adelman, the need to take remedial education courses reduces the probability of achieving a degree. Yet it is also instructive to look at the ratio of students who did not need remedial education and those who did. Students who did not take remediation courses had a graduation rate of 60%. But even the least academically prepared students—those who took five or more remedial education courses–had a 35% graduation rate. Therefore, remediation allowed the academically weakest students to perform almost three-fifths as well as the students who did not need any remediation. Further, students who needed two remedial courses performed almost three-quarters as well as the academically strongest students. These data seem to indicate that remediation is, in fact, quite effective at improving the chances of collegiate success for underprepared students.

## Financial Costs

Hard evidence regarding the costs of remediation nationwide is elusive. The most recent analysis of the cost, authored by Breneman and Haarlow (1998) suggest that nationally remedial education absorbs about $1 billion annually in a public higher education budget of $115 billion—less than 1% of expenditures. This estimate, derived by conducting a survey of all 50 states along with individual site visits to five states, includes the costs associated with remediation for both traditional age first-year students and returning adult students.

Among states and between higher education segments, the percentage of remedial education expenditures to the total budget showed wide variance. In FY1996, 1.1% of the direct salary budget of public universities in Illinois was dedicated to remediation, while it took 6.5% of the community college direct salary budget. In FY1995, the percentage of expenditures for remediation in Maryland was 1.2% of the total expenditures for the public campuses. In Washington, 7% of total expenditures was earmarked for remedial education in 1995–1996. Focusing on the appropriation per full-time equivalent (FTE) student for individual states, the cost to California for remediation is about $2,950 per FTE student and the cost to Florida is about $2,409.

It is important to note what the total national cost estimate of $1 billion does *not* entail. First, this estimate does not include the remediation budget of private colleges and universities. Second, costs borne by students through foregone earnings and diminished labor productivity were not calculated. Third, there was no effort to figure the costs to society as a whole by failing to develop the nation's human capital to its fullest potential. These limitations notwithstanding, the Breneman and Haarlow report compiles the most comprehensive, accurate information to date.

There are several impediments to collecting reliable data about the costs of remediation:

- There is no universally accepted definition of what constitutes remedial education within the academic community.
- How "costs" are distributed among the several activities within a college or university can, and do, vary widely.
- Even if the functions to be included in determining the cost of remediation were understood, higher education institutions have difficulty supplying precise breakdowns of remediation costs.

- It is not always clear whether reported cost figures include expenditures or appropriations. As Breneman and Haarlow point out, "These are two different measures of cost, and ideally, one would want all the figures on both bases, but what one gets is a mix of the two" (1998, pp. 12–13).
- Because states do not compute remediation education costs regularly, financial data can either be relatively current or several years old.

Perhaps the most intractable barrier to collecting valid and reliable data on remediation is that noted by commentators like Astin and Steinberg: Official estimates of the extent and cost of remediation are often understated for a variety of reasons—not the least of which is the perceived damage to the "reputation" of a college or university. Unfortunately, there are many incentives for agencies and institutions to underreport remediation. Thus, we can reasonably conclude that the costs of remediation are higher than reported. Our estimate is that the figure is probably closer to $2 billion. However, if $2 billion—which amounts to 2% of higher education expenditures—is the actual cost of remediation, it is still a relatively modest amount to be spent on an activity of such importance to the nation. If remedial education were terminated at every college and university, it is unlikely that the money would be put to better use.

A useful case study is the Arkansas Department of Higher Education's comprehensive study over several years that compares direct and indirect instructional costs of academic programs for the state's public colleges and universities. In 1996–1997, the total cost of remediation in Arkansas colleges and universities was $27 million—approximately 3% of the total expenditures. At community colleges, 9% of the total expenditures went to remedial education compared to 2% at four-year institutions. The total state subsidy for remedial education was almost $14 million. The state subsidy for community colleges was 59% of the total expenditures compared to 40% at four-year institutions. These data show that, although remediation is provided at both four-year and two-year institutions, community colleges commit substantially more resources toward remedial education—which is not surprising given their open-admissions policies.

The Arkansas cost study shows that the cost per FTE student for remedial education at the four-year institutions was $7,381. The average program costs per FTE student at four-year institutions ranged from $7,919 for psychology, to $8,804 for English, to $9,320 for mathematics, to $12,369 in music. The cost per FTE student for remedial education at the community colleges was $6,709. The average program costs per FTE student at the community colleges ranged from $6,163 for general studies, to $7,730 for business, to $8,235 in nursing.

These data illustrate that remediation costs per FTE student generally are lower than the costs per FTE student for core academic programs—English, mathematics, etc.—that lead to an associate or bachelor's degree. Knowing the cost per FTE student for remediation vis-à-vis the cost per FTE student for academic programs provides another viewpoint in the remediation debate. One issue that most institutions grapple with is resource reallocation: How can the institution use limited resources to the greatest benefit? What is the cost/benefit of providing remediation? Many institutions are targeting "low-demand programs"—programs with few graduates—for elimination. How does the cost of low-demand programs compare to remedial education costs, and can resources be better used elsewhere? How is the cost per FTE student in academic programs affected by remedial students who are successful and who participate in college-level courses? These and other questions can frame the public policy debate regarding the cost of remediation.

In addition to examining the financial cost of providing remedial education in higher education, it is helpful to look at the other side of the coin. More explicitly, what are the financial gains of a successful remedial education program for a specific institution? A remedial education program that enables a significant proportion of remedial students to continue their education after completing remedial courses is beneficial for the institutional bottom line since it enhances revenue that can partially offset costs associated with providing remediation.

## Social and Economic Costs of Not Providing Remediation

What does the nation get for its $1 to $2 billion investment in remedial education? There is considerable evidence that the nation cannot afford to disfranchise even a small portion of the population who has the potential of succeeding in college from participating in some form of postsecondary education. Therefore, the costs and benefits associated with providing access to underprepared students and helping them succeed in higher education must be measured accurately.

Ponitz, as cited in Breneman and Haarlow, points out that 80% of sustainable jobs today require some education beyond high school (Breneman & Haarlow, 1998). Currently, 65% of the nation's workers need the skills of a generalist/technician, including advanced reading, writing, mathematical, critical thinking, and interpersonal group skills. Twenty years ago, that figure was only 15% (Breneman & Haarlow, 1998).

According to a Lehman Brothers report (citing Bureau of Labor Statistics data), the growth rate in jobs between 1994 and 2005 will be the greatest for categories that require at least an associate's degree (Ghazi & Irani, 1997). Jobs requiring a master's degree will grow the fastest (at a rate of 28%), followed closely by those requiring a bachelor's degree (27%), and an associate's degree (24%). "All jobs requiring postsecondary education and training of an associate's degree or better are projected to grow significantly higher than the average, and all those with lesser levels of training are expected to grow below the average," summarizes the Lehman Brothers' report. "In our opinion, this is a clear indication that the transformation to a knowledge-based economy will require a more highly skilled, more adept, and more knowledgeable work force" (Ghazi & Irani, 1997, p. 71).

A report from The Institute for Higher Education Policy (1998b) summarizes four types of benefits of going to college: private economic benefits, private social benefits, public economic benefits, and public social benefits. While much of the recent public policy focus has been on the private benefits, the public benefits of going to college are extensive. Since going to college results in greater benefits to the public as a whole—increased tax revenues, greater productivity, reduced crime rates, increased quality of civic life, etc.—then students who benefit from the remedial instruction provided by higher education also must be contributing to the public good.

However, not all agree with these findings. Rubenstein (1998) argues that the economic return of higher education to the graduate is an illusion. Significant factors relating to higher wages of college graduates when compared to high school graduates include the higher socioeconomic background of college graduates, in addition to their higher motivation and, probably, higher IQs. He further notes that too many colleges are chasing many marginal students and that the United States has an abundance of college graduates, not a deficit. As a consequence, in 1995 approximately 40% of people with some college education—and 10% of those with a college degree—worked at jobs requiring only high school skills. In 1971, the figures were 30% and 6% respectively. Rubenstein concludes that functionally literate graduates are in short supply. College graduates who do not have the functional literacy traditionally associated with college degrees are taking jobs that had previously gone to employees with high school diplomas.

Rubenstein's argument is alarming and, if accurate, poses a challenge to educators in both the K-12 and higher education sectors. The obvious challenge is to ensure that college graduates are functionally literate and possess the skills necessary to compete in a global society. Few would argue, it seems to us, that there can be too many functionally literate people, whether they are college graduates or not. As a society, we have little choice about providing remediation in higher education, with the goal of increasing functional literacy. Abandoning remedial efforts in higher education and therefore reducing the number of people gaining the skills and knowledge associated with postsecondary education is unwise public policy. Thus, it is appropriate to confront the causes of underpreparation and try to reduce the necessity for remediation as much as possible. In addition, policies should be explored to improve the effectiveness of remediation programs, and cost efficiencies should be implemented wherever needed.

## Recommendations

The evidence is compelling that remediation in colleges and universities is not an appendage with little connection to the mission of the institution but rather represents a core function of the higher education community that it has performed for hundreds of years. Although the financial data are not as reliable as some would like, there is sufficient reason to assume that the cost is minimal when compared to the total higher education budget. Also, the case has been made that attempts to eliminate remediation completely from higher education are both unrealistic and unwise public policy. Realizing this, where do we go from here?

It is important to recognize that not all remediation is delivered effectively or efficiently. Like any educational process, remedial education must be continuously examined and revised to meet prevailing conditions and needs. Therefore, good public policy must focus upon two mutually reinforcing goals: (1) implementing multiple strategies that help to reduce the need for remediation in higher education, and (2) improving the effectiveness of remedial education in higher education. It is evident that a piecemeal approach to addressing the problem of remediation in higher education has not worked. Intermittent schemes to "correct" remedial education are stop-gap solutions at best. Only a systemic design at the state level comprised of a set of interrelated strategies will succeed.

The discussion below presents a set of strategies that states and institutions can use to achieve the public policy goals outlined here. We emphasize that there is a positive relationship between the number of implemented strategies and the probability of meeting the public policy goals. Implementing one or two of the strategies may be helpful, but fundamentally addressing the issue requires using the entire range of strategic options.

The importance of collaboration cannot be understated. Borrowing the realtor's mantra—location, location, location—reducing the need for remediation in higher education will require collaboration between and among: colleges and universities and high schools; states and their colleges and universities, as well as state departments of education, K-12 public and private schools, public and private two- and four-year colleges and universities, businesses, and philanthropies. We have no illusions that the various players in the educational enterprise will welcome cooperation and abandon their traditional turf. We simply state that a lack of a true, invested collaborative effort among the parties will doom any effort to fully address the issue of remediation.

## Reducing the Need for Remediation in Higher Education

Strategies for reducing the need for college remediation include: (a) aligning high school requirements and course content with college competency and content expectations; (b) offering early intervention and financial aid programs that target K-12 students by linking mentoring, tutoring, and academic guidance with a guarantee of college financial aid; (3) tracking students and providing high school feedback systems; and (4) improving teacher preparation. Many of these approaches are found in the K-16 movement occurring in many states.

1. *Aligning High School Requirements with College Content and Competency Expectations.* Several state initiatives are underway to define specifically what a first-year college student needs to know and be able to do. These initiatives often are identified in terms of content and competency levels rather than Carnegie units or high-school class rank. College entry-level content standards and competencies apply across the curriculum to all first-year students who are recent high school graduates. They do not target students enrolling in a specific course or a specific major. The competency categories parallel college general education categories and align with the content standards being adopted in school districts.

2. *Early Intervention and Financial Aid Programs.* Some states have developed, or are considering developing, early intervention strategies in the high schools, often beginning in the ninth grade. These techniques are designed to correct student academic deficiencies before the students reach college. Also, a number of states have established early intervention financial aid programs modeled after the Taylor Plan in Louisiana, which in addition to enhancing access, contain provisions to increase the ability of students to succeed in college. Although details vary from state to state, the programs guarantee low-income K-12 students admission to college if they meet certain criteria, including completion of a college-preparatory curriculum, achieving a minimum grade point average, and participating in a counseling program. The federal government has enacted the Gaining Early Awareness and Readiness for Undergraduate Programs (GEAR UP) for low-income students. This program encourages states and university-school partnerships to provide support services to students who are at risk of dropping out of school by offering them information, encouragement, and the means to pursue postsecondary study.

3. *Student Tracking and High School Feedback Systems.* An effective tool for enhancing collaboration between high schools and colleges, in addition to identifying areas of mutual concern, is to provide feedback to high schools regarding the success of their students in college. Several

states provide high schools with information on student admission exemptions; remedial course work in mathematics, English, and reading; performance in the first college-level courses in English and mathematics; cumulative grade point averages; and persistence (Wallhaus, 1998).

4. *Improved Teacher Preparation.* Teacher education reform is now on the national agenda, as evidenced by the 1998 reauthorization of the Higher Education Act of 1965. The legislation replaces several small teacher education programs—which were not funded—with a three-part grant: 45% of the funding will go to states to improve the quality of its teachers; 45% will go to partnerships between colleges and secondary schools; and 10% will go to recruiting more students to teach in low-income school districts (Burd, 1998).

Initiatives in several states include: (a) reexamining teacher certification and licensure requirements based on specific standards of what teachers should know and be able to do, (b) emphasizing academic disciplines in the teacher education curricula, and (3) establishing performance-based career advancement opportunities for veteran teachers.

## Improving the Effectiveness of Remediation in Higher Education

What can be done to improve the effectiveness of remediation in higher education? We have identified three core strategies: (a) creating interinstitutional collaborations, (b) making remediation a comprehensive program, and (c) utilizing technology.

1. *Interinstitutional Collaboration.* Astin makes a strong case for interinstitutional collaboration between institutions of higher education in a region or state. The opportunities for collaborative research—given that there are hundreds of remedial programs of all types and perhaps thousands of individual courses—are remarkable. Research on programs for underprepared students and faculty preparation to teach such students should be a collaborative effort among colleges and universities in a system or state. Although admitting that such collaboration would be difficult to achieve because of threats to institutional "reputation," interinstitutional conversations hopefully would be successful in leading the participants to agree that (a) "developing effective programs for lower-performing students at *all levels of education* is of vital importance not only to our education system, but also to the state and the society at large" and (b) "finding and implementing more effective programs for underprepared students is a 'systems' challenge that must be accepted and shared by all institutions at all levels of education" (Astin, 1998, pp. 29–30; emphasis ours).

2. *Making Remediation a Comprehensive Program.* Substantial research has been conducted to identify essential components of an effective remedial education program. One recent study by the Massachusetts community colleges provides an excellent overview of best practices in remedial education (Massachusetts, 1998). These practices include:

   - *Assessment and Placement.* All incoming students are evaluated and, where necessary, placed in remediation according to a mandatory comprehensive instrument for assessing reading, writing, and mathematics.
   - *Curriculum Design and Delivery.* The goals and objectives of the remedial program must be defined clearly so that all students understand them.
   - *Support Services.* Underprepared students require individualized help. Effective programs use "intrusive" advising to identify and solve problems early.
   - *Evaluation.* The remedial education program's effectiveness is assessed according to how many students complete remedial education programs, how many excel continue on to college-level courses, how many complete college-level courses, and how many reach their academic goals.

3. *Utilizing Technology.* In the past decade or so, computers have enhanced the teaching-learning process, particularly in remedial courses that are hierarchical, linear, and stable in their structure and content. Many private companies have developed, or are developing, remedial software. One such company, Academic Systems Corporation, has generated computer-assisted remedial courses in mathematics and writing that are being used in hundreds of colleges and universities nationwide. Several controlled studies in colleges and universities have indicated that this type of pedagogy has great potential for remedial education (Academic Systems, 1997). The applied nature of the courses and the fact that the software is geared to adults is especially appropriate for students in remedial courses. Although the student can work at his or her own pace, mediated learning allows the instructor to intervene whenever the student is having difficulty.

## Next Steps

The previous strategies promote the two public policy goals of reducing the need for remediation in higher education while at the same time improving its effectiveness. In effect, these strategies provide a checklist of initiatives that have a positive effect on the two policy objectives. If our thesis is correct, the degree to which a state or region implements these strategies will determine the extent to which it will meet the policy goals.

One way to test this premise would be to conduct a set of case studies in key states. The strategies in the checklist can be used as criteria for making objective judgments about a state's commitment to reducing and improving remediation. Correlating a state's "score"—the extent of its active strategies—with its success in attaining the dual public policy objectives would contribute illuminating information to the national dialogue on remediation. The case study method could further the dialogue about what works in remedial education and could address the need for more accurate and timely data.

The need for remediation and its core function in higher education will not be eliminated by controversy and criticism. Unfortunately, much of the recent discussion on remedial education has tended to produce more heat than light. Public policy efforts would be more productively focused on determining what works in remedial education, for whom, and at what cost. These efforts would propel the nation's higher education institutions toward reaching the dual goals of reducing the need for remediation while ensuring its continued effectiveness.

*Jamie P. Merisotis* is President of The Institute for Higher Education Policy in Washington, D.C. *Ronald A. Phipps* is Senior Associate at The Institute. This article is based in part on a 1998 report published by The Institute, *College Remediation: What It Is, What It Costs, What's at Stake*, available at www.ihep.com. The authors thank Christina Redmond, Research Assistant, and Mark Harvey, Project Assistant, for editorial and research support for this article and the prior report. Address queries to Jamie P. Merisotis at The Institute for Higher Education Policy, 1320 19th Street NW, Suite 400, Washington, D.C. 20036; telephone (202) 861-8223; fax: (202) 861-9307; e-mail: institute@ihep.com. See also: www.ihep.com

# References

Academic Systems. (1997). *Working paper: The economics of mediated learning.* Mountain View, CA: Academic Systems. From the Academic Systems website <www.academic.com>.

Adelman, C. (1998, Summer). The kiss of death? An alternative view of college remediation. *National Crosstalk,* 6(3), p. 11. San Jose, CA: National Center for Public Policy and Higher Education.

Arkansas Department of Higher Education. (1998). *Arkansas academic cost accounting.* Little Rock: Arkansas Department of Higher Education.

Astin, A. (1998, June 19). *Higher education and civic responsibility.* Paper presented at the American Council on Education's Conference on Civic Roles and Responsibilities, Washington, D.C.

Breneman D., & Haarlow, W. (1998). *Remediation in higher education.* Washington, D.C.: Thomas B. Fordham Foundation.

Burd, S. (1998, October 16). The higher education amendments of 1998: The impact on college and students. *Chronicle of Higher Education,* A39. From the Chronicle of Higher Education website <www.chronicle.com.>

Colorado Commission on Higher Education. (1998). *K-12/postsecondary linkage initiatives.* Denver: Colorado Commission on Higher Education.

Crowe, E. (1998). *Statewide remedial education policies.* Denver, CO: State Higher Education Executive Officers.

Ghazi K., & Irani, I. (1997). *Emerging trends in the $670 billion education market.* New York: Lehman Brothers.

Ignash, J. (1997, Winter). Who should provide postsecondary remedial/developmental education? In J. Ignash (Ed.), *New Directions for Community Colleges, No. 100* (pp. 5–19). San Francisco: Jossey-Bass.

The Institute for Higher Education Policy. (1996). *Life after 40: A new portrait of today's—and tomorrow's— postsecondary students.* Boston: Institute for Higher Education Policy and The Education Resources Institute.

The Institute for Higher Education Policy. (1998a). *College remediation: What it is. What it costs. What's at stake.* Washington, D.C.: Institute for Higher Education Policy.

The Institute for Higher Education Policy. (1998b). Reaping the Benefits: Defining the public and private value of going to college. *The new millennium project on higher education costs, pricing, and productivity.* Washington, D.C.: Institute for Higher Education Policy.

Maryland Higher Education Commission. (1996). *A study of remedial education at Maryland public campuses.* Annapolis: Maryland Higher Education Commission.

Maryland Higher Education Commission. (1998). *College performance of New Maryland high school graduates.* Annapolis: Maryland Higher Education Commission.

Massachusetts Community College Development Education Committee (MCCDEC). (1998). Access and quality: Improving the performance of Massachusetts community college developmental education programs. Boston: MCCDEC.

National Center for Public Policy and Higher Education. (1998, Summer). The remedial controversy. *National Crosstalk, 6*(3), p. 2.

Payne, E., & Lyman, B. (1998). *Issues affecting the definition of developmental education.* From the National Association of Developmental Education website <www.umkc.edu/cad/nade/index.htm>.

Rubenstein, E. (1998, Fall). The college payoff illusion. *American Outlook,* 14–18. (Published in New York by the Hudson Institute.)

Ruppert, S. (1996). *The politics of remedy: State legislative views on higher education.* Washington, D.C.: National Education Association.

U.S. Department of Education. National Center for Education Statistics (NCES). (1996). *Remedial education at higher education institutions in fall 1995.* NCES 97-584. Washington, D.C.: U.S. Government Printing Office.

Wallhaus, R. (1998). *Statewide K-16 systems: Helping underprepared students succeed in postsecondary education programs.* Denver, CO: State Higher Education Executive Officers.

Weissman, J., Bulakowski, C., & Jumisco, M. (1997, Winter). Using research to evaluate developmental education programs and policies. In J. Ignash (Ed.), *New Directions for Community Colleges, No. 100* (pp. 73–80). San Francisco: Jossey-Bass.

# Accounting for Student Success: An Empirical Analysis of the Origins and Spread of State Student Unit-record Systems

JAMES C. HEARN

*University of Georgia*

MICHAEL K. MCLENDON

*Vanderbilt University*

CHRISTINE G. MOKHER

*CNA*

**Abstract**   This event history analysis explores factors driving the emergence over recent decades of comprehensive state-level student unit-record [SUR] systems, a potentially powerful tool for increasing student success. Findings suggest that the adoption of these systems is rooted in demand and ideological factors. Larger states, states with high proportions of students of traditional college-going age, and states subject to federal civil-rights monitoring, were more likely to adopt SUR systems, suggesting influences of demands posed by size and legal constraints. In addition, states with more liberal citizen ideology were more likely to adopt the systems. Interestingly, the strength of private colleges and universities in a state worked against the adoption of SUR systems, suggesting that privacy and autonomy concerns were important deterrents to adoption. The results of this analysis illuminate the factors that inhibit and enhance SUR systems' organizational and philosophical acceptance, and thus ideally can contribute to future policymaking in this arena.

**Keywords** State policy • Database systems • Student success • Accountability • Policy adoption

## Introduction

Integrated, inclusive, longitudinal student-level data systems have long been a virtual holy grail for many educators and policymakers seeking to improve postsecondary students' chances for educational success. Large numbers of students disappear from institutional rolls from year to year (Adelman et al. 2003; Ewell et al. 2003; Goldrick-Rab 2006), for destinations usually unknown to those institutions and policymakers. When only institution-level data are available, it is impossible to know which of a school's departed students have dropped out of higher education altogether, and which have simply gone on to complete their educations elsewhere. For this reason, it is hard for institutions and policymakers at the state and federal levels to ascertain students' rationales and destinations, and thus determine whether existing policies should be reformed. Programmatic databases, such as those compiled for a state merit-aid program, cannot redress the problem, because they tend to be specialized, limited to program participants, and unconnected to many aspects of student careers. Periodic national surveys tend to be insufficiently timely and inclusive to address many student-success issues.[1] Clearly, educational leaders, policymakers, and analysts can benefit from a capacity to comprehensively track large numbers of students as they move from enrollment in one institution to enrollment elsewhere, full-time employment, or other activities.

Accordingly, many policymakers and postsecondary leaders have urged the development of student unit-record [SUR] systems. Employing a *consumerist* rationale, US Secretary of Education Margaret Spellings (2006) has focused on the marketplace benefits of SUR databases, stating that her agency would work to build a database "capable of addressing concerns such as: How much is this school really going to cost me? How long will it take to get my degree?" SUR systems can also aid policymakers' efforts to promote access, choice, and persistence for all students. Employing this *equity* rationale, a recent annual report of the State Higher Education Executive Officers (SHEEO 2006) stated that "Many of the questions about student progress and success can only be addressed with unit record data that report on students' activity regardless of where and when they attend college." Finally, there is a *managerial* rationale: student unit-record data can efficiently integrate information systems for philosophically related but operationally distinct programs, can reduce data duplication, and can limit fraud and abuse in student-aid systems.

Why, then, are SUR data not already available to all key stakeholders in higher education? For one thing, these systems raise technical and cost concerns, especially in the developmental stage but also in the ongoing maintenance of a database necessary to adequately capture the postsecondary careers of students (Ewell et al. 2003; NCES 2005).[2]

The most prominent resistance to SUR systems, however, has arisen out of anxieties about whether government should have access to these kinds of data and about how such data might be used. These concerns stem not only from philosophical and political objections to "Big Brother" data accumulation but also from worries over the dangers of potentially breached personal data systems. The stance of the National Association of Independent Colleges and Universities [NAICU] (2007a) regarding a national student-record database is illustrative:

> The most significant concern is its threat to student privacy. We do not believe that simply enrolling in college should trigger permanent entry into a federal registry, and we fear that the existence of such a massive registry will prove irresistible to future demands for access to the data for non-educational purposes.

In support of this stance, NAICU cites results from a commissioned national poll, conducted in June 2006 by Ipsos Public Affairs. The poll found that "By a factor of more than two to one (68–27%), Americans think that enough information is already collected at the college and university level. They believe that dredging for more data would be a breach of students' privacy that could result in the misuse of their personal information" (NAICU 2007b). In addition, the poll respondents expressed worries over the ultimate returns to such data aggregation: "Sixty percent of Americans believe that collecting individual student data is costly, intrusive, and does not address a pressing public policy issue" (ibid.). NAICU argues that these sentiments "have been echoed in editorials and student newspapers throughout the country and are reflected as well by the prohibition against the implementation of a student unit record data system in higher-education legislation approved by the House of Representatives in March 2006" (NAICU 2007a).

Partly in response to such concerns at the national level, some analysts have urged consideration of a bottom-up rather than top-down approach to the problem (Bailey 2006). That is, a more feasible goal might be working toward construction of a national database through the progressive integration of SUR databases from the fifty states. It is those state databases that are the focus of the present analysis.

## Study Purpose and Conceptualization

The number of SUR databases has grown notably since the first systematic national survey of state systems (Russell 1999). Now, at least 40 states have SUR systems in place, giving them some capacity to track students moving from one institution to another within state boundaries (Ewell and Boeke 2007). All of these databases contain, at minimum, basic information on enrollment, major, degrees granted, race/ethnicity, and gender (i.e., the core data elements sought annually in the federal IPEDS data collection) for all students enrolled in public institutions. Some states adopted some form of a SUR system over three decades ago, while others did so only in recent years, and some continue to resist altogether. Yet, virtually nothing systematic is known about the origins and the spread of these programs across the states. In the current climate, with arguments for improved understanding of student success often centering on improving databases (e.g., see Bailey 2006; Spellings 2006), it is important to build empirical knowledgability of the forces driving governments toward or away from student unit-record data. This is so for several reasons.

First, understanding the conditions associated with state adoption of SURs may better equip institutional leaders to anticipate potential policy change in their own states. Although leaders and institutions may be unable to directly influence most of the factors within their states that spur the creation of new governmental policies for higher education, appreciating the conditions under which such change is most likely to occur may permit them to more effectively influence the substance and the timing of debates surrounding adoption of those policies. From a more conceptual perspective, analyzing the factors associated with the spread of SUR databases affords researchers an exceptional opportunity to test how well theories of governmental behavior "travel" in the domain of higher education, where until very recently such theorizing had largely been overlooked. Because not all states have adopted SURs, inevitably questions arise as to which factors drove certain states to adopt these policies at the times at which they did. The determinants of state policy for higher education have begun attracting substantial, new scholarly attention (e.g., Doyle 2006; Lowry 2007; McLendon and Hearn 2007; McLendon et al. 2006; Weinstein and Krause 2006). To what extent does the growth of SURs align with what the field is learning about the factors driving other state postsecondary policies? To what extent do SURs stand as an anomalous case of policy adoption? Our work adds to emerging research in this vein by focusing on state adoption of policies holding important implications for students, institutions, and states.

Our study hypotheses were directed toward understanding the dynamics of whether and when individual states would adopt SUR systems. Our conceptualizing draws on three closely related but distinct bodies of research literature: the comparative-state politics literature (e.g., Barrilleaux et al. 2002; Soss et al. 2001), the literature on state policy innovation and diffusion (Berry and Berry 1990, 1992, 2007), and the growing body of related empirical work on factors associated with adoption by state governments of various *postsecondary* policies (e.g., Doyle 2006; Hearn and Griswold 1994; McLendon et al. 2006; McLendon et al. 2005; Zumeta 1996).

Based on this literature, we propose an explanatory model with four components, reflecting four sources of potential influence on SUR adoption. Hypotheses 1–3 focus on *socioeconomic* factors influencing SUR initiation: to what extent do the state's size, population distribution, and economic conditions drive this innovation? Hypotheses 4–6 focus on *structural and legal* factors: to what extent is SUR adoption influenced by the strength of the state's private higher-education sector, the nature of the state's postsecondary governing arrangements, and federal legal pressures concerning segregation in colleges and universities? Hypotheses 7–9 focus on influences stemming from state *political* systems: how does SUR adoption relate to citizens' governmental ideologies, citizens' partisan voting patterns, and the party composition of state government? Finally, hypothesis 10 focuses on the potential *diffusion context* surrounding state decision making on SUR systems: how might a state's regional neighbors influence its adoption of this innovation? The research and professional literature suggests specific directions for each of these 10 hypothesized relationships.

*Hypothesis 1: States with large populations will be more likely to initiate SUR systems* Populous states may need SUR systems to deal with the complexities of greater enrollments and greater arrays of institutions. States with larger populations also tend to adopt policies and programs of greater technical sophistication (Berry and Berry 2007). SURs, with their heavy demands of information collection, may be viewed as one such kind of state policy.

*Hypothesis 2: States with high proportions of citizens aged 18–24 will be more likely to initiate SUR systems* States with younger populations may tend to invest more heavily in policies directed to ensuring those populations are well educated and employed. Because SUR systems may improve students' chances for postsecondary success and eventual occupational placement, they may attract greater support in such states.

*Hypothesis 3: States with weak economic climates will be more likely to initiate SUR systems* Economic conditions, as indicated by such factors as gross state product per capita, can shape state policy initiation (e.g., Berry and Berry 1990), and in higher education, economic disadvantages appear to be associated with some forms of policy experimentation (Mingle 1983; McLendon et al. 2006).

*Hypothesis 4: States with high proportions of students in private institutions will be less likely to initiate SUR systems* Among the more outspoken opponents of SUR systems are some leaders of private institutions, who express concerns over impending governmental threats to student privacy and institutional autonomy (e.g., see NAICU, 2007a,b). It follows that SUR establishment may be less likely in states with proportionately large independent-college sectors.

*Hypothesis 5: States that employ consolidated governing boards will be more likely to initiate SUR systems* Consolidated governing boards represent the most centralized form of higher-education governance, and often have greater staff and analytic resources than their counterparts in coordinating boards and state planning agencies (McGuinness 1997; McLendon 2003; Zumeta 1996). Perhaps as a consequence, centralized systems appear to generate more policy innovation (Doyle 2006; Hearn and Griswold 1994; McLendon et al. 2005). Thus, states with more centralized governance may be more likely to innovate in data integration in the pursuit of student success.

*Hypothesis 6: States that have been subject to federal litigation for maintaining segregated higher-education systems will be more likely to initiate SUR systems* States whose higher-education systems were judged segregated and unequal over the years since the 1950s faced greater challenges than others in documenting the success, or lack of it, of African-American and other students (Ewell et al. 2003). These states were required to submit periodic reports to the Office of Civil Rights on their progress toward integrating their public colleges and universities. Because SUR systems enhance states' capabilities to provide such documentation, those states may have been especially likely to adopt such systems.

*Hypothesis 7: States whose citizen ideology is more liberal will be more likely to initiate SUR database systems in higher education* Broadly speaking, political ideology may be understood as a coherent and consistent set of orientations or attitudes toward politics (Berry et al. 1998). States with more liberal citizenries—understood as the citizenry's mean position on a liberal-conservative continuum of the electorate in a state—historically have been prone to support more generously funded social services and bigger government (e.g., Barrilleaux et al. 2002; Berry et al. 1998). These states also tend to engage in more policy innovation (Berry and Berry 2007). Extending this logic, we believe that more ideologically liberal states also may be more likely to support the building of an encompassing database to track student progress.

*Hypothesis 8: States in which popular support for Libertarian presidential candidates is greater will be less likely to initiate SUR systems* The most persistent objection to SUR systems has come from those worried over threats to individual privacy. No political party is more attentive to privacy issues than the Libertarian party, so states with greater affinity for the party may be especially resistant to the privacy threats inherent in SUR systems.

*Hypothesis 9: States with Republican control of legislatures and the governorship will be more likely to initiate SUR systems* Partisan strength can influence state policy outcomes (Alt and Lowry 2000; Berry and Berry 1990; Squire and Hamm 2005; Wong and Langevin 2006). Republicans may be not only more suspicious of public bureaucracy but also more oriented to efficiency and accountability in government programs (McLendon et al. 2006). Thus, states with Republican-controlled legislatures and governorships may be more likely to adopt SUR systems.

*Hypothesis 10: States whose regional neighbors have already adopted a SUR system will themselves be more likely to adopt one* Presumably propelled by regional associations and other formal and informal informational and peer contacts, state-to-state diffusion effects have been shown to occur in higher education (Doyle 2006; Doyle et al. 2005; McLendon et al. 2005). Data-system innovations might also diffuse along regional lines. That is, states whose regional neighbors have already enacted a SUR system may be more likely to do the same.

## Research Design

Event history analysis [EHA] was used to examine the factors that influence the timing of a state's adoption of a SUR system. Although this analytic technique originated in the biomedical sciences, social scientists in fields such as political science increasingly have utilized event history models to understand the occurrence of dynamic social phenomena (e.g. Berry and Berry 1990; Mooney and Lee 1995). Event history analysis has also been incorporated into the study of state adoption of certain education policies, including performance-accountability initiatives in higher education (McLendon et al. 2006), merit-based student grant programs (Doyle 2006), prepaid tuition and college savings plans (Doyle et al. 2005), charter school legislation (Renzulli and Roscigno 2005; Wong and Langevin 2005; Wong and Shen 2002), and school choice measures (Mintrom 2000). Event history analysis provides several advantages over traditional logistic regression models by allowing for the analysis of time-dependent variables, taking explicitly into account the length of time until the event occurs, and providing an estimate of the risk of an event occurring at any given time period (DesJardins 2003; Bennett 1999; Box-Steffensmeier and Jones 2004; Box-Steffensmeier and Bradford 2004).

The sample for the analysis includes a total of 42 states. Alaska and Hawaii were omitted due to their geographic isolation, which precludes the analysis of the effects of regional diffusion. Nebraska was omitted since the effects of partisan control of the government could not be tested due to the state's unicameral legislative system. California was excluded from the analysis because it adopted a SUR in 1970, and longitudinal data for the values of many of the independent variables were not available for the year of adoption. Lastly, Maine, North Dakota, West Virginia, and Wyoming could not be included in the analysis because accurate information was not available regarding the exact year of SUR adoption.

The data for the dependent variable, the year in which each state first adopted a SUR system, were collected from a student unit-record survey conducted by Peter Ewell and his colleagues at NCHEMS (Ewell and Boeke 2007). These databases all share at least three common characteristics: (1) they contain electronic records for every student in at least one sector of public institutions in the state, (2) they represent "snapshots" at specific periods of time, typically a semester or quarter of the academic year, and (3) they are centrally maintained by the state or each institution submits its own records to one electronic system. Although the type of information in each database may differ slightly, at a minimum all "databases can consistently track students on the basis of seven core pieces of information: enrollment (at a given institution), degree awarded, program/major, sex, race/ethnicity and date of birth" (Ewell et al. 2003, p. 3). In the event that the exact year of policy adoption was unclear, state and system officials were contacted to verify the information.

The independent variables used in this analysis reflect the 10 hypotheses presented earlier in the paper: total population (logged), percentage of the population aged 18–24, GSP per capita (logged), percentage of higher-education enrollments in private institutions, a dichotomous variable for whether the state had a consolidated governing board, a dichotomous variable for whether the state was under federal litigation for segregated higher-education systems,[3] citizen ideology (Berry et al. 2004), percentage of votes for a Libertarian presidential candidate in the most recent national election, unified Republican control of the government, and the number of neighboring states with a SUR system.

The data for these variables were collected from a variety of reliable secondary data sources, such as the Bureau of Economic Analysis and the Inter-University Consortium for Political and Social Science Research (ICPSR). Table 1 provides a description of each of these variables with the source of the data.

## Table 1. Variable descriptions and sources

| Variable | Description | Source |
|---|---|---|
| State adoption of a student unit-record [SUR] system | Dummy variable (yes = 1; no = 0) indicating whether a state adopts a student unit record [SUR] system in this year. These systems all: (1) contain electronic records for every student in at least one sector of public institutions in the state, (2) represent "snapshots" at specific periods of time, and (3) are centrally maintained by the state or each institution submits its own records to one electronic system. At a minimum all databases can consistently track students on the basis of seven core pieces of information: enrollment (at a given institution), degree awarded, program/major, sex, race/ethnicity and date of birth | Ewell and Boeke (2007); Personal communication with state and system officials |
| Total population (logged) | Annual measure of total population (logged) | Census/Southern Regional Education Board [SREB], yearly totals and decennial census |
| % Population aged 18–24 | Annual measure of the percentage of the total population between the ages of 18 and 24 | Census/SREB |
| GSP per capita (logged) | Annual measure of the gross state product per capita (logged) | Bureau of Economic Analysis |
| % Higher education enrollments in private institutions | Annual measure of the percentage of higher education enrollments in private institutions | National Center for Education Statistics/SREB |
| Consolidated governing board | Dummy variable (yes = 1; no = 0) indicating whether the state has a consolidated governing board | McGuiness' *State Structures Handbook* and Education Commission of the States [ECS] |
| States under federal litigation for segregated higher-education systems | Dummy variable (yes = 1; no = 0) indicating whether the state was subject to federal litigation for maintaining segregated higher-education systems | Southern Educational Foundation (1995, 1998) |
| Citizen ideology | Index of citizen ideology; continuous variable with higher values indicating higher levels of liberalism | Berry et al. (2004) data from the Inter-University Consortium for Political and Social Research (ICPSR) |
| % Libertarian vote | Four-year measure of the percentage of votes for a Libertarian candidate in the last presidential election | Leip's *Atlas of US Presidential Elections*, at http://uselectionatlas.org/RESULTS/index.html |
| Unified republican control of government | Dummy variable (yes = 1; no = 0) indicating whether the republican party controlled both chambers of the legislature and the governorship in the state | Klarner data at *State Politics & Policy Quarterly* [SPPQ] data archive, Book of the States, Council of State Governments |
| Diffusion of SUR system | Number of neighboring states with a SUR system | Authors' calculations using data from the dependent variable and maps |

For our event of interest, we accepted the minimal SUR definition employed by Ewell and Boeke (2007) in their comprehensive survey: an integrated data system containing core IPEDS student data at the individual level and giving a state the capability to track students across at least the public institutions in the state. Time is measured discretely as the year in which a state first adopted a SUR system. Our data set begins in 1973, when Texas and Wisconsin first adopted a SUR system, and continues until a total of 33 states had adopted systems in 2005. States that had not yet adopted a SUR system by the end of the observation period are right censored observations. Event history analysis uses information about both censored and non-censored cases to predict the risk of event occurrence at a point in time.

The dependent variable expresses the duration of time in years ($t$) until a state ($i$) adopts a SUR system. First, we calculated the survival function, representing the probability that a unit will "survive" (or fail to experience the event) longer than time $t$ (Box-Steffensmeier and Jones 2004; Box-Steffensmeier and Bradford 2004; DesJardins 2003; Singer and Willett 2003). Next, we calculated the hazard function, our primary dependent variable of interest. The hazard function represents the instantaneous rate of change in the probability of experiencing an event at time $t$, conditional upon "survival" up to the specified period of time. For our analysis, the hazard function indicates the probability that a state without a SUR system would adopt one in a particular year, given its values of the independent variables that influence change.

Because the probability that a state adopts a SUR system may change over time as these policies become more popular, the risk of experiencing the event must be allowed to vary in different time periods. In order to account for these changes over time, we used a specific type of event history model known as the Cox proportional hazards model. The Cox model focuses on the relationship between the outcome and the covariates of theoretical interest, without the need for specifying the functional form of the duration dependence (Box-Steffensmeier and Jones 2004). For each year of the analysis, any state that has not yet adopted a SUR system is included in the "risk set" of observations that are eligible to have an event at that point in time. Information about the order of the events is used to estimate the conditional probability that a state will adopt a SUR system for each time period, given the number of states at risk and the values of those states on important covariates. Maximum partial likelihood estimation is used to calculate the parameter estimates using information about these ordered failure times to predict the likelihood of observing the data that we have in fact observed. These estimates characterize how the hazard distribution changes as a function of the covariates, without making any assumptions about the underlying nature or shape of the baseline hazard rate.

"Tied" events occur when multiple states adopt a SUR in the same year. Since maximum partial likelihood estimation uses information about the rank ordering of failure times, tied events make it difficult to determine which states should be included in the risk set because the exact order in which the events occurred is undetermined. In this analysis, the exact discrete method was used to construct the partial likelihood estimates when tied events occurred. This method assumes true discrete time by calculating all of the possible risk sets at each tied failure time. Although this technique is still an approximation of the actual order in which the events occurred, it provides an accurate estimate as long as a large number of ties do not occur in a single time period (Box-Steffensmeier and Jones 2004). In our sample, less than 10% of states adopted a SUR in any 1 year.

The final model for the adoption of a SUR system can be expressed as:

$$h_i(t) = h_0(\text{t}) \exp(\beta'x),$$

where $h_i(t)$ is the proportional hazard of adopting a SUR system for state $i$ in year $t$, and $\beta'x$ is the matrix of regression parameters and covariates (Box-Steffensmeier and Jones 2004; Hosmer and Lemeshow 1999). The coefficients are exponentiated to make it easier to interpret them substantively in the form of hazard ratios. A hazard ratio greater than one indicates that the risk of adopting a SUR increases as the values of the covariate increase, indicating that the state is more likely to adopt a SUR. Conversely, a hazard ratio of less than one indicates that the risk of adopting a SUR decreases as the values of the covariate increase, indicating a longer time to event.

The Cox model is a "proportional hazards" model, which means there is an assumption that the ratio of the hazard rates between any two observations or groups is constant over time. In order to test this assumption, Schoenfeld residuals were calculated to determine whether the effect of any of the covariates changed disproportionately over time (Grambsch and Therneau 1994). The results indicated that there is no evidence that any of the variables in our final model violated the proportional hazards assumptions. Additional diagnostic methods were conducted including an assessment of the overall model fit using Cox-Snell residuals and an examination of the deviance residuals to identify any outlier values.

## Findings

Table 2 presents descriptive data for the independent and dependent variables in the analysis during 1973 and 2005 for the 42 states in our sample. Citizen ideology remained relatively stable with a value just below the middle of the conservative-liberal continuum in both years, and the average percentage of votes for a Libertarian presidential remained less than 1%. The variable that indicated the greatest change during this time period was unified Republican control of the government. Republicans had control of both chambers of the legislature and the governorship in 17% of states in 1973 and 63% of states in 2005. The percentage of higher-education enrollments in private institutions increased slightly from 22.0% to 24.2% during this time. In both years, approximately one-third of states had a consolidated governing board and one-third of states had been subject to federal litigation for maintaining segregated higher-education systems. In terms of demographic characteristics, the average total state population increased slightly over time, while the percentage of the population aged 18–24 declined from 12.6% to 9.9%. Economically, state wealth increased slightly over time as indicted by the rise in the GSP per capita. The descriptive statistics also indicate that by 2005, states had an average of approximately 3 neighboring states that had adopted a SUR system.

Table 3 lists the states that adopted a SUR system during each year of the analysis, the number of states in the risk set at each time period, the survivor function, and the hazard rate. Over time, the survivor function declines at a fairly steady rate with no more than four states adopting a SUR in a single year. The final survivor function of 0.214 indicates that only 21% of the states in the sample had not adopted a SUR system by the end of 2005. The hazard rate provides an estimate of the likelihood that a state without a SUR would adopt one in a particular year. In all years the hazard rate is less than 6%, indicating that there was no sudden time period in which there was a rapid change in the likelihood of adopting a SUR. As illustrated in Fig. 1, the hazard rate peaks around the mid-1990s, and then begins to decline slightly. This decline results from the process of censoring, rather than the event process itself. Over time as more states adopt SUR systems, the number of states remaining to adopt SURs declines, so the likelihood of adopting a SUR system in a given year also declines.

**Table 2. Descriptive statistics for the sample (N = 42 states)**

| Variable | 1973 | | 2005 | |
|---|---|---|---|---|
| | Mean | Standard deviation | Mean | Standard deviation |
| State adoption of a student unit-record [SUR] system | 0.05 | 0.22 | 0.00 | 0.00 |
| Total population (logged) | 14.91 | 0.94 | 15.27 | 0.88 |
| % Population aged 18–24 | 12.61 | 0.84 | 9.85 | 0.64 |
| GSP per capita (logged) | 10.15 | 0.12 | 10.58 | 0.16 |
| % Higher-education enrollments in private institutions | 21.98 | 12.50 | 24.17 | 12.20 |
| Consolidated governing board | 0.33 | 0.48 | 0.33 | 0.48 |
| States under federal litigation for segregated higher-education systems | 0.33 | 0.48 | 0.33 | 0.48 |
| Citizen ideology | 46.42 | 16.64 | 48.96 | 12.71 |
| % Libertarian vote | 0.01 | 0.02 | 0.29 | 0.19 |
| Unified republican control of government | 0.17 | 0.38 | 0.63 | 0.50 |
| Number of neighboring states with a SUR system | 0.14 | 0.35 | 3.05 | 1.53 |

**Table 3. States adopting a student unit record [SUR] system with Kalpan–Meier survivor function and hazard rate**

| Year | States adopting SUR systems | Number of adoptions | Cumulative adoptions | Risk set | Survivor function | Hazard rate |
|------|------|------|------|------|------|------|
| 1973 | TX, WI | 2 | 2 | 42 | 0.952 | 0.003 |
| 1974 | | 0 | 2 | 40 | 0.952 | 0.000 |
| 1975 | | 0 | 2 | 40 | 0.952 | 0.000 |
| 1976 | | 0 | 2 | 40 | 0.952 | 0.000 |
| 1977 | MD, OK | 2 | 4 | 40 | 0.905 | 0.003 |
| 1978 | NC | 1 | 5 | 38 | 0.881 | 0.002 |
| 1979 | IN | 1 | 6 | 37 | 0.857 | 0.002 |
| 1980 | KY | 1 | 7 | 36 | 0.833 | 0.002 |
| 1981 | | 0 | 7 | 35 | 0.833 | 0.000 |
| 1982 | | 0 | 7 | 35 | 0.833 | 0.000 |
| 1983 | GA, IL, MN | 3 | 10 | 35 | 0.762 | 0.007 |
| 1984 | MS | 1 | 11 | 32 | 0.738 | 0.003 |
| 1985 | FL, MA, NJ | 3 | 14 | 31 | 0.667 | 0.008 |
| 1986 | | 0 | 14 | 28 | 0.667 | 0.000 |
| 1987 | CO | 1 | 15 | 28 | 0.643 | 0.003 |
| 1988 | CT, LA, MO, NY | 4 | 19 | 27 | 0.548 | 0.015 |
| 1989 | | 0 | 19 | 23 | 0.548 | 0.000 |
| 1990 | OR | 1 | 20 | 23 | 0.524 | 0.004 |
| 1991 | TN | 1 | 21 | 22 | 0.500 | 0.005 |
| 1992 | VA | 1 | 22 | 21 | 0.476 | 0.006 |
| 1993 | AR, SC | 2 | 24 | 20 | 0.429 | 0.012 |
| 1994 | NM, WA | 2 | 26 | 18 | 0.381 | 0.014 |
| 1995 | | 0 | 26 | 16 | 0.381 | 0.000 |
| 1996 | | 0 | 26 | 16 | 0.381 | 0.000 |
| 1997 | | 0 | 26 | 16 | 0.381 | 0.000 |
| 1998 | AL, AZ, OH, SD | 4 | 30 | 16 | 0.286 | 0.051 |
| 1999 | UT | 1 | 31 | 12 | 0.262 | 0.016 |
| 2000 | NV | 1 | 32 | 11 | 0.238 | 0.019 |
| 2001 | | 0 | 32 | 10 | 0.238 | 0.000 |
| 2002 | KS | 1 | 33 | 10 | 0.214 | 0.031 |
| 2003 | | 0 | 33 | 9 | 0.214 | 0.000 |
| 2004 | | 0 | 33 | 9 | 0.214 | 0.000 |
| 2005 | | 0 | 33 | 9 | 0.214 | 0.000 |

Table 4 presents the results of event history analysis using the broadest definition of SUR system, as defined in the previous section. While political party strength, governance arrangements, economic conditions, and actions in neighboring states seem irrelevant to the adoption of these systems,[4] contrary to our initial expectations, a number of our hypotheses were upheld.

Viewing the results as a whole, we infer two major themes in the effects: "demand" influences and "ideological" influences. The significant "demand" influences uncovered suggest that the adoption of SUR systems may be driven by states' needs for more data on their postsecondary education systems. First, controlling for other factors, states with larger overall populations have been more likely to adopt SUR systems. Larger states may face additional complexities as they attempt to track and serve great numbers of students across multiple institutions and systems, and may be particularly likely to benefit from integrated databases. Next, the percentage of the population aged 18–24 is positively associated with the adoption of an SUR system. Since states may need to allocate a greater proportion of their resources to higher education if there is a relatively large college-age population, they may be especially concerned about monitoring student careers and outcomes.

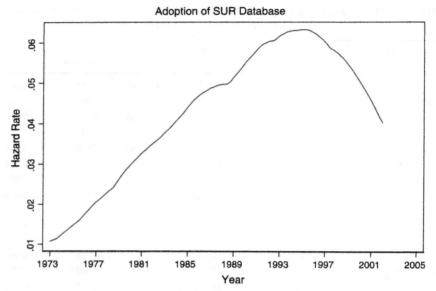

Figure 1. Smoothed Hazard Rate

**Table 4. Results from Cox proportional hazard model for state adoption of a SUR system (standard errors in parentheses)**

|  | Coefficient | Exp (Coefficient) |
|---|---|---|
| Total population (logged) | 0.96** (0.30) | 2.62** |
| % Population aged 18–24 | 0.77** (0.25) | 2.16** |
| GSP per capita (logged) | 1.59 (1.66) | 4.89 |
| % Higher education enrollments in private institutions | −0.07** (0.02) | 0.93** |
| Consolidated governing board | 0.74 (0.59) | 2.09 |
| States under fed. litigation for segregated higher-education systems | 1.66** (0.63) | 5.27** |
| Citizen ideology | 0.05* (0.02) | 1.05* |
| % Libertarian vote | −0.85 (0.76) | 0.43 |
| Unified republican control of government | −0.02 (0.77) | 0.98 |
| Number of neighboring states with a SUR system | −0.41 (0.24) | 0.67 |
| Log likelihood | −74.92 |  |
| Likelihood ratio | 34.68 |  |
| Degrees of freedom | 10 |  |
| Sample size | 42 |  |

\* $p \leq 0.01$, \*\* $p \leq 0.01$

Third, states facing desegregation litigation have been especially likely to establish SUR systems. These states faced strict monitoring from the Office of Civil Rights and may have needed better mechanisms for tracking enrollment and retention rates for students of color in order to meet legal requirements.

The graph of the smoothed hazard function in Fig. 2 illustrates the relative magnitude of the effect of each of these "demand" influences. The solid line indicates changes over time in the hazard function of an "average" state, representing an observation with average values for all of the independent variables in the analysis. The various dotted lines indicate how the estimated hazard rate changes, given hypothetical values of each of the demand characteristics. The demand characteristic with the greatest effect on the hazard of adopting a SUR is the dichotomous variable indicating whether the state was subject to federal litigation for maintaining a segregated higher-education system. On average, the hazard of adopting a SUR system is 5.3 times greater for states

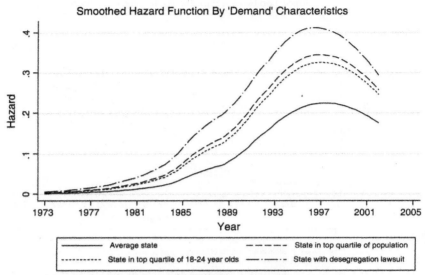

Figure 2.  State Adoption of a SUR System

with a desegregation lawsuit compared to states without a lawsuit. In addition, states in the top quartile of total population and states in the top quartile of the percentage of the population aged 18–24 both have a similar effect in magnitude on increasing the likelihood that a state will adopt a SUR system in a given year. The graph also illustrates that the difference in the hazard rate appears to be proportional between groups with these different demand characteristics over time, as assumed in the Cox proportional hazards model.

The significant "ideological" influences uncovered suggest that, to the extent ideology is involved in decisions regarding SUR systems, it appears to be reflected in how states resolve the tension between their citizenry's underlying public-policy values and the interests of private higher education in preserving institutional autonomy. Our findings indicate that states whose underlying citizen ideology is more liberal have been more likely to establish a SUR system than more conservative states. Yet interestingly, the expressed partisan political preferences of the population did not appear to influence decision-making regarding SUR systems: neither unified Republican control of government nor popular support for Libertarian presidential candidates affected SUR system adoption.

While underlying liberal values were positively associated with initiating SUR systems, the strength of private colleges and universities in a state worked in opposition to such systems. As hypothesized, states with greater proportions of students enrolled in private institutions have been less likely to initiate a SUR system. This finding may signal either ideological or demand-based sentiment. Perhaps ideologically based interest-group opposition from private institutions to SUR systems may have been successful in thwarting their initiation. Alternatively, because the benefits of SUR systems shrink to the extent that large numbers of students remain absent in the database, and because only a handful of states thus far have been able to incorporate significant data for students in private institutions into their SUR systems (Ewell and Boeke 2007), it may be that policy leaders perceive the returns to investing in start-up, public-institutions only, SUR systems insufficient in states with small public-institution enrollments.

Figure 3 illustrates the relative magnitude of the effect of each of these "ideological" influences by comparing the hazard rate for an "average state" to states with hypothetical values for each of the ideological characteristics. As indicated in the graph, the likelihood of adopting a SUR system in any given year is smaller for states in the top quartile of enrollments in private higher education relative to the "average" state. A one percent increase in higher-education enrollment in private institutions leads to an estimated 6.6% decrease in the hazard of adopting an SUR, holding other factors constant. In addition, states in the top quartile of values for liberal ideology have a relatively greater risk of adopting a SUR compared to an "average state." The graph also indicates

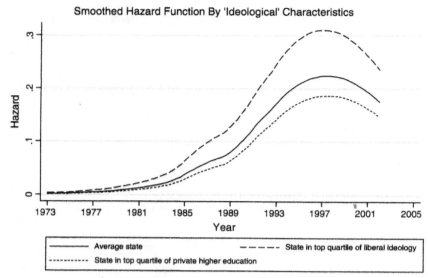

**Figure 3.  State Adoption of a SUR System**

that the ratio of the hazard rates between states with these different ideological characteristics is constant over time, which is consistent with the proportional hazards assumption.

Beyond the adoption of *any* SUR system lies the question of the particular kind of SUR system adopted. As noted earlier, the analysis presented in Table 3 adopted the broadest operationalization of a SUR presented in the work of Ewell and Boeke (2007). What might be the implications for our analysis, however, of *alternative* definitions of SUR systems, moving beyond the minimal criteria?

Two elaborations of SUR datasets merit empirical attention in future studies on this topic. First, 14 of the 40 states with SUR systems incorporate what Ewell and Boeke (2007) suggest is a full range of information, encompassing sex, race/ethnicity, date of birth, geographic origin, high school attended, high school graduation date, program/major, financial aid, full-time/part-time status, credits attempted, credits earned, cumulative GPA, and degree awarded. What factors might drive a state to invest in building such a comprehensive system?[5]

Second, the most ambitious and potentially most useful SUR systems incorporate data for students in *both* public and private institutions. This scope provides state policymakers a far more complete picture of student pathways and success (Hearn and Anderson 1989, 1995). At the same time, it is potentially the most difficult to achieve, given private-college leaders' resistance to these systems (noted earlier, and empirically supported in our results). Which states then, have achieved some measure of integration across the public and private institutions in their states? As of Ewell and Boeke's survey (2007), 17 states incorporated at least some data from independent institutions into their SUR systems, a gain of five states since 2002. Of those 17 systems, only seven incorporate data from all independent colleges and universities in their states. What factors might drive a state to commit to efforts to secure private institution participation in SUR database development?

## Implications

For SUR advocates, the movement toward building integrated unit-record databases promises significant breakthroughs supporting some longstanding goals of researchers, leaders, and policymakers. Bailey (2006, p. 10), for example, has stated that,

> These data sets offer consistent unit record longitudinal data across public institutions and, in some cases, private institutions, within states. Sample sizes are also large enough to allow analyses of individual institutions, and in large states there are enough colleges to provide significant variation in college policies and practices. Moreover, it is also possible to collect data on college practices to supplement the more superficial measures found in IPEDS. Linking these data to the cross-sectional surveys such as NSSE [the National Survey of Student Engagement] and CCSSE [the Community College Survey of Student Engagement] could offer important new insights.

Bailey focuses mainly on the need to integrate various data sources in the service of institutional policies affecting postsecondary student success. SUR advocates also note the benefits of three related forms of data integration. First, many states are moving toward building integrated unit-record data for P-12 education (Redden 2007). P-12 preparation is critical to postsecondary success, and these state efforts are focusing on such indicators as unique statewide student identifiers connecting student data across key databases across years; student-level enrollment, demographic and program participation information; the ability to match individual students' test records from year to year to measure academic growth; information on untested students and the reasons they were not tested; a teacher-identifier system with the ability to match teachers to students; student-level transcript information, including information on courses completed and grades earned; student-level college readiness test scores; student-level graduation and dropout data; a state data-audit system assessing data quality, validity and reliability; and, most importantly for the present analysis, building capabilities to match student records between the P-12 and higher-education systems (National Data Quality Campaign 2007). Achieving these goals at the P-12 level could arguably serve students both before and during their postsecondary years.

Second, students' chances for success may benefit from not only better integrated local data systems but also better coordination between individual states and federal data systems. As St. John et al. (2001), have argued, simultaneous and more comprehensive knowledgability about students' financing status in institutional, state, *and* federal systems can help direct student-aid awards more precisely toward serving student success. Notably, effective federal policymaking depends on knowledgability about students' status in state systems, and about the various policy linkages between federal and state policies of different kinds.

Finally, advocates argue that across-state data integration can have significant benefits: because single-state SUR systems cannot address the dynamics of student migration in and out of state (NCES 2005), they provide imperfect information on the factors shaping student attainments. Crossing the frontier to multi-state SUR systems will be a daunting challenge. Ewell and Boeke (2007) note that, as of their survey, only five states secured data from neighboring states to allow consideration of patterns of student mobility. Given the currently lagging support for a federal SUR system, integrating state systems at the regional or consortial level appears to be a more achievable goal.

What, in fact, are the prospects for building a national SUR database by accretion, that is, sector by sector and state by state? Inclusive longitudinal student data could potentially serve prominent quality and accountability agendas (Miller and Ewell 2005; National Commission on Accountability 2005), and calls for unit-record data are increasing, but resistance to such systems at the national level continues to be strong among privacy advocates and others.[6] In this context, support for state-level SURs appears to be the key to change, so it is important to understand the factors favoring the emergence of state SUR systems.

Toward that end, it is regrettable that currently available data do not allow the assignment of adoption dates to SUR systems of different extensiveness. Importantly, were data available on adoption dates for the extensive systems that incorporate and integrate data on a wide range of factors, including age, sex, and race/ethnicity enrollment histories, grades, credit accumulation, program/major, financial aid awards, and degree awards, it would be possible to more precisely discern key factors in the adoption of partial and extensive SUR systems. Because no adoption dates were available here for the various potential elements of SUR systems, the dependent variable for the analysis was necessarily operationalized in a more inclusive way.[7]

The analysis here nevertheless does provide intriguing results. The findings suggest that the emergence of state unit-record systems flows from a complex combination of demographic, structural, and ideological forces that lie, to some degree, beyond the capacity of policymakers to influence very directly. The factors that appear to have been shaping state policy trajectories appear to be deeply rooted in the organizational, societal, and cultural complexions of states. From a social-scientific standpoint, this is not necessarily a limitation: evidence on the social, political, and economic bases of an event is important in and of itself for building fundamental knowledge about the workings of central institutions in the society. Along these lines, event history analyses of the kind undertaken here have been contributing importantly to recent developments in the fields of political science and sociology (Berry and Berry 2007; Box-Steffensmeier and Bradford 2004; DesJardins 2003; McLendon et al. 2006; Singer and Willett 2003; Strang 1994).

But the present analysis was not aimed toward that level of contribution alone. While most of the influential factors uncovered in the present study indeed may lie largely beyond policymakers' immediate control, this research provides some new, across-state evidence hinting at how policymakers have framed SUR debates, and how they might frame future debates on these issues. While state and institutional leaders may be unable to change their citizenries' underlying ideological predispositions, for example, they may nonetheless be able to use those predispositions to shape policy discussions in ways that support desired policy ends. Thus, knowing that liberal ideology is associated with SUR adoption, institutional leaders may wish to argue for SURs in terms that help mobilize liberal leaders and citizens toward active support. SURs, in this framing, can be seen to represent valued government action in helping ensure social well-being, equity, and fair market competition.

It should be noted that some prospective policy developments are central to the future of SUR systems. Specifically, that future depends significantly on the resolution of some ambiguities across the states in the legal interpretation of the national Family Educational Rights and Privacy Act [FERPA]. The Act, passed in 1974, requires schools to obtain formal permission from the student or parent before releasing any student educational data. As Ewell et al. (2003) note, FERPA has been interpreted variously by states' attorneys general, sometimes allowing construction of SUR databases and sometimes restricting such efforts. Institutions and states violating FERPA provisions become vulnerable to the withholding of all federal funding (ibid.). Clearly, states and institutions will be reluctant to participate in the construction of SUR systems at the state, regional, and national levels if they perceive substantial financial or legal risks, so any policymaker efforts to lessen the ambiguities in this arena will enhance public debates concerning SUR database construction.

Resolving legal questions addresses only one of the questions surrounding adopting these policies, however. Ideally, the analysis presented here will provide a useful addition to knowledgability regarding the core influences shaping state SUR systems. These systems are increasingly being touted as foundational for emerging national efforts to improve student success, so it seems essential for advocates and opponents alike to understand better what factors inhibit and enhance their organizational and philosophical acceptance, as well as their ultimate utility.

**Acknowledgments** We are indebted to Peter Ewell and his colleagues at NCHEMS for sharing their student unit-record survey data and providing additional information and suggestions for our analysis. Several state and system officials were also helpful in answering questions about their state systems. Finally, we appreciate insightful suggestions and comments from Carol Frances and Scott Thomas.

## Notes

1. Importantly, sampling limitations limit the utility in this domain of the otherwise very valuable national longitudinal surveys of the National Center for Education Statistics, precluding studying state-level questions and questions relating to racial-ethnic and socioeconomic sub-populations.

2. Focusing on prospects for a national SUR database, Ewell et al. (2003), using work by Adelman (1999), estimate that 10 years of data would be necessary to encompass the educational careers of an adequate proportion of US students.

3. The variable for federal litigation is a time-invariant indicator because data for the exact year in which the desegregation lawsuit began and OCR monitoring ended were not readily available. Although it would have been preferable to have time-varying values for this variable, the indicator does provide valid information on the pressures faced by these states. States with strong indications that they were about to come under federal scrutiny and states just released from federal scrutiny are arguably just as sensitive as states under formal scrutiny, perhaps even more so, to the need for data gathering and dataset construction of this kind.

4. To explore the possibility that states may be responding to changing trends in these characteristics over time, we tried different specifications of several independent variables in our model. Since support for Libertarian candidates likely begins prior to an election, we substituted the percent Libertarian votes in the last presidential election with values from the 2 years leading up to and 2 years following each elec-

tion. Also, as the growth or decline of GSP per capita may affect a state's economy slowly over time, we tried using a 1-year lag and a 3-year moving average for this variable. In all models the results were essentially unchanged.

5. In the present study, this analysis was precluded because no available data identify the dates of modifications and expansions in state SUR systems.

6. See Hearn (2006) for a review of some of the issues on both sides of the student unit records debate.

7. According to Ewell and Boeke (2007), such "super" SUR systems may be found in at least one postsecondary system in 18 states, including California, Florida, Kansas, North Dakota, Ohio, and South Carolina. It is unclear, however, how much of the data collected in these current systems was also gathered when SURs were first initiated in these states.

# References

Adelman, C. (1999). *Answers in the tool box: Academic intensity, attendance patterns, and bachelor's degree attainment.* Washington, D.C.: US Department of Education.

Adelman, C., Daniel, B., Berkowitz, I., & Owings, J. (2003). *Postsecondary attainment, attendance, curriculum, and performance: Selected results from the NELS:88/2000 Postsecondary Education Transcript Study (PETS), 2000.* Washington, D.C.: National Center for Education Statistics.

Alt, J. E., & Lowry, R. C. (2000). A dynamic model of state budget outcomes under divided partisan government. *Journal of Politics, 62*(4), 1035–1069.

Bailey, T. R. (2006). *Research on institution-level practice for postsecondary student success.* Report prepared under contract for the National Symposium on Student Success, National Postsecondary Education Collaborative. Washington, D.C.: US Department of Education.

Barrilleaux, C., Holbrook, T., & Langer, L. (2002). Electoral competition, legislative balance, and state welfare policy. *American Journal of Political Science, 46*(2), 415–427.

Bennett, D. S. (1999). Parametric models, duration dependence, and time-varying data revisited. *American Journal of Political Science, 43,* 256–270.

Berry, F. S., & Berry, W. D. (1990). State lottery adoptions as policy innovations: An event history analysis. *American Political Science Review, 84*(2), 395–416.

Berry, F. S., & Berry, W. D. (1992). Tax innovation in the states: Capitalizing on political opportunity. *American Journal of Political Science, 36*(3), 715–742.

Berry, F. S., & Berry, W. D. (2007). Innovation and diffusion models in policy research. In P. Sabatier (Ed.), *Theories of the policy process* (2nd ed.). Boulder, CO: Westview Press.

Berry, W. D., Ringquist, E. J., Fording, R. C., & Hanson, R. L. (1998). Measuring citizen and government ideology in the American state, 1960–93. *American Journal of Political Science, 42*(1), 327–348.

Berry, W. D., Ringquist, E. J., Fording, R. C., & Hanson, R. L. (2004). *Measuring citizen and government ideology in the United States. ICPSR Study No.: 1208.* (Data file). Available from Inter-University Consortium for Political and Social Research Web site, http://webapp.icpsr.umich.edu/cocoon/ICPSR-PRA/01208.xml.

Box-Steffensmeier, J. M., & Bradford, S. J. (2004). *Timing and political change: Event history modeling in political science.* Ann Arbor: University of Michigan Press.

Box-Steffensmeier, J. M., & Jones, B. S. (2004). *Event history modeling: A guide for social scientists.* Cambridge, New York: Cambridge University Press.

DesJardins, S. L. (2003). Event history methods. In J. Smart (Ed.), *Higher education: Handbook of theory and research* (Vol. XVIII, pp. 421–472). London: Kluwer.

Doyle, W. R. (2006). Adoption of merit-based student grant programs: An event history analysis. *Educational Evaluation and Policy Analysis, 28*(3), 259–285.

Doyle, W. R., McLendon, M. K., & Hearn, J. C. (2005). *The adoption of prepaid tuition and savings plans in the American states: An event history analysis.* Paper presented at the Association for the Study of Higher Education (ASHE), Philadelphia, PA.

Ewell, P. T., & Bocke, M. (2007). *Critical connections: Linking states' unit record systems to track students' progress. New agenda series, Lumina foundation.* Indianapolis, IN: Lumina Foundation.

Ewell, P. T., Schild, P. R., & Paulson, K. (2003). *Following the mobile student: Can we develop the capacity for a comprehensive database to assess student progression?* Research Report, Lumina Foundation. Indianapolis, IN: Lumina Foundation.

Goldrick-Rab, S. (2006). Following their every move: An investigation of social-class differences in college pathways. *Sociology of Education, 79,* 61–79.

Grambsch, P. M., & Therneau, T. M. (1994). Proportional hazards tests and diagnostics based on weighted residuals. *Biometrika, 81*(3), 515–526.

Hearn, J. C. (2006). *Student success: What research suggests for policy and practice*. Report prepared under contract for the National Symposium on Student Success, National Postsecondary Education Collaborative, Washington, D.C.: US Department of Education.

Hearn, J. C., & Anderson, M. S. (1989). Integrating postsecondary education financing policies: The Minnesota model. In R. H. Fenske (Ed.), *New directions for institutional research: Studying the impact of student aid on institutions* (Vol. 62, pp. 55–73). San Francisco: Jossey-Bass.

Hearn, J. C., & Anderson, M. S. (1995). The Minnesota financing experiment. In E. St. John (Ed.), *New directions for higher education: Rethinking tuition and financial aid strategies* (Vol. 89, pp. 5–25). San Francisco: Jossey-Bass.

Hearn, J. C., & Griswold, C. P. (1994). State-level centralization and policy innovation in US postsecondary education. *Educational Evaluation and Policy Analysis, 16*(2), 161–190.

Hosmer, D. W., & Lemeshow, S. (1999). *Applied survival analysis: Regression modeling of time to event data*. New York: Wiley.

Lowry, R. C. (2007). The political economy of public universities in the United States. *State Politics and Policy Quarterly, 7*(3), 303–324.

McGuinness, A. C. (1997). *State postsecondary education structures handbook*. Denver, CO: Education Commission of the States.

McLendon, M. K. (2003). State governance reform of higher education: Patterns, trends, and theories of the public policy process. In J. Smart (Ed.), *Higher education: Handbook of theory and research* (Vol. XVIII, pp. 57–143). London: Kluwer.

McLendon, M. K., & Hearn, J. C. (2007). Incorporating political indicators into comparative-state research on postsecondary policy: Opportunities and limitations of space and time. In K. Shaw & D. E. Heller (Eds.), *The challenges of comparative state-level higher education policy research*. Sterling, VA: Stylus.

McLendon, M. K., Hearn, J. C., & Deaton, R. (2006). Called to account: Analyzing the origins and spread of state performance-accountability policies for higher education. *Educational Evaluation and Policy Analysis, 28*(1), 1–24.

McLendon, M. K., Heller, D. E., & Young, S. (2005). State postsecondary education policy innovation: Politics, competition, and the interstate migration of policy ideas. *The Journal of Higher Education, 76*(4), 363–400.

Miller, M. S., & Ewell, P. T. (2005). *Measuring up on college-level learning*. San Jose, CA: National Center for Public Policy in Higher Education.

Mingle, J. (Ed.). (1983). *Management flexibility and state regulation in higher education*. Atlanta: Southern Regional Education Board.

Mintrom, M. (2000). *Policy entrepreneurs and school choice*. Washington, D.C.: Georgetown University Press.

Mooney, C. Z., & Lee, M. H. (1995). Legislative morality in the American states: The case of pre-Roe abortion regulation reform. *American Journal of Political Science, 39*, 599–627.

National Association of Independent Colleges and Universities. (2007a). Re: Student unit record data. http://www.naicu.edu/HEA/UnitRecord.shtm. Downloaded 29 March 2007.

National Association of Independent Colleges and Universities. (2007b). American public gives low marks to proposed federal database on students. http://www.naicu.edu/news_room/id.249/news_detail.asp. Downloaded 20 July 2007.

National Center for Education Statistics. (2005). *Feasibility of a student unit record system within the Integrated Postsecondary Education Data System*. Report NCES 2005–160. Washington, D.C.: US Department of Education, Institute of Education Sciences.

National Commission on Accountability in Higher Education. (2005). *Accountability for better results: A national imperative for higher education*. Boulder, CO: State Higher Education Executive Officers (SHEEO).

National Data Quality Campaign, The. (2007). Data quality campaign—Just for the Kids/NCEA. Downloaded 20 July 2007 from http://www.dataqualitycampaign.org.

Redden, E. (2007). State leaders tackle unit records, remediation. Inside higher education, 12 July 2007. Downloaded 12 July 2007 from http://insidehighered.com/layout/set/print/new/2007/07/12/ecs.

Renzulli, L. A., & Roscigno, V. J. (2005). Charter school policy, implementation, and diffusion across the United States. *Sociology of Education, 78*(4), 344–265.

Russell, A. B. (1999). *The status of statewide student transition data systems: A survey of SHEEO agencies*. State Higher Education Executive Officers (SHEEO): Denver, CO.

Singer, J. D., & Willett, J. B. (2003). *Applied longitudinal data analysis: Modeling change and event occurrence*. Oxford: Oxford University Press.

Soss, J., Schram, S., Vartanian, T. P., & O'Brien, E. (2001). Setting the terms of relief: Explaining state policy choices in the devolution revolution. *American Journal of Political Science, 45*(2), 378–395.

Spellings, M. (2006). An action plan for higher education. Remarks delivered to the National Press Club, September 6. Washington, D.C. Downloaded 29 March 2007 from http://www.ed.gov/news/speeches/2006/09/09262006.html.

Squire, P., & Hamm, K. E. (2005). *101 chambers: Congress, state legislatures, and the future of legislative studies* (1st ed.). Columbus: Ohio State University Press.

St. John, E. P., Hu, S., & Weber, J. (2001). State policy and the affordability of public higher education: The influence of state grants on persistence in Indiana. *Research in Higher Education, 42*(4), 401–428.

Strang, D. (1994). Introduction to event history methods. In T. Janoski & A. Hicks' (Eds.), *The comparative political economy of the welfare state: New methodologies and approaches* (pp. 245–253). Cambridge University Press.

State Higher Education Executive Officers. (2006). *Annual report*. Boulder, CO: State Higher Education Executive Officers.

Weinstein, M. A., & Krause, G. A. (2006). *Institutional reputation and peer diffusion of administrative innovations: Evidence from technology transfer office adoptions by public research universities in the American states*. Paper presented at the Midwest Political Science Association annual meeting, Chicago, IL.

Wong, K. K., & Langevin, W. E. (2005). *The diffusion of governance reform in American public education: An event history analysis of state takeover and charter school laws*. Nashville, TN: National Center on School Choice.

Wong, K. K., & Langevin, W. (2006). Policy expansion of school choice in the American states. http://www.vanderbilt.edu/schoolchoice/publications.html. Downloaded 15 May 2007.

Wong, K. K., & Shen, F. X. (2002). Politics of state-led reform in education: Market competition and electoral dynamics. *Educational Policy, 16*(1), 161–192.

Zumeta, W. (1996). Meeting the demand for higher education without breaking the bank: A framework for the design of state higher education policies for an era of increasing demand. *Journal of Higher Education, 67*(4), 367–425.

# Because the Numbers Matter: Transforming Postsecondary Education Data on Student Race and Ethnicity to Meet the Challenges of a Changing Nation

KRISTEN A. RENN AND CHRISTINA J. LUNCEFORD

*In 1997, the Office of Management and Budget revised guidelines for treatment of racial and ethnic data, adding a requirement to allow respondents to indicate more than one race and mandating a change in all federal data collection and reporting by January 1, 2003. Nearly 2 years after the deadline for implementation, however, higher education institutions had not yet been required by the National Center for Education Statistics to make the change. This article discusses the policy context for collecting and reporting data on student race and ethnicity in higher education and challenges created by the addition of the multiple race option. This article describes the current status of postsecondary racial/ethnic data collection, predicts challenges in aggregating and bridging data, and makes recommendations for policy and practice.*

**Keywords:** *biracial; higher education; racial/ethnic data*

IN OCTOBER 1997, the United States Office of Management and Budget (OMB) issued revisions to its Directive 15, changing the federal racial identification process to expand the number of racial categories and to include the option for respondents to indicate more than one race (OMB, 1997). The 2000 census marked the first time in U.S. history that individuals had the option to self-identify in more than one of the five racial categories (American Indian or Alaska Native, Asian, Black or African American, Native Hawaiian or Other Pacific Islander, White) in addition to indicating Hispanic or Latino ethnicity.[1] Of all respondents, 2.4% indicated more than one racial category; although these respondents represent a small minority of the total population, it is important for higher education policy that 4.0% of those under age 18 and 7.7% of those under age 18 reporting Hispanic or Latino ethnicity indicated more than one category (U.S. Census Bureau, 2001). Analyzing 30 years of data from the Cooperative Institutional Research Program's (CIRP) annual freshmen

EDUCATIONAL POLICY, Vol. 18 No. 5, November 2004 752–783
DOI: 10.1177/0895904804269941

survey, Szelényi and Martínez (2004) found an increase in the number of bi- and multiracial students to 4.8% of respondents in 2000.[2] Without a change in data collection procedures, institutional record keeping based on the monoracial assumption that instructions to "check one box only" would accurately capture racial demographics would soon be confounded by individuals for whom the one-box option is inappropriate. In fact, OMB mandated an immediate change in federal data collection and the full implementation of the change in data reporting by January 2003.

On the surface, the inclusion of an option to indicate more than one racial category seems a minor change in data collection, to be accomplished with a word processor and new forms; beneath this simple change lays a political minefield from institutional to national levels. It involves the National Center for Education Statistics (NCES) and the Office of Civil Rights (OCR), state legislatures and higher education coordinating boards, institutional policy and legal compliance, and a societal trend away from self-reporting racial and ethnic categories. Anticipating the challenge of implementing the changes and the political consequences of such changes (e.g., implications for congressional redistricting, incomparability of data pre- and post-revisions, etc.), representatives from a number of federal agencies have been working to develop guidelines for collecting racial and ethnic data under the revised standards, to create "crosswalks" from old data to new, and to keep stakeholders informed of the changes. Representatives of postsecondary institutions and organizations have been involved in the process, and the stakes for this constituency are high.

In a culture of legal challenges to affirmative action, racial statistics matter more than ever. The implementation of revisions to OMB Directive 15 could have a significant effect not only on how data are collected but also on the numbers themselves. It is not clear that data collected before, during, and after the transition can be compared in any meaningful way, yet these data will become very important in assessing the effect of California's Proposition 209, the *Hopwood* decision in the fifth circuit, and the "One Florida" plan on enrollments and graduation rates of various racial and ethnic group members. In Adams-Fordice states, such as Oklahoma, that remain under court orders to comply with the Civil Rights Act of 1964 but receive less publicity than California, Texas, or Florida, the OMB's shift is considered premature (Stroup, 1998). Finally, there are questions about how the shift might run afoul of the Federal Educational Records Privacy Act (FERPA) in cases where individuals might be identified by a unique combination of race and ethnic categories. Clearly, there is more at stake than revising and reprinting institutional forms to meet the new federal standards. Issues of how data collection will be transformed intersect with what the new data will say about the status of racial and ethnic groups in postsecondary education.

Elsewhere (Renn & Lunceford, 2002, 2004), we discuss in detail the policy environment in which data on race and ethnicity have been and are currently collected. In this article, we briefly review federal policy changes and describe their effect on institutional data collection as illustrated by data from two studies of data collection practices at national samples of institutions. We then propose strategies for comparing data from before and after the policy change and topics for future research in the area.

## Background and Policy Environment in Which Data on Race and Ethnicity are Collected

The U.S. Bureau of the Census has counted individuals by race since the 18th century, although definitions and methods of identifying members of racial categories have varied substantially over time (Lee, 1993). Figures based on a complex system of labels for individuals with varying levels of Black and White "blood" (e.g., "full-blooded Negroe," "mulatto," "quadroon," "octoroon"), all based on observation of skin tone, were admitted by the 1890 census report to be "of little value" (Spickard, 1989, p. 433, note 27). By the 1950 census, this system had given way to three racial categories: White, Black, and Other (U.S. Census Bureau, 1957).

During the 1960s, the federal government began collecting racial data for reasons other than the decennial population count. Title VII of the Civil Rights Act of 1964 directed the Census Bureau to collect registration and voting information by race, color, and national origin and is believed to be "the first Civil Rights era instance of Congress mandating the collecting of racial data" (Farley, 2001, p. 3). In addition, the use of racial ratios and busing to integrate public school students and teachers (*Swann v. Charlotte Mecklenberg County*, 1971) de facto required the collection of racial data, and the Department of Health, Education and Welfare (HEW) Office of Civil Rights was using Title IV of the Civil Rights Act of 1964 to collect information about the race of public school students. Title VII of the Civil Rights Act of 1965 established the Equal Employment Opportunities Commission, requiring data on race and sex to ensure employers' compliance.

The 1970s brought additional changes to federal record keeping related to race and national origin. In 1973 the Federal Interagency Committee on Education (FICE)[3] began the process of creating government-wide standards for racial classification. In 1977, the OMB issued Directive 15, which mandated that federal agencies gathering demographic data must use four major racial categories (White, Black, Asian or Pacific Islander, American Indian or Alaska Native), with only one per person. Spanish heritage (yes or no) was also to be determined for each individual either by a separate question or as a fifth "racial/ethnic" category (OMB, 1977). A rider amended to a military appropriations bill by Congressman Robert Matsui delineated the Asian or Pacific Islander category on the 1980 census as Japanese, Chinese, Filipino, Vietnamese, Asian Indian, Hawaiian, Guamanian, and Samoan (Farley, 2001).

Prompted by an emerging political movement of mixed-race people and parents of multiracial children, in 1993, OMB began a formal review of the standards for collecting, analyzing, and reporting government data on race and ethnicity. The resulting OMB standards, issued in October 1997, apply to "all federally collected data and reporting, including all levels of education, the national census, medical research, disease statistics, drawing boundaries for Congressional districts, the Voting Rights Act, and compliance with federal law and statutory regulations" (Davis-Van Atta, 1998, Summary, ¶3). The new standards included the change from five "acceptable racial and ethnic categories" (American Indian or Alaskan Native, Asian or Pacific Islander, Black, Hispanic, White) to "five minimum categories for data on race: American Indian or Alaska Native, Asian, Black or African American, Native Hawaiian or Other Pacific Islander, White" and "two categories for data on ethnicity: Hispanic or Latino, Not Hispanic or Latino" (OMB, 1997, Summary, ¶2). The new standards also stipulated that there be no "multiracial" or "multiethnic" option but that respondents be offered the option of indicating more than one category. The preferred method of racial/ethnic data collection is through a two-question format that asks first about ethnicity and then about race, although a one-question format is permissible. Self-identification is the preferred mode for collecting racial and ethnic data, although "observer-collected" data on race and ethnicity are permitted, in which case the observer should use six categories, combining the racial and ethnic categories as in the one-question format (OMB, 1997).

Reporting requirements were also changed to include the minimum of reporting in the five racial groups and two ethnicities when data were collected by self-identification or the six racial/ethnic groups when data were collected by observation. In addition,

> data producers are strongly encouraged to report detailed distributions, including all possible combinations, of multiple responses to the race question. If data on multiple responses are collapsed, at a minimum, the total number of respondents indicating more than one racial category must be provided (NCES, 2000).

OMB directed all changes to be effective "as soon as possible, but not later than January 1, 2003" (OMB, 1997, Effective Date, ¶1) (see appendix for a timeline of events related to the development of policy related to racial/ethnic data collection in postsecondary education).

## Collection and Reporting of Racial and Ethnic Data in Postsecondary Education

Although the new standards apply legally only to data collection and reporting by federal agencies, multiple interfaces among postsecondary institutions, related organizations, and the federal government all but mandate changes in institutional data collection and reporting.

> Not adopting the new methodologies at the institutional level would lead to fundamental incompatibility not only between one's institutional data and all federal data (e.g. census data, IPEDS [Integrated Postsecondary Education Data System] data) but also to lack of comparability between

institutions that have adopted the new standards and those that have not. Further, the result of not adopting the new standards would mean an inability to report institutional racial and ethnic data that more accurately reflect the U.S. population and would also forfeit an opportunity to provide prospective and current students, faculty, and alumni with options to capture for their [sic] racial and ethnic backgrounds more fully and accurately. (Davis-Van Atta, 1998, Implications for Institutions, ¶2)

Furthermore, it was expected that "adopting the new standards will result in not only new data, but also in a different *structure* for national and institutional databases" (Davis-Van Atta, 1998, Implications for Institutions, ¶3, emphasis in original). For example, rather than use a single data field with a limited set of single values to represent one racial/ethnic background per person, databases might have to include multiple permutations of possible racial/ethnic combinations, each with its own data field and dichotomous values. Overhauling institutional, state, and national databases to reflect the new OMB standards was predicted to be "likely to require considerable investment of both time and money" and "very different analytic treatment of racial and ethnic data, as well as of all other data associated with racial and ethnic backgrounds" (Davis-Van Atta, 1998, Implications for Institutions, ¶3).

To address these issues, the National Postsecondary Education Cooperative (NPEC), NCES, and the National Science Foundation (NSF) cosponsored a Policy Panel on Racial/Ethnic Data Collection. In 1999, the Policy Panel issued recommendations for data collection and data reporting. Based on the assumption that it would take 2 years to create and adopt appropriate software and 2 years to become consistent in collecting and maintaining racial/ethnic data across institutions, the panel predicted that "it would probably take institutions 4 years to have complete, consistent data, beginning from the time of their commitment to make the changes" (Westat, 1999, p. 5). Furthermore, in terms of readiness as of 1999 to comply with the revised OMB Directive 15, according to the Policy Panel report,

Institutions of higher education are generally aware of the classification changes, but they are all waiting on official, definitive guidance from OMB and NCES before they begin implementing the changes. However, not all information technology staff are aware of these changes, especially since many institutions are focusing their technology resources on Y2K efforts. (Westat, 1999, p. 4)

So by February 1999, it was already fairly clear that it would not be possible for institutions to meet the directive's January 1, 2003, deadline for implementation, even if guidelines for collecting and reporting racial/ethnic were immediately forthcoming from OMB.

Because of the central role of IPEDS in postsecondary data collection and reporting, a consensus emerged among higher education stakeholders (e.g., NCES, NSF, institutions, national testing organizations, etc.) that a planned redesign of the IPEDS survey could serve as both model and method for facilitating institutional conversion to the new standards. The Policy Panel recommended a timeline for transformation of the process, proposed to begin March 1999 with NCES issuing written recommendations from the Policy Panel and to end in fall of the 2002–2003 academic year with the IPEDS Fall Enrollment survey. The Policy Panel further recommended that "implementation of the changes should occur simultaneously in all institutions" (Westat, 1999, p. 9), with the exception of the Graduation Rate Survey, which should be phased in because of difficulty in ascertaining under the new standards the race and ethnicity of students who left institutions prior to graduation.

## Data Collection

In response to Directive 15's allowance for a one- or two-question format for collecting data, the Policy Panel recommended the one-question format, unless states required the two-question format. Use of this format would result in six racial/ethnic categories: American Indian/Alaska Native, Native Hawaiian and Other Pacific Islander, Asian American, Black/African American, White, and Hispanic/Latino. The Policy Panel further recommended that institutions use eight data fields—these six categories plus a "bridge field" from the old coding scheme or the new data and a "flag field" to indicate whether the bridge field was from old or new data (Westat, 1999, p.6).

**Table 1. One- and Two-Question Formats for Obtaining Data on Race and Ethnicity**

| Two-Question Format (Preferred) | One-Question Format |
|---|---|
| 1. Which best describes you? (Choose one.)<br>　a. Hispanic/Latino<br>　b. Non-Hispanic/Latino<br>2. Which of these best describes your background (Choose one or more.)<br>　a. American Indian/Alaska Native<br>　b. Asian<br>　c. Black/African American<br>　d. Native Hawaiian/other Pacific Islander<br>　e. White | Which of these best describes your background? (Choose one or more.)<br>　a. Hispanic/Latino<br>　b. American Indian/Alaska Native<br>　c. Asian<br>　d. Black/African American<br>　e. Native Hawaiian/other Pacific Islander<br>　f. White |

*Source:* NCES Taskforce for IPEDS Redesign (1999, pp. 25-26)

The NCES Taskforce for IPEDS Redesign (1999) ultimately recommended that institutions could choose either the one- or two-question format for obtaining race/ethnicity data and a modified version of the Policy Panel's two-table reporting format. The two-question format for collecting data better meets the OMB requirement that ethnicity be reported independently from race (see Table 1 for the two acceptable data collection formats).

In either case, institutions would have sufficient information to report respondents of single racial groups, multiple combinations of races, and either Hispanic/Latino or non-Hispanic Latino (either by choosing the appropriate response in the first question of the two-question format or by choosing or not choosing Hispanic/Latino in the one-question format). Both formats clearly meet the requirements of OMB Directive 15 (1997) for collecting data on race and ethnicity.

## Data Reporting

The Policy Panel accepted the Taskforce's recommendation of a 16-category table, including both unduplicated and duplicated counts of respondents by race, and IPEDS made plans to move ahead with the format. The table specified reporting in the following categories:

1. Nonresident aliens (U.S. citizens and resident aliens)
2. Unknown race/ethnicity
3. American Indian/Alaska Native only
4. Asian only
5. Black/African American only
6. Native Hawaiian/other Pacific Islander only
7. White only
8. Hispanic/Latino only
9. Hispanic/Latino and one or more races
10. Non-Hispanic and more than one race (Computed unduplicated total count [sum of 1 through 10 above])
11. American Indian/Alaska Native alone or in combination
12. Asian alone or in combination
13. Black/African American alone or in combination
14. Native Hawaiian/other Pacific Islander alone or in combination
15. White alone or in combination
16. Hispanic/Latino alone or in combination

Categories 11 through 16 are for reporting maximum counts of individuals with a particular racial/ethnic background. For example, white alone or in combination includes all individuals who report "white only" and white and any other race/ethnicity. (NCES Taskforce, 1999, p. 26)

This proposal, however, was effectively overridden by an alternate reporting plan that emerged from the Department of Education Office of Civil Rights (see Renn & Lunceford, 2004, for an analysis of this policy process).

While the IPEDS proposal for a 16-category framework was put on hold, OMB issued a bulletin titled *Guidance on Aggregation and Allocation of Data on Race for Use in Civil Rights Monitoring and Enforcement* (OMB, 2000) to assist various federal agencies in their efforts to work with data on race used in relation to civil rights. OCR stipulated a framework for reporting race only (i.e., not including information on Hispanic/Latino ethnicity), including the five single races, the four most common double race combinations from the 2000 census, any additional combinations that represent 1% or more of the population in a jurisdiction and the balance of individuals reporting more than one race.[4] The issuing bulletin provides this example:[5]

1. American Indian or Alaska Native
2. Asian
3. Black or African American
4. Native Hawaiian or Other Pacific Islander
5. White
6. American Indian or Alaska Native *and* White
7. Asian *and* White
8. Black or African American *and* White
9. American Indian or Alaska Native *and* Black or African American
10. > 1 percent: Fill in if applicable_____
11. > 1 percent: Fill in if applicable_____
12. Balance of individuals reporting more than one race
13. Total (OMB, 2000, Aggregation Guidance, ¶2)

The specificity of the four most common combinations—as well as any others that might apply in particular circumstances—could not be met in aggregated data by the 16-category framework proposed by NCES, although it could be met at the individual respondent level. For example, a respondent who marked Asian and White would be counted in three items (10, 12, and 15) of the NCES framework and in only item (7) of the new OMB framework. Once the data from multiple respondents were aggregated at the institutional level, it would not be clear from the NCES table how to allocate those individuals in the OMB table. Asian-White mixes would be indistinguishable from other Asian mixes, and the presence of individuals indicating three or more races would further confound the data. This example illustrates the importance of developing guidelines for aggregating data on race and ethnicity so that data can be compared within and across institutions and agencies. Although the OMB guidelines were imposed from outside the postsecondary education data community, they provide a more clear system for obtaining an unduplicated count that captures more of the specific racial backgrounds of individuals than does the NCES 16-category framework and may ultimately prove more useful, especially if they are adopted as the standard by other agencies for reporting data on race.

While the OMB issued its guidance on data aggregation in 2000 and full compliance with OMB Directive 15 was mandated by January 1, 2003, by late 2004, NCES had not specified how institutional data on race and ethnicity were to be reported to IPEDS. The most recent communication from NCES (2002) noted,

> NCES strongly recommends that institutions do nothing at this time to change their current race and ethnicity reporting systems and formats; it would be best to wait until more definitive decisions have been made. We will advise the postsecondary education community as soon as resolution is reached, as well as the time frame for implementation.

The Association for Institutional Research further instructed institutions that the "deadline is no longer in effect," aggregate reporting decisions have not been made, and "reporting for postsecondary institutions is currently 'on hold'" (Sapp & Fuller, 2002). Given the time from a decision for IPEDS reporting to implementation by institutions (estimated to be up to 4 years, Westat, 1999), the postsecondary sector may not implement the 1997 revisions to racial and ethnic data collection by even a full decade after their adoption. And once the changes are implemented, substantial challenges remain for data analysis and interpretation.

## Challenges for Data Analysis: Bridging Old (1977) and New (1997) Data Formats

If the changes were only a matter of data collection and aggregate reporting, the delay in adopting them would not seem to be more than a bureaucratic inconvenience. But racial/ethnic data are needed to inform important public policy questions in a number of arenas, including higher education. The need to "provide the most accurate and informative body of data" to "those Federal Government officials charged with carrying out constitutional and legislative mandates, such as redistricting legislatures, enforcing civil rights laws, and monitoring progress in anti-discrimination programs" (Tabulation Working Group, 1999, pp. 8–9) is identified repeatedly in OMB documents related to the development of guidelines for implementation of revisions to Directive 15. For the higher education community, the ability to compare data within and across institutions and state systems and nationally is essential to understanding issues of access, equity, and success in the postsecondary education sector. As with proposals to collect and report data, proposals for bridging data have been put forward by a number of stakeholders, culminating in recommendations from the Interagency Committee for the Review of Standards for Data on Race and Ethnicity's Tabulation Working Group (2000) in *Provisional Guidance on the Implementation of the 1997 Standards for Federal Data on Race and Ethnicity*. In this section, we briefly summarize these recommendations as they apply to postsecondary education data.

The Tabulation Working Group's guidelines provide for a "bridge period" during which agencies are permitted to use both the new data collected under the 1997 standards and a "bridging estimate," which is "a prediction of how the responses would have been collected and coded under the 1977 standards" (Tabulation Working Group, 2000, p. 85). This process allows for new data to be compared more meaningfully to the older format, although it does not attempt to estimate how old data might be seen under the new standards (which would not be possible, since respondents could indicate only one racial category and there is no way to determine how many individuals might have done so). In essence, the bridging estimates attempt to collapse the new data, with multiple race responses, into the old categories for race and ethnicity.

Several acceptable bridging methods were proposed, all of which involve the use of individual-level responses. The methods fall into two major types: "whole assignment," which places each individual into a single racial category, and "fractional assignment," which places individuals indicating more than one race into multiple categories (Tabulation Working Group, 2000, p. 87). Within whole assignment methods, individuals can be assigned on a deterministic set of rules (e.g., all White and Black/African American responses are assigned to the Black/African American category) or a probabilistic rule that randomly assigns a certain percent of multiple race responders to specific single race categories (e.g., 75% of White and Black/African American responders are assigned to Black/African American and 25% are assigned to White). A fractional assignment method could either assign a straight fraction of each response to the appropriate categories (e.g., a White and Asian respondent is assigned .5 to White and .5 to Asian) or in some ratio representing the amount of time that individual might identify with one group compared to another (e.g., a White and Asian respondent could be assigned .25 to White and .75 to Asian). Attempting to estimate how often an individual might identify in different groups is a messy and political business and therefore not likely to be incorporated often in strategies for reporting data on race and ethnicity.

Although whole assignment methods may be easier to manage statistically and fit better with a sense of one-body-one-response (avoiding the "half a person" effect of fractional assignment), they fail to meet a primary goal of the OMB's revision to Directive 15—that is, the ability of respondents to self-identify. Fractional assignment promises to better meet this goal, although the identities of mixed race college students are not necessarily well represented by simple division (see Harris & Sim, 2002; Renn, 2000, 2003, 2004; Rockquemore & Brunsma, 2002; Wallace, 2001). Allen and Turner (2001) offered strategies for fractional assignment based on 1990 census responses regarding ancestry. Allen and Turner's strategies hold promise for those institutions that want to engage in probabilistic fractional assignment when reporting aggregate data while representing, to the best extent possible, the identities of mixed-race respondents.

It is crucial that institutions determine a common method to bridge data across time and sources. In an analysis of six different bridging methods using race data from Census 2000, Grieco (2002) found that the various methods did not produce consistent estimates for all race groups. The NPEC/NCES/NSF Policy Panel recommended that NCES should build a 2 to 3 year bridge from new to old data, in part because a national bridge would be useful to institutions needing to bridge their own data. The need to bridge institutional data would continue unless and until institutions resurveyed continuing students for IPEDS compliance and staff for equal employment opportunity (EEO) reporting requirements; the Policy Panel therefore recommended that "institutions should be *strongly* encouraged but not required to resurvey continuing students" (Westat, 1999, p. 14). Resurveying all students using a common data collection format is also supported by the recent finding of Monzo (2004) that even within institutions, there may be variances across data collection methods (e.g., different terms or instructions on paper and online admissions applications). The Policy Panel further recommended that NCES should report data in only one format, that institutions report all data to NCES using only one format in a given year, that institutions should convert old data to the new format before reporting it, and that new data should be reported as new data rather than attempting to collapse it back into the old formats (p. 14). These recommendations were made with the suggestion that the 16-category framework be adopted and work less well with the 2000 version of *Provisional Guidance*, but they convey in clear terms the recommendation that NCES provide leadership to institutions in bridging between new and old data.

With the derailment of the plan for the 16-category framework and the subsequent silence from NCES regarding revisions to race and ethnicity data collected and reported for IPEDS, institutions are left with no additional guidance on collecting, reporting, or analyzing data. Although this silence hardly represents a crisis of national policy, there are a number of important cases around the country that would benefit from resolution of this issue. Even where data on race and ethnicity are not evidence for public policy debates and civil rights monitoring, institutions attempting to track their own progress in terms of access, participation, and success across racial and ethnic categories wait in statistical limbo for guidance from NCES.

In February 1997, the State Survey on Racial and Ethnic Classifications was conducted for NCES and the Office for Civil Rights (OCR) to review OMB's Directive 15 and assess the quality and efficacy of the use of the K-12 school data collected by the state departments of education using the five standard federal categories for race and ethnicity (Carey, Rowand, & Farris, 1998). The results included information in every state except Hawaii. In this study, eight states reported using categories other than the five standard categories mandated by the federal government; some states included a "multiracial" category, while others added separate categories to identify specific populations within one of the five categories requested by the government (e.g., "Filipino" was a separate category in California). Seventeen states reported that changing to meet the Directive 15 standards would affect their ability to project enrollment and may even "prevent comparisons across time." In addition, 31 states reported requests from schools and parents to add a "multiracial" category; 20 states agreed with these requests to add a "multiracial" category to "reflect the nation's increased diversity" or to "reflect the growing population of mixed-race individuals." Since 1997, primary and secondary school systems have been working with NCES and OCR to represent their student populations and comply with new federal standards; evidence suggests that similar cooperation in the postsecondary sector has been lacking. Indeed, little has been known about how postsecondary institutions collect and report data related to race and ethnicity or how the 1997 changes will affect them. In the next section, we use findings from a study of data collection and reporting practices to illustrate challenges of interstate and interinstitutional comparisons of racial/ethnic data in education.

## Practices In Data Collection and Reporting: Evidence From the Field

In fall 2002, we conducted a preliminary study of how institutions of higher education obtain and report data on students' race and ethnicity. We randomly selected 10% of the doctorate-granting institutions, master's colleges and universities, and baccalaureate colleges under the Carnegie Classification of Institutions of Higher Education (public and private) and 5% of the public associate's colleges (Carnegie Foundation for the Advancement of Teaching, 2002). Our final sample was 5% ($N$ = 127) of our selected categories (15% of doctorate-granting institutions, 4% of master's colleges and universities, 4% of baccalaureate colleges, and 4% of public associate's colleges).

We obtained applications for undergraduate admission from sample institutions through the Internet, in portable document format (PDF) or an online version. If an application was not available from an institution's Web site, we contacted the office of admissions or institutional research via telephone or e-mail to find out how they collected students' racial and/or ethnic information. We collected, from institutional Web sites or via telephone, data on the percentage of students of color at each institution. Finally, we contacted relevant officials at a subsample of institutions ($n$ = 32) to find out what influenced their determination of data collection categories.

For the purpose of this preliminary study, we categorized institutions into two groups ("old" and "expanded") on the basis of how students' race and ethnicity data were collected and reported. The "old" category included institutions that used the 1977 OMB Directive 15 racial categories, which are American Indian or Alaska Native, Asian or Pacific Islander, Black, and White (single selection only, sometimes including Hispanic/Latino as an additional category). The "expanded" category included institutions that had implemented the 1997 revisions to OMB's Directive 15 (at a minimum) and/or had further expanded on the broad race and ethnicity categories (e.g., one institution expanded its old "Asian or Pacific Islander" category into 10 new categories: Chinese, Japanese, Korean, Asian Indian, Other Asian, Laotian, Cambodian, Other Southeast Asian, Thai, and Vietnamese).

For data analysis, the institutions were further categorized into eight regions of the United States (see Table 2). Data were analyzed by Carnegie classification, region, institutional type (public vs. private), and the percentage of students of color per institution. Demographics of the sample are summarized in Table 3.

## Findings and Discussion of Preliminary Study

Ninety-eight percent of the institutions collected racial/ethnic data on their application for admission. The remaining schools reported that they collect the information when students register for courses. Only two institutions did not collect racial and/or ethnic data via application for admission. Both of these schools were historically Black colleges or universities. In fall 2002, the majority (62%) of institutions had not yet implemented the 1997 revisions to OMB's Directive 15 or expanded the 1977 racial/ethnic categories. Data collection and reporting categories varied by Carnegie classification, region, and institutional type, although only variations across regions were found to be statistically significant (see Table 4). The average percent of students of color at institutions using the old categories was 20.7%, whereas the percentage of students of color at those using expanded categories was 22.4.

In exploring why institutions had or had not made changes to their racial/ethnic collecting categories, we found that institutions in the "old" category were guided primarily by adherence to IPEDS reporting standards. Institutions that had expanded categories beyond those in the 1997 revision to Directive 15 did so to be more inclusive of the demographic of their student population. For example, two institutions located in the same region used a "Cape Verdean" category to represent better their local community and student body.

Although institutions expanded the categories for data collection, they typically collapsed the categories back to the single, "old" categories on publicized institutional reports as observed on institutional Web sites. The California State University (CSU) system was an example of a single system that had strategically created categories to be easily collapsed for IPEDS reporting yet strived to represent student demographics at individual campuses. The CSU system used the CSU Mentor for application to any CSU institution. The application had one set of 27 options for students to choose their "ethnic identity." These data were collapsed into nine categories for the CSU system statistical reports and were further collapsed into five categories for IPEDS reporting (California State University, 2002, see Table 5). Web sites of individual institutions in the CSU system revealed variations in how these data were reported. Individual campuses reported data (collapsing ethnicities into different categories) based on their student demographics and institutional preference.

**Table 2. Regions**

| Region 1 | Region 2 | Region 3 | Region 4 | Region 5 | Region 6 | Region 7 | Region 8 |
|---|---|---|---|---|---|---|---|
| Connecticut (3.83) | Delaware (1.30, 1986) | Kentucky (2.31) | Alabama (2.98) | Illinois (3.18) | Iowa (2.58) | Arizona (3.80, 1996) | Alaska (16.54) |
| Maine (3.53) | West Virginia (4.05) | Maryland/Washington DC (5.32) | Arkansas (4.40) | Indiana (3.88) | Kansas (5.18) | Colorado (7.32) | California (10.15) |
| Massachusetts (4.06) | Pennsylvania (3.56) | North Carolina (4.14) | Florida (5.94) | Michigan (4.02) | Minnesota (2.38) | Montana (2.38) | Hawaii (18.8, 1999) |
| New Hampshire (6.64) | | South Carolina (2.87) | Georgia (5.78) | Ohio (3.41) | Missouri (3.75) | New Mexico (8.20) | Idaho (6.45) |
| Rhode Island (4.52) | | Virginia (4.76) | Mississippi (2.15) | Wisconsin (3.55) | Nebraska (5.41) | Texas (6.29) | Nevada (5.90, 1995) |
| Vermont (2.65) | | | Tennessee (3.99) | | North Dakota (1.77) | Utah (2.38) | Oregon (9.02) |
| New York (4.57) | | | Louisiana (5.02) | | South Dakota (1.19) | Wyoming | Washington (7.29) |
| | | | | | Oklahoma (9.21) | | |

*Note*: Numbers in parentheses indicate the percentage of biracial and multiracial college students, including Latinas/Latinos, responding to the Cooperative Institutional Research Program (CIRP) Survey in 2000 according to Szelényi and Martínez (2004).

### Table 3. Demographic Characteristics of Institutions (N = 127)

| Characteristic | n | % of N |
|---|---|---|
| Carnegie classification | | |
| Doctoral/research universities—extensive | 22 | 17.3 |
| Doctoral/research universities—intensive | 16 | 12.6 |
| Master's colleges and universities I | 22 | 17.3 |
| Master's colleges and universities II | 4 | 3.1 |
| Baccalaureate colleges—liberal arts | 14 | 11.0 |
| Baccalaureate colleges—general | 8 | 6.3 |
| Associates colleges | 41 | 32.3 |
| Region | | |
| 1 | 19 | 15.0 |
| 2 | 5 | 3.9 |
| 3 | 15 | 11.8 |
| 4 | 15 | 11.8 |
| 5 | 22 | 17.3 |
| 6 | 10 | 7.9 |
| 7 | 16 | 12.6 |
| 8 | 25 | 19.7 |
| Type | | |
| Public | 92 | 72.4 |
| Private | 35 | 27.6 |
| Data collection/reporting categories | | |
| Old | 79 | 62.2 |
| Expanded | 48 | 37.8 |

The overall finding that by 2002, only a few months before the federal deadline for compliance, 62.2% of institutions had not yet implemented OMB's 1997 revisions to its Directive 15 was striking. The Policy Panel estimated that it would take institutions 4 years to implement changes to their methods of data collection (Westat, 1999). More than 5 years after OMB issued the 1997 revisions to the standards for data collection and reporting, fewer than 40% of institutions had made changes. In addition, only 17.3% of institutions in our study offered students the option of marking more than one category for race and/or ethnicity (depending on the one- or two-question format)—a critical element of the new standards. Four out of five institutions had yet to make this substantial change to comply with Directive 15.

## Further Evidence of Disparate Institutional Practices

A recent study (Monzo, 2004) targeting the five states with the highest percentage of census respondents indicating more than one race (Hawaii, Alaska, California, Oklahoma, and Nevada) and the five states with the lowest percentage of respondents indicating more than one race (South Carolina, Alabama, Maine, West Virginia, and Mississippi)[6] found that collection of data on student race and ethnicity in higher education continued to vary widely. Monzo noted that institutions in states with either very high or very low percentages of more-than-one-race respondents in their population did not differ significantly in the frequency with which they offered applicants the option to indicate more than one race on a college application. Yet each group differed significantly on this question—and both were more likely to offer the more-than-one-race option—from institutions in the other 40 states (categorized as the "middle" group).

Additional findings from the study (Monzo, 2004) indicated differences among institutions from states in the high-, middle-, and low-percentage groups in frequencies of offering an option to indicate "other" as a racial category and an option to indicate "biracial or multiracial." Neither option is acceptable by the OMB, NCES, or IPEDS data collection or reporting standards, which mandate the use of five racial and two ethnic categories (or a combined six category format). It was not clear from this study how these data would be aggregated and reported to IPEDS. Monzo also found that within many individual institutions, there were multiple ways that data were collected on admissions forms; some institutions used different options on the online and paper versions of the application, for example, further complicating the data aggregation and reporting questions. While

**Table 4. Data Collection/Reporting Category by Demographic**

| Data Category | Old | | Expanded | | p |
|---|---|---|---|---|---|
| | n | Percentage of Category | n | Percentage of Category | |
| Carnegie classification | | | | | |
| Doctoral/research universities—extensive | 10 | 45.5 | 12 | 54.5 | .672 |
| Doctoral/research universities—intensive | 10 | 62.5 | 6 | 37.5 | |
| Master's colleges and universities I | 15 | 68.2 | 7 | 31.8 | |
| Master's colleges and universities II | 3 | 75.0 | 1 | 25.0 | |
| Baccalaureate colleges—liberal arts | 8 | 57.1 | 6 | 42.9 | |
| Baccalaureate colleges—general | 5 | 62.5 | 3 | 37.5 | |
| Associates colleges | 28 | 68.3 | 13 | 31.7 | |
| Region | | | | | |
| 1 | 12 | 63.2 | 7 | 36.8 | .000* |
| 2 | 2 | 40.0 | 3 | 60.0 | |
| 3 | 14 | 93.3 | 1 | 6.7 | |
| 4 | 13 | 86.7 | 2 | 13.3 | |
| 5 | 10 | 45.5 | 12 | 54.5 | |
| 6 | 8 | 80.0 | 2 | 20.0 | |
| 7 | 13 | 81.3 | 3 | 18.8 | |
| 8 | 7 | 28.0 | 18 | 72.0 | |
| Type | | | | | |
| Public | 55 | 59.8 | 37 | 40.2 | .361 |
| Private | 24 | 68.6 | 11 | 31.4 | |

*$p < .001$.

**Table 5. Race and Ethnic Data Collection and Reporting of the California State University (CSU) System**

| Application for Admission | CSU System Statistical Reports | Integrated Postsecondary Education Data System (IPEDS) Reports |
|---|---|---|
| African American | African American | African American |
| American Indian | American Indian | American Indian |
| Chinese<br>Japanese<br>Korean<br>Asian Indian<br>Other Asian<br>Laotian<br>Cambodian<br>Other Southeast Asian<br>Thai<br>Vietnamese | Asian American | Asian/Pacific Islander |
| Filipino<br>Guamanian<br>Hawaiian<br>Samoan<br>Other Pacific Islander | Filipino<br>Pacific Islander | |
| Mexican American<br>Central American<br>South American<br>Cuban<br>Puerto Rican<br>Other Latino | Mexican American<br>Other Latino | Latino |
| White, non-Latino | White, non-Latino | White, non-Latino |
| Other<br>No response<br>Decline to state | Unknown | Unknown |

*Source:* California State University (2002).

additional research is necessary to address the reasons underlying these findings, it seems clear that institutional practices vary in ways that are not necessarily predictable based on institutional classification, type, or student composition, although some evidence suggests that regional and state differences in the general population may have an influence on institutional practices.

## Changing Social Contexts for the Collection of Data on Race and Ethnicity

Often omitted from discussions on racial classification is why individuals self-identify as they do and how self-identification changes over time and across contexts. It is outside the scope of this article to describe all of the influences on racial/ethnic self-identification, but it is important to understand some particular challenges to the reliability of data on race and ethnicity in postsecondary education. Many mixed-race adolescents and college students do not identify unilaterally across social contexts (e.g., Renn, 2000, 2003, 2004; Rockquemore & Brunsma, 2002; Wallace, 2001). Instead, they may identify situationally according to a range of sociocultural influences. In a school-based survey with a nationally representative sample of adolescents, Harris and Sim (2002) found that 12% of middle and high school children provided inconsistent answers to almost identical questions asking them to indicate their race and/or ethnicity. School-based surveys were conducted with 83,135 high school and middle school children and 18,924 interviews were conducted at home with the same students. While 8.6% of the adolescents reported being multiracial at home or in school, only 1.6% reported multiracial in both contexts, and only 1.1% selected the same combination of two or more racial groups in both contexts. As a result, there were discrepancies in multiracial reporting in school and at home—54% of those reporting as multiracial at home were not multiracial in school data, and 75% of the school multiracial population was not multiracial in home data.

Fluidity in racial identification may be influenced by an individual's age and place or region of residence. For example, individuals who grew up when law or common practice dictated that anyone with any African American heritage, even a very small fraction, was classified as Black may still continue that classification or pass their views to family members; multiracial individuals may thus be influenced to identify in only a single monoracial category. Differences between socially distinct monoracial groups may also cause fluidity of self-identification (e.g., Renn, 2000, 2003, 2004). Harris and Sim (2002) found different patterns of those who provided inconsistent self-reported data on race by different racial/ethnic groups. While a larger percentage of individuals who identified as both "White" and "Black" at school identified as only "Black" at home, a larger percentage of individuals who identified as "White" and "Asian" at school identified as "White" at home. There is no common understanding or practice of self-identification of race or ethnicity, especially among multiracial individuals or in families that have multiracial children who may identify differently from one another.

Over a lifetime, individuals may change how they identify in terms of race and ethnicity (see Farley, 2001; Harris & Sim, 2002; Lopez, 2003; Renn, 2004). When collecting data from one census to the next, if the person who completes the information for an entire household has a different view of race from that of the person who completes the next census, racial classifications, even in this single household, may be vastly different. In the attempt to determine the best method to collect and bridge data across time and sources, it is important to understand that concepts of race and ethnicity change over time and context, and methods of treating and interpreting data must account for or at least acknowledge these changes.

## Implications for Policy, Practice, and Research

### Implications and Recommendations for Postsecondary Education

It is clear that higher education is in the early process of a major change in policies and procedures surrounding the collection, analysis, and reporting of data related to race and ethnicity. It is also clear that the postsecondary sector as a whole did not meet the January 2003 deadline of the OMB's 1997 Directive 15 nor had it done so nearly 2 years later. The consequences of missing that deadline do not appear dire; there is nothing in the directive and no indication elsewhere that institutions or agencies will be penalized for failing to meet this deadline. Given the advance time required to implement such a shift in educational institutions, it would have been a fairly close call to implement the changes by the deadline in any case, but the apparent disconnect between NCES and other stakeholders rendered the task unfeasible by January 2003. And although the deadline came and went without systemic changes in postsecondary data collection and reporting, the changes are inevitable and will affect data at the institutional, state, and national level.

Decisions about data collection seem reasonably solid; there has been no public discussion of changing from the option of a one-question or two-question format for collecting data from students and employees. These formats are compatible with the 2000 census and should yield data that can be made comparable across data from a number of federal sources. It is not clear whether or not institutions will be required to resurvey all students and employees. We anticipate that the number of individuals who refused to answer would be significant and could have an adverse effect on the value of data collected. Still, a requirement to resurvey could provide valuable information for institutional data bridging purposes, and we concur with the NCES Taskforce on IPEDS Redesign that institutions should engage in this process. Students should be encouraged to reidentify themselves prior to registration, and employees should be encouraged to do so as well, perhaps in conjunction with annual benefits review and subscription. At many institutions, an online process would not be difficult to implement or manage. In all cases, an individual institution ought to keep the wording of items requesting information on race and ethnicity identical across all data collection instruments it employs (paper, online, admissions and employment applications, subsequent requests for information, etc.).

The current situation for data collection, as evident through our survey of 127 institutions (Renn & Lunceford, 2002), is nearly consistent in timing of data collection (all but two collect from students on application and do not resurvey) but quite divergent in how questions are asked, how many responses students may supply, and what categories are available, even within some institutions (see also Monzo, 2004). Although there will certainly remain some diversity among categories available, standardization of how the information is requested will be an asset to the data community, institutions, and students themselves. Institutions have by and large heeded the NCES call to stay the course and have not changed questions in anticipation of the new standards; indeed, the majority still requires students to indicate only one racial category.

Because it is clear that some method of reporting by respondents who indicate more than one race will be mandated in the relatively near future, we strongly recommend that institutions begin to collect data in a format that at a minimum permits more than one response for race, that uses the 1997 racial category definitions, and that also includes information on Hispanic/Latino or Not Hispanic/Latino ethnicity. These categories are not in question, nor is there debate about the one- or two-question format for collecting data. If necessary, data could be collected in both old and new formats so that IPEDS data could be submitted under current ("old") guidelines, and bridging could be accomplished fairly easily to whatever new guidelines are issued. Having recommended this change, however, we recognize that the realities of institutional record keeping work against us in this matter, and we are not optimistic that our recommendation will be adopted over the urging of various agencies and organizations that institutions make no changes until NCES mandates changes in IPEDS data collection (e.g., NCES, 1999, 2002; Sapp & Fuller, 2002).

Data aggregation and reporting, however, represent much more complex tasks that must be coordinated within and across institutions. Comparability of data is critical to conducting peer analyses; to analyzing institutional, systemic, and national trends; and to civil rights monitoring and enforcement. Two options have been in discussion in the postsecondary education community—the 16-category framework and the OMB civil rights format. Although there are certainly other formats for reporting data, we will discuss the strengths and weaknesses of these two.

The OMB format has been adopted and is in use nationally; there are strong arguments for having postsecondary data reported in this format. It facilitates comparisons across agencies and purposes; it is a fairly straightforward approach that includes an unduplicated count; it can be adapted to specific populations whose racial combinations may vary from the national norm; it provides specificity in racial combinations in ways that the 16-category framework does not. Furthermore, bridging from pre-1997 data is not terribly complicated using this format. What it lacks, however, is any accounting for ethnicity. It is a race-only framework that requires additional tabulation to indicate Latino or Hispanic heritage. It also fails to recognize the specific combinations of races falling below 1% of the total, which, although not appearing to be a significant disservice to individuals, does violate the "self-determination" philosophy of OMB Directive 15 (OMB, 1997). While OMB very clearly stated that this framework was for the purposes of civil rights monitoring and enforcement only, the adoption of this policy across agencies indicates that it will be a presence and a precedent for federal agencies.

The NCES 16-category framework could still be adopted for IPEDS and other purposes. It is especially useful to higher education because it includes nonresident aliens, who constitute an important segment of the postsecondary population; it includes an "unknown" category, which can be important in understanding the relative proportion of other individuals counted; and it includes ethnicity. Although somewhat bulky, the combination of unduplicated total (lines 1 through 10) and duplicated figures (lines 11 through 16) provides a more accurate picture of campus populations and, more so than the OMB unduplicated format, meets the spirit of self-determination. What it lacks, however, is specificity. It is not clear from this framework how many of the "alone or in combination" respondents are "in combination" with other specific races. There is no way without examining individual records to determine the number of, for example, Asian-White respondents.

On some campuses, this information could be important, as could the ability to compare this information across institutions, especially within state systems.

Although neither is perfect and there are undoubtedly other models, we recommend the adoption of the OMB model. It includes more specificity than the NCES framework, it is less confusing than the unduplicated-duplicated dual system, and from it, the duplicated information could easily be constructed if it were of interest. We recommend, however, that the OMB model be modified to include Hispanic/Latino as an equal category to the five "races" and to include Hispanic/Latino as appropriate in the four most common combinations reported in the table. Because 7.7% of those under age 18 indicating more than one race also reported Latino or Hispanic ethnicity (U.S. Census Bureau, 2001), it is critical to provide a means to express this identity in educational demographics. Our recommendation challenges OMB's differentiation between race and ethnicity and, although we again acknowledge the contested nature of the discussion, asserts that the lived experience of students identified as Latino or Hispanic constitutes an experience on par with students identified with so-called racial groups.

Current practices vary widely, with no consistent method for institutional presentation of data outside the IPEDS process. Even within systems that collect data through common admissions applications (e.g., the California State Universities), data presentation is inconsistent. There will always be reasons for institutional variation in data presentation, and some institutions will want to present far more detail than the 16-category or OMB formats. We recommend, however, that institutions make available data in whatever format is adopted by IPEDS, as well as institutional reporting formats, with information on how individuals who indicated more than one race were assigned to categories (if this is not apparent from the final model adopted by IPEDS). At present, it is difficult to compare data across institutions from information available at a glance on institutional Web sites, for example. It is even more difficult to determine how multiracial individuals are represented in the data presented.

Recommendations for bridging and analyzing data hinge, in part, on the framework adopted for aggregation and reporting. Some important philosophical elements, however, apply to any plan for bridging old and new data. These bridge calculations involve highly charged political stakes and personal identities as the process essentially involves reassigning individual responses from the categories indicated by individuals into the "old" single-response categories.

As Allen and Turner (2001) indicated, there are a number of ways to assign the responses of mixed-race individuals to single categories that are acceptable under the OMB's *Provisional Guidance* (Tabulation Working Group, 2000). We are least comfortable with "whole assignment" models that call for unilateral assignment of all individuals with White and other racial heritage into the category of that other race. This is, in fact, the OMB's method in civil rights monitoring and enforcement calculations, and we are troubled by the ways this model inflates the number of people in racial categories other than White, no matter how those individuals might look, feel, or act.

We support Allen and Turner's (2001) recommendations for "fractional assignment," although in responding to the individual's right to self-determination they interfere somewhat with the institution's need to have data that are readily analyzed by whole numbers. If institutions adopted an overlapping data collection process (e.g., collecting data with "old" and "new" questions for a few years), an institution-specific scheme for fractional assignment could be determined that would account for regional racial and ethnic history and trends in self-determination. In the absence of the resources or will to conduct such a bridging study, many institutions could rely on Allen and Turner's work for guidance on fractional assignment. Once the final IPEDS categories are established, this issue should be revisited for further clarification.

## Recommendations for Future Research

Our article represents two strands of work—the policy context and current practices—on the topic of postsecondary data collection and reporting related to race and ethnicity. Yet we are left with a number of questions and a number of suggestions for future research in each of the study's areas. And of course, we are eager to see what will happen when NCES issues final recommendations for IPEDS revisions in the area of race and ethnicity. The research represented in this paper could be expanded in a number of interesting ways, some of which we suggest here.

First, an in depth qualitative study of the change process would be useful and interesting. More information on decisions within the NPEC/NCES/NSF Policy Panel and the NCES Taskforce on IPEDS Revision could reveal insights into political processes and stakeholder influences. How, for example, was the 16-category framework developed, whom would it benefit, and why was it abandoned? Can a resolution be reached that meets the same needs yet also meets OMB and other agency concerns and mandates? How can similar situations (such as developing and then abandoning a solution) be avoided in the future? What can be learned from the process followed in the K-12 arena (see Carey et al., 1998; Lopez, 2003) that would benefit this analysis and future change efforts? After NCES issues new IPEDS guidelines, a follow-up study to see how these guidelines were ultimately developed and are being received by a number of stakeholders would be in order.

A broader study placing the postsecondary data community in the context of a larger federal data community could also be useful in understanding how postsecondary education is seen and how it might exert its influence at the federal level. Certainly, every agency within the government and the many external constituencies that must collect and report data on race and ethnicity are affected by OMB Directive 15 (OMB, 1997). Whose concerns are being heard most clearly? How do their concerns match or conflict with those of higher education? Should members of the postsecondary sector form political alliances differently to achieve mutually beneficial outcomes? How might they do so? A thorough document review of other agencies' processes related to Directive 15 and subsequent interviews with key informants could provide useful information for future decision making around interagency initiatives and cross-agency mandates. And once the changes are in place, a thorough review of the place of NCES and NPEC in the final decision would be instructive as well.

With regard to current practices for data collection and reporting, there are several questions that would benefit from additional research even before changes are finalized. For example, why specifically have some institutions changed from "old" to "new" and/or "expanded" data collection? What forces operate on institutions to cause them to make these changes? How do institutions respond to local constituencies in this regard? How are they aggregating and reporting data that do not fit the prescribed IPEDS categories?

Once changes are mandated by IPEDS, a follow-up study of how institutions ask for data on race and ethnicity (the one- or two-question format or other variation), as well as how they aggregate and report data would be important to understanding the national picture of data collection and reporting. It may be the case that after the changes are made, data remain incomparable across institutions, systems, and states. While many data analysis needs can be met without exactly comparable data, the needs of the postsecondary community and the public may not be best served if data cannot be aligned for easy comparison.

The issue of bridging will require further research to ascertain the effectiveness of different proposed bridging methods. The ability to compare old and new data sets for purposes of tracking access, retention, and completion is critical. The ability to compare trends across broad historical time frames is already impeded by inconsistent data collection methodologies and terminologies, but it will be impeded further by inconsistent bridging practices. It will be important to examine bridging proposals and then actual bridging practices to determine the viability and effectiveness of various methods.

## Conclusion

At the outset, we stated that when it comes to data on race and ethnicity in higher education, "the numbers matter." The numbers matter at the individual, institutional, state, and federal levels. The ability to track access, retention, completion, and employment by race and ethnicity is important as our loosely coupled "system" of postsecondary education attempts to meet educational, workforce, and research needs of a nation that is changing rapidly in terms of demography and economics. At a time when some institutions have abandoned (or been forced to abandon) affirmative action, others are still under legal orders to meet racial desegregation mandates; the ability to assess the effect of the former and progress toward the latter depends on the reliability of data collection and reporting across time. Although OMB's Directive 15 (OMB, 1997) was an important step toward allowing individual self-determination of multiple racial categories, it came at a time when the reliability of racial data was more important than ever in postsecondary education.

The outcomes of the changes remain to be seen. It is not clear how or even when Directive 15 will be fully implemented in higher education. While we are hopeful that this change will provide an impetus for higher education institutions to align themselves fairly uniformly with whatever new guidelines IPEDS requires, we are even more hopeful that institutions will voluntarily adopt some uniform means of collecting and reporting data. Where they choose to be more descriptive than required by IPEDS (e.g., the California State University system), we hope that they will be explicit about how they are collapsing data into IPEDS categories so that comparisons across categories can be made easily by any interested party. Most of all, we are hopeful that the current change process, bureaucratic and incomplete as it may now be, might serve as a model for future changes to data collection—changes that will almost surely be required as the U.S. population continues to become more diverse and less easily confined to "one box only."

# Appendix

Timeline of Events Related to Development and Implementation of Office of Management and Budget (OMB) Directive 15 and Subsequent Revisions

*1973:* Department of Health, Education and Welfare (HEW) Secretary Casper Weinberger asks the Federal Interagency Committee on Education (FICE) to begin process of creating government-wide standards for racial classification

*1977:* OMB issues Directive 15, mandating that federal agencies gathering demographic data use four major racial categories (White, Black, Asian or Pacific Islander, American Indian or Alaska Native). Spanish heritage (yes or no) was also to be determined for each individual.

*1980:* U.S. census includes a delineation of the Asian or Pacific Islander category as Japanese, Chinese, Filipino, Vietnamese, Asian Indian, Hawaiian, Guamanian, and Samoan

*1993:* OMB begins formal review of standards for collecting, analyzing, and reporting federal data.

*1994:* OMB creates Interagency Committee for the Review of Race and Ethnic Standards (ICRRES), representing more than 30 federal agencies.

*October 1997:* OMB issues revision to Directive 15; changes from "five acceptable racial and ethnic categories" to "five minimum categories for data on race: American Indian or Alaskan Native, Asian, Black or African American, Native Hawaiian or Other Pacific Islander, White" and "two categories for data on ethnicity: Hispanic or Latino, Not Hispanic or Latino)." There is no multiracial or multiethnic option, but respondents must be offered option of indicating more than one racial category; mandated to take effect for Census 2000 and for all federal data by January 1, 2003.

*March 1998 and February 1999:* National Postsecondary Education Cooperative (NPEC), National Center for Education Statistics (NCES), and National Science Foundation (NSF) sponsor meetings of a joint Policy Panel on Racial/Ethnic Data Collection (Policy Panel).

*February 1999:* Tabulation Working Group of Interagency Committee for the "Review of Standards for Data on Race and Ethnicity" (formerly ICRRES) issues "Draft Provisional Guidelines on the Implementation of the 1997 Standards for Federal Data on Race and Ethnicity" for comment and review by interested parties and agencies.

*April 1999:* Policy Panel issues final report, including the 16-category framework for reporting data on race and ethnicity; recommendations incorporate recommendations of Tabulation Working Group's "Draft Provisional Guidance" report.

*August 1999:* NCES Taskforce for Integrated Postsecondary Education Data System (IPEDS) Redesign accepts 16-category framework for use in IPEDS data collection and reporting.

*November 1999:* NCES puts hold on recommendation for 16-category framework and tells institutions not to make any changes until additional guidance is forthcoming from federal government.

*March 2000:* OMB issues bulletin on the collection and reporting of racial data for civil rights monitoring and enforcement; it contains a format for reporting race that is incompatible with NCES 16-category framework.

*December 2000:* Interagency Tabulation Working Group issues "Provisional Guidelines on the Implementation of the 1997 Standards for Federal Data on Race and Ethnicity"; it includes the March 2000 OMB format for reporting race.

*July and August 2002:* Postsecondary Statistics Division of NCES informs postsecondary education community that "the status of the changes in race and ethnicity reporting that were to be implemented with the 2002 IPEDS Fall Enrollment Survey is currently being revisited" and "is strongly recommending that institutions do nothing at this time to change their current race and ethnicity reporting systems and formats." January 1, 2003, deadline no longer applies.

## Notes

1. Definitions of *race* and *ethnicity* vary by source and interpretation. For the purposes of this article, we are using the federal governments' terminology and categories (five races and two ethnicities), which we acknowledge to be highly contested constructs.
2. A figure of 4.8% was calculated using Latino as a race. Removing Latino as a race yields 3.5% count of bi- and multiracial students.
3. The Federal Interagency Committee on Education (FICE) was established in 1964 by executive order (Office of Management and Budget, 1994, Background, ¶1), and members have included the Departments of Education, Agriculture, Commerce, Defense, Energy, Health and Human Services, Housing and Urban Development, Interior, Transportation, and Treasury, as well as a number of non-cabinet agencies (Army Information Paper, n.d.).
4. Office of Management and Budget (OMB) (2000, Allocation Guidance, ¶1) also provided guidelines for the allocation of multiple race responses for use in civil rights monitoring and enforcement as follows:

   Responses in the five single race categories are not allocated.
   Responses that combine one minority race and white are allocated to the minority race.
   Responses that include two or more minority races are allocated as follows:

   - If the enforcement action is in response to a complaint, allocate to the race that the complainant alleges the discrimination was based on.
   - If the enforcement action requires assessing disparate effect or discriminatory patterns, analyze the patterns based on alternative allocations to each of the minority groups.

5. Although the bulletin was issued before the four most common racial combinations could actually be determined from the 2000 census, the combinations provided in the Office of Management and Budget (OMB) example were, in fact, the four most common reported by census respondents. Therefore, the bulletin's example represents OMB's actual final guidance on the matter.
6. States in these lists based on the U.S. census differ from those containing the highest and lowest percentages of biracial and multiracial college students responding to the Cooperative Institutional Research Program (CIRP) survey as reported by Szelényi and Martínez (2004) as indicated in Table 2. Census figures include all ages of respondents and do not include Latinas/Latinos.

## References

Allen, J. P., & Turner, E. (2001). Bridging 1990 and 2000 census race data: Fractional assignment of multiracial populations. *Population Research and Policy Review, 20,* 513–533.

Army Information Paper. (n.d.). Federal Interagency Committee on Education information paper. Retrieved October 20, 2002, from http://www.army.mil/features/educationsummit/infopaperFICE.doc

California State University. (2002). *Analytic studies/Chancellor's office information technology services: Data element dictionary.* Retrieved October 28, 2002, from http://www.calstate.edu/cim/data-elem-dic/APDB-Transaction-DED.pdf

Carey, N., Rowand, C., & Farris, E. (1998). State survey on racial and ethnic classifications (NCES 98034). Washington, D.C.: National Center for Educational Statistics. Retrieved August 3, 2004, from http://nces.ed.gov/pubsearch/pubsinfo.asp?pubid=98034

Carnegie Foundation for the Advancement of Teaching. (2002). *Carnegie classification of institutions of higher education: 2000 edition category definitions.* Retrieved online August 18, 2002, from http://www.carnegiefoundation.org/Classification/

Davis-Van Atta, D. (with Arnold, C., & Lyddon, J. W.) (1998, June). New federal standards for racial and ethnic data collection and reporting. *AIR alert: A briefing on emerging issues in higher education from the Association for Institutional Research* (No. 6). Retrieved April 23, 2002, from http://www.fsu.edu/air.alert6.htm

Farley, R. (2001). *Identifying with multiple races: A social movement that succeeded but failed?* (PSC Research Report No. 01–491). Ann Arbor: Population Studies Center at the Institute for Social Research, University of Michigan. Retrieved October 17, 2002, from http://www.psc.isr.umich.edu/pubs/papers/rr01-491.pdf

Grieco, E. M. (2002). An evaluation of bridging methods using race data from Census 2002. *Population Research and Policy Review, 21*, 91–107.

Harris, D. R., & Sim, J. J. (2002). Who is multiracial? Assessing the complexity of lived race. *American Sociological Review, 67*(4), 614–627.

Lee, S. (1993). Racial classifications in the U.S. census: 1890–1990. *Ethnic and Racial Studies, 16*(1), 75–94.

Lopez, A. M. (2003). Mixed-race school-age children: A summary of Census 2000 data. *Educational Researcher, 32*, 25–37.

Monzo, J. C. (2004, August). *I am Race-Unknown, Other, and Unspecified: An investigation of the methods and practices that colleges and universities use to collect and report data on multiracial students.* Paper presented at the 2004 Ronald E. McNair Post-Baccalaureate Achievement/Student Research Opportunity Program Symposium. Michigan State University, East Lansing.

National Center for Education Statistics (NCES). (1999, November 5). *What's new in racial/ethnic reporting for IPEDS.* Retrieved April 17, 2002, from http://nces.ed.gov/ipeds/newracereport.html

National Center for Education Statistics (NCES). (2000). *Appendix L: Revisions to the standards for the classification of federal data on race and ethnicity.* Retrieved online April 23, 2002, from http://www.nces.ed.gov/pubs2000/studenthb/append_L.asp

National Center for Education Statistics (NCES). (2002, June 21). *What's new in racial/ethnic reporting for IPEDS.* Retrieved August 3, 2004, from http://nces.ed.gov/ipeds/newracereport.asp

NCES Taskforce for IPEDS Redesign. (1999, August 31). *Integrated postsecondary education data systems (IPEDS): An improved system. Final report.* Washington, D.C.: National Center for Education Statistics. Retrieved April 17, 2002, from http://nces.ed.gov/ipeds/pdf/redesign/redesign.pdf

Office of Management and Budget (OMB). (1977). *Standards for the Classification of Federal Data on Race and Ethnicity* (Statistical Policy Directive No. 15). Washington, D.C.: Office of Management and Budget. Retrieved October 28, 2002, from http://www.whitehouse.gov/omb/fedreg/notice_15.html

Office of Management and Budget (OMB). (1994). Standards for the Classification of Federal Data on Race and Ethnicity. Retrieved October 28, 2002, from http://www.whitehouse.gov/omb/fedreg/notice_15.html

Office of Management and Budget (OMB). (1997). *Revisions to the Standards for the Classification of Federal Data on Race and Ethnicity.* Retrieved April 23, 2002, from http://www.whitehouse.gov/omb/fedreg/ombdir 15.html

Office of Management and Budget (OMB). (2000, March 9). *OMB Bulletin No. 00-02: Guidance on aggregation and allocation of data on race for use in civil rights monitoring and enforcement.* Retrieved April 22, 2002, from http://www.whitehouse.gov/omb/bulletins/print/b00-02.html

Renn, K. A. (2000). Patterns of situational identity among biracial and multiracial college students. *The Review of Higher Education, 23*(4), 399–420.

Renn, K. A. (2003). Understanding the identities of mixed race college students through a developmental ecology lens. *Journal of College Student Development, 44*, 383–403.

Renn, K. A. (2004). *Mixed race students in college: The ecology of race, identity, and community on campus.* Albany, NY: SUNY Press.

Renn, K. A., & Lunceford, C. J. (2002, November). *Because the numbers matter: Transforming racial/ethnic reporting data to account for mixed race students in postsecondary education.* Presented at the Annual Meeting of the Association for the Study of Higher Education, Sacramento, CA.

Renn, K. A., & Lunceford, C. J. (2004, April). *Making meaningful comparisons: Transforming racial and ethnic data in education, pre- to post-Directive 15.* Presented at the Annual Meeting of the American Educational Research Association, San Diego, CA.

Rockquemore, K. A., & Brunsma, D. L. (2002). *Beyond Black: Biracial identity in America.* Thousand Oaks, CA: Sage.

Sapp, M., & Fuller, C. (2002, August). Follow up to Alert #14, Update on federal race and ethnicity reporting changes. *AIR alert: A briefing on emerging issues in higher education from the Association for Institutional Research* (No. 14). Retrieved September 7, 2002, from http://www.airweb.org/page.asp?page=364

Spickard, P. R. (1989). *Mixed blood: Intermarriage and ethnic identity in twentieth-century America.* Madison: University of Wisconsin Press.

Stroup, K. (1998). *Summary proceedings for the policy panel on racial/ethnic data collection March 17–18, 1998.* Retrieved April 10, 2002, from http://www.nces.ed.gov/npec/papers/race-ethnic3.asp#overview

Swann v. Charlotte-Mecklenberg County Board of Education, 402 U.S. 1 (1971).

Szelényi, K., & Martínez, F. (2004). *Multiracial college students in the United States: Multilevel modeling of recent historical trends.* Paper presented at the annual meeting of the American Education Research Association, April 2004, San Diego, CA.

Tabulation Working Group, Interagency Committee for the Review of Standards for Data on Race and Ethnicity. (1999, February 17). *Draft provisional guidance on the implementation of the 1997 standards for federal data on race and ethnicity.* Washington, D.C.: Office of Management and Budget. Retrieved April 20, 2002, from http://www.whitehouse.gov/omb/inforeg/race.pdf

Tabulation Working Group, Interagency Committee for the Review of Standards for Data on Race and Ethnicity. (2000, December 15). *Provisional guidance on the implementation of the 1997 standards for federal data on race and ethnicity.* Washington, D.C.: Office of Management and Budget. Retrieved April 20, 2002, from http://www.whitehouse.gov/omb/inforeg/r&e_guidance2000update.pdf

U.S. Census Bureau. (1957). *Statistical abstract of the United States.* Washington, D.C.: Government Printing Office.

U.S. Census Bureau. (2001). Mapping census 2000: The geography of diversity. Retrieved March 15, 2002, from http://factfinder.census.gov

Wallace, K. R. (2001). *Relative/outsider: The art and politics of identity among mixed heritage students.* Westport, CT: Ablex.

Westat. (1999, April 2). *Recommendations of the Policy Panel on Racial/Ethnic Data Collection, February 11–12, 1999.* Rockville, MD: Author.

*Kristen A. Renn is an assistant professor of higher, adult, and lifelong education at Michigan State University. Her research interests include identity in higher education, mixed-race college students, and gender issues in higher education.*

*Christina J. Lunceford is a Ph.D. candidate in higher, adult, and lifelong education at Michigan State University. In addition to studying issues related to mixed-race students in the United States, she is conducting fieldwork on students' role in organizational change in post-Apartheid South African higher education institutions.*

AUTHORS' NOTE: Some ideas and arguments in this article were presented in papers at meetings of the Association for the Study of Higher Education, the American Educational Research Association, and the Association for Institutional Research. In addition to appreciating the comments and questions of discussants and audiences at those meetings, the authors wish to acknowledge Katalin Szelényi, Jamie C. Monzo, and the journal's anonymous reviewers of this manuscript.

# Institutions, Accreditors, and the Federal Government

## Redefining Their "Appropriate Relationship"

### JUDITH EATON

For almost two years, accrediting organizations and higher-education institutions have been confronted with a most serious challenge from the federal government, one that goes to the heart of the role and purposes of colleges and universities. The government has been taking action that could result in its assuming unprecedented direct control over standards of quality and the academic offerings of higher education.

The central aim of this effort is enhanced accountability, and the key target has been accreditation. Why accreditation? Because it is the primary means by which higher education ensures and improves its quality—and, crucially, accreditation is also subject to federal control.

The challenge is fundamental: Who, going forward, will have the primary authority and responsibility for academic quality?

This is emphatically not just another of those periodic dust-ups between higher education and the government in Washington. At stake is the longstanding "appropriate relationship" that has prevailed among government, accreditors, and institutions. Institutions and accreditors have historically had primary responsibility for academic quality, and the federal government has long relied on their judgment when making policy determinations regarding the use of federal funds. But if the current governmental challenge is successful, the authority for defining and judging academic quality would shift from institutions and accreditors to the federal government. This would amount to a "federalizing" of accreditation and affect all accredited colleges and universities, subjecting them to considerable additional federal control.

The challenge goes beyond a shifting relationship to include substantive matters as well, with the government focused on four accountability issues. Institutions and accreditors are to be accountable to the federal government:

- To provide more evidence of student achievement and institutional performance;
- To make this information easily accessible to the public;
- To develop means to compare institutions or groups of institutions;
- To establish threshold standards for collegiate learning.

What follows is an examination of how the federal accountability challenge is putting pressure on the relationship among institutions, accreditors, and the government. It concludes with five suggestions, designed to preclude the federalizing of accreditation by creating a new relationship based upon (1) federal reaffirmation that institutions and accreditors have primary responsibility for academic quality; (2) a federal commitment to eliminate or overhaul the federal recognition function; (3) a significant ratcheting up of action from institutions on the four accountability issues; (4) a significant strengthening of accreditation practice to address these issues; and (5) the creation of a new and compelling symbol of the responsibility institutions and accreditors have for leadership regarding academic quality, such as a searchable national database designed to help answer questions about academic quality.

A new relationship among the three parties would mean that they would all increase their investment in accountability, but the shift of responsibility to monitor and evaluate academic quality away from institutions and accreditors to the federal government would not occur. Instead, institutions and accreditors would acknowledge and act on the federal demand for enhanced accountability, provided that the government defer to institutional leadership for oversight of academic quality, with accreditors confirming that this oversight has in fact been exercised.

# How Did We Get Here?

Throughout much of their history, U.S. colleges and universities and accrediting organizations have enjoyed the benefits of independent—yet accountable—operations, based on their success with both self-governance and self-regulation. Elected or appointed governing boards of colleges and universities, rather than government, were entrusted with ensuring that institutions provided a high-quality education, maintained fiscal integrity, and served the public interest. Colleges and universities have long relied not on government but rather on accreditation's collegial, yet rigorous, system of self study and peer review to examine and enhance their teaching and learning, research, and service roles.

## Accountability and the Role of the Federal Government

At the same time, the federal government has had a significant stake in higher education, driven by many years of financial investment. The Veterans Readjustment Assistance Act (GI Bill) of 1952 launched the current federal investment, providing extensive tuition assistance to returning veterans of World War II. Later in the 1950s, the federal government again turned to higher education for a major expansion of the research needed for scientific and defense purposes. Some 50 years later, this federal funding now amounts to some $100 billion annually—a significant sum to be sure, although not the majority of funding for higher education.

Despite its major expansion of investment, the federal government deliberately chose not to directly regulate collegiate quality. Instead, it turned to higher education's private, self-regulatory accreditation bodies as "reliable authorities" to assure that federal funds were spent appropriately. In 1952 the U.S. Commissioner of Education began to publish a list of "nationally recognized accrediting agencies" to affirm the quality of the institutions at which veterans used their grant aid.

In agreeing to rely on colleges and universities for high-quality teaching, learning, and research while not regulating them directly, the federal government effectively defined what would come to be considered "the appropriate relationship" among itself, higher education, and accreditors. Institutions and accrediting organizations, working together, assured accountability for academic quality. In extending deference to them, the government was endorsing the value and effectiveness of the U.S. higher-education enterprise, including its traditions of self-governance and self-regulation, with accreditation as a reliable and respected means to assure students and society of its worth.

The relationship was characterized by mutual respect and acknowledgment of mutual gain among equals. The top-down, government-based regulatory or "ministry-of-education" approach to higher education that characterized much of the rest of the world was thought not to be needed in the United States. Subsequently, the United States has been lauded for its absence of a national "system" of higher education and for its restraint with regard to government control, with many observers pointing to the independence of U.S. higher education as a key factor in its national and international preeminence with regard to access and quality.

In 1965, the system of self-governance and self-regulation by institutions and accrediting organizations, accompanied by federal investment in higher education, was codified in the Higher Education Act (HEA). Although there have been a number of changes in the law over time, the fundamental features of the relationship have remained pretty much intact.

## Accountability and the Commission on the Future of Higher Education

But recently, a series of forces have been in play that could radically alter that relationship. Of greatest significance, in September 2005, the U.S. Secretary of Education established a Commission on the Future of Higher Education, a body composed of business, policy, and higher-education leaders that scrutinized the accessibility, affordability, and accountability of higher education. The work of the commission has constituted the most significant federal attention to higher education in the past 25 years.

The commission's final report was issued in September 2006, and its most dramatic impact to date has been on accreditation. It criticized accreditation severely, maintaining that it lacks rigor, fails to adequately address student achievement, does not encourage innovation, fails to provide a basis for comparisons among institutions, and does not effectively inform students and the general public about academic quality.

To remedy these perceived deficiencies, the commission offered several recommendations regarding accreditation. If enacted, the recommendations would call for institutions and accreditors to:

(1) Provide more evidence of student achievement and institutional performance and make this evidence primary when judging academic quality;
(2) Make this information easily understandable and readily accessible to the public;
(3) Develop various means to compare institutions or groups of institutions regarding their success in student achievement and institutional performance.

The commission's report did not address how the recommendations related to accreditation would be implemented. But the U.S. Department of Education was not content either with issuing the commission's report and then allowing it to suffer the sit-on-the-shelf fate common to similar documents, or with leaving action on its various recommendations to the higher-education community. Instead, the department chose to force the accountability issue. It is this decision, more than the substance of the commission's recommendations, that could upend the historic institution-accreditor-government relationship.

The Education Department turned to two readily available federal vehicles or levers for action. The first was the National Advisory Committee on Institutional Quality and Integrity (NACIQI, pronounced NaSEEkee), a body of individuals from outside government established in law to advise the Secretary of Education on the quality and effectiveness of accrediting organizations and recommend which organizations should be federally "recognized." Over the years, NACIQI members have included business leaders and state officials, as well as college and university presidents and students. Second, the department proposed changes in the regulations that it uses to implement the Higher Education Act's provisions that focus on federal recognition of accreditors. Because only institutions that are accredited by federally recognized accrediting organizations are eligible for the $100 billion in federal funds dispensed annually to colleges and universities, NACIQI and the accreditation regulations are indeed powerful levers through which the federal government can pressure higher education.

## Strengthening the Government's Role: NACIQI

Until recently, NACIQI's scrutiny of accrediting organizations proceeded within the framework of the relationship I described above. This included acceptance of the basic values on which accreditation operates: primary emphasis on mission when judging quality, the value of self study and peer review, and respect for institutional autonomy and academic freedom. Accrediting organizations themselves were free to meet the federal standards in various ways. In short, NACIQI accepted the collegial, peer-based features that had been part of accreditation since its inception.

But NACIQI's scrutiny is quickly becoming a key means by which to implement the commission's recommendations. Accreditation's emphasis on institutional mission as the appropriate driver of expectations regarding student achievement is being diminished by insistence that institutions are to be held accountable for at least a core group of "outcome indicators" for purposes of comparisons. These indicators are to be developed by accreditors but must be approved by NACIQI. In addition, and going beyond the commission's recommendations, deference to the academic judgment of institutions with regard to student achievement is being replaced by a demand that accreditors establish—and that NACIQI approve—minimum standards for student achievement that apply to all institutions reviewed by any accreditor. NACIQI has thus become the primary arena for a discussion of what counts as threshold quality.

Moreover, NACIQI is questioning the adequacy of the information given the public about accreditation reviews. The customary zone of discretion in which accrediting organizations work confidentially with their institutions is giving way, under NACIQI pressure, to demands that institutions and accreditors make public all information generated in the course of a review. There is discussion of accrediting organizations' providing more information about the reasons for decisions about accredited status, including both the strengths and weaknesses of an institution under review. While NACIQI has been emphasizing these issues for some time, there is—coincident with the commission's deliberations, papers, and report—a significant escalation in the pervasiveness and the intensity of NACIQI's focus on them.

Congress has taken exception to NACIQI's role in implementing the commission's recommendations in a way that bypasses the reauthorization of the Higher Education Act. At this writing, the Senate Health, Education, Labor, and Pensions Committee has just proposed a Higher Education Act measure that would replace NACIQI with a new body called the Accreditation and Institutional Quality and Integrity Advisory Committee. Its members would be appointed not by the Secretary of Education alone but rather jointly by the department, the Senate, and the House of Representatives.

## Strengthening Government Oversight: Negotiated Rulemaking

In addition to ratcheting up accountability expectations through the work of NACIQI, the Education Department also launched a process known as "negotiated rulemaking," to further expand the regulations to which federally recognized accreditors are subject. "Negotiated rulemaking" convenes individuals from the department and the higher-education community to address changes that the government would like to see in current regulations, in this case those used to implement the federal recognition standards and to review accrediting organizations.

A rulemaking panel was convened in February, approximately five months after the release of the commission's report in September 2006, and it concluded in June. It was, from the start, a means to reinforce the shift in NACIQI scrutiny and provide the department with stronger and additional tools by which to control accreditation, propelling the conversion of a collegial system answerable to the higher-education community into a regulatory system answerable to the federal government. If the department succeeds in establishing these new rules, the federalizing of accreditation will have advanced dramatically.

The department proposed rule changes that would position accreditors to replace quality indicators developed by colleges and universities with ones developed by accreditors and, most important, subject to federal control through NACIQI. The department also sought changes to enable the federal government to become directly involved in setting academic policy through rules that address, for example, how institutions deal with transfer of credit. Additionally, the rule changes would reaffirm NACIQI's broad scope of authority vis-à-vis the accrediting organizations that it reviews.

An accrediting organization coming before NACIQI in the future must be prepared for an extensive range of potential recommendations on subjects lying within the committee's purview— anything from instant renewal of recognition for the maximum of five years to instant removal of recognition. In a shot across the bow, NACIQI has already recommended the removal of recognition for one accrediting agency, the New England Association of Schools and Colleges' Commission on Technical and Career Institutions. At a prior meeting, the committee also recommended that the American Academy of Liberal Education be constrained from accrediting any additional institutions— a recommendation adopted by the Secretary of Education.

The use of NACIQI and the negotiated-rulemaking process are positioning the department to hold institutions and accreditors directly accountable to the government for academic quality, bypassing the accountability of institutions through their governing boards and accrediting organizations.

The rules of negotiated rulemaking stipulate that a failure to come to consensus on any proposed changes in the regulations means that the department can do what it likes with those regulations. No consensus having been reached in the negotiated-rulemaking process this year for accreditation and despite Congressional warnings that it was overstepping its authority in issuing rules that should be negotiated during the reauthorization of the Higher Education Act, the department at first seemed inclined to proceed with the rule changes. But at this writing, Education Secretary Margaret Spellings has just assured Sen. Lamar Alexander (R-TN) that she will not, at this time, issue rules that put in place department proposals on student learning, transparency, and other issues considered in negotiated rulemaking.

## Where Are Higher Education and Accreditation Going?

### The Accountability Climate Has Changed

The commission's report, however troublesome to some institutions and accreditors, does capture a public sentiment that goes well beyond the views of some commission members and the Education Department. It reflects the essentially utilitarian approach to the value of a higher-education degree that is now common in public discourse. Higher education is viewed as an increasingly and unreasonably costly investment in time and money, and earning a credential is seen as a necessary return on this investment, given the growing importance of at least some higher-education degrees for economic success and safety in contemporary society.

The report has also tapped into the strongly held beliefs of at least some government officials and others that higher education, long respected and even revered in this society, must be more accountable to the public. Indeed, our society is in the midst of a substantial escalation of expectations with regard to the accountability of many social institutions, including government itself, charities, churches, and corporations, as well as elementary and secondary education. It is becoming more and more difficult for colleges and universities, which spend hundreds of billions of public and private dollars annually, to argue persuasively that they should not be more accountable for what they produce with those dollars.

Finally, that many of the calls for accountability, as well as proposed solutions, are coming from the federal level is consistent with a growing perception that accountability requires federal intervention.

To the extent that we ignore anxiety over access and price, the escalation of accountability, and growing emphasis on federal solutions, we may imperil our future.

### Higher Education's Response

A great deal has been done by institutions and accreditors in recent years that is innovative, far-sighted, creative, and effective in responding to the call for enhanced accountability. These efforts, while various, share important features: They are voluntary, emphasize institutional mission as the basis for determining quality, engage faculty, and preserve institutional responsibility for academic quality.

Many colleges and universities have been focusing on greater accountability for a number of years. At the same time, all accreditors have embraced standards that call for institutions to report on student-learning outcomes and institutional performance. The accreditors' approach to learning outcomes varies, from holding institutions responsible both for identifying and collecting evidence of outcomes based on their missions, to accreditors making their own judgments about effectiveness of institutions, to accreditors and institutions voluntarily establishing shared student-achievement expectations. In response to these demands from accreditors and sometimes states, institutional activities have clustered around developing outcomes-based approaches to judging institutional effectiveness, including student achievement in general education and in the majors.

Currently, a number of institutions are working through their national associations to identify indicators about which they will all collect evidence and make comparisons. (See George Kuh's article in this issue mentioning the Voluntary System of Accountability being fashioned by the National Association of State Universities and Land-Grant Colleges and the American Association of State Colleges and Universities.) Other institutions are using national testing vehicles such as the Collegiate Learning Assessment or the Measure of Academic Proficiency and Progress, or measures of student engagement such as the National Survey of Student Engagement. Still others have created institutional profiles that contain information about performance and other dimensions of institutional operation, which are often shared with the public via Web sites and electronic portfolios.

Accreditors provide extensive information about how accreditation operates and are explicit about their standards, policies, and practices. A number offer aggregated information about the major characteristics of the institutions they accredit (e.g., degree levels, mission, and enrollment). A small number of accreditors require institutions to provide outcomes information to the public, although most do not provide this information themselves, and most do not make the reasons for their accreditation decisions public.

The fourth accountability issue, the establishment of threshold learning standards, has not yet been addressed by institutions or accreditors. Much work remains to be done in this area to sustain, on one hand, the primacy of institutional mission and, on the other, to establish some common expectations of when claims of quality based on mission are less than acceptable.

## Strengthening the Community Response to Accountability

However valuable, the current good work by institutions and accreditors concerning accountability is not enough. A significant escalation of effort by institutions and accrediting organizations is essential to address the current accountability challenges—a response that is more robust, immediate, and self-reflective. And more institutions and accreditors need to engage in this work.

More of them could, for instance, develop templates of student achievement and institutional performance. Additional programs that emphasize outcomes, public information, comparability, and threshold quality could be launched. More institutional funds could be invested in special accountability initiatives. Action-based research into student achievement could be ramped up. Search engines could be designed that assist students and the public in obtaining information about institutional performance. More work could be done to share effective practices across the higher-education community.

A more robust response to accountability demands also requires that institutions no longer assert that academic quality is solely a faculty issue and not under the purview of institutional leadership. Faculty engagement and judgment are vital, but the institution's leaders need to ensure swift action to improve any lackluster results, as well as participate in the development of quality indicators and the determination of what counts as success at, and for, their institutions.

Finally, a more robust response means that institutions and accreditors need to accept that any future claim to leadership regarding academic quality requires more investment in accountability.

## A New Relationship

Based on events of the last 20 or so months, what has been considered the appropriate relationship of institutions, accreditors, and the federal government is unlikely to continue. Concerns about access, demands that all social institutions be more accountable, and the growing societal investment in federal solutions to social concerns all require that the relationship be redefined.

Acknowledging that the federal government will continue to place greater emphasis on evidence of student learning and institutional performance, improved information for the public, comparability among institutions, and learning standards, I offer five suggestions as the basis for a new relationship to help preclude the federalizing of accreditation and the ensuing harm to institutions.

- *The federal government* needs to publicly reaffirm, whether through a resolution or in law, the leadership role of higher education in defining and judging academic quality and to acknowledge the importance and value of self-governance and the self-regulatory system of accreditation.

- *The federal government* needs to reconsider its oversight role in accreditation, either eliminating that role entirely or overhauling the recognition function. That overhaul would include rethinking how NACIQI members are selected and the extent to which its membership is representative of both higher education and the public, as well as auditing NACIQI's policies, procedures, and scope of operation. (As mentioned earlier, a Congressional panel has already proposed an alternative to NACIQI that may be included in the reauthorization legislation.)
- *Institutions* need to accelerate and enrich current efforts to produce evidence of performance, make this evidence available to the public, and accelerate efforts to address comparability among institutions and threshold expectations of quality.
- *Accrediting organizations* also need to quickly address these accountability issues and strengthen practices needed to ensure that accreditation standards addressing them are rigorously enforced.
- *Institutions and accrediting organizations* need to join forces to launch a compelling new symbol of their leadership in defining and judging quality in order to demonstrate their commitment to public accountability.

This last might be achieved through institutions and accreditors developing a national, voluntary, searchable database containing the performance profiles of accredited institutions across the country. This database should enable users to obtain immediate and reliable information about the quality of individual colleges or universities, as well as of groups of similar colleges and universities.

These suggestions for a new relationship assume that the federal government will continue to strengthen its expectations concerning accountability. However, these expectations would be met through institutions and accreditors that strengthen their investment in accountability as the warrant for their academic leadership. The federal government would not usurp higher education's primary responsibility for defining and judging academic quality, but rather would hold institutions and accreditors accountable for doing this work.

## Conclusion

For almost two years, a major effort has been under way to redistribute responsibility and authority for ensuring academic quality in higher education among the federal government, accreditors, and institutions. The primary target for these efforts has been the community of federally recognized accrediting organizations, and the primary goal has been to establish federal standards for defining and judging academic quality, a task heretofore left to institutions working with accrediting organizations. If successful, this effort will fundamentally undermine key features of higher education, especially its long history of self-governance and self-regulation.

A newly calibrated relationship is needed, and the five suggestions offered above provide a foundation on which to establish it. It will take courage and creativity on the part of institutions, accreditors, and the federal government, but it will be worth it. If the suggestions are adopted, the strength of American higher education will be sustained, even as its accountability is enriched.

*Judith Eaton is president of the Council for Higher Education Accreditation (CHEA). She previously served as chancellor of the Minnesota State Colleges and Universities and president of the Council for Aid to Education, the Community College of Philadelphia, and the Community College of Southern Nevada.*

# Called to Account: Analyzing the Origins and Spread of State Performance-Accountability Policies for Higher Education

MICHAEL K. MCLENDON, JAMES C. HEARN,
AND RUSS DEATON
*Vanderbilt University*

*Employing a theoretical framework derived from the policy innovation and diffusion literature, this research examines how variations over time and across state sociopolitical systems influence states' adoption of accountability policies in higher education. Specifically, factors influencing the adoption of three kinds of performance-accountability policies for public higher education in the period 1979–2002 were investigated. Findings from the event history analysis supported the authors' original hypotheses only in part; the primary drivers of policy adoption were legislative party strength and higher-education governance arrangements, but the direction of these influences varied across the policies studied.*

**Keywords:** *accountability, event history analysis, governance, higher education, policy adoption, state politics*

Over the past 20 years, the concept and practice of accountability in U.S. public higher education have undergone marked change. In an earlier era, accountability often referred to the design of statewide governance structures capable of accommodating the simultaneous need for institutional autonomy and external oversight of campus decision-making. The central question before policy-makers in this earlier era was: Precisely which activities and functions of public colleges and universities (e.g., academic programs, budgets, tuition setting, and so forth) should be dictated by the state and which should be left to the discretion of campuses? The accountability focus, therefore, was on the design of governance systems capable of effectively and efficiently regulating the flow of campus resources and the decisions of campus officials (Berdahl, 1971; McLendon, 2003; Volkwein, 1987). In the past two decades, however, accountability has begun to acquire new meaning and to assume different form.

The rhetoric of the "new accountability" movement in public higher education has called for a refocusing of attention on outcomes of campus activities, rather than the traditional focus on inputs alone (Burke, 2002, 2005a; National Commission on Accountability in Higher Education, 2005; Zumeta, 1998). In this new accountability era, no longer are structural arrangements or resource inputs the primary focus of state policymakers; increasingly, states are demanding performance by public colleges and universities. In scrutinizing outcomes, state policymakers have sought to influence institutional behavior for the purpose of improving institutional performance. For example, many states began experimenting in the 1980s and 1990s with new incentives systems designed to link campus resource inputs with desired performance outcomes. Under some of these new accountability regimes, the awarding of state financial resources became conditioned upon institutional performance in specified areas, such as student retention and graduation rates, undergraduate access, measures of institutional efficiency, student scores on licensure exams, job placement rates, faculty productivity, and campus diversity.

These new programs have taken three distinct forms. *Performance funding* is an approach that links state funding "directly and tightly to the performance of public campuses on individual indicators" (Burke & Minassians, 2003, p. 3). Under these policies, the relationship between performance and funding is predetermined and prescribed: if an institution meets a specified performance target, it receives a designated amount or percentage of state funding. The premier source of comparative data on the programs, Burke and associates' seven annual surveys of state performance-accountability policies, found that by 2003, 25 states had adopted a performance-funding program (Burke & Minassians, 2001, 2002, 2003; Burke & Modarresi, 1999; Burke, Rosen, Minassians, & Lessard, 2000; Burke & Serban, 1997, 1998). By contrast, *performance budgeting* permits governors, legislators and state board officials, "to consider campus achievement on performance indicators as one factor in determining allocations for public campuses" (Burke & Minassians, 2003, p. 3). In other words, the prospect of financial reward for institutional performance depends solely on the discretion of appropriators. By 2003, 35 states had established performance-budgeting programs. Recently, states have initiated a third performance-based policy for higher education, *performance reporting*. Performance reports provide for policymakers and the public indicators on institutional and statewide performance; unlike the other programs, however, performance reporting has no formal link to allocations. Thus, this third mechanism relies "on information and publicity rather than funding or budgeting to encourage colleges and universities to improve their performance" (Burke & Minassians, 2003, p. 5). As of 2003, 42 states had adopted a performance-reporting policy. The popularity of all three performance-accountability policies soared in the 1990s.

Close observers have attributed this new focus on performance accountability in higher education to a variety of factors. These factors include (a) structural changes in the U.S. economy (e.g., globalization), which brought pressure from the business community for campuses to maximize productivity and efficiency; (b) recent shifts in the theory and practice of public-sector governance, which, in the name of "reinventing government," valued decentralization, entrepreneurship, and a greater emphasis on markets, competitiveness, and the measurement of performance[1]; (c) the extreme financial pressures placed on state governments in the 1990s, which intensified higher education's competition with other budget priorities for increasingly limited state discretionary dollars; (d) the reform movement in K–12 education, which ratcheted up pressures for accountability across all educational sectors; (e) changes in state political leadership, which brought to office a new breed of elected official, one purported to be more sympathetic to the call for increased accountability in higher education; and (f) the failure of the earlier "voluntary assessment" movement in higher education to satisfy for these elected officials that public universities are capable on their own of meeting growing accountability demands (Burke, 2005b; Burke & Serban, 1997; Zumeta, 1998).

Yet nothing of a systematic, empirical nature is known about the roots or spread of performance policies in higher education. Indeed, with few exceptions the literature remains largely descriptive in nature, prescriptive in tone, and anecdotal in content.[2]

There are compelling reasons for rigorous empirical analysis of the determinants of state performance-accountability policies for higher education. By all accounts, the "new accountability" movement represents a milestone in the evolving campus-state relationship, one holding important implications for the financing and governance of public higher education and for the ways in which elected officials and citizens assess the value of the larger higher-education enterprise. Clearly, recent changes in the concept and practice of higher-education accountability have not been uniform across states, yet in initiating these new accountability regimes, many states have increased their institutional oversight in ways unprecedented in U.S. history.[3] The recent accountability movement in higher education also tracks closely with trends in other governmental domains that some observers have characterized as fundamentally reshaping the design and delivery of public-sector programs, both in the United States and abroad (Thompson & Riccucci, 1998). Along more academic lines, the recent proliferating of performance policies affords researchers an excellent opportunity to test general theories of governmental behavior in the specific context of higher education, where such theories have rarely been tested. Not all states have undertaken these reforms, nor have states pursued identical reform trajectories. Inevitably, therefore, questions arise as to which factors drove certain states to take the important step of adopting performance-oriented approaches to higher education. Which characteristics of the states and of their higher-education systems account for differences in the policy postures of the states? Why do states adopt performance policies for higher education at the times at which they do? To what extent do conventional explanations of policy adoption in the states hold in the specific case of the adoption of higher-education performance policies?

This article reports the results of an empirical investigation into these questions—that is, into the factors that have influenced the states to adopt performance-funding, performance-budgeting, and performance-reporting policies. We develop and test a theoretical model derived from the comparative state policy and politics literature. The model focuses on how variations over time and across state sociopolitical systems influence policy adoption in the higher-education arena. Specifically, we employ event history analysis (EHA) to examine how certain demographic, economic, organizational, and political characteristics of individual states, in concert with diffusion processes among states, influenced the adoption of performance policies during the period 1979–2002. Although this particular longitudinal analytic technique is relatively new to higher-education research, it is ideally suited for studying the kinds of dynamic social and political processes that often are at work in the adoption by states of new public policies (Berry & Berry, 1990; Box-Steffensmeier & Jones, 1997; DesJardins, 2003). In the sections to follow, we present our theoretical framework, study hypotheses, research design, analytic findings, and the conceptual implications of those findings.

## State Policy Innovation and Diffusion: A Theoretical Framework

Our investigation builds conceptually on the comparative state policy and politics literature, particularly theory and research on policy innovation and diffusion.[4] Policy innovation and diffusion research draws on theories of U.S. federalism in viewing the 50 states both as individual policy actors and as agents of potential mutual influence within a larger social system (Dye, 1990). It holds that states adopt the policies they do in part because of their internal sociodemographic, economic, and political characteristics and in part because of their ability to influence one another's behavior. In other words, any satisfactory explanation of state policy behavior must seek to account for both the intrastate (i.e., within-state) and the interstate (among-state) determinants of the behavior.

Social scientists have studied the determinants of state policy comparatively and systematically for at least 50 years. Most early investigations, those of the 1950s and early 1960s, examined levels of state expenditure on social services, focusing on the political correlates (e.g., malapportionment or political culture) of expenditures. In the mid-1960s important studies by Dye (1966), Hofferbert (1966), and others tilted debate in favor of economic-development interpretations of state policy. Regardless, however, of their specific explanatory focus, studies of this era generally shared the assumption that the critical drivers of state policy resided within individual states.

This assumption was first seriously challenged with the publication in 1969 of Walker's landmark study of policy diffusion among the states. Reasoning that levels of public expenditure alone were an inadequate measure of state governmental activity, Walker turned to a more fundamental decision of government: whether to initiate a policy in the first place. Observing that some states (e.g., New York, California, Wisconsin) had long held reputations as policy innovators, or as states to which their neighbors looked for ideas when crafting their own policies, Walker argued that state officials have good reason to emulate the policies of their neighbors, resulting in the spread of policies along regional lines. His rationale was twofold. First, building on the work of March and Simon (1958), Walker asserted that the lack of time, the absence of information, and the cognitive constraints of human beings might lead policymakers to borrow ideas (to "satisfice") in an attempt to simplify the process of choosing among complex alternatives. Second, Walker pointed to interstate competition as a source of policy emulation; states might compete with one another to achieve a competitive advantage or to avoid being disadvantaged relative to their peers. Consistent with his hypothesis, Walker's analysis of nearly 90 different policies adopted prior to 1965 revealed a pattern to the spread of public policies among states in which a regional leader adopted a given policy first, followed by neighboring states within the same geographic region. Walker's findings helped redirect scholarship away from models that focused solely on the internal attributes of states.

Berry and Berry (1990, 1992) reinvigorated research with their pioneering use of a powerful new analytic technique, EHA. In two influential studies, Berry and Berry applied event history analysis in predicting the probability that a state would adopt a lottery (1990) or a new tax (1992) in a given year. The studies yielded similar results: internal determinants and regional diffusion both proved to be statistically significant predictors of adoption. Berry and Berry's work sparked renewed interest in understanding the conditions that lead state governments to adopt new policies, and an impressive body of empirical work has accumulated in recent years on the determinants of state policy adoption. For example, Mintrom (1997) and Wong and Shen (2002) examined the spread of charter school policies. Mooney and Lee (1995) analyzed the adoption and spread of abortion regulation and death penalty laws. And Hays (1996) assessed the determinants of state reform of various civil and criminal statutes.

Yet, it is worthwhile to note that, overall, the empirical evidence in support of diffusion effects is mixed. Mooney's (2001) review of the literature, for example, found that only 50% of the 24 EHA models reported in studies of state policy diffusion published in "top political science journals in the 1990s contained positively and statistically significant coefficients" (p. 107) for the diffusion variable. Mooney (2001) also found that the early, landmark studies by Berry and Berry (1990, 1992) were biased toward finding a positive diffusion effect because they failed to use time controls to stabilize the hazard rate. Our application of the policy innovation and diffusion framework to study policy outcomes in public higher education provides an additional empirical test of diffusion in a domain where diffusion processes have rarely been studied (McLendon, Heller, & Young, 2005).

## Study Hypotheses

Our analysis of the adoption of higher-education performance policies in the states follows in the tradition of the studies by Walker (1969), Berry and Berry (1990, 1992) and others in conceptualizing state policy as arising potentially both from the internal characteristics of the states and the external diffusion forces among them. Specifically, we distilled from the literature 10 potential explanations for state adoption of new performance policies in higher education. In order of their presentation, these hypotheses point to various distal and proximal influences, including (1) long-term demographic conditions, (2) short-term economic climates, (3) legislative professionalism, (4) party strength in the legislature, (5) gubernatorial power, (6) partisan control of the governor's office, (7) growth in public-sector tuition levels, (8) growth in undergraduate enrollment levels, (9) centralized governance structures for higher education, and (10) interstate diffusion. As indicated in our following discussion, we chose some of the hypotheses (e.g., demographic and economic conditions, partisanship, and higher-education governance) because previous research on state policy innovation and diffusion has found them to be associated with patterns of governmental activity in other policy arenas. We selected other hypotheses (e.g., higher-education tuition and enrollment levels) in an effort to test specific assertions made in the higher-education literature about the origins of recent accountability mandates.

### Hypothesis I: States With Lower Levels of Educational Attainment Will Be More Likely to Adopt New Higher-Education Performance Policies

One of the early, robust findings of the comparative state policy literature was that socioeconomic development patterns seemed to account for much of the interstate variation in public policy (Dawson & Robinson, 1963; Dye, 1966; Walker, 1969). Classically, researchers associated higher levels of development, such as educational attainment, wealth, or industrialization, with higher levels of public expenditure. In the context of the adoption of new policies, often the rationale advanced was that higher levels of development provided states the requisite capacity (both human-capital and fiscal) for undertaking policy experimentation. Although recent studies seem to have dispelled the myth of economic determinism, our first hypothesis concerning the adoption of performance policies in higher education builds on previous research in asserting that development patterns may indeed help explain adoption.

We reconceptualize the relationship, however, as one in which states with lower (rather than higher) levels of educational attainment will be more likely to adopt new performance policies. Whereas previous research tended to treat educational attainment as a generic measure of a state's capacity or propensity to innovate, we view it as an indicator of the economic development needs in a given state and of the corresponding demands the state may place on higher education institutions to help remedy a development deficit. Over the past 20 years, policymakers increasingly have turned to higher education as an engine of economic development. Public colleges and universities are expected to contribute to economic development in part through their production of human capital. Because rising educational attainment levels correlate highly with economic growth and diversification, the twin tenets of many states' development strategies (Beeson & Montgomery, 1993), we hypothesize that pressures on public higher education to demonstrate its performance will be greatest in those states where levels of educational attainment are lowest.

## Hypothesis 2: States With Poorer Economic Climates Will Be More Likely to Adopt New Higher-Education Performance Policies

Whereas the previous explanation focuses on the long-term demographic patterns of states, our second hypothesis points to near-term economic conditions. Numerous studies have found evidence of a relationship between short-term economic conditions and the probability of states adopting certain new policies (Berry, 1990, 1992; Stream, 1999). What is more, many observers of the recent accountability movement in higher education have surmised that the new mandates may be driven in part by fluctuating economic conditions in the states (e.g., Burke, 2002). We hypothesize that states with poorer economic climates will have heightened incentive for ensuring that public agencies are making wise use of limited public resources, and thus will be more likely to initiate new performance regimes for higher education.

## Hypothesis 3: The More Professionalized a State Legislature, the Greater the Probability of the State Adopting New Higher-Education Performance Policies

Our third hypothesis points to the role of legislative professionalism as influencing the adoption of performance policies in higher education. Professionalism refers to certain institutional attributes of state legislatures, particularly session length, member pay, and number of staff. Legislatures that, like the U.S. Congress, meet in extended session, pay their members well, and provide ample staff, are deemed as professional institutions. Legislatures with session lengths of brief duration, low pay for members, and few staff are considered non-professionalized or, "citizen legislatures" (Squire, 2000).

The variation that exists in the professionalism of legislatures holds important implications for state policy. Professionalism can directly influence policy in that greater analytic capacity (i.e., more staff with which to study problems and find solutions and longer sessions in which to do so) tends to produce a higher volume of legislation. Professionalism also may influence policy innovation indirectly: professionalized settings tend to attract better-educated legislators, ones who may be more inclined to consider novel policy approaches (Barrilleaux, Holbrook, & Langer, 2002; Squire, 1992, 2000). Only a few studies have empirically examined the effects of legislative professionalism on state higher-education policy (Doyle, 2005; McLendon et al., 2005; Nicholson-Crotty & Meier, 2003). Because the formulating and implementing of new performance policies for higher education, however, would require state officials to consider complex, technical information about the performance of campuses and systems (e.g., indicators of institutional quality, student achievement, or administrative costs), we hypothesize that states whose legislatures possess greater analytical capacity will be more likely to adopt the policies.

## Hypothesis 4: The Higher the Proportion of Seats in a Legislature Held by Republicans, the Greater the Probability the State Will Adopt New Higher-Education Performance Policies

Although some keen observers of the performance-accountability movement in higher education have expressed skepticism concerning a relationship between partisanship and the emergence of the new accountability policies (e.g., Burke, 2002), we believe a reasoned argument can be made that party control of government institutions may help explain the policy behaviors of states. At a very broad level, a substantial literature indicates that party control can influence state policy outcomes, at least in some areas (Alt & Lowry, 2000; Barrilleaux & Bernick, 2003; Barrilleaux et al., 2002; Berry & Berry, 1990; Holbrook & Percy, 1992; Stream, 1999). Democratic Party strength, for instance, has been linked with higher levels of overall state spending, with higher levels of spending on education and welfare programs, and with abortion access and gay rights initiatives. Republicans, on the other hand, have been associated with regulatory and tax policies that are viewed as favorable to business interests and with opposition to lotteries and abortion access.[5] What is more, Republicans often are characterized as being ideologically suspicious of public bureaucracy, and as associated more closely than Democrats with themes of holding government to account. Because performance policies in higher education accord closely with these broader accountability themes, we hypothesize that states whose legislatures have a higher proportion of Republican members will be more likely to adopt new performance policies.

## Hypothesis 5: States Whose Governors Hold Stronger Institutional Powers of Office Will Be More Likely to Adopt New Higher-Education Performance Policies

Whereas our previous two hypotheses examined the role that legislatures may play in determining the performance-accountability policies of the states, our fifth and sixth hypotheses focus on the policy influence of governors. Although governors exert considerable influence in the separation-of-powers system that characterizes American state government, the precise extent of their influence on public policy processes and outcomes can vary from one state to the next, depending in part on the institutional powers governors possess (Beyle, 1999). In some states, governors wield relatively strong authority in the form of the line-item veto, broad appointment powers, and robust tenure potential; in other states, governors possess fewer formal instruments of policy control, thus limiting their influence. Some research finds that variation in the institutional powers of governors helps explain policy outcomes in the states (e.g., Beyle, 1999; Dometrius, 1987; Yates & Fording, 2005).

Although empirical research on the policy impacts of governors in higher education is sparse overall, there is limited case-study and survey research indicating that governors may have played an important role in the emergence in some states of performance-accountability policies (Burke, 2002, 2005a; Zumeta, 1998). This involvement seems reasonable on a number of levels. In the 1980s, many governors began charging that public college and university systems had neglected undergraduate education and had failed to be responsive to public concern over administrative bloat, faculty productivity, and college costs (Burke, 2005a; Mumper, 2001). In an era of increasing pressures on state budgets, governors would have had ample incentive to improve the performance of all executive agencies, including higher education. Whereas the performance programs of the 1990s may have provided governors a potential tool for turning these general concerns into concrete policy goals, their capability of doing so, we believe, would have depended on the extent of the governors' institutional powers to further those policy aims.[6]

## Hypothesis 6: States With Republican Governors Will Be More Likely to Adopt New Higher-Education Performance Policies

We believe that states whose governors are Republican will be more likely to establish new performance policies for higher education for much the same reason that Republican-leaning legislatures may be inclined toward adopting the policies. Namely, Republicans tend to be more closely associated than Democrats with policies that are implicitly suspicious of public bureaucracy or critical of the performance of public-sector organizations. Our sixth hypothesis, therefore, builds on our previous ones in asserting that Republican gubernatorial party control is likely to be an important source of influence in the establishment of new performance policies for higher education.

### Hypothesis 7: States Experiencing Rapid Growth in Undergraduate Tuition Levels Will Be More Likely to Adopt New Higher-Education Performance Policies

Whereas our previous propositions pointed to the socioeconomic and political landscapes of states as the primary drivers of adopting new performance policies, this seventh hypothesis identifies the first of two potential sources of influence within the higher-education arena: rapid growth in public-sector tuition levels. Tuition levels throughout higher education have risen steeply in recent decades, but tuition in some states has risen more sharply than in others (Hearn, Griswold, & Marine, 1996; Heller, 2001). We surmise that state officials may view escalating tuition levels as one indicator of the higher-education sector's lack of accountability and, thus, as a problem for which new accountability mandates seem a suitable solution. As noted, many elected officials believe that public higher education has failed to live within its means (i.e., failed to control costs and curtail administrative bloat) or to perform adequately its core mission (Heller, 2001; Mumper, 2001). State leaders, therefore, may interpret rapid tuition increases as tantamount to higher education placing untenable demands both on state budgets and on citizens, who worry they will be unable to afford college. In effect, rapid growth in undergraduate tuition levels may persuade state officials of the need for new performance policies to ensure institutional accountability.

### Hypothesis 8: States Experiencing Rapid Growth in Undergraduate Enrollment Levels Will Be More Likely to Adopt New Performance Policies

As is the case with tuition levels, states have experienced substantial increases in undergraduate enrollments, although the rate of growth across states has varied considerably. Because enrollment is weighted heavily in most states' funding formulas for higher education (Layzell & Lyddon, 1990), enrollment increases portend additional financial demands to be placed on the state. This condition may in turn ratchet pressures for higher-education institutions to demonstrate their wise use of limited public resources. We reason that the probability of a state adopting a new performance regime for higher education will be greater in those states experiencing rapid growth in undergraduate enrollment levels.

### Hypothesis 9: States With More Highly Centralized Higher-Education Governance Structures Will Be More Likely to Adopt New Performance Policies

Typologies typically portray the states as practicing one of several basic models of statewide governance of higher education. These models tend to be arrayed along a continuum representing the degree of centralized control by the state. Toward one end of the continuum lie consolidated governing boards, which analysts regard as the most centralized form of governance because they possess line authority over the academic and fiscal affairs of campuses. Toward the other end of the governance continuum lie several kinds of statewide coordinating boards, whose precise authority over institutional budgets and programs varies according to type but, in all cases, represent less direct control over local campuses. Importantly, these less powerful coordinating boards tend to have fewer staff resources than do their empowered counterparts. The extant literature conceptualizes the different higher-education governance structures as affording states different analytic capabilities for formulating higher-education policy (Berdahl, 1971; Hearn & Griswold, 1994; McGuinness, 1997; McLendon, 2003; Zumeta, 1996). Consolidated boards sometimes are theorized to increase the likelihood of a state "innovating" because such boards provide policymakers an abundance of analytic resources (i.e., more professional staff holding expertise in higher-education policy and finance) with which to search for new ideas and solutions (Hearn & Griswold, 1994). Several studies have found empirical support for a relationship between centralized governance and policy innovation in higher education (Hearn & Griswold, 1994; McLendon et al., 2005). Our ninth hypothesis draws on this literature in proposing that states with more centralized governance arrangements will be more likely to adopt new performance policies.

### Hypothesis 10: States Whose Neighbors Have Already Adopted a Higher-Education Performance Policy Will Be More Likely to Adopt the Same Policy

As we have noted, interstate diffusion is a particularly fertile area of research on comparative-state policy. Several distinct diffusion models exist. The most prevalent holds that states are most likely to emulate their immediate neighbors, meaning those with which they share a border (Berry & Berry, 1990; Mintrom, 1997). For example, Berry and Berry (1990) found that the probability a state would adopt a lottery was positively related to the number of states bordering it that had already adopted one. Although several studies have examined the relationship between geography and state higher-education policy (Hearn et al., 1996; Hearn & Griswold, 1994; Volkwein, 1987; Zumeta, 1996), only a single study—by McLendon et al. (2005)—has empirically assayed interstate diffusion pressures in higher education. Leading observers have suggested that diffusion-like forces also may have been at work in the emergence of performance policies for higher education. Notably, Burke (2002, p. xiv) has pointed to Tennessee's 1979 performance-funding program, the nation's first, as an "attractive and available model . . . ready-made for borrowing" by other states. Burke, in observing that "legislation by fax" was common practice in higher-education policymaking during the 1980s and 1990s, characterized the Tennessee program as a model that spread to "state capitols across the country" (p. 18). Our final hypothesis seeks empirically to assay this claim.

## Research Design

The purpose of our study was to examine the factors that influenced states to establish new higher-education performance policies. Because our interest was in examining governmental behavior across states and over time, our investigation demanded a dataset that could accommodate both the spatial and temporal dimensions of the behavior (i.e., the adoption of new accountability mandates). We therefore developed a longitudinal dataset that incorporated annual indicators of the conditions we hypothesized would influence adoption of the policies over the period 1979–2002.

### Variables and Measures

Our analysis employed a 47-state dataset. Consistent with similar studies in the field (Berry & Berry, 1990; Mintrom, 1997), we dropped Alaska, Hawaii, and Nebraska from our analysis. We excluded Alaska and Hawaii because their noncontiguity to other states precludes a meaningful assessment of diffusion, a key conceptual interest of ours. We excluded Nebraska because the state's unique nonpartisan legislature poses problems for the testing of some political variables. The practice of omitting Nebraska from analyses in which partisan control is a critical theoretical consideration is commonplace in the literature.[7]

We assembled data on the 47 states from a variety of secondary sources. The study's dependent variables were whether a state adopted a performance-funding, performance-budgeting, and performance-reporting policy in a given year. We gleaned the adoption dates of these policies from the seven national surveys conducted by Burke et al. From 1979 to 2002, 25 states adopted performance-funding policies, so our total number of dependent observations for this policy category was 25. The total number of dependent observations for the performance-budgeting policy category was 34. The total number of dependent observations for the performance-reporting policy category was 42.

The independent-variable indicators included in our analysis correspond to the 10 hypotheses presented earlier in the article. Those variables are educational attainment, change in gross state product, legislative professionalism, percentage of Republicans in the legislature, gubernatorial power, Republican gubernatorial control, change in tuition at state flagship universities, change in public higher-education enrollment, the presence of consolidated governing boards, and neighbor diffusion.

The independent variable *educational attainment* is a time-dependent variable indicated by the percentage of a state's population age 25 and higher that had completed 4 or more years of college. This variable was lagged 1 year. We used decennial U.S. Census Bureau data for 1990 and 2000, and data from Current Population Surveys for other years. The data can be found at http://www.postsecondary.org. Because data were not available for all states for all years, values for years prior to 1989 were held constant at their 1989 levels.

*Change in gross state product* is an annual time-dependent variable that measures the 3-year average change in a state's gross product, lagged 1 year. The source for gross state product is the U.S. Department of Commerce Bureau of Economic Analysis, found at http://www.bea.gov.

*Legislative professionalism* is a time-dependent variable that measures the degree of professionalism of a state's legislature. Legislative professionalism is a metric combining salary levels, staff size, and legislative session length; higher values indicate a higher level of professionalism. Professionalism is calculated in year *t*, and therefore is unlagged. Our data source for years 1979–1987 is King (2000). For years 1988–1994, we used Squire (1992). The source for years 1995–2001 was Squire (2000). Squire also provided data for 2002 directly to us.

*Percent Republican legislature* is an annual time-dependent variable that indicates the proportion of major party legislators across both chambers of a state's legislature that is Republican.[8] Percent Republican membership, like legislative professionalism, was calculated in year *t*, and thus unlagged. Data for years 1979-2000 came from Klarner's data set, "Measurement of Partisan Balance of State Government," which is available at http://www.unl.edu/SPPQ/journal_datasets/klarner.html. Klarner provided data for 2001–2002 directly to us.

*Gubernatorial power* is a time-dependent variable that measures the degree of a governor's institutional powers. This variable is a metric combining scores on six individual indices of gubernatorial power, including the governor's tenure potential, appointment power, budget power, veto power, extent to which the governor's party also controls the legislature, and whether the state provides for separately elected executive branch officials. Gubernatorial power is unlagged. Data for this variable came from Beyle's ratings of gubernatorial power for the years, 1980, 1988, 1994, 1998, and 2001. These data can be found at http://www.unc.edu/~beyle/gubnewpwr.html.

*Republican governor* is an annual time-dependent variable that indicates whether a state had a Republican governor in a given year. Republican governor, like previous political variables, was calculated in year *t*, and thus unlagged. The source for this variable was the Klarner dataset.

*Change in public tuition* is an annual time-dependent variable that measures the 3-year average change in tuition at each state's flagship institution, lagged 1 year. The source for the tuition variable was Postsecondary Education Opportunity, a periodical series that tracks annual changes to tuition at state flagship institutions. The source for these data is http://www.postsecondary.org/.

*Change in public enrollment* is an annual time-dependent variable that measures the 3-year average change in public higher-education enrollment, lagged 1 year. The source for the enrollment variable was the National Center of Education Statistics. These data can be found at http://nces.ed.gov/programs/digest/d02/lt3.asp#c3a_1.

*Consolidated governing board* indicates whether the state had this type of statewide higher-education governance arrangement, according to McGuinness's (1985, 1988, 1994, 1997) five-fold typology of governance (i.e., planning agency, advisory coordinating board, regulatory coordinating board without budget authority, regulatory coordinating board with budget authority, and consolidated governing board). We used a dummy variable indicating the presence of a consolidated governing board.[9]

*Diffusion of performance policy* is an annual time-dependent variable defined as the percentage of a state's contiguous neighbors that had already adopted a particular policy in the year in which a given state adopted the policy, with a 1-year lag. The variable was hand calculated by the researchers based on the adoption dates of each dependent variable.

## Analytic Methods

We conducted our analysis across state-year units using EHA, a regression-like technique that has grown increasingly prevalent in the social sciences (particularly in political science) for use in studying dynamic change processes (Allison, 1984; Box-Steffensmeier & Jones, 1997, 2004;

DesJardins, 2003; Yamaguchi, 1991). EHA examines both whether and when a particular event occurred. Specifically, the method permits the researcher to study how the units of analysis make transitions from one state of being to another, and how variation in the values of the independent variables influence that change. In EHA, the dependent variable measures the duration of time that units spend in a state before experiencing some event. A model can be created that permits the analyst to make inferences concerning the influence of certain independent variables on the length of the duration and the occurrence of the event (Box-Steffensmeier & Jones, 1997; DesJardins, 2003). For those interested in modeling state-level policy phenomena, EHA's distinct advantages are that the method effectively addresses problems of right-censoring and that the coefficient estimates EHA generates can be used to calculate predicted probabilities that a state with certain attributes will adopt a policy in a given year (Berry & Berry, 1990; Box-Steffensmeier & Jones, 2004; Mintrom, 1997).

We employed a particular kind of EHA model, a discrete-time logit model for nonrepeatable events (Alison, 1984; Box-Steffensmeier & Jones, 1997; DesJardins, 2003; Yamaguchi, 1991). In our analysis, we divided time into distinct units, measured in calendar years, within which the event (a state's adoption of each of the three policies) either occurred or did not. We were then interested in tracking the history of what happened to a state $i$ in year $t$. We assumed that a state's adoption of a performance policy was a case of nonrepeatable one-way transition, meaning a transition from one state of being to another state of being that occurs at most once for each subject in the dataset. Once a state adopted a performance policy, the state could not repeat the event or take it back.[10] Our use of years as a measure of time and our assumption of nonrepeatable events made the discrete-time logit model of EHA an appropriate analytic choice.

Two essential features of EHA are the risk set and the hazard rate. The risk set is the set of states that are at risk of event occurrence at each point in time (Allison, 1984; Box-Steffensmeier & Jones, 1997; DesJardins, 2003). Following the classic work of Berry and Berry (1990, 1992) and others (e.g., Mintrom, 1997), we assumed that a state was not at risk of adopting a particular policy until at least one state had adopted it. Therefore, our dataset on performance-funding policies began in 1979, the year Tennessee adopted the nation's first such program. Our data set on performance-budgeting policies began in 1984, the year Illinois established its program.[11] Our dataset on performance-reporting policies began in 1982, the year Alabama adopted the first such program. For each of the three policies we studied, the risk set began with the total number of states and was reduced each year by the number of events (i.e., states adopting the particular policy) that occurred the previous year. When a state adopted a policy, it was no longer at risk of adopting and we removed it from the data set. The risk set, therefore, shrank over time.[12]

Once we determined the risk set, we then calculated the hazard rate. The hazard rate is the fundamental dependent variable in an event history model. It is an unobserved variable that controls both the occurrence and timing of events (DesJardins, 2003). Formally, therefore, the discrete-time EHA models we employed attempted to explain the hazard rate of adoption or, the probability that a state would adopt a particular policy (i.e., experience the "event") in year $t$, given that it had not adopted the policy (i.e., "survived") up to that point in time. We estimated the hazard rate by dividing the number of events in year $t$ by the risk set in a given year $t$.

To estimate our coefficients and to test the predictive power of our various hypotheses, we specified separate models for performance funding, performance budgeting, and performance reporting. Because of the relatively small number of events in each of our three analyses, we used the complementary log-log link function (Buckley & Westerland, 2004). All three of our models took the simple form of

$$h(t) = 1 - \exp\left(-e^{x\beta}\right),$$

where $h(t)$ is the hazard rate of adoption and the array $x\beta$ represents the independent variables.

We expanded the array of independent variables, represented by $x\beta$, to the full equation below, allowing us to predict the effect of the explanatory variables on the hazard rate of adoption for each of the three performance-accountability policies we studied:

$$ADOPT_{i,t} = b_1 EDATTAIN_{i,t} + b_2 CHANGEGSP_{i,t}$$
$$+ b_3 LEGPROF_{i,t} + b_4 LEGREPUB_{i,t}$$
$$+ b_5 GOVPOWER_{i,t}$$
$$+ b_6 GOVREPUB_{i,t}$$
$$+ b_7 CHANGETUITION_{i,t}$$
$$+ b_8 CHANGEENROLL_{i,t}$$
$$+ b_9 GOVERNANCE_{i,t}$$
$$+ b_{10} DIFFUSION_{i,t}$$
$$+ TIMECONTROLS_{i,t}$$

where $ADOPT_{i,t}$ is the hazard rate of adoption in year $t$ for state $i$.

Two potential problems sometimes associated with discrete-time event history models are spatial and temporal dependence. We therefore undertook several established procedures and performed a series of diagnostic tests to ensure that our modeling did not violate any of the assumptions of the particular form of EHA that we employed. To address the potential problem of spatial dependence, for example, our models employed robust standard errors. We also corrected for temporal dependence using the spline technique developed by Beck, Katz, and Tucker (1998) and the code developed by Tucker (1999) for use with STATA 8. The Beck, Katz, and Tucker method uses a series of cubic splines to correct for potential problems associated with the temporally dependent nature of observations in state-year data sets. We detected none of the problems that would have been associated with temporal dependence.

## Empirical Findings

Using the models specified above, our analysis reveals an interesting and somewhat surprising set of findings that support our hypotheses only in part. Our first finding involves the power of our theoretical framework to explain adoption respectively for the three different state higher-education performance policies. While our analyses of influences on the adoption of performance-funding and performance-budgeting policies produced statistically significant and substantively interesting results, as described below, we found no statistically significant evidence of influences on the adoption of performance-reporting policies. It appears that, whereas select propositions from our theory of state policy adoption are significant predictors of performance funding and performance budgeting, performance-reporting policies are insensitive to all of the hypothesized influences. Therefore, no descriptive data or EHA results are presented for performance reporting in the following material.

Table 1 reports definitions, measures, and descriptive statistics for the study's independent-variable indicators and for the two remaining dependent outcomes: performance-funding and performance-budgeting policies. Table 2 presents the intercorrelations for the variables in our performance-funding model. Table 3 contains data on the risk sets and hazard rates for performance-funding policies, and Figure 1 presents the performance-funding hazard rate in graphical form. Table 4 presents the intercorrelations for the variables in our performance-budgeting model. Table 5 contains data on the risk sets and hazard rates for performance budgeting; Figure 2 presents graphically the performance-budgeting hazard rate. Finally, Table 6 reports the statistical results of our EHA of performance-funding and performance-budgeting policies.

Our second key finding pertains to the specific explanations for performance-funding and performance-budgeting policies. Overall, the model results indicate that the primary drivers of state adoption of the two policies were legislative party strength and higher-education governance arrangements. For both policies, the percent of a state's legislature that was Republican and the presence of a consolidated governing board affected the probability of adoption in statistically significant ways. Notably, however, the direction of the two variables' effects were opposite for the two outcomes. For the category of performance funding, higher percentages of Republican legislators in a state and the absence of a consolidated governing board increased the probability of a state adopting such a policy in a given year, at statistical significance levels of $p \leq .05$ and of $p \leq .01$, respectively. By contrast, lower percentages of Republican legislators and the presence of a consolidated governing board significantly increased the probability of a state adopting a performance-budgeting policy. Expressed in somewhat different terms, states in which Republicans held a greater number of seats in the legislature and where campus governance was less centralized were more likely to adopt new performance-funding policies, whereas states in which Republicans held a fewer number of legislative seats and where higher-education governance was more centralized were more likely to adopt performance-budgeting policies.[13]

## Discussion and Implications

This study began as an effort to understand the conditions under which state governments adopt new performance-accountability policies for public higher education. We conceptualized the adoption of the policies to be a function of certain demographic, economic, and political characteristics of the states, enrollment and tuition pressures within the higher-education sector, higher-education governance arrangements, and interstate diffusion forces. Using EHA, we tested the predictive power of these hypothesized influences on the adoption of performance-funding, performance-budgeting, and performance-reporting policies during the period 1979–2002. Our analysis revealed several conceptually provocative findings as well as a few surprises. Because those findings have few parallels in the higher-education literature, the discussion below focuses on the conceptual implications of our work and on promising avenues for research.

Of course, one important question involves the inability of our explanatory variables to predict the emergence of performance-reporting policies, while successfully predicting performance-funding and performance-budgeting policies. One interpretation might hold that performance-reporting requirements are products of universally increasing pressures for accountability, an exogenous trend unrelated to our specific model. Alternatively, given the very recent emergence of these policies, one might view the lack of relationships as revealing performance-reporting mandates as artifacts of failed reform efforts toward either performance funding or budgeting, that is, as a political compromise acceptable to proponents and opponents of performance funding and budgeting. Either scenario might explain the absence of statistical influences here, in the face of detectable influences on our other two performance policies.

Turning to the results associated with performance funding and budgeting, one finding with important conceptual implications involves the intriguing effects of Republican legislative strength and higher-education governance structure on policy-adoption patterns. With respect to party strength, why might a larger Republican presence in state legislatures be associated with the adoption of new performance-funding programs but a smaller Republican presence be associated with performance-budgeting initiatives? And, given those findings, why might levels of Republican membership be unrelated to performance-reporting policies? We believe the answer may rest partially in the differing natures of the three policies and in underlying differences in the beliefs of the two parties.

We were somewhat naive to suggest in our initial hypotheses that partisanship and other independent variables would have uniform directional influences on the three performance policies. In fact, the policies differ substantively from one another in important ways, which, we now believe, hold implications for their attractiveness to the parties. Of the three policies, performance funding is said to have the sharpest "teeth" because this program ties budget allocations tightly to campus performance—to the extent that campuses may actually lose funding should they fail to

## Table 1. Variable Descriptions and Summary Statistics

| Variable | Description | Performance funding | | Performance budgeting | |
|---|---|---|---|---|---|
| | | Mean | Standard deviation | Mean | Standard deviation |
| State adoption of account-ability policy | Dummy variable (yes = 1; no = 0) indicating whether a state adopts an account-ability policy in this year | 0.03 | 0.16 | 0.05 | 0.21 |
| Educational attainment | Percentage of state's popu-lation age 25 and higher that completed 4 or more years of college | 21.05 | 4.36 | 21.37 | 4.53 |
| Gross state product change | Annual measure of 3-year average change in amount of gross state product (millions of dollars), lagged 1 year | 6.98 | 3.05 | 6.43 | 2.63 |
| Legislative professionalism | Index of legislative profes-sionalism; continuous variable with higher val-ues indicating higher level of professionalism | 22.04 | 14.52 | 21.62 | 14.69 |
| Percent Republican legislature | Annual measure of percent-age of seats across both chambers of state's legis-lature that is Republican | 42.11 | 17.85 | 43.52 | 16.38 |
| Gubernatorial power | Index measure indicating degree of governor's in-stitutional powers | 3.56 | 0.60 | 3.55 | 0.53 |
| Republican governor | Annual dummy variable in-dicating whether Republi-can held governor's office | 0.47 | 0.50 | 0.48 | 0.50 |
| Tuition change | Annual measure of 3-year average change in tuition at state's flagship univer-sity, lagged 1 year | 8.27 | 4.58 | 8.65 | 4.64 |
| Enrollment change | Annual measure of 3-year average change in public higher education enroll-ment, lagged 1 year | 1.62 | 2.27 | 1.42 | 2.42 |
| Consolidated governing board | Dummy variable (yes = 1; no = 0) indicating whether state has consoli-dated governing board | 0.45 | 0.50 | 0.39 | 0.49 |
| Diffusion of performance policy | Proportion of neighbors with performance policy, lagged 1 year | 11.44 | 18.39 | 13.99 | 23.24 |

*Note.* See the section "*Variables and Measures*" for a thorough description of the corresponding data sources for each variable. The summary statistics for these policies are different because the performance-funding and performance-budgeting sample commencement years are different.

perform adequately. Performance budgeting, by contrast, is a comparatively weaker program that may offer elected officials a "political escape" (Burke, 2002, p. 25) from implementing a system of high-stakes rewards and punishments for higher education: "Governors and legislators can claim credit for considering performance in budgeting without the controversy of altering campus allo-cations." Lastly, performance reporting relies solely on information as a lever for encouraging

**Table 2. Intercorrelations for Performance Funding**

| Correlations—Performance funding dataset | Educational attainment | % change GSP | Legislative professionalism | % Republican legislature | Gubernatorial power | Republican governor | % change tuition | % change enrollment | Consolidated governing board |
|---|---|---|---|---|---|---|---|---|---|
| Educational attainment | 1.000 | | | | | | | | |
| % change in gross state product | 0.064 | 1.000 | | | | | | | |
| Legislative professionalism | 0.169 | 0.043 | 1.000 | | | | | | |
| % Republican legislature | 0.271 | −0.030 | −0.101 | 1.000 | | | | | |
| Gubernatorial power | 0.173 | 0.035 | 0.326 | 0.184 | 1.000 | | | | |
| Republican governor | 0.021 | −0.094 | 0.054 | 0.205 | −0.036 | 1.000 | | | |
| % change in tuition | −0.029 | −0.134 | 0.126 | −0.074 | 0.080 | 0.009 | 1.000 | | |
| % change in public enrollment | −0.133 | 0.183 | −0.194 | −0.013 | −0.116 | −0.090 | −0.230 | 1.000 | |
| Consolidated governing board | −0.207 | −0.021 | −0.352 | 0.208 | −0.086 | 0.011 | −0.153 | 0.118 | 1.000 |
| Diffusion | 0.035 | −0.188 | −0.151 | −0.142 | −0.205 | 0.118 | 0.170 | −0.123 | 0.132 |

**Table 3. Risk Sets, Hazard Rates, and States Adopting Performance-Funding Policies**

| Year | States Adopting performance funding | Number of adoptions | Cumulative adoptions | Risk set | Hazard rate |
|---|---|---|---|---|---|
| 1979 | TN | 1 | 1 | 47 | 0.021 |
| 1980 | | 0 | 1 | 46 | 0.000 |
| 1981 | | 0 | 1 | 46 | 0.000 |
| 1982 | | 0 | 1 | 46 | 0.000 |
| 1983 | | 0 | 1 | 46 | 0.000 |
| 1984 | | 0 | 1 | 46 | 0.000 |
| 1985 | CT | 1 | 2 | 46 | 0.022 |
| 1986 | | 0 | 2 | 45 | 0.000 |
| 1987 | | 0 | 2 | 45 | 0.000 |
| 1988 | | 0 | 2 | 45 | 0.000 |
| 1989 | | 0 | 2 | 45 | 0.000 |
| 1990 | | 0 | 2 | 45 | 0.000 |
| 1991 | MO | 1 | 3 | 45 | 0.022 |
| 1992 | KY | 1 | 4 | 44 | 0.023 |
| 1993 | | 0 | 4 | 43 | 0.000 |
| 1994 | FL, CO, MN | 3 | 7 | 43 | 0.070 |
| 1995 | OH | 1 | 8 | 40 | 0.025 |
| 1996 | SC | 1 | 9 | 39 | 0.026 |
| 1997 | WA, SD, OK, LA, IN | 5 | 14 | 38 | 0.132 |
| 1998 | CA, IL | 2 | 16 | 33 | 0.061 |
| 1999 | KS, TX, NY, NJ, VA | 5 | 21 | 31 | 0.161 |
| 2000 | OR, ID, PA | 3 | 24 | 26 | 0.115 |
| 2001 | AR | 1 | 25 | 23 | 0.043 |
| 2002 | | 0 | 25 | 22 | 0.000 |

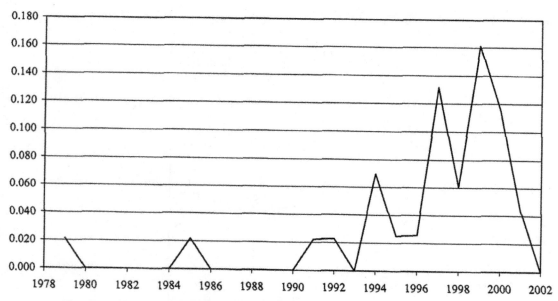

**Figure 1. Empirical Hazard Rate of Performance-Funding Policy Adoption**

campus performance. Because these policies provide state officials no real increased authority, Burke (2002) has characterized them as a symbolic rather than substantive reform that, once adopted, have been ignored in many capitols.

Building on our earlier argument, that Republicans tend to be ideologically suspicious of public bureaucracy and thus ally themselves (more than do Democrats) with themes of government

**Table 4. Intercorrelations for Performance Budgeting**

| Correlations—Performance budgeting dataset | Educational attainment | % change GSP | Legislative professionalism | % republican legislature | Gubernatorial power | Republican governor | % change tuition | % change enrollment | Consolidated governing board |
|---|---|---|---|---|---|---|---|---|---|
| Educational attainment | 1.000 | | | | | | | | |
| % Change in gross state product | 0.058 | 1.000 | | | | | | | |
| Legislative professionalism | 0.188 | 0.086 | 1.000 | | | | | | |
| % Republican legislature | 0.294 | −0.047 | −0.093 | 1.000 | | | | | |
| Gubernatorial power | 0.135 | 0.019 | 0.302 | 0.108 | 1.000 | | | | |
| Republican governor | 0.001 | −0.067 | 0.047 | 0.212 | −0.056 | 1.000 | | | |
| % change in tuition | −0.044 | −0.103 | 0.137 | −0.152 | 0.128 | −0.029 | 1.000 | | |
| % change in public enrollment | −0.192 | 0.101 | −0.214 | −0.051 | −0.178 | −0.108 | −0.237 | 1.000 | |
| Consolidated governing board | −0.247 | −0.025 | −0.310 | 0.216 | −0.055 | 0.089 | −0.098 | 0.132 | 1.000 |
| Diffusion | 0.035 | −0.155 | −0.142 | 0.109 | −0.143 | 0.132 | −0.270 | −0.089 | −0.133 |

**Table 5. Risk Sets, Hazard Rates, and States Adopting Performance-Budgeting Policies**

| Year | States Adopting performance budgeting | Number of adoptions | Cumulative adoptions | Risk set | Hazard rate |
|---|---|---|---|---|---|
| 1984 | IL | 1 | 1 | 47 | 0.021 |
| 1985 | | 0 | 1 | 46 | 0.000 |
| 1986 | | 0 | 1 | 46 | 0.000 |
| 1987 | | 0 | 1 | 46 | 0.000 |
| 1988 | IN | 1 | 2 | 46 | 0.022 |
| 1989 | | 0 | 2 | 45 | 0.000 |
| 1990 | | 0 | 2 | 45 | 0.000 |
| 1991 | NE, OK | 2 | 4 | 45 | 0.044 |
| 1992 | MS | 1 | 5 | 43 | 0.023 |
| 1993 | GA | 1 | 6 | 42 | 0.024 |
| 1994 | FL | 1 | 7 | 41 | 0.024 |
| 1995 | KS, WV | 2 | 9 | 40 | 0.050 |
| 1996 | CO, ID, NC, IA | 4 | 13 | 38 | 0.105 |
| 1997 | SD, LA, RI | 3 | 16 | 34 | 0.088 |
| 1998 | OR, ME | 2 | 18 | 31 | 0.065 |
| 1999 | WA, NM, MO, MI, VA, NJ, CT, MA | 8 | 26 | 29 | 0.276 |
| 2000 | CA, NV, UT, WI, AL, MD | 6 | 32 | 21 | 0.286 |
| 2001 | | 0 | 32 | 15 | 0.000 |
| 2002 | VT, AR | 2 | 34 | 15 | 0.133 |

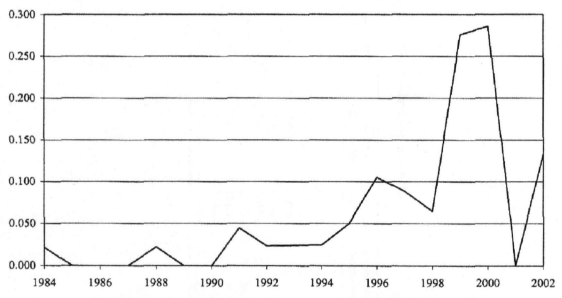

**Figure 2. Empirical Hazard Rate of Performance-Budgeting Policy Adoption**

accountability, Republicans may favor performance-funding policies because these initiatives offer elected officials the strongest leverage for ratcheting up accountability pressures within the large public bureaucracy of higher education. On the other hand, Democrats, being less fundamentally inclined to a government-accountability agenda, may favor performance-budgeting policies because these policies demonstrate a rhetorical commitment to accountability without the triggers that mechanically penalize campuses. Hence, one finds adoption of performance-funding policies in states where Republicans exert greater legislative influence, and adoption of performance-budgeting policies in states where Republican influence is weaker (and Democratic influence, by definition,

**Table 6. Event History Analysis of State Adoption of Performance-Funding and Performance-Budgeting Policies**

| Variable | Performance funding | | Performance budgeting | |
|---|---|---|---|---|
| | exp(B) | SE | exp(B) | SE |
| Educational attainment | 0.936 | 0.057 | 1.044 | 0.044 |
| % change in gross state product | 1.106 | 0.076 | 1.027 | 0.099 |
| Legislative professionalism | 1.004 | 0.016 | 1.005 | 0.010 |
| % Republican legislature | 1.033* | 0.014 | 0.970** | 0.011 |
| Gubernatorial power | 1.318 | 0.574 | 0.749 | 0.268 |
| Republican governor | 1.575 | 0.742 | 0.884 | 0.327 |
| % change in tuition | 1.043 | 0.026 | 0.934 | 0.052 |
| % change in public enrollment | 1.171 | 0.122 | 1.037 | 0.069 |
| Consolidated governing board | 0.111** | 0.078 | 2.630* | 1.180 |
| Diffusion | 0.984 | 0.024 | 1.000 | 0.013 |
| Number of observations | 975 | | 715 | |
| −2 × log likelihood | 175.92 | | 219.68 | |
| Chi-squared (df) | 66.9 (9) | | 46.8 (11) | |
| P > chi-squared | 0.000 | | 0.000 | |

** $p > .01$; * $p > .05$.

is greater). Because performance-reporting policies are so insubstantial, they may offer neither party the substantive or rhetorical advantages associated with passage of a performance regime for higher education, and thus are linked exclusively with neither party.

We offer another potential explanation for our partisanship finding, here drawing on the growing literature on congressional oversight of the executive branch (Aberbach, 1990; Ogul & Rockman, 1990). Congressional oversight refers to efforts by Congress, its committees, or its members to learn about and to control executive-branch behavior. Research has built heavily on theories of bureaucracy and principal–agent relations. Legislatures (principals) inevitably must delegate authority to bureaucracy (agents) for the implementing of policies. Yet, those to whom power is delegated acquire advantages, such as the latitude to implement in ways that are more or less consistent with the wishes of the principal.

Although assessments vary as to the precise nature of the trend, most scholars agree that Congressional oversight of the bureaucracy has increased substantially in recent decades. One explanation is the changing party control of Congress. Smith (2003) notes that Democrats, because of their majority status, were able to control the legislation that resulted in the creation and growth of the modern federal bureaucracy, along with the implementation process that followed. He reasons that Republicans, when they control Congress, might be more aggressive in their oversight of that Democratic-shaped bureaucracy. The assumption in this argument appears to be, while all principals share a vested interest in monitoring independent-minded agents, principals previously in the Congressional minority will, once they achieve the majority, seek to oversee more actively the programs of the opposition, the former majority. Phrasing it differently, we might posit that new principals are likely to oversee the policies and programs established by old principals more rigorously than the old principals oversaw their own policies and programs.

We see conceptual leverage in these ideas for explaining partisan effects on higher-education performance policies. Clearly, the three policies we studied can be viewed as a form of legislative oversight of the public higher-education bureaucracy: to varying degrees, the policies represent efforts by legislators to monitor the activities of higher education for purposes of learning about the bureaucracy's behavior and, possibly, of remedying deviations from legislative preferences. The proposition, developed above, that parties should be expected to conduct increased oversight of their opponent's policies, also seems quite plausible in this context. Measured in terms of appropriations and enrollments, the higher-education bureaucracy grew most rapidly from the late 1950s through the mid-1970s, when Democrats' share of state legislative seats was at its peak. Thus, it seems reasonable that legislative interest in more stringent forms of oversight of public higher education (i.e., performance-funding policies) began growing in the 1980s and 1990s, when Republican state legislative membership climbed appreciably.

Our conceptualizing, therefore, has led us to two different interpretations of our empirical finding regarding political parties and performance policies in higher education. Whereas the former explanation emphasizes differences in the ideological dispositions of the two major parties, the latter explanation focuses on the conditions under which parties may increase their oversight of bureaucracy. These interpretations are admittedly speculative. Yet the finding seems to us sufficiently interesting to merit additional scholarship. To date, researchers largely have ignored the relationship between partisan control of government institutions and higher-education policy outcomes in the states; our findings suggest that such focus is warranted indeed.

We turn to the equally curious relationships we found between governance structures and policy adoption; namely, that states without consolidated governing boards were more likely to adopt performance-funding policies, whereas states with the boards were more likely to adopt performance-budgeting policies. Our initial governance hypothesis was grounded in a higher-education literature that tends to differentiate between governance structures on the basis of the analytic capabilities they afford policymakers (i.e., centralized arrangements provide greater analytical resources, which in turn spur policy innovation). Our analysis suggests, however, that scholars may need to rethink the underlying assumptions linking governance structures with state policy outcomes for higher education. Specifically, theory and research may need to shift focus from the *information* boards provide to the *interests* boards protect. In reconceptualizing governance effects, we build on Lowry's (2001) application of principal–agent theory to state higher-education policy.

Lowry hypothesized that statewide governance structures for higher education should help explain variation in the tuition pricing and spending behaviors of public universities because governance arrangements "affect the ability of different actors to influence decisions . . ." (p. 846). He reasoned that, because either the state legislature or governor appoints their membership, coordinating boards are in effect extensions of elected officials' capacity to supervise. As such, these boards should behave in a manner that is more consistent with the preferences of elected officials and voters, resulting in lower tuition and in higher spending on student services. By contrast, because consolidated boards tend to institutionalize the preferences of faculty and administrators, their existence in a state should lead to policies that are more consistent with the preferences of academic stakeholders (i.e., higher levels of tuition and lower levels of spending on student services) (p. 847). Lowry's analysis, using data on 407 public universities for a single year, produced evidence consistent with these hypotheses.

Building on this logic, we propose a reformulated view of state governance of higher education that diverges from the familiar analytic-capacity perspective with which we began our study. We now view governance arrangements as serving to institutionalize the preferences of different sets of stakeholders, which seek to shape policy consistent with their preferences. Consolidated governing boards are distinctive organizationally because they represent a kind of academic cartel in which a central group of university-system administrators directs the affairs of campuses on a statewide basis (Zumeta, 1996). This condition may help explain why states with consolidated boards tend not to adopt performance-funding policies, opting instead for performance-budgeting schemes: the preference of consolidated boards, which are dominated by academic stakeholders, is to avoid rigorous performance regimes that would firmly hold constituent campuses to account. Consistent with those preferences, the academic cartels that are consolidated governing boards leverage their centralized resources in support of their states adopting the programmatically weaker performance budgeting because those programs lend the appearance of accountability, but lack the enforcement teeth that accompany performance funding. Governance, therefore, "matters" because organizational and authority structures help determine whose interests will prevail.

Again, we are speculating here in an effort to reconceptualize complex relationships defying straightforward explanation. The underlying logic of this particular explanation, however, provides a plausible rationale upon which future research might build.

Of comparable importance is what our analysis failed to show. Specifically, we found no evidence that educational attainment levels, economic climates, the professionalism of legislatures, gubernatorial powers and partisanship, conditions within higher-education systems, or diffusion influences from neighboring states increase the probability of states adopting new performance-funding, performance-budgeting, or performance-reporting policies for higher education. The absence of connections to socioeconomic conditions speaks against interpretations of these policies as "bootstrapping" efforts by poor or threatened states, just as the nonassociation with certain characteristics of the nation's governors appears to counter the claim that these policies are gubernatorially driven. Also, the absence of connections to the professionalism of legislatures or to university tuition and enrollment patterns seems to argue against construing performance mandates as a rational policy response to contemporary problems within state systems of higher education. Rather, as we argued earlier, the emergence of the "new accountability" in higher education appears to have been driven in good part by patterns of power and influence at the intersection of legislative and campus preferences.

Of the various nonassociations we noted, the absence of a diffusion effect struck us as particularly interesting, and led us to delve deeper into our initial finding. As we previously observed, several studies have documented regional influences on state higher-education policies (Hearn & Griswold, 1994; Hearn et al., 1996; Zumeta, 1996). What could account for these regional differences, besides variation from one part of the country to the next in demography, economic climates, politics, or higher-education governance patterns? In higher education, region-based policy consortia, such as the Southern Regional Education Board and the Western Interstate Commission on Higher Education, have long served as conduits for disseminating information about higher-education policies among states within different regions. The question of which states are relevant to another's policymaking depends on the underlying relationships believed to drive the policy behavior in question. Because our original specification of diffusion (i.e., contiguous neighbors) may have failed to capture influences that occur among states that reside within a common geographic region but that do not share a contiguous border, we developed a second diffusion measure.

In this alternative specification, we coded each state according to its affiliation with one of the four regional higher-education consortia: the Midwestern Higher Education Compact, the New England Board of Higher Education, the Southern Regional Education Board, and the Western Interstate Commission for Higher Education. We then measured regional diffusion as an annual time-dependent variable defined as the percentage of a state's regional neighbors that had already adopted the accountability policy in the year in which a given state adopted the policy, with a 1-year lag. Our substituting of regional diffusion for the contiguous-diffusion variable produced remarkably little change in the results reported in Table 6; models containing regional diffusion yielded coefficients of roughly the same size and produced the same significant variables in the same directions at nearly the same significance levels. Although this second specification provides few new statistical insights, we believe the line of inquiry merits further attention. Prominent spatially related factors for future consideration might include political-geographic connections not typically modeled (e.g., distances between state capitols). Also worth future investigation are economic connections (e.g., the Dakotas and Montana have long been closely tied to Minnesota economically via trade, although those states are often considered to be in different regions) between and among states.

We can point to other prospective avenues of research, as well. Researchers, for example, would do well to consider the role of policy entrepreneurship in accountability reforms in higher education. Policy entrepreneurs often are defined as individuals whose actions promote dynamic policy change. In their study of large-scale policy change, Baumgartner and Jones (1993) found that the structural features of American federalism help shape policy trajectories, but individual actors also matter. Entrepreneurs facilitate change by redefining problems, refashioning policy images, developing potential solutions, and mobilizing the previously disinterested. Incorporating the policy entrepreneurship literature into future research could deepen understanding of the causal mechanisms that lie behind adoption of performance-accountability policies for higher education. Mintrom's (1997) work on the diffusion of state school-choice policies provides an important step in this direction. Using EHA and survey data on the roles played by entrepreneurs in advancing school-choice legislation, Mintrom found that the presence and actions of entrepreneurs significantly raised the probability of a state enacting the reforms. In what ways do entrepreneurs facilitate adoption of accountability reforms in higher education? Although we found no evidence linking certain institutional characteristics (e.g., formal powers) of the nation's governors to the emergence of new accountability mandates, our research cannot address the more nuanced question of the extent to which specific governors (or other entrepreneurs) may have promoted policy change in their states. Melding survey research or interview-based field-work with longitudinal analysis such as the kind we have pursued could yield rich insights into the dynamics of higher-education policy entrepreneurship within and among states.

Along similar lines, future research on policy adoption and diffusion in both the K–12 and higher-education arenas would benefit from a more fine-grained operationalizing of policy and a closer analysis of policy change over time. Much of the research on the determinants of state education policies fails to differentiate between similar policies on the basis of their scope or content. Yet, states rarely adopt policies of the precise same dimensions. In the context of our study, for example, few states' performance-funding policies look just alike; the policies vary both in terms of the number and nature of codified performance dimensions.

Quite aside from the issue of how such differences should be meaningfully scored in a study such as ours, the question holds other important implications. Treating as identical policies that in fact are only conceptually or practically similar to one another may be sufficient for the purpose of identifying factors associated with distinctive types or classes of public policy. But analyzing change in policy design and content as policies germinate would afford quite a different set of insights. To what extent are the factors associated with the adoption of more robust performance-funding policies similar to the factors associated with the adoption of less robust ones? What accounts for the broadening—or narrowing—of policy scope over time? To what extent do late-stage adopters learn from the past successes (and failures) of early-stage adopters? In terms of the politics of policy adoption, to what extent does the degree of controversy that is associated with a policy influence subsequent behavior by government? Controversial policies can mobilize and energize political opposition in other states, and proponents in those states may seek to stanch political opposition by putting forth less comprehensive, more nuanced policy proposals (Hays, 1996; Mooney & Lee 1995).

Building on this observation leads us to a final set of questions meriting future consideration, questions involving the dynamics of policy morbidity and mortality. Our study, like most others of its kind, focuses on the correlates of policy creation and commencement, rather than on the determinants of policy decline and death. Yet policies sometimes do meet with death, as when policymakers slash program funding, reduce agency authority, or simply strike a policy from statute. As we noted earlier, there are somewhat fewer fully operational performance-funding and budgeting programs today than a few years ago. What explains this recent decline? To what extent do the factors explaining the initial adoption of performance programs in higher education differ from those associated with the programs' demise? Which theoretical and methodological perspectives best expand our understanding of performance policies—and other education policy reforms, for that matter—over the later stages of their life span? Addressing these questions would broaden the scope of research to encompass the full life span of an education policy, including its birth, maturation, decline, and death. Ideally, our study provides at least a modest early contribution to a robust future research agenda.

## Notes

1. Several variants of public-sector reform were at work during this period, both in the United States and abroad. In the United Kingdom, Canada, Australia, and New Zealand, the reforms became known as the New Public Management. In the United States, Osborne and Gaebler's (1992) *Reinventing Government* was deeply influential. Both reform thrusts, however, emphasized a more flexible model of public-sector organization that stressed the role of markets, productivity, decentralization, and accountability (Kettl, 1997; Thompson & Riccucci, 1998).

2. A few studies, however, provide important insights into the evolution and impacts of the policies. For example, Zumeta (1998) distills a series of insightful observations from the experiences of four states that experimented with performance funding. Burke (2005a) reports the results of several surveys of state and campus leaders on their perceptions of the impacts of performance programs. Richardson and Smalling (2005) examine the implications of governance arrangements for the implementation of performance accountability. In a different vein, Dunn (2003) links developments in higher-education accountability with theories of democratic governance.

3. Whereas there is evidence that a few of the states that previously adopted these initiatives may now be retreating from them (Burke, 2005b), the very emergence of the new accountability approaches and their variability across states make the phenomenon important, conceptually and empirically.

4. We follow convention in defining an innovation as a policy or program that is new to the state government adopting it (Hearn & Griswold, 1994; Mintrom, 1997).

5. These relationships may not be clear-cut. Barrilleaux, Holbrook, and Langer (2002), for example, identify several conditions that may mediate party effects on state policy outcomes. Because party effects on state policy for higher education have rarely been tested, we pursue a fairly straightforward analysis, reserving consideration of joint effects for future study.

6. Governors may also have an electoral incentive to support adoption of new performance policies in higher education that many legislators do not share. Because governors compete for office at a statewide level, rather than at the district level, "running against" public bureaucracy (including public higher education) may prove politically appealing. By contrast, because legislators compete for office at the district level, they may be wed to more parochial interests and, thus, may be disinclined to support new mandates that campuses located in their districts view as onerous.

7. We lost relatively few events (dependent observations) as a result of our decisions: the three states accounted for only four adoptions across the three policy categories.

8. The variable is measured as the percentage of legislators who are Republican out of the total of Democratic and Republican legislators in a state, thus the percentage of seats held by Republicans is directly and inversely related to the percentage of seats held by Democrats, and vice versa.

9. Our use of a categorical variable reflects our core research interest: we sought to examine the impact of consolidated governing boards on performance-accountability policies given the strength of previous findings linking this particular structure with adoption of other postsecondary policies.

10. Our focus was on the determinants of a state's initial adoption of the policies, thus what happened to the policy after it was initiated was of no concern to us analytically.

11. Because we excluded Hawaii from our analysis, our dataset on performance-budgeting policies began with Illinois' program in 1984, the second such to be adopted nationally, rather than with Hawaii's program, the nation's first in 1975. Because a gap of 9 years separated the Hawaii and Illinois program adoptions, our omitting of Hawaii had no significant effect on our results. The rationale for omitting select events on conceptual, empirical or data-related grounds may be found in leading EHA studies (e.g., Berry & Berry, 1992; Mintrom, 1997).

12. See Box-Steffensmeier and Jones (2004) and Petersen (1991) for discussion of approaches to structuring event history data sets.

13. To probe these relationships further, we tested several alternative specifications of the partisanship and governance variables. For partisanship, we created a variable (using the Klarner dataset) to represent Republican control of both the legislature and the governor's office in a given year. We also developed alternative specifications of governance using the consolidated governing board as the excluded category, including one with governance as a categorical variable. These operationalizations yielded results confirming of our original specification.

# References

Aberbach, J. (1990). *Keeping a watchful eye: The politics of Congressional oversight.* Washington, D.C.: The Brookings Institution.

Allison, P. D. (1984). *Event history analysis.* Beverly Hills, CA: Sage Publications.

Alt, J. E., & Lowry, R. C. (2000). A dynamic model of state budget outcomes under divided partisan government. *Journal of Politics, 62*(4), 1035–1069.

Barrilleaux, C., & Bernick, E. (2003). "Deservingness," discretion, and the state politics of welfare spending, 1990–1996. *State Politics and Policy Quarterly 3,* 1–18.

Barrilleaux, C., Holbrook, T., & Langer, L. (2002). Electoral competition, legislative balance, and state welfare policy. *American Journal of Political Science, 46*(2), 415–427.

Baumgartner, F. R., & Jones, B. D. (1993). *Agendas and instability in American politics.* Chicago: University of Chicago Press.

Beck, N., Katz, J., & Tucker, R. (1998). Taking time seriously: Time-series-cross-section with a binary dependent variable. *American Journal of Political Science, 42*(4), 1260–1288.

Beeson, P., & Montgomery, E. (1993). The effects of colleges and universities on local labor markets. *Review of Economics and Statistics, 75*(4), 753–761.

Berdahl, R. O. (1971). *Statewide coordination of higher education.* Washington, D.C.: ACE.

Berry, F. S., & Berry, W. D. (1990). State lottery adoptions as policy innovations: An event history analysis. *American Political Science Review, 84*(2), 395–416.

Berry, F. S., & Berry, W. D. (1992). Tax innovation in the states: Capitalizing on political opportunity. *American Journal of Political Science, 36*(3), 715–742.

Beyle, T. (1999). The governors. In V. Gray, R. Hanson, & H. Jacob (Eds.), *Politics in the American states: A comparative analysis* (pp. 191–231). Washington, D.C.: CQ Press.

Box-Steffensmeier, J., & Jones, B. (1997). Time is of the essence: Event history models in political science. *American Journal of Political Science, 41*(4), 1414–1461.

Box-Steffensmeier, J., & Jones, B. (2004). *Event history modeling.* Cambridge University Press.

Buckley, J. B., & Westerland, C. (2004). Duration dependence, functional form, and corrected standard errors: Improving EHA models of state policy diffusion. *State Politics and Policy Quarterly, 4*(1), 94–113.

Burke, J. C. (2005a). Reinventing accountability. In J. C. Burke (Ed.), *Achieving accountability in higher education.* (pp. 216–245). San Francisco, CA: Jossey-Bass.

Burke, J. C. (2005b). The many faces of accountability. In J. C. Burke (Ed.), *Achieving accountability in higher education.* (pp. 1–24). San Francisco, CA: Jossey-Bass.

Burke, J. C. (2002). *Funding public colleges and universities for performance: Popularity, problems, and prospects.* Albany, NY: Nelson Rockefeller Institute Press.

Burke, J. C., & Minassians, H. P. (2001). *Linking resources to campus results: From fad to trend, the 5th annual survey.* Albany, NY: Rockefeller Institute of Government.

Burke, J. C., & Minassians, H. P. (2002). *Performance reporting: The preferred "no cost" accountability program—Sixth annual report.* Albany, NY: Rockefeller Institute.

Burke, J., & Minassians, H. (2003). *Real accountability or accountability "lite": Seventh annual survey, 2003.* Albany, NY: Rockefeller Institute of Government.

Burke, J. C., & Modarresi, S. (1999). *Performance funding and budgeting: Popularity and volatility—the 3rd annual survey.* Albany, NY: Rockefeller Institute of Government.

Burke, J. C., Rosen, J., Minassians, H. P., & Lessard, T. (2000). *Performance funding and budgeting: The 4th annual survey.* Albany, NY: Rockefeller Institute of Government.

Burke, J. C., & Serban, A. (1997). *State performance funding and budgeting for public higher education.* Albany, NY: State University of New York, Rockefeller Institute.

Burke, J. C., & Serban, A. (1998). *Current status and future prospects of performance funding and budgeting for higher education.* Albany, NY: Rockefeller Institute of Government.

Dawson, R. E., & Robinson, J. A. (1963). Inter-party competition, economic variables, and welfare policies in the American states. *Journal of Politics, 25*(2), 265–289.

DesJardins, S. L. (2003). Event history methods. In J. Smart (Ed.), *Higher education: Handbook of theory and research.* (Vol. XVIII). (pp. 421–472). London: Kluwer.

Dometrius, N. C. (1987). Changing gubernatorial power. *Western Political Quarterly, 40,* 320–328.

Doyle, W. R. (2005). The adoption of merit-based student grant programs: An event history analysis. Unpublished manuscript.

Dunn, D. (2003). Accountability, democracy, & higher education. *Educational Policy, 17*(1), 60–79.

Dye, T. R. (1990). *Competition among governments.* Lexington, MA: Lexington Books.

Dye, T. R. (1966). *Politics, economics and the public.* Chicago: Rand McNally.

Hays, S. P. (1996). Influences on re-invention during the diffusion of innovations. *Political Research Quarterly, 49*(3), 631–650.

Hearn, J. C., & Griswold, C. P. (1994). State-level centralization and policy innovation in U.S. postsecondary education. *Educational Evaluation and Policy Analysis, 16*(2), 161–190.

Hearn, J. C., Griswold, C., & Marine, G. (1996). Region, resources, reason: A contextual analysis of state tuition and student aid policies. *Research in Higher Education, 37*(1), 241–278.

Heller, D. E. (Ed.). (2001). *The states and public higher education policy: Affordability, access, and accountability.* Baltimore, MD: The Johns Hopkins University Press.

Hofferbert, R. I. (1966). The relation between public policy and structural and environmental variables in the American states. *American Political Science Review, 60*(1), 73–82.

Holbrook, T., & Percy, S. (1992). Exploring variations in state laws providing protections for persons with disabilities. *Western Political Quarterly, 45,* 191–220.

Kettl, D. (1997). The global revolution in public management: Driving themes, missing links. *Journal of Policy Analysis and Management, 16*(3), 446–462.

King, J. D. (2000). Changes in professionalism in U.S. state legislatures. *Legislative Studies Quarterly, 25*(2), 327–343.

Layzell, D. T., & Lyddon, J. W. (1990). *Budgeting for higher education at the state level.* ASHE-ERIC Report No. 4. Washington, D.C.: Association for the Study of Higher Education.

Lowry, R. C. (2001). Governmental structure, trustee selection, and public university prices and spending. *American Journal of Political Science, 45*(4), 845–861.

March, J. G., & Simon, H. (1958). *Organizations.* New York: Wiley.

McGuinness, A. C. (1985). *State postsecondary education structures handbook.* Denver, CO: Education Commission of the States.

McGuinness, A. C. (1988). *State postsecondary education structures handbook.* Denver, CO: Education Commission of the States.

McGuinness, A. C. (1994). *State postsecondary education structures handbook.* Denver, CO: Education Commission of the States.

McGuinness, A. C. (1997). *State postsecondary education structures handbook.* Denver, CO: Education Commission of the States.

McLendon, M. K. (2003). State governance reform of higher education: Patterns, trends, and theories of the public policy process. In J. Smart (Ed.), *Higher education: Handbook of theory and research.* (Vol. XVIII) (pp. 57–143). London: Kluwer.

McLendon, M. K., Heller, D. E., & Young, S. (2005). State postsecondary education policy innovation: Politics, competition, and the interstate migration of policy ideas. *The Journal of Higher Education, 76*(4), 363–400.

Mintrom, M. (1997). Policy entrepreneurs and the diffusion of innovation. *American Journal of Political Science, 41,* 738–770.

Mooney, C. Z. (2001). Modeling regional effects on state policy diffusion. *Political Research Quarterly, 54*(1), 103–124.

Mooney, C. Z., & Lee, M. H. (1995). Pre-Roe abortion regulation reform in the U.S. states. *American Journal of Political Science, 39,* 599–627.

Mumper, M. (2001). The paradox of college prices. In D. Heller (Ed.), *The states and public higher education policy.* Baltimore, MD: Johns Hopkins University Press.

National Commission on Accountability in Higher Education. (2005). *Accountability for better results.* Boulder, CO: State Higher Education Executive Officers Association.

Nicholson-Crotty, J., & Meier, K. J. (2003). Politics, structure, and public policy: The case of higher education. *Educational Policy, 17*(1), 80–97.

Ogul, M., & Rockman, B. (1990). Overseeing oversight. *Legislative Studies Quarterly, 15,* 5–24.

Osborne, D., & Gaebler, T. (1992) *Reinventing government.* Reading, MA: Addison-Wesley.

Petersen, T. (1991). The statistical analysis of event histories. *Sociological methods and research, 19,* 270–323.

Richardson, R. C., Jr., & Smalling, T. (2005). Accountability and governance. In J. C. Burke (Ed.), *Achieving accountability in higher education.* (pp. 55–77). San Francisco, CA: Jossey-Bass.

Smith, K. W. (2003, September). The growth of Congressional oversight. Paper presented at the annual meeting of the American Political Science Association, Philadelphia, PA.

Squire, P. (1992). Legislative professionalization and membership diversity in state legislatures. *Legislative Studies Quarterly, 17*(1), 69–79.

Squire, P. (2000). Uncontested seats in state legislative elections. *Legislative Studies Quarterly, 25*(1), 131–146.

Stream, C. (1999). Health reform in the states. *Political Research Quarterly, 52*(3), 499–525.

Thompson, F. J., & Riccucci, N. M. (1998). Reinventing government. *Annual Review of Political Science, Vol. 1,* 231–257.

Tucker, R. (1999). BTSCS: A binary time-series cross-section data analysis utility, Version 4.0.4. http://www.fas.harvard.edu/rtucker/programs/btscs/btscs.html.

Volkwein, J. F. (1987). State regulation and campus autonomy. In J. Smart (Ed.), *Higher education: Handbook of theory and research.* (Vol. III). New York: Agathon Press.

Walker, J. L. (1969). The diffusion of innovations among the American states. *American Political Science Review, 63*(3), 880–899.

Wong, K. K., & Shen, F. X. (2002). Politics of state-led education reform: Market competition and electoral dynamics. *Educational Policy, 16*(1), 161–192.

Yamaguchi, K. (1991). *Event history analysis.* Newbury Park, CA: Sage.

Yates, J., & Fording, R. (2005). Politics and state punitiveness in black and white. *Journal of Politics, 67*(4), 1099–1121.

Zumeta, W. (1996). Meeting the demand for higher education without breaking the bank. *The Journal of Higher Education, 67*(4), 367–425.

Zumeta, W. (1998). Public university accountability to the state in the late twentieth century: Time for a rethinking? *Policy Studies Review, 15*(4), 5–22.

## Authors

MICHAEL K. McLENDON is an Assistant Professor of Public Policy and Higher Education, Department of Leadership, Policy, and Organizations, Peabody College of Vanderbilt University. His areas of specialization are state governance, politics, and public policy of higher education.

JAMES C. HEARN is a Professor of Public Policy and Higher Education, Department of Leadership, Policy, and Organizations, Peabody College of Vanderbilt University. His area of specialization is postsecondary education organization and policy.

RUSS DEATON is a Ph.D. candidate, Department of Leadership, Policy, and Organizations, Peabody College of Vanderbilt University. His area of specialization is higher education finance.

*We thank Joseph Burke, Stephan DesJardins, Will Doyle, David Leslie, Bruce Oppenheimer, Karen Paulson, Richard Tucker, and William Zumeta for their comments and suggestions on this manuscript and on the ideas contained herein. We thank William Berry, Peverill Squire, and Carl Klarner for sharing select data with us. We bear all responsibility for errors.*

# Assessing the Connection Between Higher Education Policy and Performance

MARIO C. MARTINEZ, MICHELLE NILSON

*University of Nevada–Las Vegas*

In 1997, the state of South Dakota instituted an incentive program to reward institutions for performance related to state policy priorities. The program had a specified starting and ending point, running its course in 2002. This program provides a unique opportunity to study the connection between higher education policy and performance, an issue of central concern in most states as they try to maximize their use of existing state resources. The analysis uses literature and concepts from existing higher education studies as a guide to conduct the case study. The article outlines those areas where policy was most strongly connected to performance and speculates on why other areas may not have yielded such a link.

*Keywords: policy; performance; South Dakota; case study*

In 1997, the South Dakota University System Board of Regents adopted nine state policy goals: (a) access for all qualified South Dakotans, (b) enrollment in economic growth programs, (c) improvement in academic performance, (d) attraction and retention of qualified professionals, (e) development of faculty professionals, (f) collaboration among the universities, (g) enhancement of current technological infrastructure, (h) maintenance of current facilities and equipment, and (i) generation of external funds. The board adopted these goals after a series of roundtable meetings that included state policy makers, higher education administrators, and business leaders from around the state. The regent-led roundtables were intended to define higher education priorities with input from the various higher education stakeholders across the state.

South Dakota's approach to higher education policy offers a unique opportunity to study a policy effort that had a predetermined starting and ending point. The nine goals had a 5-year life that ended in 2002. In addition, data exist, both within and outside the system, on measures of performance that tie to select policy goals. The study of South Dakota, then, raises important research questions that address the intersection between higher education policy and state-level higher education performance:

*Authors' Note: The research reported here was funded by the Alliance for International Higher Education and Policy Studies, a 6-year study of higher education policy and performance. The Alliance for International Higher Education and Policy Studies project is managed out of New York University with support from the Ford Foundation and encourages dissemination of research relevant to policy and performance within and across states and countries.*

- Was higher education performance in South Dakota tied to the state policy goals defined in 1997?
- Did higher education reach the state policy goals by 2002?
- Did some policy goals more effectively influence higher education performance than did others?

These questions have significance beyond South Dakota. Ruppert's (2001) national survey of state policy makers found that legislators often look to other states and their policies for guidance. Perhaps the best example of this is Georgia's HOPE scholarship. In addition, states often initiate policy-level changes in governance (Marcus, 1997) or finance with little evidence that such policies have worked elsewhere.

We were interested in answering the research questions in the context of policy-related scholarship and chose to focus on South Dakota's university system because explicit policy has been directed at this sector. Although there are several tribal colleges and technical institutes throughout the state, the focus on the university system offers a chance to get beyond a descriptive case study and investigate whether there is evidence to suggest that policy influenced performance in the state. Our research also surfaced individual differences among the six universities that compose the South Dakota University System, but given the necessity for focus, we chiefly analyze our findings at the system level.

We start this article by reviewing literature relevant to our study and outlining the methodology, which includes a brief description of how we used conceptual tools and defined performance for purposes of the study. Next, we present a synopsis of the case study to highlight information that helps address our research questions. We conclude by returning to the research questions and offering our thoughts on the connection between policy and performance in the state.

## Perspectives on State Higher Education Policy

Policy research in higher education has been largely concentrated on issues of governance and state funding. The study of financial aid currently dominates the landscape of state policy research as scholars have taken a particular interest examining need-based and merit-based state aid programs (St. John, Musoba, & Simmons, 2003), loans and grants (Hauptman, 1997), and the effects of different types of aid on different populations (Heller, 1999). Some efforts have examined state funding in general (Callan & Finney, 1997), and a few have concentrated on the effects of state appropriations on enrollments (Hossler, Lund, Ramin, Westfall, & Irish, 1997). Others, such as Robst (2001), have looked at how reductions in state appropriations affected institutional efficiency. Burke's research (Burke & Associates, 2002; Burke & Modarresi, 2000) has concentrated on performance funding and primarily describes problems and promising prospects associated with performance funding. This work offers important lessons to states considering performance funding or currently using it. In general, however, the scholarship on state funding and aid is descriptive or exploratory and lacks a systematic conceptualization.

The governance literature has a long descriptive history with conflicting opinions about the desirability of centralization and its effect on institutions. Glenny's (1959) groundbreaking work seemed to favor centralization, whereas that same year, Moos and Rourke (1959) spoke against regulation and its effect on institutional autonomy. Berdahl (1971) and Millet (1984) articulated the purpose of governance structures and continued to study higher education autonomy in relation to the state. McGuinness, Epper, and Arrendondo (1994) established a widely used classification scheme for identifying the various governance structures found throughout the 50 states.

Recent research on governance has charted governance reform throughout the states (Marcus, 1997), but studies that have sought to explore the relationship between governance and performance have produced mixed results. Volkwein (1989) found that the degree of state regulation was unrelated to administrative expenditures. Lowry (2001) associated more centralization with higher tuition, whereas Hearn, Griswold, and Marine (1996) concluded just the opposite. In another study, Hearn and Griswold (1994) found that in general, centralized governance structures were associated with more innovative policy. But a study by McLendon, Heller, and Young (2001) found no relationship between centralization and state financing innovation. As the literature on state higher education policy has matured, the focus has been on investigating possible linkages between governance structures and performance. The findings are mixed, but they establish a precedent for thinking about how policy influences higher education governance and subsequent performance.

Some studies have moved toward the conceptual development of higher education policy. Clark (1983) and Williams (1995) described a relationship between state authority and academic interests. Clark spoke of rules of the game that help to define the ways in which higher education goods and services are developed and exchanged, altering the relative strength of market forces, state regulation, and institutional autonomy. McLendon's (2003) work has pursued an inquiry into the process of policy making, which has definite overlap with the *rules of the game* concept so prominent in Clark's work. The process of policy making cannot be completely separated from examining the outcomes of a policy nor can those who are involved in defining the rules and championing the policies be separated from examining the outcomes. For example, Green's (1994) explanation of the policy process involves policy analysis, policy formation, policy decision, and political analysis, all of which are separate but overlapping and each of which can inform the other. All of these concepts have implications for our work in South Dakota. Although we did not seek to employ a framework on policy processes, it is through the investigation of people and processes that we come to a better understanding of policy and outcomes.

There are numerous approaches to policy analysis. Cost-benefit analysis (Nas, 1996), welfare economics, public choice, and information processing (Bobrow & Dryzek, 1987) are all frames of reference that may for a given situation apply to higher education policy analysis. For example, the information processing frame sometimes relies on the case study method to understand how judgments are made and problems solved. However, we found one of Weimer and Vining's (1992, p. 258) suggestions for policy analysis very applicable to our study: review literature, gather data and statistical sources, conduct field research, and apply common sense and logic to explain the data in light of an analytical framework. Given this advice and our focus on policy and performance, we turned to Richardson, Reeves-Bracco, Callan, and Finney's (1999) framework on higher education systems as a guiding theoretical lens. Developed from research within the higher education domain, this is perhaps the most ambitious conceptual model of state higher education policy. These researchers conducted an intensive, seven-state case study investigation to examine the relationship among state-level policy, governance, and the performance of each state's higher education system. This study stands as significant, especially in light of McLendon's (2003, p. 93) assertion that case studies of governance and policy are largely characterized as single-case studies with virtually no comparative case designs.

There are other models from outside disciplines—such as the institutional analysis and development framework devised by Ostrom, Gardner, and Walker (1994)—that can inform higher education policy. Ostrom and her colleagues suggest the use of multiple levels of analysis when examining policy-type structures. Their framework is based on a nested structure of rules within rules in which actors at each level interact according to the resources and constraints established by rules at higher levels. Still, we focused on the Richardson et al. (1999) framework because it is specific to higher education and because, in many respects, it is conceptually aligned with work such as Ostrom et al.'s work in that it calls attention to different actors, different rules at different levels, and different levels of decision making.

Richardson et al.'s (1999) grounded framework derived three levels of a state higher education system. The first level, the policy environment, includes characteristics of the state and state government that are a product of history and current events. Variables that shape a state's relationship with and its ability to support higher education include relative authority of the executive and legislative branches and the constitutional status of higher education institutions or systems. The system design is the second level and includes higher education capacity, organizational designs of higher education institutions and governance structures, and assignment of responsibilities for achieving higher education goals. Although the system design gives shape to work processes that occur within the system, Richardson et al. define the third level as a separate work process level because many policies explicitly target some factor within this domain. The four major work processes that the authors identified were information management, state-budgeting methodology, program planning, and articulation and collaboration.

We were particularly interested in Richardson et al.'s (1999) summaries of how state higher education systems equated to results of information, cost, access, and affordability. According to the authors, states with unified, bureaucratic systems were more likely to engage in planning and less likely to provide information that supported such planning to those outside the system. In addition, high-cost systems (measured as appropriations per student) did not necessarily produce more access, but lower cost systems tended to limit student choice by requiring a majority of first-time freshmen to enroll in a community college. Finally, affordability seemed to fare best in states where it was obvious that a public entity took responsibility for addressing issues that affected the prices that institutions charged.

## Procedures

We gathered case data before the site visit to update our understanding of South Dakota's context. The case data included state documents, state higher education generated data, U.S. Census data, and consulting sources. Twelve on-site interviews were conducted in April of 2003. All interviewees were knowledgeable about higher education and included administrators, board members, legislators, and analysts within the legislative and executive branches. In addition, we conducted telephone interviews with three institutional-level administrators. Every interview started with a brief introduction, and respondents were free to address any significant higher education issues related to policy and performance. We drafted an interview protocol for reference, but we tended toward the open-ended interview approach. This approach, best characterized by Merriam (1998) as semistructured, accommodates the informant's unstructured responses. All interview and case data were entered into a qualitative software package for analysis.

The interviews were coded according to themes that were based on the literature and our initial data-gathering efforts. We used the Richardson et al. (1999) framework to identify categories and themes to arrange the written case study in a logical format. This conceptualization identifies players (governor, legislators, administrators) and entities (legislature, boards) and the many levels on which interactions take place (within their particular state contexts, the higher education system), which proved helpful to the development of our case. This process also helped us to move toward conclusions and to make comparisons of the case results to Richardson et al.'s summary findings.

Richardson et al. (1999) also identify performance categories, but we used other sources for coding this data as well. For example, the National Center for Public Policy and Higher Education's (NCPPHE) report card (NCPPHE, 2002) identifies five state-level performance categories. There were also several reports generated in South Dakota that addressed performance. In addition, the interviews called attention to several areas of performance that are not easy to define or quantify—such as learning, quality, and efficiency—and these areas also were important in the analysis. For some areas of performance, there is no single agreed-on definition, so we tried to use multiple sources of evidence where possible. The categories we focused on were those that surfaced as most prominent in our case data: participation, affordability, quality, learning, and efficiency. The definitions (and sometimes competing definitions) will unfold with the analysis.

It is important to note that we used the NCPPHE's performance measures as one source of information. The NCPPHE measures have received much press but limited academic scrutiny (Martinez, Farias, & Arellano, 2002), and our intent was not to comment on the validity of the measures or to use them as an all-encompassing assessment of South Dakota's performance. Rather, they serve as one piece of information. Other information was equally if not more important to the study. We now describe South Dakota and then move to the results.

## The Policy Environment

Public universities in South Dakota operate as a unified system. There is one board of regents for all six universities. University presidents do not approach the legislature individually and typically raise issues through the board of regents. The increased emphasis on unification since the 1980s is attributed to multiple factors, although one legislator said increased collaboration is "primarily driven by limited resources."

The board of regents and its executive director have unified the institutions and involved state policy makers via what are known as roundtables. The roundtables were initiated in 1995 by the board of regents and continue to provide a forum whereby higher education stakeholders discuss issues of state concern. The board of regents provides direction for the roundtable discussions, but it has commonly used a third party to moderate the meetings to create an atmosphere of goodwill and objectivity.

Participation in the early roundtables culminated in the nine state policy goals referred to at the beginning of the article. The board of regents guided the process, but there is near unanimity in the state that all roundtable participants had the opportunity to provide input. The board of regents, in its annual fact book, has provided a quantitative assessment of each of these goals. Although there were nine state policy goals that guided South Dakota higher education from 1997 to 2002, it is clear that policy makers are most mindful of goals dealing with participation, efficiency, and collaboration.

## The Governor and Legislature

Governor Mike Rounds took office in January 2003. Governor Rounds was previously in the legislature and succeeds Governor Bill Janklow. Governor Janklow served four terms as governor of South Dakota and is credited by many for establishing the foundation for a strong board of regents through his appointments. Governor Janklow, during his tenure, actively participated in higher education–related discussions and was described as supportive. One legislator said that Governor Janklow was often critical of higher education in public but praised it in private. Governor Rounds's initial approach somewhat contrasted with his predecessor. Janklow had very specific solutions in mind; Governor Rounds, according to several sources, gathered different ideas and input. No matter who is governor, higher education policy will, according to several sources, continue to require the governor's approval to be successful.

The legislature in South Dakota is part-time and meets from 35 to 40 days per year. What was true 5 years ago is still true today: There is little staff, so legislators rely on information from the governor's office or from the various state agencies. In the case of higher education, the majority of information the legislature receives is from the board of regents. The credibility legislators attach to the regent-generated information has increased over time. One staff member on the board said that the continuing dialogue and relationship that higher education leaders have built with legislators translates into trust and credibility with regard to the information the board offers.

Higher education respondents described legislative involvement in current roundtables as excellent. One regent staffer said that the roundtables have become an entitlement whereby people expect to be invited to discuss the issues. Currently, there is one major roundtable every year, usually at the end of the year. Invitees include the governor and some of his staff, legislators, regents, and presidents. In the summer, four regional mini-roundtables are held throughout the state. The executive director for the board of regents (hereafter referred to as the executive director) estimated that 40% of legislators respond to invitations to attend the mini-roundtables. The legislative role in closing one of the original seven institutions is a clear indication of policy maker involvement and of interest in public higher education, particularly from a cost perspective.

The board has used an additional mechanism to engage legislators and the public in higher education discussions. The board recently began sponsoring town meetings. The board of regents' staff arranges a town meeting at a local venue and invites community leaders and the public. The local state legislator is asked to run the meeting, which has the added benefit for the legislator of providing a forum to communicate with constituents. According to the executive director, the town meetings have been successful and are important because "they simply get people talking about higher education."

## System Design

South Dakota's University System dominates the postsecondary landscape in the state in terms of funding, enrollment, and public attention. There are four technical institutes but no community colleges in the state. The South Dakota University System Board of Regents governs the six public, 4-year institutions and comprises nine members who are appointed by the governor and confirmed by the senate. The board is responsible for system-wide and state-level planning initiatives, and it sets tuition at the six universities. Administrators and legislators alike indicated that the board was effective in the 1990s largely because of Janklow's appointments.

One of the most critical duties of the board is to appoint an executive director. In 1994, the board laid the groundwork to increase its power by granting the executive director increased responsibility relative to the institutional executive officers. This change roughly coincided with the current executive director's tenure. The current executive director has presided over the implementation of the roundtables in the state, the shift away from enrollment-driven formulas, and the use of incentive funding. He is viewed almost unanimously as an effective leader who has built bridges with policy makers, K-12 leaders, and institutional presidents. Many respondents in South Dakota believe that the university system has made great strides since 1995 and attribute much of the success to the executive director's leadership and the capable staff he has built during his tenure.

## Work Processes

### Fiscal Policy

The evolution of fiscal policy in South Dakota is chronicled in Martinez's (1999) report on policy-driven change in South Dakota. In 1997, the board, in consultation with the legislature, approved and implemented a funding approach that is really a product of two components. The majority of appropriations are part of the first component, called base-plus. The base-plus appropriation to the institutions is no longer predicated on enrollment, is guaranteed, and is adjusted for inflationary increases over time.

From 1997 to 2002, South Dakota also had a performance-based funding component. This component was called the State Policy Incentive Funding component because it corresponded to five of the nine state policy priority areas: access, economic growth programs, academic improvement, collaboration, and an increase in nonstate funds. Each incentive goal was tied to 1% of the institution's budget. In total then, 5% of each institution's budget was at risk. Institutions that met all five incentive goals retained the entire 5% of their annual budgets; those that did not meet one or more of the goals lost the corresponding percentage from their budgets.

South Dakota's State Policy Incentive Funding program has easily been the vehicle most responsible for increasing visibility of higher education priorities in the state. One respondent said that the incentives have improved legislative, executive, and public perceptions of higher education. Table 1 details the five goals, the measures, and the outcomes for the entire six-university system from 1997 to 2002. The incentive goals corresponded with direct measures that were quantified by the institutions and the board of regents' system office. There were performance variations within the six universities, but the results in Table 1 provide a system-level indication of performance from 1997 to 2002, which is the primary focus on this research.

Table 1 shows that, as a system, higher education improved by every measure. Almost every institution met its academic improvement goals as well, although this detail is not shown on the table. Each institution consulted with the board of regents to set its baseline measures and expected goals for each year. In the early phase of the new funding approach, there were different opinions as to whether the incentive portion of the new fiscal policy would be effective. Now that the program has run its course, the general opinion from respondents is favorable. Even those who are not fully convinced that the incentive funding was as effective as it might have been still believe that the state is better off than it was in 1997. One legislator said that the 5% probably was not enough and that higher education could have been pushed further, but this legislator also said that the state was probably better off today because of the incentive funding. Board of regents staff indicated mostly positive response from policy makers, and symbolically it appears that the incentive funding has done much to elevate higher education's image.

South Dakota's willingness to implement change to align with state policy goals is impressive, but noticeably absent from state fiscal policy is student financial aid. The state has never had a strong record of providing financial aid to its students. In the early 1990s, the state had a small scholarship program championed by former Governor Mickelson. The program accounted for only 1% of total student aid in the state and was 21% need based and 79% merit based. The program was phased out in 1999.

**Table 1. State Incentive Funding Goals, Associated Measures, and System Results**

| Goal | Measures | 1997 to 2002 |
|---|---|---|
| South Dakota resident enrollment | Change in fall enrollment | 2.99% increase in resident enrollment |
| Students enrolled in economic growth programs | Change in fall enrollment in targeted programs | 44.50% increase in enrollment |
| Academic improvement | Comparison of student improvement on the Collegiate Assessment of Academic Proficiency to national norms; universities whose student improvement equals or surpasses national norms retain the incentive | Students made expected or better progress (fall and spring 2001, systemwide) in writing, mathematics, reading, and science reasoning |
| Collaboration | Track the number of institutions sharing faculty or facilities and high school students (full-time equivalent) | 183.00% increase |
| External funds | Yearly external funds | 2000: $51,794,683; 2002: $56,769,880 |

Source: South Dakota Board of Regents (2002, 2003).

Policy makers in South Dakota are more concerned with the lack of state-funded financial aid today than they were in 1997. Two scholarship programs were introduced in the 2003 legislative session. Only one program passed, and although it was not funded, observers view the passage as significant because the infrastructure will be in place when the funding becomes available. It is significant that the governor himself introduced one of the bills. Many in higher education feel this is an indication of a growing sense that student aid must somehow figure into the higher education–funding equation in the state.

One regent described a successful institutional effort to provide financial aid to students. South Dakota State University implemented a private scholarship program to award $1,000 to students based on ACT scores. The awards continue if students maintain their grades. The program, according to several interviewees, has helped students and stimulated demand. It has also generated good publicity for the institution.

## The Importance of Collaboration

Communication between state policy makers and higher education leaders is high. Starting in 1995, the board of regents laid the groundwork for communication through the roundtables. The board-sponsored town meetings have been yet another effective mechanism to bring people together to talk about higher education-related issues. The roundtables can be declared a success to the extent that higher education stakeholders bought into the nine state policy goals that emerged from the roundtables. The board of regents' staff led the effort and incorporated input from the roundtables to develop the nine state policy goals, and buy in was widespread across the state.

University presidents are included in the yearly roundtable, but the board of regents serves as the interface between state policy makers and the institutions. State-level or even national information is converted to action for the institutions, said one administrator, once the board of regents translates such information into policy goals or action items. In the early roundtables in the mid-1990s, policy-maker concern was focused on efficiency. Efficiency concerns were largely driven by resource constraints, and it is safe to say that these initial conversations have played a role in many of the priorities the board has pursued. This, in turn, has led to communication and collaboration between and among institutions.

In 1995, the legislature passed a resolution calling on higher education to be more efficient. Higher education did not receive initial budget cuts, but the board pushed for a unified approach to manage academic resources. Institutions were asked to achieve savings through a number of strategies including cutting low enrollment programs, consolidating administration, and changing business practices. One policy, called the 7/10 rule, stipulated that the board would not fund graduate courses with fewer than 7 students or undergraduate courses with fewer than 10 students. These policies encouraged collaboration among institutions. Interinstitutional programs have been developed in certain areas where it is clear that one institution cannot maintain a program on its own but where demand from multiple institutions signals that the program should continue. Institutions have also shared facilities to offer courses that draw on the strengths of the different universities.

Collaboration played a key role in the eventual definition of the nine policy goals. The concept of *collaboration* also was formalized as a policy goal to encourage such behavior between and among institutions in its incentive goals. The number of formal and systematic contacts as actually counted and measured is shown in Table 1. Collaboration can take the form of sharing resources or faculty or perhaps of institutions meeting together to discuss how to more effectively use state resources.

An important collaboration among institutions manifests in what are known as discipline councils. The discipline councils are organized by academic discipline. Each institution has two representatives for a certain discipline (education, business, etc.). The discipline council representatives meet during the year to discuss a range of issues including how to meet state needs and improve student learning. The executive director travels to each institution for campus visits and during these visits meets with faculty representatives from the discipline councils. At one meeting, it appeared that some representatives felt their discipline council was on task and making progress whereas other councils appeared to be struggling. According to one regent staff member, the discipline councils on the whole have been successful. Every undergraduate course has been reviewed, and 3,100 courses have been merged into 1,600 common courses.

Communication between K-12 education and higher education has improved during the past few years. Legislative and higher education respondents both indicated that K-12 regional and state leaders were not very amenable to collaboration with the universities in the past. One legislator described K-12 education as the stumbling block to collaboration. Much of that has changed during the past 2 years. The board of regents meets with the state board of education, and the executive director for the board of regents meets with K-12 leaders once a month. The board of regents' staff is now located in the same government building as the state board of education. The physical proximity has, according to some, enhanced communication between higher education and K-12 representatives because they see each other more often. Some of the regents themselves also have led prior state-level task forces that involved K-12 and higher education, which further enhanced communication between K-12 and higher education.

## Assessing Policy and Performance in South Dakota

In this section, we draw on the case study results to gain a better understanding of why South Dakota performed as it did with respect to select measures. The performance discussion roughly follows the incentive funding goals listed in Table 1, although we discuss multiple goals when it appeared that there was significant overlap between the goals and their results. After the performance discussion, we conclude by returning to the Richardson et al. (1999) framework and our research questions.

### Participation and Collaboration

In the latter half of the 1990s, state leaders in South Dakota were very aware that the slow growth in the population could affect future postsecondary enrollments. Most in the state saw participation as a future challenge because demographic growth could not be expected to fuel demand. One of the five state policy goals gave credit to each institution that increased its resident enrollment. According to the executive director, the incentive encouraged institutions to find ways to increase participation among graduating high school seniors. Because the universities were judged on total enrollment, there was also an incentive to help students return to the university.

South Dakota received an improved grade for participation in *Measuring Up 2002* (B-) as compared to *Measuring Up 2000* (C; NCPPHE, 2002). Participation, as measured by the NCPPHE (2002), is the extent to which young adults and working-age adults enroll in postsecondary programs in their state. According to *Measuring Up 2002*, the primary improvement for South Dakota participation occurred in the percentage of high school freshmen who enrolled in college within 4 years.

Actually, the improvement in participation is related to a combination of factors. The incentive goal that directly encouraged institutions to increase in-state enrollment was, according to one university president, simply a tool to help draw attention to enrollment to attract quality South Dakota students. The president said his university put a lot of emphasis on recruiting and retention initiatives, admissions counselors, and even marketing. An advisor from the governor's office said that recruitment has been an area that higher education has targeted, and from his perspective, they have been successful.

From 1997 to 2002, institutions also were rewarded for building enrollments in programs that were designated as economic growth programs. All of the institutions built enrollment in their designated programs, although the growth rates were different across the campuses. This funding incentive goal, although important in concept, is subject to some question. When this incentive goal is coupled with the incentive goal that rewarded overall enrollment increases, institutions could have been rewarded twice for the same enrollment growth. Perhaps a better goal for the economic growth programs would have been to reward institutions for the number of students who completed such programs. This would have spoken to a performance indicator that has not been addressed in South Dakota higher education policy—completion and degree attainment.

Enrollment growth was not just a function of the incentive goals. The funding changes South Dakota instituted in 1997 also help explain why enrollment has continued to climb even in the face of demographic challenges. Because the current funding process provides a pool of money that supplies a base level of funding for each institution, policy makers are not as concerned about efforts to increase out-of-state enrollments. As a result, barriers for students from neighboring states have been eased. For example, it is now easier for Iowa and Nebraska residents to qualify for in-state tuition rates than it was in the past. South Dakota State University believes that institutional scholarships have been another means to help build enrollment. Institutional believers point to the growth in enrollment coinciding with the university's offering of institutional aid as their evidence.

Collaboration between universities is perhaps the biggest factor that has helped build participation in the state. Collaboration itself was a state incentive goal, and the board actually measured the increase in interactions between and among institutions and K-12 education (183% from 1997 to 2002 according to the regent reports). Collaboration and the increases in participation are very much connected. One influential state representative said that collaboration is driven by policy but that the policy pushing collaboration is driven by limited resources. The state representative cited as successful a collaboration that involves three universities and one technical institute. The Sioux Falls Center in Sioux Falls, the largest city in the state, is a collaboration whereby three universities (University of South Dakota, South Dakota State University, and Dakota State University) offer courses on the campus of a technical institute. The combined campus has experienced strong growth in undergraduate and graduate education. Participation will increase, said one regent staff member, if a university takes the programs to the people. If a university offers a course at the Sioux Falls Center, it will receive enrollment credit for the students taking the course.

The Electronic University Consortium (EUC) is another effort that has encouraged enrollment. The EUC was created in 2000 by the board of regents to coordinate the distance education course offerings of the six public universities. The mission of the EUC is to leverage state technology investments and to draw on the individual strengths of the different universities. Internet course offerings through the EUC started off strong and have continued to rise. These enrollments are part of the system increases for the enrollment incentive goals shown in Table 1.

South Dakota leaders feel confident that the many policy efforts to improve postsecondary participation have worked. The enrollment incentive goals, the new state-funding methodology, and the many collaborative undertakings have all helped the state not only to maintain but also to build enrollment in the face of anemic demographic growth.

## The Role of Affordability on Participation

Though affordability was not a state incentive funding goal, higher education leaders and policy makers in South Dakota equate affordability with low tuition and low tuition with participation. South Dakota received an F in *Measuring Up 2002* for affordability, which was a decline from its D+ in 2000 (NCPPHE, 2002). Affordability in *Measuring Up* looks at measures of tuition and state aid and the extent to which students rely on loans to finance their education. In South Dakota, the only state aid program was phased out by the time *Measuring Up 2002* was released. In addition, students in South Dakota have always financed more of their education with loans than do students in other states. By most measures, however, tuition at public 4-year institutions in the state is very reasonable, even in the national report card subcategories. In one regional comparison of eight states, an analysis by the board of regents found that South Dakota's undergraduate tuition for 2001 was lower than five of its seven peer states, and there was no peer state with lower graduate tuition.[1] One legislator said that tuition in South Dakota is very affordable and that students have access to grants and loans, although he did add, "A state aid program may be useful because it would help us retain some of our best students." Two university administrators, although stressing that they could always use more state resources, acknowledged that the state "makes efforts to fund higher education." A former state senator said that students should have a partnership in financing their education. He said that the NCPPHE's affordability grade for South Dakota was short sighted and that policy makers have always made sure that tuition is affordable. Finally, a current legislative leader cited a publication by *U.S. News & World Report* when he said that despite whatever grade a national report card assigned South Dakota, the state is perceived as a bargain given quality and tuition. A higher education leader said that the state's national grade on affordability is not really a big issue but that the grade can be used as a way to start conversation. He continued,

> We may end up addressing a particular issue that doesn't get us any points on the report card, but that is not an issue in my view. As long as we are doing something that is effective for our state in a particular area, that is what counts.

## Efficiency and Collaboration

Although the NCPPHE (2002) does not have a measure for it, efficiency is an important component of South Dakota higher education policy. It is also an important measure to most policy makers around the country. South Dakota policy makers very much equate indicators such as cost per capita with what they term as *efficiency*. Policy makers also use the term *efficiency* when they speak of generating savings, encouraging lower program costs, or making the best use of state resources. State leaders have been squarely involved in decisions meant to improve efficiency and hence maximize the state's higher education investment. The state's emphasis on efficiency through the years makes it an important topic when studying the link between policy and performance. Many of the collaborations, including those mentioned in the section on participation, also were consciously instituted to realize efficiencies within the system. Thus, collaboration was not only a goal itself but also enabled the state to improve participation and efficiency.

There are indications that South Dakota's higher education is efficient or is at least making efforts to become efficient. In 2001, South Dakota appropriated the least amount of tax dollars per resident for higher education operating expenses and student aid of the five study states in the Alliance for International Higher Education and Policy Studies project (New York, California, South Dakota, New Jersey, and New Mexico).[2] One might expect that a measure containing costs in the numerator and population in the denominator might artificially increase the result for South Dakota, a state with a small population of about 755,000, but this is not the case. From a different perspective, some might guess, based on this information, that higher education is underfunded, but with rising enrollments despite a declining population, this is a difficult case to support. The state has managed public resources efficiently and has given attention to cost efficiency.

Institutions also have been cost conscious. The board of regents' decision to proactively instruct institutional administrators to find efficiencies and generate a 10% savings in the last half of the 1990s was a successful attempt to persuade policy makers that higher education was efficient.

Institutions have shared facilities, have teamed to reduce duplication, and have consolidated course offerings, activity that has been pushed by policy makers and rewarded by the collaboration incentive goal in Table 1. A portion of the collaboration goal also rewards institutions for the number of high school students who are enrolled in their courses. The board considers such enrollment important because it demonstrates collaboration between the university and area high schools and may allow students to earn their degrees sooner, which reduces the cost of higher education. Policy makers also believe that efficiency is important because it is one way for institutions to maintain affordable tuition.

If South Dakota were graded on its efforts to find efficiencies, the state would receive high marks. The universities have demonstrated that they can generate savings and work together, sure evidence that efficiency is a priority throughout higher education. The centralized governance structure of the state allows the board of regents to translate policy priorities into action for the institutions. The authority of the executive director creates an environment that ensures institutions take system priorities seriously.

## Quality and Learning

Quality and learning are difficult to measure, but South Dakota's policy goals speak to both of these areas. In the state, quality is measured from a faculty and student perspective. On the faculty side, one of the nine state policy goals sought to attract and retain the highly qualified professionals needed to carry out the teaching, research, and service of the university. The regents believe that competitive salaries are critical if the state is to attract quality faculty. In 1998, the state began a salary competitiveness program to close the gap between salaries for South Dakota professors and those for professors from surrounding public state universities. South Dakota's salaries were consistently at or near the bottom of such comparisons. The 3-year plan did not require additional state appropriations and was funded through a combination of employee reductions, savings from previous years, and increases in tuition and fees. As of 2001, faculty salaries moved to within 9.4% of similar faculty salaries in surrounding states, a marked improvement from previous levels.

Student quality was measured by one of the incentive goals that spoke to academic improvement. The board awarded institutions if their students showed expected or better-than-expected improvement on the Collegiate Assessment of Academic Proficiency. The percentage gains in achievement for any student can be compared against national norms in the areas of writing, math, reading, and science. Table 1 does not show the details for each institution, but overall the institutions did very well and retained their incentive goal each year. The executive director felt that this measure needed some work because he was not confident that the Collegiate Assessment of Academic Proficiency improvement was the best way to capture learning.

South Dakota has also attempted to address quality from an institutional standpoint. In the mid-1990s, institutions successfully met a savings goal, and the governor bought into the board's recommendation that the institutions keep the savings to establish what have become known as centers of excellence. Each institution was allowed to reinvest its efficiency savings into a priority area to allow it to further increase its excellence in that area. Some institutions have focused on technology, and others have focused on business or other areas. The centers were meant to highlight how savings could be reinvested in a priority area to increase quality and expertise at each university, but there were no measures put in place to assess such quality or excellence. The only information available to assess the centers of excellence was in the form of interview feedback. Legislative and board comments regarding the centers were mixed, and their assessments were based on constituent feedback or on their own subjective perceptions. Despite this, a common feeling is that some of the centers have done very well and that others are languishing and need to be closed. One state representative said that the direction and success of each center is more a function of the individual faculty member leading it. Another policy maker said that the centers of excellence have for the most part been a good thing, but he was not sure exactly how they matched specific state goals. Perhaps the verdict on the centers is mixed because they do not directly tie to any of the nine policy goals, and it is no surprise that state leaders seem to have trouble understanding the purpose of the centers.

## External Funding

One of the incentive funding goals explicitly rewarded institutions for increasing nonstate financial support. Table 1 shows that, overall, the system increased nonstate funds between 1997 and 2002, although there were some fluctuations within those years. There have been questions in other states as to the appropriate proportion of public university revenues that should come from outside sources, but in South Dakota, this has not been an issue. The state's documented support for this goal suggests that external funding can improve educational experiences for students and contribute to capital improvements. Some respondents who referenced the funding goal emphasized the more pragmatic side of external giving: It is possible to save state resources if the universities increase outside funds.

Institutional and board of regent respondents were in agreement that it was difficult to set university targets for this goal. It is possible that a target was set but that a university had already met or was close to meeting its goal. Policy has encouraged the institutions to increase their external funding, but the connection between policy and performance in this area is not entirely clear. Goals that require quantifiable evidence of improvement assume that such quantification is accurately established from the start. In reality, data-gathering techniques for new goals gain credibility as they are refined over time. It is possible, as one state-level official put it, to game the system in some areas but not others. Perhaps it is not so important that some of the universities may have already achieved their goals when the initial target for external funds was established. The state, through the policy goal, encouraged a starting point for documenting and encouraging external giving. In fairness, from a system perspective, it appears that external funding is on the rise and that institutional presidents have made this a priority.

## Conclusion

One of Richardson et al.'s (1999) summary findings was that unified states were more likely to engage in planning and less likely to provide information that supported such planning to those outside the system. Our evidence supports the former premise but not the latter. The South Dakota University System is best characterized as a unified system, and the board of regents used several different vehicles (roundtables, town meetings, meetings with university administrators) to promote planning and proactively shape policy priorities. However, higher education leaders have shown a willingness to publish and publicize system- and institutional-level descriptions and performance data on a yearly basis. The state's legislative capacity to perform such an assessment is almost nonexistent, and policy makers have come to view the system office's information as credible. In this sense, the information provided by the institutions and the regents has helped policy makers feel that there exists a link between performance and policy.

Although Richardson et al. (1999) found that high cost systems did not necessarily produce more access, we found that it is possible to achieve steady improvement in participation in a relatively low-cost system such as South Dakota's. By South Dakota's own measures and those of the NCPPHE (2002), the state has improved its participation levels in spite of a declining 18- to 24-year-old population. Finally, Richardson et al. state that affordability is best maintained when a public entity is responsible for monitoring it. There is much disagreement about what defines affordability. The NCPPHE's result is clearly different from how South Dakotan's define affordability. Regents, policy makers, and even institutional administrators all believe higher education is affordable in South Dakota, and they point to not only low tuition but also rising participation as evidence. The regents and policy makers both believe they play a role to ensure affordability, which from their perspective means that they would agree with the premise that affordability is maintained when a public entity (or perhaps entities) works to ensure it. Given the case evidence, we support this view.

With the backdrop of the theoretical framework, we more fully address our first two research questions: Were policy and performance linked, and did the state accomplish its goals by 2002? There is strong evidence from the case study that performance was tied to the state policy goals. In particular, by most measures and by most accounts, state policy had a positive effect on both participation and efficiency throughout the 5-year period that we studied. We agree with Richardson et al. (1999) that the role of a strong public entity (in this case, the board of regents) is central to planning, policy, and measurement. In South Dakota, the board's strong role also enhanced the state's ability to link certain policies to performance, although quality, learning, and external fund raising were less easy to assess.

This brings us to our final research question, which was whether some policy goals were more effective than others. After our analysis of the state, it is our conclusion that the most influential state policy was that of collaboration. The state formally rewarded institutions for sharing faculty and facilities. In addition, policy makers and the board have encouraged institutions to collaborate with each other and with K-12 schools. The policy of collaboration has been effective because it ties to multiple, positive institutional outcomes. First, institutions have become more efficient because of collaboration. Institutions have collaborated on course offerings and consolidated other courses, and they have worked with K-12 schools to enroll seniors in select offerings. Perhaps the largest manifestation of collaboration is the Sioux Falls Center, which is an effort involving four universities.

Direct policy also has targeted participation. Institutions responded to the incentive funding to encourage state resident participation and increase enrollment in targeted economic growth programs. The policies of collaboration and participation probably worked in concert as well because institutions that participate in the Sioux Falls Center and the Electronic Consortium University have yet another means of increasing student credit hour production.

The State Policy Incentive Funding program, which accounted for a possible 5% of institutional funding, was the centerpiece of South Dakota's strategy to draw attention to policy priorities. Pfeffer (as cited in Morgan, 1997) has suggested that it is the use of marginal funds that creates disproportionate influence on behavior, and we believe this to be true in South Dakota as well. Pfeffer's assertion also squares with higher education research on performance funding. Burke and Modarresi (2000) advise that performance funds need only be a marginal proportion of funding to have the intended effect. These researchers also summarized that successful states that used performance measurements had neither too few nor too many measures and that the measures were easy to understand. South Dakota met these conditions for most of its measures. The combination of incentive funding and the board's ability to draw institutional attention to the priorities embodied in the incentives means that, overall, the program was effective.

On the whole, South Dakota developed a coherent higher education policy agenda during our period of study. Policy makers and higher education administrators worked together to build policy priorities. Several respondents agreed that the trust between higher education leaders and policy makers has increased and allowed people to work together toward common objectives. There is no substitute for developing relationships, which is something that takes place over time, according to one regent staff member.

The case of South Dakota demonstrates that policy can affect higher education performance. The board of regents drove the process from 1997 to 2002, but there has been involvement and consensus along the way. Policy makers and institutional administrators had a voice in the process, which led to the buy in of the priorities. This buy in was apparent from the various stakeholder transcripts. To be sure, there were some priorities that were difficult to measure, and there were some specific areas where it was not obvious that a particular policy influenced an actual change. The board of regents' staff and the executive director are forthright about those policy areas that may not have been as effective as originally hoped (e.g., learning and quality). Policies that continue to target these areas may require refinement in the future. South Dakota leaders will learn how to strengthen the tie between policy and performance as they refine policy priorities and the ways they measure the effect of those priorities. The system in the state allows policy and educational decision makers to learn from their past efforts. This means the state can build on policies that were successful and learn from those that fell short.

## Notes

1. The *Regents Fact Book* for 2002 (South Dakota Board of Regents, 2002) shows a regional analysis comparing South Dakota University tuition to surrounding states within the region.

2. The Alliance for International Higher Education Policy Studies has used Grapevine and census data to calculate cost per capita of higher education in its six study states. The least expensive system is in South Dakota, with a cost per capita at $187.60; the most expensive system was in New Mexico, with a cost per capita of $334.20.

# References

Berdahl, R. O. (1971). *Statewide coordination of higher education*. Washington, D.C.: American Council on Education.

Bobrow, D. B., & Dryzek, J. S. (1987). *Policy analysis and design*. Pittsburgh, PA: University of Pittsburgh Press.

Burke, J. C., & Associates (2002). *Funding public colleges and universities for performance: Popularity, problems, and prospects*. Albany, NY: Rockefeller Institute Press.

Burke, J. C., & Modarresi, S. (2000). To keep or not to keep performance funding: Signals from stockholders. *Journal of Higher Education, 71*, 432–453.

Callan, P. M., & Finney, J. E. (Eds.). (1997). *Public and private financing of higher education: Shaping public policy for the future*. Phoenix, AZ: American Council on Education and Oryx Press.

Clark, R. B. (1983), *The higher education system: Academic organization in cross-national perspective*. Berkeley: University of California Press.

Glenny, L. A. (1959). *Autonomy of public colleges: The challenge of coordination*. New York: McGraw-Hill.

Green, T. F. (1994). Policy questions: A conceptual study. *Education Policy Analysis Archives, 2*(7). Retrieved November 1, 2004, from http://epaa.asu.edu/epaa/v2n7.html

Hauptman, A. M. (1997). Financing American higher education in the 1990s. In J. L. Yeager, G. M. Nelson, E. A. Potter, J. C. Weidman, & T. G. Zullo (Eds.), *ASHE reader on finance in higher education* (2nd ed., pp. 118–119). Boston: Pearson.

Hearn, J. C., & Griswold, C. P. (1994). State-level centralization and policy innovation in U.S. postsecondary education. *Educational Evaluation and Policy Analysis, 16*(2), 161–190.

Hearn, J. C., Griswold, C. P., & Marine, G. (1996). Region, resources, and reason: A contextual analysis of state tuition and student aid policies. *Research in Higher Education, 37*(1), 241–278.

Heller, D. (1999). The effects of tuition and state financial aid on public college enrollment. *The Review of Higher Education, 23*(1), 65–89.

Hossler, D., Lund, J. P., Ramin, J., Westfall, S., & Irish, S. (1997). State funding for higher education. *The Journal of Higher Education, 69*(2), 173.

Lowry, R. C. (2001). Governmental structure, trustee selection, and public university prices and spending. *American Journal of Political Science, 45*, 845–861.

Marcus, L. R. (1997). Restructuring state higher education governance patterns. *Review of Higher Education, 20*, 399–418.

Martinez, M. (1999). *South Dakota: Developing policy-driven change in higher education*. San Jose, CA: The National Center for Public Policy and Higher Education.

Martinez, M. C., Farias, J., & Arellano, E. (2002). State higher education report cards: What's in a grade? *The Review of Higher Education, 26*(1), 1–18.

McGuinness, A. C., Epper, R. M., & Arrendondo, S. (1994). *State postsecondary education structures handbook*. Denver, CO: Education Commission of the States.

McLendon, M. K. (2003). State governance reform of higher education. In J. C. Smart (Ed.), *Higher education: Handbook of theory and research* (Vol. 18, pp. 57–143). Dordrecht, Netherlands: Kluwer Academic.

McLendon, M. K., Heller, D., & Young, S. (2001, April). *State postsecondary policy innovation: Politics, competition, and interstate migration of policy ideas*, Paper presented at the annual meeting of the Midwest Political Science Association, Chicago.

Merriam, S. B. (1998). *Qualitative research and case study applications in education*. San Francisco: Jossey-Bass.

Millet, J. D. (1984). *Conflict in higher education: State government coordination versus institutional independence*. San Francisco: Jossey-Bass.

Moos, M. C., & Rourke, F. E. (1959). *The campus and the state*. Baltimore: Johns Hopkins University Press.

Morgan, G. (1997). *Images of organization* (2nd ed.). Thousand Oaks, CA: Sage.

Nas, T. F. (1996). *Cost-benefit analysis: Theory and application*. Thousand Oaks, CA: Sage.

The National Center for Public Policy and Higher Education. (2002). *Measuring up 2002: The state-by-state report card for higher education*. San Jose, CA: Author.

Ostrom, E., Gardner, R., & Walker, J. (1994). *Rules, games, and common pool resources*. Ann Arbor: University of Michigan Press.

Richardson, R. C., Reeves-Bracco, K., Callan, P. M., & Finney, J. E. (1999). *Designing state higher education systems for a new century*. Phoenix, AZ: American Council on Education and Oryx Press.

Robst, J. (2001). Cost efficiency in public higher educational institutions. *Journal of Higher Education, 72,* 730–751.

Ruppert, S. S. (2001). *Where do we go from here? State legislative views on higher education in the new millennium.* Washington, D.C.: National Education Association.

South Dakota Board of Regents. (2002). *Fact book 2002: South Dakota public universities and special schools—Your future is here.* Retrieved July 9, 2004, from http://www.sdbor.edu/publications/

South Dakota Board of Regents. (2003). *Fact book 2003: South Dakota public universities and special schools—Your future is here.* Retrieved July 9, 2004, from http://www.sdbor.edu/publications/

St. John, E. P., Musoba, G. D., & Simmons, A. B. (2003). Keeping the promise: The impact of Indiana's Twenty-first Century Scholars Program. *The Review of Higher Education, 27*(1), 103–123.

Volkwein, J. F. (1989). Changes in quality among public universities. *The Journal of Higher Education, 60*(2), 136–151.

Weimer, D. L., & Vining, A. R. (1992). *Policy analysis: Concepts and practice.* Englewood Cliffs, NJ: Prentice Hall.

Williams, G. L. (1995). The marketization of higher education reforms and potential reforms in higher education finance. In D. Dill (Ed.), *Emerging patterns of social demand and university reform: Through a glass darkly* (pp. 170–171). Tarrytown, NY: Elsevier Science.

**Mario C. Martinez** is an associate professor at the University of Nevada–Las Vegas and has worked for 6 years on the Alliance for International Higher Education and Policy Studies project administered out of New York University.

**Michelle Nilson** is a doctoral candidate at the University of Nevada–Las Vegas. She has worked as a graduate assistant with the Ford Foundation's Bridging Higher Education to the States project at University of Nevada–Las Vegas for 2 years.

# Accountability in Higher Education: Bridge over Troubled Water?

JEROEN HUISMAN

Center for Higher Education Policy Studies,
University of Twente

JAN CURRIE

School of Education, Murdoch University

**Abstract.** *This article discusses the impact of accountability on higher education policies in Europe and the United States. We describe how the accountability movement relates to other policy trends in higher education, providing empirical data on how accountability was implemented and how academics and managers in four universities perceived these policies. We close the article with a reflection on the observed shift from professional to political accountability that uses 'soft' mechanisms that seem to offer little change in the quality of education in these countries.*

**Keywords:** *academics, accountability, higher education policy, university management*

## Introduction

Accountability is on the higher education policy agenda in many systems. In a number of countries accountability is institutionalized and commonly accepted, in others it is a recent phenomenon, and in others it is a contested issue on the higher education agenda. Some analysts think that governments and other stakeholders do not have the right to make academics formally accountable for their performance. To support their view most of these analysts refer to the concepts of academic freedom and professional autonomy. Others believe that the increasing attention to public, measurable accountability is the logical consequence of governments retreating from closely monitoring higher education and allowing an increase in institutional autonomy. Moreover, others are preoccupied with the intended and unintended consequences of the growing attention to accountability. Given these concerns many interesting questions arise regarding accountability.

This article has five aims. First, we present a conceptual exploration of the concept of accountability. Second, we investigate the rise of accountability: why and how has accountability entered higher education? Third, we review what has happened at the national policy level regarding accountability in France, the Netherlands, the United States and Norway. Fourth, we report on how accountability is actually implemented and perceived by staff members and managers in four universities in France (University of Avignon), the Netherlands (University of Twente), Norway (University of Oslo) and the United States (Boston College). Fifth, we discuss the paradox emerging from the empirical data: despite growing attention to accountability at the national level, at the shop-floor level staff members are to some extent cynical about the ability of current accountability mechanisms to improve quality. Although some of our respondents stated that accountability could lead to greater improvements, they felt that the current mechanisms were not very beneficial. At the extreme end there were those who disliked external forms of accountability preferring instead to rely on internal motivation to improve their teaching and who counted on the professional integrity of their colleagues for quality improvement. There was a noticeable gap between policy rhetoric demanding harsher, managerial forms of accountability and the lack of its implementation in our four case studies. This is explored in the conclusion.

## Conceptual Exploration

Analysts of accountability generally agree that it is the "answerability for performance" (Romzek 2000, p. 22) or "the obligation to report to others, to explain, to justify, to answer questions about how resources have been used, and to what effect" (Trow 1996, p. 310). Both Romzek and Trow supplement these definitions with the question: who is to be held accountable, for what, to whom, and through what means? Trow (1996) also questions the consequences (see Wagner (1989) for a similar approach, and Kogan (1986) for a slightly different method).

Romzek (2000) offers the most comprehensive framework for analyzing types of accountability relationships. She identifies four basic types: hierarchical, legal, professional and political. The last two are the types that are more often found in higher education currently. In some countries there has been a movement from professional to political accountability as national governments begin to 'steer from a distance' (Kickert 1991; Marceau 1993), allowing institutions greater autonomy at the same time as making them more accountable.

Professional and political accountability systems reflect situations "where the individual or agency has substantially more discretion to pursue relevant tasks than under legal or hierarchical types. And the review standards, when they are invoked, are much broader" (Romzek 2000, p. 25). Romzek notes that the difference between professional and political accountability is the *source* of the standard for performance. "Professional accountability systems are reflected in work arrangements that afford high degrees of autonomy to individuals who base their decision-making on internalized norms of appropriate practice" (2000, p. 26). Political accountability relationships afford managers the discretion or choice to be responsive to the concerns of key interest groups, such as elected officials, clientele groups, and the general public.

Trow (1996) adds to Romzek's framework by more explicitly pointing to the functions of accountability and more specifically focusing on the higher education context. Regarding the functions, he first maintains that accountability is a constraint on arbitrary power, thereby discouraging fraud and manipulation, and strengthening the legitimacy of institutions that are obligated to report to appropriate groups. Second, accountability is claimed to sustain or raise the quality of performance by forcing those involved to examine their operations critically and to subject them to critical review from outside. Third, accountability can be used as a regulatory device through the kind of reports and the explicit and implicit criteria to be met by the reporting institutions.

## Accountability in Higher Education: Where Does it Come From?

Why has there been an increased emphasis on accountability in the 1980s and 1990s in both Europe and the United States? Here we explore some globalizing practices which have led to this increase and the shift towards more public, political accountability. A number of writers (Henry et al. 2001; Rhoades and Sporn 2002; Vidovich 2002) have argued that a global model of quality policy in higher education has emerged through professional mechanisms, such as annual conferences and the international circulation of professionals, as well as through the influence of international organizations, such as the Organisation for Economic Cooperation and Development (OECD) and the International Network of Quality Assurance Agencies in Higher Education (INQAAHE). Rhoades and Sporn convincingly demonstrate the diffusion of quality assurance models between two 'core' regions, the USA and Europe. Quality assurance in Europe as in most parts of the world emerged in the 1990s whereas it existed in a variety of forms in the USA since the late 1800s. However, the global model that is emerging and influencing most countries differs to some extent from the accreditation of institutions common in the USA. It resembles more the quality issues introduced at the state level by state boards and legislatures emphasizing "quality review processes . . . in the context of strategic management efforts to refocus institutions" (Rhoades and Sporn 2002, p. 361). These forms of quality management have been taken from business and the federal government in the USA and are related to the efficient and effective use of public resources. Similar trends which had already existed in the USA for at least two decades prior to the 1990s began impacting on higher education in Europe. However, as much as it is clear that "the cross-Atlantic and intra-European patterns of influence are evident in the professional discourse of higher education" (Rhoades and Sporn 2002, p. 369), there are also local differences and resistance on the part of some European policy makers to following the American model. Furthermore, there are countries that are taking the lead in Europe, such as England and the Netherlands, and developing their unique brands of quality assurance systems. In coining the term 'glonacal' Marginson and Rhoades state that "at every level—global, national and local – elements and influences of other levels are present" (2002, p. 289). There are policy networks at every level that are influencing the creation of quality agendas that are similar to each other, yet have unique attributes that significantly relate to their geographic and historical contexts. At the same time, there are overriding influences that determine major shifts in higher education policies. The ideological shift towards the New Right led to greater privatization of higher education and was a major influence bringing market forces to bear on universities. In addition, the following global trends influencing higher education systems from the 1980s to the present have affected the type of quality assurance programs (and thus accountability mechanisms) established in different national systems (see also e.g., De Boer et al. 2002; World Bank 2002).

- *Changing relationships between governments and universities:* In most systems there was a relatively strong bond between government and higher education institutions through funding, legislation, and planning mechanisms. However, governments have retreated and opened the arena for greater autonomy and market mechanisms (Gornitzka et al. 1999). In this context, Neave's (1988, 1998) analysis of developments in Western Europe is revealing. He points to the striking change from *ex ante* governmental control by legislation and procedures to *ex post* justification by quality assurance and accountability measures. This development was particularly visible in Western Europe in the 1980s and in Central and Eastern Europe in the 1990s. The change occurred earlier in the United States where public policies combined with market mechanisms particularly in the 1970s and 1980s when political accountability overtook professional judgment in universities as the quality mechanism. According to Trow (1996), accountability began to replace trust in professional integrity in the USA during this period.
- *Efficiency and value for money:* A related, yet autonomous development is the growing trend of governments to document value for money. This is partly due to the massification of higher education around the world pressuring government budgets. With increasing student numbers the cry for efficiency and effectiveness became louder, for instance parents and tax-payers began to challenge the presumed quality of higher education. During the past decade in many countries, a specific element of the value for money issue shifted from considering higher education as a public or quasi-public good towards considering higher education as more of a private good. Within this context debates occurred regarding the introduction of tuition fees and student grant systems or interest-bearing loans. Understandably such debates influenced the accountability issue. Students confronted with increased private costs for higher education became more critical of the services delivered in exchange.
- *Internationalization of higher education and globalization:* National borders were once evident; however today, globalization of the economy, the free flow of goods, services, ideas, and people, blurs these boundaries. Globalization facilitates the entrance of foreign higher education institutions and business organizations into national arenas and alters the previously homogeneous cultural and normative expectations concerning the nature of higher education. This cultural change, which may only be a gradual long-term change, raises questions related to

accountability. Should foreign institutions be treated in a similar manner to national institutions or should they be treated differently according to their position, possibilities, and duties within the higher education landscape? Additionally, should foreign institutions be accountable to the government in their home country or to the government in the country where they preside? In this context the current debates regarding the inclusion of education in the General Agreement on Trades and Services (GATS) are also relevant (see Altbach 2001). If higher education is included in the WTO agreement, does this imply that such global arrangements supersede national or supra-national, for instance European, agreements on accountability?

- *Information and communication technology developments:* The increasing technological possibilities particularly in the context of information and communication technology have hastened globalization processes. This adds to the previous point in two ways. First, the actual location of a higher education institution becomes less relevant as technologies allow institutions to work globally and easily across national boundaries. Second, questions regarding legal and political control over less tangible or virtual institutions become more urgent and complex.

In sum, various interrelated trends are affecting higher education and the role and instruments of accountability in higher education. However, its role will differ depending on the historical context and the way national governments decide to implement accountability mechanisms and how they are approaching globalization as a neo-liberal economic ideology.

## Accountability in National Contexts

On the basis of an analysis of developments in the four countries (see Currie et al. 2003 for more details), we observed that accountability and globalization were particularly visible in policies that stressed the importance of higher education in its competitive role, that is, supporting the nation in the global economy. This challenges national governments to keep a close watch on the effectiveness and efficiency of higher education institutions and make them more accountable.

Our conclusions for universities are rather similar to those of Leithwood et al. regarding accountability at the school level: "The current preoccupation with educational accountability appears to have begun in most developed countries in the 1960s, acquiring significant new energy during the mid-to-late 1980s. The reasons for these calls for greater accountability, furthermore, are to be found in the wider economic, political, and social context of which schools are a part. These contexts are not uniform across all countries" (1999, p. 11).

There are some noteworthy differences among the countries we examined. In Norway, new public management ideas and the country's position in the European political landscape, that is part of Europe, but not of the European Community, were triggers for introducing greater accountability. The government intended to introduce accountability mechanisms, such as activity planning and quality assurance; however, concurrently the government decentralized a number of activities, thus initiating greater institutional autonomy. As a result, the accountability policies were stripped of their thorns during the implementation process and in practice became less effectual than the government planned

Dutch universities also gained greater autonomy in a number of areas. This general trend requires two qualifications. First, the government maintained its power over a number of aspects of higher education. Second, in some areas it was not so much a question of more or less autonomy but of shifting responsibilities and accountability mechanisms, in other words, 'steering from a distance'. The most important development in practice was the introduction of a national quality assurance system. The original intentions of the government seemed far-reaching. But, similar to the Norwegian case and due to the Dutch corporatist model of policy making, the actual implementation of accountability turned out to be more modest.

The face of accountability in the United States changed over time. Broadly speaking, there was a shift from an internally-oriented system of accountability aimed at improvement towards an explicit, externally-oriented one. The reasons for the change lie significantly in the fact that the costs of higher education grew enormously with consequences for national and state budgets and the general public's view that higher education was not delivering value for money. These changes clearly saw a movement from professional to political accountability as universities sought to gain greater public approval for their quality.

The French higher education system is still largely controlled by the Ministry, despite some developments towards deregulation and decentralization. The efforts of the government to implement formal accountability mechanisms were not accepted wholeheartedly and turned out to focus mainly on monitoring developments in higher education. The quality assurance through the *Comité National d'Evaluation* (CNE) was introduced as a voluntary scheme and there have been few consequences for the institutions involved, other than increasing their prestige and reputation.

## Accountability in Institutional Contexts

We now take a further step in our investigation of accountability by looking at how it was implemented within four universities. We describe the impact that national debates and policies actually had on daily practices and on the views of academics and administrators, summarizing the main findings according to three central themes/questions we discussed with the interviewees: the accountability measures at the government and university levels, the measures at the individual level, and the effectiveness of these measures.

### Sample

We gathered qualitative data through in-depth interviews with academics and managers from four diverse universities in France, the Netherlands, Norway, and the United States. It is important to emphasize that this research was not a strictly comparative study because we did not control the sample of institutions or the interview respondents to enable a statistical or explanatory comparison of our findings. However, we chose a similar set of participants in each of the universities and they were asked a similar set of twenty questions about governance, accountability, competition and generating funds, and new technologies, ending with a few questions regarding the role of tenure and the future of the university. Thus, this allowed us to observe the similarities and differences in the trends that existed during 1998 and 1999 across the four universities. In this article, we focus on the three questions asked about accountability.

There were 131 interviews with a small number of senior managers and an approximately equal number of academic staff from professional schools (education, applied languages, and/or law), sciences, and social sciences (arts). The interviews were conducted face-to-face, almost entirely by one of the authors, ensuring consistency in questioning and depth of probing. The sample included 37 individuals from Boston, 32 from Avignon, 31 from Oslo, and 31 from Twente. The academics interviewed ranged from professors to assistant professors, consisting of more men than women, particularly at Avignon and Twente, with a more equal representation at Boston College and Oslo. The senior managers interviewed included presidents, vice rectors/vice presidents, provosts, and university secretaries/registrars.

We chose particular universities that were not representative of universities in their countries but were chosen to represent different types of universities (large/small; capital-based/provincial; public/private; research-oriented/teaching-oriented; managerial/collegial). Boston College is a medium-sized (12,500 students), private, Jesuit university located in the United States, which became highly managed due to a brush with bankruptcy in the early 1970s. The University of Avignon is a small (7,100 students), provincial, liberal arts university located in southern France and is mainly an undergraduate institution. The University of Oslo is a large (34,400 students) university located in the capital of Norway and is mainly research focused. The University of Twente is a small (5,500 students), entrepreneurial university located in the eastern part of the Netherlands and combines technology and social sciences. Oslo and Twente determine their futures, having greater autonomy than Avignon, yet not as much as Boston College with its need and capacity to garner private funds. However, Twente is less dependent on government funding, becoming an 'entrepreneurial' university by building up money from research and consulting contracts. Avignon and Oslo staff members are beginning to embrace and serve local community economic interests, yet their traditional nature and reliance on government funding remains intact more than Boston

College or Twente. Students at Oslo did not pay tuition fees; at Avignon, they paid a few hundred dollars in administrative costs; at Twente they paid about $1,500; and at Boston tuition fees were about $21,500 (US dollar equivalents in 1999).

## Accountability Measures in Force at University and Department Level

Here respondents were asked to mention the accountability measures, for example research indices, quality reviews, and teaching evaluations that were introduced by the government to monitor universities and departments. The University of Avignon seems the least preoccupied with accountability requirements by the government. A small number (16 percent) of responses indicated that there is no control or monitoring in place and a little less than a third (29 percent) of the responses stated that there is no change or only debates taking place on the issue of accountability. In sum, almost half of the responses stated that there was a lack of accountability mechanisms or a lack of change other than the monitoring of student numbers which was seen as a traditional form of accountability.

> I would say that the structures of evaluation haven't really changed much. As for your examples, I am not really convinced that the Minister takes much notice of the pass rates; however the percentage of students enrolled, yes, evidently. But the only thing that this is used for is so that the Minister can establish a budgetary notation to allocate credits to the university, but after this has been done, we are the ones who decide what we are going to do with the funds and whether or not we are going to cut certain courses or keep them. So the Minister in a way rids himself of this responsibility. Otherwise I would say that in this area, nothing has really changed. There has been a change in the Minister's discourse, a change of methods, but not a change in the procedures of evaluation. (Avignon, Junior, Male, Academic, Professional School)

About half (47 percent) of the responses indicated that accountability exists 'out there' but no immediate effect was noticeable. Most of the elements of accountability, for instance monitoring of student choice, pass rates, required qualifications of academics, and performance related funding for small parts of the university budget seemed relatively harmless. Whereas the general tendency in the responses was that accountability mechanisms were not necessary, a few responses (8 percent) mentioned that there should be some external scrutiny from the government. The following quote identifies that the evaluation should be on the content of the course, not on the performance of the professor, which seems to be an important distinction that the French would want to maintain.

> We are in the middle of an important transformation at the moment, which is based on the English and American systems. Up until now, we had no student course evaluations at all, and I feel that this was missing from our system. The students should be allowed to evaluate the contents of their courses, (as opposed to evaluating or making criticisms of the actual professors) and to make an evaluation of the overall way in which their choice of subject has been presented to them—they should be given an opportunity to say which areas of the course could be improved, or what needs to be added, etc. I think that this is a very good idea, however some of my more traditionalist colleagues have a very negative attitude towards this kind of thing, saying that it would undermine their authority and prestige, which may I add, I think is quite far from the truth. (Avignon, Senior, Male, Academic, Social Sciences)

Boston College could be positioned at the other end of the spectrum. It must be stressed that although the university, being private, is not monitored by the state legislature, 74 percent of the responses indicated that accountability is all around the place, mainly by external reviews. Nevertheless, a number of responses indicated that external reviews were a fairly recent monitoring device, introduced to improve the performance of some departments and used to reward others.

> The university puts together an evaluation for the department as a whole. There are sticks and carrots with respect to monitoring. The university has just come out with an award for teaching for faculty with a little cash prize of $4000, not much. It's more recognition than a monetary reward. Our performance is measured individually but also departmental wise. In the university's opinion, are we allocating too many resources to the graduate program versus undergraduate? Do we have enough electives on the book? (Boston College, Senior, Male, Academic, Social Sciences)

In addition to the external review mechanisms, 15 percent of the responses named explicitly the internal scrutiny of class sizes and other elements of the educational process. The attention paid to accountability does not always mean that respondents are seriously 'bothered' by accountability.

*The academic vice president and deans do not seem to monitor departments all that directly. There is an annual report that's put in, but I don't know exactly what happens to these. It goes up to the dean, and I have never had any feedback.* (Boston College, Senior, Male, Academic, Professional School)

Most of the responses in this category, however, accepted external reviews and stated that these were helpful for improving their programs and procedures. Also a number of responses indicated that there were departments that were hardly evaluated or held accountable to management at a higher level. In addition to the accountability measures described above, some responses (6 percent) related to national rankings of their university. This should not be literally taken as a direct accountability measure, for external organizations use university data to rank institutions, indirectly implying that the university could be asked to explain or justify its performance vis-à-vis its regulatory bodies (in this case, its Board of Trustees). Others (5 percent) mentioned direct action by the department chair (exhortations to do better) or dismissing a department chair if reports were very negative.

The University of Twente and the University of Oslo took middle positions between Boston College and the University of Avignon. At Twente almost all respondents (78 percent) referred to external reviews of different aspects, teaching and research separately, by national visiting committees. The compulsory participation in these quality assurance processes implies that each study program for education and each department/faculty for research would write a self-evaluation and a peer review committee would visit the program to assess the reports and makes recommendations on areas that may need improvement.

*The university is fairly well set up in terms of quality assurance procedures and accountability procedures. The faculties are reviewed twice yearly, and all that is done in terms of performance indicators, reviews, student evaluations—everything you can imagine.* (Twente, Senior, Male, Academic, Social Sciences)

A number of responses (15 percent) mentioned the funding mechanisms that partly took into account the performance of the university based on the number of graduates at the Masters level, time to complete a degree, and number of PhDs granted. A small number (7 percent) of the responses related to the internal monitoring practices of the university, partly as a preparation for the national quality assurance system, and partly as a preparation for obtaining accreditation. At the time of the survey, this was a voluntary activity, soon to become part of the obligatory accreditation mechanisms.

At the University of Oslo, most responses (57 percent) reported the role of completion rates in accountability procedures and about a third (31 percent) mentioned the annual productivity forms. A minority of responses (7 percent) mentioned discipline reviews. It was clear from responses that completion rates and annual productivity reporting practices did not lead to severe consequences in terms of the budget, as these indicators determine only a small part of the budget.

*Completion rates of students were introduced several years ago by the government, so part of the funding is related to credit points. It is still not a major element, but it is there. Research indices are still rather primitive. It is essentially a question of publications and the number of doctoral candidates we produce. It's not sophisticated, and so far it is not specifically linked to the budgets or any rewards or punishment. Quality reviews are done not on an extensive, regular basis, but the government asks the Research Council to conduct periodic reviews on the state of a discipline. It is done on a national basis. And teaching evaluations, again there has been a consistent push I would say from the Ministry, even supported by prizes, for those who do this the way the former Minister would like it to be done. So yes, again there are really no heavy sanctions for those who don't use these evaluations. The pressure so far has been essentially to use course evaluations on a regular and a fairly systematic basis. The results of the evaluations have few consequences for those involved. As yet, there is no mechanism for translating the results of these reviews into decisions about budgets.* (Oslo, Senior, Male, Academic, Social Sciences)

There is a push to pay attention to quality monitoring and quality reviews, but there are no mechanisms for translating the results of the reviews into decisions about budgets. Some parts of the university appear to take the accountability mechanisms seriously.

*There is a lot of evaluation, and that's new. We didn't have that at all many years ago, and of course, I think that it is quite useful. We have had international committees evaluating our research. And as to teaching, this institute has been doing that for a longer time than other institutes. The student organization picks out a couple of different teaching units every semester to evaluate. Together with the teacher in charge they choose the questions, and one of the students is given some money to do the statistics. I think it works quite well.* (Oslo, Senior, Female, Academic, Sciences)

Given the fact that many interviewed at the University of Oslo were not aware of all the mechanisms in place to monitor their activities, the accountability practices seem rather ceremonial without any real sanctions that might threaten the survival of departments.

## Accountability Measures in Force at the Individual Level

Although there is some overlap in the responses on accountability measures at the organizational and the individual levels, we decided to discuss them separately.

At the University of Oslo, teaching evaluations (43 percent of the responses) and annual reports (40 percent of the responses) were mentioned the most as accountability mechanisms at the individual level. For many respondents, there appears to be some frustration expressed about the amount of time the various reports take and the amount of overlap in demands for the same information.

> We have, of course, now an increased amount of reporting: that you record your plans for teaching for the term, then after each term, then after each year, you report what you have been doing. How much teaching you have done. What kind of research you have carried out. Also all sorts of publications and things like that. This is new to the university. It is not something that happened in that format earlier on. And the head will have a conversation with each member of the staff once a year. (Oslo, Senior, Male, Academic, Professional School)

Eleven percent of the responses related to the international peer reviews of their research, such as grant applications and journal articles. A small number of responses (7 percent) regarded university prizes and dialogue meetings between central administration and the faculties as other monitoring mechanisms. The latter can easily be interpreted as 'soft' monitoring, that is, discussing problems and raising possible solutions; the former is more difficult to directly connect to accountability. One should interpret the mention of prizes, however, as a mechanism through which individuals are not so much held accountable, as rewarded on the basis of a comparison of their merits or achievements. In sum, the following quote suggests that quality is not so much the game as quantity at the University of Oslo.

> Maybe we should call it countability, because it is always a question of quantity not quality. They are counting teaching hours, articles written, conferences attended and projects planned. We use quite a lot of time to report about what we are doing. (Oslo, Senior, Male, Academic, Professional School)

At Boston College, 62 percent of the responses referred to the annual reviews, built on the evaluation of each individual's teaching, research, and community service.

> Everybody has to submit an annual report. In collaboration, the department chair, dean and associate dean scrutinize that annual report. So we look at the publications, the teaching evaluations, and the service. And the assumption is that everybody will be given a small raise, and then on top of that somewhere between one and maybe up to two percent in merit pay can be added to that depending on our judgment. So faculty members are aware that they are expected to be productive. I think the criteria for productivity are fairly well known. We tend to rely on some quantitative measures across the board and the chair can add the voice that looks at quality as well. (Boston College, Senior, Male, Academic, Professional School)

A minority of responses (13 percent) mentioned mentoring programs and peer teaching evaluations and another 13 percent mentioned tenure reviews. With respect to the latter: those without tenure go through the tenuring process, as has always happened traditionally, and those who are going for promotion to full professor are scrutinized in great detail. There is now also discussion of post-tenure reviews at Boston College, which could involve sanctions for those whose productivity is below the norm or whose teaching is evaluated as below average. A small proportion (10 percent) identified no formal evaluation mechanisms, suggesting some discrepancy between departments at Boston College. Others are not particularly satisfied with the feedback they get as individuals.

> I don't think they are very effective at all. The sanction or reward of a salary increase is I think effective. It will tell you pretty directly what the institution thinks of you, but the lack of any kind of formative evaluation I think shows and the institution would be better off if it did a better job of that. (Boston, Senior, Male, Academic, Professional School)

At the University of Twente, four direct methods of monitoring the performance of academics were mentioned. Over a third (35 percent) of the responses reported that annual individual reviews were used without sanctions, 28 percent of the responses mentioned teaching surveys, 20 percent mentioned annual reports given to the department chair, and 13 percent of the responses identified annual reviews with bonuses, task reassignments, or performance assessment plans. Only four percent mentioned indirect measures, such as counting the number of PhD students and formula funding.

> *We have some system of personal interviews every year linked to the annual report. There may be some sort of task reassignment, and some departments don't seem to have any system. This is a major policy issue that the board of the university wants to deal with, and it is in favor of a systematic approach of academic management by the dean and the department chairs. This would enable departmental chairs or group leaders to implement a system of interviews every half a year and link these to an assignment of tasks and results of the tasks, looking back and looking forward. (Twente, Senior, Male, Manager)*

The personal interviews were criticized for their lack of usefulness, that is, they did not result in salary increments or even promotion unless an academic asked for specific advice in this regard. Thus the annual review meetings were not usually used to discuss career development. Regarding the teaching surveys, respondents indicated that these were mostly applied to first year courses and that the focus was to a larger extent on the courses and the programs rather than on the individual academic participating in a program. A good example of a rather effective method of evaluating a course is described by a female academic in the sciences.

> *Our favourite type of evaluation is the oral method, evaluating the course with a small group of students. We have representatives of each of the student project groups, say about five or six students, and one of my colleagues and I meet with them about once every month or so. Because this way when something is going wrong you can immediately change things. We prefer that to having the written evaluation after the course because then the changes can only be made the next year. (Twente, Senior, Female, Academic, Sciences)*

At the University of Avignon, the pattern was similar to that of accountability at the organizational level. Altogether 68 percent said there was no evaluation; although out of this percentage, 20 percent reported that there were discussions on this issue and evaluations may occur in the future. This latter response is expressed in the following quote:

> *For the moment, there are none at all, but I know that there is talk of establishing accountability measures during the new reform and that these measures will include student evaluation of courses. This has been planned for sometime this year, but up until now, nothing has materialized. (Avignon, Senior, Male, Academic, Sciences)*

Some felt there was a need for indirect and/or informal evaluations (15 percent), and clearly some actually felt that some type of individual accountability measures (17 percent) would be of benefit to the university.

> *I would very much like to show the inspectors a piece of paper with a list of all my accomplishments, all the things that I am proud of, because nobody takes into account what actually happened during the year. Quality goes unnoticed in this system/quality is sacrificed for quantity. Figures are used as an indication of quality. (Avignon, Senior, Male, Manager, Professional School)*

## How Effective are These Measures?

Here the respondents were asked to react to the question of whether the accountability mechanisms in place were effective in either monitoring quality or improving the quality of teaching and research within the university. Do accountability measures improve the quality of teaching and research?

Almost half (44 percent) of the responses at the University of Oslo indicated that accountability measures do not improve the quality.

> *In lots of instances, you can see that this has been a major source of stress and resulted in somewhat unproductive adjustments. When you reward a specific kind of activity and not something else, which may be equally important, you can see unintended consequences. (Oslo, Senior, Male, Academic, Social Sciences)*

About a similar percentage (47 percent) thought that they improved as a result of accountability, although a fair share of this percentage qualified their comments. Examples of these comments include that the improvements in quality were mainly a result of a person's internal motivation or that it was necessary to encourage but not to punish staff to improve quality. There were a few responses (8 percent) suggesting that they were not sure about the impact or found it difficult to assess.

At Boston, College the responses were in general more negative than positive. About 56 percent of the responses stated that the measures were not effective.

> The annual review in which the dean sends you a letter about your strengths and weaknesses, I don't get a sense that this is used to improve the quality of teaching or research. I have never heard of people acting on these things. I don't have a sense that this method has been used to create new ways or better ways to teach. (Boston College, Junior, Female, Academic, Professional School)

They described the kind of evaluation that they thought would be more effective. It appears that most want more formative rather than summative evaluations, more collaborative and peer-review types of evaluations and more one-on-one feedback, in a developmental, supportive atmosphere. A few respondents felt that the current mechanisms were not harsh enough. Also some commented on the fact that formal mechanisms were not as important as having a culture in which teaching was taken seriously. About 44 percent of the responses saw the current mechanisms as effective. They felt that the teaching surveys gave good feedback and the rewards and sanctions may make people more productive, also that the tenure and promotion processes helped to focus attention on teaching and research.

> I felt the efforts to do internal teaching observations and meetings with faculty were really good. I really enjoyed those. At the suggestion of the chair I have gone to the Academic Development Center and had that person observe my class and make suggestions. Actually she came back twice and that was very helpful. I find fewer avenues with regard to research for mentorship but there are some good teaching avenues. (Boston College, Senior, Female, Academic, Sciences)

No one felt that the salary increments were enough to really change behavior, but receiving a negative increment or even just an average increment would signal disapproval of performance and may effect a change. Teaching and research awards were also seen as beneficial. Only one response indicated that trying to judge the effectiveness of these measures was really too difficult.

At the University of Twente there is a more positive picture of the impact of accountability measures. Slightly over half (54 percent) of the responses indicated that the measures were effective.

> Yes, I think they do have positive influences in the long run. I've been working at the university for twenty years, and in the beginning there were few monitoring activities in research or in teaching. And now I would say that these monitoring activities have improved the quality of teaching and research. (Twente, Junior, Male, Academic, Social Sciences)

A little over a third (38 percent) of the responses showed that there were doubts about the effectiveness of accountability measures. The comments made were about the lack of effectiveness of the current mechanisms, because they did not think that these mechanisms really changed the motivation to research, and they believed that there might be other mechanisms that could have greater impact.

> It is a difficult question to answer, because the quality of education has for sure improved in the last decade and research the same. But I'm not sure if the major impact of this improvement is due to the measures we have been discussing or pressure from outside, such as international competition for funding, national competition for students and so on. (Twente, Senior, Male, Manager)

A few responses in this category also doubted whether the quality of research or the effectiveness of teaching could be assessed. A small number (8 percent) of the responses explicitly indicated that the mechanisms in force needed to be changed. They suggested introducing more collaborative, non-individual measures, peer reviews, and more formative evaluations.

Given the lack of accountability mechanisms at the University of Avignon, people responded to a general question of whether they thought these measures could potentially be effective in improving the quality of teaching and research in their university. About a fifth (22 percent) of the responses implied a positive response. They argued that the university needed to be more efficient and open-minded to the scrutiny of external demands. Over a half (56 percent) of the responses were doubtful, but in a positive sense. They qualified their responses by saying that internal motivation was also necessary and that there was a risk if assessment would only take into account quantitative indicators. In this category of responses, there were also academics and administrators indicating that it would be difficult to develop accountability mechanisms.

> *I believe that academics should have the responsibility for evaluating their own work; it is part of their job. But it is difficult to know exactly which mechanisms should be put into place to make sure that this procedure is put to use effectively, and that it actually does become part and parcel of their role in the university.* (Avignon, Junior, Female, Academic, Professional School)

Some arguments related to the choice of criteria or what specifically should be evaluated. A minority of responses (14 percent) indicated that accountability would not improve academic performance. A further 8 percent felt that they did not know enough to comment. In sum, some might suggest that there is an anarchistic tendency at the University of Avignon. If this is more widespread than just this university, then it will make it difficult for the government to impose 'hard' accountability mechanisms on academics. The solution may be to implement 'softer' mechanisms that are more formative, using peer reviews and voluntary teaching evaluations.

## Discussion

When we look at the type of mechanisms in use, both at the organizational and the individual level, it is striking that most mechanisms would be categorized as 'soft' measures: monitoring and explanation, and a few of them would be described as strong measures: justification. Regarding the effects of accountability mechanisms, many academics in this study were skeptical about the effectiveness of current measures. There was some opposition to the bureaucratic procedures, the amount of work involved and the focus on quantifiable indicators. Many respondents doubted whether the procedures would indeed have the presumed impact. Across the four countries, many respondents argued for less formal, more individualistic procedures, and pleaded for a culture in which informal procedures were accepted as part of the working environment. On the other hand, there were also arguments from a minority of respondents who wanted to introduce accountability mechanisms that rewarded good practices and punished low quality performance.

The responses clearly were influenced by the contexts in which the accountability debate took place and the experiences gained with accountability. The four universities apparently were in different stages of development. Boston College and the University of Twente seemed to be the two institutions in which accountability measures were to an extent institutionalized, although the Boston case showed considerable variety by department. Another difference was the fact that in the Dutch case, the university followed the national quality assurance requirements, whereas in the United States case, there was much more variety in procedures used by the departments. Aside from regional accreditation agencies in the United States, there is no national body to monitor accountability mechanisms and most universities set up their own accountability procedures. The University of Oslo seemed to be representative of universities in which accountability was to some extent implemented, but at the same time practices were mostly ceremonial. At the University of Avignon accountability was least visible, debates were taking place, but in practice not many mechanisms were implemented. In particular, the practices at the European institutions were reflections of developments at the national levels.

Connecting the findings at the case study level to those at the national levels and the theoretical framework, there are some interesting relationships. Romzek's (2000) types of accountability most found in professional organizations were true of these universities with a slight movement towards greater political accountability. The use of performance indicators by state level authorities in the United States—to show 'value for money' illustrates this shift towards political accountability. Another type of dynamism is shown in most national cases that illustrate legitimate authorities' shift from invoking one type of accountability, proactive by legislative requirements, towards other output-oriented forms, such as accreditation, performance-based funding and reporting performance indicators. Most accountability mechanisms belonged to the category of 'soft' mechanisms. They were not set up to sanction individuals or their activities.

The national and institutional case studies seem to indicate that the changing relationship between government and universities is the most important factor affecting the rise of accountability. The shift in types of steering relationships towards more institutional autonomy and to some extent increasing market mechanisms invoked accountability mechanisms or new types of accountability mechanisms. Neither administrators nor academics wholeheartedly welcomed many of these.

## Conclusion: Are Accountability Policies Failing Universities?

One of the striking findings was that 'soft' accountability measures were favoured over 'hard' measures that would involve rewards and sanctions. This implies a deviation from the contents of most of the policy proposals (either at the national or institutional level). How is it possible that strong cries for more accountability from higher education's stakeholders in various countries have—seemingly—no direct, severe impact on the day-to-day practices of academics? There are different explanations for this paradox; some of these were evident in our empirical data. We address these briefly.

### Shift from Professional to Political Accountability

One could maintain that despite the governments' attempts to bring about change by implementing accountability mechanisms, the academic professionals within the organizations were able to resist— and possibly subvert—these policies because they saw them as a sort of 'window dressing'. The shift from professional to political accountability has allowed universities to satisfy the accountability requirements demanded by their public stakeholders and legislatures by introducing accountability mechanisms that for the most part count existing activities. Sometimes they introduce new measures which take the time of academics but they do not necessarily exact new activities upon them. They generally use those measures that are already in existence, such as teaching evaluations and annual reviews which count grants and publications of academics. These do not change the day-to-day behaviour of academics and do not necessarily lead to any increased quality for the clients of the universities, namely the students.

Within universities, as highly professionalized sites, there is internal control over the processes of education and research as in most public bureaucracies. Governments at a great distance from these processes are not able to get a grip on the internal workings of universities. For one reason, they lack the specialized knowledge or the ability to judge the quality of education given to students. For another reason the cost of gaining such knowledge is usually considered to be too great.

This argument explains why even in cases where the government has been able to implement some elements of accountability mechanisms (e.g., in the Netherlands and Norway), the ultimate impact is less than expected. Research on the impact of quality assurance mechanisms and activity planning in Norway seems to be in line with this contention; for example, activity planning was merely experienced as a ritual with hardly any harmful effects (Bleiklie et al. 2000) and the universities merely turned the quality assessment procedures into processes that suited their strong bottom-up traditions (Stensaker 1997). The Dutch experience seems to be a case where the academics and their representative bodies have been able to strip the intended accountability mechanisms of their thorns. Already in the corporatist policy process, specific university organisations were able to influence the debate. For example, the Association of Dutch Universities (VSNU) was able to gain control over the quality assurance system and to 'convince' the government not to collect performance indicators to gain insight into the quality of the universities (Huisman 2003).

### Policy Rhetoric

One interpretation of the subversion of accountability mechanisms could be that the government policies simply failed to implement more severe policies. This would not be surprising, for there are many examples of policy failures or partly successful policies in higher education (Cerych and Sabatier 1986). On the other hand, it would be surprising, given the variety of contexts in which the policies were formulated and the variety of instruments suggested, that all attempts across the countries and institutions to implement harsher forms of accountability.

Another explanation could be that most attention to accountability in (government) policy papers is merely rhetoric. That is, governments plead for accountability measures but actually refrain from enforcing specific policy instruments. It is actually difficult for them to monitor whether higher education institutions really account for their performance. There is also usually an emphasis on processes rather than outcomes and rarely are sanctions applied.

## Value of 'Soft' Mechanisms and Professional Accountability

A third line of reasoning points to the management of higher education institutions as the weakest link in the accountability chain. Governments may have been successful in putting forward accountability policies, but if institutional leaders do not 'translate' the policies into institutional mechanisms, then nothing changes. There are some indications in the empirical material that indeed institutional management was hesitant to implement such measures. An important explanation—at least in the European continental context—is that university management is still in its infancy. That is, only recently have institutional leaders been granted the power to really manage their institutions. Before the mid-1980s (in some countries earlier or later) institutional leadership to a considerable extent implied ceremonial behavior and routine leadership. Since the 1990s, the roles and functions of these leaders became much stronger and from the late 1990s on, we began to see a new generation of leaders in power (again: there are important differences between the countries). These new leaders still have to get used to their new roles, which could imply that stronger leadership is emerging, but only gradually. Some leaders have grasped the opportunity to lead and implemented far-reaching changes in their institutions. Others have tended to stay in a more traditional role and decided against managing in an overt and aggressive way. This could explain the rather weak implementation of accountability measures in the European countries.

Another explanation of the hesitancy of university leaders is not so much based on a lack of managerial skills, but based on a positive reading of their current leadership: purposively the managers side-step stronger accountability measures for softer ones which they believe are more effective in leading in a collegial and collaborative manner. Thus they gain greater professional integrity from their staff. In the case of Boston College, which has a strong managerial culture and where a range of accountability mechanisms exist, there may be good reasons why the case for more punitive measures has not been made. The managers there may have recognized that 'soft' mechanisms are more effective in a professional environment. Based on Romzek's types, universities are places of high autonomy where the kind of monitoring that would suit them best is one based on professional expertise. This is why qualitative judgments made by one's peers are preferable to hierarchical assessments based on efficiency and hard quantitative indicators that often eschew qualitative judgments.

There is already considerable judgment exercised in universities that is dependent upon peer expertise, for example in peer reviews of grants, articles, promotion applications, and teaching awards. There are limits to the type of managerial accountability imposed from above. It may be effective for some type of workers, but for university scholars 'soft' monitoring may be better because they are more often motivated by intrinsic rather than extrinsic rewards. Managers in these four case studies may be intuitively in touch with this idea and have avoided the worst excesses of hierarchical or managerial accountability or 'hard' monitoring, which would use quantifiable performance indicators and sanctions that may not produce the most effective results in a university environment. If this explanation holds, the university managers have been able to build a bridge over troubled (accountability) water, easing the minds of their academics. If the managers' strategy seems effective, policy makers at national levels may want to heed the advice of university managers and especially academic researchers who may be best placed to assess the type of accountability mechanisms most suited to universities.

## References

Altbach, P. G. (2001). 'Higher education and the WTO: Globalization run amok', *International Higher Education*, 23, 2–4.

Bleiklie, I., Høstaker, R. and Vabø, A. (2000). *Policy and Practice in Higher Education. Reforming Norwegian Universities*. London: Jessica Kingsley.

Boer, H. de, Huisman, J., Klemperer, A., Meulen, B. van der, Neave, G., Theisens, H. and Wende, M. van der (2002). *Academia in the 21st Century. An Analysis of Trends and Perspectives in Higher Education and Research.* The Hague: Advisory Council for Science and Technology Policy.

Cerych, L. and Sabatier, P. (1986). *Great Expectations and Mixed Performance.* Stoke-on-Trent: Trentham Books.

Currie, J., Boer, H. de, DeAngelis, R., Huisman, J. and Lacotte, C. (2003). *Globalizing Practices and University Responses.* Westport: Greenwood Press.

Gornitzka, Å., Huisman, J., Klemperer, A., Maassen, P., Heffen, O. van, Maat, L. van de and Vossensteyn. H. (1999). *State Steering Models with Respect to Western European Higher Education.* Enschede: CHEPS.

Henry, M., Lingard, B., Rizvi, F. and Taylor, S. (2001). *The OECD, Globalisation and Education Policy.* London: Pergamon.

Huisman, J. (2003). 'Institutional reform in higher education: Forever changes?', in Denters, B., Heffen, O. van, Huisman, J. and Klok, P-J. (eds.), *Interactive Governance and Market Mechanisms.* Dordrecht: Kluwer, pp. 113–128.

Kickert, W. J. M. (1991). 'Steering at a distance: A new paradigm of public governance in Dutch higher education'. *Presented at the European Consortium for Political Research, University of Essex.*

Kogan, M. (1986). *Education Accountability. An Analytic Overview.* London: Hutchinson.

Leithwood, K., Edge, K. and Jantzi, D. (1999). *Educational Accountability: The State of the Art.* Gütersloh: Bertelsmann.

Marceau, J. (1993). *Steering from a Distance: International Trends in the Financing and Governance of Higher Education.* Canberra: Australian Government Publishing Service.

Marginson, S. and Rhoades, G. (2002). 'Beyond national states, markets and systems of higher education: A glonacal agency heuristic', *Higher Education, 43*(3), 281–309.

Neave, G. (1988). 'On the cultivation of quality, efficiency and enterprise: An overview of recent trends in higher education in Western Europe', *European Journal of Education, 23*(1/2), 7–23.

Neave, G. (1998). 'The evaluative state reconsidered', *European Journal of Education, 33*(3), 265–284.

Rhoades, G. and Sporn, B. (2002). 'Quality assurance in Europe and the U.S.: Professional and political economic framing of higher education policy', *Higher Education, 43*(3), 355–390.

Romzek, B. S. (2000). 'Dynamics of public accountability in an era of reform', *International Review of Administrative Sciences, 66*(1), 21–44.

Stensaker, B. (1997). 'From accountability to opportunity: The role of quality assessments in Norway', *Quality in Higher Education, 3*(3), 277–284.

Trow, M. (1996). 'Trust, markets and accountability in higher education: A comparative perspective', *Higher Education Policy, 9*(4), 309–324.

Vidovich, L. (2002). 'Quality assurance in Australian higher education: Globalisation and 'steering at a distance'', *Higher Education, 43*(3), 391–408.

Wagner, R. (1989). *Accountability in education: A philosophical inquiry.* New York/London: Routledge.

World Bank (2002). *Constructing Knowledge Societies: New Challenges for Tertiary Education.* Washington: World Bank.

# The Bologna Club:
## What U.S. Higher Education Can Learn from a Decade of European Reconstruction

## C. ADELMAN

## Introduction

The global economy changed a while ago. We all know it. U.S. corporations and organizations conduct core business and operations (and not merely marketing and sales) in other countries. Foreign corporations and organizations reciprocate in the United States. Ownership obviously knows no borders. Physical location has given way to cyber-location. Yes, physical goods (from aircraft to apricots) move from place to place; yes, retail and personal care services are local. But knowledge services know no place, and knowledge services determine what quantities of what physical goods will move from here to there, determine what qualities of human life can and will be enhanced, determine what materials and processes will be discovered, shaped, and adopted in the rhythms of life. These knowledge services, and every facet of their distribution, draw up the level of learning across populations everywhere. Culture and language ensure that the world is not flat, but in the matter of knowledge it is, and the world's knowledge content is rising.

And so the world is learning more—or appears to be learning more. It is not surprising, nor should it be disappointing. The level of learning which we judge adequate to participate in knowledge services (from creation to management) begins after students pass through the various structures known as secondary education. Crossing that border, nation states deliver—and make room for others to deliver—courses of study (in a variety of forms, structures, and processes) that culminate in the award of higher credentials. The rates at which populations enter postsecondary education (called "tertiary education" in many countries) and complete these credentials are used as proxies for learning.

But it ain't necessarily so, and nowhere in recent years have public authorities, academic leaders, faculties, and students wrestled more with the knots of credentials and learning than in the old nations of Europe, "from Cork to Vladivostok," as they put it (stretching the continent a bit).

This report-essay brings to a broad academic, policy-making, and general audience in the United States:

- The most important core features of the reconstruction of higher education across 46 countries on the European continent known as the Bologna Process. Twenty nine of these countries have been involved since the Bologna Declaration was signed by education ministers in 1999, with others joining the effort at later dates. The original timetable called for all the provisions of the Declaration to be implemented by 2010, but subsequent experience, inevitable inertia and resistence, new provisions, and additional partners have pushed back the realization of objectives probably by a decade. In terms reaching across geography and languages, let alone in terms of turning ancient higher education systems on their heads, the Bologna Process is the most far reaching and ambitious reform of higher education ever undertaken.

650

It is still a work in progress, but as it has attracted both considerable attention and imitation of some of its features by former colonial countries in Latin America, Africa, and Australasia, it has sufficient momentum to become the dominant global higher education model within the next two decades.

- Highlights of what European higher education authorities, academic leaders, faculty, and students have accomplished and learned in the course of their efforts, particularly in the challenging matters of student learning outcomes (set in what are called "qualification frameworks"), the relationship of these frameworks to credits and curriculum reform, and the reflection of all of this in the documentation of student attainment called "Diploma Supplements." These highlights help clarify what Bologna is and what it is not. They have been selected because they are extraordinarily relevant to challenges that face U.S. higher education, and this document urges us to learn something from beyond our own borders that just might help us rethink our higher education enterprise.

Based on what we can learn from the experience of our European colleagues, this report makes some very concrete suggestions for change across the U.S. higher education system, all of them following a student-centered story line of accountability, including

- Developing detailed and public degree qualification frameworks for state higher education systems, and, for all institutions, in students' major fields;
- Revising the reference points and terms of our credit system;
- Introducing a new class of intermediate credentials;
- Expanding dual-admission "alliances" between community colleges and four-year institutions;
- Developing and expanding "bridge" access programs between stages of higher education;
- Refining our definition and treatment of part-time students; and
- Developing a distinctive version of a diploma supplement that summarizes individual student achievement.

That is a tall order for an essay of this length and style, and might have been taller had we sought a complete review and analysis of Bologna along with an account of the status of access, participation, internal and cross-border mobility, financing, and governance of higher education systems in the 46 participating countries. Those are subjects for another day—in fact, for many other days, and principally by the hands of scholars in the participating countries. Behind this document—and for those who are interested in more detail—we provide:

- A longer, more formal research-oriented monograph, with conventional citations, covering a slightly expanded territory, and
- An information resources library of some 500 documents gathered and either reviewed, read, scanned, and/or translated in the course of this project, and organized in 25 topical bins.

The information resources library will be posted on the Institute for Higher Education Policy Web site's "Global Performance Initiative" silo at www.ihep.org/Research/GlobalPerformance.cfm in July 2008. The research monograph will follow, on the same Web site, after review by European colleagues is completed in September. Prior to that time, a shorter, more policy-oriented version of this document will be published and distributed by the Institute for Higher Education Policy and the sponsor of this project, the Lumina Foundation for Education.

## Sources of Information

As noted, 46 countries are participating—to a greater or lesser extent—in the Bologna Process, some of them prior to its plenary event in 1999. There is an enormous amount of information available to the Web researcher, principally from:

- The Bologna Process committees and Follow-Up Groups,
- European University Association's *Trends* reports (there have been five of these), and the *Stocktaking* reports (sponsored by the European Commission, and now bi-annual),
- The European Students Union's, *Bologna Through Student Eyes* (bi-annual),
- Annual Bologna progress reports submitted by each participating country,

and from individual Ministries and their statistical arms, national associations (e.g. Rectors' Conferences), transnational organizations such as the European University Association, research centers (e.g. CHEPS in the Netherlands, CIPES in Portugal, CHE in Germany), transnational surveys ("Eurostudents" and "Eurobarometers"), and individual institutions of higher education themselves. While this essay will cite a few statistics and provide some reflections on the current state of European data on higher education, the major topic of comparative international data on higher education participation and attainment will be addressed in a second report from the Institute for Higher Education Policy's Global Performance project early in 2009.

In addition to a substantial selection of this Web-based information (both in English,[1] and translated from Dutch, French, German, Polish, Portuguese, Spanish, and Swedish documents), the background for this essay included

- Interviews and discussions with faculty and administrators in institutions of higher education, research institutes, ministries, and national higher education organizations in a selection of Bologna-participating countries: Austria, France, Germany, the Netherlands, Scotland (whose higher education authority is separate from that for the rest of the United Kingdom), Slovenia, and Sweden.
- E-mail interviews and document exchanges with ministries and research centers in Portugal and Poland.
- Participation in forums and seminars devoted to Bologna Process issues of the Academic Cooperation Association in Brussels, and the European Association for Institutional Research, and follow-up exchanges and assistance from attendees and presenters from Denmark, Norway, Spain, Switzerland, and the United Kingdom.

Other Bologna-participating countries should not feel slighted by the list: it is what we were able to accomplish in a condensed and intense effort between June 2007 and February 2008.

Appendix A lists the individuals (and their organizational affiliations) who so generously gave of their time, efforts, and wisdom to enlighten this undertaking. We hope our readers join us in gratitude.

## Bologna: What is it, and Where Did It Come From?

In our view, the Bologna Process came about as a delayed by-product of European integration in its third phase. That integration started with economics in what we once called the Common Market (technically, the European Economic Community, or EEC, born in the merged governance of the steel and coal industries in 1950), moved to political tasks of reconciliation and development with the fall of the Berlin Wall, then back to economics with the Maastricht Treaty of 1992 and its establishment of the European Monetary Union under the eventual flag of the Euro. Though the treaty didn't have much to say about higher education, it recognized that the European economy was knowledge-based and hence fed by the system that generates and distributes knowledge. That recognition led to considerable improvements in the education systems of countries whose industries and finances were already interlocked, and to the importance of recognizing shared history and culture. Given the timing of efforts spinning out of this recognition in the late 1990s, a period of notable bloodshed in the Balkans, the Bologna Process explicitly acknowledged a peace-motivation in intensifying European integration through education reform. In this reading, educational cooperation and enhanced cross-border mobility of students and faculty were seen as an inoculation against spreading tensions. The existing student mobility programs (e.g. ERASMUS) could not, in themselves, be turned into a broader structure of reform, and no pan-European organization had the legal authority to impose reform.

It is important for U.S. readers to be reminded that the European Union does not cover all the countries in Europe (there are 27 countries in the EU in 2007; there were 15 at the time of the Bologna Declaration in 1999), and that the Euro is a dominant, but not universal, currency. Despite considerable variance in language and culture (which remains, as it should), Europe began to resemble a quasi-federal arrangement: a set of states with no economic borders yet a common workforce that was ironically stuck behind political borders because these countries, united in other ways, and despite agreements, did not yet fully recognize—or even understand—their neighbors' education credentials. In order to recognize credentials across borders and thus to provide mobility for the advanced knowledge workforce, some convergence of education practices and standards was called for, and broad consensus sought at the European level. Bologna offered national systems of higher education the opportunity to join a "club" exercising similar (though not identical) forms of educational development.[2] Eventually, they all joined, though with varying degrees of enthusiasm. It was the only game in town, so to speak. And its members now include 4,000 institutions of higher education and 16 million students, an enterprise comparable to the size and scope of higher education in the United States.

Looking backward, one can identify a number of steps toward this convergence, each of which is named for the setting in which the meeting of the minds took place:

- **The Lisbon Recognition Convention** of 1997, at which, under the aegis of UNESCO, 29 European countries agreed to a set of principles for mutual recognition of education credentials, from grade school to graduate school, and articulated eight (8) broad levels on which these credentials should sit. A total of 39 countries have ratified the agreement as of 2007.

- **The Sorbonne Declaration** of 1998, at which the education ministers of the four largest countries in the European Union (France, Germany, Italy, and the United Kingdom) agreed to design and lead a broad and cooperative reconstruction of the basic terms of higher education to create a common European degree structure, to remove barriers to cross-national mobility, and to take advantage of the potential of university systems across the Continent. In its rhetoric of frameworks, cycles, credits, flexibility, shared culture, and transparent "readability" of processes and standards, the Sorbonne Declaration contains all the seeds of Bologna.

- **The Bologna Declaration** itself in 1999, in which 29 countries' ministers of education agreed to a process that would bring their higher education systems into greater harmony and transparency in matters of degree cycles, quality assurance practices, and credit mechanisms so as to realize mutual recognition of course work and degrees and hence enable their students to move more easily through the borderless economic landscape of Europe. Such actions, they reasoned, would create a European Higher Education Area that would also be attractive to students from other continents. The ministers set a goal of completing all the revisions to existing systems so that they were singing in the same key—though not necessarily with the same melodic line—by 2010. It is important to note that the Bologna Declaration was a ministerial level statement—with no legal obligations attached—and that each country's national legislature subsequently could choose to revise the laws and regulations under which its higher education system operated so as to realize the objectives agreed to. Some of these legislative revisions did not occur until 2005 (Poland) or 2006 (Sweden); and some have yet to take place.[3] The ministers agreed to meet every other year to review progress, evaluate and adjust the dimensions and boundaries of the core processes, add new emphases, and welcome new partners. These meetings have taken place in Prague (2001), Berlin (2003), Bergen (2005), and London (2007). The next meeting is scheduled for Leuven and Louvain, Belgium in 2009.

- **The Lisbon Strategy** of 2000—not part of the Bologna Process, but intersecting it. The second trip to Lisbon was like the first in that its purposes transcended higher education. Think of it as 15 countries that then constituted the European Union, in the face of declining economic clout, setting out a strategy for lifelong learning and workforce development so that their aging labor forces could be renewed and Europe become, also by 2010, "the most competitive and the most dynamic knowledge-based economy in the world."[4] While the lifelong learning objectives of Lisbon 2000 intersect those of the Bologna Process, the Lisbon agenda placed major emphases on innovations in economic, environmental and social development that go well beyond the role of formal education in their respective societies. In matters of education, the Lisbon Strategy focused not on higher education, rather on reducing school drop-out rates, increasing upper secondary school graduation rates, and improving literacy levels among teenagers. Sound familiar? As in the case of Bologna, the 2010 target is not likely to be met, but much is being learned along the way.

- **In Prague** (2001), and following the Lisbon 2000 example, lifelong learning was added to the major policy themes of Bologna, and students, a core stakeholder group, were solicited to participate on the committees and in the processes of reshaping higher education (we will note that student groups enthusiastically took up this invitation). Students urged the inclusion of a "social dimensions" component of the Bologna agenda, though that took time to develop. The import of Bologna had now filtered through governments, academic authorities, and faculties, so this was a process with momentum.

- **In Berlin** (2003). If the Prague meeting was largely a "let's see where we are" discussion, the Berlin Communique was more specific with respect to expansion of the existing "action lines" of the Bologna Process. Establishing compatible qualifications frameworks for degrees at both European and national levels became a core tool. The general outlines of a Qualifications Framework for the European Higher Education Area were agreed to, and sent off to committees for elaboration. The two-cycle degree (undergraduate/graduate) of the original declaration became three (a Bachelor's/Master's core, plus doctoral education—in order not to lose the connection between higher education and research). With these changes, the objectives of degree recognition and mobility of students across borders were fortified. Lifelong learning, and system flexibility to accommodate it, was reenforced as a goal of the process, and more vigilant quality assurance (what we call accreditation processes, but in Europe a more far reaching practice) was highlighted.

- **In Bergen** (2005) the most significant additions to the portfolio of Bologna objectives were focused on the development and recognition of joint degrees (involving institutions from more than one country), the reinforcement of the flexibility theme, and the establishment of procedures for the assessment and recognition of prior learning (something we do in our external degree institutions such as Empire State in New York, Charter Oak in Connecticut, and Thomas Edison in New Jersey, and for which Europeans give us great credit). The Bergen meeting also witnessed the full articulation of the "social dimensions" theme of the Bologna Process, that is, enhanced attention to students from disadvantaged groups. While each country has its own definition of "disadvantaged groups," the most common features of the European definitions include geographically isolated (principally rural) populations, students with disabilities, children of immigrants, and children of the working class.

- **In London** (2007), the ministers took action to bolster standards in accreditation and quality assurance by endorsing the establishment of a formal "register" of Quality Assurance Agencies (now a reality), spent considerable energy on steps to promote the attractiveness of the European Higher Education Area in a global market, and pushed lagging member countries to complete their national qualification frameworks. While pressing forward on the portfolio of objectives initially targeted for completion by 2010, there was no doubt in the official communiques following the London meeting that these developments would continue well beyond 2010, and that considerable improvement in data systems for tracking and reporting student academic histories is necessary to mark progress and change across all the reform lines of Bologna.

Along the way, associations of universities, disciplinary and professional associations, conferences of higher education administrators, student organizations, and other stakeholder groups have held hundreds of meetings and seminars and have issued even more hundreds of declarations, studies, reports, and proposals that have fed, modified, and expanded the evolution of the original Bologna design. Everybody has had something to say and contribute.

## Background for Judging What We Are Looking At

### Types of Institutions of Higher Education (IHEs)

No matter how each European higher education system presents itself, there are basically four kinds of public institutions in play on the field of what is known, internationally, as "tertiary" education:

- Universities, which award doctoral degrees, conduct research as a core activity, and offer programs in traditional academic fields, some occupationally-oriented fields (e.g. business), and those fields which are regulated by licensure or certification requirements (e.g. Law, Medicine, Engineering, Architecture).
- Occupationally-oriented institutions, which do not offer doctoral degrees, do not conduct research as a core activity, do not usually offer degrees in traditional academic fields, rather offer Bachelor's and Master's degrees in fields such as tourism and hospitality management, biotechnology, design, management information systems, social work, and some of the regulated professional fields. When a system includes these institutions as a distinct class, it is called a "binary system." These institutions are sometimes termed "polytechnics" (Portugal), *högskolen* (Sweden), *Fachhochschulen* (Germany and Austria), *hogescholen* (the Netherlands), and Institutes of Technology (Ireland). This essay will use the European label, "of applied sciences," to describe these institutions. Indeed, we have hundreds of them in the U.S., colleges in which the vast majority of enrollments and degrees are in occupationally-oriented fields and in which the Master's degree is the highest offering.

- Free-standing specialty institutions, many of which offer Master's and doctoral degrees, and some of which offer *only* Master's and doctoral degrees (e.g. the 18 *grands etablissements* in France). There are free standing medical schools (e.g. Innsbruck in Austria), degree-granting music conservatories (e.g. the Royal Academy of Music in Stockholm), and institutes of fine arts, dance, and theater (more prominent on the European landscape than in the U.S.). Most (but not all) of the institutions specializing in the fine, performing, and applied arts are on the "south side" of the binary line, so to speak, i.e. they are classified with the polytechnics, the *hogescholen* and other "applied science" institutions (even though they are specialized).
- Institutions offering programs that can overlap the lower levels of tertiary education and the upper levels of secondary education. "Further Education" institutions in England and Scotland illustrate this phenomenon, as do the *Ciclos Superiores* in Spain. While designed for what we would call continuing education and with no admissions requirements, they award certificates and diplomas that, with assessment, allow students to transfer into universities in ways analogous to those in which our community college students move into four-year institutions.

A European national higher education system can call itself "unitary" (as opposed to "binary"), and still contain all four types of schools—and some include hybrid institutions that span upper secondary/postsecondary/university levels (found principally in the UK, though the German *Berufsakademien,* originally postsecondary vocational schools, but now with Bachelor's degree programs offered on contract with specific employers on a cooperative education model, also illustrate this phenomenon). Some disciplines and programs are offered in more than one type of institution, depending on national system. The education of teachers for elementary and secondary schools is a prime example. What we in the U.S. would describe as liberal arts colleges, awarding only Bachelor's degrees in arts and sciences fields, are very rare in Europe.[5]

Where private institutions have entered the tertiary domain (principally as for-profit institutions in Eastern Europe, and in Portugal, where their share of enrollments is shrinking), the typology of institutions becomes more complex. But private higher education is otherwise a minor phenomenon in Bologna territory.

European education also includes non degree-granting vocational trade schools comparable to those in the U.S. that offer certificates. While we classify these institutions as "postsecondary," they are not considered "tertiary" education in Europe, and are not part of the Bologna universe.

## Student Paths and Demographics

In many European systems of primary and secondary education, students need a Global Positioning Device just to figure out where they are sitting. There are lower secondary schools and upper secondary schools, and multiple types of each, with vocational pathways, general pathways, and academic pathways running through them. Connections between paths are sometimes possible, sometimes not. We would call this a tracking system, but to an outside observer, the diagrams of these tracks bear some resemblance to Jackson Pollock's fractal paintings: ultimately there is a different kind of order in apparent chaos, but it takes concentration to determine where that order lies.

In most of the 46 Bologna countries, the principal route to entering degree-granting institutions is determined by high school leaving examinations or university entrance examinations. The best known of these to U.S. audiences are the A-levels in the United Kingdom, the *Baccalaureat* in France, and the *Abitur* in Germany (though each of the 16 German states—or *Länder*—has its own version of the *Abitur*). In general, for traditional-age students coming out of upper secondary schools, pass the exam(s) and you can enter either universities or applied science institutions. There.are variations in which secondary school grade point average is weighted more heavily than the examination (e.g. Portugal, where the admissions process is centralized), or in which the examination score becomes part of the student's grade point average, hence, where one's choice is thus limited by performance (Germany). And there are other cases, e.g. the Czech Republic, where admission itself is limited by the capacity of the system (some 40 percent of applicants in the Czech Republic are rejected on those grounds).

Since, in most European systems, you enter a specific major program (e.g. anthropology, business, mechanical engineering), you may encounter a cap on enrollment in your preferred field. Depending on country and field, admission to that program may be determined by exam score and/or lottery (or, in the UK, by something called "tariff points," the explanation of which is best set aside). Medicine is always a case of selection or combination of selection and lottery; music requires an audition; fine arts, a portfolio. For applied science institutions, labor market conditions and projections may also determine caps, and programs such as Tourism and Hospitality Management are usually designed and adjusted on the basis of feedback of representatives and experts from the industry in question. In all this, and contrary to conventional wisdom in the U.S., students in Europe can change majors (in some countries and universities more easily than others): Gillian Mackintosh, Deputy Academic Registrar of Aberdeen University in Scotland reports a 40 percent change of major rate among undergraduates (in the U.S., it's about 50 percent, i.e. there is not much difference).

There are other routes into the higher education systems of Europe, and the Bologna Process has inspired countries to develop multiple paths, e.g. from vocational secondary schools to applied science institutions of higher education, and for older beginning students, through recognition of prior learning in non-formal settings and bridge programs (we will talk about these options later in the essay). This inspiration emerges from both the flexibility objectives of Bologna and its increasing emphasis on the "social dimension" of participation in higher education, i.e. increasing access.

The average age at which students enter higher education varies from 19 (UK and France) to 23 (Finland). In Germany and Austria, 18 year-old males are required to perform six to 12 months of either military or civil service, and that obviously delays entrance to higher education.[6] It will not surprise U.S. readers that the age distribution of European students is older in the applied science institutions and among part-timers. Some demographics are universal.

## Status of European Systems Prior to Bologna

Not everybody started from the same pole position to realize the initial and evolving objectives of the Bologna Process, and some countries' higher education systems had undergone dramatic changes of their own in the 1990s, to wit:

- Finland expanded its higher education system by a *third,* creating a new sector of 11 polytechnic institutions known as AMKs. For the U.S. to engage in a similar expansion would require the creation of about 600 new bachelor's degree-granting schools, and the addition of 3 million undergraduate students.
- Poland saw the birth of 300 private institutions of higher education between 1990 and 2001, with enrollment in this sector growing from 29 thousand to nearly 600 thousand (roughly 30 percent of total higher education enrollments) in that period. Some of these institutions were small; some were very specialized; many were located in comparatively isolated areas of the country.

Less dramatic experiments and steps toward what became Bologna ideals were underway in other countries[7] and in professional disciplines. Most of these might have withered without the visible direction, broad stakeholder involvement, and ferment of Bologna dynamics. The 2005 evaluation of the Scottish Credit and Qualifications Framework introduced in 2001 used the concept of "additionality" to highlight this phenomenon. That is, we should always be asking the extent to which Bologna added to what was already happening, and whether it matters that participants knew all the details of Bologna if they were already living analogues to those details. For national systems that were "stuck," as Jurgen Enders of the Center for Higher Education Policy Studies in the Netherlands noted, Bologna was "an icebreaker, a discourse" that created educational realities within "an acceptable range of difference." In this broader discourse, Bologna played a facilitative role—not the cause or origin but the platform for innovation.

Special consideration of large scale changes should be marked for countries in the former sphere of the former Soviet Union. As Pavel Zgaga of the University of Ljubljana in Slovenia remarked, "when the dictator disappears, everything becomes problematic." That is, students and faculty moved from a position in which everything was decided for them by a central authority to one in which nothing was pre-determined. Whole societies were walking around in a daze after the dissolution of the Iron Curtain in 1989, seeking to find their footing amidst vacuums of organization and protocols. New institutions and rules had to be created, and higher education was swept up in the dynamics of this environment.

Credit systems existed in a number of countries, e.g. Scotland, Spain, Sweden, Finland and the Netherlands before Bologna, though based on different units of analysis (e.g. Spanish credits were based on faculty teaching hours, not student effort hours; Finnish credits were based on a "study week," not hours). The European Credit Transfer System (ECTS) was in use broadly in the 1990s, but only for purposes of transfer for students from one country studying in another country under the rubrics of the ERASMUS student mobility programs. In general, ECTS was not used for purposes of credit *accumulation* until Bologna. While some of the pre-Bologna credit systems are still in use, all of them translate their metrics into ECTS.[8] That credits are attached to courses with set subject boundaries is second nature to the U.S. system, but the classical model of European university education was not presented in course modules with taxonomies, prerequisites, credits, and sequences. With the advent of Bologna, everything is modularized, but only two-thirds of higher education institutions had adopted ECTS as an accumulation currency as of 2006, even though ECTS is one of the pillars of the European Higher Education Area.

## Notes

1. The reader should note that when documents in English are quoted, the original European English spellings are used, e.g. "specialised" (for specialized), "competences" (for competencies), "programme" (for program), etc.

2. Under the economic theory of "convergence clubs," Bologna is a form of technology transfer that brings nations from different platforms of educational development to a point of embracing similar paradigms.

3. For a spreadsheet prepared by Aditi Banerjee (former policy intern at the Institute for Higher Education Policy), including the major recent higher education legislation in each participating country, click on *www.ihep.org/assets/files/countrystatus2007.pdf*

4. Using a combination of higher education attainment and such factors as corporate investment in R&D, creativity of scientific community, and internet penetration rates, the World Economic Forum's 2004–05 "competitiveness" rankings placed the then 25 countries of the EU, collectively, on the 15th rung. The U.S. was ranked second, something you usually don't hear about in the complaints about our slippage in the world.

5. The three "university colleges" in the Netherlands (at Utrecht, Roosevelt Academy, and Maastricht), targeting foreign students and domestic students from international and bilingual secondary schools, represent an acknowledged revival of classic arts and sciences education. With support from the European Commission, this core group of institutions in the Netherlands is planning an expansion to a European network of similar schools.

6. The average age of entry in Germany will fall after 2012, as the pre-college system moves from 13 years to 12. What otherwise might have been a decline in the entering postsecondary population due to a flattening of the baby boom curve will remain stable to 2020.

7. Starting in 1998, Germany, for example, set up the structures and labels for what became the Bologna Bachelor's and Master's degrees, but left it up to individual institutions to add these to the existing system.

8. One notable exception is that of the UK, which is in process of finalizing its own credit system, and will subsequently confront articulation between that system and ECTS.

# CHAPTER 7:
# TEACHER PREPARATION

# Who's in Charge Here?
## The Changing Landscape of Teacher Preparation in America

CHARLES R. COBLE, ROY EDELFELT AND
JAN KETTLEWELL

## Introduction

As former vice president of university-school programs with the University of North Carolina, one of my responsibilities was to meet periodically with all 15 deans of the colleges, schools and departments of education. The meetings were always lively, full of debate, and sometimes contentious. It was often my duty to share bad news, usually related to actions taken at a recent State Board of Education meeting or about a new bill introduced by the General Assembly that, if passed (which they often were), would negatively impact the state's teacher education programs in some way . . . at least from the dean's point of view. One particular meeting was especially tense and one of the most accomplished deans and, heretofore, a close ally on most matters slammed his hands on the table and shouted, "Charlie, you are not my boss!"

Jack's admonition that I was not his boss (which was absolutely true) stimulated my thinking about the deans' role and their bosses. As a former dean for 13 years, the answer came easily. A day later, I sent the following e-mail missive to the deans:

> I think we clearly established at the last deans' meeting that you do not work for me. But for whom do you work? Who is your boss?

> - For sure you work for your **chancellor** since he or she is the CEO of your campus.
> - However, on a daily basis, you work more closely with your **provost/vice chancellor for academic affairs** since he/she controls your positions and budgets.
> - However, you also work for the **vice chancellor for institutional development and/or grants and contract offices** since this individual helps you identify the people and services that provide the grants, contacts and gifts that help establish higher standards of excellence in your unit.
> - However, you also work for your **faculty and staff** since without their support you can accomplish very little.
> - However, you also work for the **governor** since we have elected a long series of "education governors" in North Carolina who run a positive education platform.
> - However, you also work for the **general assembly** since they pen laws affecting education and teacher preparation, specifically at times, and they fund the university budget.
> - However, you also work for the **state board of education** since it sets licensure, program approval and accreditation standards, and establishes numerous other policies and guidelines that directly and deeply affect your program, faculty and curricula.

- *However, you also work for the* **board of governors** *since this board establishes policies and approves programs and budgets that dramatically affect your programs, i.e., the second major, the program length, community college transfer agreements, outreach policies with the public schools and program budgets.*
- *However, you also work for the* **president of the university** *since the President has been willing to identify teacher preparation and professional development as issues for which she has pledged her full support and on which her success will, in part, be judged.*
- *However, you also work for the cadre of* **professional educators** *who have helped us all by identifying best practices based on research; since, after all, we do not operate in isolation but are committed to the ethics and standards that guide our profession.*
- *However, in a larger sense, you work for the* **parents and communities across the state** *since they establish the expectations and provide most of the financial support for universities in general and professional preparation specifically.*
- *However, on a moral level, we work for the* **young people of the state** *since we have agreed to a mission statement that commits us to "produce professional educators of the highest quality and to support their continued development on behalf of the children in North Carolina."*

*In this environment of multiple "bosses" with multiple agendas, we nevertheless must work together to do the very best we can to maintain our focus on our "core" business: to prepare high-quality professional educators for our public schools. My best, Charles Coble, June 5, 1998.*

This true vignette helps frame the issues we attempt to address in this paper: who governs teacher preparation? Are there some new ways of thinking about how this complex, divided, semi-profession of teaching should be professionally prepared?

Newer research knowledge strongly links the quality of the teacher to student's academic success—something that seemed self-evident to many, but not until recently validated in research. The No Child Left Behind Act of 2000 builds upon this research base by calling for "highly qualified teachers" for every classroom in America by 2006. Since public education has now become a national imperative, and now we know teachers make a difference in student achievement, it is not surprising that the preparation of teachers is, again, coming under greater scrutiny.

We have started where we thought we should—at the beginning of teacher preparation in the United States. We have not attempted to provide a complete history, but enough to lay out as clearly as we could how we arrived at where we are, why teacher preparation is organized the way it is and some of the many problems associated with the current structure of teacher preparation. We also have attempted, in brief, to describe the history of teacher approval and licensure, which parallels the development of teacher preparation.

We then attempted to show some promising signs of change, primarily the movement toward increased clinical practice in partnership schools and professional development schools that are changing the roles and relationships between universities and the public schools. We include three different state partnership models, which describe the different manifestations of school-university teacher preparation partnerships that are developing across the nation. Many feel this "movement" is the only viable strategy for preparing effective teachers in our economically and ethnically diverse society.

In this paper, we have not addressed the growing involvement of community colleges in teacher preparation. Nor did we say much about alternative licensure. These omissions may fatally flaw the paper, but we did not have in mind simply describing all the possible iterations in teacher preparation. Rather, we have attempted to provide a broad look at the development of teacher preparation and its changing links to the larger teaching profession, not so much the many possible providers.

Finally, we tried to think about where might the future take us. Where do we want it to take us? We also provide a brief glimpse of an entirely different model for professional credentialing that is becoming a reality in America. We invite you to think with us about the future of teacher preparation as well, and what kinds of organizational structures would most support increased student learning and achievement in the public schools.

## A Brief History of Teacher Preparation

Teacher preparation in the United States is about 175 years old.[1] The term as used in this paper means preservice preparation that equips a teacher with the special knowledge and skills he or she needs to teach. It began in the 1830s as a small amount of study beyond the 8th grade, focused on pedagogy and offered in private schools. Not until 1974 – about 140 years later – did every state require certification of teachers based on four years of college preparation, including specified amounts of general education, specialization in a subject field and pedagogy.

In colonial times before the 1830s, little theoretical or practical attention was given to preparing teachers. Going to school was not expected of the young. Provision of schooling was a local option, often dependent on the availability of a teacher. Usually, school was held for only a few months in winter. The curriculum was limited to "the Bible, reading and writing, and less arithmetic" (Frazier et al., 1935, p. 2) because time, money and personnel were not available to teach more than the essentials of literacy.

Until the 1860s, when the Civil War intruded, most teachers were men. They were generally ignorant, ill prepared, punitive and narrowly focused on pouring facts into children's minds. Perhaps no more could be expected in a new, rough country whose adults were not well educated. Teaching was often a part-time job and seldom pursued as a career. Men usually used it as a steppingstone, often to the ministry. Women used it as employment between schooling and marriage.

Before the 1830s, most elementary school teachers had little education beyond their own six or eight years in elementary school. High school teachers were better educated, some being graduates of Latin grammar schools, "English" schools or academies, a few being graduates of four-year liberal arts colleges. A rare teacher had taken a course or received some instruction in teaching.

In the 1830s, America, then a fledgling nation of 23 states, was just beginning to develop "common" (public) schools. Europe was a strong influence in the new land. In Prussia and France, teacher-training institutions were developing, many built on the educational philosophies of a Swiss educator, Johann Heinrich Pestalozzi. Pestalozzi believed that teaching should heed a child's instincts, not impose learning on them. He thought it should be oriented to what a child could see, hear and touch in his or her immediate environment. For teaching to do that, Pestalozzi asserted, teachers needed special training in the nature of the child. Hence, the special teacher training institutions emerged. The French dubbed it "ecole normale," "ecole" meaning school, "normale," coming from the Latin "norma," literally meaning a carpenter's square, figuratively meaning a model, a principle. To the French this was a school in which the rules or principles of teaching were taught. The Americans translated the term to "normal school."

The philosophies and practices of Prussia and France attracted attention from Americans. In 1823, Samuel R. Hall established the first private normal school in America, in his home state, Vermont. Four years later, James G. Carter established the second private normal school, in Massachusetts.

It took 12 more years and the political efforts of many citizens and educators, chief among them Horace Mann, to see the first public normal school established, in July 1839, in Lexington, Massachusetts. A second Massachusetts public normal school was established the same year at Barre, a third in 1840 at Bridgewater. All three were designated state normal schools in 1845.

Slowly the idea of publicly supported state institutions for teacher training took hold beyond Massachusetts. New York, which had set a precedent in 1834 by appropriating money to support teacher-training departments in the academies, established its first normal school in 1844. Michigan and Connecticut followed in 1849, Rhode Island in 1854, New Jersey in 1855, Illinois in 1857 and Minnesota in 1858. From this base, the institution spread rapidly within and across states in the last four decades of the 19th century and the first two decades of the 20th century.

The early normal schools offered a few weeks to a year of study. Later, two years and then three years became the rule. Students studied the subjects that they would teach (at first, the Bible, orthography, reading, etc.), how to teach them and general pedagogy. They also practiced teaching in model schools.

Normal schools trained elementary school teachers. Initially, students were admitted directly from elementary school. Gradually, schooling beyond the 8th grade became a requirement. Massachusetts had another first in 1894 when it made high school graduation an entrance standard in normal schools.

Two other Europeans, whose ideas had a substantial effect on normal school training, were Johann Friedrich Herbart, a German philosopher and psychologist, and Friedrich Froebel, a German educator. Herbart's contribution was teaching methods. His belief in the importance of association in learning led him to formulate a five-step process of learning and teaching: preparation (orientation), presentation, association, generalization and application. "In the hands of some the new methods led to a vital professionalizing of education; in the hands of others they were formalized into a stiff and unchanging pattern that saddled rigid 'lesson plans' upon generations of teachers and their students" (Butts 1947, p. 439). Froebel's contribution was kindergarten education, to foster the "mental, moral and expressive powers" of young children before they entered elementary school (Butts 1947, p. 426).

Trailing the development of normal schools by some years was the beginning of teacher training in the colleges and universities, directed largely at secondary school teachers. (By 1870 there were only 80,000 students enrolled in the nation's high schools.) It first took the form of occasional lectures on pedagogy. Then it became recognized by a chairman in education with a more systematic program of lectures and instruction. The first permanent chairman in education was established at the University of Iowa in 1873, the second at the University of Michigan in 1879. By the turn of the century, the number of permanent chairmen in education had reached almost 250.

A recurring issue during the foregoing developments was the degree to which education in the subject matter the person was going to teach was adequate preparation and the degree to which training in pedagogy was an essential complement to subject matter. The issue has never been fully resolved for all levels of public school teaching. The normal schools clearly represented a swing to professionalism and general pedagogy. Today, training in pedagogy is not an issue in the education of elementary school teachers, but it still is a topic for debate in the preparation of secondary school teachers (as demonstrated by their very limited training in education).

Another issue was whether the college was the appropriate place to train teachers. James P. Wickersham reported in 1886 that, "'the experiment of educating teachers in colleges failed . . . [T]he general work of a college and the special work of a teachers' school can never be made to harmonize" (Frazier et al., 1935). The issue then was resolved by the decision to train elementary school teachers in normal schools and secondary school teachers in colleges. Nonetheless, the trend was toward more training.

Still another issue was whether teacher preparation should take place in a college separate from general collegiate education. The issue today is whether schools or colleges of education should be identified as professional schools and have the autonomy that goes with such status, or whether departments, schools or colleges of education should serve or work with other departments, schools or colleges in providing a program of teacher education. In normal school and teachers college days, the issue was resolved dually: education of elementary school teachers in a less-than-collegiate professional institution, education of secondary school teachers in a liberal arts college or university, with support from small departments of education.

Finally, there was the issue of public support for teacher preparation. For preservice teachers, the issue was hard fought in Massachusetts in the 1830s, but finally won decisively there and later elsewhere. The level of public support, however, for teacher preparation and their deferral to professionals to prepare teachers has never been comparable to that granted to other professions.

The number of normal schools peaked around 1920 at 326. Then, in increasing numbers, normal schools began to become teachers colleges. The evolution occurred for many reasons:

- The average level of education of the population was rising
- More and more jobs had begun to require high school graduation
- The public and the profession itself were demanding more training for teachers
- Teacher preparation was gaining respectability
- A good general education had become recognized as essential for all teachers
- Specialization in a major field required more time
- Certification or licensure authority was becoming centralized in state departments of education, causing rapid and more uniform raising of preparation standards.

Data from the early years of World War I show the state of teacher preparation at the time. Of the roughly 600,000 teachers then in service, it was estimated that 5% had no education beyond the 8th grade, one-third had less than four years of education beyond the 8th grade, and one-half had no professional preparation for teaching (Evenden 1935).

That condition had improved only slightly as the early 1920s were reached. A 1922 report found, and a 1923 report confirmed, that about 55% of American teachers did not have the equivalent of two years of training beyond high school (Evenden 1935).

The evolution of normal schools into teachers colleges began as early as 1897 with the designation, of Michigan's state normal school at Ypsilanti, as Michigan State Normal College. By 1920, as normal schools reached their peak in number, 46 teachers colleges had been established, public and private. Over the next 20 years, the number of teachers colleges increased fourfold while the number of normal schools diminished by two-thirds. By 1950 only five normal schools remained; by 1960, none.

The differences between teachers colleges and normal schools were several:

- A four-year curriculum (ultimately) versus one that was two or three years
- Study of subjects well beyond what was to be taught
- The addition of a general education program more comparable to the liberal education provided for any baccalaureate degree
- Increased requirements in a major field
- A full program of professional studies in history and foundations of education, and curriculum and teaching methods
- Several practica, culminating in student teaching (which in most colleges became full time for eight or more weeks during the 1950s).

But even as the single-purpose teachers college eclipsed the normal school, it began itself to be superseded. Many state teachers colleges became state colleges, and some of the latter became state universities as their mission was broadened. A few teachers colleges affiliated with universities. Within universities, departments of education became schools and colleges. The changeover began in a major way in the 1940s and continued through the 1960s. Today there are no teachers colleges in the United States. There are, however, more than 1,200 institutions that prepare elementary and secondary school teachers.

The transitions in institutional organization of teacher preparation occurred for many reasons. First, teacher educators saw the value of preparing teachers along with students preparing for other fields. The multipurpose institution, it was argued, would be less parochial. Second, after World War II, due largely to the GI Bill, there was a greater demand for public higher education, and expanding the academic scope of existing colleges was easier than building entirely new institutions. Third, some thought a strong liberal arts label would add respectability to teacher preparation. This argument was another configuration of the battle between subject matter and pedagogy. Finally, teacher preparation needed strong faculties in the arts and sciences both for general education and for greater depth in teaching specialties, particularly for secondary school teachers.

With the changeover came further improvement in standards of preparation and the academic status of teacher education. Study of the liberal arts became a major part of the preparation of all teachers, and specialization in teaching areas was mandated for high school teachers. Practica or student teaching and internships in actual school situations for specified numbers of days and weeks became standard. Teacher preparation became more accepted as a university function (though it still is disdained by many academics and others). Graduate schools of education began to blossom and proliferate in many cases focusing more on research and less on preparing teachers—and, thus, become less connected to actual classroom teachers.

For teacher preparation, the price of becoming an accepted part of higher education has proved to be high, however, and the effects on quality are no less questionable now than when the movement began. Becoming a part of higher education has subjected curriculum and course changes to scrutiny and approval by academic senates, many of which have no interest in or knowledge of teacher preparation. It has saddled colleges of education with university reward systems that do not always fit the program priorities of a college in which field-based practica and technical assistance to schools are important. It has locked faculties of education into staffing justifications based on full-time-equivalent ratios that may serve standard course-producing departments but hardly accommodate the diverse and complex duties of education faculties. It has drawn graduate professors of education further and further away from the practical concerns of schools, under the compulsion to conduct research and train researchers.

Most ironic of the results of the marriage of teacher preparation to academe is the money drain from tuition-producing continuing education programs. Income from such programs typically reverts to the general fund of the college or university after instructional costs are paid. The result has been major support from education tuition for other programs in the college or university, while teacher education itself operates on the lowest budget of any professional school.

## Teacher Certification, Program Accreditation and Professionalism

The evolution of teacher certification and state certification paralleled the evolution of normal schools to state teachers colleges and finally to comprehensive universities. While closely aligned in many ways, those who grant degrees to teach (universities) and those who grant certificates to teach (state departments of education and/or teaching standards boards) are in different organizations. Therein lies a source of tension and conflict within the profession and from external critics as well.

Though Indiana became the first state to require a high school diploma as a minimal requirement for teachers. New York, however, was the real leader in the movement toward certification of teachers. At first ministers or town officials determined who could teach, which they based largely on the applicants personal and moral characteristics. But, by 1812, local examinations of teacher candidates (with or without formal preparation) came into general use as a way of helping to select teachers for the local schools. By 1834, the responsibility for testing teachers was placed into the hands of the newly approved county superintendents who were granted the authority to develop and administer certification (except to normal school graduates). Then by 1899, the state superintendent for education was given the authority, by state legislation, to set the questions, establish cut-scores and oversee testing of teacher candidates. The New York state superintendent also was granted authority over all teacher preparation institutions, thus becoming the first state to have a uniform system of certification under state control. That set a trend for the states that spread rapidly in the next century (Angus 2001).

After professional organizations formed in the 19th and early 20th century, the National Education Association, the National Society for the Study of Education, the National Society of College Teachers in Education and the American Association of Teacher's Colleges began to develop and push for more and higher standards for both the preparation of teachers and for the granting of teacher certificates by states. Critics of teacher certification and teacher preparation, such as Diane Ravitch, have been highly critical of this move toward professionalism of teaching, claiming that it has split pedagogy and the liberal arts disciplines (Ravitch 2002).

In 1946, the National Education Association (NEA) created the National Commission on Teacher Education and Professional Standards (TEPS) in large part to give teachers more power within the teaching profession, which had largely been dominated by faculty in schools of education, school administrators and state department employees. In national conferences and in state chapters, TEPS officials attacked many of the prevailing practices and helped raise the voice of teachers in increasing the standards for entry and in advancing program approval standards over teacher preparation programs. TEPS (thus the NEA) became an equal partner with the American Association of Colleges for Teacher Education (AACTE) and the National Association of State Directors of Teacher Education and Certification (NASDTEC) in forming the National Council for the Accreditation of Teacher Education (NCATE) in 1952. Currently, approximately half of the teacher preparation programs in America are NCATE accredited, but the influence of practicing teachers on the NCATE board has been reduced over time (Angus 2001). Ravitch and other critics of the education bureaucracy assume more unanimity in the profession than may actually exist.

Clearly, one of the outcomes of professionalizing teaching was a close relationship between the standards required for certification, and the pedagogical and content courses offered by the institutions to prepare a person to meet those requirements. This led, inevitably to friction between the departments of public instruction, which were both issuing standards and approving institutions to prepare teachers: an external agency was essentially dictating the curriculum of the preparation institutions. Again, critics of teacher preparation view this development as an unholy alliance between the education professors and their former students in the departments of education. Critics see the "three-legged stool" of preparation, certification and accreditation that grew rapidly in the 20th century as a self-serving strategy to intrude more and more intellectually deficit pedagogical training courses at the expense of traditional liberal arts courses. (For a full account of these criticisms, see Diane Ravitch, *The Troubled Crusade* and *Professionalism and the Public Good: A Brief History of Teacher Certification* by David L. Angus.)

## The Disconnect Between Higher Education and the Public Schools

The critics of the "education establishment" seem largely unaware of the internal power struggles that are still very much a part of the tension within the education community. There are also significant internal disagreements within the "family" of K-12 education that pits teachers against administrators at all levels, from schools, to districts to departments of education. Teachers feel largely marginalized by these groups and from the process of school reform and the reform of their own profession—and disconnected from their own professional school (Angus 2001). The transformation of the nation's largest organization for teachers, the National Education Association (NEA), to a union and the subsequent expulsion of administrators from its ranks ended the "politics of consensus" within the profession. The growing militancy of the fast growing AFT (American Federation of Teachers), which is linked to the AFL and CIO, and NEA's increased militancy also has greatly alienated both the education and liberal arts faculties, fracturing the once unified profession (Angus 2001).

As previously discussed, in the earliest colonial years in America, teachers learned their practice through serving as apprentices to other "school masters" who, after a period of time, declared the apprentices to be qualified. There was no liberal arts or pedagogical preparation within colleges and universities. As normal schools developed into teachers colleges, students developed their beginning skills in teaching in laboratory schools, which expanded rapidly after 1900. Laboratory schools were owned by their host institutions and were not, therefore, governed by local boards of education. This relationship changed over time as the laboratory schools survived the transition of normal schools to teachers colleges, and then to state teachers colleges. Laboratory schools were largely populated by the sons and daughters of the college faculties and by the more privileged. The dramatic social changes, however, that followed *Brown vs. Board of Education*, the civil rights movement, school desegregation, and the Vietnam War rendered the laboratory schools more and more unlike other public schools and the larger society. As the last of the laboratory schools became regular public schools, they were slowly abandoned by the teacher education faculties (Hopkins 1995).

The demise of the laboratory school coincided with the transition of the state teachers colleges to state colleges and universities. Concurrently, teacher education faculties became more and more distant from the realities of the public schools. Teacher education faculties became more like the arts and sciences faculties and less focused on preparing teachers to do the work of the public schools. Research and writing about how to prepare teachers has become more professionally rewarding to faculty than to actually prepare effective teachers. The irony of this development is the still thin research base underlying the practices of teacher preparation (Allen, M., 2003).

But, with the release in 1983 of the report by the National Commission on Excellence in Education, *A Nation at Risk*, criticisms of education and of teacher preparation (which had been underway in repeated cycles since World War II), grew louder. The 1985 report titled *A Call for Change in Teacher Education* produced by the National Commission for Excellence in Teacher Education and the more influential Carnegie Commission's 1986 Report of the Task Force on Education and the Economy, *Teaching as a Profession*, called increased attention to the disconnect between university teacher preparation and the schools populated by their graduates. These reports also were critical of the lack of rigor in teacher preparation generally.

More recently, some are proposing "radical" changes to the rules for how teachers are licensed and how they are recognized for additional achievement in a way that bypasses teacher educators wholesale and significantly alters the governing norms of state departments of education. Proponents of a "market model" are creating parallel structures for the licensure of teachers, for advanced teacher licensure and for the accreditation of teacher education programs. The National Council on Teacher Quality and the Education Leaders Council have joined together to create the American Board for Certification of Teacher Excellence (ABCTE) *(http://www.abcte.org/)*.

ABCTE will offer college graduates – with at least a bachelor's degree – the opportunity to earn a Passport Certificate if: they can pass a criminal background check; pass a series of examinations demonstrating subject-area competency, written language skills and a fundamental knowledge of teaching; and "document participation in a high-quality professional development preservice experience that is classroom focused." ABCTE also will offer a Master Teaching Certificate for experienced teachers who pass a "rigorous" examination and who have a track record of teaching excellence as demonstrated by student achievement.

The success of the ABCTE process will depend ultimately on state recognition of the non-state-specific Passport credentials and of the Master Teacher Certification through state salary structures. Efforts currently are underway to have the U.S. Department of Education grant the same level of federal support to the ABCTE Master Teacher Certification process as is awarded to the existing National Board for Professional Teaching Standards (NBPTS).

## Toward the Reconnection of Higher Education and the Public Schools

In recent years several groups and organizations have joined forces toward what is becoming a movement to reconnect higher education and the public schools, and to strengthen teacher preparation, teaching quality and student success through increased collaboration. Some of these groups or organizations have featured connections between higher education and the schools to strengthen teacher preparation; other groups have expanded the scope of the connections between higher education and the schools with teaching quality (as opposed to teacher preparation) as the centerpiece; and others, still, have emphasized the broader alignment of P-12 schools and higher education with teacher preparation as one component of what has come to be called preschool (P) through college (16), or P-16 initiatives.

### Theme 1: School-university Partnerships with a Primary Focus on Teacher Preparation

Many rightly credit John Goodlad for the seminal work that has led to the resurgence of school-university partnerships across the country. Following Goodlad's extensive research on the public schools (most recently chronicled in *A Place Called School* 1984), he focused intently on teacher preparation beginning in the last half of the 1990s. Goodlad and his colleges studied sample institutions—each representing one of the six types of colleges and universities that prepare teachers—collecting surveys, reviewing case histories, conducting interviews and reviewing documents about the teacher preparation programs. In *Teachers for Our Nation's Schools* (1990) Goodlad explains the substance of his research—describing teacher preparation as "one of our nation's neglected enterprises" (p. xv).

Goodlad's major premise in *Teachers for Our Nation's Schools* is that the connection between good teachers and good schools is fundamental, and this connection has been ignored. He laid out 19 postulates—described as necessary conditions—that need to be in place if teacher preparation is to be improved. Through a competitive process, Goodlad invited colleges and universities that prepare teachers to join him in a National Network for Educational Renewal (NNER) committed to implementing the 19 postulates.

Two of these postulates, in particular, emphasize the fundamental connection between higher education and the public schools. (1) There must be a clearly identifiable group of academic and clinical faculty members with full authority, responsibility and accountability for teacher preparation. (2) There must be an identified group of partner schools—parallel to teaching hospitals—that are settings of best practice and that accept dual responsibility for the children in their charge and for the preparation of future teachers.

In the first of these two postulates, Goodlad emphasized the importance of arts and sciences and education faculties sharing responsibility for teacher preparation—but not in some abstract way that describes teacher preparation as an "all-university" responsibility. Rather, Goodlad emphasized the importance of "particular" faculty members being identified with responsibility for teacher preparation. Goodlad once asked the following questions during a visit to a university campus: If the president of this university were to call a meeting of the teacher preparation faculty to discuss the teacher preparation curriculum, who would come? Would faculty members in the arts and sciences even know if they are a part of the teacher preparation faculty?

In the second of these two postulates, the concept of an identifiable group of schools as necessary "partners" in teacher preparation was described as needing to replace the scattergun approach to field placements in schools that had characterized teacher preparation in previous decades. He introduced the concept of "partner schools."

In *Educational Renewal: Better Teachers, Better Schools* (1994), Goodlad expanded on the work described in *Teachers for Our Nation's Schools*. Here he drew on the progress of the NNER sites in implementing the 19 postulates—and emphasized the importance of the simultaneous renewal of teacher preparation and the public schools. He described Centers of Pedagogy as the necessary structures within which the identifiable group of faculty members from the arts and sciences, education and partner schools would engage in the simultaneous renewal of teacher preparation and the public schools. Goodlad included all 19 postulates in his description of Centers of Pedagogy and listed their functions as:

- Preparing new teachers
- Engaging in inquiry
- Establishing connections among public schools where field placements occur in teacher preparation (a defined network)
- Bringing coherence to all program components of teacher preparation
- Working concurrently on improving public schools and teacher preparation.

The seminal contributions of Goodlad to school-university partnerships are that they must be purposeful—with a clear and substantive agenda, that the partnership cannot be considered two-way (universities and schools), but three-way and specific—particular faculty members from the arts and sciences and education within universities, and particular schools as partners—all focused on the simultaneous renewal of teacher preparation and the public schools. The American Association of Colleges for Teacher Preparation also embraced the simultaneous renewal of P-12 education and the education of educators in the first goal of its strategic plan AACTE, 1995). Illustrations of three of the NNER partnerships are described in *Centers of Pedagogy* (Patterson et al. 1999).

Three additional groups emerged within the same approximate time period as the NNER: Project 30, the Renaissance Group and the Holmes Group. Project 30–30 institutions committed to arts and science/education collaboration in the redesign of teacher preparation—added definition to the substance of the arts and science/education collaboration (Murray 1996). The Renaissance Group, also a consortium of higher education institutions with a major commitment to teacher education, established 11 principles for member institutions that featured teacher preparation as the shared responsibility of university faculty and school practitioners *(http://www.emporia.edu/rengroup/)*. The Holmes Group (invited research universities) developed three reports: (1) *Tomorrow's Teachers* (1986), (2) *Tomorrow's Schools* (1990) and (3) *Tomorrow's Schools of Education* (1995). In these reports, well-prepared teachers are described as the key ingredient to school reform; professional development schools (similar to what Goodlad calls partner schools) are described as the type of laboratory needed for teacher preparation; and the quality of teacher preparation teachers receive is described as fundamental to the quality of teachers. Holmes Group institutions committed to the following:

a. To make education schools accountable to the profession and to the public for the trustworthy performance of their graduates at beginning and advanced levels of practice
b. To make research, development and demonstration of quality learning in real schools and communities a primary mission of education schools
c. To connect professional schools of education with professionals directly responsible for elementary and secondary education at local, state, regional and national levels to coalesce around higher standards
d. To recognize interdependence and commonality of purpose in preparing educators for various roles in schools, roles that call for teamwork and common understanding of learner-centered education in the 21st century
e. To provide leadership in making education schools better places for professional study and learning
f. To center work on professional knowledge and skills for educators who serve children and youth
g. To contribute to the development of state and local policies that give all youngsters the opportunity to learn from highly qualified educators (http://www.holmespartnership.org).

Building on the third report of the Holmes Group, *Tomorrow's Schools of Education*, the Network of Innovative Colleges of Education was formed under the leadership of the University of Tennessee. This network featured the efforts of five education deans to restructure colleges of education (Innovative Colleges of Education 1996).

Partner or professional development schools are a common feature in all the preceding networks and organizations. Most organizations agree on at least four common purposes of partner or professional development schools:

1. Provide a clinical setting for preservice teachers
2. Engage in professional development of practitioners
3. Promote and conduct inquiry that advances knowledge of schools
4. Provide exemplary education for the P-12 students in attendance (Clark and Smith 1999).

The National Council for the Accreditation of Teacher Education has created standards for professional development schools (NCATE, 2001). Nancy Zimpher (2001) describes the learning of teachers as important as that of children in professional development schools.

## Vignette—The University of North Carolina

While teacher preparation institutions across the country strengthened school-university partnerships throughout the 1990s in directions similar to those described above, few, if any, university systems have made as much progress as the University of North Carolina system in reconnecting higher education and the schools to strengthen the preparation and development of teachers. In 1997, the 15 colleges/schools/departments of education in the University of North Carolina and the public schools entered into partnerships to work toward five "guiding principles" for school-university partnerships approved by the University of North Carolina Board of Governors (Coble 1998):

1. Increased time for preservice teacher to experience earlier, longer and more intensive field-based placements in the public schools, connected to methods classes and clinical teachers at school sites
2. Jointly crafted professional development programs for teachers, administrators and others in the public schools and universities
3. Increased communication between public schools and higher education for the purpose of sharing and disseminating best practices
4. Generated and applied research and knowledge about teaching and learning
5. Involved university and school personnel in curriculum planning and program improvement.

Some of the lessons learned in the University-School Teacher Education Partnerships are:

- *Partnerships are beneficial.* Results are produced that are only possible through collaboration.
- *Thoughtful selection of partnership participants is an important first step.* Involve both university and public school faculty in the selection of partnership sites to ensure buy-in.
- *It is important to take time up front to lay a foundation for teamwork.* Building relationships among key participants at the beginning will help build trust and establish ties for open communication.
- *All stakeholder groups should be involved throughout program development and implementation.* All stakeholder groups should be given opportunities to contribute ideas, communicate their interests and ask questions before decisions that affect them are made.
- *Cultural differences between partners must be acknowledged and addressed.* Building mutual understanding of differences (e.g., priorities and reward systems) can strengthen partnerships.
- *Partnerships must create value for all parties.* Partnerships require shared ownership of the responsibility for teacher preparation.
- *The scope of activities undertaken must be realistic with respect to available resources.* To do too many things at one time can dilute the overall effectiveness of the partnership.
- *Planning ahead and training are necessary prior to implementation.* Failure to do so will lead to inevitable disappointment of the outcome.
- *Evaluate, document and communicate program performance.* To build a culture of mutual respect and accountability, the successes and failures of the partnership must be documented and reported.

## Theme 2: Teaching Quality as the Centerpiece of School-university Partnerships

The National Commission on Teaching and America's Future (NCTAF), chaired by Governor James B. Hunt of North Carolina and directed by Linda Darling-Hammond, further documented the importance of teaching quality in improving student learning in the public schools (NCTAF, 1996). But the contributions of the commission extend the connections between higher education and public schools beyond a primary focus on teacher preparation and recommended the following:

1. Importance of standards for both students and teachers
2. Reinvention of teacher preparation and professional development around standards for teachers (performance-based licensure, using the Interstate New Teacher Assessment and Support Consortium Standards for beginning teachers and National Board for Professional Teaching Standards as benchmarks for accomplished teaching)
3. Major emphasis on teacher recruitment and bringing an end to out-of-field teaching to provide every child with a competent, caring and qualified teacher
4. Career continuums for teachers that encourage and reward knowledge and skills
5. Reorganization of schools to better support teacher and student success, with school principals who understand teaching and learning and who can lead high-performing schools.

Twelve states became "partner states" and have been leading efforts to put these five recommendations in place. A central contribution of NCTAF is that "teaching quality" rather than "teacher preparation" moved to the centerpiece of school-university partnerships. In addition to teacher preparation, work in partnerships broadened to include policy development on conditions of practice, shared induction and mentoring programs, teacher recruitment initiatives, and an emphasis on the preparation and development of educational leaders who put conditions in place to support student and teacher success.

The National Governors Association (NGA) and the National Conference of State Legislatures (NCSL), with funding from the Carnegie Corporation, are currently working with five states to take policy action on matters of teaching quality. As with the National Commission on Teaching and America's Future, this NGA/NCSL collaborative is focusing more broadly on teaching quality, encouraging policy action to define teaching quality, to incorporate student learning into teacher evaluation, to embed teacher professional development in the work of school improvement (perhaps through partner or professional development schools), to focus evaluation policy on improving teaching practice, to create career ladders for teachers with performance-based compensation for successful teachers, and to incorporate multiple stakeholders—especially teachers—in the design of a teacher evaluation system.

An emphasis on "teaching quality" rather than "teacher quality" also has become prominent in the work of other professional organizations on teacher professional development. For example, the National Foundation for the Improvement of Education (1996) offers six recommendations to help teachers assume responsibility for their own professional development:

1. Professional development should be school centered – based on the needs of students in the schools where teachers are teaching.
2. Standards for student learning and for professional practice should guide the design of professional development.
3. Individual teachers should design their professional development to fulfill their school's needs for expertise.
4. Teachers and administrators should create peer assistance and review procedures, and collaborate in counseling out of the profession any teacher who does not meet professional standards of practice despite sustained assistance.
5. Teachers who have additional expertise should have opportunities to provide schoolwide leadership.
6. Every school should provide a yearlong induction program for first-year teachers.

With recommendations such as these, the role and responsibility of universities in teacher professional development is changed. Rather than serving as "provider" of professional development, university faculty members assist individual teachers (as appropriate) in meeting their individual goals through partner or professional development schools, and they become participants in shared learning within learning communities.

# Vignette—Texas A&M University System

To illustrate one example of comprehensive school-university partnerships, the work of the Texas A&M University System is featured. In 1999 the Texas A&M University System approved six objectives:

1. Expand and refine the successful school-university partnerships underway, particularly in educator preparation
2. Elevate the status of educator preparation and school-university partnerships within the A&M System
3. Increase the quality and effectiveness of all educator preparation programs with the A&M System
4. Strengthen curriculum alignment and instructional transition between public high schools, community colleges and universities within the A&M System
5. Promote collaborative research and development that advances state education policies
6. Provide a comprehensive and continuous improvement system for educator preparation and student preparedness within the A&M System (Texas A&M University System's Board of Trustees, March 1999).

Through collaboration between the Texas A&M University System and the Texas Education Agency, an Institute for School-University Partnerships has been created to provide leadership toward achieving these six objectives. A&M institutions that achieve the highest level of institutional commitment to partner with Texas public schools will be designated as "Regents' Centers for Excellence in Education."

The Institute for School-University Partnerships also is leading the school-university collaborative to develop an "Academic Roadmap" for K-12 students, parents, teachers, counselors and school administrators—guiding access and success routes to the baccalaureate degree in any field. Likewise, the institute sponsors an academy for higher education faculty to learn more about the public schools and to facilitate increased investment of faculty in field-based education preparation programs. Faculty members selected for this academy are given high status with A&M institutions. Finally, the institute is promoting formal partnerships between A&M institutions and community colleges to strengthen the program alignment in teacher preparation between community colleges and A&M institutions and to recruit increased numbers of potential teacher candidates through the community colleges.

## Theme 3: Preschool through College (P-16) School-university Partnerships

The Education Trust, under the leadership of Kati Haycock, has played the seminal role in promoting and leading kindergarten through college (K-16) or preschool to college (P-16) school-university partnerships. The Education Trust was created to promote high academic achievement for all students at all levels, kindergarten through college, with special emphasis on schools and colleges that serve predominantly Latino, African American, American Indian and low-income students (*Thinking K-16* 2002). The work of the Education Trust features two key leverage points for K-16 partnerships: Alignment of student standards, assessments and curricula to ensure all high school graduates are "college ready" should they choose to attend; and the preparation of teachers with the knowledge and skill set to help all P-12 students become "college ready."

The State Higher Education Executive Officers (SHEEO) and the Education Commission of the States (ECS) also have launched a collaborative PK-16 initiative with a similar focus (Zimpher 1999; Tafel and Eberhart 1999, and O'Bannon, et al. 2002). More than half of the states now report some form of K-16 or P-16 partnerships (Callan et al. 2001)

The National Association of System Heads (university system chancellors with a single governing board for multiple institutions), which is an affiliate of the Education Trust, developed a K-16 Square to reflect the commitments needed by both K-12 education and university systems (NASH 1999). Two corners of the K-16 Square reflect commitments needed from K-12 school systems; the other two corners show commitments needed from colleges and universities.

## The K-16 SQUARE

The simplicity of the K-16 Square shows clearly the interdependence of the K-12 and university systems. K-16 or P-16 partnerships that embrace the vision described above from NASH move work on teaching quality (and its foundation, teacher preparation) away from the center of school-university partnerships and add equal emphasis on aligning systems–standards, assessments and curricula–for students as they move from one level to the next, preschool through college. P-16 or K-16 partnerships thus have two main strands of work that together are central to the partnership, with both dependent upon the success of the other (Henry and Kettlewell 1999).

 Moreover, within a K-16 or P-16 framework the two major partners—schools and universities—cannot make the commitments to the other partner and then do the work independently. The standards set for students, aligned preschool through college, are used as a basis for determining if teacher candidates' content knowledge is sufficient to bring P-12 student performance to high standards. Commitment D (from the K-16 Square) calls upon universities that prepare teachers to base their recommendations for certification on evidence of teacher candidates' accomplishment in bringing P-12 student performance to high standards. This commitment shifts work on teaching quality from the performance of what the teacher knows and can do to the impact of the teacher's performance on P-12 student learning in schools. Increasing student learning is at the core of both strands of K-16 or P-16 work.

## Vignette—University System of Georgia

Georgia launched a statewide P-16 agenda dedicated to the commitments outlined in the NASH K-16 Square in 1995 (http://www.usg.edu/p16). Early work on aligning standards, assessments and curricula was done by regional P-16 councils. Using the regionally based P-16 standards as a guide, the Board of Regents of the University System of Georgia (two-year colleges and all baccalaureate-, master's- and doctoral-level public institutions) adopted a results-based set of Regents' Principles for the preparation of teachers and school leaders, with a similar set of principles for the preparation of school counselors pending approval. The focus of all three sets of principles is

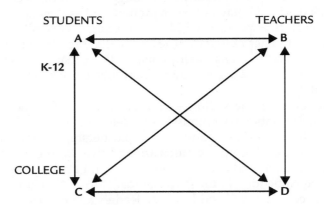

**STATE SYSTEMS K-16**

COMMITMENT A: We will ensure that all high school graduates meet high standards.
COMMITMENT B: We will accept only teachers who can bring all students' performance to high standards.
COMMITMENT C: We will accept into college only students who meet high standards
COMMITMENT D: We will ensure that all teacher candidates we produce are prepared to bring student performance to high standards

on outcomes—the educator's impact on improving children's learning in the public schools. In all university system institutions that prepare teachers, responsibility for educator preparation is vested in a shared governance structure, including faculty from the college of education, college of arts and science, and partner schools. To be recommended for certification beginning in May 2002, universities must have evidence that each teacher candidate:

- Is able to bring diverse students to high levels of learning (at point of initial certification)
- Shows advanced levels of accomplishment in bringing diverse students to high levels of learning (after two-years of teaching)
- Can demonstrate in their work with children that they:
  - Have sufficient depth in content fields
  - Organize teaching around high standards
  - Use data to improve student learning
  - Customize instruction for individuals and groups
  - Use technology to advance student learning
  - Manage classrooms effectively
  - Diagnose difficulties in reading and mathematics and know what to do about them (early childhood education).

Because teacher attrition is such a problem in Georgia and with school administrators and state and school system policies responsible for the conditions in schools that contribute negatively to teacher retention in the classroom, the Leadership Institute for School Improvement was created in 2001–02. The institute is an incubator for policy change and is a unique provider of preparation and development programs for educational leaders. Georgia's Leadership Institute operates as a four-way partnership among business, higher education, K-12 education and state government.

Currently, under the leadership of the Georgia Department of Education (K-12 education) in partnership with the University System of Georgia, Department of Technical and Adult Education (technical colleges), and the Office of School Readiness (preschool programs), P-14 student-learning standards are under development in the four core academic areas. The level 12 standards define what it means to be college ready; the level 14 standards are intended to make clear what students must know, be able to do and understand to matriculate from lower- to upper-division work in college and to transfer from a two-year to a baccalaureate degree-granting institution.

All the research networks, and work in the three states featured in the vignettes, point to the need for strong school-university partnerships. Although the authors recognize that distinctions among the partnerships described may not be as pronounced as they appear here, the intent has been to make clear at least three primary emphases in school-university partnerships: (1) those focused predominantly on teacher preparation, (2) those that broaden the emphasis from teacher preparation to an emphasis on "teaching quality" and (3) those that focus on both the student side of progression from preschool through college and from college back to schools in educator preparation and development.

From the experience of one of the authors – who has participated in the NNER, under the leadership of John Goodlad; the National Commission on Teaching and America's Future, under the leadership of Linda Darling-Hammond; and in P-16 partnerships, under the leadership of Kati Haycock—it is clear the clusters of partnerships are additive. Both Goodlad's emphasis on the simultaneous renewal of schools and teacher preparation, and Darling-Hammond's emphasis on teaching quality must be embedded in the P-16 agenda. P-16 or K-16 partnerships complete the loop—K-12 students are college ready and teachers, leaders and counselors (in terms of preparation and policies that support student and teacher success) are able to bring K-12 students to be college ready.

## Conclusions and Recommendations

Initiatives to create stronger links between the public schools and colleges and universities are welcome signs of renewed focus on better preparing teachers and have a clearer focus on school improvement and student success. These, however, are still best characterized as initiatives that are not fully embedded and, as noted, not fully codified into a uniform professional standard.

School-university partnerships and K-16 or P-16 councils are options, not expectations for universally accepted practice.

If the school-university partnership, PDS's, and/or K-16 or P-16 councils take hold in America and become codified as the norms of practice in preparing teachers, then different governance and finance structures will have to emerge simultaneously. One of the "lessons learned", from the three state vignettes included in this document and from the literature, is that school-university partnerships work when responsibility for them is shared. Agreements have to be reached and the leaders of different organizations and institutions have to "sign off" on those agreements if the partnerships are to have a chance at succeeding.

But, for teacher preparation to improve systemically, partnerships between higher education and the public schools have to go beyond the *chance* that they will develop. The higher education community of professionals and the precollege professional community will have to accept partnerships as the way that teacher preparation will happen and happen by a set of "rules" that have been codified by accrediting boards and licensing agents in the state departments of education, professional standards boards or new entities that emerge over time.

Educators, policymakers and other decisionmakers must work together to better assure longevity, stability and sustained interdependence of school-university partnerships. Such partnerships would:

1. Identify the mutual benefits derived from partnerships, such as productivity gains, service innovations, improved conditions and satisfaction with work and outcome results
2. Establish reward structures that recognize the commitments and contributions of professional employees in public schools and higher education who work to achieve positive outcomes across traditional organizational boundaries
3. Promote shared knowledge and a culture of mutual dependency where time, money, technology, special expertise and facilities are devoted to the partnership
4. Build stronger organizational linkages that promote the integration of resources, information and professional social networks.

Five action steps are recommended to facilitate the development of the new structures—structures that will fill the "white spaces" between the current K-12 and higher education organizational charts. These recommended actions are pre- or co-requisite to the building of university-school partnerships as described above.

1. There must be a focus on educating policymakers and on why the current separation between K-12 and higher education is insufficient to improving schools, teachers, teacher preparation and student achievement.
2. Joint planning is required between K-12 and higher educators at all levels to make the multiple layers of decisions required to build sustainable partnerships.
3. The K-16 partners and policy community must create the appropriate measures to assure the public assessment and accountability of their performance and results.
4. Cross-functional teams must be developed to access new knowledge among the partners, build social networks grounded in professional experience, and to support the stability of the partnership as players change over time.
5. Technological barriers that separate the K-12 and higher education communities must be eliminated. There must be increased access to data related to the identified success indicators—primarily student achievement—but also documenting partnership activities and reports.

## Summary Statement

All the research, networks and work in the three states featured in the vignettes point to the need for strong school-university partnerships. Although the authors of this paper recognize that distinctions among the partnerships described may not be as pronounced as they appear here, the intent has been to make clear at least three primary emphases in school-university partnerships: those focused predominantly on teacher preparation, those that place primary emphasis on "teaching quality," and those that focus on student learning by highlighting both the student side of progression from preschool through college and from college back to schools in educator preparation and development.

# References

Allen, Michael. *Eight Questions on Teacher Preparation: What Does the Research Say?* Denver, CO: Education Commission of the States, 2003.

American Association of Colleges for Teacher Education. *Long-range and Strategic Plan 1994-2004.* Washington, D.C.: AACTE, 1995.

American Board for Certification of Teacher Excellence. *Certification Programs.* http://www.abcte.org.

Angus, David L. *Professionalism and the Public Good: A Brief History of Teacher Certification.* Thomas B. Fordham Foundation, January 2001.

Butts, R. F. *A Cultural History of Education: Reassessing Our Educational Traditions.* New York: McGraw-Hill, 1947.

Callan, Patrick, Gene Maeroff and Michael Usdan. *The Learning Connection: New Partnerships Between Schools and Colleges.* New York: Teachers College Press, 2001.

Clark, Richard and Wilma Smith. "Partnerships, Centers and Schools." In *The Beat of a Different Drummer: Essays on Educational Renewal in Honor of John I. Goodlad* edited by Kenneth Sirotnik and Roger Soder. New York: Peter Lang Publishing, Inc., 1999.

Coble, Charles. "Overview of University-school Teacher Education Partnerships." In *University-school Teacher Education Partnerships* edited by Roy Edelfelt. Chapel Hill: University of North Carolina System, 1998.

The Education Trust. *Thinking, K-16*(6), 1, 2002.

Evenden, E. S. *National Survey of the Education of Teachers, Vol. 6, Summary and Interpretations.* Bulletin 1933, No. 10. Washington, D.C.: U.S. Government Printing Office, 1935.

Frazier, B. W., G. L. Betts, W. J. Greenleaf, D. Waples, N. H. Dearborn, M. Carney and T. Alexander. *National Survey of the Education of Teachers, Vol. 5, Special Survey Studies.* Bulletin 1933, No. 10. Washington, D.C.: U.S. Government Printing Office, 1935.

Goodlad, John. *A Place Called School.* New York: McGraw-Hill Book Company, 1984.

Goodlad, John. *Educational Renewal: Better Teachers, Better Schools.* San Francisco: Jossey-Bass Publishers, 1994.

Goodlad, John. *Teachers for Our Nation's Schools.* San Francisco: Jossey-Bass Publishers, 1990.

Henry, Ronald and Jan Kettlewell. "Georgia's P-16 Partnerships." *Metropolitan Universities,* (10), 2, 1999.

Holmes Group Web site: http://www.holmespartnership.org.

Hopkins, Scott. "Using the Past: Guiding the Future." In *Emerging Trends in Teacher Preparation* edited by Gloria Appelt Slick. Corwin Press, Inc., 1995.

California Council on Teacher Education. "Innovative Colleges of Education." *Teacher Education Quarterly,* (23), 1, 1996.

Murray, Frank. "Building a Knowledge Base for the Preparation of Teachers." In *The Teacher Educator's Handbook.* Washington, D.C.: American Association of Colleges for Teacher Education, 1996.

National Association of System Heads. *A Statement of State Education CEOs, K-16: With Renewed Hope—and Determination.* Washington, D.C.: NASH, 1999.

National Commission on Teaching and America's Future. *What Matters Most: Teaching for America's Future.* New York: NCTAF, 1996.

National Conference of State Legislatures Web site: http://www.ncsl.org.

National Council for the Accreditation of Teacher Education. *Standards for Professional Development Schools.* Washington, D.C.: NCATE, 2001.

National Foundation for the Improvement of Education. *Teachers Take Charge of Their Learning.* Washington, D.C.: NFIE, 1996.

National Governors Association Web site: http://www.nga.org.

O'Bannon, Frank, Gary Locke, Sharon Kagan, Spud Van de Water and Stephen Portch. "P-16: The Next Great Education Reform." *State Education Leader* (20), 1. Denver: Education Commission of the States, 2002.

Patterson, Robert, Nicholas Michelli and Arthur Pacheco. *Centers of Pedagogy.* San Francisco: Jossey-Bass Publishers, 1999.

Ravitch, Diane. *A Brief History of Teacher Professionalism.* Paper presented at the White House Conference on Preparing Tomorrow's Teachers, 2002. http://www.ed.gov/admins/tchrqual/learn/preparingteachersconference/ravitch.html.

Ravitch, Diane. *The Troubled Crusade.* New York: Basic Books, 1983.

Renaissance Group Web site: http://www.emporia.edu/rengroup/.

Tafel, Jonathan and Nancy Eberhart. "Statewide School-college K-16 Partnerships To Improve Student Performance." In *State Strategies that Support Successful Student Transitions from Secondary to Post-Secondary Education.* Denver: State Higher Education Executive Officers (SHEEO) and ACT, Inc., 1999.

Texas A&M University System Board of Regents. *Regents' Initiative for Excellence in Education.* College Station: Board of Regents, 1999.

University System of Georgia Web site: http://www.usg.edu/p16.

Zimpher, Nancy. "Creating Professional School Sites." *Theory into Practice,* (29), 1, 2001.

Zimpher, Nancy. "Teacher Quality and P-16 Reform: The State Policy Context." In *State Strategies that Support Successful Student Transitions from Secondary to Post-Secondary Education.* Denver: SHEEO and ACT, Inc., 1999.

*This summary of the history of teacher preparation is adapted from "A History of the Professional Development of Teachers" by R.A. Edelfelt and M. Johnson, 1980, in C.E. Feistritzer and C. Dobson (Eds.), The 1981 Report on Educational Personnel Development, Washington, D.C.: Feistritzer Publications; and A Brief History of Standards in Teacher Education by R.A. Edelfelt and J.D. Raths, 1999, Reston, VA: Association of Teacher Educators.*

# Community Colleges and Teacher Preparation: Roles, Issues and Opportunities

## Tricia Coulter, Ph.D. and Bruce Vandal, Ph.D.

## Overview

The role of community colleges in preparing the next generation of teachers in U.S. classrooms continues to evolve. In many states, community colleges are no longer playing an informal or tangential role in teacher preparation and instead are becoming critical leaders in efforts to develop a pool of highly effective teachers for states and regions that have demand which far exceeds supply.

In August of 2006, the Education Commission of the States and the National Center for Teacher Transformation convened representatives from a variety of national organizations representing state higher education executive officers, community colleges, teacher preparation programs, teacher accreditation and K-12 education to discuss the role of community colleges in teacher education. The meeting focused on how community colleges can meet the needs of an increasingly diverse teaching industry and catalyze reform in teacher education. The following paper describes a variety of forces in education policy and reform that are providing an important context to the role of community colleges in teacher education. In addition, the paper articulates how community colleges can capitalize on their unique attributes as responsive institutions that serve a diverse population of students and industry needs to meet critical workforce demand in local and regional communities and positively impact the field of teacher education.

## Forces Impacting Community Colleges and Teacher Education

As states continue to struggle with the challenges of educating their citizens for a knowledge-based, global economy, it is no surprise that teacher quality and effectiveness are viewed as critical components of an effective state education reform strategy. Policymakers and teacher educators engaged in the development of state policy governing teacher preparation are encountering three significant forces which impact their ability to identify and train teachers who are prepared for the 21st century classroom. Among the forces shaping the future of teacher preparation are:

- Continuing demand for quality teachers, especially in specific subject shortage areas
- Recognition that retention and ongoing training of teachers is needed to maintain an effective teaching force
- Increasing economic and cultural diversity of students in U.S. classrooms requiring schools to find teachers who have the capacity and commitment to educate students who come to school with a wide range of educational needs.

In several states profoundly affected by these forces, community colleges have proven to be uniquely suited to addressing these challenges and, as a result, have seen their role in teacher preparation expand.

A closer examination of each of these forces viewed through the lens of teacher education provides insight into how community colleges are well-positioned for this role.

## High Teacher Demand

While there is some disagreement on whether there is a national teacher shortage, there is no question that in certain regions of the country and specific disciplines, many schools are having great difficulty finding highly qualified teachers for their classrooms.[1] These difficulties exist in some states for teachers in general and in most states for teachers in specific subject areas.

The demand for teachers in all subject areas can be linked to enrollment increases in the general student population. According to the National Center for Education Statistics, 23 states will experience enrollment increases through 2014. Thirteen of those 23 states will see enrollment increases of between 5 and 15%.[2] In many states facing enrollment increases, the demand for teachers outstrips the capacity of traditional university-based teacher preparation programs and consequently community colleges have become more involved in meeting growing demand.

In **Nevada**, which projects enrollment increases of over 28%, the state responded by enabling Great Basin College to offer baccalaureate degrees in teacher education as a means of providing teachers for the largely rural communities that Great Basin serves.[3] In **Florida**, which predicts a 10% increase in student enrollment, the state department of education projects that for the 2006-07 school year there will be a shortage of over 32,000 teachers and that the state will need to produce 20,000 new teachers a year for the next ten years to meet growing demand.

At present, 52% of the teachers graduating from "traditional" teacher education programs from Florida state universities are community college transfers.[4] Florida has responded to the incredible demand for teachers by taking advantage of the large number of teacher education candidates who are entering teacher education programs from community colleges by allowing community colleges to confer baccalaureate degrees in teacher education, and by developing one of the nation's most aggressive alternative certification programs at the state's community colleges.

The demand for teachers in many regions becomes more complicated when you consider the level of demand in specific high need teaching disciplines. Of the 64 fields in which teacher education programs are offered, 29 have shortages and none of the fields report having a large surplus.[5] Areas that have the greatest demand include: special education, mathematics, physical sciences, English as a second language, foreign languages, and vocational or technical education. According to the National Center of Education Statistics, over 25% of all schools in the United States "found it very difficult or were not able to fill the vacancies in these fields" for the 2003-04 school year.[6]

Greater concern about U.S. competitiveness has led to an array of responses to the shortage of math and science teachers. In a review of recent reports on U.S. economic competitiveness, teacher preparation and teacher quality were named as important components of a national strategy.[7] Reports from such diverse organizations as the National Defense Education and Innovation Initiative of the Association of American Universities, the National Academies, The National Summit on Competitiveness and The Business Roundtable suggest that academic researchers, business and policymakers alike believe teacher preparation is a critical component of a national strategy for meeting long term economic goals.[8]

Community colleges have been quick to recognize the opportunity presented by the level of interest in science, technology, engineering and mathematics (STEM) education among policymakers. The American Association of Community Colleges (AACC), through a grant from the National Science Foundation, identified steps community colleges should take to improve the capacity of teachers to teach in the STEM fields.[9] As a result of their efforts, many community colleges have developed a variety of strategies for attracting students with skills and interest in STEM fields into teaching. Strategies implemented by community colleges include curriculum development, improving instruction in STEM classes at the community college, aligning student and community services in support of students with an interest in teaching in STEM fields, and building partnerships with K-12 and teacher education programs to create seamless transitions for students into community college and ultimately to a teaching license.

Community colleges, because of their history of providing responsive solutions for business, are well positioned to provide the customized programs and strategies that are needed to meet the specific workforce needs of the regions they serve. As policymakers and K-12 school districts advocate for multifaceted approaches to preparing teachers beyond the traditional model, community colleges can be powerful players capable of meeting the expectations of policymakers and K-12 leaders.

## Recruiting and Retaining Highly Effective Teachers

Some argue the number of teaching candidates produced by colleges is not as much a problem as the ability of school districts to attract those candidates to their schools and to retain them. Only 60% of students who complete teacher education programs move directly into teaching jobs. Of those who do go into teaching, only 50 to 60% are on the job five years later.[10]

As schools and school districts are faced with the challenge of finding and retaining teachers that meet new federal and state requirements, it is more important than ever to invest in the capacity of teachers through professional development opportunities designed to improve their effectiveness. The use of technology in the classroom, data-driven decisionmaking and enhancing content knowledge are just a few of the areas in which teachers must continually develop new knowledge and skills. These opportunities need to be available and customized to meet the unique needs of specific schools and school districts.

Community colleges can play a critical role in providing customized professional development for teachers that is available and accessible. In many communities, the community college provides not only the expertise, but also the facilities that are conducive to providing quality training opportunities for teachers. At Anne Arundel Community College in Maryland, the Teacher Education and Childcare (TEACH) Center within the institution's customized training division has created an innovative model for developing customized training opportunities for teachers from surrounding schools. The ability of the community college to offer solutions that directly respond to the needs of local area educators is viewed as a critical economic development strategy for providing the support teachers need to persist in their positions and to provide the best possible education opportunities for their children.

## Economic and Racial/Ethnic Diversity of Students

In addition to the rapid increases in enrollment in many states and the subsequent demand for teachers it generates, many more states are seeing their K-12 enrollments become more racially, ethnically and economically diverse. In 2004, 41% of all students enrolled in U.S. schools were either Hispanic, black or Asian/Pacific Islanders. In areas experiencing the greatest enrollment increases, minority students make up an even larger percentage of enrollments. In southern states, 46% of students were from minority groups and in western states, 57% of enrollments were from minority groups.[11]

These changing demographics will require schools to hire more teachers in specialty areas such as English as a second language. In addition, the low number of teachers from minority and immigrant communities creates another complication for many classrooms that seek to create differentiated instruction for children of various backgrounds, skills and dispositions.[12]

Community colleges have traditionally been a primary access point for minority and low-income students. Over 40% of students enrolled in community colleges were from a racial/ethnic minority group. In addition, over 28% of dependent students at community colleges came from families with annual incomes of less than $32,000, and 46% of independent students earned less than $25,000 per year.[13] As a result, the community college has a unique understanding of students from diverse backgrounds and can be a source of teachers who are well equipped to meet the needs of minority and low-income students. At many community colleges that serve urban communities, the college is directly impacted by the quality of the education provided to low-income and minority students who ultimately enroll in the community college. As a result, the college has both a unique understanding of the circumstances of students as well as an opportunity to become actively involved in both the preparation and professional development of teachers from urban K-12 schools.

At Miami-Dade College in **Florida**, where 88% of students are either Hispanic or African American, they offer a BS in teacher education, with a large percent of the students who earn a degree staying in the immediate area to teach.[14] As a result, the college is not only receiving students from Miami's diverse K-12 schools, they are actively engaged in preparing the teachers that will educate the Miami-Dade students of the future. All of these forces are having a tremendous impact on both the supply of teachers and the demand for their services. As the teaching industry becomes more complicated, it is more important than ever for states to consider diversified approaches to preparing teachers. The traditional four-year university experience may be too narrow an approach for preparing the wide range of candidates that could meet the precise needs of schools and districts.

## Community Colleges: Providing Diverse Approaches to Teacher Education

The flexibility and responsiveness of community colleges in teacher education is evidenced by the many different approaches to teacher preparation they pursue. Throughout the country, community colleges have implemented a variety of strategies ranging from offering introductory education courses to awarding baccalaureate degrees in teacher education. The most prominent approaches to teacher preparation involving community colleges fall into the following four categories:

- 2 + 2 arrangements with teacher education programs at traditional baccalaureate granting colleges and universities
- Alternative certification programs for post-baccalaureate students
- Baccalaureate programs offered by the community college
- Customized professional development programs created in collaboration with local school districts.

Each of these approaches show great promise for meeting teacher education needs in states. However, there is also much to be learned about how to ensure that these efforts ultimately produce highly effective teachers. Following are brief descriptions of each approach along with some of their strengths and weaknesses.

### 2 + 2 Programs

2 + 2 programs are the most common approach taken by community colleges involved in teacher preparation. Providing core general education courses for students who intend to transfer to a baccalaureate granting institution is a key aspect of the traditional mission of most community colleges. The more specific goal of preparing students for transfer into traditional teacher education programs has led to a myriad of strategies ranging from providing relevant general education courses and possibly one or two teacher education courses to more sophisticated partnerships with traditional teacher education programs. Examples of the latter include: Associate of Arts in Teaching degrees that are aligned with public four-year teacher education programs; joint admission programs where a course of study is designed by the community college and teacher education program for students they jointly admit; common course numbering agreements at the state level which ensure courses will transfer from the community college to a four-year institution; and finally entrance exams for community college students (such as Praxis I or College Learning Assessment [CLA]) which ensure students are academically prepared for teacher education coursework.[15]

The strength of the 2 + 2 approach is that virtually every community college can become a feeder into teacher education programs by coordinating with the degree granting program. A community college that has a strong general education curriculum and is able to offer an introduction to teaching or another similar intro-level course can attract a viable pool of teacher candidates, particularly students who cannot afford more expensive four-year programs. The challenge of this approach is that detailed and binding articulation agreements between colleges are hard to negotiate and sustain.[16] Agreements between a community college and a teacher education program at a private college or even a four-year public institution can often be a difficult give-and-take in which students are caught in the middle.

## Alternate Certification Programs for Post-Baccalaureate Students

Community colleges in many states offer opportunities for individuals to complete the credits neces-sary for teacher licensure through a post-baccalaureate program. While post-baccalaureate programs are also offered by traditional teacher education programs, community college programs often differ in many respects. While most post-baccalaureate programs at four-year institutions provide the oppor-tunity for post-baccalaureate courses to apply toward a master's degree, community college pro-grams may only provide coursework on a non-credit basis and, as a result, not provide progress toward a master's degree or any other advanced credential.[17] There are exceptions, like Rio Salado of the Maricopa Community Colleges in **Arizona**, where master's credit is available through partnerships with master's-level universities. By and large this is rare and consequently most students enrolled in community college alternate certification programs are not able to earn graduate-level credit.

The strength of the community college post-baccalaureate program is it provides a low cost option for earning a teaching license, which is particularly attractive to displaced workers who require additional training to shift careers. While a non-credit alternative certification program may not lead to a master's degree, it can be argued that a non-credit program meets the demands of a specific seg-ment of the teacher preparation market that community colleges are ideally suited to serve.

Offering a program that is such a departure from traditional four-year teacher education programs—at institutions that do not have long track records in providing teacher education—make post-baccalaureate programs at community colleges subject to scrutiny. Consequently, these programs need to go to great lengths to establish their credibility. An example of this is the Educator Preparation Institutes (EPIs) created by the **Florida** State Legislature, which provide a variety of teacher education services to include post-baccalaureate licensure. In addition to seeking the same level of approval through the state as other teacher education programs, the EPIs work with the state of Florida to develop a common competency-based curriculum, appropriate pre- and post-learning assessments, agreements with state teacher education agencies on establishing appropri-ate quality controls, training for faculty in scientifically based instruction techniques, standards for field experiences, and a sound program evaluation and accountability system.[18]

## Community College Baccalaureate Programs

Despite the controversy that surrounds it, the community college baccalaureate program has become a very important option for states with teacher shortages in particular fields or geographic regions.

Opponents often argue that offering baccalaureate degrees is outside the scope of the community college mission. Community college leaders from baccalaureate-granting institutions respond that offer-ing these programs is consistent with their mission – to meet the needs of the surrounding commu-nity. According to those who run these programs, baccalaureate-level teacher education programs at community colleges do not replicate what occurs at established traditional teacher education programs and instead create programs more customized to the needs of the communities they serve. Likewise, the programs tend not to be steeped in the traditional curriculum of many teacher education programs, but model their programs around emerging theory, research and practice in education.[19]

Most community colleges add the baccalaureate option after a careful analysis which deter-mines whether the program will meet a critical need in the community or state in which the insti-tution resides. According to Tom Furlong, senior vice-president of Baccalaureate Programs and University Partnerships at St. Petersburg College, the community college will first determine whether an existing college which offers baccalaureate degrees can meet the need in the community. Next, if existing baccalaureate-granting colleges cannot meet the need on their own, the community col-lege will pursue a partnership with the degree-granting college to offer the program jointly. It is only after these two avenues are exhausted that St. Petersburg College would develop its own baccalaureate program.[20]

Typically, community colleges will offer baccalaureate degrees in one of the following circum-stances:

- Offering new degree pathways for existing occupational programs offered by the community college
- Creating new degree capacity in high demand career programs

- Developing programs in areas where there are no four-year programs or limited offerings
- Offering degrees in areas where no other higher education institution exists within hundreds of miles
- Providing a low-cost choice in an area that serves high numbers of low-income students
- Meeting a region's bachelor degree needs by offering a flexible option that enables students to take courses at night, online or on weekends
- Ensuring that the state's residents are proximate to a low-cost baccalaureate degree choice.[21]

The challenge for community college baccalaureate teacher education programs is changing negative perceptions about community college capacity and earning acceptance from those who employ their teacher candidates. Many still question the quality of community college offerings and the students they enroll. The systems and processes established by community colleges to ensure they provide a high-quality option that meets a clear community need are intended to counter these concerns. To further demonstrate their quality, many community colleges go to great lengths to earn accreditation for their program as soon as possible.[22]

## Community College Professional Development Programs

Professional development programs are yet another way community colleges provide teacher education. Like many of the other community college teacher education strategies, professional development programs are often tied to the needs of the communities in which colleges are located. Unlike the other approaches, professional development programs involve a much more intimate relationship with the schools and districts within those communities. Community colleges provide a venue and a means for providing customized professional development for teachers based on specific expectations outlined by school districts.

The types of professional development programs offered by community colleges can range from courses required for recertification to cutting-edge courses focusing on the use of technology in the classroom, and pragmatic sessions on how to meet the needs of the growing diversity of students in classrooms.[23]

The unique capacity of community colleges to provide customized training to employees in various industries ranging from manufacturing to health care makes the community college a logical location to offer innovative professional development opportunities to meet the specific needs of schools and districts. For this reason, many feel professional development programs at community colleges could benefit from being viewed as part of the economic and workforce development efforts of community colleges. Anne Arundel Community College has applied a workforce development/customized training model to its professional development efforts by consolidating all its education-related services under one umbrella called the Teacher Education and Childcare Institute (TEACH). This approach has made all of the college's teacher education services more accessible to students, current teachers and school systems.[24]

Unlike other customized training programs at community colleges, professional development programs for teachers are not a source of revenue for the college.[25] School districts typically have limited funds for professional development and colleges are not able to charge rates consistent with their private sector partners. Instead, community colleges view their professional development efforts as part of their community service mission and not as a growth sector for the college. As a result, these programs may not be optimized as true engines of innovation in teacher education.

# Challenges and Opportunities for Community Colleges in Teacher Preparation

Community colleges are well positioned to be innovators in teacher education. As with all other systems of teacher preparation in this age of increased accountability, there are areas that need to be addressed to ensure their effectiveness and credibility. These areas provide an opportunity for community colleges to leverage their assets and mission:

1. Achieving quality
2. Moving from articulation to alignment

3. Establishing mission differentiation
4. Responsiveness to the education industry
5. Capacity to generate and analyze data.

## Quality

Whether or not a community college is required to adhere to federal, state or accreditation standards of quality, they should seek to design their programs with these definitions of quality in mind. Baccalaureate and alternative licensure programs should strongly consider seeking accreditation from organizations like the National Council for Accreditation of Teacher Education (NCATE). In addition, programs that do not confer degrees or recommend students for licensure and therefore are not required to adhere to established government or accreditation standards should nevertheless set quality standards for their efforts that are consistent with those identified by state departments of education and accrediting bodies.

As community colleges have expanded their role in teacher preparation, they have taken the challenge of ensuring quality in course offerings seriously. In many states, community colleges are under the same state-level requirements for program approval as four-year institutions. This requirement can be invaluable for the purpose of statewide acceptance of community college-based teacher preparation programs.[26] Additionally, community colleges often use boards and advisory committees that include members of the K-12 education system to review and approve the quality and variety of course offerings. At Great Basin College in **Nevada**, for example, this takes the form of the Teacher Education Committee which serves as the formalized structure for program evaluation, review and modification.[27]

There are challenges remaining in the quality arena, however, for both community colleges and teacher preparation programs based at four-year institutions. Issues of quality have intensified with the increased accountability resulting from the No Child Left Behind Act (NCLB). Although the primary focus of NCLB is at the K-12 level, it is expected that its focus on accountability will extend to postsecondary education through the reauthorization of the Higher Education Act, and specifically Title II of the Act which deals with institutions responsible for teacher preparation.[28] Additionally, the federal government is considering changing their requirements from the more degree- and knowledge-based standards of highly qualified teachers to an outcomes-based system of highly effective teachers. These new standards will require a shift in how teachers are assessed throughout the system, including their preparation programs. One way to respond to this challenge would be to create a more outcomes-based system including a common definition of quality and a consensus on standards for what potential teachers should know and be able to do at the end of their preparation programs. With all providers of teacher education required to meet these standards, the assumption about quality based solely on the type of institution at which preparation was received should be eliminated.

As the federal government, states and accrediting agencies continue to create greater clarity in their standards for teacher preparation, it will become easier for community colleges to become a more credible player in teacher preparation. No longer will the sole purview of teacher education standards fall within the realm of four-year teacher education programs. The result could be a proliferation of postsecondary institutions that offer teacher education opportunities.

## Moving from Articulation to Alignment

The use of articulation agreements between community colleges and four-year institutions are one method through which community colleges are engaged in quality teacher preparation. Articulation agreements take many forms. Four common types are:

- *2 + 2 programs,* where successfully completing a specified core curriculum at a two-year institution guarantees junior status transfer to a four-year institution
- *Joint admissions programs,* where students choose both the two- and four-year institutions they will attend before they begin their program, and work with both institutions to design a seamless transition

- *Common course numbering agreements,* which ease transfer of credits by allowing students to take the same courses, by number, at a two-year institution as would be required of students in the four-year institution's program
- *Externally validated criteria for transfer,* where students must pass an exam external to the two-year institution (such as PRAXIS I or CLAs) in order to be admitted to the four-year institution.[29]

One challenge with articulation agreements is the perception by community colleges that the system is more top-down because of university mandates on what it will or will not accept than collaborative where the objective is to create an integrated four-year program. The top-down model results in a bifurcated system of teacher preparation whereby only basic education courses are taken at the community college and content and pedagogical specific courses are taken at the university.

Cheri St. Arnauld from the National Association of Community College Teacher Education Programs (NACCTEP) argues that 2 + 2 programs must move from negotiating articulation agreements to creating and sustaining curricular alignment.[30] According to St. Arnauld, colleges must recognize that it is more important than ever for community colleges and traditional teacher education programs to shift from working as two separate entities negotiating articulation agreements to deeper partnerships where the goal is a sustained commitment to curriculum alignment between the community college and the teacher education program.

To fully utilize community colleges, teacher preparation must be viewed as a four-year process including content and pedagogical training continuously throughout the four years. A change to a fully integrated system would also respond to the continuous call—among those advocating for teacher preparation reform—for earlier field and teaching experience in teacher preparation programs.

## Establishing Mission Differentiation

"Mission creep" is a term often used in connection with the practice of community colleges' expanded role in teacher education, specifically if these institutions offer a four-year teaching degree. In these situations, four-year institutions have claimed that community colleges are extending outside of their missions into the traditional territory of universities. In the face of this accusation, it is important to remember the primary mission of community colleges is to respond to the needs of the community in which they are situated, both as these needs relate to serving the students residing in the community and the needs of the business or other industry of that community. The expanded role of community colleges in teacher education is a direct reflection of that mission.

Community colleges often structure course offerings at times and formats more amenable to a working individual's schedule, through evening or compressed weekend courses. For example, teacher preparation programs at Great Basin College in Nevada serve students in a variety of classroom settings from traditional live lectures to technologically based interactive classrooms to integrated seminar sessions utilizing multi-faculty teaching teams from a variety of academic disciplines. Courses can also be delivered to branch campuses and satellite centers to serve the needs of regionally bound students thereby providing rural students wishing to remain in their community the opportunity to pursue a baccalaureate degree.[31]

In addition to focusing on student needs, community colleges usually have close ties with the business community in which they reside and are able to design courses and degree programs tailored to the needs and opportunities available. In teacher preparation programs at community colleges, this function is often formalized through committees or advisory councils, which include principals, superintendents and other members of school districts.[32]

It is important to note that the "mission creep" argument opposing the expansion of community colleges' roles in teacher education is most strident in systems where public funding is attached to student attendance and less so where the community colleges and universities maintain a focus on serving the needs of the students and workforce. In addition to maintaining this focus, policymakers who advocate for greater collaboration throughout the education system can promote positive working relationships between community colleges and traditional teacher education programs by supporting teacher education programs at community colleges. Creation of high quality policy can also help. States that have authorized community colleges to offer four-year degrees have done so with state workforce needs in mind, and as a result often include language in legislation and policy that preserves the community colleges' core mission as responsive, community-based institutions.[33]

As they say, the genie is out of the bottle with regard to community colleges and their role in offering baccalaureate degrees. Due to the leadership of several key states that have ventured into this new territory of offering opportunities to earn licensure at their community colleges, other states now considering how to meet their future teacher preparation needs will have a growing base of knowledge by which to consider an expanded role for their community colleges.

## Responsiveness to the Education Industry

As mentioned above, an essential part of the mission and history of community colleges is to respond to the needs of the surrounding community and the industries employing its residents. Current needs in the teaching workforce include increasing the racial/ethnic diversity and experience of teachers, ensuring that high-quality teachers are equitably distributed to rural and hard-to-staff schools, and making available high-quality pre-service and in-service programs tailored to the needs of the education community. Community colleges provide access to a population typically under-served by universities—people with racial/ethnic diversity, older adults, first generation college students and individuals who are place-bound. These are the same people who are underrepresented in the K-12 teaching force.

### Increasing diversity

There are currently over 1,000 community colleges across the country enrolling 11.6 million students. Forty-five percent of all undergraduate students are enrolled at community colleges and they represent a broad array of racial, ethnic and age diversity – 47% of black undergraduate students, 55% of Hispanic undergraduate students, 47% of Asian/Pacific Islander undergraduate students and 57% of Native American undergraduate students attend community colleges. Additionally, the average age of a community college student is 29.[34] Providing these students with the opportunity to gain teacher preparation in a student-focused environment in which they feel comfortable could encourage them to complete teacher preparation programs and join the teaching force.

### Equitable distribution

There is some evidence that teachers remain geographically close to where they were trained when they enter the workforce.[35] Community colleges often serve geographic areas not served by universities. Great Basin College in Nevada, for example, serves a 62,000-square-mile service area in rural north-east Nevada not served by any university. Providing the opportunity for individuals already living in these areas to participate in teacher education programs without requiring them to leave their homes and families increases the supply of well-prepared teachers in these areas.

### Tailored pre-service and in-service programs

The close working relationships community colleges maintain with their communities allows them to customize both pre-service and in-service training for the needs of the education industry. One example of this is the creation of alternative preparation programs based at community colleges. At St. Petersburg College in Florida this has taken the form of Educator Preparation Institutes (EPIs), which are competency-based alternative certification programs for individuals with non-education baccalaureate degrees.

As discussed above, community colleges also offer professional development tailored to the needs of the industry. In 1998, Anne Arundel Community College and Anne Arundel County Public Schools collaborated on a technology training model for teachers. The T3 Project served the needs of teachers in the area and has evolved beyond its original function to include new initiatives such as a credit program for teaching assistants in response to new requirements articulated in NCLB.[36]

The market community colleges serve and the business models they employ provide a new and valuable resource for generating a more numerous and diverse teaching force, as well as a responsive model that provides customized professional development solutions to local schools and school districts. States should consider how they might provide resources to support further innovation and collaboration between K-12 education and community colleges to further develop this source of innovation.

## Capacity to Generate and Analyze Data

An institution must be able to collect and utilize appropriate data in order to improve practice and sustain high-quality programs. Community colleges are continuously challenged by difficulties in gaining access to data on student performance. State licensure examinations and credentialing requirements typically serve as the standard by which quality is determined. Unfortunately, data on student performance is often not shared with the community college system, thereby blocking that means of obtaining feedback on community college programs. Community colleges often do not receive feedback on the performance of transfer students once the student is enrolled at the four-year institution. An example of quality use of data for improvement community colleges should monitor is *Achieving the Dream,* a multi-year national initiative that uses data to drive change and help community college students achieve success.[37]

Making the data available is only one challenge, however. Community colleges often do not have the resources for trained analysts or other personnel to translate these data into information for program improvement. *Achieving the Dream* is demonstrating the importance of having trained institutional researchers on campus.

Federal and state-level debates over longitudinal data systems from pre-K through postsecondary education may provide some relief to community colleges as they seek to engage in continuous improvement strategies; however, it is more important than ever for community colleges to build their own capacity to collect and analyze data. This may require difficult decisions on how to prioritize resources, but in the end may prove critical to their efforts to be seen as credible players in the teacher preparation field.

# Courses of Action

Community Colleges are a valuable partner in meeting the needs of teachers and the K-12 education sector (because of their history and ability to respond to the needs of the students and communities they serve). There are steps that can be taken and challenges that need to be addressed in order to take full advantage of the expanded role of community colleges in teacher preparation:

- Teacher preparation should be viewed as a four-year process that includes content and pedagogical training continuously throughout the four-years
- Outcomes-based standards of what teachers should know and be able to do at all levels of preparation should be created, and all pathways to teacher preparation should be assessed against these standards
- Program and course development should be a collaborative process including representation from universities, community colleges and the K-12 sector that is focused on needs and goals of the teaching workforce
- Common data components focused on program improvement should be agreed upon and shared among all institutions involved in teacher preparation
- Each state department of education should encourage ongoing "collaboration and communication" among legislators, community colleges, universities and the K-12 sector on how the community college teacher preparation model can be used to improve the quality of teacher preparation and ameliorate state teacher shortages
- Policymakers and institution leaders should consider providing resources to either community colleges or K-12 school districts to support customized training for teachers through negotiated contracts and/or partnerships between community colleges and school districts.

# Endnotes

1. American Association of State Colleges and Universities, "The Facts and Fictions about Teacher Shortages", *Policy Matters*, Volume 2, Number 5, May, 2005.

2. National Center for Education Statistics, *Projections of Education Statistics to 2014. Thirty-third edition*, U.S. Department of Education Institute of Education Sciences, 2005.

3. Danny Gonzales, Working Paper Prepared for the Education Commission of the States, July, 2006.

4. Judith Bilsky, *Florida's Community College System Collaborates Cross-sector to Produce Highly-Effective Teachers*, Working Paper Prepared for the Education Commission of the States, July, 2006.

5. American Association for Employment in Education, *Educator Supply and Demand in the United States*, 2005.

6. National Center for Education Statistics, *Schools and Staffing Survey 2003–04*, United States Department of Education, 2005.

7. Kyle Zinth, *A Synthesis of Recommendations for Improving Math and Science Education*, Education Commission of the States, 2006.

8. Association of American Universities, *National Defense Education and Innovation Initiative: Meeting America's Economic and Security Challenges in the 21st Century*, January 2006: http://www.aau.edu/reports/NDEII.pdf; National Academies Press, *Rising Above the Gathering Storm: Energizing and Employing America for a Brighter Economic Future*, October 2005: http://fermat.nap.edu/catalog/11463.html; The National Summit on Competitiveness, *Statement of the National Summit on Competitiveness: Investing in U.S. Innovation*, December 2005: http://www.usinnovation.org/pdf/National_Summit_Statement.pdf; The Business Roundtable, *Tapping America's Potential: The Education for Innovation Initiative*, July 2005: http://www.businessroundtable.org/pdf/20050803001TAPfinalnb.pdf.

9. Madeline Patton, Lynn Barnett, and Faith San Felice, *Teaching By Choice: Community College Science and Mathematics Preparation of K-12 Teachers*, American Association of Community Colleges, 2005.

10. American Association of State Colleges and Universities, "The Facts and Fictions about Teacher Shortages", *Policy Matters*, Volume 2, Number 5, May, 2005.

11. National Center for Education Statistics, *The Condition of Education 2006*, United States Department of Education, 2006.

12. Leslie Ann Roberts, *Baccalaureate Degree Programs and the Community College Mission*, Working Paper prepared for the Education Commission of the States, July, 2006.

13. National Center for Education Statistics, 2003-04 National Postsecondary Student Aid Study *(NPSAS:04)*, United States Department of Education, 2005.

14. *Miami Dade College Strategic Plan 2004-2010: The Creative Engine For Our Community's Future*, 2004. Miami Dade College.

15. Martha Smith, *Community College Teacher Preparation*, Working Paper prepared for the Education Commission of the States, July, 2006.; Shamila Basu Conger, *Effective Articulation Between Two and Four Year Teacher Preparation Programs: A State Higher Education Policy Perspective*, Working Paper prepared for the Education Commission of the States, July, 2006.

16. Cheri St. Arnauld, *Setting Quality Standards for 2+2 Community College Teacher Education Programs*, Working Paper prepared for the Education Commission of the States, July, 2006.

17. Donna Gollnick, *Community Colleges and Teacher Education: Roles, Issues, Opportunities for Accreditation*, Working Paper prepared for the Education Commission of the States. July, 2006.

18. Judith Bilsky, *Florida's Community College System Collaborates Cross-sector to Produce Highly-Effective Teachers*, Working Paper Prepared for the Education Commission of the States, July, 2006.

19. Danny Gonzales, Working Paper Prepared for the Education Commission of the States, July, 2006.

20. Thomas Furlong, Comments made at Education Commission of the States meeting: Community Colleges and Teacher Preparation: Roles, Issues and Opportunities, August 8-9, 2006.

21. Jean Floten, Upper Division Enrollment Planning Discussion for Washington State, November 10, 2004.

22. Thomas Furlong, Comments made at Education Commission of the States meeting: Community Colleges and Teacher Preparation: Roles, Issues and Opportunities, August 8-9, 2006.

23. Martha Smith, *Community College Teacher Preparation*, Working Paper prepared for the Education Commission of the States, July, 2006.

24. Ibid.

25. Thomas Furlong, Comments made at Education Commission of the States meeting: Community Colleges and Teacher Preparation: Roles, Issues and Opportunities, August 8-9, 2006.

26. Judith Bilsky, *Florida's Community College System Collaborates Cross-sector to Produce Highly-Effective Teachers,* Working Paper Prepared for the Education Commission of the States, July, 2006.

27. Danny Gonzales, Working Paper Prepared for the Education Commission of the States, July, 2006.

28. Public Law 105-244, Amendments to the Higher Education Act 1965, http://www.ed.gov/policy/high-ered/leg/hea98/index.html.

29. Shamila Basu Conger, *Effective Articulation Between Two and Four Year Teacher Preparation Programs: A State Higher Education Policy Perspective,* Working Paper prepared for the Education Commission of the States, July, 2006.

30. Cheri St. Arnauld, Comments made at Education Commission of the States meeting: Community Colleges and Teacher Preparation: Roles, Issues and Opportunities, August 8-9, 2006.

31. Danny Gonzales, Working Paper Prepared for the Education Commission of the States, July, 2006.

32. Terri Schwartzbeck, *School Districts, Community Colleges, and Teacher Education,* Working Paper prepared for the Education Commission of the States, July, 2006.

33. Leslie Ann Roberts, *Baccalaureate Degree Programs and the Community College Mission,* Working Paper prepared for the Education Commission of the States, July, 2006.

34. American Association of Community Colleges Web site, "Community College Fact Sheet," http://www.aacc.nche.edu/Content/NavigationMenu/AboutCommunityColleges/Fast_Facts1/Fast_Facts.htm. Accessed 30 October 2006.

35. Lyn Cornett, *Teacher Supply and Demand in Tennessee, 2003,* Southern Regional Education Board, 2003.

36. Martha Smith, *Community College Teacher Preparation,* Working Paper prepared for the Education Commission of the States, July, 2006.

37. Achieving the Dream, http://www.achievingthedream.org/_images/_index03/FS-Dream.pdf. Accessed 30 October, 2006.

# Appendix 1

Participants in Community Colleges and Teacher Preparation:

**Roles, Issues and Opportunities Meeting. August 8-9, 2006, Washington, D.C.**

*Sharmila Basu Conger,* Policy Analyst, State Higher Education Executive Officers (SHEEO)
*Judith Bilsky,* Vice-Chancellor, Florida Community College System
*Kay Burniston,* Associate Vice-President, Baccalaureate Programs, St. Petersburg College
*Tricia Coulter,* Director, Teacher Quality and Leadership Institute, Education Commission of the States (ECS)
*Tom Furlong,* Senior Vice-President, Baccalaureate Programs and University Partnerships, St. Petersburg College
*Donna Gollnick,* Senior Vice-President, National Council for Accreditation of Teacher Education (NCATE)
*Danny Gonzales,* Deputy to the President, Great Basin College
*Adeniji Odutola,* Director, National Center for Teacher Transformation (NCTT)
*Leslie Roberts,* President-Elect, Board of Directors, National Association of Community College Teacher Education Programs (NACCTEP)
*Faith San Felice,* Senior Program Associate for Teaching and Learning, American Association of Community Colleges (AACC)
*Terry Schwartzbeck,* Policy Analyst, American Association of School Administrators
*Martha Smith,* President, Anne Arundel Community College
*Cheri St. Arnauld,* Executive Director, National Association of Community College Teacher Education Programs (NACCTEP)
*Bruce Vandal,* Director, Postsecondary Education and Workforce Development Institute, Education Commission of the States (ECS)

# Appendix 2

## Featured Community College Teacher Preparation Programs

### Florida Educator Preparation Institutes

Educator Preparation Institutes at accredited postsecondary institutions provide professional development for teachers for classroom improvement and for recertification, training for substitute teachers, paraprofessional instruction, and competency-based instruction for Bachelor Degree holders leading to temporary and full teacher certification. EPIs provide an alternate route to certification for mid-career professionals and college graduates who were not education majors. The EPIs choosing to offer competency-based post-baccalaureate certification must meet the same standards and the same accomplished educator practices as any 4-year teacher education program, including field experience and a passing score on each of the Florida Teacher Certification Examinations (FTCE). All twenty-eight community colleges have implemented EPIs. Twenty-five community colleges collaborated on a common teacher preparation curriculum in submitting a joint EPI application to DOE, and all received full DOE approval.

### Great Basin College, Nevada Baccalaureate Teacher Education Program

As the first of the baccalaureate programs offered by Great Basin College, the Elementary Education degree pioneered the unique integrated curriculum that has set Great Basin College apart from peer institutions across the nation. Held up as a national model for innovation and efficiency, the program creates a learning experience that integrates knowledge, skill and methods of inquiry from several disciplines.

Students create an e-Portfolio demonstrating competencies in meeting or exceeding the state teaching standards. The e-Portfolio includes sample lesson plans research, and videos of student teaching experiences.

The program collaborates with five school districts in northeastern Nevada, to coordinate field and student teaching experiences.

### St. Petersburg College Baccalaureate Teacher Education Program

St. Petersburg College in Florida offers six areas of concentration in their bachelor's degree program in teacher education. In addition, the IMPACT programs allows students with a bachelor's degree to earn their teacher certification.

### T3, Anne Arundel Community College

Anne Arundel Community College's (AACC) Total Teacher Training (T3) develops and offers courses to meet specific instructional and technological professional development needs of Anne Arundel County Public School (AACPS) employees in all job categories. The T3 Project, a joint venture of the college and the school system began in 1998 as a training model that melded two county institutions utilizing the strengths and infrastructure of one to advance the professional development goals of the other. The T3 Project, originally titled Teacher Technology Training, has become a link between the two institutions that has evolved beyond its original function to include new initiatives such as credit programs for conditional teachers and teaching assistants in response to No Child Left Behind legislation, as well as non-credit training in Building Quality Relationships with Parents, Internet Safety and Spanish for Educators. T3 programs provide instruction for all audiences, including classroom teachers, administrators, school and central office support staff. The partnership involves collaboration among directors and coordinators of both institutions in order to assess specific professional development needs and determine the most efficient and effective delivery model.

TEACH Institute, Anne Arundel Community College

The TEACH Institute of Anne Arundel Community College (AACC) provides a continuum of educational programs for those who currently are or who plan to become professionals that work with children from birth through grade12 in learning environments and child care settings. The vision of the TEACH Institute is to enrich the lives of the children of Anne Arundel County by supporting and informing the adults who have chosen as their careers to educate and care for them. In 2003, AACC combined three areas of the college, the traditional credit Education Department, the non-credit Child Care Training and the contract T3 Project, to create the Teacher Education and Child Care (TEACH) Institute. *The mission of the TEACH Institute is the preparation and continuous development of educators who meet the diverse needs of learners in all educational settings. Full-time and part-time faculty members are certified professionals who model effective teaching practices and provide relevant student-centered learning experiences to prepare future educators. Family care providers, licensed centers and the county school system rely on the TEACH Institute to provide pre-service and in-service training for those in the field of early childhood education and care.*

Teaching By Choice Initiative, American Association of Community Colleges

With support from the National Science Foundation (NSF), AACC, in partnership with the National Association of Community College Teacher Education Programs (NACCTEP) and the American Mathematical Association of Two-Year Colleges (AMATYC), developed Teaching by Choice (TBC): Addressing the National Teacher Shortage. TBC is a two-part initiative focusing on the increasing demand for K-12 teachers and community college faculty in science, technology, engineering and mathematics (STEM). The project resulted in two reports:

*Teaching by Choice: Cultivating Exemplary Community College STEM Faculty*
is a 34-page report of recommendations and promising practices in the recruitment, retention, and professional development of exemplary, diverse community college faculty in science, technology, engineering and mathematics, outlined during the Teaching by Choice National Leadership Summit on Community College Faculty, convened in Washington, D.C., December 12-14, 2005.

*Teaching by Choice: Community College Science and Mathematics Preparation of K-12 Teachers*
is a 35-page report of recommendations for community college K-12 teacher preparation programs developed during the Teaching by Choice national conference, convened in Washington, D.C., September 9, 10 & 11, 2004.

# Appendix 3

## Resources on Community Colleges and Teacher Preparation

### National Center for Teacher Transformation

The National Center for Teacher Transformation (NCTT) at St. Petersburg College in Florida was created in 2003 by a congressionally authorized grant through The Fund for the Improvement of Postsecondary Education. The goal of NCTT is to identify solutions for critical issues affecting education through the establishment of creative partnerships that will result in the education workforce excellence. *http://www.spcollege.edu/nctt/*

### State Higher Education Executive Officers

The State Higher Education Executive Officers (SHEEO) is a nonprofit, nationwide association of the chief executive officers serving statewide coordinating boards and governing boards of postsecondary education. *http://www.sheeo.org/default.htm*

### National Council for the Accreditation of Teacher Education

The National Council for the Accreditation of Teacher Education (NCATE) is the teaching profession's mechanism to help establish high-quality teacher preparation. Through the process of professional accreditation of schools, colleges and departments of education, NCATE works to make a difference in the quality of teaching and teacher preparation today, tomorrow and for the next century. NCATE's performance-based system of accreditation fosters competent classroom teachers and other educators who work to improve the education of all P-12 students. NCATE believes every student deserves a caring, competent, and highly qualified teacher. *http://www.ncate.org/*

### National Association of Community College Teacher Education Programs

The National Association of Community College Teacher Education Programs (NACCTEP) is an organization of community colleges, staff and students involved in teacher education programs; universities involved in teacher education programs; and industry partners and professional associations who work as partners with community college teacher education programs.

NACCTEP serves as a voice for community colleges in national discussions about teacher education. It works to enhance current community college teacher education programs and serves as a resource for those looking to develop new programs. NACCTEP facilitates connections between and among community college teacher education programs and community college teacher education faculty. *http://www.nacctep.org/*

### American Association of School Administrators

The American Association of School Administrators (AASA), founded in 1865, is the professional organization for more than 13,000 educational leaders across America and in many other countries. The mission of AASA is to support and develop effective school-system leaders who are dedicated to the highest quality public education for all children. *http://www.aasa.org/*

### Education Commission of the States

The Education Commission of the States (ECS) is an interstate compact created in 1965 to improve public education by facilitating the exchange of information, ideas and experiences among state policymakers and education leaders. As a nonprofit, nonpartisan organization involving key leaders from all levels of the education system, ECS creates unique opportunities to build partnerships, share information and promote the development of policy based on available research and strategies. *http://www.ecs.org/*

### American Association of Community Colleges

Founded in 1920, the American Association of Community Colleges (AACC) has, over four decades, become the leading proponent and the national "voice for community colleges." AACC is the primary advocacy organization for community colleges at the national level and works closely with directors of state offices to inform and affect state policy. AACC supports and promotes its member colleges through policy initiatives, innovative programs, research and information, and strategic outreach to business and industry and the national news media. *http://www.aacc.nche.edu/*

# Federal Role in Teacher Quality: "Redefinition" or Policy Alignment?

## LORA COHEN-VOGEL

*Although state attention to teacher preparation and professional development began more than 150 years ago with the provision of teacher education in Massachusetts, the federal government did not get involved in teacher preparation and development until the late 1950s. Even then, Washington lawmakers generally restricted their activities to financial assistance for in-service training and college aid for teachers. Over time, the federal approach to teacher education has expanded in shape and scope, even as some continued to characterize it as peripheral to core issues of instruction. Today, with the passage of the No Child Left Behind Act of 2001, the federal government claims to have redefined its role. By tracing the evolution of federal involvement in teacher education over time, this study finds that the act's provisions may reflect an ongoing attempt beginning in the 1990s to align teacher preparation and professional development activities with K-12 educational reform efforts.*

*Keywords:* governance; federal policy; teacher education

ALTHOUGH STATES, BY ESTABLISHING programmatic requirements for postsecondary institutions that train teachers and by certifying new entrants to the field, have largely defined the shape of preservice teacher preparation and professional development, the federal government has on occasion intervened. Since its genesis[1] in 1958 with the National Defense Education Act (NDEA), federal involvement in education in general has been modest and sporadic, swelling in response to perceived workforce shortages or other national crises (e.g., the Sputnik launch; Johnson & Borkow, 1985). Scholars have described federal efforts as "of little consequence" to the direction of teacher preparation (Clark & McNergney, 1990). Arguably, however, media exposés and highly politicized debates about teacher education among professional associations and private foundations have over the past 20 years attracted the attention of Congress and the White House, stoking legislative activity at the federal level. The belief that schools and schooling in general should be left to the states with minimal federal involvement has been replaced with a new, more complicated governance norm wherein federal, state, and local authorities share control of education.

Apart from the surge in activity by the federal government, the nature of its involvement in teacher education and development may be changing. Historically, according to Earley and Schneider (1996),

EDUCATIONAL POLICY, Vol. 19 No. 1. January and March 2005 18-43

DOI: 10.1177/0895904804272246

Federal attention to the recruitment, preparation, and continuing professional development of educators has been a policy instrument rather than the target of federal policy. That is, although programs related to special education, bilingual education, mathematics and science education, and vocational education include modest funds for educator recruitment, preparation, or retraining, the teacher-education components of these programs are tools to achieve a broader policy objective, such as a more technologically literate workforce, or to ease the transition of children with special needs into traditional elementary and secondary school settings. (p. 306)

Reticent to take up key issues within the teacher-education field, federal officials focused their efforts exclusively on governance reform (e.g., deregulation of credentialing), altogether avoiding fundamental disputes over the components of appropriate teacher preparation. By failing to address teacher education directly, federal support "was characterized by a patchwork of programs that were small, categorical, or of short duration, and peripheral to school improvement" (Earley & Schneider, 1996, p. 306).

Signaling a change in its approach to teacher-education policy, however, federal legislation in the 1990s, namely the Higher Education Amendments of 1992, the Goals 2000: Educate America Act of 1996 (Goals 2000), and the 1994 reauthorization of the Elementary and Secondary Education Act (ESEA), began to attend to core conflicts that had in earlier eras been sidestepped (Earley & Schneider, 1996). The 1990s witnessed the standards era in educational reform. As shall be shown, its focus on outcomes and accountability at the K-12 level increased pressure for concomitant attention to teacher education. As efforts ensued to align standardized student tests and school and district accountability mechanisms with new content standards, it would not be long until teacher education became a focal point for the standards movement as well. Indeed, for this wave of reform to work, teachers would have to be well-trained in the content areas represented on the tests.

With the sixth reauthorization of the ESEA, the No Child Left Behind Act of 2001 (NCLB), the federal government claims to have redefined its role. By tracing the evolution of federal involvement in teacher education over time, this study finds that the bulk of NCLB's teacher-education and development initiatives instead continue on a path set in the early 1990s with the development of eight national education goals. NCLB provisions that pertain to the preparation of new teachers and the development of the current teacher workforce depart from previous legislative initiatives insomuch as they shift (or extend) accountability from postsecondary institutions that prepare teachers to districts and schools themselves. But, they do not represent significant changes in the central goals, assumptions, and fiscal patterns that have typified federal teacher-education and development policy during the last decade.

## Goals, Instruments, and Funding in Teacher-Education and Development Policy: an Analytical Approach

Through content analysis of federal legislation, government and budget documents, and appropriations bills, this article tracks the role of the federal government in teacher education and development across 50 years. The terms *teacher education* and *teacher preparation policy* describe legislation, rules, agency guidelines, and court decisions that are issued by or on behalf of an authoritative person or body to guide who will teach, what teacher candidates must know and be able to do, and how their preparation is to be structured (Hawley, 1990). Policy makers often define the delivery systems or instruments through which they hope to affect change. With regard to teacher-education policy, such instruments might "include financial aid and other recruitment tools, various screening tests and procedures, curriculum requirements and mandated learning experiences" (p. 136–137). As used herein, teacher professional development policy seeks to influence the amount and type of development activities for the existing teacher workforce, the model for professional advancement in the field, and the criteria by which teacher practice is evaluated (and teachers terminated). The delivery systems or instruments designed to advance these policy objectives include monetary assistance for in-service programs, targeted funding for key curricular topics, funds for a specified set of providers, tiered licensure systems, and prescribed evaluation schedules.

Thirteen federal departments and several semiautonomous agencies (e.g., the National Science Foundation) provide some support for educator recruitment, preparation, and development (Shaul,

1999). A review of the more than 100 federal teacher-education programs in the United States is beyond the scope of this article. Instead, beginning with the NDEA of 1958, the major bills for federal aid to schools are analyzed to trace the level and nature of federal involvement in teacher preparation and professional development over time and to assess the extent to which recent legislation seeks to redefine that involvement. The following laws are examined: the NDEA of 1965, the Higher Education Act of 1965, the Educational Professional Development Act of 1967, the Higher Education Amendments of 1992, the Improving America's Schools Act of 1994, Goals 2000 of 1996, the Higher Education Amendments of 1998, and NCLB of 2001.

The analysis of the legislation is organized around three dimensions: (a) the goals and assumptions upon which the policy is based; (b) the policy instruments developed to deliver the goals; and (c) the funding of federal teacher-education policy over time. Key findings within each section are presented in Table 1.

## Teacher Preparation for What? Tracking Core Goals and Assumptions

To illustrate a shift in the core goals and assumptions embedded in federal initiatives related to teacher education, this section begins in the 1950s, the decade that changed Congress' hands-off approach to schooling in America (Ramirez, 2004). In 1957 in the midst of the Cold War with the Soviet Union, Americans were awed as they watched the Russian launch of the spacecraft Sputnik:

> As a technical achievement, Sputnik caught the world's attention and the American public off-guard.... The public feared that the Soviets' ability to launch satellites also translated into the capability to launch ballistic missiles that could carry nuclear weapons from Europe to the U.S. (Garber, 2003, p. 1)

As its name suggests, the NDEA of 1958 was passed in response. The general provisions of the act read as follows: "An educational emergency exists and requires action by the federal government. Assistance will come from Washington to help develop as rapidly as possible those skills essential to the national security." By providing new instructional tools for teachers, its core assumption[2] was that our global competitiveness and the nation's defenses would be secured by strengthening instruction in math, science, and foreign languages (see Table 1).[3]

Introduced 7 years (and more than 25 Soviet Union and U.S. space flights) later by the Johnson Administration, the Higher Education Act primarily created a system of federal grants and loans to help poor students attend postsecondary institutions.[4] Most of the programs intended to improve teacher training did not emerge until later through more recent amendments, and when they did, they were placed in Title V of the Higher Education Act. According to Earley (1998), "Title V became the home for many very small programs that rarely were funded and that were only indirectly connected to the preparation of educators" (p. 1). The original Higher Education Act did establish two programs for the improvement of teaching, a teacher fellowship program, and Teacher Corps. But, these programs, according to some, were advanced not for the reform of teacher education but primarily as employment policies (Earley & Schneider, 1996). Facing a shortage of teachers and a returning army of Peace Corps volunteers, Teacher Corps offered incentives to individuals who entered the teaching profession. Later, after the shortage began to fill, the program was reconstituted to encourage persons to teach in schools located in low-income neighborhoods.

The Education Professions Development Act of 1967 (EPDA) symbolized what some have called the federal government's peak involvement in teacher education (Clark & McNergney, 1990). The EPDA amended the Higher Education Act of 1965 purportedly for the purpose of improving the quality of teaching and helping to meet critical shortages of adequately trained educational personnel. As with the Higher Education Act, however, researchers have argued that the primary purpose for the initiative was a matter of economics (Earley & Schneider, 1996). In fact, the peak level of involvement mirrored the greatest shortage of teachers on record. It is little wonder that the federal role in teacher recruitment and development dropped off by the early 1980s after the shortage had become a surplus.

The teacher surplus was only partially responsible for federal neglect of teacher education during the 1980s. President Ronald Reagan believed that educational authority belonged to the states

**Table 1. Key Goals, Instruments, and Funding Patterns of Teacher Education and Professional Development Provisions in Federal Legislation**

| | Goals and Assumptions | Policy Instruments | Funding Patterns |
|---|---|---|---|
| National Defense Education Act (1958) | Compete globally and secure nation's defenses. (Assumption: Improving instruction in science, math, and foreign languages will advance the goals.) | Upgraded instructional tools for teachers; training institutes. | Special-purpose aid provisions; money directed to programs that prepare teachers in certain subjects and for certain students. |
| Higher Education Act (1965) | Solve teacher shortage and employ returning Peace Corps volunteers. | Incentives to teach; district and school site training. | Funds have limited reach; even Teacher Corps, with its relatively large appropriation, reaches only 10% of institutions that prepare teachers (Earley, 1994). |
| Education Professions Development Act (1967) | Fill teacher shortage and improve teaching. | Fellowships; training complexes. | Categorical approaches for the distribution of federal aid continues. |
| Higher Education Act (1992) | Promote concurrent reform of K-12 schools and postsecondary institutions that prepare teachers. (Assumptions: Good schools require good teachers; good teachers will be produced in institutions committed to renewing teacher education and K-12 needs.) | Partnerships between K-12 and institutions with schools, colleges, and departments of education (SCDEs); expanded preservice and professional development service providers; programs to ease transition to teaching from outside fields. | Unfunded. |

| | | | |
|---|---|---|---|
| Goals 2000: Educate America Act (1994) | Set forth a framework to guide federal education policy; upgrade teachers' opportunities to acquire the knowledge and skills necessary to prepare all students for the 21st century. (Assumption: All children can meet high content and performance standards.) | Improvement plans; partnerships between K-12 and institutions with SCDEs. | Moves away from categorical approaches targeting individual children, instead focusing on reform of schools with poor children; 90% of each state's share is reserved for local educational agencies and schools; grants are awarded to districts that partner with postsecondary institutions to improve preservice and continuing teacher education. |
| Elementary and Secondary Education Act Improving America's Schools (1994) | Ensure that teachers are prepared to teach to high standards. (Assumption: Teaching matters to student learning.) | High-quality professional development aligned to state standards; ongoing teacher preservice and continuing education should include subject area content and pedagogy. | Despite renewed federal efforts, appropriations to teacher education and professional development, in particular, did not improve much from their 1980s levels. |
| Higher Education Act (1998) | Improve teacher preparation programs at postsecondary institutions. (Assumptions: SCDEs are not preparing teachers adequately; Test performance is a valid measure of teacher quality.) | Reporting requirements by institutions with SCDEs (e.g., test scores of teacher candidates). | Money flows to schools and districts (not to SCDEs); block grant. |
| Elementary and Secondary Education Act No Child Left Behind (2001) | Ensure that all children are taught by highly qualified teachers. (Assumptions: Teachers with demonstrated content knowledge will lead to improved instruction which will lead to improved student achievement.) | Teacher subject matter knowledge and certification requirements; alternative training providers; school-level accountability. | Funding levels characterized as insufficient to achieve requirements within the time allotted; appropriations to develop and expand alternative routes into teaching. |

and attempted unsuccessfully to abolish the Department of Education. By the time President George H. W. Bush had been in office for 2 years, however, the pressure to reform the nation's public schools was so great that it was he, Reagan's former vice president, who called together the nation's governors and hosted the first ever national summit on education, urging participants to join him to define national goals in education.[5]

Among the final pieces of legislation that President Bush signed before leaving office in 1992 was a bill to reauthorize of the Higher Education Act. Reform documents released during the 1980s by various professional associations, foundations, and government agencies had argued that the creation and maintenance of good schools required good teachers. The purpose of Title V (wherein teacher provisions were housed) then was to encourage institutions of higher education to focus more of their attention on their teacher preparation programs and the needs of K-12 schools. Though Title V never received an appropriation, it was significant for two reasons. First, it addressed the conflict over the meaning of good teaching, asserting that professional education should include both subject area content and how to teach it. Second, it recognized that the reform of K-12 and higher education could not proceed on independent tracks (Earley & Schneider, 1996).

Title V of the 1992 reauthorization of the Higher Education Act, coupled with key assumptions that were and continue to be embedded within the ongoing national dialogue surrounding teacher quality, "helped set the education policy agenda for consideration of education reform legislation that would occur 2 years later" (Earley & Schneider, 1996, p. 312). The first of these assumptions is that teacher quality matters (Wayne, 2000). It has been nearly 40 years since the Coleman report questioned the capacity of school inputs to affect student achievement. The ensuing scholarly debate about whether money matters has only recently abated as both sides have agreed it is how money is spent that counts. Money disbursed to improve teaching, research suggests, is money well spent. Congressional proponents of the teacher quality provision pointed to the Tennessee STAR experiment (Finn & Achilles, 1990) as evidence that teaching matters and to Sanders and Rivers (1996) who demonstrated that 3 years in a classroom with high-quality teachers can boost students' achievement on statewide tests by as much as 50 percentile points. In 1996, the National Commission on Teaching and America's Future (1996) placed teacher quality at the center of the education reform agenda in its report *What Matters Most: Teaching for America's Future,* stating that the most important influence on students' learning is what their teachers know and do.

Second is the assumption that new recruits enter the teaching profession with deficits. Whether they believe that low teacher salaries stymie the recruitment of the nation's best and brightest or that traditional teacher-education programs do not adequately prepare the workforce, federal lawmakers agree that many teachers enter the classrooms without the skills necessary to exact high student achievement. According to Wayne (2000), "The recent, widely publicized failures on a new teacher licensure test in Massachusetts confirmed lawmakers' intuition that major quality deficits exist early in the teacher pipeline" (p. 3; see McDermott, this issue, for a full discussion of the Massachusetts case).

Third, it is widely assumed that teacher quality is inequitably distributed among our nation's schools (Wayne, 2000). Teacher shortages are largely the blight of high-poverty schools, and shortages force school leaders to hire less-qualified applicants and to distribute faculty assignments in ways that exacerbate out-of-field teaching (Ingersoll, 1996; Jennings, 2003).

These dominant assumptions were embedded in Goals 2000, in the 1994 reauthorization of the ESEA, and in Title II of the Higher Education Act of 1998. As its premise, Goals 2000 was intended to help all students to achieve their full potential. To do so, according to Richard Riley (1996), then Secretary of Education under President Clinton, "teachers must have access to high-quality preservice and continuing professional development opportunities" (p. 1). Among the eight national education goals, Goal 4 promised America's teachers access to programs for the continued improvement of their professional skills and the opportunity to acquire the knowledge and skills needed to instruct and prepare all American students for the next century.

The 1994 reauthorization of ESEA, Improving America's Schools Act (IASA), attempted to integrate Title I into the overall structure of Goals 2000. IASA encouraged states to develop curricular content and performance standards to help ensure that all children have access to quality education. Recognizing the importance of a good teacher in this endeavor, the Clinton administration's approach to educational reform, and IASA in particular, was to focus both K-12 and school, college, and department of education (SCDEs) activities around challenging content and performance standards. Observers, nevertheless, have characterized the approach to teacher education reflected in the 1994 reauthorization as enabling rather than transforming. That is, funding for teacher professional development was intended to be used to upgrade individual teacher's skills, "not to transform the nature of teacher preparation in a fundamental way" (Earley, 2000, p. 27).

Although the teacher-education provisions in Title II of the 1998 Higher Education Act, authorizing teacher recruitment programs and programs for the preparation and development of teachers that developed both subject area knowledge and pedagogical skills, mirrored those of IASA, they also called for a radically new approach to SCDE accountability:[6] "The underlying assumption in this legislation was that schools and colleges of education were failing to prepare teachers well" (Hitz, 2004, p. 4). As amended, the Higher Education Act authorized

> programs intended to improve the quality of training and preparation that prospective K-12 teachers receive from teacher-education programs at the postsecondary level. The Congress acted out of concern that the quality of the K-12 teaching force was a critical element in the successful implementation of federal initiatives to raise the academic performance of K-12 students. (Stedman, 2003, p. 13)

Through provisions that held teacher-education programs accountable for graduate's scores on a state exam, lawmakers hoped to motivate institutions with programs in teacher preparation to reform. In addition, the amendments were directed toward alleviating inequities by raising teacher quality in high-poverty schools to propel the educational and lifelong opportunities of all children.

Symbolically named NCLB, the recent reauthorization of ESEA was intended to increase student achievement for all kids by requiring their assessment in Grades 3 through 8, demanding annual performance improvements, and upgrading instructional quality. By the start of the 2002 school year, teachers and paraprofessionals hired with Title I funds had to have met a specified set of criteria, namely the demonstration of content knowledge in the fields in which they teach.[7] In addition, Title I of NCLB mandated that all teachers teaching core academic subjects (i.e., English, reading or language arts, mathematics, science, foreign languages, civics and government, economics, arts, history, and geography) be highly qualified by the end of the 2005–2006 school year. *Highly qualified* has been defined in the legislation as a teacher who

> has obtained full state certification as a teacher (including certification obtained through alternative routes to certification) or passed the state teacher licensing examination, and holds a license to teach in such state, except that when used with respect to any teacher teaching in a public charter school, the term means that the teacher meets the requirements set forth in the state's public charter school law; and (ii) the teacher has not had certification of licensure requirements waived on an emergency, temporary, or provisional basis. (Title I, section 9101)

By permitting teachers to become highly qualified through alternative routes into teaching, NCLB presumes that content knowledge is sufficient for quality teaching; that is, the possible effectiveness of content experts with little or no coursework in education is equal to that of traditionally prepared teaching candidates (Kaplan & Owings, 2003).

## Delivering the Promise: The Levers of Change

As the goals and assumptions behind the federal intervention in teacher education have changed, so have the policy instruments employed to achieve them (see Table 1). NDEA (1958), through Titles III and IX, aimed to upgrade science and math instruction by disseminating improved instructional materials to teachers through summer and year-long institutes (Clark & McNergney, 1990). Such institutes became the model for improving teacher effectiveness for the first decades of federal involvement in teacher education (Earley, 1998).

To fill the shortage of teachers during the 1960s, the Higher Education Act of 1965 established the Teacher Corps. In addition to providing incentives for returning Peace Corps volunteers to teach, Teacher Corps was significant for promoting a school or district site model of teacher training. It signified a shift in traditional notions of where teacher education should occur because the training of the Teacher Corps would take place in schools and district offices, not at colleges of education.

Through the 1967 enactment of EPDA, programs were added to improve teacher training and to continue to recruit more teachers. They ranged from fellowships for teachers to teacher- and administrator-training complexes. But, federal monies dedicated through EPDA to teacher education were reduced in 1970, just 3 years after the authorization, and

> most of the training complexes did not materialize. As late as 1974, several EPDA projects were still in existence, though funding by that time had been drastically reduced, and much of the training complex activity had evolved to teacher centers. (Jenkins, 1997, p. 276)

According to Clark and McNergney (1990),

> The last-gasp effort of the United States Office of Education and its successor agency the Department of Education in major program involvement in teacher education was lost with the demise of the Teacher Centers Program [and Teacher Corps] after 1980. (p. 102)

Under the Reagan Administration, the expansion of federal involvement in teacher education and education in general ceased. It was Reagan's Department of Education, however, that convened the National Commission on Excellence in Education (1983) that in 1983 released what was arguably one of the most influential education reports of the 20th century, *A Nation at Risk: The Imperative for Educational Reform.* Among its recommendations, the Commission called for judging teacher preparation programs by the ability of their graduates to meet high standards (see National Commission on Excellence in Education, 1983, Recommendation D).

Although no federal initiatives emerged to deal with the problems raised in the report, it did nonetheless stir national efforts to reform teacher education among nongovernmental organizations. Numerous educational reform documents from such national groups as the National Commission for Excellence in Teacher Education, the Carnegie Forum on Education and the Economy, the Center for Educational Renewal, the National Governors' Association, and the Holmes Group converged around key recommendations: Teacher preparation should consist of a full academic major in the subject to be taught and should be supplemented by opportunities to develop professional knowledge and skills through professional education courses and through an internship (Jordan, 1986).

In addition to the growing activity among nongovernmental organizations, states beefed up their efforts as both legislative activity and spending on elementary and secondary education by the federal government decreased markedly (see Sonnenberg, 2004). Legislation and programs dealing with teacher education at the state level surged during the 1980s, producing "a cacophony of often contrary . . . initiatives. For example, efforts to recognize and reward excellence in teaching among the ranks of the experienced . . . conflicted with the need to attract and keep a talented pool of neophytes" (Clark & McNergney, 1990, p. 103). A decade of state reform of teacher education, according to Darling-Hammond and Berry (1988), was marked by efforts to establish or increase admission requirements to teacher-education programs, to regulate programs' curricula to focus on the acquisition of knowledge in core content areas, to discover alternative routes to certification, and to test teacher competency.

Numerous reform documents of the 1980s, most notably *A Nation at Risk* (National Commission on Excellence in Education, 1983), set the stage for federal intervention during the 1990s and beyond (Earley & Schneider, 1996). Prodded on by a public weary over bad news about America's schools, President George H. W. Bush in 1989 called together the nation's governors for the first ever summit on education. Although the new president was firm in his commitment to the development of "national but not federal" goals for education, the summit would mark renewed federal involvement in teacher preparation and development and in education issues generally.

The subsequent Higher Education Amendments of 1992, Goals 2000 (enacted in 1994), and IASA, the fifth reauthorization of the ESEA, signaled a different approach to teacher-education policy, addressing core policy conflicts that had in earlier eras been avoided. To improve the professional competence of teachers and administrators, those on one side of the policy conflict support heavier reliance on professional standards in the form of accreditation, licensing, and certification. As in medicine, law, and engineering, it is argued, candidates should graduate from accredited institutions, pass licensing examinations that include both content and performance components that simulate practice in the field, and be certified when they obtain advanced levels of competence (e.g., master certification by the National Board for Professional Teaching Standards). Leading this agenda is the National Commission for Teaching and America's Future, which regards professional standards as a necessary lever not only for raising the quality of teacher practice but also for ensuring equity. In their view, proposals to reduce or abandon preservice training and certification would exacerbate disparities between advantaged and disadvantaged students "by removing requirements for even minimally equitable treatment of less advantaged students in the allocation of teachers and other resources, and by reducing teachers' access to knowledge that might help them to become more effective" (Darling-Hammond, 2000, p. 2). On the other side of the policy conflict, opponents portray increased licensure and certification requirements as the problem, not the solution (Ballou & Podgursky, 2000). This argument is made succinctly in the Thomas B. Fordham Foundation's (1999) *The Teachers We Need and How to Get More of Them: A Manifesto.* The manifesto argues that additional requirements, specifically so-called Mickey Mouse courses that focus on how to teach a subject, have no proven link to student learning and will only constrain the potential supply of new teachers. Quality teaching, in their view, is not produced in schools of education. Instead, teaching will improve only when regulations over who can teach are limited to a bachelor's degree in an academic field and when principals are empowered to hire from the open market (Ballou & Podgursky, 2000).

To the relief of professionalists, Title V of the Higher Education Amendments in the early 1990s signaled that teacher education should include both subject area content and pedagogy. The 1992 reauthorization was perhaps more significant, however, because it upset the traditional practice of exclusively supporting college education programs that train prospective teachers. The new title would grant states, public schools, and postsecondary institutions awards to recruit, train, and develop teachers (Earley & Sneider, 1996). Consisting of more than 20 programs, Title V also promoted partnerships between K-12 schools and institutions of higher education, a policy lever that would be emphasized in subsequent legislation. Further, the Higher Education Act authorized efforts to ease the transition of persons moving from another occupation into teaching (Institute for Higher Education Policy, 2003).

To prepare and develop the knowledge and skills needed to instruct all American students for the 21st century, Goals 2000 directed the governor and chief state school officer in each state along with a panel of other state, school, business, community, and higher education leaders to design a state improvement plan for elementary and secondary education. Each state's plan had to include strategies to improve its system of teacher recruitment, preparation, and professional development delivery. For system improvement, the act again encouraged school districts to partner with postsecondary institutions that have SCDEs. Indeed, in awarding federally funded grants, states were required to prioritize proposals from school districts that have formed partnerships with college educators (Earley & Schneider, 1996).

The levers through which Title I of the 1994 reauthorization of the ESEA would improve teachers' knowledge and skills included requiring that teachers and other members of a school's staff participate in professional development. The Title II Eisenhower Professional Development program provided that such efforts be aligned to challenging state content and performance standards, moving away from one-shot in-service workshops toward sustained professional development activities incorporated into the daily life of the school. Other programs within IASA funded efforts by higher education institutions and other organizations to develop their capacity to offer high-quality professional development and upgrade preservice teacher preparation programs. Finally, funds could support clearinghouses, professional-development institutes, and formal networks of teachers and administrators.

As Congress prepared to reauthorize the Higher Education Act, members decided to streamline Title V and eliminate mention of unfunded programs. A new Title II authorized programs aimed at recruiting and preparing teachers (Earley, 1998). "To stop the flow of low-quality teachers" into the profession, the Higher Education Amendments of 1998 also demonstrated that Congress was "willing to intervene in the affairs of institutions of higher education as never before" (Wayne, 2000, p. 5). The 1998 amendments to the Higher Education Act required all states and postsecondary institutions that directly or indirectly received federal aid through the act to "provide the secretary of education with data on teacher preparation standards and licensure procedures" (Earley, 2000, p. 33).

Moreover, teacher-education programs were to be held accountable by their relative outcomes. The act called for test scores for all teacher candidates to be reported by institution and compared to those of other teacher preparation programs. In addition, the accountability provisions required that institutions report the number of students enrolled in their teacher preparation programs, the number of supervised hours candidates spend in practice-teaching positions, their faculty-to-student ratios, and whether their programs are accredited by the state (Earley, 2000). Under the amendments, if a teacher education program is determined, on the basis of its pass rate, to be low performing (a term similarly applied to K-12 schools that fail to make yearly progress) and ultimately loses state funding as a result, its eligibility to receive federal funds will be revoked, as will federal assistance disbursed to its students. Finally, the act required that new institutions of higher education and K-12 partnership programs aimed at improving teacher quality and the recipient of 45% of Title II funds be evaluated on various measures including whether the partnerships improved student achievement, increased entry standards for programs that prepare teachers, and enhanced candidate performance on teacher licensure examinations.

In NCLB, the primary policy instrument through which federal lawmakers plan to improve teacher quality is requiring the demonstration of subject area knowledge. To be highly qualified, a teacher must have a bachelor's degree, be fully certified or licensed, and demonstrate competence in the subjects he or she teaches. A paraprofessional must possess 2 or more years of postsecondary education or pass a state test. As such, the teacher-quality provisions within NCLB intimate that certification, a college degree, and subject matter competence will translate to higher student achievement. Having gained credibility at the national level, the assumption nonetheless has been questioned by, for example, some in the standards movement who would prefer to define teachers' quality based solely on the outcomes achieved with their students (Ballou & Podgursky, 2000).

Under NCLB, teacher certification may be obtained through traditional or alternative routes. The hefty appropriation to alternative certification programs like Transition to Teaching and Troops-to-Teachers[8] mirrors the tenor of recent reports out of the U.S. Department of Education characterizing university-based teacher training programs as ineffective in the production of quality teachers. A 2002 report by Secretary Rod Paige (2002) states, "Formal teacher training programs are failing to produce the types of highly qualified teachers that NCLB demands" (p. viii). The report recommends making attendance at schools of education and practice teaching optional through the development and promotion of alternative certification programs.

New accountability requirements within NCLB compel states to establish measurable objectives for each local education agency (LEA) and school to include a minimum annual increase in the percentage of highly qualified teachers and in the percentage of teachers receiving high-quality professional development (section 1119 (a)). The penalties for LEAs and schools that fail to meet their annual goals, however, seem relatively weak. Should an LEA fail to meet the objectives for 2 consecutive years it will be required to develop an improvement plan to enable the district to overcome the obstacles that prevented it from reaching its goals. If, after the 3rd year, the LEA fails both to make progress toward meeting the highly qualified teacher objectives and fails to make adequate yearly progress for 3 consecutive years, the state in conjunction with district and school staff will prescribe professional development activities in which the school's teachers must participate (section 2141 (c)).

Washington has little leverage to enforce the teacher quality requirements in NCLB at the state level. If, in combination with failing to demonstrate progress toward proficiency by all student subgroups on standardized tests, the state educational agency fails to meet its teacher quality targets, the U.S. Department of Education can withhold federal funds dedicated to state administrative functions, but the amount is relatively insignificant (i.e., up to 1% of Title I allocations). If the department determines that a state continues to be out of compliance with the act's provision, it can make broader cuts in a state's federal funding. However, because most of these funds are dedicated to disadvantaged children and students with disabilities, deeper cuts may be viewed as "politically risky" by elected officials in Washington (Jennings, 2003).

## Trends in Federal Funding

Apart from shifts in the goals, assumptions, and instruments of federal teacher-education policy, federal funds for education and teacher education, specifically, have varied in type and amount.[9]

Though the bulk of its attention is directed toward NCLB, this section uses historical texts, publicly available budget reports, and other documentation to trace patterns of federal funding for teacher recruitment, preparation, and development over time.

## Types of Federal Funding

Leading up to the passage of the NDEA, political debates about federal aid to education during the 1940s and through 1957 were fought over general-purpose aid. These general-purpose aid initiatives would have appropriated monies to school districts without specifying how funds were to be spent. But, bills introduced before 1958, like the Senate proposal to supplement local dollars to establish a national minimum per-pupil expenditure sponsored by Taft, Thomas, and Hill in 1947, all failed. It was not until 1958 and NDEA with its special-purpose aid provisions did advocates of federal aid to K-12 education finally score their first big victory (Kaestle, 2001).

Since then, federal funds for education have in general been disbursed categorically with aid tied to the needs of particular subpopulations of schoolchildren or specific purposes. Funding for teacher-education programs is no exception: "Before 1990, federal policy targeted only a small percentage of teacher preparation institutions, such as those offering bilingual, vocational, or special education programs" (Earley & Schneider, 1996, p. 318). Moreover, federal funds were directed toward the recruitment and development of the workforce in certain teaching fields.[10] Over time, federal funds for teacher preparation and development were spread somewhat more broadly among student populations and additional content areas.

## Levels of Federal Funding

Funding for federally established teacher-preparation programs and partnerships fall within the domestic discretionary budget. Monitoring budget requests, appropriations, or outlays can provide a snapshot of the level of federal support for teacher preservice preparation and professional development across time. Tracking these funds is difficult, however, as at least 13 federal departments receive money for teacher preparation or development. Limiting the analysis to appropriations to or outlays by the Department of Education eliminates some, though not all,of the complexities. Because the Department of Education was created in 1980, budget reports are available only for that time forward. Moreover, although some programs have been eliminated, others have been renamed or revised and their funds rolled into new programs. Although it is not the objective here to overcome these obstacles and conduct a conclusive, longitudinal budget analysis, this section does report some observations about budget and appropriation levels beginning in 1980 and derived from information in select appropriations bills, budget tables, and secondary reports.[11]

In 1980, the discretionary funds appropriated to elementary and secondary education totaled just more than $7 billion. The amount appropriated to postsecondary education was $5.6 billion. A year later, with President Reagan in the White House, Congress reauthorized the ESEA, known as the Education Consolidation and Improvement Act of 1981. Consolidated into the State Block Grants and National Discretionary Programs were 26 programs. As such, the little money for teacher education was folded into grants that allowed states and districts unprecedented flexibility in program expenditures.[12]

Funded at more than $700 million in 1980, the Professional Development Program did receive a 1981 appropriation, though it was significantly scaled back. Weathering a $250 million cut in just 1 year, the program's appropriation never again reached its pre-Reagan levels. Later in the decade, Congress seeded $9 million to the Eisenhower Professional Development Program (federal activities)[13] beginning in 1985, but total appropriations never topped $23.5 million (in 1999).[14]

As the 1980s came to a close and as the first Bush Administration came into office, federal activity in education began to rebound. For 2 consecutive years beginning in 1990, President Bush proposed federal funding for the Alternative Certification for Teachers and Principals Program authorized the year before.[15] When Congress failed to fund it, President Bush proposed that $20 million be appropriated to Partnerships for Innovative Teacher Education. It too was never funded. However, nearly $1 million annually was dedicated to the Mid-Career Teacher Training through the 1990 and 1991 appropriations bills. Authorized through the Higher Education Act, the program was designed to encourage institutions of higher education with schools or Departments of Education to establish programs to provide teacher training to individuals moving to a career in education from another occupation. All 10 of the projects funded were intended to reduce financial and duplicative coursework barriers to teacher training and certification. The projects offered 6 to 24 months of training and included mentoring by skilled teachers and on-the-job instruction leading to teacher certification. The program was discontinued in 1992 when President Clinton came into office.

After the 1994 enactment of Goals 2000 and IASA, President Clinton proposed shifting professional development funds into the Eisenhower Professional Development State Grants Program. He zeroed-out the Professional Development Program, which had been funded at $620 million 1 year earlier, proposing $750 million for the new program. Congress, however, appropriated only $250 million, $500 million short of the President Clinton's request and a sum that represented half of the previous year's commitment. The 1995 Department of Education Appropriations Act did fund the Systemic Improvement Program (authorized through Goals 2000 the year before), which could be spent on teacher development, at $362 million, though President Clinton had proposed almost twice that much. Although President Clinton had in his budget proposal requested $1.42 billion for the Eisenhower Professional Development State Grants Program and Goals 2000 Systemic Improvement Program combined, the 1995 appropriation did not even reach the $620 million appropriated to the old Professional Development Program 1 year before. The request-appropriations pattern between President Clinton and Congress continued at approximately these levels throughout the 1990s.[16]

As the Republican Party stumbled in the 1998 elections, some members in Congress began to question their hard-line stance (following their sweep in 1994). As they did, the federal appropriation to education and teacher education began to increase, though its impact remained limited. Authorized at $300 million, Title II in the Higher Education Act received only $75 million in 1999, or one half of 1% of the total appropriation for education that year. The centerpiece of the legislation, the State and Local Programs for Teacher Excellence, used a block grant to distribute funds. At least 50% of a state's allocation was required to be sent to school districts for recruitment and professional-development activities.

For the 1999 fiscal year, President Clinton proposed and was able to secure from Congress more than $1.1 billion for the Federal Class-Size Reduction Program (CSR). States were required to allocate 100% of the funds to school districts, distributing them through a formula using poverty and enrollment data. To reduce class size in early grades, the school districts were to use no less than 82% of the funds for recruiting and training new teachers and for teacher salaries. A small portion of the total, no more than 15%, could be used for professional development and associated costs. One year later,

> The appropriation [for CSR] totaled $1.3 billion . . . and the proportion of funds potentially available for professional development increased from 15 percent to 25 percent, whereas the portion required to be used on teacher salaries correspondingly decreased from a minimum of 82 to 72 percent. The FY 2001 appropriation rose to $1,623 billion. (Millsap et al., 2004, p. 1)

As part of NCLB in 2001, the CSR program and the Eisenhower Professional Development program were folded into Title II, Part A, to fund the Teacher Quality Grants program. When the federal government began requiring major improvements in the qualifications of all teachers, new and existing, and of paraprofessionals working in schools, they broadened the instruments through which districts could spend federal funds to help improve teacher quality. Through the act, LEAs may use their Title II, Part A funds to recruit highly qualified teachers, to provide financial incentives for teachers in high-need areas, to offer professional development in core academic areas, to retain teachers through mentoring, induction, and other support programs, to reduce class size, to reform tenure, to provide merit pay, and to test teachers. Despite the increased flexibility, more than 80% of district Title II, Part A spending goes toward teacher salaries to reduce class size and toward professional development (U.S. Department of Education, 2003).

Title II also required states to use their allotments to develop new programs to reform teacher certification and licensing requirements and to establish programs that recruit professionals from fields outside of teaching. In 2003, Congress appropriated nearly 20% more money than 1 year earlier, a total of $41.7 million, to assist midcareer professionals to obtain certification through the Transition to Teaching program. Congress also appropriated another $28.8 million (or 55% over 2002) for Troops-to-Teachers.

Because labor-related expenditures account for the vast majority of all educational spending, the budgetary impact of the teacher-quality requirement, especially in some states (like California with the largest percentage of uncertified teachers), will likely cost more than any other single requirement within NCLB. Congress authorized more than $3 billion for preparing, training, and recruiting high-quality teachers and principals with the passage of NCLB in December 2001. When the President's budget request for the Department of Education and the subsequent appropriations bill fell far short of expectations,[17] many accused the federal government of delivering an unfunded mandate that would tax states and districts already facing severe budget crises. Calling the requirement for a highly qualified teacher in every classroom the single most important step to implementing NCLB, they admonished the administration for cutting federal resources for teachers by 4% and for eliminating training for 18,000 teachers (Kennedy & Miller, 2002). Others suggested that without federal dollars to implement the requirements NCLB would likely exacerbate inequities in the system. Although some districts would have a healthy property base upon which to draw revenue, many districts, especially those that include the country's poorest schools, will simply be unable to raise the additional monies needed to hire and develop more qualified teachers.

The real test of the federal government's commitment to teacher improvement may come this year as Congress works to pass the 2005 appropriations bills. Monies appropriated this fall will fund the 2005–2006 school year, a year that, under NCLB, encapsulates two significant deadlines.[18] First, states and school districts must begin testing all students in Grades 3 through 8 in reading and mathematics. Second, by the end of the 2005–2006 school year, all teachers must be highly qualified. Overall, President Bush's 2005 budget request includes $57.3 billion in discretionary appropriations for the Department of Education, representing an increase of $1.7 billion (3%) over the 2004 level. President Bush is proposing that $2.9 billion, an amount that is nearly equal to the 2003 and 2004 appropriation, be dedicated for Title II, Part A. An additional $14 million and $45 million was budgeted for Troops-to-Teachers and Transition to Teaching, respectively. In July 2004, the House Appropriations Committee marked up a bill that would provide for an overall increase of $2 billion over fiscal year 2004, for a total of $57.7 billion. Nearly $3 billion would provide states and districts with funds to improve teacher quality. The House Appropriations Committee version also provides almost $50 million for the Transition to Teaching program and $269 million for math and science partnerships to increase the pool of teachers trained in these fields. As of mid-October 2004, the Senate was yet to act.

## Discussion

The goals of federal teacher-education and development policy have, since initial involvement by Washington, expanded from upgrading science and math instruction to requiring high-quality teachers in every core subject and for all students. The instruments through which the policy goals were to be carried out have also seen a distinctive shift. Summer institutes and training centers have largely fallen away to mechanisms that hold states, districts, schools, and institutions that prepare teachers accountable for ensuring their teachers are highly qualified. Finally, patterns in the type and amount of federal funding for teacher preparation and development have evolved. In the first years of federal intervention in teacher education, federal dollars flowed largely to postsecondary institutions that trained teachers and to other organizations like the National Science Foundation. These funds dropped off considerably in the 1980s during the Reagan administration. Today, recipients of federal aid for teacher preparation and development are largely districts and schools themselves. Moreover, federal funds are supporting efforts to develop and promote alternative routes to teacher education provided by a range of public and private providers.

Many of the observed shifts have occurred incrementally over the past dozen years. Starting in the early 1990s, federal policy broke with its traditional role of attempting to fill teacher shortages and began to directly address what teachers should know and be able to do. By striving to link teacher knowledge and skills to K-12 curriculum standards, by encouraging SCDEs to partner with schools, and by holding preparation programs to account, policy makers hope to focus content and practice within preparatory and development programs.

NCLB, adopted nearly a decade later, has not as much redefined teacher preparation-and-development policy as extended recent assumptions that teaching quality matters. The federal focus on upgrading teacher practice to prepare all students for the 21st century economy predates NCLB having commenced in 1994 with Goals 2000. Moreover, according to studies by the U.S. Department of Education (2002b, 2002c) and others, NCLB has not led to significant shifts in how states and districts spend federal funds to improve teaching. Although some states are offering limited incentives to teachers who work in their poorest schools, "none is offering the higher salaries and other benefits that are likely to be needed to fill every classroom in the most challenged schools with highly qualified teachers" (Jennings, 2003, p. 307).

Where a gap exists between NCLB and previous legislation is with the instruments of reform. NCLB demands that every school ensure that all of its teachers have met federally defined quality standards. The onus of reform, therefore, has been extended from programs that prepare teachers to individual schools in which teachers teach.

Elsewhere scholars have argued that policy making in general favors incremental change over radical innovation because policy makers are more likely to lend their support to policy solutions for which risks and costs are known (Lindblom, 1959; Tyack & Cuban, 1995). An alternative or additional explanation for the tinkering that characterizes federal involvement in teacher education is a will for tighter policy alignment.

Policy alignment seeks to minimize inconsistencies and reduce obstacles to reform. Among the stated purposes of Goals 2000, the law that established the national education goals and embraced the movement for standards-based reform, was "to create a 'template' or framework for other federal education legislation" (Earley & Schneider, 1996, p. 313). To focus federal education policy, the legislation authorized monies for state and local education agencies to establish guidelines that would provide a model through which federal education programs could be integrated. Its ultimate goal was system-wide reform.

The standards movement, as it would become known, focused education policy at all levels of government on performance outcomes, replacing an exclusive interest in schooling inputs (e.g., student-teacher ratios, number of textbooks). Outcomes were to be measured by performance on state-standardized examinations. In the 1990s, attention turned to aligning exams with the state content standards through the use of criterion-referenced tests. Reforming teacher preparation and development was the next logical step. Secretary of Education Richard Riley emphasized in 1995 that federal education legislation was being designed to get states and districts to create plans to align the curriculum, assessment systems, and teacher preparation and development with core content standards. Amendments to the Higher Education Act in 1998 required all states to report, among other information, the degree to which K-12 content standards align with teacher licensure requirements. In the provision of professional development, NCLB required that funds be spent on activities in core academic subjects including the utilization of challenging state content standards (section 2134 (a)).

Though its pace has been incremental, the increasing federal role in teacher education and development has meant that "power to influence teacher education [is] accumulating at all the operating levels in the system" (Clark & McNergney, 1990, p. 115). Cohen (1982) has argued that power accumulates in all levels at once because higher level governments (e.g., states) have to rely on lower level governments (e.g., districts) to implement their ideas, and these lower level governments set up subunits to handle some of the administrative work. With the responsibility of policy coordination left to the subunits, street-level bureaucrats tend to amass influence, improvise responses, and discourage uniformity. Learning to teach is a complex and lifelong process, requiring opportunities to connect preservice preparation to new teacher induction and new teacher induction to ongoing professional development (Feiman-Nemser, 2001). Multilevel power accumulation, what some have called garbage-can governance, makes this kind of coordination unlikely. Future research must consider the teacher-quality implications of a system in which the federal government defines teacher quality, states certify teachers through accreditation and licensure, colleges of education control preservice training, schools themselves provide new teacher induction, and professional development is "everybody and nobody's responsibility" (Feiman-Nemser, 2001, p. 2).

# Notes

1. Prior to 1958, federal involvement in education was limited mostly to food programs.
2. Moreover, the act's provisions stressed schooling as a means for intellectual development (not for social-ization) and a focus on gifted children, a view that tends "to prevail during periods of heightened inter-national competition" (Kaestle & Smith, 1982, p. 393).
3. However, through the analysis of archival documents, Kaestle (2001) discovered that a Department of Health, Education, and Welfare task force had written a bill that was almost identical to NDEA in 1957 before the launch of Sputnik. According to political scientist John Kingdon (1984), an available set of pol-icy alternatives floats around Washington at any given time waiting for a problem to which it can attach. A perceived crisis, in this case the Sputnik launch, can provide the necessary though not sufficient agent for adoption.
4. That same year, as a response to poverty and racial discord, the Elementary and Secondary Education Act (ESEA) of 1965 was enacted. The purpose of ESEA was to improve the basic skills of children living in low-income neighborhoods (Kaestle, 2001). With regard to teacher education, ESEA directed funds to the continuing education of existing teachers whose students had special needs (e.g., limited English proficiency).
5. Initiatives were advanced by both Republican and Democratic members of Congress during the first Bush Administration, although none became law.
6. Although the approach was codified into law in 1998, an amendment to the Higher Education Act was introduced in 1985 (but not enacted) that would have required any institution that prepared teachers to offer a warranty plan to their graduates (Earley, 2000).
7. The U.S. Department of Education (2002a) *Desktop Reference of the No Child Left Behind Act* describes the pro-vision as ensuring "that Title I schools provide instruction by highly qualified instructional staff" (p. 19).
8. Transition to Teaching disburses grants to eligible organizations to recruit, train, and place talented indi-viduals into teaching positions. Troops-to-Teachers provides funds to recruit, train, and support former members of the military to teach in high-poverty schools.
9. A more comprehensive analysis of federal funding of teacher education over time might consider addi-tional issues. For example, there is evidence that the Department of Education under President Clinton was moderately successful in shifting the target of federal dollars from LEAs to schools themselves.
10. The National Defense Education Act of 1958, for example, directed funds to states and local agencies to strengthen curriculum and instruction in mathematics, science, and foreign languages.
11. Outlays, or the amount actually spent on teacher education and development, was not available.
12. As such, it is difficult to track how much of the funds went to improving teacher recruitment, training, and development.
13. Funds projects of national significance that contribute to the design and implementation of high quality professional development.
14. At that time, the state grants were funding the Eisenhower National Clearinghouse for Math and Science Education and the National Board for Professional Teaching Standards.
15. The program was authorized through the Educational Excellence Act of 1989, Part C, but was never funded.
16. A small Minority Teacher Recruitment program, authorized through Title V of the Higher Education Act, was funded in 1993 at approximately $2.5 million.
17. Some analysis suggested that the budget would cut $90 million from elementary and secondary school programs covered by NCLB.
18. There is a growing consensus that Congress will delay passage until after the November elections.

# References

Ballou, D., & Podgursky, M. (2000). Gaining control of professional licensing and advancement. In T. Loveless (Ed.), *Conflicting missions* (pp. 69–109). Washington, D.C.: Brookings Institution.

Clark, D. L., & McNergney, R. F. (1990). Governance of teacher education. In R. W. Houston (Ed.), *Handbook of research on teacher education* (pp. 101–118). New York: Macmillan.

Cohen, D. K. (1982). Policy and organization: The impact of state and federal educational policy on school governance. *Harvard Educational Review, 52*(4), 474–499.

Darling-Hammond, L. (2000). Reforming teacher preparation and licensing: Debating the evidence. *Teachers College Record, 102*(1), 28–56.

Darling-Hammond, L., & Berry, B. (1988). *Evolution of teacher policy.* Santa Monica, CA: RAND.

Earley, P. M. (1998). *Teacher quality enhancement grants for states and partnerships: HEA, Title II. An AACTE issue paper.* Retrieved June 21, 2004, from http://www.edpolicy.org/publications/documents/hea.htm

Earley, P. M. (2000). Finding the culprit: Federal policy and teacher education. *Educational Policy, 14,* 25–39.

Earley, P. M., & Schneider, E. (1996). Federal policy and teacher education. In J. Sikula, T. Buttery, & E. Guyton (Eds.), *Handbook of research on teacher education* (2nd ed., pp. 306–319). New York: Simon & Schuster.

Feiman-Nemser, S. (2001). From preparation to practice: Designing a continuum to strengthen and sustain teaching. *Teachers College Record, 103*(6), 1013–1055.

Finn, J. D., & Achilles, C. M. (1990). Answers and questions about class size: A statewide experiment. *American Educational Research Journal, 27*(3), 557–577.

Garber, S. (2003). *Sputnik and the dawn of the space age.* Retrieved May 25, 2004, from http://www.hq.nasa.gov/office/pao/History/sputnik/

Hawley, W. D. (1990). Systematic analysis, public policy-making and teacher education. In R. W. Houston (Ed.), *Handbook of research on teacher education* (pp. 136–156). New York: Macmillan.

Hitz, R. (2004). Editorial: Teacher education reform. *Educational Perspectives, 36*(1). Retrieved August 9, 2004, from http://www.hawaii.edu/edper/pages/vol36n1-2.htm

Ingersoll, R. M. (1996, August). *Teacher quality and inequality.* Paper presented at the annual meeting of the American Statistical Association, Chicago, Illinois.

Institute for Higher Education Policy. (2003). *Reauthorizing the Higher Education Act: Issues and options.* Washington, D.C.: Author.

Jennings, J. (2003). From the White House to the schoolhouse: Greater demands and new roles. In W. L. Boyd & D. Miretzky (Eds.), *American educational governance on trial: Change and challenges* (pp. 291–308). Chicago: University of Chicago Press.

Jordan, K. F. (1986, July 18). *Teacher education recommendations in the school reform efforts* (Rep. No. 86–780 S). Washington, D.C.: Congressional Research Service.

Jordan, K. F., & Borkow, N. B. (1985). *Federal efforts to improve America's teaching force* (Rep. No. 85–644 S). Washington, D.C.: Congressional Research Service.

Kaestle, C. F. (2001). Federal aid to education since World War II. In J. Jennings (Ed.), *The future of the federal role in elementary and secondary education.* Washington, D.C.: Center for Education Policy.

Kaestle, C. F., & Smith, M. S. (1982). The federal role in elementary and secondary education, 1940–1980. *Harvard Educational Review, 52*(4), 384–408.

Kaplan, L. S., & Owings, W. A. (2003). No Child Left Behind: The politics of teacher quality. *Phi Delta Kappan, 84*(9), 687–692.

Kennedy, E. M., & Miller, G. (2002). *Letter to President George W. Bush.* Retrieved August 10, 2004, from http://edworkforce.house.gov/democrats/rel31802.html

Kingdon, J. (1984). *Agendas, alternatives, and public policies.* New York: HarperCollins.

Lindblom, C. (1959). The science of muddling through. *Public Administration Review, 19,* 79–88.

Millsap, M., Giancola, J., Smith, W., Hunt, D., Humphrey, D., Wechsler, M., et al. (2004). *A descriptive evaluation of the federal class-size reduction program.* Retrieved June 3, 2004, from http://www.ed.gov/about/offices/list/ods/ppss/reports.html

National Commission on Excellence in Education. (1983). *A nation at risk: The imperative for educational reform.* Washington, D.C.: U.S. Department of Education.

National Commission on Teaching and America's Future. (1996). *What matters most: Teaching for America's future.* New York: Author.

Paige, R. (2002). *Meeting the highly qualified teachers challenge: The secretary's first annual report on teacher quality.* Washington, D.C.: U.S. Department of Education.

Ramirez, H. (2004). The shift from hands-off: The federal role in supporting and defining teacher quality. In R. Hess, A. Rotherham, & K. Walsh (Eds.), *A qualified teacher in every classroom?* Cambridge, MA: Harvard Education Publishing.

Riley, R. (1996). *Achieving the goals: Goal 4 teacher professional development.* Washington, D.C.: U.S. Department of Education.

Sanders, W. L., & Rivers, J. C. (1996). *Cumulative and residual effects of teachers on future student academic achievement.* Knoxville, TN: University of Tennessee Value-Added Research and Assessment Center.

Shaul, M. (1999, May 5). *Testimony presented to the Subcommittee on Postsecondary Education, Training, and Life-Long Learning.* Washington, D.C.: U.S. House of Representatives.

Sonnenberg, W. (2004). *Federal support for education: FY 1980 to FY 2003* (Rep. No. NCES 2004–026). Washington, D.C.: National Center for Education Statistics.

Stedman, J. (2003). *The Higher Education Act: Reauthorization status and issues.* Retrieved July 13, 2004, from http://usinfo.state.gov/usa/infousa/educ/files/hiedact.pdf

Thomas B. Fordham Foundation. (1999). *The teachers we need and how to get more of them: A manifesto.* Retrieved February 4, 2004, from http://www.edexcellence.net

Tyack, D., & Cuban, L. (1995). *Tinkering toward utopia: A century of public school reform.* Cambridge, MA: Harvard University Press.

U.S. Department of Education. (2002a). *Desktop reference of the No Child Left Behind Act.* Washington, D.C.: Author.

U.S. Department of Education. (2002b). *Helping teachers through high-quality professional development.* Washington, D.C.: Author.

U.S. Department of Education. (2002c). *Outline of programs and selected changes in the No Child Left Behind Act of 2001.* Washington, D.C.: Author.

U.S. Department of Education. (2003). *Improving teacher quality in U.S. school districts: Districts' use of Title II, Part A, funds in 2002–2003.* Washington, D.C.: Author.

Wayne, A. J. (2000). *Federal policies to improve teacher quality for low-income students.* Unpublished doctoral dissertation, University of Maryland, College Park.

*Lora Cohen-Vogel is an assistant professor in the College of Education at Florida State University. Her research interests include the political antecedents of education policy and the governance structures that facilitate or impede policy adoption, implementation, and effectiveness.*

# Appendix

## Additional References and Resources

While we made every attempt possible to include as many related readings as space would allow, however, it was impossible to include everything. Many great references are noted below that the editors suggest you consider reading to expand your knowledge base. The first section of these additional resources includes readings that are directly related to the sections and topics we cover in this Second Edition. The second section provides many more additional readings that are related to the general public policy and higher education topics that go beyond the scope of the topics covered in this Second Edition. The third section includes several key policy reports that were just too large (or long) to include in this Section Edition. We believe these additional references and resources provide substantial support to the reader in learning more about public policy and higher education. One important point to note is that we tried to limit our inclusions in these three sections to research published since the First Edition (1997), so we believe these additional resources are very timely and current.

## I. Additional references to support our sections and topics covered in this Second Edition

## Part I: Foundations of Public Policy and Higher Education

### Arenas of Policymaking

Baumgartner, F. R., & Jones, B. D. (1991). Agenda dynamics and policy subsystems. *Journal of Politics, 53*, 1044–1074.

Crosson, P. H. (1984). State postsecondary education policy systems. *The Review of Higher Education, 7*(2), 125–142

Doyle, W. R. (2007). Public opinion, partisan identification, and higher education policy. *Journal of Higher Education, 78*(4), 369–401.

Frost, S. H., Hearn, J. C., & Marine, G. (1997). State policy and the public research university. *Journal of Higher Education, 68*(4), 363–397.

Hearn, J. C. & Griswold, C. P. (1994). State level centralization and policy innovation in US postsecondary education. *Educational Evaluation and Policy Analysis, 16*(2), 161–190.

Martinez, M. C. (1999). The uneasy public policy triangle in higher education. *The Review of Higher Education, 22*(3), 247–263.

McLendon, M. K. (2003). The politics of higher education: Toward an expanded research agenda. *Educational Policy, 17*(1), 165–191.

McLendon, M. K., & Eddings, S. (2002). Direct democracy and higher education: The state ballot as an instrument of higher education policy making. *Educational Policy, 16*(1), 193–218.

McLendon, M. K., & Hearn, J. C. (2005). Mandated openness and higher-education governance: Policy, theoretical and analytical perspectives. In J. C. Smart (Ed.), *Higher education: Handbook of theory and research* Vol. XXI (pp. 39–97). New York, NY: Kluwer Academic Publishers.

McLendon, M. K., & Hearn, J. C. (2003). Introduction: The politics of higher education. *Educational Policy, 17*(1), 3–11.

McLendon, M. K., Heller, D., & Young, S. (2001). State postsecondary policy innovation: Politics, competition, and interstate migration of policy ideas. Paper presented at the annual meeting of the Midwest Political Science Association, Chicago, Ill.

Nicholson-Crotty, J., & Meier, K. J. (2003). Politics structure and public policy: The case of higher education. *Educational Policy, 17*(1), 80–97.

Wildavsky, A. (1979). *The politics of the budgetary process* (3rd ed.). Boston: Little Brown. (Chapters 2 and 5)

Zumeta, W. (1992). State policies and private higher education: Policies, correlates, and linkages. *The Journal of Higher Education, 62*(4), 363–417.

## Policy Inquiry/Analysis

Martinez, M. C. (2008). Competencies and higher education policy analysts. *Educational Policy, 22*(5), 623–639.

Sabatier, P. A. (2001). Toward better theories of the policy process. *Political Science and Politics, 24*(2), 144–156.

Shakespeare, C. (2008). Uncovering information's role in the state higher education policy-making process. *Educational Policy, 22*(6), 875–899.

Shaw, K. M. (2004). Using feminist critical policy analysis in the realm of higher education: The case of welfare reform as gendered educational policy. *Journal of Higher Education, 75*(1), 56–79.

True, J. L., Jones, B. D., & Baumgartner, F. R. (1999). Punctuated equilibrium theory: Explaining stability and change in American policymaking. In P.A. Sabatier (Ed.), *Theories of the Policy Process* (pp. 155–188). Boulder, CO: Westview Press.

Weis, L., Nozaki, Y., Granfield, R., & Olsen, N. (2007). A call for civically engaged educational policy-related scholarship. *Educational Policy, 21*(2), 426–433.

# Part II: Current Issues in Public Policy & Higher Education

## Access, Success, Attainment, P-16

Anderson, G., Sun, J., & Alfonso, M. (2006). Effectiveness of statewide articulation agreements on the probability of transfer: A preliminary policy analysis. *The Review of Higher Education, 29*(3), 269–291.

Bottoms, G., & Young, M. (2008). *Lost in transition: Building a better path from school to college and careers.* Atlanta, GA: Southern Regional Education Board.

Callan, P. M., & Finney, J. E. (2003). *Multiple pathways and state policy: Toward education and training beyond high school.* Boston, MA: Jobs for the Future.

Callan, P. M., Finney, J. E., Kirst, M. W., Usdan, M. D., & Venezia, A. (2006). Claiming common ground: State policymaking for improving college readiness and success. Palo Alto, CA: The Institute for Educational Leadership; The National Center for Public Policy and Higher Education; & The Stanford Institute for Higher Education Research.

Contreras, F. E. (2005). The reconstruction of merit post-Proposition 209. *Educational Policy, 19*(2), 371–395.

Corwin, Z. B., & Tierney, W. G. (2007, January). *Getting there - and beyond: Building a culture of college-going in high schools.* Los Angeles, CA: University of Southern California Center for Higher Education Policy Analysis. Retrieved April 29, 2008, from http://www.usc.edu/dept/chepa/working/Getting%20There%20 FINAL.pdf

Gandara, P., Horn, C., & Orfield, G. (2005). The access crisis in higher education. *Educational Policy, 19*(2), 255–261.

Goldrick-Rab, S., & Shaw, K. M. (2005). Racial and ethnic differences in the impact of work-first policies on college access. *Educational Evaluation and Policy Analysis, 27*(4), 291–307

Hamrick, F. A., & Stage, F. K. (2004). College predisposition at high-minority enrollment, low-income schools. *Review of Higher Education, 27*(2), 151–168.

Heller, D. E. (1999). The effects of tuition and state financial aid on public college enrollment. *The Review of Higher Education, 23*(1), 65–89.

Hu, S., & St. John, E. P. (2001). Student persistence in a public higher education system: Understanding racial and ethnic differences. *The Journal of Higher Education, 72*(3), 265–286.

Hurtado, S., Dey, E. L., Gurin, P. Y., & Gurin, G. (2003). College environments, diversity and student learning. In J. C. Smart (Ed.), *Higher education: Handbook of theory & research* Vol. XVIII (pp. 145–189). New York, NY: Kluwer Academic Publishers.

Mazzeo, C. (2002). Stakes for students: Agenda-setting and remedial education. *Review of Higher Education, 26*(1), 19–39.

Merisotis, J. P., & Phipps, R. A. (2000). Remedial education in colleges and universities: What's really going on? *Review of Higher Education, 24*(1), 67–85.

Mumper, M. (2003). Does policy design matter? Comparing universal and targeted approaches to encourage college participation. *Educational Policy, 17*(1), 38–59.

Mumper, M. (2001). The paradox of college prices: Five stories with no clear lesson. In D. Heller (Ed.), *The states and public higher education policy* (pp. 39–63). Baltimore, MD: Johns Hopkins University Press.

Nettles, M., & Cole, J. (1999). *State of higher education assessment policy.* Stanford, CA: National Center for Postsecondary Improvement.

Paulsen, M. B., & St. John, E. P. (2002). Social class and college costs: Examining the financial nexus between college choice and persistence. *Journal of Higher Education, 73*(2), 189–236.

Perna, L. W., & Titus, M. A. (2004). Understanding differences in the choice of college attended: The role of state public policies. *Review of Higher Education, 27*(4), 501–525.

Perna, L. W. (2006). Studying college access and choice: A proposed conceptual model. In J. C. Smart (Ed.), *Higher education: Handbook of theory & research volume XXI* (pp. 99–157). New York, NY: Kluwer Academic Publishers.

Perna, L. W., Rowan-Kenyon, H., Bell, A., Thomas, S.L., & Li, C. (2008). A typology of federal and state programs designed to promote college enrollment. *Journal of Higher Education, 79*(3), 243–267.

Perna, L. W., Rowan-Kenyon, H., Thomas, S. L., Bell, A., Anderson, R., & Li, C. (2008). The role of college counseling in shaping college opportunity: Variations across high schools. *Review of Higher Education, 31*(2), 131–159.

Perna, L. W., Steele, P., Woda, S., & Hibbert, T. (2005). State public policies and the racial/ethnic stratification of college access and choice in the state of Maryland. *Review of Higher Education, 28*(2), 245–272.

Perna, L. W., & Titus, M. A. (2005). The relationship between parental involvement as social capital and college enrollment: An examination of racial/ethnic group differences. *Journal of Higher Education, 76*(5), 485–518.

Renn, K. A., & Lunceford, C. J. (2004). Because the numbers matter: Transforming postsecondary education data on student race and ethnicity to meet the challenges of a changing nation. *Educational Policy, 18*(5), 752–783.

St. John, E. P., Paulsen, M. B., & Carter, D. F. (2005). Diversity, college costs, and postsecondary opportunity: An examination of the financial nexus between college choice and persistence for African Americans and whites. *Journal of Higher Education, 76*(5), 545–569.

Stampen, J. O., & Hansen, W. L. (1999). Improving higher education access and persistence: New directions from a "systems" perspective. *Educational Evaluation and Policy Analysis, 21*(4), 417–426.

Thomas, S. L., & Perna, L. W. (2004). The opportunity agenda: A reexamination of postsecondary reward & opportunity. In J. C. Smart (Ed.), *Higher education: Handbook of theory & research volume XIX* (pp. 43–84). New York, NY: Kluwer Academic Publishers.

Tierney, W. G. (2002). Parents and families in precollege preparation: The lack of connection between research and practice. *Educational Policy, 16*(4), 588–606.

Titus, M. A. (2006) No college student left behind: The influence of financial aspects of a state's higher education policy on college completion. *Review of Higher Education, 29*(3), 293–317.

United States Department of Education. (2008, May 21). *Protecting student access and affordability in higher education: The secretary's plan for ensuring access to federal student loans for the 2008–09 school year.* Washington, D.C.: Author.

Venezia, A., Callan, P. M., Finney, J. E., Kirst, M. W., & Usdan, M. D. (2005). *The governance divide: A report on a four-state study on improving college readiness and success.* Retrieved April 30, 2008, from http://www.stanford.edu/group/bridgeproject/8-26-05%20Governance%20Divide.pdf

Venezia, A., & Kirst, M. W. (2005). Inequitable opportunities: How current education systems and policies undermine the chances for student persistence and success in college. *Educational Policy, 19*(2), 283–307.

Venezia, A., Kirst, M. W., & Antonio, A. (2003). *SchoBetraying the college dream: How disconnected K-12 and postsecondary education systems undermine student aspirations.* Retrieved April 1, 2007, from http://www.stanford.edu/group/bridgeproject/betrayingthecollegedream.pdf

Wellman, J. V. (2002). *State policy and community college-baccalaureate transfer.* Palo Alto, CA: National Center for Public Policy and Higher Education and the Institute for Higher Education Policy

Wolff, R. A. (2004). Accountability and accreditation: Can reforms match increasing demand? In J. C. Burke (Ed.), *Achieving accountability in higher education: Balancing public, academic and market demands* (pp. 78–103). San Francisco, CA: Jossey Bass.

Wolniak, G. C., & Engberg, M. E. (2008). The effects of high school feeder networks on college enrollment. *Review of Higher Education, 31*(1), 27–53.

## Access, Success, Attainment and P-16 for Colleges/Universities with Special Populations

### Accountability, Assessment, Accreditation

#### Accountability

Alexander, F. K. (2000). The changing face of accountability: Monitoring and assessing institutional performance in higher education. *The Journal of Higher Education, (71)*4, 411–431.

Burke, J. C. (2004). The many faces of accountability. In Burke, J. C. (Ed.), *Achieving accountability in higher education: Balancing public, academic and market demands,* (pp. 1–24) San Francisco, CA: Jossey Bass.

Burke, J. C. (2004). The three corners of the accountability triangle: Serving all, submitting to none. In Burke, J. C. (Ed.), *Achieving accountability in higher education: Balancing public, academic and market demands,* (pp. 296–324) San Francisco, CA: Jossey Bass.

Callan, P. M., & Finney, J. E. (2004). State-by-state report cards: Public purposes and accountability. In Burke, J. C. (Eds.), *Achieving accountability in higher education: Balancing public, academic and market demands,* (pp. 198–215) San Francisco, CA: Jossey Bass.

Huisman, J., & Currie, J. (2004). Accountability in higher education: Bridge over troubled water? *Higher Education, 48*(4), 529–551.

Kezar, A. J. (2004). Obtaining integrity? Reviewing and examining the charter between higher education and society. *Review of Higher Education, 27*(4), 429–459.

Lane, J. E. (2007). The spider web of oversight: An analysis of external oversight of higher education. *Journal of Higher Education, 78*(6), 615–644.

Martinez, M. C., Farias, J., & Arellano, E. (2002). State higher education report cards: What's in a grade? *Review of Higher Education, 26*(1), 1–18.

Martinez, M. C., & Nilson, M. (2006). Assessing the connection between higher education policy and performance. *Educational Policy, 20*(2), 299–322.

McLendon, M. K. (2003). Setting the governmental agenda for state decentralization of higher education. *The Journal of Higher Education, 74*(5), 479–515.

McLendon, M. K., Hearn, J. C., & Deaton, R. (2006). Called to account: Analyzing the origins and spread of state performance-accountability policies for higher education. *Educational Evaluation and Policy Analysis, 28*(1), 1–24.

Minor, J. T. (2008). The relationship between selection processes of public trustees and state higher education performance. *Educational Policy, 22*(6), 830–853.

National Commission on Accountability in Higher Education. (2005). *Accountability for better results: A national imperative for higher education.* Boulder, CO: State Higher Education Executive Officers.

Sabloff, P. L. W. (1997). Another reason why state legislatures will continue to restrict public university autonomy. *The Review of Higher Education, 20*(2), 141–162.

United States Department of Education. (2006, September 26). *Action plan for higher education: Improving accessibility, affordability and accountability.* Washington, D.C.: Author.

#### Accreditation

Dunn, D. (2003). Accountability, democratic theory, and higher education. *Educational Policy, 17*(1), 60–79.

#### SURDs (Data Unit Section):

Griswold, C. P. (1999). Political turbulence and policy research: The national commission on student financial assistance. *The Review of Higher Education, 22*(2), 143–164.

# Finance & Student Aid Policy

Advisory Committee on Student Financial Aid. (2007). *Turn the page: Making college textbooks more affordable.* Washington, D.C.: Author

Advisory Committee on Student Financial Aid. (2006). *Mortgaging our future: How financial barriers to college undercut America's global competitiveness.* Washington, D.C.: Author

Advisory Committee on Student Financial Aid. (2005). *The student aid gauntlet: Making access to college simple and certain.* Washington, D.C.: Author

Advisory Committee on Student Financial Aid. (2002). *Empty promises: The myth of college access in America.* Washington, D.C.: Author

Advisory Committee on Student Financial Aid. (2001). *Access denied.* Washington, D.C.: Author

Cohen-Vogel, L., Ingle, W. K., Levine, A. A., & Spence, M. (2008). The "spread" of merit-based college aid: Politics, policy consortia, and interstate competition. *Educational Policy, 22*(3), 339–362.

DesJardins, S. L. (2001). Assessing the effects of changing institutional aid policy. *Research in Higher Education, 42*(6), 653–678.

DesJardins, S. L., Ahlburg, D. A., & McCall, B. P. (2002). An integrated model of application, admission, enrollment & financial aid. *Journal of Higher Education, 73*(5), 381–429.

Dickeson, R. C. (2004). *Collision course: Rising college costs threaten America's future and require shared solutions.* Indianapolis, IN: Lumina Foundation for Education.

Ehrenberg, R. G., Zhang, L., & Levin, J. M. (2006). Crafting a class: The trade-off between merit scholarships and enrolling lower-income students. *Review of Higher Education, 29*(2), 195–211.

Hearn, J. C., Griswold, C. P., & Marine, G. (1996). Region, resource, and reason: A contextual analysis of state tuition and student aid policies. *Research in Higher Education, 37*(3), 241–278.

Heller, D. E. (2002). The policy shift in state financial aid programs. In J. C. Smart (Ed.), *Higher education: Handbook of theory and research* Vol. XVII (pp. 221–261). New York, NY: Kluwer Academic Publishers.

Henry, G. T., Rubenstein, R., & Bugler, D. T. (2004). Is HOPE enough? Impacts of receiving and losing merit-based financial aid. *Educational Policy, 18*(5), 686–709.

The Institute for College Access and Success. (2008, April). *Comparison and analysis of financial aid pledges: How much would families actually have to pay?* Retrieved April 29, 2008, from http://www.ticas.org/files/pub/Pledges_Analysis.pdf

Johnstone, D. B. (1998). Patterns of finance: Revolution, evolution, or more of the same? *The Review of Higher Education, 21*(3), 245–255.

Marcus, L. R., Pratt, B., & Stevens, J. L. (1997). Deregulating colleges: The autonomy experiment. *Educational Policy, 11*(1), 92–110.

Oberg, J. H. (1997). Testing federal student-aid fungibility in two competing versions of federalism. *Publius, 27*(1), 115–134.

Robst, J. (2001). Cost efficiency in public higher education institutions. *The Journal of Higher Education, 72*(6), 730–750.

Serow, R. C. (2004). Policy as symbol: Title II of the 1944 G.I. bill. *Review of Higher Education, 27*(4), 481–499.

St. John, E. P., Musoba, G. D. & Simmons, A. B. (2003). Keeping the promise: The impact of Indiana's twenty first century scholars program. *Review of Higher Education, 27*(1), 103–123.

Somers, P., Hollis, J. M., & Stokes, T. (2000). The federal government as first creditor on student loans: Politics and policy. *Educational Evaluation and Policy Analysis, 22*(4), 331–339.

Tienda, M., & Niu, S. X. (2006). Flagships, feeders, and the Texas top 10% law: A test of the "brain drain" hypothesis. *Journal of Higher Education, 77*(4), 712–739.

Turner, S. E. (2001). Federal financial aid: How well does it work? In J. C. Smart (Ed.), *Higher education: Handbook of theory and research* Vol. XVI (pp.341–363). New York, NY: Kluwer Academic Publishers.

Zumeta, W. (1996). Meeting the demand for higher education without breaking the bank: A framework for the design of state higher education policies for an era of increasing demand. *The Journal of Higher Education, 67*(4), 367–425.

## Appropriations/Funding

Alexander, F. K. (2000). The silent crisis: The relative fiscal capacity of public universities to compete for faculty. *Review of Higher Education, 24*(2), 113–129.

Cheslock, J. J., & Gianneschi, M. (2008). Replacing state appropriations with alternative revenue sources: The case of voluntary support. *Journal of Higher Education, 79*(2), 208–229.

Davies, G. K. (2006). *Setting a public agenda for higher education in the states: Lessons learned form the national collaborative for higher education policy.* Palo Alto, CA: The National Collaborative for Higher Education policy

Dowd, A. C., & Grant, J. L. (2005). Equity and efficiency of community college appropriations: The role of local financing. *The Review of Higher Education, 29*(2), 167–194.

Doyle, W. R. (2007). The political economy of redistribution through higher education subsidies. In J. C. Smart (Ed.), *Higher education: Handbook of theory and research volume* Vol. XXII (pp. 335–409). New York, NY: Kluwer Academic Publishers.

Doyle, W. R. (2006). Adoption of merit-based student grant programs: An event history analysis. *Educational Evaluation and Policy Analysis, 28*(3), 259–285.

Heller, D. E. (2005). Public subsidies for higher education in California: An exploratory analysis of who pays and who benefits. *Educational Policy, 19*(2), 349–370.

Hossler, D., Lund, J. P., Ramin, J., Westfall, S., & Irish, S. (1997). State funding for higher education: The Sisyphean task. *The Journal of Higher Education, 68*(2), 160–190.

Kaplan, G. E. (2006, September). *State fiscal crises and cuts in higher education: The implications for access, institutional performance, and strategic reengineering.* Boulder, CO: Western Interstate Commission for Higher Education.

Leifner, I. (2003). Funding, resource allocation, and performance in higher education systems. *Higher Education, 46*(4), 469–489.

Leslie, D. W., & Berdahl, R. O. (2008). The politics of restructuring higher education in Virginia: A case study. *Review of Higher Education, 31*(3), 309–328.

McLendon, M. K. (2003). State governance reform of higher education: Patterns, trends, and theories of the public policy process. In J. C. Smart (Ed.), *Higher education: Handbook of theory and research volume* Vol. XVIII (pp. 57–144). New York, NY: Kluwer Academic Publishers.

McLendon, M. K., Deaton, S. B., & Hearn, J. C. (2007). The enactment of reforms in state governance of higher education: Testing the political instability hypothesis. *Journal of Higher Education, (78)*6, 645–675.

Mills, M. R. (2007). Stories of politics and policy: Florida's higher education governance reorganization. *The Journal of Higher Education, 78*(2), 162–18.

Novak, R. J. (1996). Methods, objectives, and consequences of restructuring. In T. MacTaggart (Ed.), *Restructuring higher education* (pp. 16–50). San Francisco, CA: Jossey-Bass.

Sav, G. T. (1997). Separate and unequal: State financing of historically black colleges and universities. *The Journal of Blacks in Higher Education, 15,* 101–104.

St. John, E. P., Chung, C. Musoba, G. D., Simmons, A. B., Wooden, O. S., & Mendes, J. P. (2004). *Expanding college access: The impact of state financing strategies.* Indianapolis, IN: Lumina Foundation for Education/Indiana Education Policy Center at Indiana University.

## Affordability

American Association of State Colleges and Universities and SunGard Higher Education. (2008). *Cost containment: A survey of current practices at America's state colleges and universities.* Retrieved April 29, 2008, from http://www.aascu.org/policy/media/cost.pdf

Baird, K. (2006). The political economy of college prepaid tuition plans. *The Review of Higher Education, 26*(2), 141–166.

Dowd, A. C., & Grant, J. L. (2006). Equity and efficiency of community college appropriations: The role of local financing. *The Review of Higher Education, 29*(2), 167–194.

Fethke, G. (2005). Strategic determination of higher education subsidies and tuitions. *Economics of Education Review, 24*(5), 601–609.

Finney, J. E., & Kelly, P. J. (2004). Affordability: Obtaining and making sense of information about how students, families, and states pay for higher education. *Change, 36*(4), 54–59.

Immerwahr, J., & Johnson, J. (2007, May). *Squeeze play: How parents and the public look at higher education today.* Palo Alto, CA: National Center for Public Policy and Higher Education. Retrieved April 29, 2008, from http://www.highereducation.org/reports/squeeze_play/index.html

Johnstone, D. B. (2004). The economics and politics of cost sharing in higher education: Comparative perspectives. *Economics of Education Review, 23*(4), 403–410.

National Center for Public Policy and Higher Education. (2002). *Losing ground: A national status report on the affordability of American higher education*. Retrieved April 29, 2008, from http://www.highereducation.org/reports/losing_ground/affordability_report_final_bw.pdf

Paulsen, M. B., & John, E. P. S. (2002). Social class and college costs: Examining the financial nexus between college choice and persistence. *The Journal of Higher Education, 73*(2), 189–236.

Shin, J., & Milton, S. (2006). Rethinking tuition effects on enrollment in public four-year colleges and universities. *The Review of Higher Education, 29*(2), 213–237.

## Teacher Preparation

Coble, C., Edelfelt, R., & Kettlewell, J. (2004). *Who's in charge here? The changing landscape of teacher preparation in America*. Denver, CO: Education Commission of the States.

Colbeck, C. L. (2002). State policies to improve undergraduate teaching: Administrator and faculty responses. *The Journal of Higher Education, 73*(1), 3–25.

Coulter, T., & Vandal, B. (2007). *Community colleges and teacher preparation: Roles, issues and opportunities*. Denver, CO: Education Commission of the States.

Lasley, T. J., Siedentop, D., & Yinger, R. (2006). A systematic approach to enhancing teacher quality: The Ohio model. *Journal of Teacher Education, 57*(1), 13.

Levine, A. (2006). *Educating school teachers*. Washington, D.C.: Education Schools Project.

Zimpher, N. L. (1999). *Teacher quality and P-16 reform: The state policy context*. Boulder, CO: State Higher Education Executive Officers.

## II. Other related issues and references not addressed in this Second Edition:

Bradshaw, T. K., Kennedy, K. M., Davis, P. R., Lloyd, L., Gwebu, N., & Last, J. A. (2003). Science first: Contributions of a university-industry toxic substances research and teaching program to economic development. *Journal of Higher Education, 74*(3), 292–320.

Payne, A. A. (2003). The role of politically motivated subsidies on university research activities. *Educational Policy, 17*(1), 12–37.

Siegfried, J. J., Sanderson, A. R., & McHenry, P. (2007). The economic impact of colleges and universities. *Economics of Education Review, 26*(5), 546–558.

Taylor, M., Plummer, P., Bryson, J. R. & Garlick, S. (2008) The Role of Universities in Building Local Economic Capacities. *Politics & Policy, 36*(2), 216–231.

US Congress. (2000). Campus sex crimes prevention act: Section 106 of Public law 106–386. Washington, D.C.: Author.

US Congress. (2007). College cost reduction and access act of 2007

United States Department of Education. (2006). *A test of leadership: Charting the future of US Higher education*. Washington, D.C.: Author.

Weerts, D. J., & Ronca, J. M. (2006). Examining differences in state support for higher education: A comparative study of state appropriations for research in universities. *Journal of Higher Education, 77*(6), 936–967.

## Emerging Issues

Higher Education Center for Alcohol and other Drug Abuse and Violence Prevention. (2006). Complying with the drug free schools and campuses regulations: A guide for university and college administrators. Washington, D.C.: United States Department of Education.

Oliverez, P. M., Chavez, M. L., Soriano, M. & Tierney, W. G. (2006, October). The college and financial aid guide for AB540 undocumented immigrant students. Los Angeles, CA: University of Southern California Center for Higher Education Policy Analysis. Retrieved April 29, 2008, http://www.usc.edu/dept/chepa/pdf/AB_540_final.pdf

Perry, A. M. (2006). Toward a theoretical framework for membership: The case of undocumented immigrants and financial aid for postsecondary education. *Review of Higher Education, 30*(1), 21–40.

Security on Campus (n.d.) The Jeanne Cleary Act. Retrieved May 1, 2008 from http://www.securityoncampus.org/schools/cleryact/cleryact.html

US Congress. (2000). Crime awareness and campus security act (Cleary Act). Washington, D.C.: Author

US Congress. (1994). Communications Assistance for Law Enforcement Act of 1994: Public law No. 103–414, 108 Stat. 4279. Washington, D.C.: Author.

United States Department of Education. (2007). Balancing student privacy and school safety: A guide to the family educational rights and privacy act for colleges and universities. Washington, D.C.: Author.

## Governance

Bastedo, M. N. (2005). The making of an activist governing board. *The Review of Higher Education, 28*(4), 551–570.

Berdahl, R. O. (2000). A view from the bridge: Higher education at the macro-management level. *The Review of Higher Education, 24*(1), 103–112.

De Give, M. L., & Olswang, S. G. (1999). The making of a branch campus system: A statewide strategy of coalition building. *The Review of Higher Education, 22*(3), 287–313.

Hearn, J. C., McLendon, M. K., & Gilchrist, L. Z. (April 2004). *Governing in the sunshine: Open meetings, open records, and effective governance in public higher education.* Retrieved April 30, 2008, from http://www.usc.edu/dept/chepa/pdf/Sunshine%20Final%20Report%2020040212.pdf

Lingenfelter, P. E. (January/February 2007). How should states respond to a test of leadership? *Change, 39*(1), 13–17.

Toma, J. D. (2007). Expanding peripheral activities, increasing accountability demands and reconsidering governance in U.S. higher education. *Higher Education Research and Development, 26*(1), 57–72.

## General Higher Education Policy

Blackwell, E. A., & Cistone, P. J. (1999). Power and influence in higher education: The case of Florida. *Higher Education Policy, 12*(2), 111–122.

Marcus, L. (1997). Restructuring state higher education governance patterns. *Review of Higher Education, 20*(4), 399–418.

Martinez, M. C. (2002). Understanding state higher education systems: Applying a new framework. *The Journal of Higher Education, 73*(3), 349–374.

Martinez, M. C. (1999). The states and higher education: Legislative views on the governance of public colleges and universities: Enhancing the public interest. *The Review of Higher Education, 22*(3), 247–263.

McDaniel, O. C. (1996). The paradigms of governance in higher education systems. *Higher Education Policy, 9*(2), 137–158.

Mills, M. R. (2007). Stories of politics and policy: Florida's higher education governance reorganization. *The Journal of Higher Education, 78*(2), 162–187.

Pusser, B. (2003). Beyond Baldridge: Extending the political model of higher education organization and governance. *Educational Policy, 17*(1), 121–140.

Wellman, J. V. (2002). *State policy and community college baccalaureate transfer.* Palo Alto, CA: National Center for Public Policy and Higher Education and the Institute for Higher Education Policy. Retrieved April 28, 2008, from www.highereducation.org/reports/transfer/transfer.pdf.

## International Perspectives

Abraham Lincoln Study Abroad Fellowship Program (2005). *Global competence & national needs: One million Americans studying abroad.* Washington, D.C.: Author.

Altbach, P. G. & Knight, J. (2007 Fall/Winter). The internationalization of higher education: Motivations and realities. *Journal of Studies in International Education,* 290–305

Eckel, P. D. (2001). A world apart? Higher education transformation in the US and South Africa. *Higher Education Policy, 14*(2), 103–115.

Fisher, G. (1998). Policy, governance and the reconstruction of higher education in South Africa. *Higher Education Policy, 11*(2–3), 121–140.

Gornitzka, Å., & Maassen, P. (2000). National policies concerning the economic role of higher education. *Higher Education Policy, 13*(3), 225–230.

Huisman, J., & Morphew, C. C. (1998). Centralization and diversity: Evaluating the effects of government policies in U.S.A. and Dutch higher education. *Higher Education Policy, 11*(1), 3–13.

Huitema, D., Jeliazkova, M., & Westerheijden, D. F. (2002). Phases, levels and circles in policy development: The cases of higher education and environmental quality assurance. *Higher Education Policy, 15*(2), 197–215.

Knight, J. (2004 Spring). Internationalization remodeled: Definition, approaches, and rationales. *Journal of Studies in International Education,* 5–31.

Leifner, I. (2003). Funding, resource allocation, and performance in higher education systems. *Higher Education, 46*(4), 469–489.

Reiko, Y. (2001). University reform in the post-massification era in Japan: Analysis of government education policy for the 21st century. *Higher Education Policy, 14*(4), 277–291.

Tierney, W. G. (2004 January). Globalization and educational reform: The challenges ahead. *Journal of Hispanic Higher Education,* 5–20.

## Affirmative Action

Rendon, L. I., Novack, V., & Dowell, D. (2004). Testing race-neutral admissions models: Lessons from California State University – Long Beach. *The Review of Higher Education, 28*(2), 221–243.

## Adult Literacy/Remedial Education

Mazzeo, C. (2002). Stakes for students: Agenda-setting and remedial education. *The Review of Higher Education, 26*(1), 19–39.

## Distance/Online Education as Vehicle for Increasing Access

Epper, R. M. (1997). Coordination and completion in postsecondary distance education: A comparative cast study of statewide policies. *The Journal of Higher Education, 68*(5), 551–587.

Mendivil, J. L. I. (2002). The new providers of higher education. *Higher Education Policy, 15*(4), 353–364.

## Data and Information Management (Data-Driven Decision Making)

Ewell, P. (2001). Statewide testing in higher education. *Change, 33*(2), 20–27.

Institute for Higher Education Policy. (2007). *The measuring global performance initiative.* Retrieved April 25, 2008, from http://www.ihep.org/research/featured-projects.cfm.

## Training/Educating Workforce and Leaders and Higher Ed as Engine of Economic Opportunity

Siegfried, J. J., Sanderson, A. R., & McHenry, P. (2007). The economic impact of colleges and universities. *Economics of Education Review, 26*(5), 546–558.

## Business Incubation and Research & Development

Feller, I. (2000). Social contracts and the impact of matching fund requirements on American research universities. *Educational Evaluation and Policy Analysis, 22*(1), 91–98.

## Spellings Commission Recommendations

Green, K. C. (2006). Bring data: A new role for information technology after the Spellings Commission. *Educause Review, 41*(6), 30–46.

## III. Reports and Research from Higher Education Associations and Agencies

Achieve, Inc. (2007, April). *Closing the expectations gap 2007: An annual 50-state progress report on the alignment of high school policies with the demands of college and work.* Retrieved April 29, 2008, from http://www.achieve.org/files/50-state-07-Final.pdf

ACT, Inc. (2007). *Aligning postsecondary expectations and high school practice: The gap defined.* Retrieved April 29, 2008. from http://www.act.org/research/policymakers/pdf/NCSPolicyBrief.pdf

ACT, Inc. (2004). *The role of academic and non-academic factors in improving college retention: ACT policy report.* Retrieved April 29, 2008, from http://www.act.org/research/policymakers/pdf/college_retention.pdf

American Association of State Colleges and Universities. (2008). 2008 Public Policy Agenda. Retrieved April 30, 2008, from http:/www.aascu.org/media/pdf/08_ppa.pdf

American Association of State Colleges and Universities. (2008, April). *The public realities of private student loans* (A Higher Education Policy Brief). Retrieved April 29, 2008, from http://www.aascu.org/media/pm/pdf/pmapril08.pdf

American Association of State Colleges and Universities. (2008, January). *Top 10 state policy issues for higher education in 2008* (A Higher Education Policy Brief). Retrieved April 30, 2008, from http://www.aascu.org/media/pm/pdf/topten2008.pdf

American Council on Education (2007). Redefining the golden years: How adults aged 55+ are changing our ideas about work, learning, and retirement. Retrieved April 25, 2008, from http://www.acenet.edu/AM/Template.cfm?Section=Search&template=/M/HTMLDisplay.cfm&ContentID=20109

Association of American Colleges and Universities. (2007). *College learning for the new global century.* Retrieved April 29, 2008, from http://www.aacu.org/advocacy/leap/documents/GlobalCentury_final.pdf

Association of Governing Boards of Universities and Colleges. (2007, April). *Ten public policy issues for 2007 and 2008* (Public Policy Paper Series No. 07–01). Washington, D.C.

Association of Governing Boards of Universities and Colleges. (2005, May). *Ten public policy issues for 2005 and 2006* (Public Policy Paper Series No. 05–01) [Electronic version]. Washington, D.C.

Breton, A. (1966). A theory of the demand for public goods. *The Canadian Journal of Economics and Political Science / Revue Canadienne d'Economique Et De Science Politique, 32*(4), 455–467.

Colorado Children's Campaign & the Donnell-Kay Foundation. (2007). The high cost of not graduating from high school. Retrieved April 29, 2008, from http://www.dkfoundation.org/pdf/highcostofnotgraduatinghighschool-2005.pdf

Colorado Children's Campaign, Donnell-Kay Foundation, & the Piton Foundation. (2006). *State accountability report 2005–2006 school year.* Retrieved April 29, 2008, from http://www.reportcardcolorado.com/files/reportcard_2006.pdf

De la Rosa, M. L. & Tierney, W. G. (2006). *Breaking through the barriers to college: Empowering low-income communities, schools, and families for college opportunity and student financial aid.* Los Angeles, CA: University of Southern California, Center for Higher Education Policy Analysis. Retrieved April 29, 2008, from http://www.usc.edu/dept/chepa/pdf/Breaking_through_Barriers_final.pdf

Educational Testing Service (2007, June). *Standards, accountability and flexibility: Americans speak on No Child Left Behind reauthorization.* Retrieved April 29, 2008, from http://www.ets.org/Media/Education_Topics/pdf/5884_Key_Findings.pdf

Kennedy, B., Oliverez, P. M., & Tierney, W. G. (2007, February). *Cashing in or cashing out: Tools for measuring the effectiveness and outcomes of financial aid events.* Los Angeles, CA: University of Southern California Center for Higher Education Policy Analysis. Retrieved April 29, 2008, from http://www.usc.edu/dept/chepa/pdf/Evaluating_Events_FINAL.pdf.

Lumina Foundation for Education. (2007). *What we know about access and success in postsecondary education.* Retrieved April 29, 2008, from http://www.luminafoundation.org/research/what_we_know/index.html

Lumina Foundation for Education. (2007). *A voice from the middle: Highlights of the 2007 NASSP/PDK middle school student poll.* Retrieved April 29, 2008, from http://www.pdkintl.org/ms_poll/07ms_poll_highlights.pdf

Miller, M. A. & Ewell, P. T. (2005, April). *Measuring up on college-level learning* (National Center Report No. 05–8). Palo Alto, CA: National Center for Public Policy and Higher Education. Retrieved April 29, 2008, from http://www.highereducation.org/reports/mu_learning/Learning.pdf

National Center for Public Policy and Higher Education. (2005, July). *State capacity for higher education policy: The need for state policy leadership.* Retrieved April 29, 2008, from http://www.highereducation.org/crosstalk/ct0305/news0305-insert.pdf

National Center for Public Policy and Higher Education Research. (2004, April). *The educational pipeline: Big investment, big returns.* Retrieved April 29, 2008, from http://www.highereducation.org/reports/pipeline/pipeline.pdf

National Center for Public Policy and Higher Education. (2004, January). *Responding to the crisis in college opportunity.* Retrieved April 29, 2008, http://www.highereducation.org/reports/crisis/crisis.pdf

National Center for Public Policy and Higher Education Research. (2003, February). *Purposes, policies, performance: Higher education and the fulfillment of a state's public agenda.* Retrieved April 30, 2008, from http://www.highereducation.org/reports/aiheps/AIHEPS.pdf

National Conference of State Legislatures. (2007, Dec. 14). *NCSL: State legislatures face unsettling conditions in 2008.* Retrieved April 25, 2008, from http://www.ncsl.org/programs/press/2007/prl21407.htm.

National Conference of State Legislators. (2006). *Engaging Latino communities for education: A model for student achievement.* Retrieved April 29, 2008, from http://www.ncsl.org/programs/pubs/summaries/013159-sum.htm%20%20%20

Paving a new path to and through postsecondary education. (2007, Spring). *The Navigator, 6*(2), 1–3.

Richardson, R. C., Bracco, K. R., Callan, P. M., & Finney, J. E. (1998). *Higher education governance: Balancing institutional and market influences.* Palo Alto, CA: National Center for Public Policy and Higher Education. Retrieved April 30, 2008, from http://www.highereducation.org/reports/governance/governance.pdf

State Higher Education Executive Officers (2005). *Accountability for better results: A national imperative for higher education.* Retrieved April 29, 2008, from http://www.sheeo.org/account/accountability.pdf

United States Department of Education: The Secretary of Education's Commission on the Future of Higher Education (2006, September). *A test of leadership: Charting the future of U.S. higher education.* Retrieved April 30, 2008, from http://www.ed.gov/about/bdscomm/list/hiedfuture/reports/pre-pub-report.pdf

USC Center for Higher Education Policy Analysis. (2006). *Student success in college: Puzzle, pipeline or pathway?*

Wolanin, T. R. (2003). *What to expect in the reauthorization of the Higher Education Act* (AGB Public Policy Paper Series, No. 03–04). Washington, D.C.: Association of Governing Boards of Universities and Colleges.